ABOUT THE EDITOR

Duane Champagne has been teaching at the University of California at Los Angeles since 1984. In 1986, he became editor of the *American Indian Culture and Research Journal* and went on to be named associate professor in 1992.

Dr. Champagne received a postdoctoral award from the Rockefeller Foundation in 1982–83 and, during this time, completed fieldwork trips to the Tlingit of southeast Alaska and to the Northern Cheyenne in Montana.

Most of Dr. Champagne's writings focus on issues of social, cultural, and political change in American Indian societies as they adapted to European political, cultural, and economic incorporation. He has published in both the sociology and American Indian studies fields, including *American Indian Societies: Strategies and Conditions of Political and Cultural Survival* (1989), *Social Order and Political Change: Constitutional Governments Among the Cherokee, the Choctaw, the Chickasaw, and the Creek* (1992), and *The Native North American Almanac* (1994).

Dr. Champagne is also the director of the UCLA American Indian Studies Center, which carries out research, conducts a master's degree program in American Indian studies, and publishes books for both academic and Indian communities.

Chronology

OF NATIVE
NORTH AMERICAN
HISTORY

HIGHLIGHTS

The Chronology of Native North American History is a reference source designed for users seeking information on important people, places, and events in the history of Native peoples from pre-Columbian times to the present. Chronologically arranged entries cover all fields of endeavor, including:

- Activism
- Administration
- Agriculture
- Art
- Cultures
- Education
- Engineering

- Environment
- Law and legislation
- Literature
- Politics
- Religion
- Science
- Sports

The Chronology of Native North American History provides an abundance of information, and its orderly format makes it easy to use. Special features include:

- Introductory essay surveying Native cultures, history, and religions
- Historical timeline
- Tribal chronologies
- Short biographical sketches of Native Americans
- Annotated bibliography
- Excerpts from significant speeches, documents, and legal cases
- Keyword index listing important names, tribes, events, and locations
- Over 170 photos and maps

Chronology

OF NATIVE NORTH AMERICAN HISTORY

FROM PRE-COLUMBIAN TIMES TO THE PRESENT

DUANE CHAMPAGNE

EDITOR

 Gale Research Inc. • *DETROIT* • *WASHINGTON, D.C.* • *LONDON*

Gale Research Inc. Staff

Jane Hoehner, *Developmental Editor;* Kelle S. Sisung, *Associate Developmental Editor;* Lawrence W. Baker, *Senior Developmental Editor;* Christine Nasso and Leah Knight, *Acquisitions Editors*

Mary Beth Trimper, *Production Director;* Evi Seoud, *Assistant Production Manager;* Mary Kelley, *Production Associate*

Cynthia Baldwin, *Art Director;* Barbara J. Yarrow, *Graphic Services Supervisor;* Pamela A.E. Galbreath, *Cover and Page Designer;* Todd Nessel, *MacIntosh Artist;* C.J. Jonik, *Desktop Publisher;* Willie F. Mathis, *Camera Operator*

Benita Spight, *Data Entry Services Manager;* Gwendolyn Tucker, *Data Entry Supervisor;* Nancy Sheridan, *Data Entry Associate*

Front cover illustration: From Two Piegan tipis (1910). Courtesy of the Library of Congress; Chief Joseph.

Back cover illustration: Okanagan Larry Pierce. Courtesy of Canapress Photo Service. Photo be Rod McIvor.

Library of Congress Cataloging-in-Publication Data
1. Indians of North America—History—Chronology
E77.C555 1994
970.004'97'00202—dc20
94-18455
CIP

ISBN 0-8103-9195-3
Printed in the United States of America by Gale Research Inc.
Published simultaneously in the United Kingdom
by Gale Research International Limited
(An affiliated company of Gale Research Inc.)

10 9 8 7 6 5 4 3 2 1

The trademark **ITP** is used under license.

EDITORIAL TEAM

Editor: Duane Champagne, *Director, American Indian Studies Center,* and *Associate Professor of Sociology, University of California, Los Angeles*

Associate Editor: Troy Johnson, *American Indian Studies Center,* and *History Department, University of California, Los Angeles*

Assistant Editors: Theodore Binnema, *History Department, University of Alberta, Edmonton, Alberta, Canada*; Carla Gentry, *American Indian Studies Center, University of California, Los Angeles*; Derrick Milne, *American Indian Studies Center,* and *Anthropology Department, University of California, Los Angeles*

Permissions Editor: Roselle Kipp, *American Indian Studies Center, University of California, Los Angeles*

TABLE OF CONTENTS

PREFACE xi
ACKNOWLEDGMENTS xiii
TRIBAL CHRONOLOGIES xv
INTRODUCTION xviii
HISTORICAL TIMELINE lvi

Part 1: NATIVE NORTH AMERICAN HISTORY BEFORE 1500
CHAPTER 1 50,000 B.C. TO A.D.1499 3

Part 2: NATIVE NORTH AMERICAN HISTORY 1500–1959
CHAPTER 2 1500 TO 1599 35
CHAPTER 3 1600 TO 1699 50
CHAPTER 4 1700 TO 1799 79
CHAPTER 5 1800 TO 1849 118
CHAPTER 6 1850 TO 1899 175
CHAPTER 7 1900 TO 1959 250

Part 3: NATIVE NORTH AMERICAN HISTORY 1960–1994
CHAPTER 8 1960 TO 1969 339
CHAPTER 9 1970 TO 1979 367
CHAPTER 10 1980 TO 1994 424

AMERICAN INDIAN ORATORS 503
DOCUMENTS OF HISTORY 511
EXCERPTS FROM SIGNIFICANT LEGAL CASES 525
GENERAL BIBLIOGRAPHY 533
ILLUSTRATIONS CREDITS 541
INDEX 547

PREFACE

The Chronology of Native North American *History* presents a comprehensive listing of historical and cultural events about the Native peoples of North America and Canada. It was our intention to create the most comprehensive and sympathetic chronology about Native issues and events available today. Considerable emphasis was given to recent historical events, since they are the least well-published and understood by the general public. Furthermore, *The Chronology* provides considerable historical information about the many cultures that lived before Columbus's landing in 1492. It is our sincere hope that this volume will contribute to the general understanding of the contributions and situations of Native peoples in contemporary and historical life.

Within the scope of *The Chronology*, it was our intention to cover many issues and topics that affected Native peoples, were important to Native peoples, and which influenced U.S. and Canadian society. Consequently, *The Chronology* contains strands of historical events in law, legislation, art, politics, tribal history, religion, health, education, film, theater, literature, and other fields. We have tried not to emphasize one field of events over the other, but rather to provide a short and readily digestible summary of major events in a variety of areas that captures the diversity and depth of Native historical experiences. The numerous illustrations—including maps, line drawings, and photographs—were designed to complement and augment the chronological entries and should help the reader further understand their significance and meaning. The introduction serves as an initial summary to those readers who have little knowledge of Native history. The book is divided into ten chapters and supplemented with short sections containing Native speeches and excerpts from important historical legal documents. An extensive index provides quick access to numerous people, places, and events. We expect our readers not only to use the volume as a reference work, but also to enjoy reading and browsing through the illustrations.

SUGGESTIONS ARE WELCOME

A work the size of *The Chronology of Native North American History* may contain oversights and errors, and we appreciate any suggestions for correction of factual material or additions that will make future editions more accurate, sympathetic, and useful. Please send comments to:

Editor
The Chronology of Native North American History
Gale Research Inc.
835 Penobscot Bldg.
Detroit, MI 48226
Phone: (313) 961-2242
FAX: (313) 961-6741
Toll-free: 1-800-347-GALE

Duane Champagne
May 1994

ACKNOWLEDGMENTS

The compilation of *The Chronology* was an interesting and rewarding task for everyone involved. Many people played important roles during the inception and production of the book: I give great thanks to associate editor Troy Johnson, who carried most of the day-to-day management of the project during the summer of 1993. Troy supervised the assistant editors, Carla Gentry and Derek Milne, who were often asked to accomplish more than they thought possible. Special thanks go to Theodore Binnema, who provided most of the information on Canadian history. Without his contribution, the Canadian parts of *The Chronology* would surely be lacking.

The staff at Gale Research Inc. pursued this project with their usual diligence. Chris Nasso and Leah Knight must be recognized for developing the concept of the book and for having the foresight to see its great value. Jane Hoehner, our editor, greatly contributed to strengthening and clarifying untold aspects of the text.

Our recognition and thanks also go to the numerous people who helped secure illustrations and permissions. I am greatly indebted to our permissions editor, Roselle Kipp, who spent considerable time managing the heavy load of correspondence necessary to locate and obtain the illustrations; special thanks go out to Vee Salabiye, our American Indian Studies Librarian, who spent many hours searching for difficult-to-find historical facts, and whose efforts greatly contributed to the accuracy of *The Chronology*; Paola Carini, who helped organize the placement of illustrations within the text; Ned Blackhawk, who contributed early on in the project until his graduate examinations forced him to turn back to full-time study; and Viviana Quinteros, who helped put the final entries together, and who helped prepare the index.

Again I find myself seeking absolution from my family, who bravely carried on throughout my numerous absences. All three of my children, Talya, Gabe, and Demelza, deserve my special thanks for their understanding. In some small way, I hope this book will repay their patience.

Duane Champagne
May 1994

Tribal

CHRONOLOGIES

APACHE: Arrive in Southwest, c. A.D. 800–1000; European contact, 1540; acquire horses, early 17th century; Spanish-Apache warfare, 1786–1821; Mexican-Apache warfare, 1830–50; San Carlos Indian Reservation established, 1875; Apache ordered to San Carlos, 1876; Geronimo confined to San Carlos, 1877; escapes, 1878; returns 1880. Geronimo surrenders and with his Chiricahua warriors is exiled to Florida prison, 1886.

CHEROKEE: Arrive in Southeast, c. 10,000 B.C.; European contact, 1539–43; Cherokee sold as slaves, 1681; fight on the side of the British, War of 1776; land cessions 1721–1835; Cherokee syllabary, 1821; Cherokee Constitution, 1828; Trail of Tears (removal) 1838–39; fought for Confederacy in Civil War, 1861–65; Cherokee rolls prepared, 1900–02; dissolution of Cherokee State, 1906; tribal government reestablished, 1970s.

CHEYENNE: Migrate to Great Plains, 1775; division into Northern and Southern nations, 1850; Fort Laramie Treaty, 1851; Sand Creek Massacre, 1864; Cheyenne-Arapaho War, 1864–65; War for the Bozeman Trail, 1866–68; Medicine Lodge Treaty, 1867; Fort Laramie Treaty, 1868; Red River War, 1874–75; some Northern Cheyenne fight with Sioux against Custer at Battle of Little Bighorn, 1876; removal to Indian Territory, 1877; North-

ern Cheyenne led by Dull Knife and Little Wolf escape Indian Territory, 1877; eastern Montana Northern Cheyenne Reservation established in early 1880s.

CHICKASAW: European contact, 1540; war with French colonies and their Indian allies, 1729–60; treaties between the United States and the Chickasaw, 1801, 1805; fight with Andrew Jackson against Creek Red Stick warriors, 1813–14; land cessions 1828–37; Chickasaw migrate to Indian Territory, 1838–50; Chickasaw Constitution, 1856; dissolution of Chickasaw State, 1906; tribal government reestablished, 1970s.

CHIPPEWA (OJIBWAY): Arrive in Lake Michigan/Lake Superior area, 1615; Beaver Wars, 1649–1700; some migrate into Great Plains area, 1700–1800; land cessions, 1837, 1842, 1854; relocated to reservations, 1850s; lands allotted, 1889; fishing/hunting treaty rights protests, 1980s.

CHOCTAW: European contact, 1540; Choctaw uprising, 1755; first land cession, 2.5 million acres, Treaty of Fort Adams, 1801; Treaty of Hopewell, 1876; Treaty at Treaty Ground, 1820; Treaty of Dancing Rabbit Creek, 1830; removal to Indian territory, 1831–33; Choctaw Constitution, 1860; land allotted, 1902; dissolution of Choctaw State, 1906; tribal government reestablished, 1970s.

COMANCHE: Arrive in southern Plains, c. A.D. 1300; acquire horses, c. 1680–1700; Quanah Parker born, 1835; battle of Adobe Walls, 1874; battle of Palo Duro Canyon, 1874; surrender at Fort Sill, 1875; assigned to reservation, 1875.

CREEK: Arrive in Southeast, c. 10,000 B.C.; European contact, 1540–42; Red Stick War, 1812–13; battle of Horseshoe Bend, 1814; Treaty of Indian Springs, 1825; removal to Indian Territory, 1820-40; Creek Constitution, 1867; dissolution of Creek State, 1906; tribal government reestablished, 1970s; Poarch Band of Creek federally recognized, 1984.

CROW: Arrive on Great Plains (known as Hidatsa), c. 1430; acquire horses, c. 1680; Crow tribe splits from Hidatsa, 1776; Crow establish Sun Dance, 1840; land cessions, 1846–51; Fort Laramie Treaty, 1851; U.S. Army Scouts, c. 1850–80; battle of Rosebud, 1876; proposed $5 million settlement for Crow lands vetoed by President Eisenhower, 1956; state of Montana orders Crow to open access to fishing on Bighorn River, 1981.

FOX: Beaver Wars, 1638–84; move from Michigan to Wisconsin to avoid war with Iroquois, 1654; war between Fox and French, 1712–18, 1727–37; sign Treaty of St. Louis ceding sections of Illinois, Wisconsin, and Missouri for $2,000, 1804; begin mining lead in southwestern Wisconsin, 1810; Black Hawk War, 1831–32; relocated to Indian Territory, 1833–40; Fox land in Indian Territory opened to U.S. settlement, 1884–94.

HOPI: Hopi emerge from Anasazi culture, 1200–1400; establish the village of Oraibi, c. 1150; Spanish contact, 1539; Hopi revolt against Spanish, 1541; Spanish missions established among Hopi, 1629; Pope's rebellion, 1680; Spanish reconquest, 1693; Hopi evict Spanish friar, 1776; Navajo-Hopi Rehabilitation Act signed, 1950; Hopi and Navajo Relocation Act, 1974 and 1980.

KIOWA: Arrive on Great Plains, c. 1430; acquire horses, c. 1680; Medicine Lodge Treaty, 1867; reservation created in Indian Territory, 1867; Fort Laramie Treaty, 1868; battle of Soldier Springs, 1868; battle of Adobe Walls, 1874; Red River War 1874–75; Kiowa surrender, 1875; Chief Satanta dies in prison, 1878; *Lone Wolf v. Hitchcock,* 1903.

MODOC: Arrive in Columbia Plateau, c. 6,000 B.C.; ceded lands, 1854; relocated to Klamath Reservation, 1869; left reservation, 1870; Modoc War 1872–73; surrender, 1873; General Canby killed, 1873; sent to Indian Territory, 1873; return to Klamath Reservation, 1909; federal tribal recognition terminated, 1961; federal tribal recognition restored, 1986.

MOHAWK: Arrive in Northeast, c. A.D. 1000–1300; cofounded Iroquois League, c. 1300–1570; European contact, 1534; Caughnawaga reservation established, 1676; American Revolution, align with British, 1774–84; protest blocks St. Lawrence Seaway International Bridge, 1968; Mohawk, New York/Canadian confrontation, 1990.

NAVAJO: Arrive in Southwest, c. 13th century; Treaty at Canyon de Chelly, 1849; war between Navajo and U.S., 1862–67; Kit Carson campaign against Navajo, 1863; "The Long Walk," removal to Bosque Redondo, 1864; Treaty of Bosque Redondo, Navajo Reservation created, assignment to reservation, 1868; Navajo Tribal Council formed, 1922; reject Indian Reorganization Act (IRA) government, 1934; serve as "Code Talkers" during World War II, 1941–45; Navajo-Hopi Rehabilitation Act signed into law, 1950; *Navajo Times* begins publication, 1960; California State Supreme Court upholds right of Navajo use of peyote in religious ceremonies, 1964; establish Navajo Community College, 1971.

NEZ PERCÉ: Acquire horses, c. 1740; contact with Lewis and Clark Expedition, 1805; Walla Walla Council, 1855, 1863; Wallowa set aside as Nez Percé Reservation, 1873; Wallowa opened to U.S. settlers, 1875; Nez Percé ordered to Lapwai Reservation, 1877; Flight of the Nez Percé, 1877; Chief Joseph's surrender, 1877; consigned to Colville Reservation (Washington), 1878.

ONONDAGA: Arrive in Northeast, c. A.D. 1000–1300; cofounded Iroquois league, c. 1300–1570; Beaver Wars, 1649-1700; ally with Dutch/English, 1664; Canandaigua Treaty establishes reservation, 1794; claim 175,000 acres in New York State, 1978; win victory for jurisdictional sovereignty, 1979; twelve wampum belts returned by New York State, 1989.

PAIUTE: European contact, 1776; influx of gold-seekers, 1850s; Pyramid Lake War, 1860; Snake War, 1866–68; Wodziwob starts first Ghost Dance, 1869–70; relocate to Yakima and Malheur reservations, 1878; Wovoka starts second ghost dance movement, 1890; file claim with U.S. Indian Claims Commission for $1 billion as Indian share of Comstock Lode silver mine, 1951; federal tribal recognition terminated, 1957; federal tribal recognition restored, 1980.

PAWNEE: Arrive in Great Plains, 1300; European contact, 1541; acquire horses, c. 1700; serve as Indian scouts for U.S. army, 1866–90; removal to Oklahoma Territory, 1874–75; adopt Ghost Dance teachings, 1890s; attempt to repatriate remains of six Pawnee scouts decapitated in late 1860s, 1970–present.

SEMINOLE: Split from Creek, settle in Florida, c. 1750; attacked by Andrew Jackson, 1817; Seminole wars, 1835–42; removal to Indian Territory, 1838–41; fight for Confederacy in Civil War, 1861–65; reservations established in Florida, 1930s; bingo parlor opens, 1970s.

SENECA: Arrive in Northeast, c. A.D. 1000–1300; cofounded Iroquois league, c. 1300–1570; Beaver Wars, 1649–1700; Pontiac's War, 1763; Handsome Lake and the Longhouse Religion, 1799–1815; establish Handsome Lake Church,

1830s; removal to Indian Territory, 1830s; protest building of Kinzua Dam, 1940s–50s; agree to dispute settlement over taxes levied by State of New York, 1989.

SHAWNEE: Driven out of Cumberland Valley by Iroquois, Chickasaw, and Cherokee, 1675–1700; Covenant Chain of Friendship with British colonies, 1748; form alliance with Delaware to prevent westward colonial expansion, 1750s; Little Turtle's War, 1791–95; Treaty at Fort Greenville, 1795; Tecumseh and Tenskwatawa (the Shawnee Prophet) rise to prominence and forge a powerful pan-Indian alliance, 1808–12; cede land in Kansas, 1867; federal government appropriates remaining lands, 1865–67; relocated to Indian Territory, 1867.

SIOUX: European contact, 1678; Sioux uprising, 1862; Fetterman battle, 1866; Fort Laramie Treaty, 1868; battle of Little Big Horn, 1876; Crazy Horse surrenders, 1877; massacre at Wounded Knee Creek, 1890; annuities denied the Minnesota Sioux in 1863 are restored, 1917; two Sioux tribes displaced by the Oahe and Fort Randall Dam are authorized to receive more than $10.8 million in compensation, 1954; three additional Sioux tribes displaced by the Oahe and Fort Randall Dam receive $14.8 million; Oglala Sioux and members of American Indian Movement occupy Pine Ridge reservation hamlet of Wounded Knee from February 27 to May 8, 1973; in *U.S. v. Sioux Nation*, Sioux win a $122 million judgment for the illegal taking of the Black Hills, 1980.

TLINGIT: Arrive on Northwest Coast, c. B.C. 8,000; European contact, 1741; fur trade with Russia, 1783; drive Russians out of fort at Sitka, Alaska, 1802; Russians retake fort, 1804; Tlingit attack Russians, 1806, 1809, 1813; U.S. Navy shells Tlingit island, 1882; Alaska Native Brotherhood founded, 1912; win land claims, 1965; Sealaska Corporation formed, 1970s; seek an official apology from U.S. government for shelling of Tlingit island, 1982.

INTRODUCTION

CREATION STORIES

Virtually all Native North American societies account for their origins with creation histories. In many ways these histories are analogous to the Judeo-Christian account of the world's creation and the beginning of humanity in the story of Adam and Eve. The stories usually contain characters—like the Coyote in the West and Raven in the Northwest and Arctic—whose roles are both creative and destructive. Trickster figures account for the presence of death, illness, imbalance, and moral disorder in the world, while the Great Spirit is considered to be a benevolent gift giver to the earth's people and other beings. Evil events that happen to a Native community are not attributed to the wrath of the Great Spirit but are seen as being caused by the immoral acts of community members, the breaking of sacred rules, or the improper performance of ceremonies to honor the Great Spirit.

At the time of creation, many Native cultures received from the Great Spirit, often through intermediary spirits, the arts of culture, ceremonials, sometimes clan organization, and political organization. For example, the Great Spirit gave the Cherokee seven clans. These seven clans were the primary social units in Cherokee society, and many of its major ceremonials required the presence and participation of members from all the clans. Similarly, the trickster figure Raven bequeathed the clan and moiety (two major divisions called Raven and Eagle) organization to the Tlingit people of present-day Alaska and gave them their central potlatch tradition. At a potlatch ceremony, clans related by marriage gathered to give away food, sacred items like copper plates, and artwork as a way of honoring their ancestors and repaying relatives for their help and material support, such as performing funeral obligations on the death of a close relative.

In other societies, the Great Spirit often bequeathed a sacred bundle of objects for the entire nation. The sacred bundle of the Arapaho, for example, included a sacred pipe, with which the elders of the nation smoked sacred tobacco and prayed to the Great Spirit for assistance. The Arapaho creation story was considered so sacred that only certain priests were allowed to repeat it to a small group of elders for fear that a mistake made in the retelling would bring bad luck to the entire nation. One Arapaho man and his lineal descendants were assigned the task of protecting and caring for the sacred creation bundle.

Native North Americans lived in a world of sacred beings, sacred laws, and sacred social and political orders. They strongly emphasized the preserving of their traditions and worked to ensure that their laws and institutions were carried on by the younger people of the cultural community. To do otherwise was considered a course bereft of spiritual blessings and aid—one that threatened serious harm to the entire community through natural events such as drought, disease, death, poor hunting, or tribal discord. This emphasis on tradition has informed and sustained Native people over many centuries, both before and after the arrival of Europeans. Much of Native North American history can be understood only from the premise that Native individuals and communities often consider their way of life as sacred, given by the Great Spirit, and for that reason have resisted attempts to change their cultures. This Native orientation differs profoundly from the contemporary Western practice of removing the sacred from everyday life and from major economic and political actions, and relegating them to church and specific religious ceremonies.

Most archaeologists believe that people first arrived in North America by migrating over the present-day Bering Strait between Alaska and Siberia between 15,000 and 20,000 years ago. Native creation stories do not confirm such migrations, although the Cherokee, Delaware, Choctaw, Chickasaw, and others have stories within their traditions that tell of long marches, usually from west to east. The Creek people have a story that says they migrated continuously to the east in search of the abode of the sun. Upon reaching the great ocean, now called the Atlantic, they gave up their quest and settled in what is now the southeastern United States. The Delaware have a migration story, the *Walam Olum*, in which the Algonkian-speaking nations of North America traveled from west to east, many stopping along the way to populate the middle interior of North America. The Delaware, the grandfather nation or leading Algonkian-speaking nation, finally reached the Atlantic Ocean in present-day southern New England and decided to settle.

The migration stories provided Native nations with records of traditional relations with other tribes, and also gave them claims to the land where they settled. The sacred claim to territory is most easily seen in the migration stories of the Choctaw, Chickasaw, and Creek. In each case, a sacred pole pointed the direction in which the people were to march each day. When the pole stood still, the people considered it a sign from the Great Spirit that he had led them to the land that

he intended for their occupation and livelihood. In later years, when Europeans attempted to claim Native land, many Native nations were reluctant to move elsewhere or to sell the land because it had been given to them by the Great Spirit.

Some Native cultures do not have migration stories, but hold that their people emerged from worlds beneath the earth. The Navajo, Pueblos, Coushatta, some Choctaw, and others have such traditions. For the Navajo and Pueblos, the current world is the fifth world: people, in different physical form than in the present-world, traveled through four underworlds, but on each occasion committed unruly acts against the spirit beings there and were forced to flee through small openings in the roof of the underworld into the next higher world. Migrations through the lower worlds were moral journeys during which the all too human follies of people were revealed and caused disruption and disorder. Through the journey within the first four underworlds, the people learned how to maintain order, harmony, and balance between males and females and with the spirit beings— lessons that are necessary in order to preserve the present fifth world from destruction. If the people are immoral, and do not practice their ritual and sacred obligations, then the harmony of the present world will be disrupted and the world destroyed; the people will be forced to escape to the next world, the sixth world. (According to the Pueblo tradition there are nine worlds.) Social and moral harmony is thus closely tied to the preservation of cosmic order.

The Native culture's emergence stories also provide a strong sense of place, and a sacredness of place. In both Navajo and Pueblo cultures there are sacred mountains, sacred lakes, and other sacred places. Ceremonials are held in these sacred places, and their performances recall the stories that define the meaning of the land and locations in ways that were not generally known or understood by most European explorers, travelers, or comprehended by contemporary general public or government officials.

For many Native North Americans, the creation stories account for their origins and help to define their relationship to the rest of the world. The view offered by archaeologists that Native peoples came across the Bering Strait from Asia 15,000 to 20,000 years ago has little meaning to many Natives. While archaeologists disregard Native creation stories as unscientific, many Native people will not accept the archaeologists' argument as to how the American continents were populated. This debate is analogous in various ways to the debate between Creationists and Evolutionists. The Creationists believe in the Christian Bible and in the story of Genesis where God made the earth and its people in six days. Evolutionists argue that the Earth and the universe are billions of years old and that the development of life and of people took several billion years. In this Chronology, considerable archaeological evidence is presented, adding to our knowledge about the early peoples who inhabited North America. However, the Native world view should always be kept in mind.

While archaeologists might doubt the scientific value of the creation stories, many Native people still honor the stories and the moral, social, and religious obligations that are associated with them. Because the Natives act in ways that are informed by their creation stories and religions, their historical actions, strong commitment to preserving tradition, resistance to European political and economic change, and struggle to endure are not easily understood from a string of chronological events. With Native Americans, as well as for all peoples of the world, familiarity and interpretation of their cultures greatly enhances an understanding of history.

50,000 B.C.–A.D. 1499

The earliest people to live in North America are called Paleo-Indians, or Old Stone Age Indians. Perhaps as early as 27,000 B.C. Asian migrants were living in present-day Alaska, though some students of prehistoric cultures suggest that people came and spread throughout North America thousands of years before that. The periodically expanding glaciers may have absorbed enough water to dry up the Bering Strait and allow land passage for people and animals during several periods. Geologists suggest that the Bering passage was open for intervals ranging from a few thousand years to 10,000 years at least four times in the last 50,000 years. It is difficult to know conclusively, however, since our primary information about these early groups derives almost entirely from stone and sometimes bone implements.

By the end of the last ice age, about 10,000 to 12,000 years ago, the Native peoples had settled throughout North America. The climate was colder than it is today, but it was slowly heating up. North America was then populated by horses, camels, saber-toothed tigers, woolly mammoths, large bison, and other large game. The Paleo-Indians lived by gathering plant food, such as berries and roots, and by hunting. Their primary hunting weapons were a spear with a stone point, and the *atlatl*, a spear thrower in which the spear is attached to the top of a handle to provide greater thrust.

About 10,000 B.C. a warming period emerged, and the glaciers rapidly receded north. Over the next two millennia, the climate changed rapidly, and many of the large game animals perished. The Paleo-Indians were forced to adapt to the new climatic conditions by hunting smaller game, fishing, and migrating to exploit roots and fruits over large areas. By 7,000 B.C. the migratory big game hunting of the Paleo-Indian period was over, and the Archaic, or foraging, period began. Around 4,000 B.C. Archaic Indian populations grew, and more reliance on fish and more efficient exploitation of foraging resources occurred. The Archaic Indians adapted to many of the ecological areas of North America, and, by 2,000 B.C., some ancestral groups of contemporary Natives can be identified. It also appears that at this time, the introduction of Latin American plants and farming technology greatly stimulated efforts to domesticate local plants. Many small societies in the eastern woodlands settled into sedentary villages supported in part by domestic horticulture, which used hand implements to turn the earth rather than domesticated animals and plows. Plants cultivated at this time included sunflowers, squash, goosefoot, knotweed, and maygrass. In addition, the pipe, which is sacred in many Native societies, appeared among some of the sedentary villages in the present-day Illinois region.

By 1,500 B.C., many groups in the present-day southwestern and southeastern United States were cultivating corn, squash, beans, and other plants. Traders or travelers from present-day Mexico or central America probably introduced corn to northern Natives, who added it to their diet of domestic food plants. Corn, squash, and beans were called the "three sisters" by the Iroquois, and became the most popular crops in eastern North America. The peoples living along the Mississippi and Ohio valleys increasingly cultivated plants, although hunting, fishing, and gathering of roots and wild fruits remained the primary source of food and added variety to the people's diets.

An early major mound site, from about 1,200 B.C., was found at what is now Poverty Point, Louisiana. It would take a large number of people to build the mounds, indicating that a central leadership was capable of organizing such vast quantities of labor. The largest mound is seventy feet high and 600 feet across. Some crude pottery has been found, and it appears that squash was cultivated, but there is no evidence of corn production. The Poverty Point community did not endure, however, and the people returned to a more decentralized political order and economy. The Poverty Point mound builders appear to have been a brief elaboration of southwestern archaic culture, and not strongly influenced by Mexican or the later Adena culture.

From 500 B.C. to 100 B.C., the small horticultural communities of the central Ohio Valley formed a similar culture and built mounds, usually with cone-shaped tops and intended primarily for burial. The Adena culture was supported largely by hunting, gathering, and horticulture and was characterized by large earthworks and several symbolically sculptured icons, such as the famous serpent mound that was 1,254 feet long and 4 to 5 feet high. Although some Adena mounds may

have been built earlier, the major mounds and symbolic sculptures were built after 500 B.C. Apparently, the Adena people lived in villages of ten or more small houses and gathered at the mounds for ceremonial purposes according to their annual ritual cycle, of which we know very little. Many of the conical Adena mounds were burial mounds, where people were interred with utilitarian objects such as scrapers, drills, and stone knives. Burial patterns indicate that Adena culture was stratified, perhaps with priests and chiefs.

About 100 B.C., the Adena culture was transformed into the Hopewell culture, which flourished until approximately A.D. 800. The Hopewell tradition originated in present-day Illinois and may have had trade and other ties with the Adena people for several centuries. Large earthworks and lavish grave goods characterized the Hopewell culture. Like the Adena people, the Hopewellians depended greatly on hunting and gathering of wild plants, and horticulture remained a secondary and limited food source. The Hopewellians also built their ceremonial mounds within a sacred circle. Important leaders were buried in more extensive mounds, with more elaborate goods, than in the Adena culture. Extensive trade networks are indicated by many of the funeral objects, since obsidian rock from Yellowstone Park has been found as well as objects from Florida, the Southeast, and present-day North Dakota. The Hopewell culture influenced cultures throughout many of the middle and eastern sections of what is today the United States. Mound construction, pipes, pottery styles, and armor were Hopewellian characteristics that were widely adopted. In what is now Louisiana, the Marksville culture shares similarities with the Hopewellian cultures to the north. Marksville towns are characterized by ceremonial mounds, cultivation of corn, and burial of important leaders in mounds. They continue to hunt, fish, and gather wild plants to supplement their crops of corn, squash, beans, and other plants. The spread of Hopewellian culture seems to indicate increased political and ceremonial centralization and stratification among Native southeastern and midwestern peoples. Mounds require considerable organization of labor to build; there also must be powerful and persuasive leaders who are deemed worthy of elaborate burials. The Hopewell culture started to decline after A.D. 400, perhaps owing to population pressures or to the emerging widespread use of bows and arrows, which replaced the *atlatl* in warfare. Some Hopewell towns were fortified, indicating increased warfare after A.D. 400. Nevertheless many of the southeastern Hopewell towns survived and merged with the Mississippi culture after A.D. 700.

The Mississippi culture flourished from about A.D. 700 to about 1600. In contrast to the Hopewell and Adena cultures, there was more reliance on corn and agricultural production; a stratified social hierarchy lived on platform mounds, unlike the conical burial mounds characteristic of the Hopewell and Adena cultures. Mound-building Mississippi cultures developed in the major river valleys of the central United States, including the Mississippi, Tennessee, Cumberland, and lower Ohio. Some Mississippi culture towns, such as Cahokia, a site across the river from present-day St. Louis, Missouri, grew large with perhaps as many as 30,000 residents. The towns and sacred mounds were laid out with reference to major cosmic events like the summer and winter solstices. A priesthood and political leadership apparently was considered divine and lived in houses on top of the platform mounds. The Mississippi culture also was characterized by extensive trade networks throughout central and eastern North America, and there may have been trade connections with the civilizations of Mexico. Much of the trade consisted of items for ceremonial use, such as copper from the northern nations and pipestone and other stone from quarries to make pipes and art objects. Native traders used a simplified language called the Mobilian trade jargon, named after the Mobile people, who lived in present-day southern Alabama. Specific clans may have had an exclusive right to engage in the trade, as was the case among the Huron people of the lower Great Lakes.

When French explorers met the Natchez of present-day Louisiana in the early 1700s, they got a glimpse of a Mississippi culture. The Natchez were led by a man called the "Great Sun," who was considered sacred and who led ceremonial and political activities. A group of "nobles" and priests was closely associated with the Great Sun, and a class, or perhaps more accurately certain clans, of "stinkards" were the common people. According to tradition, the Great Spirit ruled on earth for many years and then returned to the sky above. Before going he designated a man and his wife, sometimes a sister, to carry on in his place. Thus the Great Sun and his lineage ruled by the direct command of the Great Spirit, and represented the will and leadership of the Great Spirit on earth. The Natchez later told traders that at one time as many as 500 Great Suns ruled separate nations up and down the Mississippi Valley and its tributaries. Similarly, when Hernando de Soto marched through the Southeast, he encountered many Mississippi culture communities. De Soto's associates reported that among the Chickasaw, the "king," who was honored as a sacred being, was carried about by men. The Mississippi culture appears to have been highly stratified in religious, political, and social terms. The bow and arrow was in common use, and corn and squash were major items of horticultural production. The great mounds were ceremonial centers around which many people lived, and those who resided around an extensive area might owe allegiance to a sacred mound. Among the Choctaw, for example, the sacred mound Nanih Waiya was considered the ceremonial center of the Choctaw Nation.

Many of the Native nations that we know today probably participated in the Mississippi culture. Certainly the Natchez, Caddo, Pawnee, Choctaw, Creek, Illinois, Cherokee, Shawnee, Chickasaw, Hidatsa, Crow, and perhaps the Sioux were part of this culture or were strongly influenced by it. The centralized and ceremonially stratified organization of their towns seems very different from the view that colonists had of Natives. The Mississippi culture disintegrated very quickly in the 1500s, perhaps because of epidemics that were carried by Europeans and spread from the coastal areas through networks of Native populations. Thus even de Soto in 1540 reported empty villages, and some archaeologists have found evidence of massive population declines, as much as 90 percent, among Mississippi culture communities. Such devastating epidemics virtually destroyed communities, including many priests and other knowledgeable individuals. As a result, much historical, medicinal, and ritual knowledge gathered by the Mississippi culture has been lost. Archaeological evidence also indicates that warfare intensified among the Mississippi communities, which led to fortifications of villages and towns. By the 1700s, when European traders regularly visited the interior regions, the Mississippi cultures were no longer there. Most decentralized into loose confederacies of villages or clans, with only a few exceptional remnants such as the Natchez.

A second major horticultural society arose in the southwestern United States, largely in what is now New Mexico and Arizona. The Hohokam peoples migrated from Mexico around 300 B.C. and settled along the Gila River in Arizona. Between A.D. 550 and A.D. 900, Mexican civilization exerted considerable influence over the Hohokam, and incorporated them into its trade and cultural expansion. The Hohokam grew corn extensively, constructing canals and using irrigation to support their crops. They also borrowed the Mesoamerican tradition of building ball courts, which have great religious and social significance for the Mesoamerican culture and ceremonial cycle.

The Hohokam constructed trade centers and sedentary villages, but by 1300 were forced to abandon their large-scale horticultural practices and larger settlements owing to a severe drought in the late 1200s. Thereafter many Hohokam were forced to exploit the sparse resources of the desert environment and river areas. The Hohokam are the ancestors of the present-day Pima-speaking tribes. The Pima people have continued to farm the land with irrigation into the twentieth century.

The Mesoamerican-inspired Hohokam culture appears to have fostered considerable change among the Mogollon peoples, who were hunters and gatherers living in what is today Arizona and New Mexico. Over the period 250 B.C. to A.D. 1150 the Mogollon peoples borrowed from the Hohokam such items as pottery art, farming methods, and domestic crops, while after A.D. 700 the Mogollon peoples came under the influence of the Anasazi, or early Pueblo, culture. The Mogollon had an early form of the *kiva* (underground or partially underground chambers used for ceremonials or councils), indicating that they adopted a religion and ceremonial cycle similar to the Pueblos, rather than the ball court games and rituals of the Hohokam and Mesoamerican civilizations. By A.D. 1150 the Mogollon peoples were merged with the Pueblo peoples, who were migrating into Mogollon regions.

The ancestors of the Pueblo peoples were farming and building multi-story houses as early as A.D. 900. By this date, corn was a major crop in the Southwest, and southwestern farmers were building irrigation canals and dams and using various planting methods to preserve scarce rainfall. Over the next several hundred years, until about 1250, the Pueblo peoples built large towns and large irrigation networks. Trade with Mexico developed and Mesoamerican mounds and ball courts were built in the region of present-day Arizona. Several trading towns were connected to the coastal peoples of what is now California and to the Toltec civilization of Mexico. Between 1000 and 1180, Anasazi communities emerged and built large structures and towns using stone blocks. Chaco Canyon in present-day northwest New Mexico served as a central trade and ceremonial center to many smaller communities throughout the Southwest. The largest structure in Chaco Canyon was Pueblo Bonito, which had 800 rooms and 35 kivas arranged around a central plaza. The kivas are considered to be similar to the ones the Pueblo people use today. Toward the end of the thirteenth century, however, droughts caused the residents of Chaco Canyon to disperse. Some of the Chaco Canyon residents probably migrated to Mesa Verde, in present-day Colorado. There they constructed multi-story houses for communities of 200 to 500 people and built numerous kivas for religious ceremonies. Furthermore, in part because the Southwest is an arid environment, rain and ceremonies to welcome and attract *Kachinas*, or benevolent rain spirits, made up an important part of the Pueblo annual ceremonial cycle, which is very much tied to ensuring that the crops and corn grow and help feed the people. During the drought of the late thirteenth century, the Pueblo peoples were forced to migrate to areas with more reliable water sources. By 1300, most Pueblo communities had moved to sites along the Rio Grande Valley and its tributaries in present-day eastern New Mexico, while others relocated along the Little Colorado River in what is now Arizona. A few communities stayed on until about 1400, but they too were forced to move because of the harsh dry environment. The western Pueblo constructed about ten villages along the Colorado River and eventually came to be known as the Hopi, while the Rio Grande Pueblos comprised numerous villages, perhaps as many as 40, before their first contact with Spanish explorers and missionaries in about 1540.

Around the twelfth and thirteenth centuries, numerous bands of Athapascan-speaking bands migrated into the Southwest and southern plains areas. The Athapascan-speaking peoples migrated from present-day western Alaska and northwest Canada, where most contemporary Athapascan-speaking peoples live. They traveled down through the plains area, eventually entered the Southwest, and continued to migrate farther west during the eighteenth and nineteenth centuries. The more western Athapascan-speakers eventually formed the Navajo people, while the more eastern bands, who migrated first to the southern plains, formed a variety of Apache tribes. The Athapascan-speakers were hunters and gatherers, but started a period of prolonged exchange, and sometimes warfare, with the Pueblo peoples and eventually adopted many aspects of Pueblo ceremonial life.

On the eve of the European intrusion of Christopher Columbus in 1492, there were hundreds of Native North American societies that were generally economically and politically independent from one another. The major horticultural societies consisted of the Mississippi culture and southwestern Pueblos, while others exploited the varying environments of their regions. Anthro-

pologists have devised a series of regional culture areas where the ecological conditions are generally similar. These major culture areas are known as the Northeast, Southeast, Plains, Southwest, Great Basin, California, Plateau, Pacific Northwest, Subarctic, and Arctic.

Within these regions, there was considerable diversity in Native cultures and social and political institutions. The peoples of the Pacific Northwest formed elaborate clan and moiety structures that varied from group to group but shared the creation stories of the culture hero and trickster figure Raven. Similarly, the potlatch ceremony was a central feature, but its meaning and relations to other institutions varied considerably from society to society. For the Tlingit, the potlatch honored the clan ancestors, ended the period of mourning for a deceased relative, marked new ranks and titles, and paid off members of the opposite moiety for services rendered during a blood relative's funeral. Among the Kwakiutl, the potlatch was associated with marriage, and noted the new wealth and status brought to the marriage by the bride's lineage. The Pacific Northwest groups developed an elaborate artistic and material culture based on the area's abundance of salmon. Artistic items included totem poles, elaborately woven blankets, carved clan and house crests, and carved chests that always portrayed mythical themes and other traditional stories. The Pacific Northwest region extended along the coastal regions from the panhandle of present-day Alaska to northern California.

The Yupik and Inuit, commonly called Eskimos, of Alaska and the Canadian Arctic Circle did not have clans or moieties, but were organized into small villages of related families, where social relations were more egalitarian than those of the symbolically stratified peoples of the Pacific Northwest. The peoples of the subarctic hunted and gathered in spare and harsh environments and tended to live in dispersed bands or villages, which occasionally came together in larger bands or regional ceremonial gatherings. Shamen, or individual ritual specialists, were the primary ceremonial leaders and healers. By 1500, in western

Canada, the subarctic people were mainly of Athapascan-speakers such as the Dogrib, Slave, Carrier, Hare, Chipewyan, and others. The eastern Canadian subarctic was populated by Algonkian-speakers such as the Cree, Naskapi, Montagnais, and Beothuk.

By 1500, the peoples of the northeastern part of the present United States had adopted horticulture, and were growing corn, squash, and beans, among other crops. The northeastern peoples did not take up mound building, or burial in mounds, but lived in large fortified towns. The Iroquois, a major northeastern group, adopted long houses that were divided into compartments for nuclear families. The Iroquois long house was usually occupied by members of a lineage from the same clan. Reckoned through the mother, the clans and lineages were the most important social, political, and economic institutions within Iroquois culture.

The precise dates are unknown, but probably between 1000 and 1450, five nations of Iroquois (Seneca, Oneida, Onondaga, Mohawk, and Cayuga) formed a confederacy. Living in what is now Ontario, Deganawida, a member of the Iroquoian-speaking Huron Nation, had a vision and was instructed by the Great Spirit to bring peace to the warring Iroquois peoples. Conflicts arose among the Iroquois nations because clan members were obligated to seek a death for any death caused by someone outside their clan and nation. The blood revenge applied even if a death was accidental. Deganawida sought to secure an agreement among the Iroquois nations that would peaceably solve such issues. Unable to secure agreement from his own people, he traveled to seek peace among the other Iroquois-speaking nations. One of the five nations, the Onondaga, were reluctant to join, so the Peacemaker agreed to make Onondaga, near present-day Syracuse, New York, the seat of the new Iroquois Confederacy, and to name an influential Onondaga clan leader as a leading member of the new federation. Thus the Iroquois league, or Iroquois Confederacy, was born, and served to ameliorate wrongs and misunderstandings that developed among the five nations.

At the first meeting, 49 lineages from the five nations attended, and each was given an hereditary seat on the council. Deganawida was the fiftieth leader, but no one was allowed to succeed him, while the other 49 chiefs were succeeded by males within their lineage and clan. The eldest able-bodied clan matron had the right to nominate and to impeach the lineage chief within the confederate council. Women played very important and powerful political and economic roles within Iroquois society and within the confederacy. Women held their own councils, and advised the confederate council of their decisions. In general, the members of the confederate council paid very close attention to the wishes of their mothers, aunts, and sisters. The Iroquois Confederacy played an important role in history and it continues to the present day in modified form. According to Iroquois tradition, the Great Spirit bequeathed the organization and peacemaking mission to the Iroquois, and therefore many Iroquois are greatly reluctant to adopt any changes to it.

Other northeastern nations, such as the Algonkian-speaking Delaware, Wampanoag, and Passamaquoddy did not have clan organizations similar to the Iroquois, rather they formed loose political confederacies according to alliances of bands or local villages. The Algonkian-speaking peoples lived in small settlements composed of relatives or related families, and had gardens and hunting and fishing territories that were recognized and respected by the members of other bands. They grew corn, squash, beans, and other domesticated plants.

The western part of the present-day United States and southwestern Canada, the Great Basin, Plateau, and California cultural areas were populated by hunters and gatherers. The Great Basin is a high area within the Rocky Mountains (mainly Nevada and east-central California), where the Paiute, Ute, Shoshoni, and other nations exploited sparse hunting and gathering resources in the valleys. In northern California, the culture resembled those of the Northwest Coast; the central region was greatly influenced by the Great Basin cultures, while the southern California Natives had many affinities to the desert peoples of northern Mexico and the southwest region. In the Plateau region, netting or spearing salmon along the rivers, especially the Columbia and the Fraser, was a long-time source of subsistence. Winters were spent in earthen lodges; during the warm weather, the Plateau peoples moved about to exploit salmon fishing runs, to hunt game, and to collect roots and berries in the canyons and uplands. Nez Percé, Kalispel, Flathead, and Wenatchee were some of the Native nations living in the Plateau region of present-day northeastern Washington and southern British Columbia.

Special mention should be made of the plains area, since the general image of Native Americans is that of the buffalo-hunting, horse-riding, eagle-feathered, vision-seeking plains hunter and warrior. While this view of Native Americans is almost universal, there were no such peoples living anywhere in North America before the 1700s. In the several centuries before 1500, relatively few peoples lived on the plains. Some nomadic groups followed the buffalo herds and hunted them by using buffalo hide camouflages to approach the animals. Along some of the eastern plains river valleys, there were small horticultural communities. They probably hunted buffalo with spears and bows and arrows, but they also grew corn, and most likely were greatly influenced by the woodland-horticultural cultures of the northeast or by the Mississippi cultures along the Mississippi River and some of its tributaries. In North America, horses became extinct around 8,000 B.C. with the receding of the last major glacier. Only when horses were reintroduced to North America by the Spanish after A.D. 1540 did herds of wild horses reemerge on the plains and some Native groups capture and domesticate them. Native nations such as the Sioux, Cheyenne, Kiowa, Gros Ventre, and others now closely identified with the plains culture, did not live in the plains before the 1700s. The Sioux were in what is now Minnesota, where they hunted and planted crops. The Cheyenne lived in present-day central Ontario, and the Kiowa lived in the mountains of western Mon-

tana. The Gros Ventre farmed along the Red River Valley in southern Manitoba. The well-known and idolized plains culture was developed by Native peoples who migrated into the plains relatively late in history and who had for thousands of years before lived in different ways.

1500–1599

By 1500 there may have been about seven to 15 million people living in the present-day United States and perhaps as many as one million Natives living in what is now Canada. Hundreds of distinct languages, cultures, ceremonial cycles, traditions, and social-political orders dotted the landscape.

European exploration during the sixteenth century caused considerable disruption to these Native peoples. Many Native cultures disappeared or suffered massive losses of life from epidemics and military actions. The loss of life was so great during the 1500s that we have relatively little knowledge of Native life before that time except for a few stories and the remnants found by archaeologists. During the 1500s, Natives also developed new trade relations, competitive political relations, and foreign cultures introduced by the Europeans, all of which created rapid change. Over the next 500 years, Native life was predominantly determined by its political, economic, and cultural ties to the European colonists.

As early as Christopher Columbus's second voyage in 1493, the European crews and settlers had transmitted diseases that were unknown to Native healers and usually not curable by European doctors. Over the centuries European populations had been ravaged by plague, smallpox, and influenza and the survivors had gained some immunity, but few North American Natives had built up any resistance to the new diseases. The reports of tens of millions of people dying in Mexico during the 1520s and 1530s, soon after the Spanish conquest, are difficult to comprehend. Similar epidemics seem to have spread through the eastern and southern parts of North America where early colonies were established. Many contacts with Europeans went unrecorded during this period, but it appears that Europeans regularly fished off present-day Newfoundland and traded with the Natives. Along the eastern seaboard, European ships established intermittent trade, and some sought Native slaves, which they took by force. Contacts with fishermen, explorers, and slavers presented opportunities for exchange of diseases, which appear to have spread quickly to the interior. Some archaeological evidence indicates that population losses to some communities were in the order of 90 percent, leaving only a remnant to carry on.

By 1514, at least one unknown disease had reached the Natives of Florida. When Hernando de Soto traveled the Southeast between 1539 and 1543, his army visited many Mississippi culture groups, but noted that some villages were abandoned. In 1559, when a second Spanish expedition reached present-day Pensacola Bay, Florida, its members found that the large towns noted by de Soto had coalesced into small villages. This major decentralization resulted in a reorganization of Native life. In most cases, the southeastern Natives abandoned the flat-top mounds, where priests and sacred leaders lived and ruled. The old ruling priesthoods declined in political authority and influence, and local villages and kinship groups reasserted political and economic independence. The decentralized political and ceremonial coalitions of villages formed the remnant Mississippi culture nations which became known as Cherokee, Creek, Chickasaw, Choctaw, Natchez, Coushatta, and the other southeastern nations.

In the Northeast, Jacques Cartier, a French explorer, visited the Iroquois of the St. Lawrence River, and his crew transmitted a lethal disease to them. The full effect of the epidemic is not known, but before the end of the sixteenth century, the Iroquois were forced to abandon their homeland. Algonkian-speaking nations such as the Chippewa, Ottawa, Potawatomi, and others migrated from the eastern Canadian coast and occupied the St. Lawrence River region held by the Iroquois earlier

in the century. Most likely rampant disease and early colonial settlement of French New France dispersed the Iroquois and Algonkian-speakers, and induced them to move inland.

The Native nations of present-day Virginia did not escape the outbreak of smallpox in 1564, as the disease spread among the Native nations over a region ranging from Chesapeake Bay to Florida. The Timucua, a major Florida nation, was affected, and the Powhatan, Pamunkey, and Mattaponi nations suffered incredible losses. The same epidemic was spread by traders and travelers to the Susquehannock people, who were living in what is now Pennsylvania. In 1585, English settlers brought diseases to the Roanoke Island Natives of present-day North Carolina. Also in 1585, a major epidemic spread through the North Carolina Native population, probably killing one quarter of the population. In 1586, the English explorer Francis Drake attacked St. Augustine of Florida, and introduced an unidentified but deadly disease to the Timucua Natives.

The Southwest peoples also experienced various epidemics throughout the sixteenth century. The Hopi villages along the Little Colorado River were reduced from ten to four. More epidemics in the 1620s and 1630s caused the Hopi to abandon the Little Colorado River villages and join the five Hopi villages at Black Mesa in present-day northern Arizona. Many other Pueblo peoples along the Rio Grande Valley in eastern New Mexico suffered 70 to 80 percent reductions in population due to disease.

For the many regions of North America such as California, the Pacific Northwest, the Arctic and Subarctic, there is little information about diseases or trade relations that might have affected the peoples living there. For the rest of the Native peoples who were nearer to European settlements and contacts, the sixteenth century was a period of demographic disaster. For the next four centuries, until about 1900, Native populations steadily declined, and non-Indian policymakers predicted that Natives would eventually disappear. Each succeeding century carried more diseases to the uncontaminated interior Native nations, and caused enormous losses of Native lives. The sixteenth century also saw the first attempts to create permanent European settlements in North America; these efforts significantly intensified during the next century.

1600–1699

The seventeenth century saw the establishment of a variety of major European colonies, Native incorporation into the fur trade, and the beginnings of massive losses of land and political independence among many of the coastal Native nations. During this century, the French expanded their settlement of New France, or present-day eastern Canada; the Swedes, Dutch, and English established colonies in what is now New Jersey, New York, Virginia, Pennsylvania, South Carolina, and New England. The Spanish held and expanded their colonies in Florida and West Florida (present-day Alabama and Mississippi), and supported their royal colony in present-day New Mexico. In 1699, the French established Louisiana Colony. While throughout the century epidemics continued to take a heavy toll among Native nations, the establishment of rival European colonial empires presented a different kind of threat to Native land, hunting, and trade resources. Many coastal Native nations were forced to migrate into the interior in order to gain relief from colonial land expansion and political domination.

While the fur trade between the Europeans and Native nations began in the sixteenth century, it became the primary economic tie between many Natives and newcomers during the seventeenth century. Native peoples quickly saw the utility of metal axes, knives, needles, and traps, as well as textiles and other goods. A farmer with a metal axe could clear the same amount of land as ten men with stone axes. Trading with the Europeans for metal goods and textiles, many Natives stopped making stone and bone implements. Soon most Natives preferred to hunt and trap, and then trade for metal goods and other manufactured goods.

Furthermore, slave trading was still rampant in the seventeenth century, and Native people were captured and sold in the colonies. Consequently, some Native nations began to supply captives to the Europeans for trade. Europeans organized Native slave raids on interior nations and supplied their Natives with guns, powder, and lead. The slave raids were especially fierce among the Choctaw of present-day Mississippi and Louisiana during the 1680s and 1690s. So many Choctaw were carted off to slavery that it is now almost impossible to reconstruct their social and political organization for the period before 1650; at least two major social and political divisions were so depleted of people that they joined other Choctaw districts. After 1670, Cherokee, Creek, and Chickasaw participated with Englishmen from Charlestown in the slave raids and trade. The Cherokee and Chickasaw also heavily raided the Shawnee of what is now Kentucky and Ohio, and by the 1690s the Shawnee decided to move out of the area and seek refuge among the Creek in present-day Alabama, in Georgia along the Savannah River (which is named after the Shawnee), and among the Delaware near present-day Philadelphia. Slave raiding continued into the 1700s, but by the early eighteenth century, Indian slaves were difficult to contain within the lands they know well and where they had many potential allies. Furthermore, many Natives died in captivity. Consequently, by 1720, the Indian slave trade declined and was supplanted by the fur trade as the primary economic tie between Natives and the southern colonies. Indian slaves were shipped to the Caribbean Islands, where they were easier to control, and black slaves imported from Africa became the preferred labor of the southern plantation owners.

The fur trade brought many changes to Native economies. Native hunters, who once gathered only enough animal meat and skins to supply their subsistence needs, now became specialized hunters and trappers. Some spent considerable time, sometimes up to six months, hunting and trapping in order to trade for European manufactured goods. Beaver and deerskins were the primary pelts traded, with deerskins made into leather and beaver pelts valued by Europeans for making hats. European demand for furs led to the overexploitation of fur-bearing animals in many coastal regions by the 1640s.

The Iroquois Confederacy sought trade and diplomatic agreements with the Iroquois nations of the lower Great Lakes, including the Neutral Nation, Petun, and Huron, but these nations traded with the French, while the Five Nations traded with the Dutch at Fort Orange (Albany) in New Holland. The French did not wish to lose their trade, and prevented their Iroquoian and Algonkian-speaking allies from making trade agreements with the Iroquois. With the help of weapons and ammunition from Dutch traders, the Iroquois initiated the Beaver Wars, a series of battles marked with intermittent periods of peace, that lasted from about 1649 to 1700. The Iroquois warriors, supported by the Dutch, destroyed the Iroquoian nations of the lower Great Lakes and either adopted their survivors or sent them farther into the interior to the upper Great Lakes. English and Dutch traders continued to support the Iroquois trade expansion into the interior region in order to gain access to the Native nations there. The French were reluctant to supply their Native trade allies with more than a few weapons, and hence the Iroquois had a clear military advantage. The other French-allied Algonkian-speaking nations, the Chippewa, Ottawa, and Potawatomi, also were pushed farther west into the Great Lakes region, where they encountered and fought the local nations such as the Winnebago, the Illinois, and the Sioux. Thereafter, the Ottawa became the major trade partners with the French at Quebec and Montreal.

The Native nations along the eastern seaboard encountered considerable difficulties with the European colonists, and soon were struggling to maintain their territory and political independence. Relatively small coastal nations such as the Delaware exhausted their supplies of beaver, and, unable to move into the interior because of powerful Iroquoian peoples, were reduced to selling game, baskets, and land to the Europeans in order to gain trade goods. By 1675, most Delaware had migrated to present-day eastern Pennsylvania to land granted to them by the Iroquois. Members of other remnant coastal Algonkian-speaking nations such as the Munsee joined the Delaware, as well as segments of the Shawnee and a remnant of the Iroquoian-speaking Susquehannock from southern Pennsylvania, who were decimated by war and disease. Through the next several centuries, the Delaware were constantly forced to migrate further into the interior until the main group settled in present-day Oklahoma in the late 1860s.

The Natives of New England rapidly lost political independence to the Puritans of Massachusetts Colony, which was founded in 1630. In 1636–37, the Pequot of present-day Connecticut were induced to war with the English and suffered badly. Some Pequot left New England and joined the Shawnee, but a few stayed and were subject to Puritan and later Connecticut law. Similarly, the other Massachusetts Natives, especially the Wampanoag Confederacy, were subdued in King Phillip's War of 1675–76. The Wampanoags were unable to tolerate the political and economic abuses of the Puritans and rose in arms to preserve their culture and political freedom. The Wampanoags were defeated, and most Natives in Massachusetts and southern New England were forced to abide by Puritan rule. After 1690, the government of England took control of the Puritan colonies because of religious excesses and political abuses. The Natives of New England were made subject to English law, and led economically and politically marginal lives on the edge of New England society. About 16 Native communities became Christians and formed "praying towns," which adopted New England Protestantism and town hall government.

The Natives of Virginia fared no better than those of New England. Soon after the establishment of Jamestown Colony in 1607, the English hoped to expand their farming activities and to appropriate the cleared fields and farms of the Mattaponi, Chickahominy, Rappahannock, and other members of the Powhatan Confederacy. By the 1620s tensions broke into war, with the colonists gaining the upper hand. By the 1640s, the Powhatan Confederacy again went to war against English territorial expansion and other political and economic abuses. Again the English gained more ground as a result of war. In the 1670s, during Bacon's Rebellion, another war was carried on by the Virginians against the Natives, and more land and political freedom was lost. By the late 1690s, the Native nations of Virginia and Maryland were subject to colonial law, and to a large extent dispossessed of their coastal lands. Disease and war caused their populations to decline significantly, and the colonists outnumbered the Natives. By 1700, the colonial governments largely ignored the Native peoples of the middle Atlantic colonies. The Natives, though politically and economically marginalized, endured as small communities but remained targets of land speculators, who tried to acquire the remnants of land the Natives continued to hold.

During the late 1600s many Native groups began migrating westward, out of the way of colonial expansion and other Native nations that were pushed west because of the Beaver Wars. The Cheyenne living in central Ontario started moving west, and by the late 1600s were living in present-day Minnesota; in the next century, they migrated onto the plains. Some of the first Sioux people, now called the Assiniboine, began to migrate onto the plains in the late 1600s, where horses and buffalo were in good supply. During the late 1600s and 1700s, Chippewa bands, armed with French trade weapons, attacked Sioux settlements in Minnesota, and pressured more Sioux toward the plains. The Athapascan-speakers, later known as Apache, began raiding Caddoan settlements in the lower Mississippi Valley and the Pueblo and Spanish settlements in present-day eastern New Mexico. The Apache acquired horses, which made them extremely mobile and enabled them to raid horticultural peoples along the river valleys. Some Athapascan-speakers took up farming, and obtained sheep and learned to pasture and breed them, along with horses. These

peoples were later identified by the Spanish as "Navajo."

The sixteenth century was a difficult one for the Pueblo peoples of the Southwest. At the beginning of the century, the Spanish had established New Mexico, a royal colony. Since precious metals were not found in New Mexico, the king of Spain declared the area a missionary field and subsidized soldiers and missionaries to live there and to subdue the Natives. The Spanish demanded labor, political submission, and acceptance of Catholicism from the Pueblos. Natives were commandeered to work on the ranches and farms of military officers and Spanish land grantees, as well as to build churches and to provide farms and food for the mission priests and their staffs. These requirements, similar to feudal European serf labor, were alien to the Pueblos and very much resented by them.

In 1609 the Spanish established their headquarters at Santa Fe, a location near many of the Pueblo villages. An uneasy peace reigned, and, while some Pueblos were willing to accept Christianity, many continued to practice Pueblo religions. The Spanish authorities arrested about 30 leading Pueblo religious leaders and accused them of witchcraft. After this incident, one of the Pueblo leaders, known as Popé, organized a rebellion. In 1680, they killed many of the Catholic priests and attacked the Spanish garrison at Santa Fe. For the next 12 years, the Pueblos remained free. In 1692, however, the Spanish returned and fighting soon erupted when many Pueblos refuse to vacate Spanish-built compounds in Santa Fe. By 1696, most Pueblos were subdued. Many migrated; in particular some Tewa joined the Hopi at First Mesa in present-day Arizona and some Jemez joined the Navajo. The Navajo learned much of Pueblo culture from the war refugees, and Navajo pottery, ceremony, and sacred stories owe much to Pueblo influence. As a result of the 1680 revolt, and negotiations leading to peace in the 1690s, the Pueblos gained from the Spanish rights to territory, the end of labor demands, and greater tolerance of Pueblo ceremonies and religion. Many Pueblo believe that the revolt of 1680 helped ensure the survival of Pueblo communities, land bases, and religions.

1700–1799

In the eighteenth century, intensified colonial economic competition and military conflict involved many eastern North American Native nations. The struggle for control of Indian fur trade, and political alliance by French, English, and Spanish colonies, directly or indirectly affected most eastern Native societies by the end of the century. During this time, many Native peoples had their first regular contact with European traders or colonists. This was the case in California where Spanish missions were established after 1768; in Alaska where Russian missionaries, traders, and officials established a colony; in the Canadian North; and in the plains where Native peoples maintained trade relations with French and other traders. In the eastern portion of North America, there was almost constant warfare among the European colonies, and the eastern Native peoples were drawn into the conflicts because they were dependent on trade for manufactured goods and for weapons for hunting and defense. This dependence deepened throughout the century. Some Native nations, like the Winnebago, Chippewa, and perhaps the Menominee, abandoned older forms of matrilineal clan organization and began to hunt, trap, and live in small patrilineal bands that were suited to the European traders' preference for dealing with male heads of households. Diseases continued to rage among the Natives, causing a steady decline in population and disruption of Native economic, political, and social relations.

EASTERN NATIVE NATIONS

In 1699, the French established Louisiana Colony and initiated a plan to contain the English colonies to the Atlantic seaboard by creating a chain of forts and alliances with Native nations along the Mississippi and Ohio valleys. There emerged an active trade and military competition to control the Mississippi River, a competition in which the Chickasaw became a major English ally and trading partner and ultimately prevented the French from completing their plan. The major colonial conflicts were Queen Anne's War (1702–13), King William's War (1744–48), the French and Indian War (1754–60) known as the Seven Years' War in Europe (1756–63), and the American Revolutionary War (1775–83).

After the Revolutionary War, peace was not established with the Natives on the Ohio and southern frontiers until 1795, when both the British and the Spanish decided not to provide their Native allies with weapons and military supplies to resist U.S. expansion into the interior of the continent. The eastern Native nations were then forced to recognize the United States as the major power in the region.

As the European colonies grew more powerful, the Native peoples were required to defend their territorial and trade interests. Many of the northern Algonkian-speaking nations of present-day southern Canada were allied closely with the French and only reluctantly accepted English alliance after 1760. The Cherokee developed a long-standing trade relation with South Carolina, while most Choctaw preferred trade and military alliance with the French in the Louisiana Colony. The Creek and Iroquois Confederacy both built alliances among Native nations and remnant groups. The Iroquois offered the alliance of peace granted by the peacemaker Deganawida, and after 1700 went about creating trade and diplomatic ties with many of the interior Algonkian-speaking nations that they had fought during the Beaver Wars (1649–1700). By the late 1690s, the Iroquois were severely beleaguered from their wars with the French and their Native allies.

The English began settling the Mohawk Valley, land which the Iroquois considered their own. The chiefs of the confederacy decided that the English were as big a threat to their people as the French. Thereafter, the Iroquois tried to avoid wars and worked to balance their trade and political relations between the French and English. By making treaties with both European colonies, the Iroquois hoped to gain trade, diplomatic, and material advantages. In addition, the Iroquois claimed to have created an alliance of over 50 Native interior nations and stated they could muster their warriors if necessary. Most likely this Iroquois claim was primarily a bargaining point, for it seems doubtful that the Iroquois ever commanded such a large force of men from other Native nations. The Iroquois plan was based on offering the interior nations, such as the Chippewa, Illinois, Wyandot, and others access to the trade at Albany (New York) where English goods were cheaper, more varied, and of better quality than those of the French. This plan unraveled in the 1740s, when Pennsylvania traders followed the Delaware and Shawnee to the Ohio Valley and began to trade in the Native villages. Thereafter the Iroquois fortunes steadily declined, although the English supported the confederacy in order to gain trade and diplomatic access to the interior nations.

During the 1750s, the Delaware and Shawnee, unhappy with Iroquois leadership and greatly interested in halting further colonial expansion, took the initiative in forming and leading a confederacy of Indian nations from the Ohio and Great Lakes regions. At the end of the French and Indian War, the English assumed control of trade and military supplies, and many Native nations were fearful that English restrictions on trade in guns and the discontinuance of diplomatic gifts of trade goods meant that they were planning to retaliate against the Natives for their part in the war. Therefore, Pontiac, an Ottawa leader, started to organize an alliance of nations to prevent the English from occupying the formerly French forts in the Great Lakes region. At the same time, a prophet emerged among the Delaware, preaching that the Great Spirit in heaven had instructed him to tell the Native people that they must return to the lifestyle of hunting and living of their forebears, and must throw off all that they had taken from the Europeans, including their clothes and goods. Furthermore, the Natives must drive the Europeans from the continent before the Natives could achieve salvation in heaven. Pontiac associated himself with the Delaware prophet and mustered forces to attack the British-occupied forts in 1763. Although the Natives did not drive out the British, they were able to gain better trade and diplomatic relations.

The Native confederation was revived during Lord Dunmore's War (1773–74), when Virginia settlers threatened Shawnee land in the Ohio Valley. After the American Revolutionary War, Little Turtle, a Miami war chief, led a confederacy of Native nations against the United States during a series of battles in 1790 to 1794. After the battle of Fallen Timbers in 1794, the Native confederates realized that the English would not support their fight against the U.S. invasion of the Ohio Valley. Late in 1794, the United States and Britain signed Jay's Treaty, after which the British retreated from the forts in the Old Northwest and relocated in southern Canada. The Natives were left to negotiate a treaty with the United States at Greenville (present-day Indiana) in 1795.

In the Southeast, the Creek followed a strategy of balancing off the French in Louisiana and Fort Toulouse (present-day Jacksonville, Alabama), the Spanish in Florida, and the English in Carolina and later Georgia. The Creek first challenged the English colonists by supporting the Yamasee in a war with Carolina in 1715, but defeat led the Creek to adopt a new strategy of playing off each colonial power to secure trade goods and diplomatic gifts. The Creek also adopted remnant nations that were retreating from coastal conflicts with the colonists. Many small villages and tribes joined the Creek Confederacy and were allowed to retain their own traditions, language, religion, and local government, but were obligated to adhere to the laws and participate in the sacred rituals of the Creek. The Creek Confederacy continued its balance of power strategy until 1795, when the Spanish withdrew their military support for containing the expansion of the U.S. colonies. Thereafter, the Creek, as well as the Cherokee, Choctaw, and Chickasaw, were obligated in treaties to recognize U.S. dominance within the southeastern area.

After the defeat of the French in late December 1759 at Montreal, the British won control of New France. At the end of the Seven Years' War, they also won control of Florida from the Spanish. During the 1760s, the British gained European-recognized domination of eastern and northern North America and moved to establish law over its new territories with the Royal Proclamation of 1763. The proclamation restricted settlers to the eastern divide of the Appalachian Mountains, and reserved for the Native peoples the land west of the divide. British manufacturers and fur trading interests persuaded the British government to protect the lands and rights of Native hunters and trappers. In Canadian Native law, the Proclamation of 1763 became an important legal document, creating the doctrine that the Crown, or regent of England, owned the land and that the Natives had land rights largely at the pleasure of the Crown.

Before the British could establish administrative control over the Natives in eastern North America, however, the Revolutionary War started. The restriction on settlements west of the Appalachian Mountains was a major concern of the colonists, since settlers were streaming into Native territories such as present-day Ohio, Kentucky, and Tennessee and causing considerable conflict with the Native peoples. The Revolutionary War saw the revival of rival colonial powers and intense military and diplomatic conflict, and many Native nations were called upon to choose sides between the British and the colonists. The Iroquois Confederacy in 1777 was divided: Some under the leadership of the Mohawk Joseph Brant sided with the British; the Seneca, Cayuga, and Onondaga preferred neutrality; the Oneida and Tuscarora favored the colonists. According to the laws of the confederacy, if a decision was not unanimous, then nations, clans, lineages, and individuals were free to choose their own paths. The confederacy split, and was never fully restored. When the British lost the war, the Iroquois under Brant settled permanently in present-day southern Ontario, where they were given a small reservation, now called Six Nations Reserve. The leaders of the Turtle division of the Delaware favored the colonists and signed the first Native treaty in 1778 with the Continental Congress, but members of the Turkey and Wolf divisions feared that the colonists could not supply trade goods, weapons, and ammunition and therefore allied with the British. The Creek and the Cherokee also were divided over whose side to take, although toward the end of the war the Creek gravitated toward the British due to lack of supplies and ill treatment at the hands of the colonists. The Chickamauga, a group of Cherokee villages, sided with the British, but most Cherokee leaders wished to maintain neutrality, remembering that in 1760 they fought a war with the colonists in which many Cherokee villages were destroyed and many people killed.

The wars of Napoleon and the signing of the Treaty of San Lorenzo (1795) with the United States caused the Spanish to turn their attention to Europe and away from the poor and financially draining Florida colonies. Without Spanish support the major southern nations signed treaties with the United States in the late 1790s. The peace, however, was extremely tenuous. Settlers could not be controlled by the U.S. government or the army and continuous land encroachments created border hostilities. The United States did not secure authoritative control over the eastern portion of the country until 1820.

SOUTHWEST NATIVE NATIONS

During the eighteenth century, the Pueblos worked out stable political and economic relations with the Spanish in New Mexico. The Pueblo Revolt of 1680 had secured their freedom from forced labor and some political and religious freedom. The Pueblos accepted missionaries into their villages on condition that they did not interfere with traditional beliefs and ceremonies. The Hopi, living farthest away from the Spanish, were most reluctant to take up Spanish Catholicism, and destroyed the mission at Awatowi in 1700. The Spanish and Pueblo established regular trade relations with the Navajo and Apache, who lived in mobile bands and were starting to move into New Mexican Territory. During the 1700s and 1800s, the eastern Apache migrated across New Mexico, and many settled in what is now Arizona. The Navajo incorporated sheep herding into their economy and continued to trade with the Spanish and Pueblos.

Between 1769 and 1820, many Spanish missions were also built in California, with the first at San Diego. The Franciscan priests induced thousands of Natives to join the missions, and used severe disciplinary methods to maintain control. The Natives were required to live and work within the society of the mission and to give up traditional cultures. Heavy work for building the missions caused great strain among the Natives and diseases spread rapidly, killing many of them. Many surviving Natives became Christians and most lost major parts of their traditional religions and cultures.

PLAINS CULTURE

Many new groups entered the plains area during the 1700s, and firmly established the well-known features of the Plains culture consisting of horseback riding, the Sun Dance, sacred bundles, large-scale buffalo hunting, mobile tipis, and soldier societies. From the eastern woodlands around Lake Superior, the Cheyenne and the Lakota Sioux migrated to the northern plains. They were woodland people who grew corn, gathered wild plants, and hunted, but they soon adopted the plains culture.

At the same time, the sedentary plains peoples who lived in the lower Missouri Valley—the Pawnee, Oto, Hidatsa and others—declined in population and were subject to raids by the migratory plains people. The cornfields were difficult to defend and the raids forced many farmers like the Pawnee to adopt the horse-raiding style that was emerging. The Hidatsa and Arikara migrated up the Missouri River and settled near present-day Bismarck, North Dakota. The Crow, a segment group of the related Hidatsa and Arikara, broke away on a religious quest to find a place for themselves, as seen in a vision by their leader. The Crow migrated northward into present-day western Canada, but again turned southward and even-

tually settled in what is now southern Montana. The Kiowa and Comanche migrated to the southern plains from the Rocky Mountains and eventually settled in present-day northern Texas and Oklahoma.

ARCTIC AND SUBARCTIC NATIVE CULTURES

During the 1700s, trade goods from the Hudson's Bay Company reached into the Arctic and Subarctic regions. An extensive network brought trade goods to the Rocky Mountains and the Great Basin. Horses became more available, primarily through raiding, and the Ute in the southern Great Basin and the Nez Percé in the Columbia Basin gained greater mobility for gathering food, defense, fighting their enemies, and trading with their friends.

Russian explorers began sailing along the Alaska coast by 1741 and reported good prospects for trade in seal and otter skins. During the 1700s, these skins were in high demand in China, where they were used to make clothing. By the 1760s, Russian traders and Russian Orthodox priests were extending political and cultural influence over the Aleutian Islands and along the southern coastal regions of Alaska. Russian forts and trading establishments eventually were located as far south as northern California. The Aleut people, in particular, suffered at the hands of the Russians; many were forced to hunt and secure furs for the Russian trading company—The Russian-American Company. Aleutian population declined and the culture disintegrated under the force of Russian political and cultural domination. The Tlingit, however, living on the panhandle, kept their political and cultural independence, although the Russian colonial headquarters was located at New Archangel, or present-day Sitka, Alaska, the site of a long-time Tlingit village. The Tlingit quickly joined in the fur trade with the Russians, and added new-found wealth to their traditional potlatch ceremonies. The Tlingit established trade networks with the Athapascan-speaking Natives of the western subarctic, and served as lucrative middlemen between the Russian, and later the British and American, trading companies. By 1785, many Pacific Northwest peoples including the Haida, Nootka, Tsimshian, Tlingit, and Bella Coola were trading seal and otter skins to the Russians, British, and "Boston Men," as the Americans were called. Missions often accompanied the establishment of major Russian trade posts, and many Natives in the Aleutian Islands and along the southern coast of Alaska converted to the Russian Orthodox religion.

The eighteenth century saw expansion of European trade networks to even the most isolated Native North Americans. The colonial wars, colonial expansion, and the emergence of the United States all contributed to the disruption of Native life. Native groups like the Chippewa pushed into present-day Minnesota and in turn pressured many Sioux to move onto the plains; the Coushatta sought refuge under Spanish protection in present-day Texas; and the newly formed Seminole, who were composed of Hitchiti and Muskogee peoples, sought refuge in Florida. The Seminole had since the 1750s been drifting southward into Florida, in part because of differences with the English colonial officials and with the actions and policies of the Creek Confederacy. Groups of Shawnee, Delaware, Peoria, and Piankashaw sought economic security and peace by migrating across the Mississippi River to lands offered to them by the Spanish.

By the end of the century, many eastern Native nations were forced to reconcile themselves to life under an expansionist United States. The U.S. government initiated policies of assimilation and hired missionaries to teach Natives farming and to educate and Christianize their children. Congress appropriated funds and by the late 1790s Quaker missionaries were at work among the Seneca on the northern Pennsylvania reservation of the influential war chief, Cornplanter.

1800–1899

During the 1800s, Canada emerged as an independent dominion within the British Empire, and the United States expanded across the conti-

nent. By the 1890s most Native North American peoples were relegated to small portions of land under heavy administrative control by the U.S. or Canadian government. Throughout the century Native peoples were severely pressed as settlers, land speculators, gold miners, and, after the 1870s, railroads, pushed across the continent. During the eighteenth century the pace of expansion was so rapid that most Native societies had little time to react or adjust. Not only did the Native North Americans face daunting political obstacles, but diseases continued to take a considerable toll, especially in the plains area. Toward the end of the century Native population declined to its lowest point since the landing of Columbus in 1492.

UNITED STATES

During the first years of the 1800s, U.S. policy toward Natives continued to focus on assimilation. It was thought that if the Natives adopted farming and Christianity, they would more willingly surrender the vast lands needed for hunting and trapping, and more willingly accept eventual U.S. citizenship. When the United States purchased the Louisiana Territory from the French in 1803, the plan to remove all Natives across the Mississippi River was born. Although the United States had limited success inducing Natives to voluntarily migrate west, treaty commissioners, nevertheless, maintained an active campaign to buy land from the Natives, to make way for settlers in the Old Northwest and in the South. Nearly every year Native leaders were pressed to sell land. These land sales, especially among the Natives of the Old Northwest, were the cause of considerable resentment against the United States.

EARLY RELIGIOUS MOVEMENTS Throughout the century a series of Native religious movements emerged under the rapidly changing political, economic, and cultural climate of North America. Some major movements became established religions, including the Peyote Church, the Dreamer religion, the Kickapoo Prophet's community, the Shaker Church, and the Handsome Lake Church. Other movements like the two Ghost Dances of

1870 and 1890, the Winnebago Prophet, the Cherokee religious movement of 1810–12, and the Shawnee Prophet of 1806–11 did not have lasting effects on Native cultures. All the movements, nevertheless, were attempts to create cultural solutions to evolving conditions that endangered the Natives' traditional ways or threatened to leave them politically and economically marginalized.

The Cherokee movement was very short-lived. In 1811 and 1812, several Cherokee saw visions that said the spirits were unhappy with the Cherokee for leaving their sacred sites and towns and for abandoning many of the ancient customs in favor of mills, U.S. dress, farms, and plantations. Several prophets emerged and predicted that all unbelievers would perish in a fiery hailstorm, while believers would be saved if they congregated at certain mountain tops. After the predictions did not come to pass, the prophets were discredited and the movement died out.

The most enduring of the early religious movements were created by the Seneca Handsome Lake and Kenekuk of the Vermillion band of Kickapoo. In 1799, Handsome Lake started having visions that gave instructions to the Seneca and Iroquois about how to change their religion and lives. By the late 1790s, the New York Iroquois were separated from their brethren at Six Nations Reserve in Ontario, and had sold nearly all their land except small reservations in upstate New York and Cornplanter's private reserve in northern Pennsylvania. The Iroquois were socially and economically depressed and were having a difficult time adjusting to the sedentary and restricted life of a small reservation. Considerable alcohol abuse, unwillingness to adopt agriculture, family breakups, and internal political disunity were making life increasingly difficult for them. Handsome Lake taught that the Iroquois must change or they would perish as a people. He said that the Great Spirit had instructed him to teach the people, and he established a new religion that incorporated selected traditional ceremonies and Christian beliefs such as personal salvation, reward in heaven, and punishment in hell. The new moral code, or

the "Good Word," of Handsome Lake gave religious assurances to the Iroquois to abandon abuse of alcohol, allowed men to take up farming, introduced a new code of personal responsibility, and ended some family and moral abuses. Handsome Lake's new religion helped the Iroquois to become a nation of farmers. It also combined traditional and Christian concepts that were acceptable and believable within the Seneca and Iroquois communities, and that enabled the Iroquois to construct farming communities within the economic and political situation of small reservations. After Handsome Lake's death in 1815, the religion was carried on. In the 1830s, it took on the form of a church, which continues to serve Iroquois peoples to the present day.

By the early 1800s, Kenekuk of the Vermillion band of Kickapoo was dismayed at the destruction that had befallen his people. He began preaching a religion that contained traditional, Protestant, and Catholic elements, but which remained uniquely Kickapoo. Like Handsome Lake of the Senecas, Kenekuk taught nonviolence, and created a set of moral teachings based on individual responsibility, advocated adoption of farming, and strongly resisted removal. He introduced concepts of heavenly reward, personal salvation, and confession of sins. The prophet enforced strict regulations against drinking and other activities he considered detrimental to group cohesion, discipline, and survival. Nevertheless, after considerable resistance, his community was forced to remove from their homeland in present-day Illinois. In 1833, he and his followers moved west to Indian Territory, in present-day Kansas. In 1851 the prophet's community was joined by a band of Potawatomi. Kenekuk died in 1853, but he left a religion which has continued providing his people with an enduring spiritual legacy that has enabled them to survive as a community and to accommodate to changing economic and political circumstances.

Another major movement was initiated by Tenskwatawa, "The Open Door," who in early 1806 had visions of the Great Spirit giving him instructions for the Native people. While living among the Delaware villages in present-day Indiana, Tenskwatawa was influenced by the Munsee Prophetess who initiated ceremonial and religious changes among the Munsee and Delaware. Tenskwatawa and his brother Tecumseh were Shawnee, who for many years lived with and allied themselves to the Delaware. The Shawnee Prophet taught that the unfortunate condition of the Natives was due to their ready acceptance of European trade, material goods, and lifestyle. He instructed people to reject fur trading, and to return to the religion, bows and arrows, and lifestyle of their forebears, then the Great Spirit would provide them with peace and plenty. Many Natives believed that Tenskwatawa was a personification of a great creator figure. As such, many Natives believed that Tenskwatawa had great powers and provided a solution to the declining economic, demographic, and political conditions of the Native peoples. While Tecumseh was traveling among the Chickasaw, Creek, and Choctaw in the south to rally their support for a Native alliance against the United States, in November of 1811 a U.S. army force led by future U.S. president William Henry Harrison approached the prophet's village of Tippecanoe in present-day Indiana. The prophet told his men that he would perform ceremonies that would protect them from the weapons of the U.S. soldiers. However, when the Natives of several nations attacked the U.S. camp, they suffered significant casualties. After the battle, many Native warriors were understandably angry with the prophet and abandoned his teachings.

REMOVAL TRENDS AFTER 1812 The War of 1812 marked a major watershed for the Natives of eastern North America. At the 1814 Treaty of Ghent, which ended the war, the British agreed to refrain from interfering with the Native peoples. The British would no longer supply trade or diplomatic goods and would make no alliances of mutual military support with the Native nations within the sphere of influence of the United States. In return, the British insisted that the Natives be restored to their territories. Furthermore, by 1819 and 1820, the Spanish believed they could no longer hold onto Florida within the crumbling Spanish Empire, and in treaty yielded present-day

Florida, Alabama, and Mississippi to the United States. Consequently, by 1820, the United States had gained undisputed domination over the eastern part of the country.

Until the administration of President Andrew Jackson (1829–37), the government used persuasion to induce the Natives to migrate west—with little success. After 1829, the Jackson administration launched a concerted effort to remove Natives from the East. This effort culminated in the Indian Removal Act of 1830, which provided funds and authorization to remove Native people west of the Mississippi River. The southern Native nations were well aware of U.S. intentions, and actively sought to remain in their territories. The Cherokee in northwest Georgia, eastern Tennessee, and northern Alabama resisted by adopting a constitutional government in 1828. The constitution stated that the Cherokee people were not willing to cede their homeland. The state of Georgia greatly disliked the declaration of the Cherokee constitution, and after Jackson's election declared Georgia law over the Cherokee Nation within Georgia chartered limits, and abolished the Cherokee government except for the purpose of negotiating a removal treaty. Furthermore, the Georgians gave away Cherokee land by lottery, and many Cherokee were dispossessed of their farms and plantations. The discovery of gold in Cherokee country brought more Georgians and more abuses. The Cherokee had no legal or property rights in Georgia courts and were not citizens of the United States. At least one Cherokee was executed under Georgia state law before the Cherokee government could appeal his conviction in federal court.

The Cherokee government, with the aid of President Jackson's political opponents, appealed to the U.S. Supreme Court under a clause in the Constitution that allows foreign nations to sue for damages caused by U.S. citizens or governments. The court ruled in *Cherokee Nation v. Georgia* (1831) that the Cherokee were not a foreign nation, but more like a "domestic dependent nation" and therefore could not sue for redress under the U.S. Constitution. The decision, a landmark case in Indian law, restricts the foreign status of Native nations. Since the Cherokee were not U.S. citizens, they did not have rights in federal or state courts. The Cherokee government and allies circumvented this ruling by asking several U.S. missionaries to challenge Georgia laws. Two finally agreed. Samuel Worcester and an associate Presbyterian missionary named Butterick carried on Cherokee Nation business and were arrested when they refused to recognize Georgia law in the Cherokee Nation. They were tried and sentenced to several years' hard labor in a Georgia prison. The Cherokee government appealed the sentence in a case known as *Worcester v. Georgia* (1832). It was the opinion of the court that Georgia did not have the right to extend its laws over the Cherokee Nation. According to the commerce clause of the Constitution, only the federal government had the right to regulate trade and relations with the Indian nations. The decision was considered a great victory in the Cherokee Nation, but the court did not order an injunction against Georgia and did not prevent Georgia from eventually forcing the Cherokee from their homeland.

President Jackson would not enforce the ruling, fearing that the enforcement of federal rights over Georgia would fracture the already fragile U.S. union. Consequently, he advised the Cherokee to remove. After six months in prison, Worcester and Butterick were freed, and Worcester moved his mission west of the Mississippi River, believing that the Cherokee could no longer safely live in the East. Most Cherokee refused to move, but, by 1835, many Cherokee planters believed that the nation could not survive in the East. They signed the Treaty of New Echota and agreed to move to Indian Territory. Most Cherokee resisted, but, in the summer of 1838, U.S. troops rounded up the majority and induced them to migrate west in the fall and winter of 1838–39. A small group escaped to the mountains, and their descendants now comprise the Eastern Cherokee living in Qualla Boundary Reservation and other Cherokee communities in North Carolina. In the march west, called the Trail of Tears, about a quarter of the Cherokee, mostly very old or very young, died. This greatly embittered the surviving Cherokee against the signers of the Treaty of New Echota, and political conflict prevailed for the rest of the century, if it does not persist to the present. After some conflict and negotiation, the Cherokee reestablished their constitutional government in 1839, only to have it abolished by the United States in 1907.

The Choctaw formed a constitutional government in 1826, and retained three regional chiefs as executive. An attempt to centralize the government failed in 1830, and in the same year at Dancing Rabbit Creek, the Choctaw leaders were coerced into signing a removal treaty. Most Choctaw migrated west to Indian Territory in the early 1830s, while others remained and formed the Mississippi Choctaw, as they are known today. Between 1834 and 1860, the Choctaw incrementally formed a constitutional government, which they lived under until it was abolished in 1907 to make way for the state of Oklahoma. The Chickasaw signed a removal treaty in 1836 and after 1837 migrated west to settle with the Choctaw. They separated from the Choctaw in 1855 and formed their own constitutional government in 1856. The Chickasaw government was also abolished in 1907.

The Creek tried desperately to remain in their home territories in Georgia and Alabama, but by 1836 were overwhelmed by settlers. After a conflict called the Creek War of 1836, caused by starving members of several villages, most Creek leaders decided to migrate to Indian Territory. A few Creek communities remained behind, and in recent years one of the eastern Creek communities, the Poarch Creek band, gained federal recognition as an Indian tribe. In Indian Territory, the Creek continued their traditions. In 1867 after the Civil War, the former Creek planter class insisted on abolishing the traditional government of a council of village chiefs and demanded a constitutional government, which was adopted. The first elections resulted in controversy, and the Creek conservatives repudiated the constitutional government. Disagreement over the form of government continued until 1907, when the constitution was abolished.

The removal policy affected mostly those nations in the present-day eastern United States. Indian Territory was established in what is now Kansas and Oklahoma, and during the 1840s and 1850s there was talk of creating an Indian state that would have representatives in Congress. The plan of Indian statehood was never achieved, and soon after the Civil War, train companies and settlers clamored for the opening of Indian Territory. Native peoples such as the Delaware, Shawnee, and Pawnee were removed from Kansas and resettled in Oklahoma. Other groups also were removed to Indian Territory including the Northern Cheyenne, some rebellious Modoc, Geronimo, some of his Apache associates, and his family, a group of Papago, and others. Many northern plains groups, such as the Northern Cheyenne, did not want to live in Indian Territory, and in 1877 made a daring escape led by Lone Wolf and Dull Knife to return to their homeland. They eventually were captured, and in 1883 were granted a reservation on the Tongue River in eastern Montana. After this and other desperate escapes, the U.S. government ended its policy of removal to Indian Territory and left most Native peoples to live on small reservations nearer to their traditional homelands.

After 1870, railroad companies built tracks through Indian Territory and soon U.S. citizens outnumbered the Natives. During the 1880s and 1890s, land in Indian Territory was opened to U.S. settlers. After Congress passed the General Allotment Act of 1887, much of the land in Indian Territory was parceled to individual Indians, who according to government policy were to farm the land. The surplus lands were opened to U.S. settlers. Many Indian Territory nations including the Comanche, Kiowa, Southern Cheyenne, Southern Arapaho were affected by allotment policies, and lost most if not all of their communal lands. The Cherokee, Choctaw, Chickasaw, and Seminole escaped the 1887 Allotment Act because of alliances to powerful Texas cattlemen who rented their land for grazing, but were included in the 1898 Curtis Act, which set the stage for the allotment of their lands and abolishment of their

governments in 1907. In 1907, Indian Territory became the state of Oklahoma. Most of the Native peoples were settled onto allotments and little remained of communal tribal land, although Native governments continued to operate, primarily to manage the remaining landed estate. The principal chiefs, or governors, were appointed by U.S. officials. Oklahoma statehood did not abolish the culture and community of Oklahoma Indians, but over the next 50 years many lost their allotments by fraud, poverty, and failure to pay taxes or mortgages. During the twentieth century, however, Oklahoma Indians would make a political and cultural resurgence.

SOUTHWEST NATIVE NATIONS In the Southwest, the Spanish continued to interact with the cultures and peoples in the region until they were ousted by the Mexican Revolution of 1820 and many Franciscan missionaries were sent back to Spain. After 1820, Mexican control and interest in the distant New Mexico was weak, and there was little financial support from the new Mexican government. In the early 1820s, New Mexico opened the Santa Fe trail, which invited U.S. merchants and trade and initiated U.S. interest in the region. Sporadic conflicts continued between the Mexicans and various Navajo and Apache bands. In general, the Pueblo peoples accepted Christianity, but during this time of loose Mexican administrative control, they maintained their religions and communities. The Mexican-American War of 1846–48 brought U.S. conquest of present-day New Mexico, Arizona, and California, and the Gadson Purchase of 1853 completed the contemporary map of the Southwest. Soon thereafter many U.S. businessmen, merchants, speculators, and settlers moved into the area. Subsequently, government forces attempted to subdue the Navajo and Apache bands. Between 1846 and 1849, the U.S. government sent five expeditions against marauding Navajo bands. In 1858 a band of Navajo, who were led by Manuelito, attacked Fort Defiance, but were quickly subdued. The Navajo claimed that the U.S. soldiers were grazing their horses on Navajo land. Between 1861 and 1863, a band of the Pinal Apache led by Cochise became embroiled in conflict with U.S. soldiers over Apache cattle rustling and the kidnapping of a U.S. rancher's stepson. Some of Cochise's party were captured, held hostage, and executed in retaliation for his execution of nine hostages taken in raids on a wagon train and Butterfield station. Cochise vowed to continue fighting, although U.S. soldiers were withdrawn to fight in the Civil War. Cochise and his Apache band, in alliance with the Apache leader Mangas Coloradas, battled U.S. forces until 1872, when Cochise agreed to settle on a reservation in eastern Arizona.

From summer through the winter of 1863–64, U.S. forces led by Kit Carson rounded up Navajo bands in an effort to force them to locate in one place and to take up U.S. culture and civilization. About 10,000 Navajo were captured and marched 350 miles to Bosque Redondo in eastern New Mexico, where they were held until Navajo leaders signed a treaty in 1868. The march is known as "The Long Walk" by the Navajo, who felt they were being led to prison. About 40 percent of the Navajo died during the march and imprisonment. The Treaty of 1868 established the large Navajo Reservation on lands in present-day New Mexico and Arizona. The Hopi people and lands in northern Arizona were completely surrounded by the Navajo Reservation, and a large amount of unoccupied Hopi land was settled by Navajo sheepherders. Only in 1882 was a Hopi reservation created by order of the Bureau of Indian Affairs. The overlapping territorial claims led to many controversies, and conflicts over land between the Hopi and Navajo continue during the twentieth century. After 1868, the Navajo resettled on their reservation and raised cattle and sheep and farmed. They became one of the most populous Native people in North America, and by 1990, there were at least 160,000 Navajo.

Apache resistance flared again between 1875 and 1886 when the U.S. decided to consolidate the Apache bands on the reservation at San Carlos in Arizona. In 1881, unrest at San Carlos Reservation was led by a medicine man called Nakaidoklini. Eighty-five scouts arrested Nakaidoklini at Cibecue Creek, and while the prophet submitted quietly,

his followers opened fire. In the ensuing fight, the Apache suffered significant casualties including Nakaidoklini himself. The prophet's death led to outbreaks among the Apache for the next several years. The Apache leader Geronimo and Naiche, son of Cochise, and others left the San Carlos Reservation for Mexico, but returned on raids to exact revenge for the Cibecue Creek deaths. Intermittent raids were carried out over the next several years, and U.S. Army forces were mustered to pursue Geronimo's people. He and his associates surrendered in 1886. Five hundred Apache were shipped to prison in Florida and Alabama. Geronimo was not allowed to return to Arizona and he died in prison at Fort Sill, Oklahoma, in 1909.

California Natives suffered considerably during the nineteenth century. From 1800 to 1820, the expanding mission system attempted to destroy their culture, and organized many California Natives to work and live within mission communities. The Franciscan padres exerted considerable control over the Natives and severely restricted their lifestyle, using excessive corporal punishment to correct Native offenders of mission administration. California Native populations within the missions significantly declined because of disease and overwork. In 1818, the missions reported 64,000 baptized Natives, with 41,000 deaths. California mission Indians were effectively insulated from Native culture, and much knowledge of the old ways was lost. After the Mexican Revolution of 1820, the California missions were disbanded and many padres sent back to Spain. In 1834, 30,000 Natives were living in Catholic mission communities.

After the U.S. conquest of California in the Mexican-American War (1846–48), the fortunes of California Natives quickly soured. In 1848, Maidu Indians working for James Marshall, a miller, discovered gold at Sutter's Mill near what is now Sacramento, and in 1849, the California Gold Rush began, (although between 1848 and 1850 many miners were California Natives). Non-Native miners, who were interested in the gold for themselves, turned abusive toward northern California Natives. Militia groups waged a war of extermination against "Digger Indians," and the populations of many California Native groups dropped from 100,000 in 1850 to about 16,000 in 1880. During the middle 1850s, Office of Indian Affairs officials signed treaties with many of the Native groups in California, under which they ceded all but 8 million acres of land. California miners, however, afraid that Native reservation lands contained valuable gold deposits, were powerful enough to prevent ratification of the treaties. Without the treaties most Native groups in California did not have rights to land, and they fell into poverty. By the end of the century, Native Californians were largely dispossessed and marginalized socially, politically, and economically on the land that they had called their own only decades earlier.

PACIFIC NORTHWEST NATIVE CULTURES The Natives of the Pacific Northwest in Washington and Oregon enjoyed early trade relations with the Europeans and Americans. In the Plateau region the Salish, Shuswap, Lillooet, and Thompson Natives traded with the North West Company, which by 1820 merged with the Hudson's Bay Company. By 1827, the Nootka, Haida, and Tsimshian in present-day British Columbia also traded with the Hudson's Bay Company. Thereafter, Hudson's Bay trading posts reached the Pacific Coast people, whose cultures featured creation, hoarding, and redistribution of wealth in potlatches or "give aways." Trade introduced new sources and avenues for gaining wealth, and intensified social and cultural competition. Some enterprising formerly lower status clans, houses, and individuals sought to advance their social positions by trade and middleman bartering with isolated Native villages and peoples. During the 1840 to 1890 period, Northwest culture art flourished as trade introduced many new materials for artistic expression—materials that were used to make and adorn blankets, clan and house crests, totem poles, and ceremonial masks. Potlatches became more elaborate, competitive, and frequent. In 1884 the Canadian government banned the potlatch, because missionaries and officials believed the Natives were wasting their talents and energies preparing for and participating in the potlatch ceremonies.

In 1854 and 1855, many of the western Oregon and Washington Natives, such as Puyallup, Muckleshoot, Duwamish, Nisqually signed treaties ceding land to the United States, while retaining fishing rights to their accustomed places and agreeing to settle on reservations. These treaties would form the basis of the Native treaty and fishing rights struggles of the Pacific Northwest in the 1960s and 1970s.

The Northwest was the scene of two religious movements during the latter decades of the nineteenth century. Smohalla was the founder of the Dreamer religion, reported to have about 2,000 adherents among the Oregon and Washington Natives by 1870. A chief among the small nation of Wanapum or Columbia River Indians, Smohalla started preaching his strongly anti-U.S. message about 1850. He announced that he had traveled widely in the spirit world, and by divine command had been sent back to teach a new religion to the Natives, one which apparently combined Catholic and Mormon teachings with aspects of traditional Native beliefs and ceremonials. Smohalla taught that the Natives should not take up farming, or sell their land, and should return to the life of their ancestors and reject U.S. lifestyles. Smohalla preferred that his followers spend their time seeking spiritual knowledge through dreams, rather than attending school and working farms. His people were to live off nature's bounty by fishing, hunting, and gathering plants, all which were granted by the Great Spirit. Smohalla's movement spread among many Native peoples in Oregon, Washington, and northern California. It may have been a force for motivating Native resistance in several northwestern conflicts such as the Yakima War of 1855–56 and the Nez Percé War of 1877.

The second religious movement originated in the Puget Sound area of Washington about 1881 and is often called the Indian Shaker Church. In this movement, John Slocum, a member of the Squaxim people, purportedly died, went to heaven, received a message for the Native people, and returned to preach the message of the Great Spirit. The Indian Shaker belief borrowed certain Christian beliefs, such as the doctrine that behavior determines whether an individual goes to heaven or hell and that Jesus Christ is the savior. Slocum's mission was to teach the Native people by encouraging moral behavior, very similar to Christian ethics. The Shaker Indians were taught to stop drinking alcohol, gambling, betting, horse racing, or using tobacco, and to renounce the practices of shamen and medicine men of the old religion. The strong Christian emphasis of the Indian Shaker religion led the Presbyterian Church to adopt it as a special part of its own church. The term "shaker" is used because of a characteristic trembling among the Indian Shakers when they were praying. This Native religious order should not to be confused with the Christian Shaker church from the eastern and midwestern United States. The Indian Shaker Church spread among the eastern Washington peoples such as the Skokomish, Squaxim, Chehalis, Nisqually, Cowlitz, and Columbia River Indians, as well as to the Yakima Reservation. The Indian Shakers continue to practice their religion.

Like the Dreamer religion, the Shaker Church emerged during a period of rapid political and economic decline, when the solutions of the old culture and religion were not proving helpful. The new religions created cultural, religious, and moral accommodations to the rapidly changing conditions of the late nineteenth century, and provided new cultural communities for those Native peoples who did not find Christianity and the abandonment of tradition a completely satisfactory way to live.

ARCTIC AND SUBARCTIC NATIVE CULTURES As before noted, the Russian-American Company traded with the Natives of Alaska. In 1867, the Russian-American Company sold Alaska to the United States for $7.5 million. Protestant missionaries found converts and established schools among the Tlingit, Tsimshian, Haida, Yupik, Inuit, and Athapascan. Many Native communities formed local chapters of religious societies, which provided models, organization, and resources for broader political organization among Alaska Natives during the twentieth century. U.S. adminis-

tration in Alaska was very weak and only a few special case reservations were created. Natives were in the majority until after World War II, and many Native communities were extremely isolated. The isolation of most Alaska Native communities allowed them to avoid much of the direct political and economic contact with the outside world that had marginalized most of the Native communities in the lower forty-eight states.

Canning companies and non-Native fishermen soon appropriated most of the salmon fishing runs traditionally held by the Tlingit, who were forced to fish on the open sea. Tlingit fishermen marketed their catch to the canning companies, and many Native women began seasonal employment in the canning factories. Until about 1900, much of the new income continued to be invested in the potlatch ceremonies, although by this time young Tlingit families started moving out of the traditional communal houses and into U.S.-style frame houses. By 1900, the Tlingit population had dropped to about 5,000, and more houses and families were forced to pool their resources in order to give respectable potlatches. These ceremonies were banned from about 1915 until the early 1950s, but many Tlingit continued to celebrate potlatch traditions, although often thinly disguised within Christian or U.S. secular holidays.

PLAINS CULTURE During the nineteenth century, the plains area was subject to rapid change and continued epidemics, and the century ended with the buffalo almost extinct, farmers and railroad companies owning the plains, and most Native people relegated to small reservations under the strict control of U.S. agents and administration. In the early 1800s, many plains nations such as the Osage, Pawnee, Ponca, and Kaw were disturbed by Native nations being pushed onto the plains, or, after the 1830s, by the nations that removed from the East under government policy. These early resettlements resulted in conflict as the plains nations considered the Native newcomers as invaders and threats to their accustomed hunting territories. The Pawnee, for example, soon found themselves fighting with the expan-

sionist Sioux and with the Delaware, who originally lived on the Atlantic Coast and suffered
repeated removals to settle in present-day Kansas
in the early 1830s. U.S. settlers soon followed and
added to the woes of the Pawnee, who were
increasingly unable to defend their homeland from
numerous contenders. Similarly, the Cherokee
had to defeat the Osage in several battles to ensure
their place in present-day northeastern Oklahoma. The Chickasaw and Choctaw were continually harassed on their western frontier by mobile
plains warriors such as the Comanche and Kiowa.

The situation on the plains changed quickly
after the Civil War. In 1866, the plains culture of
buffalo hunting, large summer communal gatherings for buffalo hunting and ceremonies, intermittent warfare, Sun Dance and sacred bundle ceremonies, and frequent migrations was in full swing.
By 1880, however, most buffalo were gone, and
U.S. policy turned toward pacification of Native
peoples and resettlement onto reservations where
the Natives could be Christianized, turned into
farmers, and eventually become U.S. citizens. The
post-war period also brought many newcomers
onto the plains, including traders, merchants, and
hunters. By 1870 railroads were in place across the
country, and the U.S. Congress provided incentives to companies to build more rail lines, lines
that were considered essential to unifying a large
domestic national economy. Railroads were often
offered every alternate section (640 acres) of land
on each side of the tracks that were laid in the
West. If the land was still owned by Native people,
acquisition had to wait for them to surrender it to
the United States. Consequently, during the 1880s
and 1890s, many railroad companies maintained
strong lobbies and pressured Congress to extinguish Native lands in the West and on the plains.

The railroads brought people to the plains in
numbers that far overshadowed the Native populations of the area, which continued to decline
because of disease, poor economic conditions, and
war. Many of the newcomers hunted buffalo for
sport, or for their tongues, heads, or horns. These
hunters came equipped with repeating rifles, newly introduced toward the end of the Civil War,
which made them more efficient at killing buffalo
and other animals. U.S. officials and army officers
encouraged slaughter of the buffalo as a means of
destroying the subsistence of the plains peoples,
making them more vulnerable and less resistant.

Numerous battles, wars, and conflicts were
fought with the newcomers. U.S. Army units were
stationed throughout the West to keep the peace
and to battle with Native nations. Some Sioux fled
from the Minnesota Sioux Uprising of 1862–64 to
their Santee relatives in North Dakota, while
about 3,000 under leadership of Little Crow sought
refuge in southern Canada, and in 1874 were
granted a reserve by the Canadian government.
Massacres such the 1864 Sand Creek killing by
Colorado militia of about 150 Southern Cheyenne
embittered the Cheyenne and their Sioux allies.
Black Kettle, the Cheyenne leader at Sand Creek,
survived only to be killed in another massacre led
by Col. George Armstrong Custer in late 1869. In
early 1865, and as retaliation for the Sand Creek
murders, 1,000 Sioux and Cheyenne attacked and
looted Julesburg, Colorado. The Sioux and Cheyenne attacked Forts Mitchell and Laramie, and
attacked points on the Oregon-California Trail
and the North Platte River crossing. The Sioux
were defeated in battle by U.S. forces on the
Powder River, and they retired to wait out severe
winter weather.

Gold discovered in Montana brought miners into Montana through the Bozeman Trail
between Fort Laramie, Wyoming, and Virginia
City, Montana. The Oglala and Cheyenne put
considerable military pressure on the miners traveling up the trail between 1866 and 1868. In 1868
the United States was forced to sign the Treaty at
Fort Laramie and agreed to close the Bozeman
Trail, since it was in Indian territory. The major
Sioux leader Red Cloud agreed to settle on a
reservation in present-day northern Nebraska and
southern South Dakota, which once bore his name,
the Red Cloud Agency, but is now known as Pine
Ridge. In 1874, Colonel Custer led a expedition to
the sacred Black Hills of the Sioux and discovered
gold. More miners came into the region, violating
the 1868 Fort Laramie Treaty, and causing the

Sioux and their Cheyenne allies to go to war. The Sioux and Cheyenne, under the leadership of the medicine man Sitting Bull and the warrior Crazy Horse, defeated Colonel Custer at the famous battle of the Little Bighorn in the summer of 1876. After the battle, however, the Sioux and Cheyenne fled from stronger and better supplied U.S. Army units, and most migrated to Canada. Within a few years, the Sioux, near starvation from the lack of buffalo to hunt, surrendered and reluctantly settled on reservations.

Agreements worked out with the Sioux in 1876 and the late 1870s provided them with a reservation, the Great Sioux Nation, which included most of South Dakota and parts of North Dakota. Contrary to the guarantees of the 1868 Fort Laramie Treaty and late 1870s agreements, in 1889 the land base of the Great Sioux Nation was significantly reduced to very nearly size of the contemporary Sioux reservations. The Sioux could no longer hunt or live on the plains, they were reduced to provisions guaranteed by treaty and agreement, and they were constrained by strict regulations enforced by U.S. agents at each of the reservation agency offices. Nevertheless, the U.S. Congress did not fulfill all the treaty conditions and agreements, and started to allocate fewer provisions than were needed to feed the Sioux; property lost during the wars was not compensated as agreed upon.

In the southern plains, the last major Indian campaign was the Red River War of 1875–76, which the Kiowa, Southern Cheyenne, Arapaho, Kiowa-Apache, and Comanche fought against the traders who were using repeating rifles to slaughter the buffalo. The Kiowa and Comanche knew they could not maintain their way of life without abundant buffalo herds to hunt. The Kiowa were led by Lone Wolf and the Comanche by Quanah Parker. The Native forces were unable to withstand the better equipped U.S. forces and were forced to surrender and to live on reservations in what is now Oklahoma. After surrender, 71 leaders were sent to prison in Florida.

In the late 1870s, the Ute, Bannock, and Nez Percé fought wars with the United States, but were subdued and relegated to reservations. By the late 1880s, most major Native groups on the plains were on reservations. Great misery was felt by the Native peoples over the transition to reservation life—largely a life of captivity, dependence, and control by the U.S. administration—and the loss of economic and political independence. Under these conditions many Native peoples looked for ways to restore the old order, or to change and adapt to the new economic and political conditions. Missionaries provided a solution for some, by conversion to Christian faith. For many, however, Christianity did not preserve tradition and a Native view of the world. Several significant religious movements arose during the late nineteenth century, chiefly the Ghost Dance of 1870, the Ghost Dance of 1890, and the Peyote religion.

LATE NINETEENTH-CENTURY RELIGIOUS MOVEMENTS The Ghost Dance of 1870 was formed by the Paiute prophet Wodziwob from the Walker Valley in present-day Nevada. During the post-Civil War period, the Paiute of the Great Basin were in economic and social transition. Many worked for U.S. farmers and ranchers as wage laborers, although they continued to live in their traditional lodges and hunted and gathered wild plants in the high desert. Wodziwob taught the people the round dance, or Ghost Dance, where people danced around in a circle and sang songs, often until they collapsed. While unconscious, the dancers sought visions that gave knowledge of dead relatives, the spirit world, and future events. In the early 1870s, Wodziwob taught that if the Native people practiced the dance a great upheaval or earthquake would destroy the Euro-Americans and leave their houses and their wealth to the surviving Natives. Furthermore, departed dead Natives would be resurrected and live to claim the goods of the earth and the wealth of the Euro-Americans. This revelation, in particular, was appealing since there had been great losses of life over the years. Wodziwob's predictions, however, did not come to pass and he died shortly thereafter.

In 1889, Wovoka, a Paiute from Walker Valley Reserve, again taught the Ghost Dance, and predicted that within a few years many dead ancestors would be returned to life, a great cataclysmic event would destroy the Euro-Americans, and the land and animals would be restored so that the Natives would live in a paradise of plenty, freedom, and peace. This doctrine and prediction spread quickly through the Bannock, Arapaho, Shoshoni, Goshute, and Ute, and onto the plains where some Sioux bands, a Cheyenne band, the Southern Cheyenne, Kiowa, and others embraced it. In the south the Walapai, Chemehuevi, Havasupai, and Mohave adopted the dance and religion, but the Apache, Navajo, Pueblos, and Papago did not. Even though Wovoka did not travel, his doctrine spread from tribe to tribe.

For Wovoka, the religion did not require active military or political resistance to U.S. authorities. It was his belief that the great restoration of Native life, peace, and happiness would occur by divine intercession. Hence Wovoka encouraged the Native peoples to attend school, comply with government demands, and wait for the great day of change. Although some Ghost Dancers among the Sioux taught that the Ghost Dance shirts, worn mainly by Sioux dancers, gave protection against bullets, this was not a doctrine of Wovoka. After the Wounded Knee Massacre of 1890, when about 300 Sioux were murdered by army troops, U.S. authorities attempted to suppress Ghost Dancing because they feared a general uprising. Wovoka also discouraged further dancing, but held to the belief that the great day of resurrection was coming. The Paiute, Kiowa, and Southern Cheyenne, and others adopted a similar view, but, as the predictions did not come true in the early 1890s and government suppression prevailed, many Natives abandoned the movement, although a few small groups secretly kept it up well into the twentieth century.

The Peyote religion found a wide following on the plains after 1875. As with the Ghost Dance, many of its adherents were seeking spiritual and social answers to the distressing conditions of early reservation life, and to the looming realization that their former lives and culture were no longer possible. The peyote button taken to induce visions and communication with the spirit world spread across the plains from Mexican Native sources. Quanah Parker, the former Comanche leader in the Red River War, took up the Peyote religion. Parker traveled from reservation to reservation telling people about the peyote button and religion. A Caddo-Delaware medicine man, John Wilson, took up the Peyote religion, introduced various rituals and doctrines, including belief in Jesus Christ, and created many of its contemporary ceremonies and doctrines. The Peyote religion combined traditional and Protestant Christian doctrines and belief; it was nonpolitical and flexible enough to appeal to the varied cultural traditions on the plains and elsewhere in Native North America. Heavy emphasis was placed on individual moral responsibility, public confession of sins, avoidance of drinking, family unity, and healing. In 1918, under pressure to legitimate themselves as an official religious organization, Peyote leaders incorporated the Native American Church in Oklahoma.

CANADA

Ever since the days of New France, French traders traveled, lived, and traded among the Natives of the interior, especially the Algonkian-speaking nations. Relations were developed between the traders and Native women for convenience, for protection gained from the women's family, and for trade connections. The children of these marriages are called Métis or, literally, mixed-bloods. After 1760 when British men engaged in trade and made similar arrangements, the offspring were called Country-born. Most French-speaking Métis were Catholic, while many English-speaking Country-born favored the Anglican church. A number of Métis worked for the large trading firms such as Hudson's Bay Company and the North West Company. By the early 1800s, Métis were hunting buffalo on the northern plains and selling hides and meat to trading posts in both Canada and the northern United States. If good trade agreements could not be made with the Canadians, the Métis usually were willing to trade in Minneapolis as borders at this time were not well defined.

In 1812, Lord Selkirk established Red River Colony near what is now Winnipeg, Manitoba. The Métis saw the settlement as a threat to their trading way of life, but supplied the colonists with buffalo meat anyway. In 1816, at the battle of Seven Oaks, Métis employed by the North West Company defeated the Red River colonists, who tried to prevent the Métis from transporting pemmican (dried buffalo meat) to their camp at Lake Winnipeg. This particular event created a sense of nationhood among the Métis, and was even commemorated in song.

In 1821, the Hudson's Bay Company and North West Company merged into a reorganized Hudson's Bay Company. Many Métis were no longer needed as employees and, as a cost cutting measure, the Hudson's Bay Company tried to induce them to settle and farm along the Red River, but the Métis were not willing farmers at this time, and preferred to hunt on the plains. The Métis thus developed into a labor pool for the Hudson's Bay Company, supplying up to 50 percent of the work force. They hunted buffalo, sold pemmican, and acted as guides, interpreters, and boatmen. With their own language composed of many Algonkian, English, and French words, but with Algonkian grammatical construction, the Métis increasingly formed a separate identity and culture with their own songs, music, and folklore that was neither entirely European nor entirely Native.

In 1830, when Natives were no longer considered important as military allies, the Canadian government transferred jurisdiction of Native affairs from military to civilian administration. Early Canadian civilian policies emphasized assimilation of Natives directly into Canadian society, not isolated on independent reserves as Lord Francis Bond Head had suggested in the early 1830s. In 1839, ministers such as Judge James Macaulay rejected Bond Head's plan, pointing to the farmers among the Mississauga on Credit River Reserve near Toronto as a successful example of Native assimilation. In 1860, the British Crown turned

over financial responsibility for Canadian Natives to Canada. Since the Native population was steadily declining and government assimilation programs sought to bring Natives into Canadian society, the financial burden was expected to be short-lived, because it was thought the Natives would soon assimilate or die off.

In 1867, Britain granted Ontario, Quebec, New Brunswick, and Nova Scotia Dominion status, which allowed Canada to form a government and eventually to annex the western and northern territories. By this time, only some Native groups in Ontario had signed treaties of land cession. In the other provinces, reserves were set aside for Natives but not as part of a treaty agreement. All provinces handed over control of Native reserve lands to the federal Canadian government. In the United States, court cases and policy specify that Natives have certain rights to land ownership, while in Canada, according to the Royal Proclamation of 1763, the Crown, or British monarch, owns the land and allows the Natives to live on special reserves at the Crown's pleasure. In 1867, there were about 23,000 Natives in Canada, but thousands more lived in the western and northern regions later annexed to Canada.

In 1869, the Canadian parliament passed the Gradual Enfranchisement Act, which imposed elected band councils over traditional Native governments, gave Canadian officials power to depose traditional leaders for cause, and stipulated that the children of Native women married to non-Native men were considered citizens and could not claim Indian status. The act continued the assimilationist policies of the Canadian government, and attempted to promote ways in which to change Native government practices and incorporate Natives into Canadian society as citizens.

Conditions over the next 15 years changed rapidly. The northern plains were depleted of buffalo, and the Métis and Canadian Native plains peoples, the Cree, Assiniboine, Blackfoot, Métis, and others, were increasingly impoverished and diseases killed many children. The government pressured the plains groups to settle onto reserves, but most preferred their independent life.

In June of 1884, Louis Riel was asked by the Métis and some Native groups of the North-West Territories to present their grievances to the federal government. In 1873 and 1874, Louis Riel was elected to Parliament from Manitoba, but he lived in exile in the United States and did not take his seat out of fear of political and legal retaliation from the Canadian government. A provisional government was established at Batoche (present-day Saskatchewan) in 1885, and the Canadian government moved quickly and forcefully to crush it. The impoverished Natives and Métis of the plains did not have enough military supplies to mount a sustained and powerful resistance to the Canadian government forces, and the Métis rebellion soon ended. Riel was captured, tried, and executed as a traitor in 1885. He quickly became a political martyr for the Métis. His execution was controversial in Canada, and later writings, plays, and movies reexamined Riel's life and the Métis rebellion.

In 1871, the Canadian government initiated a series of 11 numbered treaties with Native groups. Two major land cession treaties, the Robinson-Huron and Robinson-Superior treaties, negotiated in 1850 by a British agent, were the model for the numbered treaties. The Robinson treaties gained land primarily in Ontario from Chippewa bands. From 1871 to 1923, the Canadian government negotiated treaties of cession for lands in present-day Manitoba, Ontario, Saskatchewan, Alberta, the North-West Territories, and other provinces.

The Indian Act of 1876 addressed Canadian legislation concerning Natives. Natives were encouraged to adopt elected band councils and to settle on privately owned farms; self-supporting Native farmers were encouraged to take Canadian citizenship. Only one Native had adopted Canadian citizenship since 1857, and between 1876 and the end of the century, few voluntarily became citizens. As in the United States, after 1883 many Canadian Native children in the western provinces and territories were sent to residential schools away from their parents. Their Native language and cultures were forcibly discouraged, and strong pressures for assimilation were imposed on the children.

By the end of the nineteenth century, most Native peoples in North America were under heavy state control on reservations or reserves. Both the United States and Canada supported assimilationist policies that discouraged traditional religion, culture, customs, political organization, and language, while encouraging boarding schools, the English language, elective governments, farming, and Western culture. In the 1890s, U.S. Native population declined to 250,000, its lowest level since the landing of Columbus. Many predicted that Native peoples and cultures were doomed, and anthropologists and art collectors rushed to collect ethnographic materials and art objects.

1900–1994

UNITED STATES

In the United States, the assimilationist policies continued until the early 1930s. U.S. agents assumed dictatorial control over Native reservation communities, and traditional governments often were ignored in favor of "business councils" which functioned to sign contracts enabling non-Natives to exploit reservation resources. The commissioners of Indian affairs, as late as 1924, instructed their agency superintendents to ban tribal religious ceremonies, although some ceremonies, such as the plains Sun Dance, continued out of official view. Until the end of World War II, many Native children were sent to government or church-run boarding schools, where U.S. culture was emphasized. Until 1934, the Office of Indian Affairs (later the Bureau of Indians Affairs) annually surveyed and allotted lands according to various allotment acts and treaties. Surplus Native lands were offered to non-Native settlers. Between 1887 and 1934, U.S. Natives lost over 90 million acres to the allotment process.

In 1924, in part because of Native service in World War I and lobbying by the Alaska Native

Brotherhood, the United States granted citizenship to Native peoples. The General Citizenship Act stated, however, that unless specifically prohibited by Congress, U.S. Natives were to retain rights to self-government and to treaty benefits. The act enabled Natives to vote in federal elections, but some states, such as Arizona, New Mexico, and Alaska, refused to allow them to vote until lengthy legal action was taken.

In 1928, the Meriam Report provided details on the unfavorable economic conditions on Native reservations, stating that Natives were among the poorest, least educated, least healthy, and most depressed populations in the United States. The report urged a major change in government administration and policies. Many of the recommendations were realized in the 1934 Wheeler-Howard Act, or the Indian Reorganization Act (IRA). Indian rights activist John Collier, who admired the culture, art, and social-religious organization of the Pueblo peoples, became commissioner of Indian affairs and served until 1946. Collier sought to implement the New Deal mission with emphasis on elected tribal governments, tribal business corporations, and freedom of cultural expression. Eventually 92 Native groups accepted the IRA, while considerably fewer adopted an IRA tribal business corporation. The IRA governments were modeled after U.S. political institutions, and few Natives understood them; many, such as most Pueblos and some Iroquois reservations, preferred their traditional forms of government. In the end, however, the IRA did not live up to its goals due to lack of funds, some Native resistance, the intrusion of World War II, and Congressional movement toward assimilationist policies in the late 1930s. IRA governments and most Native governments generally functioned as appendages to the Office of Indian Affairs.

In 1936, Congress passed the Indian Arts and Crafts Board Act, which promoted the economic welfare of Natives by developing markets for Indian works. Art exhibitions, publicity, and other events were carried out to promote both traditional and contemporary Native art and crafts. In 1962, the Institute of American Indian Art was opened in Santa Fe, New Mexico, and fostered both traditional and modern art. Kevin Redstar, Fritz Scholder, Allan Houser, T.C. Cannon, and many other famous contemporary Native artists and sculptors have been influenced by the institute's training and tradition. In the early 1990s, the institute planned to build a new facility on donated land near Santa Fe.

During World War II many Natives served in the U.S. armed forces or migrated to cities to work in defense-related industries. When they returned to the reservations after the war, they often were unhappy with the economic, health, and education conditions they found and the everyday prejudices they experienced. Having fought for the nation during the war, the soldiers and workers expected equal treatment in business and government. Many veterans joined tribal governments in efforts to help their communities develop economically and work more effectively with government agencies.

U.S. government policies after the war turned toward terminating federal and Native relations and assimilating Natives into the general population. During the 1950s and early 1960s, the Bureau of Indian Affairs terminated over 100 Native communities, many of them small California groups. Termination implied that the government no longer upheld treaty agreements to protect Native land and to provide services such as health, education, and sometime subsistence. Reservation lands were to be taken over by county and state organizations, and the terminated Native communities would no longer carry the status and benefits of a federally recognized Indian tribe. Native opposition to the plan was organized by the National Congress of American Indians (NCAI), founded in 1944 by Indian administration employees. The NCAI played the role of lobbyist and watchdog regarding legislation and government Indian policy. By 1960, Native opposition ended the termination program for most reservations. During the 1970s and 1980s, terminated groups such as the Menominee, Klamath, and others petitioned Congress, which on separate occasions passed acts to restore their communities to federal recognition.

Many other terminated groups now are engaged in the difficult task of convincing Congress to pass a bill restoring them to federal recognition as Indian tribes.

During the 1950s, the Bureau of Indian Affairs (BIA), created a relocation program that helped reservation residents migrate to urban areas to live and work. During the 1950s, the BIA aided thousands of Natives in moving to Denver, Los Angeles, Chicago, Minneapolis, and other large cities. Los Angeles became the city with the largest Native population and, until the 1990 census, California had the largest Native population. According to the 1990 census, Oklahoma now has the largest Native population. Both the 1980 and 1990 census also showed that most Natives, at least two-thirds in the 1990 census, were living in urban areas and not on reservations.

Urban life and the ability to travel by car, airplane, and train provided Native peoples of many cultures the opportunity to meet and to take part in powwows, crafts markets, art exhibits, fairs, national political gatherings, and other events. Some observers note that a pan-Indian culture has emerged, exemplified by the congregation of Natives of many different cultures at powwows. Since most of the powwows are danced for entertainment, non-Natives usually are welcome to see them. Nevertheless, some dances, such as the Kiowa Gourd Dance, are considered traditional and sacred, and a respectful audience is expected.

The 1960s saw the beginning of the contemporary self-determination policy. By the middle 1960s, many Native communities were benefiting from community block grant programs and Community Action Programs (CAP), which were administered by the Office of Economic Development (OEO). These programs provided direct access to financial aid and funds for hiring tribal government administrators and covering expenses. Previously, reservation governments worked only with the Bureau of Indian Affairs (BIA), and when the Great Society programs of the Johnson administration became available, the BIA offered to administer them if Natives proved eligible. The OEO was highly suspicious of BIA paternalism

and control over reservation communities, and consequently decided to avoid the BIA structure and deliver its programs directly to reservation communities. Elections and tribal administration became much more serious, and there was rapid turnover of tribal leadership. As additional federal agencies offering housing, education, and economic development services became accessible, BIA began to compete, but as a smaller share of overall funding administered by tribal governments.

Zuni Pueblo, not wishing to remain under BIA administration, found an obscure rule allowing them to contract for services offered by the BIA and to have a stronger hand in administering programs that affected their community. The Zuni example greatly influenced the Indian Self-Determination and Education Act of 1975, where mechanisms were created for reservation governments to contract for delivering BIA programs.

The 1960s and 1970s were a period of great activism in U.S. society, with the civil rights movement and the Vietnam War. Native groups participated only marginally in the civil rights movement because Native rights often were based on treaty and on national sovereignty, rather than on equal rights under the U.S. Constitution. In 1968, the American Indian Movement (AIM) was founded in Minneapolis by Dennis Banks, Clyde Bellecourt, and others. At first AIM sought to reduce police harassment and to provide alternative, culturally sensitive education for Native children who were having difficulties in the public school system. The period from 1970 to 1975 saw a rapid rise in activist movements, and hundreds of protests and takeovers occurred. The most prominent were protests at BIA offices, the Longest Walk, the takeover and destruction of BIA headquarters in Washington, D.C., the Alcatraz occupation of 1969–71, and the takeover of Wounded Knee II in 1973. In the middle 1970s AIM efforts turned to treaty issues and serving elders on reservations. AIM also has cooperated with other indigenous peoples around the world in bringing rights issues before the United Nations and a U.N. subcommittee is examining and will recommend human rights guidelines to member nations.

In 1969, the Navajo Community College, the first to be tribally owned and operated, opened on the Navajo Reservation. A few years later Deganawida-Quetzalcoatl University (DQ University) was established in northern California. Other Native community colleges followed, and Congress provided funding in the 1970s. In the early 1990s there were 28 community colleges on reservations in the United States and a few in Canada. Some were aspiring to move to four-year accredited programs. These colleges have provided many Native peoples the opportunity to begin their higher education while living in their home communities.

The 1970s saw significant action in the return of Taos Blue Lake, a place central to Taos Pueblos ceremonies and Creation stories. In 1970, Congress passed the Taos Blue Lake Act, returning the lake and surrounding 48,000 acres to Taos Pueblo. The act ended an over half-century struggle by the Taos community to regain control of the lake. The return of Taos Blue Lake represented one of the few occasions when the U.S. government returned land to the Indians. The Alaska Native Claims Settlement Act was passed in 1971, securing 44 million acres of land, $962.5 million, and 13 profitmaking corporations and over 200 village corporations for the Alaska Natives. The twelve regional Alaska Native corporations (the thirteenth was located in Seattle for at-large Alaska Natives) have become major sources of employment for some Alaska Native regions. The act became a model for Native claims settlements around the world and influenced policy in Canada, New Zealand, Australia, and elsewhere. Similarly, the Maine Indian Settlement Act of 1980 provided the Passamaquoddy, Penobscot, and Maliseet with $81.5 million and the right to purchase 300,000 acres of land. The Rhode Island Natives also won a land claim, and many other northeastern Native communities have sued to reclaim land or to gain monetary compensation for land lost.

The Native American culture experienced a literary renaissance during the decades following the 1960s with Native writers such as N. Scott Momaday *(House Made of Dawn)*, Leslie Silko, *(Ceremony)*, and James Welch *(Winter in the Blood)*, as well as Paula Gunn Allen and Joy Harjo. Louise Erdrich wrote the well-known trilogy, *Love Medicine, Beet Queen,* and *Tracks,* while Sherman Alexie entered the stage with *The Business of Fancy Dancing* and *Old Shirts and New Skins*. In addition, the critical analysis of Native American literature emerged in college curriculum and has spawned a literature of analysis among college English professors.

Funding for Native programs decreased in the 1980s and early 1990s, although greater economic self-sufficiency was encouraged. In over 200 Native communities, income is generated by gambling establishments. The Seminole of Florida began the current emphasis on gambling, opening a casino on their reservation and inviting retired Floridians to play; in the 1970s, the tribe began to make millions of dollars in profit. Other tribes followed suit with their own bingo and gambling establishments. State legal challenges to Native gambling activities have not succeeded in closing them down. Native communities reportedly are grossing about $6.5 billion (1993) in gambling business, although that compares to over $300 billion nationally. Nevertheless, income generated from Native gaming exceeds government allocations of funds from both the Bureau of Indian Affairs and the Indian Health Service. Many Native communities use the income to support housing projects, protect traditional art and ceremonial objects, operate museums, aid elders, and carry out programs for which there are no other funds. While there is some debate among Natives about the morality of earning money from gambling establishments, the income and employment generated is welcomed in communities suffering from high unemployment rates and few resources.

In the late 1980s and early 1990s, many issues have continued to confront Native communities in the United States. Water rights issues occupy the attention of communities in the Southwest, where Native reservations must compete with states and powerful interests to gain a share of water for reservation economic purposes. Land rights and land claims are concerns in other Native communities. The Sioux have refused to accept a monetary settlement for loss of the Black Hills and want the return of land instead. The Hopi and Navajo dispute overlapping land claims in Arizona; the government has relocated some Navajo from Hopi land, with unhappy economic and health effects on many of the Navajo. At least 150 Native communities have petitioned for federal recognition, a process that is made difficult, costly, and time-consuming by the BIA. In 1990, Congress passed the Native American Graves and Repatriation Act, which directs federally funded institutions and museums to catalog and return Native human remains, funerary objects, and tribal cultural objects, but which exempts private collections. Economic development, retention of culture and ceremonies, education, high unemployment, and health all remain major challenges for U.S. Native reservation communities.

CANADA

In Canada, as in the United States, the Native population was relegated to reserve lands and communities. The Native population reached a low of 110,000 in 1910, after which the count began to slowly rise. (The Canadian census of 1993 listed 626,000 status Indians, 212,650 Métis, and 49,255 Inuit.) Canadian Native policy was strongly assimilative until the 1970s, and involved strong emphasis on education, the English language, Christianity, and eventually entry and participation in Euro-Canadian society. As part of the assimilation strategy, in 1924 Native governments were abolished and elective band governments were imposed on most Native band communities. Only 20 percent of Native voters participated in early band elections and the Iroquois strongly resisted new elective band governments, while appealing to the League of Nations for recognition of national sovereignty. Nevertheless, the Iroquois and other Canadian Natives were forced to accept the new Canadian government reorganization of Native political life.

A major move away from the Canadian government's assimilation strategy followed a sequence of government events that began in 1969, when Jean Crétien, minister of Indian affairs, released the federal government's White Paper. This government policy paper, entitled *Statement of the Government of Canada on Indian Policy, 1969,* rejected the Hawthorn Report (1968), which recommended that Natives be treated as "Citizens Plus," having both citizen and Native rights. Crétien argued that special status for Natives hindered their social, economic, and political development. The Indian Act and Indian Affairs Department were to be abolished in five years, while reserves were to be held in trust before confederation (adoption of a Canadian constitution) could pass on wardship. The White Paper rejected Native land claims as too unrealistic for resolution. The plan was similar in intent to the termination policy of the 1950s in the United States, recommending that Natives become fully incorporated into Canadian society and that special legal or treaty rights for Native peoples be ended.

Substantial Native opposition to the White Paper quickly developed, on the grounds that it ignored Native views and previous agreements and treaties. In 1970, however, some Native support for the White Paper came from William Wuttunee, Cree, who wrote *Ruffled Feathers,* a reply to *Unjust Society* and a defense of the White Paper. *(The Unjust Society: The Tragedy of Canada's Indians,* denouncing Canada's assimilationist policies, was written in 1969 by Harold Cardinal.)

In 1970, Cardinal, president of the Alberta Indian Association, was a main force behind *Citizens Plus* (the Red Paper) a major Native response to the White Paper. The Red Paper denounced the White Paper as an assimilationist attempt to abolish the Indian Act and Native legal status and treaty rights. Incorporating the views of many Native organizations across Canada, the Red Paper demanded that Native treaty, land rights, and legal rights be honored by the Canadian government. The Red Paper called for reorganization of the Indian Affairs Department in order to make it more effective and for a Claims Commission with power to settle Native land claims. Under the pressures of Native criticism, Prime Minister Pierre

Trudeau withdrew from the policies outlined in the White Paper.

In 1971, the Union of British Columbia Indian Chiefs released the Brown Bag, *A Declaration of Native Rights—The British Columbia Indian Position Paper*, which rejected the White Paper as an attempt by the government to avoid fulfilling its obligations to Natives. The Brown Bag put more emphasis on the resolution of outstanding Native Land claims than did the Red Paper, probably because British Columbia Natives were having a difficult time getting land claims recognized and resolved. Also in 1971, Quebec's Dorian Commission, commissioned in 1966, declared that Natives deserve compensation for land lost. The report recommended that Quebec province take responsibility for Indian and Inuit affairs.

A major land claim issue began in 1970 when Quebec announced plans for the James Bay Hydroelectric Project, which would flood about 4,000 square miles of Native land. In 1972, the Cree and Inuit of northern Quebec gained a permanent court injunction against Quebec building the dam. The James Bay project was halted by November 1973, and a year later the Northern Cree and Inuit bands signed the James Bay Agreement, which enabled the province to continue building the dam and reservoir in return for financial, service, and political considerations. As time went on, however, the Quebec government failed to provide the agreed-upon compensation to the Cree and Inuit.

In November 1975, the East Main Cree, Montagnais, and Inuit bands of northern Quebec signed the James Bay and Northern Quebec Agreement, the first land surrender agreement in Canada in 50 years. The Natives received 410,000 square miles of land, $225 million in compensation, and significant rights to manage their own political, economic, and social affairs. In 1977, the Quebec and Canadian governments passed James Bay Settlement Acts, affirming the 1975 agreement. In 1978, the Naskapi and Inuit of northeastern Quebec signed the Northeastern Quebec Agreement, similar to the James Bay and Northern Quebec Agreement of 1975.

In 1980, however, Cree of northern Quebec filed suit against Quebec for failure to honor the James Bay and Northern Quebec Agreement. In 1982, reports found that the federal government was not living up to the James Bay settlement agreements. On May 10, 1989, the northern Quebec Cree filed a suit to stop the $7.5 billion Great Whale Project (Phase II of the James Bay Hydroelectric Project). Late in 1992, a Canadian Federal Court of Appeals ruled that the federal government did not have to do an environmental assessment because the project was authorized by the 1975 agreement.

The James Bay agreements set a precedent for numerous negotiated land agreements between Native peoples and the Canadian government. Further legal support came from the 1973 Canadian Supreme Court case, *Calder v. Attorney General*, which forced British Columbia to give greater recognition to Native land rights. British Columbia had a long history of legal and political conflict over land with Natives of the province. In 1916, the McKenna-McBride report recommended adding some land and cutting off land to other reserves which were created between 1880 and 1910. In 1919 and 1920, the province acted to appropriate land from some Native reserves. In 1927, British Columbian courts ruled that Natives had not established claims to land based on aboriginal title, and $100,000 was given annually to British Columbian Natives, instead of treaty money.

In 1973, the federal government announced the establishment of an Office of Native Claims, a branch of the Department of Indian Affairs and Northern Development. The office would handle only six comprehensive claims at a time. The *Calder v. Attorney General* case is credited by federal officials for influencing a reversal of the White Paper policy position of 1969. Many Native organizations welcomed the new policy, but some Native leaders expressed more caution. In 1975, British Columbia agreed to negotiate land claims for the land taken in 1919–20 without consent of the Native bands.

During the 1960s and 1970s, many new and revived Native organizations emerged in Canada.

The Inuvialuit Organization was formed in 1969, as well as COPE, the Committee for Original People's Entitlement, formed to represent the Inuvialuit of the lower Mackenzie Valley. The Northwest Territories Indian Organization was organized by the Dene people in 1970. In 1971, the Northern Quebec Inuit Association was organized to oppose the James Bay Hydroelectric Project. In 1975, George Manuel, president of the National Indian Brotherhood, organized a conference of the World Council on Indigenous Peoples in British Columbia. The Inuit Circumpolar Conference (I.C.C.), formed in Alaska in 1977, represented the Inuit peoples of the United States, Siberia, Canada, and Greenland. Most groups were involved in national Canadian politics over Native rights issues, and others were concerned with land settlement negotiations.

In 1976, the Inuit Tapirisat of Canada (ITC) presented a claim for most of northern Canada and proposed establishment of Nunavut, "Our Land." The new territory would have 80 percent Inuit residents. Because western Canadian Natives decided to make an independent claim, in 1977 the ITC presented a revised land claim for the central and eastern Arctic. In 1980, ITC agreed to set aside demands for Nunavut Territory in order to get its land claim started, since the Canadian government refused to negotiate demands for territorial status. In 1982, the ITC organized the Tungavik Federation of Nunavut (TFN) to represent it in negotiations, and in 1990 TFN completed negotiations for land settlement in the central and eastern Arctic. The Inuit retained 350,000 square kilometers and gained $580 million in exchange for surrender of the rest of the north-central and eastern Arctic. Residents of the Northwest Territories narrowly approved the boundary of Nunavut, which is to be established by 1999.

Native rights were further defended in the 1976–77 Berger Report. The report recommended a 10- to 15-year delay in the building of a pipeline to ship northern Alaska oil southward, after discovery of oil in Prudhoe Bay in 1968. The report recommended that Native land rights be settled before construction of the pipeline through the Mackenzie Valley begins. Most Native organizations supported the report, but the Northwest Territories Métis Association favored more rapid economic development.

During the 1970s and 1980s numerous land claims were made by Native groups across Canada. In 1976, the Dene land claim in the Northwest Territories sought much of the land in the western sector of the Northwest Territory and powers of provincial government. In 1977 the government rejected separate Dene and Inuit governments in the Northwest Territory. These proposals stalled negotiations of northern land claims. The Métis of Northwest Territories presented its own land claim, and in 1976 withdrew from the Dene land claim for the NWT. Also in 1977, Métis land claims in Saskatchewan reached a preliminary agreement. In 1978, COPE signed an agreement-in-principle with the Canadian government for a land claim settlement in the western Arctic. COPE represented 2,500 Inuvialuit of the Mackenzie Valley in a comprehensive land claim settlement. The Inuvialuit retained 32,000 acres, 5,000 acres of subsurface rights, and 5,000 square miles of wilderness area for hunting, trapping, and fishing. By 1984, however, COPE represented only the Inuvialuit.

Major efforts at Native political, legal, and policy reform occurred during the 1980s in Canada. In 1979, The Native Council of Canada issued a *Declaration of Native and Indian Rights*, which argued that Natives have rights to self-determination, representation in legislatures, and constitutional reform, and sought recognition of Native rights within confederation. Canada's prime minister and provincial premiers agreed in 1980 that Native groups can participate in constitutional talks that affect them. In September 1980, however, Native groups filed suit to prevent adoption of a Canadian Constitution without Native consent. Canadian officials wished to write a constitution that would put the country exclusively under its own control, and out of the orbit of British government. Canadian Native leaders appealed to Britain, and Prime Minister Trudeau agreed to include a provision in the proposed Canadian constitution that would secure Native rights, if the provincial premiers agreed. Native leaders also favored entrenchment of provisions of the Proclamation of 1763 into the constitution, thus affirming Native land rights. On April 24, 1981, Saskatchewan Natives rejected constitutional reform, because it did not go far enough to protect their rights. Nevertheless, in November 1981, Canadian premiers deleted Native rights passages from the proposed Canadian Constitution. Native leaders angrily denounced the action. Canadian Native rights took a further blow, when in January 1982 a British court decided that Canadian Native affairs belong to the jurisdiction of Canada rather than Britain, and that therefore Canadian Natives cannot appeal to British courts for protection of their treaty or land rights. The Canadian Constitution Act of 1982 was passed over the strong opposition of Native groups. The act expanded the definition of Indian by including Métis and Inuit. The act also upheld treaty rights and guaranteed Native participation in First Ministers Conferences with the prime minister and provincial premiers to consider further constitutional amendments on Native rights.

In June 1985, the Canadian Parliament passed C-31 (the Indian Amendment Act), removing sections of the Canadian Indian Act that discriminate against women and restoring Indian status to those whose mothers had married non-Natives. The Canadian legal definition of Indian status had been challenged in the early 1980s by the U.N. Human Rights Commission, which ruled that the Indian Act discriminated by gender. Many Indian bands refused to accept C-31, because it could bring an influx of new status Indians and put a strain on already meager band funds.

During the 1980s, the First Ministers Conferences were held with the participation of major national and regional Native organizations. Georges Erasmus, Dene, leader of the Assembly of First Nations (1985–1991), was spokesman for the group at the Constitutional Conferences on Native constitutional rights in 1983, 1984, 1985, and

1986. Louis (Smokey) Bruyere, Ojibway, president of Native Council of Canada, also was active in several constitutional conferences between 1981 and 1988. The 1985 and 1986 constitutional conferences failed to define Native rights to self-government, and the Canadian government announced it would negotiate self-government with individual bands.

In 1987, the Meech Lake Accord was worked out by the prime minister and provincial premiers as a new constitutional reform package for Canada, but no reference was given to Native rights. Native leaders denounced the new constitutional proposal and objected that they had not provided input into the agreement. Ovide Mercredi, a Cree who did not legally gain Indian status until the passage of Bill C-31 in 1985, was involved in opposition to the Meech Lake Accord. In 1990, the Accord failed, because Elijah Harper, a Cree-Ojibway and a member of the Manitoba Legislative Assembly, used complex procedural tactics to block its consideration in the provincial legislature. (The accord needed unanimous consent among the provinces and federal government, and therefore Manitoba's inability to vote in favor caused the defeat of the proposal.)

In April 1992, an informal constitutional agreement was made among the provinces, the federal government, and Native leaders to recognize the inherent right of Native self-government. As grand chief of the Assembly of First Nations, Mercredi took a central role in negotiating the Charlottetown Accord. Some Native leaders, however, were unhappy about not being invited to the discussions. In August 1992, Native, provincial, and federal officials reached agreement within the Charlottetown Accord to entrench Native rights to self-government in the Canadian Constitution. Nevertheless, in a national referendum on October 26, 1992, the Charlottetown Accord was defeated. Some Natives argued the self-government provisions were not clear enough. Native leaders declared they will continue their struggle to protect Native rights to self-government within Canadian law and the Constitution.

NATIVE NORTH AMERICA AT THE END OF THE TWENTIETH CENTURY

For the past 500 years, Native North Americans have faced a myriad of troubles, including disease, migration, political and cultural subjugation, and economic distress. Nevertheless, many Native American communities have survived and in fact have made a significant effort in recent years to restore and extend cultural traditions and communities. This work is far from over, and most likely will continue well into the twenty-first century. Native languages are on the defensive, and many are in danger of being lost, but many Native people retain Native identity. A minority of Natives hold strong nationalist orientations based on treaties and sovereign rights, but most

Native North Americans are comfortable living, working, and even serving in the armed forces of the United States or Canada. Most Native peoples wish to retain their identities and cultural traditions, treaty rights, and rights to self-government within the context of contemporary U.S. or Canadian law and society. Many problems remain, however. Poverty, land claims, political sovereignty, Native rights, international indigenous rights, Native law, water rights, fishing rights, hunting rights, and other issues will occupy the attention of Native peoples, the United States, and Canada for years to come. Native North American peoples, through their hundreds of varied cultures and historical experiences, can help us better understand today's struggles for freedom, cultural diversity, and human rights.

Historical Timeline

50,000 B.C. Bering land bridge exposed in what is now the Bering Strait.

45,000 B.C. Cave bear cult in Europe.

40,000 B.C. Modern *Homo sapiens* well established in Europe.

28,000 B.C. Cave paintings in Europe.

27,000 B.C. Paleo-Indian societies migrate south following ice-free corridors.

25,000 B.C. Earliest known oil lamps in France.

25,000 B.C. New technologies appear among the Paleo-Indian societies of North America.

24,000 B.C. Sculptured clay figurines in Europe.

15,000 B.C. Solutreau culture in Europe.

15,000 B.C. Clovis stone points become used in every mainland state of what becomes the United States.

11,000 B.C. Small bands of hunters make their way across the Bering Sea Land Bridge from Siberia.

10,000 B.C. Bow and arrow in use in Europe (earliest certain use).

10,000 B.C. Glaciers start to thaw, and the Pleistocene ice age wanes.

9,200 B.C. Folsom culture in New Mexico emerges.

9,000 B.C. Jericho established; among earliest known towns.

9,000 B.C. Earliest fired pottery in Japan (Jomon period).

8,500 B.C. Sheep are domesticated in Near East.

8,350 B.C. Cold-hammered copper in use in Turkey.

8,000 B.C. Plano culture, also known as the Plainview, emerges.

c. 7,000 B.C. Grinding stones are widespread in Near East.

7,000 B.C. Copper-casting in Near East.

| 40,000 B.C. Modern *Homo sapiens* well established in Europe. | 25,000 B.C. New technologies appear among the Paleo-Indian societies of North America. | 11,000 B.C. Small bands of hunters make their way across the Bering Sea Land Bridge from Siberia. | 7,000 B.C. Paleo-Indian period characterized by big game migratory hunting ends. |

| 50,000 B.C. | 30,000 | 10,000 | 5,000 |

7,000 B.C. Paleo-Indian period characterized by big game migratory hunting ends.

3,000 B.C. Oldest pottery in New World, Colombia.

3,000 B.C. First bronze artifacts in Middle East (arsenic; tin alloys).

3,000 B.C. At Umnak and other islands in the Aleutian chain, people skilled at hunting seals, sea lions, and whales build villages with small oval houses, three to five meters in diameter.

2,500 B.C. Pyramid construction begins in Europe.

2,500 B.C. Beginnings of Indus River civilization in India.

2,500 B.C. Windmiller cultural pattern emerges. Many scholars believe that the Windmiller peoples are the ancestors of the five major cultures of the Central California Valley: the Yokut, Miwok, Maidu, Wintun, and Ohlone.

c. 1,000 B.C. First extensive use of wool clothing (Scandinavia).

1,000 B.C. Earliest rotary hand mills for grain in Middle East.

1,000 B.C. Unique cultures develop throughout the Midwestern and Eastern regions, described comprehensively as Woodland culture. This includes Adena, Hopewell, Mississippian, and others.

776 B.C. First recorded Olympiad in Greece.

750 B.C. Assyrian Empire establishes world's first highway system.

700 B.C. Dorset Inuit culture develops in the region north of Hudson Bay.

c. 400 B.C. Peak of classical Greece.

c. 400 B.C. Democritus introduces concept of atom.

400 B.C. People of the Adena Culture build a huge earthwork today called Serpent Mound. The body of the serpent measures 382 meters (1254 feet) long.

250 B.C. Cultivation of locally domesticated plants begins in present-day northeastern United States.

c. 240 B.C. Initial phases of construction of Great Wall of China.

226 B.C. Colossus of Rhodes destroyed by earthquake.

A.D. 1 Roots of the Hohokam cultural tradition emerge in the Sonoran Desert of south-central Arizona and adjacent regions of Chihuahua and Sonora in Mexico.

c. A.D. 30 Crucifixion of Jesus of Nazareth; establishment of Christian faith.

A.D. 64 Burning of Rome.

c. A.D. 200 Construction of Cholula pyramid mound in Mexico begins.

A.D. 200 Small sedentary villages develop in the Southwest. The first evidence for the Mogollon cultural tradition is defined. Pottery first appears in the Southwest.

A.D. 200 Classic Mayan period begins.

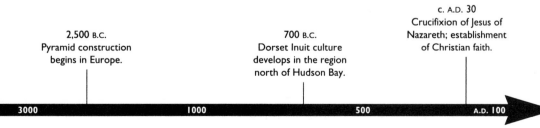

2,500 B.C. Pyramid construction begins in Europe.

700 B.C. Dorset Inuit culture develops in the region north of Hudson Bay.

c. A.D. 30 Crucifixion of Jesus of Nazareth; establishment of Christian faith.

3000　　1000　　500　　A.D. 100

A.D. 300 Construction of massive irrigation systems begins in the Hohokam culture; Hopewellian societies give way to cultures of the Late Woodland period.

A.D 313 Constantine's Edict of Milan legalizes Christianity in Rome.

A.D. 330 Constantinople founded at Byzantium.

c. A.D. 400 Invention of stern post rudder in northern Europe.

A.D. 400 The Anasazi tradition emerges in the Four Corners region of Arizona, New Mexico, Colorado, and Utah.

A.D. 410 Romans withdraw from England.

A.D. 450 The people of the Lower Mississippi Valley build conical burial mounds and some of the first flat-top platform mounds in North America.

A.D. 700 *Beowulf* written in northern Europe.

A.D. 700 Polynesian Triangle (Hawaii, Easter Island, New Zealand) now settled.

A.D. 700–1000 Most Anasazi villages make the transition from subterranean pithouse dwellings to above-surface masonry dwellings, later called "pueblos."

A.D. 711 Moors (Saracens) invade Spain.

A.D. 725 Earliest known mechanical clock.

A.D. 750 The cultures of the Late Woodland period begin transformation into the societies of the Mississippian period.

c. A.D. 800 First porcelain produced in China.

A.D. 800 Charlemagne, king of Franks, proclaimed Holy Roman Emperor by pope.

A.D. 825 Northern Athapascan groups, ancestors to modern-day Apache and Navajo, migrate from their homeland in northern subarctic into the plains and toward the southwest.

A.D. 875 Pottery of the type later used by Navajo and Apaches appears in Gobernador Canyon, New Mexico.

A.D. 900 Agriculture is commonly practiced in most areas. Maize becomes a major crop.

A.D. 900 Mississippian culture takes shape in the eastern United States.

A.D. 900 In the Ohio Valley and Great Lakes regions, civilizations now classified as Hopewell develop.

A.D. 900 Navajo and other Apachean groups are believed to separate from their linguistic relatives in Canada at this time. They arrive in the Southwest sometime in the early sixteenth century.

A.D. 900–1450 Consolidation and expansion of many major Hohokam sites occurs. Above-ground adobe structures come into use, irrigation canal systems are greatly expanded, and Mesoamerican-style platform mounds and ball courts are constructed. The Hohokam build Casa Grande in the Phoenix Basin.

A.D. 910 First paper currency (China).

A.D. 969 Cairo, Egypt, founded.

A.D 313
Constantine's Edict of
Milan legalizes
Christianity in Rome.

A.D. 450
The people of the Lower
Mississippi Valley build conical
burial mounds and some of
the first flat-top platform
mounds in North America.

A.D. 800
Charlemagne, king of
Franks, proclaimed Holy
Roman Emperor by pope.

200   400   600   800

c. 1000 Arabic numerals begin to replace Roman numerals in Europe.

1000 Norsemen settle in southern Greenland.

1000 Pueblos develop in central and southern New Mexico around central plazas in the region of the Mogollon cultural tradition.

1000 In New York and the St. Lawrence River Valley people build small villages; the first clear evidence for cultivation of maize, beans, and squash occurs.

1000–1130 The Mimbres culture flourishes in southwestern New Mexico.

1000–1180 By the 11th century, the center of Anasazi culture is Chaco Canyon, a 32-square mile area in present-day northwest New Mexico.

1004 Thorvald Erickson killed in first Indian-European skirmish in New World.

1007 Leif Eriksson makes one of the first documented contacts with Native Americans.

1025 Ancestral Navajo migrate into Southwest.

1027 Second Mayan empire begins.

1050–1250 Mississippian trading and ceremonial center reaches its highest level of complexity.

1054 Break between churches in Rome and Constantinople.

1054 Chinese observe nova forming today's Crab Nebula.

1100 Shone Kingdom in East Africa, centered at Great Zimbabwe, emerges.

1100–1300 Mesa Verde site in southern Colorado reaches its cultural height.

1100–1804 Use of shell money becomes widespread throughout the California area.

1145 Second Christian crusade begins.

1242 Roger Bacon describes gunpowder.

c. 1250 Earliest development of cannons in Europe.

1250 The Hohokam way of life is replaced by a pueblo-building culture and by modern Pima-Papago culture.

c. 1300 Invention of spinning wheel.

c. 1300 Beginning of the Renaissance in Italy.

c. 1300 Deganawida, Huron spiritual leader, establishes the Iroquois Confederacy.

1300–1600 Great Temple Mound (Middle Mississippi) civilizations flourish in the river valleys of Arkansas, Mississippi, Alabama, Tennessee, Missouri, Kentucky, southern Illinois, southern Indiana, and Ohio. Caddoan-speaking peoples develop village societies in the Texas-Louisiana-Arkansas-Oklahoma border region.

c. 1350 Cast-metal type developed in Korea.

1350 One of the largest Mississippian period ceremonial centers is built, consisting of twenty mounds and an associated village, located 40 miles south of present-day Tuscaloosa.

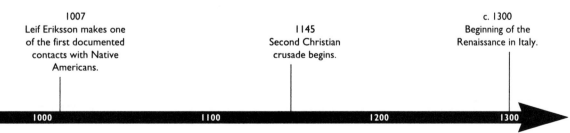

1007
Leif Eriksson makes one of the first documented contacts with Native Americans.

1145
Second Christian crusade begins.

c. 1300
Beginning of the Renaissance in Italy.

1000   1100   1200   1300

1350 Paiute, Ute, and Shoshoni replace the earlier Fremont culture.

1379 Venice effectively ends Genoese power in battle of Chioggia.

1449 Last Byzantine emperor crowned.

1450 Groups related to the Pawnee migrate north to the Missouri River in South Dakota. Their descendants are recognized as the present-day Arikara.

1453 End of Hundred Years War.

1492 On an island in the Bahamas called Guanahani by Natives and San Salvador by Europeans, the expedition led by Christopher Columbus touches ground. In December, Columbus lands on an island similar to Castile, and names it Hispañola.

1493 On November 3, Christopher Columbus begins his second voyage to the "new world." Returning to Hispañola, Columbus discovers that the Navidad colony disbanded shortly after his departure.

1493 Pope Alexander VI issues Inter Caetera II, granting to Spain all lands west of line running 100 leagues west of the Cape Verde Islands.

1494 Christopher Columbus imposes gold tax on Natives 14 years of age and older; Columbus initiates the enslavement of American Indians, capturing over 500 and sending them to Spain to be sold.

1494 Treaty of Tordesillas divides new lands between Spain and Portugal.

c. 1500 Beginnings of empirical science in Europe.

1500 The sixteenth century marks the beginning of a widespread decline in Native population, which continues until about 1900.

1500 Columbus and his successors consolidate Spanish control of the Caribbean and begin a period of exploration in North and Central America.

1500 Up to a million people from a wide variety of cultural groups occupy the area that will become Canada.

1501 Gaspar Corte Real, supported by Portugal, explores eastern coast and kidnaps more than 50 Indians, returning them to Lisbon where they are sold into slavery.

1503 Ottoman Turks seize control of Greece.

1504 Columbus returns from last voyage.

1508 Sebastian Cabot reaches Hudson Bay in search of Northwest passage.

1508–11 Caribbean Indian population is devastated by disease, warfare, and over-work. In Puerto Rico the Indian population is 200,000 in 1508 and 20,000 in 1511.

1509 Henry VIII becomes king of England.

1510 "Las Casa de Contractacion" sanctions importation of Negro slaves from Africa to America.

1511 Bartolome de las Casas writes *Destruction of the Indies,* in which he chronicles the Spanish conquistadors' cruelty against Native

1449
Last Byzantine
emperor crowned.

1453
End of Hundred Years War.

1400   1425   1450   1475

Americans. These cruelties include butchering men, women, and children like "sheep in the slaughter house."

1512 Laws of Burgos passed, giving New World Natives legal protection against abuse and authorizing Negro slavery.

1512 Juan Ponce de Leon, the governor of Puerto Rico, given license by the Spanish king to explore and settle Florida.

1514 "Requerimiento" orders New World Natives to surrender their hearts, souls, and bodies to the church and Spanish Crown or face devastation.

1517 Martin Luther lights fuse of Protestant Reformation.

1517 Cordoba discovers Yucatan and the Maya.

1519–21 The Aztec Empire falls.

1520–22 First circumnavigation of globe by Magellan's crew.

1526 Tyndale prints first Bible in English; executed for heresy.

1528–36 Narváez Expedition. In 1528 Panfilo de Narváez lands at Tampa Bay on the west coast of Florida with 400 colonists.

1530–1600 Spanish explore Baja California.

1534 Cambridge University Press established.

1534–41 Jacques Cartier of France explores the St. Lawrence River.

1539 Marcos de Niza, Estevanico, and the Zuni explore the region now known as the American Southwest, searching for the fabled "Seven Cities of Cíbola."

1542 Juan Rodriguez Cabrillo and Bartolome Ferrelo explore the Pacific Coast and encounter numerous California Indian tribes.

1542 Portuguese traders reach Japan.

1542 Copernicus (1473–1543) publishes theory of sun-centered solar system.

1564 William Shakespeare (d. 1616) and Galileo Galilei (d. 1642) are born.

1565 Spanish found St. Augustine, oldest European settlement in the United States.

1570 The Spaniards unsuccessfully attempt to gain a foothold in Virginia within the territory of the Powhatan Confederacy.

1578–79 Francis Drake of England explores the California coast and encounters such groups as the Coastal Miwok.

1582–98 The Spanish begin settlement of New Mexico.

1585–1607 Roanoke Colony founded.

1587 Virginia Dare born at Roanoke, first child of English parents in America.

1588 Defeat of Spanish Armada by England.

1595 Pocahontas is born.

1597 Shakespeare's *Romeo and Juliet* is published.

1603–15 Samuel de Champlain's voyages in the Northeast lead to extensive contacts with various Algonquin and Iroquois tribes.

1492	1512	1542
The expedition led by Christopher Columbus touches ground.	Juan Ponce de Leon, the governor of Puerto Rico, given license by the Spanish king to explore and settle Florida.	Copernicus (1473–1543) publishes theory of sun-centered solar system.

| 1500 | 1525 | 1550 | 1575 |

1605 Cervantes publishes *Don Quixote.*

1607 Jamestown, Virginia, the first English colony in the New World, is founded.

1609 Galileo builds first effective telescope.

1609 Henry Hudson, sailing for the Netherlands, opens lucrative fur trade with the Lenape, Wappinger, Manhattan, Hackensack, Munsee, and Mohican nations of New Netherlands (present-day New York).

1613–14 Marriage of Pocahontas and John Rolfe.

1620 Pilgrims arrive in New World.

1622 First Indian rebellion in Virginia.

1626 Purchase of Manhattan.

1630 Construction begins in India on the Taj Mahal.

1630 The Puritans arrive.

1636–37 The Pequot War.

1637 Emperor of Japan expels foreigners and closes nation to trade.

1642 Pascal builds early mechanical calculating device.

1645–1700 The Beaver Wars.

1648 Taj Mahal is completed.

1660 Stuart restoration in England.

1661 The Spanish raid the sacred kivas of many Pueblo Indians, destroy hundreds of *kachina* masks, and attempt to further suppress Pueblo religion.

1665 First microscope-based description of living cells (Hooks).

1665 Great plague in London kills 68,000 people.

1670 Newton develops the principles of calculus.

1670 Hudson's Bay Company is chartered.

1675 Charles II founds Royal Observatory at Greenwich, England.

1675–76 King Philip's War.

1675–77 Bacon's Rebellion.

1680–92 The Pueblo Revolt expels Spanish from American Southwest.

1687 Newton publishes *Principia Mathematica.*

1687 Newton formulates law of gravity.

1691 Yorktown, Virginia, is founded.

1692 Salem witch trials.

1692 Reconquest of the Pueblos.

1700–1800 Rise of modern national states in Europe.

1702–13 Queen Anne's War.

1712 Newcomen invents first practical steam engine.

1712–34 The Fox (Mesquakie) Wars.

1716–27 The Creek and Cherokee War.

1595
Pocahontas is born.

1622
First Indian rebellion
in Virginia.

1665
Great plague in London
kills 68,000 people.

1600   1625   1650   1675

1717 Halley shows that solar system moves through space.

1726 Swift publishes *Gulliver's Travels*.

1729 Destruction of the Natchez Nation.

1735 Linnaeus publishes first edition of *Systema Naturae*.

1737 The Delaware "Walking Purchase."

1740 Bering (Danish) discovers Alaska for Russia.

1740–1867 Russian exploration and fur trade.

1744–48 King William's War.

c. 1750 Beginning of the Industrial Revolution.

1751 The Albany Plan, a plan of union for the British colonies, is proposed by Benjamin Franklin.

1752 Benjamin Franklin proves lightning is electrical; develops lightning rod.

1754–63 French and Indian War (known as Seven Years' War in Europe).

1755 Samuel Johnson's English Dictionary is published.

1760 New France falls to the British.

1760–63 The Delaware Prophet establishes a new religion designed only for the Delaware.

1763 On October 7, at the height of Indian resistance to the British, British king George III issues the Royal Proclamation of 1763, which asserts title to all land in the territory claimed by the British, but declares that Indians have the right to use all land outside established colonies until the Crown has negotiated land cession treaties.

1763–64 Pontiac's War.

1765 Watt develops first efficient steam engines.

1766 Rediscovery of ancient site of Olympia.

1768 Treaty of Fort Stanwix.

1769 Daniel Boone discovers Cumberland Gap; opens a path to the West.

1769–1835 The California mission system begins with Juniperro Serras' founding of the San Diego mission in 1769. Between 1769 and 1835, the Spanish establish 19 more missions and several presidios (military posts) along the California coast, with devastating effects on the California Indian population.

1770 Boston Massacre.

1773 Boston "Tea-party."

1773–74 Lord Dunmore's War.

1774 First Continental Congress assembles.

1776 First "scientific" study of race (Blumenbach).

1776–81 The American Revolution.

1777 Articles of Confederation are signed.

1777–83 The Iroquois Confederacy is dispersed.

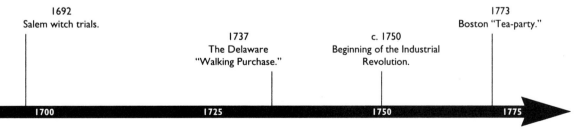

1692
Salem witch trials.

1737
The Delaware
"Walking Purchase."

c. 1750
Beginning of the Industrial
Revolution.

1773
Boston "Tea-party."

1700   1725   1750   1775

1778 Treaty between the United States and the Delaware Tribe—first United States-Indian Treaty.

1782 England recognizes United States independence.

1782 Christian Delaware Indians are massacred at Gnadenhutten, Ohio.

1783 Massachusetts supreme court outlaws slavery.

1785 The Virginia Assembly decrees that every mixed person with one-quarter or more "Negro blood" is to be deemed a mulatto.

1786 On August 7, the first federal Indian reservation is established.

1786–95 Little Turtle's War.

1787 The Northwest Ordinance calls for the division of lands north of the Ohio River into territories that can eventually become states.

1789 French revolution begins.

1789 U.S. Constitution in effect; George Washington elected president.

1789 Indian Affairs moved to War Department; Henry Knox becomes first Secretary of War.

1790 On July 22, the first "Trade and Intercourse Act" is enacted in order to establish firm relations with Indian tribes.

1793 Louis XVI and Marie Antoinette of France are beheaded.

1793 Eli Whitney invents the cotton gin.

1794 Jay Treaty.

1799 Napoleon seizes control in France.

1799 Handsome Lake begins new religious revitalization movement.

1803 Louisiana Purchase.

1804 Aaron Burr kills Alexander Hamilton in duel.

1804 Napoleon crowns himself emperor.

1804 First flight of glider with a fixed wing and tail (Sir George Cayley).

1804–06 Lewis and Clark explore the Missouri River.

1806 Zebulon Pike "discovers" Pike's Peak.

1806–09 Tecumseh and Tenskwatawa attempt to unite Indian people from numerous tribes in an effort to halt westward expansion of U.S. settlers and further loss of Indian land.

1809 Treaty of Fort Wayne. Approximately three million acres of choice land long the Wabash River is given up for $8,200 by the Delaware, Potawatomi, Miami, Kickapoo, and Eel River tribes.

1809 The "Phoenix," first seagoing steamship, sails from New York to Philadelphia.

1810 Hall invents breech-loading rifle.

1811 Battle of Tippecanoe.

1812 Napoleon captures Moscow.

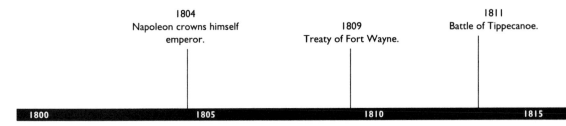

1804
Napoleon crowns himself emperor.

1809
Treaty of Fort Wayne.

1811
Battle of Tippecanoe.

1800   1805   1810   1815

1812 The Russians establish Fort Ross (Rus) at Mad Shiu-miu in Pomo Indian country on the present-day California coast.

1812 The War of 1812 begins. The Treaty of Ghent brings an end to the war in 1814.

1813–14 The Red Stick War.

1815 The battle at Waterloo brings an end to the Napoleonic era.

1817–18 The First Seminole War.

1818 First U.S. passenger railroad (Baltimore and Ohio, horse-drawn).

1819 *Savannah* makes first part-steam, part-sail Atlantic crossing.

1819 Commercial preservation of food begins in United States.

1820 Missouri Compromise divides the United States into two parts regarding legal slavery.

1821 Sequoyah finishes work on the Cherokee syllabary.

1823 Monroe Doctrine is proclaimed.

1823 In *Johnson v. McIntosh*, a case before the U.S. Supreme Court, Chief Justice John Marshall recognizes that Indian tribes have the right to land by their prior use, but rules that Indian have no power to grant lands to anyone other than the federal government.

1824 *The Life of Mary Jemison*, one of many Indian captivity stories, is published in the U.S.

1825 First steam railroad locomotive (Stephenson).

1825 A census taken among the Cherokee tribe in Georgia reveals that the Cherokee possess 33 grist mills; 13 sawmills; one power mill; 69 blacksmith shops; 2 tab yards; 762 looms; 2,486 spinning wheels; 172 wagons; 2,923 plows; 7,683 horses; 22,537 black cattle; 46,732 swine; and 2,566 sheep.

1825 After visiting the United States, Alexis de Toqueville writes "They kindly take the Indian by the hand and lead them to a grave far from the lands of their fathers."

1826 Geronimo (Goyathlay), Chiricahua Apache tribal leader, is born.

1827 Cherokee Nation adopts its constitution.

1828 The *Cherokee Phoenix* newspaper is published.

1829 Gold is discovered on Cherokee land.

1829 On June 6, Shanawdithit, the last known Beothuk, dies. The Beothuk, reclusive inhabitants of Newfoundland, have been gradually killed off by disease and by Micmac, Inuit, and European attacks.

1829 Braille introduces printing system for the blind.

1830 Upper Canada establishes a system of reserves for Indian people.

1830 Congress votes in favor of the Indian Removal Act and authorizes $500,000 to relocate Indians to Indian Territory.

1830 Treaty at Dancing Rabbit Creek.

1831 Colt develops the revolver.

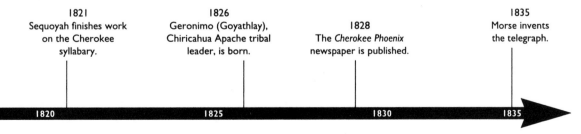

| 1821 Sequoyah finishes work on the Cherokee syllabary. | 1826 Geronimo (Goyathlay), Chiricahua Apache tribal leader, is born. | 1828 The *Cherokee Phoenix* newspaper is published. | 1835 Morse invents the telegraph. |

1820   1825   1830   1835

1831 Sitting Bull, Hunkpapa Sioux tribal leader, is born.

1831 *Cherokee Nation v. Georgia.* The U.S. Supreme Court recognizes Indian tribes as "domestic dependent nations with an unquestionable right to the lands which they occupy, until that right shall be extinguished by a voluntary cession to our government...."

1832 Black Hawk War.

1832 In *Worcester v. Georgia,* the Supreme Court strikes down Georgia law, arguing that only the federal government has the right to regulate affairs in Indian country and that states cannot extend their laws over Indian governments.

1835 Morse invents the telegraph.

1835 Oberlin College opens to all races, first in the United States.

1835 Treaty of New Echota.

1835 The *Cherokee Phoenix* is denied freedom of the press when the newspaper incurs the displeasure of the Georgia governor.

1835–41 The Second Seminole War.

1836 Creek removal.

1836–70 Smallpox epidemics on the plains, decimating the once numerous Mandan and Hidatsa. Both tribes lose as much as 90 percent of their population, leaving only a few hundred survivors.

1837 In June, Assiniboine visiting the American Fur Company's Fort Union contract smallpox from infected traders; up to three-quarters of

the Siksika, Peigan, Kainai (Blood), Sarcee, Atsina, and Assiniboine are killed.

1838–39 Cherokee removal, "Trail of Tears."

1841 First immigrant wagon train for California.

1841 Methodist hymnal published using Cree syllabics.

1842 Settlement of Oregon begins via Oregon Trail.

1842 Joseph Howe appointed Canadian Indian commissioner.

1843 Hudson's Bay Company establishes Fort Victoria in Canada.

1846 With the annexation of Texas, more than 100,000 Indian people are added to the U.S. population.

1846–48 Mexican-American War.

1847 A monument is erected in honor of Uncas, a fictional Mohegan, memorialized in the book, *The Last of the Mohicans,* written by James Fenimore Cooper.

1848 Mexico cedes most of present U.S. Southwest to the United States.

1848 California Gold Rush.

1849 Marx and Engels publish *Communist Manifesto.*

1849 Treaty with the Navajo at Cheille.

1850 World population reaches one billion.

1850 Quechan uprising.

1841 Methodist hymnal published using Cree syllabics.	1846 With the annexation of Texas, more than 100,000 Indian people are added to the U.S. population.	1850 World population reaches one billion.
1840	1845	1850

1850 Ojibway sign Robinson Treaty.

1850–60 Non-ratification of California Indian Treaties. In California, 18 treaties are negotiated; however, California's government, U.S. congressmen, and non-Indian Californians prevent the treaty ratifications in Congress.

1850–80 Genocide of California Indians. Fearing widespread Indian uprisings, non-Indian Californians kill and terrorize California Indians. By 1880 the Indian population in California declines to 16,000, from 100,000 in 1850.

1852 *Uncle Tom's Cabin* published by Harriet Beecher Stowe.

1853 The Gadsden Purchase.

1854 Indian Commissioner George Manypenny calls for the abandonment of the Indian removal policy.

1855 *Songs of Hiawatha* published by Longfellow.

1855 Chippewa treaty.

1855 Salish and Kutenai land cessions.

1855 Yakima War.

1855 Rogue River War.

1855 Fort Belknap Reserve is established.

1856 Discovery in Germany of first recognized fossil of Neanderthal.

1857 Pawnee treaty.

1858 Navajo war.

1859 First commercial oil well drilled in Pennsylvania by Edwin Drake.

1859 The silver rush period in Nevada, Arizona, and part of California brings prospectors, miners, and adventurers, as well as a large lawless element, into remote Indian areas.

1859 *On the Origin of Species* published by Charles Darwin.

1860 The Paiute War.

1860 Pony Express begins, operates 18 months.

1861 First transcontinental telegraph line.

1861 Gatling hand-cranked machine gun is invented.

1861–63 Apache uprising.

1861–65 American Civil War.

1862–64 The Minnesota Sioux uprising.

1863 The Navajo Long Walk.

1863 Emancipation Proclamation is issued by President Abraham Lincoln.

1864 Sand Creek Massacre.

1865 Sioux-Cheyenne uprising.

1865 Abraham Lincoln is assassinated.

1866–68 War for the Bozeman Trail.

1866–74 The Montana Black Hills Gold Rush.

1867 The United States buys Alaska.

1868 Treaty of Fort Laramie.

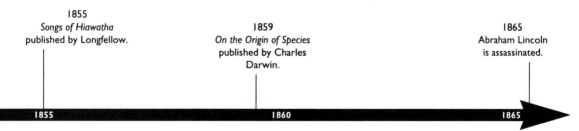

1855
Songs of Hiawatha
published by Longfellow.

1859
On the Origin of Species
published by Charles
Darwin.

1865
Abraham Lincoln
is assassinated.

1855   1860   1865

1868 Navajo Indian Reservation is created.

1868 Plains Warfare begins.

1868 Sioux Treaty of 1868.

1868 Cro-Magnon remains found in France.

1868 Refrigerated railroad cars for food transport are invented.

1869 Transcontinental railroad is completed in the United States.

1870 Jules Verne publishes *Twenty Thousand Leagues Under the Sea.*

1870 *McKay v. Campbell.* The U.S. Supreme Court holds that Indians born in tribal allegiance are not born "in the United States" and are therefore not citizens.

1870 Grant's Peace Policy.

1871 Charles Darwin publishes *The Descent of Man.*

1871 U.S. Congress formally ends treaty-making with American Indian tribes.

1871–79 Wholesale destruction of the buffalo begins. Between 1870 and 1885, more than 10 million buffalo are slaughtered. By 1878 the southern herd is virtually wiped out. The northern herd's demise follows a similar pattern.

1872 U.S. Congress establishes first national park (Yellowstone).

1872 The Modoc War.

1874–75 The Red River (Buffalo) Wars.

1874–81 Warfare on the Northern Plains.

1876 Alexander Graham Bell invents the telephone.

1876 Battle of the Little Big Horn.

1877 Newspaper *Cheyenne Transporter* begins publication.

1877 The Nez Percé War.

1878 The Bannock War.

1879 Sheepeater War.

1879 Ute War.

1879 *Standing Bear v. Crook.* A federal judge rules that "an Indian is a 'person' within the meaning of the laws of the United States."

1879 Sequoyah Convention.

1879–90 Founding of Carlisle Indian Boarding School.

1880 Sun dance is banned by U.S. government.

1881 President James Garfield is assassinated.

1881 Alexander II of Russia is assassinated.

1881–84 Helen Hunt Jackson publishes *A Century of Dishonor*, an indictment of U.S. Indian policy.

1881–85 Religion and customs forbidden. Despite safeguards in the Bill of Rights of the Constitution, President Chester A. Arthur authorizes the Secretary of the Interior to give official approval to rules forbidding "rites, customs...contrary to civilization." In the same action, dances, religious rites, and traditional rituals were likewise forbidden.

1870 *McKay v. Campbell.*	1876 Battle of the Little Big Horn.	1881 President James Garfield is assassinated.

1870	1875	1880

1882 Creation of "Indian Territory" by U.S. Congress.

1882 An act to civilize Pueblo Indians is passed on May 17, containing a provision embodying first assumption of federal responsibility of "civilizing" the Pueblo Indians.

1882 Establishment of Papago (Tohono O'Odham) Reservation.

1882 Hopi Reservation is set aside.

1883 *Ex Parte Crow Dog.* The U.S. Supreme Court rules that Congress had never passed any law extending the federal criminal code to reservation Indians, even though the Sioux had agreed to be subject to any laws Congress might impose on them.

1883 Courts for Indian offenses on Indian reservations are established.

1884 Opening of Haskell Institute.

1884 Chilocco Industrial School is established.

1884 Pueblo Industrial School is established.

1884 Northern Cheyenne Reserve is established.

1885 The Indian Major Crimes Act is passed, allowing U.S. officials to arrest Indians on reservations who have committed one of seven serious crimes (later amended to 10 crimes and then to 14).

1886 Apache resistance under Geronimo.

1886 *United States v. Kagama. Kagama* is a test of the constitutionality of the Major Crimes Act and an affirmation of Congress' power to enact that act. In *Kagama* the court finds that protection of the Indians requires withholding the power of such protection from the individual states.

1887 The General Allotment (Dawes) Act is passed by the U.S. Congress.

1888 James Francis Thorpe, Sauk and Fox athlete, is born.

1888 White Men and Indian Women Marriage Act. On August 9, an act is passed to regulate legal effects of marriages between white men and Indian women, prohibiting white men of intermarrying to obtain tribal rights and to protect property.

1889 Elimination of reservations and tribes recommended by Lake Mohonk reformers of Indian policy.

1889 Minnesota Chippewa Allotment Act.

1889 Oklahoma is opened for settlement.

1889 The Second Ghost Dance Religion.

1890 Wounded Knee Massacre.

1890 Territory of Oklahoma is created.

1890 Ellis Island immigration depot is opened.

1891 Sioux Indian Act allows the Secretary of Interior to divide the reservation of the Sioux Nation of Indians in Dakota into separate reservations.

1891 Fort Berthold Reservation is established.

1883
Ex Parte Crow Dog.

1890
Wounded Knee
Massacre.

1895
Discovery of X-rays
by Roentgen.

1885   1890   1895

1891 Discovery of first fossils of Homo erectus in Java by E. Dubois.

1893 San Carlos Reservation is established.

1893 U.S. troops forcibly gather Hopi children and punish their parents for resisting enforced education.

1894 The company of Thomas A. Edison, Inc. films "The Sioux Ghost Dance" in its West Orange, New Jersey, movie studio.

1895 Discovery of X-rays by Roentgen.

1897 The Intoxication in Indian Country Act is passed forbidding the transportation of ardent spirits, ale, beer, wine, or intoxicating liquor or liquors of whatever kind, under any pretense, into Indian country.

1898 The United States annexes Republic of Hawaii.

1898 USS *Maine* is destroyed; Spanish-American War follows.

1898 The United States annexes Republic of Hawaii.

1899 In *Stephens v. Cherokee Nation* the U.S. Supreme Court holds that Congress has a "plenary power of legislation" over Indian tribes "subject only to the Constitution of the United States."

1901 President William McKinley is assassinated.

1901 Citizenship Act for the Five Civilized Tribes passed by Congress.

1902 Congress passes Cherokee, Choctaw, and Chickasaw land allotment acts.

1903 Wright brothers fly first successful heavier-than-air aircraft.

1903 *Lone Wolf v. Hitchcock* decision.

1905 *United States v. Winans* decision.

1905 Provinces of Alberta and Saskatchewan are created.

1906 Taos Blue Lake is seized.

1906 Burke Act passes.

1906 Alaska Allotment Act.

1907 U.S. "Great White Fleet" circles globe.

1907 Indian Territory becomes Oklahoma.

1908 *Winters v. United States* decision.

1911 Ishi, the "last wild Indian in America," emerges.

1911 First transcontinental flight.

1911 Society of the American Indian is organized.

1912 Jim Thorpe wins Olympic decathlon.

1912 Alaska Native Brotherhood is founded.

1914 Archduke Ferdinand of Austria is assassinated; World War I begins.

1915 Liner *Lusitania* is sunk by German U-boat.

1917 Russian revolution.

1917 Indian births exceed deaths.

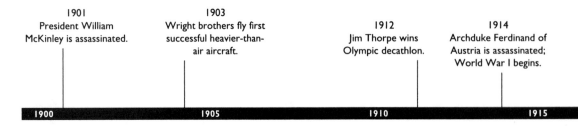

1901	1903	1912	1914
President William McKinley is assassinated.	Wright brothers fly first successful heavier-than-air aircraft.	Jim Thorpe wins Olympic decathlon.	Archduke Ferdinand of Austria is assassinated; World War I begins.

| 1900 | 1905 | 1910 | 1915 |

1918 Native American Church is established.

1919 Treaty of Versailles ends WWI (and sets up WWII).

1919 U.S. citizenship for Indian veterans of WWI.

1920 Non-Indian women gain the vote in the United States.

1920 League of Nations is established.

1921 Potlatch celebrants are arrested.

1922 Federation of Mission Indians is founded.

1922 Indian Welfare League is founded.

1922 U.S.S.R. is established.

1922 Insulin is discovered.

1923 Hitler's "beer-hall putsch" fails; writes *Mein Kampf* while in jail.

1923 Formation of Navajo Tribal Council.

1923 American Indian Defense Association is formed.

1924 Indians are given citizenship.

1924 Stalin seizes power in Soviet Union.

1925 *The Vanishing American* premieres.

1926 Indian Defense League is organized.

1926 National Congress of American Indians is formed.

1927 Longhouse religion is revived.

1928 Charles Curtis is elected vice-president.

1928 Meriam Report is published.

1929 Collapse of stock market in the United States triggers world depression.

1930s Navajo stock reduction.

1930 Kidnapping of Navajo children.

1930 World population reaches two billion.

1931 Native Brotherhood of British Columbia is formed.

1932 *Black Elk Speaks* is published.

1932 Métis Association of Alberta is formed.

1933 Hitler proclaims the Third Reich.

1933 John Collier is appointed Commissioner of Indian Affairs.

1934 Congress repeals the General Allotment Act, replaced by Johnson-O'Malley Act.

1934 Indian Reorganization Act (Wheeler-Howard Act) is passed.

1934 Mao Tse-Tung leads "Long March."

1934 Hitler assumes power in Germany.

1936 Pacific Coast Native Fisherman's Association is formed.

1936 Alaska Native Reorganization Act is passed.

1936 Indian Arts and Crafts Board Act is passed.

1939 World War II begins.

1940 Indian men register for draft for first time.

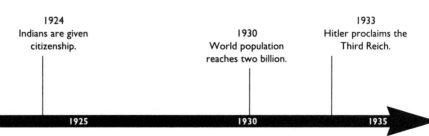

1941 The United States enters World War II following attack on Pearl Harbor.

1941 *Handbook of Federal Indian Law* is published.

1942 Atomic age begins with first controlled atomic chain reaction.

1942 Pacific Coast Native Fisherman's Association merges with Native Brotherhood of British Columbia.

1942 Iroquois declare war on Germany.

1943 Kateri Tekakwitha is declared venerable.

1944 National Congress of American Indians is established.

1944 Canadian Social Security is extended to Natives in northern Canada.

1946 Arapaho Sun Dance held.

1946 Indian Claims Commission Act is passed.

1947 Radiocarbon (carbon-14) dating developed by Libby.

1947 British India partitioned into independent nations of India and Pakistan.

1948 State of Israel is established by United Nations.

1949 Communists establish People's Republic of China.

1949 Hoover Commission report.

1950s Relocation of Indian people into urban areas.

1950 Sun Dance revived among the Sioux.

1953 Termination resolution passes.

1953 Public Law 280 is passed. The law allowed greater state jurisdiction over criminal cases occurring in Indian country in several states including California, Wisconsin, Minnesota, Oregon, Nebraska, and later, in 1959, Alaska.

1954 Ellis Island Immigration depot closed.

1954 World's first nuclear submarine launched (USS *Nautilus)*.

1957 World population reaches three billion.

1958–68 Approximately 200,000 Indians relocate to urban areas.

1959 Mounties attack council house at Six Nations.

1960s Renaissance in Northwest Coastal Art.

1961 National Indian Youth Council is founded.

1962 Institute of American Indian Art is founded.

1963 John F. Kennedy is assassinated.

1963 Native American Movement started.

1963 State of Washington rules against Indian fishing rights.

1964 American Indian Historical Society is founded.

1964 American direct military action begins in Vietnam.

1965 Social inequality triggers Watts riot.

1943
Kateri Tekakwitha is
declared venerable.

1949
Communists
establish People's
Republic of China.

1957
World population
reaches three billion.

1940   1945   1950   1955

1966 Medicare begins in the United States.

1968 Dr. Martin Luther King, Jr., is assassinated.

1968 Robert F. Kennedy is assassinated.

1968 California Indian Legal Service founded.

1968 N. Scott Momaday's novel, *House Made of Dawn*, is published.

1968 National Council on Indian Opportunity is established.

1968 American Indian Civil Rights Act is passed.

1968 Poor People's march on the Bureau of Indian Affairs (BIA).

1968 American Indian Movement (AIM) is founded.

1968 United Native Americans is organized.

1968 Mohawk block traffic from the United States to Canada.

1969 Native American Student Union is formed.

1969 Navajo Community College opens.

1969 North American Indian Traveling College developed.

1969 Senator Edward Kennedy calls for White House conference on Indian problems.

1969 National Indian Education Association is organized.

1969 Alcatraz Island occupied by Indians of All Tribes, Inc.

1969 The Union of British Columbia Indian Chiefs holds founding convention.

1969 Neil Armstrong becomes first human to set foot on the moon.

1970 Indian Brotherhood of the Northwest Territories (Dene Nation) is established.

1970 First Arctic Winter games are held in Yellowknife, Northwest Territories.

1970 Indian Elementary and Secondary Education Act is passed.

1970 North American Indian Unity Convention.

1970 Nixon announces policy of Indian self-determination.

1970 Taos Blue Lake returned to Taos Pueblo.

1970 First "Earth Day."

1970–75 Indian groups demonstrate throughout the United States; occupy numerous government facilities.

1971 Native American Rights Fund (NARF) is founded.

1971 Deganawida-Quetzalcoatl University is founded.

1971 The Alaska Native Claims Act signed.

1971 Indian occupation of Alcatraz Island ends, other occupations continue.

1971 Wallace Black Elk holds Sun Dance at Wounded Knee, South Dakota.

1972 Trail of Broken Treaties (march on Washington, D.C.) begins.

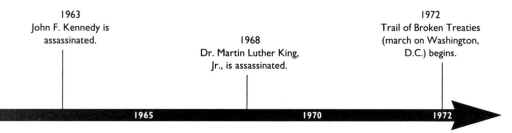

1963
John F. Kennedy is
assassinated.

1968
Dr. Martin Luther King,
Jr., is assassinated.

1972
Trail of Broken Treaties
(march on Washington,
D.C.) begins.

1960   1965   1970   1972

1972 Indians from Trail of Broken Treaties occupy Washington, D.C., BIA headquarters.

1973 Occupation of Wounded Knee II, led by AIM.

1974 Richard M. Nixon resigns U.S. presidency.

1974 Women of All Red Nations is founded.

1974 *United States v. Washington* (Indian treaty fishing rights) is decided.

1974 Hopi and Navajo Relocation Act is signed.

1975 Council of Energy Resource Tribes (CERT) is formed.

1975 Indian Self-Determination and Education Assistance Act signed.

1975 Shootout on Pine Ridge Reservation between AIM members and Federal Bureau of Investigation (FBI) agents results in death of two FBI agents. Leonard Peltier convicted of the murders.

1975 James Bay and Northern Quebec Agreement signed.

1976 World population reaches four billion.

1977 Smallpox eradicated.

1977 American Indian Policy Review Commission Report released.

1978 The Longest Walk begins on Alcatraz Island and proceeds to Washington, D.C.

1978 American Indian Religious Freedom Act (AIRFA) signed.

1978 Indian Child Welfare Act (ICWA) signed.

1978 Congress awards Lakota Nation (Sioux Nation) $122 million for illegal taking of the Black Hills. Lakota Nation refuses the award.

1979 Nuclear accident at Three Mile Island power plant.

1980 New York State sends 70 police to Akwesasne, the St. Regis Mohawk Reservation, to quell local political unrest.

1980 Indian and Federal Trade Act signed.

1980 Kateri Tekakwitha beatified.

1980 *United States v. Sioux Nation* decided. The U.S. Supreme Court upholds the $122 million judgment against the United States for illegal taking of the Black Hills.

1980 Hopi-Navajo Relocation Act signed.

1980 U'Mista Cultural Center opened in Alert Bay.

1980 Helsinki conference reviews U.S. treatment of American Indians.

1980 Eruption of Mt. St. Helens in Washington.

1981 U.S. Supreme Court gets first woman justice (Sandra Day O'Connor).

1981 Indigenous Women's Network founded.

1981 Navajo-Hopi Joint Use Area partitioned.

1982 Canada Constitution Act of 1982 proclaimed.

1982 James Bay agreement reached to deal with problems with James Bay and Northern Quebec agreement.

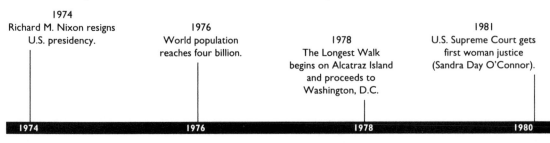

1974	1976	1978	1981
Richard M. Nixon resigns U.S. presidency.	World population reaches four billion.	The Longest Walk begins on Alcatraz Island and proceeds to Washington, D.C.	U.S. Supreme Court gets first woman justice (Sandra Day O'Connor).

| 1974 | 1976 | 1978 | 1980 |

1982 National Navajo Code Talkers day is established.

1982 Jim Thorpe's Olympic medals are restored.

1982 Indian Claims Limitation Act of 1982 signed.

1983 American Indian Registry is established.

1984 Wilma Mankiller sworn in as principal chief of Cherokee Nation.

1986 National debt passes the $2 trillion mark.

1986 Major nuclear power plant accident at Chernobyl in Soviet Union.

1986 Smithsonian Museum of Natural History agrees to return Indian skeletal remains.

1987 *California v. Cabazon Band of Mission Indians* decision is handed down. California may not regulate bingo and gambling on the Cabazon and Morongo Reservations.

1987 Meech Lake Accord signed in Canada.

1987 Pope John Paul II addresses American Indian leaders in Phoenix, Arizona.

1988 *Lyng v. Northwest Indian Cemetery Protective Association* decision handed down. The decision limited American Indian free exercise of religion and curtailed Indian ability to protect sacred sites.

1988 Congress passes Indian Gaming Regulatory Act.

1988 Native Hawaiian Health Care Act of 1988 signed.

1989 *Employment Division v. Smith* decision handed down regarding use of peyote.

1989 *Mississippi Choctaw Band v. Holyfield,* a landmark Indian Child Welfare Act (ICWA), decision is reached.

1989 FBI and New York troopers raid St. Regis Indian Reservation casinos.

1989 Congress approves construction of National Museum of American Indian.

1989 Exxon supertanker Valdez runs aground in Alaska.

1990 Mohawk blockade proposed golf course on sacred burial site near Oka, Quebec.

1990 Native film and video production is established in Edmonton, Alberta.

1990 *Oregon v. Smith* Supreme Court ruling against use of peyote.

1990 Self-Governance Pilot Program announced.

1990 White House Conference on Indian Education.

1990 Native American Graves Protection and Repatriation Act signed.

1990 Indian Child Protection and Family Abuse Prevention Act signed.

1990 Indian Arts and Crafts Act signed.

1990 Census reports Indian population to be 1,959,234.

1991 Tribal Self-Governance Demonstration Project Act signed.

1992 Native Americans demonstrate in response to the Columbus Quincentenary.

1993 1993 is designated the International Year of Indigenous Peoples.

1993 Ada Elizabeth Deer appointed assistant secretary of Indian Affairs.

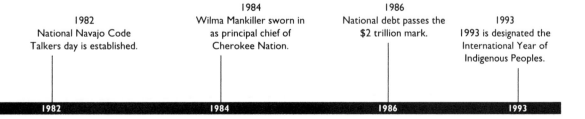

1982
National Navajo Code
Talkers day is established.

1984
Wilma Mankiller sworn in
as principal chief of
Cherokee Nation.

1986
National debt passes the
$2 trillion mark.

1993
1993 is designated the
International Year of
Indigenous Peoples.

1982   1984   1986   1993

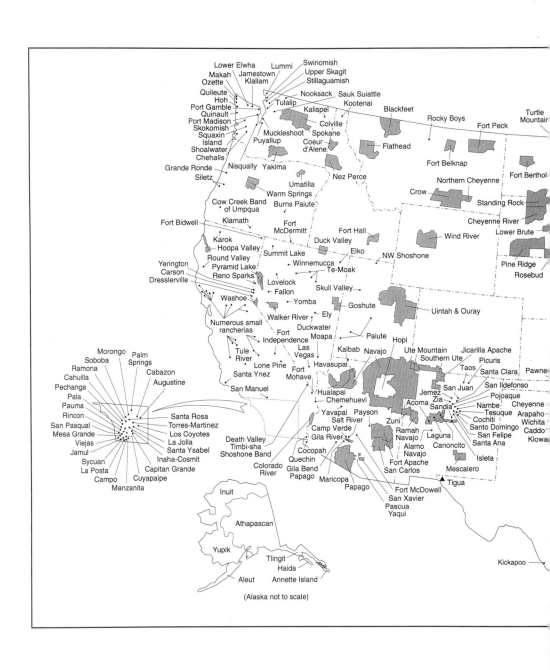

Lower Elwha
Makah
Ozette
Quileute
Hoh
Port Gamble
Quinault
Port Madison
Skokomish
Squaxin
Island
Shoalwater
Chehalis
Grande Ronde
Siletz
Jamestown
Klallam
Lummi
Swinomish
Upper Skagit
Stillaguamish
Nooksack
Sauk Suiattle
Tulalip
Kalispel
Muckleshoot
Puyallup
Nisqually
Yakima
Kootenai
Colville
Spokane
Coeur
d'Alene
Blackfeet
Rocky Boys
Fort Peck
Turtle
Mountain
Flathead
Fort Belknap
Fort Berthol
Umatilla
Warm Springs
Burns Paiute
Nez Perce
Northern Cheyenne
Crow
Standing Rock
Cow Creek Band
of Umpqua
Fort Bidwell
Klamath
Fort
McDermitt
Duck Valley
Fort Hall
Elko
NW Shoshone
Wind River
Cheyenne River
Lower Brute
Karok
Hoopa Valley
Round Valley
Pyramid Lake
Reno Sparks
Yerington
Carson
Dresslerville
Summit Lake
Winnemucca
Te-Moak
Pine Ridge
Rosebud
Lovelock
Fallon
Skull Valley
Washoe
Yomba
Goshute
Uintah & Ouray
Walker River
Ely
Numerous small
rancherias
Fort
Independence
Duckwater
Moapa
Paiute
Hopi
Tule
River
Lone Pine
Santa Ynez
San Manuel
Fort
Mohave
Las
Vegas
Kaibab
Navajo
Ute Mountain
Southern Ute
Jicarilla Apache
Picuris
Taos
Santa Clara
Pawne
Havasupai
Hualapai
Chemehuevi
Jemez
San Juan
San Ildefonso
Pojoaque
Nambe
Tesuque
Cheyenne
Arapaho
Wichita
Caddo
Kiowa
Morongo
Soboba
Ramona
Cahuilla
Pechanga
Pala
Pauma
Rincon
San Pasqual
Mesa Grande
Viejas
Jamul
Sycuan
La Posta
Campo
Manzanita
Palm
Springs
Cabazon
Augustine
Santa Rosa
Torres-Martinez
Los Coyotes
La Jolla
Santa Ysabel
Inaha-Cosmit
Capitan Grande
Cuyapaipe
Yavapai
Salt River
Camp Verde
Gila River
Payson
Acoma
Sandia
Zuni
Ramah
Navajo
Alamo
Navajo
Zia
Cochiti
Laguna
Canoncito
Santo Domingo
San Felipe
Santa Ana
Isleta
Death Valley
Timbi-sha
Shoshone Band
Colorado
River
Cocopah
Quechin
Gila Bend
Papago
Maricopa
Papago
Fort Apache
San Carlos
Fort McDowell
San Xavier
Pascua
Yaqui
Mescalero
Tigua
Inuit
Athapascan
Yupik
Tlingit
Haida
Aleut
Annette Island
Kickapoo

(Alaska not to scale)

Federal Indian Reservations
● Federal Indian Reservations
▲ State Indian Reservations

Bois Forte
Deer Creek
Vermillion Lake
Red Lake
Red Cliff
Bad River
Grand Portage
L'Anse
White Earth
Leech Lake
Lac Vieux Desert
Hannahville
Bay Mills
Sault Ste Marie
seton
Fond du Lac
Ontonagon
Sandy Lake
Mille Lacs
St. Croix
Lac du Flambeau
Grand Traverse
Lac Courte-Oreilles
Prairie Island
Sokaogan Chippewa
Potawatomi
pper Sioux
Shakopee
Menominee
Oneida
dreau
Lower Sioux
Yankton
Winnebago
Stockbridge-Munsee
Isabella
Sac and Fox
Potawatomi
ntee
ioux
Winnebago
Omaha
c and Fox
Iowa
ckapoo
awatomi
Peoria
Quapaw
nkawa
Shawnee
Ottawa
nca
Kaw
Wyandot
le
Osage
Seneca Cayuga
Miami
E. Shawnee
Modoc
Cherokee
Creek
Seminole
Choctaw
va
Chickasaw
Shawnee
Mississippi Choctaw
Potawatomi
Sac and Fox
Coushatta
Kickapoo
Poarch Creek
Tunica-Biloxi
Alabama-Coushatta
Chitimacha

Micmac
Houlton Maliseet
Indian Township
Pennocook
Pleasant Point
Ganienkeh
Penobscot
St. Regis
Abnaki
Nipmuk-Hassanamisko
Tonawanda
Oneida
Onondaga
Tuscarora
Oil Springs
Shagticoke
Paugusett
Allegheny
Cattaraugus
Wampanoag
Narragansett
Mashantucket Pequot
Paucatuck Pequot
Shinnecock
Poosepatuck

Mattaponi
Pamunkey

Cherokee
Catawba

Brighton Seminole
Big Cypress Seminole
Dania
Miccosukee

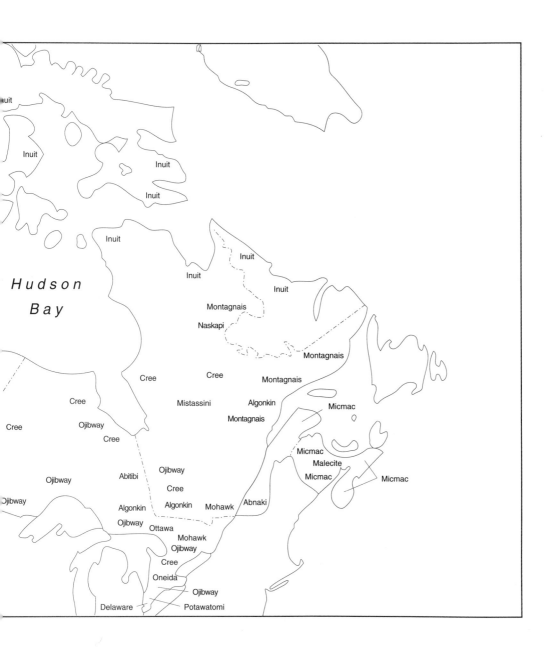

Inuit

Inuit

Inuit

Inuit

Inuit

Inuit

Inuit

Inuit

Inuit

Hudson Bay

Montagnais

Naskapi

Montagnais

Cree

Cree

Montagnais

Micmac

Cree

Mistassini

Algonkin

Cree

Montagnais

Micmac

Cree

Ojibway

Malecite

Micmac

Micmac

Cree

Ojibway

Abitibi

Ojibway

Ojibway

Cree

Algonkin

Algonkin

Mohawk

Abnaki

Ojibway

Ottawa

Mohawk

Ojibway

Cree

Oneida

Ojibway

Delaware

Potawatomi

Chronology

OF NATIVE NORTH AMERICAN HISTORY

Part 1

NATIVE
NORTH AMERICAN
HISTORY BEFORE 1500

Chapter 1

50,000 B.C. TO A.D. 1499

50,000–10,000 B.C.

50,000 B.C. **Beringia.** At various times during the latter part of the Pleistocene epoch of the Ice Age, lands now submerged in the Bering Strait are intermittently exposed. The stretches of tundra are possibly 1,000 miles wide and create the Bering Strait Land Bridge, known as Beringia, between North America and Asia. Large animals of the Ice Age migrate across these vast areas into North America, followed by groups of humans. The Paleo-Siberians, or Paleo-Indians, thus become the first individuals to inhabit North America.

The migration of humanity from Asia gradually proceeds for many millennia, as does the ensuing dispersal of peoples throughout North and South America. Once in North America, early humankind follows various ice-free corridors south throughout the continent. From these corridors, for example, Paleo-Indians, also known as Lithic Indians, disperse along major river valleys and mountain passes and eventually cover the Western Hemisphere. Even after the final submersion of Beringia, migrations to North America from Asia continue. As late as 3000 B.C., Eskimos, Aleuts, and possibly, Athapascans use wooden dugouts and skin boats to cross the Bering Sea and establish societies and cultures in North America.

38,000 B.C. **Texas.** During the long stretch of

centuries after human migration to North America begins, and until the end of the Ice Age, big-game hunting is the dominant way of life. Most hunting societies track large Pleistocene game such as woolly mammoths, mastodons, saber-toothed tigers, American lions, camels, bighorn bison, short-faced bears, and other mammals for sustenance. In Lewisville, Texas, the concentration of human and animal remains indicates the presence of early societies in this area. Since, technologically, these societies rely on bone implements and wooden spears, the period from about 50,000 B.C. to 25,000 B.C. is often referred to as the Pre-Projectile Point Stage.

27,000 B.C. **Yukon.** During the Pleistocene period, while nearly all of northern North America is heavily glaciated, much of western Alaska and the Yukon River drainage of central Alaska are not ice covered. Sealed off from the rest of the continent by western Canadian ice, this area is known as the "Alaskan Refuge." As the glaciers thaw, sea levels increase and cover much of the land bridge. At Old Crow Flats in the northern Yukon Territory, a caribou bone scraper is one of the earliest artifacts that reveals the process of settlement in this region.

25,000 B.C. **North America.** New technologies appear among the Paleo-Indian societies of North America. Workable stone—especially flint, chart, and obsidian—is crafted into functional tools such as knives, scrapers, choppers, and, most importantly for hunting, spear points. The introduction of stone spear points dramatically alters the subsistence patterns of Paleo-Indians. Different periods of Paleo-Indian history are classified by the types of spear points used and normally bear the name of the site at which a particular stone point has been found, such as Sandia, Clovis, Folsom, and Plano. The fact that these stone points are not found in Asia indicates that the technological adaptations occurred only within North American Indian societies.

25,000 B.C. Sandia Mountains, New Mexico. Paleo-Indian societies that develop in the Southwest use the Sandia stone point. From two to four inches long, the Sandia points have rounded bases with a bulge on one side for greater stability. The development of this point, first uncovered in the Sandia Mountains in New Mexico, is limited to the societies of the Southwest. The length and width of the point reveals a reliance on large game for sustenance.

15,000 B.C. North America. The Clovis culture, also referred to as Llano, becomes much more widespread than the Sandia. Although named after the original Clovis site in New Mexico, Clovis stone points are used in every mainland state of the United States. Characterized by its slender point with lengthwise channels on both sides, the Clovis points are crafted by pressure-flaking, and used to hunt numerous Pleistocene animals, especially mammoths and mastodons. Widespread use of Clovis stone points disappears around 9200 B.C.

11,000 B.C. Alaska. Over a period of years small bands of hunters steadily make their way across the Bering Sea Land Bridge from Siberia. Eventually these people and their descendants spread throughout North and South America to become the ancestors of all subsequent generations of Native Americans. (Some archaeologists believe the first people came across well before 18,000 B.C. Although of

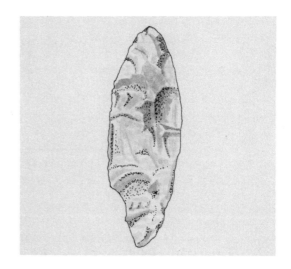

Sandia stone point. Courtesy of Molly Braun.

questionable validity, possible bone artifacts found along the Old Crow River in Canada's Yukon Territory were dated at 27,000 B.C. to 24,000 B.C.)

11,000 B.C. Lindenmeier Site, Colorado. The Paleo-Indians live a nomadic life based on hunting many types of animals and collecting wild plants. Located in Colorado, just south of the Wyoming border, the Lindenmeier site was the first Paleo-Indian camp to be studied. It helped verify the antiquity of humans in the Americas.

10,200 B.C. North America. The remains of animals closely related to wolves but about three-fourths their size are found at the Jones-Miller site in Colorado and other Paleo-Indian sites in the western United States, indicating that dogs are integral parts of many cultures.

10,000 B.C. North America. Throughout the continent glaciers rapidly begin to thaw, and the Pleistocene epoch comes to an end. According to the most widely held theories, dramatic climatic changes occur within the next few millennia. Because of the increasing temperatures, many big-game species and mam-

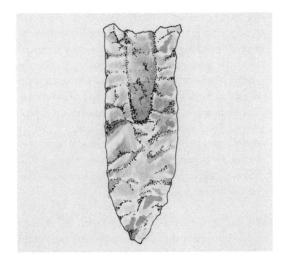

Clovis stone point. Courtesy of Molly Braun.

mals start to become extinct. Consequently, Paleo-Indian societies are forced to create new subsistence patterns.

10,000 B.C. Southwest. As big-game animals begin to die off, societal economies in the Southwest become more diversified. People begin to rely on wild plants as well as nomadic hunting, and use vegetable-grinding tools such as manos, milling stones, and, later, mortars and pestles. Human burials also appear in specific locations, revealing the growing sedentary nature of many societies in this region. The *atlatl* becomes a primary tool for hunting. The atlatl is also called a spear thrower and consists of a spear point held on top of a long handle. By holding the handle and propelling the spear forward, the hunter can achieve a lever effect and greater throwing power.

9999–6000 B.C.

9200 B.C. North America. Following the Clovis societies, a new Paleo-Indian culture emerges across the continent. Named after the Folsom site in New Mexico, the Folsom people are hunters and gatherers, but make smaller spear points than their Clovis ancestors. Folsom points are generally shorter than Sandia and Clovis points with leaflike grooves along both sides. Evidence of Folsom hunters has been found over much of North America, particularly in the Great Plains, and the Lindenmeier site in Colorado contains many Folsom remains. Folsom stone points are fluted like Clovis points, but are even more carefully fashioned, with tapered edges. The smaller Folsom points suggest that toward the end of the Clovis period, around 8000 B.C., many of the North American Pleistocene mammals, such as the mammoth, are already extinct. With smaller stone points, the Folsom cultures begin to diversify their economies, hunting many smaller animals and adapting their societies to better exploit their physical environments. Many new hunting techniques emerge, such as large-scale cooperative group activities like stampeding herds over cliffs or into swamps.

9000 B.C. Arctic. In areas untouched by glaciers, people of the Paleoarctic tradition develop an effective hunting system and are the first people in the Americas to find ways of living in the harsh arctic environment. Their tools include scrapers, spear points, and very small, razor-sharp stone tools called microblades. They live in small, highly mobile groups that move over wide territories to take advantage of the best hunting conditions. The development of different Paleo-Indian societies in the Arctic and throughout North America highlights the range of cultural and societal developments in addition to the major Sandia, Clovis, and Folsom cultures.

9000 B.C. Blackwater Draw, New Mexico. A large oval, spring-fed pond in eastern New Mexico, Blackwater Draw is the site of many Clovis campsites and bison kills. Along its western shore, numerous drives and kills are conducted by Clovis and then later Folsom hunters. The remains at this site have helped archaeologists understand the changing nature

Stone projectile point found at Folsom, New Mexico. Photo by Thane L. Bierwert. Courtesy of the Department Library Services, American Museum of Natural History.

of Paleo-Indian societies and to better date their time in history. Its now-dried strata containing artifacts of different periods and societies help reveal the changing conditions and peoples of the region.

9000 B.C. Great Basin. Another example of the development of unique societal organizations other than the dominant Paleo-Indian cultures is the Desert culture found in the Great Basin. With the dramatic climatic changes and increasing aridity of the region, the Indians of the Desert culture adapt remarkably to their environment. Artifacts from the Danger Cave archaeological site in western Utah, such as small, leaf-shaped projectile points and knives, scrapers, and engraving tools, reveal a heavy reliance on hunting. Woven containers and grinding stones found at the site show the emergence of hunting and gathering societies. Many archaeologists believe that the Danger Cave artifacts may represent a transitional period between the earlier Clovis Paleo-Indians and the later Archaic period cultures in this region.

9000 B.C. Great Plains. Although there are competing interpretations of the extinction of many of the big-game mammals, it is accepted that the end of the Pleistocene age and the warming climatic changes had drastic effects on these animals. With the extinction of predators like lions and short-faced bears, the species of bison *Bison antiquus* increase dramatically in the Great Plains. The climatic changes also foster an expansion of shortgrass prairie. The bison becomes a major food source for the people of the plains.

8500 B.C. Great Plains. Located in eastern Wyoming near the Cheyenne River, the Agate Basin site is one of a growing number of places that reveal the changing hunting strategies of the Paleo-Indian cultures. In this location bison are driven into an *arroyo*, or gully, where they are surrounded and killed. During the same period, at the Bonfire Shelter site in western Texas, herds of bison are driven over a cliff. Another major site is the Olsen-Chubbock site in Colorado where, like the Agate Basin, bison are driven down into an arroyo and then killed. These bison drives have sparked numerous scholarly debates over the extent and effects of such large-scale hunting techniques. According to widely accepted theories, these societies do not know how to preserve excess meats and could consume only limited quantities. Some scholars argue that the drives helped bring about the extinction of many of the big-game mammals, a process sometimes referred to as Pleistocene Overkill; this view, however, is generally not accepted since it fails to explain the extinction of big-game mammals in other regions.

8500 B.C. Pacific Northwest. Along the Columbia River system in the Plateau region, Paleo-Indian societies have a more diversified subsistence pattern. Artifacts and remains from the Marmes Rock Shelter on the lower Snake River in southeast Washington and from other cave sites detail an economy based on a broad range of plants and animals. The absence of large open kill sites and stone points for big-game mammals suggests smaller societal organizations and less cooperative hunting by groups.

8000 B.C. California. Although no artifacts or remains indicate the development of major Paleo-Indian societies in this region, many postglacial societies emerge in southern California during this time. Findings from the Lake Mojave region in the southeast, as well as from the San Dieguito complex near the southern coast, reveal many similarities with the Desert culture of the Great Basin, such as small-game hunting tools.

8000 B.C. Columbia River, Oregon. Along the great rivers of the Plateau region, societies emerge that rely increasingly on the natural food resources of the rivers. At sites where the Columbia River cuts through the Cascade mountain range, people camp and take advantage of the rich salmon resources. The archaeological site at this location, called the Dalles, holds the remains of thousands of salmon bones as well as a wide variety of tools. Demonstrating the diversifying economies in the region, the emergence of fishing societies indicates less reliance on hunting and gathering. As the glaciers retreat, many of these societies move from the interior plateau into coastal regions to fish in the area. According to some archaeological theories, the peoples of this region even collect tolls from other societies to extract resources from the river. This hypothesis suggests a major transition in the development of many of these societies, arguing that established trade networks and interdependent societal relations exist at this early date.

8000 B.C. Holcombe Site, Western Great Lakes. At the Holcombe site, just north of Detroit, early Archaic period foraging peoples develop tools such as gravers, scrapers, and

A monolithic stone axe from Georgia engraved with Southeastern ceremonial complex iconography. Courtesy of the National Anthropological Archives, Smithsonian Institution.

various projectile point forms, replacing earlier styles used by Paleo-Indian groups.

8000 B.C. North America. Across the continent as new, more diverse, post-Ice Age environments emerge, the Plano culture, also known as the Plainview, signifies a transition between the Paleo-Indian period and the new Archaic period. The Paleo-Indian period, characterized by migratory big-game hunting using chipped-stone weapons, changes as societies begin gathering wide assortments of fauna and flora. Located principally in the Great Plains, the Plano societies employ stone spear points but begin to further exploit their natural environment, developing more elaborate hunting techniques. Displaying a more diversified economy, the Plano societies often are referred to as a Proto-archaic society representing a continuation of many big-game hunting or Paleo-Indian characteristics but also displaying some traits of the emerging Archaic period. This new period is also known as the Foraging period.

7500 B.C.   Danger Cave, Utah. Because of the arid environment, many cave sites in the Great Basin and Southwest contain preserved remains of wood, leather, fur, basketry, and other items that usually decay at more exposed sites. Archaeologists found remains of baskets at the Danger Cave site in Utah, suggesting that Desert culture people from this region are weaving twined baskets.

7500 B.C.   Southeastern United States. Towards the end of the Paleo-Indian period in the Southeast, societies develop a unique point style called Dalton, which is often used as a projectile as well as a knife and is found in association with stone scrapers and woodworking tools. Evidence of this tradition comes from major archaeological sites throughout the area, particularly the Brand, Lace, and Sloan sites. Findings from these sites suggest that as deciduous forests expand throughout the region, the Dalton cultures begin adapting their hunting techniques.

7000 B.C.   California and Great Basin. Seashells are used to trade by the Great Basin societies through complex networks extending from Nevada to the California coastal tribes and interior California peoples. The seashells are probably valued as ornaments, and exchanged for items such as furs, food, or stone found naturally in the interior regions.

7000 B.C.   North America. With the growing diversification of subsistence patterns throughout North America, the Paleo-Indian period characterized by big-game migratory hunting ends. Societies emerging across the continent selectively exploit natural resources at frequent, seasonal intervals. This new period of subsistence adaptation is known as the Archaic, or Foraging, period. During this time subsistence patterns are based on regional ecological and environmental conditions, but generally societies are technologically more advanced and versatile. As people hunt many different animals and gather many different plants, societies become more stable and adapt better to rapidly changing circumstances. With growing economic productivity, populations increase and diversify within smaller regions. Archaic societies are often categorized as Eastern and Western, divided by the Mississippi River.

7000–6500 B.C.   Great Basin. The use of caves or rock-shelters, bark or grass beds, twined basketry, netting, matting, fur cloth, sandals, the atlatl, small projectile points, flat milling stones, scrapers and choppers, digging sticks, fire drills, hearths, wooden clubs, smoking pipes, seashell ornaments, deer-hoof rattles, medicine bags, and bird-bone whistles among many societies, especially those in the Great Basin, demonstrates the growing complexity of economic life in these periods. Basketry, sandals, and grass beds illustrate numerous processes of adaptation to the physical environment while medicine bags, rattles, and ornaments highlight complex aesthetic and religious values. Many of these remains have been unearthed at the Danger Cave and Hogup Cave sites in Utah.

6500 B.C.   Southeast. Freshwater mussels and other river resources become a major part of the diet for Archaic period peoples.

6400 B.C.   Hogup Cave, Utah. People living along the edges of ancient lakes, in the region west of present-day Salt Lake City, collect pickleweed and hunt a variety of waterfowl.

The remains of nets and traps also indicate the hunting of rabbits and other small game.

6000 B.C.   Moorehead Cave, Texas. Artifacts from the Moorehead Cave in the Great Bend region of Texas indicate the presence and long history of an Archaic hunting and gathering society that exists in this region until the period of European contact. These peoples have many cultural similarities with the Coahuiltecan peoples who live in small bands that hunt and gather over a vast region of southwest Texas and northern Mexico. Because of the aridity of the region, these related Coahuiltecan peoples never adopt agriculture.

6000 B.C.   North America. In many regions, groups adapt to smaller ranges as populations increase. Local cultural differences multiply due to decreased interaction.

5999–2500 B.C.

5500 B.C.   North America. Grinding stones called *manos* and *metates*, used for processing seeds and other plant products, become important tools in many societies and have been found in Archaic period sites. These food processing tools and techniques indicate the presence of gathering economies throughout both Eastern and Western Archaic societies.

5500 B.C.   Southern California. Archaic cultures referred to as the Encinitas tradition develop along the California coast from Paleo-Indian ancestors. Grinding stones and abundant shellfish remains provide evidence of an economy based on collecting marine coastal resources. In the San Diego area, the Encinitas tradition lasts until A.D. 1000.

5000 B.C.   Arctic and Subarctic. By this time hunting and foraging groups of the Northern Archaic tradition begin exploiting the increasingly ice-free environments. They live in small camps and hunt throughout the tundra and

forests. On the northern forest fringes, caribou hunting is a primary occupation. In the dense woodlands slightly farther south, elk, deer, and moose are important. At Aberdeen Lake, about three hundred miles west of Hudson Bay, hunters camp to intercept the seasonal migrations of vast caribou herds. These hunts continue at Aberdeen Lake for the next four thousand years.

5000 B.C.   Northwestern Great Plains. For the next 2,500 years, a drier climate prevails, causing a reduction in prairie grasses and a dwindling of the bison herds. The presence of fewer archaeological sites for this period indicates that human populations probably move out of the region.

5000 B.C.   Southern Great Basin. For nearly 4,000 years, the Pinto Basin cultures develop during the Archaic period throughout the southern Great Basin. Practicing a hunting and gathering subsistence economy, these people possess an incredible knowledge of their desert environment. Certain evidence of small circular houses suggests that they are semisedentary. They trade with other Archaic Desert culture societies.

5000 B.C.   Southwest. Of the many Western Archaic culture groups, the Cochise culture develops out of the Desert culture in Arizona and New Mexico. As the environment becomes predominantly arid, the Cochise societies constantly adapt their economic and societal organization to the local conditions. Seasonally migrating throughout the region, the Cochise peoples build homes in cliffs, caves, and in desert valleys. Gathering many different plants, the Cochise cultures are believed to pave the way for the extensive agricultural development in the region by later peoples.

4500 B.C.   Northeastern California. People of the Menlo phase (4500–2500 B.C.) are the first to build sturdy, semisubterranean earth lodges in this region. From these relatively permanent

Stenciled handprints designed on a shelter wall at Sliding Rock, Canyon de Chelly, Arizona. Photo by Earl H. Morris and A.V. Kidder. Courtesy of the Department Library Services, American Museum of Natural History.

hamlets, they exploit environments ranging from the mountains to the river valleys. Later, the climate becomes drier and the people are forced to move more often to find food. They respond by shifting to lighter, easier-to-build dwellings made of brush.

4000 B.C.   Koster Site, Illinois. Throughout the Midwest during the Archaic period population settlements begin to grow and their economies continue to diversify. Hunters and gathers build permanent shelters at base camps. In southern Illinois at the Koster Site, there is evidence of repeated use of the same encampment.

4000 B.C.   Ocean Bay, Kodiak Island, Alaska. As the sea level begins to stabilize in Alaska at Kodiak Island, about 215 miles south of the modern city of Anchorage, Arctic hunters begin adapting their skills to exploit mammals and fish in the area. Societies rely extensively on coastal hunting and fishing and develop numerous tools that facilitate the rise of a marine economy. Multiple-person kayaks, harpoons with long stone points, and knives for processing large sea animals become integral aspects of these Kodiak tradition societies.

4000 B.C.   Onion Portage, Alaska. Some of the earliest Northern Archaic tradition artifacts are found at Onion Portage on the Kobuk River in northeast Alaska. They give evidence for increasingly diverse subsistence strategies, including a shift to caribou hunting. Evidence from this site indicates that this region is used as a major village campsite for nearly 5,000 years. Accordingly, the Onion Portage site has helped archaeologists more accurately date changes in the cultural groups living in the area.

3111 B.C.   Middle America. This is the earliest date in the great Maya calendar, from which all later Maya dates are counted. The existence of a complicated, precise calendar system based on celestial observation gives indication of the complex knowledge about and recordings of time kept by North American Indian societies. It is not known exactly what happened on this date.

3000 B.C.   Southern California. In some areas along the coast, the Encinitas tradition is replaced by the Campbell tradition, which has a greater orientation toward hunting deer and other game animals. Artifacts of the Campbell tradition include leaf-shaped points and stone mortars and pestles. These food processing tools are used to help grind acorns, which are first used by people of the Campbell tradition in this area. The Campbell tradition trades extensively with other California peoples, particularly in shells and obsidian, and is predecessor of the modern Chumash of the Santa Barbara area.

3000 B.C. Southwest. Beginning about this time, favorable conditions for widespread trade and interaction develop, permitting the eventual spread of important domesticated plants from Mexico, especially maize, beans, and squash. Around the same time, four regional Archaic period traditions of hunting and gathering peoples, known collectively as the Picosa culture, take shape. In the west little is known about the San Dieguito-Pinto tradition. Its best-known artifact is the small Pinto Basin projectile point, but there are a variety of others, including small grinding slabs and choppers. In the north, the Oshara tradition shows many connections in artifact styles with the western San Dieguito-Pinto tradition. In the east, the Hueco and Coahuiltecan cultural complexes are known to include many wooden and other perishable objects, such as nets and sandals, recovered from dry caves. In the south, during the Chiricahua and San Pedro phases of the Cochise tradition, people use a wide variety of plant processing and hunting tools. Many scholars believe that these southwestern Archaic cultures are ancestors to later Hohokam and Mogollon peoples.

3000 B.C. Umnak Island, Alaska. At Umnak and other islands in the Aleutian chain, people skilled at hunting seals, sea lions, and whales build villages with small oval houses, three to five meters in diameter.

2600 B.C. Southeast. During the Middle Archaic period, throughout the Southeast, river valley populations rely heavily on fish and other river foods. Evidence from the sites of many river bank encampments reveals the increasing reliance on fish, shellfish, and other water-based foods. During the same period, it is believed that long distance trading expands. As larger populations form, more interdependent relationships are established. Shell remains indicate that expanding populations use trade as a means of maintaining good relations with a growing number of neighboring groups. It is also possible that exotic items, such as shells and rare stone, are becoming important as markers of wealth and status.

2500 B.C. Central California. For the next 2,000 years people of the Windmiller period (also called the Windmiller pattern) cultures live in permanent villages and practice a wide variety of hunting and gathering activities in California's Central Valley. Maintaining a seasonal migratory economy, the Windmiller peoples develop their own unique cultural traditions. They are the first peoples of the region to bury their dead in small mounds. They make beads and other shell ornaments, indicating their interdependency and trading networks with coastal peoples. They also design bowls, pipes, and baskets. Many scholars believe the Windmiller peoples are ancestors of the five major cultures of the Central Valley—the Yokuts, Miwok, Maidu, Wintun, and Ohlone—based on evidence of a common language in the region dating to this period.

2500 B.C. Charles River, Massachusetts. Several large fish traps, called weirs, are positioned at the mouth of the Charles and other rivers as they feed into the Atlantic Ocean. The peoples of the Northeast rely heavily on sea and river resources and continue to use weirs until European contact. This adaptation to marine resources represents a transition from the Archaic period to a more sedentary cultural tradition.

2500 B.C. Southeast. Evidence of early pottery is found at sites in Georgia and Florida. The styles are constructed using plant fibers as

Mississippian marble mortuary figure. Courtesy of Molly Braun.

tempering material to strengthen the vessels. These and later pottery indicate a major technological advance in the preparation and storage of food and other resources. The introduction and development of pottery also represents a transition from the Archaic cultural tradition to a more diversified and specialized tradition.

2499–1 B.C.

2000 B.C.   Alaska. The Arctic Small Tool tradition develops and spreads east as far as Greenland. These hunters and fishers are the first humans to live in the eastern Arctic, which other than Antarctica is the last uninhabited region of the world. The people of the Arctic Small Tool tradition are the ancestors of the modern-day Inuit. They develop remarkable hunting techniques and tools to survive and adapt in the world's harshest environment, including special harpoons and other devices for hunting seals, walrus, and whales.

2000 B.C.   Eastern United States. By this date, four major native plants are being domesticated in this region. The introduction and cultivation of agricultural products transforms many societies, as hunting and gathering groups are replaced by more sedentary, horticultural societies. The transformation brings rapid population increases, and these foods serve as major staples in the region well into European contact. Two of the four plants, squash and sunflowers, are still used today. The other two, marsh elder and chenopodium, are no longer cultivated and are now thought of only as weeds.

2000 B.C.   Great Lakes. From about this time into the period of European contact, people mine copper in the Lake Superior area. The copper is obtained in relatively pure chunks and is cold-hammered into a variety of tools and ornaments. Over time, this highly crafted copper is traded widely across the eastern woodlands and serves as a major resource of exchange.

2000 B.C.   Labrador. A type of chalcedony known as Ramah Chalcedony, a translucent type of stone easily worked into a variety of tools, becomes an important trade item after the arrival of Inuit peoples into far eastern Canada. This stone, along with black slate, is traded from Labrador throughout the Northeast. As populations increase in the Middle and Late Archaic periods, diverse cultures emerge in more localized regions and come to specialize in the extraction and production of natural resources. These materials serve as commodities of exchange throughout the Eastern Archaic cultures and signify status and prestige in many different societies.

2000 B.C.   Northern Nevada. During this time the Late Archaic cultures within this area undergo a series of changes to take advantage of the many large lakes in the area. Duck decoys, nets, fishhooks, leather robes, cordage, snares, twined bags, twined and coiled baskets, and stone, bone, and wood tools are manufactured.

2000 B.C.   Northwest Coast. Beginning as early as 2000 B.C. archaeological remains, called the

Adena burial ground in Miamisburg, Ohio. Courtesy of Dean R. Snow. (See entry, **500 B.C. Midwest**, p. 16.)

Strait of Georgia tradition, point to coastal and interior societal adaptations that eventually lead to the development of complex societies like the present-day Coast Salish and Bella Bella. Initially, artifact styles are very similar to those from Kodiak Island, Alaska, and include a wide variety of harpoons and fishing equipment. By A.D. 400 distinctive Strait of Georgia tradition artifacts include ground slate spear points, barbed points made of bone, and spindle whorls used to make cloth.

2000–1500 B.C. Ocmulgee Mounds. Archeological evidence from Ocmulgee Mounds east of present-day Macon, Georgia, indicates that Indians in Florida and Georgia are making fired earthenware ceramics.

2000 B.C.–A.D. 300 Berkeley Pattern. Utan-speaking peoples move into the San Francisco Bay area in California, eventually spreading along the Central Coast and the Monterey Bay region. Capitalizing upon the diverse resources of woodland, grassland, and marshland environments, these people utilize both shore and inland locations. It is believed that early settlements located in harvest spots with smaller

satellite communities later establishing themselves nearby.

1500 B.C. Central California. Flexed burials, some cremation, coiled basketry, wooden mortars, barbed harpoons, and the bow and arrow appear. Village sites become larger and "shell mounds" and other burial sites are built. The evidence of more concentrated, economically diversified, and culturally complex societies indicates the growth of unique and dynamic cultures with their own specialized modes of production and ideological systems. The emergence of these larger and politically organized societies during the Formative period *(See* next entry) is referred to regionally as the Pacific period, and lasts until European contact.

1500 B.C. North America. Pottery making, horticulture, village communities, ceremonial structures, trade, and weaving begin to characterize most societies throughout North America. Despite the many regional variations, this period is called the Formative period and lasts in most areas up to European contact. Also often referred to as the post-Archaic or Classic period, the Formative refers broadly to the increasing diversification of cultures and diffusion of cultural traditions throughout North America. In different regions these transformations take different linguistic, economic, religious, and political forms.

1500 B.C. Subarctic. A period of increasing cold causes the southward retreat of forests. Northern Archaic tradition hunters who are accustomed to forest environments follow the migratory caribou herds. Shortly after the Northern Archaic tradition hunters move south, Inuit (Eskimo) peoples begin living in these northern regions. Many of their communities still exist today.

1400 B.C. Louisiana. By this date, people living along the lower Mississippi River and its tributaries are constructing large mounds and living in planned communities. The best-known example from this period is the Poverty Point site, located 55 miles west of Vicksburg, Mississippi, where a massive semicircle of concentric mounds stands. Some archaeologists believe Poverty Point is the first chiefdom north of Mexico. There are approximately a hundred smaller sites with cultural connections to Poverty Point.

1400 B.C. Midwestern and Eastern Regions. Development of unique cultures throughout these regions is described comprehensively as Woodland culture and refers to Formative cultures and stages such as Adena, Hopewell, Mississippian, and others.

1000 B.C. Central California. Cultures of the Cosumnes period grow out of the earlier Windmiller culture. Artifacts suggest these peoples rely more on harvesting acorns and fishing than their Windmiller ancestors, although hunting continues to be important.

1000 B.C. Northeast. Vessels carved from a stone called steatite are a common trade item from New England to the southern Appalachian Mountains.

1000 B.C. Southwest. Evidence at Bat Cave and Jemez Cave in southwest New Mexico suggests that maize becomes an integral part of many different cultures at this time. Societies begin to incorporate the cultivation, harvesting, and planting of maize into their religious, social, and economic institutions.

1000–800 B.C. Western Arctic. Moving from the Bering Strait region and eventually spreading into the Eastern Arctic, the Norton tradition appears, introducing clay vessel and oil-burning lamp technologies.

1000–500 B.C. Choris Peninsula, Alaska. Along coastal sites north of the Bering Strait, the first pottery in Alaska appears in this area of Kotzebue Sound. Its fiber-tempered production and linear stamp style of adornment reflect recent contact with Asia.

1000 B.C.–A.D. 1100 Southern California Coast Middle Period. Increasing emphasis on maritime exploitation occurs. Shell beads and ornaments originally conceived of as ornamental decoration begin to function as currency and as a symbol of social status. Bone remains of deepwater fish suggest the development of more sophisticated water craft during the Middle Period.

900 B.C. Alaska. Thule culture begins to spread east, replacing and acculturating already existing Dorset groups. Mobile Thule technology such as umiaks, kayaks, and dog sleds allow a wider range of resource exploitation in the harsh tundra environment, providing numerous advantages over the more sedentary and locally based culture of the Dorset.

700 B.C. Foxe Basin and Baffin Island, Canada. In this vast region north of Hudson Bay, Dorset Inuit culture develops, eventually spreading to many parts of the eastern Arctic. Excavations at the Kapuivik site, near Igloolik, reveal the oldest documented occurrence of Dorset

The Serpent Mound, an effigy mound of the Adena or Hopewell culture, about the first century B.C. Courtesy of the Archives-Library Division, Ohio Historical Society. (See entry, **100 B.C. Locust Grove, Ohio**, p. 17.)

culture. Dwellings used by the Dorset people include skin tents, sod houses, and pit houses.

700 B.C. St. Lawrence and Bering Strait Islands. Technology, such as toggling harpoons, polished slate, elaborately carved bone and ivory tools, revolutionizes sea mammal hunting and forms the initial basis for the Thule or Northern Maritime tradition. The high efficiency of Thule innovations prompts the development of a specialized maritime culture with a new emphasis on whale hunting.

550 B.C.–A.D. 1100 Eastern Arctic Dorset Tradition. Climate and population changes cause the Dorset culture of the Canadian Arctic and Greenland regions to shift from caribou to seal hunting as a means of subsistence. The development of new ice-hunting techniques, such as triangular projectile points, notched slate knives, and distinctive forms for harpoon heads, allows the new emphasis on seal hunting.

500 B.C. Eastern Great Plains. Throughout the eastern border of the Great Plains for the

Hohokam stone palette, fashioned in impressionistic human figure, used for mixing pigments. Courtesy of the Photographic Collections, Arizona State Museum, University of Arizona, Tucson. (See entry, **A.D. I Southwest**, p. 18.)

next 1,500 years, many small mounds are built by people of the Plains Woodland tradition.

500 B.C.   Midwest. In the Ohio River Valley and surrounding regions, an Early Woodland cultural complex, called Adena, develops from late Archaic antecedents. The Adena people build burial mounds and live in small villages of circular semipermanent dwellings.

500 B.C.   Southeast. The older practice of using plant fiber as a tempering agent in pottery is replaced by the use of sand and limestone. At about this time, there is a large increase in the variety of decorations used on pottery throughout the region. This increase corresponds with expanding cultural diversity and the shift from a hunting and gathering way of life to the establishment of small permanent villages and the cultivation of native plants like sunflower, marsh elder, may grass, and squash. The seeds from the sunflower, marsh elder, and may grass are collected and ground to produce flour.

500 B.C.   Southwest. Beans make their first appearance in the Southwest about this time,

becoming more common after A.D. 300. Beans contain vital amino acids, which corn lacks. They also return nitrogen to the soil, which corn depletes. Consequently, by growing beans and corn in tandem, Southwestern farmers could improve their health and increase the soil's longevity.

250 B.C.   Eastern Great Plains. A variety of cultures referred to as Plains Woodland develop in this region. They differ markedly from earlier cultures in their use of pottery, sedentary villages, and mounds as places for a variety of religious purposes, including burial of the dead.

250 B.C.   Northeastern United States. People cultivate locally domesticated plants.

200 B.C.   Cape Denbigh, Alaska. Evidence from a site in present-day Cape Denbigh, Alaska, indicates that people in the Arctic are manufacturing pottery at this time.

150 B.C.   The Gunther Pattern. Located in the Humboldt Bay area, including the lower Eel and Mad rivers, this pattern shows special-

Reconstruction of a Mogollon pithouse village from the Pine Lawn phase. Courtesy of the Field Museum of Natural History, Chicago. (*See entry,* **200 New Mexico,** p. 18.)

ized adaptation to riverside and coastal environments. Noted for their use of a distinctive barbed projectile point, these ancestors of the Wiyot and Yurok peoples depend on marine resources, local hunting, and acorn harvesting for subsistence. The presence of obsidian in Gunther Pattern sites indicates long-distance trading takes place.

100 B.C.   Locust Grove, Ohio. People of the Adena or the Hopewell culture build a huge earthwork known today as the Serpent Mound.

The body of the serpent is 382 meters (1,254 feet) long and 20 to 3 feet high. Its symbolism and meaning are unknown.

100 B.C.   Midwest. Centered in Ohio and Illinois, Hopewell societies develop from local roots. The Hopewell people are especially noted for constructing massive, geometric-shaped earthworks and are among the first in North America to develop societies in which people's status is determined by the standing of the family they are born into, rather than by their own personal achievements. Hopewell societies are also known for participating in trade networks extending from the Great Lakes to the Gulf of Mexico. Some of the items traded are conch shell, shark teeth, mica, lead, copper, and various kinds of stone.

A.D. 1–500

A.D. 1   Eastern Kansas. For the next 500 years, Hopewellian communities with affinities to the east live in the area of Kansas City. Their semipermanent villages provide evidence for the early cultivation of maize.

A.D. 1   Eastern Woodlands. In many parts of the eastern United States, small-scale groups develop more complex social hierarchies with leaders whose authority is derived from group consensus.

A.D. 1   Southwest. The roots of the Hohokam cultural tradition emerge in the Sonoran Desert of south-central Arizona, especially near the modern-day Phoenix area, and in adjacent regions of Chihuahua and Sonora in Mexico. The earlier Hohokam people are hunters and gatherers, but later they develop agriculture and build massive irrigation systems to water their fields. The tradition continues until after European arrival. The ancient Hohokam may be ancestral to the present-day Pima and Papago.

A.D. 1–450   Southeast. Mortuary customs become more elaborate, and throughout the region small oval mounds are built for the burial of important members of society. This seems to indicate that certain individuals and lineages are achieving greater political, economic and social prominence in what had been more egalitarian societies.

100   Alaska. Remains ancestral to modern Inuit peoples have been identified in eastern Siberia and western Alaska. By about A.D. 1000 all northern Native Americans from Alaska to Greenland are part of a similar cultural heritage, called the Thule or Northern Maritime tradition. Archaeologically, the Thule tradition is consistently recognized for the use of polished slate and elaborately carved bone and for ivory tools used for hunting sea mammals.

100   Louisiana. Sharing similarities with the Hopewellian peoples farther north, the Marksville culture becomes an important regional variant of the Woodland period. The Marksville people develop an economy based on hunting and cultivation of native plants. They also build mounds for ceremonial purposes, including the burial of important individuals.

100   Pacific Northwest. There is a general increase in the use of larger woodworking tools in the Pacific Northwest, perhaps indicating that the carving of monumental and ceremonial woodworks in the region begins about this time.

100   Southwest. Although maize was known and used in the region at least since 1000 B.C., it does not become significant as a food crop until after A.D. 100.

200   New Mexico. The first evidence for the Mogollon cultural tradition is defined in the mountainous areas of southern New Mexico, eastern Arizona, and adjacent portions of Chihuahua and Sonora, Mexico. Like their neighbors to the north and south, the Mogollon people first build small villages of earth-covered houses and later develop multistoried pueblos and techniques for cultivating crops in a dry environment. Some people of the modern Western Pueblos are believed to be descended from the Mogollon.

200   Southwest. As farming and permanent villages increase, pottery first appears in the Southwest, becoming more widely used after 400. Most pottery in the Southwest is made by coiling strips of clay to build up the body of the vessel. Both fragile and heavy, early pottery is too cumbersome for mobile hunting bands, and clay pots become practical and common only after village settlement occurs.

200 **Southwest.** Small sedentary villages develop, marking the end of nomadic hunting and gathering societies in many parts of the region. Also during this time, the Patayan tradition has its origins in southwestern Arizona, but is primarily associated with the Colorado River region and occupies a vast area extending from northern Baja California to northwest Arizona. The Patayan people are among the first pottery producers in the Southwest. Several sites excavated south of the Grand Canyon in Arizona give some information on dwellings and subsistence. Their early dwellings are small and made of wood or masonry, usually with an attached *ramada* or open-air porch. They probably grow corn and squash and hunt a variety of local animals.

200–1000 **Weeden Island Culture.** The proto-Mississippian Weeden Island culture arises and flourishes among the people of the Gulf coastal plain between Florida, Alabama, and Georgia. Social organization of Weeden Island society seems to lie somewhere between the more egalitarian Archaic hunter-gatherer groups and the chiefdom that characterizes the Mississippian climax. Like their Hopewellian predecessors, for example, Weeden Island peoples build low platform mounds, often supporting civic or religious structures. Weeden Island sites show increasing complexity throughout their history, finally becoming part of the Mississippian tradition when the advent of maize agriculture occurs throughout much of the Southeast between A.D. 800 and 1000.

300 **The Augustine Pattern.** Evolving out of the Berkeley Pattern, the Augustine is noted for such technological innovations as the bow and arrow, tubular formed tobacco pipes, and the practice of burning ceremonial objects prior to the burial of a deceased person. Support of more densely populated communities requires intensified hunting, fishing, and gathering of acorns and other wild vegetable foods. Increased intercommunity relations prompt the spread of cults and secret societies. Around 200 the Augustine Pattern spreads to the Eel and Russian river areas in northern California. By 1400 the Augustine evolves to meet the social and cultural demands of many highly concentrated population centers, producing elaborate ceremonies and social stratification.

300 **Midwest.** Around this date Hopewellian societies give way to cultures of the Late Woodland period. The reasons for the decline of Hopewell in the Midwest are not known, but may be related to the breakup of long-distance trade connections, increased warfare, and climate change.

300 **Southwest.** Archaeological evidence indicates that by this time the prehistoric peoples of the American Southwest are weaving flat-braided sashes from the hair of dogs and other animals, employing a finger-weave technique still used today.

400 **Southwest.** The Anasazi tradition emerges in the Four Corners region of Arizona, New Mexico, Colorado, and Utah. The Anasazi practice agriculture and through time move from pithouse villages to the construction of large multiroomed apartment buildings, some with more than 1,200 rooms. The pueblos in Chaco Canyon in western New Mexico are examples of Anasazi dwellings. The Anasazi produce many distinctive styles of pottery; especially recognizable are the black on white geometric designs. The people of the modern pueblos of Arizona and New Mexico are descended from different branches of the Anasazi.

400–550 **North America.** The bow and arrow are in use in several regions, including the plains, spreading rapidly throughout the continent as a major technological advance for hunting and warfare. Although the bow and arrow become very popular, the spear and *atlatl* still receive some use.

400–1350   Fremont Culture. In about A.D. 400 the first sedentary horticultural Great Basin communities appear in eastern Nevada, western Colorado, and much of Utah. The Fremont culture includes a number of discernibly southwestern characteristics, including cultivation of maize, pottery, pit houses, and later stone architecture. Like their southwestern counterparts, the Fremont peoples disperse when prolonged droughts eliminate maize agriculture as a viable means of subsistence. By the time of European contact, corn is grown only by a few Great Basin groups and only on a relatively limited scale.

450   Lower Mississippi Valley. The people of the Lower Mississippi Valley build conical burial mounds and some of the first flat-top platform mounds in North America. The flat-top platform mounds probably are used as substructures for temples or residences for important people. Platform mounds become a hallmark of the later Mississippian period.

500   Central Arizona. Large oval courts are built for ball games and are similar to those found throughout Mesoamerica such as the famous Mayan ceremonial center of Chichén Itzá on the Yucatan Peninsula.

500   Central California. Hotchkiss period cultures develop out of the earlier Cosumnes period. Hotchkiss period economy is based heavily on acorn gathering, but also fishing, fowling, and hunting.

500   Eastern United States. Compared to earlier cultures in the eastern woodlands, Late Woodland peoples build very few mounds and participate little in long-distance trade. The Late Woodland groups are organized differently than their Poverty Point, Adena, or Hopewell ancestors.

500   Florida and Georgia. Hopewellian cultures along the Gulf Coast continue to thrive after those of the Midwest disintegrate. One of the largest sites is Kolomoki in southern Georgia, with numerous burial mounds and a large rectangular flat-top mound. The site may have had a population of about a thousand people.

500   Southeast. Pottery manufacture flourishes throughout most of the Southeast by this time.

501–999

700   Crenshaw Site, Arkansas. This site, near Texarkana, Texas, is the earliest known ceremonial center linked to the modern Caddo people. The Caddo occupy the area of western Arkansas, eastern Louisiana, eastern Texas, and eastern Oklahoma. Between A.D. 900 and 1100, at least six mounds are constructed at the Crenshaw site. One of the mounds contains the remains of more than 2,000 deer antlers.

700–1000   Southwest. Most Anasazi villages make the transition from subterranean pithouse dwellings to above-surface masonry dwellings, later called "pueblos" by the Spanish who first encounter them. The change from pithouse to pueblo occurs at different times throughout the Southwest, and is likely caused by increased dependence on agriculture. As farming corn becomes the principal means of subsistence, southwestern peoples become more sedentary and permanent structures more practical. It is thought that the first above-ground buildings served as storage facilities for food surpluses. As pueblo architecture becomes standard, the pithouse structure evolves into the *kiva*, the subterranean ceremonial and communal chamber found throughout the Southwest. Among the Anasazi, pottery manufacture commences.

750   Eastern United States. The cultures of the Late Woodland period begin transformation into the societies of the Mississippian period. In some areas there is a dramatic shift in subsistence and societal structures, and many groups intensify agriculture based on maize cultivation. This is associated with the growth of elaborate status hierarchies and hereditary leadership.

750 Range Site, Southern Illinois. This site, near East St. Louis, provides some of the first tangible evidence for centralized, large-scale storage of food and settlements planned around a plaza. This may represent evidence for the further development of social hierarchies responsible for the distribution of shared resources.

800 Toltec Site, Arkansas. The Toltec site, near Little Rock, Arkansas, consists of ten mounds arranged around a plaza, enclosed by a two-meter-high earth embankment. This is the most complex settlement known in the Southeast at this time. Although named for the Toltec people of Mexico, the site is the outgrowth of local social developments and not the result of a migration of people from Mexico.

800 Zebree Site, Arkansas. At this site, about 55 miles north of Memphis, Tennessee, some of the first evidence for larger storage pits corresponds with the increased importance of maize throughout the region as an easily stored food resource.

825–900 Athapascan Migration. Different bands from northern Athapascan groups begin migrating from their homelands toward the present-day American Southwest. They begin moving as a single group or set of closely related bands, later becoming the linguistically and culturally differentiated modern-day Apache and Navajo.

850 Great Plains. Throughout the region, cultures of the Plains Village tradition develop along major and minor river valleys. They practice agriculture in conjunction with bison hunting and wild plant gathering. In the northern and central plains they build large, well-insulated earth lodges. In the south they construct houses with grass roofs.

875 New Mexico. Pottery of the type later used by Navajo and Apaches appears in Gobernador Canyon, New Mexico. The pottery is associated with villages of a "developmental pueblo" type.

880 Spiro Site, Oklahoma. On the uplands near the Arkansas River, twelve miles west of Fort Smith, Arkansas, Caddoans build a series of large, square ceremonial buildings around a plaza. Over the next 200 years these buildings are periodically destroyed and rebuilt as part of an elaborate ceremonial cycle. By A.D. 1100, Spiro becomes a major ceremonial center known for its extensive trade connections.

900 Alaska. Thule Inuit (Eskimo) culture begins to spread east, replacing and acculturating existing Dorset groups.

900 Eastern United States. In many areas, cultures referred to as Mississippian take shape. These cultures are organized as chiefdoms, with an economy based on maize cultivation and locally domesticated crops. Mississippian chiefdoms participate in long-distance trade and a widespread religion termed the Southeastern Ceremonial Complex, which includes elaborate burial customs such as mound building. Although most Mississippian communities are impermanent and small, some like Cahokia on the Mississippi River near St. Louis and Moundville in Alabama act as centers of commerce and ceremony for many hundreds of years.

900 Kincaid Site, Ohio. One of the major regional mound centers of the Mississippian period, this site is occupied for 500 years. The Kincaid Site is located at the confluence of the Ohio, Tennessee, and Cumberland rivers, near the town of Paducah, Kentucky. It contains two mound groups, a large village, and a palisade.

900 Midwest. In the Ohio Valley and Great Lakes regions, civilizations now classified as Hopewell develop. Characterized by mound building, agriculture cultivation, and extensive metal and pottery production, these societies remain extremely interdependent and connected with greater regional economies.

900 Mississippi Gulf. In the Lower Mississippi Valley, numerous societies consistently de-

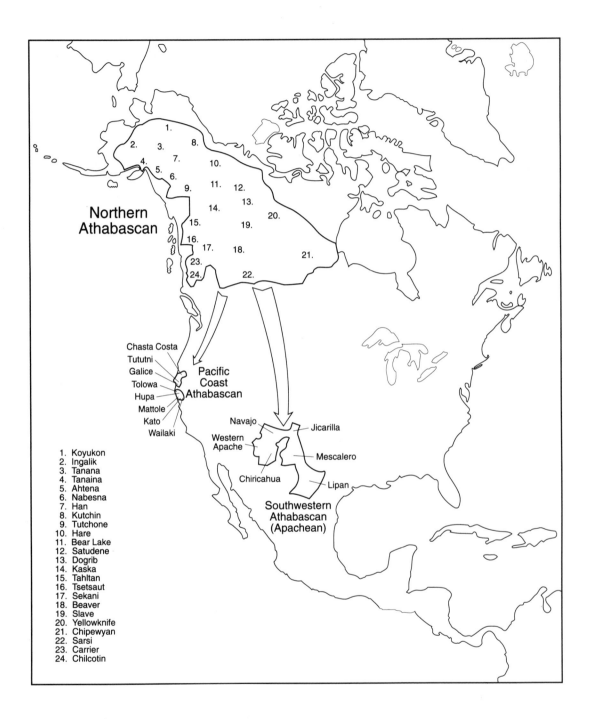

Northern
Athabascan

Pacific
Coast
Athabascan

Chasta Costa
Tututni
Galice
Tolowa
Hupa
Mattole
Kato
Wailaki

1. Koyukon
2. Ingalik
3. Tanana
4. Tanaina
5. Ahtena
6. Nabesna
7. Han
8. Kutchin
9. Tutchone
10. Hare
11. Bear Lake
12. Satudene
13. Dogrib
14. Kaska
15. Tahltan
16. Tsetsaut
17. Sekani
18. Beaver
19. Slave
20. Yellowknife
21. Chipewyan
22. Sarsi
23. Carrier
24. Chilcotin

Navajo   Jicarilla
Western
Apache   Mescalero

Chiricahua   Lipan

Southwestern
Athabascan
(Apachean)

Map of the Athabascan migrations from the sub-Arctic to the Southwest and Pacific Northwest. Courtesy of Duane Champagne.

22

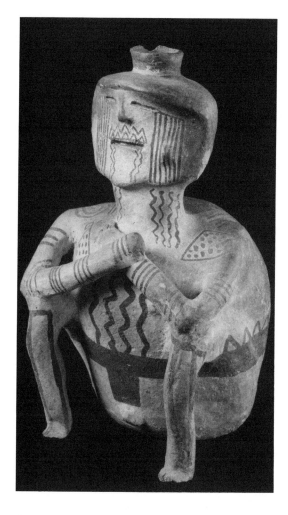

Anazasi human effigy jar (A.D. 900–1150) from Chaco Canyon, New Mexico. Photo by Hillel Burger. Courtesy of the Peabody Museum, Harvard University.

Pottery of the Casas Grande people. Courtesy of the National Anthropological Archives, Smithsonian Institution.

velop and create regional economies comparable to the Hopewellian peoples of the Ohio Valley. Combining hunting and agriculture and set in community villages, these civilizations maintain extensive trade networks and develop complex religious and cultural institutions. Because of their dramatic religious centers, archaeologists have identified three successive stages of these civilizations: (1) the Marksville Culture (Burial Mound II Period, A.D. 900–1100); (2) the Troyville Culture (Burial Mound II, A.D. 1100–1300); and (3) the Coles Creek Culture (Temple Mound I or Middle Mississippi, A.D. 1300–1500). These stages illustrate the constantly changing religious structures and values of these societies.

900   Southwest. By this date, agriculture is commonly practiced in most areas. Maize becomes a major crop. Although maize contains less food value than some wild plants, it produces higher and more predictable yields. Southwestern farmers use a variety of irrigation canals, dams, and planting methods to conserve scarce rainfall.

900–1100   Thule Expansion. Extending throughout the northern regions from Alaska to Greenland, the Thule or Northern Maritime tradition develops out of the older Norton tradition, providing the foundation for modern Inuit and Eskimo cultures.

900–1300   Northern Alabama. Related to the Hopewell culture to the north, the Copena civilization develops within the larger Mississippian cultures. Building large conical burial

One of the two ball courts excavated at Snaketown, Arizona. The court is 100 by 130 feet and was constructed between A.D. 600 and 900. Courtesy of the Photographic Collections, Arizona State Museum, University of Arizona, Tucson.

mounds, the Copena people use many different ornamental objects such as shells, polished stones, copper, and sheet mica for ceremonial and religious purposes. Part of much larger trading networks and regional economies, the Copena are one of many different but interrelated civilizations in the southern regions.

900–1450 Snaketown, Casa Grande, and the Hohokam Climax. During the Colonial and Classic periods, consolidation and expansion of many major Hohokam sites occurs. Above-ground adobe structures come into use, irrigation canal systems are greatly expanded, and, in several places, Mesoamerica-style platform mounds and ball courts are constructed. One of the largest Hohokam settlements, Snaketown, serves as an important trading center during this time, linking the Southwest with Mesoamerica groups like the Toltec and distributing the acid-etched shell work the Hohokam export to Mogollon and Anasazi groups. Also during their Classic phase, the Hohokam build Casa Grande on the Gila River in the Phoenix Basin. The main building at the Casa Grande site is four stories tall and made with caliche-adobe walls, reflecting pueblo-style architectural in-

fluences. The structure may have served as a chief's house.

947 Topiltzin Is Born. Topiltzin was raised by his grandparents and then sent to a school for priests at Xochicalco, in present-day Mexico, where there was a pyramid to the god Quetzelquatl. He later became the leader of the Toltec and founded the great city of Tula (A.D. 968). He gathered together many people of the former great city of Teotihuacan who also worshipped Quetzelquatl, and they provided the skill to build Tula. Topiltzin tried to reform the religion of his own people, stopping human sacrifices and replacing them with gifts of tortillas, flowers, incense, butterflies, and snakes. He also taught new agricultural methods and new ways to work silver, gold, and copper.

950 South Dakota. People identified as the Middle Missouri tradition migrate to the Great Plains from Minnesota and Iowa. They bring with them a heritage of farming and settle along the fertile bottomlands of the Missouri River in South Dakota where maize, squash, and other crops grow in spite of the cold winters and often dry summers. They are rec-

A series of doorways joining the multi-storied rooms and ceremonial chambers of Pueblo Bonito at Chaco Canyon. Courtesy of Troy Johnson. *(See entry, 1000–1180, p. 26.)*

ognized as the ancestors of the modern-day Mandan and Hidatsa.

985   Greenland. Thule Inuit encounter the first expedition of Norsemen to reach North America.

1000–1274

1000   Central and Southern New Mexico. Some of the earliest compact villages, later called pueblos by the Spanish, develop around central plazas in the region of the Mogollon cultural tradition.

1000   Kansas and Nebraska. Along the major rivers in this region, cultures grouped as the Central Plains tradition develop a farming lifestyle based on maize, beans, squash, tobacco, and sunflowers. They live in large, multifamily, earth-covered houses.

1000   New York and St. Lawrence River Valley. During the Owasco period (A.D. 1000–

1300), people build small villages throughout this region and the first clear evidence for cultivation of maize, beans, and squash occurs. By the end of the Owasco period, dwellings consist of multifamily longhouses, some more than 200 feet long, and villages are surrounded by fortifications, indicating the prevalence of warfare. People of the Owasco period are ancestors of the Iroquois.

1000   Owens, Panamint, and Death Valleys, Utah. From numerous archaeological remains, similar cultural and economic patterns help identify ancestors of modern Paiute.

1000–1130   Mimbres Climax. The Mimbres culture flourishes in southwestern New Mexico. The Mimbres people live in settlements of up to 150 contiguous rooms built of river pebbles and adobe and are best known for their elaborate pictorial pottery designs.

1000–1180   Rise and Fall of the Chaco Phenomenon. By the eleventh century, Anasazi communities are characterized by settlements of large multiroom above-ground pueblos, constructed of masonry blocks. The center of Anasazi culture is a 32-square mile area in present-day northwest New Mexico. Chaco Canyon contains 12 separate towns, including the largest, Pueblo Bonito, with 800 rooms and 35 kivas arranged in a D-shape around a central plaza. Dominant among the monumental architecture are the omnipresent great kivas, huge circular, semisubterranean structures sometimes more than 50 feet in diameter. Chacoan settlements like Pueblo Bonito are built in very short amounts of time, probably less than a few decades, and require careful planning and an almost inestimable amount of labor to construct (over a million shaped stones are required to build Pueblo Bonito alone). Interestingly, it has been calculated that the canyon has only enough arable land to feed about 2,000 people, far fewer than the towns are capable of housing. Moreover, Chaco Canyon is connected to a number of outlying communities by a complex

system of roads, some stretching up to 50 miles in length, indicating that it functions as the center of a ceremonial and trading network. Other evidence, such as the paucity of burials and the huge quantities of imported turquoise, ceramics, and other materials also support this conclusion. The most impressive architectural achievement in Native North America, the "Chaco Phenomenon," as archaeologists have called it, is short-lived. Prolonged droughts and other factors force its quick decline in the twelfth century. Building ceases by 1130 and the canyon is abandoned within 50 years, the resident population probably dispersing to Mesa Verde and other more hospitable areas.

1007   Leif Eriksson. This Norwegian explorer makes one of the first documented European contacts with Native Americans on mainland North America. Eskimo, Beothuk, and Micmac peoples encounter him and members of his party.

1025   Pacific Northwest and Southwest. Ancestral Navajo bands break from northern Athapascans and migrate into the Southwest.

1050–1250   Cahokia Region, Southern Illinois. The Mississippian trading and ceremonial center at Cahokia, near present-day St. Louis, reaches its highest level of complexity. More than 100 mounds of various shapes and sizes are constructed at Cahokia, whose population may reach 30,000. The principal mound, Monks Mound, is the largest pre-Columbian construction north of Mexico, containing over 21 million cubic feet of earth and covering 16 acres.

1060   Chihuahua, Mexico. At the Casas Grande site (also called Paquime), 200 miles southwest of El Paso, a large settlement is built, similar to those on the west coast of Mexico. Traders from Mexico establish the site to improve trade between the civilizations of Mexico and those of the Southwest. About 1205 the settlement is destroyed, possibly by a revolt.

Etowah Mound, important Mississippian center in present-day Georgia. Courtesy of Molly Braun.

1097 Southwest. A Chaco pueblo, called Kinya'a by the Navaho, is inhabited at this time by the Kinya-ani people (Tall House People). The Navaho and Apache Kinya-ani clan is believed to be descended from this group.

1100 Eastern United States. Over-reliance on starchy foods, particularly maize, in the diet is linked to the poorer health of Mississippian period populations, especially those living in larger villages.

1100 New York Region. By this date, the archaeological remains linked to the cultural development of the modern Iroquois can be recognized.

1100 Northeast. Beginning about this time many groups construct fortifications around their villages, indicating widespread warfare.

1100–1300 Mesa Verde Climax. Inhabited continuously from A.D. 600 to 1300, the Mesa Verde site in southern Colorado reaches its height after 1100. At about this time, the Anasazi residents of Mesa Verde begin to move off the mesas and into sheltered areas in the cliffs below, apparently for defensive reasons.

By the time the move is completed, the Fewkes Canyon settlements consist of over 33 cliff dwelling sites, with more than 500 living and storage rooms and 60 kivas. The largest of these, Cliff Palace, contains some 220 rooms and 23 kivas and houses as many as 350 people. In general, the Mesa Verde settlements differ from those at Chaco Canyon in that the focus is on individual communities as opposed to large-scale regional integration. By about 1300 the entire San Juan drainage, including the Mesa Verde area, is abandoned by the pueblo peoples living there, who migrate to the Hopi/Zuni and Rio Grande areas to the south and southeast.

1100–1400 Classic Thule. Settlement expands throughout the High Arctic with Thule villages along the coastlines of the Hudson Strait, Foxe basin, the Mackenzie Delta down to Melville Peninsula, and across Greenland's northern and eastern shores. At this time, whale hunting is the Thule's primary means of subsistence. Contact with other Arctic communities provides for the exchange of iron and copper, increasing the effectiveness of Thule tools.

1100–1804 Southern California Coast Late Period. Use of shell money becomes wide-

Cahokia Mounds, c. A.D. 1100–1150. This painting by Lloyd K. Townsend is a reconstruction of the site from across Twin Mounds and Central Plaza to Monk's Mounds. Courtesy of the Cahokia Mounds State Historic Site.

spread throughout the southern California area, indicating the growing complexity of cultures in this region. The people of this time are Hokan-speaking Chumash and others, ancestors to the coastal groups who would later meet European explorers and missionaries. Studies of shell beads and other artifacts suggest that Chumash society may have developed continuously for over 7,000 years in the area now known as the Santa Barbara Channel.

1150   Great Basin. Shoshonean-speaking peoples are pushed into the Colorado River Valley north of present-day Needles, probably displacing Yumans who then migrate east.

1175   Awatovi Site, Arizona. Located 75 miles north of Winslow, Arizona, the Hopi call this site "Place of the Bow Clan People." At one point the pueblo consists of 1,300 ground-floor rooms with a population of more than a thousand. About 1450, a large two-story pueblo is built. The Franciscans build a church here in the sixteenth century.

1200   Oklahoma. In central Oklahoma the people of the Washita River phase (1200–1450)

develop villages based on an economy of maize cultivation and the hunting of deer and bison.

1200   Southwest. According to Navaho tradition, the Quacka'n (Yucca people) come from a desert area west of San Francisco Peaks and are nonagricultural food gathering people. They then become absorbed into Navajo 38 years after the origin of the first clan.

1220   Texas and Oklahoma Panhandles. Groups move from New Mexico to take advantage of better agricultural conditions that result from a moister climate.

1250   South-Central Arizona. The Hohokam way of life is gradually replaced by a pueblo-building culture and by modern Pima-Papago culture. Colorado River Indians later preserve many elements of Hohokam culture.

1275–1499

1275   Southwest. Tree rings indicate a period of severe drought in the Southwest during this

Great Kiva, Chetro Ketl community, Chaco Canyon, New Mexico. Courtesy of Dean R. Snow.

time, causing the abandonment of most of the San Juan River basin.

1276–1299 Southwest. The Cestcine, Tlastcine, and Tsejinciai groups are incorporated into the Navajo bands from nearby related Apache populations.

c. 1300 Deganawida, Huron Spiritual Leader, Flourishes in the Eastern United States. Deganawida is the founder of the Iroquois Confederacy. Its origin is unknown, but is generally dated before the landing of Columbus in

1492. In Iroquois history, Deganawida lives in a time when there is little peace among the Iroquois-speaking nations, of which the Huron, Deganawida's tribe then residing in Ontario, is one. Deganawida has a vision from the Great Spirit that instructs him to give the Great Law, a set of rules and procedures for working out differences and settling hostilities between nations. Hiawatha becomes the spokesperson for the message of Deganawida and the Great Spirit. Both Deganawida and Hiawatha travel among the Iroquois nations, and convince them to form

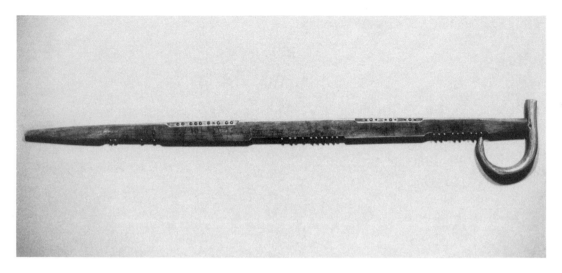

Notched staff used by Iroquois sachem to list the members of the Great Council. Each peg represents a council member. Courtesy of the Cranbrook Institute of Science.

a confederacy of 49 chiefs. Through ceremonies and agreements they settle their disputes and form the Iroquois League. The purpose of the league is to create peace and to spread the Great Law of peace to all nations in the world.

1300   Eastern United States. Common beans are present by at least 1070. They do not, however, come into wide usage until 1300. Although beans are an important nutritional addition to maize-based diets, they are not adopted in all areas.

1300–1500   Louisiana. The Coles Creek culture of Louisiana builds large and elaborate temple mounds. Some pyramids are as high as 80 feet with flattops for numerous temples.

c. 1300–1600   Southwest. Although dating from about 1000, Anasazi mural painting reaches its apex between 1300 and 1600 in two separate regions, the Jeddito Valley in the Hopi region of Arizona and the Rio Grande drainage in present-day central New Mexico. In these areas, pueblo walls are sometimes covered with up to 100 superimposed layers of painted plaster murals.

1300–1600   Midwest. Great Temple Mound or Middle Mississippi civilizations flourish in the river valleys of Arkansas, Mississippi, Alabama, Tennessee, Missouri, Kentucky, southern Illinois, southern Indiana, and Ohio. These societies are organized into republics dominated by a large city surrounded by smaller cities. Each city consists of a plaza, one or more pyramid-like temple mounds, temples, chief's houses, and other houses.

1300–1600   Southern Mississippi. Caddoan-speaking peoples develop village societies in the Texas-Louisiana-Arkansas-Oklahoma border region. These civilizations are variants from the Temple Mound civilization found further east. The Caddoans become part of extremely complex, interdependent trade networks throughout the Midwest and South.

1316   Southwest. According to Western Apache tradition, Apache live at Dance Camp with Navajo and Hopi bands.

1320–1400   Southwest. Pueblo people abandon pueblos at Kinishba, Point of Pines and Dewey Flat.

1346–1375 Southwest. Living as cliff dwellers, the Western Apache develop hostilities with their neighbors in the Cibecue region of Arizona. Tuzigoot Pueblo abandon areas in upper Verde Valley Arizona, which are then occupied by Yavapai and Walapai.

1350 Eastern Great Basin. Hunting and gathering peoples associated with the modern southern Paiute, Ute, and Shoshoni replace the earlier Fremont culture.

1350 Moundville, Alabama. One of the largest Mississippian period ceremonial centers is located 40 miles south of present-day Tuscaloosa. By this date, the site consists of 20 mounds and an associated village. It is probably the center of a chiefdom that includes a number of other sites situated along the Black Warrior River and adjacent areas in west-central Alabama.

1400 Midwest. Throughout a broad section of Missouri and Illinois, including the once densely populated Cahokia region, an "empty quarter" develops, possibly as a result of a poorer climate for agriculture.

1400 Southern California. Archaeological remains of the Chumash, a tribe that lives in the vicinity of modern-day Santa Barbara, date through the period of European contact. The Chumash are known archaeologically by the term Canaliño.

1400 Southwest. The last Pueblo settlement in southern Arizona, Casa Grande is abandoned. Its destruction is due in part to Apache raids.

1400–1600 Little Ice Age. Climate changes in the far North become severe, creating what scientists call the "Little Ice Age" and causing the advance of glaciers near Greenland and Baffin Island. Whaling and other kinds of boat hunting are limited, resulting in migration out of the High Arctic area during this time.

1450 Nebraska. Groups related to the Pawnee migrate north to the Missouri River in South Dakota. Their descendants are the Arikara, who live today in North Dakota and are members of the Three Affiliated Tribes, along with their neighbors, the Mandan and Hidatsa.

1450–1650 The South. A new religious-ceremonial movement spreads throughout the South from Texas to Georgia. Influenced by Mexican and Huasteca, much of the movement's imagery has Mexican Indian-style designs.

1492 The Caribbean. On October 12, on an island in the Bahamas called Guanahani by Natives and San Salvador by Europeans, the expedition led by Christopher Columbus touches ground.

1493 Columbus's Second Voyage. On November 3, Christopher Columbus begins his second voyage to the "new world." Returning to Hispañola, Columbus discovers that the Navidad colony disbanded shortly after his departure. The Navidad colonists begin to harass the local Taino and subsequently attack a neighboring *cacique* (leader), Caonabo, who retaliates and kills all of the Spanish raiders. Columbus's party uses this event as justification to mount their own military campaign against the Indians. Fighting continues for several years and by 1496 Bartolome de las Casas, a Spanish priest and scholar, claims that a mere third of the Native population remains from the time of Columbus's first contact.

1493 Line of Demarcation. Following Spain's exploration of North America, the pope establishes a Line of Demarcation between Spain and Portugal which divides the territories in the

Earthen pyramids in Moundville, Alabama. Courtesy of Dean R. Snow.

Western Hemisphere and gives to Spain all lands 370 leagues west of the Cape Verde Islands.

1494 Taino Slavery. Christopher Columbus initiates the enslavement of American Indians, capturing over 500 and sending them to Spain to be sold.

1497 Cabot Kidnaps Micmac. Sailing for England, Italian John Cabot visits Cape Breton Island off the eastern shore of Canada and kidnaps three Micmac Indians.

1497–1505 Vespucci's Voyages. Supported by Spain, Florentine merchant Amerigo Vespucci explores the West Indies and South America. A chronicle of his navigations, *Mundus Novus,* is published between 1504 and 1505. He is given credit for the discovery of the new world mainland (America is named after him), though whether he even went ashore is still debated.

Part 2

NATIVE NORTH AMERICAN HISTORY 1500–1959

Chapter 2
1500 TO 1599

1500–1520

c. 1500 The Abandonment of Key Marco. Prior to its mysterious abandonment around the year 1500, the port town of Key Marco is a thriving ceremonial and trading center for the Calusa Nation of southwestern Florida. Situated in a swampy coastal area, it is constructed on an artificial base made mostly of shell and bisected by a complex system of canals which create several artificial lagoons. In spite of its grandeur, the historical existence of Key Marco is unknown until 1895, when a team of archaeologists finds an enormous cache of wood carvings, tools, bowls, cups, and numerous ceremonial artifacts, almost perfectly preserved by the mud of the swamp in which they were deposited. The variety and concentration of such ritual and daily artifacts seems to indicate a sudden and involuntary evacuation, but, in spite of the wealth of the evidence found there, the mystery of the Calusa island town remains unsolved.

1500 Canada. Up to a million people from a wide variety of cultural groups occupy the area which will become Canada. Perhaps 40 percent live near the Pacific Coast, where a warm, moist climate and abundant resources (particularly salmon) allow the development of substantial villages near sheltered bays and along river valleys. Residents in these villages live in large houses of log and plank construction. The

coastal groups have developed hierarchical, chiefdoms, in which social status and wealth are primarily inherited. The only other societies in the area of present-day Canada which approach such complexity are the tribal agricultural societies of the Iroquoian peoples, including the St. Lawrence Iroquois, Huron, Petun, and Neutral. These groups, residing along the St. Lawrence River and in the Great Lakes region south and east of Lake Huron, live in longhouses in semipermanent, palisaded villages (which are relocated every 10 to 30 years when the soil is exhausted) surrounded by fields of corn, beans, squash, and tobacco. All other societies are centered around wandering groups of extended families known as residential bands of hunter-gatherers (they rely on gathering wild food and hunting game rather than planting and harvesting a crop). While many bands might share important cultural attributes such as language, customs, rituals, and folklore, they are not united by any political or economic institutions or leadership. Thus, terms like "Micmac," "Cree," and "Sekani" refer to groups of bands, not tribes. Similarly, various groups speak related languages. For example, various groups from the Micmac on the East Coast to the Peigan along the Rocky Mountains speak an Algonkian language. All Inuit (Eskimo) speak a dialect of Inuktitut, and Indians throughout the northwestern interior of the continent speak a Dene (Athapascan) language. These

---

groups are not united by any particular sense of community.

The size of residential bands varies according to the time of year and the environment in which they are found. Indian bands may number as few as 10 family members during the winter when resources are scarce, or over a thousand members during the summer when food is more plentiful. They live in portable skin or bark tents (tipis or wigwams). Most Inuit, who occupy regions north of the treeline, gather in larger bands during the winter and separate into smaller ones in the summer, living in snow houses (igloos) in winter and sod hunts or skin tents in the summer. Because they move their camps frequently, they do not accumulate more possessions than necessary. There are extensive trade networks among different groups.

1500   The Caribbean. Columbus and his successors consolidate Spanish control of the Caribbean and begin a period of exploration in North and Central America with repercussions to the present day.

1500   Native Population Decline. The sixteenth century marks the beginning of a widespread decline in Native population. Over the next four centuries, perhaps as many as 60 million people die, primarily of European imported diseases such as smallpox and scarlet fever. In the United States, the population decline continues until about 1900, when Indian populations begin to recover.

1501   East Coast. Gaspar Corte Real, supported by Portugal, explores the East Coast and kidnaps more than 50 Indians.

1502   Newfoundland. English fishermen begin making regular trips to the waters off Newfoundland.

1503   European Fishermen and Whalers. Various groups along the East Coast begin occasional trade with European fishermen and whalers. They frequently exchange furs and food for metal goods and cloth. The Beothuk,

who reside on the island of Newfoundland, are one of the few groups that balk at this opportunity although they do trouble some fishermen who dry their fish on land, by taking some of their goods.

1506–1518   St. Lawrence River. The French unsuccessfully attempt to explore and establish colonies along the St. Lawrence River in eastern Canada.

1508–1511   Decimation of the West Indies. After Spanish invasions, the Caribbean Indian population is devastated by disease, warfare, and labor. In Puerto Rico, the Indian population is at 200,000 in 1508 and at 20,000 in 1511.

1511   Responses to Spanish Colonial Exploitation. Spurred by the suffering and death of the peoples of the West Indies, Antonio de Montesinos, a Catholic priest, gives a stirring sermon to the Spanish leaders of Hispaniola, condemning them for their treatment of Native Americans. Another priest, Bartolome de las Casas, writes *Destruction of the Indies*, in which he chronicles the Spanish conquistadors' cruelty against Native Americans. These gruesome acts include butchering men, women, and children like "sheep in the slaughter house."

1512   Laws of Burgos. Spanish Dominican priest Bartolome de las Casas and others attempt to stop the atrocities and begin a reform movement to alter the Spanish Indian policies. The result of this courtly debate is the enactment of the Laws of Burgos, a series of reforms that outlaws Indian slavery and orders the owners of large tracts of land—land taken from the Indians and known as *encomiendas*—to improve the treatment of their Indian laborers. The Spanish conquistadors cannot legally invade, enslave, or exploit Indians without first reading them the *Requerimiento*, a document outlining the Christian interpretation of creation and the hierarchy of the Catholic Church. Indians are told to surrender their hearts, souls, and bodies to the Church and Spanish crown or face utter devastation. "We ask and require . . . that you acknowledge the Church," the document reads. If the Indians do not obey, the Spanish promise to "make war against you . . . subject you to the yoke and obedience of the Church [and Crown] . . . take you, and your wives, and your children, and . . . make slaves of them . . . take away your goods and . . . do you all the harm and damage we can."

The *Requerimiento* is intended to offer Native Americans a chance to surrender and submit peacefully to Spanish rule. But as with the Laws of Burgos, the Spanish ignore the substance as well as the spirit of the *Requerimiento*. The Laws of Burgos fail to end Spanish abuses, which continue throughout Latin America for 400 more years.

1512   Pope Julius II Decree. Pope Julius II decrees that Indians are descended from Adam and Eve.

1513   Vasco Nunez de Balboa. Vasco Nunez de Balboa crosses Middle America and sights the Pacific Ocean.

1513–1521   Ponce de Leon and the "Fountain of Youth." European belief in the existence of mythic waters capable of regenerating the old and infirm predates Columbus's explorations of North America. By 1481 Sir John Mandeville had already written of the existence of such a "Fountain of Youth" in Asia. Later, when the Arawak slaves brought back to Spain by Columbus and other explorers tell the Spanish of certain life-giving waters among Florida's Timucua people, the Spanish believe their stories to be proof that the fountain exists. In 1512 Juan Ponce de Leon, the governor of Puerto Rico, is given license by the king to explore and settle Florida, which the Spanish name *Bimini*, meaning "life source." Though one stated goal of de Leon's mission is to obtain slaves, it is his search for the fountain for which he is best known. He reaches Florida for the first time in 1513 and has extensive contact with the peoples of that region. The Saturiwa

and Ai nations both greet the expedition with hostility, as do the Calusa, who, in 80 war canoes, drive de Leon's ships away from the coast. These receptions do much to deter Spanish designs on Bimini, and they return to the land of the Calusa only in 1521, after conquests by Cortés in Mexico reignite Spanish interest in the region. This time de Leon fares little better—shortly after landing, he is shot in the thigh by a Calusa arrow and later dies in Havana from the wound, never having seen the fabled Fountain of Youth.

1519–1521   The Aztec Empire Falls. The Spanish adventurer, Hernando Cortés, accompanied by a few hundred Spaniards and large numbers of Tlaxcala and other anti-Aztec Indian allies, encounters the Aztecs at Tenochtitlan (present-day Mexico City). The men are received cordially, and are housed in a sumptuous palace put at their disposal by the Aztec emperor, Moctezuma. Cortés responds by seizing Moctezuma, while his notorious captain, Pedro de Alvarado, leads an attack on a religious gathering which leaves 600 Mexican citizens dead. The Aztecs mobilize their army and besiege the Spanish. Cut off from their Tlaxcala allies, Cortés and his men are forced to abandon Mexico City, escaping via a causeway suspended above the lake surrounding Tenochtitlan. The retreat is costly for Cortés—his men, laden with the gold they have looted, are easy targets. By the time he escapes Tenochtitlan, two-thirds of his men are lost. The surviving members of the expedition find safety among the neighboring Tlaxcala, and for the next year Cortés and his allies rebuild their forces. Dissension within the Aztec Empire further assists Cortés when Texcoco, a major city-state located just east of Tenochtitlan, allies itself with the Spanish. A new expedition is launched against the Aztec capital, and after four months Tenochtitlan is finally subjugated. After defeating the Aztec Empire which controls most of southern Mexico, Cortés establishes himself as ruler of Mexico. The Spanish thereafter control the Indians once subject to Aztec rule. The colony of New Spain is founded.

1520–1534 Taino Rebellion. Within three decades of the establishment of the Spanish colony on Hispañola, the population of the island drops from estimates of over a million people to just a few thousand. One of the survivors is Guayocuya, a man the Spanish call Enrique. Like all the people of Hispañola in the era of Spanish colonization, the land of Enrique's birthright, as well as the labor of its residents, is given away by the crown to a Spanish overseer. When smallpox makes Indian labor in his village unavailable, Enrique is held responsible and imprisoned three times. Finally, when Enrique's wife is raped by the overseer, he calls for action. Enrique and his hundreds of supporters hide in the mountains and conduct a guerrilla war against the Spanish. Unable to trap or defeat the Taino rebels, the Spanish attempt to negotiate with Enrique, offering him a pardon if he will give up his struggle and submit to the Spanish authorities. Enrique repeatedly refuses Spanish overtures, until finally, after 14 years of fighting, the Spanish submit and Enrique and the other refugees are granted land upon which to live in freedom. The Taino rebellion is one of the few instances in the history of North America of a successful Indian revolt against colonial oppression.

1521–1540

1523 The First Indian "Informant." A Spanish expedition to America's southern coast returns to Spain with Chicora, a captured Indian. Interviewed by the historian Peter Martyr, Chicora gives first recorded Indian perspective.

1523–1524 Verrazzano Explores the East Coast. Backed by France, Giovanni da Verrazzano explores the Atlantic Coast. Wampanoag, Narragansett, and Delaware Indians encounter the explorer and his party.

1528–1536 Narváez Expedition. In 1528 Panfilo de Narváez lands at Tampa Bay on the west coast of Florida with 400 colonists. Already familiar with the benefits of Spanish "exploration," the Florida Indians are immediately hostile and a quarter of the original group turns back with the ships. The rest of the colonists are attacked by different Indian groups as they advance west and north, and their numbers further decrease. At Appalachia Bay the colonists can stand no more. They kill their horses and construct small boats from the hides, while subsisting on horse flesh and the corn they find in abandoned Indian towns. With their force reduced to 242 men, the colonists take to the sea, hoping to reach Mexico. The expedition is shipwrecked near present-day Galveston, Texas, and fewer than a hundred survive. Having never encountered Europeans, the local Karankawa and Atakapa Indians treat the Spanish well, initially. But as food becomes scarcer and European diseases begin taking a large toll on their Indian hosts, the colonists succumb to a number of misfortunes until only five remain. These five, including the expedition's treasurer Álvar Nuñez Cabeza de Vaca and a Black slave named Estevánico, live among the Indians of the Texas coast for six years before four of them escape to an interior tribe which de Vaca had encountered on a trading trip sometime earlier (the fifth elects to stay with the coastal Indians). They continue heading west through southern New Mexico and Arizona before turning south through the Sonora Valley. Escorted by Yaqui Indians, they meet up with a Spanish slaving expedition on the Sinaloa River. The group finally reaches Mexico City in July 1536, and their stories of rich cities to the north fuel Spanish desires for gold and wealth, leading to the Coronado expedition three years later.

1530–1600 Spanish Explore Baja California. Spanish expeditions explore Baja California and California but are unable to establish a permanent foothold. Cortés is defeated by Baja Natives.

1533 The Yaqui Repel Guzmán. Leading a party of soldiers on a slaving mission, Diego de Guzmán explores the Sea of Cortés. When he reaches the northernmost river of this region, he is greeted by Yaqui Indians ready for battle, who draw a line in the dirt and warn the Spaniards not to cross it into their territory. Guzmán defies the Indians and in the battle that ensues, the Spanish are driven back.

JULY 7, 1534 Micmac at Chaleur Bay. Bands of Micmac at Chaleur Bay, in the Gulf of St. Lawrence along North America's East Coast, attract the attention of the French explorer, Jacques Cartier, by waving furs on sticks. Friendly trade between the Micmac and the French follows. The Micmac gather along the coast each summer to fish, after spending the winter hunting in the interior.

JULY 16, 1534 St. Lawrence Iroquois. On a fishing trip to the Gaspé Peninsula, about 300 St. Lawrence Iroquois from the agricultural village of Stadacona (Quebec City), meet Cartier's party near the end of the peninsula. The group has no furs to trade. Cartier takes two sons of Donnacona, the chief at Stadacona, back to France with him.

1534–1541 Cartier Explores the Northeast. Cartier explores the St. Lawrence River in three voyages, making contact with Algonkian- and Iroquoian-speaking tribes in the Northeast. On his second voyage, Cartier reaches the Indian settlements of Stadacona (Quebec City) and Hochelaga (Montreal). Donnacona's two sons, Domagaya and Taignoagny, are reunited with their kin at Stadacona. The village of about 500 people, residing in longhouses, engages in peaceful trade with Cartier, whom Donnacona's sons have guided to this point, but they are angered when Cartier's party sails farther up the St. Lawrence River toward Hochelaga. The Stadaconans claim the right to control the flow of traffic past their village. The agricultural village of Hochelaga, occupied by between 1,500 and 3,500 people, trades with

Cartier. Cartier's party returns to a site near Stadacona to winter. Many of the crew develops scurvy, a disease caused by a deficiency in ascorbic acid (vitamin C). Twenty-five die and 75 more fall ill. Despite their suspicions, the Stadaconans teach Cartier's party how to cure scurvy by drinking a vitamin C-rich brew made of the bark of the white cedar. In the spring, perhaps with the encouragement of Donnacona's rivals in Stadacona, Cartier seizes the chief and nine other Iroquois and takes them to France. Donnacona speaks to Cartier of the Kingdom of Saguenay to the west, said to be rich in gold and silver and inhabited by white men. Some historians suggest that Donnacona knows of the Spanish in Mexico, but most are of the view that Donnacona is embroidering facts about copper deposits around Lake Superior and is possibly referring to the Huron in present-day Ontario. Donnacona is presented to King Francis I, who is impressed by Donnacona's description of the Kingdom of Saguenay and decides to challenge Spanish claims to North America by establishing a French settlement on the St. Lawrence. Although Cartier has promised to return Donnacona to his homeland, Donnacona dies while still abroad.

1537 Indians Declared Worthy of Christian Conversion. Pope Paul III issues a formal declaration asserting that Indians of the New World are people, and can become Christians. The Church is seeking to curb the abuses which Indians are facing.

1539 Francisco de Vitoria. Francisco de Vitoria, a lawyer whose work foresaw the idea of "human rights" in international law, lectures in Spain and advocates that Indians are free men and exempt from slavery.

1539 Marcos de Niza, Estevánico, and the Zuni. As reconnaissance for the impending Coronado expedition, a Franciscan friar named Marcos de Niza explores the region now known as the American Southwest, searching for the

The Micmac were among the earliest Indians to meet the European traders. This painting of a Micmac encampment completed between 1820 and 1830 suggests that they retained much of their earlier culture. The guns provide the clearest evidence of cultural adaptation. Courtesy of the National Archives of Canada.

fabled "Seven Cities of Cíbola." A veteran of service in both Guatemala and Peru, de Niza is accompanied by an escort of Mexican Indians from the Opata region as well as the slave Estevánico, who as a survivor of the Narváez expedition had travel through the region several years before. Estevánico and the Opata contingent travel some distance ahead of de Niza. Near the six pueblos of Zuni, de Niza meets fleeing members of the advance party who inform the Franciscan that the Zuni had killed

Estevánico and many others. Although de Niza would return to Mexico claiming that the Zuni pueblos had wealth greater than the Aztecs or Incas, it is unlikely that he ever actually saw them himself.

1539–1543 De Soto in the Southeast. Only three years after returning from Pizarro's conquest of the Inca Empire in Peru, Hernando de Soto is granted license from the king of Spain to "conquer, pacify, and people," the territory of

An early view of Native Americans in Florida, rowing a canoe and showing a communal house for storage of food, c. 1590. These engravings were based on watercolors by Jacques Le Moyne, now lost. Courtesy of the Rare Books & Manuscript Division of the New York Public Library—Astor, Lenox, and Tilden Foundations.

La Florida. On May 30, 1539, de Soto lands on the western coast of Florida in the land of the Ocita Nation. He begins his march heading north, then west through the territory of the Timucua and Appalachia. At the town of Napetuca, de Soto seizes the Timucuan chief; when the chief's men attempt to rescue him, they are defeated and enslaved by the Spanish. Continuing northward, de Soto next visits the Creek town of Cofitachequi, where, although given mica, freshwater pearls, and hundreds of bushels of corn for his army to eat, he plunders graves for gold and other valuables. Continuing on to what is now Alabama, he abducts chiefs and terrorizes populations at Chiaha, Coosa, and the fortified town of Mobile (Mabila). When the Mobile people resist, a fierce battle ensues and the fort is burned, with hundreds perishing in the flames and hundreds more killed in the fighting. The Spanish suffer significant losses and de Soto rests for a month before advancing on Chickasaw territory, where he spends the winter of 1540–41. There the Spanish inhabit another of the many abandoned towns they would encounter on their voyage. Delayed by almost constant Chickasaw

attacks, the expedition crosses the Mississippi River in June 1541. De Soto continues searching for treasure for over a year, moving from town to town among the Natchez and Tunica peoples, finding little he considers valuable. De Soto falls ill and dies in May 1542. He is succeeded by Luis de Moscoso, who explores westward as far as the territory of the Tonkawa in present-day eastern Texas. There the Spanish encounter turquoise stone and cotton mantas traded from the Rio Grande Pueblos. Finding the region inhospitable, they return to the Mississippi, build barges, and sail toward the Gulf of Mexico. Pursued by a flotilla of 100 Natchez war canoes, the Spanish are forced to kill their horses to lighten their load. They reach Panuco, Mexico, in September 1543, empty-handed after almost four and a half years of plundering.

1540 Big Eyes Taken Captive. A Wichita woman, Big Eyes, is taken captive near the Red River of eastern Texas by Tejas Indians around 1535. She is later sold to Tiguex Indians and moved to Arizona where she comes into contact with Spanish explorer Francisco Vásquez de Coronado in 1540. In a battle between the Tiguex and the Spanish, Big Eyes becomes a prisoner of Spanish captain Juan de Zaldivar. She accompanies the exploration party in their search for the Seven Cities of Cíbola and gold. In 1541, the group reaches the panhandle area of Texas. Familiar with this territory, Big Eyes escapes and returns to her Wichita people.

In 1542, some of Hernando de Soto's people arrive and question the woman's contact with Coronado. Pressed for detailed information, she draws a crude sketch of Coronado's route from the Rio Grande to the Tule Canyon. A copy of this map eventually reaches Europe and is incorporated into the cartography of that time. Big Eyes herself serves as a connection linking the western Coronado expedition with the eastern de Soto exploration party, thereby providing the first estimate of the North American continent span.

1540–1542   Coronado in the Southwest. Simultaneously with de Soto's swath through the Southeast, Coronado explores the Southwest, searching for the Seven Cities of Cíbola and the wealth described by Marcos de Niza. Behind him is an army of more than 300 men, 4 Franciscan friars, and hundreds of Mexican Indians. After establishing their first garrison in the territory of the Opata, Coronado's army reaches Zuni and demands submission in July 1540. The Zuni draw a line of cornmeal on the ground, forbidding the Spaniards to cross it. A battle ensues and the Spaniards storm the pueblo. From the upper stories of their city, the Zuni shower their attackers with arrows and stones, but eventually superior weaponry wins out and the Zuni are defeated. From Zuni, Coronado orders an expedition sent northwest into Hopi territory. Again a line of cornmeal is drawn on the ground and again a battle follows in which the defenders are defeated. Another expedition is sent east. After making a brief but peaceful stop at Acoma pueblo, it continues into Pecos territory. There, under Pedro de Alvarado, the Spanish encounter several plains Indians who tell them of the fabulous riches of Quivira, a

land farther to the east. When the Indians are unable to provide the proof of Quivira's grandeur that Alvarado seeks, the Spaniard has them put in chains. Instead of proceeding, however, Alvarado returns to Coronado's camp, recently moved from Zuni to the populous Tiquex region along the Rio Grande, south of modern-day Albuquerque. There Spanish demands for submission and tribute spark a revolt in the winter of 1540–41, but it is brutally suppressed and 200 Tiwa are burned at the stake for resisting. With Tiguex virtually destroyed, Coronado sets out on April 25, 1541, to find Quivira. Once on the grasslands of the southern plains, Coronado and his army are led in circles by their Pawnee slave guide before reaching Quivira in July. Instead of the palaces he had imagined, Coronado finds only the beehive-shaped grass houses of the Wichita. Disappointed, he orders his guide strangled to death. Later that year Coronado returns to his base in Tiguex and the following spring the expedition ends, like de Soto's, empty-handed.

c. 1540–1600   Southwest. The use of wool is introduced in the Southwest when Indians of that region begin raising sheep brought to North America by the Spanish. At about this same time, Pueblo Indians begin weaving on flat looms. The Navajo begin weaving around 1700, learning the skill from their Pueblo neighbors.

1540–1600   De Soto and the Mississippians. De Soto and other Spaniards encounter the remnants of the southeastern Mississippian culture, which consists of politically and ceremonially centralized chiefdoms, or small city-states, often managed by priests or sacred chiefs. Diseases transmitted by European explorers, fishermen, and slave raiders decimate Mississippian culture populations. By 1600, most Mississippian ceremonial centers are abandoned and the formerly Mississippian culture groups move up and down the Mississippi Valley and into the southeastern United States, dispersed into decentralized political alliances and confederacies of villages or local kinship groups. By the early

A five-story Pueblo building. Courtesy of the National Anthropological Archives, Smithsonian Institution.

1700s much of the Mississippian culture has disappeared. Some of the remnant Mississippian culture nations are known today as the Creek, Cherokee, Natchez, Chickasaw, Caddo, Pawnee, and Choctaw.

1541–1599

AUGUST, 1541–SPRING 1543 St. Lawrence Iroquois. Faced with the hostility of the St.

Lawrence Iroquois at Stadacona, French efforts led by Jacques Cartier and Jean-François de La Rocque, Sieur de Roberval, the newly commissioned Lieutenant-general in Canada, to establish a settlement in the region fail. The party spends much of its time exploring for precious metals. This marks the last known contact between Europeans and the St. Lawrence Iroquois.

1542 Cabrillo Explores the Pacific Coast. Juan Rodriguez Cabrillo and Bartolome Ferrelo explore the Pacific Coast and encounter numerous California Indian tribes.

1542 Indians Fight from Horseback. In Mexico, Spanish are forced to allow their Indian allies to fight on horseback in order to suppress a serious rebellion. These are the first mounted Indian warriors in the Americas.

1542–1600 Turmoil in the Northeast. The Iroquoian-speaking nations (Huron, Five Nations, and others) who live along the St. Lawrence River are invaded and displaced by Algonkian-speaking nations (Montagnais, Ottawa, Algonquin, and others) from the north and west. The Iroquoian-speaking nations retreat south and to the lower Great Lakes area.

1543–1588 Trade with European Traders. Trade between various groups along the North American East Coast and Europeans becomes increasingly common. Up to 50 ships visit the Montagnais trade center at Tadoussac, at the mouth of the Saguenay River on the lower St. Lawrence River. The Montagnais are hunter-gatherers occupying the rugged region north of the St. Lawrence. By refusing to trade until competing European parties are on hand, they are able to acquire goods at steadily lower costs. Then, as European goods are incorporated into existing trading networks, groups residing as far away as Hudson Bay and the Great Lakes acquire iron tools. To protect their role as middlemen, the Montagnais work to prevent direct trade between most of other Indian groups and the Europeans. As an exception, bands of Algonquin, hunter-gatherers occupying areas east of Montagnais territory, are allowed to trade with Europeans at Tadoussac, perhaps as part of an alliance. The Algonquin (a group of proto-Ojibway bands) should not be confused with the Algonkian-speaking peoples, which includes the Algonquin (sometimes spelled Algonkian or Algonkin), as well as the Micmac, Montagnais, Ottawa (Odawa), Cree, Ojibway (Ojibwa, Chippewa, or Anishinabe), Miami,

Illinois, and many other Indian peoples who speak related Algonkian dialects.

c. 1550 Powhatan (Wahunsonacock), Powhatan Tribal Leader, Is Born. In the late 1500s and 1600s, the Indian chief Wahunsonacock presides over the Powhatan Confederacy, an alliance of Indian tribes and villages stretching from the Potomac River to the Tidewater region of Virginia. The English call the chief Powhatan (Falls of the River), after the village where the Indian leader dwells. He is an important figure in the opening stages of English efforts to settle in the Tidewater, in particular the Jamestown expedition of 1607. The English government knows that maintaining friendly relations with the Powhatan people is a key to establishing a foothold in the region. For this reason, Powhatan is courted by several colonial leaders. In 1609, he is offered a crown from the king of England and reluctantly agrees to have it placed ceremoniously on his head. In return, Powhatan, sends the king of England his old moccasins and a mantle. In 1614, a degree of harmony is achieved after the marriage of Pocahontas, Powhatan's daughter, to John Rolfe, a leading citizen of the Jamestown colony. After the marriage, Powhatan negotiates a peace settlement that produces generally friendly relations with the English until a few years after his death in 1618.

1559 Tristan de Luna and the Demise of the Southeastern Tribes. In 1559 the Spaniard Tristan de Luna explores Florida's Gulf Coast, covering some of the same ground as de Soto did 20 years earlier. His objective is the establishment of three colonies, the last of which is to be located in the inland province of Coosa, a Muskogean-speaking group of Indians then living in present-day Alabama. Although he had visited it, de Soto had left Coosa relatively intact, and his stories of its wealth grew after his return. By the time Luna and his company arrive in Coosa in the summer of 1560, their supplies had been lost in a hurricane and they are desperate and starving, the wealth of Coosa their last hope of survival. But they are surprised to discover the main Coosa village, formerly a town of 500 houses, is now but 50 houses, a small remnant of this once-thriving center. Ironically the destruction to Coosa and other towns like it came not at the hands of de Soto, but in his wake. A sick slave the Spanish left behind became the point of origin for a series of epidemics that swept the Southeast, leaving many tribes depopulated. By 1600 the survivors of towns either destroyed by de Soto or reduced in his wake, including Abihka, Kashita, Coweta and Coosa, coalesce to form the new Creek confederacy.

1563–1565 Huguenots in Florida. Protestants known as Huguenots flee Catholic France. Led by Jean Ribaulty, they attempt to colonize an area from South Carolina to St. Augustine, in present-day Florida. During this time French artist Jacques le Moyne draws some of the earliest known European representations of Native North Americans. The colony is destroyed in 1565 by Spanish warships under Pedro Menéndez de Avilés.

1565–1568 Menéndez Establishes St. Augustine. The first permanent European settlement in North America is established at St. Augustine, Florida, by Pedro Menéndez de Avilés. Small posts are established up the Atlantic coastline to Georgia; the area is called Guale. With Menéndez come Jesuit missionaries, though they are replaced in 1573 by the Franciscan order.

1568 Jesuit Indian School Organized. Jesuits organize a school in Havana for Indian children brought from Florida, thus establishing the first missionary school for North American Indians.

1570 Contact with Powhatan Confederacy. The Spaniards unsuccessfully attempt to gain a foothold in Virginia within the territory of the Tsen-Akamak (the Powhatan Confederacy). It is likely that Mexican or West Indian Natives came with the Spanish and perhaps joined the Powhatan in their attacks on the Spanish. In later years, it is said that both Wahunsonacock (Powhatan) and Opechancanough (Pamunkey) were of Mexican or West Indian origin.

1576–1578 Baffin Island Inuit. Bands of Baffin Island Inuit, hunter-gatherers who inhabit the tundra regions of North America, have unfriendly confrontations with the English explorer, Admiral Martin Frobisher, along Frobisher Bay on Baffin Island in the eastern arctic. Several Inuit are captured by Frobisher and taken to London. There the Inuit, with remarkable clothing and a distinctive skin boat called a kayak, cause a sensation. All die in London. Aside from Frobisher's three expeditions in 1576, 1577, and 1578, at least 14 other expeditions, most sponsored by the English, visit Inuit and Cree lands as far southwest as James Bay between 1576 and 1632. As the expeditions are intended to find precious metals and a passageway to the Orient, the Inuit and Cree, hunter-gatherers who reside along the southern Hudson Bay, meet few of them and the encounters are usually hostile. The Inuit and Cree make use of iron and wood discarded or wrecked along the coasts.

1578–1579 Drake Explores California. Francis Drake of England explores the California coast and encounters such groups as the Coastal Miwok.

1580 Massasoit, Wampanoag Tribal Leader, Is Born. Massasoit, a principal leader of the Wampanoag people in the early 1600s, encourages friendship with English settlers. As leader of the Wampanoag, Massasoit exercises control over a number of Indian groups that occupy lands from Narragansett Bay to Cape Cod in present-day Massachusetts, and he negotiates friendly relations with the recently arrived Pilgrim (1620) and Puritan (1630) settlers. As early as 1621, with the aid of Squanto, a Wampanoag who speaks English, Massasoit

An early view of American Indians in the Southeast and Florida. Courtesy of the Rare Books & Manuscript Division of the New York Public Library—Astor, Lenox, and Tilden Foundations.

carries on communications with the Pilgrims at their Plymouth settlement. Massasoit helps the settlers in a number of ways, including donations of land and advice on farming and hunting. The Wampanoag chief becomes close friends with Roger Williams, a progressive-minded theologian, and, according to many accounts, influences Williams's relative understanding and favorable view of New England Indians' lives and right to territory. Massasoit eventually comes to resent the growing encroachment of English settlers and his son, Philip, turns this resentment into war in 1675–76. Massasoit dies in 1661.

1582–1598 The Spanish Begin Settlement of New Mexico. Spanish expeditions begin to enter the southern Plains and Pueblo territory by way of the Rio Grande Valley, in eastern New Mexico. Although at first repelled by Pueblo and Apache Indians, by 1598 a Spanish colony is established at San Juan Pueblo, in northern New Mexico.

1583 English Fishermen Visit Newfoundland. An English visitor to St. Johns, Newfoundland,

records how the frequent visits of European fisherman are causing the abandonment of the area by local Indians. Many are being enslaved, while others are dying of the new diseases.

1585–1607 Roanoke Colony Founded. The Spanish are not alone in their desire for lands in North America. In 1585, Sir Walter Raleigh founds an English colony on Roanoke Island, North Carolina, but the settlement does not survive. What happened to the English settlers at the Roanoke colony remains a mystery.

1588 Fur Trade Monopolies Granted. The French king, Henry III, begins a policy of granting a fur trade monopoly to certain parties. The policy arises because competition has reduced the profits for Europeans to very low levels, and because the beaver furs from North America have suddenly come into great demand in Europe. The *castor gras* (literally "greasy beaver"), beaver pelts which Indians have used for clothing for a season or two, thus the English term, "coat beaver," are particularly valuable in the felting process because they have shed the long guard hairs, retained the shorter

On April 30, 1562, two small French ships cast anchor and met with Indians near present-day St. Augustine, Florida. Courtesy of the Rare Books & Manuscript Division of the New York Public Library—Astor, Lenox, and Tilden Foundation.

barbed hairs (beaver wool), and absorbed perspiration and body oils. Indian traders may be somewhat confused to find that Europeans increasingly want their worn beaver furs rather than the soft luxury furs they had sought before.

1590 Samoset, Pemaquid Tribal Leader, Is Born. Samoset is a sachem of the Pemaquid band of Abenaki, living on Monhegan Island off the coast of Maine. He greets the Pilgrims at Plymouth in English (which he has learned from contact with traders) and becomes an instrumental liaison between the Pilgrims and Indians. Samoset and Squanto, the Wampanoag Indian who had been taken to England as a slave, arrange a meeting between the colonists and Massasoit, grand sachem of the Wampanoag Confederacy. Squanto, who returns to North America in 1619, and Samoset help negotiate the first treaty with the Wampanoag chief Massasoit in 1621. In 1625, Samoset signs the first land deed in America, ceding close to

An early view of American Indians, cooking fish. Courtesy of the Rare Books & Manuscript Division of the New York Public Library—Astor, Lenox, and Tilden Foundation.

12,000 acres to the Englishmen William Parnell, Thomas Way, and William England. Samoset dies that same year.

1595   Pocahontas, Powhatan Cultural Mediator, Is Born. Pocahontas is the daughter of Powhatan and the niece of Opechancanough, both leaders of the Powhatan Confederacy that occupies much of the state of Virginia. In 1612, Pocahontas is abducted by English settlers and held hostage. During this time she learns English and converts to Christianity (*See also* entry, 1612). In 1614, Pocahontas marries John Rolfe, an English settler in Virginia, and is credited with helping early English settlers maintain peaceful relations with the Powhatan. Although the actual events are undocumented, it is widely believed that Pocahontas intervenes to prevent the execution of John Smith, the Jamestown leader captured by Powhatan allies because he is thought to have commanded raids on several Indian villages. In 1616, Pocahontas and her husband make a widely publicized trip to England. For the Virginia colonists, Pocahontas is good publicity. She is offered as proof that the struggling colony can survive and maintain good Indian relations. For Pocahontas, however-

er, the trip proves deadly—she dies a year later of a European disease.

1598–1599   The Subjugation of Acoma. Made governor of New Mexico in 1598, Juan de Oñate leads an expedition through pueblo territory with the primary mission of subduing the peoples of that region and establishing a Spanish colony. His initial contact with Acoma, a pueblo situated on a 300-foot mesa, is peaceful, but when Juan de Zaldivar brings reinforcements, diplomacy turns to hostility. Badly in need of food, Zaldivar and his men attempt to purchase some cornmeal from the Acoma people. Upon gaining admittance to the pueblo, however, the soldiers' demands increase, fueling pueblo resentment. Although the exact chain of events is unknown, the men of the town attack the Spaniards, and all but five men are killed, including Zaldivar himself. There is no record of the number of Acoma dead. One month later, on January 21, 1599, Vincente de Zaldivar arrives with a force of 70 men to avenge his brother's death. Although Acoma's location would seem to make it impregnable, Zaldivar and his army manage to gain access to the village when a cadre of 12 men scale the rear access while the bulk of the Spanish force distracts the Indians with maneuvers on the other side. Once on top they burn buildings and slaughter people indiscriminately. By the end of the three-day battle, 800 Acoma are dead. Another 570 are put on trial. Women between the ages of 12 and 25 are indentured to 20 years' servitude at the Spanish capital of San Juan. Men are also condemned to servitude, but as an added punishment are publicly mutilated as well. In the plazas of other pueblos, males over 12 years of age each have one foot chopped off. Two Hopi visitors to Acoma during the time of the punitive expedition are sent home with their right hands severed, in order to show their people what resistance to the Spanish crown will bring. Although both Zaldivar and Oñate are later tried and found guilty of excessive cruelty, there is little consolation in the verdict for their numerous pueblo victims.

1 6 0 0 – 1 6 1 9

1600–1615 French Trade Networks. Along the St. Lawrence seaway, the French begin active fur trading. Numerous attempts are made to establish settlements, such as the outpost at Tadoussac.

1603–1615 Champlain Explores the Northeast. Samuel de Champlain's voyages in the Northeast lead to extensive contacts with various Algonkian-speaking and Iroquois tribes. Champlain established Quebec on July 3, 1608. There was no sign of the former village of Stadacona (at Quebec) or Hochelaga (at Montreal). Expanding trade relations with different Algonkian-speaking peoples, Champlain sides with the Huron in a war party against the Onondaga in 1615, thus turning the mighty Five Nations of the Iroquois Confederacy against the French

1604–1607 Trade Established at Port Royal. Led by Membertou, a band of Micmac establish trade with the French at Port Royal, at the mouth of the Annapolis River along the shores of the Bay of Fundy (a large bay separating New Brunswick from the peninsula of Nova Scotia). Port Royal is the first attempt by Europeans to establish a permanent trading post in North America. Relocated from a less suitable island site, Port Royal is in *Megumaage* (the name the

Micmac attach to their territory), which extends east from the St. John River Valley to include todays provinces of Nova Scotia and Prince Edward Island (called Abegweit, or "Cradled on the Waves," by the Micmac), most of New Brunswick, and the Gaspé Peninsula of Quebec. The Micmac are able to use their access to European goods, including weapons, to take the offensive against Abenaki enemies to the west. The French abandon Port Royal in 1607 but resettle shortly afterward. Membertou and over a hundred other Micmac are baptized by a French missionary, Jessé Fléché, at Port Royal on June 24, 1610, foreshadowing the long connection between the Micmac, the French, and Roman Catholicism. The relationship is symbolized in 1610 by a wampum belt given by Membertou to the French.

1606–1614 War between Spanish and New Mexico Indians. Continual warfare between Spanish and Indians in New Mexico, especially Navajo, Jemez, and Pueblo refugees, develops. Indians capturing herds of horses are among some the earliest reports of Native use of these animals in North America.

1607 English Settlement in Virginia. The British Virginia Company, a monopoly granted by the English king, James I, establishes a settlement at Jamestown on the lands of the Pamunkey Indians, a subgroup within the Powhatan Confederacy. Like those from other European na-

French artist's view of American Indians used as illustration to *Les Voyages du Sr. de Champlain*, c. 1615–18. Reprinted by permission of the Houghton Library, Harvard University.

tions, English citizens come to America to exploit its resources and get rich. When the colonizers arrive, they spend much of their time exploring the James River and gathering rocks believed to contain gold. The "gold" turns out to be pyrite or "fool's gold," and the English cast about for another resource.

Wahunsonacock (*See* biography, c. 1550), the leader of the Powhatan Confederacy (referred to simply as Powhatan by the English), warmly receives the colonizers. During the first winter, the Indians save the Englishmen from starvation. George Percy, one of the Jamestown settlers, writes that English rations are reduced to "but a small can of barley, sodden in water, to five men a day." Percy praises God who "put the terror into the sauvages' hearts" so that the "wild and cruel pagans" would not destroy the English. Percy proclaims that God sent "those people which were our mortal enemies, to relieve us with victuals, as bread, corn, fish, and flesh in great plenty." Without the help of Powhatan and his people, they would have "all perished."

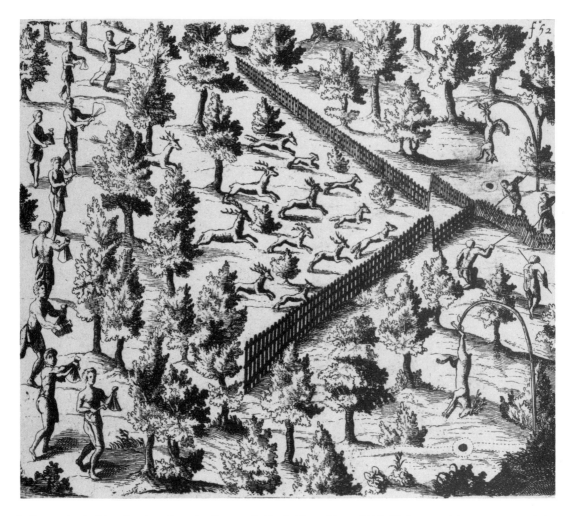

Indian method of hunting deer, from *Les Voyages du Sr. de Champlain*, c. 1615–18. Reprinted by permission of the Houghton Library, Harvard University.

The English soon repay the Pamunkey by demanding their submission to English rule and the payment of an annual tribute of corn. John Smith, the leader of the Jamestown settlement, advocates an aggressive policy toward the Indians, which causes conflicts between the settlers and the Indians of Chesapeake Bay. At first, Powhatan aids the colonists, but after a few years he becomes disillusioned with the English. He asks, "Why will you destroy us who supply you with food? What can you get by war?" He cannot understand the English animosity toward the Indians nor can he truly understand the full extent of European desire for material gain.

1609   Henry Hudson Opens Fur Trade. Henry Hudson, sailing for the Netherlands, opens a lucrative fur trade with the Lenape, Wappinger, Manhattan, Hackensack, Munsee, and Mohican nations of New Netherlands (present-day New York).

1609   Santa Fe Founded. The Spanish found Santa Fe in New Mexico.

JUNE–JULY 1609   Huron Visit Quebec City. With the reluctant agreement of the Algonquin, a group of Huron (who call themselves Wyandot or Ouendat) of the Arendaronon (Rock People) visit the newly established French trading post at Quebec City. The St. Lawrence Iroquois have disappeared from the region since 1543. Champlain joins a party of Huron, Algonquin, and Montagnais in a raid on villages of the Iroquois Five Nations Confederacy (Mohawk, Oneida, Onondaga, Cayuga, and Seneca) near Lake Champlain in New York. Equipped with muskets, Champlain is very successful in the battle. He joins other raids in 1610 and 1615. Because of these raids, and because they are attracted to European traders who also have become active on the Hudson River, the Iroquois Confederacy end, until 1633, their forays into the St. Lawrence River region.

1612   Dutch Traders on the Hudson River. Dutch traders expand their trade on the Hudson River, especially with the Iroquois.

1613   The Kidnapping of Pocohontas. The daughter of the powerful leader Powhatan, Pocohontas is kidnapped by the English and held captive in Jamestown, where she meets her future husband, the settler John Rolfe. Baptized by the Church of England the following year, she is renamed "Rebecca." *(See also* biography, 1595*).*

1613   Near-Extinction of Beothuk. In response to a shooting attempt on their tribesmen by a Frenchman, the Beothuk Indians in Newfoundland kill 37 fishermen. In retaliation, the French arm the Micmac, the traditional enemies of the Beothuk, and offer them bounties for scalps, leading to the virtual extinction of the Beothuk tribe.

1614   Dutch Fur Trade in North America.

This portrait of Pocahontas was made in London in 1616, one year before her sudden death. Courtesy of the National Anthropological Archives, Smithsonian Institution.

United New Netherland Company begins developing the Dutch fur trade in North America.

1615   Impact of the Fur Trade. The confederacy of Algonkian-speaking nations (Ottawa, Potawatomi, Chippewa, and possibly Cree) continue a migration starting near the Atlantic Coast, then through the St. Lawrence River basin, and finally to the Lake Michigan and Lake Superior area. These nations have a tradition of political and ceremonial unity, although they begin to separate into small bands because of the demands of the fur trade economy. Indians trade furs for European-manufactured goods such as rifles, metal hatchets and knives, cloth, beads, alcoholic drinks, and other items. The Indians quickly recognize the value of the goods and find that the Europeans are willing to trade for skins and furs, most often deerskins and beaver skins, which are made into leather and hats. Indians begin to hunt for furbearing animals more often, for longer periods of time, and for the market, instead of for necessity. Consequently, some nations, like the Potawatomi, Ottawa, and Chippewa, migrate into the interior in search of territories that support furbearing animals. The fur trade defines the primary economic relation between Europeans and Indians until about 1800.

AUGUST 1, 1615 Huron Welcome Samuel de Champlain. Huron villagers welcome Samuel de Champlain, leader of New France, who will be their guest until the spring of 1616. The Huron and French conclude an alliance during Champlain's visit to Huronia. The Huron, numbering some 30,000 people, occupy longhouses in several palisaded villages of up to 3,500 people in the region between Lake Simcoe and Lake Huron. Aside from the Arendaronon tribe there are also the Attignawantan (Bear), Attigneenongnhac Cord Makers), Tahontaenrat (Deer), and Ataronchronon (Swamp). The villagers grow corn, beans, squash, and some sunflowers and tobacco in neighboring fields. Because they are the northernmost agricultural group in the region, they are at the focus of an extensive trade network. Their agricultural produce and that of the neighboring Iroquoian Petun (Tobacco People), who are centered in villages just south of Georgian Bay, and the Neutral People, who occupy villages east of Lake Ontario, are exchanged for the dried fish and meat produced by hunter-gatherers to the north. The Huron language is the main language of trade. The Petun and the Ottawa, hunter-gatherers of the Bruce Peninsula and Manitoulin Island which separate Georgian Bay from Lake Huron, also meet Champlain during this trip. In September Champlain joins a Huron raid on Iroquois Five Nations villages south of Lake Ontario. Champlain leaves Huronia on May 22, 1616.

1615–1640s Northeastern Trading Networks. The Huron, an Iroquoian-speaking nation of 30-35,000 people living near Lake Huron, in alliance with other Iroquoian-speakers—Tobacco, Attiwandaronk (Neutral Nation), and Erie of present-day Ohio—establish a vast trade network in the eastern interior of North America. Goods are exchanged through trade networks that extend into Mexico, to the Gulf

of Mexico, and as far west as Minnesota. By the early 1600s these networks are distributing manufactured goods, metal knives, guns, tools, cloth, and other items gained in trade with the French in New France (southeastern Canada). By 1635, beaver supplies in the Huron homeland are depleted because of European demand for fur. The Huron are forced to trade with other nations or to hunt on the territories of other Native nations. In the late 1640s the Five Nations, with Dutch supplies of guns, ball, and powder, destroy the Huron and allied nations' trade empire. Under French influence, the Huron and their allies refuse to grant the Five Nations trade access to the interior from the early 1620s to 1649.

1615–1649 The Huron Trade Empire. Through Huron and Algonkian-speaking middlemen, Indian groups as far north as James Bay and as far west as Lake Michigan acquire European goods. These middlemen profit by transporting the furs of various bands to the trade centers at Quebec City, Trois Rivières (established 1634), and Ville Marie (Montreal, established 1642), and European goods from these centers to other Indian groups. The Huron accept French Roman Catholic (Récollet) missionaries and young French boys as part of their alliance with the French, but work to prevent direct trade between the French and other groups such as the Petun and Neutral. Access to metal tools, and wealth made possible by increased trade enable the Huron to develop a more elaborate cultural life. This is evident in the much more elaborate Feast of the Dead, Iroquoian reburial ceremonies, held every 10 to 20 years when villages were relocated.

1616–1620 Smallpox among the New England Natives. A smallpox epidemic ravages the New England Indians who live along the coastline from present-day Massachusetts to Maine.

1617 Micmac and European Disease. Many Micmac are killed in a devastating epidemic. Because Native groups have not built up immunities, when a European disease strikes a certain band, all of its members become ill. With no experience in dealing with the disease, and with few healthy band members to care for the sick, many Natives die because of ineffective and even counterproductive responses and because starvation or dehydration complicates their condition.

1618–1631 Powhatan Confederacy Declares War. When Wahunsonacock dies in 1618, his brother Opechancanough assumes leadership of the tribal confederation. In 1619 colonists establish a school for Indian children in order to convert them to Christianity. Relations between the colonists and Indians grow more hostile, and in 1622 Opechancanough moves against the English, who suffer 350 deaths, losing more than one-third of their colony, and nearly leave Virginia. The English Crown takes over Jamestown and Virginia, providing aid and protection to the settlers.

Some English believe that the war of 1622 ultimately will be good for the colony. John Smith writes that the conflict "will be good for the Plantation, because we have just cause to destroy them by all means possible." Another Englishman writes that the English are "now set at liberty by the treacherous violence of Sauvages." By right of war, the English can now invade Indian lands and thereby "enjoy their cultivated places . . . and possessing the fruits of other labours. Now their cleared grounds in all their villages (which are situated in the fruitfullest places of the land) shall be inhabited by us, whereas heretofore the grubbing of woods was the greatest labour."

The first Virginia War intermittently lasts nearly ten years, with many deaths among the Natives and colonists. The territory of the Chickahominy Nation, an ally nation within the Powhatan Confederacy, is ravaged by colonial attacks throughout the 1620s. The Native population in Virginia begins to decline significantly, mostly because of disease, warfare, and, most likely, migration. In 1608, about 30,000

Natives live around Chesapeake Bay, but by 1669 only 2,000 remain.

1620–1639

1620 Arrival of the Pilgrims. The Pilgrims arrive aboard the *Mayflower* at Plymouth, Massachusetts. Before landing, they sign a compact calling for self-rule. The Pilgrims barely survive their first winter in Massachusetts but are helped by several friendly Indians, one of whom was Tisquantum, more commonly known as Squanto. He is captured sometime between 1605 and 1614, when an English ship abducts several Indians and carries them off for sale in Europe. Tisquantum is taken to Malaga Island, Spain, and sold. He makes his way back home by way of England and Newfoundland, only to find that his home village has been wiped out by disease. He lives with the Wampanoag and their chief, Massasoit, who extends influence over much of present-day Massachusetts and Rhode Island. During his travels, Tisquantum learns some English.

Tisquantum, like other Native Americans, aids the colonists, showing them where to hunt and fish and how to grow and prepare crops such as squash, corn, and beans. After a disastrous first winter, the Pilgrims learn quickly from the Indians' lessons. In the autumn of 1621 they invite Massasoit to a feast to give thanks; he arrives with 90 people. When the Pilgrims do not have sufficient food, Massasoit asks his people to provide food as well.

1624 Dutch Settlement. Having established the Dutch West India Company in 1621 to open trade routes through treaties, the Dutch settlers found Fort Orange (present-day Albany, NY) in New Netherlands. Two years later, the Dutch and Mahican allies march against the Iroquois and are defeated. Fort Orange is largely abandoned.

1626 Purchase of Manhattan. Peter Minuit, governor of New Netherlands, trades 60 guilders of goods—legend says worth twenty-four dollars—for Manhattan Island. Minuit buys the land from a band of Shinnecock Indians, but later has to buy it again from the Reckgawawanc, a Manhattan band which claims hunting rights to the island.

1627 Carib Indian Slaves. Carib Indians are brought to Virginia as slaves and flee to the Powhatan Confederacy for safety.

1627 New France Company Chartered. The Company of New France is chartered to colonize New France and further develop the fur trade with Indians.

JULY 1629 English Pirates Take Control of New France. Perhaps aided by Montagnais who are frustrated by French trading behavior, a party of English pirates led by David Kirke takes control of New France and Acadia. The Treaty of Saint Germain-en-Laye (March 29, 1632) returns New France and Acadia to France.

1629–1633 Establishment of Pueblo Missions. Spanish missionaries establish Catholic churches at Acoma, Hopi, and Zuni pueblos.

1629–1633 Zuni Missionization and Revolt. Only in 1629, after the Rio Grande pueblos had experienced missionization for almost two decades, did the Spanish church turn its attention to the Zuni and Hopi to the west. Missionaries accompanied by military guards are sent to these areas between 1629 and 1633, but they are so strongly opposed by the Native religious leaders in Zuni that in 1633 the soldiers and two of the four missionaries there are killed. Expecting Spanish reprisal, the Zuni retreat to the top of Corn Mesa, where many stayed as long as ten years before returning to the village.

1630 The Puritans Arrive. Ten years after the Pilgrims' arrival, the Puritans (a Protestant religious sect) led by John Winthrop arrive in Massachusetts. The Puritans believe that they are on a mission from God to establish a "City Upon the Hill," a perfect Christian society in which the Puritans form a covenant among themselves and with God to live a holy life. Outsiders are not invited into the covenant unless they agree to subjugate themselves to the rules of the religious community. Most Native Americans do not want to join this covenant and are considered outside of God's law. In fact, Puritan minister Cotton Mather maintains that Indians are the "accursed seed of Canaan" who have been dispatched by Satan "in hopes that the gospel of Jesus Christ would never come here to destroy or disturb his absolute empire over them." Reverend Mather points to the devastating disease that ravages Native populations to prove English superiority. He calls the smallpox epidemic of 1633–35, which kills thousands of Natives, a "remarkable and terrible stroke of God upon the natives." The Puritans argue that God sent the disease to kill Satan's children and to clear the land for his true flock.

1631 James Bay Region Explored. Thomas James and Luke Fox of England explore the James Bay region near the Hudson Bay.

1631–1642 Roger Williams and Indian Rights. Roger Williams of the Massachusetts colony contends that the royal charter for the colony illegally expropriates tribal lands. He urges a humane policy towards Indians. In 1636, he founds Rhode Island and insists that settlers there buy land from Indians. In 1642, Williams's Indian-English dictionary is published in London.

1632–1643 Period of Truce. Negotiations with the Pamunkey and Chickahominy Indians in central Virginia bring brief peace. Despite the treaties and negotiations, English settlers continue to advance on Indian lands while Indian slavery continues on English farms and tobacco plantations.

1633 Land Allotment Precedent Set. The general court of the Massachusetts colony sets a precedent of land allotment to Indians and of central rather than local governments handling Indian affairs.

1633–1635 Smallpox Epidemics. Smallpox epidemics among Indians of New England, New France, and New Netherland decimate already weakened populations. The disease may have spread inland to groups who have not yet met Europeans.

1633–1650 Jesuits among the Huron. The Jesuits attempt to convert the Huron people to Catholicism. Despite limited successes, eventually all of the missions are destroyed by the Five Nations.

1634 Nicolet Explores the Northeast. A Frenchman, Jean Nicolet, travels up the Ottawa River to Georgian Bay and then to Sault Ste. Marie and Wisconsin. Meeting different Algonkian-speaking peoples, such as the Winnebago, he learns of many powerful societies. The Winnebago, for example, have over 3,000 warriors and already trade European goods with the Huron, Ottawa, and Nispissing.

SPRING 1634 Trois-Rivières Established. The French establish Trois-Rivières as a trading post and military fort upstream from Quebec City at the mouth of the St. Maurice River. The settlement is intended to help protect Quebec City. The Iroquois Confederacy have recently begun frequent attacks on New France and upon French Indian allies in the St. Lawrence Valley area. The Iroquois appear to seek access to the valuable fur resources of the North, perhaps because their own lands are depleted of furs. Algonquin and Attikamek groups residing near Trois-Rivières begin trading at that site rather than traveling to Quebec City.

JUNE 1634 Smallpox among the Montagnais, Algonquin, and Huron. Smallpox spreads from the St. Lawrence Valley, killing many Montagnais, Algonquin, and Huron.

SEPTEMBER 19, 1634 Jesuits Choose Huron

Village as First Mission. The Jesuits choose the Huron village of Ihonatiria as the site of their first mission to the Huron and their neighbors. The Jesuits, who began their missionary efforts in New France in 1626, have replaced the Récollets as the principal missionary order in the colony. Unlike the Récollets, the Jesuits adopt a strategy in which they live among Indian groups rather than encouraging Indians to settle among the French.

1635 First Indian School Established in New France. The Jesuits establish the first school for Indians in New France. Instruction is in French, Latin, Huron and Montagnais.

1635 Over-Hunting of Beaver. Nearly all of the beaver are over-hunted in the Huron country. To maintain their trade relations with the French and other Indian tribes, the Huron must now get all of their furs elsewhere.

1635–1640 Smallpox and Other Epidemics in New France and New England. Several epidemics, the worst a 1639 smallpox epidemic, reduce the populations of Huronia from about 20,000 to 10,000. The epidemics also affect the Algonkian-speaking nations, as well as the Petun and Neutral. The diseases spread from non-Native settlements in New France and New England.

1636–1637 The Pequot War. Along with the Narragansett, the Pequot and their allies are the most powerful tribal group in the New England area in the sixteenth and early seventeenth centuries. Their location has the effect of making them strategically important—the Connecticut Valley is an ample producer of fur and wampum, two of the region's most important commodities. Not long after arriving, the Puritans assert their authority over the Pequot, who resist English encroachment. In 1634, Indians kill John Stone and eight companions who are hunting for Native slaves. Puritans use Stone's death to claim jurisdiction over the Pequot and to demand their surrender of land, valuable goods, and Stone's killers. The Narragansett, living to the east of the Pequot, are believed to have committed the murders, but the Pequot agree to the Puritan demands. However, they do not abide by the terms of the agreement, and relations with the English grow steadily worse. In 1636, several Narragansett kill an English trader and then flee into Pequot country. When the English demand the return of the Narragansett, the Pequot refuse and a fight ensues. In May 1637 the Massachusetts General Court, the colony's legislature, drafts articles of war and raises an army against the Pequot. Primarily through the diplomacy of Roger Williams, the colonists are able to enlist the powerful Narragansett and other tribes against the Pequot. In May 1637, Puritans, Pilgrims, and their Indian allies attack and set fire to the palisaded Pequot fort at Mystic River, killing as many as 700 men, women, and children. By the following year, the shattered remnants of the once-powerful Pequot Nation are forced to agree to harsh peace conditions, and the balance of power in the New England area shifts from the Indians to the Euro-Americans.

1636–1640 Iroquois and Huron Hostilities. While the Pequot War rages in New England, the Iroquois and Huron erupt in small-scale fighting. Although not very extreme, a perpetual state of hostility characterizes the relations between the two most powerful Indian nations in the St. Lawrence region.

1637 Pequot War. During the Pequot War, the Mohawk help the English against both the Pequot and Narragansett.

JULY 1637 Jesuits among the Montagnais. Jesuits begin an attempt to settle Montagnais in an agricultural community at a place they call Sillery, a favorite Montagnais fishing site near Quebec City. Several families whose hunting grounds have been depleted settle at the site, but this first Indian reserve in present-day Canada has limited success. The effort is made

French engraving of a 'Sauvage Iroquois.' Courtesy of the Library of Congress.

in the belief that Indians must be settled in order to be evangelized.

1637–1641 The Ute Acquire the Horse. The Spaniards of New Mexico attack the peaceful Ute of the Great Basin to get slaves. Many of these Ute escape and introduce horses among their people. The Ute then become one of the most powerful people of the region.

1638 Early Reservations. The Puritans establish what would now be called a "reservation" for the Quinnipiac Nation living near what is now New Haven, Connecticut. Under the terms of their agreement, the Quinnipiac retain only 1,200 acres of their original land on which they are subject to the jurisdiction of an English magistrate or agent. Under English rule, Quinnipiac people cannot sell or leave their lands or receive "foreign" Indians. They cannot buy guns, powder, or whisky. They must accept Christianity and reject their traditional spiritual beliefs, which Puritans feel are the teachings of Satan.

1638 Sweden Claims Land along Delaware Bay. Sweden lays claims to land along the Delaware Bay and maintains a trading post there until 1655.

1639 Philip (Metacom), Wampanoag Tribal Leader, Is Born. Philip is the grand sachem of the Wampanoag Confederacy, an alliance of Algonkian-speaking peoples living in New England. Philip finds peace with the New England colonists impossible, and he leads a revolt against them. Fighting erupts on June 16, 1675, at the frontier settlement of Swansea. The conflict quickly escalates across southern New England, involving the colonies of Plymouth, Massachusetts, Connecticut, and, to a limited extent, Rhode Island. Some tribes, including the Narragansett and Nipmuck, support Philip; others give assistance to the English. On December 19, 1675, a decisive battle in southern Rhode Island results in the deaths of approximately 600 Indians; 400 are captured.

In August 1676, Philip himself is killed after being betrayed by his own warriors. His body is mutilated and displayed publicly.

1639–1649 Sainte - Marie - Among - the - Hurons, Jesuit Missionary Center. Sainte-Marie-Among-the-Hurons, a missionary center constructed near the southeast shores of Georgian Bay in central Huronia, develops as the nucleus of Jesuit missionary efforts among the Huron, Petun, Nispissing, Ojibway, and Ottawa.

1639–1662 Taos Indians Abandon New Mexico Pueblo. The Taos Indians abandon their pueblo in New Mexico and flee to the Apaches in western Kansas where they build a new pueblo. Some are brought back by the Spaniards before 1642, but others stay until 1662. The Taos take horses with them, thus introducing horses in the central plains by 1640 at the latest.

1640–1649

c. 1640 Dakota Migration. Following a dispute, members of the Dakota in northern Minnesota separate from their kin and move toward the Lake of the Woods region, beginning a series of migrations which will take them to Lake Winnipeg region by the 1680s and as far west as the valleys of the Rocky Mountains by 1800. Bands become known to Europeans as the Assiniboine, and near the Rocky Mountains as the Stoney. (*Assiniboine* means something like "those who cook using hot stones" in an Ojibway dialect.) The Dakota (Sioux) and Assiniboine are hunter-gatherers who speak a Siouan language.

c. 1640 Northeast. Art historians trace the origin of floral designs in Northeast Indian art to about this time, when French Ursuline nuns in Canada teach Indian converts embroidery at their convent in Quebec City. Floral design eventually spreads westward across the continent.

1640 Five Nations Exhaust Local Beaver Supplies. The Five Nations of the Iroquois Confederacy are no longer able to supply their trade requirements by hunting and trapping on their home territory in upstate New York. The Five Nations have come to depend on trade with the Dutch at Fort Orange to supply knives, axes, cloth, beads, and guns and powder. After 1640, they look to the interior nations to supply them with trade ties or allow them access to beaver territories. During the 1640s, the Iroquois try to negotiate trade and diplomatic agreements with the Huron, Neutral Nation, and Erie, but the French move to prevent permanent trade agreements. With 12,000 people and 2,200 warriors, the people of the Five Nations are far less numerous than their Huron rivals.

1640–1641 Potawatomi and Winnebago Hostilities. On their way to attack the Potawatomi, the Winnebago lose 500 warriors during a terrible storm near Green Bay, Wisconsin. Tensions between the Winnebago and Potawatomi exist from Potawatomi migration into Winnebago territories. After fleeing the Attiwandaronk in Michigan, the Potawatomi are forced toward Mackinac by Winnebago attacks.

1640s English Settlement of Maryland. By this decade the English are settling in Maryland and to the south, along the James River, and are now coveting more territory.

1641 Huron and Algonkian-Speaking Traders Receive Firearms. For the first time, Huron and Algonkian-speaking traders, who have been baptized as Christians, are given firearms in trade by the French. This change in policy follows an intensification of attacks by the Iroquois after they acquire significant numbers of firearms from Dutch traders on the Hudson River.

1641 Iroquois Confederacy. The Five Nations of the Iroquois Confederacy seek to make peace with the French and the Huron to gain greater access to furs. Short of guns and in need of resources to trade, the Five Nations face growing dependency, and French are not interested in any treaties which would divert trade from them to the Dutch in New York.

1641 Raritan Indians. In reaction to the killing of a Staten Island farmer by a group of Raritan Indians, the Dutch offer bounties for Raritan scalps or heads.

1641–1642 Spanish Civil War. Civil war among Spaniards in New Mexico devastates Pueblos and other Indians on both sides.

1642 Founding of Montreal. Founded by Sieur de Maionneuve and Paul de Chomedey, Montreal is located in the heart of the St. Lawrence region and constructed at the site of the former Indian village of Hochelaga. Begun as a mission, the site quickly develops into an important military outpost and the center of the expanding French fur trading empire in North America. Iroquois attacks on the French and on Huron and Algonkian-speaking trading parties are disrupting fur trade in the region.

1642 Iroquois Attack Huron. The Iroquois step up their attacks on the Huron and their allies.

1642–1649 Illinois and Winnebago War. The Winnebago face an extremely hard winter and epidemic. According to neighboring Illinois tradition, the Illinois send food to the Winnebago, who accept it but also attack the Illinois. The Illinois Confederacy then launches a major war against the Winnebago and defeats them. Southern Wisconsin thus falls under the control of the Illinois and their ally, the Miami. The Winnebago move inland towards Green Bay.

1643 Mohawk Alliance with the Dutch. The Mohawk, along with the other members of the Iroquois Confederacy, sign a treaty with the Dutch. Consequently, the Five Nations become stronger and are able to disrupt the French-Huron trading network.

1643–1645 Kieft's War. At the time of its greatest extent, New Netherland extends from present-day southern Delaware to western Long Island and along the Hudson River into what is now New York State. This area is home to about 25,000 Indians from 40 different nations, including the Montauk, Esopus, Mahican, and Raritan peoples. As the Dutch colony grows, relations between the colonists and the Indians of the region worsen. After a series of incidents and retaliations, Gen. William Kieft blames a robbery perpetrated by his own men on the Raritan Indians. Angry settlers then burn the Raritan fields, kill three Raritan, and abduct the chief's brother. The Raritan respond by attacking a Dutch plantation. Kieft calls for the extinction of the whole tribe. That same year a Dutchman is murdered by a Wecquaesgeek Indian, and Kieft calls for their extinction, too. He orders an attack on a multitribal Algonkian-speaking village, killing 80 and capturing 30. Eleven nations retaliate by declaring war on the Dutch. Although the Indian effort meets with some initial success, the Dutch are able to conclude a peace with the Long Island groups, splitting the alliance. With support from the English, they relentlessly pursue the remaining nations. Over 500 men, women, and children are killed when the combined Dutch-English force discovers a winter camp near present-day Stamford, Connecticut. In the two years before the conclusion of Kieft's War in August 1645, more than 1,600 Indians are killed.

1643–1654 Michigan Tribes Forced Westward. The Sauk, Kickapoo, and Fox nations are forced to leave their homes in Michigan and southern Ontario under extreme pressures from first the Attiwandaronk and then the Five Nations. They gradually migrate to Wisconsin as part of a larger migration of Indian nations fleeing constant trading wars.

1644–1646 The Second Virginia War. The Powhatan Confederacy stages a second war against Virginia colony. After the war of 1622, the Indians try to live in peace with the settlers, but the English continue expanding onto Indian lands. Some Indians are held as slaves or servants. By 1641, the English have settled in Maryland and south of the James River and covet the land of the Rappahannock, a major Powhatan ally. By 1642, the English are selecting land sites, even some that include Indian villages. The war of 1644–46 temporarily prevents English territorial expansion.

Opechancanough, now old and feeble, is carried to the battlefield where he wants to die a warrior's death rather than submit to the English. After two years of warfare, the Indians and colonists negotiate an agreement defining a boundary between the two. The Treaty of 1646 prohibits English land expansion; however, the Indians are left with only a portion of their former lands. The colonists agree to respect Native rights to these territories. Indians become subject to the rule of the colonial Virginia courts and must provide an annual tribute of beaver pelts. Nevertheless, by 1649 English colonists are disregarding the treaty and moving farther into Indian territory.

1645–1700 The Beaver Wars. Tensions between the Five Nations of the Iroquois Confederacy and the French-Huron Alliance continue to escalate. Attempts to reach a peace or negotiated settlement continue to fail. A limited agreement to allow equal access to existing fur resources is reached in 1645 but appears to break down following the summer of 1646, when the Huron bring to Montreal the greatest fur fleet ever. As the powerful and wealthy Huron continue to exploit tremendous amounts of furs, the Iroquois face dire consequences. Lacking the trade resources to obtain essential European goods, such as iron, guns, and power, the Five Nations launch an enormous attack of over a thousand warriors against the Huron in the spring of 1649. Catching the Huron by surprise, the Five Nations force them and their allies to flee. Many starve away from their homes, and some attempt to join other nations. Eastern Canada and the Great Lakes region is now plunged into warfare as the Five Nations attempt to assert hegemony over the region.

After failing to gain a reliable trade agreement with the Huron and their trading allies, the Iroquois, with Dutch support and guns and powder, initiate a series of intermittent wars against the Susquehannock, Huron, Neutral Nation, Erie, Ottawa, and other French trading nations. By 1650, the Huron trade empire is destroyed by the Iroquois Confederacy. The Ottawa (whose name means "to trade") then assume the role of middlemen traders between the interior nations of the Great Lakes area and the French. Thereafter, the Confederacy carries its wars and diplomacy to the Indian nations of the interior, attacking the Chippewa, the confederated tribes of the Illinois, and the Ottawa, and pushing these nations farther into present-day Michigan and Wisconsin. The Five Nations are generally successful in these wars and are able to supply the Dutch, until 1664, with trade goods. After 1664, the English capture New Netherland and rename it New York. The English continue the policies of the Dutch traders by supplying the Iroquois with weapons to carry on their trade wars with the interior nations. The French are reluctant to supply their trading partners with guns, putting the interior nations at a disadvantage against the better supplied Iroquois.

1648–1669 Shawnee Migration. Separating from other Algonkian-speaking groups such as the Sauk, Fox, and Kickapoo, the Shawnee migrate into the Ohio River Valley away from growing trade wars in the Great Lakes regions.

1649 Virginia Colonists and Indian Land. Despite the previous treaty negotiations and settlements, Virginia colonists continue to pour into Indian lands and villages. The Rappahannock are surrounded by hundreds of settlers who arrive in their lands and begin organizing administrative counties.

MARCH 16, 1649 Iroquois Confederacy Attacks Huronia. The Iroquois Confederacy initiates a concerted attack on Huronia that kills or scatters the entire Huron population. Some survivors are integrated into neighboring groups, including the tribes of the Iroquois Confederacy; some resettle in mission settlements such as Lorette near Quebec City, retaining their Huron name; and others migrate throughout the Great Lakes area where they become known as Wyandot (Wyandotte, Wendat, derived from *Ouendat*, their own name for themselves). By 1652 the Iroquois also destroy the Petun and Neutral.

1650–1659

c. 1650 Tomochichi, Creek Tribal Leader, Is Born. Tomochichi is born in the mid-1600s and lives at the Creek village of Apalachukla, along the Chattahoochee River in present-day Alabama. He moves to Georgia in the early 1700s when a new English colony is rapidly being settled. In 1733, Tomochichi is visited by a party of colonists led by James Oglethorpe, the founder of the Georgia colony, at which time he signs a peace treaty on behalf of the Creek Nation. In return for massive land grants, the Creek are accorded privileges, such as protection under English law and liberal trading rights. Tomochichi is praised for his peacemaking efforts and, in 1734, heads a Creek delegation to England, where he and his family are presented to King George II and Queen Carolina. Tomochichi's friendship with the English leads to a long-term Cree-British trade relationship, and he remains a friend to the English for the remainder of his life. Tomochichi dies in 1739.

1650 Catawba Emergence. In the Southeast, the Catawba Indian tribe emerges out of a combination of previously related groups. Facing the devastating effects of diseases, growing economic dependency on Europeans, and the threats of constant warfare, fractions of previous groups come together and create a new society for themselves. Although combining previous traditions and values, the new society comes to have its own distinct cultural and societal structures.

1650 Cheyenne Migration Begins. Because of the expanding Iroquois trade empire, the Cheyenne, probably living in southern Ontario or Quebec, are forced to migrate westward. By 1775, they reach the Great Plains of what is now Montana and the Dakotas, where they adopt Plains culture with buffalo hunting, an original Sun Dance ceremony, and sacred bundles given to them by the prophetic figure Sweet Medicine.

1650 Inunaina Arapaho Become Buffalo Hunters. The Inunaina Arapaho leave the Red River of the North, abandon agriculture, and become buffalo hunters. The Aaninena (Atsina or Gros Ventre) split off and go due west into Montana while the Inuaina turn southwesterly towards the Black Hills and Great Plains.

1650 Pueblo Resistance. The Tiwa of Isleta, Alameda, and Sandia, along with the Keres of Cochiti and San Felipe and the Towa of Jemez, plan to revolt against the Spanish tyranny. The plot is disclosed and the Spanish crush it, hanging nine leaders.

1650 Tribal Migrations. Numerous Indian tribes migrate from their villages due to expanding trade wars. The Wyandot and many Algonkian-speaking tribes flee their homes to the western edge of the Great Lakes.

1650–1665 Apache and Spanish at War. The Salinero Apache of the Zuni Mountains and the Spanish are in open warfare.

1650–1671 Nispissing Migrations. The Nispissing, an Algonkian-speaking group, flee from Lake Nispissing northwesterly to Lake Nipigon where they develop trade relations with the Cree. By 1670 the Nispissing have moved to Lake Superior but begin returning to Lake Nispissing.

1651 The Five Nations Defeat the Atti- wandaronk. Following the defeats of the Huron, the Attiwandaronk, a subgroup of the Huron, emerge as leading rivals to the Iroquois. The Five Nations now attack and destroy an entire Attiwandaronk village, and the Attiwandaronk retaliate by destroying a Seneca town. Following several years of warfare, the Iroquois Confederacy consolidates its control over the Attiwandaronk, forcing many to flee southward.

1651–1653 Iroquois Raids in the Great Lakes Region. The Iroquois continue their raids into the Great Lakes region. As far west as Green Bay, Wisconsin, they attack and further prevent the Wyandot and their allies from recovering. The Iroquois begin securing trade relations with many Algonkian-speaking tribes who previously had traded with the Wyandot.

1651–1665 Iroquois Expand Influence. The Iroquois use former Huron, Petun, and Neutral lands as hunting grounds and raid Ottawa, Nispissing, and Montagnais, as well as the French in New France, as far away as the Saguenay River, James Bay, and Lake Superior. The Ottawa move west toward the site of Sault Ste. Marie to escape the raids. Ottawa and Wyandot trading parties must use circuitous routes to reach French trading centers. Indian groups formerly supplied by Indian middlemen trade increasingly with *coureurs de bois* (literally "woods runners"), itinerant Frenchmen who trade directly with trapping Indians. These men depend on the birchbark canoe, snowshoes, and clothing of the Indians. Some Indian women marry them following the customs in Indian societies (*à la façon du pays* or "according to the custom of the country"). The Iroquois are threatening the very survival of the European colony in New France by the end of these years. New France has fewer than 2,000 non-Native residents.

1652 Morattico Indians. Morattico Indians move their village from the Corotoma area to present-day Morattico Creek in Virginia because of English settlers' pressure.

1652–1653 Attiwandaronk Indians. Some Attiwandaronk winter at Skenchio-e, near Windsor, Ontario. They later join the Iroquois.

1653 Erie and Iroquois Hostilities Commence. Hostilities begin between the Erie and the Iroquois. The Erie, sheltering many Huron refugees burn a Seneca town and kill 80 Seneca returning from Lake Huron.

1653 The Five Nations Make Peace with France. In the spring the Seneca and Cayuga are ready to make peace with the French. By June the Onondaga are willing, and in August the Mohawk reluctantly agree to peace. The Iroquois, having established themselves as the dominant power in the St. Lawrence and eastern Great Lakes regions, no longer have reason to war with the French. In autumn a partial peace is agreed to, but many Iroquois are still concerned with French ties to other Algonkian-speaking nations.

1653 Pamunkey and Chickahominy Indians. The Pamunkey and Chickahominy in Virginia continue to be pressured by English settlers. Realizing the growing tensions, the Virginia government orders some settlers to move back.

1654 The Iroquois Attack the Erie. An Erie war party penetrates to within a day's journey of Onondaga and kills three hunters. The Five Nations are planning major assaults on the Erie. In the summer, an Iroquois army of 1,800 warriors is organized to attack the Erie, who have about 2,000 warriors in all. A Five Nations army of 700 men attacks the main Erie town successfully, killing or capturing the inhabitants.

1654 Michigan Peninsula. Almost the entire lower Michigan peninsula is uninhabited due to intertribal wars.

1654–1656 Wyandot and Ottawa Attempt to Reopen Fur Trade. In June 1654, a great canoe fleet of Wyandot and Ottawa reaches Montreal from Green Bay via the Ottawa River with a great quantity of furs. Hoping to reopen the old fur trade shattered by the Five Nations, their daring voyage reveals the centrality of European trade for many societies. In 1656, Ottawa and Wyandot traders bring a great canoe fleet of furs to Montreal, angering the Five Nations. In December, 1,200 Iroquois warriors attack the Ottawa in order to disrupt the revived French fur trade.

1654–1657 Warfare between Iroquois and Erie. Warfare between the Iroquois and the Erie rages on, with the Erie retreating southward to the upper Ohio River where they later become known as the Black Minquas (Mingo). Many of the Erie, however, are captured and enslaved by the Five Nations.

1655 The Timucua Rebellion. In the hundred years following de Soto's expedition, the Timucua of northern Florida experience unceasing hardship. Increasing Spanish military presence under Pedro Menéndez de Avilés is followed in 1609 with the creation of the first mission in Timucua territory. Then, between 1613–17, a violent epidemic claims over half of the Timucua Nation. Dependent on Spanish trade goods, the much-weakened Timucua easily fall under mission control, and, by 1633, the Spanish can claim that virtually all of the Timucua are converted. In the next several decades, the Spanish greatly increase their labor demands on the Timucua, and a second epidemic halves the population again in 1655. Then, as corrupt colonial officials illicitly trade away supplies and goods earmarked for the Timucua laborers, discontent grows. When Spanish fears of an English invasion cause Governor Pedro Rebolledo to order the Timucuan militia activated, open resistance is ignited. Under their chief Lucas Menendez, the Timucua rebel, killing some soldiers and other civilians at the San Pedro mission. The Spanish retaliate, overwhelming the Timucua forces with the help of some Appalachia converts. Eleven Timucua, including Lucas Menendez, are paraded through the mission towns and publicly hanged. Other leaders are sentenced to forced labor, while much of the remaining Timucua population is relocated in order to better serve the needs of the Spanish Empire.

1655–1656   Powhatan Confederation. Totopotamoy, leader of the Powhatan Confederation, is persuaded to lead 100 warriors against hostile Indians gathered above the fall line on the James and Pamunkey rivers. The English side with the Powhatan and they are both defeated, with the loss of Totopotamoy and all or most of his warriors.

1655–1659   Ottawa and Wyandot Migrations. The Ottawa and Wyandot abandon Green Bay and move west to the Mississippi River. They then move north, finally reaching Lake Superior.

1655–1664   Peach Wars. In September 1655 Hendrick Van Dyck, formerly a commanding officer during the campaigns of Kieft's War, kills a woman for picking peaches in his orchard, setting off a cycle of violence and revenge which eventually causes the destruction of the Esopus Nation, in what is now Pennsylvania. After Esopus warriors burn farms and houses, and the Dutch destroy Indian settlements, a delegation of Esopus tribal leaders comes to the town of Wiltwyck in order to attend peace negotiations with Peter Stuyvesant, the governor-general. While the delegation sleeps, they are slaughtered by Stuyvesant's men. The Esopus retaliate by burning eight Dutch soldiers and maintaining a siege on Wiltwyck for three years. In 1660 a large Dutch force captures several hundred Esopus of all ages and both sexes. When Esopus leaders refuse to negotiate for their release, Stuyvesant sells the hostages into slavery in the Caribbean. The Peach Wars continue for another four years, until the decimated Esopus are forced to cede their homeland to the Dutch. Stuyvesant celebrates the occasion by proclaiming "a day of general thanksgiving to the Almighty." Later

that year the English troops invade New Netherland and the Dutch presence in North America comes to an end.

1655–1670   Sioux Incorporate European Trade Goods. Introduced to European goods by the Wyandot and Ottawa, the Sioux who live along the upper Mississippi River in Minnesota quickly incorporate these goods into their lifestyles. Wyandot and Ottawa traders begin to take advantage of the Sioux and warfare develops, driving the Wyandot and Ottawa farther north.

1656   Queen Anne Assumes Leadership of Pamunkey. With the death of her husband, Totopotomoi, Cocacoeske (or "Queen Anne") assumes leadership of the Pamunkey Indians, a tribe allied with the Powhatan Confederacy. Initially siding with the English colonists of Virginia, in 1675 she renounces Governor William Berkeley's council for neglect of her people, many of whom have been killed by forces commanded by Berkeley's cousin, Nathaniel Bacon. Securing promises of future compensation from the council, she provides Pamunkey warriors to quell Bacon's rebellion; she subsequently receives a silver badge for her support.

1656   Virginia Assembly and Indian Land Policies. The Virginia Assembly issues numerous Indian land policies. Land granted to Indians would not be alienable except with the consent of the assembly. Two years later, the assembly rules that no patents will be issued to English settlers until each Indian town receives 50 acres for each Indian "bowman." These policies, however, are challenged and disobeyed by the settlers.

1657–1660   Iroquois and French Fur Trade. The Iroquois are unable to destroy their enemies in the west and resort to blockading the Ottawa River. This technique effectively halts much of the French fur trade.

1658   French and Cree Trade. Cree Indians come to Chequamegon Bay on the south shore of Lake Superior to trade with the French. The Chippewa have abandoned the region. The

French traders, led by Pierre Radisson and Sieur de Groseillers, also visit the Ottawa at Lac Court Oreilles and then visit Cree and Sioux to the west at the end of Lake Superior.

1658 Rappahannock Land Cessions. The leaders of the Rappahannock Indians enter into an agreement with Col. Moore Fantleroy and cede some 8,000 acres to Fantleroy, including Morattico Town and Mangorite. The Morattico, consequently, are forced to move their town to the east side of Totuskey Creek. In short, both the Rappahannock and Morattico are again forced to concede lands to aggressive English settlers.

1660-1669

1660 The Chippewa-Sioux Wars. The Chippewa (Ojibway) living in the upper Great Lakes region start to move west, armed with guns and trade goods. Pushed by colonial and Iroquois expansion, the Chippewa invade Sioux territory in present-day Minnesota. After much fighting with the Chippewa, many Sioux move onto the plains in the 1700s, where they adopt the buffalo-hunting horse culture for which they are well known in U.S. history. Before this time, the Sioux were a settled horticultural people living in the woodlands east of the plains area.

1660 Western Apache in the Southwest. Western Apache have control over the area from Sonora and Pima north to the lands of Coninas and to the Hopi Area and are said to wage war on all other Indian groups in surrounding areas.

MAY 2–9, 1660 Iroquois Attack Long Sault. A group of 800 Iroquois defeat a party of 44 Huron and Algonquin and 16 Frenchmen at Long Sault on the Ottawa River near Montreal. All but one Huron are killed.

1660s–1670s Algonkian-Speaking Indians. Many Algonkian-speaking tribes, such as the Menominee, Sauk, and Fox, concentrate in the Green Bay-Fox River region of Wisconsin. Devastated by warfare, disease, and economic dependency, these tribes are far away from their traditional homes.

1660s–1670s The Ottawa and Wyandot Establish Trading Center. The Ottawa and Wyandot establish a trading center at Chegnamegon Bay on Lake Superior. In 1665 the Jesuit priest, Father Allonex, meets 800 warriors of many different nations here. By 1670, there are over 50 villages on the bay.

1661 The Chickahominy Are Dispossessed. The Chickahominy Nation, part of the Powhatan Confederacy, moves from the Pamunkey River to the Mattaponi River. The Chickahominy sell 2,000 acres of land to an Englishman named Hammond. Phillip Mallory buys 743 acres from the Chickahominy, the beginning of the Mallory family's two-century effort to acquire Chickahominy lands in Virginia.

1661 Spanish Attacked in Georgia. Spanish posts in Guale (Georgia) are attacked by northern Indians. The missions north of the Savannah River are abandoned by the Spanish.

1661 Spanish Suppression of Pueblo Religions. The Spanish raid the sacred kivas of many Pueblo Indians, destroy hundreds of *kachina* masks, and attempt to further suppress Pueblo religion.

1661 Susquehannock Attack Seneca Trading Parties. The Susquehannock Indians, anxious to secure a share of the Great Lakes fur trade, begin ambushing Seneca trading parties in western New York. The unity of the Iroquois Confederacy becomes threatened by Mohawk indifference to Seneca problems.

MARCH 1662 Virginia Assembly Land Policy. The Colonial Assembly in Virginia declares that no Indian king or other person may sell or alienate any land justly claimed by the Indians. Attempts to ensure Indian property rights reveals the extreme pressures exerted on the Indian communities by Virginia settlers.

1662–1680 Iroquois League Under Attack. After the defeat of a large body of Iroquois warriors at Mackinac by a coalition of Algonkian-speaking tribes and the Wyandot, the Algonkian-speaking tribes and Wyandot begin invading areas held by the Iroquois tribes. Supported by the French, these attacks, along with continued Susquehannock aggression, begin to weaken the Iroquois empire. Slowly, through alliances with the French and different Algonkian-speaking tribes, a coalition of tribes pushes the Five Nations eastward out of the Great Lakes. Many tribes are thus able to return to their present communities around the Great Lakes.

1663 New France Becomes a Colony. The Company of the New France is disbanded, and New France becomes a colony with a royal governor. French colonization in Canada thus is established permanently.

1664 The English Take Over New Netherland. The English gain control of New Netherland from the Dutch and become allies and partners with the Iroquois League. New Amsterdam on Manhattan Island becomes New York.

1664 New Mexico Pueblo Policy. Governor Peñalosa of New Mexico issues an edict stating that all Indians, even those at peace with the Spanish, will not be allowed inside the pueblos except at certain times and only in certain numbers. This edict attempts to prevent Apache-Pueblo trade and reveals the growing threat and burden of Apache raids on Spanish outposts in Indian territories.

1666–1667 Five Nations Communities. Two French armies invade the homelands of the Five Nations in 1666, and by 1667 many Five Nations communities agree to peace settlements. In the same year, the Five Nations make peace with the Nispissing, Ottawa, Mahican, and other groups so that they can concentrate on their war with the Susquehannock and send fur-trading embassies among the western Algonkian-speaking nations.

1667 Apache and Spanish Peace. By February 10, all of the Apache near New Mexico are forced to accept peace with the Spanish except those of Chiquito and El Chilmo.

1667 The Spanish Suppress Pueblo Resistance. The Piros, Tompiros, Mansos, and Chihuahua tribes and the Apaches of the Gila and Pecos Rivers plan a revolt against the Spaniards. The Spanish hear of the plans and prevent the revolt.

1667 Susquehannock War against Seneca and Cayuga. The Susquehannock, with Shawnee and Black Minqua (Erie) allies, take the offensive against the Seneca and Cayuga, driving many Cayuga to the north of Lake Ontario. The Swedes and English of Delaware and Maryland are helping to arm the Susquehannock.

JULY 7, 1667 Iroquois and French Peace Agreement. The Iroquois conclude a peace agreement with the French following French attacks on Mohawk villages in October 1666. Iroquois numbers have been much depleted by disease and war. The peace agreement opens the Great Lakes for the fur trade.

1667–1680 Apache and Navajo Raids on Spanish Settlements. The Apaches and Navajo begin continuous warfare against the Spanish settlements in New Mexico. They carry off large numbers of horses and begin trading them throughout the regions to the north and east.

1668 Canadian Natives and Jesuits. Encouraged by Jesuits, a number of Oneida and Mohawk families take up residence at La Prairie (Kahnawaké, Caughnawaga) near Montreal. In the belief that French colonists will corrupt the Indians, the Jesuits establish the village at some distance from European settlement.

SEPTEMBER 29, 1668–AUGUST 1669 Cree Fur Trade on Hudson Bay. About 300 Cree trade a considerable amount of fur with English traders at the mouth of the Rupert River along the shores of James Bay. The event marks the beginning of organized trade focused on the Hudson Bay.

1668–1669 Canadian Exploration. Pierre Esprit Radisson and Sieur de Groseilliers explore west of the St. Lawrence River as far as Lake Superior, as well as the Hudson Bay region, for France.

1669–1673 Joliet and Marquette Expedition. Louis Joliet and Jacques Marquette explore the Great Lakes and the Mississippi River for France.

1670–1679

1670 Cree and Ojibway Traders. Cree and Ojibway (Chippewa) traders begin traveling to Hudson's Bay Company (H.B.C.) posts established at the mouths of the Rupert, Moose, and Albany rivers. The Ojibway, who identify themselves as *Anishinaabe,* are Algonkian-speaking hunter-gatherers occupying the area north and east of Lake Superior. By taking advantage of the competition between the French traders centered on the St. Lawrence, and the H.B.C. posts, the Indians are able to improve trade terms and acquire a wider range of higher quality goods than had been available before. While Indian groups are forced to travel to James Bay in order to trade with the H.B.C., several hundred French *coureurs de bois* bring trade goods to the Indian groups each year. A number of Indian bands are induced to stay near H.B.C. fur trading posts all year in order to provide various goods and services to the traders. These "Home Guard" Indians also intermarry with H.B.C. traders according to Native customs.

1670 Hudson's Bay Company Chartered. The Hudson's Bay Company is chartered by the English.

1670 Miami Trade at Fox River. Coming from the south and west, the Miami gather in the Fox River area of Wisconsin. They come to trade in European goods and number over 8,000 warriors out of 24,000 individuals.

1670s Awashonks, Woman Chieftain. Woman chieftain of the Saconnet band of present-day Little Compton, Rhode Island, Awashonks initially lends warriors to support King Philip's War of 1675–76. A meeting with British captain Benjamin Church causes her to change sides and ally the Saconnet with the English colonists. Hence, Saconnets battled their former confederacy allies, the Wampanoag. However, Awashonks's political positioning allows her to maintain the integrity of her own band; she leads her people to the settlement of Sandwich, Massachusetts.

1670s Chickahominy. Chickahominy Indians are reported living on the "frontier" of Virginia with no English settlers living to the west. The Chickahominy are able to trade regularly with the Susquehannock as well as with the Manakin, Occaneechi, Saponi, and other groups to the Southwest.

1670–1710 Carolina Colony and the Early Southern Indian Slave Trade. Charles Town, in present-day South Carolina, is established. Early encounters lead to conflict with local tribal groups such as the Cusabo and Westo. The English attempt to enslave many Indians for plantation work and enlist other nations such as the Creek and Cherokee to raid interior nations, like the Choctaw in Mississippi and Louisiana for slaves. During the 1680s and 1690s, the Choctaw are under considerable pressure and lose many people to slave raids. In 1699, the French establish Louisiana colony, and supply the Choctaw with weapons, that they use to protect themselves from the English, Creek, and Cherokee slave raids. Some Choctaw regions thereafter are strongly allied to the French in gratitude for their help in preserving the Choctaw Nation. By 1710, the

Indian slave trade declines; Indians made poor slaves since they knew the local area and escaped often. Thereafter, the fur trade becomes the primary economic relation of the southern Indians to the colonists.

1671 Chippewa Treaty. Sieur St. Lusson makes a treaty with the Chippewa at Sault Ste. Marie for France.

JUNE 24, 1671 Apache Attack. The new governor of New Mexico, Miranda, is attacked on a wagon train to Albuquerque by "Seven River" and Gila Mountain Apache. Miranda swears to mount a new campaign against the Apache and to exterminate them.

1671–1679 French Forts in Great Lakes. The French begin establishing forts in the Great Lakes region as far northwest as Kaministikwia (Thunder Bay, Ontario) near the western edge of Lake Superior and at *Bawating* (Place of the Rapids), which the French call Sault Ste. Marie, an important fishing site on the St. Mary's River (the river which drains Lake Superior). The forts are erected for purposes of defense, trade, missions, and diplomacy. Ojibway at these sites benefit from their role as traders and middlemen. Frequent intermarriage between the French and Ojibway has led to the growth of a mixed-blood population.

1671–1680 Apache Migration. Apaches begin migrating to the Southwest from the southern plains. They raid Spanish settlements and Indian pueblos; sheep, horses, and trade goods are stolen. By this time, the Apache are well equipped with guns and horses and are able to elude and challenge Spanish armed forces.

1672 Indians as Mail Couriers. Colonial postal clerks use Indians to carry mail between New York City and Albany because winter weather is considered too severe for non-Indian couriers.

1672–1680 Apache Raid Pueblos. Because of continuous warfare between the Apache and

Spanish, numerous Pueblo communities are raided. Six pueblos are depopulated in the Piro-Tompiro-Eastern Tewa region.

1673 Sioux and Chippewa Warfare. A delegation of Sioux is sent to the newly established French outpost at Sault Ste. Marie. They are killed by a Chippewa party, perhaps to keep the Sioux isolated from European trading partners.

1673 Tamahita Indian Raids. Tamahita Indians, living just north of the Cherokee, raid as far south as Appalachia and Carolina. The increased English presence in the region precipitates many Indian societies to vie for control over different regions in order to secure a stable trading base.

1673–1674 Iroquois-Susquehannock War. The Seneca and Cayuga gradually gain the support of the other members of the Iroquois Confederacy for a full-scale war against the Susquehannock. Supported by English colonists in Maryland, the Susquehannock are able to repel Five Nations attacks. At peace with their other neighbors, however, the Five Nations begin to concentrate their forces more heavily on the Susquehannock adversaries.

1673–1679 Miami Migration. The large and powerful Miami Confederacy migrates out of Wisconsin to the eastern side of Lake Michigan. With Five Nations attacks subsiding, many Algonkian-speaking nations aided by the French are able to move into previously war-torn regions.

1673–1680 Illinois Confederacy. The great Illinois Confederacy occupies a strong position in Illinois. With hostile relations with the southern tribes of the Osage, the Chickasaw, and the Quapaw, the Illinois constantly attempt to solidify their position with the French.

1673–1681 Miami and Illinois Confederacies Become Hostile. Because of heightened trading relations, the Miami and Illinois confederacies become hostile and threaten to dis-

Ojibway shelter frame. Courtesy of the American Indian Studies Center, University of California at Los Angeles.

rupt much of the French fur trade in the Great Lakes. Although war is avoided, the fragile alliance between the Algonkian-speaking nations and the French in the Great Lakes is forced to adapt itself to the constantly changing nature of Algonkian-speaking societies.

1673–1720　Oto Migration. The Oto Indians gradually move west from the Des Moines River to the Blue River in Iowa, then across the Missouri River to the mouth of the Platte. Facing the increasingly powerful alliance between the Algonkian-speaking nations and the French in the Great Lakes region, the Oto migrate to secure their own resources.

1674–1680　English-Westo Alliance. The Westo Indians, living on the Savannah River and armed with guns from Virginia, dominate the interior of South Carolina. The English become their allies and trade deerskins, furs, and Indian slaves with them.

1675　Indian Use of European Trade Goods. European goods replace many indigenous goods throughout eastern North America and Canada, as nations incorporate the new products into their existing lifestyles. For example, glass beads replace much of the porcupine quill work done by eastern tribes. European glass beads are imported from Venice and Prague to decorate clothing.

1675　Secretary of Indian Affairs. The English establish a Board of Commissioners and a Secretary of Indian Affairs in Albany.

1675　Sioux Wage War against Illinois and Muskwakiwuk. Competing for trade resources and access to the French, the Sioux begin to wage war against the Illinois and Muskwakiwuk.

1675–1676　King Philip's War. The Puritans proceed to concentrate Indians on reservations and open former Indian lands to Puritan resettlement. By 1671, the Puritans have established 14 reservations and have forced many Indians from their homelands. Metacom, the Wampanoag son of Massasoit known to the English as King Philip, protests Puritan policies. He argues that the English set out to destroy Native American cultures and steal Indian lands. In 1671, Puritans arrest Metacom, but later release him. He continues to move among the tribes, telling them that the settlers are destroying Indian culture and sovereignty. By 1675, Metacom has a sufficient following to launch a war against the English. Abenaki, Nipmuck, Narragansett, and Wampanoag Indians join forces and attack more than half of the 90 English settlements in New England. The Indians, however, do not stand long against the English. Upon conclusion of hostilities, the English General Court decreases the number of reservations from 14 to 5 and places all Indians they can find upon these reserves. The Puritan government has Metacom executed and his wife, son, and hundreds of followers sold into slavery. Many of King Philip's allies, such as the Wampanoag, Nipmuck, and Narragansett, are enslaved or flee to the Mahican, in New York, or to the Abenaki Confederation in present-day Maine. The remnant northeastern Indian nations settle down to English rule in small communities, and over the next few centuries establish about 15 "praying towns" of Christian Indians, whose local government is much like the rest of New England. The "praying" Indians become socially and economically marginalized in New England society.

1675–1677 Bacon's Rebellion. In 1675 and 1676, a third major war erupts between Indians and Virginia settlers. This time, Maryland settlers are drawn into the battles with Virginia rebels and disrupted Indian nations. The Rappahannock flee their villages, and their land is taken by Virginia settlers. The colonists defeat the Susquehannock, who are pressed in the North by the expanding Iroquois trade empire, and who move into Virginia territory only to be abused by Virginia traders. The colonists are led by Nathaniel Bacon, who leads a rebellion to free Virginia colony from English rule. The English restore order, but not before Bacon's army kills and enslaves many Susquehannock, Occaneechi, Appomatuck, Manakin, and members of the Powhatan Confederacy. The Indians lose heavily in the war.

In 1677, a treaty of peace is signed between some Indian nations and Virginia colony. This treaty guarantees the signing Indians at least three miles of land in each direction from each of their villages. This leaves the remainder—most—of the land open to Virginia settlements and plantations. The Indians of Virginia are forced to acknowledge English law and courts, are subject to Virginia rule, and are left without significant land resources.

1675–1677 The Iroquois Defeat the Susquehannock. The Iroquois launch an all-out war on the Susquehannock, driving them south into Virginia and Maryland colonies where they encounter hostilities with colonists there. The Susquehannock are attacked by settlers also and are pushed further south. Thoroughly defeated, they split up; some go further south, while others are forced to join the Seneca. A few survive as "Conestogas" living near Lancaster, Pennsylvania, until 1763. With the expulsion of the Susquehannock from their territories, the Iroquois next begin major campaigns throughout the inland region along the eastern coast, known as the Piedmont.

1676–1677 Pueblos Abandoned. Spanish-held pueblos of Las Salinas Senecu, Cuarac, and Chilili in New Mexico are abandoned because of Apache attacks. These attack engender vicious atrocities in retaliation for Apache attacks.

1677 Five Nations Seek Control of Fur Trade. With the Susquehannock defeated, the Five Nations seek control of the fur trade of the Ohio Valley and attack major French allies such as the Illiniwek (Illinois). Meanwhile, French traders raid Iroquois parties.

1677–1731 Shawnee Migrations and Regroupings. The Shawnee probably occupy what is now northern Kentucky and southern Ohio before European contact. During the late 1600s Chickasaw and Cherokee slave raiding and fur trading expeditions force the Shawnee to retreat from their homeland. Some Shawnee migrate south to Georgia to live on the Savannah River, which is named after them, while others move to western Virginia and Pennsylvania. Others join the Creek Nation in Alabama, where they establish a permanent village within the Creek Nation. Sometime before 1680 the Five Nations grant the Delaware, Susquehannock, Shawnee, and other remnant coastal nations the right to occupy territory in eastern Pennsylvania, and many locate near what is now Philadelphia. Most of these nations are now landless, and the Iroquois use the landless Indian nations to create a buffer zone between themselves and the English colonies.

1678–1679 Treaty between Chippewa and Sioux. Daniel Greyson Duluth of France explores Great Lakes and negotiates treaties between warring Chippewa (Ojibway) and Sioux.

1679 Spanish Attempt to Convert Creek. Spanish attempt to convert Lower Creek (Apalachicola) to Catholicism but are rejected by the "Emperor" of Coweta. Spanish missionary attempts in the following years are repelled by the Creek.

---

1 6 8 0 – 1 6 8 9

1680 Five Nations and Miami Hostilities. Approximately 500 Iroquois warriors enter the Illinois country while most of the Illinois warriors are away hunting. Returning homeward after their attack, the party falls upon two lodges of Miami, who pay 3,000 beaver pelts for the return of some captured Miami. The Five Nations are hostile toward the Miami for trading with the French.

1680 Fur Trade. The Ottawa now control about two-thirds of the fur trade with the French, while the Chippewa and related groups supply most of the rest. The Iroquois are unsuccessful in persuading or forcing the Algonkian-speaking Indian allies to trade with them or with the English in New York. The Iroquois make

greater inroads for hunting and trading south of the Great Lakes area, using both diplomacy and armed forces to attain their commercial ends.

1680 Iroquois Attacks. Ottawa and Ojibway trips to New France, which have been declining over the last decade, end when the Iroquois intensify their attacks in the St. Lawrence region. Itinerant French traders replace them.

1680 King Hendrick, Mohawk-Mahican Tribal Leader, Is Born. King Hendrick is born among the Mahican, an Algonkian-speaking nation living in present-day eastern Connecticut. Hendrick is adopted by the Mohawk, one of the Five Nations of the Iroquois Confederacy. He is an important leader of his people and liaison to British settlers when he make his famous trip to England in 1710 as a result of a royal invitation. After he returns to North America, Hendrick becomes a spokesman for the Iroquois League and is a key English ally in their battles against the French in New France (Canada). In 1754, Hendrick is invited to the Albany Congress where he consults with the colonists on their plans for unification. Perhaps as a result of Hendrick's relationship with colonial leaders, the colonial and later U.S. government in many ways reflects the structure of the Iroquois League. Early in the fighting that leads to the French and Indian War, Hendrick leads Mohawk warriors against French forces and dies in 1755 from wounds suffered at the battle of Lake George.

1680–1681 La Salle Urges an Algonkian-Speaking Confederacy. Rene Cavalier de La Salle, a French explorer, winters among the Miami at the mouth of the St. Joseph River. Among the Miami are some Mahican led by Nanagoucy. He proposes the creation of a confederacy of western tribes to resist the Five Nations, offers to undertake the organization of such a confederacy, and says more eastern Algonkian-speaking groups would gladly join. Although the Miami support the idea but do not want to go to war, anti-Iroquois sentiments pervade most Algonkian-speaking nations throughout the region.

1680–1683   The English Attack the Westo. English colonists of South Carolina decide to destroy their allies, the Westo, in order to obtain slaves for themselves and to gain better access into the interior. Aided by some Shawnee, the English kill all but 50 Westo by 1683. These survivors later join the Creek. The English plan to open trade from South Carolina with the Chisca (Yuchi), Shawnee, and Coweta (Creek), as the Westo control of the interior is being removed.

1680–1684   Spanish Lose Control of Georgia. Spanish control of Guale (coastal Georgia) is shattered by English and Indian attacks. In 1684, the Indians of Guale, the Yamasee, rebel against the Spanish. The Yamasee begin raiding Florida to sell slaves to the English.

1680–1693   The Pueblo Revolt. After he and 46 other religious leaders are arrested and publicly whipped for "idolatry" by the Spanish, Popé, a Native American visionary from San Juan Pueblo, leads an armed revolt against the Spanish. Popé claims he is visited by the spirit world and given a holy charge to rid his homeland of the Spanish. His message brings about a Native revitalization movement that demands an end to the 80-year Spanish occupation and a return to traditional life. Runners are sent to all of the pueblos with knotted cords, which measure the days until the revolt is to take place. The Spanish are forewarned, but the resistance leaders accelerate their timetable. The revolt begins several days early at Taos pueblo on August 10, 1680, and spreads quickly to the other pueblos. After besieging the new capital at Santa Fe, the Indians drive the Spanish first to Isleta (one of the few pueblos not participating in the revolt) and then to El Paso del Norte (El Paso, Texas). The Indian patriots kill 21 friars and more than 400 people to recover their homelands and religious rights. The resistance leaders do away with virtually all traces of the Spanish presence.

Crosses and rosaries are destroyed or burned and neither Christian deities nor names are spoken. The Spanish language is forbidden and records of the Spanish government are burned in the Santa Fe plaza. Plants introduced from Europe are taken from the ground. With the expulsion of the Spanish from New Mexico, access to Pueblo communities is opened. Many Athapascan raid the pueblos, facilitating the spread of the horse.

Though causing great damage, several attempts at reconquest end in failure and Pueblo autonomy continues for 12 years. In autumn of 1692, the Spanish military commander Diego de Vargas begins the bloody recovery in earnest, and it ends four years later. Revolt and reconquest create great turmoil in the Southwest and, rather than live under Spanish rule, many Pueblo people flee west to live either among the Hopi or with small Navajo bands in the North. Many other pueblos are destroyed or abandoned. By the end of the eighteenth century, only 19 of more than 60 pre-revolt Rio Grande villages survive.

1681   Five Nations and Miami Hostilities. The Five Nations send an embassy to the Miami to persuade them to join their alliance, but the Miami remain disinterested. Because of previous Five Nations attacks, as well as the presence of the party of French explorer Rene Cavalier de La Salle in a Miami village, Five Nations attempts to ally themselves with the Miami are unsuccessful.

DECEMBER 6, 1681   Otermín Attempts to Put Down Pueblo Revolt. Spanish forces under Governor Antonio de Otermín reach Isleta Pueblo and force the submission of that pueblo's people, numbering 511 persons. This first attempt at reconquest in the aftermath of the Pueblo Revolt fails, however, when Otermín is unable to conquer the pueblos farther north. He must settle instead for the sacking and burning of ten abandoned pueblos south of Cochití. Other failed attempts at reconquest of the pueblo region occur in 1688 under Governor Pedro Reneros de Posada and in 1689 under Domingo Jironza Petriz de Cruzate.

1681–1682 Nanagoucy Advocates an Intertribal Confederacy. Nanagoucy, a Mahican leader, travels among the tribes of the Ohio country, advocating an intertribal confederacy. The French support the idea, and by 1683 300 lodges of Illinois, Miami, and Shawnee are gathered on the Illinois River near a fort the French are building. Soon there are 1,200 Illinois, 1,300 Miami, 500 Wea, 300 Kilatica, 200 Shawnee, 100 Pepikokia, 150 Piankashaw, and 70 Ouabona (Wappano or easterners, probably Mahican).

1682 Canadian Native Traders. Western Cree and Assiniboine bands begin trading at York Factory, a new Hudson's Bay Company (H.B.C.) post at the mouth of the Nelson and Hayes rivers on the western shores of Hudson Bay. These bands spend the winters in the region surrounding Lake Winnipeg, traveling to the post only once a year. Expert canoemen, they act as middlemen between other Indian bands in the west (many of which do not use canoes) and the H.B.C. As many as 550 Indians travel to York Factory each year. By 1730 the Siksika, Kainai (Blood), Peigan, and Atsina (Gros Ventre) have acquired European goods, including guns from Cree and Assiniboine traders. These groups are Algonkian-speaking buffalo hunters whose lives center on the migrating buffalo herds of the northern prairies. These pedestrian hunters kill buffalo by luring them into enclosures (pounds) or by driving them over cliffs (jumps). The buffalo provide Indians with food and the raw materials for clothing and tipis. Cree prevent enemy Chipewyan bands residing to the north from trading at York Factory or acquiring European weapons. The Chipewyan are Dene (Athapascan) hunter-gatherers of the western subarctic forests. They depend heavily on migrating herds of caribou, often luring them into pounds or driving them into deep water where they are killed. Cree bands residing near the H.B.C. posts act as Home Guard, providing mostly goods and services, rather than furs, in return for trade items.

1682 La Salle Claims Louisiana for France. Rene Cavalier de La Salle claims the Mississippi Valley (Louisiana) for France. Three years later, he establishes a settlement on Matagorda Bay on the Gulf of Mexico.

1682 Pennsylvania Colony and Delaware Treaty. William Penn purchases the present site of Philadelphia, Pennsylvania. The treaty is negotiated with a leading Delaware chief, sometimes called Tammany. A long period of peaceful relations begins between Quakers and the Indians, although relations are not always peaceful with Pennsylvania colony, especially after the 1730s.

1683 Five Nations Attacks Increase. Following their defeat of the Susquehannock, the Five Nations increase their raids throughout the East. Facing Seneca attacks, the Rappahannock are asked by the English to join with the Nanzattico or to move to the new Rappahannock fort, both in Virginia. It appears that they move to the Nanzattico fort. This same year, the Five Nations send an army to attack Mackinac but the French, Ottawa, Potawatomi, and Wyandot are so strongly entrenched that the Iroquois are forced to retire with only the capture of five Wyandot scouts.

1683 Lacrosse Described. French missionaries describe an Ojibway sport called *baggataway* (lacrosse).

1683–1690s Shawnee Slave Trade. The Shawnee of the Savannah River dominate trade with South Carolina, getting guns in exchange for furs and slaves. The Shawnee capture their slaves by raiding the Winyah, Appomatuck, Cherokee, and Chatot peoples.

1684 Five Nations Alliance Rejected. The Ottawa and other northern tribes reject a proposed alliance with the Five Nations, even

1775 engraving of William Penn, founder of Pennsylvania, concluding a treaty with the Delaware Indians. Courtesy of the Library of Congress.

though the English trade goods offered by the Iroquois are lower-priced than those of the French. The Ottawa are apprehensive about Iroquois control over the fur trade.

1684 Western Algonkian-Speaking Nations Repel the Iroquois. The Five Nations send an army against the Illinois Confederacy and other Algonkian-speaking allies and the French at Fort St. Louis on the Illinois River. The Iroquois are forced to retreat with considerable losses after a six-day siege. The defeat begins the end of Iroquois efforts to gain a monopoly over the northern and western fur trade.

1684–1688 Five Nations Neutrality Policy. Following their defeats in the west, a shift in Five Nations policy occurs. The Mohawk now recognize that the English at Albany are taking advantage of them and that they need peace and opportunity to trade with the French. In 1687 the Seneca are defeated by the French and the Mohawk do not come to their aid. In 1688 the Onondaga, Oneida, and Cayuga sign a treaty in Montreal guaranteeing Five Nations neutrality, commencing a series of Iroquois attempts to play off competing British and

French interests in the shifting balance of power in the Great Lakes and St. Lawrence regions.

1685–1686 English Influence among the Creek. English traders gain influence in the main Lower Creek towns of Coweta and Kashita, angering the Spanish who have been attempting to gain control of the region for years.

1686 Hostilities In the Southeast. With heightened Spanish-English rivalries in the Southeast, both sides and their respective Indian allies become targets of attacks. The Spanish, with their Timucua and mulatto allies, attack South Carolina settlements and destroy a Scottish settlement.

1688 Pima Revolt. Pima Indians are in full revolt because of slave raids by the soldiers of Sinaloa to obtain forced labor for the silver mines in the area.

1689 Mississippi Claimed for France. Nicholas Perrot formally claims the upper Mississippi region for France.

AUGUST 5, 1689 Iroquois Attack French Settlement. More than one thousand Iroquois attack a French settlement at Lachine, near Montreal. Approximately 100 French settlers are killed or captured. This intensifies French-Iroquois hostilities.

1689–1697 King William's War and Other Colonial Conflicts. King William's War initiates a series of colonial wars that last until the end of the War of 1812. During this time, there is an undeclared war on the frontier, first between the English and French and their respective Indian allies until 1763, or the end of the French and Indian War. Frontier conflict starts again with the Revolutionary War in 1776; war on the borders continues until 1795. The War of 1812 is the last conflict before the United States finally establishes its military control over the eastern coastal states and their frontiers. During this period of more than 125 years of intermittent warfare, Indian nations attempt to maintain trade relations with one or more European colonies and to retain their territory and political independence from colonial domination. Since Indian nations cannot produce metal goods or guns and powder, they depend on trade with European powers to supply these and other more domestic economic requirements. The Indian nations thus are forced to side with one or another European power in order to have access to trade and weapons, which become increasingly important for defense during the nearly constant colonial struggle and warfare. Indians nations often sell themselves as mercenaries to a European power as a means of obtaining goods other than by trapping furs and trading. In the North, the Algonkian-speaking nations often side with the French, until their defeat in 1763, while the Five Nations, especially the Mohawk, often side with the English, at least until 1755, when some Seneca begin to favor the French. After 1763, the western Algonkian-speaking nations (Ottawa, Chippewa, Potawatomi, Miami, and others) side with the British against the United States until the end of the War of 1812. Some nations, like the Five Nations and the Creek in the South, try to balance power diplomatically among the European colonies by not taking sides and by threatening an opponent with defection in order to gain political or trade concessions from the Europeans.

1690–1699

1690 English Open Trade with Cherokee. The English open up regular trade from South Carolina to the Cherokee; however, trade with the Shawnee, Creek, Yuchi, and Yamasee remains more lucrative.

1690–1700 Settlers Seek Indian Lands. In Virginia, settlers seek ways to acquire still more Indian lands. The Virginia government continuously breaks existing treaties with Indian nations, such as the Treaty of 1677. Although the British Crown often upholds Indian rights, colonists and Virginia officials keep infringing upon Indian lands, acquiring them "by hook or crook."

1690–1701 Ojibway Expansion. Ojibway formerly centered around Sault Ste. Marie expand southeast throughout what is now southern Ontario, where they become known as the Mississauga; west beyond the Great Lakes, where they become known as the Saulteaux; and south into the present-day United States, where they become known as Chippewa. At the same time, mixed-blood residents in Great Lakes settlements such as Sault Ste. Marie and Kaministikwia begin to develop a separate identity and lifestyle that will become known as Métis. The French word *métis*, like the Spanish word *mestizo*, refers to mixed-blood people, especially those of mixed European and American Indian ancestry.

1690–1705 Powhatan Cultural Survival. Despite their political subjugation and economic reliance on European goods, many of the Powhatan still maintain their traditions. Housing styles, religious practices, dress styles, language, and ceremonies reveal the continuities in cultural traditions.

1690–1715 Trade Alliance between Lower Creek and English Established. The Creeks begin raiding Spanish settlements and their Indian allies to capture slaves to sell to the English. The Yamasee also become allies of the English and carry raids into Florida.

1690–1720s Apache Setbacks. Formerly dominant on the High Plains, the Apaches now begin to suffer defeats primarily for two reasons: first, their eastern enemies (Pawnee, Skidi, Wichita, and other Caddoan) are receiving guns from the French, and secondly, the Ute and Comanche are attacking them from the west and the northwest.

1690–1776 Spread of the Horse to Southern California. The use of the horse gradually spreads from northwestern Sonora, beginning in the 1690s, to the Tohono O'Odham and Pima of Arizona in 1700, to the Colorado River in 1744, and to the southern California desert by 1774.

1692 Reconquest of the Pueblos. On August 16, the governor of New Mexico, Diego de Vargas, leaves Guadalupe del Paso to begin preliminary military pacification of the pueblos. Although his small force is nearly annihilated at Santa Fe, Jemez, and Hopi, during a four-month campaign he succeeds through diplomacy in restoring 23 pueblo villages to the crown, while the padres who accompany him baptize more than 2,000 Indians. The following year, beginning on October 13, 1693, the recolonization of New Mexico begins. When the expedition of 100 soldiers, 70 families, 18 friars, and some Indian allies reaches pueblo country, they discover that the people are again ready to resist Spanish intrusion. Only Santa Ana, Zia, San Felipe, and Pecos demonstrate loyalty to the Spanish, while the Tewa, Tano, Picurís, Taos, Jémez, Acoma, and Hopi remain hostile. However, the unity of 1680 is gone,

and, while some of the pueblos fight against the Spanish, others (particularly the Keresan groups) join them. With Pecos assistance, de Vargas retakes Santa Fe on December 30, 1693. Other pueblos continue to hold out, and considerable force is used to subjugate groups such as Jemez, whose villages are destroyed and people scattered. Within two years of the Spanish return, another major pan-Pueblo revolt occurs.

1692–1694 Shawnee and Five Nations Make Peace. New York Dutch and English traders join a group of Shawnee and return with them to the Ohio Valley. Several hundred Shawnee settle with the Munsee between the Delaware and Hudson rivers. These Shawnee are welcomed as "grandsons" by the Delaware and are at peace with the Five Nations, ending an extended period of intermittent warfare.

1692–1699 South Carolina Slave Trade. English traders from South Carolina gain temporary control of the Indian trade throughout Georgia, Tennessee, Alabama, and Mississippi and even reach Arkansas. Throughout the regions the traders manipulate their influence over the different peoples to provoke warfare for the acquisition of slaves.

1693–1697 Pima and Apache Warfare. The Sobaipuris Indians (Pima) of the San Pedro River are pressured by the Spanish into fighting their former allies, the Apache. Because of escalating Apache hostilities, the Pima vacate their land in the 1760s.

1696 Pueblo Resistance Continues. On June 4, following the reestablishment of Spanish authority under de Vargas, a second major revolt occurs among the pueblo groups. Only Pecos, Tesuque, San Felipe, Santa Ana, and Zia remain loyal to the Spanish. Missionaries at Taos, San Ildefonso, Nambé, San Cristóbal, and San Diego de Jémez pueblos are murdered, and 21 soldiers are killed. Unable to force the Spanish out of Santa Fe as they had done 16 years before, the various pueblos cannot withstand Spanish counterattacks that destroy villages and food supplies. By the end of the year, the revolt is successfully put down. Following the defeat of the pueblos, the Picurís under Luis Tupatu abandon their home and join their Jicarilla Apache allies at Cuartelejo (east of Pueblo, Colorado, today in western Kansas), where they live until August 1706 when they are returned through the efforts of the acting governor, Francisco Cuervo y Valdez.

1698 Newfoundland Settlement Prohibited. The British Parliament bans all permanent settlement on the island of Newfoundland. Nevertheless, European settlers move onto the island.

1698 Sobaipuri Pueblo Attacked. On March 30, 600 Athapascan attack a Sobaipuri pueblo near Quiburi and are victorious. The Sobaipuri then counterattack and repel most of the Athapascan force. Following this defeat, the Janos and Sumas Apache make peace at El Paso.

1699–1702 French Influence in the Southeast. Because of increased English and Indian raids, the French gain influence among many tribes in the South. During this time, for example, the Acolapissa of the Pearl River, west of present-day Biloxi, become French allies for this reason. Likewise, the Choctaw-English alliance is shaken because the English continue to buy Choctaw slaves captured by other tribes. The French consolidate their influence in the Southeast by establishing posts at Biloxi in 1699 and in Mobile in 1702.

Chapter 4
_____
1700 TO 1799

_____
1700–1719

1700 The Missions. Native Americans influence the Spanish in many areas, particularly with their gifts of foods, natural resources, and architecture. In return, American Indians acquire horses, cattle, sheep, mules, and other livestock. In California and Texas, Indians become skilled cowboys and cowgirls in their own right. They also learn to cultivate wheat to make bread, especially fry bread, a traditional bread made by frying wheat dough. Some Indians learn the new religion and Christianity spreads widely among the American tribes. Spanish priests, generally of the Jesuit and Franciscan orders, establish missions from the Atlantic to the Pacific. The priests oversee Indian life at the missions where Indians supply the labor to build the beautiful structures so admired today.

The mission system is not always a positive influence for most Native Americans. Indians often die from the meager diet and hard work, and sometimes go unattended following injuries or disease. When they refuse to work, priests or Christian Indians whip them, including the women and children, into submission. When families flee the missions, presidio soldiers hunt them down and force them to return. Native Americans also die in large numbers from disease and unsanitary conditions. Epidemics occur periodically in California under

the Spanish occupation, the first recorded one in 1777 at Mission Santa Clara. An epidemic of diphtheria and pneumonia occurs in 1802, ravaging the young from Mission San Carlos to San Luis Obispo. Still another epidemic decimates Native Americans from San Francisco to Santa Barbara, and more than 1,600 die from measles. Children under the age of ten are almost wiped out in this epidemic. The Native American population declines by as much as 45 percent under the Spanish occupation of California as the direct result of introduced sickness and disease.

c. 1700–1760 Early Migration onto the Plains. The Shoshoni, buffalo hunters on the western plains between the Missouri and the Red Deer Rivers, acquire horses for the first time. This gives them an important military advantage over their northern enemies. As a result, the Siksika, Kainai (Blood), Peigan (Blackfeet in Montana, but Blackfoot in Canada), and Atsina retreat toward the Northeast. Horse ownership spreads to most plains groups by 1760, bringing important changes to Indian societies and to relations among Indian groups. For example, horses make buffalo hunting and transporting goods much easier. Thus, the size of residential bands grows, and horse ownership becomes a symbol of prestige and wealth in formerly egalitarian societies. Possession of horses and guns allows the Blackfoot Confederacy and

_____
79

the Atsina to force the Shoshoni to retreat toward the Southwest.

AUGUST 4, 1701 Iroquois and French Peace Agreement. After almost a century of mostly hostile relations and two years of negotiations, the Iroquois and French conclude a peace agreement. The Iroquois, much affected by battle losses, agree to remain neutral in wars between the French and the English. The peace agreement opens the door for the Mohawk at Caughnawaga near Montreal to begin (with the tacit approval of the French who suffer a glut of furs) a trade in contraband furs from Montreal to Albany.

1701–1755 The Iroquois Adopt Neutrality. The Iroquois shift their policy from alliance with the English to neutrality between the French colonies in New France and the English colonies. Late in the 1690s the English begin to occupy Iroquois territory in the Mohawk Valley; this, along with the burden and losses of warfare with the French and their Indian allies, convinces the Iroquois that their English ally is as much a threat to them as were the French. During the 1690s the Iroquois suffer from a series of military setbacks and the new English land threats. In response they slightly centralize the Confederate Council, composed of 49 chiefs from the Five Nations, and develop a new policy of a united front against the Europeans. This centralization takes the form of having one chief speak for the entire confederacy of Five Nations, rather than five chiefs speaking for their individual nations.

After a treaty of peace with the French in 1701, the Iroquois Confederacy negotiates commercial agreements with the Ottawa, Chippewa, Illinois Confederacy, and other interior nations. In exchange for allowing the Iroquois to hunt and trade in the interior and Great Lakes area, the interior nations are allowed to travel to Albany, New York, to trade with the English, who have cheaper, better quality goods and a better selection than the French. This agreement bolsters Iroquois domi-

Green quartzite effigy found in east-central Alberta that hints at the central role that buffalo played in Plains Indian societies. The buffalo was the source of food, clothing, and shelter. Courtesy of the Glenbow Museum, Calgary, Alberta.

nance in the region until the 1740s, when Pennsylvania traders follow the retreating Delaware and Shawnee into the Ohio Valley and beyond. The Iroquois restrict English trade to Albany, but the Pennsylvania traders go directly to the interior villages. Thus, the Iroquois lose their strong trade position, and their power and influence decline. The English continue to support the Iroquois Confederacy until the Revolutionary War, as a means to gain trade relations and diplomatic influence over the interior nations. By the 1750s, however, the Iroquois empire is a political puppet for British colonial designs.

1702–1713 Queen Anne's War. Queen Anne's War, pitting the English against the French and Spanish, starts in Europe but is also fought in the American colonies. Between 1702 and 1704, the English and Indian allies (Creek and probably Cherokee) attack the Florida mission Indians of Guale (Georgia) and nearly annihilate the entire population of Apalachee Indians, a remnant of which later joins the Creek. The area from the Savannah River to St. Augustine, Florida, is depopulated of Indian people and the Spanish missions are destroyed. Some Yamasee Indians, many being mission Indians in Guale, migrate to Spanish protection in Florida. The Spanish are unable or unwilling to protect them from English expansion into Florida.

APRIL 19, 1710 Four "Kings" Visit London. Hailed and celebrated as Indian "Kings," four Mohawk diplomats visit London. There the four receive royal treatment, gaining a celebrity status unknown among previous Indian visitors to Europe and even meeting with Queen Anne before their return to North America.

1711–1722 Tuscarora War and Migration. The Tuscarora, an Iroquoian-speaking nation living in what is now North Carolina, become involved in war with the English over trade disputes. Many Tuscarora become indebted to English traders, who give them credit in the form of goods in the autumn of the year and collect the credit in the spring after the hunt. Many Tuscarora cannot pay back the credit, and some traders confiscate the hunters' children and wives to sell as slaves. This manner of collecting the debts leads to war in 1711, and the Tuscarora are defeated by 1713. Many migrate out of eastern North Carolina and travel north, where they find, to their surprise, that the Tuscarora and the Iroquois (Five Nations) speak very closely related languages. The Tuscarora are invited by the Oneida, one of the Five Nations of the Iroquois Confederacy, to live with them and join the confederacy. Between 1715 and 1722, many Tuscarora settle in New York with the Iroquois and are adopted into the confederacy. Nevertheless, the 49 chiefs do not wish to create new Tuscarora chiefs, which would violate the sacred constitution of the confederacy, and so the Oneida chiefs speak and represent the Tuscarora, at least until the 1800s, when the confederacy was greatly disrupted. After 1715, the Iroquois Five Nations becomes known as the Six Nations.

1712–1734 The Fox (Mesquakie) Wars. In the early years of the fur trade, the Fox or Mesquakie Nation of western Wisconsin and Illinois is powerful enough to exact a tribute from foreigners traveling through their territory. French fur traders resent this tax, and the French begin arming the Chippewa, traditional enemies of the Mesquakie. The Mesquakie respond by raiding the Chippewa and the French, becoming the same kind of hazard to French fur trading efforts that the Iroquois had been in the previous century. When a large group of Mesquakie move nearer to Detroit for their own trading purposes, the camp they share with their Mascouten allies is attacked and besieged by a combined French and multitribal Indian force. After 19 days, the Mesquakie escape, but are pursued and forced to surrender after a fierce four-day battle. They suffer the loss of 1,000 men, women, and children. Believing the unruly Fox finally subdued, the French are surprised to learn that about a year later they are reportedly repelling French traders in Wisconsin. The French respond by sending a force which attacks the main Fox village at Butte des Morts. After a three-day siege, the Fox are forced to agree to French terms, cede all of their land to the crown, and hunt to pay the costs of the war. By 1728, the indomitable Fox regroup and begin forging an anti-French alliance with neighboring tribes, including the Sauk, Mascouten, Kickapoo, Winnebago, and Dakota. In 1730, the French attack Fox again, and the repeated assaults force them to seek refuge among the Seneca. On the way there, the Fox are attacked; more than 400 are killed and another 500 sold into slavery. Again the French consider the Fox eliminated, and again the Fox regroup. Another 300 are killed or captured in 1731. The remaining Fox seek protection among the Sauk, who refuse to relinquish them, killing a French commander who brazenly demands their surrender. The two tribes are then pursued by the French and their Indian allies, but escape into Iowa where they continue living to this day.

1713   Micmac Resistance to the French. The Micmac and Maliseet refuse to recognize the terms of the Treaty of Utrecht (April 4, 1713), by which the French cede their homeland to the English. Ile Royale (Cape Breton) and Ile St Jean (Prince Edward Island) are the only parts of the territory which the French retain. In response to the English refusal to dispense annual presentations of gifts as the French had done, the Micmac begin their resistance to the English. The Iroquois also refuse to recognize terms of the treaty that place them under English rule. The population of Micmac at this time has been estimated at 1,500.

1715–1717   The Yamasee War and Creek Neutrality. The Yamasee of present-day Georgia, in alliance with the Creek and other smaller coastal nations such as the Hitchiti, Yuchi, and Mikasuki, rise up against the English because of a series of trade and other abuses. The Yamasee and allies are defeated, and many tribes migrate south into Florida, ultimately forming part of the Seminole, while others join the Creek Confederacy, then occupying what is now central Georgia and Alabama. This defeat convinces the Creek leaders that war against the English is not profitable, and the Creek embark on a policy of neutrality between the English colonies in the Carolinas, the Spanish in Florida and West Florida (now southern Alabama and Mississippi), and the French colony of Louisiana. The Creek play balance of power between the rival European powers and attempt to maximize trade and diplomatic concessions from the colonists.

MAY 7, 1716   Chipewyan and Cree Peace. A party of Chipewyan arrives at York Factory after making peace with Cree Home Guard at that post. The event encourages the establishment of a post at the mouth of the Churchill River which will be more accessible to the Chipewyan. The peace is arranged by Thanadelthur, a young Chipewyan woman who, after escaping from Cree captors in 1714, fled to York Factory.

1716–1727   The Creek and Cherokee War. In the Yamasee War, the Cherokee side with the English against the Creek and their allies. This leads to bloodshed and several failed attempts to reestablish peace. In 1716, an English-allied Cherokee kills a delegation of visiting Creek and Yamasee emissaries, which initiates the war. Thus, in the period after the end of the Yamasee War, the Creek and Cherokee carry on raiding parties and revenge attacks against one another.

1716–1738   Micmac Induced to Move to Missions. French Roman Catholic missionaries induce Micmac residing near the French fortress at Louisbourg on Cape Breton to move to missions such as Antigonish and Shubenacadie in Nova Scotia, Malpeque on Ile St. Jean (Prince Edward Island), and Merligueche on Ile Royale. All but Merligueche are established in territory claimed by the British. The missions serve French and Micmac desires to maintain contact, although the Micmac do not establish sedentary communities as the missionaries hope.

JULY 1717   Chipewyan Become Trade Middlemen. The establishment of a Hudson's Bay Company post at the mouth of the Churchill River enables the Chipewyan to establish themselves as middlemen to other Dene groups as far west as Great Slave Lake and the Coppermine River. Traveling mostly on foot, they rely heavily on caribou for food. Their position as middlemen allows them to expand their hunting territories at the expense of Inuit and Indians to the west.

1720–1739

1720   Indian Education. The first permanent Indian school is created in Williamsburg, Virginia.

1720–1760   French Wars on the Chickasaw. The Chickasaw are attracted to an English alliance because they are enticed by the low-priced, high-quality English trade goods. The English, in turn, seek a Chickasaw alliance because they wish to disrupt the French plan to control the Mississippi Valley by erecting a series of forts and making alliances with the Indian nations along the Mississippi River. In general, the Chickasaw favor the English, although there is a small party of Chickasaw who favor French alliance. Between 1729 and 1752, the French launch four major military expeditions against the Chickasaw villages near the Mississippi River in western Kentucky and northwestern Mississippi. The Chickasaw survive all these attacks, although at times are desperate for supplies and ammunition. In 1739, some Chickasaw migrate to South Carolina for English protection, while others, many of whom are survivors of the Natchez nation who sought Chickasaw protection from the French in 1729, move to live among the western Creek. The Chickasaw are a major military obstacle to the French plan of enveloping the British colonies and restricting them to the Atlantic seaboard.

1722   Six Nations Confederacy Formed. The Tuscarora conclude an agreement with the Iroquois Five Nations to form the Six Nations Confederacy. The Tuscarora moved to the region from North Carolina in 1714 after being displaced by war, conflict over trade debts, and European agricultural expansion.

1723–1725   Dummer's War. Although initially an ally and trading partner of England, the Abenaki of northern New England (a group of tribes including the Pigwacket, Arosagunacook, Kennebec, and Penobscot in the east, and the Sokoki, Penacook, Cowasuck, and others in the west), launch an attack on the encroaching English colonies, precipitating a conflict known as Dummer's War. Due to their location, the western Abenaki under the charismatic leader Grey Lock are able to lead guerrilla-like attacks on their British foes with great success and little possibility for reprisal. In the east, however, many villages are attacked and destroyed. The most notable is the populous Kennebec settle-

ment at Norridgewok, whose destruction in August 1724 forces the Abenaki to negotiate a peace early the following year, bringing Dummer's War to an end.

1725   Anne (Queen Anne), Powhatan Tribal Leader, Dies. During her lifetime Anne is a forceful defender of her people's rights. Anne's husband, Totopotomoi, has allied himself with Virginia colonists to fight an alliance of inland tribes. Upon his death in battle about 1655, Anne assumes leadership of her husband's band. She and her people live at the junction of the Pamunkey and Mattapony rivers in Virginia. Anne plays a pivotal role in the Virginia colony's internal dispute known as Bacon's Rebellion. She remains a forceful advocate for her people in negotiations with the Virginia colonists during her rule. In 1715, Anne addresses the Virginia legislature and outlines the interests of her people within the Virginia colony.

1725   John Logan (Tachnechdorus), Mingo (Cayuga) Tribal Leader, Is Born. John Logan is the leader of the bands of Iroquois-speaking Mingo who live near the headwaters of the Ohio River in western Pennsylvania. Logan is a Mingo leader during the Lord Dunmore's War of 1774, when the Mingo and Shawnee nations try to block Virginia settlers from crossing the line set by the Proclamation of 1763 (forbidding colonial settlement beyond the crest of the Appalachian mountains). After moving to Ohio in 1774, when members of his family are massacred by settlers for no apparent reason, Logan adopts a militant stance and begins a series of raids against settlers throughout the trans-Appalachian region. Logan's forces are defeated at the battle of Point Pleasant, Pennsylvania, in 1774, and Logan refuses to attend a peace conference at present-day Sciota, Ohio. It is believed that he delivers an eloquent letter much admired at the time and later cited by Thomas Jefferson. Logan continues his attacks during the American War for Independence and is killed in 1780.

1726 Boston Treaty. Representatives of the Micmac, Maliseet and Passamaquoddy gather at Annapolis Royal (in Nova Scotia) to ratify a treaty (known as the Boston Treaty because it was negotiated there) that acknowledges British sovereignty in Nova Scotia. The British promise to respect Indian hunting and fishing rights.

1729 Destruction of the Natchez Nation. The Natchez Nation is a Muskogean-speaking society with a centralized sacred chieftain, "The Great Sun." A remnant society of the Mississippian culture, the nation rebels against French attempts to impose taxes and confiscate land in its central village, Natchez. The French at Natchez plantation, in the Louisiana colony, are wiped out. The French and their Choctaw allies counterattack and destroy the Natchez villages. The Great Sun is captured and, along with several hundred other captives, is sold into slavery in the Caribbean Islands. The Natchez descendants still live there. Other Natchez escape, some seeking refuge among the Chickasaw, who give them shelter, but this intensifies warring relations between the Natchez and the French and Choctaw.

1729 Kanesataké Established. Four Hundred Iroquois from Caughnawaga settle at the Lake of Two Mountains (Kanesataké or Oka).

1737 The Delaware "Walking Purchase." In the years following William Penn's famous treaty with the Delaware (Lenape) Indians, relations between the Pennsylvania colonists and the Delaware deteriorate. By the 1730s the Delaware are being pushed out of their lands with increasing frequency. At this time, Thomas Penn, son of the colony's founder, discovers a treaty signed by three Delaware chiefs, ceding to Penn's father all of the Delaware lands "as far as a man can go in a day and a half." After gaining agreement from several Delaware chiefs how this distance should be determined, the colonists select three of their best athletes, offering money and land as incentives to the runner who could travel the greatest distance. When the day of the walk arrives, August 25, 1737, settlers bearing refreshments line the route to cheer on the runners. So much did the three exert themselves that only one of the runners survived the walk, collapsing after clearing 65 miles in the allotted day and a half. Victims of one of the strangest episodes in Indian-colonial relations, the Delaware are forced westward. Since the time of their removal, the authenticity of the deed "discovered" by Thomas Penn has been called into question.

1737 Matonabbee, Chipewyan Leader, Is Born. Born near the Hudson's Bay Company (H.B.C.) Prince of Wales Fort (Churchill), Matonabbee's early years are spent among a Chipewyan band which hunts for the traders at that post. His familiarity with the traders, and his ability to speak Cree and some English in addition to his native Chipewyan Dene dialect, enables him to take a prominent role as ambassador for the H.B.C. among other Dene Indians and to Cree bands near Lake Athabasca. Greeted with lavish gifts at every visit to Churchill, Matonabbee occasionally leads several hundred Chipewyan to the post, proving his value as trading captain.

After drawing a remarkable map which portrays the region from the Hudson Bay westward to beyond Great Slave Lake, including the location of a copper mine (at the mouth of the Coppermine River on the Arctic Ocean), Matonabbee and his several wives guide H.B.C. employee Samuel Hearne on a two-year journey to the mouth of that site. This service again increases Matonabbee's prestige with the traders.

Apparently distraught at the destruction of Prince of Wales Fort by the French in 1782, Matonabbee commits suicide shortly after.

1739 Arikara Migrate North. About this time, the group of Indians known now as the Arikara (a group closely related to the Pawnee) begin to migrate north from the Loup River in Nebraska. They travel up the Missouri River to settle eventually in central North Dakota.

Miniature model showing Natchez life, with a house for corn storage on the left, and a mound temple in the back. Photo by Thane L. Bierwert. Courtesy of the Department of Library Services, American Museum of Natural History.

1740–1749

c. 1740   John Deserontyon, Mohawk Chief, Is Born. John Deserontyon (popularly known as Captain John Deserontyon) is born in a Mohawk village in New York. As a Mohawk chief in New York state in the 1770s, he decides to fight for the British against their rebellious American colonies. Undefeated in the War of Independence, yet finding that his people's homeland has been ceded to the new republic, Deserontyon, together with Joseph Brant *(See* biography, 1742), another Mohawk chief, negotiates with the British for a new homeland in British North America. Deserontyon's group settles on a reserve near the Bay of Quinte, north of Lake Ontario. The nearby town of Deseronto is named after this important ally. Deserontyon dies about 1811.

c. 1740   Mikak, Labrador Inuk, Is Born. The young Mikak is first encountered by Europeans in September 1765, when her party of Labrador Inuit offer emergency shelter to some Moravian missionaries, including Jens Haven, who establishes the first mission among the Inuk. In

November, Mikak is captured by a party from Newfoundland and impresses her captors with her intelligence. She is brought to London, England, in 1768 where current ideas regarding "noble savages" ensure that she receives a friendly welcome. (The "noble savage" idea is based on a belief that simple societies escape the problems of violence and crime which plague more complex societies.) In London Mikak meets Haven once again. The Moravians are granted permission to establish missions in Labrador in 1769, in part because of Mikak's good reports concerning Haven. The Moravian missionaries return Mikak to her family in 1770, and she helps them choose the site for their first mission at Nain in 1771. She marries a prominent Inuk religious leader and resumes living among her people, but keeps a costly dress given to her while she was in England and assures Moravian missionaries that she has accepted Christianity. Mikak is the subject of a painting by John Russell that hangs in Göttingen University in Germany. She dies in 1795.

1740–1751   Southwestern Resistance. The Indian nations of present-day northern Mexico continue their resistance against the Spanish government and religion through the mid-eighteenth century. In 1740, the Yaqui and Mayo of the Sonoran desert attempt to rid themselves of Spanish oppression, losing thousands of lives in the process. Along the Sonoran coast, starving groups of Seri Indians raid the missions for food. Spain attempts to prevent this by constructing a garrison on Seri land, but when soldiers take the best farming land from the Seri, they protest. The Spanish respond by selling the women of 80 Seri families into slavery in Guatemala. The Seri revolt, but before a force is sent to subdue them, they withdraw to the Cerro Prieto mountains; when the force arrives, they are nowhere to be found. Then, when the Lower Pima revolt under Luis Oacpicagigua in 1751, the Seri are temporarily forgotten by the Spanish. The Pima are successful in forcing the Spanish out of Tubatama, where they had built a garrison and a mission, but after the victory, repeated Spanish offensives eventually force the Pima to surrender in 1752. The subjugation of the Pima allows the Spanish to refocus their attention back on the Seri, who had continued their guerrilla attacks throughout the Pima revolt. But the Seri are tenacious, and four major campaigns in ten years fail to bring their acquiescence. In fact, Seri groups and their allies wage war against the Spanish sporadically for over 20 years before finally being subdued.

1740–1753   Cree and Assiniboine Trade with French. Cree and Assiniboine bands near Lake Winnipeg begin trading with French traders who have come to the region. After abandoning some posts in the western Great Lakes region earlier, the French have renewed their westward expansion. By 1753 they have established posts as far west as the Fort à la Corne on the lower Saskatchewan River. Indian traders bring most of their most valuable furs to the French in exchange for the most sought-after European goods. They bring the bulkier furs, which the French do not want, to Hudson's Bay Company posts along Hudson Bay. Cree and Assiniboine bands apparently resist efforts

of fur traders to establish direct trade with other groups upstream.

1740–1867   Russian Exploration and Fur Trade. The first Russian explorers sail over to Alaska and explore the entire Alaska coastline, encountering many Pacific Northwest Coast tribal groups like the Haida, Tlingit, Aleut, and others. In the 1740s and 1750s, following Vitus Bering, who in 1741 sighted the North American continent and explored the Bering Sea and Bering Strait, the Russians open trade with Natives for sea otter pelts. Russian fur traders, called *promyshlenniki*, expand their enterprises in the far Northwest and by 1805 reach San Francisco, California. The Russians establish colonies primarily to exploit the rich resource in fur. To accomplish this, they virtually enslave Native village populations, often by taking women as hostages and forcing men to trap furs. Native resistance efforts, such as the Aleut rebellion of 1761–62, meet with harsh reprisal, and the Russian effect on the Native Alaskans is striking. After 50 years of Russian contact, the Aleut groups number only a tenth of their original population. Cultural effects are also felt. In exchange for furs, the Russians trade guns, powder, lead, pots and pans, knives, fishhooks, beads, and cloth. As is the case with the fur trade elsewhere in North America, the groups the Russians trade with alter their traditional lives to obtain furs to exchange for these items; in doing so, their cultures change and many become dependent on the European supply of manufactured goods. At the same time, the fur trade has a disastrous effect on the animals being hunted, and populations of sea otter, seal, Arctic fox, and numerous other species are devastated during the Russian period.

In the second half of the eighteenth century, the Russian government sends over many Russian Orthodox priests both to convert the Native Alaskans and to protect them from the excesses of the *promyshlenniki*. Many of these Russian Orthodox churches and their Native congregations—sometimes singing mass in archaic Russian—can still be found in several places in Alaska.

1742 Joseph Brant (Thayendanegea), Mohawk Tribal Leader, Is Born. Joseph Brant is the son of a full-blooded Mohawk chief, but there are claims that his mother is half-European. Brant attends a Christian school in Connecticut and masters spoken and written English. In the early 1760s and 1770s, as a translator and diplomat, he helps the English to negotiate with Iroquois tribes. When the American Revolution breaks out, Brant aligns himself with the Loyalist cause and travels to England in 1775. He participates in a number of battles directly, and insists on using his own military tactics and stratagems. In appreciation of his military services, the English give him a retirement pension and a large tract of land along the Grand River in Ontario, Canada. Like many others, Brant is an Indian who lives between two worlds. He is credited with having translated the Bible into the Mohawk language. He dies in November 1807.

1744–1748 King William's War. King William's War is initiated in Europe but also fought by the European colonies in North America. This war pits the French against the English, and each side persuades its Indian allies to fight. It is cheaper and more efficient for colonial governments to hire Indian fighters to engage in war than to import troops from Europe, where they are badly needed. In North America the war is inconclusive; the Treaty of Aix-la-Chapelle, negotiated in Europe, restores all original boundaries.

AUTUMN/WINTER 1746 Typhus Epidemic among Micmac. Typhus spreads from a Micmac party visiting with a group of their French allies at Chebucto Bay (Halifax Harbor), killing up to a third of the Micmac.

1748–1751 Choctaw Civil War. The Choctaw Nation is divided during the 1730s and 1740s between loyalty to the French and cheap trade goods given by the English. One region, the central and northeast villages, favors English trade, while the western and southern villages favor French alliance. Civil war erupts between the regions when Red Shoes, the head warrior of the eastern allied towns, is assassinated for a bounty by a pro-French Indian. Both sides rely on their allies to supply weapons and ammunition, but the British fail to provide enough support for their allies and the pro-British eastern villages are defeated by the opposing forces. After 1751 Choctaw political relations are organized into three autonomous political regions: the conservative Six Towns district (or *iksa*, a Choctaw term for a matrilineal descent group) in the south favors the French; the western villages, called "people of the long hair," also favors the French; and the northeastern villages, called the "potato people," favor the British. Each district has a chief and a council, and each decides its own internal matters, rarely meeting with the other two districts to discuss national business. The basic three-district political system lasts among the Choctaw until 1907, when the U.S. government abolishes the government of the Choctaw Nation.

1749 Creek Mary. Coosaponakeesa, the daughter of mixed Cree heritage, is baptized "Mary" and formally educated according to British dictates; she returns to Creek country as a girl of 16. In 1733, James Oglethorpe, founder of the Colony of Georgia, hires Mary as his interpreter. Her negotiations among the Indians allow her to advocate support of the English over the Spanish for political control of the American Southeast. In 1749, Mary proclaims herself to be the "empress" of the Creek. She then lays claim to a tract of Georgia mainland plus several coastal islands: St. Catherine's, Sapelo, and Ossabaw. Land-holdings aside, Mary and her third husband, the Creek Indian agent Thomas Bosomworth, are in debt. They request payment from the Georgian colonists for past services, a request which the colonists ignore. Then, leading a force of Creek warriors,

Mary and her husband advance upon the colony. Their rebellion, however, fails; they are taken captive and their warriors bought off. The couple eventually take their claims to the court of England, resulting in a small settlement decision in their favor in 1759.

JULY 1749 Halifax, Nova Scotia, Established. The British show their intention to gain control of lands occupied by Micmac by establishing the town of Halifax at Chebucto Bay, Nova Scotia. The action prompts Micmac attacks.

1750–1759

c. 1750 Ozette Preserved by Landslide. Sometime around 1750, a massive landslide buries the town of Ozette covering at least four full houses in the Makah fishing and whaling village on the southern coast of Cape Flattery in what is now Washington State. The mud preserves the village almost perfectly—even fragile organic materials such as intricate wood carvings, hides, and netting are not lost. The preservation gives modern archaeologists a remarkably accurate picture of Makah life at that time.

c. 1750 Sarcee Indians Emerge as Tribe. A group of Beaver bands inhabiting the forested Lesser Slave Lake region, present-day northern Alberta, move to the northern prairies where, as equestrian buffalo hunters, they become known as the Sarcee.

1750 Canassatego, Onondaga Tribal Leader, Dies. Canassatego is a strong supporter of the Iroquois League of Nations, the government of the Mohawk, Oneida, Onondaga, Tuscarora, Cayuga, and Seneca of what is now upstate New York. He represents the league in a number of important conferences, alliances, and agreements with English diplomats. Canassatego works to ensure that no treaties are signed by members of the league without full consent of the league's governing body. By 1742, Canassatego, with translator Conrad Weiser, negotiates an alliance between the Iroquois League and Pennsylvania officials who are anxious to ally themselves with the Indians in order to prevent French encroachment. During these negotiations, Canassatego demonstrates a keen understanding of republican principles and urges the English colonists to respect the pledges and concepts of the league and its "league of friendship" with the colonists. Canassatego is an impressive speaker, with a presence that commands attention from all persons in a room with him. It is believed that Canassatego is killed by a fellow Iroquois allied with the French.

1750–1850 Chickahominy Nation Disperses. The Chickahominy nation of Virginia breaks into several smaller communities. Some join the Pamunkey, Mattaponi, and other remaining nations living near the Chesapeake Bay area, while others hang onto their lands, living by hunting and fishing. By the 1760s and later, the Chickahominy people are no longer mentioned in Virginia records.

1751 Albany Plan. Benjamin Franklin, a prominent citizen and statesman from Pennsylvania, proposes a plan of union for the British colonies. Franklin has several times visited the Iroquois Confederacy (Six Nations) and suggests their model for unifying the colonies. He remarks that it is strange that the Six Nations could form an apparently indissoluble union, while 10 or 12 British colonies could not. The plan fails in 1751—for want of interest by more than a few colonists—but is revived later in the Articles of Confederation (1777–88), the first laws of U.S. government, and in the U.S. Constitution (implemented in 1789).

1752 Old Briton, Miami Tribal Leader, Dies. Old Briton is a member of the Piankashaw band of Miami. He originally lives in what is now northwestern Indiana. In the early 1700s, Old Briton is an important trading ally of the British. The Miami leader helps to establish the trading center at Pickawillany, near present-day Piqua, Ohio. Old Briton also repulsed a number of French military attacks to maintain his control of the Miami territory in Indiana. In 1748, a treaty between Old Briton and the British formalizes a trading partnership between the Piankashaw and the British. To better accommodate his new trading partners, Old Briton moves his people eastward to the village of Pickawillany. Old Briton is killed during a French attack on the village of Pickawillany in 1752.

November 22, 1752 Micmac and British Treaty. The Shubenacadie band of Micmac, led by Jean-Baptiste Cope, and the British agree to sign a peace treaty (the Halifax Treaty) in an elaborate ceremony at Halifax, easing hostility between the two groups. The Micmac have been resisting the British occupation of their territory since 1713. The treaty follows British military action against the Micmac as well as British agreements to dispense gifts to the Micmac each October and to recognize Micmac hunting and fishing rights. The peace is broken the following May when a Micmac party destroys a British ship. Nevertheless, the treaty becomes the basis of some twentieth century claims.

October 11, 1754 Blackfoot Meet with Hudson's Bay Officials. At a meeting near the Red Deer River on the western prairies, a Blackfoot Confederacy chief tells Hudson's Bay Company envoy Anthony Henday that the tribe will not travel to the Hudson Bay to trade because they are satisfied with acquiring European goods through Cree and Assiniboine middlemen. As equestrian buffalo hunters, not expert in canoe travel and not accustomed to eating fish and fowl, the Plains Indians seek to avoid traveling to the Bay. Henday has been brought to the prairies by a Cree band. The Blackfoot probably have encountered Europeans before this meeting.

1754–1763 French and Indian War. Although precipitated by French construction of Fort Duquesne on land already claimed by the British colony Virginia, the so-called French and Indian War (known as the Seven Years' War in Europe) is actually the climax of a series of wars between England and France, both vying for supremacy in North America. For Native North Americans, objectives in these colonial conflicts are somewhat different, and their alliances with one power or another are influenced by a number of complex factors, including trading relationships and colonial expansion. The Cherokee nation, for example, initially sides with the British, largely to halt the incursion of displaced Shawnee into their territory, but later, mistreated by their English allies, turns against them. In general, although France is not without its Indian enemies (for example, the Mohawk, who have close trading ties to the British and support them in spite of a league neutrality stance), the less extensive French settlements mean that most Indian groups fight against England whose colonies had already caused the demise or destruction of numerous Indian nations. The many nations aligning themselves with France include the Wyandot, Shawnee, Chippewa, Potawatomi, Ottawa, Miami, Abenaki, Micmac, and Lenape. At first the war goes well for the French and their Indian allies, the western Algonkian-speaking tribes playing an important role in numerous conflicts, including the celebrated defeat of Edward Braddock in 1755. As the war drags on, however, greater English numbers and resources begin to have their effect, and in the end the French lose nearly all of their claims in the Americas, including Canada and the Illinois-Mississippi River valleys. With the French exit from North America, the Indians who fought with them find themselves at the mercy of the British for trade goods and supplies.

1755 Akwesasne Reserve. Iroquois settle at St. Regis (Akwesasne), a Roman Catholic missionary settlement south of the St. Lawrence River near Montreal. Today the Akwesasne

By 1750 the horse had spread throughout the plains, greatly easing the quest for food. Particularly in western regions, where steep river valleys and cliffs abounded, large herds of buffalo were driven over 'buffalo jumps,' to be butchered by the women. Courtesy of the National Archives of Canada.

reserve straddles the border between the United States and Canada.

1755 Johnson Appointed Indian Superintendent. Sir William Johnson is named British superintendent of Indian Affairs, Northern Department. Johnson is respected by the Iroquois, eventually marrying Molly Brant *(See* biography, 1759), brother of Joseph Brant *(See* biography, 1742). He serves until 1774.

1759 Alexander McGillivray, Creek Tribal Leader, Is Born. McGillivray is born near the upper town Creek village, Little Talisee, located in present-day Alabama. He is sent by his father, a British trader, to school in what is now Charleston, South Carolina, and receives additional private tutoring from a relative. The American Revolutionary War interrupts his studies, and he returns to the Creek nation, where the upper towns generally favor British alliance. In late 1778, political leadership of Little Talisee is transferred to McGillivray, who is only about 18 years old. The choice of McGillivray as upper town principal chief is unusual, since Creek leaders are generally older

men who have acquired considerable training in ritual and religious knowledge. McGillivray, however, speaks English and knows colonial institutions, which are great advantages in treaty and diplomatic negotiations. Following the war, McGillivray enters into a business partnership with the British trading firm, Panton, Leslie & Company. He works a plantation at Hickory Ground, a sacred white village in the upper town regions. As chief, McGillivray tries to protect Creek lands from U.S. settlers, and tries to reorganize the Creek national council by replacing the elderly town chiefs with the village head warriors. In 1790, he negotiates a treaty with George Washington in New York City. McGillivray dies in 1793.

1759 Molly Brant, Mohawk, Is Born. At the age of 23, this Mohawk woman becomes the mistress of William Johnson and an important Indian diplomat. Johnson is the man in charge of the British Indian Department's Northern District. In addition to her role as Johnson's political consort and estate hostess, Brant also raises several children. Her influence with the Iroquois enables Johnson to advance his own diplomatic agenda. Throughout the American Revolution, Brant provides information to the British regarding the movement of rebel troops stationed in Mohawk Valley. Ultimately, Brant's power proves instrumental in her people's continued support of the British Crown.

OCTOBER 4, 1759 British Attack Abenaki. British troops attack the Abenaki settlement at Odanak on the south shore of the St. Lawrence River between Quebec City and Montreal, burning homes and killing about 30 people. The Abenaki of Odanak, long-time allies of the French, moved to New France from the south around 1670.

1760–1769

SEPTEMBER 9, 1760 New France Falls to the British. Following the fall of Montreal, New France surrenders to the British. According to the surrender terms, the British agree to respect land which the French have reserved for use by Indians. Nevertheless, Indian groups, who do not consider themselves defeated, quickly come to resent the British decision to end the French practice of dispensing annual gifts to Indians. Indian trappers who have been trading with the French find that they are briefly cut off from supplies of European goods from Montreal. The trade resumes very quickly, however.

1760–1763 Delaware Prophet. After the French defeat in the early 1760s, and while the British threaten domination, several prophets emerge among the Delaware people. Two major figures teach very different messages. One brings a militant message, involving borrowed Christian concepts of personal salvation in heaven; the other "domestic" Delaware prophet teaches a message also borrowed from Christian ideas of heaven and a central god, but establishes a new religion designed only for the Delaware, not for any of the other Indian or European nations.

The "militant" prophet emphasizes that the Europeans will have to be driven off the continent and that the Indians must return to the customs of their ancestors before they can be restored to their former prosperous and happy state. This message greatly influences the Ottawa leader Pontiac, who uses it to mobilize warriors from different nations to strike at the English in 1763. The "domestic" Delaware prophet creates a new national religion, reorganizes the disrupted kinship system, and creates new and permanent chiefs for the three reorganized kinship-religious divisions of the religiously-politically unified Delaware nation.

1760–1775 British in Sole Control of Eastern North America. The French defeat changes the situation of the eastern Native nations. Since about 1600, there have been at least two major European powers fighting for control of trade and land. Now only the British remain, and only one nation controls trade relations, the supplies of goods, and the weapons and ammunition. The British try to regulate the distribution of trade and weapons, which makes the formerly French-allied Indians suspicious of British intentions. Furthermore, the British intend to occupy the old French forts, such as Detroit and Chicago, in the Great Lakes area, which are on territory the Indians claim and have not granted British occupation. Ottawa, Wyandot, Miami, Great Lakes nations, and Shawnee Indians living north of the Ohio River fear the British political domination. In the 1760s and early 1770s, the British administration plans to regulate the Indians' trade and activities, but these plans are disrupted by the emergence of the Revolutionary War in 1775.

JULY 25, 1761 Native and British Peace Agreement. The terms of a peace agreement between the Micmac, Maliseet, and Passamaquoddy and the British are formally signified in an elaborate ceremony in Halifax. French aid has allowed the Micmac to resist the British since

1713, but the final French defeat has cut them off from their suppliers.

FEBRUARY 10, 1763 Treaty of Paris. By signing the Treaty of Paris, the French formally cede New France and Acadia (except St. Pierre and Miquelon, two small islands near Newfoundland) to Britain. St. Pierre and Miquelon provide a base from which the Micmac and French can maintain contact.

MAY 1763 Pontiac Seeks Pan-Indian Alliance against British. Pontiac, an Ottawa headman seeking a pan-Indian alliance against the British, follows a militant Delaware prophet and leads a group of Delaware, Ottawa, Wyandot-Petun, Potawatomi, Ojibway, Seneca, and others in an attempt to prevent the British from controlling the lands surrounding the Great Lakes. They take all British forts west of Niagara Falls, except Detroit and Fort Pitt (Pittsburgh). Some groups, including the Iroquois settled near Montreal, side with the British. The conflict between the British and these Indians reaches a stalemate by autumn.

OCTOBER 7, 1763 Royal Proclamation of 1763. At the height of Indian resistance to the British, the British king, George III, issues the Royal Proclamation of 1763. In it the British Crown asserts title to all land in the territory claimed by the British, but declares that Indians have the right to use all land outside established colonies until the crown has negotiated land cession treaties (treaties in which aboriginal groups surrender land rights to the government in exchange for other rights or payments) with Indian groups who use the land. The proclamation results in the drawing of a boundary, the Proclamation Line of 1763, running along the crest of the Appalachian Mountains. Indian country is west of the line from the Appalachian Mountains to the Mississippi River, while the colonists can settle lands east of the line. Within months, the British begin signing land

cession treaties with Indian groups on the Niagara Peninsula, between Lakes Ontario and Erie. The proclamation, which will become enshrined in Canada's 1982 Constitution, will form the basis of many aboriginal land claims in later years. *(See also* map of Indian Treaty Areas in Canada, p. 394.)

1763–1764 Pontiac's War. Pontiac follows the precepts of the militant Delaware prophet and, through this religious revitalization movement, forms an Indian confederacy of the Ottawa, Delaware, Wyandot, Seneca, Potawatomi, Kickapoo, Shawnee, and Miami tribes. Pontiac leads the confederacy in a short-lived war, which does not prevent the British from occupying the old French forts of the Ohio and Great Lakes area.

1763–1774 Pre-Revolutionary Policy. During this time, most of the nations in the eastern portion of North America reassess their relationship with the British government and the colonists. Native Americans realize that a rift has developed between the British homeland and the colonists, and many seek positions of neutrality; however, as the British government and the colonists drift closer to war, some of the nations favor alliance with the British. Many Indians believe that in the event of war, the British will win. Many Indians also believe that the colonists, who are interested in acquiring more land, are a greater threat to the Indians than the British government.

1765 Menawa, Creek Tribal Leader, Is Born. Menawa, also called Hothlepoya, is a war chief of the upper town Creek. He is born along the Talapoosa River in Alabama and establishes his reputation as a daring warrior through numerous raids for horses on settlements in Tennessee. Menawa earns the title "Crazy War Hunter" for his exploits in battle, including his bravery at the battle of Horseshoe Bend in 1814. Menawa is opposed to removal of the Creek to land west of the Mississippi, and leads an armed force that executes William McIntosh

Cherokee visitors to London in 1762. Courtesy of the National Anthropological Archives, Smithsonian Institution.

in 1825. McIntosh has been sentenced to death by the Creek council after having signed the Treaty of Indian Springs in 1825, ceding 25 million acres of Creek land to the United States. Menawa leads warriors in support of U.S. troops early in the Seminole War of 1835–42. He relocates to Indian Territory, present-day Oklahoma, in 1836, and dies in 1865.

DECEMBER 14, 1765   Paxton Boys' Massacre.
Frustrated by the failure of Pennsylvania's Quaker-dominated assembly to take more aggres-

sive action against the Indians of that state, a group of 75 Presbyterians from Paxton in Lancaster County take matters into their own hands. They attack a village of Conestoga Mission Indians (Christianized Susquehannock and others) and violently murder six people, scalping them all. The remaining Conestoga, who had been away from the village at the time, are moved to the Lancaster jail for their own protection. Governor John Penn issues a proclamation denouncing the incident and ordering the violence to stop, but in spite of his orders

Ottawa chief Pontiac encountering Robert Rogers on his way to occupy Detroit in November 1760. This engraving shows the two men smoking the calumet, or the so-called peace pipe. Courtesy of the Library of Congress.

the Paxton Boys strike again, breaking into the jail on December 27 and murdering the remaining 14 Conestoga.

JULY 23, 1766 Pontiac Concludes Peace Agreement with British. Pontiac and about 40 other chiefs conclude a formal peace agreement with the British, ending a three-year Indian resistance to the British. Pontiac and other groups have already made peace a year or more ago, but a weaker resistance has continued. The British have al-

ready agreed to recognize certain Indian land rights.

1767 Black Hawk, Sac (Sauk) Tribal Leader, Is Born. During his lifetime Black Hawk resists the expansion of U.S. settlement into his homeland, located near the Rock River in what is now Illinois. As a young man, Black Hawk shows interest in forming a confederation of Indian tribes to protest the many dubious treaties that were the basis of U.S. settlement in the region. In 1832, he fights a series of ill-fated engagements with U.S. forces, known as the Black Hawk War *(See* entry, 1832). Following the war, he is imprisoned at Fort Monroe, Virginia. In 1833, he is taken to Washington, D.C., where he meets President Andrew Jackson. In the ensuing years, Black Hawk becomes something of a celebrity. Many authors vie to write his biography, which he dictates in 1833. Black Hawk dies in 1838.

JULY 23, 1767 St. John's Island. In a one-day lottery, the British government grants the land of *Abegweit* (St. John's Island, Prince Edward Island) in the Gulf of St. Lawrence to British proprietors. No land is set aside for the Micmac inhabitants of the island.

1768 Tecumseh, Shawnee Tribal Leader, Is Born. Tecumseh is born in a Shawnee settlement known as Old Pique (near the present-day city of Springfield, Ohio) in the Ohio Valley. Tecumseh (meaning "goes through one place to another") learns warfare early in life. In his early teens he takes part in the American Revolution on the side of the British. Following the revolution, the Shawnee regularly take up arms to defend their Ohio land against U.S. settlers. Tecumseh refuses to recognize land cessions agreed to in the 1795 Treaty of Greenville and emerges as a spokesman for the Midwest Indians. He attends councils, studies treaties, and learns all that he can about the historical and legal status of American Indians. Tecumseh unites with his brother Tenskwatawa (meaning "the open door") to forge an intertribal confederacy, which they hope will contain U.S. territorial expansion into Indian lands. Tecumseh and his brother urge their people to forgo the sale of Indian land, to reject European ways, and to renew Indian traditions. In particular the brothers warn against the use of alcohol, which is devastating many Indian communities. Within a few years, the two have assembled a growing community of believers in Prophetstown, located at the junction of the Wabash River and Tippecanoe Creek in Indiana. At the battle of Tippecanoe in November

1811, Tenskwatawa and his followers fight U.S. Army units. Tenskwatawa has told his followers that his spiritual power will protect the Indians from army bullets, but when the Indians suffer significant casualties in the battle, he loses prestige and his followers abandon him. Many members of Tecumseh's alliance disperse as well. Tecumseh joins the British to fight against the Americans in the War of 1812 and is killed at the battle of the Thames on October 5, 1813.

1768 Treaty of Fort Stanwix. Bowing to British insistence, the Six Nations cede land ranging from south of the Ohio River into northern Kentucky. Most of this land comprises the traditional Shawnee homeland, and the Shawnee do not recognize the right of the Six Nations to sell it to the British. Thereafter, the Shawnee and their ally, the Delaware, both nations then residing in Ohio, organize a pan-Indian confederacy without the leadership of the Six Nations, now seen as puppets of the British. The Six Nations, since about 1700, have gained informal leadership of a broad coalition of Indian nations, once boasting that they could muster warriors from 50 nations. Now the influence of the Six Nations declines, and the loose confederacy of western Indian nations is led by the Shawnee, Delaware, and Miami. The confederation tries to keep settlers out of the Old Northwest—the land west of the Ohio River and including the Great Lakes area. This confederacy defends the Old Northwest until the end of the War of 1812.

1769 California Indian Mission System. The San Diego mission is established, the first in a series of 21 religious agrarian settlements to be built approximately a day's journey apart along El Camino Real, the Spanish land route from San Diego to San Francisco. The mission is moved in 1774 and completed by 1823. The missions supports two Franciscan friars as overseers, a protective military garrison, and hundreds of "Christianized" Indians, who are impressed for mission work and religious conversion.

Tribal ties are suppressed. This mission is attacked by Indians in 1775, secularized in 1835, and sold in 1846, and the property is returned to the church.

1769 Dartmouth College Established. Eleazor Wheelock moves his school for training Indian ministers, started in 1743, to New Hampshire and establishes Dartmouth College. Samson Occum, Wheelock's Mohegan student and an ordained Presbyterian minister, travels to England to preach and raise funds for the school from 1765–67. Soon, however, Occum and Wheelock disagree over the purpose of the school as Wheelock turns to training non-Indian missionaries. Occum leaves to minister and teach among the Brotherton Indians.

1769–1835 Missions Established in California. The California mission system begins with Juniperro Serra's founding of the San Diego mission in 1769. In the half-century before the Mexican government secularizes them in 1835, the Spanish establish 17 more missions and several presidio military bases along the California coast, with devastating effects on the California Indian population. The missions bring Indian groups once living in small, scattered village sites into a central location. Once in the missions, the neophytes, as converted Indians are called, are not permitted to leave and remain under the control of the Spanish authorities. Those who do not obey are subject to a number of punishments, including solitary confinement, lashing, branding, and even execution. Within the "gentle yoke of Catholicism," the neophytes are taught trades ranging from blacksmithing and candlemaking to farming, in the process serving the economic interests of their oppressors. Mission Indians find life very difficult; the Spanish forbid any practice of traditional cultures and religions, and many Indians die of disease and hardship. The death registries at Mission Santa Barbara alone list 4,000 names, while the coastal California Indian population at large is reduced during the mission period from an estimated 70,000 to less than 15,000.

In response to this invasion of their territory, California Indian groups begin almost immediately to resist. The Ipai and Tipai Indians, in whose land the San Diego mission is built, attack the Spanish camp within a month of its establishment. Six years later on November 4, 1775, under the leadership of two baptized village headmen, a force of 800 Ipai and Tipai destroys the mission there, killing the resident padre. Other acts of rebellion also take place, most notably the 1824 revolt at Missions La Purísima and Santa Barbara when mistreated neophytes capture both missions for a short time. In the end, though, these revolts are all defeated.

1770–1774

c. 1770 Horses. By this time, virtually every modern plains tribe in North America has obtained the horse.

1770 California Indian Mission System. Mission San Carlos is founded at Monterey, but moved in 1771 to a new site near Carmel to avoid the neighborhood of the military garrison at Monterey. The presence of the soldiers is considered by Father Serra as "injurious to the spiritual work of the priests." The mission is secularized in 1834.

1770 Sequoyah, Cherokee Linguist, Is Born. Sequoyah is born in Taskigi (Tuskegee), near present-day Vonore, Tennessee. His mother is Cherokee and his father a U.S. trader. Sequoyah's early life is varied. He is a skilled farmer, hunter, and trader. He also serves under General Andrew Jackson in the Creek War of 1813 and 1814. Sequoyah is justly celebrated for his development of the Cherokee syllabary *(See entry, 1821)*, which is a set of symbols for each syllable sound in the Cherokee language, rather than an alphabet in which symbols represent fewer but shorter sounds. Although Sequoyah's achievement is initially met with some skepticism by his fellow Cherokee, his syllabary serves the Cherokee people admirably for many decades and is the genesis of several Cherokee publications. In subsequent years, Sequoyah continues to play an active role in politics and linguistics. In the late 1830s, as president of the western Cherokee, he sponsors the Cherokee Act of Union, which unites eastern and western parts of the Cherokee Nation. In 1842, Sequoyah sets out on an expedition to locate a lost band of Cherokee who have emigrated westward during the American Revolution. He hopes to locate them by cross-referencing languages. When he fails to return from the expedition, a fellow Cherokee named Oonoley searches for him. Sequoyah dies in 1843, during his quest for the lost band.

MARCH 5, 1770 Boston Massacre. The British perpetrate the Boston Massacre when they fire into a crowd gathered outside the Boston Customs House in defiance of British policy, killing Crispus Attucks, a man of African-American and Massachusetts Indian extraction.

DECEMBER 7, 1770 Matonabbee Guides Samuel Hearne. Matonabbee, a prominent Chipewyan trader of Chipewyan-Cree extraction, begins guiding Hudson's Bay Company employee Samuel Hearne from Churchill toward a fabled copper mine in the interior *(See also* biography, 1737).

1771 California Indian Mission System. Mission San Antonio de Padua is founded near present-day King City in California. Moved in 1773, the mission is the site of the poisoning of several padres in 1801. In 1834, the mission is secularized and offered for sale in 1845. The property is returned to the Catholic church in 1862.

1771 California Indian Mission System. Mission San Gabriel is founded. The mission is moved in 1775, attacked by Indians in 1834,

and offered for sale in 1846. The property is returned to the Catholic church in 1862.

1771 Major Ridge, Cherokee Tribal Leader, Is Born. In his younger days, Major Ridge goes by his Cherokee name, Nunna Hidihi (He Who Stands on the Mountaintop and Sees Clearly); a name of great respect for a man who shows wisdom and understanding in the Cherokee councils. As a young man, Ridge fights as a warrior in the numerous border wars with U.S. settlers until peace emerges in 1795. Thereafter, Ridge and a small group of Cherokee leaders decide that agriculture and political change are the only means of ensuring Cherokee national survival from U.S. pressures for land cessions. Between 1797 and 1810, Ridge is a leading advocate for abolishment of the law of blood, the rule whereby clans exacted a death for a death in cases of murder. During the Creek War of 1813–14, many Cherokee fight with the U.S. Army and lower town Creek villages. Ridge rises to the rank of major, and thereafter is called Major Ridge. Between 1810 and 1828, the Cherokee incrementally form a constitutional government, modeled after the U.S. government. In 1835, Ridge and a minority group of Cherokee planters sign the Treaty of New Echota, thereby agreeing to migrate to Indian Territory (Oklahoma). The treaty signers fear that remaining in the East is impossible because American settlers are confiscating Cherokee property and the Cherokee government is outlawed. Many conservative Cherokee consider Major Ridge and the others traitors for signing the treaty and are embittered by the significant loss of life during the ensuing forced removal, the Trail of Tears, during the winter of 1838–39. Major Ridge and several others are assassinated in 1839.

JULY 17, 1771 Chipewyan and Dogrib Attack Copper Inuit. A group of Chipewyan and Dogrib warriors led by Matonabbee attack a band of Copper Inuit camped near the mouth of the Coppermine River. Hudson's Bay Company employee Samuel Hearne, who is accompanying Matonabbee, notes that the Copper Inuit and the Yellowknife Indians of the region make tools from the small amount of copper found near the river. By this time, Indians who reside along the Coppermine River and the Great Slave Lake already have access to European goods. Although some Dogrib and Yellowknife, Dene (Athapascans) who inhabit the region surrounding Great Slave Lake and Great Bear Lake, have visited Churchill, they usually acquire European goods through Chipewyan middlemen such as Matonabbee at much higher prices than the company asks. *(See* biography, 1737.) Indians residing farther west, near the Mackenzie River, do not have access to European goods.

AUGUST 9, 1771   Inuit Show Missionaries Location for Trading Post. Labrador Inuit, led by Mikak *(See* biography, c. 1740), show Moravian (*Unitas Fratrum,* United Brethren) missionary Jens Haven a suitable location to establish Nain, a trading and missionary post along the northern Labrador coast. For many years, the Labrador Inuit have treated outsiders with hostility, but because of the efforts of Mikak, they are now willing to allow the missionaries and traders to settle among them. This begins a relationship between the Labrador Inuit and the Moravian missionaries that is to endure into the twentieth century.

1772   California Indian Mission System. Mission San Luis Obispo is founded. The chapel is built first of logs, but, because of damage caused by hostile Indians, the mission has to be rebuilt. In time, fire-resistant tile roofs are added here and to other missions as well. In 1776 the mission survives a fire raid by Indians. It is secularized in 1835, sold in 1845, and finally the property is returned to the Catholic church in 1859.

1772   Earliest American Indian Writing Sample. A sermon by Samson Occum, preached at the execution of Indian Moses Paul, is the earliest example of American Indian writing

published in English. It is a work influenced by the Christian missionary activity of the time. Occum also produces *Choice Collection of Hymns and Spiritual Songs* in 1774.

1773–1774   Lord Dunmore's War. Increasing numbers of settlers from Virginia move into the territory around the forks of the Ohio River. Although this area had been ceded by the Six Nations by the Treaty of Lancaster (1744) and the Treaty of Fort Stanwix (1768), the principal occupants at this time are the Shawnee, who refuse to acknowledge Iroquois entitlement or British possession. Settler-Indian relations deteriorate and mutual depredations occur, including the murder of the family of Logan, a Cayuga Indian married to a Shawnee woman, on April 30, 1774. Logan vows to avenge the deaths of his family, and the Shawnee under Cornstalk attack the intruding settlers. Lord Dunmore, governor of Virginia, musters an army and fights a series of skirmishes with the Indians along the Virginia and Pennsylvania frontier. At Point Pleasant, near the mouth of the Kanawha River, one of Dunmore's columns defeats the Shawnee, and they are forced to accept the settlement of their lands.

AUGUST 9, 1774   Nootka Trade with Juan Pérez Hernandez. The Nootka (Nuu-chah-nulth), of Nootka Sound on western Vancouver Island trade with Spanish explorer Juan Pérez Hernandez. On July 15, Haida near the Queen Charlotte Islands had a similar meeting with the explorer. For both these groups, this is probably their first contact with Europeans. The Indians give up otter furs and a variety of skillfully crafted items in exchange for clothing, beads, and knives. Some of the Nootka trade items are carved by professional artists employed by wealthy chiefs. The abundant fish resources of the Pacific Coast allow for the development of remarkably populous and complex societies.

SEPTEMBER 3, 1774   Cumberland House Established. The Hudson's Bay Company (H.B.C.)

April 1778 drawing of the interior of habitation at Nootka Sound by John Webber. Photo by Hillel Burger. Courtesy of the Peabody Museum, Harvard University.

establishes Cumberland House on the Lower Saskatchewan River near the present site of The Pas, Manitoba. This marks the end of the H.B.C.'s policy of building posts only on the shores of Hudson Bay. The change comes about because Cree and Assiniboine bands are taking fewer and fewer furs to the H.B.C., preferring instead to trade with traders from Montreal who are taking European goods directly to them. The fur traders from Montreal had renewed contact with western Indians within a few years of the fall of New France in 1760. The H.B.C. move foreshadows the rapid spread of fur trade posts which will see every Indian group east of the Rocky Mountains and south of Lake Athabasca have at least one fur trade post established in or near its territory by 1800.

1774–1775 Formation of the Indian Departments. During the First Continental Congress in 1774, the delegates, worried about Indian loyalties, commit £40,000 to Indian affairs and appoint a Committee on Indian Affairs to negotiate terms of neutrality or support from the Indians. In 1775, the First Continental Congress assumes control over Indian affairs, not leaving the issue to the individual colonies

as had the British. Northern, southern, and middle departments are created, with commissioners appointed to the head of each. Indian affairs are considered of such importance at this juncture in U.S. history that Benjamin Franklin, Patrick Henry, and James Wilson, all central leaders in the Revolution, are named the first commissioners of the Indian departments. The commissioners are authorized to make treaties and to arrest British agents. They open negotiations with the Six Nations in order to win their neutrality in the impending war, if not their alliance. The commissioners offer trade goods and blacksmith services as a part of a treaty of alliance, but the Six Nations decline the offer.

1774–1821 Fur Trade Competition. Indian groups throughout the subarctic forest from Labrador to the Mackenzie River basin and from the northern plains are able to use competition among fur traders to demand low prices for European goods, and a higher quality and range of these goods. Increased access also allows Indian bands to acquire more European goods, although this leads to resource depletion in much of the subarctic forest by 1821. Various

Indian groups assume specialized roles in the fur trade. Most northern Indians acquire European goods by supplying furs, particularly beaver furs. Cree and Assiniboine bands that, because of the spread of fur trade posts, have lost their role as middlemen become suppliers of the large amount of buffalo meat required to provision fur traders. Many plains bands primarily trade wolf and fox furs, horses, and buffalo meat. Traders also depend on Natives, including mixed-blood (Métis), for diverse goods and services, from birch bark canoes and snowshoes to guiding and interpreting services. Larger numbers of traders increases the mixed-blood population considerably. Plains Métis become provisioners and seasonal workers for the fur trading companies. At this time, the term Métis refers specifically to the French-speaking, Roman Catholic mixed-blood community with primarily French Canadian and Ojibway or Cree ancestry. The English-speaking, Protestant mixed-blood are known as "Country-born." The Métis form a stronger, more cohesive identity than the Country-born.

1775–1779

1775 The Cheyenne Receive the Sacred Law. According to Cheyenne tradition, at about this time the Cheyenne are granted their sacred law and covenant with the Creator through the prophet Sweet Medicine. Sweet Medicine receives the law directly from the Creator on a sacred mountain, present-day Bear Butte in South Dakota. Sweet Medicine then gives the Cheyenne instructions to form a council of 44 chiefs—40 chiefs elected from the ten traditional Cheyenne bands and four chiefs appointed to represent the four sacred directions. Sweet Medicine also gives the Cheyenne their most sacred bundle, composed of four arrows and their particular version of the Sun Dance. Along with the sacred bundle, Sweet Medicine also teaches the Cheyenne the Sacred Arrow Bundle Dance, which renews the covenant

relation between the Cheyenne nation and the Creator. The covenant relation obliges the Cheyenne people to uphold the sacred law and ceremonies, and in return the Creator preserves the Cheyenne nation from physical and cultural destruction.

1775 William McIntosh, Creek Tribal Leader, Is Born. William McIntosh, a mixed-blood, rises to political influence as head warrior of Coweta. Coweta is the central red or war village among the Creek lower towns, located in present-day western Georgia. McIntosh comes to prominence during the Red Stick War (1813–14), when mainly upper town Creek villages, those in Alabama, rebel against U.S. influence over the leaders of the Creek council. During the war, McIntosh zealously leads the lower towns and cooperates with U.S. forces to secure the Red Stick's defeat in 1814. In 1814 at Fort Jackson, present-day Jackson, Mississippi, General Andrew Jackson demands 22 million acres of Creek national territory. The Creek resolve not to cede land again to the United States and to punish with death any person who sells land without national council authority. Nevertheless, in 1818 and 1821, McIntosh leads Creek delegations that cede more land to the United States. After the second treaty, McIntosh is warned by the council that further unauthorized treaty cessions will result in his trial for treason. In the Treaty of Indian Springs of 1825, McIntosh and a dozen other chiefs cede the last Creek holdings in western Georgia. In 1825, McIntosh is condemned for this act and executed by order of the Creek council.

1776 California Indian Mission System. Mission San Francisco de Asis is founded. The mission has a population of 1,100 Indians in 1804. A measles epidemic in 1806 kills 236 Indian people. Abandonment of the mission is proposed in 1822, the mission is secularized in 1834, and undergoes a smallpox epidemic in 1838. The property is returned to the Catholic church in 1857.

A group of Plains Cree driving buffalo into a 'pound.' Mounted hunters and a row of waving Indians guide the herd toward the enclosure (constructed of branches), where the buffalo can be slaughtered. Notice that the bow and arrow remains the weapon of choice even though the Cree own guns. Courtesy of the Glenbow Archives, Calgary, Alberta.

1776   California Indian Mission System. Mission San Juan Capistrano is founded near what is now San Clemente. Refounded in 1776, the mission has an Indian population of 765 in 1790. The Indians are emancipated in 1833, the mission is sold in 1845, and restoration of the mission is attempted in 1860.

1777   The American Revolution. The American Revolution continues. The Shawnee chief Black Fish, fighting on the side of the British, conducts numerous attacks on Harrodsburg and Boonesboro, Kentucky. In mid-summer 1777, Wyandot, Mingo, Cherokee, and Shawnee warriors, led by Cornstalk, the Shawnee chief, raid the area of Wheeling, West Virginia. Cornstalk is killed on November 10, while at Fort Randolph at Point Pleasant under a flag of truce.

1777   California Indian Mission System. Mission Santa Clara is founded, then moved twice because of heavy flooding. The mission moves in 1779 and is rededicated by Father Serra in 1784, just before his death. By 1801 the Santa Clara Indian population rises to 1,200. The

mission is secularized in 1836 and acquired by Jesuits in 1851.

1777   Indian Land Purchases. The New York state government incorporates an article into its constitution which declares invalid all purchases of territory from the Natives since October 17, 1774, and forbids all cessions in the future without the permission of the state legislature.

1777–1783   The Iroquois Confederacy Is Dispersed. The Revolutionary War permanently disrupts the unity of the Iroquois Confederacy. At the beginning of the war, many Iroquois, especially the Seneca and Onondaga, favor neutrality and do not wish to join with either of the warring parties. Some Mohawk, led by Joseph Brant, a close family friend to the British agent William Johnson, fight with the British. The Oneida and Tuscarora, because of local trade and friendship ties with settlers, side with the United States. This absence of agreement about how to handle the war does not allow the confederacy's council to arrive at a binding plan of action through consensual agreement. (All six nations of the confederacy must agree to all decisions, otherwise each nation acts independently.) Since there is no agreement, the individual nations, villages, even families make their own decisions about alliance or neutrality. This causes a deep rift within the confederacy, which is not effectively restored even after the Revolutionary War. The pro-British Iroquois move to Canada during and after the war and eventually form their own confederacy, and the Iroquois remaining in New York do likewise. Thus, by the early 1800s, two independent Iroquois confederacies emerge.

1777–1787   Articles of Confederation. Under the Articles of Confederation—the first U.S. laws of national government—Native Americans are treated as sovereign nations. Under the terms of the Peace of Paris (1783), the United States receives claim to all the land from the Atlantic to the Mississippi River, and from the Great Lakes to the Florida border. Congress has administrative authority over these lands, but most of them belong to Indians. The British had long followed the precedent that Native Americans had a "natural right" to the land but that they could relinquish title to the lands through agreements. For the most part, the United States follows this principle, although the country will claim vast areas of land from the Indians by right of conquest. In 1779, the Continental Congress passes a law asserting that only the national government can transfer ownership of Indian lands, and, by the Northwest Ordinance of 1787, the United States promises that Native Americans' "land and property shall never be taken from them without their consent; and in their property, rights and liberty, they shall never be invaded or disturbed, unless in just and lawful wars authorized by Congress."

1778   American Revolution. The Shawnee chief Blue Jacket captures Daniel Boone, who escapes in May, and warns of an impending raid on Boonesboro, Kentucky. The Shaw-

Mohawk Chief Thayendanegea (Joseph Brant). Courtesy of the National Gallery of Canada, Ottawa.

nee chief Black Fish lays siege to Fort Randolph. The fort holds out and Black Fish withdraws, but Shawnee, Wyandot, Mingo, Delaware, Miami, and some Kickapoo continue to raid throughout the West. In September 1778, the Pennsylvania militia sets out to destroy Susquehannock River Indian towns, Joseph Brant, the Mohawk chief, raids the valleys of the Neversink and Mamakating, and in November Brant and the Seneca chiefs Little Beard and Gucinges attack Cherry Valley.

1778 Shawnee Prophet Tenskwatawa (The Open Door) Is Born. Tenskwatawa is born at Old Piqua, near Springfield, Ohio, son of a Shawnee war chief and his Cherokee-Creek wife. Better known as the Shawnee Prophet, Tenskwatawa is the brother of Tecumseh, the famous Indian leader who tries to rally Indian forces against U.S. expansion before and during the War of 1812. Tenskwatawa becomes an alcoholic early in his life and loses the sight in his left eye in a hunting accident. In 1806, while living in the Delaware villages in Indiana, stretching from Indianapolis to Munsee, Tenskwatawa is influenced by the cultural and ceremonial revival created by the Munsee Prophetess, who in 1804–05 reforms the Delaware Big House religion, the main religious ceremony of the Delaware people. In February 1806, Tenskwatawa has an out-of-body experience and a vision that he dies and goes to heaven to see the Great Spirit, and brings back a message to the Indian people. Tenskwatawa, the prophet, begins to preach a return to traditional Shawnee customs, condemns intermarriage with Europeans, and rejects contact with them. He promotes claims that he can cure sickness and prevent death. The brothers Tenskwatawa and Tecumseh envision a vast Indian confederacy strong enough to keep the colonists from expanding any further west. They found Prophetstown along the confluence of the Wabash River and Tippecanoe Creek in Indiana, and many Indians come to live there. While Tecumseh is absent from Prophetstown in 1811, Tenskwatawa ignores his caution to avoid confrontation with Indiana governor William Henry Harrison's troops. Tenskwatawa performs rituals that he promises will prevent bullets from harming his followers, and convinces them to attack Harrison's troops. Called the battle of Tippecanoe in November 1811, the Indians fight an inconclusive battle with significant casualties on both sides. Following the battle the prophet is left without influence and can no longer command believers. Tenskwatawa flees to Canada, returns 15 years later in 1826, and eventually settles in Wyandotte County, Kansas. He dies in 1837.

SEPTEMBER 17, 1778 United States and Delaware Tribe Treaty. At Fort Pitt (present-day Pittsburgh, Pennsylvania), the Delaware, (actually primarily the Turtle people, one of three Delaware divisions), sign a peace treaty with the United States that offers the Delaware the right to send representatives to Congress and become part of the U.S. nation. This clause, however, is never implemented. The signing of this treaty establishes treaties as the primary legal basis for federal policies toward the American Indian. The practice continues until 1871 when Congress prohibits further treaty making by means of a provision attached to an appropriations act. Between 1778 and 1871, the Senate ratified 370 treaties with Indian tribes; since 1871, agreements with Indian groups have been made by act of Congress, executive orders, or executive agreements. These treaties, orders, and agreements stand on essentially the same footing as treaties with foreign nations.

1778–1800 Native Bands Acquire Access to European Goods. Dogrib, Yellowknife, Slave, and Beaver bands residing in the area surrounding Lake Athabasca acquire access to European goods for the first time when Indian guides lead Montreal trader Peter Pond to the lower Athabasca River. There, on July 2, 1778, he establishes a fur trading post, the first in the Arctic Ocean watershed. The relationship between these Indians and the Chipewyan bands which had until now been their only source of

European goods, becomes more friendly. Chipewyan bands begin to gravitate more toward the Athabasca River region than toward the Hudson's Bay Company post at Churchill on Hudson Bay. This, coupled with the company's decision to begin trading guns with the Inuit along the Hudson Bay, allows bands of Inuit to move southwest into regions vacated by Chipewyan bands. These Inuit, who come to depend almost wholly on the large migrating caribou herds of the region, become known as the Caribou Inuit. Hostilities between the Inuit and the Chipewyan are further reduced after the Chipewyan are hit by smallpox in the early 1780s. Indians of the Athabasca region introduce Peter Pond to pemmican, a type of preserved meat and fat which is compact, nutritious, and high in energy. Though used mostly as an emergency food supply among Indians, pemmican quickly becomes an essential staple among fur traders. Most of the pemmican is made by Indian women at fur trade posts from meat supplied by Plains Indians and Métis.

1779   American Revolution. George Washington, commander in chief of the colonial army, orders General John Sullivan to attack the Iroquois Confederacy. Many Indian towns are burned. In April, Oneida chief Hanyerry, an American ally, helps destroy Onondaga, capital of the Iroquois Confederation. On July 10, the continental army and militiamen destroy Chilicothe, the Shawnee "capital," and mortally wound Chief Black Fish.

1780–1784

c. 1780   Northeast Craftwork. Decorative ribbonwork comes into use among the southern Great Lakes tribes, who enhance their clothing by cutting the colorful ribbons of silk and satin into strips and sewing them in intricate patterns on various garments.

1780   American Revolution. American colonel Daniel Brodhead destroys Mingo, Wyandot,

and Seneca towns. Mohawk, Seneca, and Cayuga push the American-allied Oneida back to Schenectady. In June 1780, Delaware, Wyandot, Ottawa, Mingo, Ojibway, Tawa, Miami, and Potawatomi join with British and Canadian forces to invade Kentucky. Cherokee, Chickamauga, and Creeks continue to raid American southern settlements until October 7, when forces under John Sevier and Andrew Pickens devastate Indian settlements. On October 15, Sir John Johnson, Joseph Brant, and the Seneca chief Cornplanter descend upon the Scoharie Valley, burning everything they encounter over the next few days and destroying a small militia force. Johnson and Brant are driven out of the valley in October by a militia force led by General Robert Van Rensselaer, augmented by Oneida.

1780   California Indian Mission System. Spanish presidios, or forts, are established at Santa Barbara, San Diego, Monterey, and San Francisco. Smaller military garrisons are kept at each mission. Two military colonies are established on the Colorado River, the main river crossing for the land route to Sonora, Mexico, within Quechan (Yuma) territory.

1780–1782   Smallpox Epidemic. Up to half the Siksika, Kainai (Blood), Peigan, Cree, Assiniboine, and Atsina (Gros Ventre), and an even higher percentage of some Chipewyan bands, are killed as smallpox spreads north from the Shoshoni in the upper Missouri River region. This smallpox epidemic spread northward from Mexico affecting the entire plains area.

1780s   Indian Treaties. In the 1780s several unsuccessful treaties are signed between small Indian groups and the U.S. government. The U.S. commissioners negotiate these treaties at Fort Stanwix with the Six Nations (1784); at Fort McIntosh with the Wyandot, Delaware, Chippewa, and Ottawa (1785); at Fort Finney with the Shawnee (1786); and at Fort Hopewell with the Cherokee, Choctaw, and Chickasaw (1786). The treaties typically contain several articles, including those that cede certain lands to the United States. Not all of the Indian leaders of the various nations agree with or sign the treaties. Trouble results when settlers move onto western lands they purchase from land companies. In Ohio, Kentucky, and Tennessee, settlers often find Native Americans still residing on and laying claim to lands that the settlers have bought. Although some settlers and Indians live peacefully beside one another, there is continued conflict over land ownership.

Land disputes result in intermittent skirmishes along the frontier between 1790 and 1794. President George Washington answers the Indian challenge by directing General Josiah Harmer and 1,500 troops to engage the Indians. Kickapoo, Shawnee, and Miami snipers harass the soldiers as they march south of the Maumee River in Ohio. In September 1790 the Indian alliance launches a successful battle that defeats Harmer and provokes Washington into sending Governor Arthur St. Clair and 3,000 troops to the Maumee River in Indiana to confront the Indians. Once again Native American forces strike hard, killing and wounding more than 900 soldiers. Still determined to destroy the Indian alliance in the Old Northwest, Washington orders General Anthony Wayne into Ohio. In August 1794 the confederated nations, led by Little Turtle of the Miami Nation, go into battle against Wayne, known to the Indians as "Blacksnake," at the battle of Fallen Timbers, near present-day Fort Wayne, Indiana. In part, because the British fail to come to the Indians' aid at the battle, the Indians are forced to retreat. The Indians' political position further erodes when, in late 1794, the United States and Britain sign Jay's Treaty; the English depart to Canada and withdraw their military support for their Indian allies.

1780s U.S. Settler Expansion in the South.
In the South, parts of the Cherokee, Creek, Choctaw, and Chickasaw nations side with the Spanish in order to curtail U.S. settler expansion into their territories. Like the British in the

North, the Spanish in Florida and West Florida (present-day southern Alabama and Mississippi) provide the southern Indians with trade and weapons. This leads to intermittent warfare between the westward-moving settlers and the Indian nations, who are intent on defending their territory. Several of the southern nations form a confederacy against U.S. intrusion and choose Alexander McGillivray to lead them. McGillivray at first sides with the Spanish against the Americans. Then, after meeting President Washington in New York in 1790, McGillivray becomes a brigadier general in the U.S. Army; he continues to deal with both the Spanish and U.S. governments until his death in 1793. The loose-knit confederacy McGillivray led did not last long after his death; most Cherokee, Choctaw, and Chickasaw try to live peacefully with the settlers, but some antisettler Indians, particularly within the Creek nation and among the Chickamauga Cherokee, maintain their pro-Spanish stance.

Like the British, the Spanish hope to prevent the territorial expansion of the young United States. In 1795, when the Napoleonic Wars begin in Europe, the Spanish turn their attention to Europe and ignore their relatively unprofitable Florida colonies. Thus, the southern Indian nations, in a series of treaties in the middle 1790s, are forced to recognize the United States as the major non-Indian power in the South.

In the Southwest, Spanish forces are withdrawn from the Colorado River area because of concerted Indian resistance. The overland connection between Sonora, Mexico, and Spanish California is severed for many years.

April 1781 American Revolution.
Joseph Brant, Mohawk leader, attacks Cherry Valley. American fortunes are at a low ebb when Colonel Marinus Willett is assigned command of the region. He successfully quells raiding for most of the summer of 1781.

July 1781 Quechan War of Independence.
The Quechan (Yuma) Indians of the lower

Colorado River revolt. The warriors of the Colorado are generally successful in most of their struggles with the Spaniards and are ultimately successful in 1783 when the provinces of Sonora and California are cut off from each other.

1782   California Indian Mission System. Mission San Buenaventura, near present-day Ventura, is founded. Extensive orchards and gardens are planted. The mission is burned in 1792, rebuilt, and has an Indian population of 1,297 in 1800. The mission is sold in 1846, and the property is returned to the church in 1862. Three Spanish soldiers are granted ranchos nearby for service to the Spanish crown—the first of the large individual land grants.

1782   Christian Indians Massacred. Christian Delaware Indians are massacred at Gnadenhutten, Ohio. Upon the advice of the English, to avoid conflicts with frontier farmers, the Indians move away to Sandusky in Ohio country in October 1781. Because of a severe winter famine it is necessary for some members to return at harvest time. Colonel Daniel Brodhead, commander of the Continental Army's Western Department, dispatches Colonel David Williamson to "punish" the Delaware. Ninety men, women, and children are killed by mallet blows to the back of the head. Although the massacre is roundly condemned, Williamson is not punished. When the Delaware seek revenge for the Gnadenhutten massacre, Colonel Crawford undertakes the "Second Moravian Campaign," destroying Moravian, Delaware, and Wyandot towns.

c. 1783   Keokuk, Sac (Sauk) Tribal Leader, Is Born. Keokuk is born in the village of Saukenuk in present-day Illinois. He obtains a position of power among his people by demonstrating bravery against the Sioux, although he is not a hereditary chief. By the early 1800s, the official policy of the U.S. government has become one of forced treaties and acquisition of Indian land. Keokuk, though not recognized as

a chief among his own people, is selected by the U.S. government as the official representative of the Sauk because of his refusal to support the British in 1812 and his friendly overtures to the United States. Keokuk signs a number of treaties that include an exchange of Sauk land in the Rock River country for a tract located westward and an annual cash compensation, which is to be administered by Keokuk. In the 1830s, Keokuk redeems himself in the eyes of some Sauk by his skillful defense of Sauk land interests against Sioux territorial claims in Washington, D.C. In 1845, however, he cedes Iowa lands in exchange for a reservation in Kansas. Keokuk dies three years later, amid reports that followers of Black Hawk killed him.

1783–1784   Loyalists Settle on Canadian Native Lands. The arrival of a large number of settlers marks the beginning of a new era for the Micmac, Maliseet, and Passamaquoddy along the Atlantic Coast north of the United States. Most of the settlers are Loyalists who have left the United States following its War of Independence. With the war over, the British place less value on Indians as military allies. For this reason, beginning in 1784, the office of superintendent of Indian Affairs in Nova Scotia is not filled. Land grants promised to the Micmac are not surveyed. The new colonists settle predominantly around bays and inlets and in the St. John River Valley—all important sites for Micmac and Maliseet. Most of the Passamaquoddy move into the United States to the area of northern Maine.

1783–1790   Indian Land Sales. The U.S. government has little money with which to operate, but it claims all of the Indian land west to the Mississippi River. The new nation makes considerable money by selling western lands in Ohio, Indiana, Kentucky, and Tennessee. In the north, the Wyandot, Delaware, Shawnee, Miami, Chippewa, Potawatomi, Kickapoo, Ottawa, and some Iroquois warriors join to defy the U.S. invasion of the Old Northwest, bringing war to the settlers in Ohio in their attempt to drive them out. Between 1783 and 1790 perhaps a thousand settlers lose their lives; there are no estimates regarding Indian deaths north of the Ohio River caused by war and disease.

1783–1795 Intermittent Border Wars. The Treaty of Paris formally ends the Revolutionary War in 1783. Following the war the political and military situation remains extremely unstable. Between 1783 and 1795 the British continue to occupy the forts of the Old Northwest, at Detroit and Chicago, although by treaty they are to be evacuated. The United States has neither the military strength nor the will to dislodge the British soldiers. The British occupy the forts and supply their Indian allies west of the Ohio River with goods and weapons, hoping that the Indian nations will create a buffer zone between the United States and Canada. The Indian nations (Delaware, Miami, Shawnee, Ottawa, and others) hope to use British support to keep U.S. settlers from streaming across the Ohio River and taking Indian land. As the Revolutionary War comes to an end, Congress believes it is "essential to the welfare and interest of the United States" to keep a "friendship with the Indians." To prevent conflicts, Congress forbids "all persons from making settlements on lands inhabited or claimed by Indians, without the limits [outside the boundaries] of any particular State, and from purchasing or receiving any gift or cession of such lands or claims without the express authority and directions of the United States in Congress assembled." Like previous proclamations, this is designed to centralize control of land purchases.

c. 1784 Sacajawea, Lemhi (Shoshoni) Guide, Is Born. Sacajawea is kidnapped by Hidatsa Indians when she is ten years old and taken to a village near present-day Mandan, North Dakota. In 1804 she is purchased, or won, by French-Canadian fur trader Toussaint Charbonneau. In the early 1800s, entertaining hopes that she will be reunited with the Shoshoni nation, Sacajawea accompanies Meriwether Lewis and William Clark on their historic expedition from St. Louis, Missouri, to the Pacific Ocean. Sacajawea proves to be a valuable liaison for the U.S. explorers, since she speaks a number of languages, including Shoshoni and Siouan. Sacajawea is responsible in large part for the success of the expedition, due to her navigational, diplomatic, and translating skills. During the expedition Sacajawea reveals to Lewis and Clark important passageways through the wilderness and also provides the expedition with valuable information about edible plants.

MAY 22, 1784 Mississauga Agree to Sell Land to British. Mississauga (southeastern Ojibway) bands led by Wabakinine agree to sell land to the British so that Britain's Iroquois allies in the United States can relocate to British territory. The Iroquois are upset by the terms of the Treaty of Versailles which has granted their territory to the United States. Mohawk captain Joseph Brant (See biography, 1742), a veteran of the U.S. War of Independence, and over 1,800 members of all six groups within the Iroquois Confederacy (Mohawk, Oneida, Onondaga, Cayuga, Seneca, and Tuscarora) settle on the Six Nations reserve along the Grand River near present day Brantford, Ontario. Captain John Deserontyon (See biography, c. 1740), who fought on the side of the British in the Seven Years' War, the Pontiac uprising, and the U.S. War of Independence, settles with another group of about 200 Iroquois on a reserve near the Bay of Quinte on the north shore of Lake Ontario. The new border between the United States and British North America cuts across the St. Regis (Akwesasne) Iroquois settlement. Despite the terms of the Treaty of Versailles, many Indian residents of the United States maintain contacts with the British at British forts maintained within U.S. territory. The relationship between the Mississauga and the Iroquois, long hostile, becomes friendly.

1785–1789

1785　Congress and the Southeastern Tribes. A resolution of Congress in this year asks the Creeks to meet with the Congress on October 1 but Congress refuses to negotiate when only two towns are represented and instead meets with the Cherokee at Hopewell. A mutual return of all prisoners is agreed to and the Cherokee acknowledge the sovereignty of the United States *(See* entry, November 18, 1785).

1785　Kenekuk, Kickapoo Tribal and Spiritual Leader, Is Born. Kenekuk is the religious and political leader of a community of Kickapoo, which is later joined by some Potawatomi. The Kickapoo live in Illinois, while the Potawatomi occupy part of Michigan, but a small group of them go with Kenekuk and his Kickapoo community when they are removed to Kansas after 1833. Kenekuk is influenced by the Shawnee Prophet, who before the War of 1812 advocates strong and overt military resistance to U.S. settlers and territorial expansion. The War of 1812 leaves the Kickapoo and other northern Great Lakes Indian nations in a state of disarray and destitution. Kenekuk, like the Shawnee Prophet before him, claims he had a vision containing a message from the Great Spirit for the Indian people, and for the Kickapoo in particular. Kenekuk's vision differs from the Shawnee Prophet's message in that it preaches accommodation to U.S. culture and land demands. The Kickapoo prophet works to create a new moral and religious community for his followers, one that draws on elements of Catholic, Protestant, and traditional Kickapoo religious beliefs. He advocates the taking up of agriculture and the formation of self-sufficient Indian farming communities. He bans alcohol, instructs his followers to maintain friendly relations with U.S. settlers, and develops a self-contained religious moral community, that tries to preserve its land and identity from the onslaught of U.S. settlers and the demands of the U.S. government. In 1832, Kenekuk's commu-

nity does not join with Black Hawk in his war to regain parts of Illinois. In Kansas, Kenekuk continues his preaching, and he attracts some converts from the Potawatomi. Kenekuk dies in 1852, but his community survives until this day, and the people retain the distinct religious teachings of the Kickapoo prophet.

1785　Virginia Assembly. The Virginia Assembly decrees that every mixed person with one quarter or more "Negro blood" is to be deemed a mulatto. This means that all Indians who are one quarter or more African are longer legally Indian but are now to be subject to all of the laws aimed at controlling Blacks.

NOVEMBER 18, 1785　The Hopewell Treaty Signed. Within a year of its treaty of peace with Great Britain, the new government set out to restore peace with the tribal confederacies that still controlled its frontiers. The Treaty of Hopewell is typical of the period from 1784 to 1798. The Cherokee acknowledged themselves to be "under the protection of the United States of America and of no other sovereign whatsoever," and agreed that the United States would henceforth "regulate trade with the Indians." In case of any serious crimes by Cherokee against U.S. citizens, the offenders were to be tried under Cherokee rules. If U.S. citizens offended a Cherokee, then the offender was to be surrendered to the United States for punishment. Neither nation would engage in retaliation for injuries except after a diplomatic demand for satisfaction had been made and refused. By this means, the Cherokee and other eastern tribes come under the exclusive "protection" of the United States, without surrendering their right to govern themselves within their own boundaries.

1785–1812　Canadian Sea Otter Trade. With news that sea otter pelts can be sold at a high price in the Orient, traders from Britain, France, Spain, Russia, and the United States (after 1788) arrive in the Northwest in increasing numbers. The maritime trade on the West Coast peaks between 1792 and 1812. Haida,

Nootka, Tsimshian, Tlingit, and Bella Coola (Nuxalk) of the Pacific Coast use the competition among different European shipborne traders to acquire European goods at low prices. Early trade is centered on the islands and outer coast where sea otter are plentiful. Coastal groups, especially those at the mouths of large rivers such as the Ksan (Skeena), Nass, Stikine, and Taku, incorporate these goods into already existing inland trade networks. They have long traveled to interior rendezvous sites where they have traded products such as eulachon (candlefish) oil, dentalium shells, and blankets to interior groups in exchange for moose and caribou hides, goat wool, and small furs. Because of the importance of eulachon oil in this trade the routes are known as "grease trails." In order to protect their position, powerful coastal groups prevent inland groups from reaching the coast where these goods could be had. Incorporation of European goods into this network adds to Coastal Indian prosperity and dominance. Certain leaders along the outer coast, such as Yuquot leader Maquinna and Clayoquot leader Wickanish, use fur trade wealth to consolidate their influential positions. With access to metal tools, Coastal Indians create more intricate wooden artifacts, from totem poles to canoes, and the Haida begin carving argillite (a black stone). Potlatch ceremonies also became more elaborate. Potlatches are Northwest Coastal Indian ceremonies in which a large amount of accumulated wealth is given away in order to enhance the status of the donors. Prominent Indian leaders employ professional craftsmen to produce materials for potlatches. Soon inland groups that have access to major salmon rivers also establish substantial seasonal settlements and trade goods with other bands farther inland. In this way, European goods are conveyed as far east as the Rocky Mountains. The dominant position of the coastal groups induces inland groups to adopt some aspects of nearby coastal cultures, such as language and potlatch ceremonies. In this developing trade, the Chinook jargon, derived from several lan-

guages, becomes the language of trade. Blankets act as a currency. Already proficient in large dugout cedar canoes, the Coastal Indians soon adopt the use of sails.

1786 California Indian Mission System. Mission Santa Barbara is founded by Father Serra's successor, Father Lasuen. The mission undergoes an earthquake in 1812 and an Indian uprising in 1824. The mission is secularized in 1834 and sold in 1846, and the property is returned to the church in 1865.

1786 Indian Land. Thomas Jefferson states: "It may be regarded as certain, that not a foot of land will ever be taken from the Indians, without their own consent. The sacredness of their rights is felt by all thinking persons in America as much as in Europe."

JUNE 28, 1786 Indian Department. Congress passes a measure to reorganize the Indian Department so that Indian relations may be more effectively regulated to curb the independent actions of the states and to control irresponsible traders and settlers.

AUGUST 7, 1786 Federal Indian Reservations. The first federal Indian reservation is established. Congress establishes two departments: the Northern, with jurisdiction north of the Ohio River and west of the Hudson River, and the Southern, which covers the area south of the Ohio River. A superintendent is appointed to head each of the departments, reporting to the Secretary of War. Each of these officials has the power to grant licenses to trade and live among the Indian people.

1786–1795 Little Turtle's War. Little Turtle (Miami), Blue Jacket (Shawnee), and other bands of Shawnee and Miami repudiate an agreement which declares the Ohio country to be U.S. territory. During negotiations, Kekewepellethe (Shawnee) attempts to retain possession of the land; however, William Butler and George Rogers Clark, U.S. negotiators prevail. Kekewepellethe agrees to relinquish the entire Miami Valley. Little Turtle responds by intensifying hit-and-run raids that had not stopped following the Revolutionary War. George Washington responds by assigning Josiah Harmar, militiamen, and a small number of regular army troops to the area. Little Turtle proves himself a skilled warrior by drawing soldiers far from their bases of supply and attacking when they are at their weakest.

1787   California Indian Mission System. California Mission La Purísima is founded. In 1804 the mission has an Indian population of 1,522; in 1810 it has 20,000 livestock on hand. It is destroyed by an earthquake in 1812. A new church, built at a new site in 1818, is secularized in 1834 and sold in 1845. In the 1870s some property is returned to the Catholic church.

1787   Indians and the U.S. Constitution. The Constitutional Convention meets in Philadelphia, Pennsylvania, to plan a new government. Benjamin Franklin suggests that the leaders seriously consider a study of Iroquois law, which unifies northeastern Indian groups for many years. He recommends inclusion of certain egalitarian concepts within the planned Constitution.

Some Native Americans and scholars argue that the delegates learn much about representative government from the Iroquois and that the Constitution is patterned after the political ideas of the Iroquois and the political structure of their league. Furthermore, ideas of individual political freedom, free speech, political equality, and political community are recorded in sixteenth- and seventeenth-century encounters with Native societies. Many of these observations are incorporated into the Enlightenment philosophy of the 1700s by such men as Jean-Jacques Rousseau and Voltaire. The Enlightenment philosophy in turn influences contemporary political thought and the organization of democracy in Western nations.

After much debate, the states ratify the Constitution and it becomes the supreme law in the United States. The constitutional delegates want Indian policy to be centralized and determined by Congress. Article 1, Section 8, of the Constitution, often called "the Commerce Clause," empowers Congress to make all laws pertaining to the Indian trade and diplomatic relations. This clause prohibits the original 13 colonies from negotiating treaties directly with Indian nations and also leaves control over Indian land in federal hands, outside individual states' jurisdictions. Through treaty-making, which requires ratification by the Senate with a two-thirds vote and signature by the president, the Indian nations form a legal relationship with the U.S. government. The adopted Constitution gives the government the power to "regulate commerce with foreign nations and among the several states and with the Indian tribes within the limits of any states, not subject to the laws thereof." This clause, along with the power to enact other laws and to negotiate treaties, provides the basis for subsequent laws and decisions regarding Indians.

1787   Northwest Ordinance. The Northwest Ordinance of 1787 calls for the division of lands north of the Ohio River into territories that can eventually become states. In this way, the Congress establishes the mechanism by which territories and states will be created. In order to open lands for settlement, Congress passes the Ordinance of 1785, which calls for the survey of "Public Land" into townships of 6 miles square divided into 36 sections of 640 acres each, costing $640. This method favors land speculators with money to invest. Real estate companies emerge, buying large tracts of land and subdividing them to make purchases more affordable for smaller farmers. Yet, in order for the two ordinances to work, the United States must secure Indian title to the land. The government establishes this through treaties. Additionally, the Northwest Ordinance pledges to provide an education for the Indian people. The act states: "Religion, morality, and knowledge, being necessary to good government and the happiness of mankind, schools, and the means of education shall forever be encouraged."

The Northwest Ordinance is prominent in creating the basis for U.S. settlements beyond the Alleghenies and in the formulation of Indian policy. Ironically, the ordinance states: "The utmost of good faith shall always be observed toward the Indians; their land and property shall never be taken away from them without their consent; and their property, rights and liberty shall never be invaded by Congress; but laws founded in justice and humanity shall from time to time be made for preventing wrongs to them, and for preserving peace and friendship with them."

OCTOBER 26, 1787 Treaty Claims. The federal government instructs the governor of the Northwest Territory to investigate claims by the northwestern tribes regarding illegal treaties made in 1785. The governor is instructed to examine the treaties, but not to alter them unless a change of boundary beneficial to the United States can be obtained.

1788 Seattle (Sealth), Duwamish-Suquamish Tribal Leader, Is Born. Seattle, a principal chief of the Duwamish people, encourages friendship and commerce with the U.S. settlers pouring into the Pacific Northwest region, and avoids being drawn into the ongoing regional conflicts between settlers and Indians that are permeating the Northwest during this time. Throughout the Gold Rush era of the 1850s, Seattle maintains peace, despite the influx of miners and settlers. By 1855, tensions between settlers and the other Indians in the area are mounting, and the breaking of treaty terms finally leads to the Yakima War of 1855–56. Seattle chooses not to fight and signs the Fort Elliot Treaty, in which he agrees to relocate his people to a reservation. Chief Seattle and his people remain allied with American forces and withstand an attack by the neighboring Nisqually Indians. He and his people later relocate to the Port Madison Reservation, near present-day Bremerton, Washington. The city of Seattle, Washington, is named after the Duwamish chief, who dies in 1866.

1789 Indian Affairs Moved to War Department. Since 1784 Congress has delegated negotiation of treaties to the War Department. In 1786, the Secretary of War assumes management of Indian affairs, and in 1789, with the creation of the new War Department, Indian affairs are delegated to the first Secretary of War, Henry Knox. Because many Indian nations on the frontier are allied with the British or Spanish and resist U.S. settlement, the War Department is seen as the most appropriate agency to manage Indian relations.

JANUARY 9, 1789 Treaty of Fort Harmar. A treaty is negotiated between the Wyandot, other Indian tribes, and the United States, in which the provisions of the agreement of 1785 are renewed except that the boundaries of the Indian lands are changed to include new land that has been ceded to the United States. The Indians are allowed to possess their lands but may not dispose of them to any nation except the United States. For this cession the Indians receive $6,000 in goods. This treaty did not settle land controversy over Americans settling in the Ohio country, however, and the battle of Fallen Timbers follows in 1794.

JULY 7, 1789 Purchase of Indian Land. Secretary of War Henry Knox urges Congress to purchase Indian lands before U.S. settlers seize the lands. Congress votes $20,000 to be spent to defray the costs of negotiating land cessions with the Indians. Between 1789–1850, the U.S. negotiates and ratifies 245 treaties with the Indians in which the government secures over 450 million acres of land for less than $190 million.

SEPTEMBER 17, 1789 Ratification of Treaties. President Washington affirms the requirement of Senate ratification of treaties. Soon after the adoption of the new Constitution, doubts arose as to whether Indian treaties require Senate ratification. "It is said to be the general understanding and practice of nations, as a check on the mistakes and indiscretions of ministers or commissioners, not to consider any treaty negotiated and signed by such officers, as final and conclusive, until ratified by the Sovereign or Government from whom they derive their powers," the president wrote, "This practice has been adopted by the United States respecting their treaties with European nations, and I am inclined to think it would be advisable to observe it in the conduct of our treaties with the Indians." After a lengthy inquiry, the Senate ultimately agrees with the President.

SUMMER 1789   Kutchin Tell of the Existence of the Yukon River. Several groups, including eastern Kutchin (Gwich'in, Loucheux) and Hare, Dene (Athapascan) hunter-gatherers that reside along the *Deh-cho* ("Big River," Mackenzie River), meet Alexander Mackenzie's party descending that river. The Kutchin who hunt west of the Deh-cho tell Mackenzie of a large westward flowing river (Yukon River) to the west of the mountain range along the Mackenzie River. The Hare, who reside in the harsh environment north and northwest of Great Bear Lake, depend heavily on the snowshoe hare for food and clothing.

1790–1794

1790   John Ross, Cherokee Tribal Leader, Is Born. While a young man, Ross becomes a successful merchant and slave owner. He strongly advocates agricultural and political change for the Cherokee as a means to preserve the nation from U.S. demands for land cessions and from Cherokee migration west of the Mississippi River. In 1811, he is appointed to the standing committee that meets to transact Cherokee

government business while the national council, composed of about 50 village headman, is not in session. During the 1820s, the Cherokee incrementally adopt a constitutional government and become an agricultural nation. During much of the 1820s, Ross serves as secretary to the Cherokee principal chief, Path Killer, who is very influential among the conservatives that constitute a large majority within the nation. Most conservatives prefer to remain in their eastern homelands and resist U.S. pressure to migrate west. Following Path Killer's death in 1827, Ross inherits his great influence among the conservatives. In 1827, he serves as chairman of the Cherokee Constitutional Convention and in 1828 is elected principal chief by the Cherokee National Council. Between 1828 and 1866, Ross leads the Cherokee conservatives, who form the National party. The conservative majority consistently reelects Ross as principal chief, and in return he works to preserve Cherokee national and territorial independence from U.S. encroachments.

1790   Trade In California. Artillery companies are stationed at the main California ports to discourage foreign trade and commerce in the Spanish province. The northwestern fur trade causes new European interest and attracts foreign vessels to Spanish areas.

JULY 22, 1790   Trade and Intercourse Act. The first "Trade and Intercourse Act" is enacted in order to establish firm relations with the Indian tribes. The act exemplifies this trend by attempting to regulate commercial relations with the various tribes. Early U.S. laws affecting Indian people generally seek to establish direct legal, political, and trade relations between the federal government and the Indian nations. The act reads, in part, "That no sale of lands shall be made by any Indians, or any nation or persons, or to any state, whether having the right of preemption to such lands or not, unless the same shall be made and duly executed at some public treaty, held under the same authority of the United States." This is the first in a series of four such acts regulating trade and intercourse with Indian tribes. The act makes virtually all interaction between Indians and non-Indians come under federal control. The federal government must give its approval to the transference of lands held in trust, by Indians to non-Indians. The act regulates commercial trade with the Indians, establishes penalties for violations by traders, and provides for criminal provisions for murder and other crimes against Indians in Indian country. One of the crucial provisions that is the basis of current eastern land claims is the requirement that Indian land cannot be sold by the tribe without federal control. This statute remains in effect and is the basis for claims of various Indian tribes to lands taken without such consent.

1791   California Indian Mission System. Mission Santa Cruz is founded. Abandonment of the mission is proposed in 1805. Father Quintana is murdered at the mission in 1812. The mission is secularized in 1834, the mission tower collapses in 1840, and the church is destroyed by an earthquake in 1857.

1791   California Indian Mission System. Mission Soledad is founded. The mission experiences an epidemic in 1802, and in 1810 has the lowest Indian population of all the missions. The mission is secularized in 1835, and the property is returned to the church in 1859.

OCTOBER 1791   Northwest Territory. U.S. military forces suffer their worst defeat in all of the Indian wars, when General Arthur St. Clair, governor of the Northwest Territory, leads a "punitive expedition" against the Shawnee and allied tribes. Little Turtle attacks St. Clair and his force of 1,400 untrained militia on a vulnerable plateau above the upper Wabash River. Six-hundred-twenty-three officers and men, along with 24 civilian teamsters, are killed and 172 soldiers are wounded, making Custer's

later loss of 211 at the Little Big Horn in 1876 seem small in comparison. In 1792, George Washington replaces St. Clair with former Revolutionary commander "Mad" Anthony Wayne.

1792–1827   Indian Slavery. A number of persons of part-Indian or Indian descent are liberated from slavery by the Virginia courts since it was "discovered" that any person descended from a female Indian enslaved after 1703 or 1691 was legally a free person. Many other such persons continue to be held as slaves because of their ignorance or lack of access to the courts.

c. 1793   Cuthbert Grant, Métis Leader, Is Born. Perhaps the first leader of the Métis, Grant plays an important role in the development of Métis nationalism. Born on the northern plains, he is educated in Montreal, returning west in 1815. He works first for the North West Company and then, after that company's merger with the Hudson's Bay Company, for the reorganized Hudson's Bay Company. Grant's superiors in the North West Company name him "Captain of the Métis" in 1814, and he leads the Métis resistance to the Red River Colony in 1814 and 1815. He also leads the Métis party that confronts and kills 20 Red River colonists at the battle of Seven Oaks in 1816. Although the Hudson's Bay Company brings charges against Grant for these and other actions, the charges are dropped. For some time, the company considers him the "Warden of the Plains." In this capacity Grant works to uphold the company's trade monopoly. This task, however, puts him at odds with most of the Métis for whom private trading is important. After the Sayer Trial of 1849 the company concedes that it is unable to enforce its monopoly, and, therefore, Grant's period of influence ends. He dies on July 15, 1854.

1793   Indian Treaty Rights. Federal agents meet with Delaware and 12 other Indian tribes but are unable to come to terms. The Indians insist that boundaries remain in accordance with treaties negotiated and ratified by the U.S. government, but the government says it cannot comply and that settlers illegally squatting on Indian land cannot be moved.

MARCH 1, 1793 The Second Trade and Intercourse Act. Congress enacts the second "Trade and Intercourse Act," restricting anyone without a license from having "any interest or concern in any trade with the Indians," and to be subject to a fine and/or imprisonment. Congress, in the Second Intercourse Act, authorizes an expenditure of not more than $20,000 annually for the purchase of domestic animals and farming implements for the Indian nations. (It proved to be an insufficient sum to be effective, despite President Washington's advice to the Indians to stop warring and adopt the U.S. life ways). The act also provides for presidential appointment of temporary agents among the Indian tribes.

MARCH 2, 1793 Treaty Negotiations. Under the "Appropriation Act for Expenses of a Treaty with Northwest Indians," Congress authorizes a sum not to exceed $100,000 for commissioners to negotiate a treaty with hostile Indian tribes northwest of the Ohio River.

JULY 17, 1793 Alexander Mackenzie Reaches Bella Coola Village. Members of a Bella Coola (Nuxalk) village trade with Alexander Mackenzie, after trading with Captain George Vancouver a short time ago. They exchange fish and furs for iron, copper, knives, and trinkets. Mackenzie reaches the Bella Coola village after several Indian groups guides him on a search for a route from the Peace River to the Pacific Ocean. The final leg of the trip follows an important "grease trail" used by Bella Coola, Chilcotin, and Carrier. Most of the Indians along Mackenzie's route, including the Sekani, Athapascan hunter-gatherers centered around the Finlay and Parsnip rivers, are already familiar with

European goods that have reached them from the west through Indian trading networks.

OCTOBER 1793–JUNE 1794 Atsina and Siksika Attack Hudson's Bay Company. Frustrated by their inability to protect themselves from their Cree and Assiniboine rivals, Atsina and Siksika bands attack nearby posts on the North Saskatchewan River. On June 24, 1794, they attack Hudson's Bay Company and North West Company posts on the South Saskatchewan River. The attacks, apparently intended to acquire guns, serve to intensify Cree and Assiniboine hostility, and the Atsina begin a gradual withdrawal from the Saskatchewan River region. This retreat will see the Atsina centered around the Milk River, in present-day Montana, by 1850.

1794 Indian Education. The first Indian treaty is signed with the United States with provisions to provide education. In this treaty, the Oneida, Tuscarora, and Stockbridge gain agreements that the United States will provide them with teachers, who will be employed to "instruct some young men of these three nations in the arts of the miller and the sawer."

JUNE 1794 Little Turtle's War. Twelve hundred warriors under Blue Jacket and Tecumseh route one of "Mad Anthony" Wayne's pack trains. Blue Jacket and Tecumseh, victorious, attempt to call off their warriors, but Ottawa and other Indian allies advance on Wayne's Fort Recovery, where they are repelled. Wayne builds two more advance posts, Fort Adams and Fort Defiance, the latter in the midst of abandoned hostile villages. In preparation for battle, Blue Jacket's warriors fast. Wayne pauses on August 17 to build Fort Deposit, where he caches all that is unnecessary for combat. On August 20 Wayne resumes his advance. Many of Blue Jacket's now-famished warriors are out looking for food; those who remain are weak from hunger. The battle is inconclusive, but the Indians find that their British allies offer no aid.

After Jay's Treaty in November 1794, the British withdraw from the Northwest, and the Indians are forced to treat with the United States at Fort Greenville (Indiana) in 1795.

NOVEMBER 11, 1794 Six Nations Treaties. A treaty is signed between the federal government and the Six Nations, confirming all previous treaties. Certain reservations are secured for the Indians forever, with the stipulation that the tribes are never to claim any lands in possession of the United States. Any offenses made against the Natives are to be reported to the government, and no retaliations are to be made by the Natives. The federal government is to pay the Six Nations in goods valued at $10,000 and an annual annuity of $4,500 forever.

NOVEMBER 19, 1794 Jay's Treaty. The Treaty of Amity, Commerce, and Navigation between Great Britain and the United States (Jay's Treaty) is signed. Most tribes do not yet recognize the new international border between the United States and Canada, nor do they see any reason to respect it. Tribes continue to conduct diplomacy with both the United States and Great Britain. The Jay's Treaty restores trade between the former British colonies and British North America (present-day Canada), but also guarantees Indians' freedom of movement between the two countries: "nor shall the Indians passing or repassing with their own proper goods and effects of whatever nature, pay for the same any impost or duty whatever. But goods in bales, or other large packages, unusual among Indians, shall not be considered as goods belonging bona fide to Indians." This provision is included in U.S. customs laws until 1897, and, in 1928, Congress enacts legislation exempting Canadian Indians from the provisions of U.S. immigration laws.

In late 1794, the British agree to withdraw from fur trade and military posts they occupy in U.S. territory. The posts have been important for maintaining contact between the British and their Indian allies in the United States. The terms of the treaty guarantee Indians free passage across the U.S.-British North American border. Deprived of fur trade contacts within the United States, British traders are encouraged to increase trade toward the northwest.

DECEMBER 2, 1794 Revolutionary War Compensation. Treaty between the federal government and the Oneida, Tuscarora, and Stockbridge Indians, the government agrees to compensate the tribes for property losses that occurred during the Revolutionary War, because they were the allies of the colonies. They are paid $5,000 for their losses, plus $1,000 for rebuilding a church that was burned by the British. They are also to get grist mills, sawmills, and millers to operate them. In return, the tribes are to forgo all other claims, except individual ones, against the central government. They are also to receive any form of education they need.

1795–1799

OCTOBER 27, 1795 Mississippi River Open to Anglo-American Trade. The Treaty of San Lorenzo is signed between the United States and Spain which opens up the Mississippi River to Anglo-American trade and also places the larger portion of the four major southern tribes (Creek, Cherokee, Chickasaw, and Choctaw) into the domain of the U.S. federal government.

APRIL 18, 1796 Trading Houses Act. The federal government experiments by establishing factories (a federal store or Indian trading house) among the Indians; 28 in all, run by government agents, under control of the president of the United States. They are primarily created to control trade with Indian people and to counteract the influence of French, Spanish, and British traders. The factories, which sell American supplies to Indians on credit, are to ensure a good price for furs and supply the

Indians with cheaper and better goods. The act expires and is renewed numerous times between 1796 and 1822. Trading houses were abolished by an act of May 6, 1822.

1797 California Indian Mission System. Mission San Fernando is founded. The mission sustains earthquake damage in 1812, is secularized in 1834, and the property is returned to the church in 1861.

1797 California Indian Mission System. Mission San Jose is founded. The mission experiences uprisings by Indian people in 1805, 1817, and 1826. In 1824 the Indian population of the mission is 1,806. The mission is secularized in 1834 and sold in 1846, and the property is returned to the church in 1858.

1797 California Indian Mission System. Mission San Juan Bautistais is founded. The mission is secularized in 1835, and a steeple is added in 1865.

1797 California Indian Mission System. Mission San Miguel is founded. In 1830 mission livestock total 12,400. In 1831 Indians are offered freedom. The property is sold in 1849, and the property is returned to the church in 1859.

1797 Mangas Coloradas, Mimbreno Apache Tribal Leader, Is Born. Coloradas is a member of the Mimbreno Apache, a tribe closely related to the Chiricahua Apache, and is a leader in the early years of the Apache Wars of the 1860s. In 1846, the United States takes possession of the New Mexico Territory, and Coloradas's enemy becomes the U.S. Army. In the 1850s, American miners begin pouring into the region. Coloradas is captured and whipped by a group of miners, then released as a message to other Indians to stay away. Coloradas, who is probably close to 60 years old at the time of the beating, survives and steps up his warring against U.S. and Mexican miners. In the early 1860s,

when the U.S. cavalry leaves the southwest region to fight in the Civil War, military protection of settlers and miners is taken on by governor of California, who dispatches troops to the region. In 1862, Coloradas and his Apache ally, Cochise, attack the California troops in southern Arizona at a place known as Apache Pass. Coloradas is wounded, but continues to press his attacks. As a result, in 1863, he is invited to a peace parley by U.S. military authorities. The parley is a ruse. Coloradas is murdered at Fort McLane, although U.S. authorities report that he is killed while trying to escape.

1799 Religious Revitalization and Handsome Lake. Handsome Lake, a Seneca clan leader, becomes ill and his family and friends gather to pay their respects before he dies. Not long after apparently dying, Handsome Lake recovers and tells everyone that his soul left his body and went outside, where he met three Native angels. The angels tell Handsome Lake that he is to end his drinking, live a good life, and follow the teachings of the Creator who would reveal himself in the months ahead. In the autumn of 1799 Handsome Lake has a second vision, in which he meets the Creator and learns lessons that become the hallmark of the revitalized Longhouse religion. Handsome Lake dies in 1815, but his teachings are kept by his many Iroquois followers. By the late 1830s the religion becomes the Handsome Lake Church. His visions and teachings are known as the *Gaiwiio*— the good word. He teaches that Native Americans should live in peace with the United States, but that they should spiritually and culturally be Iroquois. His doctrines stress peace within the family and among all people.

FEBRUARY 19, 1799 Appropriation Act. The Appropriation Act for Treaties with Indians is passed by Congress, appropriating a sum of not

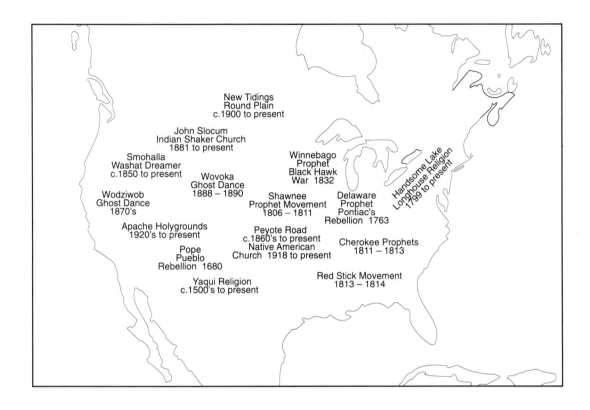

Native American revitalization movements. Courtesy of Duane Champagne.

more than $25,000 for expenses to negotiate treaties with Indian tribes.

MARCH 3, 1799 Trade and Intercourse Act. The Trade and Intercourse Act is passed, regulating trade and political relations with Indians until 1802. The act calls for a penalty to unlicensed persons dealing with Indians. The act also establishes boundaries in the area of Lake Erie, Tennessee, Alabama, and Florida.

AUTUMN 1799 Peigan Trading. The Peigan, Algonkian-speaking buffalo hunters residing just east of the Rocky Mountains in present-day Alberta, begin trading at North West Company and Hudson's Bay Company posts near the headwaters of the North Saskatchewan River. The Peigan prevent the Kootenay (Kutenai)—who are accustomed to using resources on either side of the Rocky Mountains, including the buffalo herds—from reaching the fur trade posts, and force them to stay west of the mountains.

$$Chapter\ 5$$

1800 TO 1849

1 8 0 0

c. 1800 Northwest Coast. The Russians introduce silver engraving to the Tlingit. Although little is known about early Indian uses of silver engraving, later in the century many Northwest Coast artists decorate jewelry and other objects.

JANUARY 18, 1800 Peace Preservation Act Passed. This act is aimed at the "preservation of peace with the Indian tribes" and is passed to prevent European settlers from inciting Indian tribes on the western frontier to attacks against the United States. Anyone convicted of acts that incited Indians to attack settlers could be fined $1,000 or $2,000. Anyone found guilty of alienating the loyalty of Indian people from the U.S. government could be imprisoned.

1 8 0 1

SUMMER 1801 Smallpox Epidemic. Many Atsina (Gros Ventre) on today's southern Canadian prairies die after contracting smallpox from their Arapaho relations south of the Missouri River. The same epidemic spreads via the Columbia Plateau in the United States to the Coast Salish of the Lower Fraser River Valley and Vancouver Island. The Coast Indians may have been exposed to smallpox in an earlier epidemic during the 1770s.

1 8 0 2

1802 Early Indian Map of Western Regions. Siksika headman Ak ko makki (Old Swan) draws a map for the Hudson's Bay Company employee, Peter Fidler, that shows the entire Missouri River drainage system from its headwaters to beyond the confluence of the Yellowstone and Missouri rivers. His drawings will become the source of the map used by U.S. explorers Meriwether Lewis and William Clark to explore the region between 1804 and 1806.

1802 Loisel's Second Trip to the Middle Missouri. In 1801, Regis Loisel, co-organizer with Clamorgan of the Missouri Fur Company, makes a trip up the Missouri, of which little is known. On a second trip, in 1802, he is accompanied by Pierre-Antone Tabeau, who leaves a narrative account of the journey. Tabeau's journal provides one of the first written histories of Indian people west of the Mississippi: "Some Yincton hunters whom I see every day and who knowing some French, traded more than a hundred beaver skins each when they hunted in the territory of the St. Peter's River, brought me fifteen skins this year after having scoured all the fall the east bank of the Missouri and having visited the sources of all the little rivers and streams emptying into it in a space of more than a hundred leagues. The assembled Sioux number at least 4,000 men bearing arms and with the exception of two weak tribes, who are tillers of the soil near the St. Peter's River, are all migratory. Spring and summer they follow the cow over the vast prairies that separate the St. Peter's River from the Missouri and, in the autumn they follow her still by approaching again with her the great rivers where each tribe fixes its winter encampment."

1802 Osceola, Seminole Tribal Leader, Is Born. Osceola is born near the Tallapoosa River along the border between present-day Georgia and Alabama. In the 1830s, he leads a resistance movement to prevent the relocation of his people from their homeland in Florida to Indian reservations west of the Mississippi in what is now Oklahoma. While still a teenager, Osceola fights in the First Seminole War of 1817–18. Seven years later he fights in a Second Seminole War for his people, this time in the role of leader. On December 18, 1835, Osceola leads a party that ambushes Wiley Thompson, an Indian agent working to gain Seminole compliance with the removal treaty of 1830. For the next two years, Osceola spearheads a relocation resistance movement. His capture in 1842 marks the official end of the Third Seminole War, although many Seminole continue to resist U.S. removal efforts by retreating to the isolated swamp regions of Florida. Osceola dies in 1842.

JANUARY 1, 1802 Peter Jones (Kahkewaquonaby, "Sacred Feathers") Is Born. Jones, who became a Mississauga chief, farmer, and Methodist missionary, is born of a non-Native father and a Mississauga (Ojibway) mother, and is raised among the Mississauga. In June 1823 he is converted to Methodist Christianity and devotes the rest of his life to missionary work among the Indians of Upper Canada. In 1826 he establishes the Credit Mission (Mississauga, Ontario), a village in which the Mississauga are encouraged to adopt a settled, agricultural way of life. He becomes chief of this band. Jones and some of his followers move to a new settlement (New Credit) donated by the Six Nations Reserve near Brantford, Ontario, in 1847.

Jones becomes renowned among Indians and non-Indians as a preacher and tours Upper Canada, the United States, and England to raise funds. Through Jones, a large proportion of the Mississauga become Methodist. He and his brother John translate portions of the Bible into Ojibway.

Jones firmly believes that Christianity is the only true religion, and that Indians ought to be completely assimilated into European civilization. Thus, he downplays his aboriginal roots, and opposes Sir Francis Bond Head's 1836 proposal to relocate all of Upper Canada's Indians to Manitoulin Island. Head's proposal stems from a belief that Indians cannot be assimilated into Upper Canadian society, a position which Jones, whose work plays a crucial role in the Mississauga adaptation to the new ways of life being introduced by non-Natives, rejects.

In his lifetime, Jones published an Ojibway spelling book, hymn book, and translations of Bible books. His *Life and Journals* (1860) and *History of the Ojibway Indians* (1861) were published after his death on June 29, 1856.

FEBRUARY 1802 Northern Fur Trade. The Atsina, who reside near fur trading posts at Chesterfield House near the confluence of the South Saskatchewan and Red Deer rivers, kill several Iroquois who are on their way to the Cypress Hills to trap beaver. Since the 1790s a number of Iroquois, most of them from Kanesataké (Caughnawaga, Oka), have come to the foothills of the Rockies where many have become important trappers.

MARCH 30, 1802 Trade and Intercourse Act. Congress passes the Trade and Intercourse

Act, regulating trade and activities with Indians and authorizing the president to impose measures preventing the vending or distribution of spirituous liquors among any Indian tribe. Made at the request of trading posts competing with the Spanish for Creek and Cherokee business, the act incorporates the first four temporary Trade and Intercourse Acts and restricts liquor consumption among tribes.

1 8 0 3

1803   Black Kettle, Southern Cheyenne Tribal Leader, Is Born. Black Kettle is a Cheyenne tribal peace leader whose band is attacked in the infamous Sand Creek Massacre during the Cheyenne and Arapaho War of 1864–65. Black Kettle is actively engaged as a warrior against the Ute and Delaware, who are enemies of his tribe. Black Kettle, however, advocates good relations with the Americans and ratifies a treaty maintaining peace in Colorado and along the Santa Fe Trail. After traveling to Washington, D.C., in 1863, he meets with President Abraham Lincoln. Black Kettle is killed on November 27, 1868, when Lt. Col. George Armstrong Custer and the Seventh Cavalry attack his encampment on the Washita River, in Indian Territory (Oklahoma). Black Kettle rides out with his wife in a blinding snowstorm hoping to prevent the attack by parleying with the soldiers. Both are shot dead on sight and their bodies trampled by the advancing columns, while the regimental band plays "Gerry Owen" as Custer and his men kill another hundred Cheyenne, mostly women and children.

1803   Indian Education. Congress appropriates $3,000 to civilize and educate the "heathens." By the terms of a treaty with the Kaskaskia Indians of present-day Illinois, the U.S. agrees to provide an annual contribution of $100 for seven years to pay for the services of a Roman Catholic priest who, among his other duties, will instruct the children in literature.

1803   Louisiana Purchase. Napoleon sells Louisiana to the United States for $15 million. With no constitutional authority to do so, President Thomas Jefferson concludes the deal in 1803, purchasing 800,000 square miles of land stretching from the Mississippi River to the Rocky Mountains, thereby paving the way for the American government to explore the new lands west of the Mississippi. The president immediately dispatches two U.S. Army officers, Meriwether Lewis and William Clark, on an expedition to explore the largely unknown lands. With the purchase of these western lands, President Jefferson proposes that many of the Indian nations living east of the Mississippi River be removed west to lands where they will be "out of the way" of U.S. settlers, and the eastern land will be open to settlement. The western lands contain large numbers of Indian nations, many of whom have yet to have extended political relations with a European or U.S. government.

MARCH 22, 1803   Nootka Attack. Members of a Yuquot Nootka (Nuu-chah-nulth) village led by Maquinna (c. 1786–1817) attack and kill all but two traders on the U.S. ship *Boston* at Nootka Sound on the west coast of Vancouver Island. The attack may be related to the fact that Europeans are increasingly trading with Indian groups that have inland connections because the valuable sea otter are largely depleted along the outer Pacific Coast where the Nootka reside. Indian attacks on fur traders in this region are rare.

1803–1806   Western Land Acquisition. President Thomas Jefferson directs the governor of Indiana Territory, William Henry Harrison, to acquire vast tracts west of the Greenville Treaty boundary. As Indian lands dwindle, the Shawnee warrior Tecumseh emerges as a powerful political force bent on forging an Indian union from the Great Lakes to the Gulf of Mexico.

1 8 0 4

1804   California Indian Mission System. Mission Santa Ines is founded. The mission suffers earthquake damage in 1812 and an Indian uprising in 1824. The mission is secularized in 1834, sold in 1846, and the property is returned to the church in 1862.

1804   Washakie (Gambler's Gourd), Flathead-Shoshoni Tribal Leader, Is Born. Washakie is born in Montana's Bitterroot Mountains. When his father dies, Washakie goes to live with his mother's eastern Shoshoni family in the Wind River mountain chain of Wyoming. He becomes the principal head of his band in the 1840s. The Shoshoni are known for their hospitable relations with the United States, and few Indians are as helpful to the westward passage of immigrants as Washakie, who provides regular patrols of his men to guard and assist travelers along that region of the Oregon Trail. During this time he becomes friends with Brigham Young and spends part of one winter at the Mormon leader's home. In honor of his help toward the U.S. military in 1876 and 1877, following the battle of the Rosebud, Camp Brown is renamed Fort Washakie. On a trip to Yellowstone Park in 1878, President Ulysses S. Grant gives him a silver saddle. In 1897, Washakie becomes a Christian and is baptized as an Episcopalian. He dies three years later.

SUMMER 1804   Fort Good Hope Established. Hudson's Bay Company traders establish Fort Good Hope on the Mackenzie River not far downstream from its confluence with the Great Bear River. The post attracts Hare, Eastern Kutchin (Gwich'in), and Mountain Dene. The Mountain Dene live on the eastern slopes of the Mackenzie Mountains west of the Mackenzie River. In 1823, Fort Good Hope is relocated to just south of the Arctic Circle at the request of Kutchin traders. It remains the northernmost trading establishment until 1840.

1804–1806   Lewis and Clark Explore the Missouri. On May 14, U.S. Army officers Meriwether Lewis and William Clark and their company of 28 soldiers, a half-Indian interpreter, and an African-American slave named York set off up the treacherous, sandbar-filled Missouri River in three boats. They arrive at the James River in southeastern South Dakota on August 27. They are charged by President Jefferson to explore and map this largely unknown realm and beyond, an expedition Jefferson has them preparing for even before the 1803 Louisiana Purchase. The winter of 1804–05 is spent in North Dakota with friendly Mandan Indians where they acquire a valuable addition to the party, a 16-year-old Lemhi (Shoshoni) Indian woman named Sacajawea, the pregnant wife of French-Canadian trapper Toussaint Charbonneau. Sacajawea proves invaluable when she guides the Lewis and Clark expedition up the Missouri River and through the Rocky Mountain passes of Montana and Wyoming to the land of the Shoshoni people from whom she had been taken at age 13. Sacajawea (*See* biography, c. 1784) interprets for the explorers, rescues their equipment when a canoe capsizes, and obtains horses from local Indians. The expedition is gone four months and ten days, and covers 7,689 miles of uncharted land. Their topographical sketches show how people can reach the Pacific Ocean, and their report of the rich beaver supply in the rivers sets off a rush of trappers heading westward. Their encounters are generally peaceful, although they have a hostile encounter with the Peigan in July 1806. Following the return of Lewis and Clark, U.S. trappers move into the upper Missouri drainage.

1 8 0 5

1805   The Munsee Prophetess. In the early 1800s U.S. officials in Indiana pressure leaders

Shoshoni arriving at camp for at meeting at the Green River, 1837. Courtesy of the Walters Art Gallery, Baltimore.

of the Delaware, Shawnee, and other Old Northwest Indian nations into selling significant tracts of land, resulting in considerable tension and dismay among most members of the Indian nations. Between 1803 and 1805, while the Delaware and Munsee are living in the present-day areas of Indianapolis and Muncie, several Delaware have visions. But in 1805, a female, now known only as the Munsee Prophetess, has a vision and consequently introduces modifications to the Delaware Big House Religion, the Delaware national religion since the Delaware

Prophet of the 1760s. The Munsee Prophetess teaches that the Indians must retain their traditions and reject farming, Christianity, trade, and European clothing, otherwise the Delaware Nation will continue to decline politically, economically, and spiritually. When Tenskwatawa (*See* biography, 1778), the Shawnee Prophet who lives in the Delaware and Munsee villages, emerges in February 1806, the prophetess defers to him. The brother of Shawnee chief Tecumseh, Tenskwatawa preaches a return to the Indian religion and way of life and denounces the European customs, dress, and use of alcohol.

1805   North West Company Posts Established. Northern Sekani and Kaska bands greet the establishment of North West Company posts in the Liard River drainage. The Liard River is a large river flowing eastward toward the Mackenzie River west of Great Slave Lake. The Kaska are Athapascan hunter-gatherers of the plateau region surrounding the upper Liard River drainage.

1805–1807   Sekani and Carrier Begin Direct Trade with Euro-Americans. Sekani and Carrier bands occupying plateau areas in present-day central British Columbia begin direct trade with Euro-American fur traders when the North West Company establishes posts west of the Rocky Mountains (New Caledonia) for the first time. These Indians also retain access to European goods via Gitskan middlemen. A site at Bear Lake, near the headwaters of the Skeena River, is an important Gitskan, Carrier, and Sekani trading center. These facts, and the increasingly hostile relations with the Beaver and Cree, induce the Sekani to avoid the eastern slopes of the Rocky Mountains, which they are accustomed to visiting for part of each year. Kootenay House, established near the headwaters of the Kootenay River just west of the Rocky Mountains in 1807, provides the Kootenay (Kutenai) with their first secure access to European goods. By 1805 the North West Company has established posts throughout much of the forested area east of the Continental Divide. Nearby bands serve as provisioners at these fur trade posts.

1 8 0 6

1806   Office of Superintendent of Indian Trade. The Office of Superintendent of Indian Trade is established. The duties of this newly created bureau include the purchase and charge of all goods intended for trade with the Indian nations.

1806   Stand Watie, Cherokee Tribal Leader, Is Born. Stand Watie is born near present-day Rome, Georgia. He receives his education in mission schools, and then returns to his homeland to work with his brother, Elias Boudinot, on the *Cherokee Phoenix* newspaper. During this time Stand Watie becomes a pro-removal supporter and embraces the Treaty of New Echota in 1835, which forces the Cherokee to leave their homeland in western Georgia, eastern Tennessee, western Carolina, and eastern Alabama. From 1845 to 1861, Stand Watie builds and maintains a successful plantation in Indian Territory (Oklahoma), using Black slave labor, and serves on the Cherokee Council, including stints as speaker of the lower Cherokee legislative house. He joins the Confederate forces during the Civil War in 1861 and organizes a cavalry regiment. He is commissioned a colonel in the First Cherokee Mounted Rifles in October 1861 and plays major roles in several battles. In the 1862 battle of Pea Ridge, Arkansas, Stand Watie's troops capture Union artillery positions that have been a major obstacle to Confederate strategy. In 1865, Stand Watie surrenders to Union forces, the last general in the Confederate Army to do so. After the war, he acts in his new capacity as principal chief of the southern Cherokee, rebuilding tribal assets during Reconstruction. Stand Watie dies in 1871.

JULY 1806   Siksika and Cree Warfare. The death of 28 Siksika at the hands of a band of Cree foreshadows the almost continuously hostile relations between the Cree and the Siksika, Kainai (Blood) and Peigan, Atsina, and Sarcee that will follow. Mostly friendly relations start to deteriorate in the 1790s with the increase of Cree and Assiniboine raids on Blackfoot Confederacy and Atsina horse herds.

1806–1809   Tecumseh and Tenskwatawa Try to Halt Expansion. The brothers (*See* biography, 1768 and 1778) attempt to unite Indian people from numerous tribes in an effort to halt westward expansion of U.S. settlers and further loss of Indian land. In February 1806, while living among the Delaware and Munsee, Tenskwatawa reportedly dies. While his family prepares him for burial, he regains consciousness, saying that he has died and visited the Master of Life. Tenskwatawa reports that through him, "The Open Door," Native Americans can learn "The Way." Thousands of Indians gravitate toward Tenskwatawa and his teachings, flocking to hear him preach in a village called Prophetstown. So many Native peoples come to the village that resources are depleted, and the prophet is forced to move his town west, settling near the junction of the Tippecanoe and Wabash Rivers in eastern Indiana. Through his religious revitalization movement, Tenskwatawa unites many tribes to stand against the United States.

Using his brother's spiritual movement, Tecumseh forges a pan-Indian confederacy that is both political and military. Tecumseh, Tenskwatawa, and their followers reject the Treaty of Fort Wayne (1809), in which some Indian leaders cede 3 million acres to the United States. At the treaty council, Tecumseh tells Governor William Henry Harrison (the future U.S. president) that he rejects any agreement with the United States "on the ground that all the land belonged to all the Indians, and that not even the whole membership of a single tribe could alienate the property of the race."

1 8 0 8

1808 Canadian Timber Industry. A dramatic increase in British demand for wood brings a rapid expansion of the Canadian timber industry particularly in New Brunswick and in the Ottawa River Valley. Some Indians find seasonal employment, however the practice of transporting logs by river results in drastic reduction of fishstocks, which are important to Native inhabitants.

APRIL 6, 1808 *The Indian Princess* Produced. *The Indian Princess*, an operatic melodrama, is the original play about an Indian, written by James Nelson Barber, and produced on April 6 at the Chestnut Theatre in Philadelphia.

MAY 28–JULY 2, 1808 Salish Trade with North West Company. Shuswap, Lillooet, and Thompson (Ntlakapamux), all Interior Salish groups residing along the Fraser River, meet and trade with Simon Fraser of the North West Company. Suspicious Cowichan (Coast Salish) near the mouth of the river prevent Fraser's party from actually reaching the Pacific Coast.

1 8 0 9

1809 Ganado Mucho, Navajo-Hopi Tribal Leader, Is Born. Ganado Mucho is a young man when the Navajo carry out particularly vehement strikes on Mexican troops in the 1830s. From 1846–49, five expeditions of U.S. troops attempt to subdue the marauding Navajo. Because of his large herds of cattle Ganado Mucho is accused of cattle theft, but he successfully denies the charges. In 1858, Ganado Mucho signs an agreement with other peaceful Navajo ranchers to report any thefts of livestock and to return any livestock found. Mucho becomes the head of his local band, but possesses no authority outside his own group. Despite the ratification of a peace treaty between some Navajo bands and the U.S., other Navajo bands continue their raids and clashes with U.S. Army troops. Col. Kit Carson leads U.S. forces through the heart of Navajo county in 1863–66. During the war, Mucho loses two daughters and a son to raids by the Ute and Mexicans. His band surrenders, and he leads them along with others on the brutal "long walk" from Fort Defiance in Arizona to Fort Sumner at Bosque Redondo in New Mexico. The Navajo are held as prisoners until a peace treaty is signed by Ganado Mucho and others in 1868. Until his death at age 84, Mucho lives on the Navajo Reservation.

1809 Treaty of Fort Wayne. Approximately 3 million acres of choice land along the Wabash River are given up for $8,200 by the Delaware, Potawatomi, Miami, Kickapoo, and Eel River tribes. A portion of the land had belonged to the Shawnee, and Shawnee chief Tecumseh declared the transaction to be illegal, stating: ". . . this land that was sold, and the goods that was given for it, was only done by a few. . . . Sell a country! Why not sell the air, the great sea, as well as the earth? Did not the Great Spirit make them all for the use of his children?"

1 8 1 0

1810 Billy Bowlegs, Seminole Tribal Leader, Is Born. Billy Bowlegs is the leader of the last group of Seminole Indians to remain in Florida against the will of the U.S. government. During the Seminole War of 1835–42, following the death of Seminole leader Osceola and the surrender of other leaders, Bowlegs leads 200 Seminole warriors in an attack on a government trading post that has been opened on Seminole land, killing most of the garrison. Following the attack, Bowlegs and his band live in the Florida Everglades for almost a year, hiding during the day and raiding during the night. Bowlegs and members of his band agree to emigrate to Indian Territory in 1858. Bowlegs fights for the North in the Civil War in 1861 and dies in 1864.

1810 Buffalo Hump, Comanche Tribal Leader, Is Born. Buffalo Hump proves himself as a war chief of the Comanche in his many raids into Texas and Mexico for horses and slaves. He becomes principal chief of the Penateka Band of Comanche in 1849, following the cholera epidemic that sweeps through the southern Plains. In October 1865, Buffalo Hump,

with chiefs from other southern Plains tribes, attends a treaty council with U.S. commissioners along the Little Arkansas River in present-day Kansas. As a result of the treaty, the Comanche, Kiowa, Kiowa-Apache, Southern Cheyenne, and Southern Arapaho are forced to relinquish claims to territory north of the Arkansas River. Buffalo Hump dies in 1870 and his son, also named Buffalo Hump, carries on the fighting under the new Comanche chief Quanah Parker.

1810 Dull Knife, Northern Cheyenne Tribal Leader, Is Born. Dull Knife and his warriors are active in the Cheyenne-Arapaho War in Colorado in 1864–65 and the Sioux Wars for the Northern Plains in 1866–67 (including the Fetterman Fight), and also join the Sioux under Sitting Bull and Crazy Horse in the War for the Black Hills of 1876–77. Dull Knife and Little Wolf, another Cheyenne war chief, successfully avoid capture, even during the massive government retaliation following the Little Bighorn defeat of 1876. In May 1877, Dull Knife and his followers surrender at Fort Robinson following an attack at Dull Knife's camp at the Powder River in Wyoming; the Indians suffer 25 deaths; 173 tipis are destroyed, along with food and clothing; and 500 ponies are captured. Dull Knife dies in 1883, shortly before the Northern Cheyenne are officially granted the Tongue River Reservation in Montana as their home.

1810 Little Crow, Santee Sioux Tribal Leader, Is Born. Little Crow is a Santee Sioux and son of a chief of the Kaposia Band of Mdewakanton Santee, who live in western Minnesota. In 1851 Little Crow signs the Treaty of Mendota that transfers much of the Santee land to the United States in exchange for a reservation on the upper Minnesota River, plus annuities in an annual payment. In 1858, Little Crow is part of a Sioux delegation that travels to Washington, D.C., for further negotiations with the U.S. government. His participation in the signing of the Treaty of Mendota angers many members of his tribe, and he is not nominated as a tribal representative to the general council. In August 1862 Little Crow joins in the Santee Sioux uprising against settlers of Minnesota when the government annuity, guaranteed by the treaty of 1851, is delayed. The Santee open their war with raids on trading posts and settlements. Little Crow leads an assault on Fort Ridgely where he loses a large number of warriors before calling off the siege. After a protracted battle at Birch Coulee, 13 miles from Fort Ridgely, many of the surviving Santee withdraw to Dakota Territory or Canada. Little Crow dies in July 1863 on a horse-raiding expedition out of Canada into Minnesota.

1810   Satank (Sitting Bear), Kiowa Tribal Leader, Is Born. Satank is born in the Black Hills and becomes a prominent war chief among the Kiowa and a leader among the Principal Dogs military society. Satank is instrumental in establishing peace between the Kiowa and Cheyenne, thus producing a formidable fighting force against the U.S. settlers on Indian lands in the southern Plains. Though respected by his tribe, his vengeful personality breeds fear among even his own people. In 1867 Satank is one of the principal spokesmen for the Kiowa at the Medicine Lodge Council. This council is called by advocates of President Ulysses S. Grant's peace policy and cites the Sand Creek massacre as an example of heavy-handed military tactics. The resulting Medicine Lodge Treaty of 1867 assigns the Kiowa to a combined reservation (with the Arapaho) in Indian Territory (Oklahoma). In May 1871, Satank joins Satanta and Kicking Bird, two other Kiowa leaders, in an attack on an army wagon train traveling along the Butterfield Southern Stage Route in Young County, Texas. In the ensuing battle, the Kiowa kill eight of the twelve defenders, rout the rest, and plunder the wagons. Satank is arrested and then killed in an attempted escape from army guards while en route to trial at Fort Richardson, Texas. Satank is buried in the Fort Sill military cemetery.

1 8 1 1

SUMMER 1811   Salish Trade with North West Company. Okanagan and other Interior Salish groups in the Plateau region along the Columbia River system meet and trade with the North West Company representative, David Thompson. Several groups in the region are eager to have a more secure supply of European weapons in order to better defend themselves when they go to the western plains for occasional buffalo hunts. The Peigan have been making such hunting trips dangerous for several decades.

NOVEMBER 7, 1811   Battle of Tippecanoe. With a Creek medicine man named Seekaboo, Tecumseh travels to the southern Indian nations seeking support for his confederacy. On November 7, taking advantage of Tecumseh's absence, William Henry Harrison and his force of 1,000 men engage Tenskwatawa and his warriors in battle two miles from Tippecanoe. Tenskwatawa encourages his warriors by telling them they will go into battle protected by a magical fog and that the Great Spirit is urging them to fight. While losses on both sides are heavy, the Indians withdraw from the battle. The most significant casualty is Tenskwatawa's credibility as a seer and a prophet. Many among the Delaware, Miami, and Shawnee desert the Prophet's movement and the defeat severely damages Tecumseh's hopes of holding back the westward flood of U.S. settlers.

1 8 1 2

1812   California Indian Mission System. Approximately 50 Indians are killed at the San Juan Capistrano mission in California when an earthquake destroys the church while they are attending mass.

1812   Cochise, Chiricahua Apache Tribal Leader, Is Born. In 1861 Cochise is falsely accused of abducting a rancher's child and is imprisoned

Comanche feats of horsemanship. Courtesy of the National Museum of American Art, Washington D.C./Art Resource NY.

by an American lieutenant. Cochise escapes, but in the ensuing years, from 1863 to 1872, he leads a series of conflicts known as the Apache Wars. From his stronghold in the Dragoon Mountains (located in southern Arizona), Cochise and his ally, Mangas Coloradas, lead an effective guerrilla campaign against U.S. and Mexican forces. In 1871, Cochise repudiates efforts to relocate his people to a reservation in New Mexico. In 1872, he agrees to abstain from attacks in exchange for reservation land in eastern Arizona. Peace comes to the region for the few short years prior to Cochise's death in 1874.

1812 Fort Ross. The Russians establish Fort Ross (Rus) at Mad Shiu-miu in Pomo Indian country on the California coast about 100 miles north of San Francisco. Among the Russian fur traders and settlers are 85 Aleuts, brought from their native Alaskan areas. The new colonists make efforts to befriend the Kashaya Pomo and Hukueko Indians.

1812 Spanish Florida. A unit of the Georgia militia invades Seminole Indian land in Spanish Florida but is nearly annihilated. In 1813

Tennessee volunteers raid and burn their way through Seminole villages in northern Florida for three weeks. Alleged slave raiding and cattle rustling by the Seminoles are cited as provocations for the raids.

JUNE 19, 1812 The War of 1812. The United States declares war on Great Britain, ostensibly over the British policy of waylaying American ships in international waters and seizing sailors deemed to be British subjects, for forced service in His Majesty's Navy. The declaration of war comes three days after the British government has agreed to suspend the objectionable practice. On August 12, Tecumseh crosses the Detroit River with 24 warriors and three days later ambushes 150 Ohio militiamen sent to escort a supply train. Gen. William Hull, a hero of the Revolutionary War and now governor of Michigan Territory, sends 600 more men to escort the pack train. The party is ambushed a second time and Hull withdraws to Fort Detroit.

The War of 1812 devastates the land and populations of the Indians of the Old Northwest. At the Treaty of Ghent, which ends the war, the British agree that all the territory south of the Great Lakes belongs to the United States, and that they agree not to give aid to Indian allies there. This leaves the Indian nations living east of the Mississippi River entirely within the sphere of the U.S. government's influence. The Indians no longer have the supplies or alliance of a rival European power to balance against the United States. By 1819, the Spanish sell Florida and West Florida to the United States, and U.S. claims to the land east of the Mississippi River are undisputed, except by the Indian nations still living there. After 1817 to 1819, however, the political and diplomatic position of the Indian nations rapidly deteriorates, and they have less ability to retain territory and political independence.

AUGUST 1812   Red River Colony Established. The Hudson's Bay Company (H.B.C.) establishes the Red River Colony (Selkirk Settlement) near today's Winnipeg, Manitoba. Many H.B.C. employees see the settlement as a place to which they can retire with their Indian and mixed-blood wives and children. Most North West Company employees, and their Métis employees and allies, see the establishment of the colony as a threat to their livelihood. Still, Métis do provide essential pemmican (dried meat) to the colony in these early years.

WINTER 1812   Indian Attack on Fort Nelson. An Indian attack at Fort Nelson, in today's northern British Columbia, prompts the North West Company to withdraw from posts in the Liard River basin.

1 8 1 3

OCTOBER 5, 1813   Death of Tecumseh. Shawnee tribal leader Tecumseh *(See biography, 1768)* dies in a battle with U.S. forces. An important leader among Britain's Indian allies in battles with the United States, Tecumseh worked to forge a pan-Indian alliance against U.S. expansion. Many Indian groups (among

them Wyandot, Iroquois, and Ottawa) have allied with Britain in the War of 1812 in the hope that the British will work to establish an Indian buffer state between the U.S. and British Territory.

1813–1814   The Red Stick War. During the War of 1812, the Creeks fight their own civil war, principally between villages strongly allied to the United States (the White Sticks) and the Creek villages that are opposed to U. S. meddling in Creek political, cultural and economic life (the Red Sticks). Angry over U.S. interference and control within the Creek government and influenced by Tecumseh's message of resistance to the United States, Red Sticks attack Creek villages allied with the United States. On August 30, the Red Sticks also attack Fort Mims, killing most of the U.S. citizens there and bringing the United States into the Creek civil war. Gen. Andrew Jackson, with 5,000 troops and a number of Indian scouts, marches against the Red Sticks at the village of Tohopeka at Horseshoe Bend on the Tallapoosa River in March 1814. Surrounded and assaulted by cannon, the Creek suffer losses of more than 800 men, women, and children. With Red Sticks' resistance at an end, the Creek Nation is forced to accept the 1814 Treaty of Ft. Jackson, which cedes 22 million acres of Creek land in Georgia and Alabama to the U.S. government.

1 8 1 4

1814   Treaty of Ghent. The Treaty of Ghent brings an end to the War of 1812, which in North America has largely been fought in Indian territory with tribes participating on both sides. Discussion of the future status of Indian tribes occupies British and American negotiators for nearly two months. The Americans insist that the tribes, as "subjects" of the United States, are no longer any concern of the king, while Great Britain accuses the United States of contemplating the removal and "extinction of those nations." The Americans argue that their practice of acquiring Indian land only by treaty demonstrates their "humane" policy, but British negotiators say this merely shows that the United States recognizes the tribes as sovereign nations. In the end, the British and Americans simply agree to restore the rights of the tribes on each side of the international border as they existed prior to the war. By backing down, Great Britain has accepted the Americans' contention that Indian tribes within the boundaries of the United States could make treaties and sell their land only to the United States (the principle of "preemption"). The end of the War of 1812 closes off future possibilities of alliances between European countries and Indian tribes.

JANUARY 8, 1814 The Pemmican Proclamation Issued. Worried by a shortage of food at the Red River Colony, Miles Macdonnell, governor of the colony, issues a proclamation banning the export of pemmican (dried meat) from the Red River Colony. The Pemmican Proclamation angers the North West Company and the Métis because the pemmican supply of the region is essential to their business and livelihood. The proclamation leads the Métis to harass settlers over the following two years.

1 8 1 5

1815 British Indian Allies. Britain's Indian allies are upset to learn that the Treaty of Ghent (December 24, 1814) ending the War of 1812 has no provisions for the establishment of an Indian territory between the United States and British territory. Some of these Indians have negotiated a separate peace with the United States in July 1814.

1815 Handsome Lake, Seneca Spiritual Leader, Dies. During his lifetime, Handsome Lake is the sachem of the Turtle Clan among the Seneca, the westernmost nation of the Iroquois Confederacy. The Iroquois Confederacy consists of 6 nations and 49 sachems, or chiefs, chosen from historically privileged families. Handsome Lake obtains his title sometime before 1799 and holds it until his death in 1815. As a young man, Handsome Lake participates in the forest wars of the period: the French and Indian War (1755–59), Pontiac's War (1763), and the American Revolutionary War (1775–83). By the late 1790s, the once powerful Iroquois have lost most of their territory and are relegated to small reserves in upstate New York. In 1799 Handsome Lake reports a series of visions and preaches the Gaiwiio or "Good Word" to the Iroquois. He quickly attracts many followers and teaches that the Iroquois must reorganize central aspects of their economic, social, and religious life. Under Handsome Lake's guidance, Iroquois communities adopt new moral codes, men take up agriculture and construct family farms, and many individuals adopt new religious ceremonies and beliefs. Handsome Lake's message combines elements of Quakerism, Catholicism, and traditional Iroquois beliefs. The new religion helps the Iroquois make the transition from a hunter society to a reservation agricultural community. In the 1830s, Handsome Lake's followers formalize his teachings into a church, known as the Handsome Lake Church. His teachings are still practiced today by many Iroquois.

1815 Pocatello, Shoshoni Tribal Leader, Is Born. Pocatello becomes headman of the northwestern band of the Shoshoni Indians in 1847. This band is blamed for much of the violence along the California Trail, Salt Lake Road, and Oregon Trail as westward expansion and the California gold rush brings more and more settlers onto traditional Shoshoni lands in the northwestern corner of present-day Utah. Pocatello is captured and imprisoned in 1859, but works to maintain a delicate neutrality among the different Indian bands, Mormons, miners, ranchers, and missionaries who come into the Idaho region. In 1863, he signs the Treaty of Box Elder. From 1867 to 1869, he travels and hunts with Washakie's Wild River Shoshoni. By 1872, Pocatello's band is forced to relocate to the Fort Hall Indian Reservation in Idaho when the Union Pacific and Central Pacific railroads connect and bring further U.S. settlement into the region. Pocatello lives on the Fort Hall Reservation until his death in 1884. The town of Pocatello, Idaho, is named after this Shoshoni leader.

1815   Smohalla, Wanapum Spiritual Leader, Is Born. Smohalla is a member of the Wanapum Indian tribe that lives along the upper Columbia River in present-day eastern Washington State. He leaves this area around 1850 after a dispute with a local chief. Smohalla travels for several years and, despite being influenced by Catholic missionaries, becomes a warrior. He is wounded and left for dead during an encounter with a Salish war party. When he returns to his homeland he claims to have visited the spirit world during his near-death ordeal. He brings a message that, to the Wanapum, has the ring of authenticity due to his death-and-resurrection experience. Smohalla's preaching is a combination of nativism, cultural purity, and resistance to the U.S. government and Christianity. His popularity comes at a time when the Indian population of the region is declining due to diseases and land losses to U.S. settlers. According to Smohalla, religious truths came to him in dreams, thus the name of his religion: "Dreamer Religion." Among Smohalla's teachings are the repudiation of U.S. culture, including alcohol and agricultural practices. Smohalla spreads his message throughout the region and has many converts, including Old Joseph, a former Christian. His teachings influence a number of later prophets who also preach a message of resistance and cultural identity. Smohalla dies in 1907.

SEPTEMBER 8, 1815   Treaty of Spring Wells Signed. In the Treaty of Spring Wells and in 19 other treaties concluded with Indian tribes of the Great Lakes and Ohio Valley between 1815 and 1825, the U.S. complies with its obligation under the Treaty of Ghent to restore the prewar rights and status of Indian tribes that fought on the British side in the War of 1812. Omitted from this restoration were the Red Stick segment of the Creek who had been were forced, in 1814, to give up approximately 22 million acres of land in Alabama and Georgia in the Treaty of Fort Jackson. The Treaty of Ghent requires the U.S. to sign a separate peace treaty with each of the Indian tribes allied with the British in the war.

1815–1830s   Indian Migrations. Many Indian groups from the North and East migrate into Texas to escape from the United States. In 1812, Chief Bowles leads the Cherokee to the same area and to the Trinity and Neches rivers. In 1815 Kickapoo settle on the Sabine and Angelina rivers. They are joined by the Shawnee and Delaware nations. Together they form a loose confederacy that prospers exceedingly well in alliance with the Mexicans. In the 1830s, however, Anglos in Texas begin trying to destroy them.

---

1 8 1 6

1816   Piapot (Payepot), Cree Tribal Leader, Is Born. Piapot is a respected leader and warrior during a time of conflict for the Cree. Piapot and his grandmother are captured by the Sioux and live among the Sioux people for 14 years until a Cree raiding party frees them. Following his rescue, Piapot becomes an important source of information for the Cree, because of his knowledge of the ways of the Sioux. Following his selection as chief of his community in Manitoba, he leads a number of successful raids against the Sioux and the Blackfoot. In 1870, he takes approximately 700 warriors into Blackfoot territory and destroys several lodges. The Blackfoot, with the assistance of their allies, the Peigan, counterattack and kill at least half of Piapot's warriors. Piapot is also known for his resistance to Canadian settlement of the western Plains, and, in 1874, he refuses to sign a treaty with Canadian authorities that would have resulted in his people moving to a reserve. He reluctantly signs the treaty a year later but continues to resist the containment that its terms impose. Piapot is eventually "deposed" as chief of the Cree by Canadian authorities, but, the Cree remain loyal to him until his death in 1908.

JUNE 19, 1816   Battle of Seven Oaks. A group of Métis led by North West Company employee, Cuthbert Grant *(See* biography, c. 1793) kill 21 Red River residents in the battle of Seven Oaks, near the Red River Colony. One Métis is killed. The skirmish results after the Métis are discovered trying to transport pemmican taken from the Hudson's Bay Company's Brandon House to North West Company traders at Lake Winnipeg. This event promotes the growing sense of nationhood among the Métis and is commemorated by Métis troubadour Pierre Falcon (1793–1876) in "La Chason de la Grenouillère" (The Ballad of Frog Plain).

I 8 I 7

1817   California Indian Mission System. Mission San Rafael is founded and granted mission status in 1823. In 1828 San Rafael has an Indian population of 1,140. The mission is secularized in 1834 and sold in 1846, and the property is returned to the church in 1855. The mission was originally an assistencia of San Francisco and became a health center and sanitarium for the neophytes.

MARCH 3, 1817   Punishment of Crimes and Offenses within Indian Boundaries Act. The Punishment of Crimes and Offenses within Indian Boundaries Act is passed by Congress. The act states that Indians and other persons committing crimes within the exclusive jurisdiction of the United States will be tried and punished accordingly. The act gives federal courts jurisdiction over Indians and non-Indians in Indian territory, specifically excluding crimes committed by one Indian against another.

JULY 18, 1817   Ojibway, Saulteaux, and Cree Land Cessions. Peguis, headman among the Saulteaux (Ojibway) at Red River, and other Saulteaux and Cree headmen, sign a land cession treaty with the Hudson's Bay Company. The treaty covers land along the Red and Assiniboine rivers used by the Red River colonists. The Saulteaux, recent migrants to the region, are promised annual payments in exchange for the land. This is the first land cession treaty made in the western interior of British North America. The Peguis band has been providing the Red River colonists with vital assistance since its establishment in 1812.

NOVEMBER 21, 1817   The First Seminole War Begins. In Florida, a U.S. attack on a the former British Fort Negro, called Fowltown by the Seminoles and home of the Seminole chief Neamathla, officially begins the war in November 21, 1817. U.S. forces directed by Gen. Andrew Jackson destroy Seminole villages and farms in northern Florida, leading to the cession of Florida to the United States by Spain. The Spanish-American treaty, ratified in 1821, notes among its requirements that: "The inhabitants of the territories which his Catholic Majesty cedes to the United States, as soon as may be consistent with the principles of the Federal Constitution, (will be) admitted to the enjoyment of all privileges, rights, and immunities of the citizens of the United States." Some defeated Red Stick Creek join the Seminole in Florida and continue resistance to the U.S. with the help of English trade companies.

1817–1819   Cherokee Migration. Several thousand Cherokee emigrate beyond the Mississippi into Arkansas, forming a Cherokee Nation West, because of continuing harassment from U.S. settlers. These early Cherokee migrants later become known as Old Settlers, since they were the first Cherokee to settle in Arkansas

Mounted warriors rout a party of Red River colonists at a shootout at Seven Oaks. The Métis victory, captured in song, did much to crystallize a Métis sense of nationhood on the northern plains. Courtesy of the National Archives of Canada.

and to migrate, in the late 1820s, to Indian Territory (Oklahoma).

1 8 1 8

1818   British Land Policy. The British government begins its practice of acquiring Indian lands in exchange for promises of annual payments rather than for lump-sum payments.

1818   California Indian Mission System. Governor Vicente de Sola of California reports that 64,000 Indians have been baptized but 41,000 of them have died. Heavy work conditions, strict rules, and disease take a heavy toll on California mission Indians.

1818   Josiah Francis (Hillis Hayo) Dies. During Francis's life he is a leader in the Creek War of 1813–14. In 1811, Francis travels with Tecumseh, helping him to spread his message of Indian confederation and unity and opposition to U.S. expansion to southeastern Indian nations. During the Creek War, Francis, with William Weatherford, another upper town Creek leader, leads the Red Sticks against U.S. and Indian forces headed by Gen. Andrew Jackson. In 1815 Francis travels to England in search of support for his struggle against the United States. In 1818, he is captured by U.S. forces at St. Marks, a trading post in northern Florida, after General Jackson lures him onto a gunboat flying a British flag. Jackson has Francis executed.

1818   Manuelito, Navajo Tribal Leader, Is Born. Manuelito is born in southeastern Utah. He becomes a powerful warrior in raids against the Mexicans, Hopi, and Zuni and rises to prominence within his band. Unlike the peaceful Navajo leader, Ganado Mucho, Manuelito carries out a number of attacks and maintains resistance against U.S. Army troops. Manuelito succeeds Zarcillas as the head of his band in the 1850s when the latter resigns over failure to control his warriors' reprisals against U.S. soldiers. Along with headmen of other bands, Manuelito travels to Washington, D.C., to petition for the return of the Navajo homelands taken during the Navajo War. Troops and Ute scouts and allies under Col. Kit Carson conduct a scorched-earth policy culminating in the relocation of all Navajo prisoners to Bosque Redondo near Fort Sumner in present-day eastern New Mexico. A peace treaty is ratified by both sides in 1868. Manuelito returns to serve as principal Navajo chief and chief of tribal police. He travels to Washington and meets President Ulysses S. Grant. Manuelito dies in 1894 at the age of 76.

OCTOBER 3, 1818 Delaware Treaty. In a treaty with the United States, the Delaware cede all of their land in Indiana for a promise of land west of the Mississippi, supplies, and an annuity.

OCTOBER 6, 1818 Miami and Chippewa Treaty. The Miami and the Chippewa sign treaties with the United States. The Miami cede land in Indiana and Ohio to the United States for a promise of annuity and supplies, while the Chippewa cede land for the promise of an annuity and the right to hunt and make sugar on the land they are giving up. The treaty proclamation is made on January 15, 1819. The Chippewa holdings are further reduced by treaties in 1820, 1821, 1825, 1827, 1837, 1854, 1855, and 1863.

OCTOBER 20, 1818 British, United States Land Boundaries. The boundary between British North America and the United States is set from the Atlantic Coast to the Rocky Mountains. Indian groups along this boundary line will learn to use the line to evade law enforcement officers on either side of the border.

1 8 1 9

1819–1823 Mackenzie River Valley Depopulation. Measles spreads from the northern interior of the United States to the Ojibway and from them throughout the Northwest as far as the Mackenzie River Valley. Many Indians are killed. Over the next decade various epidemics, starvation related to game deple-

tion, and population displacements severely depopulate the Indians of the Mackenzie River drainage system, from the Beaver to the Kutchin.

1 8 2 0

c. 1820 British Columbia. The carving of argillite, a black shale quarried in the Queen Charlotte Islands off the coast of British Columbia, commences among the Haida who inhabit these islands.

1820 Barboncito, Navajo Tribal Leader, Is Born. Barboncito is born at Canyon de Chelly in present-day Arizona. Barboncito becomes both a military and religious Navajo leader and in 1846 signs a treaty pledging friendship with the United States. In early 1962 he makes peace overtures toward the federal government. In return the military chooses a barren parcel of land located in eastern New Mexico, called Bosque Redondo, as a Navajo reservation. The relocation plan pushes Barboncito into open warfare with the United States. He is taken prisoner in 1864 and escapes in 1865. Barboncito surrenders in 1868 and signs a treaty that establishes the Navajo Reservation in New Mexico and Arizona. He dies in 1871.

1820 Guardianship of Indians. John C. Calhoun, the southern senator and states' rights fire brand, advocates the destruction of tribes and a "guardianship" status for Indians. The Office of Indian Affairs adopts this policy after the Civil War.

1820 Indian Removal. Jedidiah Morse, appointed by President Monroe to survey Indian removal problems and to furnish Secretary of War John Calhoun with a report, writes: "To remove these Indians from their homes . . . into a wilderness among strangers, possibly hostile, to live as their neighbors live, by hunting, a state to which they have not been lately accustomed, and which is incompatible with civilization, can hardly be reconciled with the professed object of civilizing them."

1820   Little Wolf, Northern Cheyenne Tribal Leader, Is Born. Little Wolf is a chief of the Cheyenne military society known as the Bowstring Soldiers and, along with Dull Knife, is a war leader of the Northern Cheyenne. Little Wolf establishes his reputation as a war chief in his battles against the Comanche and Kiowa. During the 1866–68 War for the Bozeman Trail, Little Wolf fights alongside the Sioux leaders Crazy Horse and Gall in an attempt to protect Sioux lands in Montana and Wyoming. In May 1868, Little Wolf is one of the signers of the Fort Laramie Treaty, which obligates the U.S. government to vacate the forts along the Bozeman Trail. Little Wolf is one of the most active war chiefs in the War for the Black Hills of 1876–77. He is shot seven times during the battle of Dull Knife (in present-day Wyoming) in November 1876 but survives the wounds. He surrenders to federal troops in March 1879. Little Wolf becomes an army scout for Gen. Nelson Miles and is allowed to remain in the Tongue River country of Montana. In 1880, he kills a fellow Cheyenne and loses his standing as a chief. In keeping with Cheyenne tradition, he goes into voluntary exile for ten years. Little Wolf dies in 1904.

1820   Lone Wolf (Guipago), Kiowa Tribal Leader, Is Born. During the 1860s and 1870s, Lone Wolf becomes one of his tribe's most respected band chiefs and warriors. He is one of the signers of the Medicine Lodge Treaty of 1867 and later fights a series of military campaigns against U.S. forces. During the first part of his life, Lone Wolfe negotiates with U.S. agents in a spirit of peace and hope for close, friendly ties. In 1863, he visits President Abraham Lincoln as part of a delegation of southern Plains Indian leadership. Although Lone Wolf travels to Washington, D.C., in 1872 to negotiate a peace settlement, the death of his son at the hands of federal soldiers in 1873 pushes

him into war. For the next two years, he and other tribal leaders of the southern Plains meet federal and state troops in a number of consequential engagements. Lone Wolf participates in the Red River War (1874–75) fighting alongside Quanah Parker, the Comanche leader. Lone Wolf is forced to surrender at Fort Sill in the Indian Territory in 1875 and along with Mamanti, a Kiowa spiritual leader, is sent to Fort Marion in Florida. Lone Wolf is allowed to return to his homeland in 1878 and dies one year later of malaria.

1820   Ouray, Ute Tribal Leader, Is Born. Ouray is born in what is now Taos, New Mexico, and becomes a leader of the Ute, a nomadic tribe living in present-day Colorado. As a young man, Ouray is revered as a cunning and dangerous warrior, but his career shifts as he comes to realize that United States settlement in his tribe's territory is inevitable. With the growth of the mining frontier in western Colorado, the Ute are forced by miners to cede more and more of their territory. In 1863, Ouray helps negotiate a treaty with the federal government at Conejos, Colorado, in which the Ute cede all lands east of the Continental Divide. In 1867, Ouray assists Kit Carson, a U.S. Army officer, in suppressing a Ute uprising. In 1868, he accompanies Carson to Washington, D.C., and acts as spokesman for seven bands of Ute. In the subsequent negotiations, the Ute retain 16 million acres of land. In 1872, Ouray and eight other Ute again visit Washington, D.C., and cede 4 million acres of Ute land for an annual payment of $15,000. For his services, Ouray receives an additional annuity of $1,000. Ouray travels to Washington, D.C., again in 1880, where he signs the treaty by which the White River Ute are to be relocated to the Unitah Reservation in Utah. Soon after his return from Washington, Ouray dies while on a trip to Ignacio, Colorado, where the Southern Ute Agency has been relocated.

AUGUST 1820   Anglican Mission Established. John West of the Anglican Church Missionary

Society (C.M.S.) establishes a mission to convert and "civilize" Natives near the Red River Colony two years after Joseph Norbert Provencher, the first Roman Catholic missionary to the colony, arrives. To this point the Hudson's Bay Company has resisted the idea of sending missionaries to the region, believing that missionaries will interfere with the fur trade, but pressure within Britain has led the company to alter this policy. The C.M.S. and the Roman Catholics become the dominant missionaries in the colony. The English-speaking mixed-blood (Country-born) of the colony gravitate toward the Anglican Church while the French-speaking Métis lean toward the Roman Catholics.

OCTOBER 18, 1820   Treaty at Doak's Stand. The boundaries of the Choctaw Nation are established by the Treaty at Doak's Stand, concluded between the U.S. government and the Choctaw Nation. This is the first treaty to refer to "civilizing" the Indians as its main purpose, and it anticipates both the "Indian removal" policy and the individual allotment of Indian lands. The treaty specifies that all Choctaw "who live by hunting and will not work" are to be moved west, and their lands sold by the president to finance a school fund. The U.S. Indian agent is to pay for organizing a corps of Indian police, and, "in order to promote industry and sobriety amongst all classes of the Red people," is empowered to confiscate liquor. Once the Choctaw have become "so civilized and enlightened as to be made citizens," the United States will subdivide their remaining lands into family farms, and will abolish the boundary line separating them from neighboring settlements. Thus the Choctaw territory is viewed, for the first time, as a temporary, federally administered enclave, rather than as a separate country.

In accordance with the treaty, the Choctaw ceded more than 5 million acres of land. The treaty states that the boundaries "shall remain without alteration." In 1830, however,

the Choctaw are forced to exchange this land for territory in Indian Territory (Oklahoma).

1820–1821   Chipewyan, Inuit, and Dogrib Warfare. A group of Yellowknife (Chipewyan) led by Akaitcho aid British Royal Navy Officer John Franklin in his attempts to explore the Arctic coast. Akaitcho and his band of Yellowknife are known as an aggressive group, often attacking their Inuit and Dogrib neighbors.

----

1 8 2 1

1821   Cherokee Syllabary. Sequoyah (*See* biography, 1770), a Cherokee who is without formal education or knowledge of English but who has seen materials written in English, finishes work on the Cherokee syllabary. Deciding that his language should have its own writing system, Sequoyah removes himself from the main village in order to work without interruption. Fellow tribesmen scorn his efforts at first; then their feelings change to fear. Believing that Sequoyah is involved with witchcraft, they burn his cabin and all of his records, studies, and investigations. Undaunted, he reconstructs his work, which is interrupted only by tribal requirements to travel and to serve in the Cherokee army. In the Cherokee syllabary, each symbol indicates a combination of consonant plus vowel. The new syllabary is studied by the Cherokee people until thousands learn to read within a few months. In 1824 and 1828 parts of the Bible are printed in Cherokee, and in 1828 a weekly newspaper, the *Cherokee Phoenix*, begins publishing in Cherokee and English. Sequoyah's syllabary serves the Cherokee people admirably for many decades and is the genesis of several Cherokee publications.

1821   Mexican Independence. Mexico declares its independence from Spain, and thereby ushers in a new set of overlords for the Indians in what is now parts of California, Arizona, and New Mexico. Spanish colonists do not take part in the Mexican struggle for independence from Spain. When it is learned that an independent government had been formed the previous year, Governor de Sola, after meeting with eight presidio officers and religious representatives, declares allegiance to the new Mexican government. The California province becomes a Mexican state and remains a military colony.

1821–1822 Inuit Assist William Perry Expedition. A group of Iglulik Inuit provide food and information regarding the Northwest Passage for members of William Perry's expedition, which is locked in the ice near the Melville Peninsula.

1821–1825 Seminole and Creek Land Cession. William McIntosh (*See* biography, 1775), the head warrior of Coweta—a major lower town Creek village, claiming to represent the Seminole and Creek, cedes 25 million acres. The Creek national council repudiates the cession.

1821–1840 Hudson's Bay Company and North West Company Merge. The Hudson's Bay Company (H.B.C.) and North West Company merge to form a reorganized Hudson's Bay Company. About half the H.B.C. employees, including many Métis, lose their jobs. Many departing employees settle in the Red River Colony, ensuring that a large majority of the colony's inhabitants would remain mixed-blood (either English-speaking Country-born or French-speaking Métis). As a result of the reduced level of competition and the depletion of resources, Indian groups throughout the subarctic forests find that they are less able to influence the terms of the fur trade. Red River's predominantly mixed-blood population evolves into the main labor pool for the H.B.C., and by 1850 supplies half of the company's work force. The Métis economy at Red River centers on small-scale farming, buffalo hunting, and seasonal employment in the fur trade where Métis

act as guides, interpreters, and boatmen. Their sense of separate identity is strengthened by their annual buffalo hunts, unique Métchif language derived from European and Indian languages, and by their own folklore, music, dances, and flag. They develop a unique two-wheeled cart (Red River Cart) to carry their possessions and provisions.

1 8 2 2

1822 Indian Trading Houses. Congress abolishes the system of Indian trading houses, often called factories. The goods on hand are sold at public auction. Private trading companies prefer that the government withdraw from trade with Indians.

1822 Red Cloud, Oglala Sioux Tribal Leader, Is Born. Red Cloud is born in present-day north-central Nebraska near the forks of the Platte River. He is a war chief and leader of the Oglala subdivision of the Teton Sioux. Red Cloud is raised by an Oglala headman, Smoke, his mother's uncle and quickly gains a reputation for bravery and cunning in raids against the Pawnee and Crow. When he is about 19, Red Cloud shoots his uncle's rival, the most powerful Oglala chief, Bull Bear, at Fort Laramie in eastern Wyoming. Because of his exploits, he is chosen to be leader of the Iteshicha (Bad Face) band over Man Afraid of His Horses, the hereditary leader. Red Cloud is the architect of a number of attacks against U.S. settlers and miners who are traveling the Bozeman and Oregon trails. The Sioux employ guerilla-like tactics to harry soldiers and would-be settlers. Battles such as the Fetterman Fight, the Wagon Box Fight, and the Hayfield Fight lead the army to evacuate the region in 1868 and then agree in the Treaty of Fort Laramie to relinquish the Bozeman Trail in exchange for the cessation of further Indian raids. In 1870, Red Cloud travels to Washington, D.C., to meet with President Ulysses S. Grant and then goes

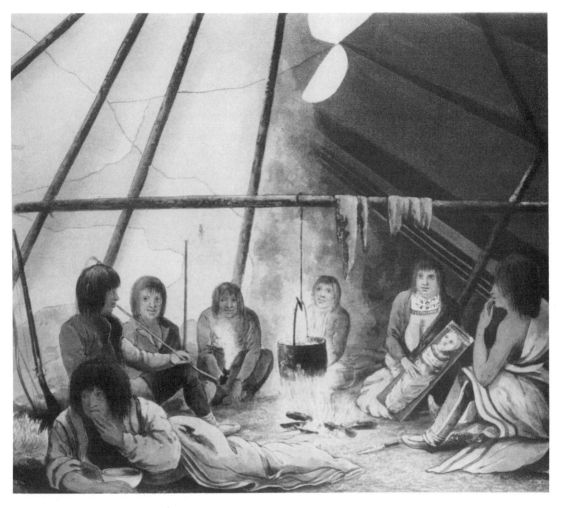

Interior of a Cree Tent, by Robert Hood, 1820. The painting shows a Creek party near the important fur trade post at Cumberland House. A number of the most sought-after trade items are evident in the tipi: a gun, a metal kettle, and tobacco. Courtesy of the National Archives of Canada.

on to New York City, where he gives a public speech. A Sioux agency bearing his name is established in southern South Dakota, but the name is changed to the Pine Ridge Reservation after government officials accuse him of secretly aiding the Sioux and Cheyenne bands that defeat Col. George Armstrong Custer at the Little Bighorn in June 1876. During his later years, Red Cloud loses his sight. He is baptized in the Catholic Church, and dies in his home on the Pine Ridge Reservation.

1822 United States Military Academy. David Moncock of the Creek tribe of the territory of Alabama is graduated from the U.S. Military Academy, after having been the first Indian to be admitted. He becomes a major and is killed in the Creek War of 1836.

JUNE 1822 Alexander Kennedy Isbister, Country-Born Fur Trader, Educator, and Lawyer, Is Born. Alexander Isbister is born at Cumberland House (Saskatchewan) of mixed Cree-

Scottish blood. He is schooled in the Orkney Islands, the home of his father, and at the Red River Colony. In 1837 he returns to North America to work for the Hudson's Bay Company. He works for the company at Fort Simpson on the Mackenzie River and at the Peel River post near the Mackenzie delta, but leaves the company in 1841 because he believes that he is being denied advancement due to racial prejudice. He returns to Britain and by 1851 he becomes headmaster of a school. He writes over 20 school textbooks in his career and becomes, in 1862, the editor of *Educational Times*.

Isbister also furthers his own education in Scotland. He attends Aberdeen University and Edinburgh University, emerging in 1858 with a graduate degree. After studying law he becomes a lawyer in 1866.

Although he remains abroad for the rest of his life, Isbister maintains his interest in the country of his birth. He represents the concerns of the Indians and mixed-blood and opposes the rule of the Hudson's Bay Company before the British government in London. Testifying in 1857 during a parliamentary inquiry regarding the Hudson's Bay Company lands, he recommends that the region be annexed by Canada. At his death on May 28, 1883, he wills his library to the newly established University of Manitoba.

1 8 2 3

1823   California Indian Mission System. Mission San Francisco, the last of the California missions, is founded. The mission is attacked by Indians in 1826. The mission is secularized in 1834, the church is razed in 1838, a new chapel built in 1841, and the mission is sold by the church in 1880.

1823   Looking Glass, Nez Percé Leader, Is Born. Looking Glass is the son of Apash Wyakaikt, who is also called Looking Glass because of the small trade mirror he wears as a pendant. The pendant is passed on to Looking Glass the younger. Looking Glass the elder participates with Old Joseph in the Walla Walla Council of 1855 as one of the chiefs who refuses to sign the treaty proposed by Gov. Isaac Stevens of Washington Territory. Looking Glass the younger, leader of the Asotian Band of the Nez Percé, refuses to sign a second treaty in 1863 that would further reduce the tribe's land. He hopes to avoid war with the United States, but he turns militant on July 1, 1877, when a combined force of army regulars and volunteer militia attack his camp near the forks of the Clearwater Creek in present-day Idaho. Looking Glass's band joins with the band of Nez Percé leader Joseph, who was attacked on June 17. United, they fight Gen. Oliver Howard at the battle of the Clearwater on July 11, 1877. Following the battle of Clearwater, the majority of the Nez Percé choose to head east through the Bitterroot Mountains to seek a military alliance with the Crow. Looking Glass is given overall command of the journey and decides to lead his band northward through Montana Territory to Canada. They now plan to seek the assistance of Sitting Bull, the famous Sioux leader, who escaped across the border earlier the same year. During the next two weeks, the trail-weary and battle-weary Nez Percé outmaneuver and outfight the army while they wind their way through the Montana wilderness toward the Canadian border. Finally, army troops led by Col. Nelson Miles catch up to Looking Glass and the Nez Percé near the Bear Paw Mountains, where they lay siege to the Indian camp. Looking Glass, who refuses to surrender, is struck by a stray bullet and killed.

1823   Office of Indian Affairs. The Office of Indian Affairs is created within the War Department. The office is created without Congressional authorization, although, it is formally recognized by Congress in 1831. Thomas L. McKenney is appointed to head the office.

1823 *Poor Sarah.* This fictional account of an Indian girl's religious conversion is considered the first work of American Indian fiction. *Poor Sarah* is written by Elias Boudinot, a Cherokee who becomes editor of the *Cherokee Phoenix* in the late 1820s and is assassinated over political issues in 1839.

FEBRUARY 28, 1823 *Johnson v. M'Intosh.* In *Johnson v. M'Intosh,* a case before the U.S. Supreme Court, Chief Justice John Marshall recognizes that Indian tribes have the right to land by their prior use, but rules that Indians have no power to grant lands to anyone other than the federal government. Marshall stresses a theory of Indian subservience to the federal government. He reasons that conquest gives the U.S. government ownership and title to Indian lands subject to the continued right of Indian occupancy and use. This case creates a landlord-tenant relationship between the government and the Indian tribes and is the first instance in which a judicially recognized federal responsibility over Indian affairs is articulated. Marshall's decision curtails Indian control over the use and sale of their own territory.

The case actually involves a dispute between two claimants: one has obtained a deed from the Piankashaw Nation, while the other has obtained a patent from the United States after the Piankashaw ceded the area by treaty. Chief Justice Marshall bases the Court's decision on the traditional understanding, among European nations, that the discoverer of a territory has the exclusive right to purchase it from the Native inhabitants (preemption). "However extravagant the pretension of converting the discovery of an inhabited country into conquest may appear," Marshall argues, it has become "indispensable" to the system of laws and government adopted by the United States. Since it limits tribes' ability to sell land to whomever they wish, their "rights to complete sovereignty are necessarily diminished." Marshall carefully adds, however, that the United States has "in no instance, entirely disregarded"

tribal sovereignty, and has left tribes free to manage their internal affairs among themselves.

OCTOBER 1823 **Dogrib Attack Yellowknife.** A Dogrib band attacks Akaitcho's Yellowknife near Great Bear Lake. The attack leads the Yellowknife to withdraw from the vicinity of the caribou herds in that region, and many starve. In the following years the Yellowknife will be absorbed into neighboring Chipewyan bands. Over the next several decades the Dogrib, Hare, and Slave from the vicinity of Great Bear Lake begin to forge a separate identity as the Sahtu Dene (Bear Lake People). The Sahtu Dene commonly use one fine fishing site on the Keith Arm of Great Bear Lake, which remains ice free almost constantly, and trade at nearby H.B.C.'s Fort Franklin (established in 1825), both of which help foster a sense of common identity and frequent contact among the bands.

1 8 2 4

1824 **Captivity Narratives.** *The Life of Mary Jemison,* one of many Indian captivity stories, is published in the United States. The account, as told to author James E. Seaver, is of Jemison's life among the Seneca for nearly 70 years and covers her marriage to two Seneca husbands.

1824 **Mexican Constitution.** The Mexican Constitution of 1824 guarantees equality of citizenship to all under Mexican jurisdiction. This ostensibly includes California Indian people.

1 8 2 5

c. 1825 **Big Bear (Mistahimaskwa), Ojibway-Cree Chief, Is Born.** Big Bear is born in a Plains Cree encampment near Fort Carlton on the North Saskatchewan River. By the 1870s, he is the head man of the largest Plains Cree band, consisting of about 2,000 members. His exploits, however, extend his influence beyond his own band, to all the Cree. During the 1870s he advocates a strategy of nonviolence, while working to reconcile differences among Plains Indian groups. Convinced that acceptance of a treaty and movement to reserves will destroy his people, he seeks a pan-Indian alliance to present a united front to the Canadian government. While the Canadian government negotiates treaties with most Plains groups by 1877, Big Bear steadfastly resists until he is forced by threat of starvation to sign Treaty 6 in December 1882. By that time the buffalo have disappeared from the Cypress Hills region, and the Canadian government is in a position to force the band to accept the treaty by refusing to bring food aid to that region. Even after signing, however, Big Bear continues his attempts to unite the Plains Cree and to force the Canadian government to renegotiate. He encourages various bands to ask the Canadian government to grant them adjoining reserves in the region surrounding the Cypress Hills. In the summer of 1884 he meets with other Plains leaders such as Poundmaker (Pitikwahanapiwiyin) and Little Pine (Minahikosis) at Thirst Dances, major Plains Indian religious, social, and political ceremonies. By this time, however, aging advocates of nonviolence like Big Bear are losing their influence while younger, more militant leaders such as Little Bad Man (Ayimisis) and Wandering Spirit (Kapapamahchakwew) attract a larger following. By April 1885 Big Bear is unable to prevent his own band from participating in attacks associated with the North-West Rebellion of 1885. Following the defeat of the Indian rebels at the hands of Canadian forces, Big Bear surrenders in July. He is convicted of inciting the attacks and sentenced to three years in prison but is released from Stony Mountain Penitentiary on March 4, 1885, a sick and broken man. He dies on the Poundmaker Reserve on January 17, 1888.

1825   Alexis de Toqueville. After visiting the United States, Alexis de Toqueville, French

nobleman and political scientist, writes, "They kindly take the Indian by the hand and lead them to a grave far from the lands of their fathers." According to de Toqueville, this is "accomplished with felicity, tranquility, legality, philanthropy and all without the shedding of blood. It is impossible to destroy mankind with more respect for the laws of humanity." De Toqueville predicts the Indian will be undisturbed in his new home for virtually no time at all, and that exposed to the "most grasping nation on the globe" would be driven from one "final" location to another "until their only refuge is the grave."

1825   Cherokee Census. A census taken among the Cherokee tribe in Georgia reveals that the Cherokee possess 33 grist mills, 13 sawmills, 1 power mill, 69 blacksmith shops, 2 tab yards, 762 looms, 2,486 spinning wheels, 172 wagons, 2,923 plows, 7,683 horses, 22,537 black cattle, 46,732 swine, and 2,566 sheep. The adoption of U.S. lifestyles makes them less, rather than more, acceptable to the U.S. settlers establishing themselves on Cherokee land. U.S. settlers petition the federal government to remove all Cherokee west of the Mississippi River.

1825   Hole-In-The-Day, Chippewa (Ojibway), Is Born. Hole-In-The-Day is born and lives near the mouth of the Mississippi River in what is now Minnesota. In 1846, Hole-In-The-Day becomes chief among the Chippewa and continues the efforts of his father (who had the same name) to prevent encroachment by Sioux living west of the Mississippi. Hole-In-The-Day negotiates a number of important treaties and agreements with the U.S. government, and his relations with the U.S. government jeopardize his standing among his own people, including tribal leaders who think he is using his influence in Washington for personal aggrandizement. In 1862, the U.S. government accuses him of planning an uprising among the Chippewa. This accusation is fueled by general unrest among Indians, such as the 1862 Sioux uprising in western Minnesota, and U.S. officials are fearful that more Indian nations will join in the hostilities. Beginning in 1864, Hole-In-The Day signs a series of treaties that cede large amounts of Chippewa land in Minnesota. Consequently, by 1868, most of Hole-In-The-Day's band are settled on the White Earth Reservation, a small plot of land in western Minnesota. In the same year Hole-In-The-Day is murdered, most likely for his role in negotiating treaties with the United States.

1825   Victorio (Beduiat), Mimbreno Apache Tribal Leader, Is Born. As a young man, Victoria fights with Mangas Coloradas, a leader in the early Apache war of the 1860s. Upon Coloradas's death in 1863, Victorio assumes control of his followers. The fighting groups consist of warriors from many tribes and collectively come to be known as Ojo Caliente (Warm Springs), since their agency is located near Ojo Caliente in present-day southwest New Mexico. Throughout the 1870s, Victorio and his followers alternate between sporadic raiding and confinement to reservation lands. In 1877 Victorio agrees to end the fighting if he and his followers are allowed to settle at Warm Springs. When these negotiations break down, Victorio and his followers are moved to the San Carlos Reservation in present-day Arizona. Finding reservation life unbearable, Victorio and about 300 followers escape on September 2, 1877. Though the majority of the Apache give themselves up a month later, Victorio and about 80 warriors remain in mountain hideouts where they wage a war of resistance for several years. His strategically placed encampments force U.S. soldiers to fight in small groups, allowing Victorio's forces to make good use of their limited numbers. In October 1880, Victorio is surprised by Mexican forces on the plains of Chihuahua. He fights until his ammunition is almost gone, and then kills himself.

JUNE 9, 1825   Treaty with the Ponca at White Paint Creek. By the 1820s, U.S. settlement has reached the Mississippi, and the United States negotiates a series of 14 treaties with Plains Indian tribes, many of which it has not dealt with diplomatically before. The main object of the treaties is to secure peace on the frontier, not to acquire western land, which is still regarded as having little value. The Ponca treaty is a typical example. The Ponca "admitted that they reside within the territorial limits of the United States, acknowledge their supremacy, and claim their protection." The tribe also recognizes U.S. authority to regulate trade with them and promises to return stolen property and "deliver up" Ponca, who may have committed crimes against U.S. citizens. The United States, in turn, promises to punish any citizens who injure, rob, or murder Ponca people.

JULY 15, 1825   Tahltan Band. Sekani headman Methodiates introduces Hudson's Bay Company employee Samuel Black to a Tahltan band in a pass between the Finlay and *Schadzue* (Stikine) river basins in north-central British Columbia. Other Tahltan bands who have access to the salmon of the Stikine River and European traders on the Pacific Coast have forced these Tahltan into this severe region. Because of the sparse fur resources of the area, however, the meeting does not lead the Hudson's Bay Company to establish posts there.

OCTOBER 1825   Micmac Homeland Burned. A large fire in northeastern New Brunswick devastates the homeland of about 450 Micmac north of the Miramichi River. The subsistence activities of Indians in New Brunswick already have been undermined by farmers and by the booming timber industry. Few Indians have found employment in the province's timber industry. Instead, Indians supplement subsistence activities through the sale of handicrafts.

1825–1860   Plays on Stage. Plays about Indians are popular on the U.S. stage during the pre–Civil War era. More than 50 are produced, including *Indian Wife* and *Pontiac, Or the Siege of Detroit*.

A hunter family of Cree Indians at York Fort, Manitoba, c. 1821. Courtesy of the National Archives of Canada.

1 8 2 6

1826   California Indian Mission System. The Mexican government secularizes the California missions with the intent of eventually turning them into Indian pueblos. Secularization is not completed until the 1840s; for some of the missions, ruin and desolation follow. The Indians who receive land allotments from the mission lands are few in number and are often forced to leave or sell the land because of lack of supplies or the actions of unscrupulous officials.

1826   Geronimo (Goyathlay), Chiricahua Apache Tribal Leader, Is Born. One of the most feared and respected of Apache leaders, Geronimo's early years are drenched in violence and warfare. His wife and children are killed by Mexican soldiers. From this point onward, his life is filled with a succession of military raids, captures, escapes, and brief attempts to live on Indian reservations. Although pursued relentlessly, Geronimo eludes the larger U.S. forces until 1886, when he is forced to surrender. Newspapers, presidents, and politicians call for

Geronimo's execution but instead he is imprisoned. In 1894, Geronimo and many of his close Apache comrades are moved to Fort Sill, Oklahoma, where he dies in 1909, still a prisoner of war.

JANUARY 24, 1826   Treaty at Buffalo Creek. After being coerced by the Ogden Land Company, the Seneca sign a treaty at Buffalo Creek and sell a portion of their land. On January 15, 1838, a similar agreement is reached with some New York Indian groups who earlier had ceded their land and moved west.

JULY 7, 1826   John Franklin Expedition. A large group of Kittigazuit Inuk camped near the mouth of the Mackenzie River in Canada have a hostile meeting with British Captain John Franklin and his party traveling through the area. An Inuit interpreter traveling with Franklin helps avoid bloodshed. Franklin's British expedition is exploring the Arctic coast from the mouth of the Coppermine River to Prudhoe Bay.

AUGUST 5, 1826   Fond du Lac Treaty. The Fond du Lac Treaty is negotiated and the Chippewa cede rights to explore and take away the native copper and copper ores and to work the mines and minerals in the country. Treaty proclamation is made on February 7, 1827.

1 8 2 7

1827   Ancient History of the Six Nations. Considered to be the first historical work by an American Indian author, the *Ancient History of the Six Nations* is published by David Cusick, a Tuscarora Indian.

MARCH 19, 1827   John Rollin Ridge, Cherokee Journalist and Author, Is Born. John is the son of John Ridge (1803–39) and the grandson of Major Ridge (*See* biography, 1771), both Cherokee leaders who favor Cherokee removal from Georgia in the 1830s. Both older

Ridges are assassinated in 1839, in part because they lead the Treaty party, a group of economically well-off Cherokee slave holders, merchants, and plantation owners who agree to migrate west to present-day Oklahoma by signing the Treaty of New Echota in 1835. John Rollin Ridge grows up in the ensuing internal political disturbances among the Cherokee. In 1849, he kills a member of the conservative National party and is forced to flee for his life. He travels to California and works as a newspaper editor and author. Ridge often writes in defense of the political rights of the Cherokee, Creek, and Choctaw. Although California Indians of his day suffer greatly from political oppression and genocide, Ridge does not take up a consistent defense of the California tribes. His life is eventful, but short. Ridge dies in 1868, leaving a legacy of writings in politics, fiction, and poetry.

JULY 27, 1827   British Columbia, Land-Based Trade Begins. With the establishment of the Hudson's Bay Company post at Fort Langley on the Fraser River about 30 kilometers (20 miles) from its mouth, land-based trade in the area of present-day British Columbia begins. During the era of ship-based trade, Indians of the outer coast, especially, the Haida, Nootka (Nuu-chah-nulth), and Tsimshian are the primary Indian traders. Fort Langley places the nearby Halkomelem Coast Salish villages in an advantageous position. Villagers attempt to control the trade of the post from their nearby fishing villages.

1827–1828   The Cherokee Republic. The Cherokee watch the drift toward a policy of forced removal and decide upon a unique course of action in their attempt to prevent their own removal. In the early 1820s the Cherokee establish a capital in New Echota (Georgia). In 1827, they write a constitution calling for three branches of government, in many ways similar to the U.S. federal constitution. In 1828, the Cherokee ratify the new constitution and elect John Ross, a wealthy Cherokee slave holder, as principal chief. The Cherokee wish to establish their government and right to preserve their homeland in Georgia, Tennessee, and eastern Alabama. The Georgia legislature, wanting to remove the Cherokee from their chartered limits, passes a series of laws that abolish the Cherokee government, appropriate Cherokee territory, and extend Georgia law over the Cherokee people. The legislature also passes an act stating that Cherokee cannot testify in court against a Georgian.

1 8 2 8

c. 1828   Ely S. Parker, Seneca Tribal Leader, Is Born. Parker is educated at Yates Academy in Yates, New York and at Cayuga Academy in Aurora, New York. In 1852 he becomes a chief among the Seneca Indians and helps the Tonawanda Seneca secure land rights to their reservation in western New York State. With the outbreak of the Civil War, Parker, a close friend and colleague of Gen. Ulysses S. Grant, serves the Union cause and pens the final copy of the Confederate Army's surrender terms at Appomattox Courthouse in 1865. When Grant becomes president in 1868, he appoints Parker his Commissioner of Indian Affairs. It is the first time an Indian has held this post. As commissioner, Parker works to rid the Bureau of Indian Affairs of corruption and fraud. He is an advocate for the western Indian tribes and gains a reputation for fairness and progressive thinking. In 1871, he is falsely accused of fraud. Although acquitted of all charges, Parker resigns and moves to New York City, where he lives until his death in 1895.

1828   California and Oregon Exploration. Jedediah Smith leads an expedition exploring most of northern California to Oregon—both inland and along the coast. His party is perhaps the first group of Americans to contact the northern Indian groups.

JULY 24, 1828   Report on Upper Canada's Indians. British Maj. Gen. H.C. Darling is-

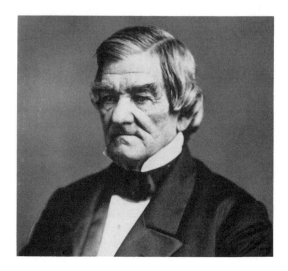

Photo of Cherokee tribal leader John Ross, taken in the 1860s. Courtesy of the National Anthropological Archives, Smithsonian Institution.

sues a report on Indian conditions in Canada. He recommends a policy of settling Indians on farms and providing them with religious and educational instruction.

AUGUST 25, 1828   Winnebago Treaty. The U.S. government negotiates a treaty with the Winnebago and the united tribes of Potawatomi, Ottawa, and Chippewa to cede lands in Michigan and Illinois. The treaty also stipulates that the Indians are not to interfere with nor molest any non-Indian person passing into Indian country for mining or other purposes. Treaty proclamation is made on January 7, 1829.

1828–1835   The *Cherokee Phoenix* Is Published. The *Cherokee Phoenix*, a weekly newspaper printed in English and in the Cherokee syllabary, is published. The newspaper's first editor is Elias Boudinot (*See also* entry, *1823 Poor Sarah*), who was educated in Cornwall, Connecticut, after attending primary school among the Moravian missionaries in Tennessee. The newspaper is discontinued when the U.S. government presses the Cherokee Nation to move west. Boudinot joins a minority group in signing the Treaty of New Echota in 1835, which, according to the U.S. government, obligates the Cherokee to move west to what is now Oklahoma.

1 8 2 9

1829   Cherokee Hymn Book Printed. The first edition of the *Cherokee Hymn Book* is printed at New Echota, Georgia. The book includes old Christian and Cherokee hymns handed down through oral tradition.

1829   *Son of the Forest*. Published in 1829, *Son of the Forest* is a personal conversion narrative by William Apes, a Pequot. The work introduces a theme of social conflict, distinguishing Indian ways from those of the recently arrived European-American. Apes identifies a theme of white injustice through Christian narratives, pointing out the hypocrisy between professed Christian attitudes and the exploitative and frequently cruel behavior directed toward Indian people. Indeed, he critiques the very use of the term "Indian," perceiving its derogatory or epithetic implications when employed by non-Natives; instead, Apes uses the term Natives as more befitting. Apes also discusses the harmful and destructive impact of alcohol upon his people, an issue which consistently affects Native individuals and their communities. Apes's later works intensify in their condemnation of U.S. society.

1829   Standing Bear (Mochunozhi), Ponca Tribal Leader, Is Born. Standing Bear is a Ponca principal chief who wins a U.S. federal case to bury his son in the Ponca homelands of Nebraska. Traditional enemies of the Sioux, the Ponca negotiate a treaty in 1858 that establishes boundaries between the two tribal groups. The treaty is abrogated when the government includes Ponca lands within the Great Sioux Reservation in the Fort Laramie Treaty of 1868. In 1876 Congress passes a law to remove the Ponca from their homeland in northern Kansas and forcibly relocates them to Indian Territory (Oklahoma). Two of Standing Bear's children perish from disease and hunger as a result of the relocation. Accompanied by 30 warriors, Standing Bear sets out to return his son's body to the old Ponca homeland. The group is spotted by settlers and Gen. George Crook orders cavalry officers to arrest them. Once the nature of the Ponca trip is understood, General Crook and others are sympathetic to Standing Bear's mission. However, federal attorneys argue that the Indians are not legally persons under the U.S. Constitution and therefore have no rights. Federal Judge Elmer Dundy rules against the attorneys, and Standing Bear's party is allowed to continue. He buries his son in northeastern Nebraska. Sympathy grows for the Ponca, and Standing Bear goes on a lecture tour of the East. Congress forms a commission to study the Ponca case and grants Standing Bear and his party land in Nebraska in 1880. Standing Bear dies in 1908.

JUNE 6, 1829   Shanawdithit, the Last Known Beothuk, Dies. The Beothuk, reclusive inhabitants of Newfoundland, have been gradually reduced by disease, by enemy (Micmac, Inuit, and European) attack, and by the harsh environment of the island.

JULY 1829   Gold Discovered on Cherokee Land. Gold is discovered on Cherokee land. The gold seekers arrive in overwhelming numbers and lawlessness prevails. Georgia increases its efforts to remove the Cherokee west of the Mississippi River.

1 8 3 0

c. 1830   Crowfoot (Isapo-Muxika) Is Born. Born among the Kainai (Blood) in southern Alberta, Crowfoot is raised among the Siksika (Blackfoot). The Kainai, Siksika, and Peigan, who are often referred to collectively as the Blackfoot Confederacy, speak the same language and have a very similar culture. Like many Indians, Crowfoot assumes different names as he matures and increases in prestige. His final name recalls his bravery in battle against enemy Crow bands.

After assuming leadership of the Big Pipes Siksika band in 1865, and becoming one of the most influential men among the entire Blackfoot Confederacy by 1870, Crowfoot guides his people through the transition from nomadic hunting days to the post-treaty reserve days. Realizing that resistance against the Canadians is futile and thankful that Canada's North-West Mounted Police have ended the whisky trade in 1874, Crowfoot signs Treaty 7 in 1877. In following years, though disillusioned by the disappearance of the buffalo, by Canadian government treatment, and by the death of many Siksika (including most of his children) in disease epidemics, Crowfoot counsels the Siksika to remain on peaceful terms with the Canadian government. As a result of Crowfoot's leadership, the Blackfoot do not join the North-West Rebellion of 1885. On April 25, 1890, Crowfoot dies at Blackfoot Crossing on his people's reserve.

1830   President Andrew Jackson Addresses Indian Removal. President Andrew Jackson, in his second annual message, addresses the question of the removal of the eastern Indian tribes to the west of the Mississippi River. ". . . Philanthropy could not wish to see this continent restored to the condition in which it was found by our forefathers. What good man would prefer a country covered with forests and ranged by a few thousand savages to our extensive Republic, studded with cities, towns, and prosperous farms, embellished with all the improvements which art can devise or industry execute, occupied by more than 12 million happy people, and filled with all the blessings of liberty, civilization and religion? The present policy of the Government is but a continuation of the same progressive change by a milder process. . . ."

1830   Roman Nose, Southern Cheyenne Tribal Leader, Is Born. Roman Nose is a leader of Indian warriors and a member of the Crooked Lance Society of the Cheyenne Indian tribe. During the wars of the 1860s, he becomes a prominent warrior and because of his bravery in battle earns the respect of a war chief. Roman Nose fights in the battle of the Platt Bridge in July 1865 during the Bozeman Trail dispute in Wyoming and Montana. In 1866, Roman Nose fights alongside the Southern Cheyenne Dog Soldiers military society. In 1867, he is present at the Fort Larned Council with Gen. Winfield Scott Hancock. Roman Nose declares to members of the Dog Soldiers that he intends to kill Hancock, but he is prevented from doing so by Tall Bull and Bull Bear. Roman Nose attends the preliminary meetings preparing for the Medicine Lodge Council of October 1867 but he does not participate in the council itself or the signing of the Medicine Lodge Treaty. He is killed in September 1868 in an engagement known by non-Indians as the battle of Beecher's Island in present-day Kansas and to Indian people as the Fight When Roman Nose Was Killed. According to Cheyenne tradition, Roman Nose's "medicine" had been broken either when his feathered war bonnet was touched by a woman or when he ate food prepared with metal utensils.

1830   Satanta, Kiowa Tribal Leader, Is Born. Satanta is born on the northern Plains, but later migrates to the southern Plains with his people. His father, Red Tipi, is keeper of the tribal medicine bundles or Tai-me. Much of Satanta's adult life is spent fighting U.S. settlers and military. He participates in raids along the Santa Fe Trail in the early 1860s, and in 1866 becomes the leader of the Kiowa who favor military resistance against U.S. military forces. In 1867, he speaks at the Kiowa Medicine Lodge Council, an annual ceremonial gathering, where, because of his eloquent speech, U.S. observers give him his nickname "The Orator of the Plains." For the next couple of years, Satanta participates in a number of raids in

Crowfoot was commemorated in a 1986 Canadian postage stamp. Courtesy of the Canada Post Corporation.

Texas where cattle ranchers and buffalo hunters are steadily pushing Kiowa and Comanche Indians onto reservations. In May 1871, he plans an ambush along the Butterfield Stage Route on the Salt Creek Prairie. After allowing a smaller medical wagon train to pass, Satanta and his warriors attack and confiscate the contents of a larger train of ten army wagons. Gen. William Tecumseh Sherman takes the attack as a sign that a more militant and coordinated offense is needed to subdue the Kiowa and Comanche, who are unwilling to settle permanently on reservations. A short time later Satanta is lured into a peace council and then arrested and sentenced to death. Humanitarian groups and Indian leaders protest the harsh sentence. In 1873, Satanta is paroled on the condition he remain on the Kiowa Reservation. In 1874, during the Comanche and U.S. conflict called the Red River War, Satanta presents himself to U.S. officials to prove that he is not taking part in the hostilities. His demonstration of loyalty is rewarded with imprisonment. Satanta dies while in prison in 1878.

APRIL 13, 1830 Canadian Indian Reserves Established. Upper Canada establishes a sys-

tem of reserves for its Indians. The move comes just as the British government transfers responsibility for Indian Affairs in Upper and Lower Canada from the military secretary to civilian administrators. This change is made because the Indians of Canada are no longer important to the British as military allies. The Indian inhabitants, primarily Iroquois and Mississauga (Ojibway), were the vast majority of the population in 1791 at the establishment of Upper Canada, but because immigrants have streamed in since then, are a small minority at this time. The changes of 1830 mark the beginning of a policy aimed at assimilating Indians into non-Native society. This policy is revealed in the Coldwater Experiment begun in 1830. In the Coldwater Experiment, Indian affairs officials induce Ojibway families to settle at a site on the southeast corner of Lake Huron's Georgian Bay. The project, aimed at training Ojibway as farmers, is abandoned by 1837. Other efforts to settle Ojibway as farmers in Upper Canada are more successful, including the Credit Mission near York (Toronto) led by Methodist Peter Jones (See biography, January 1, 1802).

JULY 15, 1830 Sauk, Fox, and Sioux Treaty.

Indian Encampment on Lake Huron, c. 1845–50, by Paul Kane. This painting shows the typical Ojibway birch bark tent and canoe. Courtesy of the Art Gallery of Ontario.

A treaty is signed with the Sauk, Fox, and Sioux, establishing title of land in Minnesota, Missouri, and Iowa, as well as authority over timber, mining, and grazing, holding the land in severalty. Not all tribes are adequately represented in the negotiations, and boundary disputes ensue. Treaty proclamation is made on February 24, 1831.

SEPTEMBER 28, 1830   Treaty at Dancing Rabbit Creek. The Choctaw sign the Treaty at Dancing Rabbit Creek, ceding more than 10 million acres of land in Alabama and Mississippi. In exchange they are promised peace, friendship, and land in the West. They are not compensated, as promised, for farm buildings, school houses, and livestock that they lose by giving up their homelands. The move takes nearly three years, and hundreds of Choctaw die during the removal. Treaty proclamation is made on February 24, 1831.

c. 1830–1850   Northern Plains. When French trader François Laroque visits the Crow Indians of the northern Plains in 1805, he discovers they are already using blue glass beads, which they obtained from the Spanish in the Southwest via

the Shoshoni. At that time, the glass beads are so prized by the Crow that 100 of them will purchase a horse. Later, beginning about 1830, distinctive styles of beadwork embroidery emerge across the plains, largely replacing the more time-consuming traditional quillwork forms. Beadwork designs decorate shirts, dresses, leggings, cradleboards, knife cases, gun cases, tobacco and medicine bags, and many other objects.

1830–1860   The Removal Era. On May 28, 1830, Congress votes in favor of the Indian Removal Act and authorizes $500,000 to relocate Indian families to Indian Territory (Oklahoma). The removal of Native Americans from their lands becomes an integral element of national Indian policy and establishes in general terms the policy (already put into practice by some treaties) of exchanging federal lands west of the Mississippi for other lands occupied by Indian tribes in the eastern portion of the United States. During the 1830s and 1840s the U.S. Army forces thousands of Indian families to leave their belongings and move to lands west of Iowa, Missouri, Kansas, Nebraska, Arkansas, and Oklahoma. The United States forces the Cherokee onto "The Trail of Tears,"

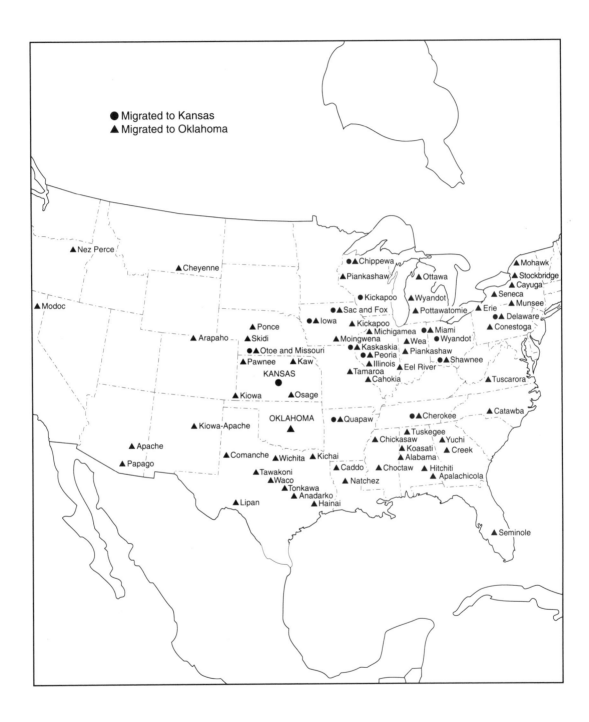

● Migrated to Kansas
▲ Migrated to Oklahoma

▲ Nez Perce

▲ Cheyenne

▲ Modoc

●▲ Chippewa

▲ Piankashaw

▲ Mohawk
▲ Stockbridge
▲ Cayuga

● Kickapoo
▲ Ottawa

▲ Seneca

● Sac and Fox
▲ Wyandot
▲ Pottawatomie
▲ Erie
▲ Munsee

▲ Arapaho

▲ Ponce
▲ Skidi

●● Iowa

● Kickapoo
▲ Michigamea
●▲ Miami
▲ Delaware
●▲ Conestoga

▲ Moingwena
▲ Wea
● Wyandot

●▲ Otoe and Missouri
▲ Kaskaskia
●▲ Peoria
▲ Piankashaw

▲ Pawnee
▲ Kaw
▲ Illinois
▲ Eel River
●▲ Shawnee

KANSAS
●

▲ Tamaroa
▲ Cahokia

▲ Tuscarora

▲ Kiowa
▲ Osage

OKLAHOMA
▲

●▲ Quapaw

●▲ Cherokee

▲ Catawba

▲ Kiowa-Apache

▲ Tuskegee

▲ Chickasaw
▲ Koasati
▲ Alabama
▲ Yuchi
▲ Creek

▲ Apache

▲ Comanche
▲ Wichita
▲ Kichai

▲ Caddo
▲ Choctaw
▲ Hitchiti
▲ Apalachicola

▲ Papago

▲ Tawakoni
▲ Waco
▲ Tonkawa
▲ Anadarko
▲ Hainai

▲ Natchez

▲ Lipan

▲ Seminole

Homelands of Indian nations that were forced to migrate after 1830 to Indian Territory in present-day Kansas and Oklahoma. Courtesy of Duane Champagne.

which directly results in the death of 4,000 to 8,000 people. One soldier writes: "I fought through the Civil War and have seen men shot to pieces and slaughtered by thousands, but the Cherokee removal was the cruelest work I ever knew."

The Cherokee are not the only southern nation to suffer removal. The army moves the Choctaw, Chickasaw, Creek, Seminole, and remnants of lesser-known peoples. Northern tribes are also removed to Indian Territory (Oklahoma and Kansas), including the Wyandot, Ottawa, Peoria, Miami, Potawatomi, Sauk, Fox, Delaware, and Seneca. The government is ill prepared to handle so many Indians along the trails and in new homes. In 1841, Maj. Ethan Allan Hitchcock investigates Indian affairs in the West and concludes that the American Indian policy is filled with "bribery, perjury and forgery, short weights, issues of spoiled meat and grain, and every conceivable subterfuge."

1 8 3 1

1831 *Cherokee Nation v. Georgia.* The U.S. Supreme Court recognizes Indian tribes as "domestic dependent nations with an unquestionable right to the lands which they occupy, until that right shall be extinguished by a voluntary cession to our government. . ." in *Cherokee Nation v. Georgia.* The court holds that an Indian tribe is neither a state nor a foreign nation within the meaning of Article III of the Constitution, so as to permit them to bring an original action in the Supreme Court. Chief Justice John Marshall combines the political and geographical aspects of Cherokee existence to create a status in law that he calls a "domestic dependent nation." Indian people reside in a state of pupilage and their relationship to the United States resembles that of a ward to a guardian. The court action is brought by the Cherokee Nation to halt Georgia's efforts to remove the Cherokee from their homeland.

1831 **Nat Turner's Rebellion.** The failure of the Nat Turner rebellion in September and October creates many hardships for non-whites in Virginia, as restrictive laws are enacted. The Eastern Shore Indians, many of whom are part Black, are driven from their homes at this time. Pressures are also put on other groups, as in 1843 when local Virginians attempt to dissolve the Pamunkey Reservation on the grounds that the Indians there are mixed with African-Americans. During the 1840s many Pamunkey move away, hoping to go "out west." Sickness forces them to spend the winter in Stafford County, where they sell the historic mantle of Queen Anne to a white man. Subsequently, this group moves to an unknown destination.

1831 **Sitting Bull, Hunkpapa Sioux Tribal Leader, Is Born.** Sitting Bull becomes a major military, spiritual, and political leader of his people in the 1800s. He is an important figure in the war for the Black Hills from 1876 to 1877 and helps to engineer the Indian victory at Little Bighorn. Sitting Bull's military and leadership abilities become evident at an early age. At age 22, he is leader of a warrior society known as the "Strong Hearts." Sitting Bull chooses not to abide by the Fort Laramie Treaty of 1868 signed by Red Cloud, a major Hunkpapa Sioux leader. Sitting Bull's adherence to traditional ways of life mark him a spiritual as well as military leader among his people. Due largely to Sitting Bull's influence, between 12,000 and 15,000 Indians gather in a camp along the Little Bighorn River in 1876 in response to U.S. presence in the area. Sitting Bull engages forces under Gen. George Crook in the battle of the Rosebud on June 17 and sends the U.S. army into retreat. Eight days later, the U.S. troops led by Col. George Armstrong Custer attack several points along the Indian encampment and are soundly defeated. From 1885 to 1886 Sitting Bull joins William Cody's Wild West Show, a traveling exhibition of "Indian fighters" and "Indian War Chiefs." In 1886, Sitting Bull leaves the show and returns to Standing Rock Reservation. In his remaining years, he continues to oppose assimilation into U.S. culture and the breakup of Sioux land. Sitting Bull is killed by government-paid Indian police in October 1890.

1831   Indian Treaties and Land Cessions.

FEBRUARY 8.   The Menominee Indians cede a large tract of land in Michigan and a smaller reservation near Green Bay in Wisconsin for a promise of an annuity, goods, and education for future generations of tribal children.

FEBRUARY–OCTOBER. In amendments to treaties set up during this time, the New York Indians of the Six Nations and the St. Regis tribe cede land at Green Bay in Wisconsin that had previously been purchased from the Menominee and Winnebago tribes. In exchange, they are given land in the West. Bribery and fraud mars the implementation of these amendments.

AUGUST 8.   The Shawnee cede their remaining land in Ohio and are transported beyond the Mississippi. Portions of the funds from the sale of their land is put into stocks for the tribe's future necessities.

AUGUST 30.   A treaty is negotiated with the Ottawa tribe in which two tracts of land are ceded. The first cession is on the Great Auglaize River in Ohio, with this branch of the tribe agreeing to move west after their cession. The second cession is on the Miami River of Lake Erie, and, although this portion of the tribe is initially unwilling to remove west, they are harassed until they finally agree to emigrate.

OCTOBER 16, 1831   Blackfoot, Atsina, and Sarcee Trade with American Fur Company. The Blackfoot Confederacy, Atsina, and Sarcee who have long traded with British and Canadian traders along the North Saskatchewan River establish peaceful trade with the American Fur

Company at Fort Piegan on the Missouri River at its confluence with the Marias River in present-day Montana, after the company agrees to trade with them rather than send its own trappers into the region. Relations have been hostile since the arrival of Americans to the region. The establishment of peaceful trade with these Indians and with the Assiniboine draws all of them southward toward the Missouri River, especially because the American traders want buffalo skins, a commodity the Hudson's Bay Company does not seek.

1831–1834   Fort Simpson Established. The Hudson's Bay Company (H.B.C.) establishes Fort Simpson at the mouth of the Nass River on the north coast of today's British Columbia. The establishment of the land-based fur trade ends the dominant position of Haida and Nootka in the fur trade. With sea otter stocks seriously depleted around the Queen Charlotte Islands, the Haida have begun growing potatoes and making argillite carvings to trade with the fur traders and with the Tsimshian. Nishga (Nisga'a) bands that have profited from the post's location at the Nass River are upset in 1834 when the post is moved to Tsimshian territory near the mouth of the Ksan (Skeena) River. Tsimshian bands now control the trade of other coastal Indian groups (including that of the Nisga'a, Southern Tlingit, Tsimshian, and Haida) at that post and of inland groups such as the Gitskan (Tsimshian) and Carrier who live up the river. Competition from Russian and American traders along the coast forces the H.B.C. to keep prices low. The low prices at the coast allow the Gitskan to offer European goods to inland Indians such as the Sekani at lower prices than those offered at inland H.B.C. posts such as Fort St. James. A series of Tsimshian headmen named Legaic come to control the trade on the Skeena River, allying themselves through marriage with senior traders at Fort Simpson. Indians at other trading posts seek to solidify their position in the same way.

1831–1839 George Catlin Paints the Plains.
Born in 1796 in the Wyoming Valley of Pennsylvania, George Catlin grows up in the Susquehanna Valley in New York, where he gains some expertise with firearms, the canoe, and fishing rods. This knowledge will prove invaluable to him when, after a move to Philadelphia in 1823, he becomes interested in the Plains Indian delegations traveling through the area on their way to Washington, D.C. Catlin thereupon decides to travel the West and create an "Indian Gallery" of portraits. In 1831 he is welcomed to St. Louis by Gen. William Clark, who is then Superintendent of Indian Affairs for the western tribes. From there he travels up the Mississippi to Prairie du Chien where he encounters the Iowa, Missouri, Sauk (Sac) and Fox, and different Sioux groups who are meeting there. Early the next year Catlin travels up the Missouri and Platte rivers and meets the Oto, Omaha, Missouri, and Pawnee. Later that spring he journeys 2,000 miles up the Missouri, north to Blackfoot and Assiniboine country. He also spends time with the Mandan, Hidatsa, and Arikara. In the approximately seven years of his project, Catlin travels by horse and canoe throughout the plains, from eastern Texas to Montana, documenting the many Indian nations he encounters. He also journeys to the Gulf states and the Southeast, where he paints the embattled Seminole and Miccosukee, among others. During his life, Catlin paints numerous important Indian leaders, including Four Bears of the Mandan; Osceola, the Miccosukee/Seminole resistance leader; Black Hawk and Keokuk of the Sauk (Sac) and Fox; Tenskwatawa (Tecumseh's brother, the Shawnee prophet); and many other Native men and women. Additionally, Catlin portrays ceremonies and lifeways of the numerous cultures he observes. Since they document an era for which no comparably extensive record exists, Catlin's observations and works are an important source of information about American Indian peoples and, particularly, the height of the Great Plains culture.

1 8 3 2

1832 Black Hawk War. Black Hawk, chief of the Sauk (Sac) and Fox (*See* biography, 1767), returns from a winter hunting trip and finds that his lodge has been invaded by U.S. settlers. He asks them to move. The settlers ignore him and the Indians retire across the Mississippi River to what is now Iowa. Black Hawk and his followers return in the spring of 1832 to reclaim their ancestral lands and to raise a crop of corn. The Illinois militia is called out to oppose the band of approximately 1,000 Sauk and Fox. Abraham Lincoln and Jefferson Davis join the militia to oppose the Indian forces. Black Hawk and his followers, are pursued through Illinois and Wisconsin by 8,000 militiamen and 150 regular army troops. On August 1, at the junction of the Bad Axe and Mississippi rivers, many of Black Hawk's followers are killed when soldiers on board the steamboat *Warrior* open fire. Black Hawk's followers suffer heavy casualties again on August 3, when Gen. Henry Atkinson and Col. Henry Dodge and their 1,300-man command arrive. The Indians who have remained on the east bank of the Mississippi, under a flag of truce, attempt to surrender, but the soldiers storm their position and massacre many of the reduced Indian force. Those who successfully make the crossing to the west bank of the Mississippi are either captured or killed by U.S.-allied Sioux. Black Hawk is captured and the remainder of his followers are returned to Iowa where they are forced to cede the eastern part of Iowa as punishment for the war. The Sauk and Fox pledge never to return, live, hunt, fish, or plant on their previous homelands.

1832 Government Health Service. Governmental health services for Indians begin when Congress authorizes funds to provide for smallpox vaccination of a number of tribes.

1832 The John Work Expedition. Expedition members note that the Cow Creek Indians of the Sacramento area express fear of slave raids

Four Bears, the last of the great Mandan chiefs. Courtesy of the National Museum of American Art, Washington D.C./ Art Resource, NY.

from the Shasta and Oregon Indians. Captured slaves are traded north to the Columbia River region. The main slave market is located at the Dalles in what is now Oregon.

1832 Worcester v. Georgia. *Worcester v. Georgia* is brought by Samuel Worcester, a U.S. citizen convicted and sentenced to a four-year prison term for refusing to swear allegiance to Georgia and for speaking out against the Indian policies of the state. In 1829, Georgia extends its laws over the portion of the Cherokee Nation within its chartered limits and demands that all U.S. citizens take an oath of allegiance to Georgia and obey Georgia law. Georgia law prohibits the Cherokee government from meeting and is intended to force the Cherokee to move west. In this case, the court strikes down the Georgia law, arguing that only the federal government has the right to regulate affairs in Indian country, and saying that states cannot extend their laws over Indian governments. Chief Justice John Marshall emphasizes the fact that the Cherokee have their own political institutions and are engaged in self-government: "The Cherokee Nation is a distinct community occupying its own territory in which the laws of Georgia can have no effect and which the citizens of Georgia have no right to enter, but with the assent of the Cherokees themselves." The ruling is based on an understanding that Indian nations have always been considered as distinct, independent political communities, retaining their original natural rights, as the undisputed possessors of the soil, from time immemorial. Indian tribes are thus sovereigns, that is, government, and state law does not apply within reservation boundaries without congressional consent. Despite Marshall's ruling in their favor, the Cherokee are forced to move west of the Mississippi between 1835 and 1839; however, *Worcester v. Georgia* now stands as a major precedent upholding Indian rights to self-government.

JULY 9, 1832 Office of Commissioner of Indian Affairs Approved. The U.S. Congress approves the "Commissioner of Indian Affairs Act" and thus creates the position of Commissioner of Indian Affairs within the Department of War, to be appointed by the president. On July 10, President Andrew Jackson appoints Elbert Herring as the first commissioner. Herring now has "direction and management of all matters arising out of Indian relations."

SEPTEMBER 15, 1832 Winnebago and Potawatomi Land Cession. The Winnebago are forced to surrender a portion of their territory near present-day Green Bay, Wisconsin, for which they receive land west of the Mississippi. This is the first land cession by the Winnebago people. On October 26, the Potawatomi cede all of their land claims in Indiana, except for specially reserved sections. In exchange they are to receive an annuity of $20,000 and goods.

1832–1834 Bodmer and Maximilian Expedition. About 30 years after Lewis and Clark explore the North American interior, a German prince named Alexander Phillip Maximilian from the principality of Wied leads a small party through the American interior. Prince Maximilian, a student of natural history, hires a young Swiss artist named Karl Bodmer to accompany the expedition and illustrate the accounts of their travels. The expedition spends two years exploring, principally in the region along the upper Missouri River. During this time the prince and his men encounter many Indian people from numerous tribes, including Dakota, Lakota, Mandan, Hidatsa, Arikara, and Crow. Bodmer's drawings and paintings of the Indian people and their costumes, objects, and customs become an invaluable record, particularly after the tribes of this region are decimated by a smallpox epidemic in 1837.

1 8 3 3

1833 *Black Hawk* Translated. The first example of the narrated Indian autobiography is the

Life of Ma-ka-tai-me-she-kia-kaik or Black Hawk. Translated by Antoine Le Claire, this "as-told-to" ethnography tells the life story of Black Hawk, the leader of the Sauk and the Fox in the Black Hawk War of 1832.

1833 *The Experiences of Five Christian Indians of the Pequot Tribe.* The second of William Apes's (Pequot) written works, this piece continues the author's critique of white behavior, especially in regard to American Indians. An autobiography, Apes details the inhumane treatment he received from whites as a child. He describes the difficulties he met with as an adolescent half-breed desiring to attend religious meetings. Apes also questions whether an Indian can truly believe in a faith and still justify its oppression of his/her very being. His use of two other Native narratives ultimately twists the concept of Christian conversion so that Indians become the "true" Christians when their conditions and behavior are contrasted to those of a righteous U.S. society.

1833 Spotted Tail, Brulé Tribal Leader, Is Born. Spotted Tail is born either along the White River in South Dakota or near Fort Laramie in Wyoming. His adult name, Spotted Tail, is associated with a raccoon and is given to him by a trapper. Spotted Tail and Little Thunder, another Brulé chief, seek revenge for the 1854 killing of the Sioux chief Brave Bear during a battle with army forces near Fort Laramie. In August 1855, at Ash Hollow, Nebraska, troops under William S. Harney overtake the Brulé Sioux and on October 18, Spotted Tail and his companions surrender. Following his release from prison, Spotted Tail takes a more diplomatic line with U.S. settlers, though he continues to struggle for Sioux land rights. Although famed as a warrior, Spotted Tail generally advises peace to his fellow Sioux. During the War for the Bozeman Trail of 1866–68, under Red Cloud, he counsels accommodation with U.S. intruders. He is one of the signers of the Fort Laramie Treaty of 1868, which establishes the Great Sioux Reservation in present-day North and South Dakota. Spotted Tail is assassinated by Crow Dog in 1881 for his willingness to accommodate to U.S. authority.

JUNE 19, 1833 Tlingit Trade Monopoly. Seeking to protect his position as middleman to inland Indians such as the Tahltan, Seix (Shakes), a Tlingit chief at the mouth of the Stikine River, forces Hudson's Bay Company trader Peter Skene Ogden to abandon plans to travel up the river to establish a fur trade post. The Russian traders at the site also threaten Ogden. The Stikine forms the basis of an important Tlingit trade route between the Pacific Northwest Coast and the interior.

1833–1836 Northern Land Cessions. By 1833 there are only 5,000 Indians left in Ohio, Indiana, Illinois, and Michigan, where the government pursues a vigorous removal policy. On September 26, 1833, the U.S. secures all of the Indian land along the western shores of Lake Michigan, as well as miscellaneous other tracts, from the Chippewa, Ottawa, and Potawatomi. In October 1834, the Miami cede their land in Indiana, and in December 1834 the Potawatomi cede land. The Ottawa, Saginaw, Chippewa, and Wyandot likewise all cede land in the spring of 1836.

1833–1843 Fort McLoughlin Established. The Hudson's Bay Company establishes Fort McLoughlin on Milbanke Sound near the site of present-day Bella Bella of British Columbia. The Bella Bella of the region control the trade of the nearby Haisla, Bella Coola (Nuxalk), and Kwakiutl (Kwagiulth, Kwakwaka'wakw). From this post, goods are conveyed along traditional trade routes to the Carrier and Chilcotin who live inland.

1 8 3 4

1834 California Indian Mission System. Governor José Figueroa rules that, in all missions not already secularized, the priests are to be replaced by civil authorities. During this period many of the Indian converts find themselves without a means of livelihood in the mission areas and move to the interior of California for survival. In the Pueblo of Los Angeles, observers note that the Indians are in worse circumstances than they had been under mission control. Former mission Indians are working on ranchos and farms and in households for mere pittances. Ranchos are rapidly encompassing the interior valleys of California and use Indian labor. Many Indian groups move into mountainous areas, often displacing other groups in a search for hunting and gathering areas.

1834 California Indian Mission System. Juan Bautista Alvarado, later a governor, is among the strongest critics of the mission system. In his opinion the missions "found the Indians in full enjoyment of their five senses, valiant in war, [and] far-sighted in their own way. . . ." But when the padres departed, "they left the Indian population half-stupefied, very much reduced in numbers, and duller than when they found them." By this date there are estimated to be 30,000 Indians living in the various California missions. Indian leaders point out that Roman Catholic church history attests to the fact that certain mission priests considered it their duty to bring the Indians under the control of the church. Some are very cruel and inhuman in their use of leg irons, wrist irons, and other means of causing submission.

1834 Indian Schools. By 1834 there are 60 schools established among the various tribes by six religious organizations and by the Indians themselves. There are 137 teachers employed and nearly 2,000 children enrolled.

1834 Marin, Miwok (Me-Wuk) Tribal Leader, Dies. During his lifetime Marin leads his people in several successful battles against the Spanish during the years between 1815 and 1824, but despite these victories he is subsequently captured and imprisoned. Later he

escapes on a balsa raft and takes refuge on a small island in San Francisco Bay. Following his recapture he is saved from execution by priests who intervene on his behalf. Marin is later converted to Catholicism and lives close to the San Rafael mission until his death

JUNE 30, 1834 Department of Indian Affairs. The "Department of Indian Affairs Act" is passed by the U.S. Congress, resulting in a reorganization of the offices charged with the administration of Indian affairs. The Department of Indian Affairs is located within the Department of War.

JUNE 30, 1834 Trade and Intercourse Act. The Trade and Intercourse Act is an attempt by Congress to update several acts which regulate trade and relations between Indians and the United States dating back to 1790. In the act, Indian territory is defined by Congress as "all that part of the United States west of the Mississippi, and not within the states of Missouri and Louisiana, or the territory of Arkansas, and, also, that part of the United States east of the Mississippi River, and not within any state to which the Indian title has not been extinguished."

1 8 3 5

1835 Caddo Land Cessions. The Caddo Indians of northwestern Louisiana cede their lands to the United States for $80,000. The Caddo move to the Brazos River area in Texas where they live as farmers and ranchers. In 1859, however, settlers drive them from Texas to Indian Territory (Oklahoma), where they are assigned to a reservation in 1872.

1835 The *Cherokee Phoenix*. The Cherokee newspaper, the *Cherokee Phoenix*, is denied freedom of the press as guaranteed by the first amendment of the U.S. Constitution when it incurs the displeasure of the Georgia governor,

Artist George Catlin portrayed the Choctaws playing games by observing them for hours in their new 'home' in Indian territory. This scene represents a ball game, c. 1834–35. Courtesy of the National Museum of American Art, Washington D.C./Art Resource, NY.

who solicits the help of the state militia in closing down the newspaper.

1835 Dat-So-La-Lee, Washo Basketmaker, Is Born. Born near Woodfords, California, this Washo woman whose Native name is "Dabuda" also comes to be known as Louisa Kizer (or Keyser). She gains great notoriety for her excellence in basket-making and for her artistic innovations. Her second marriage to Charley Kizer, a Washo-Miwok, in 1888 eventually leads to a meeting with Abram and Amy Cohn, who hire her as their laundress. Amy Cohn is fascinated by Louisa Kizer's basket weaving so the Cohns begin calling her Dat-So-La-Lee and promoting her crafts. They give Louisa Kizer room and board in exchange for the baskets she makes. The Cohns profit from her artistry, once collecting $1,400 in 1914 for one of her pieces. Louisa herself never receives money for her baskets.

In terms of Washo basket weaving, Dat-So-La-Lee introduces the in-curving *degikup* or coiled-style shape to her Native tradition. She also adds Maidu and Pomo techniques to her own Washo form. Her personal influence includes using pieces of glass and her teeth or her fingernails to scrape the basket willows. Later, she employs a tin can lid to narrow her basket splints, thereby increasing her stitches to number 30 within an inch. Her most widely recognized contribution is the two-color *degikup* frequently accompanied with either a scatter flame design, or a symmetrical or an alternating pattern of decorative bands.

1835 *Indian Nullification of the Unconstitutional Laws of Massachusetts, Relative to the Mashpee Tribe.* Clearly a work of protest literature, William Apes's text intentionally raises questions regarding Indian political rights and status. His use of the phrase "Nullification Crisis of 1832" recalls the crisis of a sovereign state pitted against the Union of the federal government, and he intends to draw parallels to the condition of American Indians. Ultimately, Apes's writing enables the Mashpee to regain their political rights in the 1830s. It is one of few Indian victories in the first half of the nineteenth century.

1835 Rain-In-The Face (Iromagaja), Hunkpapa Sioux Tribal Leader, Is Born. Rain-In-

The Face is born in present-day North Dakota at the forks of the Cheyenne River. A leading Sioux war chief, he participates in the defense of Sioux land in the 1860s and 1870s. In 1866, he fights alongside fellow Hunkpapa leaders such as Gall, and the Oglala chief, Crazy Horse, during Red Cloud's War to prevent settlement along the Bozeman Trail in Wyoming and Montana. In 1868, he leads a raid of Fort Totten in North Dakota. In 1873, Rain-In-The-Face is arrested for murder at Fort Abraham Lincoln, near present-day Bismarck, North Dakota, but he escapes to join Sitting Bull in the fight for the Black Hills in 1876. He joins with other chiefs to defeat Custer's Seventh Cavalry at the battle of the Little Bighorn in June 1876. In 1880, Rain-In-The-Face surrenders at Fort Keogh, Montana, and spends his remaining years living on the Standing Rock Reservation in North Dakota.

DECEMBER 29, 1835   Treaty of New Echota. By the Treaty of New Echota, about ten percent of the Cherokee Nation cedes all its remaining lands east of the Mississippi River for $5 million and 8 million acres of land in the West. While the Cherokee resist the illegal treaty, most are forced to move west of the Mississippi River in 1838–39, where, in the words of the treaty, "they can establish and enjoy a government of their choice and perpetuate such a state of society as may be most consonant with their views, habits and conditions." The tribe's original homeland is sold to pay for the cost of removal, and also to establish a trust fund for agriculture and education to be administered by the president. In exchange, the United States sells the tribe a tract of land in what became known as the Indian Territory, promising that it will "in no future time without their consent, be included within the territorial limits or jurisdiction of any State or Territory." The United States also promises to "secure to the Cherokee Nation the right to make and carry into effect all such laws as they may deem necessary," provided they are consistent with the U.S. Constitution, and apply only

to Indians. The Cherokee are also promised a nonvoting "delegate" in the House of Representatives. Negotiated by one Cherokee political party (the Treaty Party), and viewed as a violation of the Cherokee constitution by the majority (the National Party), this treaty leads to assassination of several Cherokee leaders in 1839. In 1846, a treaty reunites the contending political parties, which were peaceful until 1860. The rivalries reemerged during the U.S. Civil War, when the slave-owning treaty party generally sided with the South, and most conservatives eventually sided with the North.

1835–1840   Pacific Northwest Smallpox Epidemic. Up to a third of some Indian groups along the Pacific Northwest die in a smallpox epidemic. The disease is apparently brought to the region by a ship arriving at Fort Simpson. The Haida are unaffected, and Indians south of Fort McLoughlin appear to be saved by vaccination efforts by Hudson's Bay Company employees at that fort.

1835–1841   The Second Seminole War. The Second Seminole War, which begins in the winter of 1835, is brought on by Seminole reaction to the 1832 Treaty of Payne's Landing and other attempts by the U.S. to remove the Seminole from Florida. Led by the Seminole war chiefs Osceola, Wild Cat, Alligator, and Aripeka, the Seminole conduct a guerrilla-style warfare which costs the U.S. government more than $20 million and the lives of 1,500 troops. Osceola emerges as the central leader of the Seminole resistance and aligned with Philip (called King Philip), leader of the Seminoles east of St. John's River, they coordinate an assault on U.S. plantations.

In the battle of Black Point, fought west of the town of Micanopy, Osceola kills U.S. agent Gen. Wiley Thompson. Elsewhere, Seminole ambush a relief column under Maj. Francis Dade on its way to Fort King, killing 107 of 110 men. Osceola is captured while under a flag of truce in 1837 and dies in prison in 1838. The

Second Seminole War continues until 1842 at which time most Seminole are removed west of the Mississippi River.

1835–1850 Indian Funds. The federal government invests nearly all of the money that it holds for the benefit of the Indian tribes in state bonds. When some states fail to pay the interest due, Indian funds earn little money.

1 8 3 6

1836 The Aborigines Protection Society Is Founded in Great Britain. The humanitarian society seeks to convince the British government that aboriginal groups should be assimilated into societies of British heritage. The political philosophy of "philanthropic liberalism," characterized by concern for workers in Britain's Industrial Revolution, indigenous peoples throughout the British Empire, and slaves in British colonies, is strong in Britain at this time. According to this philosophy, non-Europeans are seen as "white man's burden."

1836 Cornplanter, Seneca Tribal Leader, Dies. During his life Cornplanter is a leading warrior and village leader among the Seneca, one of six nations of the Iroquois Confederacy, who live in what is now upstate New York. Following the Revolutionary War, Cornplanter argues that the Iroquois will not survive unless they adopt agriculture and U.S. forms of government. He is opposed by the nationalistic Seneca leader, Red Jacket, who thinks the Iroquois will lose their identity if they adopt U.S. lifestyles. Between 1799 and 1815, however, Cornplanter's half-brother, Handsome Lake, leads a religious and social movement that reorganizes much of Iroquois culture. Cornplanter supports this movement, which results in adoption of agriculture, small farms, and new emphases on moral and religious order within Iroquois communities. Late in his life, Cornplanter emphasizes the need to retain Iroquois culture and lifeways.

Osceola, the Black Drink, a warrior of great distinction. Courtesy of the National Museum of the American Art, Washington D.C./Art Resource NY.

1836 Creek Removal. The condition of the Creek in Alabama worsens. Intruding U.S. settlers move in on Creek land and purchase all available provisions so that the Creek are unable to acquire even corn or meat. Drought and famine combine to increase Creek difficulties. Several lower town Creeks attack Alabama settlements in search of food and ignite a brief series of skirmishes often called the Creek War of 1836. The upper town Creek aid U.S. troops in subduing the rebellious towns. Creek leaders decide that it is no longer possible to live in the East because of oppressive Alabama laws and settler appropriation of lands even on the grounds where many Creek villages stand. In 1836 the Creek agree to remove west of the Mississippi River to Indian Territory.

1836 *Eulogy on King Philip.* This published work originally begins as a series of lectures given by William Apes (Pequot) at the Odeon in Boston, Massachusetts. Apes blatantly attacks racism in the *Eulogy*, indicting the Pilgrim fathers' disgraceful treatment of Indians, he calls King Philip, or Metacom, "the greatest man ever in America." The last of Apes's literary output, he mysteriously disappears shortly after the second edition of the *Eulogy* is printed.

1836 Indian Education. There are approximately 65,000 Indians living east of the Mississippi and the Missouri rivers. By this time, another 51 schools have been established in the new locations, instructing 2,221 Indian students; 156 Indian students of advanced grades are being instructed at the Choctaw Academy in Kentucky, and 4 of the graduates are studying for the legal profession in New York, Vermont, and elsewhere.

1836 The *Walam Olum*. The *Walam Olum*, a sacred tribal chronology of the Lenni Lenape (Delaware) Indians, is first published by a French botanist, Constantine Rafinesque. The *Walam Olum* is a pictographic record of the history of the world from the time of creation to Delaware settlement near the Atlantic Coast in present-day New Jersey.

1836 Winema, Modoc Cultural Mediator, Is Born. Winema is a peacemaker and negotiator during the Modoc War of 1872–73. She is born among the Modoc Indians in northern California, in a village located along the Link River. Among her people she is well respected for her bravery. According to one story, at the age of 14 she rallies the warriors of her village to victory during a surprise attack by another California tribe. However, she tests her people's patience a year later when, at age 15, she marries a Kentucky miner. Winema's own people refuse to sanction her marriage. Eventually, however, she becomes a valuable interpreter for the Modoc in their negotiations with U.S. settlers. Over time, Winema develops a reputation as a peacemaker and diplomat—two skills that are sorely needed in the Modoc War of 1872–73. Winema and her husband serve as negotiators, interpreters, and intermediaries for the opposing sides during the Modoc War, and Winema is made a celebrity in the U.S. national media. She is escorted to Washington, D.C., for a special visit with President Ulysses S.

Grant. For the next seven years, Winema tours eastern cities in dramatic reenactments of Indian history and issues. She dies in 1920.

AUGUST 9, 1836 Manitoulin Island Reserve Established. Sir Francis Bond Head, the new lieutenant-governor of Upper Canada, believes that Indians are a "doomed race" that cannot be integrated into Euro-Canadian society. He tries to convince Ottawa (Odawa) and Mississauga (Ojibway) Indians to move to a reserve on Manitoulin Island, a large island separating Georgian Bay from the rest of Lake Huron. Head believes that the Indians are a "doomed race" that will gradually die out. Head becomes convinced that Indians are doomed after visiting Indian communities throughout Upper Canada after his arrival in the colony in January. Chief Jean-Baptiste Assiginack (1768–1865), an Ottawa who fought for the British in the War of 1812, is one of the signatories to the treaty that establishes the Manitoulin Indian Reserve. Head's policy, a reversal of Upper Canada's policy adopted in 1830 that had sought to integrate Indians into non-Native society, is abandoned when it is opposed by many Indian leaders such as Peter Jones *(See* biography, January 1, 1802), missionary groups, and humanitarian organizations such as the Aborigines Protection Society. Ojibway and Ottawa groups do move to Manitoulin Island, however, and Roman Catholics establish an Indian mission at Wikemikong and Anglicans at Manitowaning for these Indians.

SEPTEMBER 10, 1836 Sioux Land Cession. Encouraged by the state of Missouri, Zachary Taylor, the acting Indian agent, secures Sioux land in the northwestern section for $550,000.

1836–1870 Smallpox Epidemics on the Plains. The western smallpox epidemic decimates the once numerous Mandan and Hidatsa in central North Dakota. Both tribes lose as much as 90 percent of their population, leaving only a few hundred survivors. The Mandan population drops from between 1,600 and 2,000 to less than 100. Other Plains nations are also hit hard, some left with only about 20 percent of their previous numbers. Between 1836 and 1870, at least four smallpox epidemics kill thousands of people in the Plains Indian nations.

1 8 3 7

JUNE 1837 Canadian Indian Smallpox Epidemic. Assiniboine visiting the American Fur Company's Fort Union on the upper Missouri, in present-day western Montana, contract smallpox from infected traders. During the following months up to three-quarters of the Siksika, Peigan, Kainai (Blood), Sarcee, Atsina, and Assiniboine are killed after the disease spreads throughout the northern plains. Vaccination efforts by the Hudson's Bay Company between September and January help prevent the spread of the disease to the Cree or to their northern neighbors.

SEPTEMBER 29, 1837 Sioux Treaty. A treaty is negotiated in Washington, D.C., with the Sioux ceding all of their land east of the Mississippi, for which they are promised the distribution of annuities and goods each August at Fort Snelling. Problems arise over the safekeeping and distribution of payments, as graft and corruption among Indian agents and army personnel sharply reduce the annuities and goods actually received.

OCTOBER 21, 1837 Sauk (Sac) and Fox Land Cessions. The government demands more land from the Sauk and Fox, over and above that ceded in the 1832 treaty that concluded Blackhawk's War. For the new cession, the Indians are to receive goods and monies to be invested in stock. A treaty is also signed with the Sauk and Fox of Missouri for additional land cessions.

DECEMBER 1837 Gabriel Dumont, Métis Leader, Is Born. Gabriel Dumont is born at the Red River Colony, son of a Métis hunter. The

Métis are a cohesive community descended from mostly French-Cree or French-Ojibway forbearers. In 1851 he takes part in the defense of a Métis party in the battle of the Grand Coteau, and in 1862 helps conclude a peace agreement with Dakota bands that have fled north from Minnesota. Later he participates in the arrangement of peace between the Métis and the Blackfoot Confederacy.

Dumont develops into a particularly skilled guide, hunter, canoeist, and warrior, and, though he is literate in none of them, he learns to speak six languages. Dumont's skill as a buffalo hunter leads to his election in 1863 as the permanent chief of the Métis buffalo hunts, a role he holds until the last Métis hunt in 1881.

Following the Red River Resistance of 1870, Dumont emerges as the leader of the growing Métis community surrounding Batoche. Concerned that the Canadian government is ignoring their land rights, Dumont travels to Montana in 1884 to invite the exiled Louis Riel, leader of the Red River Resistance, to come to the Métis settlements of the North-West Territories to lead another resistance against Canadian authorities. Becoming "adjutant general" of the 300-member Métis army, Dumont wages successful guerrilla battles during the North-West Rebellion. Following the defeat of the Métis and the surrender of Riel, Dumont flees to the United States where he joins Buffalo Bill's Wild West Show. Granted an amnesty for his role in the North-West Rebellion in 1888, he returns to Canada. He dies at Batoche, Saskatchewan on May 16, 1906, having dictated his memoirs.

1837–1853 Kenekuk, the Kickapoo Prophet. Following the end of the War of 1812, Kenekuk, a Kickapoo, assumes leadership of a segment of the Kickapoo Nation, then living along the Osage River in Illinois. Based on Kenekuk's teachings, these Kickapoo form a community of 350 that turns to agriculture and adopts selected Protestant, Catholic, and traditional religious and moral teachings. While strongly resisting removal from their homeland, they are finally forced to migrate to Missouri in 1833 and to Kansas by 1837. There, the prophet converts a group of Potawatomi, who join the prophet's community in 1851. This community survives to the present. Kenekuk dies in Kansas in 1853, but not before promising his faithful that he will rise again after three days.

1 8 3 8

MAY 1838–MARCH 1839 Cherokee Removal. Removal of the Cherokee begins when Gen. Winfield Scott and 7,000 federal troops are sent to complete the removal of the Cherokee from the state of Georgia. Scott's troops forcibly round up the Cherokee and place them in stockades in preparation for starting them on the long trail to Indian Territory. The Cherokee remember the trek as "The Trail Where They Cried," while U.S. historians call it "The Trail of Tears." The arduous forced march begins in October 1838, and costs the Cherokee one-fourth their number, or more than 4,000 men, women, and children. The survivors reach their destination in late March 1839, reorganize themselves in the new area, and prosper despite the odds, retaining their language and alphabet to the present day. The move involves 16,000 persons and is only the first of many "trails of tears" for the eastern and southern Indian nations.

JULY 22, 1838 Tlingit, Tahltan Trade Networks. Shakes, a Tlingit chief, is dismayed to see see Hudson's Bay Company (H.B.C.) employee Robert Campbell at a Tlingit-Tahltan trade rendezvous on the lower Stikine River. The Tahltan, who escort Campbell to the rendezvous are former enemies of the Tlingit, but have made peace in order to acquire the Russian American Company and H.B.C. goods to which the Tlingit have access. Campbell has arrived in an attempt to compete with the Russian traders at the mouth of the Stikine, but the Tlingit and Tahltan understand that Campbell, who has

approached the area from the northwest via the Liard and Dease rivers (the homeland of the Sekani and Kaska), may threaten their advantageous position as middlemen. For this reason the Tahltan harass Campbell's party during the following winter after they establish a trading post at nearby Dease Lake. The post is abandoned in the spring.

1 8 3 9

C. 1839 Buffalo Bird Woman, Hidatsa Woman, Is Born. Also known by her Hidatsa name, Waheenee, Buffalo Bird Woman spends 12 years relating her personal and tribal experiences to anthropologist Gilbert Wilson beginning in 1906.

C. 1839 Charles Edenshaw, Haida Artist, Is Born. Edenshaw is born a member of the Eagle Clan at the Yatza Haida village on Graham Island in the Queen Charlotte Islands of British Columbia. He is named Takayren, or Noise-In-The-House, at birth. At a young age, Edenshaw displays a particular skill in the carving of wood and argillite (a type of black slate found naturally on the Queen Charlotte Islands). Noted for its flowing sculptural design, the popularity of his work allows him to become one of the few professional Northwest Coastal Indian carvers of his era. He frequently meets with art collectors and anthropologists (including Franz Boas and John Swanton), providing them with information about Haida art and culture and with many of his carvings, including model totem poles and drawing and sketches. This information and these carvings allow for a certain continuity in Haida art over the years. His work dramatically illustrates the intricacy of Northwest Coastal art. Though Edenshaw dies in 1924, his work continues. His great-grandson, Robert Davidson, is one of the most important contemporary carvers and a significant contributor to the post-1960s renaissance of Northwest Coastal art.

Painting of the Cherokees' Trail of Tears. Courtesy of the Woolaroc Museum, Bartlesville, Oklahoma.

JANUARY 1839 Tlingit Trade Networks. The Russian American Company agrees to lease the right to trade along the North Pacific Coast (the Alaskan panhandle) to the Hudson's Bay Company (H.B.C.). The agreement means that, rather than trying to trade directly with the Tahltan and other inland Indians, the H.B.C. will be satisfied to benefit from extensive Tlingit trading networks to convey furs to the coast. This allows the H.B.C. to direct its expansion to the area northwest of the Liard River (Yukon Territory).

APRIL 22, 1839 Canadian Indian Assimilation. Upper Canadian Judge James Buchanan Macaulay submits his report which recommends that Upper Canada's Indians be assimilated rather than sent to isolated reserves. Many Indian leaders have rejected the policy of the former lieutenant-governor of Upper Canada, Sir Francis Bond Head, which proposed to send all Indians to isolated reserves in the belief that Indians cannot succeed in non-Native society. With the help of Methodist missionaries led by Peter Jones (*See* biography, January

1, 1802), the residents of the Credit River Reserve have, since 1830, become successful farmers. Joseph Sawyer, chief of the Mississauga of the Credit River Reserve near Toronto, and other Indian leaders and missionaries welcome the report.

JULY 15, 1839   **Texas.** Texans attack the villages of Indians in northeast Texas. As a result, Cherokee, Caddo, Delaware, Shawnee, and Kickapoo peoples go north to Oklahoma. In 1840 the Cheyenne and Arapaho make peace with the Sioux, Kiowa, Kiowa Apache, and Comanche at a great council on the Arkansas River, bringing all of the High Plains tribes together in an alliance from the Black Hills in South Dakota to Texas.

1 8 4 0

1840   American Horse, Oglala Sioux Tribal Leader, Is Born. In the mid 1860s and 1870s American Horse is a Sioux leader in Red Cloud's War, which was fought for control of the Bozeman Trail, a major passage through Wyoming and Montana. He is a cousin of Red Cloud, another major Sioux leader. Until his death in 1876 American Horse remains a militant opponent to U.S. settlement of the western plains.

1840   Gall (Pizi), Hunkpapa Sioux Tribal Leader, Is Born. Raised as an orphan until his adoption by Sitting Bull, a major Sioux leader, Gall proves his abilities as a warrior early in life. During the skirmishes for control of the Bozeman Trail in 1866 and 1867, Gall establishes and hones the guerrilla techniques and decoy tactics he will use later in the struggle for control of the Black Hills. Gall is one of the principal strategists in the battle of Little Bighorn and is credited with developing the tactics that defeated Col. George Custer and some 200 U.S. soldiers in June 1876. Following the Little Bighorn, Gall leaves for Canada with Sitting Bull. In 1881, he returns to the United States

with about 300 people and surrenders at the Poplar Agency in eastern Montana. He is relocated on the Standing Rock Reservation in North Dakota. There, Gall becomes friends with Indian agent James McLaughlin and adopts a way of life more European than Indian. Gall dies in 1894.

1840   Joseph, Nez Percé Leader, Is Born. Joseph is born in the Wallowa Valley in present-day Oregon. Like his father before him, Joseph attempts to carry out a plan of passive resistance to U.S. land encroachment and to efforts by the U.S. government to relocate his people to the Nez Percé Reservation in western Idaho. The fragile peace is shattered in 1877, when U.S. settlers begin moving into the Wallowa Valley. On June 12, the inevitable fighting erupts when three young Nez Percé kill four settlers who have moved into the valley. After some initial battles, in which he demonstrates remarkable military skill, Joseph and the Nez Percé decide to escape to Canada. For the next three months they elude both U.S. troops and enemy Indian bands. In late September the Nez Percé group find themselves surrounded, only miles from the Canadian border. On October 5, 1877, Chief Joseph surrenders. In the minds of of the American public, Joseph becomes permanently identified with the courageous journey taken by the Nez Percé, largely due to his dramatic, often quoted speech made at the time of his surrender. Joseph spends the rest of his life on a number of different Indian reservations and dies on the Colville Indian Reservation in the state of Washington in 1904.

1840   Left Hand (Nawat), Southern Arapaho Tribal Leader, Is Born. As one of the principal chiefs of the Southern Cheyenne, Left Hand treads the delicate line between advocating peace and defending against U.S. encroachment. He also represents his people in negotiations with the federal government in the early 1890s. Left Hand and his warriors are present with the Southern Cheyenne leader Black Kettle at the battle of Sand Creek in November

1864, when about 150 Cheyenne men, women, and children are indiscriminately killed by Col. John Chivington's troops. The incident is considered one of the most grievous of the Civil War. Left Hand is wounded during the shooting, but refuses to take up arms and return fire against Chivington's forces. Left Hand becomes the principal chief of the Southern Arapaho in 1889, upon the death of Little Raven. In 1890, he agrees to allotment of Southern Cheyenne land in present-day Oklahoma, despite opposition from most Southern Cheyenne who prefer traditional sharing and collective ownership of land. Ultimately the allotment of land leaves most Indians in Oklahoma with a greatly reduced land base. Left Hand dies in the 1890s.

1840   Lozen, Chiricahua Apache Woman Warrior and Healer, Is Born. This swift-footed Chiricahua Apache women gains renown as a remarkable warrior and healer. A knowledgeable reconnaissance tactician, an excellent markswoman, a keen strategist, and a powerful healer, she remains single throughout her life in order to serve her people. The Chiricahua respect Lozen's uniqueness and come to rely upon her warrior ability in their battles with Mexico and the United States in the late nineteenth century. Accompanying the Apache leader Geronimo, she is one of two messengers dispatched to American troops to arrange his final surrender. In 1886, she is sent to Fort Marion and held prisoner there. Later in 1887 she is moved to Mount Vernon Barracks, Alabama, where she dies, probably due to tuberculosis.

JUNE 7, 1840   Peel River Post Established. Red Leggings and his Eastern Kutchin (Gwich'in) band, who reside in the region surrounding the Mackenzie River delta near the Arctic Ocean, induce Hudson's Bay Company traders John Bell and Alexander Kennedy Isbister (*See* biography, June 1822) to establish the Peel River Post (Fort McPherson) at a site the Kutchin have chosen on the Lower Peel River. These Kutchin protect their role as middlemen, by preventing direct trade between the fur traders and the Kutchin bands west of the Richardson Mountains, and the Inuit.

1840s   Missionaries in Red River Colony. Roman Catholic (Oblates of Mary Immaculate) missionaries, Methodist missionaries, and Anglican missionaries begin their work throughout the region west of the Great Lakes. (Missionaries started their work in the Red River Colony in 1818, but until now the Hudson's Bay Company has prevented them from spreading throughout the West.) Missionaries seek not only to evangelize Indians, but to transform their societies and lifestyles. They emerge, in the ensuing 30 years, as important intermediaries between the Indians and outside powers. Along the Pacific, the Roman Catholic missionaries and the Protestant missionaries seem to focus their efforts in separate areas (the Catholics along the south coast and the Protestants along the north coast), although in most other areas the groups appear to compete for converts.

1840–1860   Indian Territory and the Indian State. During the 1840s and 1850s U.S. officials adhere to a plan of ultimately moving all Indians to Indian Territory, in what is now Kansas and Oklahoma. By doing so, U.S. officials believe that more land can be opened to settlers, and the Indians can be incorporated into the United States by means of their own state, with elected officials representing Indian interests in Congress. In the post-Civil War period, however, this plan is abandoned because many Indian nations do not want to move to Indian Territory, and most do not want to be incorporated under one Indian political government or be included in the U.S. Congress and government.

c. 1840–c. 1890   The Golden Age of Northwest Coastal Art. With improved tools and greater wealth brought by the fur trade in the post-contact period, the art of the Northwest Coast flourishes during the mid-nineteenth century. Among the arts of the region are dancing blankets, weavings, button blankets, and a variety of sculptural forms, including ceremonial masks, rattles, and the well-known totem poles. As wealth increases and artistic forms evolve, clans seek to aggrandize their kin-groups and potlatches or give-away ceremonies become more elaborate and more frequent. Although disease greatly reduces the Northwest Coast populations, it is only with the banning of the potlatch by the Canadian government in 1884 that this artistic golden age comes to an end.

1 8 4 1

1841   Fort Ross. The Russians relinquish their northern coastal headquarters at Fort Ross, in present-day northern California, leaving the area open for occupation by Mexican authorities. The fort is purchased by John Sutter.

1841   Methodist Hymnal Published Using Cree Syllabics. James Evans, a Methodist missionary at Norway House, near the north end of Lake Winnipeg, prints a hymnal using the Cree syllabics that he has devised. This form of written Cree, later adapted to Dene and Inuit dialects, is important to missionary work but will also do much to facilitate the survival of Native languages and communication among Native peoples.

JANUARY 26, 1841   Micmac Appeal Land Loss to Queen Victoria. Queen Victoria receives an appeal from Micmac headman Paul Peminuit regarding the loss of hunting grounds, and encroachment on lands the Micmac claim as their own. The population of the Micmac at this time is declining steadily. Queen Victoria's interest prompts an investigation.

MAY 8, 1841   John Norquay, Country-Born Politician, Is Born. John Norquay is born into a Country-born family in St. Andrews, in the Red River Colony. The Country-born are

English-speaking Protestant mixed-blood peoples. The French-speaking Roman Catholic mixed-blood known as Métis form a separate community in Red River. (Later, descendants of nineteenth-century Country-born will become identified either as non-Native or as Métis.) Norquay, an excellent student, turns first to teaching and farming but eventually to politics. He is elected by acclamation to Manitoba's first legislature in 1870, becoming the minister of public works and then minister of agriculture. In 1878 he becomes the premier of the province, a position he holds for the next nine years. Though a popular premier, his government falls in scandal in 1887. Norquay dies July 15, 1889.

1 8 4 2

1842   Crazy Horse, Oglala-Brulé Sioux Tribal Leader, Is Born. Crazy Horse is born to the east of the sacred Black Hills near present-day Rapid City. While still a young man, Crazy Horse has a vivid dream of a rider on horseback in a storm, which his father interpreted as a sign of future greatness in battle. In the 1866–68 war over the Bozeman Trail, Crazy Horse joins the Oglala chief Red Cloud in raids against U.S. settlements and forts in Wyoming. On June 25, 1876, the famous battle of the Little Bighorn commences. Crazy Horse and his predominantly Cheyenne warriors attack Custer's men from the north and west. Gall and his forces charge Custer from the south and east. The U.S. troops are surrounded and completely annihilated. Despite several other brilliant campaigns against U.S. troops, the Sioux are starving and weary of battle. On May 6, 1877, Crazy Horse reluctantly surrenders with 800 followers at Fort Robinson in northwestern Nebraska. Crazy Horse is bayoneted at the Fort during an attempt to confine him to a guardhouse on September 5, 1877.

MAY 1842   Joseph Howe Appointed Indian Commissioner. The Nova Scotia government appoints Joseph Howe as an unpaid Indian commissioner. Howe's recommendations have formed the basis of Nova Scotia's Indian Act passed in March. Howe is authorized to prevent non-Natives from settling on Micmac lands, to see that money is spent to help Indians adjust to a different lifestyle, and to provide for Indian education. Howe's initial enthusiasm for the job wanes quickly. He estimates that there are only 1,300 Indians in Nova Scotia in 1843. The government finds itself unable to prevent squatting.

JULY 19, 1842 Kaska Indians Begin Trading at *Toutcho*. The Hudson's Bay Company traders at *Toutcho* (Great Water, Frances Lake), a large lake in today's southeastern Yukon, give the Kaska, Dene hunter-gatherers of the region, their first easy access to European goods. Prior to this time the Kaska apparently have had sporadic access to second-hand Russian trade goods, to valued dentalium shells conveyed to them via Chilkat (Tlingit) and Tutchone traders along aboriginal trade routes, and, recently, to goods traded at Hudson's Bay Company posts on the Liard River east of the area they inhabit. The confluence of the Pelly and Yukon rivers west of Frances Lake is an important trading site for the Coast Tlingit and the Southern Tutchone. Although the Tagish and Tutchone resent the dominance of the Tlingit, they depend on the Tlingit for access to European goods. They in turn act as middlemen to other Tutchone and Kaska bands. The Tagish of the upper Taku River are beginning to move to the region of Tagish and Marsh lakes in the upper reaches of the Yukon River in order to take advantage of the rich fur resources of that region. The close trade relationships between the Tagish and Tlingit lead the Tagish and Inland Tlingit to adopt aspects of Tlingit culture, including the Tlingit language.

1 8 4 3

1843 Eskimo Mission School. The Russian-

Greek Orthodox Church establishes the first mission school for Eskimos in Nushagak, Alaska.

1843 Horse Culture. By 1843 the Crow Indians, living in the Yellowstone and Big Horn rivers area of the Rocky Mountains, possess approximately 10,000 horses. Some of the horses were obtained in war with the Sioux and Blackfeet, others through trading and selective breading. The Crow are described as a nomadic tribe of hunters who plant only tobacco and whose dwellings number about 400 tipis.

1843 Maliseet Petition for Recognition of Land Rights. Maliseet chiefs in New Brunswick petition the New Brunswick government to recognize the same Indian land rights that the Royal Proclamation of 1763 has extended to Indians in other British provinces. Indians in New Brunswick have been affected by encroachment by farmers and foresters, and the New Brunswick government has been sympathetic to squatters.

1843 Wampum Belts. During an important tribal council meeting at Tahlequah, in present-day Oklahoma, Cherokee members make wampum belts to depict the peace they had concluded with the Iroquois prior to the Revolutionary War.

MARCH 15, 1843 Hudson's Bay Company Establishes Fort Victoria. The Hudson's Bay Company establishes Fort Victoria on southern Vancouver Island on the Pacific Coast. The Songhee Coast Salish of Cadboro Bay relocate near the trading center. By the 1860s Indians travel from as far away as the Queen Charlotte Islands and southern Alaska to trade and to find seasonal wage work at Victoria.

1 8 4 4

1844 Canadian Land Rights. Following 15 months of public hearings, a Commission on

Indian Affairs (the Bagot Commission) issues its "Report on the Affairs of the Indians of Canada." Describing the conditions among Canada's Indians (particularly in Upper Canada) as deplorable, it criticizes the lack of a coherent Indian policy in the Province of Canada (formerly Upper Canada and Lower Canada). It recommends that Indian land rights be recognized, and reserves surveyed while efforts to assimilate Indians continue. These dual recommendations of protection and assimilation become the basis of Canadian Indian policy for over a century. The commission is established on October 10, 1842, by Sir Charles Bagot, former governor-general of British North America, after he realizes that Canadian Indian policy has been unresolved since 1830.

1844 Sarah Winnemucca, Northern Paiute Activist and Educator, Is Born. Sarah Winnemucca is born near the Humboldt River in western Nevada. When she is 14, she moves in with the family of a stagecoach agent, Maj. William Ormsby, where she learns English. The Paiute War begins in 1860 and is led by Winnemucca's cousin, Numaga. She and many hostile Paiute are moved to a reservation near present-day Reno, Nevada. During the Snake War in 1866, the military requests that she and her brother, Naches, act as intermediaries. Winnemucca became the official interpreter in the military's negotiations with the Paiute and Shoshoni.

She is active as a peacemaker, teacher, and defender of her people's rights, and in 1879 lectures to sympathetic audiences in San Francisco and Sacramento, where she discusses the treatment of Indians by Indian service employees. Winnemucca commences a lecture tour of the East in 1883–84 and dresses as an Indian princess to draw crowds. While there, she meets with many important sympathizers of Indian rights and publishes *Life among the Paiutes, Their Wrongs and Claims.* Winnemucca returns to Nevada and founds a school for Indians with

money she has saved and from private donations. The school remains open for three years until funding runs out and Sarah's health falters. She dies of tuberculosis at the age of 47.

SEPTEMBER 3, 1844 New Brunswick Government Restricts Size of Land Reserves. The New Brunswick government passes legislation which restricts land reserves to a size of 50 acres (20 hectares) per family. The proceeds of the sale of additional lands are to be used for the benefit of the Indians. The money subsequently raised is very modest because of the low prices of the land.

OCTOBER 22, 1844 Louis Riel, Jr., Métis Leader, Is Born. Riel is born to a French-Ojibway (Métis) man and a French Canadian woman in the Métis community at the Red River Colony. Beginning his education in the colony, he also studies at the Collége de Montreal. After traveling through the United States for a time, he returns to the colony in 1868. The following year he leads the Métis in their resistance to the Canadian government (known as the Red River Resistance or Red River Rebellion). In August 1870 Riel flees to the United States, fearing arrest by Canadian forces. He is elected to the federal House of Commons in 1873 and in 1874, but never takes his seat. In the late 1870s he spends some time in a mental institution following a nervous breakdown and is released in 1878. He becomes a teacher at the St. Peter's mission in Montana until June 1884 when he accepts an invitation travel to Métis settlements in the North-West Territories, to represent the Métis in their grievances against the federal government. Riel's provisional government established at Batoche in 1885 prompts a strong response by the Canadian government. The North-West Rebellion is quickly crushed, and he is arrested. He is convicted of treason and executed in

Regina (Saskatchewan) on November 16, 1885. Riel is buried in St. Boniface, near Winnipeg. His execution has remained controversial, and calls for his posthumous pardon have been raised, especially by Métis. Several statues are erected in his memory. His entire writings also have been published.

1844–1845 Military Posts. Legislation is brought before the U.S. House of Representatives to secure land and build military posts to protect emigration and commerce from the East to California and Oregon. The U.S. Congress passes several enabling acts to secure the necessary land and build military forts to promote increased emigration and to protect travelers en route from the eastern and central United States to California and Oregon.

1 8 4 5

1845 Quanah Parker, Comanche Tribal and Spiritual Leader, Is Born. Parker is the son of Peta Nocona, chief of the Kwahadi band in Texas, a subgroup within the Comanche Nation, and Cynthia Parker, a non-Comanche captive. Throughout the 1860s, Parker leads numerous attacks against U.S. soldiers. He and his band escape capture longer than most Comanche in their final days living freely on the plains. In the 1870s, however, new high-powered rifles and increasing numbers of U.S. hunters are systematically killing buffalo and destroying the way of life of the Plains Indians. In 1875, after years of battle and their buffalo nearly gone, Parker and his warriors turn themselves in, defeated by hunters with repeating rifles. Parker quickly adapts to reservation life in Oklahoma where he becomes a successful rancher. He counsels his people to adapt to the

reservation without surrendering their Comanche customs and heritage. Parker adopts the peyote religion, which differs in many ways from traditional religions but offers many Indians a new form of religious belief that provides moral and spiritual support in the reservation setting. Parker becomes an appointed judge and serves in the court of Indian affairs from 1886 to 1898. He dies in 1911.

Canada Post issued this stamp honoring Louis Riel in 1970—85 years after he was executed for treason. Courtesy of the Canada Post Corporation.

1 8 4 6

1846   Annexation of Texas. With the annexation of Texas by the United States, additional Indian tribes are added to U.S. governmental control and administration. By the terms of a general peace treaty signed on May 15 at Council Springs, Texas, the Wichita, Comanche, Lipan, Kichai, and Caddo Indians recognize the jurisdiction of the U.S. government.

1846   Navajo Resistance. At the end of the Mexican-American War, U.S. settlers move into California and New Mexico where the *Diné* (Navajo for "the people," which they called themselves) face the U.S. Army. The Navajo are one of the first Indian nations in the American Southwest to deal with the United States. Between 1600 and 1846 the Navajo had confronted the *Nakai,* or Spanish, who had moved into the Rio Grande Valley of New Mexico onto lands belonging to Pueblo Indians. The Europeans introduced cattle, sheep, and horses to the Natives, and the Navajo took advantage of the innovations by sweeping down on New Mexican villages to steal stock. Comanche, Kiowa, Apache, Ute, and others followed suit, giving rise to an economy based in part on raiding. By 1846, when the United States enters New Mexico, Navajo people already have extensive holdings of cattle, sheep, and horses.

When Col. Stephen Watts Kearny enters New Mexico in 1846, he promises to end Navajo raids on New Mexican villages and, to this end, he dispatches Col. Alexander W. Doniphan to Navajo country. Doniphan meets with a group of Navajo *Naat'aanis* (headmen) at Bear Springs near present-day Gallup, New Mexico. He concludes the first treaty with the Navajo, which is ratified by the U.S. Senate and signed by the president. But the treaty means little to the Navajo who attack Doniphan's herd of horses shortly after meeting with him.

During the 1850s a number of Navajo leaders sign treaties with the United States intended to end hostilities and to establish trade relations between Indian and non-Indian communities of New Mexico. The agreements fail because the Navajo continue to raid New Mexican villages, and because New Mexicans enslave Navajo. The conflict centers on livestock and slaves, not land, since most non-Indians consider Navajo land beautiful but unproductive. In 1860, Col. Edward R. S. Canby, who had fought the Seminole in Florida, leads a campaign against the Navajo. By sending out small raiding parties and striking purposefully at civilian populations, Canby brings the Navajo to the bargaining table. In the spring of 1861 several Navajo leaders, including Manuelito, Barboncito, Armijo, Herrero, and Ganada Mucho agree to a peace treaty. Canby's campaign probably would have ended the Navajo wars had it not been for the U.S. Civil War.

JUNE 1846   Potawatomi Treaty. A series of treaties are made between the U.S. and Potawatomi bands, uniting them into the Potawatomi Nation and locating them together on land on the Kansas River. By treaties of June 5, 1846, November 15, 1861, and February 27, 1867, the Potawatomi Reserve, an area of 29.75 square miles in Kansas, is set apart for the Potawatomi.

JUNE 15, 1846   Oregon Boundary Treaty. The Oregon Boundary Treaty extends the boundary between the United States and British North America from the Rocky Mountains to the Pacific Ocean.

OCTOBER 13, 1846   Winnebago Land Cession. The Winnebago are compelled to sell to the U.S. all rights, title, interest, claim, and privileges to all land previously occupied by them, and in exchange are given land west of the Mississippi, hunting privileges, and a sum of money.

1846–1848   Mexican-American War. In California, armed settlers, aided by Capt. John C.

Fremont, who was in the area on a surveying assignment, capture Sonoma and declare California a republic. This revolt, named the Bear Flag Revolt because of the bear emblem on the California Republic flag, lasts only 26 days. Commodore John Sloat, in command of a U.S. fleet offshore, takes possession of the capital, Monterey, on July 7, 1846. The war ends in 1848 with the Treaty of Guadalupe Hidalgo. Mexico cedes to the United States any and all claims to California and the Southwest. The U.S. government thus brings American Indian policy to that region of the country and to the Pacific Northwest. As in other parts of the nation, the government considers that Indians have a "natural right" to the land; however, the Indians can also relinquish their lands through treaties. Throughout the West, the United States commissions agents to extinguish Indian title to millions of acres. Nations such as the Navajo, Sioux, Kiowa, and Modoc fight back against the U.S. Army. Others such as the Crow, Caddo, Blackfeet, Hopi, and Nespelem do not. Regardless of the policies followed by the various nations, the ultimate results are the same; the United States asserts its authority through the army and the Indian administration. Lands are taken from the Indians through treaties or by right of conquest. Western Indians secure for themselves only a minute portion of their former lands and live on lands ruled by Indian agents. Many Indians are relocated to lands controlled by their neighbors. Others are concentrated on reservations with other Indian nations, including former enemies.

1846–1858 Indian Population. More than 100,000 Indian people are added to the U.S. population by the annexation of Texas, the settlement of the Oregon boundary dispute, and the Treaty of Guadalupe Hidalgo (1848) with Mexico. Under the provisions of the 1848 treaty, the United States promises to honor the treaties and agreements made between the Indians and Mexico.

1 8 4 7

1847 *The Last of the Mohicans.* A monument is erected by the citizens of Norwich, Connecticut, in memory of Uncas, a famous Mohegan chief, memorialized in the book, *The Last of the Mohicans,* written by James Fenimore Cooper.

1847 *The Life, History, and Travels of Kah-ge-ga-bowh.* Public interest in books about Indians contributes to the publishing of *Kah-ge-ga-bowh.* Written by George Copway, an Ojibway author, this autobiography presents the writer as one who possesses both the virtues of the noble savage and western civilization. Initially raised within a traditional context, he becomes a Methodist convert at the age of 11; ergo, he demonstrates the capability of Indians to do likewise. At a time when the American public believed that the Indian must assimilate or perish, Copway's seemingly dualistic image appeals to the reading public. This image of the Native who embodies two ways of life will become a standard theme within American Indian literature.

1847 Pueblo Revolt. The Taos Pueblo Indians, angered by United States conduct of the Mexican War, attack and kill the U.S. governor of New Mexico. United States troops retaliate, attack Taos Pueblo, and kill approximately 165 Indians.

FEBRUARY 17, 1847 Petition for Removal of Hudson's Bay Company Presented to British Government. Mixed-blood (Country-born) lawyer Alexander Kennedy Isbister *(See* biography, June 1822) presents a Métis petition to the British government asking for the removal of the Hudson's Bay Company (H.B.C.) charter and the reorganization of the H.B.C. colony at Red River as a colony of the British government.

MARCH 3, 1847 Trade and Intercourse Act Passes. The act is designed to regulate trade and intercourse with the tribes and to maintain peace on the frontiers. This act defines the

Captain Cold, or Ut-ha-wah. Painting by William John Wilgus, c. 1838. Captain Cold was the Onondaga keeper of the Iroquois League Fire at Buffalo Creek. The Buffalo Creek Reservation was sold as a consequence of the Compromise Treaty of 1842, and when Ut-ha-wah died in 1847, little was left of the once powerful league. Courtesy of Yale University Art Gallery.

procedures for eliminating the liquor trade among the Indians.

JUNE 27, 1847   Kutchin Begin Direct Trade with Hudson's Bay Company. The Kutchin (Gwich'in) at the confluence of the Porcupine and Yukon rivers begin direct trade with Hud-

son's Bay Company (H.B.C.) traders who are establishing Fort Yukon at the site. These Indians, and the Han who inhabit the Yukon Valley upriver from the site, are pleased with the development because, up until now, they have depended on middlemen to bring goods upstream from Russian trading centers near the mouth of the river, or on Tutchone and Tagish bands farther upstream who acquire goods via the Tlingit on the Pacific Coast. Kutchin at the site draw maps of part of the Yukon River for the H.B.C. traders.

NOVEMBER 29, 1847   Whitman Killing. Cayuse Indians kill Oregon missionary Marcus Whitman and others. The Indians believe that the missionaries brought diseases that kill many people. In revenge, the Cayuse attack the missionaries. In February 1848, Col. Cornelius Gilliam leads 550 Oregon militiamen on an indiscriminate punitive expedition to avenge the Whitman deaths. Warfare breaks out in Oregon and, on August 14, 1848, the federal government responds to the crisis by creating the Oregon Territory.

1 8 4 8

1848   California Gold Rush. In 1848, Maidu and other California Indians working for James Marshall, a miller, discover gold at Sutter's Mill on the American River, near Sacramento, California. At first, Native Americans in California work in the gold mines, contributing significantly to their discovery and success. Between 1848 and 1850 California officials estimate that more than half the miners in California are Natives. During the 1850s some California miners abuse and kill many Indian men, women, and children. The discovery of gold at Sutter's Mill touches off a tremendous influx of people. In 1849 the gold rush begins in earnest as prospectors, ruffians, and adventurers pour into California. Widespread abuse of Indian people takes place as miners see them first as competitors in the gold field, and second, as impediments to the opening of additional land for gold exploration. Militia groups wage a war of extermination against "Digger Indians" of northern California as gold prospectors push northward and inland in search of the mother lode. The discovery of gold marks the beginning of the end for many of the California Indian tribes. In the 1850s the tribes are coerced into signing treaties with the United States, in which they cede half the state to the U.S. in return for ownership of approximately 8 million acres of land.

JUNE 1, 1848 Fort Selkirk Established. Robert Campbell of the Hudson's Bay Company (H.B.C.) arrives at the confluence of the Pelly and Yukon rivers in Canada, the location of annual Tlingit-Tutchone trading meetings. A group of Northern Tutchone are at the site. A group of Chilkat (Tlingit) that arrives in August, after the H.B.C. has established Fort Selkirk at the site, are upset to find that their ability to control the flow of European goods is threatened. Well-defended by H.B.C. employees and the Tutchone, the Chilkat do not attack the stockaded fort. In fact they agree to convey a letter from Campbell to the H.B.C. traders on the Pacific Coast.

1 8 4 9

1849 California Indian Mission System. The discovery of gold in the state of California adds to the misery of the "mission" Indians, who are already suffering because of the withdrawal of support and direction of the Spanish priests, who have, unfortunately, made them a dependent people. When Mexico becomes independent of Spain, the missions lose financial support from Europe and are forced to shut down, with consequent devastating effects on the Indians. Having surrendered possession of their own lands, many California Indians have no land on which to settle. Ultimately some mea-

ger and unsatisfactory adjustments are made, so that today there are more than 100 reservations in California, some that cover as much as 25,000 acres but others as little as two acres.

1849 Fort Rupert Established. Fort Rupert is established by the Hudson's Bay Company and becomes, until 1870, the main population center of the Kwagiulth (Kwakiutl, Kwakwaka'wakw), who reside on northeastern Vancouver Island and the nearby mainland. The post is established to exploit local coal resources, and employs Indians as miners.

MARCH 3, 1849 Indian Jurisdiction. The U.S. Congress approves the Department of Interior Act, an act establishing the Department of the Interior, and the position of Secretary of the Interior, and placing the Commissioner of Indian Affairs in the newly created department. The new department is created to manage public land, Indian land, and Indian affairs.

MAY 17, 1849 Métis Declare "Trade Is Free." Led by Louis Riel, Sr., a group of about 300 Métis surround a courthouse in the Red River Colony where fellow Métis Pierre-Guillaume Sayer has been convicted of trading furs illegally. When Sayer is released without any punishment, the Métis declare that the Hudson's Bay Company (H.B.C.) has conceded that the trade is free. During the 1840s the Métis have challenged the H.B.C. monopoly on the fur trade in the area by trading furs at centers in the nearby United States.

SEPTEMBER 9, 1849 Treaty with the Navajo at Cheille. Under Article XI of the Treaty of Guadalupe Hidalgo, the United States launches a campaign to subdue the Southwest tribes, by treaty or war. Both the Treaty with the Navajo at Cheille and a similar one made the same year with the Ute differ from earlier

Indian treaties in that the United States not only obtains authority to regulate Indian trade and protect the tribe from settlers, but also to "pass and execute in their territory such laws as may be conducive to the prosperity and happiness of [the] Indians" generally. Such broad legislative powers over tribes' internal affairs has never before been asserted by the federal government. Similar provisions are included in treaties with the Comanche, Kiowa, and Apache, as well as with many tribes of the Great Plains and the Pacific Northwest, in the 1850s.

Chapter 6

1 8 5 0

c. 1850 Central Plains. With the removal of Great Lakes tribes to the West, decoration of clothing with ribbon applique is adopted from the southern Algonkian-speaking groups by a number of central plains tribes such as the Oto, Missouri, Omaha, and Osage.

1850 Redbird Smith, Cherokee Tribal Leader and Activist, Is Born. Redbird Smith is born near present-day Fort Smith, Arkansas. His father is Cherokee and his mother is part-Cherokee. Smith becomes one of the primary leaders of the Nighthawk Keetoowah society, an old Indian religious group with a strong interest in perpetuating Cherokee culture and religion. The society has been revived as a result of the removal of the Cherokee from their ancestral homelands and relocation to Indian Territory west of the Mississippi River. Smith and the Nighthawk Keetoowah Society declare themselves a religious organization and refuse to recognize the right of the U.S. government to disperse Cherokee tribal lands. Smith leads a passive resistance movement that uses civil disobedience tactics to disrupt enrollments for distribution of allotted land. In 1902, Smith is arrested by federal marshals and forced to sign the enrollment. In 1907, Indian Territory becomes the state of Oklahoma. In 1912, Smith co-founds the Four Mothers Society, dedicat-ed to preserving and advocating the political and legal rights of Indian tribes. Redbird Smith dies in 1918.

1850 *The Traditional History and Characteristic Sketches of the Ojibway Nation.* This transcription of Ojibway traditional tales is adapted to a short-story format by George Copway, an Ojibway writer. It is the first published book-length historical treatment of the Ojibway tribe written by an Indian.

APRIL 21, 1850 Quechan Uprising. In early 1850, the Quechan Indian-operated ferry on the Colorado River is attacked and destroyed by U.S. miners and settlers. On April 21, the Quechan Indians counterattack, which triggers further militia retaliation against them. On June 1, Peter H. Burnett, the newly elected governor of California, sends troops to punish the Quechan for the counterattack. Two attacks upon other California Indian groups result in massacres, one at Big Oak Flat, where an Indian village is wiped out by miners on the Trinity River, and the other at Clear Lake, where an armed expedition raids the Indians under a peaceful guise. About 60 Pomo Indians are killed. Another 75 are believed to have been killed in Mendocino County. Governor Burnett tells the state legislature that a "war of extermination will continue to be waged between the races until the Indian race becomes extinct" and that it is "beyond the power and wisdom of man" to avert the "inevitable destiny of this race."

MAY 1, 1850 Vancouver Island Treaties. Coast Salish groups on Vancouver Island sign the first of 14 land cession treaties made with the Hudson's Bay Company colony on the island between 1850 and 1854. Each treaty covers only a small area of land in the southern half of the island. Although the treaties are intended to clear land for European settlement, the colony attracts very few settlers before 1858.

AUGUST 10, 1850 First Legal Definition of "Indian" Given. Laws designed to protect Indian reserves in the Province of Canada from encroachment by non-Indians give the first legal definition of an "Indian" in the region that will become Canada. On August 30, 1851, the definition is changed to exclude non-Indians living among or married to Indians, and descendants of Indian women who marry non-Indians. This establishes, for the first time, "status Indians" and "non-status Indians" in Canada.

SEPTEMBER 7–9, 1850 Ojibway Sign Robinson Treaty. Ojibway bands residing in the area of Upper Canada north of Lakes Huron and Superior sign the Robinson Treaties, ceding ownership of the land in exchange for a lump sum payment, annual payments, 21 reserves, and guarantees to hunting and fishing rights. The treaties, which cover twice as much land as all earlier treaties in Upper Canada combined, are the first signed to clear an area for mineral exploration rather than for settlement. Negotiations began after the Ojibway protested the presence of miners and prospectors in the region. (See map of Indian Treaty Areas in Canada, p. 394.)

1850–1851 Kwagiulth (Kwakiutl) Villages Ordered Destroyed. Richard Blanshard, governor of the newly established colony of Vancouver Island, orders the destruction of several Kwagiulth villages on northern Vancouver Island. He sus-

pects that the villagers have maliciously murdered three Hudson's Bay Company (H.B.C.) men. The H.B.C. and the British Colonial Office disapprove of the raids, and Blanshard is replaced by James Douglas in September 1851.

1850–1860 Nonratification of California Indian Treaties. In 1850, the California legislature appoints three Indian commissioners to negotiate a series of treaties with the California Indians: Reddick McKee, George W. Barbout, and Oliver Wozencraft. The next year, the commissioners negotiate 18 treaties affecting 139 separate Indian groups. These treaties will remove all Indian people from the prime mining areas and other areas of non-Indian occupation and concentrate them on reservations totaling 11,700 square miles, or 7.5 percent of the state's area. California's government, U.S. congressmen, and non-Indian Californians, who view the treaties as giving the Indians potentially valuable land, prevent the treaty ratifications in Congress. Consequently, most California Indians are not recognized by treaty, and many California Indian communities continue to seek official federal recognition.

1850–1880 California Indian Genocide. Fearing widespread Indian uprisings, non-Indian Californians kill and terrorize California Indians. The Mariposa War breaks out in northern California when Miwoks and Yokuts rise against the miners who are invading Indian homeland. California militia and self-appointed vigilantes indiscriminately hunt down and kill thousands of peaceful California Indian men, women, and children. Indian women are often kidnapped to be used as prostitutes, concubines, or, along with Indian children, sold into slavery. By the mid-1850s most of the southern and central California Indian groups have been subjugated. Only brief skirmishes occur in the San Joaquin Valley in 1857–58. In less than 30 years the Indian population in California declines from over 100,000 in 1850 to just 16,000 in 1880.

1850–1907 Religious Renewal in the Northwest. Many Indian peoples turn to their old spiritual beliefs. Indians of the Northwest Plateau (present-day western Washington) join new religious movements like the Indian Shaker Church, or Waptashi—the Feather Religion. Some Indians follow the teachings of Smohalla, the Wanapum prophet who is said to have died on two occasions and traveled to the Sky World to converse with the Creator. Smohalla was given the sacred dance and ceremony known as the Washat and told to return to his people and to remember the ceremonies of thanks for first foods and other gifts of creation. Smohalla leads a fierce resistance to selling land, and provides a new religion that mixes both Christian and traditional northwestern Indian ideas. The new religion helps individual Indians and Indian communities better cope with the rapidly changing political, economic, and social conditions in their lives. His church becomes known as the Shaker Church and continues to gather congregations among several northwestern Indian nations such the Nez Percé.

1 8 5 1

1851   Treaty of Fort Laramie. The first great treaty conference on the Great Plains is held. Approximately 10,000 Sioux, Crow, Cheyenne, Arapaho, Assiniboine, Gros Ventre, and Arikara Indians meet with U.S. officials at Horse Creek near Fort Laramie in Wyoming Territory. The purpose is to secure peace among the tribes themselves and to protect the wagon roads, including the "Mormon Trail," carrying settlers across the prairies and through Indian land. The Plains Indians define their territories and promise to stop further hostile acts. In return, the United States pledges to protect the tribes from "depredations" by American citizens, and to pay compensation for any damages suffered. The United States also promises the tribes annual distributions of goods (annuities), for a ten-year period, excluding deductions for any

injuries done to U.S. citizens. The federal government requires each tribe to select "principals or head chiefs with whom all national business will hereafter be conducted."

Failure of the United States to comply with its obligation under the Treaty of Fort Laramie precipitates 22 years of intermittent war that culminates in the battle of the Little Bighorn in 1876. Eventually the states of Colorado, Kansas, South Dakota, North Dakota, Montana, Nebraska, and Wyoming are carved from land ceded by the Fort Laramie treaty.

JUNE 1851   Tutchone and Han Meet Traders. Tutchone and Han bands camped alongside the Yukon River meet Hudson's Bay Company employee Robert Campbell as he travels from Fort Selkirk to Fort Yukon on the Yukon River. Some of the Han own few European goods, and several have never seen non-Natives before. These Han are among the last Indians in North America to make direct contact with non-Natives.

JULY 13–14, 1851   Métis/Dakota Battle. At the battle of the Grand Coteau, a small party of Métis defeats a much larger party of Dakota. The battle encourages the growing Métis sense of nationhood. As the herds of buffalo become depleted in the vicinity of the Red River Colony, the Métis are forced to travel farther in their annual buffalo hunts, even establishing winter settlements far from Red River. The competition for the declining herds of buffalo causes increasing tension among the Métis, Cree, Assiniboine, Dakota, and other Plains Indians.

1851–1880   The "Final Solution" of the Indian Problem. During these years federal bureaucrats gradually develop plans for "the final solution of the Indian problem." In essence, the plans call for the complete control of tribal affairs by colonial administrators through the Office of Indian Affairs, the complete destruction of the tribal structure, and rapid reduction of the size of the Indian land base. Commissioner Luke Lea sets forth the doctrine in 1851

Panorama of the Monumental Grandeur of the Mississippi Valley, 1850, by John J. Egan. Courtesy of the St. Louis Art Museum.

when he calls for the Indians' "concentration, their domestication and their incorporation. . ." In 1857, Commissioner Denver advocates small reservations that will force the Indians to become farmers and in which the land will be allotted individually. In 1862, Commissioner E. P. Smith states that Indians should be regarded as "wards of the government." By the 1880s this policy is in full operation.

1 8 5 2

1852 Alice Brown Davis, Seminole Tribal Leader, Is Born. Alice Brown Davis is born near Park Hill, in the Cherokee Nation in Indian Territory. She is the daughter of Dr. John F. Brown, a Scot, and Lucy Redbeard, a Seminole of the Tiger clan. During the Civil War Alice lives at Fort Gibson, and following the war she meets and marries George Davis. In 1909, she is sent as an emissary by the Indians of her nation to the Seminole still living in the Florida Everglades. She remains with them for many months, living among them, preaching to them, and endeavoring to interest

them in the advantages of civilization. In 1922, President Warren G. Harding appoints Davis as chief of the Seminole Nation, to succeed her brother, John F. Brown, Jr., who has served his people for 30 years.

1852 Dogrib Trade Center. Fort Rae, established on the north arm of Great Slave Lake, brings European goods directly to the Dogrib Dene group. Fort Rae will become the main center of the Dogrib people.

1852 Smallpox Epidemic. Smallpox strikes the Kansas Indian reservation at Council Grove, Kansas, killing in excess of 400 Indians in one winter.

AUGUST 21, 1852 Chilkat Destroy Fort Selkirk. The Hudson's Bay Company's Fort Selkirk at the confluence of the Pelly and Yukon rivers is lightly manned, and the Tutchone of the area are away on summer hunts. A group of visiting Chilkat (Tlingit) plunders the trading post, forcing the traders to abandon the site. Thus the Tlingit regain their control of the flow of European goods to the Tagish and Tutchone of the interior.

The semiannual buffalo hunt was the main event in the Plains Métis community. Note the two-wheeled Red River cart and oxen, both Métis innovations. Courtesy of the Royal Ontario Museum.

1 8 5 3

1853 California Indian Rebellion. California governor John McDougal advises President Millard Fillmore that 100,000 Indian warriors are in "a state of armed rebellion" within the state, and requests that the expenses of the irregular California militia be paid by the U.S. government. Although some funding is received, Secretary of War G.M. Conrad observes that the California troubles result far more often from "the aggressive behavior of the whites" than from the behavior of Indians. State bonds worth more than $1 million are eventually issued to pay for the "suppression of hostilities."

1853 The Gadsden Purchase. The Gadsden Purchase, an agreement between the United States and Mexico, brings to the U.S. portions of the states of Arizona, California, and New Mexico and fixes the present U.S. boundaries. The purchase brings many Indian nations in these future states under U.S. jurisdiction.

1853 The Lone Woman of San Nicholas Island. Juana Maria, a Nicoleño, is found living alone on San Nicholas Island in the Santa Barbara channel by Capt. George Nidever and his crew. Eighteen years earlier, the Indians of these islands are removed to the mainland in accord with the policies of Father Junipero Serra. Once on the mainland, the Nicoleño are employed as domestic and agricultural workers. By the time Juana Maria is "rescued" and arrives at the Santa Barbara Mission, no one can communicate with her in her language; consequently, no one learns how she managed to survive alone on the island. Shortly after she reaches the mission, she contracts dysentery and dies, the last member of her tribe. Artifacts left behind, such as a water basket, beads, a stone mortar, and a sealskin cape, have since been destroyed or lost.

1853–1856 Series of Treaties with Indians. During this period many Indian nations are induced to sell most of their remaining land and accept small parcels of land commonly called "reservations." The Chippewa in the 1850s cede most of their lands in Wisconsin and Minnesota and are relegated to small and scattered reservations. The Indian nations of present-day Washington State reluctantly do the same. Between 1853 and 1856 more than 52 treaties are made with Indian groups, and the United States acquires 174 million acres of Indian land. In many cases, the Indian communities are economically destitute and Indians are forced to trade land for goods; in some cases, for example in Washington and Wisconsin, Indians retain the right to hunt and fish on their former lands. These hunting and fishing rights are disputed and ignored by U.S. citizens.

1 8 5 4

1854   Five Civilized Tribes. A federation of Indian nations consisting of the Cherokee, Chickasaw, Choctaw, Creek, and Seminole is formed in Indian Territory, and is known thereafter as the Five Civilized Tribes.

1854   George Hunt, Tlingit Cultural Interpreter, Is Born. George Hunt is born at Fort Rupert, British Columbia. His mother is a Tlingit named Mary Ebbets, and his British father is director of the Hudson's Bay Company's trade business with Indians on the coast of British Columbia. Hunt's cultural heritage is yet more complex and enriched by the fact that he is raised among the Kwakiutl Indians (another tribe of the Northwest Coast), and he marries a Kwakiutl woman. Hunt works as a guide and cultural interpreter beginning in 1881, and for anthropologist Franz Boas, beginning in 1886. Hunt helps to organize the Northwest Coast exhibit at the American Museum of Natural History in New York City in 1903 and is instrumental in recreating Native ceremonies and other scenes shown in Edward Curtis's film, *In the Land of the War Canoes.* Hunt is eventually selected as a chief of the Kwakiutl. He dies in 1933 at the place where he was born.

1854   Indian Removal Policy. Indian Commissioner George Manypenny calls for the abandonment of the Indian removal policy, saying: "By alternate persuasion and force, some of these tribes have been removed, step by step,

from mountains to valley, and from river to plain until they have been pushed half-way across the continent. They can go no further. On the ground they now occupy, the crises must be met, and their future determined." By 1854 virtually all Indian tribes, with the exception of small isolated groups, have been removed from their ancestral homelands east of the Mississippi and relocated west of the Mississippi to Indian Territory. While most attention is directed to the tribes of the Southeast, many of the powerful tribes of the Ohio Valley and the Northeast also have been removed, or pushed westward.

1854   *Life and Adventures of Joaquin Murieta.* Although written by John Rollin Ridge, a Cherokee author, this fictional romance novel concerns a Mexican bandit and his escapades in the frontier West.

1854   Susette La Flesche (Bright Eyes), Omaha Activist, Is Born. Susette La Flesche devotes much of her life to working for women's and Indian rights. Her father is Chief Joseph La Flesche, and she is a stepsister of Francis La Flesche, the famous Omaha anthropologist. La Flesche is also known by her translated Omaha name, Bright Eyes (Inshata Theumba).

Susette is educated by Christian missionaries and later studies art at the University of Nebraska. From 1877 to 1879 she is a teacher and conducts a Sunday school for Omaha children. During that time La Flesche becomes involved in the plight of the Ponca and the controversy over their removal. In 1877, the Ponca are forced by the U.S. government to leave northern Nebraska and move to Indian Territory (Oklahoma), and settle on a 101,000-acre reservation. The Ponca are greatly dissatisfied with the forced removal and petition Congress for permission to return to their homeland in Nebraska. They are eventually granted a 10,000-acre reservation in Nebraska, but lose their Oklahoma lands to U.S. settlers. In 1879 and 1880, La Flesche makes a speaking tour of the eastern United States, with her brother

Francis and Ponca chief Standing Bear, on behalf of the Ponca. La Flesche is called Bright Eyes on the tour, which is intended to publicize the conditions and plight of Standing Bear and his people. La Flesche continues to tour the United States speaking on Indian affairs. In 1881, she marries philanthropist and journalist Thomas H. Tibbles. Throughout the late 1880s, La Flesche and her husband make numerous public appearances, including trips to England and Scotland, where they plead for improvement in the condition of the Omaha and Ponca. In 1894, La Flesche and her husband are supervising editors of *The Weekly Independent,* a populist newspaper in Lincoln, Nebraska. With Standing Bear, La Flesche co-authors *Ploughed Under: The Story of an Indian Chief.*

MARCH 1854 Jicarilla Apache. Commissioner of Indian Affairs George Manypenny compels New Mexico territorial governor William Carr Lane to discontinue federally promised rations to the Jicarilla Apache Indians. The Jicarilla respond by stealing cattle belonging to an army beef contractor. On March 5, troops under Lt. Col. Philip Cooke attack Chief Lobo Blanco's Jicarilla band on the Canadian River, killing Blanco. On March 26, Jicarilla Apache under head chief Chacón attack Lt. John Davidson's company of dragoons along the road from Taos to Santa Fe, leaving 22 troops dead. Brig. John Garland, commanding the U.S. Army's Department of New Mexico is outraged over the retaliation by the Jicarilla and states "give them neither rest nor quarter until they are humbled to the dust." Cooke employs the famous army scout Kit Carson and pursues the Jicarilla relentlessly, using a "scorched earth" policy to ensure that neither food nor shelter is available for the Indian warriors. Following a June 4 surprise attack on a Jicarilla camp of 22 lodges at the base of Fisher's Peak in the Raton mountain range, Chacón surrenders with most of his followers.

MARCH 16, 1854 Treaty with the Omaha.

The Treaty with the Omaha, signed in Washington, D.C., cedes more than 43 million acres of land to the United States. The Omaha Indians are allowed to retain only about 300,000 acres for their own use. Further, the treaty introduces three new provisions that are afterwards included in nearly every treaty made with Indian tribes. The most important is an agreement that "the President may, from time to time, in his discretion," survey parts of the tribe's territory and "allot" the parcels to individual Indians. The second provision gives the president complete control over the money paid to the tribe for land sold to the United States, including the power to withhold annuity payments for various reasons. The third provision states that the United States will have the right to build roads in Indian country without the tribe's consent. These provisions foreshadow the breakup of the reservation system, U.S. settlement, and the assimilation of the Indians, a policy that is formally adopted and applied to numerous Indian tribes by the General Allotment Act in 1887.

MAY 10, 1854 Shawnee Treaty. A treaty is signed between the U.S. government and the Shawnee Indians in which the Shawnee cede their tribal land in Kansas. The U.S. re-grants them a small tract for a reserve. The treaty is ratified on August 2, and proclaimed on November 2.

AUGUST 18, 1854 "Grattan Massacre." High Forehead, a Brulé Sioux, shoots an arrow into the flank of an ox belonging to a member of a Mormon wagon train that is passing through Indian land in the North Platte Valley of Wyoming. The owner of the ox puts in a complaint at Fort Laramie and, on August 19, Lt. John L. Grattan is dispatched to the village of Chief Brave Bear (Conquering Bear) to arrest High Forehead. When High Forehead refuses to surrender, Grattan opens fire on the Indian village, fatally wounding Chief Brave Bear. Brulé warriors, joined by Oglala Sioux, destroy

Grattan's small band of 29, leaving only one survivor. Gen. William S. Harney is sent to "punish" the Brulé. On September 3, Chief Little Thunder, successor to Brave Bear, gathers his band of 250, including those who participated in the Grattan battle. Chief Little Thunder sends a message to Harney stating that he can have either peace or war. Harney chooses war, killing 85 warriors and capturing 70 Indian women and children. While the number of casualties is relatively small, this battle begins 40 years of warfare between the United States and the Sioux Nation on the central and northern plains.

DECEMBER 26, 1854–JANUARY 22, 1855 Washington and Oregon Indian Treaties. A treaty is signed by which the Nisqually Reservation is set apart for the Muckleshoot, Nisqually, Puyallup, Skwawksnomish, Stailakoom, and five other tribes, at the Puyallup Agency in Washington. In 1854 and 1855, the territorial governor, Isaac Stevens, makes treaties with most of the tribes of Washington and northwestern Oregon. The Treaty with the Duwamish and Allied Tribes at Point Elliott, signed in January, is a typical example of these treaties. Since these tribes rely primarily on fishing for their livelihood, they sell nearly all of their lands, but reserve the "right of taking fish at usual and accustomed grounds and stations" throughout the area. Instead of referring to the reservations as the Indians' "permanent homes," as have previous Indian treaties, the Stevens' treaties state that they are for the Indians' "present use and occupation," and the "President may hereafter, when in his opinion the interests of the Territory shall require and the welfare of the said Indians be promoted," move them to any "other suitable place within said Territory as he may deem fit."

1 8 5 5

1855 Fort Peck Reserve. By treaty and execu-

tive order, the Fort Peck Reserve, 2,775 square miles in area, is set aside and occupied by Assiniboine, Brulé, Santee, Teton, Hunkpapa, and Yanktonai Sioux.

FEBRUARY 22, 1855 Chippewa Treaty. A treaty is signed with the Chippewa of the Mississippi, which cedes land in Minnesota. Ten tracts are set apart for reserves, a tract for mixed bloods, and privilege of purchase by missionaries.

MAY, JUNE, AND JULY 1855 Yakima War. Isaac Stevens, governor of Washington Territory, hastily concludes treaties binding Indians in Washington and Oregon to relinquish their lands in exchange for a reservation. Stevens promises homes, schools, horses, livestock, and generous annuities to the Nez Percé, Cayuse, Umatilla, Walla Walla, and Yakima. Stevens also pledges that removal to the reservation will not begin for two or three years following the signing of the treaty. Yakima chief Kamaiakin does not believe the word of Stevens and refuses to sign. Twelve days after the last treaty is signed, Stevens opens the country to white settlement. A group of five braves led by Kamaiakin's nephew, Qualchin, attack and kill six prospectors in September. An Indian agent sent to investigate the incident is also killed. The Yakima War is begun. In December, Col. James Kelley leads a unit of militiamen into the Walla Walla homelands and agrees to a peace parley with Chief Peo-Peo-Mox-Mox. The chief secretly orders an attack and is killed as Kelley's command endures a four-day siege. Peo-Peo-Mox-Mox's ears and scalp are displayed to fellow settlers as a triumph by the Oregon volunteers. Incensed over the display of Peo-Peo-Mox-Mox's scalp, the Umatilla, Walla Walla, and Cayuse continue to raid outlying white settlements. On February 23, 1856, raids along the lower Rogue River destroy more than 60 homes and leave 31 settlers dead. The Yakima War ends in July, following a defeat of the Walla Walla and Cayuse in the

Grande Ronde Valley by a militia led by Col. Benjamin Franklin Shaw.

JULY 16, 1855 Salish and Kutenai Land Cessions. By the Treaty of Hell Gate, signed in Montana, the Salish and Kutenai (Kootenai) cede their lands in Montana and Idaho to the United States.

SEPTEMBER 1855 Rogue River War. Takelma and Tututni (Rogue Indians), who live near the Oregon-California border, kill 10 or 11 miners along the Klamath River. In retaliation, local miners kill some 25 Indians, touching off the Rogue River War. In September, Capt. Andrew Jackson Smith offers the safety of Fort Lane, near the present-day California-Oregon border, to Indians who fear the intensifying local violence. Before Smith can admit all of the endangered Indians, however, a band of settlers raids a nearby camp, killing 23 Rogue Indians. Indian war parties take revenge, killing 27 settlers in the Rogue Valley and burning the hamlet of Gallice Creek,

OCTOBER 17, 1855 Fort Belknap Reserve. By treaty and executive order, the Fort Belknap Reserve, 840 square miles in Montana, is set aside and occupied by the Blackfeet, Assiniboine, and Gros Ventre (Atsina) nations.

1855–1858 The Seminole Form New Government. The Seminole in Florida again engage U.S. forces in what is generally called the Third Seminole War. The war begins when a party of government surveyors working in the Great Cypress Swamp vandalizes crops belonging to followers of the Seminole leader Billy Bowlegs. The Indians demand compensation or apology. Obtaining neither, they commence three years of sporadic raiding. The army cannot defeat the Seminole and their allies, who retreat to the southern Florida swamps. Eventually, the United States has to reconcile itself to leaving the Seminole in Florida. Previously, in the 1830s, some Seminole

were captured and moved to Indian Territory (Oklahoma), where they were joined with the Creek Nation. Both nations speak Muskogean languages and have a history of kindred relations. By 1855, the Oklahoma Seminole withdraw from the Creek Nation and create their own government, one that very much resembles traditional Creek government, with about a dozen politically independent villages that meet together to form a national council. The government stays in effect until 1907, when the U.S. government dissolves the major Indian governments in Indian Territory.

1855–1907 The Chickasaw Constitutional Government. In 1856, the Chickasaw Nation adopts a constitution, modeled after the U.S. Constitution, with a "governor" as chief executive, a legislature, and a judiciary. In 1834, the Chickasaw sign a removal treaty, but cannot find a new location in the West. In 1838, the Chickasaw agree to join the Choctaw government, then already in Indian Territory. Between 1840 and 1855, however, most Chickasaw do not wish to live under Choctaw law, feeling they are discriminated against. The Chickasaw appeal to the United States for a return to an independent nationality, and in an 1855 treaty the Chickasaw are granted independence. In 1856, the Chickasaw form a constitutional government, which replaces an older form of government based on clan chiefs and priests. The constitutional government manages Chickasaw affairs until 1907, when the United States abolishes it.

1 8 5 6

c. 1856 Wovoka (Jack Wilson), Paiute Spiritual Leader, Is Born. Wovoka grows up in the area of Mason Valley, Nevada, near the present-day Walker Lake Reservation. His proper name, Wovoka, means "The Cutter" in Paiute. On the death of his father he is taken into the family of a U.S. farmer named David Wilson and is given the name Jack Wilson, by which he is known among local American settlers. During the late 1880s, Wovoka becomes ill with a severe fever. In his feverish state, Wovoka receives a vision, and an account of his experience is documented by James Mooney in his book, *The Ghost Dance Religion and the Sioux Outbreak of 1890* (1896). "When the sun died," Wovoka says, "I went up to heaven and saw God and all the people who had died a long time ago. God told me to come back and tell my people they must be good and love one another, and not fight, or steal, or lie. He gave me this dance to give to my people." Wovoka's dream becomes the basis of the Ghost Dance religion. Word of the new religion spreads quickly among Indian peoples of the Great Basin and Plains regions although Wovoka himself never travels far from his birthplace. Revered by Indians while being denounced as an impostor by local settlers, Wovoka dies in 1932.

1856 Montreal Lacrosse Club. The Montreal Lacrosse Club is formed. Lacrosse gradually grows in popularity in Montreal after the Iroquois of Caughnawaga (Kahnawak') demonstrate the game to Montreal residents in 1834.

APRIL 4, 1856 Prince Edward Island Indian Commissioner. Prince Edward Island appoints its first Indian Commissioner.

AUGUST 4, 1856 Round Valley Reserve. The Round Valley Reserve is set apart in northern California. Having previously ignored the area, white settlers move in and seize the best lands, declaring them "too good for savages."

NOVEMBER 1856 Southwest Conflicts. Navajo Indian agent Henry L. Dodge disappears and is presumed dead. The Mogollon Apache are blamed, and a punitive expedition is authorized. Unable to locate Mogollon, Gen. Benjamin Bonneville dispatches Dixon S. Miles, who attacks whatever Apache bands he encounters, including friendly Mimbres, and Coyotero Apache. In a May 25 attack, six

Mimbres are killed, including Chief Chuchillo Negro, a strong peace advocate.

1857

1857 Natchez (Naiche), Chiricahua Apache Tribal Leader, Is Born. Naiche is the younger son of the great Chiricahua Apache leader Cochise. When Cochise dies and is secretly buried in the Dragoon Mountains of Arizona in 1874, Naiche assumes leadership of the tribe. Naiche guides the Chiricahua through their transition and surrender to Gen. Oliver O. Howard in 1876. In the summer of 1881, at Cibecue, in present-day Arizona, a number of soldiers and an Apache medicine man are murdered. Hundreds of U.S. troops pour into the area to quell what is perceived to be a Chiricahua uprising. In September 1881 Naiche and his followers flee the San Carlos Reservation because of the Cibecue incident. Naiche and his group later surrender and are returned to the San Carlos Reservation. In May 1884 they are removed to Turkey Creek in Arizona. Naiche flees the reservation with Geronimo and eventually surrenders to Gen. Nelson Miles. In September 1886, Naiche, Geronimo, and their followers are sent by train to Florida. From there they are transferred to Mount Vernon Barracks in Alabama, and then to Fort Sill, Indian Territory (Oklahoma). Naiche and his people are finally allotted the Mescalero Reservation east of the Rio Grande in central New Mexico. Naiche and his family move to the reservation in April 1913, and Naiche dies there in 1921.

JUNE 10, 1857 The Gradual Civilization Act. The passage of the "Act for the Gradual Civilization of the Indian Tribes in the Canadas" (Gradual Civilization Act) withholds citizenship from Canadian Indians but establishes a process called "enfranchisement" by which Indians are encouraged to abandon their legal status as Indians in exchange for citizenship. In order to do so, adult male Indians will have to demonstrate that they are educated, debt free, capable of managing their own affairs, and of "good moral character." Once enfranchised, these men and their families will lose their Indian status and be given their share of band funds and 20 hectares (50 acres) of reserve land. In order to familiarize the Indians with democratic institutions, the act encourages Indians to form elected band councils to replace their traditional councils, by granting elected band councils certain limited powers over band affairs not granted to hereditary councils. This act reflects the acceptance among British North Americans that Indians ought to be assimilated into British American society. Although most Indian leaders seek help in integrating into Canadian society, they react against the paternalistic tone of this law.

SEPTEMBER 24, 1857 Pawnee Treaty. A treaty is signed with the four confederated bands of Pawnee, in which they cede land in the Dakotas and Nebraska. In return, the United States reserves a tract of land in Nebraska. By an act of April 10, 1876, the Nebraska reserve is to be sold, and a new reserve provided in Oklahoma. An act of March 3, 1893, cedes the reserved tract in Oklahoma.

NOVEMBER 5, 1857 Tonawanda Seneca Indians. A treaty is concluded between the New York Indians and the Ogden Land Company. By the treaty provisions, the Tonawanda Seneca Indians are authorized to buy back their reservation land from the company with monies from the U.S. government.

1857–1860 Palliser/Hind Expeditions. A British expedition led by Capt. John Palliser and a Canadian expedition led by Henry Youle Hind assess the agricultural potential of the northern prairie region controlled by the Hudson's Bay Company. This is in response to the increasing interest by Euro-Americans in Canada and the United States to acquire and settle

the area. Both parties meet with and report on Native groups and missionaries in the region.

1 8 5 8

1858 Charles A. Eastman, Wahpeton (Santee) Sioux Physician and Author, Is Born. Charles Eastman is born at Redwood Falls, Minnesota, and raised in a traditional Santee Sioux setting. His mother dies shortly after his birth, and he is raised by his father's extended family. In 1874, the family moves to Flandreau, South Dakota, and Eastman is enrolled in school, which brings him into contact with U.S. culture for the first time. He comes to understand American society remarkably well and becomes a well-known Native American intellectual. Eastman attends Dartmouth College and Boston University Medical School, receiving a degree in medicine in 1890. He is the first Native American physician to serve on the Pine Ridge Reservation. A prolific author, Eastman writes about Indian culture and basic philosophical differences between Native beliefs and those of U.S. society. His autobiographical work, *Indian Boyhood* (1902), describes his childhood and reflects a concern with youth and the experience of growing up that will last throughout his career. His autobiography is followed by a series on novels on Indian life, including *Red Hunters and the Animal People* (1904), *Old Indian Days* (1907), *Wigwam Evenings: Sioux Folktales Retold* (1909), and *The Soul of the Indian* (1911). A second autobiography, *From the Deep Woods to Civilization* (1916), tells of his experiences as an adult Indian in U.S. society and is strongly critical of that society's values and the actions of the U.S. government.

MAY 15, 1858 Coeur d'Alene War. Approximately 1,000 Palouse, Spokane, and Coeur d'Alene warriors intercept a column of 158 men under Lt. Col. Edward J. Steptoe near Spokane, Washington. Steptoe and his troops are en route to impress the Indians at Colville with the power of the U.S. Army. The Indian warriors have come together to protest the building of the proposed Missouri-to-Columbia road through Indian land. Steptoe and his column turn back after being told to go home. On May 17, however, the Indians attack, killing two officers. Steptoe's command escapes by night and returns to Fort Walla Walla. On September 1, under orders by Gen. Newman S. Clarke to "make their punishment severe," and "persevere until the submission of all is complete," Col. George Wright, accompanied by Nez Percé allies, begins a vigorous, punitive campaign and defeats the Indian force at the battle of Spokane Plain on September 1 and again on September 5 at the battle of Four Lakes. Following the hanging of Kamaiakin's brother-in-law, Owhi (Kamaiakin has fled to Canada), the tribes of the Columbia basin march to the reservations prescribed by Governor Stevens's treaties.

JULY 7, 1858 Navajo War. After an argument over grazing rights, Manuelito leads Navajo in an attack on Fort Defiance. In the spring of 1858 some Navajo argue with soldiers from Fort Defiance who have been grazing their horses on land claimed by the Navajo leader Manuelito. A few months later, Manuelito defiantly sets his stock to graze on land claimed by the fort for that purpose. Maj. Thomas H. Brooks, commander of Fort Defiance, orders his men to slaughter 60 of Manuelito's animals as a warning against further grazing on land claimed by the army. On July 7, in retaliation, Navajo shoot volleys of arrows into a soldiers' camp and on July 12, a Navajo warrior murders the black servant of Major Brooks. Brooks demands that the Navajo produce the murderer or suffer retribution. Col. Dixon S. Miles is dispatched to Fort Defiance to lead a punitive expedition into Navajo land and sets September 9 as the deadline for the Navajo to turn over the murderer, or war will begin. Following the failure of the Navajo to satisfactorily comply, a nameless war commences with punitive expe-

ditions to Canyon de Chelly, Arizona, and to the village of Navajo leader Zarcillas Largos. The August 1858 raid is led by Colonel Miles and Maj. Electus Baccus wherein they burn Largos's village, mistakenly believing it to be Manuelito's village. The Navajo conduct retaliatory raids through October 1858; however, the show of force by the U.S. Army is sufficient to cause the Navajo to sue for peace.

AUGUST 2, 1858 British Columbia Gold Rush. British Columbia becomes a colony of Britain following the arrival of thousands of Euro-American gold seekers to the lower Fraser River region on the Pacific Coast. James Douglas is made lieutenant governor. This gold rush, which has disrupted the subsistence activities of the Coast Salish and Interior Salish in the region, marks the beginning of a new era in relations between Natives and non-Natives in the region. Up to this point, relations have centered on the normally mutually beneficial fur trade. From this point on the Indian residents of lower Vancouver Island and the lower Fraser Valley will be outnumbered by non-Natives. Increasingly, Indians will find seasonal wage labor as loggers, mill hands, stevedores, sailors, and farmers in order to supplement their subsistence. Intolerance and a lack of understanding leads to increasing conflict between non-Natives and Natives.

1858–1859 Mohawk Steelworkers. Mohawk from the Caughnawaga (Kahnawak') Reserve near Montreal work on the construction of the Victoria Bridge across the nearby St. Lawrence River. The Mohawk are beginning to earn a reputation as proficient and daring steelworkers.

---

1 8 5 9

1859 The Silver Rush. The silver rush period in Nevada, Arizona, and part of California again brings prospectors, miners, and adventurers, as well as a large lawless element, into the remote Indian areas. The influx brings immediate retaliation from Indian people who are now familiar with the disease, death, destruction, and loss of land associated with white miners and settlers.

FEBRUARY 28, 1859 Salt River Reserve. The Salt River Reserve, an area of 448 square miles, is established. An executive order is approved by the Congress of the United States that sets aside the first land for the Pima and Maricopa Indians in the state of Arizona. By executive orders of August 31, 1876, and January 10, 1879, additional tracts are set apart. Other additions are made on May 5, 1882, and November 15, 1883. Today, the estimated Indian population of that state is in excess of 100,000, and their recognized land area comprises 16,034,802 acres.

MARCH 30, 1859 Nova Scotia Reserves. Nova Scotia passes "An Act Concerning Indian Reserves" that permits the sale of land on Indian reserves not being occupied by Indians. The law is passed after the government finds itself unable to prevent non-Natives from squatting on reserve land. Many squatters, however, refuse to pay for the land they are occupying.

1 8 6 0

c. 1860 Nampeyo, Hopi-Tewa Potter, Is Born. Nampeyo is born at Hano (Tewa Village) on First Mesa in present-day Arizona. In 1895, Nampeyo's husband is hired to help with the excavation of Sikyatki under the direction of anthropologist J. Walter Fewkes. At Sikyatki and other ruins, Nampeyo collects shards and uses the designs in the creation of her own work. She also experiments with both ancient and modern design techniques like stippling and the use of variable line widths to approximate different shades of gray. Nampeyo develops her own style based on these traditional designs. She is a world-recognized potter who, besides develop-

ing her own style, is instrumental in bringing about a revival of traditional Native American ceramics. When Nampeyo begins losing her eyesight, her husband helps her to recreate her designs, and after his death, her daughter Fannie does likewise. After Nampeyo's death on July 20, 1942, her artistic legacy is carried on by her children and grandchildren. She has been credited with bringing about a renaissance of pottery-making among her people. Furthermore, it is her idea and inspiration that elevates pottery among her people to an art form, as it was centuries ago.

c. 1860 Navajo Silversmithing. The Navajo learn silversmithing from Mexican blacksmiths. This new art form becomes widespread later in the nineteenth century (use of turquoise in jewelry design begins about 1880), and subsequently spreads to many of the Pueblo tribes. The Zuni learn silversmithing from the Navajo in 1872, and the Hopi learn from the Zuni in 1898. These tribes and other Pueblos subsequently develop distinctive styles in jewelry-making, variations on which continue to be created today. In the twentieth century, production and sales of jewelry become more and more important in the tribal economies of the Southwest.

1860 Canada's Indians. The British government hands over financial responsibility for Canadian Indians affairs to the government of the Province of Canada. With the aboriginal population of Canada continuing to dwindle, and government policy aimed at assimilating the remaining Indians, most assume that this responsibility will be a relatively short-term one.

1860 Charles Curtis, Kaw and Osage Politician and Vice President, Is Born. Born near present-day Topeka, Kansas, Charles Curtis is only one-eighth Indian but is raised on the Kaw Reservation near Council Grove. He attends the Indian mission school on the reservation and then returns to Topeka when the Kaw are attacked by the Cheyenne. As a young man he works as a jockey during the summer seasons and attends Topeka High School. Curtis becomes a lawyer in 1881 and later enters politics as a republican, serving eight consecutive terms in the U.S. House of Representatives from 1892 until 1906. Curtis is then elected to the Senate and serves in that body from 1907 to 1913 and from 1915 to 1929. He campaigns for president and loses, then runs successfully for vice president on the ticket with Herbert Hoover. He serves as vice president from 1929 until 1933. Curtis dies in 1936.

MAY 1860 The Paiute War. Traders at Williams Station, an overland mail stop along the California Trail, abduct and rape two Indian girls. The Southern Paiute, who are already resentful of U.S. settlers, miners, and army personnel in their homeland, rescue the two girls, burn the station, and kill five Americans. An "army" of Nevada miners, under the leadership of Maj. William M. Ormsby and Henry Meredith, assemble and march on Pyramid Lake in Paiute country to seek revenge. In anticipation of a retaliatory attack, Chief Numag ambushes the miners at the Big Bend of the Truckee River Valley, causing 46 fatalities. The governor of California responds with troops under the command of Col. Jack Hayes. Leading a force of 800 men, Hayes encounters the Paiute and pursues them to Pinnacle Mountain, killing approximately 25 warriors. The Paiute sue for peace and the army establishes Fort Churchill to ensure that the California trail will remain open.

JULY 1860 Inuit Whalers. Whaling activity in the eastern Arctic picks up as whalers from the United States join the Hudson's Bay Company whalers. Netsilik, Iglulik, and Baffin Island Inuit are drawn toward the coast during the summers to work for and trade with the whalers. The Inuit, who are accustomed to whaling with large boats (umiaks) and harpoons, make proficient employees.

NOVEMBER 1860 Yakima Boarding School.

The Yakima Agency Boarding School opens, with 25 Indian pupils in residence. The original boarding school is provided for and promised under Article 5 of the Treaty with the Yakima Nation of June 5, 1855.

1860–1907 The Choctaw Constitutional Government. In 1860, after 25 years of constitutional change and amendment, the Choctaw residing in Indian Territory (Oklahoma) adopt a centralized constitutional government, with a principal chief, three district chiefs (as was the Choctaw political tradition), a national legislature, and a court system. The government remains in power until 1907, when the U.S. government abolishes it and makes Indian Territory into the state of Oklahoma.

1861

MARCH 10, 1861 E. Pauline Johnson (Tekahionwake), Mohawk Poet, Is Born. Pauline Johnson is born to a Mohawk chief and an English mother at the Six Nations Reserve near Brantford, Ontario. Educated at Brantford, Johnson begins writing poetry almost as soon as she learns to write, and as a young child she is a voracious reader. She comes to prominence in the 1890s when she begins reciting her poetry in front of live audiences. Her first collection of poetry, *The White Wampum*, is published in 1895 during a tour of England. It contains one of her best-known poems, "The Song My Paddle Sings." She returns to North America to recite her poetry across Canada and in the United States. Johnson's other books include *Canadian Born* (1903); *The Moccasin Maker* (1913); *Legends of Vancouver* (1912), based on stories told her by her Squamish Coast Salish friend, Joe Capilano; and *The Sagganappi* (1913), a novel. *Flint and Feather* (1913) is a collection of her poetry.

JULY 18, 1861 Confederate Troops Attack Arizona Indians. As Confederate Lt. Col.

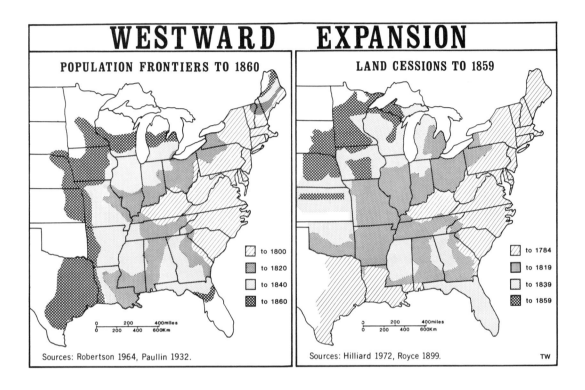

WESTWARD EXPANSION

POPULATION FRONTIERS TO 1860

to 1800
to 1820
to 1840
to 1860

0   200   400miles
0   200   400   600Km

Sources: Robertson 1964, Paullin 1932.

LAND CESSIONS TO 1859

to 1784
to 1819
to 1839
to 1859

0   200   400miles
0   200   400   600Km

Sources: Hilliard 1972, Royce 1899.   TW

Westward expansion until the 1860s. The land cessions map is based on the Indian Claims Commission Final Report, 1978. Courtesy of the University of New Mexico Press and Imre Sutton.

John R. Baylor prepares to take possession of Arizona Territory for the Confederacy, Chiricahua and Mimbreno Apache, convinced that the Union soldiers have permanently withdrawn from the region, intensify their raids. Baylor authorizes a company of Arizona Rangers to punish the Indians. Baylor takes possession of Arizona Territory for the Confederacy, proclaims himself governor, and orders the Arizona Guards to exterminate "all hostile Indians."

AUGUST 12, 1861 Kickapoo Flee Texas. The Kickapoo refuse to agree to an alliance with the Confederate States of America, because of their hostility toward Texas. The Wild Horse Creek band of Kickapoo and the Canadian band of Kickapoo move to southern Kansas.

AUGUST 21, 1861 The Cherokee Side with the Confederacy. John Ross, principal chief of the Cherokee Nation, addresses the nation requesting authority to negotiate with the Confederate States. With war between the states inevitable, Ross calls for neutrality. "While ready and willing to defend our firesides, let us not make war wantonly against the authority of the United or Confederate States, but avoid a conflict with either, and remain strictly on our own soil." At the same time, believing that "the permanent disruption of the United States into two governments is now probable," he asks for authority to enter into "an alliance with the Confederate States upon terms honorable and advantageous to the Cherokee Nation." Only this, he argues, will ensure the future of the Cherokee people. "When your nationality ceases here, it will live nowhere else. When these homes are lost, you will find no others like them." Several other tribes in the Indian Territory have signed treaties with the Confederacy when Ross speaks, and the Cherokee Nation follows on October 7. Stand Watie, a Cherokee, becomes the only Indian brigadier-general in the Confederate Army and commands two Cherokee regiments fighting in the Southwest. By 1863, however, most Cherokee abandoned the Confederacy and joined Union forces.

OCTOBER 3, 1861 Unitah Valley, Utah. By executive order the Unitah Valley in Utah is set aside for certain bands of Ute. The remaining bands claim country taken by the U.S. without formal purchase.

1861–1863 Apache Uprising. In November 1860, John Ward, a rancher near Fort Buchanan, Arizona, is raided by a group of Pinal Apache, who kidnap Ward's stepson and rustle some of Ward's cattle. Ward's wife, Jesusa Martinez, has been captured previously by Pinal Apaches and the kidnapped boy is born while Jesusa is in captivity. Ward tells the commander of Fort Buchanan that Chiricahua Apaches, led by Cochise, are responsible. Lt. George N. Bascom and 60 men set out to recover the boy and the stock and set up camp in Apache Pass on February 4, 1861. Cochise, his brother, two nephews, a woman, and a child come voluntarily to talk with Bascom, who announces that he will hold Cochise and his party captive until the boy and the stolen stock are returned. Cochise

escapes, but the rest of his party are held hostage. Cochise extracts revenge by attacking the Butterfield station and a wagon train passing by the station. He kills nine of his prisoners and offers to exchange the remaining three for the captives Bascom holds. Bascom refuses and Cochise executes his hostages. In return, Bascom hangs his prisoners. Cochise responds with a vow to exterminate all Americans in Arizona. As army troops are withdrawn from the West to fight in the U.S. Civil War, Apache-U.S. violence will be bloody and protracted and will endure for a quarter of a century.

1861–1865 The Civil War. The Civil War brings Confederate troops under Gen. Henry Hopkins Sibley to New Mexico. Most federal troops are withdrawn, except a contingent at Fort Fauntleroy. During the Civil War the Navajo continue to raid New Mexican villages left undefended when men departed to fight the Confederacy. Federal forces defeat Confederate troops near Pecos, New Mexico, and then move eastward, leaving Gen. James Carleton to administer the New Mexico Department. Col. Christopher (Kit) Carson is appointed field commander over an army of volunteers. In weeks, this force defeats the Mescalero Apache and relocates them to the Bosque Redondo of eastern New Mexico onto a bleak, windswept reservation on the Llano Estacado, or Staked Plains, near the Pecos River. It is Carleton's plan to gather the Mescalero and Navajo tribes together "little by little onto a reservation away from the haunts and hills and hiding places of their own country, and there be kind to them: there teach their children how to read and write; teach them the art of peace; teach them the truths of Christianity." Carleton represents liberal reformers who want to place Indians on reservations where they will "acquire new habits, new ideas, new modes of life: the old Indians will die off . . . the young ones will take their places . . . and thus, little by little, they will become a happy and contented people."

Although Carleton wants to "civilize" and christianize Navajo and Apache on the reservation, he is not opposed to killing them in pursuit of his goal. Under orders from Carleton, Carson pursues Navajo men, women, and children throughout the summer, autumn, and winter of 1863–64, causing the deaths of many from hardship, hunger, and exposure. Those Navajo who are captured afford Carson the opportunity to inform the tribe of the removal plans and his correspondence suggests that he does. Navajo oral history, however, indicates that they are unaware of the plans. Approximately 10,000 Navajo surrender, while perhaps several thousand others flee west to escape the army. The U.S. government forcefully removes these Navajo in its jurisdiction 350 miles to the Bosque Redondo, a place Navajo call Hweeldi (prison). There they remain until 1868, when Gen. William Tecumseh Sherman concludes a treaty with the Navajo permitting them to return to a reservation located on a portion of Dinetah.

1 8 6 2

MARCH 1862   Smallpox in the Northwest. All Indians are evicted from the Fort Victoria area after smallpox is discovered among them. Many leave for their home bands, carrying the disease as they travel. The epidemic spreads along the entire Pacific Northwest Coast and to some inland groups during the rest of the year. The epidemic prompts the Hudson's Bay Company to renew vaccination efforts.

MAY 1862   Cariboo Gold Rush. Interior Salish, Chilcotin, and Carrier in the interior of British Columbia (the Cariboo region) begin clashing with thousands of gold seekers. While many of the gold seekers leave the region soon after, some settle permanently. Gold rushes in other areas of British Columbia over the next 11 years affect most other groups there.

MAY 1862   The Civil War. Confederate Indian troops from Indian territories number 6,435 men. The Cherokee, fighting for the Confederacy in the Thomas Legion, are used to hunt

down deserters, enemy scouts, bushwhackers, and bands of Union sympathizers who are hiding in the mountains of the Carolinas and Tennessee.

MAY 27, 1862   Metlakatla Established. William Duncan of the Anglican Church Missionary Society and 50 of his Tsimshian followers leave Port Simpson (British Columbia) to establish Metlakatla, some distance from the post. Metlakatla is intended to become a model village in which the Tsimshian adopt aspects of Christianity and European lifestyles. Duncan, who arrived at Fort Simpson in 1857, seeks to remove the Indians from what he feels are the corrupting influences there. By 1880, more than a thousand residents settle in the village.

JUNE 14, 1862   Indian Property Protection Act. Congress passes the "Indian Property Protection Act." The act is designed to protect the allotted property of Indians whose tribes have signed a treaty with the United States, and who have adopted the habits of "civilized life."

OCTOBER 6, 1862   Manitoulin Island Treaty. Leaders representing Ojibway and Ottawa residents of Manitoulin Islands sign a treaty surrendering the land of the island in exchange for promises of reserves and of various rights and payments. The entire island was established as a reserve in 1836, but few Indians have moved to the island since then, and the government of the Province of Canada has abandoned its policy of relocating its Indian people there.

DECEMBER 1862   Dakota Flee North. Bands of Dakota (Siouan-speaking buffalo hunters of the northern plains) begin fleeing into Hudson's Bay Company territory after attacking settlements in Minnesota since August 17. By 1865 about 3,000 Dakota led by Little Crow will seek refuge in Canada. Many settle permanently in British North America (Manitoba) and are given a reserve in 1874.

1862–1864   The Minnesota Sioux Uprising. Because of Indian agents' corruption and incompetence in their administration of relations with the Minnesota Sioux, the Sioux almost starve from lack of supplies. In June 1862, a large group of Santee Sioux call on the Yellow Medicine Agency to receive money and rations to which they are entitled by treaty with the U.S. government. The distribution is delayed and the Sioux return on July 14, to be told once again that the food, stored in a warehouse at the Yellow Medicine Agency, cannot be released. Under the leadership of Little Crow, the Sioux attack Minnesota settlements. The uprising quickly spreads to other Santee Sioux bands living in the eastern Dakotas. At a council with the Santee, prominent trader Andrew J. Myrick declares, "So far as I am concerned, if they are hungry, let them eat grass." After another promise to distribute food is made and broken, Little Crow and a band of warriors attack Myrick in his store, kill him, and, in a symbolic gesture, stuff his mouth with grass. Raiding becomes general throughout Minnesota and approximately a thousand Minnesota settlers are killed. On September 23, Little Crow's army of about 700 warriors prepares to ambush militia Col. Henry Hastings Sibley's troops who are en route to Wood Lake. The warriors reveal themselves prematurely, attacking only a small portion of Sibley's men. Discouraged by the outcome of the battle (seven troopers and 30 Indians dead), Little Crow's forces dissolve. Beginning on September 26, Sibley accepts the surrender of 2,000 Indian warriors and the release of some 370 captives. By November 3, a military tribunal sentences 303 Santee Sioux to be hanged and the remaining 1,700 prisoners to be transferred to Fort Snelling. President Abraham Lincoln overturns most of the execution orders, but 38 Indians are hanged, the largest mass execution in U.S. history.

1862–1865 Kickapoo Migration to Mexico. Two bands of Kickapoo, about 1,300 people, migrate to Mexico, believing their bands are unfairly treated by the U.S. government and people. Both bands fight battles with Texas troops, who strongly oppose Indians settling or

traveling through the area. Both groups settle in the province of Coahiula in northern Mexico. Earlier, in 1839, a band of Kickapoo had migrated to Morelos, Mexico. They were joined by Machemanet, a Kickapoo spiritual leader, and 600 Kickapoo who leave Kansas for Mexico in the autumn of 1862, hoping for better treatment at the hands of the Mexican government. By 1865, all Kickapoo, except the band formerly led by the prophet Kenekuk, had left Kansas because of corrupt handling by U.S. Indian agents and crooked dealings by U.S. citizens. In 1867, about 100 Kickapoo return from the south and resettle near present-day Leavenworth, Kansas.

1 8 6 3

1863   The Long Walk. Kit Carson, army scout and Indian fighter, under the direction of Gen. James Carleton, leads a U.S. Army force in a campaign against the Navajo Indians of the southwestern United States to enforce a treaty signed in 1849 at Canyon de Chelly. Carson is simultaneously pursuing (also under the direction of General Carleton) the Mescalero Apache in an attempt to remove them to a 40-mile-square reservation at the Bosque Redondo on the Pecos River, in present-day New Mexico. Carleton demands that Carson carry out a "scorched earth" campaign to destroy Navajo and Apache fields, orchards, and food supplies. Contrary to normal practice, Carleton also issues an order for a hard winter campaign, stating, "Now, while the snow is deep, is the time to make an impression on the tribe." As a result of the summer scorched-earth campaign and relentless winter pursuit, the Navajo and Apache are forced to surrender and make the "The Long Walk" to the Pecos Country to be "quarantined for civilization." The March of Tears is made by 8,000 Navajo and many Mescalero Apache. Many die en route to the Bosque; some, too weak to march, are shot by the soldier escorts. Dysentery kills another 126 Navajo after they arrive at Bosque Redondo. The Navajo and remaining Mescalero Apache are held in captivity under miserable conditions until 1868.

1863   The Nez Percé and the "Thief Treaty." Throughout the West, Indians attempt to preserve their culture and live a traditional life off the reservation. For example, the Nez Percé Indians of Oregon and Idaho attempt to live in peace with the settlers and remain neutral during the Plateau Indian War of 1855–58. In 1855, the Nez Percé sign a treaty with the United States, securing nearly all of their land, but in 1860 non-Indian "traders" discover gold while prospecting on the Nez Percé Reservation in Idaho. Non-Indians flood onto Indian land; the U.S. Army is preoccupied with the Civil War and unable to prevent the invasion. Nez Percé leaders complain to the Indian Service and the government responds in 1863 by writing a new treaty reducing the reservation to one-tenth its original size. When government officials disclose the plan to Nez Percé leaders, almost all of the chiefs leave the council, refusing to accept the new treaty. Only Chief Lawyer, upon whose lands the council is held, agrees to its terms. Lawyer and 51 Nez Percé sign the document, which is ratified by the U.S. Senate and signed by the president. According to tribal law, Lawyer could speak only for his small band and not the tribe as a whole. Chief Joseph and the other Nez Percé leaders refuse to adhere to the "Thief Treaty." Chief Joseph objects: "If we ever owned the land we own it still for we never sold it."

1 8 6 4

1864   Hoopa Valley Reserve. By act of Congress, the Hoopa Valley Reserve is set apart for the Hunsatung, Hupa, Klamath River, Miskeet, Redwood, Saiaz, Sermolton, and Tishlanaton tribes, an area of 155 square miles.

1864   Indians as Witnesses. Federal law is amended by Congress to allow Indians to serve as competent witnesses in trials involving non-Indian men. Prior to this date Indian people were not allowed to testify in a court of law against white people.

APRIL 18, 1864   Round Valley Reserve. Congress establishes the Round Valley (Nome Cult) Reserve for the Clear Lake, Concow, Little Lake, Nomelaki, Pit River, Potter Valley, Redwood, Wailaki, and Yuki tribes, an area of about 50.5 square miles.

APRIL 30, 1864   Chilcotin Attacks. A group of Chilcotin, Athapascan hunter-gatherers of the arid British Columbia interior, kill 13 members of a crew building a wagon road along the Homathko River in southern British Columbia. As a result of this so-called "Chilcotin War," five Chilcotin leaders are tried and executed.

MAY 1864   British Columbia Indian Policy. Fur trader James Douglas retires as lieutenant governor of Vancouver Island. Many residents of the colony believe Douglas has been too accommodating with British Columbia's Indians. Joseph Trutch, the chief commissioner of lands and works, inaugurates the British Columbia government's policy of refusing to negotiate land cession treaties with its Indian residents—a policy that will stand for almost 130 years. The new policy provides for reserves not larger than ten acres (four hectares) for each Indian family. Indian groups, guided by missionaries, begin fighting the new policy. Non-Natives have recently begun farming in the lower Fraser River Valley, and ranching in the Okanagan region of the provinces interior.

NOVEMBER 1864   Sand Creek Massacre. Col. John M. Chivington and Gov. John Evans of Colorado allow Chief Black Kettle and his peaceful Cheyenne followers to camp near Fort Lyon for the purpose of negotiating a treaty. By night, Chivington deploys his Third Colorado

Navajo woman, with her baby in a cradleboard, at Bosque Redondo. Courtesy of the Museum of New Mexico.

Cavalry around Sand Creek, including 700 men and 4 howitzers. On November 29, Chivington leads the militia in an unprovoked attack on the Indian camp, killing up to 500 men, women, and children. The Sand Creek Massacre, as it becomes known, is one of the bloodiest and cruelest events of the Civil War and leads to public outcries against such needless brutalities. Although punishment of the parties responsible for the massacre is demanded by the public and by a U.S. congressional committee, no such action is taken.

1 8 6 5

1865 The Civil War Ends. The U.S. Army concentrates on the "Indian Problem" as it applies to Indian disturbances along regions receiving little attention up to this time—the western emigration routes and the Silver Lode areas. The government contracts with Protestant missionaries to operate schools on Indian reservations. Meanwhile, California Indians are placed under Methodist jurisdiction.

Depiction of the Sand Creek massacre by artist Robert Lindneux. His depiction includes the American flag that Chief Black Kettle raised above his tipi in a vain attempt to signal his allegiance and peaceful intentions. Courtesy of the Colorado Historical Society.

1865 Ramona, Cahuilla (Kawia) Basketmaker, Is Born. Ramona is a Cahuilla Indian who lived in what is now San Diego County, California; she was married to Juan Diego, who was murdered in dramatic fashion by a local villain named Sam Temple. Ramona becomes something of a celebrity in the late 1880s, due to the fictional story, *Ramona,* by the famous historical novelist Helen Hunt Jackson. The novel, which incorporates a romance, is an instant success and spawns a movie in the early 1900s. The real-life Ramona sells baskets and photographs of herself to eager tourists at a souvenir stand. The popularity of this work inadvertently establishes an Alta California mythos, immortalizing a falsely romantic sense of the California mission period and Spanish/Indian relations. Ramona pageants and festivals continue to this day in San Diego County.

JANUARY 1865 U.S. Army Attacks Bannock Indians. Bannock Indians camped at Battle Creek, Idaho, are attacked by U.S. Army troops. A total of 224 Indians are killed. The Bannock are guilty of raiding settlements and wagon trains for several years in a vain attempt to turn back the U.S. settlers entering their land.

JANUARY 7, 1865 Sioux-Cheyenne Uprising. A thousand Indian warriors congregate south of Julesburg, Colorado, angered over the Chivington massacre at Sand Creek. A planned attack on Fort Rankin fails, so the Indians loot Julesburg. Near the Republican River on February 2, the U.S. Army pursues Cheyenne-Arapaho raiding parties, but the Indians return to Julesburg and finish it off. Skirmishes flare up again on February 4, 5, 6, and 8 near Forts Mitchell and Laramie. Indians mass together on July 26, to attack a cavalry unit patrolling the Oregon-California Trail and North Platte River crossing. Sixty Indians die while 130 are wounded, but the attacks succeed in destroying an army supply train. In response, Gen. Patrick E. Connor dispatches 3,000 troops into Powder River country. They destroy one Arapaho village and militarily engage the Sioux. This defeat and premature winter storms bring an end to the Cheyenne-Arapaho War.

A sketch of Fort Laramie, the site of major treaties with the northern plains Indians, about 1863. Courtesy of the American Heritage Center, University of Wyoming.

MARCH 3, 1865   Colorado River Treaty. Congress enacts a proposal reserving 376 square miles located in the Colorado River Agency, Arizona, for the Chemehuevi, Walapai, Cahuilla, Cocopa, Mohave, and Yuma tribes. The corrected reserve boundaries are signed by executive order on May 15, 1876.

JULY 10, 1865   Washoe Reserve Set Aside. The secretary of the interior orders the setting aside of two reserves for the Washoe of Nevada and California as settlers claim their native territories. No "suitable land" is found "available" for these Indians, and no further governmental action is taken.

SEPTEMBER 1865   Scarlet Fever Epidemic. Up to half the Indians in the Mackenzie River Valley die when scarlet fever spreads to them from infected members of a Hudson's Bay Company supply brigade moving down the river from Fort Simpson.

OCTOBER 10, 1865   Lakota Acknowledge Authority of United States. The Minneconjou band of Lakota "officially" acknowledge the authority of the U.S. via treaty accords. In

1865–68, the U.S. attempts violation of its treaties with the Lakota, resulting in war. The Lakota succeed militarily and the United States backs down, restoring a temporary peace.

1865–1879   Kickapoo Warfare against Texas. A group of Kickapoo (Kikapuak) living in Coahiula, Mexico, wage continuous warfare against Texans settled across the Rio Grande. The Kickapoo destroy millions of dollars in property, kill hundreds of Texans, and lay waste to entire counties in south Texas.

1 8 6 6

1866   Civil Rights Amendment. Congress passes the Civil Rights Amendment. Article XIV becomes law in 1868. While the act gives blacks citizenship rights, it states that Indians are not eligible for the count that decides apportionment of United States representatives for Congress. The act specifically denies Indians the vote by the clause "excluding Indians not taxed." Any person with a quarter or more Negro ancestry is legally held to be "a colored person" in Virginia, thus threatening the Indian identity of some individuals. Henceforth, an Indian is federally defined as a person with a quarter or more Indian ancestry who was an eighth or less part-Negro. This definition is repeated in 1910, except that having one-sixteenth or more African descent defines one as a "colored person."

1866 Post-Civil War Indian Reservations. A

peace commission travels to Indian Territory in 1865 and enrages tribal leaders by arguing that "by their own acts, by making treaties with the enemies of the United States [they] had forfeited all right to annuities, lands, and protection by the United States." The Choctaw and Chickasaw eventually sign a treaty made at Washington, D.C. on April 28, 1866. Similarly, less confiscatory treaties are concluded with all tribes in Indian Territory. Slavery among the tribes is abolished, and an agreement is made giving freedmen legal rights equivalent to those accorded tribal citizens. Additional lands are sold and the proceeds used to settle freedmen on their own farms. Land tenure is individualized, but tribes maintain their own laws and representative forms of government. A federal "governor" is appointed to oversee these Reconstruction measures. In 1904 the Supreme Court upholds the constitutionality of selling tribal land for the benefit of freed slaves.

JULY 4, 1866 Delaware Land Sales. The U.S.

guarantees payment to the Delaware for land sold to the Leavenworth, Pawnee, and Western Railroad Company in accordance with an 1860 treaty. The Delaware sell their remaining reserve to the Missouri River Railroad Company.

AUGUST 1, 1866 U.S. Army Commissions

Indian Scouts. U.S. Indian scouts are commissioned within the army by order of the War Department to provide a force of Indians within the territories and Indian country. The scouts are to receive the same pay and allowances as cavalry soldiers. Within one year the number of

Indian scouts is 474, and within ten years the figure rises to 600.

1866–1868 War for the Bozeman Trail. The

U.S. begins to build forts along a trader's trail in the Powder River country so that gold seekers on their way to western Montana may pass safely through the heart of Indian hunting grounds. Reacting to these plans to refortify the Bozeman Trail, the Indians initiate raids upon American travelers and effect blockades, sometimes cutting off all passage. On December 21, 1866, the Sioux ambush a small detachment of fort troops on wood detail. Attempting to rescue the woodcutters, Capt. W.J. Fetterman leads a cavalry attack upon the Sioux; every soldier is killed. Public outrage stemming from the Fetterman battle demands a reassessment of Indian policy. Investigations are conducted and small policy innovations implemented but no equitable improvement is achieved. Subsequently, on August 1, 1867, Indians attack hay cutters near Fort C. F. Smith. The "Hayfield Fight" ends in the Indians' withdrawal. Then, on August 2, the Sioux attack more woodcutters near Fort Phil Kearny in the "Wagon Box Fight." This time Capt. J.N. Powell and his troops circle the wood wagons and are thus able to fend off the charges of the mounted Sioux until relief troops from Fort Kearny arrive. In the spring of 1868, the U.S. holds council with the Indians. On April 29, the Treaty of Fort Laramie reserves the western half of South Dakota plus a small section of North Dakota and officially designates the entire Powder River country as "unceded Indian Territory." Red Cloud refuses treaty ratification until the U.S. military abandons all posts. This treaty notably marks the event of Indians winning a war against the U.S. and dictating the official terms of peace. Under this agreement, some Sioux and Cheyenne leaders agree to move to the reservations in Montana, Wyoming, and the Dakotas. Indians secure for themselves much of the hunting grounds along the Bighorn and Powder rivers (present-day Montana).

1866–1874   The Montana Gold Rush. By the summer of 1866 non-Indians are flooding into Montana to find gold. Many miners take the Bozeman Trail from Fort Laramie, Wyoming, to the new diggings around Virginia City, Montana. The trail, however, runs though the lands of the Oglala and Brulé Sioux, who fight to keep the miners out of the region. The army establishes a series of forts along the trail for the miners' protection, but, under attack by Sioux and Cheyenne, agrees to abandon them at the Treaty of Fort Laramie in 1868. The treaty does not end U.S. incursion into Indian land, and miners, buffalo hunters, and railroad men continue to trespass on Sioux and Cheyenne country. In 1874, Lt. Col. George Armstrong Custer leads an expedition to the *Paha Sapa*, the Sioux phrase for "black hills," of South Dakota, where geologists and journalists confirm the presence of gold. A new rush commences, and the Northern Pacific Railroad moves closer to Sioux land.

1 8 6 7

1867   Cherokee National Council. The Cherokee National Council passes a law requiring U.S. cattlemen to pay ten cents for each head of cattle passing on Indian lands, as permitted by the Act of 1834. Recognizing that they would be hurt by unregulated grazing of U.S. cattle, and desiring to avoid barren ground, other tribes follow suit and erect gates for collection of tolls.

1867   Hosteen Klah, Navajo Singer and Artist, Is Born. Navajo singer (medicine man) and artist Hosteen Klah is among the most important innovators in Navajo weaving. Klah is born in 1867 and begins training in Navajo ceremonial practice at a young age. Because Klah is also a *nadle* (a man who lives as a woman, usually known as "berdache"), he learns to weave, which among the Navajo is consid-

ered women's work. During his life Klah befriends several white women who have interests in Navajo culture, including Frances Newcomb, the wife of a trader on the reservation, and Mary C. Wheelwright, a transplanted Boston aristocrat. With Wheelwright and other specialists, Klah helps preserve Navajo traditions by recording his knowledge of art and culture. He also demonstrates his weaving frequently, including appearances at two Chicago World's Fairs, in 1893 and 1933. When the Wheelwright Museum opens in 1937, it is Klah's ceremonial and artistic creations that become the core of its collection. Hosteen Klah is best known for his weaving innovations, however. He is credited with originating a pictorial style of weaving that incorporates sandpainting designs from Navajo curing ceremonies. Although a few rare examples of sandpainting weavings apparently predate Klah's work, his are the first to be done in the "whirling log" arrangement, and it is really at his instigation in 1919 that sandpainting rugs become a viable form. Klah's position as berdache, both medicine man and weaver, makes him uniquely qualified to create such a cultural and aesthetic hybrid. He teaches his nieces to weave in the sandpainting style, and this form continues to be produced by expert Navajo weavers today.

1867   The U.S. Buys Alaska. The U.S. government buys Alaska from the Russian government. The purchase does not change the situation of the Aleut, Inuit, and Indians living in Alaska. No treaties are signed, and no land ownership is determined by Alaska Natives in the sale between the United States and Alaska.

APRIL 7, 1867   Hancock's Campaign against the Cheyenne and Sioux. Gen. Winfield Scott Hancock summons Cheyenne chiefs to a conference. Bad weather results in a small turnout, however, and on April 8 Hancock disappointedly marches to a combined Cheyenne and Sioux village in order to deliver his stern mes-

Red Cloud. Courtesy of the National Anthropological Archives, Smithsonian Institution.

sage to more chiefs. The Indians flee. "This looks like the commencement of war," Hancock dryly observes. Throughout the rest of April and into July, Custer leads his Seventh Cavalry in fruitless pursuit of fleeing Cheyenne and Sioux.

JULY 1, 1867   Canadian Confederation. The British North America Act joins Canada West (Ontario), Canada East (Quebec), New Brunswick, and Nova Scotia into the new Dominion of Canada. The new federal government is given the responsibility for Indian affairs. Only Indians in Ontario have signed land cession treaties. In the other provinces, areas of land (reserves) have been set aside for the use of Indians, but not as part of a treaty. All the provinces hand over control of Indian reserve lands to the federal government to be administered on behalf of the Indians. (As wards of the government, Indians are not entrusted with direct ownership of reserve land.) Each province retains control over its remaining land and natural resources, ensuring that the federal government will have to negotiate with provincial governments if it seeks to add land to any reserves. There are approximately 23,000 Indians within the 1867 boundaries of Canada, and many thousands more in other regions of British North America later annexed to Canada.

JULY 20, 1867   The Peace Commission Act. The Peace Commission Act passes, calling for the president to appoint a commission to meet with hostile Indian tribes. The commission surveys Indian issues and recommends abandonment of the "treaty process." The commission also chooses to implement a system based upon an 1853 experiment conducted by California Superintendent of Indian Affairs Edward Fitzgerald Beale; placing a number of Indians in the Tejon Valley to become ranchers and farmers, this attempt to transform Indian to agrarian meets with extremely limited success. Regardless, this system is implemented as

national policy in the post–Civil War years. The Peace Commission meets with many tribes, concluding treaties and establishing reservations. Some of the tribes, or portions of them, agree to remain on reservations; others do not. In 1867, the commissioners reach an agreement with some Kiowa and Comanche people, creating a reservation in the southwest corner of present-day Oklahoma. Concurrently a portion of Cheyenne and Arapaho country also is recognized as a reservation. The Indian Peace Commission negotiates its final treaties with the Indians by signing the 370th pact on August 13, 1868, with the Nez Percé.

SEPTEMBER 1867   Lacrosse League. The National Lacrosse Association is formed in Kingston, Ontario. During the 1880s the game of lacrosse will briefly become very popular across Canada, even internationally. The game is derived from *baggataway*, a sport which originated among the Algonkian-speaking Indians.

1867–1883   Alaskan Missions. During this time, Christianity is brought to the Alaska Natives. Many mainland denominations establish schools in Alaska, including Congregational, Episcopalian, Moravian, Presbyterian, Roman Catholic, and Swedish Evangelical churches.

1867–1907   Creek Adopt Constitutional Government. In 1867, the Creek Nation, now living in Indian Territory, adopts a constitutional government. The first elections in 1867 are controversial, and a small majority of conservatives demand a return to the traditional Creek government based on central villages and a council composed of village leaders. The U.S. supports the constitutional government and, on various occasions, uses marshals and troops to defend it against conservative Creek opposition. Compared to the constitutional governments of the Cherokee, Choctaw, and Chickasaw, the Creek constitutional government is fraught with rebellion and political instability. In 1907, the Creek government is abolished over the

Sauk and Fox tribesmen posing for a picture with Louis Bogy, commissioner of Indian Affairs. Third from the left is Fox chief Chekuskuk, and second from the left, seated, is Sauk chief Keokuk. Bogy here pretends to read the treaty specifying that the tribes cede 157,000 acres of land along the Mississippi and Missouri rivers in exchange for $26,574 and a 750 square-mile reservation territory in present-day Oklahoma. Courtesy of the National Anthropological Archives, Smithsonian Institution.

protests of the conservative Creek, who do not wish to join U.S. society or renounce their treaty and land rights.

1 8 6 8

1868 Expense of Plains Wars. The U.S. Commissioner of Indian Affairs estimates that the cost to the government per Indian killed in the wars raging on the western plains is running very high. Between 1862 and 1867, wars with the Cheyenne, Sioux, and Navajo cost the U.S. government $100 million for several hundred Indian casualties, including women and children.

1868 *Poems*. The first volume of poetry published by an American Indian is released. *Poems* is penned by the Cherokee writer John Rollin Ridge.

APRIL 29, 1868   Treaty of Fort Laramie. The United States signs the Treaty of Fort Laramie and pledges protection of the Plains tribes, "absolute and undisturbed use and occupation" of their reservations, to remove any settlers, and to punish any U.S. citizens causing injuries to Indians, as well as providing extensive agricultural and educational aid "to insure the civilization of the Indians." Provisions include the option for individual land allotment if an Indian so wished, but the reservations as a whole are never to be sold or subdivided without the approval of "three-fourths of the adult male Indians." The United States breaks the treaty in 1874 by sending army troops under Lt. Col. George A. Custer to prospect for gold in the Black Hills, the discovery of which brings white prospectors pouring into the area. War between the Sioux and the army results. In 1969 Indian activists occupying Alcatraz Island will claim that this treaty gives them the right to claim surplus federal property.

MAY 22, 1868   Canadian Indian Legislation. The Canadian government's first legislation regarding Indians adopts the pre-Confederation assimilationist Indian policy and administration as it has been set out in Canada West (Gradual Civilization Act of 1857). It also introduces "location tickets," a means by which provisional individual title to reserve lands can be given to those seeking enfranchisement. Responsibility for Indian affairs is given to the secretary of State.

JUNE 1, 1868   Navajo Indian Reservation Created. The Navajo Reservation, the largest in the U.S., is created by the Treaty of Bosque Redondo, signed at Fort Sumner, New Mexico. Approximately 3.5 million acres of land in New Mexico, Arizona, and Utah are set aside for the Navajo, who number approximately 9,000. The land amounts to less than one-fifth of the tribe's former holdings and is mostly barren, dry, and unsuited for agriculture other than stockraising.

An important provision of the treaty stipulates: "The United States agrees that for every 30 children . . . who can be induced or compelled to attend school, a house shall be provided, and a teacher competent to teach the elementary branches of an English education shall be furnished. . . ." Years of failure and neglect follow and contribute to the result which during World War II sees the Selective Service System classify as illiterate 88 percent of Navajo males 18 to 35 years of age.

SEPTEMBER 17–24, 1868   Plains Warfare Begins. Failing to receive promised rations, Kiowa and Comanche begin raiding in northern Texas. At about the same time, Cheyenne raid settlements on the Saline and Solomon rivers. George A. Forsyth and 50 handpicked plainsmen are patrolling western Kansas when 600 to 700 Dog Soldiers and Oglala Sioux attack the small company. They are besieged for eight days on Beecher's Island (Aricaree Fork) on the Republican River. During the battle, the important Cheyenne chief Roman Nose is killed. At Sweetwater Creek in the Texas Panhandle, on March 17, 1869, Lt. Col. Custer parleys with Dog Soldiers holding two white women hostage. He seizes three chiefs and sends one back with surrender terms, demanding that the hostages be released or he will hang the others. The Cheyenne comply. Then, on July 11, under the leadership of Tall Bull, Dog Soldiers join forces with the Northern Cheyenne in the Powder River country. On this date, the Fifth Cavalry defeats the Dog Soldiers at Summit Springs, Colorado. Tall Bull is killed, and the Dog Soldiers retire to a reservation. The following winter, Sheridan proposes a three-pronged campaign. One column will approach from Fort Bascom, New Mexico; another from Fort Lyon, Colorado; and the third from Fort Dodge, Kansas. They are to converge on the Indians' winter camps on the Canadian and Washita rivers in Indian territory. On November 27, Lt. Col. George A. Custer attacks Black Kettle's

Major General William Tecumseh Sherman presides with commissioners over the signing of a treaty with chief Red Cloud at Fort Laramie, Wyoming Territory, on April 29, 1868. Courtesy of the National Anthropological Archives, Smithsonian Institution.

peaceful Cheyenne camp on the Washita River, in Oklahoma. Among the 103 Indians killed in the attack, 93 are women, old men, and children, including Chief Black Kettle and his wife. This is Custer's first major engagement with the Indian people.

---

1 8 6 9

1869   Formation of The Board of Indian Com-

missioners by Congress. An experiment in Indian administration in response to public disclosures of fraud and mismanagement within President Grant's administration, the commission sets out to be a nonpartisan voice for the Indian and is composed of ten prominent citizens. Brig. Gen. Ely Samuel Parker (Do-Ne-Ho-Geh-Weh), a chief from the Tonowanda-Seneca tribe, becomes its first commissioner on April 21. Conceived as an advisory task force, the commission investi-

Navajo prisoners of war at Fort Sumner, New Mexico, c. 1866. This picture shows Indian captives building an adobe under military guard. Courtesy of the Museum of New Mexico.

gates tribal conditions and then suggests possible reforms to federal agencies. Many of the staff members support reform, frequently putting them at odds with the Interior Department. Gen. Ely Parker, a Seneca Indian and personal friend to President Ulysses S. Grant, is appointed commissioner of Indian affairs. Parker helps initiate a policy of providing Indians with food and clothing in exchange for reconciling themselves to life on small, economically marginal reservations of land.

1869 "The Only Good Indian." Upon being introduced to a Comanche chief in Indian Territory who is referred to as a "good Indian," Gen. Philip Sherman is reported to have stated, "the only good Indians I ever saw were dead."

JUNE 22, 1869   Gradual Enfranchisement Act. The Canadian government passes the Gradual Enfranchisement Act, based on the 1857 Gradual Civilization Act. Responding to Indian resistance to the establishment of elected band councils, Indian agents are given power to depose traditional leaders for "dishonesty, intemperance and immorality," and to impose elected band councils. This act also stipulates

that when Indian women marry non-Indians, the children born of the marriage will not have legal status as Indians. Indian leaders reject the law.

AUTUMN 1869   Smallpox on Northern Plains. Thousands of Indians and Métis on the northern plains are killed in a smallpox epidemic. The disease spreads north from traders operating on the Missouri River.

OCTOBER 11, 1869   Métis Stop Survey. Worried that their rights to river lots may be threatened, 16 Métis led by Louis Riel (See biography, October 22, 1844) stop a party of Canadian surveyors near their farms. The surveyors, who have been told by the Canadian government to avoid conflict, agree not to survey on Métis farms. An agreement which would transfer the land from the Hudson's Bay Company to Canada has not yet been completed.

NOVEMBER 2, 1869   Métis Seize Fort. Métis forces led by Louis Riel take possession of Upper Fort Garry. The fort's food supply and its position at the forks of the Red and Assiniboine rivers make it the control center of the Red

Ely Parker, first Indian commissioner of Indian affairs. Courtesy of the National Anthropological Archives, Smithsonian Institution.

River Colony. The move follows the Métis eviction of William McDougall, whom the Canadian government has appointed as the new lieutenant-governor of the North-West Territories.

DECEMBER 8, 1869 Métis Provisional Government. Led by Louis Riel, the Métis at Red River establish a provisional government in order to negotiate the terms under which they will enter Canada. They deny that Canada has the right to annex the region without the residents' consent. The French-speaking Roman Catholic Métis population fears that its religion, language, and land will be threatened by an influx of English-speaking Protestant settlers from Ontario. The Country-born population, though not actively involved in the resistance, appears to be sympathetic with the Métis.

1869–1874 Whisky Trade. Whisky traders operating north from the Missouri River begin trading whisky with the Siksika, Kainai (Blood), and Peigan (Blackfoot Confederacy) north of the United States. Alcohol abuse brings serious social problems to the Blackfoot Confederacy.

The whisky trade begins in earnest during the mid-1860s in the United States after the American Fur Company collapses. Whisky traders are moving north of the border because increased law enforcement in the United States is restricting the trade there.

1 8 7 0

1870 Grant's Peace Policy. U.S. President Ulysses S. Grant gives control of the Indian agencies to various Christian dominations after the Congress passes a law prohibiting army officers from holding the post of Indian agent.

1870 Indian Education. The U.S. Congress appropriates $100,000 for American Indian education. This is the first instance of specific appropriation, as the funds are intended for the operation of federal industrial schools.

1870 Kwagiulth (Kwakiutl) Settlement. Kwagiulth (Kwakiutl, Kwakwaka'wakw) take up seasonal wage labor at a fish cannery at Alert Bay on an island near northern Vancouver Island. The subsequent establishment of a sawmill, Indian mission, government Indian agency, and schools marks the village as the chief cultural center of the Kwagiulth.

1870 *McKay v. Campbell.* The U.S. Supreme Court, in *McKay v. Campbell,* holds that Indians born in tribal allegiance are not born "in the United States: and are therefore not citizens. The Indian tribes . . . have always been held to be distinct and independent political communities, retaining the right to self-government. . . ." This U.S. Supreme Court ruling sets Indians apart from the U.S. Constitution, whose Fourteenth Amendment guarantees citizenship to "all persons born or naturalized in the United States."

JANUARY 31, 1870 California Indian Reserves. By executive order, the Mission Indian

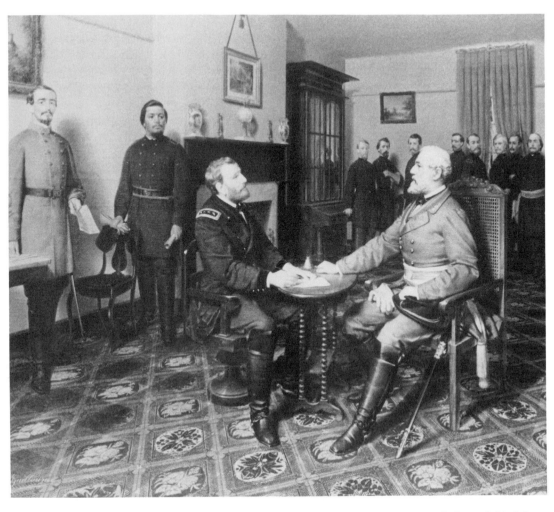

Oil painting by Louis Didier Guillaume showing Robert E. Lee (right) surrendering to Ulysses S. Grant. Behind Grant stands his chief secretary, Ely Parker, a full-blood Seneca of the Wolf Clan. Courtesy of the National Park Service, Appomattox Court House National Historical Park.

Reserve is set aside for the Diegueño, Cahuilla, San Luis Rey, Serrano and Temecula tribes.

MARCH 4, 1870 Métis Execute Prisoner. Thomas Scott, an opponent of the provisional government at Red River and an Ontario Protestant, is executed after being convicted of refusing to subordinate to the government. The execution follows the Canadian government's announcement that it is willing to negotiate with the provisional government. After the news

reaches Ontario on March 26, Ontario Protestants demand retribution.

APRIL 12, 1870 Arikara, Gros Ventre, and Mandan Reserve. A reserve is set apart for the Arikara, Gros Ventre, and Mandan at Fort Berthold, Dakota. Claims to all other lands are relinquished.

JUNE 23, 1870 Manitoba Act. Louis Riel's provisional government accepts the terms of

Members of a Blackfoot Confederacy gather in front of Fort Whoop-up (Lethbridge, Alberta), the best known whisky post in Canada. Courtesy of the Glenbow Archives, Calgary, Alberta.

the Manitoba Act. Most of the former Hudson's Bay Company lands will become the North-West Territories, administered by the federal government. The vast majority in these territories are Indian or mixed-blood (Métis and Country-born). A small area of these lands will become the Province of Manitoba. Only a very small portion of the province's population is non-Native. The Métis are given guarantees of French language rights, promises of Catholic schools, and recognition of Métis land title in the province. The federal government promises

to provide 1,400,000 acres of land for the Métis of the province. The federal government, which retains control of land and natural resources in the entire area, has also agreed to negotiate land cession treaties with the Indians of the North-West Territories and Manitoba.

AUGUST 24, 1870 Métis Flee Manitoba. Over 1,200 Canadian and British troops enter Manitoba, beginning a campaign of intimidation that prompts about two-thirds of the Métis to leave the province to join Métis settlements

Members of the Métis Provisional Government at Red River. Louis Riel is seated in the center. Courtesy of the Glenbow Archives, Calgary, Alberta.

along the North and South Saskatchewan rivers in the North-West Territories. Louis Riel flees to the United States. The troops are sent after Ontario residents who react angrily to the execution of Thomas Scott by the Métis provisional government on March 4. Many of the Métis granted scrip (certificates redeemable for land) sell their certificates at a fraction of their value.

OCTOBER 1870 Plains Indian Battle. A Kainai (Blood) and Peigan party defeat an attacking Cree-Assiniboine party led by Big Bear (*See* biography, c. 1825), Little Pine, and Piapot in the last plains war in Canada near the whisky trade post of Fort Whoop-up (at today's Lethbridge, Alberta). During the 1860s the Cree had followed the diminishing buffalo herds toward the southwest, increasing their conflicts with the Blackfoot Confederacy. Believing that smallpox had severely weakened their enemies, the Cree and Assiniboine had initiated the battle.

1870–1890 The Peyote Road. For centuries

Indians in northern Mexico have used the peyote plant in religious ceremonies. Peyote induces a mild hallucinatory state, which is said to bring the user close to the spirit world. In the late nineteenth century, the Peyote religion spreads among the Kiowa, Comanche, Cheyenne, and Arapaho. Tribal members develop their own ceremonies, songs, and symbolism, and dreams, visions, and prayers become a part of the Peyote religion. Peyote is ingested as a sacrament, and followers vow to follow the Peyote Road. They promise to be trustworthy, honorable, and community-oriented. Family, children, and cultural survival become a major emphasis of this movement. Elements of Christianity become a part of the worship service, and in 1918 the members organize themselves into the Native American Church.

The Office of Indian Affairs attempts to extinguish the religion but does not succeed. In the twentieth century, Indians introduce the church to Native peoples throughout the United States. The Native American Church has survived, but continues to face legal attacks in the twentieth century.

Comanche leader Quanah Parker. Courtesy of the National Anthropological Archives, Smithsonian Institution.

1 8 7 1

MARCH 3, 1871 The End of Treaty Making. Congress passes an act stating that it will no longer negotiate treaties with Indian nations. After this act, agreements with Indian groups are to be made by congressional acts and executive orders, which are agreements made by the president or designated official, usually by the secretary of the interior. The act is a rider attached to the Indian Appropriations Act. The act provides "That hereafter no Indian Nation of Tribes within the territory of the United States shall be acknowledged or recognized as an independent nation, tribe or power with whom the United States may contract by treaty; provided further, that nothing herein shall be construed to invalidate or impair the obligations of any treaty heretofore lawfully made and ratified, with any such Indian Nation or tribe." This ends treaty-making by the United States with Indian tribes. Between 1778 and 1871, the U.S. Senate has ratified 372 treaties with Indian tribes.

JULY 20, 1871 British Columbia Joins Canada. British Columbia enters Confederation. The government of British Columbia retains control of land and natural resources, but agrees to pursue "a policy as liberal as hitherto pursued" when transferring land (to the federal government) for use as Indian reserves. At least 25,000 of the 37,000 residents of British Columbia are Indians. With the acquisition of the Hudson's Bay Company lands in 1870 and British Columbia in 1871, the population of Indians in Canada rises to over 100,000.

AUGUST 3, 1871 Treaty 1. The first of 11 numbered treaties covering former Hudson's Bay Company lands is signed at Lower Fort Garry. Treaty 1 (The Stone Fort Treaty), covering Manitoba (including the area of the Selkirk treaty of 1817) and areas of the North-West Territories (today's southern Manitoba), is signed by Saulteaux (Ojibway) and Swampy

Plains Indians. The Great Plains travois was the principal mode of transportation used to move shelters and household and personal effects. Photo by E. Curtis. Courtesy of the International Museum of Photography at the George Eastman House.

Cree bands. The Indians will be given reserves amounting to 160 acres (65 hectares) per family of five, and annual payments of $3 per person. The government also promises farm implements and seed. *(See* map of Indian Treaty Areas in Canada, p. 394.)

AUGUST 21, 1871   Treaty 2. Treaty 2 (Manitoba Post Treaty), covering areas of the North-West Territories (today's central and southwest Manitoba, and southeast Saskatchewan), is signed by Ojibway bands. Terms are the same as for Treaty 1. *(See* map of Indian Treaty Areas in Canada, p. 394.)

1871–1879   Destruction of the Buffalo. The importance of the buffalo to plains people and their cultures cannot be overstated. Every part of the animal is put to use, and food, shelter, and clothing are all provided by the buffalo. After a market for buffalo hides develops, American leaders begin to see the destruction of the buffalo as a means to undermine Indian strength. U.S. Congressman James Garrison claims that the secretary of the interior has advised him that he would "rejoice as far as the Indian matter was concerned when the last buffalo was killed." Gen. Philip Sheridan claims that buffalo hunters did more "to settle the vexed Indian question than the entire regular army," and calls for the buffalos extermination. The slaughter doesn't take long to complete. Construction of the Union Pacific Railroad cuts the shrinking herds into northern and southern groups. Wholesale destruction begins in 1871. In one two-month period, 260,000 buffalo are killed in one section alone, and there are so many hides on the market that the price falls to a mere dollar per skin. Between 1870 and 1885, more than 10 million buffalo are slaughtered by U.S. hunters. By 1878, the southern herd is virtually wiped out. The northern group's demise follows a hauntingly similar pattern. Numbers decrease rapidly from 1876 onward, and by 1889 there are very few buffalo left.

1 8 7 3

1873   Canadian Indian Affairs. Responsibility for Canadian Indian affairs is transferred from its Department of Secretary of State to its Department of the Interior.

1873   The Modoc War. The Modoc War between the U.S. and the Modoc tribe of California is led by Chief Kintpuash (Captain Jack). The Modoc have ceded their land to the United States in 1864, but in 1872, they leave the Klamath Reservation in present-day Oregon, to which they have been assigned, and return to their ancestral lands on the Lost River in north-central California. A force of 400 soldiers, mostly regular army, drive the Modoc to take refuge in the lava beds in northeastern California. It requires several years, more than 1,000 soldiers, and the use of artillery pieces to finally dislodge the Modoc, who number about 250. During a council meeting, Captain Jack kills Gen. Edward R. S. Canby, the only general killed in an Indian war. Captain Jack and three others are tried and hanged for the murder of the general and one other member of the peace commission. The remainder of Captain Jack's band are sent to reservations in Oklahoma.

JUNE 1, 1873   Cypress Hills Killings. Ten Americans and Canadians kill up to 30 Assiniboine in what becomes known as the Cypress Hills Massacre. The Cypress Hills are in Canada's southwestern prairies. The few remaining plains buffalo herds (and the whisky trade) are centered near here.

JULY 1, 1873   Prince Edward Island Joins Canada. The province of Prince Edward Island enters the Confederation having signed no land cession treaties with Indian groups. The Micmac population of the province has fallen to about 300.

OCTOBER 3, 1873   Treaty 3. In a ceremony at Fort Frances the Saulteaux sign Treaty 3 (North-West Angle Treaty) covering today's western Ontario and southeastern Manitoba. Following long negotiations the government promises to provide reserve land of 640 acres (259 hectares) per family of five, schools, agricultural implements and livestock, annual payments of $5 per person, and hunting, trapping and fishing rights on unsettled land. The Métis of the region also

Captain Jack. Courtesy of the National Archives.

are included in this treaty. *(See* map of Indian Treaty Areas in Canada, p. 394.)

1 8 7 4

SUMMER 1874   Cassiar Gold Rush. Tahltan and Kaska subsistence activities, and the Coastal Tlingit control of the flow of European goods inland, are disrupted by a gold rush along the Dease River in the northern interior of British Columbia.

SEPTEMBER 15, 1874   Treaty 4. The Plains Cree, Assiniboine, and Saulteaux sign Treaty 4 (Qu'Appelle Treaty), covering areas of the North-West Territories (now southern Saskatchewan); its terms are similar to those of Treaty 3. *(See* map of Indian Treaty Areas in Canada, p. 394.)

OCTOBER 1874   Police in the Canadian West. Guided by mixed-blood Jerry Potts (Bear Child, Ky-yokosi, 1840-1896), the North-West Mounted Police establish Fort Macleod on an island in the Oldman River (in today's southern Alberta). The police have come to put an end to the whisky trade, prevent violence

Sitting Bull, Hunkpapa Sioux tribal leader. He was killed in October 1890 by government-paid Indian police over a dispute that erupted during a Ghost Dance ceremony at Standing Rock. Courtesy of the Library of Congress.

such as the Cypress Hills Massacre (1873), and prepare the Canadian West for peaceful settlement. Potts, the son of a fur trader and a Kainai woman, serves as a valuable interpreter and intermediary between the police and the Indians. The Indians of the Canadian West begin developing very friendly relations with the police.

1874–1875   The Red River or Buffalo Wars. As the buffalo becomes scarcer on the southern plains, many Kiowa, Kiowa-Apache, Comanche, Southern Cheyenne, and Arapaho gather on their reservations at Fort Sill, Fort Darlington, and Fort Reno to receive food. But supplies are few and far between, and the lack of food at the agencies sends parties raiding outside of the reservation boundaries. When the federal government demands that the Comanche surrender five young men accused of a raid, the Comanche refuse, and the situation escalates to war. On June 27, 1,000 warriors attack a camp of buffalo hunters at Adobe Walls in the Texas panhandle. The long-range buffalo guns are too powerful and the attack fails, but the event makes the army determined to end the military strength of the southern tribes. An ultimatum is given that all Indians not on the reservation at Fort Sill by August 3 will be considered hostile and be arrested or killed. The American forces under Gen. Nelson Miles comb the southern plains between the Canadian and Red rivers looking for off-reservation Indians. Between August and December of 1874, Miles's troops keep up a relentless pursuit. In September 1875, the army attacks and destroys the Kiowa, Comanche, and Southern Cheyenne village at Palo Duro Canyon where many of the dissidents are living. Without homes and unable to endure the hardship of a winter without supplies, the resistive bands begin surrendering at Forts Darlington, Sill, and Reno. The Kiowa, under Satanta, surrender at the Darlington Agency on October 7, 1874, and the last of the holdouts, Quanah Parker's Kwahadi Comanche, return to Fort Sill the following year, on June 2, 1875.

1874–1881   War on the Northern Plains. In the summer of 1874 an expedition under Lt. Col. George Armstrong Custer discovers gold in the Black Hills, sacred land for the Lakota Sioux, Cheyenne, and other tribes. In violation of the Fort Laramie Treaty, gold miners flood the Black Hills. The federal government attempts to solve the impending crisis by purchasing the Hills from the Lakota, but the Sioux have no intention of selling. The govern-

The first session of the General Council in Indian territory was held at Okmulgee (Oklahoma), capital of the Creek Nation, in 1870. The meeting gathered delegates from twelve different tribes, and a committee of Indian leaders framed a constitution for the new territory. This photograph shows the Creek log building and all the delegates of the council, c. 1875. Photo by Jack Hillers, C.W. Kirk Collection. Courtesy of the Archives & Manuscripts Division of the Oklahoma Historical Society.

ment issues an ultimatum: Those not reporting to their agency and reservation by January 31, 1876, will be considered hostile and be captured or killed. Several off-reservation bands fail to report and the army organizes two forces to subdue them: one under Gen. George Crook and another under Custer. Little comes of these initial expeditions; the Custer mission is delayed, and Crook's force is routed in its

cavalry attack against the Teton and Cheyenne on the Powder River. The following spring, the army sends three columns against the Sioux and their Cheyenne and Arapaho allies: Crook from the south, Col. John Gibbon from the west, and Gen. Alfred Terry, whose force includes the Seventh Cavalry commanded by Custer. As Crook's 1,000-man force advances northward along Rosebud Creek, he encounters about 700 Cheyenne and Sioux under Crazy Horse. After a six-hour fight, the Indians withdraw, but not before inflicting heavy damage on Crook's forces. But the battle of the Rosebud, as it is known, is only a prelude to a greater Indian victory.

After the battle of the Rosebud, the Indian forces regroup and establish camp in a meadow they call Greasy Grass, along the Little Bighorn River in present-day Montana. With the addition of reservation Indians who leave after spending the winter at the agencies, the camp grows quickly, swelling in size to over 7,000 people. Four days after the Rosebud fight, Terry's and Gibbon's columns unite on the Yellowstone River. After a scouting party reports the general location of the Indian encampment, Terry sends the Seventh Cavalry under Custer to the southern end of Little Big Horn Valley. On June 25, 1876, Custer divides his force for tactical purposes, and with a command of 225 men advances on the Indian camp. Warriors under Hunkpapa chief Gall confront Custer forces from the south, while Crazy Horse bears down from the north. In less than an hour, Custer and his men are killed. Only rescue by General Terry's column prevents a similar fate for the other American forces.

For the Cheyenne and Sioux Indians, the victory at Little Bighorn is short-lived. In July 1876, the army intercepts a force of 1,000 Cheyenne who have left agencies to join up with Sitting Bull and Crazy Horse, defeating them at the battle of Warbonnet Creek in northwestern Nebraska. Then, on September 8, General Crook's advance guard under Captain Miles captures American Horse's Teton band at the battle of Slim Buttes in South Dakota. Dull Knife's Northern Cheyenne are defeated by the Fourth Cavalry at the Red Fork on the Powder River, in Wyoming on November 25. Gen. Nelson Miles, recently returned from the Red River War, defeats Crazy Horse's warriors at the battle of Wolf Mountain in January 1877 and Lame Deer's Miniconjou in Montana in May.

By the spring of 1877, the Plains wars are nearly over. On May 6, Crazy Horse and over 1,000 followers surrender at Fort Robinson in Nebraska. Crazy Horse's surrender comes one day after Sitting Bull crosses into Canada. Sitting Bull stays there until July 19, 1881, when he and his starving band become the last to surrender at Fort Buford, Dakota Territory, living afterwards at the Standing Rock Reservation.

1 8 7 5

1875 Fort Marion, Florida. Following the end of the Red River War on the southern plains, 71 Kiowa, Comanche, Cheyenne, and Arapaho and one Caddo are confined at Fort Marion in St. Augustine, Florida. Many of the prisoners are young men, who depict their exploits on ledger sheets. When some of the Fort Marion ledger drawings are published on the East Coast, interest in Indian painting grows. Of particular importance among this group of ledger artists are Kiowa and Cheyenne Indians Paul Zo-Tom, Howling Wolf, Etahdleuh Doanloe, and Buffalo Meat.

1875 Navajo Rug Making. Aniline dyes, use of cotton instead of wool warp, and four-ply yarns precolored and made in Germantown, Pennsylvania, replace traditionally dyed and handspun sheep's wool in the manufacture of Navajo rugs by this time. In response to the growing non-Indian market, Navajo weavers produce thicker rugs in place of their earlier thinner, harder blankets.

MARCH 1875 The Moapa Reserve Set Aside. By an act of Congress, the Moapa River Reserve (formerly the Muddy Valley Reserve) in the Nevada Agency in Nevada, is set apart and occupied by the Chemehuevi, Kaibab, Pawipit, Paiute, and Shivwits.

APRIL 23, 1875 Camp Verde Reserve Revoked. By executive order the Camp Verde

Reserve for the Apache Mohave (Yavapai) Indians in Arizona is revoked.

SEPTEMBER 24, 1875 Treaty 5. Saulteaux and Swampy Cree bands sign Treaty 5 covering land in today's northern Manitoba and western Ontario. Treaty 1 and Treaty 2 reserve sizes and annuities are brought into line with the more liberal terms of Treaty 3 in 1875. *(See* map of Indian Treaty Areas in Canada, p. 394.)

1875–1886 Apache Resistance under Geronimo. When the government decides to consolidate the Apache groups at San Carlos in 1875, it dissolves the Apache Pass Reservation, home of the Chiricahua Apache. Following the dissolution, Geronimo lives with Juh's Nednhi band in the Sierra Madre range just over the border in Mexico. In 1876, Geronimo and the rest of Juh's band appear at the Mescalero Reservation in Ojo Caliente, and are apprehended there by the San Carlos agent who returns Geronimo and the others to Arizona. After about a year at San Carlos, Geronimo, Juh, and their followers flee the reservation again, but increased Mexican military activity forces his return to San Carlos. Unrest on the reservation grows, and many of the militants begin to follow a medicine man named Nakaidoklini, who predicts a return to power for the Apache people. On August 30, 1881, the army moves to arrest Nakaidoklini, and a fight breaks out at Cibecue Creek, during which the prophet is killed. One month later, Geronimo, Juh, Chato, Naiche (son of Cochise), and 74 others leave San Carlos for Mexico. In April 1882 they return and take revenge for the Cibecue Creek killings. A number of other attacks follow and a force under Gen. George Crook begins pursuit, entering the Sierra Madres with Mexican permission in May 1883. After an attack on Chato's camp kills nine, the remaining Apache slowly return to San Carlos, Geronimo appearing in March 1884. Another breakout occurs in May 1885, this one prompted by a reservation ban on an alcoholic beverage called *tiswin*. At that time, Geronimo, Naiche,

and more than 135 others head for Mexico, raiding and killing along the way. Despite the presence of over 3,000 U.S. soldiers, Geronimo and his band elude the American army until they are found by Crook's forces the next spring. At a conference at Canyon de los Embudos on March 25, 1886, Crook demands unconditional surrender and tells the leaders that they will be imprisoned for their actions. With some deliberation, the Apache agree to his conditions, but, while being led to Fort Bowie by Apache scouts, Geronimo, Naiche, and 24 others escape again. Furious that the Apache have been allowed to escape, the army command replaces Crook with Gen. Nelson Miles, who puts 5,000 soldiers in the field. After a summer of pursuing the tiny Chiricahua band, Geronimo is discovered at Skeleton Canyon. There, on September 4, 1886, he surrenders for the last time. After brief detention Geronimo and 500 other Apache are sent in chains to Fort Pickens in Pensacola, Florida. After a year they are relocated to the Mount Vernon barracks in Alabama, where tuberculosis and other diseases kill one-quarter of them. The Chiricahua are finally released in 1894, but they are refused entry into Arizona and are placed instead at Fort Sill in Oklahoma. There Geronimo dies in 1909, never having returned to his homeland.

c. 1875–1920s Museum Collecting. The most intensive period of museum collecting of American Indian artifacts occurs during the late nineteenth and early twentieth centuries. In 1879, the Bureau of American Ethnology (under the auspices of the Smithsonian Institution) begins its first large-scale collecting expedition to the Southwest. Between 1880–1885, 6,500 pots are taken from Zuni and Acoma pueblos alone. Art historians now believe that the removal of such large quantities of pottery undermined ceramic traditions by removing design sources. Other areas are similarly pillaged. Art historian Douglas Cole writes of the Northwest Coast region during this "scramble" for artifacts that, "By the time it ended there was more Kwakiutl material in Milwaukee than in

Geronimo and three of his warriors in 1886, after their defeat. Courtesy of the Southwest Museum, Los Angeles.

Mamalillukula, more Salish pieces in Cambridge than Comox. The city of Washington contained more Northwest Coast material than the state of Washington, and New York City probably housed more British Columbia material than British Columbia herself."

1 8 7 6

1876 British Columbia Indian Policy. Canadian governor-general Lord Dufferin protests the British Columbia government's policy regarding Indian lands. The British Columbia and federal governments have been unable to agree on the amount of land that should be provided for British Columbia Indians. The federal government wants British Columbia to establish reserves of at least 80 acres per family. The government of British Columbia insists that ten acres per family is sufficient. Indian groups in the province, supported by missionaries, have been protesting the policy of British Columbia since the 1860s. The provincial government feels that the missionaries have been inciting Indian demands for their own gain.

1876   Gertrude Simmons Bonnin (Aitkala-Sa), Sioux Author and Activist, Is Born. Gertrude Bonnin is born at the Yankton Sioux Agency in South Dakota on February 22. She is reared as a Sioux until she is eight years old, when she leaves the reservation to attend a Quaker missionary school for Indians, White's Indiana Manual Labor Institute, in Wabash, Indiana. She receives her high school diploma and goes on to Earlham College in Richmond, Indiana, where she receives recognition and prizes for her oratorical skills. Following graduation, Bonnin teaches for two years at Carlisle Indian School in Carlisle, Pennsylvania. She returns to Sioux country and in 1902 marries Raymond Talesfase Bonnin, a Sioux employee of the Indian Service. Bonnin is elected secretary of the Society of American Indians in 1916 and moves to Washington, D.C., where she carries on the society's correspondence with the Office of Indian Affairs, lectures from coast to coast as its representative, and edits its periodical, the *American Indian Magazine*. Bonnin is interested in music and one of her last undertakings is the composition, with William F. Hanson, of an Indian opera, *Sun Dance*. She dies in Washington, D.C., at the age of 61.

APRIL 12, 1876   Canadian Indian Act. The passage of the Indian Act consolidates the Canadian government's legislation regarding Indians. It continues a policy of assimilating Indians into Canadian society. It makes elected band councils voluntary and gives such councils wider powers. Location tickets, reintroduced in eastern Canada, are part of a plan to lead Indians to abandon the practice of holding land in common. Location tickets give individuals rights to 20 hectares of reserve land. Indians who farm their allotment over a period of three years are to be enfranchised and are to get absolute title to the land. (Only one Indian was enfranchised between 1857 and 1876.) The act forbids the sale of alcohol to Indians, and bars non-Indians from reserves after nightfall.

JUNE 25, 1876   Custer's Last Stand. After gold miners start working in the Black Hills, sacred to the Sioux, several bands of Sioux leave their reservations to protect the Black Hills from sacrilege. Led by Crazy Horse of the Oglala Sioux and Sitting Bull of the Hunkpapa band of Teton Sioux, the Indians gather to face U.S. troops, who are protecting the miners. Three columns converge on the Sioux, Cheyenne and their Arapaho allies. One column, led by General Alfred Terry, includes the Seventh Cavalry commanded by Col. George Armstrong Custer. Terry sends Custer to the southern end of the Little Bighorn Valley (present-day eastern Montana) where the colonel and his Crow and Arikara scouts locate a large Indian encampment. On June 25 Custer divides his force for tactical purposes and with a command of 225 men advances on the Indian camp in the Little Bighorn Valley. Sioux and Cheyenne meet his advance and kill every man, including Custer, and are only prevented from doing likewise to the other forces because they are rescued by General Terry's command. Sitting Bull and remnants of the Lakota Sioux flee to Canada and do not return until to the Dakotas until 1881.

AUGUST 23, 1876   Treaty 6. Plains Cree, Woodland Cree, and Assiniboine leaders at Fort Carlton sign Treaty 6 covering areas of the North-West Territories (today's central Alberta and Saskatchewan). Others sign the treaty at Fort Pitt on September 9. The treaty terms resemble those of earlier numbered treaties, but the Indians also secure provisions that promise assistance in case of "pestilence" or "famine" and a clause promising that "a medicine chest will be kept at the house of each Indian Agent for the use and benefit of the Indians." The great hardship facing these Indians as a result of the near extinction of the buffalo has led them to seek these guarantees. Based on the "medicine chest" provision, the Canadian govern-

The view of the Little Bighorn Valley from the position of the Seventh Cavalry looking in the direction of the Sioux, Cheyenne, and Arapaho encampments. Courtesy of Stephen Lehmer.

ment agrees by the late 1960s to provide free health care for all status Indians. Big Bear *(See* biography, c. 1825), chief of the Saskatchewan River Cree, and Poundmaker denounce the treaty's provisions. Other chiefs such as Sweet Grass had been calling for a treaty for several years. *(See* map of Indian Treaty Areas in Canada, p. 394.)

1876 AND 1878 Buffalo Calf Road Becomes Female Fighter. During the battle of the Rose-bud, then later in the "Cheyenne Breakout,"

Buffalo Calf Road, female fighter, distinguishes herself in a time recognized as one of the worst periods of Indian annihilation in the Americas.

1876–1915 Indians in the "World's Fairs." For 40 years after the Philadelphia Centennial is held in 1876 (during which the Custer "massacre" is revealed to the celebrating U.S. nation), at least ten "World's Fairs" are held throughout the United States. Among the most noteworthy are the Philadelphia event, the Louisiana Purchase Exposition in St. Louis (1904), and the Panama-Pacific International Exposition in San Francisco (1915). World's Fairs tend to glorify both past achievements and future prospects of the American nation. Reflecting the "Vanishing Indian" mentality of the time, the expositions of the late nineteenth century amply and nostalgically represent Indian peoples right alongside this past and future "progress." The World Columbian Exposition in Chicago opens on October 23, 1892, as the largest of the fairs, and provides a typical example in its treatment of Indians and their art and culture. The event, which marked the 400th anniversary of Columbus's landing in the Western Hemisphere, devotes a great deal of space to the American Indian. Organized on the theme "A Century of Progress," nearly half of the government building is devoted to American Indian lifeways, with greatest emphasis on a display testifying to the success of federal Indian education policy. The Smithsonian display is quite different, however, and includes reconstructions of traditional Indian cultures. Groups of Seneca, Penobscot, Kwakiutl, different Pueblos, Navajo, Sioux, Apache, and Nez Percé populate the Indian exhibit, offering periodic cultural demonstrations to curious onlookers. Simultaneous portrayal of the preservation and acculturation of the Indian way of life, a contradiction inherent in the displays at expositions like Chicago, reflects American ambivalence toward the American Indian at this time in history.

1 8 7 7

1877 The Nez Percé War. Between 1863 and 1876 the nontreaty Nez Percé continue to reject the Thief Treaty of 1763. After the defeat of Custer at Little Big Horn, the army orders that all nonreservation Nez Percé be placed on reservations. In 1877, Gen. Oliver O. Howard, commander of the Northwestern Department, meets with Nez Percé chiefs Hinmahtooyahlatkekt (Thunder Coming From Water Over Land, or Joseph), Ollikut, Looking Glass, Rainbow,

White Bird, and Toohoolhoolzote. Howard asks each nontreaty leader if he will move. All agree to relocate to the reservation.

On the way to their new home, a skirmish involving young Nez Percé warriors results in the Nez Percé War. The Nez Percé and their Palouse allies fight several running battles with the army as they move from their homelands to Montana. After a defeat at Big Hole, a sacred site in Montana, the Indians move into Wyoming, hoping to settle with the Crow and live like buffalo-hunting Plains people. But they are rejected by the Crow and so move farther north. When they are but 40 miles from Canada, they are attacked again by the army. After days of fighting, Joseph concludes a conditional surrender whereby the Nez Percé will not be punished for their resistance but will be allowed to settle on the reservation in Idaho. General Howard and Col. Nelson A. Miles agree to these conditions, but they are reversed by Gen. William Tecumseh Sherman. Sherman exiles the Nez Percé and Palouse to Fort Leavenworth, Kansas, as prisoners of war, before moving them to the Quapaw Agency in northeastern Indian Territory (Oklahoma) and then to the Ponca Agency.

FEBRUARY 28, 1877 Standing Rock Reserve Set Aside. By act of Congress and by treaty of April 29, 1868, the Sioux (Standing Rock) Reserve, 4,176 square miles, is set apart for the Blackfeet, Hunkpapa, and Lower and Upper Yanktonai Sioux.

MARCH 16, 1877 Zuni Land Grant Recognized. The United States, by executive order, recognizes the Pueblo grant of the Zuni holdings. On May 1, 1883, this order is amended by President Chester A. Arthur, and an executive order is reissued on March 3, 1885, defining and extending the Zuni Reservation boundaries "to except lands already settled upon and occupied in good faith by white settlers." The reservation now comprises about 440,000 acres, mostly in McKinley County in New Mexico, with a small portion in the south lying in Valencia County.

MAY 10, 1877 Carlin Farms Reservation Established. By executive order, the Carlin Farms Reserve is set aside for the Northwestern Shoshoni in Nevada.

JUNE 2, 1877 Sitting Bull in Canada. Sitting Bull (Ta-tanka-I-yotank), chief of the Hunkpapa Dakota, and about a thousand of his followers arrive in Canada after defeating United States forces at the battle of the Little Big Horn River on June 25, 1876. Dakota refugees, who began fleeing the United States in November 1876, gather at Wood Mountain near the Cypress Hills, just north of Montana. The U.S. Army burns the prairies near the Canadian border in 1879, preventing buffalo herds from moving north into Canada where they would provide food for the Dakota. Sitting Bull returns to the United States in July 1881 after many of his followers had returned. The Canadian government refuses to provide a reserve for these Dakota.

SEPTEMBER 2, 1877 Warm Springs Apache Bolt San Carlos. Victorio, an influential Apache leader, makes a break from San Carlos, leading more than 300 Warm Springs Apaches and a few Chiricahua. The Indians evade soldiers for a month before they finally surrender.

SEPTEMBER 5, 1877 Crazy Horse Is Killed. After surrendering in May to authorities at Fort Robinson in Nebraska, Crazy Horse is pressured to serve as a scout against the Nez Percé, which he refuses to do. Instead, he urges his men not to cooperate. Seeing him as a threat to peace on the reservation, General Crook orders his arrest and confinement. On the morning of September 4, eight companies of soldiers and 400 Indians set out to arrest him. Arriving at his camp, they discover that he and his wife have departed without permission for the Spotted Tail Agency. There, Spotted Tail convinces Crazy Horse to give himself up, and

he returns to Fort Robinson to surrender. After he is taken into custody the next day, Crazy Horse is led to a small cell to be confined. Once there, he is stabbed in a scuffle with guards, and dies that night.

SEPTEMBER 22, 1877 Treaty 7. The Siksika, Peigan, Kainai (Blood), Sarcee and Stoney (Assiniboine) sign Treaty 7, covering areas of the North-West Territories (today's southern Alberta). Its terms are similar to earlier numbered treaties. *(See* map of Indian Treaty Areas in Canada, p. 394.)

1877–1880 Apache Resistance under Victorio. In 1875 the government decides to consolidate all of the Apache groups west of the Rio Grande on the newly opened San Carlos Reservation on the Gila River. But San Carlos is far from the traditional homes of many of the Apache peoples, lacking game and fertile land. The difficult conditions cause Apache resentment to grow. On September 2, 1877, the Mimbreño chief Victorio and more than 300 of his followers make an escape from San Carlos. Although most of the band surrender within a month, Victorio and 80 of his men remain in the mountains, hoping to settle his people at the Mescalero Apache Reservation in western New Mexico. He attempts to negotiate this move, but is refused permission. On September 4, 1879, believing he is to be arrested, he leads his party in an attack against a cavalry camp, killing eight men. After he is joined by some Mescalero allies, Victorio's party travels into Mexico, to Texas, back into New Mexico, and finally into Arizona, raiding Mexican and American settlers throughout. Mexican and American forces cooperate to find Victorio, who manages to evade his pursuers for over a year. Finally, in the autumn of 1880, while fleeing from the Americans under Col. George Buell, Victorio is attacked in the Chihuahua desert by 350 Mexicans and their Tarahumara allies under Col. Joaquin Terrazas. On October 15–16, at the battle of Tres Castillos, Victorio's forces are defeated in fierce hand-to-hand fighting; 78

Crowfoot, the leading spokesman for the Blackfoot Confederacy, addresses representatives of the Canadian government at the negotiations for Treaty 7 at Blackfoot Crossing near Calgary in 1877. Courtesy of the Glenbow Archives, Calgary, Alberta.

Indians are killed, including Victorio. Some of the survivors will return to San Carlos to join Geronimo's attempts to escape that reservation.

1877–1883 The Northern Cheyenne Flee Indian Territory. In 1877, the Northern Cheyenne tribe, then living in present-day Montana and the western Dakotas, surrenders to U.S. troops and reluctantly agrees to migrate to Indian Territory. In 1878, Chief Dull Knife refuses to remain in Indian Territory and leads an escape of 353 of his people (60 or 70 of them fighting men) to return to their homeland in the northern plains. They subsequently travel over 400 miles, staving off constant attacks by pursuing soldiers. After the group crosses the Northern Platte, they split into two groups: one under Little Wolf goes north, the other under Dull Knife heads northwest toward Fort Robinson. Little Wolf's band spends the winter in western Nebraska, undiscovered; Dull Knife's band reaches Camp Robinson on October 25 and is detained there by the army. When the band refuses to return to Indian Territory, the post commander cuts off rations, fuel, food, and finally water. On January 9, freezing, starv-

ing, and thirsty, Dull Knife's band escapes. Pursued across the snow-covered ground by the fort's soldiers, the Cheyenne who aren't shot down run first to the White River where they relieve their thirst. Few make it much farther than that, however, and of the 149 Cheyenne, 64 are killed and another 78 are captured.

The dramatic escape of the Cheyenne receives a great deal of publicity in American newspapers, and captures the imagination of the American people. U.S. officials realize that it is extremely difficult to detain unwilling Indian nations in Indian Territory. In 1883, the Northern Cheyenne are granted a reservation in eastern Montana. U.S. Indian policymakers abandon the attempt to relocate Indian nations in Indian Territory and allow them to take reservations within their home territories.

1877–1885 The Nez Percé Exiled and Returned. Throughout the exile, Joseph presses the government to live up to the terms of the conditional surrender. In 1879, he takes his case to Washington, D.C. More importantly, he gives an interview to the editor of the *North*

Dull Knife and Little Wolf, 1880s. Courtesy of the National Anthropological Archives, Smithsonian Institution.

American Review. The resulting essay clearly reflects his feelings about the injustice of the Nez Percé exile to Eekish Pah, the Hot Place, and stirs many people to demand the Nez Percé be allowed to return to the Northwest. In 1885, the U.S. government agrees to permit the Nez Percé to return. Some Nez Percé relocate to the reservation in Idaho, but Joseph is forced to move to the Colville Reservation in north-central Washington. For years he tries to buy a portion of his homeland, the Wallowa, the Place of Winding Waters, but settlers living there refuse to sell him any land and he dies on the Colville Reservation in 1904.

1 8 7 8

1878   The Bannock War. As increasing numbers of settlers deplete their resources and reservation agencies fail to compensate for the reduction, the Bannock people are forced to raid to stay alive. On May 30, in one of these raids, two settlers are killed. Seeing retaliation as imminent, Buffalo Horn, an important Bannock chief, leads a series of raids in southern Idaho. The military campaign to subdue and return them is led by Gen. O. O. Howard. Constant pursuit through the summer of 1878 finally forces the Bannock to surrender, though a number of resisters find refuge among the Sheepeaters, a group made up of Shoshoni and Bannock living in the Salmon River Mountains of Idaho, later playing a part in the Sheepeater War.

OCTOBER 16, 1878   Mixed-Blood Premier. Country-born politician John Norquay *(See* biography, May 8, 1841) is elected premier of Manitoba, a position he holds until 1887. The Country-born are English-speaking, Protestant, mixed-blood peoples residing in Manitoba.

1 8 7 9

1879   Canadian Indian Administration. The Canadian government removes the power to grant reserve lands to individuals from band councils and grants it to the superintendent-general of Indian affairs. The move comes after some Indian bands refuse to grant parcels of reserve lands to individual Indians.

1879   Cree Reserves. The government rejects a demand by Cree bands led by Piapot, Little Pine, and Big Bear *(See* biography, c. 1825) for adjoining reserves in the Cypress Hills.

1879   *Standing Bear v. Crook.* Standing Bear and other Ponca Indians leave their reservation in the Indian Territory without the consent of the federal Indian agent, as required by federal regulations. Seized in Nebraska by the army, they sue the commanding officer, General Crook, arguing that he has no constitutional right to prevent their freedom of movement. Stating that no other case had ever "appealed so strongly to my sympathy," a federal judge rules that "an Indian is a 'person' within the meaning of the laws of the United States," and therefore has the same rights, as an individual, to personal freedom and legal protection. This is the first case to recognize Indians' individual civil rights.

1879   Ute War. Following silver strikes in their region during the 1870s, the Ute of western Colorado and eastern Utah are pressured to cede much of their territory. Ouray, an influential Ute leader, agrees to sell considerable Ute land and encourages the Ute to adopt U.S. lifestyles. The Coloradans in particular are determined to drive them out completely, going so far as to elect their governor on a "Utes Must Go" platform. At the same time, the Indian Agent at White River, Nathan Meeker, attempts to force the traditionally free-ranging Ute to become sedentary farmers, even demanding that they plow up their horses' grazing lands. These pressures make the Ute uneasy, and a frightened Meeker calls on the army for troops throughout the summer of 1879. When troops arrive on September 16, the Ute are convinced that they are to be driven off. In the fighting that follows, Meeker and nine other agency employees are killed and the agency buildings burned. This incident gives the Colorado settlers their excuse to rid themselves of the Ute, who are driven to the barren lands of Utah, where they still live on the Uintah and Ouray reservations. Only the Southern Ute remain along the southwest edge of Colorado.

MAY 1879 Sheepeater War. Shortly after Bannock fugitives join their ranks, the Sheepeaters (transplanted Bannock and Shoshoni) raid a prospectors' camp in May, killing five Chinese-American miners. Gen. O.O. Howard, fresh from his victory against the Bannock, orders the first cavalry to contain them. After a force of only 15 warriors temporarily repels the army at the Canyon of Big Creek, the tide turns against the Indians, and, like the Nez Percé and the Bannock before them, they are pursued until they can endure no more, surrendering in groups on October 1 and 2. They are subsequently placed on the Fort Hall Reservation in Idaho.

NOVEMBER 4, 1879 William Penn Adair Rogers, Cherokee Entertainer, Is Born. Will Rogers is born near Oolagah, Indian Territory (now Claremore, Oklahoma). Rogers attracts media attention in the 1920s as cowboy, writer, actor, entertainer, and unique humorist. He publishes widely read books, including *The Peace Conference* and *Rogerisms—The Cowboy Philosopher on Prohibition* (1919). Rogers raises a great deal of money for victims of a hurricane in Florida, floods in Mississippi, a drought in the Southwest, and an earthquake in Nicaragua. Rogers gains considerable fame for his witty, homespun commentaries on politics and American life. He is killed along with pilot Wiley Post in a plane crash near Point Barrow, Alaska, on August 15, 1935.

1879–1885 Friends of the Indians Organized. During these years, a number of organizations of the "Friends of the Indian" variety are established, including the National Indian Defense Association, the Indian Protection Committee, the Women's National Indian Association, and the best-known of the group, the Indian Rights Association.

1879–1885 Last Buffalo Hunt in Canada. Following the final buffalo hunt on the Canadian prairies, Canadian Plains Indian groups begin to follow buffalo herds into the northern United States. Facing famine, many begin to settle on the reserves promised them by the terms of the numbered treaties.

1879–1890 Founding of Carlisle and American Indian Education. In the autumn of 1879, Capt. Richard H. Pratt opens the Carlisle Indian School in a converted southern Pennsylvania military post. The announced purpose is to "civilize Indian children" by removing them from their homes and assimilating them into new lifestyles. "We have tried to take civilization to the Indian," Pratt often remarks, "the better plan is to take the Indian to civilization."

On the basis of Pratt's successes, the Carlisle School becomes an assimilationist model for a new Indian education policy in the United States. Other schools are quickly founded in California, Oregon, Kansas, Oklahoma, New Mexico, and Arizona, as well as on the individual reservations. By 1887, there are over 10,000 Indian students involved in the boarding school system.

U.S. reformers take Indian children from their homes and communities in the belief that it is in the interest of the children to destroy their Native culture. Children generally begin boarding school after the first grade. Government teachers force Indian children to learn English and punish them with whippings and food deprivation when they break the rules. One of the worst offenses is use of a Native language. Indian children are given haircuts and put in uniforms to further facilitate their conversion to "civilization." Luther Standing Bear, among Carlisle's first class in 1879, later recalled selecting his new American name by pointing at a list on a blackboard with a stick.

Indian student at the Carlisle Indian School before matriculation. Courtesy of the National Anthropological Archives, Smithsonian Institution.

Indian student at the Carlisle Indian School after matriculation. Courtesy of the National Anthropological Archives, Smithsonian Institution.

Curriculums are similarly assimilationist in nature, consisting of some basic academic skills and a great deal of vocational training—since Indians are not considered to be intelligent enough to learn the professions. Boys are taught blacksmithing and tailoring, while girls learn sewing, ironing, and laundering. Once they begin to show progress in learning, Indian students are placed in local homes with American families, a part of his program Pratt calls "outing."

Indian resistance to the boarding school system is strong. Many students run away, while parents of students try to protect or remove them (the famous Lakota chief Spotted Tail retrieves his children in 1880). But in general, the feelings of the Indian children and parents are given no consideration, and the price Indian peoples pay to become educated in the ways of the dominant culture is high in terms of culture and language loss. Although ideals of assimilation continue to control federal Indian education policy, financial costs and its failure to provide a quick answer to the federal government's "Indian question" eventually cause the decline of the boarding school system, especially after the turn of the century. Even the Carlisle school is closed in 1918, its barracks and buildings being used for rehabilitation of World War I veterans.

1 8 8 0

1880 Sun Dance Banned. The Indian religious practice, the Sun Dance, is banned in the United States among the Plains tribes, and their medicine men are arrested when such dances occur.

MAY 7, 1880 Indian Act Revision. The Canadian federal government revises the 1876 Indian Act to empower it to impose elected band councils on reserves east of Lake Superior. The Department of Indian Affairs is created as a separate government department, although the minister of the interior continues to serve as superintendent of Indian affairs until 1936.

JULY 31, 1880 Canada Acquires Arctic Islands. The British government transfers ownership of the arctic islands north of the Canadian mainland to the Canadian government. The Inuit inhabitants are unaware of the transfer, and the Canadian government makes no effort to administer the Inuit in the region.

c. 1880s Southwest. Most weaving of clothes and blankets in the southwestern pueblos ceases by this time.

1880–1890 Hopi Pottery. Trader Thomas Keam encourages the Hopi to mass-produce their pottery for the tourist market. Keam is responsible for the several notable design modifications in Hopi pottery, including the painting of kachinas on the pots. These changes reflect the growing importance of the tourist market in the manufacture of pueblo pottery. By 1900,

this transition from utility to commodity is nearly complete throughout the Southwest.

c. 1880–1920 Golden Age in Plains Beadwork. Although fur traders make glass beads available to Plains Indians after about 1850, it is not until the reservation era that plains beadwork reaches its artistic peak.

1 8 8 1

1881 Mungo Martin (Nakapenkim, "Chief Ten Times Over"), Kwakiutl Wood-Carver, Is Born. Mungo Martin is an important Kwakiutl wood-carver who is pivotal in reviving this art among his people late in his life. Martin is born to a family of high standing at Port Rupert, British Columbia. He is taught the art of carving by Yakotglasami and his stepfather, Charlie James. Although Martin begins carving at a young age, the prohibitions against the potlatch imposed by the federal government in 1884 cause a general decline in Northwest Coastal art late in the nineteenth century. Unable to support himself as an artist, Martin is forced to work as a commercial fisherman. In the 1940s, as museums and collectors take notice of the decline in Northwest Coastal Indian art, his talents began to be recognized. In 1947, when Martin is 66 years old, the University of British Columbia invites him to Vancouver to restore and carve totem poles. In 1952 the British Columbia Provincial Museum does likewise, and Martin's artistic skill and personal charm gain him quite a reputation, which in turn adds significantly to the growing interest in Northwest Coastal art. Through his art, Martin also contributes to the revival of Northwest Coastal ceremonialism. He builds a traditional communal house with an elaborately painted facade, the first of its kind to be raised in decades. In honor of its opening in 1953, the first public potlatch is held since the prohibition went into effect (it had been rescinded in 1951). At this potlatch traditional masked dances are held, songs sung,

Group of Omaha boys in cadet uniforms, Carlisle Indian School, Pennsylvania, 1880. Courtesy of the National Archives Trust Fund Board.

speeches made, and a copper crest displayed. In 1956, Martin raises the world's tallest totem pole in Victoria's Beacon Hill Park. Other poles carved by Martin are raised in London and in Mexico City. He continues working as a carver and artist until his death in 1962. Mungo Martin's work is carried on by his son-in-law Henry Hunt, the grandson of George Hunt (who had advised Edward Curtis in the making of his 1913 film, *In the Land of the Headhunters*). Henry Hunt later teaches his son Tony the art of carving, and in 1970–71 they carve and raise a pole at Alert Bay as a memorial to Mungo Martin. It is the first pole-raising in that village in almost 40 years and a fitting tribute to a man whose life was dedicated to Kwakiutl cultural preservation.

1881 *Nedawi.* Written by Omaha activist Suzette LaFlesche, also known as Bright Eyes, the story "Nedawi" was first published in *St. Nicholas,* a popular children's magazine. Some consider this story to be the first nonlegend short story written by an American Indian. In 1883,

Sun Dance Lodge. Each lodge had a defined structure, celestially oriented, with the entrance facing east. Courtesy of the Glenbow Archives, Calgary, Alberta.

LaFlesche's "Omaha Legends and Tent Stories" appears in the June issue of *Wide Awake.*

MARCH 3, 1881   Oto and Missouri Reserve Sold. By act of Congress, the remainder of the Oto and Missouri reserves in Nebraska and Kansas are sold off and these tribes are moved to a reservation in Oklahoma purchased from the Cherokee.

1881–1884   *A Century of Dishonor* **Published.**

Helen Hunt Jackson, in *A Century of Dishonor* (1881), writes an indictment of U.S. Indian policy and the treatment of American Indians in U.S. society. Because of her work Congress forms a special commission to investigate and suggest reforms of Indian affairs. Jackson's research on the special commission provides her with material to write a biographical novel, *Ramona,* about the life of a California Indian woman. (*See* biography, 1865.) The romanticized biography stimulates considerable interest in the United States about the plight and life of Indians.

1881–1885   Religion and Customs Forbidden. Despite safeguards in the Bill of Rights of the Constitution, President Chester A. Arthur authorizes the secretary of the interior to give official approval to rules forbidding "rites, customs . . . contrary to civilization." In the same action dances, religious rites, and traditional rituals are likewise forbidden.

1882

MAY 17, 1882   An Act to Civilize Pueblo Indians. An act passed contains a provision embodying the first assumption of federal responsibility for "civilizing" the Pueblo Indians. Included are funds for paying teachers, purchasing seeds and agricultural implements, and constructing of irrigation ditches.

AUGUST 5, 1882   Establishment of Papago (Tohono O'Odham) Reservation. By act of Congress, the Papago Reserve, an area of 43 square miles in the Pima Agency in Arizona, is set apart for the Papago tribe.

DECEMBER 8, 1882   Big Bear Signs Treaty. Big Bear's Cree band, starving in the Cypress Hills, signs Treaty 6 and promises to move to the reserve allotted to them after being told they will not be given food aid where they are. This, the last band to sign Treaty 6, has been seeking to have all Canadian plains Indians be

Masked dancers participating in a Kwakiutl winter ceremonial. Courtesy of the National Anthropological Archives, Smithsonian Institution.

given adjoining Indian reserves in the Cypress Hills region, something that the Canadian government refuses to do.

DECEMBER 16, 1882 Hopi Reservation Set Aside. By executive order, the Moqui (Hopi) Reserve is set apart for the Hopi tribe, an area of 3,863 square miles in the Navajo Agency in Arizona.

1 8 8 3

1883 Courts for Indian Offenses. Courts for Indian offenses on Indian reservations are established. The new courts are given the authority to try cases involving infractions of rules laid down by the Interior Department for the running of the reservations.

1883 *Ex Parte Crow Dog*. In 1881, when the famous Sioux chief Spotted Tail *(See* biography, 1833) is murdered by a fellow Sioux, Crow Dog, tribal leaders order the murderer to compensate the victim's family. Not satisfied with this, federal authorities bring murder charges against Crow Dog in Dakota Territory; he is

convicted and sentenced to death. Overturning the conviction, the Supreme Court explains that Congress has never passed any law extending the federal criminal code to reservation Indians, even though the Sioux have agreed to be subject to any laws Congress might impose on them. Congress has the power to impose criminal laws on Indians, the Court reasons, but has never clearly done so.

1883 Sarah Winnemucca Hopkins Publishes Book. *Life Among the Paiutes: Their Wrongs and Claims* is an autobiographical account by the writer and activist, Sarah Winnemucca Hopkins (1844–91) is published. Unlike previous Indian writers William Apes (Pequot) and George Copway (Ojibway), Winnemucca abandons the use of a Christian or missionary narrative structure. Instead, she utilizes a personal text, incorporating her own tribal history within her account. Her decision to focus upon personal experience as pertinent to Paiute ethnohistory is significant and reflects a more Native narrative influence than a religious one.

JANUARY 4, 1883 Hualapai Reservation Established. By executive order, the Hualapai

(Walapai) Reserve for the Walapai tribes is set apart, an area of 1,142 square miles in the Walapai Agency in Arizona.

MAY 1883 Railway Construction Halted. Construction of the first transcontinental railway in Canada is halted at Crowfoot's Siksika Reserve east of Calgary. Crowfoot *(See* biography, c. 1830) allows work to continue after receiving assurances that Siksika rights will be respected. The railway, constructed between 1881 and 1885, encourages significant and sudden lifestyle changes among Indian groups along the line.

JULY 6, 1883 Yuma Reservation Established. By executive order, a reserve is set apart for the Yuma of Arizona. Another executive order (January 9, 1884) returns the reserve to public domain, and a new reserve, the Fort Yuma Reservation, is established and straddles the Arizona and California border.

AUTUMN 1883 Residential Schools. The Canadian government opens several residential schools for Indians in western Canada. Since 1878 the government has supported day schools in the region. Most Indians seek education for their children but resent the coercive elements of the government's assimilationist policy. At residential schools, Indian children often are punished for attempting to maintain aspects of their Indian cultures.

1 8 8 4

1884 Alaskan Indian Education. Congress appropriates funds for education in Alaska, directing that they be distributed among the existing mission schools. The following year, Dr. Sheldon Jackson is appointed as general agent for education in Alaska.

1884 Canadian Indian Advancement Act. "An Act Conferring certain privileges on the more advanced band of Indian of Canada, with the view of training them for the exercise of Municipal Affairs" (The Indian Advancement Act), meant to be applied to Indian bands east of Lake Superior, extends the powers of elected band councils but authorizes the superintendent-general (minister) of Indian Affairs to depose Indian chiefs deemed to be unfit to lead. The amendment is made on April 19 after Indian bands elect band councils that earlier had been chosen by traditional means.

1884 *Elk v. Wilkins.* Although John Elk had left his reservation and had begun farming in a white community near Omaha, he is denied the right to vote because of his Indian ancestry. Elk challenges this as a violation of the "Equal Protection Clause" of the Fourteenth Amendment, but the Supreme Court disagrees, saying that "Indians born within the territorial limits of the United States, members of, and owing immediate allegiance to, one of the Indian tribes (an alien, though dependent, power)," are no more entitled to citizenship than the children of foreign visitors. Unlike Standing Bear, then, Elk denies that Indians are "persons" within the meaning of the Constitution, and treats them as foreigners.

APRIL 19, 1884 Potlatches Banned in Canada. Amendments are made to the Indian Act banning potlatches, elaborate ceremonies held among Indians of the Pacific Coast. Missionaries have requested the law, although it remains largely unenforced until 1921. The amendment also bans Indians from traveling off their reserves without a pass from an Indian Affairs agent. This amendment stems from a request from Indian Commissioner Edgar Dewdney for a law that will allow him to prevent "Thirst Dances" (Sun Dances), midsummer Plains Indian celebrations. Cree chiefs such as Big Bear *(See* biography, c. 1825) have been using Thirst Dances to unify Indians against the Canadian government. The amendments take effect in 1885.

JUNE 1884 Cree Council. Cree chiefs led by Big Bear *(See* biography, c. 1825) meet on the

Surveyors for the Canadian Pacific Railway meet an Ojibway band in northern Ontario in the early 1880s. The Indians are still living a nomadic subsistence and trapping lifestyle. Courtesy of Canadian Pacific Limited.

adjoining Poundmaker and Little Pine reserves near Battleford, North-West Territories (now in Saskatchewan) to discuss strategies for uniting Canadian Plains Indians in efforts to renegotiate their treaties. Another council is scheduled for 1885.

JULY 12, 1884   Chilocco Industrial School Established. By executive order, the Chilocco Industrial School Reserve (640 acres in area) is set apart in Oklahoma.

SEPTEMBER 17, 1884   Haskell Institute Opens. Haskell Institute in Lawrence, Kansas, opens to provide vocational training, marking the start of programs of education and land resource development for Indians by the government. Dr. James Marvin, former chancellor of the University of Kansas, is named superintendent. That day 22 Pawnee children are enrolled; a few days later, on September 20, eight Arapaho and Cheyenne chiefs bring an additional 80 youngsters to enroll.

Northwest Coast Indians have become famous for their totem poles. In this late nineteenth-century photograph, totem poles front the large houses of the Haida village of Skidgate, on the Queen Charlotte Island. Courtesy of the Royal British Columbia Museum, Victoria.

OCTOBER 3, 1884 Pueblo Industrial School Established. By executive order, the Pueblo Industrial School Reserve of 65.79 acres is set apart in New Mexico.

NOVEMBER 26, 1884 Northern Cheyenne Reserve Established. By executive order, the Northern Cheyenne Reserve, 765 square miles in the Tongue River Agency in Montana, is set apart.

DECEMBER 16, 1884 Métis Petition. Métis of the North-West Territories, led by Louis Riel, who has returned from exile in the United States, petition the federal government to create more provinces in the west and to deal with Indian and Métis grievances in the region. Since Treaty 3, the Canadian government has not made a treaty with the Métis.

A band of Plains Cree led by Big Bear (standing center) trade at a Hudson's Bay Company post at Fort Pitt shortly before members of the Big Bear's band join the North-West rebellion. Courtesy of the National Archives of Canada, Ottawa.

1 8 8 5

1885 Métis Defeat Police. Métis forces led by Louis Riel *(See* biography, October 22, 1844) and Gabriel Dumont *(See* biography, December 1837) seize the village of Duck Lake just up river from Batoche, North-West Territories. The next day they defeat a force of North-West Mounted Police just outside the village. Twelve police and six Métis are killed.

JANUARY 28, 1885 Métis Commission. The federal government orders the establishment of a commission to enumerate the Métis of the North-West Territories who have a legitimate claim to land. No commissioners are appointed before the North-West Rebellion breaks out in March.

MARCH 3, 1885 Indian Major Crimes Act. An act is passed listing seven serious crimes and authorizing U.S. officials to arrest Indians on their reservations who commit one of these crimes. (Later, the act is amended to cover 10 crimes and then to 14). This is in reaction to the court decision in *Ex parte Crow Dog (See* entry, 1883).

MARCH 19, 1885 Métis Provisional Government. Led by Louis Riel, the Métis at Batoche, North-West Territories (on the South Saskatchewan River), declare that they have established a provisional government to renegotiate their terms of entry into Canada. The Roman Catholic clergy at the settlement do not support Riel.

MARCH 30, 1885 Cree Ransack Homes. A group of Cree led by Poundmaker and Little Pine ransack homes in Battleford, North-West Territories. Battleford, on the North Saskatchewan River about 200 kilometers west of Batoche, is the former capital of the North-West Territories. Settlers take refuge in the community's North-West Mounted Police barracks for about a month.

APRIL 2, 1885 Cree Attack Frog Lake. Led by Wandering Spirit, warriors of Big Bear's Cree band kill nine people at Frog Lake, North-West Territories, about 400 hundred kilometers west of Batoche. The attack takes place despite Big Bear's efforts to prevent it.

APRIL 21, 1885 Peter Kelly, Haida Activist and Cleric, Is Born. Peter Kelly is born in

Poundmaker.

Skidegate among the Haida of the Queen Charlotte Islands. The son of Methodist converts, he is educated at the Coqualeetza Methodist boarding school at Sardis in southern British Columbia. In 1904, he becomes a teacher at a Methodist school in Skidegate. Later, he serves as a missionary and minister, first in the Methodist Church, then in the United Church of Canada. Later, he becomes a United Church missionary and minister. In 1916, he organizes a conference in Vancouver to address tribal rights to land. Sixteen tribal groups from across the province are represented, and the conference ends with the establishment of the Allied Indian Tribes of British Columbia. Kelly is its founding chairman. In 1919, this organization prepares what many view as the authoritative statement of Indian claims to ancestral land in British Columbia. The organization also begins lobbying the federal and provincial governments extensively regarding Indian land claims. In 1927, Kelly testifies before the special Parliamentary Committee in Ottawa established to look into Indian issues. Following the collapse of the Allied Tribes in 1927, he directs much of his energy to his work as a Methodist missionary, reemerging in the 1940s

when he joins the Native Brotherhood of British Columbia, a province-wide Indian organization. In 1946 he testifies before the Parliamentary Committee established to make recommendations regarding the Indian Act.

APRIL 24, 1885   Métis Stall Canadian Troops. Métis forces led by Gabriel Dumont stall the advance of Canadian troops toward Batoche at a battle at Fish Creek, 30 kilometers south of Batoche. Six Canadian militiamen and five Métis are killed.

MAY 2, 1885   Battle of Cut Knife Hill. Cree and Stoney warriors led by Poundmaker and the war chief Fine Day defeat Canadian forces that have attacked them at Cut Knife Creek, 50 kilometers west of Battleford, North-West Territories. Poundmaker's intervention prevents more than eight Canadian militia deaths. Five or six Indians are killed.

MAY 12, 1885   Canadian Forces Take Batoche. Following a three-day battle, Canadian government troops crush Métis and Indian forces at Batoche, North-West Territories (now in Saskatchewan). Following the collapse of this uprising known as the North-West Rebellion, many Métis disperse toward Métis settlements farther northwest or to the United States (where they become known as "Canadian Cree" and "French Chippewa").

MAY 15, 1885   Riel Surrenders. Louis Riel surrenders to Canadian troops.

MAY 28, 1885   Battle at Frenchman's Butte. Canadian forces attack Big Bear's band dug in at Frenchman's Butte, but the battle is indecisive. (Big Bear's band began moving east from Frog Lake toward Poundmaker's band near Battleford on May 1.) Frenchman's Butte is about 90 kilometers from Frog Lake and 150 kilometers from Battleford.) Following the battle, the Canadian troops withdraw, and Big Bear's band moves north into the forests.

JUNE 1885 Edward Ahenakew, Plains Cree Minister and Author, Is Born. Born at Sandy Lake, North-West Territories (now Saskatchewan), and educated at a boarding school in Prince Albert, Ahenakew begins his career as a teacher in mission schools near Sandy Lake. After becoming ordained as an Anglican priest in 1912, Ahenakew becomes a traveling missionary among reserve communities in Saskatchewan. He is best known for *Voices of the Plains Cree*, published posthumously in 1974.

JULY 2, 1885 Big Bear Surrenders. Big Bear *(See* biography, c. 1825) surrenders to the North-West Mounted Police. Poundmaker has surrendered earlier on May 26. This brings the Métis and Indian resistance known as the North-West Rebellion to an end. About 53 Canadians and 35 Indians and Métis have been killed.

JULY 20, 1885 Indians Allowed to Vote. The Dominion Franchise Act extends the right to vote to some status Indians (who meet certain qualifications) in eastern Canada. Until now, eligibility to vote in federal elections has been determined by the relevant laws in each province. Some Indians protest the extension of the franchise, fearing that they may lose some of their special rights as Indians if they vote. The law is repealed in 1898.

NOVEMBER 16, 1885 Riel Hanged. Louis Riel is hanged for treason for his role in the North-West Rebellion. The Métis consider him a martyr for their cause. French Canadians also protest the execution. Eighteen other Métis have been jailed for their part in the North-West Rebellion. The execution of Louis Riel serves to sustain Métis consciousness for the next century and the question of Riel's innocence or guilt becomes the center of one of the most controversial and divisive debates in Canadian history.

NOVEMBER 28, 1885 Indians Executed. Cree war chief Wandering Spirit and five other Cree and two Stoney Indians are hanged at Battleford, North-West Territories, for murders committed during the North-West Rebellion. Thirty-six other Indians, including Poundmaker and Big Bear are jailed.

---

1 8 8 6

1886 Maria Montoya Martinez, American Indian Artist, Is Born. Probably the best-known American Indian artist of the twentieth century, during her long career the San Ildefonso Pueblo potter Maria Martinez perfects many different styles of pottery, including the now-famous black-on-black ware she first developed with her husband around 1919. Born in 1886, Maria Montoya learns to make pottery as a child. After her marriage to Julian Martinez in 1904, the two collaborate in their work. Julian begins working on the Pajarito Plateau excavations under archaeologist Edgar Hewett in 1907, and copies many pottery and mural designs from the ruins. The Martinezes are encouraged to reproduce the designs by the Museum of New Mexico, where they work for three years after 1909. With their development of matte-and-polish black pottery in 1919, the Martinezes' reputation grows quickly. Their pottery earns numerous awards and prizes, beginning with the 1922 Santa Fe Indian Market. Although Maria and Julian prefer not to sign their work, pots made by Maria are quickly in such demand that she begins to do so. Eventually she also signs her name to the pottery of others, helping them to sell their wares. After Julian's death in 1943, Maria begins collaborating with her daughter-in-law Santana and then, in 1956, with her son Popovi Da. The ceramic renaissance Maria and her family initiate at San Ildefonso has profound aesthetic and economic effects there and at other pueblos. Though greatly elaborated on since that time, the Martinezes' black-on-black pottery remains the mainstay at both San Ildefonso and Santa Clara, with Maria's own grandchildren

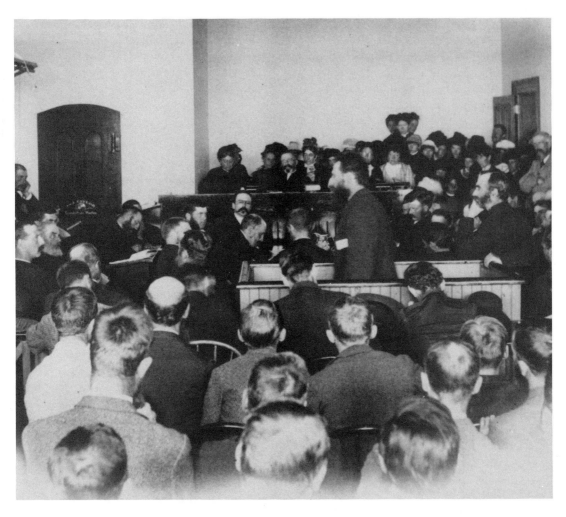

Louis Riel rises in his defense at his trial in 1885. Courtesy of the National Archives of Canada.

and great-grandchildren among its leading practitioners.

1886   *United States v. Kagama.* In response to the imposition of certain federal criminal laws on all reservation Indians under the "Major Crimes Act," two California Hoopa Indians charged with murder challenge the act's constitutionality and lose. "The power of the General Government over these remnants of a race once powerful, now weak and diminished in numbers, is necessary to their protection, as well as

the safety of those among whom they dwell," the Supreme Court reasons. "It must exist in that government, because it has never existed anywhere else, because the theater of its exercise is within the geographical limits of the United States, because it has never been denied, and because it alone can enforce its laws on all the tribes." In other words, Indian communities are dependent on the government for food, protection, and their political rights. From this arises the duty of protection, and with it the power of the federal government. Congress has not only the right, but also the duty, to exercise its power as it sees fit, to provide for the well-being of its Indian wards. *Kagama* is a test of the constitutionality of the Major Crimes Act and an affirmation of Congress's power to enact that legislation. In *Kagama,* the Court finds that protection of the Indians requires withholding the power of such protection from the individual states.

1 8 8 7

1887 The General Allotment Act. Congress passes the General Allotment Act, also known as the Dawes Act, dividing reservation land into individual parcels in severalty. The act is intended to safeguard the Indians on the land and, to this end, allotments are to be protected for 25 years. The Burke Act (1906) amends the Allotment Act of 1887, extending the original 25-year trust period for another 25 years. Supported by a coalition of eastern liberals and western land grabbers, the Allotment Act is passed in order to further civilize the Indian. The act seeks to replace collective tribal land tenure with yeoman farming, as Teddy Roosevelt defines it, "a mighty pulverizing engine to break up the tribal mass." But the misdirected good intentions of the eastern educators and politicians is only half the story. What the Allotment Act does is to open up huge amounts of Indian land for settlement. In its aftermath, millions of acres are lost through fraud, creating checkerboard ownership of tribal lands on most reservations. Exceptions to the trust period allow Indians to settle title to their land long before what the act intends. Between 1887 and 1934, when the Allotment Act is finally repealed, the U.S. government divests Native Americans of about 90 million acres, or about two-thirds of their total holdings.

1887 Metlakatla Relocated. William Duncan and his Tsimshian followers from Metlakatla move to a new village on Annette Island, Alaska.

MAY 21, 1887 James Gladstone (Akay-na-muka), Kainai Politician, Is Born. James Gladstone is born at Mountain Hill, North-West Territories (Alberta). He works at several jobs between 1905 and 1914, including stints as a typesetter for the *Calgary Herald* and as a scout and interpreter for the North-West Mounted Police. During World War II he becomes known as an excellent farmer. He farms his 800 acres on the Blood (Kainai) Reserve with the first motorized tractor in the area.

Gladstone is a founding member of the Indian Association of Alberta, serving as its president from 1948 to 1954 and again in 1956. He is a representative of Alberta Indians to the Canadian government during consultations in 1947, 1951, and 1953. He becomes Canada's first aboriginal senator in 1958, a position he uses to defend the rights of First Nations.

OCTOBER 17–19, 1887 Nishga Protest. Encouraged by missionaries, groups of Nishga from the Nass River Valley protest the loss of their land before a British Columbia government committee established to hear their grievances. The committee, though sympathetic, has no power to act on their complaints.

1 8 8 8

1888 "Destroy the Indian and Save the Individual." The Board of Indian Commissioners, which is responsible for recommending and evaluating federal Indian policy, encourages the adoption of an educational policy that in effect calls for the destruction of Indian tribal identities and the fostering of individualism among Indian students. The board concludes that 20 years is a sufficient time to accomplish this goal and withdraws government support.

1888 James Francis Thorpe, Sauk and Fox Athlete, Is Born. In 1912, King Gustav of Sweden describes Jim Thorpe as "the greatest athlete in the world." The young man from

Spring Rancheria (Cahuilla) in southern California, c. 1886. Courtesy of the Riverside Municipal Museum, Riverside, California.

Prague, Oklahoma, has just won gold medals in the pentathlon and the decathlon in the Stockholm Olympics and is on top of the sporting world. (*See also* entry, 1912.) Seven months later, however, he is stripped of the medals, and his feats are expunged from the official Olympic record book. A newspaper reporter has learned that Thorpe played semi-professional baseball for a few dollars a game. By the Olympic rules, acceptance of payment for athletic performance disqualifies Thorpe from further amateur sports and from eligibility for participation in the Olympics. Following the Olympics, Thorpe plays professional baseball from 1913–19 with a career batting average of .252. He goes on to play professional football and becomes the first president of the American Professional Football Association. He is named to both the college and professional football halls of fame. Jim Thorpe dies in 1953 at his home in Lomita, California. In 1954, a town in Pennsylvania is renamed in his honor. Many Americans from all walks of life begin a campaign to have his Olympic medals restored. Thirty-one years after his death, and seventy-two years after the Stockholm event, replicas of

his medals are returned to his daughter Charlotte during the 1984 Olympics in Los Angeles. (*See also* entry, October 13, 1982.)

JULY 2, 1888 Joseph Dion, Cree/Métis Teacher and Politician, Is Born. Dion is a status Indian and a descendent of Plains Cree chief Big Bear. He serves as a teacher on the Keehewin Reserve in Alberta, and he becomes known for organizing Indians and Métis. In 1932 he organizes l'Association de Métis d'Alberta et des Territoires des Nord Ouest (reorganized as the Métis Association of Alberta in 1940), and in 1944 he organizes the Indian Association of Alberta. Known as a relatively conservative reformer, Dion is a driving force behind the Métis Betterment Act of Alberta which establishes Métis settlements in that province. He is the author of *My Tribe the Crees*, published in 1979.

AUGUST 9, 1888 White Men and Indian Women Marriage Act. An act is passed to regulate legal effects of marriages between white men and Indian women, prohibiting white men from marrying Indian women in order to obtain tribal rights such as land. The Five

Civilized Tribes are excluded from the act, which is designed to protect Indian property and to encourage newly married Indian women to become U.S. citizens.

1889

c. 1889 Western Arctic Whaling. Between 1889 and 1907, whalers from the United States begin to operate from a base at Herschel Island in the Beaufort Sea near the mouth of the Mackenzie River. Inuit are an important labor supply for the whalers, and provide provisions to the whalers. Abuse of alcohol, the spread of disease, and starvation among the Inuit over the following years leads to the virtual extinction of the Mackenzie Inuit by 1920. Inuit caribou hunters from the interior of Alaska (who will become known as the Inuvialuit) begin moving to the Mackenzie delta region. Whaling in the eastern arctic declined during the 1880s because of depleted whale stocks. The western arctic whaling industry collapses in 1907.

1889 Elimination of Reservations and Tribes Recommended. Commissioner of Indian Affairs T.J. Morgan advocates the elimination of all Indian reservations and tribes. The Indian is to be "individualized and conform to the white man's ways, peaceably if they will, forcibly if they must. . . ."

1889 Ella Cara Deloria, Yankton Sioux, Is Born. A Yankton Sioux, Deloria studies linguistic anthropology at Columbia University (New York) under the tutelage of Dr. Franz Boas. In 1927, she becomes his research assistant and begins her work of translating and editing Sioux texts; subsequently, she publishes "Sun Dance of the Oglala" in a 1929 volume of the *Journal of American Folklore*. *Dakota Texts* is released in 1932, followed by a collaborative *Dakota Grammar* compiled with Boas in 1941. Deloria's ethnographic description of Indian, primarily Sioux, culture entitled *Speaking of Indians* is published in 1944. Her novel about a

Teton Sioux woman's life, *Waterlily*, is printed posthumously in 1988.

JANUARY 4, 1889 Minnesota Chippewa Allotment Act. An act is passed authorizing the president to appoint a commission to negotiate with the Chippewa bands in Minnesota, except White Earth and Red Lake reservations, to allot forty-acre parcels to each eligible Chippewa person.

MARCH 1, 1889 U.S. Court in Indian Territory Act. An act is passed that establishes a U.S. Court within Indian Territory under the supervision of a judge, for a four-year term, with deputy marshals and a clerk.

APRIL 22, 1889 Oklahoma Opened for Settlement. In 1885, President Ulysses S. Grant signs a bill into law which results in the withdrawal of federal troops guarding the borders of the Indian Territory, present-day Oklahoma. Four years later the area is opened for settlement. At noon on April 22, a boundary line marked by flags and stretching as far as the eye could see separates a conglomeration of wheeled vehicles, buckboards, surreys, conestogas, coaches, and bicycles from the vast Indian Territory of Oklahoma, closed by law to U.S. settlers— until that moment. With tremendous din, "boomers" and "sooners," with their horses, dogs, and cows, raise a vast cloud of dust as they race to stake their claims on choice acreage. An estimated 50,000 persons go past the line on that day, claiming 2 million acres of land. By nightfall there are tent cities, banks, and stores doing business. Each year Oklahomans commemorate the event with huge parades, rodeos, and general pandemonium in celebration of "the run of 1889."

1889–1890 The Second Ghost Dance Religion and the Wounded Knee Massacre. Wovoka, a Paiute Indian from Nevada, becomes the second Ghost Dance Prophet. In 1889, during an eclipse of the sun, Wovoka "dies" and speaks with the Creator, who advises Native Ameri-

Wovoka, the prophet of the second Ghost Dance. Courtesy of the Nevada Historical Society.

cans to live peacefully with all peoples. The Creator instructs Indians to work hard in this life and pray for an apocalypse that will restore the world to its aboriginal state. If the Indians follow the Ghost Dance path, their dead relatives will rise up and the game and plants will return.

The Ghost Dance religion spreads to many tribes throughout the West. Among the Teton Lakota, devastated by war, reservations, poverty, and disease, Wovoka's admonitions of peace are forgotten. Militant leaders like

Short Bull and Kicking Bear turn the prophet's teachings into a movement advocating violence. Although few of the Lakota participating in the dance hold such views, soldiers, settlers, government agents, and missionaries fear for their lives as rumors spread that the Ghost Dance will inspire the Sioux to fight again for their rights and freedom. In 1890, the Office of Indian Affairs outlaws the Ghost Dance, and the U.S. military strengthens its command on the northern plains. When Sitting Bull is suspected of advocating the dance, James McLaughlin, the Standing Rock agent, orders reservation policemen to arrest him. As he is being taken into custody at his cabin on December 15, a fight breaks out and Sitting Bull is killed.

Sitting Bull's death is not the end of the violence surrounding the Ghost Dance movement, however. A group of Minneconjou Ghost Dancers, led by Big Foot, travels to a site known as Wounded Knee, where Short Bull, Kicking Bear, and the more militant followers reside. They are pursued by the Seventh Cavalry under Col. James Forsyth, who is unaware that Big Foot has been asked to the reservation in order to persuade the militants to surrender. By the morning of December 28, 500 soldiers with four Hotchkiss guns surround Big Foot's camp. They begin to disarm the Ghost Dancers when a medicine man named Yellow Bird exhorts his people to resist. A rifle is discharged and the army fires on the Sioux, killing more than 300 Indian men, women, and children. This incident is known as the Wounded Knee Massacre.

1 8 9 0

MAY 2, 1890 Territory of Oklahoma Established. The Territory of Oklahoma is created out of a portion of the Indian Territory. This act also enlarges the jurisdiction of the special court created by act of March 1, 1889, and

The massacre at Wounded Knee. One hundred and forty-six bodies were interred in a mass grave on a small hill. Photo by G. Trager. Courtesy of the Nebraska State Historical Society.

places in force several general statutes of the state of Arkansas.

1890–1900 The "Vanishing Americans." At the turn of the twentieth century, most non-Indians believe that the Native peoples are the "Vanishing Americans" and will not long survive. The American Indian population declines to a low point of 237,196 in the 1900 U.S. Census. After 1900, however, the Indian population slowly recovers. In 1920, the Census Bureau records 244,437 Native Americans. This number increases to 357,499 in 1950; 1,366,676 in 1980; and 1,959,234 in 1990.

1890–1934 The Assimilationist Policy. After 1890 most Indian nations are located on reservations or are not recognized by the federal government. Reservation Indians come under direct administrative control from U.S. Indian agents. Since most reservation economies cannot support their Indian populations, Indian reservation residents become economically and politically dependent on the Office of Indian

Crow Indian woman carrying a child. Courtesy of the National Museum of the American Indian, Smithsonian Institution, Charles Rau Collection.

Affairs and its field agents. Food, clothing, medicine, education, and ceremonial life come under strict regulations. Traditional tribal governments are inhibited from operating, and ceremonies like the Plains Sun Dances are prohibited. Children are sent to boarding schools, where they are not allowed to speak their Native languages. Federal policymakers hope to reeducate Indian children and incorporate them into U.S. society, and then to abolish the reservations. This policy of assimilation is not successful. Traditional government, traditional ceremonial life, and Indian languages and lifestyle persist, despite efforts to force Indians into U.S. economic and social life.

1 8 9 1

JANUARY 19, 1891   Sioux Indian Act. An act is passed allowing the secretary of interior "to divide a portion of the reservation of the Sioux Nation of Indians in Dakota into separate reservations and to secure the relinquishment of the Indian title to the remainder." This act supersedes the 1868 Treaty of Fort Laramie and results in considerable losses of land by the Sioux.

FEBRUARY 16, 1891   Indian Schools Act. An act for the construction of suitable school buildings for Indian industrial schools in Wisconsin, Michigan, Minnesota, and other states is passed. The schools are to be based on the model of Carlisle Indian Industrial School, and to cost no more than $30,000 each.

FEBRUARY 28, 1891   Land Allotment Act. An act is passed that amends the General Land Allotment Act of 1887 to extend its benefits and the protection of the laws of the United States to Indians on various reservations.

MARCH 3, 1891   Fort Berthold Reservation Established. By an act of Congress, the Fort Berthold Reserve, an area of 1,383 square miles in North Dakota, is set apart and occupied by

In 1680, the Pueblo Indian town of Zia was destroyed by the Spanish as a result of the Pueblo's revolt against them. Hundreds of Pueblo Indians were killed in battle, and the Pueblo of Zia were thought to have 'disappeared.' This picture was taken two hundred years later in a 'kiva,' or ceremonial chamber. It shows a Pueblo Zia ceremony for the treatment of a sick boy. Courtesy of the National Anthropological Archives, Smithsonian Institution.

Arikara, Gros Ventre, and Mandan. By executive order of June 17, 1892, additional lands are set apart.

MARCH 3, 1891 Indian Depredations Act. An act is passed "providing for the jurisdiction and payment of claims arising from Indian depredations."

AUGUST 30, 1891 Elmer Jamieson, Iroquois

Educator, Is Born. After graduating from McMaster University in Hamilton, Ontario, in 1913, he enlists in the Canadian army. When Canadian army personnel are unable to decipher his letters to his family (written in Mohawk), the army approaches him to help them develop a code based on the language—the first wartime Indian communications network. (During World War II, the U.S. Army develops other very effective communications codes based on Indian languages.)

After World War I Jamieson returns to McMaster University and to the University of Toronto, eventually earning a Ph.D. in education in 1928. He is chair of the chemistry and biology department at North Toronto Collegiate from 1922–57.

1891–1915 Indian Scouts. The ending of the Indian Wars witnesses a vast decline in the number of scouts in the army. In 1891 the figure has fallen to 130, with the reduction continuing until 1915 when only 24 are on active duty. One of the many duties of scouts during the Indian campaigns is to supply the army posts with fresh meat.

1 8 9 2

FEBRUARY 6, 1892 Andrew Paull, Squamish Activist, Is Born. Born in southern British Columbia among the Squamish Coastal Salish of that region, Paull works as a longshoreman until he is hired as an interpreter for the McKenna-McBride Commission in 1913, translating the presentations of Salish people to the commission. This introduces him to many different indigenous peoples in the province. In June 1916, Paull, with Haida Peter Kelly, organizes a conference in Vancouver to address Indian land issues in the province. The Allied Indian Tribes of British Columbia is formed at this conference. The organization presents the case of British Columbia Indians for the following decade, culminating in 1927 when Paull speaks before a special Parliamentary Committee in Ottawa established to address Indian land issues in British Columbia. The organization collapses soon afterward, and Paull becomes a sportswriter for the Vancouver daily newspaper, promoting Indian social events in the Vancouver region. He reenters political life in 1942 when he joins the Native Brotherhood of British Columbia. Paull forms the rival North American Indian Brotherhood in 1945 and

serves as its president for three years. During that time he testifies before the Parliamentary Committee established to consider changes to the Indian Act. Afterward he acts as a spokesman for Salish people in the interior of British Columbia.

JULY 13, 1892 Indian Agent Act. An act is passed by Congress making appropriations for the Indian Department and for military officers to act as Indian agents.

JULY 23, 1892 Intoxication in Indian Country Act. A law is enacted forbidding the sale and transportation of alcoholic beverages in Indian country. "No ardent spirits, ale, beer, wine, or intoxicating liquor or liquors of whatever kind shall be introduced under any pretense, into the Indian country." Violation of this law is punishable by up to two years' imprisonment.

1 8 9 3

1893 Enforced Education. U.S. troops forcibly gather Hopi children and punish their parents for resisting enforced education.

1893 Haskell Institute. In order to accommodate its growing population, Haskell Indian Institute expands to nine grades. In 1896, a kindergarten is added.

1893 Reduction of Indian Agencies. The Indian Appropriations Act contains the first provision to eliminate the Indian agent, transferring control to the superintendent of schools located on the reservation. By this act, the superintendent of the Indian School at Cherokee, North Carolina, is required, in addition to his regular duties, to perform those formerly done by the agent for the Cherokee Agency. By this means, the number of Indian Agencies is gradually diminished, until in 1907 only a single one, located in Wintah, Utah, remains.

Tsimshian bear mask, Queen Charlotte Islands, British Columbia. Photo by Melinda McNaugher. Courtesy of the Carnegie Museum of Natural History, Pittsburgh.

1 8 9 4

1894 First Indian Film. The company of Thomas A. Edison films *The Sioux Ghost Dance* in its West Orange, New Jersey, movie studio. This brief recreation of several warriors in headfeathers and breechcloths was actually a kinescope viewed through a "peephole" format. It is the first known motion picture recording of American Indians, and is followed by several other Edison documentaries, including *Indian Day School* and *Serving Rations to the Indians*, both in 1898.

JULY 23, 1894 Indian Leaders Deposed. Canadian federal legislation empowers the superintendent-general of Indian Affairs to depose Indian leaders in the West. The law also makes deposed Indian leaders ineligible for election for three years. This provision is passed because Indian bands have been reelecting leaders deposed by Indian Agents.

AUGUST 15, 1894 Parent Consent for Education Act. A general appropriation act is passed "to supervise Indian affairs stressing education for Indians and prohibiting sending children to schools outside the state or territory of their residence without the consent of their parents or natural guardians."

1 8 9 5

C. 1895 Lucy Lewis, Hopi-Tewa Artist, Is Born. Lucy Lewis of Acoma ranks with the Hopi-Tewa artist Nampeyo and the Martinezes of San Ildefonso among the most important figures in the twentieth-century revival of pueblo pottery. Lewis is notable for her use of prehistoric Anasazi designs. She learns pottery-making from her great-aunt, and receives the award of merit at the first exhibition she enters, the 1950 Intertribal Indian Ceremonial at Gallup, New Mexico. She also wins first place at the Santa Fe Indian Market that same year. Before her death in 1992, she wins numerous awards and honors, and her work is shown widely. A number of her daughters and granddaughters continue to make pottery.

1895 Indian Music in Symphony. Anton Dvôrák writes "The New World Symphony," utilizing the music of the Omaha (Nebraska) Indians as a theme. Included are such selections as "Land of the Sky Blue Waters" and "At Dawning."

1895 Sanapia, Yapai Comanche, Is Born. Born near Fort Sill, Oklahoma, Sanapia is of the Yapai Comanche. Influenced by her mother, a Comanche-Arapaho traditionalist and medicine woman, Sanapia begins her own medicine training at the age of 13. By the time she reaches her 17th year, she possesses the necessary skills and knowledge to practice medicine and healing as an eagle doctor. During the 1930s, Sanapia undergoes personal experiences that prevent her from healing. She resumes her practice again in the 1940s. Her specialty is the treatment of "ghost sickness." It is believed that fearful contact with a ghost provokes the state of facial paralysis common to this sickness. Notably, "ghost sickness" frequently affected

Late nineteenth-century Iroquois false face mask of painted wood with metal eyes, human hair, and a shark's snaggle tooth. Photo by R.P. Sheridan and D. Bauer. Courtesy of the Department Library Services, American Museum of Natural History.

Comanches undergoing the acculturative process. By the late 1960s, Sanapia becomes the last surviving eagle doctor. Within traditional Comanche society, she achieves the maximum power and prestige possible for a woman. As an old woman, Sanapia wishes to transfer her power, but there is no apparent successor. Instead, she works with anthropologist David E. Jones. He formally transcribes her life story and preserves her knowledge of medicine and her doctoring practices.

1 8 9 6

c. 1896 John Slocum, Coast Salish Spiritual Leader, Dies. John Slocum is born near Puget Sound, Washington, during the early 1830s. In 1881 he becomes sick and apparently dies. Friends are summoned and preparations are being made for the funeral when suddenly he revives. He then announces that he has been to visit the judgment place of God and has received instructions about ways Indian people need to change

their lives if they want to achieve salvation. This visionary experience became the basis of Tschaddam, or the Indian Shaker Church as it is known in English. Much of Slocum's message admonished the Indian people to give up drinking alcohol, stop gambling, and to work toward developing stronger family and community ties. The teachings contain a mixture of traditional Indian cultural concepts and selected Christian views. The Indian Shaker religion still flourishes among coastal Indians of British Columbia, Washington, Oregon, and northwestern California, although it has undergone many changes since its inception. John Slocum dies between 1896 and 1898.

1896 Settlers Fill Canadian Prairies. After coming in only modest numbers since 1870, settlers start to flow into the Canadian prairies. The vast majority of the population in the region in 1870, Natives now are becoming a small minority. Settlers often view Natives as obstacles to progress and resent any special legal rights Indians enjoy, yet they also often do not accept the Natives as equals. This is an era in which ideas of scientific racism derived from the evolutionary ideas of Charles Darwin lead many Canadians to view Indians as inherently inferior to persons of European descent.

1896 *Talton v. Mayes*. *Talton v. Mayes* addresses the question of the constitutionality of the Fifth Amendment. The appellant, a Cherokee Indian, is charged with the murder of another Cherokee Indian within the Cherokee territory. The 1890 act which establishes the Territory of Oklahoma provides that the Indian nations in the Indian Territory will retain exclusive jurisdiction over crimes committed by tribal members in Indian country. Thus the crime in question is not a federal offense. The decision is that the Fifth Amendment does not operate on the power of Indian self-government.

JULY 1896 Métis Settlement. Approximately 50 Métis families begin settling at St. Paul des Métis, northeast of Edmonton. The Métis at the mission, set up by Father Albert Lacombe, disperse by 1908.

1 8 9 7

JUNE 7, 1897 Education Appropriation Act. An act is passed which mandates that Congress give funding priority to Indian day and industrial schools over sectarian schools in all cases.

JUNE 30, 1897 Indian Liquor Act. An act is passed prohibiting the sale, gift, barter, exchange, or other disposition of beer, wine, and other liquors to Indians.

1897–1930 Edward Curtis Documents the "Vanishing Race." Born in Wisconsin in 1868, Edward S. Curtis moves to Washington with his family at age 19. There he becomes interested in photography. Sometime later Curtis, an experienced mountain climber, saves an expedition from freezing on Mt. Ranier. This party includes, among others, Gifford Pinchot (chief of the U.S. Department of Forestry), C. Hart Merriam (chief of the U.S. Biological Survey), and George Bird Grinnell, at that time the editor of *Field and Stream* magazine. Grinnell later invites Curtis to spend a season with him among the Peigan tribes in northern Montana. Believing he is witnessing the passing of the traditional Indian way of life, Curtis becomes determined to preserve the Native culture through photography and ethnological notes. For 30 years, beginning around the turn of the century, Curtis attempts to systematically photograph the Indian tribes west of the Mississippi from New Mexico to Alaska. For the first nine years, he finances the project himself, but in 1905 he meets President Theodore Roosevelt at an exhibition of Indian photographs in Washington, D.C. President Roosevelt arranges for a meeting with financier J.P. Morgan, who agrees to assist Curtis's project. Much of the project's enormous cost (over $1.5 million in all) is subsequently supplied by Morgan. In the 30 years it takes Curtis to complete his project,

he studies more than 80 tribes, recording over 10,000 songs and taking 40,000 photographs. Although scholars have questioned Curtis's belief in the inevitable end of the American Indian as well as the ethnographic accuracy of some of his images, the value of his photographic record cannot be overstated.

1 8 9 8

1898 Klondike Gold Rush. Thousands of gold seekers rush to the Yukon River near Dawson City in northwestern Canada after news of a large gold find in the area reaches southern centers. In Dawson City's brief heyday, it boasts a population of 40,000. The gold is found on August 17, 1896, by two Tagish men known as Skookum Jim and Tagish Charlie and by George Carmack, a non-Native from the United States. The coming of gold seekers profoundly affects the lives of the Han who have long hunted and fished in the region. Many of the Han are drawn into the cash economy as provisioners, guides, and laborers. Many also suffer from the effects of frontier violence, introduced diseases, and alcohol abuse.

The gold rush ends the long-established trade dominance of the Coastal Tlingit. To this point the Tlingit have protected their role as the sole conveyors of trade goods from the Pacific Coast to the interior. The gold rush makes various goods of non-Native manufacture, including alcohol, more easily accessible to the Kaska, Tahltan, Inland Tlingit, Tagish, Tutchone, and Kutchin. The Inland Tlingit, who have already begun to move from the headwaters of the Taku River to the headwaters of the Yukon River to take advantage of the fur resources of the region, continue to do so, supplementing subsistence activities with wage labor. They work as packers, guides, woodcutters, and crewmen on steamships. Increased contact also encourages the spread of diseases among the Native inhabitants. When a railway is constructed from Skagway to Whitehorse, the Tagish move to a new village at Carcross (Caribou Crossing) along the rail line. The gold rush prompts the creation of the Yukon Territory, and the arrival of Canadian law enforcement. Within a few years most non-Natives leave the region but law enforcement officers, fur traders, and missionaries remain. Yukon Indians continue to supplement subsistence activities by trapping

JUNE 13, 1898 Indian Franchise. A new Dominion Franchise Act in Canada specifically makes eligibility for the vote in federal elections dependent on provincial laws. Few Canadian status Indians actually have qualified to vote since 1885 even though they were not specifically excluded. This remains the case in Nova Scotia, the only province that does not specifically exclude Indians from the franchise.

JUNE 28, 1898 Curtis Act. An act is passed extending all provisions of the General Allotment Act to the Indian Territory. Known as the Curtis Act, it also abolishes tribal courts and forbids the enforcement of tribal laws in federal court. This act allots the lands of the Cherokee, Choctaw, Chickasaw, Creek, and Seminole, and abolishes their constitutional governments.

1 8 9 9

1899 Dan George, Squamish Actor, Is Born. Dan George is born on the Burrard Indian Reserve near Vancouver, British Columbia, and begins acting only later in life. Until the age of 60, he works as a longshoreman, logger, and musician. He is chief of the Squamish band of Burrard Inlet, British Columbia, from 1951 to 1963. George is discovered as an actor in 1959, and he dedicates the rest of his life to improving the image of Indian people in film, theater, and television. He portrays an Indian elder in Canadian television and theater, including the Canadian Broadcasting Corporation's production of "Caribou Country," and the original

production of "The Ecstasy of Rita Joe," a contemporary drama about Indian people. Dan George is an accomplished and acclaimed actor, perhaps best known for his portrayal of a Cheyenne elder named Old Lodge Skins in the film, *Little Big Man.* For this role, he receives the New York Film Critics Award for best supporting actor in 1970. George refuses to endorse Indian political causes, but throughout his career he seeks to change the dominant image of Indian people in the media. Dan George dies in Vancouver at the age of 82.

1899 Indian Education. By this year, $2.5 million is expended annually for the education of 20,000 Indian students at 148 boarding schools and 225 day schools nationwide.

1889 Monument to Tomochichi. A monument is erected by the Colonial Dames of America in Savannah, Georgia, to the memory of Tomochichi, noted Creek chief who helped found the Georgia Colony.

1899 *Queen of the Woods.* *Queen of the Woods* by Chief Simon Pokagon is published. It is the first novel written by an American Indian.

1899 *Stephens v. Cherokee Nation.* The U.S. Supreme Court, in *Stephens v. Cherokee Nation,* holds that Congress has a "plenary power of legislation" over Indian tribes "subject only to the Constitution of the United States."

JUNE 21, 1899 Treaty 8. At a ceremony at Lesser Slave Lake, and through the next year, the Cree of today's northern Alberta; the Beaver, Athapascan hunters of the Peace River region of northern Alberta and British Columbia; and the Chipewyan of northern Alberta and the North-West Territories south of Great Slave Lake sign Treaty 8. The Métis of the region are issued scrip, certificates redeemable for land or cash. The Indians demanded the treaty after numbers of non-Indians pass through the region on their way to the Yukon gold fields. The Canadian government seeks the first seven "numbered treaties" to clear the way for settlement. Treaties 8 to 11 are signed to pave the way for resource exploration and development. *(See* map of Indian Treaty Areas in Canada, p. 394.)

Chapter 7

1900 to 1959

1 9 0 0

1900s Struggle and Change in the Twentieth Century. The early years of the twentieth century are difficult times for Native Americans who continue to feel the disastrous effects of the General Allotment Act of 1887. Federal, state, and county officials often work in conjunction with the private sector to divest the American Indians of their estate. Railroad, cattle, mining, timber, and oil companies take every opportunity to liquidate Indian title to lands and resources.

c. 1900 Fewkes Study of Hopi Ceremonies. J. Walter Fewkes, an ethnologist working with the Hopi Indians, commissions a group of anonymous self-trained painters to illustrate his studies of Hopi ceremonies. Although the Hopi who illustrate Fewkes's volume on kachinas are labeled witches by traditional Hopi for depicting the sacred beings, the representations are the first produced by Southwestern Indians in a nonindigenous media; it is generally thought that Fewkes's action stimulates the development of Pueblo painting. Fewkes's 1895 excavations at the ruins of Sikyatki similarly contribute to Hopi and Hopi/Tewa arts, inspiring Nampeyo, a Hopi-Tewa woman potter, to resurrect a nearly lost technique of pottery design found at that site.

c. 1900 Susan Billie Is Born. Matriarch of the Seminole Panther clan, Susan Billie is a well-known and highly respected medicine woman. The traditions she practices have been passed down from her father, her uncles, and her grandfather. She is also the sister of Buffalo Jim, one of the oldest living medicine men of the modern era. Billie's medicine combines the inherent healing properties of herbs with the spiritual power of songs and rituals. She elects to share this knowledge with her children and grandchildren, thereby ensuring the maintenance of Seminole medicine even as the tribe moves from a hunting-trapping subsistence base to a modern tribal government-business enterprising one, within her own lifetime. In 1984, Billie is featured in a public television documentary entitled "Four Corners of Earth," which focuses on the role of Indian women and their influence upon the maintenance of cultural continuity.

1900 Fred Kabotie, Hopi Artist, Is Born. Born and raised in the Second Mesa village of Shongopovi, Hopi artist Fred Kabotie is an important figure in the development of Pueblo painting and the first Hopi professional artist. In 1915, pressured by the federal government's drive to assimilate younger Hopi, Kabotie leaves Second Mesa for the Indian School in Santa Fe, where he begins painting watercolors. After graduating from public high school in 1925, Kabotie wins a prize at the Southeast Indian

Fair in Santa Fe, the forerunner of Indian Market. The following year, Kabotie is commissioned to paint a collection of Hopi ceremonial scenes for the Museum of the American Indian in New York. Beginning in 1937 he teaches art at the new Hopi High School at Oraibi, a position he keeps until the school closes, 22 years later. Kabotie's reputation as an artist continues to grow, and in 1941 he recreates the Awatovi murals for the Museum of Modern Art show in New York. Four years later he is awarded a Guggenheim Fellowship. From the 1950s on, Kabotie paints sporadically, devoting himself instead to community projects like the founding of the Hopi Cultural Center at Second Mesa, which he helps establish in 1971. Kabotie dies in 1986 in Shongopovi.

1900 *The Middle Five.* Omaha writer Francis La Flesche's autobiography, *The Middle Five,* tells the story of his experiences at a Presbyterian mission school in Bellevue, Nebraska. He primarily dwells upon the adjustments he and his friends are forced to make while attending the school. Many years before and after the publication of *The Middle Five,* La Flesche serves as anthropologist Alice Fletcher's primary resource and informant for her work on the Omaha tribe. With composer Charles Wakefield Cadman, La Flesche also writes a three-act Indian opera that is never produced

NOVEMBER 4, 1900 Oneida Indians Vote. Three hundred Oneida Indians go to the polls and vote in the New York State elections.

1 9 0 1

1901 Five Civilized Tribes Citizenship Act. Congress passes the Citizenship Act for the Five Civilized Tribes, which are the Cherokee, Choctaw, Chickasaw, Seminole, and Creek peoples.

1901 Old Indian Legends Published. Yankton Sioux Gertrude Bonnin, also known as Zitkala-Sa, writes and publishes a book oriented toward children, entitled *Old Indian Legends.*

1901 Samaria Indian Baptist Church Organized. The Samaria Indian School is established in Virginia by Chickahominy Indian people, and a teacher is hired. Later, the county school system takes over the school.

1901 Sequoyah League Founded. Primarily through the efforts of writer and reformer Charles Lummis, the Sequoyah League, a philanthropic group working for the welfare of California Indians, is organized in 1901. Before its demise in 1909, the league seeks "to make better Indians and better treated ones."

1901–1911 Cupa Indian Land Sites. Six Cupa Indian villages lose their land sites in the Warner's Ranch area in San Diego County. The Sequoyah League persuades Congress to finance the purchase of lands near the Pala Reservation so that the forcibly evicted Cupa may settle there.

1 9 0 2

1902 Aleut-Eskimo Education. Attempting to make Indian-Aleut-Eskimo education more relevant, the first local school board is established at Nome, Alaska.

1902 Alexander Posey and the "Fus Fixico Letters." Alexander Posey, a Creek writer and poet, is best known for his satirical letters. Born and raised in Creek Nation territory in Oklahoma, he graduates from Bacone University in Muskogee in 1895. He serves the Creek Nation in various capacities, and in 1902 becomes editor of the Eufaula *Indian Journal.* During his tenure as editor, the Dawes Act begins to affect the "Five Civilized Tribes" of Oklahoma; Posey wryly observes and comments upon the act's effects in his editorial column, called the "Fus Fixico Letters." Posey's writing career is cut tragically short, however, when he dies at the

Boy in traditional dress with Lacrosse stick and girl with burden basket. Seneca, Iroquois, Cattaraugus Reservation, New York, 1901. Courtesy of the National Museum of the American Indian, Smithsonian Institution.

age of 34 in a drowning accident on May 27, 1908.

1902   Civil Service Act. The Civil Service Act is extended to the Bureau of Indian Affairs.

1902   Essie Parrish Is Born. Recognized by the Kashaya Pomo as the last of their four prophet leaders, Essie Parrish is a powerful dreamer, a sucking doctor (heals by ritually extracting harmful objects from a patient's body), and a leader in both politics and religion. In 1943, she

assumes the position of official religious leader/ dreamer of the Kashaya people after her predecessor, Annie Jarvis, passes away. In the years that follow, Parrish is instrumental in preserving Kashaya traditions and tribal cohesion even as other Pomo groups feel the increasingly dominant sway of status quo America. Because of her influence, many Indian and non-Indian authorities see the Kashaya Pomo as an extremely important native source of religious and historical information.

Parrish is involved in the making of over

Chief Shake's house at Wrangell, Alaska, around the turn of the twentieth century. Courtesy of the National Anthropological, Archives Smithsonian Institution.

two dozen films documenting Kashaya culture. Awarded the Western Heritage Award in 1965, the film *Chishkle* or "Beautiful Tree" presents Essie preparing acorns, a staple food source for many California Indians; other films show her dream dancing and doctoring. *Kashaya Texts* and a Kashaya dictionary are both collaborative works written by Robert Oswalt in conjunction with Parrish. The multitalented Parrish is also a famous basket-weaver and many of her works still can be viewed at the University of California Berkeley's Lowie Museum.

1902   *Indian Boyhood*. Charles Eastman, a Wahpeton Sioux, publishes *Indian Boyhood*. A graduate of Dartmouth, Eastman earns his M.D. at the Boston University School of Medicine in 1890 at the age of 32. After graduating he becomes a government physician at the Pine Ridge Agency where in 1909 he witnesses and treats the brutalities endured by the survivors of the Wounded Knee Massacre. Frequently perceived and publicly applauded as a model of Indian success by proassimilationist progressives, Eastman embarks upon a literary career by publishing some autobiographical pieces in *St. Nicholas* magazine. These pieces are then col-

lectively published as *Indian Boyhood*. A number of other works follow, including two collections of short stories, *Red Hunters and the Animal People* (1904) and *Old Indian Days* (1907), an anthology of traditional stories; *Wigwam Evenings* (1909); and a number of books on contemporary Indian life, most notably *The Soul of the Indian* (1911) and *From the Deep Woods to Civilization* (1916). Eastman also helps found the first pan-Indian organization, the Society of the American Indian (SAI), and serves on the Committee of One Hundred that investigates and analyzes federal Indian policy in the famous Meriam Report of 1928. In the last years of his life, Eastman becomes a "show" Indian; he is touted as the "thrilling attraction" for many Indian enthusiasts at YMCA and Boy Scout camps, where he lives in a hobbyist simulation of a tipi. He dies in 1939 and is buried in an unmarked grave near Detroit.

MARCH 1, 1902   Creek Land Allotment Act. Congress passes the Creek Land Allotment Act, an act calling for the general land allotment of 160 acres surveyed and distributed to Creek members in Oklahoma, and the establishment of town sites in Oklahoma.

MAY 27, 1902 General Appropriation Act. Congress passes an act to fulfill treaty obligations, civilize Indians, and carry out allotment. The act also supports schools for Indians, covers Indian office expenses, and provides supplies to the tribes. Finally, the act allows the secretary of interior to permit heirs to sell trust-restricted lands instead of dividing them among heirs.

JULY 1, 1902 Cherokee Land Allotment Act. Congress passes the Cherokee Land Allotment Act, an act providing for the allotment of lands belonging to the Cherokee Nation in Oklahoma. The act allows for the disposition of town sites in Oklahoma, including appraisement of the land's natural resources, and the implementation of a Cherokee tribal roll to serve as documentation for federal recognition of tribal membership.

JULY 1, 1902 Choctaw and Chickasaw Land Allotment Act. Congress passes the Choctaw and Chickasaw Land Allotment Act, an act to ratify and confirm an agreement with the Choctaw and Chickasaw tribes to allot their tribal lands in Oklahoma for distribution to individual Choctaws and Chickasaws.

WINTER 1902 Epidemic Kills Inuit. Disease and starvation wipe out the Sadlermiut (Sallirmiut) of southern Southampton Island in the North-West Territory. The Inuit population of this island has been gradually reduced by disease and starvation. In the same year, a measles epidemic devastates the Mackenzie Inuit gathered at Kittigazuit, at the mouth of the Mackenzie River. For the past several centuries, up to a thousand Inuit gather at Kittigazuit each summer. Such a large village is possible because, with kayaks, the Inuit can easily drive large numbers of beluga whales into the shallow river water where the whales are then butchered. A smaller number of Inuit stay at this site all winter, living in driftwood and turf homes. The epidemic of 1902 foreshadows the end of the Mackenzie Inuit by 1920.

1 9 0 3

1903 Charles Bender, Chippewa Major League Pitcher. Charles Bender, a Chippewa, starts his major league baseball career with the Philadelphia Athletics of the American League. Considered one of the greatest pitchers of all time, he wins 212 games and loses only 28.

1903 Indian Agencies Eliminated. Many Indian agencies are eliminated and their work load shifted to the reservation schools.

1903 *Lone Wolf v. Hitchcock.* The Treaty of Medicine Lodge (1867) decrees that no part of the Kiowa-Comanche Reservation can be sold to the United States without the approval of three-fourths of the adult male Indians. Under the Dawes Act, Congress subsequently allots the reservation, selling off the "surplus" without obtaining the necessary approval. In 1902, Lone Wolf, a Kiowa leader, files a lawsuit to prevent the Interior Department from expropriating tribal land for public use. The Supreme Court rules against him in the *Lone Wolf v. Hitchcock* decision, giving Congress the authority to decide how to deal with and dispose of all Indian lands. Upholding the government's action, the Supreme Court reasons, "The power exists to abrogate the provisions of an Indian treaty, though presumably such power will be exercised only when circumstances arise which will not only justify the government in disregarding the stipulations of the treaty, but may demand, in the interest of the country and the Indians themselves, that it should do so." Lone Wolf literally creates a doctrine claiming that Congress possesses plenary power in Indian affairs, meaning that Congress has the power to abrogate, ignore, or change Indian treaties without interference from the courts. This decision is a major blow to Indian treaty rights.

1 9 0 4

1904 D'Arcy McNickle, Cree and Flathead Writer and Government Administrator, Is

Born. D'Arcy McNickle is born in St. Ignatius, Montana, of mixed-blood of Cree and Scotch ancestry. As a child he is adopted into the Flathead tribe. McNickle is one of the most highly educated Indian people of his generation, having attended the University of Montana, Oxford University in England, and the University of Grenoble in France. He works as a writer in New York City from 1925 to 1935 and then becomes involved in the Federal Writers Project in 1935 and 1936. His novel *The Surrounded* (1936) is considered a masterpiece of Native American literature for its time. Other important books by McNickle include *They Came Here First: The Epic of the American Indian* (1949), *Runner in the Sun: A Story of Indian Maize* (1954), *Indians and Other Americans: Two Ways of Life Meet* (with Harold Fey, 1959), *Indian Tribes of the United States: Ethnic and Cultural Survival* (1962), and *Indian Man: A Life of Oliver La Farge* (1971). McNickle wins several literary awards, including the distinguished Guggenheim Fellowship (1963–64). The D'Arcy McNickle Center at the Newberry Library in Chicago is one of the leading institutions for Native American historiography.

1904 Pomo Land Claims. The Yokaia Pomo Indians win a court case to keep their property intact in spite of continued encroachment.

1904 Sioux Land Allotments. The government begins allotting lands to the Sioux in South Dakota.

MARCH 11, 1904 Pipelines Act. Congress passes the Pipelines Act stating "the Secretary of Interior is hereby authorized and empowered to grant a right of way in the nature of an easement for the construction, operation, and maintenance of pipelines for the conveyance of oil and gas through any Indian reservation, through any lands held by an Indian tribe or nation in the Indian Territory," including allotted land, with compensation paid to the tribe or individual as the case may be.

APRIL 23, 1904 Practice of Medicine and Surgery in Indian Territory Act. Congress passes the Practice of Medicine and Surgery in Indian Territory Act, an act stating "no person shall practice medicine and surgery, or either, as a profession in the Indian Territory without first being registered as a physician and surgeon, or either. . . ."

APRIL 28, 1904 Arkansas Indian Territory. The Arkansas legislature passes an act that extends and continues all the laws of Arkansas heretofore put in force in the Indian Territory, so as to embrace all persons and estates therein, "whether Indian, freedmen or otherwise," and confers "full and complete jurisdiction" upon the district courts in the territory regarding "all estate of decedents, the guardianship, of minors and incompetents, whether Indians, freedman, or otherwise."

APRIL 28, 1904 White Earth Reservation Allotment Act. Congress passes the White Earth Reservation Allotment Act, calling for parcels of 160 acres to be allotted to Chippewa living on the White Earth Reservation according to provisions of the General Allotment Act of 1887.

1 9 0 5

1905 George Clutesi, Nuu-Chah-Nulth (Nootka) Chief, Artist, and Author, Is Born. Born in Port Alberni, British Columbia, Clutesi works as a pile driver until a 1940 accident prevents him from carrying out physical labor. This allows him to direct his efforts toward painting and writing. He inherits the art supplies of prominent Canadian artist Emily Carr upon her death in 1945. He subsequently emerges as a painter, writer, and spokesperson for the Nootka and for Canadian Natives in general. He contributes a mural to the Indian pavilion at Expo 67 in Montreal, and writes *Son of Raven, Son of Deer: Fables of the Tse-shaht*

Navajo riding to Tesacod Canyon, 1905. Photo by Edward Curtis. Courtesy of the Library of Congress.

People (1967), a book of legends, and *Potlatch* (1969), based on his people's oral traditions.

1905   Government Medical Services for Canadian Natives. Dr. Peter H. Bryce is appointed as Canada's first superintendent of medical services for Canada's Natives. Until now the government has depended on missionaries to provide health care for isolated Indian groups, among whom tuberculosis is epidemic.

1905   *United States v. Winans.* In *United States v. Winans,* the Supreme Court holds that a

treaty may reserve certain rights such as fishing or hunting off-reservation for an Indian tribe. The court also holds that tribal rights, including rights to land and to self-government, are not granted to the tribe by the U.S. Rather, under the reserved rights doctrine, tribes retained (reserved) such rights as part of their status as prior and continuing sovereigns.

MARCH 3, 1905   Pueblo Land Taxation. Congress passes an act exempting land held by pueblo villages or individuals within Pueblo

Earth lodge of the Hidatsa tribe, photographed at the beginning of the twentieth century. Photo by R.H. Lowie. Courtesy of the Department of Library Services, American Museum of Natural History.

reservations from "taxation of any kind whatsoever . . . until Congress shall otherwise provide." Included in this exemption are cattle, sheep, and any personal property furnished by the United States or used in the cultivation of lands.

JULY 12, 1905 Treaty 9. The Cree and Ojibway leaders of northern Ontario begin signing Treaty 9. The Métis are also issued scrip. *(See* map of Indian Treaty Areas in Canada, p. 394.)

SEPTEMBER 1, 1905 New Canadian Provinces. The provinces of Alberta and Saskatchewan are created from areas of the North-West Territories but are not given control of the land or natural resources.

1905–1906 Kickapoo Migrations. Approximately 200 Kickapoo leave Oklahoma to escape the greed and anti-Indianism of settlers there. They journey to Coahuila to be near other Kickapoo already residing in Mexico. There, they are defrauded and abused by a white man whom they mistakenly trust. In 1907, the immigrant Kickapoo are moved to Sonora, near the Arizona border. Finally, some

return to Oklahoma in 1916 but others drift in northern Mexico without any land of value.

1 9 0 6

1906 Angel DeCora, Winnebago Indian Artist, Is Born. As the director of the Leupp Art Department at Carlisle Indian School from 1906 to 1915, Angel DeCora initiates and develops an intensive art program for Indian students. She encourages them to use Indian designs in conjunction with modern art media during a time when Indian culture is perceived not only as "anti-civilized" but also as a burden to the process of Indian assimilation. Needless to say, Richard Pratt, the school's director, opposes DeCora's program. Yet the very views DeCora espouses correlate to the Southwest "San Ildefonso School" of Indian Art which begins to emerge around 1910; this school, considered the "renaissance" of Indian art, coincides with the era of the Indian New Deal and eventually spurs the development of an Indian Arts and Crafts Department in 1935. In addition to her outlook and her teaching, DeCora illustrates several Indian-authored

Virginia Rosemyre Hunt (1875–1921), a Gabrielino-Serrano. In her lifetime she completed several hundred oil paintings. Courtesy of Wallace Cleaves.

books, including Francis La Flesche's *The Middle Five,* Gertrude Bonnin's *Old Indian Legends,* Natalie Curtis's *The Indian's Book,* and Elaine Goodale Eastman's *Yellow Star.* Her affiliation with Bonnin leads to DeCora's active support of the Society of American Indians.

1906   Cutbank Canal Completed. The Cutbank Canal, serving the Blackfeet Reservation of the Peigan Indians of Montana, is completed by the Indian Service, using mostly Indian labor and teams of horses. The irrigation project encompasses 14,000 acres of land.

1906   *Geronimo's Story of His Life.* Dictated by the famous Chiricahua Apache leader, translated by Asa Daklugie, and edited by S.M. Barrett, this "autobiography" represents one of the historically most important American Indian literary productions. Barrett claims the project of writing the book is initiated by Geronimo who wishes to call attention to the plight of his people, many of whom, like Geronimo, are languishing at Fort Sill in the aftermath of the famous Apache resistance of the 1880s. By the time the autobiography is undertaken, Geronimo and the others have been prisoners of war for over 20 years. Initially Barrett's requests to do the autobiography are turned down by the army officer in charge of the military reservation. Yet Barrett eventually receives permission from President Theodore Roosevelt and, upon publication, the autobiography is dedicated to the president. Although it commences with Geronimo's rendering of the mythological origins of the Apache people, *Geronimo's Story of His Life* is primarily an historical recollection of the Apache resistance.

1906   Hotevilla Hopi Village Founded. Beginning in the late nineteenth century, pressures of acculturation begin exerting themselves on the Hopi. In 1887 a day school is built at Keams Canyon, and in 1894 schools are added at Polacca and Oraibi on First and Third Mesas, respectively. At the same time, there is an increasing Christian presence on the mesas.

In 1893, H.R. Voth builds a Mennonite church at Oraibi and sets about winning converts. Controversy builds between conservative Hopi, who reject Christianity and U.S. government administration, and Christian Hopi and those more willing to accept the presence of the U.S. government. In 1906, Lomahongyoma, a leader of the conservative Hopi, invites a number of conservative Hopi from the village of Shongopovi to live at Oraibi. This greatly upsets the residents of Oraibi, who decide ask the newcomers to leave. On September 8,300 conservative Hopi leave Oraibi. After their eviction the conservatives establish their own village, Hotevilla, seven miles northwest of Oraibi on Third Mesa. Hotevilla remains among the most conservative and traditional Hopi villages to this day.

1906 Taos Blue Lake Seized. In creating the Carson National Forest, the federal government seizes 50,000 acres of wilderness land high in the Sangre de Cristo mountains of New Mexico. Included is Blue Lake, a principal shrine for the people of Taos Pueblo; they hold the lake, as well as the land around it, as sacred.

FEBRUARY 26, 1906 Five Civilized Tribes Council Act. Congress passes the Five Civilized Tribes Council Act, designed to keep the tribal governments of the Cherokee, Creek, Seminole, Chickasaw, and Choctaw in operation in the form of the national councils. The act also empowers the president to fill the office of the principal chief in certain circumstances; abolishes all tribal taxes under tribal law or regulations of the secretary of the interior; requires presidential approval of tribal legislation and contracts affecting federal property; and provides for continuation of tribal governments until otherwise provided by Congress.

APRIL 26, 1906 Final Disposition of Affairs of Five Civilized Tribes Act. Congress passes the Final Disposition of Affairs of Five Civilized Tribes Act, which reaffirms tribal membership among the Five Civilized Tribes, provides for school funding, and payments to Indians, and acknowledges lands held in trust and recognition for the Five Civilized governments.

MAY 8, 1906 Burke Act. Congress passes the Burke Act, an act to amend the Dawes Allotment Act, extending the laws of the United States and Territories over the Indians and giving the secretary of the interior the discretionary power to shorten the 25-year trust period on allotted lands upon declaring the competency of the owner. Following the end of the 25-year trust period, every allottee is to be subject to civil and criminal laws; citizenship rights are conferred to allottees on issue of fee simple title of property. This continues the government policy of assimilation by which Indian tribal life is weakened and Indian lands alienated from Indian ownership.

MAY 17, 1906 Alaska Allotment Act. Congress passes the Alaska Allotment Act which allows Alaska Natives (Inuit, Yupik, Aleut and Indian) to claim full title to individual homesites of 160 acres of nonmineral land.

SUMMER 1906 Salish Petition. Joe Capilano, chief of the Squamish Coast Salish band near Vancouver, petitions King Edward VII of England to help British Columbia Indians gain redress of their grievances.

AUGUST 28, 1906 Treaty 10. Chipewyan and Cree bands of northern Ontario begin signing Treaty 10. They have been requesting a treaty for over 20 years. (*See* map of Indian Treaty Areas in Canada, p. 394.)

1 9 0 7

1907 Kickapoo Migrations. The Kickapoo newcomers to Coahuila move to an abandoned ranch 20 miles south of Douglas, Arizona. Some return to Oklahoma in 1916, while others wander across northern Mexico between So-

Chief Joe Capilano (center, holding robe) on the north Vancouver Ferry wharf before leaving for London in 1906. Courtesy of the City of Vancouver Archives.

nora and Coahuila, occasionally returning to Oklahoma.

1907 Mabel McKay, Cache Creek Pomo Basketmaker, Is Born. Mabel McKay is a Long Valley Cache Creek Pomo (also referred to as Patwin) basket-maker and doctor. Shortly after her birth in 1907 on a ranch in Nice, Lake County, California, McKay moves with her mother to the town of Rumsey. There she is raised by her maternal grandmother, Sarah Taylor. Taylor's brother Richard began the revivalist Bole Maru (Dream Dance) movement among the Pomo and Southwestern Wintun in 1871. Mabel McKay follows her uncle by becoming a Dream Dance doctor, as well as a prophet for her people. McKay is also one of the foremost Pomo basket-makers, a people widely known for their basket-making achievements. McKay makes basketry the old way, dreaming her basket designs and following the important cultural prescriptions associated with her art. The last weaver to create baskets in the traditional manner, McKay is especially well known for her miniatures and feather baskets, which are held in important collections throughout the United States and

Europe. She teaches basket-making for nearly 50 years, lectures widely at universities, and is a repository of cultural knowledge for her own people and for the numerous anthropologists and other scholars who seek her out. At the time of her death in 1993, Mabel McKay is the last living representative of the Long Valley Cache Creek Pomo.

1907 Sale of Indian Allotments. Congress authorizes the selling of land allotments belonging to Indian people who are declared by non-Indian courts to be incompetent individuals.

JANUARY 23, 1907 Charles Curtis Elected to U.S. Senate. Charles Curtis, a Kaw Indian from Kansas, is elected to the U.S. Senate, thereby becoming the first Indian to attain such high rank and prominence. Curtis serves from January 23 to March 13, 1913, and from March 4, 1915, to March 3, 1929, at which time he resigns his position to become vice president of the United States under Herbert Hoover.

MARCH 2, 1907 Tribal Funds Act. Congress passes the Tribal Funds Act, which authorizes the secretary of the interior "to designate any individual Indian" to be entitled to an allotment or a share of his or her tribal domain.

APRIL 19, 1907 Indian Athlete. Tom Longboat, an Onondaga athlete from the Six Nations Reserve near Brantford, Ontario, wins the Boston Marathon in record time. He has already won several long-distance races in Canada.

NOVEMBER 16, 1907 Indian Territory Becomes Oklahoma. The state of Oklahoma is admitted to the Union. Many Indians, including Benjamin Harrison, a Choctaw, help draw up the new state's constitution. Establishment of statehood for the former Indian Territory further reduces the Indians living there. Most Indian governments in the former Indian Territory are abolished, including the constitutional governments of the Cherokee, Choctaw, Chickasaw, Seminole, and Creek nations. Most Indian land is allotted to individuals, sometimes forcibly to conservative Indians who do not recognize U.S. rights to abolish their government or to take their land. In the late 1890s and early 1900s, several rebellious movements try to resist allotment and dissolution of their national governments and land, but without success. Such movements were the Creek Snake Indians under Chitto Harjo, the Nighthawk Keetoowah Society under Red Bird Smith, as well as less well-known movements among the Seminole, Choctaw, and Chickasaw. Oklahoma citizens urge that the remaining Indian lands be put on the market and that Indian landholdings be taxed. Over the next 30 years, many Indians given allotments lose their land because of debt, legal fraud, and inability to pay taxes. The tribal governments of the former Indian Territory nations are kept up informally, and some are revived starting in the late 1930s. The Choctaw, Cherokee, Chickasaw, Creek, and Seminole regain the right to elect their own governments in the early 1970s, but the governments are now under the jurisdiction of the Bureau of Indian Affairs.

1 9 0 8

1908 Chickahominy Tribe Organized. The modern Chickahominy tribe of Virginia is officially organized with William H. Adkins as chief. The tribal officers also include an assistant chief, clerk, treasurer, and council members.

1908 Indian Agent Title Abandoned. The title "Indian Agent" is abandoned and gradually replaced by the term "Superintendent." This position is usually filled through promotion of Bureau of Indian Affairs' career workers.

1908 Louis Tewanima Competes in Olympic Games. Louis Tewanima, a Hopi Indian runners from Arizona, competes in the Olympic Games held in London, finishing ninth in the marathon. In the next Olympics, he finishes second to the famed "Flying Finn," Kannes Kilehmainen. A triple medal winner in the 1908 and the 1912 Olympics, he competes in both the 5,000 and 10,000 meter events, as well as the marathon. He becomes the first athlete elected to the Arizona Sports Hall of Fame.

1908 William W. Keeler, Cherokee Businessperson and Tribal Leader, Is Born. In 1949, William Keeler is appointed principal chief of the Cherokee Nation in Oklahoma. He serves as appointed principal chief until 1971, and between 1971 and 1975 is the first elected principal chief since 1907. During his tenure, Keeler gains a reputation as an able administrator and leader. He serves on two major government task forces, investigating and reporting on major issues in Indian affairs. In 1962, Keeler works on a task force that investigates the conditions of Alaska Natives and their land claims. Keeler also helps establish the Cherokee Foundation, which endeavors to promote the welfare and culture of the Cherokee Nation and its members.

1908 *Winters v. United States.* In one of the most important cases in the twentieth-century Indian law, the U.S. Supreme Court decides

Kwakiutl maiden and her kinfolk in a canoe going to meet her intended husband, c. 1907. Courtesy of the Rare Books & Manuscripts Division of the New York Public Library—Astor, Lenox, and Tilden Foundations.

that American Indians on reservation lands retain the right to sufficient water for agricultural uses. The Winters case involves the Fort Belknap Reservation in Montana, which had been created by an 1888 agreement. This agreement set one boundary of the reservation at the middle of the Milk River, but made no mention of rights to the use of water. In the years following the creation of the reservation, non-Indian settlers off the reservation build dams that divert the flow of the river and interfere with the Indian's agricultural uses. The settlers

claim to have appropriated the water after the reservation is established but prior to any use of water by the Indians. The Supreme Court throws out the settlers' defense, holding instead that at the time the Fort Belknap lands were reserved by the 1888 agreement, water rights for the Indians also were reserved by necessary implication. This case provides the foundation of Indian water rights and is often referred to as the "Winters Doctrine." This doctrine becomes very important after the 1960s, when Colorado, Arizona, New Mexico, and California start to divide scarce water resources among themselves. Because of the Winters decision, Indian reservations in the area are guaranteed access to water for reservation development.

MAY 27, 1908 Removal of Restrictions from Some Lands of Allottees of Five Civilized Tribes Act. The Removal of Restrictions from Some Lands of Allottees of Five Civilized Tribes Act is passed, authorizing the secretary of the interior to remove restrictions from Indians of the Five Civilized Tribes who are of less than one-half Indian blood, allottees who are intermarried with whites, freedmen, and mixed-blood Indian minors of less than one-half Indian blood.

MAY 29, 1908 Allotted Lands Selling Act. The Allotted Lands Selling Act is passed extending the authority of the secretary of the interior to issue patents in fee to purchasers of Indian lands; Indian allotments may then be sold on petition of allottee. The secretary also is empowered to ascertain the legal heirs involved in such transactions.

JULY 28, 1908 *The Redman and the Child* Released. American movie pioneer D.W. Griffith releases his first western, *The Redman and the Child.* This silent film is only one reel (about 1,000 feet or 10 minutes in length) and tells the story of an Indian warrior's enduring friendship with a young white boy. It is the first of more than two dozen Indian-theme films directed by Griffith. Some of his more popular works include: *Leatherstocking* (1909), *Ramona* (1910), *A Mohawk's Way* (1910), *A Chief's Daughter* (1911), *A Pueblo Legend* (1912), and *The Battle at Elderbush Gulch* (1914).

1 9 0 9

1909 Indians Appeal. The Indian tribes of the Province of British Columbia, an alliance of 20 Indian groups, appeal to the British throne for help in settling their land claims.

1 9 1 0

1910 Annie Dodge Wauneka, Navajo Tribal Leader, Is Born. Annie Dodge Wauneka is born in a hogan in Old Sawmill, Arizona, and attends the Albuquerque Indian School. Her principal education, however, comes at the side of her father as he travels the Navajo Reservation tending to the needs of his people. The poverty and sickness she witnesses as a young child become the focus of her life's work. Wauneka concentrates her efforts on reducing death and illness from tuberculosis on the reservation. After studying with the U.S. Public Health Service, she seeks to implement a health education program in her own community. Four years after her father's death, Wauneka is elected to the tribal council, where she is equally adamant about obtaining a better education for her people. She believes that poor education is a major factor inhibiting a better life for the Navajo. She is the first woman to be elected to the Navajo Tribal Council and in 1964 is the first Native American to receive the Presidential Medal of Freedom. Wauneka receives numerous awards and honors throughout her lifetime, including Arizona's Woman of the Year Achievement Award, the Josephine B. Hughes Memorial Award, and the Indian Achievement Award.

1910 Calusa Indian Education. Captain Odock of the Calusa Indian tribe begins efforts to obtain a public school within his tribal area, and ultimately an all-Indian school district is established. Other such Indian-directed school districts are established with Calusa assistance.

1910 Indian Education. By this year, 51 percent of Indian children are attending school, but 64 percent of Indian adults still are considered illiterate.

1910 The Omnibus Act. Congress passes the Omnibus Act, which provides for the determination of heirs of allottees, holdings of trust patents on land, partition of estates, issuance of

Sewing class in an Indian boarding school in Genoa, Nebraska. Courtesy of the National Archives.

certificates of competency to individual Indians, making of Indian wills, prohibition of conveyance of trust land, protection of Indian timber, and various allotment procedures.

1910 Sun Dance Forbidden. Regulations issued by the Office of Indian Affairs forbid the Sun Dance of the Plains Indians, citing the self-inflicted "torture" by dance participants as extreme. Such regulations prove to be flagrant violations of the U.S. Constitution.

JUNE 20, 1910 New Mexico Enabling Act.

Congress passes the New Mexico Enabling Act, which contains a specific provision that "the terms 'Indian' and 'Indian country' shall include the Pueblo Indians of New Mexico and the lands now owned or occupied by them."

JUNE 25, 1910 Restricted Trust Lands Act. Congress passes the Restricted Trust Lands Act amending the sale of trust lands to improve the order of determining heirs of deceased Indians for the sale and leasing of restricted lands. This act is later amended on February

Fourth-graders in an Indian boarding school in Genoa, Nebraska, 1910. Courtesy of the National Archives.

14, 1913, to regulate Indian allotments disposed by a will.

DECEMBER 31, 1910 *The Yaqui Girl* **Produced.** *Yaqui Girl,* a love story between an Indian woman and a Mexican man, is the first film produced by Pathe Frerer's newly established West Coast studio in Los Angeles. James Young Deer, a Winnebago Indian from Nebraska, becomes the studio's head of production, and during his three-year reign supervises more than 100 western and Spanish-theme

pictures. Other popular films of Young Deer include: *A Cheyenne Brave* (1910), *The Red Girl and the Child* (1910), *Red Deer's Devotion* (1911), and *Lt. Scott's Narrow Escape* (1911).

1 9 1 1

c. 1911 Canadian Indian Population. The population of Indians in the area that has become Canada reaches its lowest level (under 110,000 persons). The aboriginal population

School band, c. 1910, at an Indian boarding school in Genoa, Nebraska. Courtesy of the National Archives.

has been steadily declining because of disease and starvation related to resource depletion.

1911   Corruption in Indian Affairs. Seeking to explain the corruption rampant in the nation's conduct of Indian affairs, Indian Commissioner Robert G. Valentine reports, "Indian Affairs are, even under the best possible administration, peculiarly a field for the grafter and other wrongdoers. The land and the monies of the Indian offer a bait which the most suited will not refuse."

1911   Hopi Children Forced to Attend Boarding School. The U.S. Army forcibly enters Hotevilla and captures 69 Hopi children, who are coerced into attending boarding school. They are taken away from their parents and families for many years and are unable to return home, even during school vacations.

1911   Ishi Emerges. After years of hiding from settlers in California's southern Cascade Mountains, a Yana Yahi Indian, known as Ishi, allows himself to be captured in Oroville, California.

Kwakiutl canoes with an upright bear effigy arriving for a festival in 1910. The Kwakiutl, of British Columbia (Northwest Pacific Coast), are predominantly fishing people. Courtesy of the Philadelphia Museum of Art; purchased with funds from the American Museum of Photography.

He creates a sensation in the newspapers, which refer to him as the "last wild Indian in North America." The only remaining member of the Yahi tribe, Ishi survives for five years, living at the University of California Museum of Anthropology in San Francisco and providing a great deal of ethnographic and linguistic material for the famous anthropologist Alfred Kroeber.

1911 Reserve Relocation. A Songhee Coast Salish band is removed from their reserve in Victoria, British Columbia. The government seeks the valuable land on which the Indians reside. The Songhee moved to the site from nearby Cadboro Bay in the 1840s after the Hudson's Bay Company established Fort Victoria. In the 1850s, settlers began agitating for the removal of the Indians.

1911 Seneca Attempt to Collect Back Rents. The Seneca Nation (Allegheny) tries to hire an attorney to press collections of back rent due

In 1911, Ishi left his homeland in the foothills of Mount Lassen in northern California and gave himself up to local townsmen. He was the last member of the Yahi tribe. Courtesy of the Phoebe A. Hearst Museum of Anthropology, University of California at Berkeley.

from Salamanca whites, but the federal government refuses to grant funds for that purpose. In 1915, the Seneca Council adopts a resolution canceling the defaulted leases, but the Office of Indian Affairs takes no action.

1911   Shoshoni Revolt. The last recorded uprising of Indians occurs when the Shoshoni revolt in Humboldt County, Nevada, murdering some stockmen. A sheriff's posse subsequently hunts down the band, killing everyone except a woman and two small children.

MARCH 1911   Chippewa Protest Indian Images in Movies. A group of Chippewa arrive in Washington, D.C., to protest the movies' alleged distortions of American Indians. They request that President William H. Taft impose congressional regulations against the industry's stereotyping of Native Americans. The Indians cite the Selig Polyscope Company's production of *The Curse of the Red Man* (1911), a story of an educated Indian who succumbs to alcoholism. Angry protesters label the film's depiction of

the tragic hero as "an untrue portrayal of the Indian."

APRIL 1911   Society of the American Indian Organized. Seven prominent American Indians meet in Columbus, Ohio, and establish a pan-Indian organization. The seven are Dr. Charles Eastman (Santee Sioux), Dr. Carlos Montezuma (Yavapai), Henry Standing Bear (Lakota Sioux), Charles Daganett (Peoria), Laura Cornelius (Oneida), Thomas Sloan (Omaha), and Minnie Kellogg (Oneida). A national conference takes place in October 1911, at which time the name Society of American Indians (SAI) is chosen. Headquartered in Washington, D.C., SAI lobbies for better educational programs and improved reservation conditions. In 1913, under the guidance of Arthur C. Parker (Seneca), SAI begins publishing the *Quarterly Journal for the Society of American Indians,* which is renamed *American Indian Magazine* in 1916. For about a decade SAI gives Indian people a new dimension of representation, providing a much-needed voice and calling for reforms in federal Indian policy. Soon, however, internal dissent over issues of representation, Indian administration policies, and peyote use proves to be the undoing of SAI. At the society's first convention, Minnie Kellogg emerges as a national Indian voice. She recommends a policy of Indian self-sufficiency and independence through the implementation of self-sustaining economic plans that are to be developed on Indian reservations. Her recommendations meet with little society support, although she does find constituency support from the Iroquois. Henceforth, she dedicates much of her political activism to the recovery of Oneida lands in New York and Wisconsin. What is noteworthy about Kellogg is that she problem-solved modern issues by using traditional Iroquois images and institutions. Her strategies have since served as precedent and have influenced all subsequent Iroquois land claims. Kellogg, however, dies in obscurity due to accusations of fraud and mismanagement of funds that purportedly occurred during her time of active leadership. The last conference of this important organization is held in 1923.

MAY 1911 Indian Act Amendment. The Canadian federal government amends the Indian Act to allow it to expropriate land on Indian reserves regardless of the terms of treaties.

JULY 7, 1911 Pacific Fur Seal Convention. A convention concerning the hunting of Pacific fur seals is held at Washington, D.C. Attended by the United States, Great Britain, Japan, and Russia, the convention ratifies the first modern international treaty to recognize the rights of Indians and other indigenous peoples to hunt and fish for subsistence. The convention attempts to reduce commercial sealing in the Bering Sea and Gulf of Alaska, but provides that its restrictions "shall not apply to Indians, Ainos, Aleuts or other aborigines dwelling on the coast of the waters mentioned . . . who carry on pelagic sealing in canoes . . . provided that such aborigines are not in the employment of other persons or under contract to deliver the skins to any person." This provision remains in force until 1986, when, under pressure from animal-rights groups, the United States allows the 1911 convention treaty to lapse.

1 9 1 2

1912 Canadian Indian Athlete. Long-distance runner Tom Longboat runs 15 miles in one hour, 18 minutes, and 10 seconds, thereby setting a new professional record. This follows a disappointment in the marathon at the London Olympics of 1908, when Longboat collapses. Longboat becomes the most celebrated Canadian athlete of this generation.

1912 Founding of the Alaska Native Brotherhood. Modeled after religious organizations of the Russian Orthodox and Protestant churches, the Alaska Native Brotherhood is formed at Juneau, Alaska, by eleven Tlingits and one Tsimshian, all strong Presbyterians, who at-

tended the Presbyterian-administered boarding school at Sitka, Alaska, an old Tlingit village. In 1915, an auxiliary organization, the Alaska Native Sisterhood, follows the same path as the Brotherhood. The Brotherhood promotes civil rights issues such as the right to vote, access to public education for Native children, and civil rights in public places, such as the right to attend movie theaters. It defends Native workers in the Alaskan canneries, defends the rights of Native fisherman, and fights a major land case for the 1911 taking of the Tongass Forest from the Tlingit and Haida tribes of panhandle Alaska. The Brotherhood wins the Tongass Forest case in the 1950s and in 1965 receives payment of $7.5 million after a struggle that starts in 1929. The Brotherhood continues to the present day as an active political force in Alaska Native issues.

1912 Jim Thorpe Wins the Olympic Decathlon. Jim Thorpe of the Sauk and Fox Tribe, represents the United States in the Olympic games in Sweden; he wins both the pentathlon and decathlon events. Thorpe's medals are later taken away from him because he had previously played semi-professional baseball. The medals are formally reinstated in 1984 after years of lobbying by Indians and the Thorpe family. (*See* entry, October 13, 1982.) Thorpe goes on to star in professional football during its early days. The Carlisle Institute graduate is frequently referred to as the world's greatest athlete.

1912 Navajo Dictionary Published. The first Navajo dictionary ever published is compiled by the Franciscan Fathers of Arizona.

1912 Robert L. Bennett, Oneida Commissioner of Indian Affairs, Is Born. Born at Oneida, Wisconsin, Bennett attends Haskell Institute in Kansas and goes on to obtain his degree in law from Southeastern University School of Law in Washington, D.C. Bennett then serves as a Bureau of Indian Affairs administrative assistant on the Navajo Reservation and remains there until serving as a marine during World War II. Bennett is appointed as commissioner of Indian affairs in 1966 and becomes known as an extremely vigorous administrator. He travels throughout the United States helping tribes to establish and direct their own social programs and fighting against the movement to exclude Indian tribes from federal assistance.

1912 *Wassaja* Founded. Dr. Carlos Montezuma, a Yavapai and one of the original members of the Society of American Indians, breaks away from that group to found his own publication, the *Wassaja*. This periodical may well be regarded as the first militant Indian journal of this century. Among his many radical positions, Montezuma advocates the abolition of the Office of Indian Affairs.

1912 Yukioma, Hopi Leader, Imprisoned. Yukioma, leader of the Hopi Hostiles, is imprisoned for resistance, exercising his freedom of speech, and refusing to obey orders from the Indian Administration's agent.

FEBRUARY 1912 *The War on the Plains* Released. Thomas H. Ince, producer with the "Bison-101" motion picture company in southern California, releases his first two-reel western, *The War on the Plains*. By an agreement with the federal government, Ince transports a large group of Oglala Sioux Indians from Pine Ridge, South Dakota, to his studio ranch in southern California's Santa Monica Mountains. For the next three years, Ince's Indian actors appear in more than 80 of his westerns. His more notable movies include *The Indian Massacre* (1912), *The Last of the Line* (1914), *The Invaders* (1912), and *The Battle of the Red Men* (1912).

MAY 15, 1912 Quebec Boundaries. Quebec is granted territory as far north as Hudson Strait on the condition it will negotiate land surrender agreements with Natives. The boundaries of Ontario and Manitoba also are extended northward.

JUNE 6, 1912 Classification and Appraisal of Unallotted Indian Lands Act. Congress passes the Classification and Appraisal of Unallotted Indian Lands Act, an act authorizing the secretary of the interior to classify or reclassify and appraise or reappraise unallotted or unreserved land within any Indian reservation opened to settlement.

1912–1920 Indian Land Leases. A dramatic escalation in leasing and sales of Indian lands occurs, caused by increasing commodity prices after World War I and termination sentiment in Congress.

1912–1928 Osage Oil. During the height of the Osage oil boom between 1912 and 1928, over $157 million in oil-rich lands belonging to the Osage tribe are auctioned off to eager non-Indian oil men, who sometimes pay as much as $1 million for a tract of 160 acres. Oil is discovered on the reservation in 1897 and ten years later, when their lands are allotted, the Osage wisely insist on tribal ownership of subsurface mineral rights. Great profits are made on the auctioned land, therefore, but the enormous sums paid to the tribe for their oil-bearing territory result in numerous attempts to defraud the Osage people of their newfound wealth.

1 9 1 3

1913 The Buffalo Head Nickel Issued. The federal government issues the famous "Buffalo Head" Indian nickel designed by James Earl Fraser. The nickel is an idealized composite portrait of 13 Indian chiefs, including John Big Tree of the Iroquois, Iron Tall of the Sioux, and Two Moons of the Cheyenne.

1913 Declaration of Allegiance to the Government of the United States by the North American Indian. This remarkable document, which many tribal leaders believe to be a treaty, is in actuality a publicity stunt by Rodman Wanamaker and a group of East Coast businessmen who had managed to obtain the blessing of President Taft for a signing ceremony at Fort Wadsworth in New York City. As Taft and the chiefs sign, newly issued Buffalo nickels are distributed to the audience. The Declaration has the Indians say: "With our right hands extended in brotherly love and our left hands holding the Pipe of Peace, we hereby bury all past ill feelings and proclaim abroad to all the Nations of the world our firm allegiance to this Nation and to the Stars and Stripes." Later the same year, the new president, Woodrow Wilson, gives Joseph Dixon, a Wanamaker associate, permission to bring this document (and souvenir American flags) to every Indian reservation in the United States. By Christmas it has been signed by more than 900 Indians from 189 tribes, encouraging Wanamaker and other "reformers" to begin the campaign for Indian citizenship.

1913 *United States v. Sandoval.* The same year as the "Declaration of Allegiance," the Supreme Court ironically upholds Congress's power to impose "Indian" status on the Pueblo of New Mexico, regarded as citizens since 1877. The court is particularly impressed by the fact that the Pueblos hold secret dances in their kivas from which non-Pueblo are excluded, considering it proof of their savagery. "Of course," the court observes, it would be unconstitutional for Congress to subject anyone to federal supervision by "arbitrarily calling them an Indian tribe." However, with respect to "distinctly Indian communities the questions whether, to what extent, and for what time they shall be recognized and dealt with as dependent tribes requiring the guardianship and protection of the United States are to be determined by Congress, not by the courts."

JANUARY 22, 1913 Nishga Land Claim. The Nishga (Nisga'a), Tsimshian-speaking Indians of northwestern British Columbia, adopt the "Statement of the Nishga Nation or Tribe of Indians" asserting their claim to land in the Nass River Valley. The Nishga, like other Indians in British Columbia, reject the position that they have no legitimate claim to land. They petition the Judicial Committee of the Privy Council, in London, England (until 1949 Canada's highest court), to hear their land claim. Later, the Privy Council refuses to hear their claim because the Canadian government will not sponsor the appeal. In September 1912, British Columbia premier Richard McBride agrees to establish a Royal Commission (McKenna-McBride Commission) to determine the appropriate size for Indian reserves in the province, but he maintains the position that these reserved lands are a privilege, not a right. On April 23, the commission begins its hearings to determine the appropriate size for each reserve in the province.

FEBRUARY 23, 1913 *The Squaw Man* **Released.** *The Squaw Man,* a moving picture based upon the play by Edwin Milton Royle, is first shown in commercial theaters. Co-directed by Cecil B. DeMille and Oscar C. Apfel, the film is also the first feature-length western to be shot in what is now Hollywood, and stars the Winnebago Indian actress "Redwing." This tragic story of a white man's marriage to an Indian woman is subsequently filmed twice, once in 1918 and again in 1931 (both remakes are produced and directed by DeMille).

DECEMBER 7, 1913 *In the Land of the Head-Hunters* **Released.** *In the Land of the Head-Hunters,* a silent feature film about life among the Northwest Coast Kwakiutl Indians, opens in New York. Written and produced by pioneer photographer and filmmaker Edward S. Curtis, *In the Land of the Head-Hunters* draws upon Native customs and a dramatic storyline of love and revenge to recreate Kwakiutl lifestyle. A reedited 1973 version of the same film, *In the Land of the War Canoes,* includes additional tribal songs and instrumental music.

1 9 1 4

1914   Allan Houser, Chiricahua Apache Artist, Is Born. Chiricahua Apache artist Allan Houser is recognized as being the outstanding twentieth-century American Indian sculptor. A grand-nephew of Geronimo, Houser's parents were taken to Fort Sill, Oklahoma, with the other Apache resisters. Houser is born in Apache Oklahoma, and there he attends school only sporadically, staying home much of the time on his family's farm. Houser begins painting in the traditional style around 1924, but he soon becomes more interested in sculpture as a medium. Like many American Indian artists, Houser studies with Dorothy Dunn at the Studio in Santa Fe. With the opening of the Institute of the American Indian Arts in 1962, Houser begins teaching sculpture and painting there, a position he keeps until his retirement in 1975. Among his numerous honors are a Guggenheim Fellowship (1949) and the Palmes d'Académiques from the French government in 1954. Houser's son, Bob Haozous, is a reputable sculptor in his own right.

1914–1918   World War I. Up to 4,000 Indians, approximately 35 percent of those eligible, fight for Canada in World War I. As noncitizens, Indians are not eligible for the draft. Neither do they qualify for all the veterans' benefits that non-Natives do.

1 9 1 5

1915   Indian Man Refused Right to Register to Vote. Ethan Anderson, an Indian, attempts to register to vote with the Lake County clerk and is refused. This case becomes a test case for the California Supreme Court and eventually leads to the granting of citizenship rights to all nonreservation Indians in California.

1915   Land Authorized for Landless Indians. Congress passes the first appropriation act authorizing the Indian Office to buy land for landless Indians in the state of California.

FEBRUARY 1915   Allied Tribes of British Columbia. Opposition to the conduct of the McKenna-McBride Commission spurs Rev. Peter Kelly *(See* biography, April 21, 1885) and Andrew Paull *(See* biography, February 6, 1892) to organize the Allied Tribes of British Columbia. It appeals to the federal government for help in settling land claims in British Columbia. The McKenna-McBride Commission travels through the province to determine the size of each Indian reserve. British Columbia Indians are the first in Canada to establish political organizations to represent them.

AUGUST 3, 1915   Frank Arthur Calder, Nisga'a Political Leader, Is Born. Born at Nass Harbour in northwestern British Columbia, Calder is adopted, according to Nisga'a customs by a prominent Nisga'a family, and trained from childhood to assume a leadership role among his people. He is sent to a residential school in Chilliwack in southern British Columbia. During the 1940s he is involved in the North American Indian Brotherhood and the Native Brotherhood of British Columbia, rival attempts to unite British Columbia Indians in one organization. After graduating from the Anglican Theological College at the University of British Columbia in 1946, he becomes involved in provincial politics. In 1949 he is elected as a representative of the Co-operative Commonwealth Federation (C.C.F.) (later reorganized as the New Democratic Party—N.D.P.) in the province's legislature, thus becoming the first Indian legislator in Canada. He serves as a member of the legislative assembly of British Columbia until 1979 (both with the C.C.F.-N.D.P. and with the Social Credit Party), briefly serving in the cabinet from September 1972 to July 1973.

In the meantime, Calder's activities in Indian organizations continue. In 1955 he founds and becomes the first president of the Nishga Tribal Council (Nisga'a Nation). The

The Quaker City banquet of the Society of American Indians, Hotel Walton, February 14, 1914. Courtesy of the National Archives.

organization becomes the model for other tribal councils in British Columbia. While Calder's belief that the reserve system has been a hindrance to Indians and his endorsement of aspects of the 1969 White Paper put him at odds with many other Native leaders in British Columbia, his work earns the respect of many of them.

A 1973 Supreme Court of Canada decision on a land claims case brought forward by Frank Calder and the Nishga Tribal Council

(the *Calder v. Attorney General* case) becomes the most important of its kind in Canadian history. (*See* entry, January 31, 1973.) Although the claimants lose the case, the decision is instrumental in leading the Canadian government to change its land claims policy and begin negotiating land claims. Since then, Native groups from across Canada have taken advantage of this new policy, although ironically British Columbia land claims remain unsettled.

In 1988 Calder becomes an Officer of

A remarkably high number of Indians enlisted for service in World War I and World War II despite their status as noncitizens. Here young men from File Hills Indian Colony in southern Saskatchewan pose with their fathers before leaving for duty. Courtesy of the National Archives of Canada.

the Order of Canada (an honor accorded no more than 46 people per year). In 1989 he earns a degree of Doctor of Divinity.

1 9 1 6

1916   Copper Inuit Trade. With the establishment of trading posts on Coronation Gulf in Canada's Arctic, the Copper Inuit on Victoria Island and the nearby mainland become the last

aboriginal group in North America to establish regular contact with non-Natives. Fur trading companies begin establishing trading posts along the Arctic coast in 1911 shortly after the whaling industry collapses.

1916   McKenna-McBride Report. The final report of a Royal Commission on Indian Affairs in British Columbia (the McKenna-McBride Commission) recommends adding land to some reserves in British Columbia and

Chief Raven, a Skidgate-Haida. c. 1915. His family emblem is carved at the center of his headgear, while ermine, feathers, and sea lion whiskers adorn the rest. Courtesy of the Rare Books & Manuscripts Division of the New York Public Library—Astor, Lenox, and Tilden Foundations.

cutting off land (of considerably greater value) from others. The commission is established in September 1912 to determine the appropriate size for each reserve. Most of the reserves in the province have been allotted between 1880 and 1910. Peter Kelly (*See* biography, April 21, 1885) and Andrew Paull (*See* biography, February 6, 1892) of the Allied Tribes of British Columbia voice the British Columbia Indians' denunciation of the report.

1916 *Myths and Legends of the Sioux* **Published.** This collection by Marie McLaughlin is the beginning of a literary tradition where the work stems directly from, or is loosely based upon, the author's own tribal culture.

1916 *United States v. Nice. United States v. Nice* illustrates the extent to which federal management of Indians' daily lives has become institutionalized, and, to a growing extent, inescapable. Overruling its own 1905 decision in the case of *In re Heff,* the Supreme Court holds that becoming a citizen—for example, by obtaining

an individual allotment of land under the 1887 General Allotment Act—does not necessarily exempt an Indian from the supervisory control of the Office of Indian Affairs. Citizenship and guardianship are not necessarily incompatible, the Court reasons, and it is for Congress to decide when, if ever, Indians will be fully emancipated. Interestingly, Nice involves special federal laws making it illegal for Indians to drink liquor. Prohibition will soon extend this social experiment, unsuccessfully, to the rest of the population.

MAY 5, 1916 Last Fight of the Indian Scouts. The U.S. Army Indian Scouts fight their last fight at the Ojos Azules Ranch, approximately 300 miles below the Mexican borderline. An Apache Scout detachment is part of the Eleventh Cavalry, which fights an indecisive battle against elements of the Mexican rebel Pancho Villa's forces. Although the main body of the Villa force escape, they leave behind 44 dead and many more wounded. There are no American casualties.

MAY 13, 1916 Indian Day Set Aside. Sponsored by the Society of American Indians, May 13 is set aside as Indian Day. The purpose of this day is to recognize and honor the American Indian and to improve the conditions of Indian people.

SUMMER 1916 Reserve Relocation. The Peguis Saulteaux band on the St. Peter's Reserve near Winnipeg are relocated a hundred kilometers north to the shores of Lake Winnipeg.

c. 1916–1920s Pueblo Artists Take Up Watercolor Painting. With the encouragement of the local Santa Fe intelligentsia, including author Mary Austin and artist John Sloan, a small group of young Pueblo artists, most of them from San Ildefonso, take up watercolor painting, marking the beginning of Indian easel painting. Principal among this group are Julian Martinez, Abel Sanchez, Romando Vigil, Fred Kabotie, and the man often called the father of contemporary American Indian painting, Crescencio Martinez.

1 9 1 7

1917   Declaration of Policy Statement Issued.
The "Declaration of Policy statement" is issued by Interior Department Secretary Franklin Land and Office of Indian Affairs Commissioner Cato Sells and states that "The time has come for discontinuing guardianship over all competent Indians and giving even closer attention to the incompetents that they more speedily achieve competency." Commissioner Sells applauds the new policy as an indication that the "competent Indian will no longer be treated as half ward and half citizen."

1917   Indian Births Exceed Deaths. Reversing an Indian demographic trend of over 50 years, for the first time in that period births exceed deaths.

1917   Indian Education. Congress abolishes the practice of payment of subsidies to religious groups for the education of Indian children.

1917   Reservation Coal Lands. Congress opens reservation coal lands to homesteading, with coal royalties reserved for the United States.

1917   World War I. The United States enters World War I. Despite not being subject to the draft law, more than 8,000 Indians serve in the war. Indian contributions to the war effort become an important factor in Congress's decision to pass the Indian Citizenship Act of 1924.

JUNE 14, 1917   Five Civilized Tribe Heirship Act. Congress passes the Five Civilized Tribe Heirship Act, an act authorizing jurisdiction of the Probate Court of the state of Oklahoma to settle the estates of deceased members of the Five Civilized Tribes and to partition lands

John Wilson, of mixed Delaware, Caddo, and French descent, was responsible for creating many of the current peyote doctrines and for helping spread the religion among the Plains Indians around the turn of the century. Photo by G.W. Parsons. Courtesy of the National Museum of the American Indian, Smithsonian Institution.

belonging to the full-blood heirs of deceased allottees of the Five Civilized Tribes.

1 9 1 8

1918   *Autobiography of a Fox-Woman.* A publication by Truman Michelson, this work is an ethnographic autobiography. Characteristic of early American Indian literary forms, this "as told to" narrative focuses upon a life story. Produced by salvage anthropologists keen on preserving traditional beliefs and customs, such writers sought isolated or culturally uncontaminated Indians, perceiving them to be the "true" Indian. This mode of thinking, while securing important tribal information, also unintentionally contributes to the antiquated history-less Indian stereotype.

1918   Dr. Carlos Montezuma Returns to Arizona. Dr. Carlos Montezuma, the Yavapai editor of the *Wassaja*, returns to Arizona, fighting not only for the destruction of the Office of Indian Affairs but also for the preservation of traditional Native identity and values. Dr. Montezuma also helps to organize the Pima and other tribes to resist government programs.

1918 Establishment of the Native American Church. In Mexico the use of the peyote cactus (Lophophora Williamsii) by American Indians predates the arrival of Europeans. Exactly how quickly it traveled north is unknown, but it does seem clear that the Lipan Apache probably obtained it from the Carrizo Indians of northeastern Mexico, later passing it on to the Mescalero Apache. By the 1880s use of peyote reaches Indian Territory, spreading quickly across the Plains tribes and reservation communities. As assimilation and Christianization become the dominant goals of both government and church during the late nineteenth century, Indian policy reformers, missionaries, and Indian Service personnel all attack the ritual use of peyote. Indian people, among them the great Comanche chief Quanah Parker, argue that peyote is an integral part of their religious experiences, but they are denied the right to worship with peyote because they do not have a church organization. Consequently, the Native American Church is organized and incorporated in Oklahoma in October 1918 by members of many Indian nations, including Kiowa, Comanche, Apache, Cheyenne, Ponca, and Oto.

1918 Pablita Velarde, Tewa Painter, Is Born. Pablita Velarde is a Tewa painter from Santa Clara Pueblo whose work, in a variety of mediums and styles, draws on ceremonial and mythic scenes of her culture. She begins attending the Santa Fe Indian school in 1932, where she is one of many students encouraged by art teacher Dorothy Dunn. In 1933 she is selected to work on a number of murals commissioned for the Chicago World's Fair. This leads to a number of other Work Project Administration art commissions. In 1936 she graduates from Santa Fe and begins teaching arts and crafts at the Santa Clara Day School. Velarde marries Herbert Hardin in 1942 and one year later, she gives birth to a daughter, Helen Hardin, who will later become a very important artist in her own right. Velarde's first major prize comes at the Philbrook Art Center's Annual Indian Show in 1948, and she is awarded the Palmes Academiques by the French government in 1954. The following year she wins several top honors at the Gallup Inter-tribal Ceremonial, including the Grand Prize for her painting "Old Father, the Storyteller." Later she collaborates with her father in writing and illustrating a book of Tewa legends, also called *Old Father, the Storyteller.* Since the 1960s Pablita Velarde has won numerous honors, including the New Mexico Governor's Award and an Honor Award from the National Women's Caucus for Art.

1918 *The Path on the Rainbow* **Is Published.** George Cronyn's *The Path on the Rainbow: An Anthology of Songs and Chants from the Indians of North America* is published. With an introduction by American Imagist writer Mary Austin, it is the first anthology of translations of Indian songs and poetry.

1 9 1 9

1919 California Indian Lands. Malcolm McDowell, appointed by the Board of Indian Commissioners to investigate California Indian affairs, reports that the legitimate methods used in other states to acquire Indian land titles legally has not been used by California officials.

1919 Indian Education. Congressional inquiry into the progress of Navajo education reveals that of an estimated 9,613 children of school age, only 2,089 are actually attending school. When the facts become known the following year, the secretary of the interior is ordered to "make and enforce such rules and regulations as may be necessary to secure the enrollment and regular attendance of eligible Indian children."

Later, investigators find that for years afterward, less than one-half of the school-age children are enrolled at any time. The celebrated Meriam Report of 1928 documents the deplorable condition of Indian education.

1919 League of Indians of Canada. Led by Iroquois Frederick O. Loft, the League of Indians of Canada becomes the first attempt to organize Canadian Indians nationally. Government resistance to the organization contributes to its eventual collapse.

1919 Society of Northern California Indians Formed. The Indians of Mendocino, Lake, and Sonoma counties in California form the Society of northern California Indians to seek justice, to publish a history of their people, and to obtain better schools for California Indian students. In 1922, the Mission Indian Federation is formed in southern California for similar purposes.

1919 U.S. Citizenship for Indian Veterans of World War I Act. Congress passes the U.S. Citizenship for Indian Veterans of World War I Act, granting U.S. citizenship to every American Indian who served in the armed services during World War I, including those honorably discharged. If desired, the discharged veteran could, by court of "competent" jurisdiction, be granted full property rights, individual or tribal.

1919–1920 British Columbia Reserves "Cut Off." Following recommendations of a Royal Commission on Indian Affairs in British Columbia (the McKenna-McBride Commission), the British Columbia government begins adjusting the size of reserves.

1 9 2 0

1920 Allotment of Indian Lands. The federal government begins curtailing allotment of Indian lands.

1920 Canadian Native Compulsory Enfranchisement. The Canadian federal government amends the Indian Act to allow for compulsory enfranchisement of Indians. Only 250 Indians are enfranchised between 1857 and 1920. Compulsory enfranchisement is in effect from 1920–22 and 1933–51. Mandatory school attendance also is made part of the Indian Act.

JANUARY 12, 1920 William Ronald "Bill" Reid, Haida Sculptor, Is Born. Born to a Haida mother in Vancouver, British Columbia, Reid grows up learning little about his aboriginal heritage. He works as a broadcaster for the Canadian Broadcasting Corporation in Vancouver (1945–48) and Toronto (1948–51). Only in the 1950s, after studying jewelry and engraving in Toronto, does Reid begin exploring Haida art and sculpture in depth. He learns his craft from Charles Gladstone, his maternal grandfather, and from prominent Haida artist, and Reid's relative, Charles Edenshaw. He also studies at the Central School of Art and Design in London, England. He quickly becomes recognized as an expert on Haida art, and an accomplished artist in his own right. One of his most famous sculptures is the four-and-a-half-ton yellow cedar *Raven and the First Men* (1980) on display at the University of British Columbia's Museum of Anthropology. Other noteworthy works include a bronze killer whale sculpture entitled *Chief of the Undersea World* (1984) displayed at the Vancouver Aquarium. In 1992, following five years of work, *The Spirit of Haida Gwaii*, a massive bronze sculpture depicting a canoe full of characters from Haida mythology, is installed in Canada's embassy in Washington, D.C. Reid also has been active in efforts to preserve the South Morseby Island, located in the Queen Charlotte Islands—the home of his Haida kin.

FEBRUARY 17, 1920 George Manuel, Shuswap Politician, Is Born. Born in the village of Neskainlith about 30 miles east of Kamloops, British Columbia, Manuel is raised more by his grandparents than his parents. He attends a residential school in Kamloops but when he becomes ill with tuberculosis, he is transferred to a hospital in Coqualeetza in the Lower Fraser Valley. His formal schooling ends with his illness, but he acquires enough literary skill to support his political efforts in later life.

After becoming chief of his people in the late 1940s he begins to organize the Interior Salish, launching in 1958 the Aboriginal Native Rights Committee of the Interior Tribes of British Columbia (reorganized as the North American Indian Brotherhood in 1960). Manuel, however, is best known for his term as president of the National Indian Brotherhood (N.I.B.) beginning in 1970. Under Manuel's leadership the N.I.B. becomes much more politically active, asserting its position regarding Indian rights before the government and forging links with indigenous peoples internationally. Early in Manuel's tenure, the Canadian government extends core funding to the N.I.B., allowing it to significantly increase its activities.

Manuel is devoted to international political action and is instrumental in organizing the World Council of Indigenous Peoples. His book written with M. Posluns, *The Fourth World: An Indian Reality* (1974), depicts indigenous peoples as a "Fourth World" of internal colonies dominated by nonindigenous governments. Manuel dies in November 1989.

c. 1920s The Kiowa Five. The American Indian plains painting tradition crystallizes with the "Kiowa Five," a group of painters from Oklahoma. The group, which includes Spencer Asah, James Auchiah, Jack Hokeah, Stephen Mopope, and Monroe Tsatoke, originates between 1917 and 1926 when an Indian Service employee named Susan Peters organizes an arts club for young Kiowa students near Anadarko, Oklahoma. After 1926, many of these Kiowa are enrolled in special courses at the University of Oklahoma, where they are exposed to the art deco aesthetic and other modern approaches to art. These are fused with traditional forms such as hide painting and ledger book drawings to

Hopi woman making pottery in Oraibi village using a coiling technique. Courtesy of the Field Museum of Natural History, Chicago.

form the distinctive Oklahoma style of painting. The Oklahoma style of the Kiowa Five, and others later, influences developments in the Southwest, where the Santa Fe Studio style develops in the 1930s.

1920–1930 Inuit Prosperity. Inuit in northern Canada increasingly take up trapping to supplement their subsistence activities because of the high prices being offered for arctic fox furs. The Hudson's Bay Company and other fur trade companies, including the Révillon Fréres, open trading posts throughout Inuit territories to acquire the furs. The competition for the white fox furs, which peaks in 1930, allows Inuit hunters to enjoy remarkable prosperity. Both the Hudson's Bay Company and missionaries act as important providers of health care and emergency assistance, a role that becomes much more important during the 1930s after the price of furs drops, and starvation and disease become serious problems.

1 9 2 1

1921 Indian All-American. John Levi, star athlete and student at Haskell Institute, becomes one of the first Indians to be named to the All-American football team.

1921 *Waheenee: An Indian Girl's Story* Is Published. *Waheenee: An Indian Girl's Story* is an "as told to" narrative recorded by Gilbert Wilson about the life of a Hidatsa, Waheenee, or Buffalo Bird Woman.

JUNE 27, 1921 Treaty 11. The Slave, Dogrib, Kutchin, and Hare, all Athapascan hunters of western Northwest Territories, begin signing Treaty 11, covering land north and west of Great Slave Lake. The Canadian government has been seeking the treaty since oil is discovered at Norman Wells, along the Mackenzie River in the Northwest Territories in 1920. Métis claimants are given $240 cash in place of land. *(See* map of Indian Treaty Areas in Canada, p. 394.)

NOVEMBER 2, 1921 Snyder Act. Congress passes the Snyder Act, which allows the expenditure of funds for Indians without regard to amount of Indian blood, membership in a federally recognized tribe, or residence (as long as it is in the United States). Funds are designated for support and civilization, including education; to improve health; to promote industrial development, building of irrigation sys-

tems; for general administration of Indian property, and to employ professionals to help Indians.

DECEMBER 1921 Potlatch Celebrants Arrested. Forty-five Kwagiulth are arrested for holding a potlatch. Ceremonial masks and other artifacts seized by police are sent to the Victoria Memorial Museum in Ottawa. This conviction marks the beginning of enforcement of an antipotlatch law passed in 1884. The law is repealed in 1951.

1 9 2 2

1922 Federation of Mission Indians Founded. The Federation of Mission Indians is organized in southern California. Because of alleged "hostility to the government," 57 of its members are arrested by the Department of Justice on conspiracy charges at the instigation of the Office of Indian Affairs.

1922 Gallup Inter-Tribal Indian Ceremonial. The annual Gallup Inter-Tribal Indian Ceremonial opens for the first time in New Mexico on the second Thursday in August. Lasting for four days, the Inter-Tribal is attended by both Indians and non-Indians from all over the United States. In 1970, the ceremonial is moved to a new location to make way for interstate traffic.

1922 Indian Welfare League Founded. California Indian delegates visit Washington in the hope of modifying the policies of the Office of Indian Affairs and the Department of the Interior. Other California citizens organize the Indian Welfare League to assist Indians in pursuing claims, finally persuading the Board of Indian Commissioners to investigate their reports.

1922 Iroquois Resist Non-Indian Government. Resisting a new non-Indian-imposed style of government, Iroquois from Ontario ask British Colonial Secretary Winston Churchill for help and appeal to the League of Nations at Geneva. The Iroquois delegates travel to Geneva on passports issued by the Six Nations.

1922 Will Rogers's Column Syndicated. Already a veteran of Ziegfield Follies and other vaudeville productions, mixed-blood Cherokee humorist Will Rogers begins syndicating a weekly column. Later he starts writing somewhat shorter "daily telegrams," now-famous snippets and reflections that are still syndicated over 50 years after his death. His popularity grows through the mid-1930s, and collections of his anecdotal wisdom regularly become bestsellers. The most popular humorist of his age, Rogers also stars in at least 15 motion pictures before his death in a plane crash near Point Barrow, Alaska, on August 15, 1935.

NOVEMBER 1922 Bursum Bill Controversy. For the first time since they drove the Spanish out of New Mexico in 1680, all of the Rio Grande Pueblos meet and join forces to resist the proposed Bursum bill, which seeks to legislate rights for U.S. squatters on Pueblo lands. If passed, the Bursum bill will award all non-Pueblo claims of title dating to 10 years prior to 1912, the year New Mexico becomes a state. The act also proposes that jurisdiction over Indian water rights and contested lands be given to hostile state courts. If passed, the Bursum bill will strip the Pueblos of as much as 60,000 acres. At Sante Domingo Pueblo, 123 leaders from 19 Pueblos meet and choose 17 leaders to represent their cause. Ethnologists, writers, the powerful General Federation of Women's Clubs, the artist communities at Taos and Santa Fe, and the *New Mexican*, an influential southwestern newspaper, all come to the Indians' defense. Widespread public support defeats the Bursum bill, and in 1924 the Pueblo Lands Board is created to safeguard Indian rights and establish an equitable method for ascertaining land ownership in areas in dispute. Bursum bill protests contribute significantly to the growing public interest in Indian affairs,

which in the next decade will facilitate a reevaluation of federal Indian policy.

1922–1929 Indian Religions Suppressed. The Office of Indian Affairs begins intensive efforts to suppress all Indian ceremonies on reservations.

---

1 9 2 3

1923 Arizona Printers, Inc., Organized. Victor Manuel (Pima), a printer, organizes Arizona Printers, Inc., a thriving publishing house in the southwestern United States.

1923 Committee of One Hundred Appointed. Reformers begin pressing the government to improve Indian living conditions, and in 1923 Secretary of the Interior Hubert Work appoints the Committee of One Hundred to survey American Indian policies and to make recommendations. The committee recommends increasing funds for health care, public education, scholarships, claims courts, and a scientific investigation into the effects of peyote usage.

1923 Formation of the Navajo Tribal Council. After the Navajo return from Fort Sumner in 1868, they are governed by a head chief, who is appointed by their government agent. When oil is discovered on Navajo lands in 1921, and various companies begin negotiating with the Navajo for oil and gas development leases, Commissioner of Indian Affairs Charles H. Burke issues a number of regulations, one of which calls for the creation of a tribal council of 12 delegates, 2 from each of the 6 Navajo jurisdictions. The first meeting takes place on July 7, 1923, in Toadlena, New Mexico, and Chee Dodge is elected the first chairman. The new tribal council is merely an arm of the Department of the Interior, and intended for little more than consultation.

1923 Indian Education. A survey conducted by the U.S. Commissioner of Education reveals that "only 14 percent of the Indian children in Oklahoma (are) enrolled in the public school system of that state."

1923　Indian Education. The Territory of Alaska tries unsuccessfully to enact a law prohibiting enrollment of Indian children in the Alaska public school system.

1923　Ira Hamilton Hayes, Pima World War II Hero, Is Born. A full-blooded member of the Pima tribe, Ira Hayes is probably the most famous Indian soldier of World War II. Hayes is born in Sacaton, Arizona, and joins the marines in 1942. He sees action throughout the Pacific as a paratrooper. In 1945, Hayes lands as part of the Fifth Marine Division assault troops on Iwo Jima. There he takes part in a forward attack on Mount Suribachi, and is one of six marines who raises the United States flag on the summit of the volcanic peak in the midst of heavy enemy fire. An Associated Press photographer captures the moment on film, and it becomes one of the most inspiring war photographs ever taken. The famous bronze monument in Washington, D.C., commemorating the battle of Iwo Jima, is based on this image.

1923　Land Purchase Act. Congress passes the Land Purchase Act, amending the General Land Allotment Act of 1887 to include allotment of lands purchased for Indians.

1923　Williams Treaties. Several disputed preconfederation treaties in southern Ontario are resolved with new treaties (Williams Treaties), several decades after the government acknowledges that, because of missing papers, unclear agreements, or misunderstandings, the Indians have legitimate claims. These claims cover some of the most valuable real estate in Canada. (See map of Indian Treaty Areas in Canada, p. 394.)

MAY 1923　American Indian Defense Association. In response to the Bursum bill threat, the American Indian Defense Association

(AIDA) is formed by John Collier, who later becomes Commissioner of Indian Affairs and the principal architect behind Franklin Roosevelt's Indian New Deal. The AIDA is distinctive among other "Friends of the Indian" groups, favoring an end to land allotment and calling for Indian cultural and religious freedom. The AIDA also seeks federal protection of Indian property and water rights, recognition of tribal claims, and the improvement of Indian health standards and medical and educational services. Supported by philanthropic contributions, the AIDA establishes branches in Albuquerque, Los Angeles, Milwaukee, Minneapolis, Oshkosh (Wisconsin), Pasadena, Portland, Salt Lake City, San Francisco, Santa Barbara (California), and Washington, D.C. In 1925 the AIDA begins publishing a newsletter, *American Indian Life*. By 1932, the AIDA has 1,700 members, but the election of Franklin Roosevelt and subsequent appointment of Collier as commissioner of Indian affairs begin the organization's decline. Most of the AIDA's financial backers withdraw support after the passage of the Indian reorganization act in 1934, considering the need for Indian reform to be satisfied. In 1937, the American Indian Defense Association merges with the National Association on Indian Affairs, and the two become known as the Association on American Indian Affairs (AAIA).

---

1 9 2 4

1924　Six Nations Pageant. The Six Nations pageant is started by Emily General to keep alive Iroquois history and philosophy and to preserve cultural and religious practices.

FEBRUARY 1, 1924　Inuit Executions. Two Copper Inuit, Alikomiak and Tatimagana, are executed on Herschel Island in the northern Yukon Territory after being convicted of the murder of several Inuit and non-Natives. The arrests and executions symbolize the intention of the Canadian government to begin enforcing Canadian law in the Arctic.

MAY 29, 1924 Indian Oil Leasing Act. Congress passes the Indian Oil Leasing Act. The act amends the Oil Leasing Act of 1891 by extending the leasing period of unallotted Indian lands involving oil and gas—other than those of the Five Civilized Tribes and the Osage Nation—until such quantities are exhausted.

JUNE 2, 1924 Indians Given Citizenship. Because of the services Indian soldiers performed during the World War I and lobbying by the Alaska Native Brotherhood, Congress grants all Indians the rights of U.S. citizenship. The General Citizenship Act makes American Indians citizens of the United States if they have not already attained that status. In theory, this removes the category of ward, but does not affect the control of the Office of Indian Affairs over the reservations. The act also allows Indians to vote in federal elections, but some states, such as New Mexico, prohibit Indians from voting in state elections. The new act is viewed with considerable skepticism by Indian groups, who fear that future land acquisitions might be the motivation.

JUNE 7, 1924 Public Schools Tuition Act. Congress passes the Public School Tuition Act, which calls for the secretary of interior to pay tuition for Indian students in public schools for the fiscal years 1922 and 1923, with remaining funds to go to Indian day and industrial schools.

JUNE 7, 1924 Pueblo Lands Act. Congress passes the Pueblo Lands Act, which establishes a "Pueblo Lands Board" to investigate Pueblo land titles and provides the means by which a solution can be made regarding the many non-Indian claims to the lands of the Pueblo Indians.

SEPTEMBER 17, 1924 Elected Band Council Imposed. The Canadian federal government passes an Order in Council imposing an elected council on the Six Nations Reserve in southern Ontario. The existing hereditary council refuses to disband. A number of World War I veterans from the reserve lead the campaign to form an elected band council. In the election held October 14, however, only about 20 percent of eligible voters turn out to cast ballots. Resistance to the imposition of an elected band council has been led by Cayuga Hereditary Chief Deskahe (Levi General) (1873–1925). In 1923, Deskahe, an adherent of the Longhouse religion, travels to the League of Nations in Geneva in an attempt to get the League to recognize the Six Nations as a sovereign nation.

1 9 2 5

1925 Forrest J. Gerard, Blackfeet Government Administrator and Assistant Secretary of the Interior, Is Born. Forrest Gerard is born in Browning, Montana, and graduates from Montana State University and the National Tuberculosis Association Training Institute. He serves as executive secretary of the Wyoming Tuberculosis and Health Association and as a staff member of the Montana Tuberculosis Association. In 1965, Gerard is awarded a fellowship in congressional operations, which allows him a year of intensive study in Washington focusing on the organization of Congress and the legislative process. In 1966 he is appointed legislative liaison officer for the Bureau of Indian Affairs (BIA) and during the late 1970s, he is named assistant secretary of the interior for Indian affairs. His administration is deeply concerned with the task of implementing the Self-Determination and Educational Assistance Act of 1975.

FEBRUARY 13 OR 14, 1925 Gerald Tailfeathers, Kainai (Blood) Artist, Is Born. Gerald Tailfeathers is born in 1925 on the Kainai (Blood) Reserve at Stand Off, Alberta. He develops his artistic talents while young, and holds his first exhibition before he turns 20. Educated at the Banff School of Fine Arts and at the Provincial School of Technology and Art in Calgary, Tailfeathers's career begins to flourish soon after. He is among the earliest Indians to work as a full-time artist in Canada.

Tailfeathers's painting style is pictorial and nostalgic. Many of his paintings depict members of the Blackfoot Confederacy in typical aspects of their nineteenth-century life, hunting buffalo, setting up camp, and celebrating certain rituals.

OCTOBER 15, 1925 *The Vanishing American* **Premieres.** *The Vanishing American,* a Paramount picture directed by George B. Seitz, premieres in New York City. The story of corruption and mismanagement on a modern-day reservation is based upon the popular Zane Grey serial in *Ladies Home Journal.* The film's indictment against current federal policies fuels an already heated debate between social reformers and government agents over the Indians' plight in America.

1 9 2 6

1926   Alaska Industrial School Founded. The government boarding school for Indians at White Mountain, Alaska, is renamed "Industrial School." This is the inception of a policy and program of industrial training for boarding school students.

1926   California Indian Land Claims. The Commonwealth Club of San Francisco, an elite California men's service organization, issues a research report on Indian affairs in California recommending that federal legislation be promoted immediately for a fair determination of Indian land claims in the state. The report receives considerable publicity.

1926   *Crashing Thunder: Autobiography of a Winnebago Indian.* Originally published in 1920 as part of the University of California Publications in American Archaeology and Ethnology, this life story of Winnebago Sam Blowsnake is expanded and revised in 1926 in order to

reach a wider audience. Blowsnake wrote his autobiography in a syllabary that anthropologist-editor Paul Radin then translated into English with the help of interpreter Oliver Lamere. Blowsnake's confessional narrative is important for its description of his practice and belief in both the traditional Winnebago religion and the Peyote cult, to which he is a recent convert at the time of his collaboration with Radin. Blowsnake's sister, Mountain Wolf Woman, is also an important autobiographer, and her self-titled life story, written in collaboration with anthropologist Nancy Ostreich Lurie, is published in 1961.

1926   Indian Defense League Organized. Clinton Rickard, a Tuscarora chief, and David Hill, a Mohawk from Six Nations Reserve in Canada organize the Indian Defense League; its principal purpose being to provide a defense for Indians who are too poor to pay for counsel. The league's first victory is securing the right of free travel between the U.S. and Canada for Iroquois people.

1926   Indian Named to U.S. Olympic Team. Philip Osif is named to the U.S. Olympic Games Team. Osif attended Haskell Institute and was also the U.S. National Six-Mile Track champion.

1926   Moravians Relinquish Trade. The Moravians give up their role as fur traders in Labrador but continue to provide religious, educational, and health care services to the Labrador Inuit.

1926   National Council of American Indians (NCAI). Zitkala-Sa, also known as Gertrude Bonnin, forms the pan-Indian NCAI after the Society of American Indians dissipates. She presides over the organization until her death in 1938.

1926   Taos Council Imprisoned. Commissioner of Indian Affairs Burke visits Taos Pueblo and throws the entire pueblo council into prison for violating the Indian administration's "religious crimes code."

1926 *Wild Harvest* **Published.** John Oskison, a one-eighth Cherokee born in Indian Territory, publishes the first of his novels, *Wild Harvest*. A Stanford graduate who pursues graduate study in literature at Harvard, Oskison later publishes *Black Jack Davy* (1926), *The Story of Sam Houston* (1929), and *Brothers Three* (1935), which is generally considered his best work. Oskison is the most prolific Indian writer of the 1920s and, although he does not focus on Indian life and identity to the extent that some of his contemporaries do, much of his work, particularly *Brothers Three*, contains characters who are all or part American Indian.

APRIL 13, 1926   Indian Insurance Act. Congress passes the Indian Insurance Act, stating that funds of Indian tribes under U.S. control are to be used to make insurance premium payments for protection of those tribes against fire, theft, tornado, hail, earthquakes, and other forces of nature.

APRIL 17, 1926   Land Lease Act. Congress passes the Land Lease Act calling for the secretary of interior to open Indian lands for leases for mining purposes.

JUNE 3, 1926   Northern Cheyenne Allotment Act. Congress passes the Northern Cheyenne Allotment Act to allot, in severalty, lands of the Northern Cheyenne Reservation in Montana.

---

1 9 2 7

1927 *Co-ge-we-a, the Half Blood* **Is Published.** In collaboration with Lucas McWhorter, Okanogan writer Mourning Dove (Humishuma) publishes *Co-ge-we-a, the Half-Blood*, a novel which focuses on the difficulties of being a mixed-blood Indian woman. It is the first fictional work to outline the clash of Indian and U.S. cultures as embodied within the character

of a mixed breed; eventually, such works form a genre within the American Indian literary canon. Incredibly, Mourning Dove, who completes school only through the third grade, pens the book while she is as a migrant worker, writing after spending her days in the field. Following the publication of *Co-ge-we-a*, Mourning Dove turns her attention to collecting the stories and legends of her Okanogan people. These are subsequently published in *Coyote Stories*, edited by Heister Dean Guie (1933).

MARCH 3, 1927   Indian Oil Leasing Act. Congress passes the Indian Oil Leasing Act recognizing Indian title to executive order Indian lands and Indian rights to the proceeds from mineral leases. The act calls for tribal consultation before expenditure of funds gained from mineral leases on Indian tribal land.

MARCH 31, 1927   Land Claims Outlawed. An amendment to the Canadian Indian Act makes it illegal to raise funds or donate funds for the prosecution of any Indian land claims. The law remains in force until 1951.

APRIL 9, 1927   British Columbia Land Claims. A Parliamentary Committee decides that British Columbia Indians "have not established any claim to the lands of British Columbia based on aboriginal or other title." In place of treaty money, the Indians will get $100,000 annually. The Allied Tribes of British Columbia, which had made submissions to the committee, collapses soon after the ruling.

OCTOBER 3, 1927   Kenojuak Ashevak, Inuk Artist, Is Born. Kenojuak is born at Ikerrasak, Baffin Island, in the Northwest Territories. When the West Baffin Island Eskimo Cooperative opens in 1959, Kenojuak is the first woman involved in the printmaking shop. Kenojuak begins making drawings and prints, primarily of birds and human beings intertwined with figures and fantasies. Her strong, colorful, richly composed and designed drawings and prints are much sought after, and Kenojuak quickly emerges as the foremost Inuk artist in Canada.

Although primarily known for her drawings and paintings, Kenojuak also carves and sculpts soapstone and other material. A mural she produces for the World's Fair in Osaka, Japan, in 1970 earns her acclaim. She travels widely throughout Canada and Europe. She is also the subject of a 1962 National Film Board film and a 1981 limited edition book. In 1967 she becomes the first Native to be awarded the Companion of the Order of Canada, Canada's highest honor. In 1986 the McMichael Canadian Collection Gallery in Kleinburg, Ontario, just outside Toronto, shows a 30-year retrospective of her art.

1 9 2 8

1928   Autobiography of Luther Standing Bear Published. The first of several autobiographical works by Luther Standing Bear, an Oglala Lakota, *My People the Sioux*, tells Standing Bear's life story with emphasis on comparative treatments of Lakota and early twentieth-century American cultures. Of particular interest is Standing Bear's account of his years at the Carlisle boarding school, beginning with his enrollment in the inaugural class there. Although his education in the American school system makes him cynical toward certain Lakota traditions, Standing Bear is also quite critical of federal Indian policy and the government's treatment of Indians. These criticisms become somewhat more pronounced in his second work, *Land of the Spotted Eagle* (1933), which also provides more detailed explication of Standing Bear's culture and people.

1928   California Indian Land Claims. Congress authorizes Indian land claim suits for the California Indians, specifying that the claims will be limited to Indian groups that signed treaties in 1851 and 1852. This is the first government recognition of the validity of California Indian claims.

1928   Charles Curtis Elected Vice President. Charles Curtis of Kansas, a Kaw Indian and a U.S. Senator for 25 years, is elected vice president of the United States to serve with President Herbert Hoover (1929–33).

1928   Influenza Epidemic in Canada. A particularly serious influenza epidemic in northern Canada kills 600 Dene. The high incidence of disease among Native Canadians keeps their population growth near zero.

1928   The Meriam Report Is Published. Supported by a grant from John D. Rockefeller, Jr., the Brookings Institute hires Lewis Meriam and nine other scholars to investigate the status of Indian economies, health, and education, and the federal government's administration of Indian affairs. Meriam and his committee publish a significant volume, *The Problem of Indian Administration*, commonly known as the Meriam Report. The study describes the conditions of Indian people as "deplorable," noting among the many health-related problems the presence of high infant mortality and deaths at all ages from tuberculosis, pneumonia, and measles. Navajo, Apache, Pima, and other Arizona nations have death rates from tuberculosis 17 times the national average. The report further details the educational failures and poor living conditions found at the boarding schools and recommends increased funding for Indian health and education. It also describes incidents of malnutrition, poverty, and marginal land tenure among American Indians. The Meriam Report urges Congress to appropriate money to fulfill its treaty obligations to the tribes in terms of health, education, and subsistence. It urges the president, secretary of the interior, and commissioner of Indian affairs to reform the Office of Indian Affairs.

1928 Navajo Mountain Chant. The first motion picture is taken of the Navajo Mountain Chant by Laura Adams Armer (Hosteen Tsosi).

1928 Peter MacDonald, Navajo Tribal Leader and Businessperson, Is Born. Peter MacDonald is born on the Navajo Reservation at Teec Nos Pos and is probably best known for his tenacious and imaginative defenses of Navajo land and energy resource rights. During World War II, he serves in the marines and becomes one of the highly esteemed Navajo code talkers, whose messages in the Navajo language confuse the Japanese military cryptographers during the Pacific campaigns. In 1963, MacDonald returns to the Navajo Reservation, first to serve on the New Mexico Economic Development Advisory Board and later to become director of the Office of Navajo Economic Opportunity. MacDonald is elected tribal chairman in 1970. During his three terms in office he fights to renegotiate the leases through which outside industrial interests gain access to minerals on Navajo land and seeks a more favorable policy for controlling Colorado River water rights. MacDonald also works to keep industrial development under tribal control and tries to expand Navajo democracy by encouraging people to participate in tribal elections. MacDonald receives numerous honorary awards and serves on many advisory boards, both in his capacity as a political leader and as an engineer.

1928 Peterson Zah, Navajo Tribal Leader, Is Born. As a youth, Zah is discouraged from entering college by his teachers at the Phoenix Indian school; nevertheless, he attends college on a basketball scholarship and graduates from Arizona State University with a bachelor's degree in education in 1963. After completing college, Zah returns to Window Rock, Arizona, on the Navajo Reservation, to teach carpentry as part of a pilot program intended to develop employment skills among Navajo adults. He then serves as a field coordinator at the Volunteers in Service to America (VISTA) Training Center at Arizona State University.

In 1967, Zah joins DNA-People's Legal Services, Inc., a nonprofit organization chartered by the state of Arizona to assist indigent and other economically disadvantaged Indian people. Under his direction, DNA lawyers take several landmark cases to the U.S. Supreme Court, winning cases that help establish the rights of individual Native Americans and the sovereignty of Indian nations. In 1987, he becomes chief fundraiser for the Navajo Education and Scholarship Foundation. In 1990, Zah is elected president of the Navajo Nation, a new position created by the Navajo Nation Council in a reorganization of the Navajo Nation governmental structure. In 1992–93, Zah is the elected chairman of the Navajo Nation, the only Navajo leader to be elected both as chairman and as president.

1929

JULY 1, 1929 Northern Air Service. Regular air service, using pontoon and ski equipped airplanes, begins to connect isolated settlements in the Mackenzie Valley with Edmonton, Alberta. Airplanes already have begun to greatly increase contact between northern Natives and southern Canadian people.

1929–1933 Indian Reforms. Reforms are introduced into the Office of Indian Affairs, somewhat improving Indian schools, partially stopping the loss of Indian land, and developing plans for reducing the power of Indian Agents on reservations.

1930

1930 Dennis J. Banks, Anishinabe Activist, Is Born. Dennis Banks is born on the Leech Lake Indian Reservation in northern Minnesota. In 1968, he co-founds, with Clyde Bellecourt, Mary Jane Wilson, George Mitchell, and Indian community members, the American Indian Movement (AIM), which protects the traditional ways of Indian people and engages legal cases involving the rights of Natives, such as treaty and aboriginal rights to hunting and fishing, trapping, and gathering wild rice. Under the leadership of Banks, AIM leads a protest in Custer, South Dakota, in February 1973 after homicide victim Wesley Bad Heart Bull's mother was pushed down stairs following a meeting with officials. *(See* entry, February 6–8, 1973.) As a result of his involvement in the 71-day occupation of Wounded Knee, South Dakota, in 1973, and his activities at Custer, Banks and 300 others are arrested. Banks is acquitted of charges related his participation in the Wounded Knee takeover, but is convicted of riot and assault stemming from the confrontation at Custer. In 1987, Banks is active in convincing the states of Kentucky and Indiana to pass laws against desecration of Indian graves and human remains. He organizes reburial ceremonies for over 1,200 Indian gravesites. Banks remains involved in American Indian issues, including AIM, and travels the globe lecturing, teaching Native American traditions, and sharing his experiences. Banks plays key roles in the films *War Party* (1989), *The Last of the Mohicans* (1992), and *Thunderheart* (1992).

1930 Indian Appointment of OIA Guidance and Placement Officer. Ruth Muskrat Bronson becomes the first guidance and placement officer in the newly created Office of Indian Affairs Education Division. In her 13 years of office, she dispenses educational loans and promotes Indian academic success in postsecondary institutions. Her experience as a OIA officer subsequently allows her to establish a Washington, D.C., bureau for the National Congress of American Indians (NCAI) in 1936.

1930 Kidnapping of Navajo Children. The U.S. Senate Investigating Committee reveals virtual systematic kidnapping of Indian children from their Navajo parents on the reservation by the Indian administration school officials.

JUNE 13, 1930 Interest of Trust Funds Act. Congress passes the Interest of Trust Funds

Act, which states that "all funds without account balances exceeding $500 held in trust by the United States and carried in principal accounts . . . shall bear the interest at a rate of 4 per centum per annum."

JUNE 13, 1930 Tax of Ceded Indian Irrigated Lands Act. Congress passes the Tax of Ceded Indian Irrigated Lands Act. The act amends procedures for the taxation of Indian lands classified under the Reclamation Act and includes taxation on ceded Indian irrigated land.

OCTOBER 1, 1930 Control of Natural Resources. Control of natural resources is passed from the Canadian federal government to Manitoba, Saskatchewan, and Alberta on the condition that their provincial governments will, when necessary, transfer "unoccupied" land to the federal government for Indian reserves in order to meet any outstanding treaty obligations, and on the condition that Indians will retain the right to hunt, fish, and trap for food in these provinces.

1930–1931 Exposition of Indian Tribal Arts. The success of Indian artists from Oklahoma and Santa Fe in the Art Students League exhibition of 1920 in New York City prompts the organization of the Tribal Arts Exposition. The show travels throughout the United States during 1930–31 and leads to the formation of the Indian Arts and Crafts Board under the Office of Indian Affairs in 1934.

1930–1931 Northern Cheyenne Reservation Allotted. Under special legislation passed in 1926, the Northern Cheyenne Reservation becomes the last to be allotted.

1930s Harrington-LaFarge Alphabet Developed. In the latter part of this decade, the Navajo system of writing, known as the Harrington-LaFarge alphabet, is devised and introduced.

1930s Navajo Stock Reduction. The latter part of this decade sees Navajo grazing allotments

Early twentieth-century Navajo sandpainting rug woven by Altnabah. Courtesy of the National Anthropological Archives, Smithsonian Institution.

reduced by the government from 1 million sheep to 750,000 because of the condition of the overgrazed and eroded lands. The reduction in the size of the sheep herd impoverishes many Navajo families.

1930s Office of Indian Affairs Criticized. Alice Lee Jemison boldly criticizes the Office of Indian Affairs for its New Deal program of the 1930s. The daughter of a Seneca mother and a Cherokee father, Jemison strongly identifies with her Seneca background. Indeed, it is due

in part to the Iroquois tradition of politically involved women that she assumes an active antigovernment stance. Her views reflect a general mistrust of non-Indian institutions that is frequently attributed to the politically conservative western New York State area where she is from. The extremity of Jemison's conservatism attempts to preserve Iroquois treaty rights as a safeguard for an independent Iroquois sovereignty; here, the distinction of an independent status is crucial for Jemison, as sovereignty at the pleasure of Congress actually negates tribal self-sufficiency. Consequently, Jemison becomes a leader of the ultraconservative American Indian Federation.

1 9 3 1

1931 British Columbia Indian Organization. The Native Brotherhood of British Columbia is formed by Haida Alfred Adams of Masset. The organization, modeled after the Alaska Native Brotherhood, is intended to be an intertribal organization but its membership comes predominantly from the Coastal Indians, the Interior Salish, and the Carrier.

1931 *Green Grow the Lilacs*. The best-known play by Cherokee dramatist Lynn Riggs, *Green Grow the Lilacs,* is produced. It is his first critical and financial success, later providing the basis for the musical *Oklahoma!* by Richard Rogers and Oscar Hammerstein. Riggs's later tragedy, *Cherokee Nights* (1936), emphasizes Indian themes to a much greater extent, exploring the difficulties of mixed-blood Cherokee assimilation in the period from 1895–1931. During his prolific career Riggs produces numerous other plays; publishes a volume of poetry, *The Iron Dish* (1930); and works as a freelance screenwriter. Riggs also serves as director of drama at Northwestern University and the University of Iowa.

FEBRUARY 1931 Indian Highway Act. Congress passes the Indian Highway Act, which amends the Federal Highway Act of 1921. The act calls for the secretary of agriculture to cooperate with state highway departments and with the Department of Interior to construct public highways within Indian reservations.

1 9 3 2

1932 Alaska Indian Education. The administration of education among the Natives of Alaska is transferred to the Office of Indian Affairs, headquartered in Juneau. Gradually the office becomes known as the Alaska Indian Service.

1932 Alaska Indian Education. The Alaska Indian Service opens the Wrangle Institute Boarding School.

1932 *Black Elk Speaks* Is Published. The autobiography of Oglala Sioux holy man Nicholas Black Elk, told through writer John G. Neihardt, is published in 1932. Called a "North American Bible of all tribes," by writer Vine Deloria in his preface to the 1979 reprint, *Black Elk Speaks* tells the story of Black Elk's life, covering events from his childhood among his plains people when he first receives his vision, his doctoring and ceremonial practices, and his travels through Europe with Buffalo Bill's Wild West Show. Black Elk also narrates the events of the Wounded Knee Massacre and the battle of Little Bighorn. In spite of its wealth of cultural and historical information, *Black Elk Speaks* has come under critical fire because of Neihardt's apparent distortion of Black Elk's words. It is important to note that the book actually was dictated by Black Elk through his son, who translated his father's Lakota words. The translation was in turn taken down by Neihardt's daughter, who acted as a stenographer, before being edited by Neihardt. Scholars working with the original manuscript also have noted Neihardt's tendency to emphasize the more tragic dimensions of Black Elk's life and the "end" of plains culture at the expense of other aspects of his life such as his pride in his military accomplishments and his Christianity. In structuring Black Elk's narrative in such a way, Neihardt goes so far as to reword, rewrite, and add passages to the text. The most notable addition is also the most quoted, Black Elk's "the sacred hoop is broken and scattered" speech which, for added emphasis, Neihardt uses to end the book. These limitations aside, *Black Elk Speaks* remains one of the most frequently taught works on American Indians, over 60 years after its first publication.

JANUARY 26, 1932 Indian Irrigation Act.
Congress passes the Indian Irrigation Act decreeing that the secretary of interior has authority to defer payment of construction charges on irrigation projects under the direction of the commissioner of Indian affairs.

MARCH 14, 1932 Norval Morrisseau (Copper Thunderbird), Ojibway Artist, Is Born.
Born near the Sand Point Reserve near Lake Nipigon in northern Ontario in 1932, Morrisseau works as a miner during his youth. He emerges in 1962 as the first Indian employing an obviously indigenous style to become well-known in the nonindigenous art world in Canada. A self-taught artist, Morrisseau's unique style of painting has been described as "X-ray art," because it appears to portray internal features rather than merely the surface of its subjects, or "legend art" because its inspiration is derived largely from Indian mythology. Morrisseau is known for his bold and brilliant use of color. Several artists who have adapted Morrisseau's style also have received international acclaim, giving rise to a genre of painting called "Woodlands art." While his art has been well received among non-Natives, some of his paintings stir up controversy among Natives themselves because they break taboos against depicting images of legendary figures outside spiritual rituals. Morrisseau writes and illustrates *Legends of My People, the Great Ojibway* in 1965.

JULY 1, 1932 Leavitt Act. Congress passes the Leavitt Act, which states that no assessments for construction costs can be made against Indian-owned lands within federal irrigation projects until Indian title has been extinguished. The secretary of interior is authorized to adjust or eliminate debts against individual Indians or tribes in consideration of the circumstances.

AUGUST 31, 1932 Alanis Obomsawin, Abenaki Filmmaker, Is Born. Born in New Hampshire, Obomsawin is raised on the Odanak Abenaki Reserve in Quebec. Her professional singing career begins in the 1960s. During that decade she tours Canada, the United States, and Europe. Obomsawin begins working at Canada's National Film Board in 1967. She appears in the Canadian film *Eliza's Horoscope* (1970) before turning to documentary filmmaking. Her first film, *Christmas at Moose Factory* (1971), reveals Cree lifestyles as seen through the drawings and paintings of Cree children. Her early films, including *Mother of Many Children* (1977), and *Amisk* (1977), celebrate the richness and diversity of Indian cultures. Later films are directed more at the struggles of Canada's Native peoples. *Incident at Restigouche* (1984) documents a police raid on a Quebec reserve; *Richard Cardinal: Cry From a Diary of a Métis Child* (1986) presents the tragic story of a young child whose abuse and neglect by the child welfare system leads to his suicide; *Poundmaker's Lodge: A Healing Place* (1987) examines an Indian drug and alcohol rehabilitation center near Edmonton; *No Address* (1988) focuses on Montreal's homeless aboriginal people; *Kanesataké: 270 Years of Resistance* (1993) describes the long struggle between the Mohawk at Kanesataké (Oka) and the Roman Catholic Church and the French, English, Canadian, and Quebec governments, and chronicles the 78-day Oka crisis that began on July 11, 1990. It earns several Canadian and international awards.

Obomsawin begins singing professionally in 1950. Her first solo record album, *Bush Lady* (1988), includes songs in Abenaki, English, and French.

DECEMBER 28, 1932 Alberta Métis Organization. Métis in Alberta led by Joseph Dion *(See* biography, July 2, 1888) form l'Association des Métis d'Alberta et des Territoires du Nord Ouest (renamed the Métis Association of Alberta in 1940). Dion, its president from 1932 to 1958, Jim Brady, and Malcolm Norris are important leaders in the organization.

1932–1937 The Santa Fe Studio Style. Beginning in 1932, Dorothy Dunn comes to the Santa Fe Indian School and begins teaching art to the students there. Similar to the Oklahoma style, the Santa Fe Studio painters use flatly laid color fields and strong definition of lines, often with Pueblo or Navajo traditions as subjects for their art. Among the over 700 students to train at "The Studio" are Pueblo painters José Vincente Aguilar, Joe H. Herrera, Ben Quintana, Juan B. Medina, Vince Mirabel, and José Rey Toledo. Many Navajo artists also attend the Santa Fe Studio, including Harrison Begay, Stanley Mitchell, Gerald Nailor, Quincy Tahoma, and Andrew Tsinahjinnie. Yankton Sioux artist Oscar Howe and Chiricahua Apache Allan Houser also train with Dunn in Santa Fe.

1 9 3 3

1933　Ben Nighthorse Campbell, Northern Cheyenne U.S. Senator, Is Born. Campbell is born in Auburn, California, and gives distinguished service in the air force during the Korean War. He attends San Jose State College during the 1950s, becoming a judo champion there and graduating in 1957. Campbell wins a gold medal in judo at the Pan-American Games in 1963, and captures the U.S. championship in his weight division three times. Campbell is also a member of the U.S. Olympic Team in 1964, and writes a judo manual, *Judo Drill Training*, in 1975. Campbell becomes the second Native American elected to the Colorado legislature, where he serves from 1983–86. A member of the Democratic party, he is elected to the U.S. House of Representatives in 1987 and serves as a member of the House Committee on Agriculture and the Committee on Interior and Insular Affairs; the latter includes a subcommittee on Indian affairs. In November 1992, Coloradans elect Campbell to the U.S. Senate, the first Native American to serve there.

1933　Vine Deloria, Jr., Standing Rock Sioux Writer, Lawyer, and Professor, Is Born. Vine Deloria, Jr., is born in Martin, South Dakota, to an unusually distinguished family. His grandfather is a Yankton chief. His aunt, Ella Deloria,

is a noted scholar of Indian ethnology and linguistics, and his father, Vine Deloria, Sr., is an Episcopal minister. Deloria, Jr., graduates from Iowa State University in 1958, and receives a degree in law from the University of Colorado in 1970. Through his widely published books, *Custer Died for Your Sins* (1969) and *God is Red* (1973), Vine Deloria, Jr., brings greater understanding of American Indian history and philosophy to a global audience. Deloria, Jr., serves as the executive director of the National Congress of American Indians from 1965 to 1967, and also provides leadership in other organizations such as the Citizens Crusade Against Poverty, the Council on Indian Affairs, the National Office for the Rights of the Indigent, the Institute for the Development of Indian Law, and the Indian Rights Association. Since 1991, he has taught political science at the University of Colorado at Boulder.

JANUARY 27, 1933　Five Civilized Tribes Restrictions Act. Congress passes the Five Civilized Tribes Restrictions Act calling for the secretary of interior to restrict all funds and securities of Indians who are of at least 50 percent Indian descent from one of the Five Civilized Tribes (Cherokee, Choctaw, Chickasaw, Creek, or Seminole); Indians enrolled as a member of one of the Five Civilized Tribes; and Indians who were once enrolled, but had abandoned tribal membership for U.S. citizenship, until April 26, 1956. Consequently, the Office of Indian Affairs directs distribution of funds gained from treaties or land sale for many members of the Five Civilized Tribes.

FEBRUARY 25, 1933　Indian Monies Due Act. Congress passes the act, ostensibly to benefit incompetent and minor Indians owed any amounts from accounts in government agencies. The act states also that amounts may be paid to the superintendent or other bonded officers of the Indian Service for the beneficiaries or heirs.

MARCH 4, 1933　Indian Timber Contracts Act. Congress passes the Indian Timber Contracts Act, modifying terms of existing and uncompleted contracts of Indian tribal timber, under the jurisdiction of the secretary of interior.

MAY 31, 1933   Pueblo Lands Board Appropriation Act. Congress passes the Pueblo Lands Board Appropriation Act to compensate Pueblo Indian communities and to meet awards made by the Pueblo Lands Board.

1933–1950   Collier and the Crusade for Indian Reform. In 1933, John Collier, longtime director of the American Indian Defense Association and a social crusader for Indian rights, is appointed commissioner of Indian affairs by President Franklin D. Roosevelt. Under his leadership the administration embarks upon a program known as the "Indian New Deal," which is tailored to strengthen unique Indian cultures by fostering tribal government and Indian arts and crafts as well as by preserving valuable tribal artifacts and customs. During the period from 1933–50, the Office of Indians Affairs is largely controlled by non-Indian reformers (headed by Collier) who wish to apply social science theory to Indian development. Collier and other reform leaders are sympathetic to Indian cultural values and desire to stop the loss of Indian land. They also try to stimulate economic development on the reservation. On the other hand, the approach of these reformers remains to some extent elitist, since they fail to turn control of Indian affairs over to Indian people themselves, advocating a kind of reform from above. The reformers do not understand the Indian desire for self-determination, and the basic relationship between Indians and the larger society really does not change during this period.

1 9 3 4

1934   The Indian Reorganization Act. The Indian Reorganization Act (IRA), or the Wheeler-Howard Act, is passed to fulfill the recommendations of the Meriam Report and to promote the well-being of Native Americans by recognizing the value of their diverse cultures, religions, languages, and economies. The IRA officially renders the General Allotment Act obsolete by prohibiting further allotment of Indian lands to individuals, while providing the means of consolidating reservation life and developing tribal government. Tribes are given the option to establish tribal governments under written constitutions, to incorporate by means of charters for the purpose on conducting business, or both. Additionally, the IRA extends indefinitely existing trust periods and restrictions on alienability of Indian lands. Appropriations are made for an Indian credit program, the restoration of lands lost during allotment to tribal ownership, and educational loans. The act is later amended to extend specified coverage to Oklahoma and Alaska Natives. While the Indian Reorganization Act supports the revival of tribal powers of self-government, other federal laws of the period authorize the continuing intrusion of state governmental authority in Indian country. For example, the Johnson-O'Malley Act (1934) provides for federally funded contracts with state governments to provide various services on reservations, principally education.

1934   The Johnson-O'Malley Act. Congress repeals the General Allotment Act, replacing it with the Johnson-O'Malley Act, which allows the federal government to contract with states and territories to provide services for Indians, including health care, social welfare, and education. As another part of the Indian New Deal, the commissioner of Indian affairs orders the Indian Service to hire more Indians and to cease interference with Native American spiritual beliefs, ceremonies, and traditions. Indians join the Works Project Administration (WPA), the Public Works Administration (PWA), and the Civilian Conservation Corps (CCC). While participating in such programs as the CCC, Indian families are introduced to modern farming, ranching, and forestry techniques and are taught English and basic mathematics. Opinions vary about the effect of the Indian New Deal, but the 1930s prove to be a watershed in American Indian history and a step toward Native American self-determination.

1934 N. Scott Momaday, Kiowa Novelist and Poet, Is Born. Momaday grows up in the Southwest, living on a number of Indian reservations and attending government Indian schools. He later attends the Virginia Military Academy and the University of New Mexico. Momaday begins writing poetry while teaching on the Jicarilla Apache Reservation. The poems he writes during this period lead to a Creative Fellowship from Stanford University where he earns his master's and doctorate degrees. Momaday teaches first at the University of California, Santa Barbara, and later at the University of California, Berkeley. Momaday is recognized as one of the premier writers in the United States. In 1969, his novel *House Made of Dawn* is awarded the Pulitzer Prize for fiction.

1934 *Sundown* Published. Best known for his biographical and historical works, John Joseph Mathews publishes his only novel, *Sundown.* Through its protagonist Challenge Windzer, Mathews's semi-autobiographical novel focuses on the difficulties of assimilation and marginality that face Indians of his generation. Mathews, who returns to Oklahoma to ranch and write after completing a bachelor's degree at Oxford University, serves for many years on the Osage tribal council and is instrumental in the opening of the Osage Museum. Among his notable works of history are *Wah'Kon-Tah: The Osage and the White Man's Road* (1932), an account of Osage life during the years 1878 to 1931, and *The Osages: Children of the Middle Waters* (1961), an important history of the Osage tribe.

1934 Will Sampson, Creek Actor, Is Born. Will Sampson, the widely known American Indian actor, is born and raised in Oklahoma. After stints as a cowboy, forest ranger, and professional artist, he receives an opportunity that will change his life. Sampson is hired for a part in the movie, *One Flew over the Cuckoo's Nest.* The film, based on a novel by Ken Kesey, wins five Academy Awards and critical praise for Sampson's portrayal of Chief Bromden. Sampson himself is nominated for an Academy Award as best supporting actor, and his career is launched. He goes on to act in a number of films, including *The Outlaw Josey Wales, White Buffalo, Buffalo Bill and the Indians, Old Fish Hawk, Orca,* and *Fighting Back.* In 1982, he is awarded best narration honors by the Alberta, Canada, film commission for his work on *Spirit of the Hunt,* a major Canadian film. Sampson also joins the American Indian Theater Company of Oklahoma and takes on the role of Red Cloud in the production of *Black Elk Speaks.* Sampson suffers with scleroderma, a chronic degenerative disease, and dies in 1987.

MARCH 7, 1934 Douglas Joseph Cardinal, Métis Architect, Is Born. Douglas Cardinal is considered one of the foremost architects in Canada. Of mixed-blood Blackfoot descent, Cardinal is born in Calgary, Alberta. Raised as a non-Native, it is not until the 1970s that Cardinal immerses himself in Native religion and Native issues. In 1954, during his second year at the School of Architecture at the University of British Columbia, Cardinal wins a prize for his innovative curvilinear and organic designs, but he is asked to withdraw from the school the very next year because these designs are considered radical. Cardinal completes his training at the University of Texas in 1963. Returning to Red Deer, Alberta, he designs several strikingly original churches and public buildings in Alberta, perhaps the finest being St. Mary's Church in Red Deer. These buildings reflect the undulating forms in Alberta's deep river valleys. He also becomes, during the 1970s, the first western Canadian architect to produce his drawings electronically.

Cardinal's national and international prominence is ensured in 1983 when he is awarded a commission to design the $93 million Canadian Museum of Civilization at a site directly across the Ottawa River from the Canadian Parliament buildings. When opened in 1989, the museum, with its unique curved lines, is hailed as an architectural masterpiece. In early 1993, Cardinal, who has been working from an Ottawa office since 1985, is named as the chief architect of the $77 million National Museum of the American Indian, to be built on the last open space on the National Mall in Washington, D.C. He also is designing buildings on the new campus for the Institute of American Indian Arts in Santa Fe, New Mexico.

MAY 7, 1934 U.S. Citizenship for Metlakahtla Indians Act. Congress passes the U.S. Citizenship for Metlakahtla (Metlakatla) Indians Act, which declares these Indians to be citizens of the United States. A group of Christianized Tsimshian, a Northwest Coast culture people, migrated from British Columbia, Canada, to Annette Island in southeast Alaska in 1887, establishing a colony known as Metlakatla, Alaska.

1934–1941 Seneca Arts Project. With funding provided by New Deal programs like the Temporary Emergency Relief Administration (TERA) and the Works Progress Administration (WPA) and operating under the direction of Arthur Parker, the Seneca director of the Rochester Municipal Museum (now the Rochester Museum and Science Center), the Seneca Arts project leads to the creation of over 5,000 works of art at the Tonawanda and Cattaraugus reservations. Both "traditional" and "nontraditional" art forms are produced under the program's aegis, including false face masks, bowls, spoons, cradleboards, moose hair and porcupine quillwork, silver jewelry, and baskets, as well as painting and sculpture.

1 9 3 5

1935 Ada Deer, Menominee Educator, Ac-

tivist, and Assistant Secretary-Indian Affairs, Is Born. Ada Deer is born at Keshena, Wisconsin, and receives her bachelor's degree in education from the University of Wisconsin-Madison, in 1957. In the 1970s, Deer plays a major role in the social and political development of her tribe. During 1972 and 1973, she is vice president and Washington lobbyist of the National Committee to Save the Menominee People and Forest, Inc. As chair of the Menominee Restoration Committee from 1973 to 1976, Deer is largely responsible for persuading Congress to restore the Menominee to tribal status following the termination of the tribe in 1954. Ada Deer is appointed assistant secretary for Indian affairs in 1993.

1935 *United States v. Creek Nation.* When the federal government surveys the lands it has promised to the Creek Nation in Indian Territory, an error is made and 5,000 acres are omitted. When the Creek demand compensation for this lost land a century after the mistake is made, government lawyers argue that the Creek should have either corrected the survey or complained earlier. In the majority opinion of *United States v. Creek Nation*, the Supreme Court disagrees, giving the Creek Fifth Amendment compensation from the government: "The tribe was a dependent Indian community under the guardianship of the United States" at the time, and as such it was entitled "to rely on the United States, its guardian, for needed protection of its interests." While the United States had broad powers and wide discretion in managing Indian tribes' affairs, it remains "subject to limitations inhering in such a guardianship," including an obligation of care in handling Indian property, the court says.

APRIL 10, 1935 Health Care for Native Americans. In the case of *Dreaver v. Regina*, Mr. Justice Angers of the Exchequer Court of Canada rules that the "medicine chest" clause of Treaty 6 entitles Treaty 6 Indians to free medicines, drugs, and medical supplies. This is the first court ruling on the legal meaning of this clause. The government had provided free medicine to these Indians between 1876 and 1919.

1 9 3 6

1936 *The Autobiography of a Papago Woman* **Is Published.** This work by Ruth Underhill is an "as told to" ethnobiography notable for its authorship by a female anthropologist. The *Autobiography* is also the first comprehensive study of Papago or Tohono O'Odham culture. Narrated by Maria Chona, the *Autobiography* is hailed as a breakthrough in its ethnographic literary style, its narrative depiction, and its portrayal of a distinctively female point of view.

1936 **British Columbia Indian Organization.** Kwagiulth (Kwakiutl, Kwakwaka'wakw) fishermen along the central coast of British Columbia establish the Pacific Coast Native Fisherman's Association. The association is absorbed into the Native Brotherhood of British Columbia in 1942.

1936 **Indian Actors Association Is Formed.** The Indian Actors Association, an organization affiliated with Screen Actors Guild in Hollywood, is formed to provide more opportunities and better benefits for its Native American members. The group works closely with the movies' Central Casting office to encourage studios to hire Indians as actors and technical advisors. Luther Standing Bear (Lakota Sioux) and Jim Thorpe (Potawatomi and Sauk-Fox) are the founders; later, Many Treaties (Blackfeet) chairs the association. By 1939, the group has 67 members.

1936 *The Surrounded* **Is Published.** This first novel by Salish writer D'Arcy McNickle deals with the bicultural difficulties of a Salishan/ Spanish mixed-blood named Archilde Leon. Later McNickle writes *Runner in the Sun: A Story of Indian Maize* (1954), a novel for young adults, and the posthumously published *Wind From an Enemy Sky* (1978). Like John Joseph

Mathews, McNickle is best known for his works of history and biography, including *They Came Here First* (1949), *Indian Tribes of the United States* (1962), and *Indians and Other Americans*, with Harold Fey (1970). McNickle, who works for John Collier's staff at the Office of Indian Affairs during the 1930s, also cofounds the National Congress of American Indians in 1944 and serves as the first director at the Newberry Library Center for History of the American Indian.

FEBRUARY 15, 1936 **Ewing Commission.** An Alberta Royal Commission to investigate the health, education, and general welfare of Alberta's Métis (Ewing Commission), submits its report. The commission, established on December 12, 1934, and conducted by Alberta Supreme Court Justice A. F. Ewing, finds that the Métis of Alberta are suffering desperate poverty during the severe economic depression. Adopting the position of the Métis of Alberta, the commission recommends the establishment of Métis settlements.

MAY 1, 1936 **Alaska Native Reorganization Act.** Congress passes the Alaska Native Reorganization Act extending certain provisions of the Wheeler-Howard Act (Public Law 383) to the Territory of Alaska to assist Native people.

JUNE 23, 1936 **Canadian Indian Affairs.** Responsibility for the Canadian Indian Affairs Branch is transferred to the Department of Mines and Resources.

JUNE 26, 1936 **Oklahoma Indian Welfare Act.** Congress passes the Oklahoma Indian Welfare Act to provide Oklahoma tribes (except the Osage) with provisions similar to those of the Indian Reorganization Act of 1934.

AUGUST 27, 1936 **Indian Arts and Crafts Board Act.** Congress passes the Indian Arts and Crafts Board Act, establishing a board of five commissioners to promote the economic welfare of Indian tribes and Indian wards of the government. This is to be accomplished through the development of Indian arts and crafts and through expansion of the market for such products.

SEPTEMBER 1, 1936 Alaska Reindeer Act. Congress passes the Alaska Reindeer Act, providing subsistence to Eskimos and other Alaska Natives by encouraging a self-sustaining economy and developing activity in the reindeer industry.

1 9 3 7

1937 Frank LaPena, Wintu-Nomtipom Painter, Is Born. Born in San Francisco, Frank LaPena is a Wintu-Nomtipom painter who works in a variety of media in a range of styles from abstract to realist. LaPena receives his bachelor of arts from California State University at Chico, his teaching credential from California State University at San Francisco, and his master's degree from California State University, Sacramento. His work is widely exhibited in the United States and abroad.

1937 Fritz Scholder, Luiseño Painter, Is Born. Born in Breckenridge, Minnesota, Fritz Scholder is a part-Luiseño painter who is among the most accomplished contemporary American Indian artists. After high school, Scholder attends Wisconsin State University before moving to California and completing undergraduate work at Sacramento State College. He receives his master of fine arts degree from the University of Arizona in 1964. At this same time, Scholder begins teaching at the Institute of American Indian Arts in Santa Fe and turns to Indian subject matter for his art for the first time. In so doing, Scholder becomes quite controversial. The expressionistic style of his works, so unlike anything seen before in American Indian painting, is misunderstood by traditional Indian painters who consider his work to be derogatory and insulting. There are even protest demonstrations held outside galleries showing his work. In spite of the controversy surrounding Scholder early in his career, he quickly becomes among the best-known Indian painters, collecting numerous awards and showing his work worldwide. Because it differs so greatly from the Plains and Santa Fe schools of Indian art, Scholder's work does much to liberate the Indian subject from earlier, more ethnographic styles of painting.

1937 Navajo Eastern Boundary Association Formed. A group of young Navajo led by Howard Gorman organize the Navajo Eastern Boundary Association. Its purpose is to obtain land for the 9,000 Navajo residing on public domain lands east of the reservation.

1937 Papago Tribal Council Organized. The Papago Tribal Council is organized and a constitution and set of bylaws adopted.

1 9 3 8

1938 Billy Mills, Oglala Sioux Athlete, Is Born. Billy Mills is born on the Pine Ridge Reservation in South Dakota. He attends government schools through high school and is offered a full athletic scholarship to the University of Kansas when he graduates. Though Mills is a member of his collegiate track team that wins the national track championship two years in a row and is the Big Eight cross-country champion, he does not gain much prominence. In his final year at the university, Mills tries out for the Olympic team, but does not qualify. Mills graduates and accepts an officer commission in the marine corps. During this time a fellow marine officer who knows of Mills's past track victories prods him into running again. On October 14, 1964, against overwhelming odds, Mills wins the 10,000-meter run at the Olympic Games in Tokyo, Japan. In so doing, he sets a world record. It is the first time that an American has won a distance race in the Olympics. His victory still is considered as one of the greatest athletic upsets of all time.

1938 Indian Mineral Leasing Act Amended. The Ninety-seventh Congress enacts legislation to amend the 1938 Indian Mineral Leasing Act to allow tribes to enter into various types of energy agreements heretofore legally prohibited.

1938 *United States v. Shoshoni.* In *United States v. Shoshoni,* the court holds that when a tribe's land title is recognized, the taking of timber or mineral rights is a compensable taking within the meaning of the Fifth Amendment. This is because the tribe's interest in the land is presumed to include timber and minerals in the absence of the relinquishment of these resources in the governing treaty or statute.

MARCH, 1938 *The Lone Ranger* Released. Republic Pictures releases *The Lone Ranger,* a 15-episode serial about the adventures of a mysterious masked rider and his Indian companion, Tonto. This is the original Lone Ranger film serial, which is closely followed by the sequel, *The Lone Ranger Rides Again* (1939, 15 episodes). Chief Thunder Cloud (Cherokee) portrays the Indian guide in both. From 1949–57, ABC airs *The Lone Ranger* television series featuring Jay Silverheels (Mohawk) as Tonto. In 1981, Michael Horse (Zuni/Yaqui/Mescalero) portrays the Indian lead in *The Legend of the Lone Ranger.*

APRIL 4, 1938 Federal Indian Irrigation Act. Congress passes the federal Indian Irrigation Act, allowing the secretary of interior to grant concessions on reservoir sites, reserves for canals or flowage areas, and other lands under his jurisdiction that have been withdrawn or acquired with respect to the San Carlos, Fort Hall, Flathead, and Duck Valley or Western Shoshoni irrigation projects.

MAY 11, 1938 Indian Lands Mining Act. Congress passes the Indian Lands Mining Act, which stipulates that unallotted lands within an Indian reservation, or lands owned by any tribe, group, or lands of Indians under federal juris-diction, may with approval of the secretary of interior, be leased for up to ten years.

JUNE 24, 1938 Deposit and Investment of Indian Funds Act. Congress passes the Deposit and Investment of Indian Funds Act authorizing the secretary of interior to deposit into banks the funds of any Indian or tribe that agrees to pay a high interest rate under the regulations of the member banks of the Federal Reserve System.

JULY 29, 1938 British Columbia Reserves. British Columbia transfers approximately 600,000 acres to the federal government for the purpose of Indian reserves, fulfilling its commitments to do this when it joined Canada in 1871.

NOVEMBER 22, 1938 Métis Settlements. Alberta passes the Métis Population Betterment Act, establishing eight Métis settlements in the province.

1 9 3 9

1939 Alberta Indian Organization. Eugene Steinhauer, Malcolm F Norris, and John Callihoo spearhead the formation of the Indian Association of Alberta.

1939 California Indian Land Claims. The attorney general of California, Earl Warren, is authorized to bring California Indian land claims against the United States. Not until 1942, however, is the question of U.S. liability settled, thus permitting the filing of lawsuits.

1939 Clyde Bellecourt, Ojibway Activist, Is Born. Clyde Bellecourt is born on the White Earth Reservation in Minnesota. Along with Dennis Banks and George Mitchell, also Ojibway, Bellecourt is one of the founders of the American Indian Movement (AIM), a national activist organization and a powerful force in major activist struggles of the early 1970s. On February 27, 1973, they and other leaders lead an armed occupation of Wounded Knee, South

Dakota. Bellecourt also helps draft 20 demands that are put before the government during the Indian occupation of the Washington, D.C., Bureau of Indian Affairs building in 1972. Although the demands are not met, the government does establish a task force to meet with the protest leaders and promises to make no arrests for the occupation.

1939 Havasupai Tribal Council. The Havasupai in Arizona organize a tribal council.

1939 Pueblos Discuss Legal Action to Obtain Vote. In a closed session of the All-Pueblo Council, the right of Indians to vote in New Mexico is discussed. A proposal is made to take legal action to obtain the vote, but fails due to Pueblo reluctance to get involved in state politics.

1939 Pyramid Lake Paiute. The Pyramid Lake Paiute tribe launches new legal efforts to oust non-Indian squatters. The Paiute secure widespread Indian support.

1939 Seneca Elect New Governing Board. The Seneca Nation at Allegheny elects a new governing board that seeks to collect rents owed by non-Indians of Salamanca, New York, living on Seneca land. Another of the board's objectives is the raising of some land rents. On March 4, the Seneca Council declares delinquent leases canceled.

1939 Sioux Museum and Crafts Center Created. The Sioux Museum and Crafts Center is created under the joint sponsorship of the federal government and Rapid City, South Dakota. The museum is administered by the Indian Arts and Crafts Board, an agency of the U.S. Department of Interior.

APRIL 5, 1939 Eskimos Considered Indians. The Supreme Court of Canada rules in *Re Eskimos* that Eskimos (Inuit) are to be legally regarded as Indians. This makes them the responsibility of the federal rather than the provincial governments.

MAY 7, 1939 Tonawanda Discontinue Recognition of New York Laws. The Tonawanda Council of Seneca Indians notifies New York Governor Lehman that all state laws will "discontinue to be recognized by the Tonawanda Board of the Seneca Nation."

1939–1945 World War II. Up to 6,000 Canadian Indians volunteer for service in World War II. Their status as noncitizens makes them ineligible for conscription or for certain veterans' benefits. The war effort includes the construction of weather stations and military airfields at places such as Fort Chimo (Kuujjuaq), Quebec; Coral Harbour, Northwest Territories; Frobisher Bay (Iqaluit), Northwest Territories; and Goose Bay, Labrador, areas in which Natives are little exposed to mainstream southern Canadian society.

---

1 9 4 0

1940 Rennard J. Strickland, Osage-Cherokee Lawyer, Is Born. Rennard Strickland is born in St. Louis, Missouri. He receives a bachelor of arts degree from Northeastern State College in 1961 and his law degree from the University of Virginia in 1965. Strickland is acting dean at the University of Tulsa from 1974–75, supervising director of the Shleppy Native American collections at that university from 1976–85, and professor of law at the University of Wisconsin at Madison from 1988–90. He serves as director of the Indian heritage Association of Muskogee, Oklahoma, 1966–84; chairman of the Indian Advisory Board of the Philbrook Art Center, 1979–83; and revising editor-in-chief of the *Handbook of Federal Indian Law* for the U.S. Department of Interior, 1975–82. Among Strickland's honors and awards are the Sacred Sash of the Creeks for Preservation of Tribal History, Fellow of the Doris Duke Foundation, Award of Merit from the Association of State and Local History, and the Distinguished Service Citation from the American Indian Coalition, Tulsa, Oklahoma. He publishes *The Indians in Oklahoma* (1980) and *Masterworks of American Indian Art* (1983). His interests include law, culture, and ethnohistories of the American Indian.

1940 Russell Means, Oglala-Yankton Sioux Activist, Is Born. Russell Means is born at Porcupine, South Dakota, on the Pine Ridge Indian Reservation. He is a rodeo rider, Indian dancer, ballroom dance instructor, and public accountant before returning to South Dakota to work in the Rosebud Agency's tribal office. In 1972, Means leads a caravan of 200 cars filled with American Indian Movement (AIM) supporters in protest over the death of Raymond Yellow Thunder, an Oglala man who is publicly humiliated, beaten, killed, and locked in a car trunk in Gordon, Nebraska. Means leads the AIM occupation of Wounded Knee, South Dakota, in 1973, the site of the previous massacre of Sioux by U.S. Seventh Cavalry troops on December 19, 1890. In February 1974, Dick Wilson barely defeats Means in an election for tribal chairman of the Pine Ridge Reservation.

Between 1973 and 1980, Means is tried in four separate cases. He spends one year in state prison in Sioux Falls, South Dakota, where he is stabbed, and survives four shootings. In April 1981, Means and a caravan of 20 cars journey to Victoria Creek Canyon in the Black Hills and establish Camp Yellow Thunder, with the intent to build 80 permanent structures. Since then, Means has traveled extensively and adopted many causes, including the Miskito Indians of Nicaragua. He leaves AIM in 1988, stating that it "had accomplished the impossible." In 1992, Means plays the role of Chingachgook in the movie, *The Last of the Mohicans.*

1940 Trapline Registration. The Manitoba government introduces a system of trapline registration to combat the serious over-trapping that has occurred in the past. The introduction of registered traplines requires some adaptation by Natives, but it serves to stabilize their in-come. The owner of a registered trapline has the exclusive right to trap in a given area; Native trappers are given priority. Other provinces and territories adopt trapline registration over the next decade.

MARCH 4, 1940 Nellie Cornoyea, Inuvialuk Politician, Is Born. Daughter of an Inuvialuk woman from Herschel Island in Canada's Arctic and a Norwegian immigrant, Cornoyea is born near Aklavik, Northwest Territories. She is educated in Aklavik, taking much of her schooling by correspondence. Spearheading the formation of the Committee for Original People's Entitlement (1970), Cornoyea presses an Inuvialuit land claim that is finally settled in 1984. She then coordinates aspects of the implementation of the agreement, and serves on the board of directors of the Inuvialuit Petroleum Corporation, the Inuvialuit Development Corporation, and the Enrollment Authority and Arbitration Board. She also is active in Inuit Tapirisat of Canada in these years.

In the meantime, Cornoyea works for the Canadian Broadcasting Corporation in Inuvik for nine years during the 1970s. In 1979 she is elected to the Northwest Territories Legislative Assembly as a representative for the Nunakput riding. Earning a reputation for tireless work, Cornoyea receives the Northwest Territories Native Women's Association Woman of the Year Award (Politics) in 1982. Then, in November 1991, she is elected government leader in the uniquely nonpartisan Northwest Territories Legislature.

JUNE 24, 1940 Indian Lumber Products Act. Congress passes the Indian Lumber Products Act establishing that forest products produced by Indian enterprises from forests on Indian lands may be sold under regulations as prescribed by the secretary of interior.

OCTOBER 1940 Haskell Institute National Guard. The Haskell Institute unit of the Kansas National Guard is mobilized and entered into one year's active federal service.

OCTOBER 1940   Indian Men Register for the Draft. American Indians register for the draft for the first time in United States history.

1 9 4 1

1941   Canadian Indian Population. A census shows that the Canadian Indian population has begun to grow steadily. Indian populations ended their centuries-old decline between 1911 and 1921. The designation of "Métis" is not included in this census.

1941   Felix Cohen's *Handbook of Federal Indian Law* Is Published. This legal treatise, originally written by one of the lawyers for the Department of the Interior as a government manual, greatly influences all subsequent thinking about tribal rights. Summarizing past court decisions, federal legislation, and administrative practice, Cohen concludes that Indian tribes retain all of their original powers of self-government, except those that have been expressly given up by a treaty or expressly taken away by an act of Congress. This becomes known as the principle of "residual Tribal sovereignty" and is quoted with biblical regularity by judges until 1978, when the Supreme Court establishes a different rule in the *Oliphant* case.

1941   Indian Art Exhibition. An Indian Art of the United States exhibition is held at the Museum of Modern Art in New York City.

1941   Iroquois Citizenship. The U.S. Circuit Court of Appeals rules that members of the Iroquois Confederacy are citizens of the United States. The case is brought about when Warren Green, an Onondaga, protests against the Selective Service Act on the grounds that the Onondaga are independent and not subject to the laws of the United States.

1941   *The United States as Guardian of Hualapai v. Santa Fe Pacific Railroad Company.* In this case, the U.S. Supreme Court restores 509,000 acres of land to the Hualapai Indians of Arizona.

MARCH 4–7, 1941   Conference on the Future of the American Indian. The Institute on the Future of the American Indian is held at the Museum of Modern Art in New York City in connection with an exhibition of Indian Art there. The conference is developed by the American Association on Indian Affairs (AAIA) without Indian involvement.

MAY 28, 1941   Santa Ysabel Indian Reservation Land Exchange Act. Congress passes the Santa Ysabel Indian Reservation Land Exchange Act, authorizing the secretary of interior to exchange, with the consent of the tribal government and satisfaction of the secretary, approximately one and eight-tenths acres of the reservation for approximately four and three-tenths acres of equal value.

MAY 28, 1941   Wind River Indian Lands Act. Congress passes the Wind River Indian Lands Act, authorizing the secretary of interior to determine and fix permanent boundaries of allotted, tribal, and ceded lands along the Big Wind River in order to establish the confines of the Wind River Reservation.

AUGUST 16, 1941   Rincon Band of Mission Indians Land Act. Congress passes the Rincon Band of Mission Indians Land Act, describing a small addition of certain public lands as a part of the Rincon band of Mission Indians of California. The act further directs that, until otherwise directed by Congress, none of said lands shall be allotted in severalty or subject to taxation.

1941–1945   World War II. On December 7, 1941, the United States enters World War II after the Japanese attack Pearl Harbor. More than 25,000 Native American Indian men and women join the armed services and are honored with 71 Air Medals, 51 Silver Stars, 47 Bronze Stars, 34 Distinguished Flying Crosses, and 2 Congressional Medals of Honor. Those who remain home participate in the war effort through work, buying of war bonds, blood drives, and collecting rubber, paper, and metal. A group of Navajo serve as code talkers in the South Pacific, devising a code based on the Navajo language but constructed in such a way that even a Navajo speaker could not decipher it without the key. The Japanese are never able to break the code. The Navajo code talkers most likely save the lives of thousands of U.S. soldiers. Many Indians gladly serve the United States in the war, but a few Papago under the leadership of a religious leader, a few Ute, six Hopi from Hotevilla, some Iroquois, and a number of Seminole refuse. The Seminole refuse to register because they are still technically at war with the United States, while the Iroquois object because they do not consider themselves citizens of the United States and, having declared war on Germany in 1917, they never made peace. In all, about 70,000 Indian men and women leave the reservations to enter military service or the defense industries.

1 9 4 2

1942 British Columbia Indian Organization. The Pacific Coast Native Fisherman's Association merges with the Native Brotherhood of British Columbia (N.B.B.C.). The N.B.B.C. consists of Protestant British Columbian Indians.

1942 Buffy Sainte-Marie, Cree Singer and Composer, Is Born. Buffy Sainte-Marie is orphaned as an infant and is raised in Massachusetts by a Micmac Indian couple. Sainte-Marie begins playing guitar and writings songs when she is 16 years old. In college, she studies Oriental philosophy. In the 1960s, spurred on by the positive reaction to her singing, Sainte-Marie goes to New York City, where she begins singing in the folk clubs around Greenwich Village. She has numerous hit singles, including "Universal Solder" and "Until It's Time for You to Go." Sainte-Marie becomes internationally known for both her folksinging and her

songwriting talents. In addition to her antiwar ballads, Sainte-Marie also writes songs about Native identity and injustices committed toward American Indian peoples. Sainte-Marie is an active supporter of the Indian occupiers of Alcatraz Island in 1969, giving many benefit concerts to raise money for their efforts. In the early 1970s, she becomes a regular member on *Sesame Street*, where she seeks to dispel misconceptions and stereotypes about American Indians and to provide a positive role model to Indian and non-Indian youth. Her most recent (1992) recording, entitled "Confidence and Likely Stories," marks a departure for the artist. The new songs include lush strings and multirhythmic textures that set them apart from her earlier pop and folk recordings. Sainte-Marie has infused both her recording career and her general life with a sense of purpose relating to Indian culture and concerns, both past and present. She is the founder of the Native North American Women's Association, a group sponsoring theater, arts, and education projects, and the Nihewan Foundation, a law school scholarship funded by her own concert performances.

1942 Kevin Redstar, Crow-Northern Plains Artist, Is Born. Kevin Redstar is born on the Crow Reservation in Lodge Grass, Montana. His father has an abiding interest in music, and his mother is a skilled craftswoman. In this nurturing environment, Redstar develops an early artistic capability. He studies at the Institute of American Indian Art in Santa Fe, New Mexico, from 1961 to 1964, then at the San Francisco Art Institute, and later at Montana State University. In 1965, Redstar wins a scholarship to the San Francisco Art Institute. As a freshman there, he is awarded the governor's trophy and the Al and Helen Baker Award from the Scottsdale National Indian Arts Exhibition. Redstar's first one-person exhibition is in 1971 at the Museum of the Plains Indian in Browning, Montana, where he draws heavily upon his Plains Indian culture, using Crow art and design concepts to inspire his own interpretation of the life force that exists beyond the surface of decorated objects. His latest works include exciting use of color and refined graphic design. Redstar continues to work daily, primarily in oils. His goal is to move to his native Pryor (Montana) area to create a studio for monotypes and ceramics and to focus on art and music.

1942 Richard Oakes, Mohawk Activist, Is Born. Richard Oakes is born on the St. Regis Reservation in New York. He attends school until he is 16 years old and then quits during the eleventh grade, because he feels the U.S. school system "never offered me anything." The early years of Oakes's life are spent in New York, Massachusetts, and Rhode Island before he moves to California. Oakes enrolls in San Francisco State College in February 1969, and becomes one of the founders of the Native American Studies program there. In November 1969, Oakes and a group of Indian students from southern California colleges and universities occupy Alcatraz Island, the former maximum security U.S. penitentiary. Despite government efforts to dislodge them, Oakes and the other occupiers, now known as "Indians of All Tribes," hold the island for 19 months. In June 1971, Government Services Administration special forces and U.S. marshals remove the last of the occupiers from the island. Oakes is shot and killed in 1972 by a YMCA campground guard, who believes that Oakes is acting aggressively when denied access to an Indian youth within the camp.

1942 *Seminole Nation v. the United States*. In *Seminole Nation v. the United States* the court addresses the issue of the payment of trust fund monies and the fiduciary responsibility of the federal government to Indian tribes. In its decision the Supreme Court refers to the federal responsibility toward managing Indian land and assets as a "moral obligation of the highest responsibility and trust." Since then it has been called "trust responsibility."

JANUARY 9, 1942 Indians in World War II. A press release reveals that 40 percent more Indians have enlisted in the armed services than have been drafted to this date.

JANUARY 29, 1942 Cheyenne-Arapaho Tribes Lands Act. Congress passes the Cheyenne-Arapaho Tribes Lands Act, which sets aside certain lands in Oklahoma for the Cheyenne-Arapaho tribes and carries out obligations to certain enrolled Indians under agreement with the United States.

FEBRUARY 20, 1942 Purchase from Indian Service Appropriations for Alaska Native Act. Congress passes the Purchase from Indian Service Appropriations for Alaska Native Act, authorizing the Secretary of Interior to make purchases from appropriations for the benefit of Alaska Natives; purchases may include food, clothing, supplies, and materials for sale to employees of the Department of Interior who are stationed in Alaska, and to Natives of Alaska and Native cooperative associations under his supervision.

FEBRUARY 24, 1942 Lands of Klamath and Modoc Tribes and Snake Indians Act. Congress passes the Lands of Klamath and Modoc Tribes and Snake Indians Act, calling for the secretary of interior to receive on behalf of the United States deeds of land from individual members of the Klamath tribe of Indians. The land is to be held in trust for the benefit of the Klamath and Modoc tribes and the Yahooskin band of Snake Indians.

MARCH–NOVEMBER 1942 Alaska Highway. The large number of workers required for the construction of the Alaska Highway from Dawson Creek, British Columbia, to Alaska brings dramatic social change and new diseases to the Kaska, Beaver, Tagish, Inland Tlingit, and Tutchone along its route. Some Indians find temporary employment, but most of the workers are non-Natives who leave the region after construction is completed. The improved transportation increases contact among Native groups in the North and encourages them to settle in villages along its route. The road makes it easier for trappers to live in permanent settlements and travel to traplines.

MAY 9, 1942 Manchester Rancheria Act. Congress passes the Manchester Rancheria Act reserving certain public lands in California for the Manchester band of Pomo Indians of the Manchester Rancheria.

JULY 18, 1942 Iroquois League Declares War. The Six Nations declare war on the Axis powers. Asserting its right as an independent sovereign nation, the Iroquois league formally declares war against Germany, Japan, and Italy. This act allows Iroquois men to fight in World War II on the side of the Allied powers.

OCTOBER 28, 1942 Electrical Lines Right-of-Way Parker Dam Project Act. Congress passes the Electrical Lines Right-of-Way Parker Dam Project Act for the acquisition of Indian lands required for the construction, operation, and maintenance of electrical transmission lines of the Parker Dam Project, Arizona-California.

NOVEMBER 24, 1942 Tribal Acquisition of Deceased Members' Land Act. Congress passes the Tribal Acquisition of Deceased Members' Land Act, which calls for trust lands or interest of estates without heirs, including accumulated revenue, to be turned over to the respective tribes.

DECEMBER 24, 1942 Probate of Deceased Indians of Five Civilized Tribes Act. Congress passes the Probate of Deceased Indians of Five Civilized Tribes Act, conferring to the secretary of interior the authority to determine heirs and to probate estates of deceased restricted Indians of the Five Civilized Tribes, enrolled or unenrolled, when such estates are valued at less than $2,500.

1942–1943 British Columbia Indian Organization. Andrew Paull *(See* biography, February 6, 1892) leads the organization of the North American Indian Brotherhood, an attempt to establish a national Indian organization. It becomes dominated by British Columbian Roman Catholics.

1 9 4 3

1943 California Indian Land Compensation. The California attorney general appeals to the U.S. Supreme Court for a rehearing on compensation to the Indians for appropriation of their lands.

1943 Helen Hardin, Santa Clara Pueblo Artist, Is Born. Daughter of the renowned Santa Clara Pueblo painter Pablita Velarde, Helen Hardin becomes an important figure in American Indian painting in her own right. Born in Albuquerque and raised at Santa Clara pueblo, Hardin graduates from high school in 1961, where her concentration is art. She studies art history and anthropology at the University of New Mexico, and attends a Special School for Indian Arts at the University of Arizona, a project funded by the Rockefeller Foundation. Through the late 1960s Hardin's reputation grows, and, along with numerous exhibitions of her work, she receives many prestigious awards at the National Indian Arts Exhibition in Scottsdale (Arizona), the Santa Fe Indian Market, the Philbrook Art Center, and the Gallup Inter-Tribal. Her distinctive art combines modern techniques with ancient designs, using a variety of media including acrylics, inks, washes, and architects' templates to create rectilinear designs in vivid colors. In the last years of her life she experiments with etching and performs arts-related community work, serving on the board of directors of the Southwest Association of Indian Affairs and Santa Fe's Wheelwright Museum. She dies of cancer in 1984.

1943 Ross O. Swimmer, Cherokee Tribal Leader, Is Born. Ross Swimmer is born in

Oklahoma. He receives a bachelor of science degree from the University of Oklahoma in 1965 and later a law degree from that university. Swimmer is general counsel and principal chief of the Cherokee Nation, 1971–85, and president of the First National Bank of Tahlequah, Oklahoma, 1975–85. He serves as cochairman of the Presidential Commission on Indian Reservation Economies, 1983–84. From 1986 to 1989, President Ronald Reagan appoints Swimmer assistant secretary of Indian affairs within the Department of the Interior. He oversees the Bureau of Indian Affairs, the major government agency concerned with Indian issues. Swimmer works to carry out the business and self-sufficiency goals of the Reagan administration, promoting economic development, and encouraging tribal governments to take more leadership and financial responsibility for their reservation communities. Swimmer is a member of the Oklahoma and American Bar Associations, the Oklahoma Historical Society, and the Oklahoma Industrial Development Commission.

1943   Thomas King, Author and Professor, Is Born. Thomas King, of Cherokee, Greek, and German descent, is born in Roseville, California. After working as an ambulance driver and a salesman, and as a photojournalist in New Zealand and Australia, King completes a Ph.D. in English literature. Only after accepting a position as Native Studies Professor at the University of Lethbridge does he take up creative writing. His first novel, *Medicine River* (1990), is set on the Kainai (Blood) Reserve in southern Alberta. Through the eyes of a Native photographer who returns to the reserve after several years' residence in Toronto, King explores what it means to be Native in contemporary society. His book wins the 1990 Writer's Guild of Alberta best novel award. His second work, *A Coyote Columbus Story* (1992), is a children's book. *Green Grass, Running Water* (1993) is another novel set in contemporary southern Alberta.

In addition to writing fiction, King pub-lishes poetry and writes and edits scholarly work, including *All My Relations: An Anthology of Contemporary Canadian Native Fiction (1990)*. He also writes the screenplay for a movie version of *Medicine River* released in 1993 and captures a minor acting role in the movie.

King is presently the chairman of the Native American Studies Department at the University of Minnesota in Minneapolis.

JANUARY 3, 1943   Kateri Tekakwitha Declared Venerable. Kateri Tekakwitha, a seventeenth-century Mohawk, is declared venerable by the Catholic Church, the first American Indian to attain such status. She is later beatified by Pope John Paul II. (*See* entry, June 22, 1980.)

1 9 4 4

1944   California Indian Land Claims. *A History of Proposed Settlement Claims of California Indians* is written by Robert W. King, attorney general for the state of California.

1944   California Indian Land Claims. Settling longstanding claims, the Federal Claims Court awards the California Indians $5 million or about $200 per person. However, in the case of the desert Cahuilla, a band also known as the Agua Caliente Indians, the results are very different because their lands are located in Palm Springs. Each Cahuilla receives a percentage of the rental from $350,000 worth of individually allotted lands as well as a share from the tribal acreage (30,000 acres).

1944   California Indian Land Fraud. According to newspaper investigations conducted from 1975 through 1978, legal frauds upon the individual Palm Springs Indians. Court appointed overseers over Palm Springs Indian lands embezzle funds from leasing agreements held by the Indians in the expensive Palm Springs resort area.

1944   Hank Adams, Assiniboine/Sioux Activist, Is Born. Hank Adams is born on the

Indian airmen performing a mock Indian dance for their fellow servicemen during World War II. Courtesy of the Archives Trust Fund.

Fort Peck Indian Reservation in Montana. In 1964, he plays a behind-the-scenes role when actor Marlon Brando and a thousand Indians march on the Washington State capitol in Olympia to protest state policies toward Indian fishing rights. Adams begins his activist career in April 1964 when he refuses induction into the U.S. Army until Indian treaty rights are recognized. In 1968, Adams becomes the director of the Survival of American Indian Association, a group dedicated to the Indian treaty-fishing rights battles. Adams is shot in the stomach by an unknown assailant in January 1971 while he and a companion set fish traps along the Puyallup River near Tacoma, Washington. Adams recovers from the gunshot wound and continues to protest violations of Indian treaty rights.

1944 Leonard Peltier, Ojibway Activist, Is Born. Leonard Peltier is born in Grand Forks, North Dakota, and spends a difficult childhood moving with his family from copper mines to logging camps. When his parents separate, he is placed in Wahpeton Indian School in North Dakota, where he encounters strict disciplinary treatment. Peltier becomes involved with the American Indian Movement (AIM) in 1970 and is soon a member of AIM's inner circle, traveling with Dennis Banks, a major AIM leader, to raise financial support for the group. Peltier participates in many AIM activities, including the takeover of the Bureau of Indian Affairs offices in the early 1970s. On June 26, 1975, two FBI agents are killed in a shootout near Oglala, South Dakota, on the Pine Ridge Reservation. Leonard Peltier is among a group of Lakota engaged in a shooting exchange with the agents. In a controversial trial at Fargo, North Dakota, from which 80 percent of the defense testimony is excluded, Peltier is sentenced to two consecutive life terms in prison. In many foreign nations, especially in the former socialist countries, Peltier is considered a political prisoner of the United States. New evidence regarding the Pine Ridge shoot-out is presented by Peter Matthiessen in *The Nations*, disputing Peltier's involvement in the murder of the FBI agents. Nonetheless, Peltier is presently serving the two consecutive life sentences in prison.

1944 The National Congress of American Indians Established. The Second World War develops a new leadership of Native Americans who are dissatisfied with the status quo. As a Bureau of Indian Affairs employee in the early 1940s, D'Arcy McNickle convinces BIA Commissioner John Collier of the need for an independent Indian organization. In 1944, tribal leaders from 27 states meet in Denver, Colorado, to form the National Congress of American Indians (NCAI), a group dedicated to guarding Indian rights and preserving Native culture, reservations, and tribal lands. Among the many notable achievements of NCAI's lobbying efforts are the creation of the Indian Claims Commission in 1946, the repeal of the liquor prohibition against Indians in 1953, the end of the termination policy in the early 1960s, and the Indian Self-Determination and Edu-

cation Act of 1975. With a current membership of nearly 200 tribes, NCAI continues to work on behalf of Indian concerns from its headquarters in Washington, D.C.

1944 Saskatchewan Indian Organization. Cree John Tootoosis spearheads the formation of the Saskatchewan Indian Association.

1944 Truckee River Decree. The Truckee River Decree is enacted to protect Indian water rights and specifically the tributaries flowing into Pyramid Lake, by returning first and second rights on the water flow to Pyramid Lake. The Pyramid Lake decreases in area from over 220 square miles to less than 50 square miles by 1944. The question of water rights initially stems from 1905, when the Truckee River Canal is built to divert water for incoming Nevada settlers.

1944 William Stigler Elected to U.S. Congress. William Stigler (Choctaw) is elected to the U.S. Congress from Oklahoma, and serves in the Seventy-eighth to Eighty-second Congresses. Born in Tahlequah, Oklahoma, on July 7, 1891, he graduates from Northeastern State College in 1912. He serves as a city attorney from 1920 to 1924, becoming state senator in 1924 and serving until 1932. Stigler dies on August 21, 1952.

FEBRUARY 18, 1944 Indian Confederation of American Indians. An important pow-wow is held in New York City by the Indian Confederation of American Indians, where Indians and friends gather with dancers from 15 tribes. The purpose is to acquaint New York people with Indian culture and to raise money to help needy Indians in the New York area.

MARCH 4, 1944 Additional Land for Havasupai Reservation Act. Congress passes the Additional Land for Havasupai Reservation Act, adding certain lands of the Gila and Salt rivers to the Havasupai Reservation, and authorizing the secretary of interior to exchange lands in Arizona to become a part of the reservation.

MAY 29, 1944 Additional Land to Navajo Reservation Act. Congress passes the Additional Land to Navajo Reservation Act, calling for the secretary of interior to exchange six acres of land within the Navajo Reservation for four and fourteen one-hundredths acres to the satisfaction of the Navajo tribe and the secretary of interior.

JUNE 29, 1944 Charlie Watt, Inuk Politician, Is Born. Charlie Watt is born in Fort Chimo (Kuujjuaq), Quebec, a small settlement destined to become the main population and administrative center of the Inuit in northern Quebec. As an adult he finds employment with the federal Department of Indian Affairs and Northern Development, but becomes increasingly frustrated by the government's policies toward the Inuit. He travels through northern Quebec to organize the Inuit. He is chosen the founding president of the resulting Northern Quebec Inuit Association in 1972 and works to found the Labrador Inuit Association the following year.

Watt leads the Inuit in northern Quebec in their negotiations with the Quebec and Canadian governments following the announcement of the James Bay Project, a huge hydroelectric project slated for northern Quebec. By 1975, the negotiations result in the James Bay and Northern Quebec Agreement, a huge land claims agreement covering much of northern Quebec and creating several Inuit government agencies to administer its complex provisions. Among them is the Makivik Corporation, the first Inuit development corporation, which Watt is chosen to head in 1978.

On a broader level, Watt is involved in the creation of the Inuit Committee on National Issues, established to represent the Inuit on constitutional matters. As president of that organization he represents the Inuit at the Constitutional Conference in 1983. In recog-

nition of his service, he is appointed to the Canadian Senate in 1984.

AUGUST 1, 1944 Canadian Social Security. The passage of the Family Allowance Act in Canada marks the first time that government-sponsored social welfare benefits are extended to many Natives in northern Canada. Regular family allowance payments are intended to help Canadian families in caring for their families. Though much reduced recently, some Dene peoples in northern Canada have used infanticide in order to control their populations even into the 1940s. A near collapse of fur prices after the high prices of the 1920s, and the expansion of Canadian government social security payments, education, and health care to all Natives of Canada after World War II leads Natives across northern Canada to take up residence at permanent settlements where government services are provided. Thus, the two decades after World War II witness almost a complete end to the nomadic subsistence economy among Natives in Canada. To deal with the sudden need for housing, the federal government introduces special programs for Native housing in these new centers. Up to this point, the Hudson's Bay Company and missionaries have been the primary providers of health care and emergency social assistance.

DECEMBER 13, 1944 Marriage and Divorce among Klamath, Modoc, and Snake Indians Act. Congress passes the Marriage and Divorce among Klamath, Modoc, and Snake Indians Act, stating the conditions for marriages involving the Klamath, Modoc, and Yahooskin band of Snake Indians. The act states that said marriages and divorces shall be solemnized according to the laws of the state of Oregon, and establishes that only a state court can decree a divorce.

DECEMBER 23, 1944 Tulalip Tribe Land Sale Act. Congress passes the Tulalip Tribe Land Sale Act, authorizing the secretary of interior, with the governing approval of the Tulalip tribe, to sell and convey to purchasers specific tidelands with the proceeds to be reinvested in other lands.

1 9 4 5

1945 Iroquois Seek Membership in United Nations. The Iroquois of the Six Nations Reservation send a delegation to the United Nations in San Francisco seeking membership. The Iroquois application, however, is denied.

1945 John E. Echohawk, Pawnee Attorney and Rights Activist, Is Born. John Echohawk is born in Albuquerque, New Mexico, and graduates from the University of New Mexico in 1967, in a special pre-law program that has just been initiated for Native Americans. He goes on to take a degree in law from the University of New Mexico in 1970. On graduating, Echohawk receives the Reginald Heber Smith Community Lawyer Fellowship to work with the California Indian Legal Services program in Sacramento, California. During the 1970s he joins the Native American Rights Fund (NARF), a national organization centered in Boulder, Colorado, that takes major legal cases for Indian tribes. Echohawk is very active in community service over the years and works to create opportunities for Indian youth. He serves on the board of directors of groups such as the Association on American Indian Affairs, the American Indian Lawyer Training Program, and the National Committee on Responsive Philanthropy. Echohawk has received several honors, including the President's Indian Service Award from the National Congress of American Indians.

1945 Michael Dorris, Modoc Novelist and Scholar, Is Born. Michael Dorris is born in Dayton, Washington, and raised in Washington, Idaho, Kentucky, and Montana. He studies English and classics at Georgetown University, graduating with honors in 1967. Dorris receives a master's degree in anthropology from Yale University in 1970. After leaving Yale, Dorris holds various teaching positions and becomes a professor of anthropology and Native American studies at Dartmouth in 1972. Dorris writes many scholarly publications, most importantly the books *Native Americans: Five Hundred Years After* (1975) and *A Guide to Research on North American Indians* 1983), co-authored with Arlene Hirschfelder and Mary Lou Byler. In later years, Dorris becomes better known as a novelist. His first novel, *A Yellow Raft on Blue Water,* is published in 1989, and he has since written a best-selling novel entitled *The Crown of Columbus* (1991) with his wife, Louise Erdrich. Dorris is also the author of *The Broken Cord: A Family's On-Going Struggle with Fetal Alcohol Syndrome (1989);* this nonfiction book describes the effects of the syndrome on the couple and their adopted son. A collection of Dorris's short stories, entitled *Working Men (1993),* is published in 1993.

1945 Ovide William Mercredi, Cree Politician, Is Born. Ovide Mercredi is born of a Cree mother and a Métis father near Grand Rapids, Manitoba. According to Canadian law as it stands in 1945, Mercredi does not have legal status as an Indian because his father is not a status Indian. Mercredi does not gain legal status as an Indian until after the passage of Bill C-31 in 1985. The struggle of the Cree near Grand Rapids against the construction of a hydroelectric and water regulation project nearby *(See* Manitoba hydroelectric projects entry, 1976) is important in Mercredi's decision to become politically active. After acquiring a law degree from the University of Manitoba in 1977, he practices criminal law in The Pas, Manitoba. During the 1980s, however, Mercredi turns increasingly to national constitutional matters. He becomes involved in Indian opposition to the Meech Lake Accord until its defeat in 1990 at the hands of his constitutional ally, Elijah Harper, Manitoba member of the legislative assembly.

Mercredi is chosen the grand chief of the Assembly of First Nations in 1991. He then takes a central role in the constitutional negotiations leading up to the Charlottetown Accord in 1992. The Charlottetown Accord includes provisions for self-government for Canada's aboriginal peoples, a central goal of Mercredi's negotiating strategy. The accord, however, fails to be accepted by the majority of Indians or by a majority of Canadians as a whole. Following the defeat of the Charlottetown Accord and the end of constitutional discussions, Mercredi promises to continue to work toward provisions that would give Canada's Natives the right to self-determination, but redirects much of his energy to issues within Native communities, establishing initiatives aimed at "healing" problems associated with alcoholism, violence, and abuse.

1945 Wilma P. Mankiller, Cherokee Tribal Leader, Is Born. Best known as chief of the Cherokee Nation, Wilma Mankiller is born at the Indian hospital in Tahlequah, Oklahoma. Mankiller becomes active in Indian causes in San Francisco in the late 1960s and early 1970s, and gains skills in community organization and program development. She earns an undergraduate degree in social work and in 1979 completes graduate work in community planning at the University of Arkansas. In 1983, Mankiller is the first woman elected deputy chief of the Cherokee Nation, and when the Cherokee principal chief resigns in December 1985, Mankiller succeeds him. In the historic 1987 election, with 56 percent of the vote, Mankiller becomes the first woman elected Cherokee principal chief. Mankiller insists that the accomplishments that take place during her terms of office could not have been achieved without the work and support of others. She frequently praises the tribal employees, the tribal council, and deputy chief John Ketcher, who work together for the success of the Cherokee Nation.

JANUARY 27, 1945 Harold Cardinal (Cree), Political Leader, Is Born. Born in High Prairie, Alberta, and raised on the Sucker Creek Reserve in north-central Alberta, Cardinal attends schools in Joussard and Edmonton, Alberta, and the University in Ottawa. A summer job with the Alberta Native Communications Society in 1968 leads to a permanent job as president of the Indian Association of Alberta.

It is as president of this group that Cardinal emerges on the national political scene. As the main force behind *Citizens Plus* (the Red Paper, 1970), an aboriginal response to federal efforts to abolish the Indian Act, and author of *The Unjust Society: The Tragedy of Canada's Indians* (1969), a denunciation of the effects and intentions of Canadian Indian policy, Cardinal leads Canadian Indians in protest against the government's 1969 *Statement of the Government of Canada on Indian Policy* (the White Paper). The protests lead to the eventual withdrawal of the policy paper.

Cardinal remains president of the Indian Association of Alberta until 1977 when he accepts a position in Edmonton, becoming the first Native regional director-general of Indian affairs. Cardinal's innovative reforms, however, lead to conflict both with Alberta Indian bands and with the Department of Indian Affairs, and he leaves the position seven months later. In the same year, Cardinal writes *The Rebirth of Canada's Indians*. Subsequently he takes on positions as consultant to northern Alberta Indian bands, chief of the Sucker Creek band (1982–83), and vice chief of the prairie region for the Assembly of First Nations. In 1992 he enters the University of Saskatchewan to study law.

JUNE 30, 1945 Sioux Claims Awards Act. Congress passes the Sioux Claims Awards Act, calling for a sum of $101,630 for payment to certain individual Sioux Indians, their heirs, or devises, in full settlement and satisfaction of their claims against the United States for personal property losses as found and determined by the secretary of interior.

NOVEMBER 1, 1945 Indian Health Services. Responsibility for the Canadian Indian Health Services Branch is transferred from the Department of Mines and Resources to the Department of National Health and Welfare. All other aspects of Indian Administration remain the responsibility of the Department of Mines and Resources. The change in jurisdiction reflects the growing concern regarding the health of Indians in Canada. The tuberculosis death rate among Indians in Canada in 1944 is 580 per 100,000 compared with 49 per 100,000 among Canadians as a whole. The Indian Health Services Branch was created by the Canadian government in 1927 to coordinate health care provided to Canada's Indian people. Before that date, health care was provided by fur trade companies, missionaries, and various private and public agencies. The government provides free health care for Indians on reserves who are unable to pay for medical treatment, but it emphasizes that it does so out of a sense of moral obligation to a less fortunate people, not out of any legislative obligation or treaty responsibility. The "medicine chest" clause of Treaty 6 contains the only formal acceptance by the Canadian government of any responsibility for Indian health care. Government sponsored medical insurance is not extended to all Canadians until 1966.

NOVEMBER 17, 1945 Carol Geddes, Inland Tlingit Filmmaker and Writer, Is Born. Born in the small Yukon village of Teslin in 1945, Geddes earns a bachelor's degree from Carleton University in Ottawa in 1978 and a communications diploma from Concordia University (Montreal) in 1981. Her first film, *Place for Our People* (1983), documents the successful Montreal Native Friendship Centre, calling for the development of similar institutions elsewhere. She compiles a report entitled *Community Profiles: The Native Community* for the National Film Board in 1986. The report highlights the needs of First Nations in Canada and evaluates the existing films on Native peoples. Between 1986 and 1991 Geddes produces 20 videos, many focusing on the tradition and art of Native peoples in Canada. Her first major film, *Doctor, Lawyer, and Indian Chief* (1986), docu-

menting the lives of five Native women, wins an award at the 1988 National Educational Film and Video Festival in San Francisco. She also wins the National Magazine's Silver Foundation Award in 1991 for "Growing Up Native," an article which appeared in *Homemaker's Magazine*. In 1990 she is appointed the first producer of the National Film Board's Studio One, located in Edmonton, Alberta, and devoted to the production of indigenous media. She has since moved to Whitehorse, Yukon Territory, to complete a film called *George Johnston, Tlingit Photographer*, although she continues to work actively with the National Film Board.

Geddes is the first aboriginal named to the board of the Canada Council, a Canadian government-sponsored funding agency for the arts.

1 9 4 6

1946 Arapaho Sun Dance. A Sun Dance is held by the Arapaho in Wyoming, and war veterans attend.

1946 Harry Fonseca, Indian Artist, Is Born. Artist Harry Fonseca is born in Sacramento, California, and is of Nisenan, Maidu, Hawaiian, and Portuguese ancestry. He attends California State University at Sacramento, majoring in fine arts. Fonseca works in numerous media, including acrylic, oils, and sculpture. He is best known for his pop art-inspired renderings of Coyote, and he often uses this traditional trickster figure to offer a social critique of the dominant culture.

1946 Navajo Delegates Travel to Washington, D.C. Twenty-three Navajo delegates under 86-year-old Council Chairman Henry Chee Dodge go to Washington, D.C., to ask for more schools, more hospitals, more land, and more irrigation facilities. It was Chee Dodge's eighth trip to the capital (his first was

During World War II, Ira Hayes took part in a forward attack on Mount Suribachi and was one of the six marines who raised the U.S. flag on the summit of the peak. Courtesy of the National Archives.

to attend the presidential inauguration of Grover Cleveland).

1946 Navajo Indian Education. Only about 6,000, or 25 percent, of the Navajo children between the ages of 6 and 18 years are in school, while an estimated 18,000 are not.

1946 R. Carlos Nakai, Navajo-Ute Musi-

cian, Is Born. Nakai is born in Flagstaff, Arizona, and is raised on the Navajo Reservation. He begins playing trumpet in the 1960s, but switches to Native flute in 1972 after failing to be accepted at the Juillard School of Music, the prominent New York City music school. Nakai blames this on "evidently being the wrong color." He is encouraged by elders of the central and northern Plains people during the time that he is learning to play the Native flute. Around 1982, Nakai meets the founder of Canyon Records and makes his first record, *Changes.* Since then, he has released a number of recordings on the Canyon label, including *Winter Dreams* and *Carry the Gift.* Nakai keeps tradition alive by defining both its presence and its haunting sound throughout his recordings.

1946 Reorganization of the Bureau of Indian Affairs. A special congressional commission investigates the administration of Indian affairs between 1946 and 1949 and recommends extensive reorganization. For years, Indian administration suffered from overcentralization at the Washington, D.C., office. All local agency offices send their requests directly to Washington, and it often takes months to get responses. The new Bureau of Indian Affairs (BIA) organization creates 12 area offices among the 90 agency offices on the reservations and the Washington office. Much of the day-to-day administrative power of the commissioner of Indian affairs is delegated to the directors of the 12 area offices.

1946 T.C. Cannon, Kiowa-Caddo Artist, Is Born. A Kiowa and Caddo Indian, T.C. Cannon is born in Oklahoma. He studies art at the Institute of American Indian Arts in Santa Fe and the San Francisco Art Institute. Well known for his pop art-influenced works, Cannon dies in an automobile accident in May 1978.

1946 *The Winged Serpent* Is Published. Margaret Astrov's *The Winged Serpent: An Anthology of American Indian Poetry* is published.

JANUARY 1946 Special Native Hospitals. In response to a shortage of hospital space in sparsely settled regions of Canada and the poor health of Natives in those regions, the Canadian government begins flying Natives from remote regions of Canada to Charles Camsell Indian Hospital in Edmonton, Alberta. This is the largest of several Indian hospitals established in response to concern about tuberculosis and other diseases among Natives in isolated regions. Following a period of resistance to treatment in such distant places, Indians and Inuit accept these hospitals as necessary. Some northern Natives, following extended treatment in Edmonton, elect to remain in the south.

MAY 28, 1946–JUNE 22, 1948 Parliamentary Committee. A Parliamentary Committee meeting to consider changes to the Indian Act listens to submissions by Andrew Paull *(See* biography, February 6, 1892) of the North American Indian Brotherhood; Peter Kelly *(See* biography, April 21, 1885) of the Native Brotherhood of British Columbia; Iroquois-Cree John Calihoo; Kainai (Blood) James Gladstone *(See* biography, May 21, 1887) of the Indian Association of Alberta; and leaders of other Canadian Indian groups, marking the first time that Indians have been directly consulted concerning the act. The commission's final report recommends that the government retain the goal of complete assimilation of Indian peoples but recommends the Indian Act be revised to eliminate its coercive elements. It also recommends that Indians be given the rights of Canadian citizenship, including the franchise, and that a commission be established to settle Indian land claims. Indian leaders reject the government policy of assimilation.

MAY 31, 1946 Devils Lake Indian Reservation Jurisdiction Act. Congress passes the Devils Lake Indian Reservation Jurisdiction Act. The act confers to the state of North Dakota jurisdiction over offenses committed by or against Indians on the Devils Lake Indian Reservation in North Dakota, to the same extent that its courts have jurisdiction generally over offenses committed within the state outside of Indian reservations.

JUNE 24, 1946 Additional Land for Kiowa, Comanche, and Apache Reservation Act. Congress passes the Additional Land for Kiowa, Comanche, and Apache Reservation Act, eliminating Rainy Mountain School Reserve in Oklahoma and vesting it in the United States in trust for the Indians of the Kiowa, Comanche, and Apache Indian Reservation.

JUNE 28, 1946 Costs Related to Crow Irrigation Project Act. Congress passes the Costs Related to Crow Irrigation Project Act, setting at $45,000 the aggregate costs of all expenditures for the construction of the Crow irrigation project on the Crow Indian Reservation in Montana with certain exclusions and providing funding from the U.S. Treasury.

JUNE 28, 1946 Fort Berthold Indian Awards Act. Congress passes the Fort Berthold Indian Awards Act, authorizing the sum of $400,000 for final settlement of all claims and demands of the Arikara, Gros Ventre, and Mandan of such reservation, based upon an unrestricted treaty of July 27, 1866.

AUGUST 8, 1946 Transfer of Power to Commissioner of Indian Affairs Act. Congress passes the Transfer of Power to Commissioner of Indian Affairs Act, allowing the secretary of interior, as he deems, to delegate powers and duties to the commissioner of Indian affairs in order to facilitate and simplify the administration of Indian affairs.

AUGUST 9, 1946 Leasing of Indian Lands in Washington Act. Congress passes the Leasing of Indian Lands in Washington Act, requiring written consent from Indian individuals, associations of Indians, or Indian tribes to lease Indian lands, including restricted lands, in the state of Washington.

AUGUST 10, 1946 Recognition of Keetoowah Indians Act. Congress passes the Recognition of Keetoowah Indians Act, stating that the Keetoowah Indians of the Cherokee Nation of Oklahoma shall be recognized as a band of Indians residing in Oklahoma according to section 3 of the Act of June 26, 1936.

AUGUST 13, 1946 The Indian Claims Commission Act. After extensive lobbying by the National Congress of American Indians, Congress passes the Indian Claims Commission Act. The act provides a forum in which tribes may sue the federal government for actions or lack of action that they consider detrimental to their welfare. Before this commission is created, claims of tribes, bands, and other groups against the United States can be brought before the court only if specifically authorized in each instance by Congress. Overcoming conservative opposition to become the final piece of Indian New Deal legislation, Congress creates a tribunal for the express purpose of providing Indian tribes an opportunity to obtain damages for the loss of tribal lands. Known as the Indian Claims Commission, this special court is authorized to hear and decide causes of action originating prior to the years of its creation. Tribes are given five years to file their claims. The deadline is extended, and by 1964–65, almost $100 million has been paid to settle 50 of the 158 claims decided. To date almost 600 claims have been filed with the Indian Claims Commission. The commission is largely ineffective, however, as cases take years to resolve and are a major cost. Although the commission makes several awards to Native Americans, no land is returned and by the time legal fees are deducted, the monetary awards given to Indian claimants are very meager. In 1978 cases not completed by the Commission are transferred to the U.S. Court of Claims, which, in 1983, becomes the Claims Court.

NOVEMBER 4, 1946 Robert Davidson (Guud San Glans, "Eagle of the Dawn"), Haida Artist, Is Born. Born in the Haida community of Hydaburg, Alaska, Davidson is raised in Masset on Canada's Queen Charlotte Islands, the center of the Haida population. A sculptor, printmaker, and jeweler, Davidson emerges as the foremost Haida artist of his generation. He is born into a family of prominent Haida artists, his great-grandfather being Charles Edenshaw. It is fellow Haida artist Bill Reid (*See* biography, January 12, 1920), however, who is most responsible for Davidson's training. During a one-year apprenticeship with Reid at the Vancouver Art School in 1966, Davidson's talent becomes evident. He is an instructor at the Gitenmaax School of Northwest Coast Indian Art at Ksan (*See* entry, August 12, 1970) during its construction, and in 1969 he carves and raises the Bear Mother Pole. The 12-meter totem pole is the first to be raised in Masset in 90 years. In the years that follow, he becomes well known as a carver of masks and totem poles and as a supporter of Native dance. Three of his totem poles are displayed in the PepsiCo International Sculpture Park in New York City, and three are displayed in the Maclean Hunter Building in Toronto.

1 9 4 7

1947 Army Indian Scouts Discontinued. The Army Indian Scouts are discontinued as a distinct element of the military forces of the United States. The last members have been serving at Fort Huachucha, Arizona. Their last duties include patrolling the boundaries of the post to keep out trespassers and serving as guides for surveying parties from the Interior Department. Numerous Indian heroes of the wars receive the Congressional Medal of Honor for their bravery. Achesay, Blanquet, Chiquito, Elaatoosu, Jim, Kelsay, Kosaha, Machol, Nannasaddie, and Nantajie, for instance, are some who are decorated during the Indian Wars for "gallant conduct during the campaigns and engagements with the Apaches."

1947 Iroquois Fight for Sovereignty. The Iroquois lead a fight against bills in Congress for state jurisdiction in civil and criminal cases. Philip Cook, Ray Fadden, and Mad Bear Anderson draw up a leaflet on the bills. Over Iroquois protests, bills are later passed in Congress for state jurisdiction in civil and criminal cases in New York. Edmund Wilson later claims this initiates the modern Iroquois protest movement.

1947 John Trudell, Santee Sioux Activist and Musician, Is Born. John Trudell is an active participant in many Native American protests of the 1960s and 1970s. He participates in the 1969 occupation of Alcatraz Island by Indians of All Tribes, Inc., an organization that symbolizes participation of all Native American Indians. Trudell joins the American Indian Movement (AIM) in the spring of 1970 and becomes a national spokesman for AIM soon thereafter. He participates in the 1972 Trail of Broken Treaties, a national car-caravan that brings together urban and reservation Indians from across the nation to present a formal list of demands on the federal government. Failure of communications results in an impasse and a 71-hour occupation of the Bureau of Indian Affairs office in Washington, D.C. Trudell is elected co-chair of AIM in 1973 and participates in the 1973 armed seizure of Wounded Knee, a small town in the heart of the Pine Ridge Sioux Reservation in South Dakota. In 1976, Trudell coordinates the AIM support of Leonard Peltier, who is convicted of murdering two FBI agents in June 1975 on the Pine Ridge Reservation. Trudell now resides in Los Angeles, California. He serves as a consultant for the documentary film, *Incident at Oglala*, and works as an actor in the film *Thunderheart*. In 1992, he releases his debut album, *AKA Graffiti Man*, in which he reads his poetry backed by rock and Indian musical styles.

1947 *Smoke Signals* Is Published. Marie Potts, a Maidu Indian woman, creates an intertribal newspaper, *Smoke Signals*; it is one of the earliest modern publications serving reservation and urban Indian populations in California. Published bimonthly, *Smoke Signals* seeks to inform California Indians of current issues and events which specifically affect them. The publication also strives to promote intertribal cooperation, its motto being "In Unity There Is Strength." Potts herself is recognized as both a pioneer and an exemplary American Indian journalist. The ideals surrounding her creation of *Smoke Signals* have since been upheld and emulated by other Indian publications.

MAY 19, 1947 Division of Shoshoni and Arapaho Trust Funds Act. Congress passes the Division of Shoshoni and Arapaho Trust Funds Act, dividing the trust funds of the Shoshoni and Arapaho tribes of the Wind River Reservation on deposit in the Treasury of the United States.

MAY 27, 1947 Memorial Museum on Fort Hall Reservation Act. Congress passes the Memorial Museum on Fort Hall Reservation Act, authorizing a sum of $150,000 for the purpose of constructing a museum in commemoration of old Fort Hall and a shop for the sale of Indian handicrafts; operation of the facility is to be by the Shoshoni-Bannock tribes of the Fort Hall Reservation under the supervision, management, and control of the Bureau of Indian Affairs.

JUNE 14, 1947 Navajo Gas Lands Lease Act. Congress passes the Navajo Gas Lands Lease Act, which authorizes the secretary of interior, acting through the Bureau of Mines, and the Navajo Tribe to enter into an agreement dated December 1, 1947, to substitute new leases for former oil and gas leases on the Navajo Reservation in New Mexico.

DECEMBER 19, 1947 Immediate Relief of Navajo and Hopi Act. Congress passes the Immediate Relief of Navajo and Hopi Act, authorizing a sum of $2 million to allow the secretary of interior to provide immediate relief for needy Navajo and Hopi Indians who are on their reservations or allotted holdings.

1 9 4 8

1948 *Harrison v. Laveen.* In *Harrison v. Laveen,* American Indians are granted the right to vote in Arizona state elections, a privilege denied them in spite of the passage of the federal Citizenship Act in 1924. Disenfranchisement of Indians is justified by states on various grounds, including their nonpayment of state taxes (even though non-Indians were not required to pay taxes in order to vote), their status as wards, and that their residence on a reservation is not residence within a state, a requirement for voting purposes.

1948 **Leslie Marmon Silko, Laguna Pueblo Novelist and Poet, Is Born.** Silko is born in Albuquerque, New Mexico, and spends her childhood at the Laguna Pueblo in eastern New Mexico, where she is surrounded with the culture and lore of the Laguna and Keres people. It is during these years that she learns about the traditions of Native American storytelling, principally through her grandmother and aunt. Silko receives a bachelor's degree in English from the University of New Mexico, at which time she writes her first short story, "The Man to Send Rain Clouds." In 1974, *Laguna Woman,* a book of poetry, is published. In 1977, *Storyteller,* a collection of short stories, and *Ceremony,* a novel, are published. *Ceremony,* the story of an inner journey that takes a young Indian back to his roots, establishes Silko's reputation as a leading U.S. author. Silko receives one of 21 "genius" fellowships awarded by the MacArthur Foundation. In 1991, *Almanac of the Dead* is published. The 700-page novel is called by one reviewer "the most ambitious literary undertaking of the past quarter century." Silko believes that "our identity is formed by the stories we hear when we're growing up. Literature helps us locate ourselves

in the family, the community, and the whole universe."

1948 **Louis (Smokey) Bruyere, Ojibway Politician, Is Born.** Born in northwestern Ontario in 1948, Bruyere establishes the Ontario Métis and Non-Status Indian Association while working in the mining and lumbering industries of northern Ontario. He becomes a nationally recognized figure during his term as president of the Native Council of Canada (N.C.C.) from 1981 to 1988. During these years he represents the N.C.C. at several Constitutional Conferences. He also works toward the passage of Bill C-31 in June 1985. This change to the Indian Act restores Indian status to those who were previously denied it because they or their mothers had married non-Indians. In 1991 Bruyere accepts a new position with the federal Department of Indian and Northern Affairs as spokesman for aboriginal trappers.

1948 **Mackenzie Highway.** The Mackenzie Highway, connecting Hay River, Northwest Territories, with southern centers, increases interaction between the Dene of the region and non-Natives.

1948 **Soapstone Carving Introduced.** Soapstone carving is introduced to the Hudson Bay Eskimo by non-Indian artist James Houston. Carving of soapstone subsequently finds great success in the collectors' market, spreading all the way to Alaska. It continues to be produced today in a number of regional styles.

1948 **Walter Echo-Hawk, Pawnee Lawyer, Is Born.** Walter Echo-Hawk is born on the Pawnee Reservation near Pawnee, Oklahoma. He receives a political science degree from Oklahoma State University in 1970 and a law degree from the University of New Mexico in 1973. Echo-Hawk is a senior staff attorney of the Native American Rights Fund (NARF), a national, Indian-interest legal organization headquartered in Boulder, Colorado, and has been admitted to practice law before the U.S.

Supreme Court, the Supreme Court of Colorado, and several courts of appeal. In 1989, Echo-Hawk represents a number of Indian tribes in negotiating the Smithsonian Institution reburial agreement, which receives national attention and is enacted into law. In 1989 and 1990, he is a national leader in the Indian campaign to obtain passage of the Native American Grave Protection and Repatriation Act. In 1992, Echo-Hawk is awarded the Civil Liberties Award from the American Civil Liberties Union of Oregon "for significant contributions to the cause of individual freedom."

FEBRUARY 5, 1948   Competency of Certain Osages Act. Congress passes the Competency of Certain Osages Act, authorizing the secretary of interior to issue certificates of competency to each member of the Osage tribe of less than one-half Indian blood and at least 21 years of age, with the legal guardian to assume business supervision if the Osage member is deemed incompetent by law.

FEBRUARY 5, 1948   Filing of Actions to Quit Land Titles Act. Congress passes the Filing of Actions to Quit Land Titles Act, stating that any person may file against an Indian or heirs of any Indian who was or were granted lands according to a treaty between the United States and Delaware Indians, October 3, 1818 (7 Stat. 188). The act contains a condition that such lands should never be conveyed or transferred without the approbation of the president of the United States.

FEBRUARY 5, 1948   Indian Lands Rights-of-Way Act. Congress passes the Indian Lands Rights-of-Way Act, allowing the secretary of interior to grant rights-of-way for all purposes across Indian lands held in trust by the United States, excluding the Pueblo Indians of New Mexico.

FEBRUARY 26, 1948   Certain Lands Sale of L'Anse Chippewa Act. Congress passes the Certain Lands Sale of L'Anse Chippewa Act,

allowing the secretary of interior to sell, for the sum of $2,015, certain tribal lands and allotted Indian lands. The proceeds of the sale are to be deposited with the village of L'Anse, Michigan.

MARCH 11, 1948   Uintah and Ouray Indian Reservation Boundaries Act. Congress passes the Uintah and Ouray Indian Reservation Boundaries Act, establishing the exterior boundary of the Uintah and Ouray Reservation in Grand and Uintah counties of Utah, for the benefit of the Ute Indian tribe of said reservation.

MARCH 29, 1948   Klamath Welfare Act. Congress passes the Klamath Welfare Act, authorizing the secretary of interior to pay loans; to purchase land; to build homes, including household equipment and furnishings; and to purchase feed, seed, and grain from the capital reserve fund on deposit for the Klamath, Modoc, and Yahooskin band of Snake Indians.

MAY 25, 1948   Costs on Flathead Indian Irrigation Project. Congress passes the Costs on Flathead Indian Irrigation Project, calling for the United States to reimburse costs for the construction of the irrigation and power systems of the Flathead Irrigation project in Montana, according to construction costs under the act of March 7, 1928, and supplemental acts.

JUNE 3, 1948   Crazy Horse Monument Dedicated. Five Indian survivors of the battle of the Little Big Horn are among participants in the dedication of the Crazy Horse monument in South Dakota, which is started by sculptor Korczak Ziolkowski, and will be completed with the help of contributions from interested private individuals and groups. The monument, which will take up an entire mountain top and be visible from all directions, is part of a plan that includes a research center, a medical school for Indians, and other development projects.

JUNE 30, 1948   Iowa Jurisdiction over Sac (Sauk) and Fox Reservation Act. Congress passes the Iowa Jurisdiction over Sac and Fox

Reservation Act, conferring to the state of Iowa jurisdiction over the Sac and Fox Reservation in that state.

JULY 1, 1948   Estate Sale of Crow Tribe Act. Congress passes the Estate Sale of Crow Tribe Act, to provide for the sale to the Crow tribe of the interests of the estates of deceased Crow Indian allottees, and to provide for the sale of certain lands to the board of county commissioners of Comanche County, Oklahoma.

AUGUST 8, 1948   Georges Erasmus, Dene Politician, Is Born. Born in Fort Rae in the Northwest Territories, Georges Erasmus becomes heavily involved in Dene organizations by 1969. He becomes president of the Indian Brotherhood of the Northwest Territories in 1976, a position he holds until 1983. During this time he guides the organization during its efforts to stop the construction of the Mackenzie Valley Pipeline and oversees the reorganization of the brotherhood as the Dene Nation in 1978. In 1983 he is chosen as vice chief of the Assembly of First Nations, and becomes the grandchief of the organization in 1985. In October of that year he is successful in persuading Greenpeace, an international environmental organization, to halt a proposed anti-fur campaign, a campaign which threatens the way of life for many of the Dene and Inuit of northern Canada who still depend on trapping for much of their income.

Erasmus leads the Assembly of First Nations until 1991. He acts as a spokesman for the Assembly of First Nations at Canadian Constitutional Conferences on Aboriginal Rights in 1983, 1984, 1985, and 1987. Upon stepping down as grand chief, he is appointed co-chair of the Royal Commission on Aboriginal Peoples. The commission has a mandate from the federal government to examine and report on a broad range of issues concerning aboriginal peoples in Canada, including self-government, treaties, and economic, social, and cultural issues of concern to aboriginal peoples as well as matters relating to the administration of jus-

tice. The first two reports of the commission are released in 1992 and 1993. Erasmus is also co-author of *Drumbeat: Anger and Renewal in Indian Country* (1989). He has been accorded honorary degrees from at least four Canadian universities.

1 9 4 9

1949   Arizona Refuses Social Programs for American Indians. The state of Arizona refuses to include Indians in any of its relief programs, nor does the state permit Indian children to be assisted by crippled children's programs, a policy which persists for years thereafter.

1949   The Hoover Commission. In 1949, the Hoover Commission, under the direction of former president Herbert Hoover, recommends that Native Americans be "integrated, economically and politically, as well as culturally." Hoover's report suggests that "when the trust status of Indian lands has ended, thus permitting taxation, and surplus Indian families have established themselves off the reservations, special aid to the state and local governments for Indian programs should end." The commission recommends that the federal government remove itself from regulation of and responsibility for Indian affairs. This program gathers considerable support from congressional leaders. Many reservations contain timber, oil, gas, coal, uranium, water, and other natural resources coveted by non-Indians and major corporations.

1949   Hopi Reject Hoover Commission Report. In a letter datelined "Hopi Indian Empire," six chiefs, four interpreters, and sixteen other Hopi from four villages write to President Truman in protest of the 1949 Hoover Commission report. Refusing to file a land claim, they reject the notion of "asking the government for land that is ours," and renounce any participation in BIA "rehabilitation" programs, the Navajo-Hopi act, NATO, and the Hoover

Commission's proposal for termination. "We have never abandoned our sovereignty to any foreign power or nation," they announce.

1949   Tom Jackson, Métis Singer and Actor, Is Born. Born of a Cree mother and a non-Native father, Jackson grows up in a rough section of Winnipeg, Manitoba, even living on the streets for a time. He becomes a moderately successful folksinger in the early 1970s. He takes up acting after being convinced to take a part in an all-Native production of *The Ecstasy of Rita Joe*, a play dealing with the struggles of Indians in contemporary society. His success leads him to accept other acting opportunities. In 1992 he takes central roles in the Canadian Broadcasting Corporation productions of *The Diviners* (1992) and *Medicine River* (1993). He also takes the role of Peter Kenidi, the chief of a Dene band in the fictional town of Lynx River, Northwest Territories, in the Canadian Broadcasting Corporation's dramatic series, *North of 60.*

MARCH 31, 1949   Newfoundland Joins Canada. The Province of Newfoundland and Labrador enters Confederation as Canada's tenth province without having negotiated land surrenders with any Natives. The Newfoundland government does not recognize the existence of any Indian bands on the island of Newfoundland. The Canadian and Newfoundland governments agree that the Canadian government will pay the Newfoundland government to administer Indian affairs in Labrador. As a result, the province's Indians are given fewer benefits than those in other provinces. For example, the Innu are never given a reserve. Newfoundland Indians are not specifically excluded from the provincial franchise.

MAY 17, 1949   Billy Diamond, Cree Chief, Is Born. Billy Diamond is born in a tent near Rupert House, Quebec, on the shore of James Bay. After completing school, Diamond is elected chief of the Rupert House Cree band in 1971 just as the Cree of northern Quebec are beginning to fight the James Bay Hydroelectric Project. After forging links with other northern Quebec Cree, he is elected the founding president of the Grand Council of the Cree of Quebec in 1974, a position he holds until 1984. The council is a province-wide organization devoted to the interests of the Cree in Quebec. As president of the Grand Council of the Cree of Quebec, Diamond leads the Cree opposition to hydroelectric development in the region, and ultimately the negotiations culminating in the James Bay and Northern Quebec Agreement (1975), which allows the James Bay Project to proceed but gives the Cree an significant degree of control over their own lives.

With the agreement signed, Diamond becomes chairman of the Cree Regional Authority, established to administer the implementation of the agreement. He also serves, beginning in 1976, as chairman of the James Bay Cree School Board, one of the first aboriginally controlled school boards in Canada. In 1980, he becomes president of Air Creebec, a Cree-owned regional airline.

Diamond thus leads the Cree from a time in which the Quebec government proposes northern development without acknowledging any aboriginal rights whatsoever, to a land claims agreement with the provincial and federal governments that is viewed as a model for many other aboriginal communities in Canada that are seeking greater autonomy and control over their lives.

JUNE 15, 1949   Provincial Franchise. British Columbia (B.C.) Indians vote in a provincial election for the first time, and Nishga leader Frank Calder *(See* biography, August 3, 1915) becomes the first Indian elected to a provincial legislature. He represents the large northwestern constituency called Atlin. The Native Brotherhood of British Columbia endorses granting the franchise to B.C. Indians while the North American Indian Brotherhood opposes it, fearing that B.C. Indians will lose their special rights. Indians in Nova Scotia and Yukon Territory have never been specifically excluded from the vote, although residence and property qualifications have served to exclude most. All other provinces specifically bar status Indians or Indians resident on reserves from voting. Status Indians are not legally considered to be citizens of Canada.

AUGUST 19, 1949 Certain Pueblo and Cañoncito Navajo Lands in Trust Act. Congress passes the Certain Pueblo and Cañoncito Navajo Lands in Trust Act. The act acknowledges the transfer, approved by the president of the United States, of certain public domain lands from the secretary of agriculture to the secretary of interior, to become trust lands for Pueblo and Cañoncito Navajo Indians.

AUGUST 19, 1949 Klamath County School Facilities Act. Congress passes the Klamath County School Facilities Act, providing funds for cooperation with the school board of Klamath County, Oregon, for the construction, extension, and improvement of public school facilities, to be available to all Indian and non-Indian children without discrimination.

SEPTEMBER 7, 1949 Exchange of Navajo Tribal Lands Act. Congress passes the Exchange of Navajo Tribal Lands Act, authorizing the secretary of interior, with the governing body of the Navajo tribe, to exchange surface rights of 640 acres in Arizona for land in Utah.

SEPTEMBER 7, 1949 Indian Schools in South Dakota Act. Congress passes the Indian Schools in South Dakota Act, stating that the schools operated and maintained by the Bureau of Indian Affairs on any reservation in South Dakota shall, by a voting majority of the parents of the children, decide on the course of study that is to meet at least the minimum educational requirements prescribed by the department of public instruction of South Dakota.

SEPTEMBER 8, 1949 Competent Crow Tribe Act. Congress passes the Competent Crow Tribe Act, stating that all Crow Indians born to "competent" parents shall automatically become "competent" members of the tribe.

OCTOBER 5, 1949 Agua Caliente Indian Reservation Jurisdiction Act. Congress passes the Agua Caliente Indian Reservation Jurisdiction Act, stating that all lands on the Agua Caliente Indian Reservation in the state of California, and the Indian residents thereof, shall be subject to the laws, both civil and criminal, of the State of California.

OCTOBER 10, 1949 Land Exchange North Carolina Cherokees Act. Congress passes the Land Exchange North Carolina Cherokees Act, authorizing exchange of lands between the North Carolina Cherokee and the state of North Carolina, involving right of way of the Blue Ridge Parkway, Mollie Gap, Wolf Laurel Gap, and Bunches Gap.

OCTOBER 25, 1949 Crow Tribe Buffalo Act. Congress passes the Crow Tribe Buffalo Act, calling for the secretary of interior to transfer to the Crow tribe of Montana the title to all the buffalo owned by the United States on the Crow Indian Reservation.

1 9 5 0

1950 California Indian Land Claims. Congress adopts legislation awarding $150 to each California Indian as a first or partial payment on long-standing land claims.

1950 Dillon S. Meyer and Termination. Dillon S. Meyer becomes commissioner of Indian affairs and actively supports the new "termination" policy of the Congress. During World War II, Meyer was the administrative head of the internment camps that contained many U.S. citizens of Japanese descent from throughout the western United States. The Japanese-Americans were considered a potential threat to U.S. security in the war with Japan.

1950   Graham Greene, Oneida Actor, Is Born. Graham Greene is born on the Six Nations Reserve in southwest Ontario. He begins his career in television, film, and radio in 1976. Before becoming an actor, Greene works at a number of different jobs, including stints as a high steel worker, a civil technologist, and a draftsman. Greene is perhaps best known for his performance in *Dances with Wolves*, a 1991 film produced and directed by Kevin Costner, which wins several Academy Awards, including the award for best picture. Greene portrays Kicking Bird, an elder who strives to protect his people from attacks by American authorities. Additionally, Greene is cast in a number of television series and is known for his work in *The Campbells, Spirit Bay, Captain Power, Running Brave, Adderley, Night Heat,* and *Pow-Wow Highway*. In 1993 he wins the lead role in *Medicine River* a movie based on a novel of the same title written by Thomas King *(See* biography, 1943).

1950   Indian Education. In the dawning years of America's entry into the space age, a Bureau of Indian Affairs survey estimates that there are 19,300 Indian children for whom there is no school training of any kind.

1950   Sioux Sun Dance. The Sun Dance is revived among the Sioux.

JANUARY 8, 1950   Indian Affairs. The Canadian Department of Citizenship and Immigration assumes responsibility for Indian affairs. Prime Minister Louis St. Laurent explains that since it is policy to have Indian affairs administered so as to bring all Indians to citizenship (enfranchisement), the Indian Affairs Branch ought to be part of this government department.

APRIL 19, 1950   Rehabilitation of Navajo and Hopi Indians Act. Congress passes the Rehabilitation of Navajo and Hopi Indians Act, providing facilities, employment, and services to the Navajo and Hopi to develop their natural resources and to help them become self-supporting.

JUNE 30, 1950   Inuit Franchise. The Canadian government extends the right to vote in federal elections to the Inuit. The government defends giving the Inuit, but not status Indians, the vote on the grounds that Inuit are not exempt from paying tax. On these grounds the new legislation allows status Indians to vote if they sign a waiver, which would make them eligible for taxation.

JULY 19, 1950   Gil Cardinal, Métis Filmmaker, Is Born. A graduate of the radio and television arts program at the Northern Alberta Institute of Technology in Edmonton, Alberta, Gil Cardinal emerges as the foremost Native filmmaker in Canada. After producing a daily live magazine-format show in Alberta and directing a series of programs called *Shadow Puppets* that portray adaptations of Cree and Blackfoot legends, Cardinal begins free-lancing with the federally established National Film Board in 1980.

With the National Film Board, Cardinal completes numerous projects including *Children of Alcohol* (1983), a documentary on the effects of parental alcoholism; *Discussion in Bioethics: The Courage of One's Convictions* (1985), an inquiry into medical/legal ethics; and *Fort McPherson* (1986), a look at a community's struggle with alcohol and suicide. *Foster Child* (1987), which features Cardinal as director, associate editor, and main subject, wins nine film festival awards. *The Spirit Within* (1990), which Cardinal co-directs with Will Campbell, focuses on the importance of spirituality among Indian inmates in Canada.

In 1990, Great North Productions of Edmonton, Alberta, helps Cardinal and Campbell launch Great Plains Productions, which in 1993 becomes totally controlled by aboriginals. *Our Home and Native Land* (1993), a documentary on the Assembly of First Nations grand chief, Ovide Mercredi, airs in Britain to enthusiastic reviews. In 1993, work begins on

An Inuit family receives its family allowance check at the Hudson's Bay Company store at Read Island (near Victoria Island) in the Canadian arctic in 1950. The extension of Canadian government social security payments and other public services to remote regions of Canada after World War II encouraged the movement of Indian and Inuit groups toward permanent settlements. Note that the 'Family Allowance' poster on the counter includes messages printed in Inuktitut syllabics. Courtesy of the National Archives of Canada.

Big Bear, based on Rudy Wiebe's 1973 novel, *The Temptations of Big Bear,* the story of the nineteenth-century Plains Cree chief, Big Bear *(See* Big Bear, c. 1825).

JULY 20, 1950   Tantoo Cardinal, Cree/Métis Actress, Is Born. Tantoo Cardinal is born in Fort McMurray and raised in Anzac, north of Edmonton, Alberta. Despite her lack of formal training as an actress, Cardinal finds employment, particularly in productions exposing life within the Native community. Following the release of *Marie Anne* in 1977, Cardinal receives greater exposure to a general audience. In 1990 she earns a supporting role as the wife of a Lakota medicine man in Kevin Costner's *Dances With Wolves* (1990), and a supporting role in Bruce Beresford's *Black Robe* (1991), a joint

Canadian-Australian production portraying a seventeenth-century French missionary's attempts to evangelize Native people. In 1993 she works on a title role in *Silent Tongue*.

AUGUST 1, 1950 *Broken Arrow* **Released.** *Broken Arrow*, a story about the friendship between the U.S. mail rider Thomas Jeffords and the Apache Indian leader Cochise, opens to widespread critical praise. The film is director Delmer Daves' first western, and its plea for tolerance and brotherhood is a timely theme for postwar American society. In 1951, Hollywood's Golden Globe Awards names *Broken Arrow* as the "Best Film Promoting International Understanding," and the Association of American Indian Affairs recommends the picture for its "bold, honest treatment of Indian history."

SEPTEMBER 15, 1950   Indian Land Jurisdiction in New York Act. Congress passes the Indian Land Jurisdiction in New York Act, conferring to the state of New York jurisdiction in civil actions and proceedings between Indians or between one or more Indians and any other person or persons.

SEPTEMBER 30, 1950   Separate Settlement Contracts for Sioux Act. Congress passes the Separate Settlement Contracts for Sioux Act, which authorizes the chief of engineers, Department of the Army, along with the secretary of interior, to negotiate contracts with the Cheyenne River Sioux and Standing Rock Sioux for the Oahe Dam and Reservoir Project.

1950s   Relocation Policy. During the 1950s the government begins the relocation program, which assists Indian families to move to urban areas. Administrators argue that with housing and employment in urban areas, Indians will find new lives away from their old lands and become integrated into mainstream America. In 1952, the Bureau of Indians Affairs establishes the Voluntary Relocation Program (also

known as the Employment Assistance Program), which pays for training, travel, moving, and assistance in finding urban work. The BIA also provides a strong vocational and academic training program for Indians who relocate. By 1960, approximately 35,000 Native Americans have relocated, but a third of these return to the reservations.

1 9 5 1

1951   Joy Harjo, Creek Poet and Educator, Is Born. Joy Harjo is born in Tulsa, Oklahoma. She graduates from the Institute of American Indian Arts in Santa Fe, New Mexico, in 1968, and in 1978 receives a master of fine arts degree in creative writing from the Iowa Writer's Workshop at the University of Iowa. Harjo has published four books of poetry, including *She Had Some Horses* (1983) and the award-winning *In Mad Love and War* (1990). In 1993, Harjo is a professor of English in the creative writing program at the University of New Mexico. She is also a screenwriter and is working on an original dramatic screenplay, *When We Used to Be Humans*, for the American Film Foundation.

1951   Navajo Woman on Tribal Council. Annie Dodge Wauneka breaks with tribal tradition when she is elected the first Navajo woman to the 74-member Navajo Tribal Council.

1951   Paiute Tribal Council. The Paiute organize a tribal council.

JANUARY 21, 1951   W. Yvon Dumont, Métis Politician, Is Born. Born at St. Laurent, Manitoba, in 1951 as the son of a noted political leader in the Manitoba Métis Federation, Yvon Dumont is drawn into political life at a young age. At the age of 16 he is elected secretary-treasurer of the St. Laurent local of the Manitoba Métis Federation. Within five years, he rises to the position of vice president of the

Native Council of Canada, a national organization representing non-status Indians and Métis.

In 1984 Dumont is elected president of the Manitoba Métis Federation, promising to pursue a complicated Métis land claim in Manitoba. As the federal government has rejected the claim, the case has gone to the courts. Dumont hires lawyer Thomas Berger, who headed the Mackenzie Valley Pipeline Inquiry in the 1970s, and who has become well known for his work in the area of Native claims. Under Dumont's leadership, the finances of the Manitoba Métis Federation are stabilized, enabling it to participate in the funding of new housing projects and other initiatives on behalf of Manitoba's Métis. He also is appointed a governor of the University of Manitoba, and a board member of the National Board of the Canadian Aboriginal Economic Development Strategy.

In January 1993, Prime Minister Brian Mulroney appoints Dumont to the position of lieutenant-governor of Manitoba, the first Native to hold that position in the province.

FEBRUARY 28–MARCH 2, 1951 Consultations on the Indian Act. Indian leaders from across Canada meet with Canadian Indian affairs officials regarding changes to Canada's Indian Act. The meetings follow the government's decision to abandon a 1950 attempt to change the Indian Act.

JUNE 20, 1951 Indian Act. A new Canadian Indian Act adopts the main thrust of the Parliamentary Committee report of 1948 by significantly reducing the powers of the Indian Affairs Department but retaining the assimilative aim of the Indian Act. The new act makes it easier for Indians to be enfranchised and for them to acquire location tickets. It also makes provisions allowing Indian children to be placed in integrated provincial schools. Various coercive aspects of the act, including sections banning potlatch and Thirst Dance (Sun Dance) ceremonies, are repealed. The government rejects the recommendation to establish a land

claims commission. Indian leaders protest the assimilationist aim of the Indian Act and the refusal to establish a land claims commission.

AUGUST 21, 1951 Ute Per Capita and Division Act. Congress passes the Ute Per Capita and Division Act, authoring the secretary of interior to use the tribal fund of the Ute tribes for a per capita payment to the Ute tribe of the Uintah and Ouray reservations and to divide the tribal funds with Southern Ute.

DECEMBER 6, 1951 Tomson Highway, Cree Playwright, Is Born. Tomson Highway is born near his father's trapline in northern Manitoba. He learns Cree as his second language when he is sent to boarding school at The Pas, Manitoba, at the age of six. He graduates with a bachelor of music honors degree in 1975 from the University of Western Ontario.

At the age of 30, Highway decides to write his first play, hoping to bring life on "the rez" (the reserve) to a mainstream Canadian audience. *The Rez Sisters* is a huge success after it opens in Toronto in December 1986, going on to win the Dora Mavor Moore award for best new play in Toronto's 1987–88 theater season and to place as runner-up for the Floyd S. Chalmers Award for outstanding Canadian play of 1986. It also is nominated for Canada's Governor General's Literary Award in 1988. It tours to sold-out audiences across Canada and is one of two plays representing Canada on the mainstage of the Edinburgh International Festival, a festival that showcases international drama. Highway's next play, *Dry Lips Oughta Move to Kapuskasing* (1988), wins four Dora Mavor Moore awards, including one for best new play, and is nominated for the Governor General's Literary Award in 1989.

In 1986, Highway becomes the Artistic Director of Native Earth Performing Arts Inc., Toronto's only professional Native theater company. He has written five other plays and continues in his efforts to celebrate Canada's Native people through his art.

1 9 5 2

1952 BIA Employment Assistance Program. The Bureau of Indian Affairs (BIA) inaugurates a program of employment assistance that gives opportunities to Indians who wish to relocate in urban communities, find work on or near a reservation, and obtain adult vocational training in school or on-the-job training programs. Included are provisions for financial help and assistance to help families adjust to a new environment. Over 62,000 Indians receive aid from this program.

APRIL 3, 1952 Transfer of Indian Health Care Act. Congress passes the Transfer of Indian Health Care Act, authorizing the Public Health Service to receive transfer of unused Indian health facilities to states and local governments to provide health needs to non-Indians. The act further authorizes the secretary of interior to contract with states and territories for health care facilities to meet Indian needs.

JUNE 12, 1952 Hoopa Valley Reservation School Act. Congress passes the Hoopa Valley Reservation School Act, allowing the secretary of interior to convey by deed to the state of California or to the Hoopa Unified School District of the state of California not more than 45 acres of the agency and school reserve on the Hoopa Valley Indian Reservation for the construction of a school for both Indian and non-Indian pupils.

JULY 3, 1952 Five Civilized Tribes Contracts Act. Congress passes the Five Civilized Tribes Contracts Act, allowing the Five Civilized Tribes to make contracts for professional legal services involving the prosecution of claims against the United States with the approval of the secretary of interior.

JULY 18, 1952 Cession of Rights-of-Way on Wind River Reservation Act. Congress passes the Cession of Rights-of-Way on Wind River Reservation Act, authorizing the secretary of interior to be paid from funds appropriated for the Missouri River Basin project, not to exceed $458,000, to convey and relinquish to the United States the property and rights of the Shoshoni and Arapaho needed for the construction, operation, and maintenance of the Boysen Unit of the Missouri River Basin Project.

OCTOBER 8, 1952 John Kim Bell, Mohawk Symphony Conductor and Composer, Is Born. Born on the Kahnawak' Reserve near Montreal, Quebec, Bell lives most of his childhood and youth in Columbus, Ohio, spending summers at Kahnawak'. Following musical training in Ohio and in Siena, Italy, and after conducting several Broadway musicals in New York City, he is appointed as apprentice conductor to the Toronto Symphony Orchestra in 1980.

Seeking to encourage Canadian aboriginal youth to seek musical training, Bell establishes the Canadian Native Arts Foundation (C.N.A.F.) in 1988. The foundation is a privately and publicly funded national charity that provides scholarships for Native youths being trained in the arts. The C.N.A.F. hands out approximately $1 million in scholarships to Native youths between 1988 and 1992. Included in its fund-raising concerts and events is Bell's 1988 production of "In the Land of the Spirits," the first Native ballet. The ballet's premiere at the National Arts Centre in Ottawa is a huge artistic and financial success. Bell also co-composes the ballet.

Bell is recipient of honorary doctorates from two universities in Canada, and is given the Order of Canada, an award granted by the governor general of Canada in recognition of exemplary merit and achievement.

1 9 5 3

1953 First Miss Indian America. Arlene Wesley James, a Yakima from Washington, becomes the first Miss Indian America as the result of winning the important featured event at the annual All American Indian Days celebration at Sheridan, Wyoming. Contestants are judged on the basis of poise, Indian characteristics, scholastic ability, and dedication to the advancement of the Indian people. They represent many tribes from throughout the United States and Canada. Winners travel widely to represent the American Indian people as goodwill ambassadors at many national and international events.

1953 Mary Crow Dog, Sioux Activist and Author, Is Born. Mary Crow Dog is born and raised on the Rosebud Sioux Reservation. Shocked at the violence and hopelessness of reservation life, she joins the Native American Movement during the late 1960s and later marries Leonard Crow Dog, a Sioux medicine man who revives the sacred but outlawed Ghost Dance. In 1990, she publishes the best-selling book *Lakota Woman* (with Richard Erdoes, a photographer and journalist). In her book, Crow Dog tells what it means to be a Sioux woman caught between the forces of tradition and the feminist movement.

JUNE 4, 1953 Indian School Property Act. Congress passes the Indian School Property Act, authorizing the secretary of interior to convey to state and local government agencies federal Indian land and school facilities no longer needed, that land to be no more than 20 acres.

JUNE 8, 1953 Provincial Franchise. Indians in Manitoba vote for the first time after receiving the provincial franchise in 1953. Nova Scotia, British Columbia, and the Yukon are the only other provinces or territories that do not specifically exclude Indians from the franchise.

SUMMER 1953 Inuit Relocation. Ungava Inuit families from Port Harrison (Inukjuak), on the eastern shore of Hudson Bay, and Iglulik Inuit from Pond Inlet on Baffin Island, in Canada's Arctic, are moved to new communities at Resolute Bay (Cornwallis Island) and Grise Fiord (Ellesmere Island), both in the high Arctic. Hundreds of Inuit have been relocated in government-sponsored relocations since in the 1930s but this relocation is destined to become the most controversial because, while it moves the Port Harrison Inuit to a much more game-rich area, it also strengthens Canada's claims to the high Arctic. Many of the Port Harrison Inuit do not feel at home in the harsh environment of the high Arctic, or with the Inuit from Pond Inlet.

AUGUST 1, 1953 The Termination Resolution. Congress initiates the policy often called "termination," a plan to end tribal sovereignty, health care, and most federal obligations to Indians as specified in past treaties or acts of Congress. Responsive to the national conservative swing in the 1950s, Congress passes a series of laws implementing the termination of Indian reservations. Between 1954 and 1962 more than 100 bands, communities, and rancherias are terminated or severed from direct relations with the federal government, losing many protections and services.

As termination is undertaken in earnest, Congress frequently blocks Claims Commission or U.S. Court of Claims awards to tribes, refusing to disperse the funds until termination is agreed to. This is the case, for example, with the Menominee tribe of Wisconsin, perhaps the best known of all the terminated tribes. In 1951 the Menominee are awarded a settlement of $8.5 million by the U.S. Court of Claims. Congress stalls distribution of the award, and, fearing its loss, the tribe reluctantly agrees to termination. In order to protect tribal assets, the Menominee decide to create their own county, which will handle nearly all public services. A corporation is also created—Menominee Enterprises, Incorporated—which gives each tribal member a bond worth $3,000 and 100 shares of stock in the corporation. The reservation-turned-county, however, is the poorest in Wisconsin, and in order to cover welfare, utilities, health services, and transportation costs, the county is forced to tax its only property holder—Menominee Enterprises, Incorporated. The corporation raises money by forcing tribal members to purchase the land they live on, which they can do only by selling their $3,000 bonds. This leaves many Menominee too poor to maintain utilities, health costs, and property taxes, and tax auctions become common. Unemployment rises and county welfare costs more than double within five years. Inadequate funds also force the closure of the county hospital, and by 1965 almost one-third of the Menominee test positive for tuberculosis. As it is for many contemporary Indian groups, termination is devastating for the health and welfare of the Menominee tribe.

Initial opposition to termination both from states and from many Indian groups fails to stem the termination policy tide. The California legislature, for example, first endorses and then forcefully opposes termination because the state would have to assume greater responsibility for the terminated Indians. Despite the cooperation of the Council of California Indians, the California Indian Congress, the Federated Indians of California, as well as the American Friends Service Committee, which leads to the defeat of a state termination bill in 1954, federal law prevails. Rancherias all over California disappear as lands are sold or allocated to individual Indian residents under the termination policy. In addition, Johnson-O'Malley funds for Indian education are phased out and not restored for many years. Slowly, however, the failures of the termination policy bring it to an inevitable end. The National Congress of American Indians (NCAI) fights against termination and by the late 1950s the movement for abrogation of federal support for Indians has lost its momentum, its failures far outnumbering its successes. Termination ends during President John F. Kennedy's administration, principally because of enduring opposition by Indians and state governments. Later, many tribes (including the Menominee) are restored to federal trust status. Most, however, suffer great losses during the termination era, and the effects are irreversible.

AUGUST 15, 1953 Public Law 280. In 1953, the same year the termination resolution is passed, Congress passes Public Law 280, which empowers certain states (California, Wisconsin, Nebraska, Minnesota, Oregon, and, in 1959, Alaska) to assume management over criminal justice on Indian reservations. This law opens the possibility of state jurisdiction over reservation courts. Previously, federal law and courts had upheld the separation of state and Indian government relations because this separation is explicitly written out in the commerce clause of the Constitution. Public Law 280 specifically excepts from state jurisdiction the regulation and taxation of trust property and the hunting and fishing rights of Indian people.

AUGUST 15, 1953 Shoshoni and Arapaho Compensation Act. Congress passes the Shoshoni and Arapaho Compensation Act, authorizing $1,009,500 in compensation to the Shoshoni and Arapaho tribes of the Wind River Reservation for the Riverton reclamation project and for a ceded portion of their reservation.

AUGUST 15, 1953 Termination of Certain Federal Restrictions Act. Congress passes the Termination of Certain Federal Restrictions Act, an act to repeal the forbidden sale, purchase, or possession by Indians of personal property that may be sold, purchased, or possessed by non-Indians, amending Section 1157 of title 18 of the U.S. Codes pertaining to livestock.

---

1 9 5 4

1954 Louise Erdrich, Turtle Mountain Chippewa Novelist and Poet, Is Born. Louise Erdrich is born at Little Falls, Minnesota, and is among the first group of Native American women to be recruited and accepted to Dartmouth College, where she graduates with a major in English and creative writing. After graduation, Erdrich returns to North Dakota and conducts poetry workshops throughout the state under the auspices of the Poetry in the School Program of the North Dakota Arts Council. As a novelist Erdrich often collaborates with her husband, Michael Dorris, and together they are writing a four-volume family saga, three volumes of which are published under Erdrich's name: *Love Medicine* (1984), *The Beet Queen* (1986), and *Tracks* (1988). Erdrich and Dorris also co-author a best-seller entitled *The Crown of Columbus* (1991), and Erdrich is the sole author of *The Bingo Palace* (1993).

MARCH 24, 1954 Rosemarie Kuptana, Inuvialuk Leader, Is Born. Kuptana is born near Sachs Harbour, a community of just over 100 Inuit on Banks Island in the Northwest Territories. During the 1970s, when satellite technology begins making it feasible for television and radio broadcasting to be extended to the isolated settlements of northern Canada, Kuptana is instrumental in ensuring that programming is extended not only to the English-speaking audience but to the Native majority. In 1979, she joins the Canadian Broadcasting Corporation's Northern Service. She hosts morning and noon Inuvialuktun-language programs on C.B.C. Western Arctic, focusing on cultural, social, and political issues relevant to the local people, including the Inuvialuit land claim and Arctic oil and gas exploration. She joins the fledgling Inuit Broadcasting Corporation (I.B.C.) in 1982 as assistant production coordinator. The I.B.C. broadcasts in Inuktitut, the language of the Inuit. By 1983 she is elected president of the corporation, a position she holds until 1988. She is awarded the Order of Canada in 1988 in recognition of her work in Native communications.

While much of her work is related to communications in the North, Kuptana is best known among southern Canadians as the president of the Inuit Tapirisat of Canada, the national political voice of the Inuit. Following her election to that position in April 1991, she gains considerable public exposure because she becomes very involved in the national Constitutional negotiations under way at that time. She plays an important part in the negotiations leading to the Charlottetown Accord in 1992. Kuptana also is active in the Inuit Circumpolar Conference, an international organization representing Inuit from Canada, Alaska, Greenland, and the former Union of Soviet Socialist Republics. She serves as Canadian vice president of the organization from 1986 to 1989, significant years for the organization in that the Inuit of the Soviet Union are allowed to join it in 1988. Kuptana continues to be involved in many areas, including communications in the North and international Inuit political organization.

Kuptana also writes *No More Secrets* in 1991. The book deals with the issue of child sexual abuse in Inuit communities. Kuptana is named Northerner of the Year in 1992 and is among the 12 chosen for *Maclean's* 1992 "Honour Roll."

JUNE 17, 1954 Menominee Termination Act. Congress passes the Menominee Termination Act, terminating the U.S. government relationship with the Menominee tribe of Indians. This act ends the federal trust relationship between the Menominee tribe and the United States, and promises to provide a per capita payment of $1,500 to members (amended September 8, 1960 to agree upon a plan for trusteeship over tribal properties, P.L. 86-733).

JUNE 30, 1954 Fort Peck Reservation Fee Patents Act. Congress passes the Fort Peck Reservation Fee Patents Act, granting oil and gas in lands to the allottee with fee patents, and if deceased, to heirs or devises. The majority of members of the Fort Peck Reservation vote to accept these conditions.

JULY 17, 1954 Lower Brulé, Crow Creek Sioux, and Yankton Sioux Act. Congress passes the Lower Brulé, Crow Creek Sioux, and Yankton Sioux Act, to authorize the negotiation and ratification of separate contracts with the Lower Brulé Sioux and Crow Creek Sioux in South Dakota for lands and rights involving the Fort Randall Dam and Reservoir, Missouri River Development, and the reestablishment of the Indians of the Yankton Indian Reservation in South Dakota.

AUGUST 5, 1954 Indian Health Care Transfer Act. Congress passes the Indian Health Care Transfer Act, transferring Indian health care supervised by the Bureau of Indian Affairs and the Department of Interior to the Public Health Service supervised by the secretary of health, education, and welfare.

AUGUST 13, 1954 Klamath Termination Act. Congress passes the Klamath Termination Act, terminating federal supervision of the property of the Klamath tribe in Oregon and of its individual members.

AUGUST 13, 1954 Western Oregon Indians Termination Act. Congress passes the Western Oregon Indians Termination Act, terminating federal supervision over the property of certain tribes and bands of Indians in western Oregon and its individual members.

AUGUST 23, 1954 Alabama and Coushatta Termination Act. Congress passes the Alabama and Coushatta Termination Act, terminating federal supervision of the property of the Alabama and Coushatta tribe of Indians of Texas and of the individual members.

AUGUST 24, 1954 Fee Patent Allotments for Mission Indians Act. Congress passes the Fee Patent Allotments for Mission Indians Act, confirming the authority of the secretary of interior to issue patents in fee to allotments of lands of the Mission Indians in the state of California.

AUGUST 27, 1954 Ute Tribe Termination Act. Congress passes the Ute Tribe Termina-

tion Act, to provide for the partition and distribution of the assets of the Ute Indian tribe of the Uintah and Ouray Reservation in Utah between the mixed-blood and full-blood members. The act also terminates federal supervision of the property of mixed-blood members, and authorizes a development program for the full-blood Ute tribal members.

SEPTEMBER 1, 1954 Certain Utah Indians Termination Act. Congress passes the Certain Utah Indians Termination Act, to provide for the termination of federal supervision over the property of certain tribes, bands, and colonies of Indians in the state of Utah and their individual members.

1 9 5 5

1955 Indian Health. The Division of Indian Health is transferred from the Department of the Interior to the new Health, Education and Welfare Department (HEW), so that all assets of HEW can be brought to bear upon and solve the health problems of the Indians.

1955 Indian Health. The Public Health Service assumes responsibility for Indian medical care, previously under the jurisdiction of the Bureau of Indian Affairs.

1955 *Tee-Hit-Ton Indians v. United States.* This crucial decision involves the nature of aboriginal Indian land rights, with catastrophic results for Native Alaskans. The United States has made no treaties with Alaskan Indians, Aleuts, or Eskimos, and Congress has set aside only one small reservation, at Metlakatla. In this case the Tee-Hit-Ton, a Tlingit clan, demand compensation under the Fifth Amendment for lands settled without their consent. Absent recognition by a treaty or Congress, the Supreme Court concludes, aboriginal title "is not a property right but amounts to a right of occupancy which the sovereign grants and protects against intrusion by third parties but which may be terminated and such lands fully disposed of without any legally enforceable obligation to compensate the Indians." This means that tribes are entitled to protection of their lands from everyone except the federal government. Native Alaskans do not give up their struggle for land rights as a result of this case, but can no longer insist on getting full compensation.

MAY 1955–JULY 1957   Northern Radar Stations. Construction of 58 Distant Early Warning (D.E.W.) radar stations (intended to warn of an attack from the Soviet Union) along the 70th parallel greatly increases the presence of non-Natives among the Inuit of the North. Some Inuit find wage labor at the construction sites and make use of the normally scarce wood and metal that is discarded at the sites. Some radar sites such as those at Frobisher Bay (Iqualuit) and Cambridge Bay become the nucleus for main settlements. Earlier construction of the Pinetree line (completed in 1954) along the 50th parallel, and the Mid-Canada line (completed in 1957) along the 55th parallel, also bring many non-Natives to other isolated regions of northern Ontario, Quebec, and Labrador. Increased interest in the mineral, forest, and water resources of the North leads to a large influx of non-aboriginals throughout Canada's northern regions. Natives find limited employment opportunities in mining and forestry.

JUNE 9, 1955   Provincial Franchise. Ontario Indians resident on reserves vote in provincial elections for the first time. Some Indians boycott the polls claiming that the extension of the franchise threatens recognition of Indians as separate nations.

JUNE 24, 1955   Papago Minerals Lands Act. Congress passes the Papago Minerals Lands Act, an act that states that "all tribal lands within the Papago Reservation are withdrawn from all forms of exploration, location and entry for minerals, and such lands are hereby

made a part of the reservation and held in trust by the United States for the tribe."

JUNE 28, 1955   Yakima Land Exchange Act. Congress passes the Yakima Land Exchange Act, which authorizes the purchase, sale, and exchange of certain lands on the Yakima Indian Reservation with the state of Washington.

JUNE 28, 1955   Yakima Land Lease Act. Congress passes the Yakima Land Lease Act, an act for leasing of certain lands of the Yakima tribe to the state of Washington for historical and for public park purposes.

JULY 1955   Indian Health. Congress orders the Public Health Service to raise Indian health to a level comparable to that of the nation as a whole.

AUGUST 9, 1955   Indian Lands Leasing Act. Congress passes the Indian Lands Leasing Act to allow the leasing of restricted Indian lands for public, religious, educational, recreational, residential, business, and other purposes for no longer than 25 years, with the approval of the secretary of interior.

AUGUST 9, 1955   Pueblo Land Sale to Navajo Tribe Act. Congress passes the Pueblo Land Sale to Navajo Tribe Act, authorizing the Pueblos of San Lorenzo and Pojoaque in New Mexico to sell certain lands to the Navajo tribe.

AUGUST 11, 1955   Five Civilized Tribes Restrictions Extension Act. Congress passes the Five Civilized Tribes Restrictions Extension Act, calling for the period of restriction on lands belonging to Indians of the Five Civilized Tribes in Oklahoma to be extended for the lives of the Indians who own said lands.

AUGUST 14, 1955   Colorado River Indian Reservation Lease Act. Congress passes the Colorado River Indian Reservation Lease Act, authorizing the secretary of interior to lease any unassigned lands on the Colorado River Indian Reservation.

OCTOBER 1955 Nishga Tribal Council. The Nishga Tribal Council (Nisga'a Nation) is formed as the first tribal council in British Columbia. Frank Calder *(See* biography, August 3, 1915) is its president from 1955–74. Several other tribal councils are formed in British Columbia in the ensuing years.

1 9 5 6

1956 Alaska Native Service. The Alaska Native Service is transferred to the jurisdiction and control of the Bureau of Indian Affairs.

1956 Indian Adult Education. The Bureau of Indian Affairs starts an adult education program aimed at, among other things, increasing adult functional literacy. By fiscal year 1967, more than 12,000 adult Indians are in formal classes for basic education or high school equivalency.

AUGUST 1, 1956 Wyandotte Termination Act. Congress passes the Wyandotte (Wyandot) Termination Act, to provide for the termination of federal supervision of the property of the Wyandotte tribe of Oklahoma and its members.

AUGUST 2, 1956 Peoria Termination Act. Congress passes the Peoria Termination Act, to provide for the termination of federal supervision of the property of the Peoria tribe of Indians in Oklahoma and its members.

AUGUST 3, 1956 Adult Indian Vocational Training Act. Congress passes the Adult Indian Vocational Training Act, to provide programs of vocational assistance to adult Indians on or near Indian reservations (amended December 23, 1963, P.L. 88-230 to exact a sum of $12,000 annually).

AUGUST 3, 1956 Ottawa Termination Act. Congress passes the Ottawa Termination Act, to provide for the termination of federal supervision of the property of the Ottawa tribe of Indians in Oklahoma and its members.

1 9 5 7

1957 League of North American Indians Formed. The Indian Defense League helps to mobilize traditionalist resistance and the League of North American Indians (LONAI) becomes active. During the 1950s, LONAI and its allies play a major role in the "Indian revolt."

1957 Mohawk Land Claims. Standing Arrow of the Mohawk leads a group of Indians onto lands claimed by non-Indians on Schoharie Creek. The Mohawk lay claim to the land under the treaty of 1784 and deny the validity of later acquisition by the state of New York. This is the first open reoccupation of land by Indians in modern times.

1957 Public Health Service. Congress orders the Public Health Service to provide additional financial assistance for the construction of community hospitals serving both Indians and non-Indians, if, in the opinion of the surgeon general, such construction would constitute a more effective way of providing hospital facilities for Indians.

1957 "We Shake Hands" Project. The "We Shake Hands" project, a demonstration project supervised by the Association on American Indian Affairs (AAIA), is established by certain Omaha, Sioux, and Winnebago leaders to overcome reactionary federal Indian policies that discourage Indians. It provides a framework for observable long-range programs of community action in Great Plains reservations. Later the project is expanded to include assistance from non-Indian volunteers.

MARCH 1957 Tuscarora Reservation Land Condemned. New York Power Authority engineers come to the house of Chief Clinton Rickard on the Tuscarora Reservation to get permission to take soil tests. Rickard and the Tuscarora Council refuse permission. In September, the Tuscarora learn that part of the reservation is to be taken for development, and 1,383 acres are condemned.

JUNE 1957 Midwestern Inter-Tribal Council Formed. The Midwestern Inter-tribal Council is organized in a meeting held at the University of South Dakota at Vermillion. Robert Burnette, the Rosebud chairman, is named president, while the council is rounded out by tribal council members from Nebraska and North and South Dakota.

1 9 5 8

1958 Miccosukee Land Claims. The Miccosukee of Florida are threatened by U.S. land grabbers and the Everglades Reclamation Project. When they hear of the success of the Tuscarora in resisting New York State's efforts to tax them, they ask Mad Bear Anderson to advise them. He travels south for a meeting with them and other tribes. They discuss a project to unite all of the Indians of North, South, and Central America, and send a buckskin of recognition to Fidel Castro, the Cuban leader.

1958 Navajo Sand Paintings. Over the protests of traditional Navajo, permanent versions of sand paintings are produced for sale by Navajo artists.

1958 Saskatchewan Indian Organization. Cree William Wuttunee spearheads the organization of the Federation of Saskatchewan Indians.

1958 Termination in California. Termination of California Indian lands brought about by the Termination Act of 1953 affects 44 rancherias during this period; however, the larger reservations are exempted. Tribal corporations are dissolved and their land divided into parcels or sold. In a move that affected only California Indians, the Bureau of Indian Affairs also withdraws such special Indian programs as college scholarship eligibility, vocational education, economic development programs, and water and

sanitation projects. Medical services are curtailed. The remaining special Indian programs in the public schools that are subsidized by Johnson-O'Malley funds are ended with state acquiescence.

1958 Termination Policy. Secretary of Interior Fred Seaton agrees to some modifications of the Termination Policy, but many Indians remain dissatisfied.

1958 *Williams v. Lee*. Under the 1934 Indian Reorganization Act, new tribal governments and tribal courts are established on most Indian reservations. Until the *Williams v. Lee* decision, however, it is unclear just how much state law applies to Indian reservations. A great deal has changed since *Worcester v. the State of Georgia* excluded state power over Indian affairs in 1832, and it is no longer realistic, state governments argue, to treat tribes as if they were totally separate from the states surrounding them. In this case, the Supreme Court holds that tribal courts have exclusive jurisdiction over the collection of debts from reservation Indians. The court does not base this on any specific treaty language or federal laws, but on its belief that it is federal policy "to encourage tribal governments and courts to become stronger and more highly organized." In light of this policy, state governments may not act in any way that "infringe(s) on the right of reservation Indians to make their own laws and be ruled by them." This "infringement test" is used to determine the scope of state and tribal powers prior to the 1978 *Oliphant decision*.

JANUARY 1958 Lumbee Repel the Ku Klux Klan (KKK). The Lumbee Indian people of North Carolina capture the admiration of Americans when they emerge from obscurity to drive hooded Klansmen off their lands with shotguns. The Lumbee have protested being forced to send their children 35 miles away to a state-run Indian school, and for six years have asked for an Indian school closer to their homes in Harnett County. The KKK attempts to intimidate them by holding a rally in Robeson Country, North Carolina, but are driven off by a large group of Lumbee.

FEBRUARY 1, 1958   Indian Senator. Kainai (Blood) James Gladstone *(See* biography, May 21, 1887), former president of the Indian Association of Alberta, is appointed as Canada's first Indian senator.

APRIL 16, 1958   Tuscarora Reservation Invaded. Surveyors and police invade the Tuscarora Reservation. The Tuscarora people respond with nonviolent resistance, under the leadership of Chief William Rickard, John Hewitt, and Mad Bear Anderson. Women lie down in front of the trucks, only to be kicked and abused. Three leaders are arrested, but the charges later are dropped. The Tuscarora go on to win a victory in the Federal Court of Appeals, refusing restitution of $13 million for the land in question.

JUNE 1958   Fidel Castro Invites Indian Delegation to Cuba. Cuban leader Fidel Castro invites the Six Nations and Miccosukee tribes to send delegations to Cuba. In July, they arrive in Havana, hoping that Cuba will sponsor their membership in the United Nations.

JUNE 12, 1958   Leo Johnson Enters Air Force Academy. Leo Johnson of Fairfax, Oklahoma, matriculates at the Air Force Academy in Colorado Springs, Colorado, thereby becoming the first Indian to enter that select body of young Americans. He is graduated and commissioned in the Air Force on June 6, 1962. Johnson attains the rank of captain and becomes an RC 135-M pilot. In his career, Captain Johnson receives seven Air Medals and the Air Force Commendation Medal.

SEPTEMBER 26, 1958   "Roads to Resources." Canadian Prime Minister John Diefenbaker promises an extensive road-building program in the North. The Canadian government's "Roads to Resources" program, introduced in

February and March during an election campaign, is aimed at improving access to northern resources. For Native groups, these roads will serve to increase mobility and contact with neighboring Native groups and with Euro-Canadian society.

DECEMBER 12, 1958   Formation of Federated Indian Tribes. The Federated Indian Tribes organize in Los Angeles to provide "a reservation social atmosphere" for urban Indian families. The objective is to allow urban Indians to live as traditionally as possible, even in the city.

1958–1968   Indian Relocation. Approximately 200,000 Indians move to urban areas, some with financial help from the federal government. The exact figure is difficult to gauge, however, since Indian immigrants to urban areas frequently return to their reservations.

---

1 9 5 9

1959   Indian Sanitation Standards. Congress authorizes the surgeon general to construct or otherwise provide and maintain essential sanitation facilities for Indian homes, communities, and lands.

1959   Maria Martinez Awarded the Jane Addanis Award. Maria Martinez of San Ildefonso Pueblo in New Mexico is given the Jane Addanis Award by Rockford College, Rockford, Illinois, one of the highest honors ever granted to an American woman. The award is given in recognition of Martinez's achievements as an artistic potter.

1959   Mounties Attack Council House at Six Nations Reserve. One hundred-thirty Indian people under Young Chief Logan, Emily General, and a number of reporters are present in the Six Nations Council house when the Royal Canadian Mounted Police (Mounties) attack. The Indian men are dragged and clubbed, and several women are injured. A photographer

Tuscarora protest against the New York State Power Authority's condemnation of their lands for a reservoir, 1958. Courtesy of the Buffalo and Erie County Historical Society.

trying to document the event has his camera smashed by a Mountie. Thirty-three arrests are made, but charges are later dropped.

1959   Ontario Indian Organization. The Union of Ontario Indians is formed as the first provincial Indian organization east of the prairies. Its membership is predominantly Ojibway.

1959   Trust Conveyance of Indian Lands. The Department of the Interior announces that it will no longer object to trust conveyances of land. The decision comes after an argument with the Pueblo of Santo Domingo, which took the position that it would not accept a particular tract of land unless it was conveyed in trust status.

MARCH 5, 1959   Iroquois Leadership. An estimated 1,300 supporters of the Iroquois hereditary chiefs march to the council house where the elective chief and his council are meeting behind locked doors. After removing the hinges from the door, the protesters take over the government. Mad Bear presides at a meeting attended by 5,000 people. The Elective Council is abolished, and the hereditary chiefs are restored. An Iroquois police force is established as part of a larger goal of self-sufficiency.

MARCH 29, 1959   Attempt to Form United Indian Nation. Six Nations delegates and others, including Chief Julius Twohy and Ella McCurely from Utah, meet with the Miccosukee Nation in the Everglades. The delegates decide to circulate three buckskins that would later be brought together again after having been witnessed by Indians across the nation. The buckskins represented a invitation to all Indian communities to form a "United Indian Nation."

SPRING 1959   Inuit Cooperatives. The West Baffin Island Eskimo Cooperative is formed at Cape Dorset, Baffin Island. While this cooperative is destined to become the best known, the Inuit in northern Quebec establish the first cooperatives, and others are established through-

out the eastern Arctic in subsequent years. The Canadian federal government is encouraging the formation of the Inuit cooperatives in the eastern Arctic to increase Inuit familiarity with a cash economy. The cooperatives are intended as consumer cooperatives, importing and exporting goods to and from southern Canada, and become best known for their role in marketing Inuit artwork.

The Inuit artists of the Northwest Territories and Quebec have been selling soapstone carvings throughout North America since shortly after World War II. Toronto artist James Houston, instrumental in the development of markets for Inuit art, introduces Inuit artists at Cape Dorset to the technique of printmaking in the winter of 1957–58. Following a show of Inuit prints in Montreal in 1959, a large market for these prints develops.

MAY 1959   Hopi Talk with United Nations Officials. In order to explain their prophecies and beliefs, a delegation of Hopi from Arizona travels to New York to talk with United Nations officials. While in New York they also visit Mad Bear Anderson and members of the Iroquois confederacy.

JUNE 25, 1959   Pit River Chief Ray Johnson Dies. Chief Ray Johnson of the Pit River Nation dies while picketing in Washington D.C. for recognition of his people's land rights. His widow and other Indians take Chief Johnson's body home after rejecting the Bureau of Indian Affair's offer to have his body sent back to California.

1959–1971   Alaska Native Land Claims. Alaska becomes a state in 1959; the federal government grants the new state the right to select 102 million acres of land from public domain within 25 years. Indian title in Alaska, however, has not been settled, and Alaska Native villages protest state land selections by making claims to land with the Bureau of Land Management. By 1964, Alaska Natives claim more than 300 million acres, and the secretary of the interior,

Stewart Udall, prohibits the state from selecting land until Indian title is clarified. Alaska Natives mobilize around land claims and issues like education, health, and jobs. They form local and regional associations of villages. In 1965 and 1966, Alaska Natives create the Alaska Federated Natives (AFN), a statewide organization empowered to pursue land claims and other community interests. The AFN leads Alaska Natives to a congressional settlement in 1971, called the Alaska Native Claims Settlement Act, which preserves for the Natives 44 million acres and awards them $962 million for giving up claims to the rest of Alaska.

Part 3

NATIVE
NORTH AMERICAN
HISTORY 1960–1994

Chapter 8
1960 TO 1969

1 9 6 0

1960   Alaska Indian Education. The first secondary level education program in an Alaskan Bureau of Indian Affairs (BIA) day school is established with the installation of the ninth grade at Uhalakle.

1960   Indian Education. When two brothers, Eugene and James Chance, Lumbee of North Carolina, persist in their attempt to enroll their children in Dunn High School, they are fined $150 and $100 respectively for "aiding, abetting and encouraging their children" to attend school in defiance of a court order. They are not protesting triple segregation (separate black, white, and Indian schools), but the refusal of the school board to build a school closer than one requiring daily 70-mile round trips for their children.

1960   Indian Population—U.S. Census. The U.S. Census shows approximately 509,000 Indians, plus some 43,000 Alaska Natives—identified as 14,500 Indians and 28,600 Aleuts and Eskimos. In this census, a self-enumeration technique is employed for the first time, allowing the reporting individual to identify his racial origin. Of those residing outside of Alaska, 453,000 are found to be in 23 Federal Indian Reservation states, and 56,100 in the remaining 25 states and the District of Columbia.

MARCH 31, 1960   Indian Franchise. A law which will give status Indians in Canada the right to vote in the next Canadian federal election is given royal assent. Some Indians protest the change, claiming that it undermines their status as independent peoples. Others feel that granting the franchise is the first step in a process that will see them lose their special rights, including their right to be exempt from taxation. (Indians who waive their tax-exempt status have been allowed to vote since 1950.) Status Indians in Canada have always been exempt from taxation. Saskatchewan and the Northwest Territories also give Indians the right to vote in 1960.

JULY 12, 1960   Indian Boundary Markers Act. Congress passes the Indian Boundary Markers Act, "to amend title 18 of the United States Code (25 U.S.C. 216) to make it unlawful to destroy, deface, or remove certain boundary markers on Indian reservations, and to trespass on Indian reservations to hunt, fish, or trap."

OCTOBER 5, 1960   Miccosukee Land Claims. After years of negotiations, a major step toward solution of Miccosukee land claims in Florida is taken, when the Interior Department and the state of Florida agree upon joint use of land that will secure for this unconquered people the use and occupancy of their Florida homeland and assign 200,000 acres of Indian Trust land to the

U.S. for administration and development for the Indians.

c. 1960s   Renaissance in Northwest Coast Art. Throughout the 1960s and 1970s, American Indians in the United States and Canada experience a resurgence in cultural pride. In the Northwest Coast region, this is manifested in an artistic renaissance. Young Haida artists Bill Davidson (the great-grandson of Charles Edenshaw), Bill Reid, Tony Hunt (also a relative of Edenshaw's), Nootka carver Joe Davidson, and others become well known for their inscriptions of classic forms. Like the work of Edenshaw, Mungo Martin, and other early carvers, the work of these contemporary artists also stimulates (and is stimulated by) a cultural renaissance.

1 9 6 1

1961   American Indian College Committee Organized. The American Indian College Committee is organized in California by Jack D. Forbes, Carl Gorman, and Mary Gorman. A proposal for an "American Indian University" is developed and widely distributed.

1961   Chicago Indian Conference. After mobilizing against the threat of termination in the late 1950s, 460 representatives from 90 tribes meet in Chicago and set out a policy agenda. The conference is endorsed and sponsored by the National Congress of American Indians (NCAI), and advised by Dr. Sol Tax, a well-known anthropologist and Indian advocate. The new policy agenda emphasizes greater academic training for Indian children, increased job training, improved housing on reservations, better medical facilities, access to loans for economic development, and increased emphasis on industrial development and employment on the reservations.

1961   Indian Education. A report on education shows that the number of young Indians from the reservations who enter college during the period 1950 to 1960 increases from 6,599 to 17,000; the number of high school students more than doubles, from 24,000 to 57,000.

1961   Janet McCloud, Tulalip Indian Fishing Rights Activist, Maintains Vigil. In Washington State, several Nisqually fishermen are arrested in early January by State officers. These arrests violate existing treaty stipulations between the state and the Indians already living there. Janet McCloud, a Tulalip, is one of many women who maintain vigilance in the Indian boats as a symbolic underscoring of Native fishing rights. Along with Puyallup Ramona Bennett, McCloud assumes a leading role in this struggle. Both an organizer and a participant in the fish-ins of the 1960s, McCloud also establishes the Survival of American Indians Association in 1964. By 1968 "outside Indians" and Hollywood celebrities begin demonstrating in the Washington State fish-ins, thereby gaining national attention and creating a media sensation, and, in some ways, overwhelming the sustained efforts of the local community. Indeed, many of the "hard-line" political tactics characteristically attributed to the Red Power movement of the 1970s owe their proactive stance to McCloud's perseverance.

1961   The National Indian Youth Council Started. An activist organization, the National Indian Youth Council (NIYC), is formed by Clyde Warrior (Ponca), Melvin Thom (Paiute), and others. The NIYC challenges the approaches of traditional advocacy groups such as Christian churches, the National Congress of American Indians, and the Indian Rights Association. The council presents a more activist and nationalist orientation to solving Indian problems, focusing attention during the 1960s on issues of education and discrimination and criticizing congressional leaders and the BIA bureaucracy. During its early period, the NIYC also conducts a number of fish-ins and operates as the Indian coordinator for the Poor People's Campaign in Washington, D.C., in 1968. As

American Indian issues receive more attention in the 1970s and 1980s, the NIYC expands its scope, initiating lawsuits and grass-roots campaigns against uranium and coal mining. In the 1980s, the NIYC begins providing more services, sponsoring the Indian Voter Project as well as job training and other vocational programs.

1961 President Kennedy Appoints Task Force on Indian Affairs. Newly elected President John F. Kennedy appoints a "Task Force on Indian Affairs" headed by Phillips Petroleum Company vice president W.W. Keeler and including no Indians. The task force, after months of study, decides that termination should be de-emphasized. Subsequently, Kennedy appoints Philleo Nash as Commissioner of Indian Affairs.

1961 Udall Task Force Recommends No Further Termination. In a publication entitled *The Indian: America's Unfinished Business,* the Udall Task Force, a federal study group, recommends against further government efforts to terminate Indian trust lands, successfully directing public attention to the matter.

1961 Washington Indian Rights. Secretary of Interior Stewart Udall launches a study of Indian rights in the state of Washington after approximately 35 Indian groups complain of a variety of encroachments of Indian rights and lands.

FEBRUARY 1961 Seneca Ask for Halt to Construction of Kinzua Dam. Basil Williams, president of the Allegheny Seneca, asks President Kennedy to stop the construction of the Kinzua Dam pending an impartial investigation. This plea is ignored and, once the dam is completed, Seneca lands are flooded, violating a 1794 treaty.

MAY 24, 1961 Haskell Institute Becomes National Landmark. Haskell Institute in Lawrence, Kansas (founded in 1884), is dedicated as a Registered National Historical Landmark.

DECEMBER 1961 Canadian Indian Organization. The National Indian Council is formed as the first truly national Indian organization. William Wuttunee and the Federation of Saskatchewan Indians are instrumental in its founding. Though it seeks to represent status and non-status Indians, most of its members are non-status Indians and Métis. By this time, the term "Métis" can include any person of mixed European and Indian ancestry.

1 9 6 2

1962 Founding of the Institute of American Indian Art. Housed in the same buildings where Dorothy Dunn's Santa Fe Studio was located during the 1930s, the Institute of the American Indian Art (IAIA) is founded in 1962. From its inception, students at the IAIA are given both traditional and modernist instruction, but as time passes the institute comes to represent the more progressive, experimental wing of American Indian art. By the late 1960s, students at the IAIA are utilizing a broad range of subjects and techniques. For its nontraditional approach, the IAIA is vocally criticized by Indians and non-Indians alike. Nevertheless, the work of students and teachers like Fritz Scholder (Luiseño), Allan Houser, and T.C. Cannon (Caddo) gains considerable recognition in spite of the controversy surrounding the school's approach.

1962 Indian Economic Report. According to Dr. Leona Baumgartner, assistant secretary of state, the average American Indian family in 1962 has an annual income of $1,500, or half the $3,000 figure considered to be the national poverty line.

1962 Indians Given Right to Vote in New Mexico State Elections. Indians become U.S. citizens in 1924, but some states, most notably New Mexico and Arizona, refuse to allow Indians to vote in state and local elections, claiming that as non-taxpayers and non-state residents,

Indians should have no say in state affairs. In 1948, *Harrison v. Laveen* gives Indians living in Arizona the right to vote in that state's elections. A similar case, *Montoya v. Bolack*, forces New Mexico to do the same for its sizable Indian population in 1962.

SEPTEMBER 12, 1962 Art Exhibit by Ojibway Artist. An exhibition of paintings by Ojibway artist Norval Morrisseau *(See* biography, March 14, 1932) at the Pollock Gallery in Toronto garners enthusiastic reviews. Over the following years Morrisseau emerges as the foremost "Woodlands School" artist in Canada.

DECEMBER 6, 1962 Indians Served by Bureau of Indian Affairs. Commissioner of Indian Affairs Philleo Nash states that the U.S. has some 575,000 Indian and Eskimo people, of whom only 380,000 are served by the BIA. "The balance of the Indian population—around 179,000—consists of people who live away from Indian country and are, for all practical purposes, indistinguishable from non-reservation Indians."

1 9 6 3

1963 Alaska Native Business Credit Fund Created. The Alaska Native Business Credit Fund is created by the Association on American Indian Affairs (AAIA) as a pilot project to enable individual Eskimos and Indians to start small businesses.

1963 Annie Dodge Wauneka Receives Medal of Freedom. Annie Dodge Wauneka, the first woman to serve on the Navajo tribal council, is presented with the Medal of Freedom Award by President Kennedy, only days before his assassination. This award is the country's highest peacetime honor, and is given to persons who have made outstanding contributions to the national interest or security or world peace, or who have otherwise made substantial contributions in public or private endeavors.

1963 *Arizona v. California*. In *Arizona v. California*, the Supreme Court is called upon to further define Indian water rights. In this major litigation over the lower Colorado River, the court must determine the water rights accruing to tribes along the river whose reservations had been established by both statute and executive order. The court views the question as one of the intention of Congress or the president, and holds that neither one could have meant to establish reservations without reserving for the use of the Indians the water necessary to make the land habitable and productive. The court holds that the water rights were effectively reserved as of the time of creation of the reservation.

1963 Indian Economic Report. According to Commissioner of Indian Affairs Philleo Nash, American Indians on and near the reservations "receive an income between one-quarter and one-third of the national average; have about four and a half times the unemployment; have an educational level about one-half that of the country as a whole, and have a life expectancy about two-thirds that of the rest of the country."

1963 Native American Movement Launched. The Native American Movement (NAM) is launched in Ventura and Los Angeles counties in California. NAM is designed to create sentiments of unity among persons of Native blood, especially Indians and Mexican Americans, in both North and South America. NAM advocates establishment of American Indian and Mexican-American universities and pride in Indian descent. NAM also advocates use of the term "Native American" in place of "Indian."

1963 Omaha Indian People Protest Discrimination in Employment. Omaha Indian people stage a "war dance" in front of the Douglas County courthouse in Omaha, Nebraska, as a public protest against discrimination in employment.

1963 Provincial Franchise. New Brunswick and Prince Edward Island Indians living on

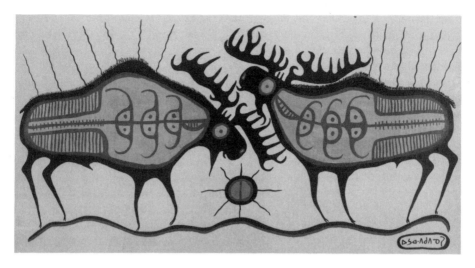

Two Bull Moose Fighting, by Norval Morisseau. In this painting Morisseau's name is signed in syllabic characters. Courtesy of the Glenbow Museum Collection, Calgary, Alberta.

reserves are given the right to vote in provincial elections.

1963 Snowmobiles Replace Dog Sleds. The introduction of the small snowmobile in the North dramatically alters the lives of the Inuit and northern Indians. Although early snowmobiles are expensive, heavy, and prone to breakdown, they are faster and carry larger loads than dog teams. The snowmobile makes it easier for trappers to live in a single village all year, since they can now quickly travel over long distances to get to hunting and fishing areas. Before snowmobiles, the Inuit and northern Indians traveled to winter villages and to other locations during the summer to take advantage of hunting, fishing, and wild plant resources. With the subsequent development of more reliable machines, dog sleds are almost completely replaced by snowmobiles.

FEBRUARY 1963 Call for Indian Unity. Francis Le Quier (Ojibway), chairman of the Committee for the Great Council Fire, calls for the unity of all North and South American Indians.

SUMMER 1963 Ojibway Band Relocation. Members of the Grassy Narrows Ojibway band in northern Ontario begin moving from their island homes to a new mainland reserve nearby. The new location makes travel to other communities much easier and helps improve their material standard of living, but makes it difficult for the band to maintain its former lifestyle, and leads to increased alcoholism, drug abuse, and violence. In this way, this move illustrates the advantages and disadvantages faced by many Indian bands across Canada as they relocate to improve access to modern conveniences and government services.

NOVEMBER 4, 1963 Revolving Loan Fund Act. Congress passes the Revolving Loan Fund Act "to establish a revolving fund from which the secretary of the interior may make loans to finance the procurement of expert assistance by Indian tribes in cases before the Indian Claims Commission."

DECEMBER 1963 American Indian Arts Center Opens. The American Indian Arts Center opens in New York City. Its purpose is to develop a broader market for the wealth of

Indian and Eskimo craftsmanship and to give evidence to the public of the high standards of Indian workmanship and excellence of American indigenous art. Within a few months of the Center's opening, the initial 35 tribes contributing grows to more than 50.

DECEMBER 1963 Indian Fishing Rights. The State of Washington Court rules against Indian fishing rights and state fisheries' wardens begin campaigning against Indian fishermen.

1 9 6 4

1964 The American Indian Historical Society Founded. Rupert Costo and Jeanette Henry Costo organize the American Indian Historical Society, a group dedicated to historical research and teaching about Native Americans. The society begins publishing *The Indian Historian*, a journal of articles on Indian history primarily from an Indian perspective. The society sponsors a series of workshops to improve teaching of or about Indians. By 1966 workshops are held at Hoopa, Beaumont, Fresno, Berkeley, and San Francisco.

1964 *The Sky Clears* Is Published. *The Sky Clears: Poetry of the American Indians*, edited by A. Grove Day, is published.

APRIL 30, 1964 Indian Timber Act. Congress passes the Indian Timber Act, "to amend the Act of June 25, 1910 (36 Stat. 857; 25 U.S.C. 406, 407), with respect to the sale of Indian timber." This act gives the secretary of the interior authority to sell timber on unallotted Indian lands on reservations and on allotments held in trust, and specifies that the proceeds be distributed to the Indian owners.

JULY 7, 1964 Appropriation of Indian Affairs Supervision Act. Congress passes the Appropriation of Indian Affairs Supervision Act, concerning appropriations for the Department of the Interior and related agencies for the

fiscal year ending June 30, 1965: Title 1– Department of the Interior Public Land Management, Bureau of Indian Affairs, an estimated $96 million for education and welfare services; $40,390,000 for resource management; $900,000 for immediate revolving fund for loans; $52,009,000 for construction, major repairs, and improvement of irrigation and power systems, buildings, and other facilities on reservations; $17 million for road construction; $4,331,000 for general administration of the Bureau of Indian Affairs; $88,000 for the Menominee School District; $3 million from tribal funds for benefit of Indians and tribes for education and land improvements.

AUGUST 31, 1964 Kinzua Dam and Seneca Termination Act. Congress passes the Kinzua Dam and Seneca Termination Act, "to authorize payment for certain interests in lands within the Allegheny Indian Reservation in New York required by the United States for the Allegheny River (Kinzua Dam) project, to provide for the relocation, rehabilitation, social and economic development of the members of the Seneca Nation."

OCTOBER 14, 1964 Billy Mills Wins Olympic Gold Medal in Tokyo. Billy Mills (*See* biography, 1938), a Sioux from South Dakota, wins the 10,000-meter run at the Olympic Games in the record time of 28 minutes and 24.04 seconds.

NOVEMBER 3, 1964 Extension of State Law onto Indian Reservations Rejected. The Sioux of North Dakota retain the right to police their reservations. On November 3, the voters of North Dakota reject a law that would extend state civil and criminal jurisdiction to the Indian reservations. The referendum is defeated by a four-to-one margin.

1964–1966 Indian Community Action Programs. President Lyndon B. Johnson's Great Society legislation for alleviating poverty is implemented with creation of the Office of

Billy Mills at the 1964 Olympic Games. Courtesy of 10K Gold.

Economic Opportunity (OEO). The OEO organizes an Indian Desk for managing antipoverty programs on Indian reservations. The Bureau of Indian Affairs (BIA) insists on administering Indian antipoverty funds, but the OEO, suspicious of paternalistic BIA management of Indian affairs, delivers antipoverty funds directly to the tribal governments. For the first time, most Indian tribal governments gain direct access to federal funds that are not administered by BIA officials. Community Action Programs (CAP) become the primary funding source and administrative organization for managing Indian antipoverty funds. During the late 1960s and 1970s many tribal governments rapidly expand in personnel, budget, and programs administered. The method of granting funds directly to tribal government control becomes the model for the Self-Determination Policy starting in the early 1970s and for the Self-Determination and Education Assistance Act of 1975.

1 9 6 5

1965   California Indian Land Claims. After many years of hearings, the descendants of the California Indians finally receive and vote to accept an award of more than $29 million for outstanding land claims. It amounts to only 47 cents an acre for 64 million acres of land, nearly two-thirds of the total state area. Since the number of eligible descendants is about 33,000, most persons receive less than $900.

1965   *Warren Trading Post v. Arizona Tax Commission.* In *Warren Trading Post v. Arizona Tax Commission*, the state of Arizona attempts to impose taxes on the Warren Trading Post, an on-reservation facility operated by non-Indians. Like most on-reservation trading posts, the Warren Trading Post is licensed by the federal government and subject to extensive federal regulation. Because of this, the Supreme Court rules against the Arizona Tax Commission, finding that state laws are preempted and that Arizona cannot tax the trading post's gross receipts.

APRIL 7, 1965   Director of National Congress of American Indians Testifies against Termination. The National Congress of American Indians (NCAI) executive director and tribal representatives testify before a U.S. Senate subcommittee against the termination of the Colville tribe of Washington, D.C. Termination began just ten years earlier in 1953 with the passage of House Concurrent Resolution 108, whose objective was to solve "the Indian problem" by assimilating Indian people into the American mainstream. This process was to be accomplished by ending the government's relationship with 109 tribes and bands that were considered to have reached a satisfactory level of economic and social achievement. Among the first tribes whose relationship with the federal government was terminated were the Klamath of Oregon and the Menominee of Wisconsin. Many other smaller groups around the nation also were terminated.

By 1965, it becomes increasingly clear that the effects of the Termination Policy on Indian communities are disastrous. The termination process leaves Indian people in a psychological and legal limbo: one day they are Indian, according to the government, and the following day they are not. Many tribal members, accustomed to the paternalism of the Bureau of Indian Affairs, are unprepared for the changes thrust upon them. Increases in alcoholism and poverty and the disintegration of the tribal unit follow. The dissolution of the reservations and reservation services results in a larger population of people dependent on state assistance.

MAY 26, 1965 Miami Indian Land Claims. The House of Representatives approves a $4.7 million award by the Indian Claims Commission to the Miami Indians of Indiana and Oklahoma for the loss of their lands in the nineteenth century.

SEPTEMBER 1965 Indian Claims Commission Rules on Blue Lake. The Indian Claims Commission rules that the Blue Lake area of Carson National Forest in New Mexico has been taken illegally and unfairly from the Taos Pueblo. The commission awards a monetary judgment, but the Indians refuse to accept it, asking Congress to return their religious sanctuary. U.S. Senator Clinton Anderson proposes Senate Bill 3085 to accomplish this objective, but it dies without action when Congress adjourns.

WINTER 1965 Five County Cherokee Organization Founded. Traditional Cherokee, led by Finis Smith, organize the Five County Cherokee organization to fight for the restoration and revitalization of the Cherokee Nation.

1 9 6 6

1966 Indian Education. A total of 150,000 Indian children in the age group 6-18 are enrolled in 216 Bureau of Indian Affairs (BIA) schools in the United States.

1966 Indian Health Statistics. A Public Health

Service report released in 1966, shows dramatic improvement in health of Indians. Random selections include a drop of 61 percent from 1954 in the death rate from tuberculosis for Indians; for Alaska Natives, it drops from 236 deaths in 1954 to 18 in 1964. Indian infant mortality declines 45 percent between 1954 and 1964, although the Indian infant death rate is still 1.5 times higher than that of the general American population.

1966 Residential Training Opportunity Center Established. The BIA signs a contract with the Radio Corporation of America to establish the first "family-centered" residential training opportunity center, which is operated at Philadelphia, Mississippi, adjacent to the Choctaw Reservation. Many "families" have since completed training and are employed as a result of this venture.

1966 Sherman Alexie, Spokane-Coeur d'Alene Poet and Novelist, Is Born. Sherman Alexie grows up in Wellpinit, Washington, on the Spokane Indian Reservation. Winner of a 1991 Washington State Arts Commission poetry fellowship and a 1992 National Endowment for the Arts poetry fellowship, Alexie publishes more than 200 poems, stories, and translations in publications such as *Another Chicago Magazine, Beloit Poetry Journal, Black Bear Review, Caliban, Journal of Ethnic Studies, Hanging Loose Press, New York Quarterly, Red Dirt,* and others. Alexie's first book of poetry and short stories, *The Business of Fancydancing,* is published in January 1992. In January 1993, he publishes a third poetry book, *Old Shirts & New Skins* (UCLA American Indian Studies Center).

1966 Value of Indian Agricultural Production. The total gross value received from agricultural production on Indian reservations is approximately $170 million. This includes crop production, livestock production, and direct use of fish and wildlife by Indians. Gross production provides Indian operators $58.6 million.

JANUARY 1, 1966 Canadian Indian Affairs. The Canadian Department of Northern Affairs and Natural Resources is given charge of Indian affairs. The reallocation of responsibility reflects the fact that the search for and extraction of resources is increasingly taking place in isolated areas where many Native inhabitants depend on hunting, trapping, and fishing for their livelihood. It also puts the minister in the difficult position of having to represent the interests of Indian groups and resource industries at the same time. The Inuit have been administered by this Department since its creation in 1953.

FEBRUARY 15, 1966 Dick Gregory Arrested in Nisqually Fish-In. Comedian Dick Gregory and his wife are arrested for illegal net-fishing, which they engage in with members of the Nisqually tribe in a protest fish-in in Washington State. The tribe, arguing that they had reserved the right to fish according to their own laws in their 1856 treaty with the federal government, is protesting the application of state game laws that dictate hook-and-line fishing, thereby preventing the tribe from fishing according to their traditional ways.

MARCH 17, 1966 Health Care. In *R. v. Johnston,* Chief Justice Culliton of the Saskatchewan Court of Appeals overturns a 1965 decision by Saskatchewan Judge J.M. Policha which found that the "medicine chest" and "pestilence" clauses of Treaty 6 entitle all status Indians in Canada to free medicine, drugs, medical supplies, and hospital care. For several years the Canadian government has provided free health care to any Indians living on reserves who are unable to pay for these services, but has always denied that it had any legal obligation to do so. Nevertheless, following the establishment of a national health insurance plan in 1966, and Indian boycotts and protests of health insurance premiums, the government does agree to pay the health premiums of all status Indians.

MARCH 17, 1966 Federal Funding. The Canadian government announces that it is embarking on a $12 million program to improve housing, sanitation, water supplies, and roads to combat poor living conditions on Canadian Indian reserves.

SPRING 1966 Indian Hunting Rights. John Chewie, a Cherokee, is arrested for killing a deer out of season on Cherokee land. When Chewie is tried in Jay, Oklahoma, 500 armed Cherokee surround the courthouse to ensure his protection.

SPRING 1966 Rough Rock Demonstration School Established. The Navajo contract with the BIA to establish the Rough Rock Demonstration School. The school is the first in modern times to be completely administered and controlled by an Indian tribe. Impetus for the school's creation comes from the realization that more than half of all reservation school students fail to complete their high school education. Studies suggest that the high dropout rate results from the teachers' lack of knowledge about Indian culture and behavior and from discriminatory treatment. The Navajos hope that, by running their own school, they will be able to reverse the dropout rate and improve the education of their children.

APRIL 1966 Trusteeship of Indian Lands. At a mid-April conference, Secretary of the Interior Stewart L. Udall calls for "foundation legislation" to give more elasticity to the trusteeship responsibility for Indian lands and to enable the Indian people to accelerate economic development of their resources.

APRIL 14, 1966 National Congress of American Indians Calls Emergency Conference. Approximately 80 tribal leaders representing 62 tribes attend an "emergency conference" called by the National Congress of American Indians to protest their not being included in a congressionally sponsored conference. The conference is called by the chairman of the House Committee on Interior and Insular Affairs,

Morris Udall, to discuss reorganization of the Bureau of Indian Affairs. Representative Udall announces the admittance of representatives to the BIA's conference and confirms that the House committee will establish a tribally comprised group to advise him on the BIA's reorganization.

APRIL 27, 1966   Robert L. Bennett Sworn In as Commissioner of Indian Affairs. At White House ceremonies to swear in Robert L. Bennett as commissioner, President Lyndon B. Johnson states, ". . . the time has come to put the first Americans first on our agenda. From this hour forward we are going to look to you to discharge that responsibility. I want . . . to begin work today on the most comprehensive program for the advancement of the Indians that the Government of the United States has ever considered. . . ."

APRIL 30, 1966   Havasupai Reject BIA Proposal to Modernize Supai. The 300 members of the Havasupai tribe, who live at the base of the Grand Canyon in Supai, reject a Bureau of Indian Affairs proposal to modernize their village. Each year, up to 2,000 visitors make the rough eight-mile trek by horseback to the only village on the 518-acre reservation. The council votes against the BIA's goals to link the reservation by roads, chair lifts, and helicopters.

APRIL 30, 1966   Robert LaFollette Confirmed as BIA Commissioner. The Senate confirms the appointment of Robert LaFollette Bennett (Oneida) as the BIA commissioner, succeeding Philleo Nash. Bennett is only the second Indian person appointed to the post of commissioner. Ely Parker, a Seneca appointed by President Ulysses S. Grant in 1869, was the first.

MAY 31, 1966   President Johnson Signs Indian Health Law. President Johnson signs into law a five-year $250,000 trachoma contact program for Indians. It comes as a result of a 1964 finding that 7,043 cases of trachoma had been reported—a 124 percent increase over

1963. In some southwestern Indian schools as many as 63 percent of the children are reported infected.

OCTOBER 1966   Alaskan Federation of Natives Conference. The Alaskan Federation of Natives (AFN) meets in Anchorage. Originally organized by Emil Notti, president of the Cook Inlet Native Association, the 300 members discuss resolutions and strategies for the preservation of their land base. The organization is particularly concerned with the halting of further state land claims until the issue of Native land rights in Alaska is resolved. Although Alaska Natives never signed treaties with the U.S. government, they are recognized by the government as possessing an aboriginal title to their lands. The exact meaning of aboriginal title, beyond a recognition that Alaskan Natives had lived on their lands for thousands of years, however, is unclear. The Alaskan Statehood Act of 1959 guarantees the Natives' hunting and fishing rights, but also gives the state of Alaska the right to appropriate 102 million acres of land for its own use. As economic development and tourism in Alaska increase, the Natives' subsistence living based on hunting, fishing, and trapping becomes increasingly endangered.

OCTOBER 1966   Hawthorn Report. The first volume of *A Survey of the Contemporary Indians of Canada* (Hawthorn Report) is released, The second volume is released in October 1967. The report, commissioned by the Department of Citizenship (Indian Affairs) in 1964, has been compiled by University of British Columbia anthropologist Dr. Harry B. Hawthorn. It criticizes Canadian Indian policy, noting that Natives are an economically, socially, and politically disadvantaged group in Canadian society. Saying that Indians have been treated as "citizens minus," the report calls for a new policy that would treat Indians as "citizens Plus." In addition to the normal rights and duties of citizenship, Indians possess certain additional rights as charter members of the

Canadian community. Indian leaders endorse the report.

NOVEMBER 1966   American Indian Affairs Association Education Conference. The 44-year-old American Indian Affairs Association holds a two-day conference on the problems of educating American Indian youths. Attended by 35 specialists, including the recently appointed chief of education in the Bureau of Indian Affairs, the group hears grim statistics concerning the lack of educational success achieved by Indian children. Coming under particular attack are the 81 boarding schools operated by the Bureau of Indian Affairs. In many instances, very young children, having no local schools, are forced to attend boarding schools 600 miles from their homes and families. Both the boarding school children and the 91,000 other Indian students who attend regular public, church, or private schools face serious problems of adjustment and discrimination, leading to a 50 percent dropout rate among Indian students.

NOVEMBER 3, 1966   Inuit and Aleut Housing. A $10 million housing program, planned to ease the substandard housing of 43,000 Inuit and Aleut citizens of Alaska living in more than 200 villages, becomes law.

1 9 6 7

1967   California Indian Education Association Formed. A conference on the education of teachers of California Indian pupils is held at Stanislaus State College. The Indian participants set up an ad hoc committee on Indian education and began regional meetings that lead to a statewide conference on California Indian education at North Fork. A new group, the California Indian Education Association (CIEA), is formed at this time and serves as a model for the National Indian Education Association (NIEA) and other states' Indian education organizations.

1967   Federal Benefits for Indian People. Federal agencies, other than the Bureau of Indian Affairs, spend more than $193 million on various programs from which Indians receive direct benefits.

1967   First All-Indian Education Association Formed. California Indian people, both resident and out-of-state, organize the first all-Indian Education Association with David Risling, Jr., as chairperson. In October 1968 this group holds the first all-Indian statewide educational conference.

1967   Indian Woman Finalist in Mrs. America Contest. Mrs. Ramona Zephier of Flandreau, South Dakota, an enrolled member of the Cheyenne River Sioux tribe, is among the ten finalists in the Mrs. America contest in San Diego. Mrs. Zephier says she regards the trip to California as an opportunity to "destroy some stereotypes" about how the Indian lives and works. "I don't go for sit-ins," she says, "and I don't presume to speak for the Indian people, but maybe this will show Indians that they can do anything if they really want to do it." Zephier received her bachelor's degree in home economics from South Dakota State University and does substitute teaching at Flandreau.

1967   Ohlone College Named. A new junior college in the San Francisco Bay Area of California is named Ohlone College, in honor of the Indian group that occupied the land now used by the school.

JANUARY 10, 1967   President Johnson Urges Self-Help Assistance for American Indians. In his State of the Union message, President Lyndon Johnson urges, "We should embark upon a major effort to provide self-help assistance to the forgotten in our midst—the American Indians."

JANUARY 16, 1967   National Indian Education Advisory Committee Established. The Bureau of Indian Affairs announces the formation of a National Indian Education Advisory

Committee to assist in the improvement of educational services to Indian students.

FEBRUARY 5, 1967 Prohibition of Sale of Liquor to Indians Repealed. The Iowa Senate approves the repeal of one of the last examples of discriminatory legislation against Indians, a law that prohibits the sale of liquor to them. Federal prohibitions against the sale of liquor to Indians were repealed by Congress in 1954.

MARCH 20, 1967 Restructuring of Indians Claims Commission. The U.S. Senate and House of Representatives approve a bill restructuring the Indian Claims Commission and extending its life through 1972. First established in 1946, the commission still has 347 unadjudicated cases on its dockets at the time of the extension.

APRIL 28–OCTOBER 27, 1967 Expo '67. Millions of visitors from Canada and around the world view the Canadian Indian pavilion at Expo '67 in Montreal. The pavilion has been planned by the National Indian Council and funded by the federal government. The Indians use the opportunity to express their grievances.

MAY 23, 1967 Provincial Franchise. Alberta Indians vote in a provincial election for the first time. They were granted the franchise in 1965.

JUNE 10, 1967 Seminole Indian Land Claims. The U.S. Claims Court upholds a 1964 decision by the Indian Claims Commission finding that the Seminole of Florida and Oklahoma have claims to 32 million acres of Florida lands under the terms of the Seminole Nation's 1823 treaty with the federal government.

JULY 1967 Apache Municipal Center and Council Hall. The White Mountain Apache tribe of Arizona dedicates a new $350,000 Municipal Center and Council Hall.

AUGUST 1967 *Indians and the Law.* *Indians and the Law,* a study commissioned by the Department of Indian Affairs and conducted by the Canadian Corrections Association, is released. The first in-depth study of the extent of Natives' problems with the law, the report finds that police and legal services have had a detrimental effect on Indians. It reports that about a one-third of Canada's prison population is of Indian origin.

AUGUST 6, 1967 Sioux Indian Land Claims. The Indian Claims Commission awards $12.2 million to eight Sioux tribes for the compensation of 29 million acres taken in fraudulent treaties during the 1800s. The illegally taken lands include half of Minnesota and parts of Iowa, North and South Dakota, and Wisconsin.

AUGUST 11, 1967 Quebec Indian Organization. The Indians of Quebec Association is formed to represent the interests of Quebec Indians.

SEPTEMBER 11, 1967 Report on Genocide of American Indians. The New York Division of the National Association for the Advancement of Colored People (NAACP) announces the preparation of a report detailing the United States' genocide of American Indians. The report is to be submitted to the United Nations.

SEPTEMBER 12, 1967 Sekani Land Flooded. Following the official completion of the W.A.C. Bennet Dam, water begins to flood Sekani homes and traditional hunting territory near the Finlay and Parsnip rivers in the interior of British Columbia. Failure to remove the trees before flooding makes the Williston Lake (reservoir) hazardous for boat travel. Many of the Sekani relocate to the villages of Ingenika and Mackenzie but find it difficult to adjust to the different lifestyle at these sites. The reservoir becomes the largest body of fresh water in British Columbia. Since 1952, the British Columbia government's "northern vision" policy has dramatically expanded rail and road mileage in the province, bringing many former isolated Indian groups in more continuous contact with non-Native society.

1 9 6 8

1968 *The Autobiography of Delfina Cuero* **Is Published.** Delfina Cuero is one of the few survivors of the Kumeyaay or Diegueño people, who were forcibly displaced by the arrival of Anglo-American and immigrant Asian settlers to the San Diego area early in this century. In the 1960s, Cuero collaborates with anthropologist Florence Shipek; she talks about her life history, revealing her personal courage and endurance when faced with the prejudice and exploitation of incoming settlers in relation to the Native Indian people already occupying the lands. Cuero's narration contributes valuable information regarding southern California coastal ecology and traditional Kumeyaay art and cultural practices.

1968 **California Indian Legal Services.** The California Indian Legal Services (CILS) is formed to assist reservation Indians.

1968 **Fairchild Semi-Conductor Announces Plans to Increase Number of Indian Workers.** The Nation's largest nonfederal employer of Indians, Fairchild Semi-Conductor Corporation, announces intentions to add another 500 workers to its production crew at Shiprock, New Mexico, thereby making a total work force of 1,200. The firm has been operating in a temporary building leased from the Navajo tribe for over a year, and begins construction on a new and larger building in December.

1968 *House Made of Dawn* **Is Published.** Written over the course of three years by Kiowa and Cherokee writer N. Scott Momaday, the novel *House Made of Dawn* receives wide acclaim upon its publication. Momaday's novel tells the story of Abel, a young Indian from San Juan Pueblo who returns from service in World War II and finds readjustment to his life difficult and painful. Abel no longer feels "at home" on the reservation, but when he attempts to relocate to Los Angeles, he experiences displacement and prejudice in the dominant urban

society. Momaday's novel is awarded a Pulitzer Prize for fiction in 1969. *House Made of Dawn* ushers in what literary critic Kenneth Lincoln has called a "Native American Renaissance." In the 25 years after the publication of Momaday's seminal work, greater and greater numbers of American Indian writers find their way into print, many of them citing Momaday as an important influence in their lives and work.

1968 **Indian Education.** Reports show that more than 90 percent of Navajo children, or more than 46,000 boys and girls between the ages of 6 and 18 years, are in school. The dramatic finding of the report is that more than 70 percent of those in school are now finishing high school, closely approximating the national average. The Bureau of Indian Affairs' operates 226 schools, with an enrollment of 51,595 Indian children, and 18 dormitories for 4,204 children attending public schools

1968 **Johnson-O'Malley Funds Restored.** Johnson-O'Malley funds for Indian education programs are restored to California Indians. The Indian Commissioner also restores other services, such as scholarship eligibility and the right to attend vocational education schools sponsored by the Bureau of Indian Affairs. This reversal of previous policy is due largely to campaigns conducted by the California Indian Education Association and Indian-controlled California Indian Legal Services, Inc.

1968 *Menominee Tribe of Indians v. United States.* *Menominee Tribe of Indians v. United States*, a court test of the "termination" of the federal protection of selected tribes, occurs in 1968. The Supreme Court upholds the power of Congress to terminate the Menominee Tribe in 1954, but gives the 1954 legislation a narrow interpretation. Treaty rights persist unless expressly legislated away, the court observes. Hunting and fishing rights reserved by the Menominee in their 1854 treaty are not mentioned specifically by Congress in 1954, and therefore are not affected. The Menominee continue to fight for restoration of those tribal rights that were expressly extinguished by Congress in 1954, and finally succeed in obtaining congressional restoration of their legal status in 1973. Many other terminated tribes win legislative restoration after 1973.

1968 *Pima Legends* **Is Published.** Anna Moore Shaw's *Pima Legends* is a collection of stories as remembered by the author from her youth. The book serves as a response to the author's sense of regret regarding the loss of traditional Pima tales.

1968 Project Own. "Project Own," launched by the Small Business Administration (SBA) and assisted by the Service Corps of Retired Executives (SCORE), is represented by BIA Assistant Commissioner for Economic Development George Hubley as a tremendous opportunity for Indians to open service businesses on their own reservations, filling basic needs for laundromats, gas stations, and so on. The formation of the fund results from changing attitudes and the willingness of banking institutions to examine minority requests for business aid more on the basis of character than on the usual criterion of collateral. The SBA will guarantee independent ventures including franchises, but not manufacturing enterprises, up to 90 percent of such loans to $350,000. However, in localities where unemployment is chronically very high, SBA may fully guarantee loans up to $25,000. With loans being made through banks rather than the SBA, credit and character checks become more personalized and realistic.

1968 Tribal Council. The Gitksan-Carrier Tribal Council (Gitksan-Wet'suwet'en Tribal Council) is formed to represent the Gitskan and the western Carrier of west-central British Columbia. The formation of tribal councils, representing status and non-status Indians of specific Indian groups, beginning with the Nishga Tribal Council in 1955, is unique to British Columbia. In other parts of Canada,

status and non-status Indians are likely to belong to separate provincial Indian organizations.

JANUARY 25, 1968 Apache Restitution. The U.S. Indian Claims Commission attempts to award the Mescalero Apaches of New Mexico $8.5 million as compensation for land taken by the United States in the nineteenth century. Mescalero elders refuse the money because U.S. law prohibits them from splitting the proceeds with the Lipan and Chiricahua branches of the Apache tribes. The House committee decides to present a bill to allow the three branches to combine present and future proceeds from the government, which are to be used for a planned massive program of investments and social improvement projects.

FEBRUARY 1968 National Indian Organization. The National Indian Council separates into the National Indian Brotherhood (N.I.B.) and the Canadian Métis Society. The N.I.B. will seek to protect benefits status Indians enjoy under treaties and the Indian Act. Walter Deiter, former leader of the Federation of Saskatchewan Indians, becomes its first president (1968–70). The Canadian Métis Society will seek to protect the aboriginal rights of Métis and non-status Indians. (The Canadian Métis Society is reorganized as the Native Council of Canada in 1971.)

FEBRUARY 3, 1968 Indian Adult Education. Congress passes Public Law 90-252, which authorizes an increase of Indian adult vocational education expenditures from $15 million to $25 million.

MARCH 6, 1968 National Council on Indian Opportunity Is Established. President Lyndon Johnson signs an executive order establishing the National Council on Indian Opportunity. Chaired by the vice president and comprised of six Indian leaders and the heads of the departments of Interior; Agriculture; Commerce; Labor; Health, Education, and Welfare; Housing and Urban Affairs; and the Office of Economic

Opportunity, the council is charged with coordinating efforts to improve programs for Indians. Although President Johnson's programs constitute one of the first efforts by the federal government to involve Indians in decision-making, the tribes continue to voice suspicion and concern that all federal programs ultimately lead to the termination of the government protection of Indian lands and the provisions of federal services—guarantees that the tribes believe Congress is obligated to provide.

MARCH 6, 1968   President Johnson's Special Message. President Lyndon Johnson delivers his "Special Message to Congress on the Problem of the American Indian: The Forgotten American." In his message announcing his request for a 10 percent increase in federal funding for Indian programs, Johnson outlines three goals: (1) "A standard of living for the Indian equal to that of the country as a whole"; (2) "Freedom of choice: an opportunity to remain in their homelands, if they choose, without surrendering their dignity; and opportunity to move to towns and cities of America, if they choose, equipped with the skills to live in equality and dignity"; and (3) "Full participation in the life of modern America, with a full share of economic opportunity and social justice." The new federal objective, according to Johnson, is "a goal that ends the old debate about 'termination' of Indian programs and stresses self-determination."

APRIL 11, 1968   American Indian Civil Rights Act Passed. Congress passes the American Indian Civil Rights Act, P.L. 90-284. This act guarantees to reservation residents many of the same civil rights and liberties in relation to tribal authorities that the U.S. Constitution guarantees to all persons in relation to federal and state authorities. The act is introduced by Senator Sam Ervin after seven years of investigations into rights denied to individual Indians by tribal and state governments and the federal government. The act is not fully supported by all tribes, especially the Pueblos, who fear that

the act will alter their traditional forms of governments and culture. The act also limits the rights of tribes to levy penalties over crimes committed on their reservations to $1,000 in fines or six months in jail. Tribal leaders are supportive of other provisions of the legislation. Other parts of the law direct the secretary of the interior to publish updated versions of Charles Kappler's *Indian Affairs: Laws and Treaties,* and Felix Cohen's *Handbook of Federal Indian Law. 82 Stat. 73 Title II—Rights of Indians.*

MAY 18, 1968   Centennial of Peace Treaty with Navajo. President Lyndon Johnson signs a bill commemorating the centennial of the federal government's peace treaty with the Navajo. The Navajo Nation, the largest in the United States, inhabits a 16 million-acre reservation located in Arizona, New Mexico, and Utah. In terms of population and acreage, the Navajo Nation is larger than 26 independent countries in the world.

MAY 19, 1968   National Congress of American Indian Tour. The National Congress of American Indians (NCAI) sponsors a tour by 49 Indian leaders from 15 western tribes. The group, which visits New York and other cities, seeks to encourage companies to establish businesses on reservations.

MAY 27, 1968   *Puyallup Tribe v. Department of Game.* A unanimous Supreme Court ruling upholds the right of Washington State to prohibit Indian net fishing for salmon in the interest of conservation. The case is an important departure from previous holdings, because it allows state regulation of certain treaty fishing rights. Three days after the decision is announced, 150 Indians march outside the plaza of the Supreme Court building in protest of the court's decision in the Puyallup case.

JUNE 21, 1968   Poor People's March on the BIA. Approximately 100 Indian participants in Martin Luther King, Jr.'s, Poor People's Campaign march on the Bureau of Indian Affairs in Washington, D.C.

JUNE 25, 1968   Indian in House of Commons. Leonard Marchand (Liberal), an Okanagan (Interior Salish) from British Columbia, becomes the first Indian elected to the House of Commons. He later becomes a member of the cabinet.

JUNE 25, 1968   Non-Indian Commission on Indian Affairs Blocked. A coalition of Indian people in California succeed in blocking the establishment of a new all-white Commission on Indian Affairs in California. The coalition persuades the Senate Finance Committee to change it to an all-Indian commission.

JULY 1968   Founding of the American Indian Movement. The American Indian Movement (AIM) is co-founded in Minneapolis, Minnesota by Dennis Banks, Clyde Bellecourt, Mary Jane Wilson and other community members. Established during a period of general civil unrest and protests by African-Americans and Mexican-Americans, the movement is organized to improve federal, state, and local social services to urban neighborhoods and to prevent the harassment of Indians by the local police. Increasingly confrontational, AIM members form patrols to monitor police activity and to demonstrate against mistreatment of Indians.

JULY 16, 1968   Dick Gregory Released from Jail. Comedian Dick Gregory is released from jail in Olympia, Washington, after fasting for six weeks to call attention to the violation of Indian treaty rights.

JULY 25, 1968   Government Consultations. Promising a "Just Society," the newly elected Liberal government led by Pierre Trudeau begins consultations with Indian groups toward establishing a new Indian policy.

SUMMER 1968   United Native Americans Or- ganized. United Native Americans (UNA) is organized in the San Francisco region. UNA seeks to unify all persons of Indian blood throughout the Americas and to develop a democratic, grass-roots organization. UNA's purpose is "to work, without compromise, for native control of native affairs at every level." Lehman Brightman is the first president. UNA publishes *Warpath*, a militant newspaper.

SEPTEMBER 7, 1968   Reverend Roe Lewis Receives Indian Achievement Award. The Reverend Dr. Roe B. Lewis of Phoenix, Arizona, of Pima and Papago blood, is named to receive the 1968 Indian Achievement Award presented annually by the Indian Council Fire. The award is established in 1933 at the Century of Progress Exposition. The Presbyterian minister is chosen because of his outstanding service in educational counseling work for the Indians, and for assisting Indian high school graduates through college and graduate school.

OCTOBER 1968   Economic Development Report. In a special report on economic development, the BIA's Indian Record states that 10,000 new jobs have been created in Indian communities since 1962 and that these new jobs are a direct result of combined efforts by the BIA and tribal groups.

OCTOBER 1968   Office of Opportunity Picketed. United Native Americans members, led by Lee Brightman, picket the Office of Opportunity (OEO) offices in San Francisco. Protesters force OEO to release $48,000 to the Neighborhood Friendship House for Indian programs.

OCTOBER 21, 1968   Supplemental Appropriation Act. Congress passes the Supplemental Appropriations Act, which includes an appropriation of $100,000 to implement the National Council on Indian Opportunity, established by Executive Order 11399 on March 6, 1968. An important piece of President Johnson's efforts to improve the plight of Indians, the council is given the following purposes: (1) to encourage the complete application of federal programs designed to aid Indians; (2) to encourage interagency cooperation in the implementation of these programs; (3) to assess the effect of these programs; and (4) to suggest ways in which these programs can be improved.

OCTOBER 24, 1968 Yavapai Land Claims. The Yavapai tribe of Arizona and the federal government agree to a $5 million settlement for the loss of over 9 million acres illegally taken from the tribe by the federal government in 1874.

NOVEMBER 1968 Indian University Pilot Project Begun. An American Indian Community University Pilot Project, directed by Dr. Jack D. Forbes, begins with a grant from the Conner Foundation, Inc.

NOVEMBER 1968 United Native Americans Conference. The United Native Americans (UNA) sponsor a conference in Oakland, California, on "Indian Power and Federal Money." The conference publicly exposes the U.S. political domination and discrimination against Indians. Speakers include Lee Brightman, Dave Risling, Jack Forbes, Tom Campbell, and Morgan Otis.

DECEMBER 18, 1968 Mohawk Block Traffic from U.S. to Canada. Mohawk from the Akwesasne Reserve block a bridge between the U.S. and Canada through their reservation in order to reassert their legal authority over their land and to protest illegal Canadian government actions, specifically the imposition of Canadian custom duties on their goods. The Mohawk claim the 1794 Jay's Treaty signed between the United States and Great Britain on behalf of Canada guarantees to the border tribes free passage and freedom from import and export taxes on goods traversing the border. Because of the failure of Canada and the United States to recognize the tribes' right to freely export and import goods, Indian families must pay taxes on goods that are carried only from one family member's house to another.

1 9 6 9

1969 Alfonso Ortiz Publishes *The Tewa World*. Alfonso Ortiz, a Tewa Indian from San Juan Pueblo, publishes *The Tewa World: Space, Time, Being and Becoming in a Pueblo Society*. With an M.A. and Ph.D. in anthropology from the University of Chicago, Ortiz's explication of his own people is immediately considered a classic in the field.

1969 BIA Structural Changes Delineated. Structural changes within the Bureau of Indian Affairs are delineated as a result of the Josephy Report, prepared by Indian author A.M. Josephy, Jr., at the request of the newly elected Johnson administration.

1969 California Indian Water Rights. The Rincon and La Jolla Indians of southern California sue to reclaim water diverted from their area.

1969 Hoopa Language Taught in Public Schools. The Hupa of the Hoopa Reservation in northern California begin teaching their language in public schools, assisted by local elders and Humboldt State University representatives, who help develop an alphabet.

1969 Indian College Site Sought. The California Indian Education Association begins a search for funding and for a physical location for an Indian college within the state.

1969 Indian Education. A U.S. Senate report entitled "Indian Education: A National Tragedy, a National Challenge" is published. The report becomes the impetus for the Indian Education Act of 1972. In 1969 the first National Indian Education Association Conference is held in Minneapolis, Minnesota.

1969   Iroquois Organization. The Foundation of Iroquois and Allied Indians is formed in Ontario.

1969   Native American Student Union Formed. The Native American Student Union is formed in the San Francisco Bay area, bringing together Indian college students. Members of the Native American Student Union will be deeply involved in the November occupation of Alcatraz Island.

1969   *The Way to Rainy Mountain* Is Published. Following the success of *House Made of Dawn*, N. Scott Momaday publishes his second book, *The Way to Rainy Mountain*, an autobiography. In it he offers multiple parallel narratives, likening his own personal journey, his evolution as an American Indian, to that of the Kiowa emergence story. His tripartite narrative structure serves to blur the lines between history, myth, and autobiography, offering the reader an innovative reworking of these traditionally distinctive genres. Holder of a Ph.D. in literature from Stanford University, Momaday has taught and lectured at numerous universities and institutions. Following *The Way to Rainy Mountain*, he publishes several collections of poetry; an autobiographical memoir entitled *The Names* (1976); and a novel, *The Ancient Child* (1989).

JANUARY 1969   Navajo Irrigation Project. Final inspection is made of the main canal and Tunnel #2 of the large Navajo Irrigation Project, designed to supply long-awaited water in Arizona to irrigate arid soils for the Indian people. This phase of the project has a construction cost of about $9 million, of which $2,750,000 goes for salaries of the workers.

JANUARY 7, 1969   Manitoba Hydroelectric Project. Over 600 Manitoba Indians and Métis protest a Manitoba Hydro project that would raise the level of Southern Indian Lake (in northern Manitoba) by almost 11 meters (35 feet) and divert much of the Churchill River. Indian homes and lands would be flooded by the project.

JANUARY 21, 1969   Navajo Community College Opens. The Navajo Community College at Many Farms, Arizona, opens its doors to students. The college is the first tribally established and Indian-controlled community college. The Navajo college, a project of tribal leader Dillon Platero, is governed by an all-Navajo board.

MARCH 1969   Provincial Franchise. Quebec Indians living on reserves become the last Indians in Canada to be given the provincial franchise.

MARCH 5, 1969   The Office of Minority Business Enterprise Established. President Richard Nixon signs an executive order to ensure that a fair proportion of all government purchases and contracts are awarded to businesses owned wholly or in part by minorities and women. Indian tribes, acting in their commercial capacity, are expressly included in the act's provisions. The act's objective is to assist tribes in the economic development of their reservations, where more than half of all families live below the poverty level and unemployment on some reservations is as high as 90 percent.

MARCH 23, 1969   Indian Life Expectancy. The Indian Health Service states that life expectancy for Indians is 64 years of age, compared with an average life expectancy of 70.5 years for non-Indians. Despite the continuing gap in life expectancy, however, the new statistics reveal a major improvement in Indian health care and standards. Twenty years earlier the average life expectancy for an Indian male was only 44 years.

MARCH 23, 1969   Trial of Mohawk Demonstrators. The trial of seven Mohawk Indian

Members of the Iroquois League protesting their right to cross the U.S.-Canadian border in accordance with 1794 Jay's Treaty, July 1969. Courtesy of the Buffalo and Erie County Historical Society.

men begins on charges stemming from demonstrations on the International Bridge between the United States and Canada.

SPRING 1969 **University of California, Berkeley, Native American Studies Program Created.** The Berkeley campus chapter of United Native Americans joins the Third World student strike, spurring the creation of a Native American Studies program. Leaders of the Indian effort are Lanada Means, Patty Silvas, Carmen Christy, Horace Spencer, and Dr. Jack

D. Forbes. Plans also are being developed for Native American Studies Centers on other California college campuses. Dr. Forbes drafts a proposal for a College of Native American Studies to be created on one of the University of California campuses. The California State Legislature endorses the idea.

APRIL 1969 **Cochiti Pueblo Signs Lease with Great Western United Corporation.** The Cochiti Pueblo in New Mexico signs a 99-year lease with Great Western United Corporation for 7,300 acres of land adjacent to the Cochiti Lake and Dam being created by the U.S. Army Corps of Engineers. Construction of thousands of resort-type homes and other recreational facilities is planned for this site, located 35 miles from Albuquerque. It is hailed as a major step in improving the economic independence of Indians.

APRIL 29, 1969   Indian Hunting Rights. Stanley Smart, a Paiute Indian from the McDermitt Indian Reservation, contests a fine imposed for shooting deer out of season on public land. The case is dismissed because of a technicality when the prosecution fails to show a county statute has been violated.

MAY 5, 1969   *House Made of Dawn* Awarded the Pulitzer Prize. Dr. N. Scott Momaday, 34-year-old Kiowa-Cherokee Indian, is awarded the Pulitzer Prize for literature, for his novel *House Made of Dawn*, becoming the first American Indian to be given this coveted recognition.

MAY 18, 1969   Klamath Win Land Claims Judgment. The Klamath tribe of Oregon wins a judgment of $4.1 million from the Indian Claims Commission for the loss of lands resulting from faulty surveys conducted by the government of their reservation in 1871 and 1888.

MAY 31, 1969   Robert Bennett Resigns as Commissioner of Indian Affairs. Robert L. Bennett resigns as commissioner of Indian affairs, concluding one of the longest tenures in office. He is only the second Indian to hold that significant post.

JUNE 1969   Carnegie Report. After analyzing the historical decline of educational attainment by Indian groups, principally that of the Choctaws and the Cherokee republics, a report issued by the influential Carnegie Corporation suggests that BIA educational officials be rewarded according to the degree that they manage

to involve the Indian community in decision making at top levels, and recommends that some of the bureau's responsibilities be transferred to the communities. Possibly the most significant proposal is for the creation of a federal commission for Indian education, limited to a five-year period, with the understanding that thereafter it would return control to Indian communities. In its projected composition there would be officials from the BIA, the U.S. Office of Education, and tribal groups, among others. The commission would be charged with the responsibility of training Indians for administering and staffing Indian schools and providing consultant support to Indian school boards as they emerged and asked for help. Further, it would supply necessary funds to revise curricula to be more reflective of Indian history, culture, and values.

JUNE 19, 1969   National Congress of American Indians Attempts to Attract Private Businesses to Reservations. The National Congress of American Indians (NCAI) hosts an exhibition and briefing sessions in New York City in an effort to attract private businesses to reservations. NCAI president Wendall Chino announces that 159 new enterprises have been started on reservations in the previous five years, with a total investment of more than $100 million.

JUNE 25, 1969   The White Paper. Following a year of consultation with Native groups, Jean Chrétien, Canada's minister of Indian affairs, releases the federal government's White Paper (Government policy paper), *Statement of the Government of Canada on Indian Policy, 1969*. The discussion paper rejects the Hawthorn Report's recommendation that Indians be treated as "citizens plus," arguing instead that Indians' special legal status has hindered their social, economic, and political development. The government proposes legislation to end all legal and constitutional distinctions relating to Indians. The Indian Act and the Indian Affairs

Department are to be abolished in about five years; reserves, held in trust by the government since before Confederation, would pass to Indian ownership. Thus, the federal and provincial governments will deal with Indians in the same way they deal with any other Canadians. During a transitional period, the government proposes to give Indians aid to alleviate social and economic problems on reserves. The policy paper dismisses aboriginal land claims as "so general and undefined that it is not realistic to think of them as . . . capable of remedy."

JUNE 25–DECEMBER 1969 Opposition to the White Paper. Indians and Indian organizations from across Canada begin to unite in opposition to the government's White Paper. As early as June 26 Walter Deiter, leader of the National Indian Brotherhood, rejects the White Paper, saying that it ignores both the views Indians expressed during the government's consultations and the guarantees given Indians in treaties. Harold Cardinal *(See* biography, January 27, 1945), Cree leader of the Indian Association of Alberta writes *Unjust Society*, a denunciation of the White Paper. During the winter it becomes a Canadian best-seller.

JUNE 30, 1969 Land for an Indian-Controlled University. Dr. Jack Forbes writes to Assistant Secretary for Housing, Education, and Welfare (HEW) Veneman to inquire into a 640-acre site between Winters and Davis, California, and requests Veneman to look into its availability for an Indian-controlled school.

JULY 1969 Margery Haury Wins Title of Miss Indian America XVI. Margery Haury, 18, a Navajo-Sioux-Arapaho-Cheyenne, wins the title of Miss Indian America XVI at Sheridan, Wyoming. She is a political science student at the University of New Mexico in Albuquerque, planning to go into law. Commenting on the importance of teaching pride in heritage, she states, "I would like to engender a closeness between all tribes. Most of the other minorities

Harold Cardinal, twenty-four-year-old president of the Indian Association of Alberta, led the Indian resistance to the Canadian government's White Paper (policy papers) of 1969. Courtesy of Canapress Photo Service.

have a common goal. We don't. We're all so different, yet we must unite."

AUGUST 1969 North American Indian Traveling College Developed. Ernest M. Benedict, a Canadian Mohawk, develops the North American Indian Traveling College. This college in a truck moves from one community to another offering training in work skills, information on how to begin consumer coopera-

View of Alcatraz Island in late November 1969 soon after the occupation by American Indian students. Courtesy of Stephen Lehmer. (*See* entry, **November 9, 1969**, p. 365.)

tives, and background on the cultural heritage of Indian people.

AUGUST 7, 1969 Louis Bruce Appointed New Commissioner of Indian Affairs. President Nixon and Secretary of the Interior Walter Hickel announce that Louis R. Bruce, a Mohawk-Oglala-Sioux Indian from New York, will be the new commissioner of Indian affairs. Bruce thereby becomes the third Indian in history to assume the high governmental post. Before him were his immediate predecessor, Robert L. Bennett, and General Ely Samuel Parker, who served during President Grant's administration. Bruce had previously served as the executive secretary of the National Congress of American Indians, and was awarded the American Indian Achievement Award and the Freedoms Award, among other honors.

AUGUST 23, 1969 Indian Representatives Call for Ouster of Interior Secretary Hickel. Representatives of 46 North American Indian nations meet at the Onondaga Reservation in New York. Representing traditional peoples, the conference passes a resolution calling for

the immediate ouster of Interior Secretary Walter Hickel. Hickel, they charge, has not been protective of Indian resources or sensitive to the needs of Indian peoples.

AUGUST 26, 1969 Quinault Tribe Closes Reservation Beaches to Non-Indians. The Quinault tribe of Washington announces the closure of reservation beaches to non-Indians, citing thefts of Indian fishing gear, littering, and defacement. The state responds that the ownership of the beaches remains in question.

AUGUST 27, 1969 Indian Youth Appear on Art Linkletter Show. Four Indian youngsters from the Pala Mission School in California are honored guests on the nationally televised Art Linkletter Show. During the show, the famous entertainer tells the audience, "This is the first time Indian children have ever appeared on my show."

AUGUST 29, 1969 New Mexico Indian Job Training Contract Renewed. The Department of the Interior announces that it has renewed its contract with Thiokol Chemical Corporation for the operation of its Indian job

Indians of All Tribes pow wow singers at Alcatraz, San Francisco, California, 1969. Courtesy of Stephen Lehmer.

training center at Roswell, New Mexico. The cost of operations for 1970 is $2,289,850. The Indians are brought to the Thiokol operation by the BIA as whole families, thus avoiding one of the problems that plagued prior Indian training endeavors, drop-outs by homesick students. Families are exposed to programs designed not only to make the Indians technically more proficient, but also to equip them for living in the mainstream of present-day America. Wives receive nutritional home economics assistance, and children are taken care of in

nurseries while the parents are away. The older children attend the regular Roswell schools. Unemployed and underemployed Indians are reported to be very enthusiastic with their new opportunities to learn "in-depth" the technical and living skills to which they are being exposed.

AUGUST 30, 1969   Indian Unity Conference Delegates Discuss Jay's Treaty of 1794. An Indian Unity conference is held near Hogansburg, New York. Delegates from 62 nations of the United States and Canada meet with Prime

Indians of All Tribes protester John Trudell at Alcatraz, San Francisco, California, 1969. Courtesy of Stephen Lehmer.

Minister Pierre Trudeau of Canada and Secretary of State William Rogers to discuss the Canadian government's refusal to recognize Jay's Treaty of 1794. Canada claims that Jay's treaty, signed by the United States and Great Britain, which states that Indians are exempt from paying custom duties and permits them to travel freely anywhere in North America, was never ratified by the Canadian government.

SEPTEMBER 1969 Alaska Pipeline. Multinational oil corporations offer hundreds of millions of dollars to acquire oil in Alaska belonging to the Inuit. They plan the development of an oil pipeline across Inuit and Dene lands. Alaska Natives organize to defeat the pipeline and to secure a fair share of the wealth from oil and land cessions.

SEPTEMBER 1969 Founder of New Mexico Uranium Industry Dies. Paddy Martinez, the Navajo sheepherder who picked up a yellow rock on Haystack Mountain and started New Mexico's multimillion-dollar uranium industry, dies in a Grants, New Mexico, hospital at the age of 78. Although his discovery of urani-

um brings riches to many, Paddy lives in a simple hogan near the shores of Bluewater Lake, grazing sheep. His strike is on property owned by the Santa Fe Railway, which rewards him by giving him a lifetime pension.

SEPTEMBER 1969 Indian Education. A follow-up of Indian high school graduates in the Southwest in 1962 indicates that almost three-fourths of those contacted continue their education. More than two-thirds of those who go on complete their programs, a majority in vocational-technical subjects. Only 7 percent complete college, while 44 percent finish vocational training programs. Another significant finding is that an overwhelming majority of the respondents note the importance of tribal languages.

SEPTEMBER 1969 Indian Employment Training Center Opens. An Employment Training Center for Indians from the northern plains states is opened at Bismarck by a corporation composed of the Indian tribes of North Dakota. The United Tribes of North Dakota Development Corporation becomes the first center initiated by Indians and having an Indian contractor. Initial enrollment is composed of 25 families, 10 solo parents, 50 single men, and 50 single women. A total of 160 people enter into the actual training program, which is funded from several federal sources.

SEPTEMBER 1969 Native Studies Program Initiated. Trent University in Peterborough, Ontario, begins the first Native studies program in Canada.

SEPTEMBER 6, 1969 Fairchild Semiconductor Factory Dedicated. National names and top political figures join the Navajos at Shiprock, New Mexico, in dedicating the largest industrial factory in the state of New Mexico. Included are David and Julie Eisenhower, Senator Joseph Montoya, newly appointed Indian commissioner Louis R. Bruce (Mohawk), and New Mexico Governor David Cargo. Fairchild Semiconductors, a subsidiary of worldwide Fairchild

Camera and Instrument Corporation, is engaged in assembling some of the components for the Apollo rocket systems. From its modest beginning, when only 50 workers are employed, it grows to a plant employing 1,200, including more Indian people than any other plant of any kind in the entire United States. Fewer than 30 key employees are non-Indian. The firm is a joint partnership involving private industry, tribal authorities, federal aid agencies, and the larger New Mexico community.

SEPTEMBER 15, 1969 Navajo Indian Irrigation Project Funding. The Senate Interior Subcommittee, prodded by U.S. Senator Joseph M. Montoya, agrees to a $2 million increase in the $3.5 million budget request of the Nixon Administration for the Navajo Indian Irrigation Project. The project, which originally was to be completed in 1979, is already far behind schedule at the time this appropriation is approved. When completed, the project will provide irrigation for 110,000 acres of land and create 1,120 new farm jobs for Navajo families, while additionally creating new jobs and economic activity for up to 80,000 Navajos.

SEPTEMBER 24, 1969 Report on Income from Indian Timber. The commissioner of Indian affairs reports that Indian timber income from sales of reservation lumber in the United States totals $32.7 million, or about twice the figure for 1967. Indian tree resources are harvested on a sustained-yield basis, to prevent overcutting and eventual depletion. The bureau official estimates that the present allowable harvest of 1.04 billion board feet may be reached in fiscal year 1970. Just as important as the income from timber sales are the job opportunities in lumbering and lumber processing created by the harvest. At the present rate, 7,000 full-time jobs are directly related, with an additional 4,000 in supporting and service employment. Commissioner Louis R. Bruce points out that several tribes are taking increased interest in developing their resources and that about 30 percent of the total volume of Indian timber is purchased by Indian and tribal enterprises.

OCTOBER 1969 AMERIND Founded. AMERIND, an organization founded to protect the rights and improve the working conditions of Indian employees, opens its Albuquerque, New Mexico, headquarters. Supported by the National Indian Youth Council, AMERIND evolves from the experiences of some Indian employees of the BIA who file discrimination complaints in Albuquerque and Gallup. In response to these and other complaints, the organization is established to fight employment discrimination and end the "second-class treatment" of Indians working for the BIA, U.S. Public Health Service, and other federal agencies serving Indian people. There are no dues or membership applications required for joining in the purposes and objectives of the new group.

OCTOBER 1969 Navajo Sign Agreement for Electric Generating Plant. Navajo Tribal Chairman Raymond Nakai signs a lease agreement for the construction of a $309 million electric generating plant to be built at Page, Arizona. Projected coal royalties, lease payments, and other contributions from the operation will exceed $1.8 million annually for the Hopi and Navajo tribes.

OCTOBER 1969 Support for Navajo Community College. The Office of Economic Opportunity (OEO) announces continued support for Navajo Community College, recently opened in January at Many Farms, Arizona. It is the first college in the country to be planned, developed, and operated by and for Indians. In awarding the grant, the OEO states that it is supporting this unique attempt to prove that a college can be responsive to the educational and economic needs of a rural community. The college serves as a laboratory for experimentation in the field of Indian education. It enrolls promising high-risk youths and undereducated adults.

OCTOBER 1, 1969 Indians Attempt to Enter Desegregated Schools in South Carolina. Indian parents seeking to enroll their children in desegregated schools in Ridgeville, South Carolina, are turned away by a line of federal marshals and threatened with a contempt of court charge. "If it takes this to get my children into the Ridgeville school, then I die," said Mrs. Gertie Creel, the mother of an eight-year-old who lives in the small Indian settlement in rural Dorchester County. The Indians and their African-American civil rights backers vow to continue a drive to close small county Indian schools.

OCTOBER 5, 1969 Albuquerque Indian Vocational Technical School. Groundbreaking ceremonies are held for the new $8 million Albuquerque Vocational Technical School for Indians. Remarks are delivered by Domingo Montoya, chairman of the All Indian Pueblo Council, Louis R. Bruce, commissioner of Indian affairs, and others. The new facility is intended to attract students from all over the United States, and is designed first by considering the curriculum needs of the future and the pupils who would be attending, and then by building the plant around these requirements. An initial 500 students will open the multimillion-dollar school, with an additional 1,000 students in years subsequent to 1971.

OCTOBER 6, 1969 NCAI Convention. American Indian people from all parts of the United States, ranging from Seminole of Florida to Yakima of Washington, and many interested non-Indians, flock to Albuquerque, New Mexico, for the opening of the annual five-day convention of the National Congress of American Indians. Political figures and office holders highlight the event, which features a colorful parade of almost 60 floats and includes tribal dancers, Indian bands, and the governors of many pueblos. Featured speakers are Secretary of the Interior Walter Hickel and Commissioner of Indian Affairs Louis R. Bruce.

OCTOBER 7, 1969 United Native Americans Call for Removal of Interior Secretary Hickel. At a National Indian Youth Conference panel, Lehman Brightman of Berkeley, California, head of an Indian group called the United Native Americans, circulates a petition calling for the removal from office of Interior Secretary Walter Hickel. To the panel audience he announces, "Hickel is the greatest enemy of the American Indian and we should get rid of such a menace. Our present Indian leadership has dwindled to talkers and rubber stamps of what the Bureau of Indian Affairs puts in front of them." He calls such Indian supporters of the BIA "Uncle Tomahawks." Outside the hotel where the meetings are in progress, a number of Indian young people carry placards calling for the removal of Hickel, but say that they are not connected with any special group.

OCTOBER 7, 1969 White House Conference on Indian Problems. U.S. Senator Edward Kennedy calls for a White House conference on Indian problems. Announcing that he will introduce a bill to authorize and finance such a project, he criticizes the Bureau of Indian Affair's handling of Native American affairs as "unsatisfactory even under the best of circumstances." He calls for the creation of a Select Committee on Human Needs of American Indians, saying, "The BIA is notorious for its resistance to reform, to innovation, and to discharging its responsibilities in a competent and sensitive fashion."

OCTOBER 8, 1969 Nixon Indian Policy. Vice President Spiro Agnew promises American Indians that the Nixon administration will not adopt a termination policy to phase out federal supervision of Indian affairs. He claims that the president will work with them on a "community-by-community and tribe-by-tribe basis." Possibly warning of a future turn of events, however, he adds that the national administration will "urge greater local leadership on the part of the Indian."

OCTOBER 12, 1969 Indian Mascot Dropped at Dartmouth College. Dartmouth College, located in New Hampshire and initially established in 1769 to educate Indians, announces that it is dropping its use of an Indian mascot in response to demands by the undergraduate body. Many students support the Indian students' views that the use of a Native American mascot degrades Indian people.

OCTOBER 13, 1969 Ford Foundation Establishes Minority Fellowships. The Ford Foundation announces the establishment of a Minority Fellowship Program for minority students, including American Indians. The program's objective is to increase the number of minority scholars obtaining doctorates in a variety of fields. The need is particularly acute in Indian country, where few Indians enter and complete college, and even fewer go on to graduate school. Without appropriate role models, educators recognize that it will be difficult to improve educational services to Indian students.

OCTOBER 29, 1969 Indian Health Care Act. Congress passes the Indian Health Care Act, an appropriations act, Title 1—Department of the Interior, calling "for expenses necessary to enable the Surgeon General to carry out the purposes of the Act of August 5, 1954 (68 Stat. 674), as amended" for Indian health care and its facilities to be administered under Public Health Services.

NOVEMBER 1969 National Indian Education Association Organized. The National Indian Education Association (NIEA) is organized in Minneapolis, Minnesota, to improve the quality of Indian education. The organization is established specifically to improve communications on Indian educational issues through national conventions and workshops; to advocate for increased funding and creative programs for the education of Indian children; and to provide technical assistance to educators in the field.

NOVEMBER 3, 1969 Senate Subcommittee Report on Indian Education Issued. The Senate Subcommittee on Indian Education issues its final report following a two-year investigation. Chaired by Senator Edward Kennedy, who took over following the death of his brother, Robert Kennedy, the committee spends two years reviewing all areas of Indian education. The report concludes that "our national policies for educating American Indians are a failure of major proportions." In comparing statistics in all aspects of education, the committee expresses its disbelief at "the low quality of virtually every aspect of schooling available to Indian children." The report enumerates 60 recommendations to improve Indian education, most importantly that Indian people be given greater control over the schooling of their children.

NOVEMBER 9, 1969 Occupation of Alcatraz Island. Fourteen Indian activists occupy Alcatraz Island in San Francisco Bay and symbolically claim the island for Indian people, offering to purchase the island for $24 worth of glass beads and red cloth. On November 20, the symbolic occupation of Alcatraz Island turns into a full-scale occupation that lasts until June 11, 1971. One hundred Indian youth, primarily California college students, representing 20 tribes occupy Alcatraz Island and demand the establishment of a center for Native American studies, an American Indian spiritual center, an Indian center of ecology, and an Indian training school. By November 28, the number of Indians on the island increases to approximately 400. They defy federal demands that they leave the island, and approximately 150 set up permanent occupancy in cell-blocks and other buildings. The federal government's actions are orchestrated directly from the White House and a "hands-off" policy toward the occupiers is adopted by President Richard Nixon. This is the result of the growing negative public image resulting from the Vietnam War and the killing of college students at Kent State University by National Guard personnel. While negotiations are conducted throughout the prolonged period of occupation, the federal government refuses to give in to the demands of the occupiers. Public sympathy for the Indians on the island decreases as time passes, and on June 11, 1971, federal marshals and Government Services Administration special forces personnel remove the 15 remaining occupiers. Following the Alcatraz occupation, Indian activists, led by former participants in the protest, occupy over 60 government facilities across the United States, demanding that Indian rights be recognized. During the occupation of Alcatraz Island, President Nixon signs legislation that returns the sacred Blue Lake to the Taos people and formally announces a government policy of self-determination for Indians. Members of the Alcatraz occupation force become leaders in the American Indian Movement (AIM) and participate in the February 1973 occupation of Wounded Knee, and the 1975 occupation of the Washington, D.C., Bureau of Indian Affairs offices.

NOVEMBER 17–22, 1969 British Columbia Indian Organization. The Union of British Columbia Indian Chiefs holds its founding convention. It is the first Indian organization in the province intended to represent all status Indians in the province. Until now smaller organizations representing status and non-status Indians in British Columbia have dominated in the province. Indians at the convention denounce the federal government's White Paper. A corresponding organization for non-status Indians, the British Columbia Association of Non-Status Indians (reorganized as the United Native Nations in 1976), was formed in March.

NOVEMBER 20, 1969 Indian Act Challenge. In the *R. v. Drybones* case, the Canadian Supreme Court strikes down sections of the Indian Act that restrict liquor sales to Indians because they contravene sections of the 1960 Bill of Rights that guarantee all Canadians equality before the law. This, the first ruling on the Bill of Rights, finds that the bill prevails over other legislation.

DECEMBER 19, 1969 Land Claims Commission. Dr. Lloyd Barber, vice president of the University of Saskatchewan, is appointed land claims commissioner according to guidelines set out in June's White Paper. The appointment is denounced by Indian groups because the commissioner has no power to negotiate settlements.

Chapter 9

1970 TO 1979

1 9 7 0

1970 American Indian Youth Council. Concern with the abysmally low economic place which Indians occupy, contrasted to an otherwise healthy and vigorous national picture, causes Indian youth groups to press for change and agitate for a "new look" for the "First Americans." Indian youth set out to accomplish change through the use of political power and activism. Because of the formal nature of treaty relations with the federal government, activist protests and demonstrations have not been considered an acceptable "Indian" option by older and sometimes more conservative Indians. Consequently, youth strategies, influenced by the civil rights movement of the 1960s, begin to adopt an overtly proactive stance.

1970 Determination of the Rights and Unity for Menominee Shareholders. In response to federal legislation terminating the Menominee, Ada Deer becomes an activist for her people during the 1960s. She helps organize the group, Determination of the Rights and Unity for Menominee Shareholders (DRUMS) in 1970; the intent of DRUMS is to repeal Congress's 1954 Termination Act. DRUMS eventually regains federal recognition for the Menominee in 1973, thereby restoring tribal health and education benefits. Subsequently, from 1974 to 1976, Ada Deer chairs the Menominee Resto-

ration Committee, where she proves instrumental in securing a new framework for the Menominee tribal government. After resigning as chair, Deer turns her attention to other issues affecting American Indians and their community.

1970 Funding for Indian Organizations. The Canadian government begins funding various Indian groups, thus marking the complete reversal of its 1927 law repressing Indian political organization. Funding helps to further strengthen organizations initiated or united by opposition to the White Paper. Funding is intended to improve communications between Native groups and the government.

1970 Indian Demonstrations. Indian groups demonstrate throughout the United States to direct attention to current Indian concerns and inequities. In California, Pit River Indians and El-Em Pomo Indians hold sit-ins on territory once belonging to their tribes in northern California.

1970 Indian Health Service. Indian health services become available to California Indians.

1970 New Indian Leader. George Manuel *(See biography, February 17, 1920)*, a Shuswap Interior Salish from British Columbia, is chosen as the new president (1970–76) of the National Indian Brotherhood (N.I.B.). His election represents a victory for the more radical wing of

First Annual War Dance Ceremony pow wow, Vancouver, British Columbia, 1970. Courtesy of Stephen Lehmer.

the organization, which opposes Walter Deiter's relatively conservative stance.

1970   Support for White Paper. William Wuttunee, a Cree lawyer and former leader of the National Indian Council, writes *Ruffled Feathers*, a reply to Cree leader of the Indian Association of Alberta Harold Cardinal's *(See* biography, January 27, 1945) *Unjust Society* and a defense of the government's White Paper. Several bands, including his own Red Pheasant band, respond by banning him from their reserves. Wuttunee, Kainai Indian senator James Gladstone *(See* biography, May 21, 1887), and a small number of other leaders voice qualified support for the White Paper.

JANUARY 1970   Deganawida-Quetzalcoatl University. Dr. Jack Forbes writes to the General Services Administration requesting information on 650 acres of land located between Winters and Davis, California, for the possible site of an Indian university. Formerly a Strategic Air Command military base, this land is incorporated as a college for Indians and Chicanos with formal title turned over by the government to Deganawida-Quetzalcoatl University trustees on April 2, 1971. *(See also* entry,

July 1970; October 29–30, 1970; November 3, 1970; January 15, 1971; and April 2, 1971.)

JANUARY 1970   Inuvialuit Organization. The Committee for Original People's Entitlement is formed to represent the interests of the Inuvialuit, who reside in the lower Mackenzie Valley region. Most of the Inuvialuit are descended from caribou hunters who moved to the area from the west between 1880 and 1920. The discovery of oil and gas reserves in the Beaufort Sea prompts them to organize.

JANUARY 1, 1970   Minority and Low Income Research. Southern California Indian tribes from the San Diego area complete a proposal under the auspices of the Wright Institute at Grossmont College; they request financing for a research and development program to uncover and implement solutions to poverty for minority and low income peoples in that area. Participating in the program are members of an ad hoc committee representing Indians, students, administrators, and the faculty of three regional community colleges—Grossmont, Mesa, and Palomar. The program is preceded by community meetings and questionnaires which gather information about the problems and needs of local Indian peoples. The proposal is sent to the Special Services Office in the Office of Health, Education, and Welfare in Washington, D.C. The implementation target date is set for September 1970.

JANUARY 17, 1970 Report on Economic Conditions on Indian Reservations. A Senate and House of Representatives joint subcommittee publishes a two-volume report on economic conditions on the reservation. Detailed in the report are charges by Bureau of Indian Affairs official William Veeder, a water resources expert, that the government has caused "irreparable damage" to the Indians and to the economic development of Indian reservations. Veeder asserts that the basic problem results from an inherent conflict of interest between the Departments of Interior and Justice, which are responsible for protecting public lands and streams as well as assuring Indian property rights. Veeder suggests that Congress create an independent governmental agency for the protection of Indian water rights.

FEBRUARY 1970 Northwest Territories Indian Organization. The Indian Brotherhood of the Northwest Territories (Dene Nation) is established.

MARCH 8, 1970 Indians March on California State Capitol. A Sacramento Indian group led by Lehman Brightman marches to the state capitol protesting the fatal shooting of Hoopa Indian Michael Ferris on December 5, 1969, in Humboldt County. Ferris, a student at UCLA, was shot to death in a Will Creek bar by a bartender.

MARCH 8, 1970 United Indians of All Tribes. United Indians of All Tribes invade Fort Lawton, pressing for their right to occupy federal lands about to be declared surplus. These Indian people believe that the invasion is critical to their cause; originally, the Indians of Seattle asked for the title to Fort Lawton. Virtually ignored by politicians, United Indians

of All Tribes dramatically points out the inefficacy that exists in governmental relations with Indians. Sen. Henry Jackson advises Seattle mayor Wes Uhlman that Fort Lawton will be deeded to the city for a park once it is declared surplus property. Protesting such land use, 14 Indian activists occupy the site, 50 miles south of Seattle, and refuse all requests to leave. A proclamation, similar to that issued from Alcatraz, states that the Indians intend to use the post as an ecological and cultural center. Indian participants in the occupation of Alcatraz Island comprise the majority of the Native occupiers. Indian Bernie Whitebear states that the group, United Indians of All Tribes, is modeled after Indians of All Tribes on Alcatraz Island. Also among the Indians participating in the demonstration is future American Indian Movement (AIM) activist Leonard Peltier. The military arrests 77 Indians and uses clubs to beat and forcibly remove the demonstrating Natives. Celebrity participant Jane Fonda is removed from the government facility along with the other occupiers. Fonda is taken into custody and given a letter of expulsion banning her from the post.

MARCH 9–14, 1970 Arctic Winter Games. The first Arctic Winter Games are held in Yellowknife, Northwest Territories. Inuvialuk Nellie Cornoyea *(See* biography, March 4, 1940) plays an important part in organizing the events, in which athletes from the Yukon, Northwest Territories, and Alaska compete in traditional Inuit and Indian games as well as sports such as basketball and hockey.

MARCH 10, 1970 Alcatraz Island. Indians of All Tribes who participated in the Fort Lawton and Fort Lewis occupations return to Alcatraz Island. Byron Harvey reports in *Thoughts From Alcatraz* that the Alcatraz protest "expanded" to Fort Lawton, thereby suggesting a larger framework to Indian protests of this time.

MARCH 13, 1970 Alcatraz Island. In a General Services Administration memorandum,

'Declaration of the Return of Indian Land,' Indians of All Tribes at Alcatraz in California. Courtesy of Stephen Lehmer.

Alcatraz caretaker Don Carroll reports, "There is a rumor on the island that the Indians are going to try to take over the military posts in Washington again this weekend." This report proves correct as Indians reoccupy Fort Lawton on March 15.

MARCH 14, 1970 BIA Office Takeovers. Indian activists take over the Bureau of Indian Affairs office in Denver, Colorado. An incident in Littleton, Colorado, incites this protest against discrimination regarding BIA anti-Indian employment policies. An Indian woman applying for a position as school counselor working with Indian children is turned down despite her qualifications for the job. There are two separate incidents in Littleton, resulting in the arrest of 21 Indians. A countrywide chain reaction is ignited: 23 arrests occur in Chicago; 12 in Alameda, California; 25 in Minneapolis; and 30 in Philadelphia. BIA offices in Cleveland, Dallas, Los Angeles, and Albuquerque become scenes of Indian protests. Those arrested in Alameda are charged with failure to leave a public building. It is unclear to what extent Indians from Alcatraz are directly involved with the occupation.

MARCH 15, 1970 Reoccupation of Fort Lawton. Indian activists reenter Fort Lawton. Federal authorities serve eviction notices upon the activists. The U.S. Army then takes 78 Indians into custody following the group's second attempt to take over Fort Lawton. Government officials identify Indians whom they consider to be leaders and agitators from the March 8 occupation and arraign these Indians before a federal commissioner. A preliminary hearing is set for April 2, but charges eventually are dropped without prosecution. Cover stories in *Time* and *Look* magazines feature the Alcatraz and Fort Lawton occupations and refer to Alcatraz as "the symbolic act of Indian awareness." The *San Francisco Chronicle* reports, "The Indians have demanded that Fort Lawton, an Army Reserve installation, be turned over to them for use as a cultural center. The Indians

Indians protesting discrimination in hiring at the Bureau of Indian Affairs (BIA), Denver, Colorado, March 1970. Photo by D.F. Barry. Courtesy of the Denver Public Library, Western History Department.

claim they have a right to the fort under the terms of an 1855 treaty. To assert their claim, the Indians, many of them veterans of the takeover of Alcatraz island, scaled steep bluffs facing Puget Sound and entered the fort by climbing over high wire fences Sunday."

MARCH 16, 1970   Ellis Island. Indians from 14 tribes attempt an assault on Ellis Island but fail when their 16-foot boat develops engine trouble. Members of Indians of All Tribes plan to claim the abandoned federal facility for an Indian commune. The coast guard invokes the Espionage Act to ward off any further attacks on the island. The Indian occupiers claim that their treaties with the government permit them to take over abandoned government land. This is a fallacious claim that also was the basis of the 1964 Indian occupation of Alcatraz Island. Mrs. Tina Robinson, whose husband was among those planning the occupation of Ellis Island, states that the occupiers are an affiliate of the group that occupied Alcatraz Island.

MARCH 22–23, 1970   Indian Sit-In Protests.

Nine Indians are arrested near Denver, Colorado, and 23 are arrested at offices of the Bureau of Indian Affairs' in Chicago, Illinois, for sit-in protests against the BIA's employment policies. Similar protests are held in Cleveland, Ohio; Minneapolis, Minnesota; Sacramento, California; and Santa Fe, New Mexico.

MARCH 23, 1970   Indians Occupy BIA Office. At an Alameda BIA office, approximately 50 Indians protest alleged job discrimination in addition to other grievances. Approximately 30 Indians hold out inside the BIA offices and eventually 12, including five from Alcatraz Island, are arrested. Richard Oakes, one of the 12 remaining occupiers, refuses to leave the office but finally submits peacefully to the police three hours later. The Indian participants are released and scheduled for a court appearance on April 3.

MARCH 23–26, 1970   Convocation of American Indian Scholars. The first Convocation of American Indian Scholars convenes at the Woodrow Wilson School, Princeton University, under the chairmanship of Dr. Alfonso Ortiz, a San Juan Pueblo Indian. The purpose of this occasion is to bring scholars, Indian students, tribal leaders and non-Indian friends together to explore issues as they bear on Indian people as a whole. The participants examine both the challenges and opportunities facing American Indian people. They also discuss the continued survival of Indians as an unique people with a distinct cultural heritage. The meeting is held under the auspices of the American Indian Historical Society.

MARCH 28, 1970   Alcatraz Island. Members of Indians of All Tribes, numbering over 40 men, women, and children, leave Alcatraz to support the Paiute protection of Pyramid Lake, Nevada. Dams stop river feeders to the lake and consequently the lake dries up 30 to 50 inches per year. Land and water are channeled to prosperous ranches and farms in the Fallon,

Nevada, area. For over a year, the Paiutes engage in a battle to preserve Pyramid Lake despite the California/Nevada agreement to divert water from the Truckee River. The Department of the Interior refuses to take any action to preserve the lake. Past actions on their part favor the rights of non-Indian farmers to whom the department has previously given portions of the Paiute tribal lands. This is precisely the nature of tribal grievances that the Indians of All Tribes hoped to publicize through their occupation of Alcatraz. The caravan to Pyramid Lake becomes a highly symbolic act. Making headlines throughout California, the caravan proves that tribal grievances are no longer isolated voices, that pan-Indian support is available for all Indian causes. Alcatraz Indians bring water from Alcatraz as a gesture of support. The Fort Lawton group states, as quoted in the Alcatraz Newsletter No. 3, "The occupation of Alcatraz has seen the beginnings of a concept of unity long dreamed of by all our people."

APRIL, 1970 Tribes and Loans Consolidation Act. Congress passes the Tribes and Loans Consolidation Act, "to provide for loans to Indian tribes and tribal corporations" This law enables the secretary of agriculture to make loans of reasonable amounts from the Farmers Home Administration direct loan account to federally recognized tribes or tribal corporations per accords within the Indian Reorganization Act of 1934, for the purpose of acquiring lands or interests within their own reservations. The 1934 act sought to prevent of further tribal land base erosion and attempted to assist tribes in the consolidation of their lands.

APRIL 2, 1970 Fort Lawton, California. Indian occupiers storm the east gate at Fort Lawton and reenter the post. This is the same date scheduled for the preliminary hearings of the Indians who occupied Fort Lawton on March 8 and 15. Fifteen more Indians are arrested and held for arraignment, including

Indian occupiers from Alcatraz Island. Charges against the group later are dismissed. Through the continuous efforts of the United Indians of All Tribes, Fort Lawton is awarded to the Indians in 1971 as an Indian cultural center. Today, Bernie Whitebear, director of the Daybreak Star Cultural Center at Fort Lawton, attributes much of their success to the occupation of Alcatraz. In 1990 Whitebear states, "Alcatraz was very much a catalyst to our occupation here. We saw what could be achieved there, and if it had not been for their determined effort on Alcatraz, there would have been no movement here. We would like to think that Alcatraz lives on in part through Fort Lawton." Ross Harden, one of the original occupiers of the island, says that the Lawton occupiers came from the different tribes on Alcatraz.

APRIL 13, 1970 Indian Elementary and Secondary Education Act. Congress passes the Indian Elementary and Secondary Education Act, which extends programs to elementary and secondary education. Title I—Amendments to the Elementary and Secondary Education Act of 1965, Part E—applies such programs to Indians on reservations, and Title II—Amendments to Public Law 815 and 874 of the Eighty-First Congress (Impact Areas Programs)—includes the construction of schools.

APRIL 15, 1970 Alcatraz Island. GSA realty officer John Peters reports that, "The Indians [on Alcatraz Island] are attempting to organize a large group to go to the Seattle area to join other Indians in invading Fort Lawton this weekend. It is reported that Stella Leach is leaving with a group of Indians on Friday, April 17, 1970, for Seattle."

APRIL 18–23, 1970 Indian Sit-Ins. Indians conduct sit-ins at several BIA offices throughout the country.

APRIL 27, 1970 Alcatraz Island. Thomas Scott, GSA realty officer, reports that, "Indians [are]

Indians of All Tribes gather for a festival during the occupation of Alcatraz Island. Courtesy of Stephen Lehmer.

leaving for another assault on Ft. Lawton, Washington."

APRIL 27, 1970 American Indian Movement.
Members of the American Indian Movement (AIM) picket the Minneapolis opening of Elliot Silverstein's *A Man Called Horse*. The Indian activists urge a boycott of the picture (the story of an Englishman and his life among the Lakota Sioux) and label its graphic portrayal of the sacred Sun Dance ceremony "humiliating and degrading." Later, the Minnesota Department of Human Rights joins the AIM members in their boycott. Reaction to the film is mixed; some Indians approve of it. Two sequels are released *Return of a Man Called Horse* (1976) and *Triumphs of a Man Called Horse* (1984).

APRIL 27, 1970 *Choctaw Nation et al. v. Oklahoma et al.* In the case of the *Choctaw Nation et al. v. Oklahoma et al.*, the Choctaw, Chickasaw, and Cherokee nations of Oklahoma win control of the lower Arkansas River, by a vote of four to three. The Supreme Court finds that the government ceded the riverbed and oil and mineral resources beneath the land to the tribes in the 1830 Treaty of Dancing Rabbit Creek, the 1832 Treaty of Pontotoc, and the 1835 Treaty of New Echota.

APRIL 29, 1970 Alcatraz Island. GSA realty officer Thomas Scott claims that he received informed army intelligence on April 28 reporting that approximately 27 Indians left [Alcatraz] island Sunday and Monday for another attempt at Fort Lawton.

MAY 1970 Mercury Poisoning. The English-Wabigoon River system in northwestern Ontario is closed to fishing after the Reed Paper Company in Dryden, Ontario, is found to have dumped tons of mercury into the river system between 1962 and 1970, causing mercury poisoning on the Grassy Narrows Ojibway Reserve 120 kilometers downstream. The ban on fishing further disrupts life in the community.

MAY 1, 1970 Rattlesnake Island, California.
Pomo Indians move onto Mu-Do-N (Rattlesnake Island) near Clear Lake, California, the ancient burial ground and village site of the El-Em Pomo. The Pomo Indians state that they have an ancestral claim to the island's 64 acres: "Our people are buried here." When the Pomo Indians declare their intention to stay on the island, the Boise-Cascade Lumber Company intervenes, saying that they intend to subdivide the island and erect a vacation condominium complex upon Pomo sacred burial grounds. Members of Indians of All Tribes, from Alcatraz Island, visit the Pomo and discuss the occupation. Boise-Cascade initially maintains that the Indians must leave the island but later relents and allows them to remain "for the time being." Philip White Eagle, a Rosebud, South Dakota, reservation Indian and a participant in the Alcatraz occupation, says that "Indians have rights and are making a broadening effort to call attention to that fact."

MAY 2–3, 1970 El-Em Pomo Occupation.
Pomo Indians and their supporters occupy a surplus army radio-transmitter base near Middletown, California. This occupation group, including Indians from Alcatraz Island, hope to reclaim a 640-acre site to use as a center for housing, education, culture, and health, a place where Pomo and other Indians could freely practice and revive their culture in natural surroundings. Sheriff's deputies cut off communications and supplies to the occupiers and subsequently arrest them on charges of entering and occupying government property. Convictions are levied against 12 of the Indian occupiers on August 16, 1970.

MAY 5, 1970 Isleta Pueblo. A tribal election at the Isleta Pueblo, located outside Albuquerque, New Mexico, grants women the right to vote.

MAY 14, 1970 Indian Claims Commission Award. The Indian Claims Commission awards

$12.2 million to the Seminole tribe for the government's illegal taking of lands in Florida. The money is to be distributed among the 1,500 Seminole in Florida and the 3,500 Seminole living in Oklahoma. The Seminole, who fought three successive wars with the federal government and resisted forced relocation to Oklahoma, successfully argue to the commission that the government had taken title to their lands in Florida under duress.

MAY 17, 1970 Mohawk Occupations. The Mohawk Indians of Akwesasne reoccupy Loon Island, which is illegally being squatted upon by non-Indian recreation-seekers. On May 9, a Mohawk group occupies Stanley Island. The Mohawks claim a total of 42 islands in the St. Lawrence River region.

MAY 21, 1970 El-Em Pomo Occupation. El-Em Pomo Indians reoccupy Mu-Do-N Island in Clear Lake, California. They claim that the Boise-Cascade Lumber Company illegally acquired the island. *(See also* entry, May 1, 1970.)

SUMMER 1970 North American Indian Unity Convention. Representatives from more than 60 Indian nations from across North America meet in Washington State where the Nisqually, Puyallup, Nooksack, and Muckleshoot Indians battle the federal government and the state over fishing rights. The meeting is named the North American Indian Unity Convention.

JUNE 1970 Hiawatha National Forest. Approximately 200 Indian men and women seize a lighthouse in the Hiawatha National Forest in Michigan.

JUNE 1970 Reclamation of Lassen National Forest. Pit River Indians head for Lassen National Forest to reclaim the land as their own. Richard Oakes brings Indian occupiers from Alcatraz Island to assist in the occupation. Marie Lego, a Pit River Indian, becomes an activist/advocate for her people. Sheriff's deputies, local police, and United States marshals armed with riot equipment and shotguns greet the caravan at the entrance to the forest. Not intending any violence, the leaders turn the caravan around and move toward their secondary goal, the Pacific Gas and Electric Company (PG&E) camp at Big Bend, California. Here, PG&E claims 52,000 acres of Pit River land. "We are the rightful and legal owners of the land," proclaims a young Indian named Mickey Gemmill. "Therefore, we reclaim all the resourceful land that has traditionally been ours with the exception of that owned by private individuals."

On June 6, the Pit River Indians occupy Lassen's fully equipped and very comfortable private campground and cabins. The campground and the national park are part of a huge section of northern California land that the Indians say was stolen from them in 1853. Some of the Pit River Indians become frightened when they are tailed from Mount Lassen to Big Bend. Among those who elect to stick it out are Richard Oakes, Grace Thorpe, and some other Alcatraz occupiers. On the second day of the occupation, U.S. marshals "armed to the teeth" inform the group that they must leave. The Indians respond by telling the marshals that it is they who are trespassers on Indian land; therefore the marshals, not the Indians, should leave. The 82 marshals counter with Black Marias, M-16s, and riot helmets, and arrest 80 women and 26 men for trespassing.

The Indians who are arrested appear in court and are sued for trespassing without having established that they owned the land. Included in the support group from Alcatraz are Oakes, Thorpe, and singer Buffy Saint-Marie. Indian lawyers make motions to dismiss the charges but the judge sustains every objection by the district attorney. The first two groups are convicted, but the case then is relocated to Sacramento, where the third group receives a trial and is acquitted in June 1971. Following the acquittal, Pit River Indians go back to the

PG&E campgrounds where more Indians are peacefully arrested. Again the Pit River Indians return to Lassen National Forest, and this time 22 are arrested on charges of building a fire without a permit. The government pursues a policy of avoidance, hoping to let the whole matter cool down and die away. The Pit River Nation resists any attempt that would let issues be "simply" forgotten. They announce their continuous claim and occupation of their ancestral lands until the lands are returned.

Throughout the trespass trials, the Pit Rivers maintain a camp at the Four Corners site near Burney and begin to cut trees that the Forest Service had left along the road; the Indians plan to use the trees to build cabins on the land. A police patrol spots them. After four days of conferences that include officials in Washington, D.C., the U.S. marshals, Forest Service personnel, and approximately 400 law enforcement personnel remove the Indians, using rifle butts, clubs, mace-guns, and trained dogs. The Indians respond by arming themselves with sticks and two-by-fours in an effort to defend themselves. One of the young Indians, Coyote, later recalls that "the day was bloody." He remembers the slow, painful ride the next day from a Susanville jail to the jail in Sacramento with "four handcuffed Indians squashed into the back of a police car with no handles on the doors."

JUNE 4, 1970   Red Paper. Two hundred Indians from across Canada present *Citizens Plus* (the Red Paper) to Minister of Indian Affairs Jean Chrétien and Prime Minister Pierre Trudeau. The Red Paper is written as the Indian Association of Alberta's response to the government's White Paper, but, following some revisions on June 3, Indian organizations from across Canada adopt it as the official Indian response to the White Paper. Taking its title from the Hawthorn Report of 1968, *Citizens Plus* condemns the government's proposal to remove Indians' special status and to transfer responsibility for Indians to the provinces. The

Red Paper demands that the special legal status of Indians be retained and that treaty obligations be kept. It calls for reorganization of the federal Indian Affairs Department in order to make it more responsive to the needs and desires of Indian peoples. The Red Paper also calls for the creation of an Indian Claims Commission with the power to settle the claims. Upon receiving the submission, Trudeau implies that the government is willing to withdraw the White Paper.

JUNE 7, 1970   Chicago American Indian Village. Police raid the "Chicago American Indian Village," a tent city behind Wrigley Field, where Indian people protest a lack of services for them in Chicago.

JUNE 29, 1970   Navajo Land Claim Victory. The Navajo Indians win a decisive court victory to prove title to 40 million acres of western land. The Indians charge that they were inadequately compensated for the lands when put on an 8 million-acre reservation in 1868. The Indian Claims Commission agrees with the Navajo, while the federal government insists that the Navajo could not prove claim to more than 10 million acres. Under court procedures, the Navajo will not ultimately receive the land. Instead the precise acreage will be determined and a value affixed to the property; the Indians are to receive a money settlement.

JULY 1970   Deganawida-Quetzalcoatl University (DQU). Members of the DQU board of trustees meet with the Yolo Native American Association to discuss the feasibility of establishing DQU. The concept of a pan-Indian university is subsequently approved.

An ad hoc committee of Indians and Chicanos prepares a preliminary proposal for DQU and the proposed site is reexamined. Kenneth Martin, Assiniboine; David Risling, Hoopa-Yurok-Karok; and Jack Forbes, Powhatan incorporate DQU as a tax-exempt, nonprofit institution. Both Risling and Forbes

Nooksack Indians gathering for a salmon bake to discuss fishing rights, Deming, Washington, 1970. Courtesy of Stephen Lehmer.

participated in the Alcatraz movement. (*See also* entry, January 1970; October 29–30, 1970; January 15, 1971; and April 2, 1971.)

JULY 8, 1970 Nixon Policy of Indian Self-Determination. The federal policy of Indian self-determination is announced. President Nixon delivers his message to Congress calling for the self-determination of Indian people without termination of federal services or status. A meeting between the president and the Taos Pueblo Indians recommends the return of

Taos Blue Lake. Other initiatives include the initiation of federal aid to urban Indians. President Nixon uses the return of Taos Blue Lake as his starting point for the federal policy of Indian self-determination. In a conversation with the President, Leonard Garment, the president's Indian affairs advisor, relates the Blue Lake issue directly to Indian self-determination: "A new Indian policy needs a starting point. Blue Lake is just that—strong on merits, and powerfully symbolic." Garment, Vice President Spiro Agnew, and Secretary of Interior

Walter Hickel all advise Nixon that "if the administration failed to keep its promise on Blue Lake, Indians across the country would regard self-determination as nothing more than the old policy of termination in some new Republican disguise." The initial request for lake title plus 48,000 acres in New Mexico was lodged by the tribe in 1906. The lake is returned to the people on December 15, 1970. Garment explained, "[W]e really have a good policy record on Indian affairs and the Blue Lake and Indian Claims (Alaska) accomplishments are down payments on the seriousness of those policies."

With this influential statement, President Nixon formally brings the "termination" policy to an end and introduces the notion of "self-determination," intended "to strengthen the Indian's sense of autonomy without threatening his sense of community." Trusteeship, protection, and Indian services moreover should not be seen as acts of generosity. "The special relationship between Indians and the federal government is the result instead of solemn obligations which have been entered into by the United States Government" in exchange for land. "To terminate this relationship would be no more appropriate than to terminate the citizenship rights of any other American," the statement says.

JULY 12, 1970 Iroquois Confederacy. Two hundred members of the Iroquois Confederacy meet in Geneva, New York, to discuss proposals for regaining political power lost to the state and federal governments. The Iroquois Confederacy, or Haudenosaunee, established more than 500 years ago, is comprised of the Onondaga, the Mohawk, the Seneca, the Oneida, the Cayuga, and the Tuscarora.

JULY 15, 1970 Sheep Mountain, North Dakota. Members of the Oglala Sioux seize an area on Sheep Mountain, North Dakota, demanding the return of a gunnery range that the military took from the tribe during World War II.

JULY 31, 1970 Washoe Land Award. Congress approves legislation transferring title to 80 acres of public domain land in Alpine County, California, to the United States in trust for the Washoe tribe of Nevada and California for use in developing community programs and housing and to improve the "deplorable situation in which they have been living for many years."

AUGUST 1, 1970 Puyallup Fishing Rights. Puyallup Indians set up a camp near the Puyallup River in Washington State and begin fishing in order to reestablish their tribal fishing rights.

AUGUST 12, 1970 Ksan Village and Art Center. Ksan, a reconstructed Gitskan (Tsimshian) village, and the Gitenmaax School of Northwest Coast Indian Art near Hazelton, British Columbia, officially open. Interest and participation on the part of Native artists in the construction of the village already has demonstrated and encouraged the renewed vigor of Northwest Coast Indian art. The following two decades witness a remarkable artistic revival among all the Northwest Coast Indians. Much of their artwork is sold to non-Native residents and visitors.

SEPTEMBER 1970 Takeover of Mount Rushmore. Approximately 50 Indians from different tribes climb to the top of Mount Rushmore and announce their takeover of the historic landmark. They intend to occupy Mount Rushmore until 123,000 acres of Indian land, unjustly taken for a gunnery range during World War II, is returned.

SEPTEMBER 1, 1970 Indian Education. A Cree band at the Saddle Lake Reserve in northeastern Alberta takes over control of the Blue Quills school from the federal government, thus becoming the first Indian band in Canada to control its own school.

SEPTEMBER 1, 1970 Tuscarora Reservation. Tuscarora Indians successfully obtain a court order allowing for the eviction of some 40 non-

Media coverage of Puyallup fishing rights protest, Tacoma, Washington, 1970. Courtesy of Stephen Lehmer.

Indian families from the Tuscarora Reservation. The court order follows a series of demonstrations staged by the Tuscarora and their supporters.

SEPTEMBER 17, 1970 Occupation of Federal Land. Army intelligence in San Francisco reports that its national office in Washington has received information regarding plans to occupy federal land there belonging either to the Department of the Army or the Interior. The action reportedly will take place sometime within the near future by a group of Indians from Alcatraz Island. Army intelligence requests all information regarding the movement of Indians occupying Alcatraz Island.

SEPTEMBER 30, 1970 Osage Land Settlement. The Justice Department announces a $13.2 million settlement with the Osage Indian Nation of Oklahoma for 28 million acres of lands purchased by the federal government in Arkansas, Kansas, Missouri, and Oklahoma between 1803 and 1819.

AUTUMN 1970–SPRING 1971 Mount Rushmore. American Indian Movement (AIM) members and a traditional group called the Oglala Sioux tribe establish a camp at Mount Rushmore enacting a symbolic Lakota claim to the Black Hills.

OCTOBER 1970 Badlands National Monument. Sioux Indian activists establish a protest camp at Badlands National Monument in South Dakota. Traditionally a religious ceremonial ground, the federal government seized Sheep Mountain to use as a bombing area during World War II. Among those erecting the camp's 23 tipis are representatives from the Alcatraz Island occupation.

OCTOBER 1970 Pit River, California. Pit River Indians and other Indian supporters, many from Alcatraz Island, occupy a site at the Four Corners area near Burney, California. The Indians erect a Quonset hut as temporary housing while they attend the trials stemming from the June 1970 occupation of PG&E lands, when approximately 80 federal officers, sheriff's deputies, and forestry employees appear. Armed with mace, clubs, shotguns, and automatic rifles, the troops surround the Indian camp. Peter Blue Cloud describes the battle: "As forest workers and officers moved toward the Quonset hut to tear it down, all hell broke

Alcatraz Is Indian Land Forever, San Francisco, California, 1970. Artist unknown. Courtesy of Stephen Lehmer.

loose, as the protectors of the law waded into the Pit River people, spraying mace, and breaking heads, swinging clubs and striking even those who already lay unconscious. Riffle butts were smashed into heads and mace filled the air. Indian women shouted and cried out in anger." Again, arrests are made but officers meet with resistance as Indians seek to defend their people's rights. A 100-year-old tribal woman witnesses police destruction and says, "I hope the white men are proud."

Of the 36 Indian people arrested at the PG&E camp near Big Bend on June 14, 1970, only seven are convicted on charges of building occupation and placed on probation. Out of 108 counts, convictions are obtained on 14. On March 30, 1972, five Indians charged with assaulting federal marshals during the battle of Four Corners are found innocent. Charges against the remaining 33 are dropped prior to or during the trial. One juror comments upon a lack of evidence in the case against the Indian people.

OCTOBER 1, 1970   Carson National Forest. Plastic explosives blow apart two Forest Service signs in Carson National Forest in protest over the development of a "ranger bill" for Taos Blue Lake rather than its return to the people. A second bombing occurs days later. The proposed ranger bill is consequently defeated and Taos Blue Lake is returned to the Taos Indian people.

OCTOBER 29–30, 1970   Deganawida-Quetzalcoatl University (DQU) Site. Sen. George Murphy's office issues a press release stating that the Davis site is to go to the University of California despite the fact that DQU submits the only legally complete request for the site. *(See also* entry, January 1970; July 1970; November 3, 1970; January 15, 1971; and April 2, 1971.)

NOVEMBER 3, 1970   CIA Listening Post Occupied. Two dozen Indian activists, including Indians from Alcatraz Island, occupy a former

Indian encampment at Pendleton Roundup (Pendleton, Oregon), September 1970. Courtesy of Stephen Lehmer.

Central Intelligence Agency (CIA) listening post near Santa Rosa, California. The CIA facility was used in the 1950s to monitor foreign broadcasts. The Indians are removed from the government property on November 6; five are arrested for trespassing. Richard Oakes, an Alcatraz leader, participates in the strategy-planning session for the occupation. Title to the land is ultimately transferred to the Pomo Indians and the Ya-Ka-Ma, "Our Land," American Indian learning center is established.

NOVEMBER 3, 1970   Deganawida-Quetzalcoatl University Site Occupied. Indians occupy a 647-acre site (a surplus military facility) near Davis, California, later the site of Deganawida-Quetzalcoatl University (DQU). "The land is ours" is the cry accompanying a claim to one square mile of the Central Valley. Slated for title by a nonprofit educational institution, the site is considered up for grabs.

A press release on October 29 indicates that the University of California at Davis will receive the land for primate research and rice farming despite its incomplete application. To gain public attention, American Indian activists, including Grace Thorpe and other former Alcatraz occupiers, climb over the site's fence and lay claim to the land. DQU receives the deed to the site on April 2, 1971. *(See also* entry, January 1970; July 1970; October 29–30, 1970; January 15, 1971; and April 2, 1971.)

NOVEMBER 4, 1970   Foreign Broadcast Information Service Station Occupied. Twelve Indians occupy the former Foreign Broadcast Information Service Monitoring Station at Healdsburg, California. All but four of the Indians leave the property at the request of the local sheriff. Indians from Alcatraz Island participate in the occupation. Aubrey Grossman, San Francisco attorney for Indians of All Tribes, appears as their counsel.

NOVEMBER 8, 1970   Army Communications Center Occupied. Approximately 75 Indians activists seize an abandoned army communications center in Davis, California. The Indians demand that the center be turned over to them for use as an Indian cultural center.

NOVEMBER 22, 1970   Pomo Indian Reservation. Richard Oakes stops motorists driving through a Pomo Indian Reservation, and charges an entry toll; he is placed under arrest for this action. The *San Francisco Chronicle* reports, "Oakes, a leader of last year's invasion of Alcatraz, allegedly posted himself, armed with a rifle, at Skagg's Springs road, after placing a fallen tree part way across the road. A sign posted there reads: "Stop pay toll ahead—$1.00. This is Indian land." California Highway Patrol officers arrest Oakes pending investigation of an armed robbery and release him from jail on his own recognizance once he agrees to a moratorium on his toll charges.

NOVEMBER 24, 1970 Wohler Bridge, California. Seven young Indians plus other Indian activists are arrested on trespassing charges when they confront federal authorities at a broadcast station near Wohler Bridge, California. Four Indians from Alcatraz Island are among those taken into custody. The Indians had been warned to leave the federal property leased to a private citizen. The occupation group claims a right to the land under a treaty made with Indians in 1865.

NOVEMBER 25, 1970 Kashia Reservation. A total of $22 is collected at the toll crossing on the Kashia Reservation near Stewart's Point-Skaggs Springs Road and Tin Barn Road, California. Charges of felony robbery levied against Richard Oakes are reduced to the charge of obstructing a public roadway. This particular incident, while mimicking Oakes's earlier actions, may not have actually included his participation. *(See also* entry, November 22, 1970.)

THANKSGIVING DAY, 1970 American Indian Movement Seizes *Mayflower II*. Members of the American Indian Movement (AIM), including Russell Means and Dennis Banks, seize control of the *Mayflower II* in Plymouth, Massachusetts. Proclaiming Thanksgiving day a national day of mourning, AIM protests against this celebration of thanks for the taking of Indian lands by white colonists. This is the first AIM attempt to extend its activism onto the national scene. Previously, AIM focused upon providing physical protection against po-

lice harassment for Indian people living in Minneapolis, Cleveland, and Washington, D.C. The names of Means and Banks, and later Trudell, become synonymous with the AIM movement.

DECEMBER 15, 1970 Nez Percé and Colville Land Claims. President Richard Nixon signs legislation authorizing the payment of $1.1 million to the Nez Percé tribe of Idaho and the Confederated tribe of Colville of Washington State. The funds are awarded to the tribes by the Indian Claims Commission for the illegal loss of tribal lands to the federal government during the nineteenth century.

DECEMBER 15, 1970 Taos Blue Lake. Taos Indians win their long battle to recover ownership of the sacred Blue Lake region of 48,000 acres.

DECEMBER 15, 1970 Taos Blue Lake Act. President Richard Nixon signs the Taos Land Bill. The legislation returns 48,000 acres of land, including Blue Lake, to the Taos Pueblo. This bill, the first legislation to restore a sizable piece of land to an Indian tribe, acknowledges that the Taos Pueblo Indians have practiced their religion at this sacred site for over 700 years. The Pueblo lost the lands in 1906 when President Theodore Roosevelt added the area to the Carson National Forest.

1971

1971 Election of Chiefs for the Five Civilized Tribes. The Bureau of Indian Affairs establishes regulations allowing for the direct election of chiefs for the Five Civilized Tribes. Comprised of the Cherokee, Creek, Seminole, Choctaw, and Chickasaw, the Five Civilized Tribes—along with more than 30 other tribes— had been relocated in the 1800s to what was then Indian Territory and is now present-day Oklahoma. Promising that the territory would always remain in Indian control, Congress re-

Dennis Banks. Courtesy of Alice M. Lambert.

Ojibway painter Norval Morisseau at work. His style and subject matter is inspired by, among other things, traditional Algonkian pictography.

verse this guarantee in the 1890s. The allotment of these lands contributes to the dissolution of tribal governments as the BIA gains the authority to appoint a chief for each of the Five Civilized Tribes. The return of electoral control to these Indians signifies an important step in the revitalization of their government.

1971   Inuit Art Exhibit. Inuit art work assembled by the Vancouver Art Gallery is exhibited in Vancouver, Copenhagen, Moscow, Leningrad, London, Philadelphia, and Ottawa.

1971   Native American Rights Fund. The California Indian Legal Services institutes a national Indian legal service, the Native American Rights Fund (NARF), with objectives to pursue the legal protection of Indian lands, treaty rights, individual rights, and the development of tribal law. NARF receives funding through the Ford Foundation and has a central office in Boulder, Colorado, and a branch office in Washington, D.C.

JANUARY 4, 1971   Inuktitut Broadcasting. Radio Tuktoyaktuk (in the village of Tuktoyaktuk, Northwest Territories), begins broadcasting in English and Inuktitut, the main Inuit dialect.

The subsequent growth of Native-language broadcasting in Canada is related to the efforts of such northerners as Rosemarie Kuptana *(See* biography, March 24, 1954) and Nellie Cornoyea *(See* biography, March 4, 1940).

JANUARY 13, 1971   Indian Education. The NAACP Legal Defense and Education Fund and Harvard University's Center for Law and Education release a 162-page report, charging state and local officials with a gross misuse of funds appropriated under the Elementary and Secondary Education Act and the 1934 Johnson-O'Malley Act. The report charges that funds that are designated for the benefit and education of Indian children are frequently used for non-Indian educational purposes. Some 250 examples of alleged impropriety are provided, such as buying expensive equipment for non-Indian schools and reducing non-Indian property taxes. "By every standard," the report emphasizes, "Indians receive the worst education of any children in the community."

JANUARY 14, 1971 Army Communications Center, Davis, California. The San Francisco regional office of the Department of Health, Education, and Welfare gives custody of a 647-acre army communications center in Davis, California, to local Indians. The Indians, who received the "care, custody, protection and maintenance" of the base, occupied the deserted base in November 1970. A spokesman for the group, Jack Forbes, announces plans to establish a college for American Indians and Mexican-Americans on the site.

JANUARY 15, 1971 Deganawida-Quetzalcoatl University. The Department of Health, Education, and Welfare assigns the army communications center site to Deganawida-Quetzalcoatl University for custody. (*See also* entry, January 1970; July 1970; October 29–30, 1970; November 3, 1970; and April 2, 1971.)

JANUARY 21, 1971 Puyallup Fishing Rights. While sleeping by the bank of the Puyallup River in Washington State, fishing rights activist Hank Adams is shot by two white vigilantes. Police imply that Adams shot himself in an effort to gain publicity for the fishing rights cause. Such protests had been going on in Washington State since 1963. In August 1970, the Puyallup Tribal Council voted to arm and maintain a camp in their traditional and accustomed fishing grounds. Adams becomes a key player in a caravan to Washington, D.C., ultimately resulting in a BIA building takeover.

Adams is instrumental in the founding of an organization called Survival of the American Indian Association (SAIA), which fights for Indian fishing and treaty rights in the Nisqually and Puyallup regions. Adams chairs a committee framing a 15-point program for a new national Indian policy "to remove the human needs and aspirations of Indian tribes and Indian people from the workings of the general American political system and to reinstate a system of bilateral relationships between Indian tribes and the federal government." These 15 points later become the foundation for a set of twenty demands presented during the Trail of Broken Treaties.

FEBRUARY 19–20, 1971 National Tribal Chairmen's Association. Tribal leaders from 50 reservations in 12 states meet in Billings, Montana, to discuss the establishment of a national association of tribal council leaders. The decision to establish the National Tribal Chairmen's Association stems from a concern by tribal reservation leaders that national Indian policy is being made in response to the actions of urban Indians and young militant reservation Indians.

FEBRUARY 22, 1971 Canadian Native Nominated for Best Supporting Actor. The Academy of Motion Picture Arts and Sciences announces the nomination of Canadian Indian actor Dan George *(See* biography, 1899) for Best Actor in a Supporting Role. George portrays the elderly medicine man, Old Lodge Skins, in *Little Big Man* (1970) and receives the New York Film Critics Award for his performance.

MARCH 3, 1971 Quebec Indian Policy. A report from Quebec's Dorion Commission notes that aboriginals have land rights in most of Quebec and that they deserve compensation for the loss of these rights. The report also recommends that the province seek to assume responsibility for Indian and Eskimo (Inuit) affairs in the province. (This would mark a complete reversal of Quebec's 1930s policy in which it took the federal government to court to force it to assume responsibility for the Inuit of northern Quebec.) The report also suggests that Indian reserves are discriminatory and counterproductive in that they segregate the Indian population. The Dorion Commission, led by geographer Henri Dorion, was commissioned in 1966 to investigate matters connected with Quebec's "territorial integrity." The commission and its recommendations reflect a Quebecois desire to be "masters in our own house."

MARCH 11, 1971   The Alaska Native Claims Settlement Act. The Alaska Native Claims Settlement Act marks the legislative beginning of the self-determination period. In their 206 villages, the 60,000 Native Alaskan people demand Indian title to 60 million acres of land following the discovery of oil on the North Slope in Alaska. On March 11, President Nixon announces through John Ehrlichman, a chief advisor on domestic affairs, that he "wanted to continue to be forthcoming on Indian affairs" and proposes a bill, later passed, that awards the Alaskan Natives title to 40,000,000 acres and one billion dollars in compensation for land taken.'"

MARCH 17, 1971   White Paper Withdrawn. Jean Chrétien, Canada's minister of Indian affairs, formally announces the retraction of the government's White Paper.

APRIL 2, 1971   Deganawida-Quetzalcoatl University. The federal government formally turns over the title to 647 acres to the trustees of DQU. The Indians and Chicanos hold a pow-wow and victory celebration. The White House feels that the establishment of DQU fulfills the demands of the Alcatraz occupiers for an Indian university. *(See also* entry, January 1970; July 1970; October 29–30, 1970; November 3, 1970; and January 15, 1971.)

APRIL 25, 1971   U.S. Census Bureau. The U.S. Census Bureau reports that the 1970 census counts 791,839 Indians, an increase of more than 50 percent from the 1960 census.

APRIL 30, 1971   James Bay Hydroelectric Project. The Quebec government announces the James Bay Hydroelectric Project in northern Quebec. Construction on phase one of the project, which would flood about 10,500 square kilometers (4,000 square miles) and divert several rivers, is scheduled to begin immediately. The Cree and Inuit of the region are not consulted before this announcement. They fear that the massive project will threaten their way of life by destroying wildlife, including the large caribou herds upon which they depend. In order to represent their interests, the Inuit form the Northern Quebec Inuit Association. Charlie Watt *(See* biography, June 29, 1944), originally from Fort Chimo (Kuujjuaq), is its first president. Quebec has not negotiated land surrender agreements with the Natives of the region despite a 1912 agreement to do so.

MAY 15, 1971   Hopi Strip Mining Suit. The Native American Rights Fund (NARF) files suit in federal court on behalf of 62 members of the Hopi tribe to stop strip-mining on 100 square miles of the Hopi Reservation. The religious leaders contend that Black Mesa is an area of sacred relevance within Hopi religion and culture. The suit is part of a larger effort by other Indians and conservationists to stop the development of a major power grid in the Four Corners area. The Hopi traditionalists' objective is to prevent mining of the coal by the Peabody Company for use in six proposed power plants.

MAY 16 AND MAY 21, 1971   Indian Intertribal Force Occupies Abandoned Naval Air Station. An Indian intertribal force takes over an abandoned naval air station near Minneapolis. The occupation force intends the station for use as an all-Indian school and cultural center. Members of AIM and other Indian organizations and tribes claim the Sioux Treaty of 1868, article 6, as their authority, just as the Indian occupiers of Alcatraz Island had done in 1964. The Indian occupiers form a governing structure and security system similar to the Alcatraz occupation structure and issue a petition to the federal government similar to that of Indians of All Tribes and the Alcatraz demonstrators. The occupiers are arrested on May 21, when members of the American Indian Movement (AIM) occupy a naval air station in Milwaukee, Wisconsin. Unlike earlier occupations of vacant land, this new occupation disrupts naval facility operations. U.S. marshal special operations group (SOG) members head towards Minneapolis to evict the occupiers, who retreat to the naval base theater and barricade themselves in. SOG members forcibly enter the theater and clash with Indians armed with clubs, knives, and other weapons.

MAY 26, 1971　Model Urban Indian Center Program. The director of the Office of Economic Opportunity (OEO) announces that $880,000 in grants will be provided to establish a Model Urban Indian Center program in Los Angeles; Minneapolis; Gallup, New Mexico; and Fairbanks, Alaska. The program intends to provide models to improve services in 40 existing urban Indian service centers. According to the 1970 census, 44.5 percent of the total Native population live in urban areas, an increase of almost 15 percent during the previous ten years. Much of this movement stems from the Bureau of Indian Affair's relocation program. In an effort to assimilate Indians into the mainstream, tribal members are encouraged to move to urban areas for work. Others move independently, forced to leave their reservation homes in search of jobs.

MAY 26, 1971　Occupation of Toyon Job Corps Center. California Pit River Indians and others join a group of Wintu Indians in occupying the 61-acre surplus Toyon Job Corps Center near Redding, California. They believe the site suits a number of Indian purposes, including housing. A settlement reached with the BIA determines that the center will be

given to the Indians in two years, during which time the Shasta Community Action Project will administer and maintain the land.

JUNE 1971　Statue of Liberty. A group of Indians, including Tom Cook (Mohawk), assistant editor of *Akwesasne Notes,* student, and former ironworker, threaten to hold the Statue of Liberty hostage in a protest demanding better treatment for American Indians. Speaking of the threatened occupation, Laurence Hauptman, in *The Iroquois Struggle for Survival,* states, "The Events at Alcatraz were a major turning point in the history of Indian activism." The takeover at Alcatraz becomes a powerful symbol to many young disillusioned Indians and stimulates a rash of similar protests.

JUNE 1, 1971　Indian Underemployment. A Canadian government census reveals that only 57 percent of the Indian labor force worked 40 weeks or more in 1970. Of those who did, 62 percent earned less than $6,000 (33 percent of the total Canadian labor force that worked 40 weeks or more earned less than $6,000).

JUNE 6, 1971　University of New Mexico Indian Law Program. Yvonne Knight, a member of the Ponca tribe of Oklahoma, receives a Juris Doctor (J.D.) degree, becoming the first Indian woman to graduate from the University of New Mexico Indian Law Program established in 1967 to increase the number of Indian lawyers.

JUNE 6–7, 1971　Mount Rushmore National Memorial. Forty Indians demand that the federal government honor the 1868 treaty with the Sioux Nation promising that all lands west of the Missouri River would belong forever to the Sioux Nation. The Indians establish a camp on top of the Mount Rushmore National Memorial. Police later arrest 20 of the protesters for climbing the monument.

JUNE 11, 1971　Alcatraz Occupation Ends. The 19-month takeover of Alcatraz Island ends when federal marshals remove the last 15 Indians (six men, four women, and five children) occupying the prison. Averaging 100 protesters from 50 different tribes, the activists announce plans to turn Alcatraz into a Center for Native American Studies, an Indian Center of Ecology, an American Indian Museum, a Great Indian Training School, and an Indian Center of Ecology. *(See* entry, November 9, 1969.)

JUNE 14, 1971 Abandoned Nike Missile Base Occupied. Indians of All Tribes (formally of Alcatraz Island) enter and occupy an abandoned Nike missile base in the Berkeley Hills overlooking San Francisco Bay; more than 100 Indians settle there. Occupiers announce their intention to remain on the base and call for the establishment of a liberation supply line. On June 17, prison buses, park rangers, marked and unmarked police cars, and army trucks loaded with military police descend upon the occupiers. The Indian occupiers, many of whom were participants in the Alcatraz occupation, are forcibly evicted.

JUNE 14–JULY 1, 1971 Abandoned Nike Missile Site Occupied. One hundred Indians occupy an abandoned Nike missile site outside of Chicago, protesting the lack of housing for Indians in Chicago.

JUNE 15, 1971 Alcatraz Indians Demonstrate. Approximately 40 Indians demonstrate in front of the federal office building in San Francisco, protesting their eviction from Alcatraz Island. The demonstrators do not attempt to enter FBI space, consequently, no arrests are made. Many protesters are veterans of the Alcatraz occupation.

JUNE 15, 1971 Pit River Nation Reclaims 900-Acre Tract. The Pit River Nation reclaims a 900-acre tract near Big Ben previously seized by Pacific Gas and Electric Company (PG&E) for collateral on bank loans. The Pit River Indians construct a round-house plus some additional structures and plant gardens. Having filed suit in Shasta County Superior

Court on June 15, the Pit River Nation seeks return of 53,000 acres of PG&E-held land and petitions the Federal Power Commission to refuse renewal of PG&E's licenses to operate dams on the Pit River. On September 22, PG&E files suit against the Pit River Indians seeking clear title to the land.

JUNE 30, 1971 Canadian Indian Education. A House of Commons committee on Indian Affairs recommends that control of education be turned over to Indians rather than to the provinces. Since 1951 an increasing number of Indians are being integrated into provincially run, off-reserve schools.

JUNE–AUGUST 1971 Wallace Black Elk's Wounded Knee Sun Dance. Calling themselves "Indians of All Tribes," a group of young Indian people come from San Francisco to Wounded Knee for a Sun Dance performed by Wallace Black Elk, John Lame Deer, and Leonard Crow Dog. This group unifies the former members of Indians of All Tribes from Alcatraz Island with the American Indian Movement (AIM), now recognized as a national Indian activist organization.

JULY 7, 1971 Deganawida-Quetzalcoatl University Opens. Deganawida-Quetzalcoatl University (DQU) opens on an abandoned army communications base. The school is on a 647-acre site seized in November of 1970 by approximately 40 Indians claiming the site as surplus property. The university itself is funded through the Ford Foundation and federal grants totaling $300,000 and is housed within ten converted military buildings. Grace Thorpe, a participant in the Alcatraz occupation, teaches a course entitled "Seminar in Surplus Land," that instructs students in "securing surplus land for education and health purposes."

JULY 17, 1971 Choctaw Voting Age Change. The Choctaw Indian Nation of Oklahoma elects to lower the eligible voting age to 18, making it the first Indian tribe to do so via tribal elections.

JULY 30, 1971 Occupation of Former Nike Missile Site. Seventy-five Indians occupy a former Nike site on the grounds of the Argonne National Laboratories in Hinsdale, Illinois.

AUGUST 1971 Onondaga, Oneida, Mohawk, and Tuscarora Protest. Approximately 100 Onondaga, Oneida, Mohawk, and Tuscarora Indians go to Interstate 81 in New York State, south of Onondaga Reservation lands, and sit down to protest the widening of the interstate highway, claiming that the initial treaty with the United States is illegal and does not provide for roadway additions. The state agrees to abandon plans for the construction of an acceleration lane on Indian lands, to drop charges against those Indians arrested, and to consult with the Council of Chiefs at all stages of the highway improvement project.

AUGUST 13, 1971 Inter-Tribal Indian Ceremonial. The Inter-Tribal Indian Ceremonial holds its 50th-year anniversary celebration in Gallup, New Mexico.

AUGUST 15, 1971 AIM Seizes Abandoned Coast Guard Lifeboat Station. A group of approximately 25 members of the Milwaukee chapter of the American Indian Movement (AIM) seize an abandoned coast guard lifeboat station at McKinley Beach, in Milwaukee, Wisconsin. The group seizes two abandoned buildings during the predawn rain, claiming a right to the property under the Sioux Treaty of 1876. The first recorded occupation of a federal facility, this is the second attempt by AIM to expand beyond its role as an urban Indian protection organization.

AUGUST 15, 1971 Return of Taos Sacred Lands, Including Blue Lake. The Taos Pueblo holds a two-day celebration, beginning August 15, marking the return of their sacred lands, including Blue Lake. Interior Secretary Rogers Morton attends the event.

AUGUST 18–28, 1971 National Inuit Organization. The Inuit Tapirisat (Inuit Brotherhood) of Canada (I.T.C.) is formed as a national alliance of Inuit organizations to protect Inuit interests. Tagak Curley, a Labrador Inuk, is elected its first president.

AUGUST 26–SEPTEMBER 1, 1971 Indian Education. The Office of Civil Rights of the Health, Education, and Welfare Department reports that 29,000 American Indians are enrolled in colleges and universities.

SEPTEMBER 16, 1971 Dedication of Southwestern Indian Polytechnic Institute. Assistant Secretary of the Interior Harrison Loesch participates in the dedication of the new $13 million Southwestern Indian Polytechnic Institute in Albuquerque, New Mexico. The school will serve 700 Indian students from 64 tribes. The 164-acre campus will offer training in business management, clerical work, drafting, radio, electronics, commercial food preparation, telecommunications, television, engineering, and optical technology.

OCTOBER 5, 1971 North Slope Alaska Claim. The Arctic Slope Native Association files suit against the state of Alaska, claiming 76,000 acres of northern Alaska. The suit claims that the state's selection of this oil-rich area in 1964 violates Native land rights in that the "Eskimo people have occupied, used and exercised dominion" over the area. The region is currently under lease to private oil companies for approximately $1 billion.

OCTOBER 8, 1971 Multicultural Policy. The Canadian government adopts a policy of multiculturalism under which grants will be given to ethnic minorities, including aboriginals, to encourage them to retain aspects of their cultures.

OCTOBER 9, 1971 Indian Education. The Senate passes a $390.3 million education bill designed to give greater control to tribes over the education of their children.

OCTOBER 13–15, 1971   AIM National Convention. The American Indian Movement (AIM) holds its first national convention. Approximately 100 delegates representing 18 chapters attend the conference at Camp Owendigo, Minnesota.

OCTOBER 26, 1971   Pit River Seek $4 Million from Shasta County and the United States. The Pit River Tribal Council files lawsuits on October 26 against Shasta County and the United States seeking $4 million in damages in connection with the Four Corners incident. The tribe charges federal and county officials with battery, false arrest, false imprisonment, and malicious mischief and seeks judicial determination that the land belongs to the Indians.

NOVEMBER 17, 1971   Brown Paper. The Union of British Columbia Indian Chiefs releases "A Declaration of Indian Rights—The British Columbia Indian Position Paper," usually known as the Brown Paper. It, like the Red Paper rejects the federal government's White Paper, (presented June 5, 1969) as an attempt on the part of the federal government to avoid fulfilling its responsibilities toward Canada's Indians, but the Brown Paper puts more emphasis on land claims issues than did the Red Paper. This reflects the fact that British Columbia Indians have had a particularly difficult time having their land claims satisfied.

DECEMBER 15, 1971   Navajo Community College Act. The Navajo Community College Act authorizes Congress to fund $5.5 million, matching other government funding, for the construction and operation of a tribal college on the Navajo Reservation.

DECEMBER 18, 1971   Alaska Native Claims Settlement Act. President Richard Nixon signs Public Law 92-203, the Alaska Native Claims Settlement Act (ANCSA).

The act extinguishes Alaska Native title to nine-tenths of Alaska in return for 44 million acres and almost $1 billion. The House passes the measure on December 14 by a vote of 307-60; the Senate passes it on a voice vote. The legislation accords the Natives title to 44 million acres in the state, to be divided among some 220 Native village corporations and 12 regional corporations established by the act to do business for profit. The regional corporations (together with a thirteenth regional corporation comprised of non-permanent Native Alaskan residents) share in a payment of $462.5 million (to be made over an eleven-year period from funds in the U.S. Treasury) and an additional $500 million in mineral revenues deriving from specified Alaska lands.

Although the Alaska Federation of Natives approves the bill by a vote of 511-56, the act remains controversial among Alaskan Natives who fear that it will destroy their traditional lifestyle centered on hunting and fishing.

1 9 7 2

1972   The Indian Education Act. Title IV, authorized by Public Law 92-318, is applied to the California educational system as a result of its acceptance and passage by Congress. This act provides for specialized programs in education for Indians and establishes the Bureau of Indian Education in the California State Department of Education.

1972   *Lame Deer: Seeker of Visions* Is Published. The first of several collaborations between Richard Erdoes and different American Indian autobiographers, *Lame Deer: Seeker of Visions* is also the best known. Anecdotal and colloquial in style, the book narrates the life and adventures of John Fire Lame Deer, a Lakota Sioux from Rosebud Reservation. More than merely a vision seeker, the autobiography tells of Lame Deer's exploits as a sheepherder, a signpainter, an inmate, a soldier, and a drunk, among many other things. Erdoes later works with Mary Brave Bird (Crow Dog), producing two separate autobiographies which narrate the life and American Indian Movement experiences of this Lakota woman from Rosebud, *Lakota Woman* (1991) and *Ohitika Woman* (1993).

1972 Native American Indian Early Childhood Education Program. Senate Bill 1258, authorizing the Native American Indian Early Childhood Education Program for ten rural school districts, is enacted. The purpose of the program is to raise the academic achievement levels of Indian students in kindergarten through grade four.

1972 Navajo Tribe and Exxon Mineral Contract. The Navajo tribe and Exxon negotiate the first Indian mineral contract providing for ownership interest.

FEBRUARY 19, 1972 Chippewa Right to Hunt, Fish, and Trap. A federal court order is issued to protect the Chippewas' right to hunt, fish, trap, and gather wild rice according to tribal laws on their Leech Lake Reservation. The Leech Lake band of Chippewa Indians win their suit against the state of Minnesota in December 1971, successfully proving that their 1855 treaty with the United States guarantees their right to hunt, fish, trap, and gather wild rice on the reservation.

FEBRUARY 19, 1972 Pit River Indians Reoccupy Four Corners Area Near Burney, California. The Pit River Indians return to the Four Corners area near Burney, California, and reoccupy the site. Authorities make no move to remove them, even when the Indians erect tents, tipis, and round-houses. By mid-April 1972, the group voluntarily moves on to more suitable sites.

MARCH 2, 1972 Stanford University. Bowing to pressure from Indian students, Stanford University in California ends a 40-year tradition of using an American Indian symbol for its athletic teams. The practice continues to the present day on other college campuses and by professional sports teams.

MARCH 4, 1972 Death of R. Yellow Thunder. In Gordon, Nebraska, five persons are charged with manslaughter and false imprisonment in the death of R. Yellow Thunder, a 41-year-old Oglala Sioux Indian. Three weeks prior, he was stripped of his clothes and forced into an American Legion Hall where a dance was in progress.

MARCH 7, 1972 National American Indian Council. Urban Indians hold a conference in Omaha, Nebraska, forming the National American Indian Council. The council commits itself to working on behalf of urban Indians nationwide.

MARCH 8, 1972 American Indians Demonstrate in Sacramento, California. Hundreds of American Indians demonstrate in front of the California State capitol in Sacramento and call for a state investigation into the fatal shooting of a 20-year-old Indian youth in December 1969. A student at UCLA, Tom Ferris was shot to death in a Willow Creek bar by a white bartender. The grand jury does not return an indictment, hence the demonstrators call for a more thorough investigation of the incident.

SPRING 1972 AIM Leaders Condemn Tribal Councils. At a convention of tribal leaders held in the spring at Cass Lake, Minnesota, AIM leaders openly condemn tribal councils for letting European Americans and BIA officials exploit tribal resources, especially fishing rights on Chippewa Lake. Bearing guns and blockading the convention center, AIM leaders demand that the Chippewa Tribal Council take a militant stand strong enough to intimidate the surrounding non-Indians into accepting tribal control of the fishing areas.

SPRING 1972 Indian Education Act of 1972. Congress passes the Indian Education Act of 1972 creating a BIA-level Office of Indian Education as well as a National Advisory Council on Indian Education, to improve the quality of public education for Indian students through grants and contracts for teachers of Indian students.

APRIL 23, 1972 AIM Members Stage Peaceful Protest on the Fort Totten Indian Reservation. Thirty Lakota and Chippewa American Indian Movement (AIM) members stage a peaceful protest on the Fort Totten Indian Reservation in North Dakota. The sit-in intends to call attention to police brutality on the reservation. In the previous few months, according to the protesters, three Indians died while in jail custody.

MAY 3, 1972 James Bay Hydroelectric Project. The Cree and Inuit of northern Quebec file for a permanent injunction to halt construction of the James Bay Hydroelectric Project. This is their first court action to stop the development, which was announced in April 1970.

MAY 20, 1972 Yakima Indians Land Restoration. President Richard Nixon signs an order restoring 21,000 acres in Gifford Pinchot National Forest to the Yakima Indians of Washington.

JUNE 1972 Lumbee Students Protect Historic Building at Pembroke State University. Lumbee students at Pembroke State University strive to prevent the destruction of a historic Indian building on the campus. In 1885, the state of North Carolina began permitting the Lumbee to operate their own school systems. The state's laws recognizes the Lumbee as "free people of color," and bars them from attending white schools while permitting them to operate their own "Indian" schools. The Lumbee started the school in 1887 and it became a four-year college in 1935. Old Main, as the building is known, serves for many years as the only building on campus. With a current enrollment of 2,500 students, the mostly non-Indian campus administration finds itself pitted against the Lumbee who are determined to save the historic building.

JULY 21, 1972 Shinnecock Indians Recognized. The U.S. government officially recognizes the Shinnecock Indians of Southampton, New York, through the inclusion of the tribe on a Bureau of Indian Affairs map that shows the locations of "federally recognized" Indian reservations and tribes.

AUGUST 24, 1972 Environmental Policy Act. The General Accounting Office issues a report charging that the Department of Interior fails to enforce the Environmental Policy Act in its regulation of strip-mining of coal on Indian and federal lands.

AUGUST 26, 1972 New Brunswick Indian Organization. The New Brunswick Association of Métis and Non-Status Indians holds its founding assembly. Indians in the Maritime provinces are the last in Canada to form formal political organizations. The process began in British Columbia early in the century. Organizations on the prairies date from the 1930s; those in Ontario and Quebec date from the post-World War II era, and in the Maritimes from the 1970s. Indian and Inuit organizations in Canada's North were established in the late 1960s and early 1970s.

SEPTEMBER 13, 1972 Indian Protest over Educational Funds. In Pawnee, Oklahoma, angry Oklahoma Indians seize a federal office for two hours in a dispute with federal and state officials over educational funds. John Trudell, one of the leaders of the 1969–71 Alcatraz Island occupation, says that the Indians won a clear-cut victory when government officials agreed to freeze all federal funds while an investigation and renegotiation of disbursements of funds, requested by the Indian occupiers, is undertaken.

OCTOBER–NOVEMBER 1972 Trail of Broken Treaties. The idea for the Trail of Broken Treaties, the march on Washington, and the occupation of the federal BIA building begins at the Sioux Rosebud Reservation in 1972.

American Indian Movement (AIM) activist Robert Burnette organizes the project in which Indians from all over the country will converge upon Washington, D.C., just before the presidential elections, to protest and draw attention to Indian issues. Caravanners coming from the Southwest follow the Cherokee Trail of Tears; the Sioux pass by the 1890 Wounded Knee massacre site.

Arriving in Washington, they find that living accommodations promised to them by their planners are not available, so the group decides to take over the Bureau of Indian Affairs office. On November 2, 1972, 600–800 Indians occupy and barricade the BIA building. They present a list of 20 civil rights demands drawn up during the march. Among them are that: treaty relations be reestablished between the federal government and the Indian nations; termination policies be repealed, including Public Law 280; the Indian land base be doubled; tribes be given criminal jurisdiction over non-Indians on reservations; and cultural and economic conditions for Indians be improved. After almost a week of occupation in which activists destroy files, furniture, and Indian art, the government promises to review the "twenty-point program," refrain from making arrests, and pay the Indians' return travel expenses. The occupation ends on November 8.

A great moral victory for the Indians, this occupation signifies the first time a national organization of Indians has faced a confrontation as a united people. The two government negotiators, Brad Patterson and Len Garment, also kept an eye on the Alcatraz occupation for the government. While many of the Alcatraz occupiers participated in the Trail of Broken Treaties, it is the first large Indian protest staged by AIM.

NOVEMBER 9, 1972 Pyramid Lake. The Paiute tribe of Nevada wins its suit against the Department of Interior for the department's management of Pyramid Lake. The court agrees that the Interior Department violated its trust responsibility by allowing water diversion from the lake, thereby threatening the economic and spiritual existence of the tribe.

NOVEMBER 14, 1972 American Indians Testify before Commission on Civil Rights. The U.S. Commission on Civil Rights hears testimony from American Indian witnesses claiming that the agency has directed its attention to the needs of African-American and Hispanic-Americans, overlooking the needs of American Indians.

DECEMBER 1972 Canadian Indian Education. The National Indian Brotherhood (N.I.B.) presents a statement titled "Indian Control of Indian Education," which advocates greater band control of Indian education. The N.I.B. statement calls attention to the fact that Indians do not enjoy parental or local control over education—rights taken for granted by most Canadians. The Department of Indian Affairs promises to work to put control of Indian education in the hands of Indian bands.

1 9 7 3

1973 Kahn-Tineta Horn, Mohawk Activist. From 1973 to 1990, Kahn-Tineta Horn serves as a program officer for the Canadian Department of Indian Affairs. Horn, a Mohawk activist, is also known for her careers as a fashion model, actress, and seller of cosmetics during the 1960s. She participated in the 1968 Mohawk protest against Canada's failure to uphold the 1795 Jay's Treaty, for which she was arrested along with 60 other demonstrators who were blockading the Canada-U.S. International Bridge located on the Akwesasne (Mohawk) Reservation in upstate New York. She loses her Indian Affairs position in 1990 for her involvement in activistic Indian affairs.

1973 *McClanahan v. Arizona State Tax Commission.* The Supreme Court makes it clear that state law will be permitted to intrude into

Indian country only if two conditions are met: (1) that there is no interference with tribal self-government; and (2) that non-Indians are involved. The Court emphasizes that Congress has the constitutional authority to preempt, or oust, state law in favor of tribal self-government.

1973 Oglala Sioux Civil Rights Organization. In Pine Ridge, South Dakota, Gladys Bissonette and Ellen Moves Camp establish the Oglala Sioux Civil Rights Organization (OSCRO). Responding to the federal government's policy of using military enforcements against the women, children, and elderly of Pine Ridge, Bissonette and Moves Camp favor armed self-defense for the Indians. This approach will distinguish Indian political tactics from previous twentieth-century policies involving disputes with the U.S. federal government.

JANUARY 9, 1973 AIM Demands Rejected. The Nixon administration officially rejects demands received from the leaders of the Trail of Broken Treaties. The demands were drawn up during the "Trail of Broken Treaties" caravan to Washington, D.C., which ended in the seven-day occupation of the BIA headquarters building. (*See* entry, October–November 1972.)

JANUARY 31, 1973 The *Calder* Case. The Canadian Supreme Court rules in the case of *Calder v. Attorney General* that aboriginal rights to land exist in law but that the rights of British Columbia Indians and Nishga claimants specifically have been extinguished by government legislation. On this basis the court rejects the claim of the Nishga of the Nass River Valley in West Central British Columbia but greatly strengthens the case for Indian land claims. The court challenge was initiated by the Nishga Tribal Council in 1967, but the Nishga have been pressing the issue since the 1860s.

FEBRUARY 6–8, 1973 AIM Protesters Clash with Police. Two hundred American Indian Movement (AIM) protesters clash with police in Custer, South Dakota. Thirty-seven Indians are arrested during a melee with police over a judge's decision to grant bail to the white man charged with the stabbing death of Wesley Bad Heart Bull. According to AIM sources, the riot erupted when after a meeting with officials the mother of the victim was pushed down a flight of stairs. Dennis Banks, AIM leader, is among those arrested.

FEBRUARY 12, 1973 Sturgis, South Dakota. Two hundred fifty Indians gather in Sturgis, South Dakota, to witness the setting of bond for Harold Withhorn, whom police have charged with the murder of a non-Indian.

FEBRUARY 14, 1973 Yukon Land Claim. Elijah Smith, chief of the Yukon Native Brotherhood (established 1968), presents the first northern land claim, *Together Today For Our Children Tomorrow,* on behalf of the 12 Indian bands of the Yukon Territory. Prime Minister Trudeau announces that a federal committee will negotiate the claim. Yukon Natives have not signed any land surrender agreements with the government.

FEBRUARY 27–MAY 8, 1973 Wounded Knee II. A group of 200 Indians, led by the American Indian Movement (AIM), congregate at the site of the 1890 Wounded Knee massacre. They demonstrate against the elected council head of the Pine Ridge Reservation, Richard (Dicky) Wilson, whose administration, they charge, is rife with corruption and nepotism and silences its critics through intimidation and violence. The Sioux traditionalists, who do not accept the Indian Reorganization Act (IRA) government as represented by Wilson, called AIM when Wilson and his administration begin beatings and shootings to enforce "Wilson rule." Tensions between the protesters and the local authorities grow until the situation becomes a siege of the town, drawing 2,000 Indians from around the area and lasting for 70 days. The Indian occupiers are surrounded by 300 federal marshals and FBI agents equipped with guns and armored personnel carriers

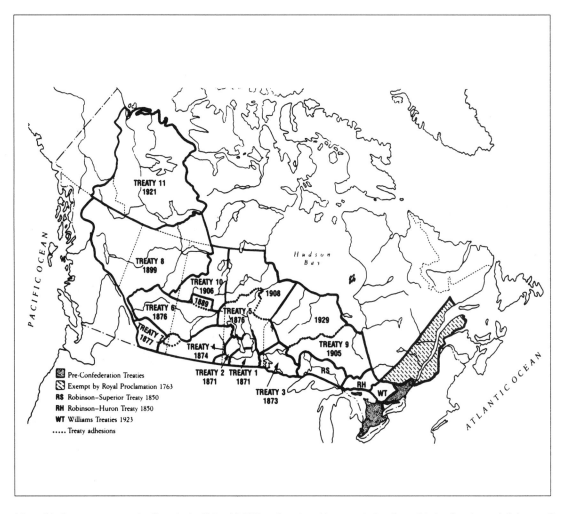

Map of Indian treaty areas in Canada, by Brian McMillan. Reprinted by permission from *Native Peoples and Cultures of Canada*.

(APCS). On March 12, the Indians declare Wounded Knee a sovereign territory of the new Oglala Sioux Nation according to the Laramie Treaty of 1868, which recognizes the Sioux as an independent nation. The siege peaks when the two sides begin firing on each other and two Indians, Frank Clearwater and Buddy Lamont, are shot and killed. The impasse ends after 67 days with a negotiated settlement and the withdrawal of both sides. The occupation calls national and worldwide media attention to the Native American civil rights movement. Al-

though an AIM occupation, former occupiers of Alcatraz Island (Indians of All Tribes) also participate.

MARCH 1973   Hopi and Navajo Clash. Clashes occur between Hopis and Navajos over the disposition of the Joint Use Area.

MARCH 27, 1973   Marlon Brando Refuses Oscar. Sacheen Littlefeather, adorned in buckskin, headband, and braids, refuses the Oscar for Best Actor on Marlon Brando's behalf.

Amidst both boos and applause, Ms. Littlefeather stands in front of the large audience at the Academy Awards presentation and announces that Brando will not accept the Oscar (for his role in *The Godfather*). She explains that the veteran actor's decision is due to "the treatment of Indians by the film industry, in television, in movie reruns, and the recent happenings in Wounded Knee, South Dakota."

MARCH 27, 1973 *Mescalero Apache Tribe v. Jones.* The Supreme Court rules in *Mescalero Apache Tribe v. Jones, Commissioner, Board of Revenue of New Mexico, et al.* that Indians are exempt from state taxation on incomes earned within reservation boundaries.

MARCH 31, 1973 **Northern Cheyenne Strip Mining Leases.** The Northern Cheyenne Tribal Council of Montana votes to instruct the Bureau of Indian Affairs to cancel strip-mining leases worth millions of dollars negotiated by the BIA on reservation lands. Lawyers for the Cheyenne tribe find 36 illegal sections in the leases that the BIA negotiates on behalf of the tribe.

APRIL 8, 1973 **Wounded Knee II.** Pollster Louis Harris reports that 51 percent of those surveyed regarding the Wounded Knee stand-off side with the Indians, while 21 percent side with the federal government.

MAY 24, 1973 **Canadian Indian Education.** The Canadian federal government announces that Indians will be given greater control of their education and that responsibility for Indian education will not be transferred to the provinces without consultation with Natives. The government cites the high dropout rate among Indians as evidence that the present system is inadequate. The National Indian Brotherhood welcomes the announcement. The policy amounts to the acceptance of the Brotherhood's December 1972 policy statement.

JUNE 14, 1973 **Unfair Trading on Navajo Reservation.** The Federal Trade Commission issues a report charging that a number of non-Indian traders, licensed by the Bureau of Indian Affairs, engage in unfair trading practices leading to a worsening of economic conditions for the inhabitants of the Navajo Reservation. The report finds that prices charged by the trading posts exceed off-reservation stores by 16.6 percent and are higher than the national average by 27 percent.

JULY 16, 1973 **Census Bureau Data on Indian Income and Education.** The Census Bureau reports that the median income for Indian families in 1969 was $5,832, compared to a national average of $9,590. Forty percent of Indian families live below the poverty level, compared to 14 percent of all families and 32 percent of black families. Education statistics indicate the greatest degree of increase since the last census. One-third of all Indians over age 25 have completed high school, with a median number of 9.8 years of school for all Indians. The number of Indian students in college has doubled since 1960.

AUGUST 8, 1973 **Canadian Land Claims Policy.** The Canadian government announces that it will establish an Office of Native Claims, a branch of the Department of Indian Affairs and Northern Development. It will negotiate "comprehensive claims," claims for land not covered by treaty, and "specific claims," claims based on treaties, the Indian Act, or other legislation. The office will deal with only six comprehensive claims at a time. Indian Affairs minister Jean Chrétien, cites the Supreme Court ruling in the *Calder v. Attorney General* case as influencing this complete reversal of the White Paper's land claims proposals. The Inuit Tapirisat of Canada welcomes the announcement. George Manuel *(See* biography, February 17, 1920), leader of the N.I.B., expresses cautious approval.

AUGUST 13, 1973 **Office of Indian Rights.** An Office of Indian Rights is created within the Civil Rights Division of the Justice Department. The office will investigate and protect individual Indian rights guaranteed under the Indian Civil Rights Act.

AUGUST 27, 1973 The *Lavell* Case. In the case of *Attorney General Canada v. Lavell,* the Canadian Supreme Court decides that provisions in the Indian Act removing Indian status from Indian women who marry non-Indians are an excusable violation of the equality guarantees contained in Canada's Bill of Rights. Most treaty Indian organizations welcome the ruling because they fear that the Bill of Rights could be used to strike down the entire Indian Act. Jeanette Lavell lost her Indian status in 1970 after she married a non-Indian.

SEPTEMBER 6, 1973 The *Paulette* Case. In *Re Paulette et al. and Registrar of Titles,* Mr. Justice Morrow of the Supreme Court of the Northwest Territories (N.W.T.) rules that the Indians of the N.W.T. have the right to file a *caveat* (a declaration that ownership of land is in dispute) on approximately one-third of the Northwest Territories, because there is significant doubt about whether Treaty 8 and Treaty 11 are legitimate land cession treaties. The case is appealed to a higher court.

OCTOBER 1973 Labrador Inuit Organization. Tagak Curley, a Labrador Inuk and the first president of the Inuit Tapirisat of Canada, spearheads the formation of the Labrador Inuit Association.

NOVEMBER 1973 James Bay Project Halted. In *Kanatewat et al. v. James Bay Development Corporation et al.,* Mr. Justice Malouf of the Quebec Superior Court grants the Cree and Inuit of northern Quebec an injunction halting development of the James Bay Hydroelectric project in northern Quebec on the grounds that Quebec has not kept provisions of the Proclamation of 1763 or its 1912 agreement with the federal government calling for the government to negotiate land surrenders with Indians. The Quebec Court of Appeals overturns the injunction a week later (November 22), but the Que-

bec government begins negotiating the Indian and Inuit claims on December 21.

NOVEMBER 17, 1973 Indictments for Wounded Knee II. The grand jury in Sioux Falls, South Dakota, returns four indictments against Indians in the Wounded Knee standoff.

NOVEMBER 19, 1973 *Department of Game of Washington v. Puyallup Tribe et al.* In a unanimous decision, the Supreme Court rules that Washington State abrogated the Puyallup Indians' treaty rights by prohibiting the tribe from commercial fishing and restricting all available fish solely to sports fishing.

NOVEMBER 22, 1973 Indigenous Peoples of the Arctic Area. Indigenous peoples of the Arctic area—Inuit, Lapps, and Indians—meet in Copenhagen, Denmark, to formulate demands for self-government and for control over land and resources. Indigenous peoples from Alaska, Canada, Greenland, Norway, and Sweden attend the four-day meeting.

DECEMBER 22, 1973 Menominee Indian Tribe of Wisconsin Restored to Full Federally Recognized Status. President Richard Nixon signs Public Law 93-197, restoring the Menominee Indian tribe of Wisconsin to full federally recognized status. Public Law 93-197 repeals the Menominee Termination Act, which imposed federal supervision over the property and members of the Menominee.

DECEMBER 28, 1973 Comprehensive Employment and Training Act of 1973 (CETA). Congress passes the Comprehensive Employment and Training Act of 1973 (CETA), Public Law 93-203, which establishes Indian Manpower Programs under Title III—Special Federal Responsibilities to help economically disadvantaged and unemployed Indians. (Later amended, the program name changes to Native American Employment and Training Programs on August 5, 1977).

1 9 7 4

1974   American Indian Higher Education Consortium (AIHEC). The American Indian Higher Education Consortium is established to provide technical assistance to developing Indian colleges.

1974   California Indian Education Centers Program. Senate Bill 2264 establishes the California Indian Education Centers Program. The intent of these centers is to improve academic achievement in basic skills such as reading and mathematics and to develop a better sense of self-concept among the Indians involved.

1974   *Winter in the Blood* Is Published. Written by James Welch, a Blackfeet and Gros Ventre writer from Montana, *Winter in the Blood* is hailed by the *New York Times* as "the best first novel of the season." With pain and humor, the books unnamed protagonist describes how he attempts to come to terms with the difficulties and boredom he experiences on a northern Montana reservation during his mid-twenties. Welch subsequently publishes several other novels that deal with questions of modern mixed-blood identity and life, *The Death of Jim Loney* (1979) and *Indian Lawyer* (1991). His historical novel of the Blackfeet, *Fool's Crow* (1986), is named "Book of the Year" by the *Los Angeles Times.*

1974   Women of All Red Nations Formed. Lorelei DeCora Means, a Minneconjou Lakota; Madonna Thunderhawk and Phyllis Young, both Hunkpapa Lakota; and others form Women of All Red Nations (WARN). These Native women participate in the American Indian Movement (AIM); from their activism, they develop an awareness of distinctive gender experiences for Indian men and women in response to a "colonialist" system. For instance, while women are only arrested, charged, and convicted for their roles in the Red Power movement, larger numbers of AIM Indian men withstand police brutality, arrest, conviction,

and or death. This more benign treatment of Indian women and misunderstanding of their power provided an opportunity for women to organize and act for the betterment of all Native people. Thus, these AIM women reestablish the political equivalent of a traditional women's society. By organizing Native women, the WARN founders feel that they can fulfill their responsibilities to establish and maintain their stance to protect and ensure Native rights for all.

JANUARY 21, 1974   Oneida Land Claims. The Supreme Court reverses a lower court decision barring the Oneida Indian Nation from suing the state of New York for rental fees on 5 million acres of land the tribe claims was illegally taken in state treaties from 1788 and 1795.

FEBRUARY 7, 1974   Oglala Sioux Tribal Council. Russell Means, leader of the American Indian Movement (AIM), is defeated by incumbent Richard Wilson in a runoff election for chairman of the Oglala Sioux Tribal Council. (In the initial vote on January 22, Means led in a field of 12 nominees by a small margin.) Means, a traditionalist who lost 1,709 to 1,530, vows to destroy the "white man's tribal government" and to reestablish "a type of government where all Indians would have a voice." Wilson, representing the more assimilationist forces on the reservation, pledges to continue full cooperation with the federal government. Charges of corruption and illegal vote counting follow the final outcome of this election.

FEBRUARY 12, 1974   *United States v. Washington*. *United States v. Washington* is the first in a series of federal court rulings on Indian treaty fishing rights in Washington State. Later upheld by the Supreme Court, this case states that the 1854–55 treaties had not been a grant of rights to the Indians, "but a grant of rights from this," and their terms should be "carried out, as far as possible, in accordance with the meaning they were understood to have by the tribal representatives at the councils, and in a spirit which generously recognizes the full obligation of this nation to protect the interests of a dependent people." While much had changed over the years, including the lifestyles of the Indians, "the mere passage of time has not eroded, and cannot erode, the rights guaranteed by solemn treaties that both sides pledged on their honor to uphold." The practical effect of the court's decision adjusts fishing regulations so that the Puyallup can catch up to half their salmon and steelhead quota in state waters and can manage the activities of their own fishermen under their own tribal laws.

FEBRUARY 16, 1974 Custer Incident Trial. Dennis Banks, co-founder of the American Indian Movement (AIM), is brought to trial for charges stemming from the 1973 riot at Custer, South Dakota. *(See* entry, February 6–8, 1973.)

FEBRUARY 20, 1974 *Morton v. Ruiz.* In *Morton v. Ruiz,* the Supreme Court unanimously upholds the right of Indians living off-reservation to receive general welfare payments from the Bureau of Indian Affairs.

MARCH 1, 1974 Adoption and Indian Status. Chief Justice Laskin of the British Columbia Court of Appeals rules in the case of *Natural Parents v. Superintendent of Child Welfare, et al.* that Canadian Indian children retain their legal status as Indians after being adopted by non-Indians.

APRIL 1974 Manitoba Hydroelectric Projects. Indian bands in northern Manitoba form the Northern Flood Committee to represent them in negotiations with the Manitoba government. The government promises to compensate them for any damage caused by hydroelectric developments planned for northern areas of the province.

APRIL 12, 1974 Indian Financing Act. Congress passes Public Law 93-262, the Indian Financing Act, making available $250 million in credits and individual grants up to $50,000.

This act provides "for financing the economic development of Indians and Indian organizations," involving the federal definition of an "Indian," "tribe," "reservation," "economic enterprise," and other terms (amended October 4, 1984).

JUNE 4, 1974 Northern Cheyenne Coal Lease. Secretary of Interior Rogers C.B. Morton announces that the Bureau of Indian Affairs (BIA) accedes to the Northern Cheyenne tribe's request that coal lease terms be renegotiated; the BIA has handled the leases on behalf of the tribe since 1969. The Northern Cheyenne seek cancellation of the leases that allow strip mining on the Montana reservation on the grounds that the terms are not favorable to the tribe. The new guidelines require that all leases meet federal environmental protection standards, follow a revised royalty schedule, and obtain the joint approval of both the tribe and the mining company.

JUNE 17, 1974 Election of Arizona County Supervisor. The Supreme Court refuses to review a lower court decision upholding the election of an Arizona county supervisor who is a member of the Navajo Nation. Non-Indian voters challenge his eligibility on the grounds that his status as a reservation Indian makes him immune from state taxes and "normal" legal processes.

JUNE 17, 1974 *Morton v. Mancari.* Responding to the backlash against affirmative action policies in the 1970s, preferential employment of Indians by the Bureau of Indian Affairs (BIA) is challenged as discriminatory. *Morton v. Mancari,* significant due to its address of employment preferences, is upheld by the Supreme Court as constitutional. The statute gives Indians an employment preference for positions within the BIA. The decision relies on the fact that preference flows from a historical trust relationship dating as far back as 1834. This trust is a governmental relationship between the U.S. and Indian nations, and not one based upon race. Hence, seeking Indians to work in the BIA "does not constitute 'racial' discrimination." Indeed, it is not even a 'racial' preference. Rather, it is an employment criterion reasonably designed to further the cause of Indian self-government and to make the BIA more responsive to the needs of its constituent groups. It is directed to participation by the governed in the governing agency." Thus, the legal status of the BIA is *sui generis* (constituting a class alone). It is important to note that employment preference for Indians is not applicable to other agencies or activities.

JULY 1974   Office of Native Claims. The Canadian federal government establishes the office to evaluate and negotiate Indian land claims.

JULY 2, 1974   Native Lieutenant-Governor. Ralph Steinhauer (b. 1905), former chief of the Saddle Lake Cree band and founder of the Indian Association of Alberta, is sworn as the lieutenant-governor of Alberta, the first Native lieutenant-governor in Canadian history. Steinhauer is descended from an Ojibway who came west as a Methodist missionary to the Cree in 1855.

JULY 22, 1974   Park Occupation. Ojibway Indians of the Ojibway Warrior Society led by Louis Cameron begin occupying the 14-acre Anicinibe Park in Kenora, Ontario. They claim that the Department of Indian Affairs sold the land upon which the park is built in 1959, without their permission. Kenora is located on Lake of the Woods in northwestern Ontario. The Ojibway Warrior Society is formed in 1972 by a number of Ojibway who have begun to believe that radical action is necessary if they are to achieve redress of their grievances. Many Natives in Canada are influenced by the same notions of "Red Power" that inspire Indians in the American Indian Movement in the United States.

AUGUST 28, 1974   Park Occupation. Ojibway Indians of the Ojibway Warrior Society end their five-week occupation of the Anicinibe Park in Kenora (in northwestern Ontario), after reaching a tentative agreement with authorities. The confrontation became an armed siege on August 13. The Ojibway, inspired by the tactics of the American Indian Movement, fail to get significant support from other Indians or from the general public.

AUGUST 28–30, 1974   U.S. Civil Rights Commission Holds Hearings. The New Mexico advisory committee of the U.S. Civil Rights Commission holds three days of hearings near Farmington, New Mexico. The hearings stem from the beating deaths of three Navajo men by three white teenagers who happen to find the victims in an intoxicated condition. The teenagers are sentenced to two to three years in a reformatory per state juvenile laws. Navajo leaders testify to a variety of abuses, ranging from commercial cheating to murder, suffered by Navajos in off-reservation towns located in Colorado, Utah, and New Mexico. Several Navajo leaders request support in obtaining the closure of off-reservation taverns.

SEPTEMBER 16, 1974   Custer Incident Trial. Dennis Banks, an American Indian Movement (AIM) co-founder, is freed following a six-month trial on charges arising from the 1973 riot over the mistreatment of homicide victim Wesley Bad Heart Bull's mother at a meeting with officials in Custer, South Dakota.

SEPTEMBER 20, 1974   "Native Caravan." Five Indians are arrested for assaulting and obstructing police officers as 200 Indians trying to storm the Parliament Buildings in Ottawa, battle with police and the military. The protest starts September 15 when the "Native Caravan" begins traveling from Vancouver to Ottawa to demand settlement of their land claims and to protest poor housing conditions and social services on their reserves.

OCTOBER 1974   Government-Native Relations. The Canadian federal government creates a

Joint Cabinet-National Indian Brotherhood Committee and a Cabinet-Native Council of Canada Committee to improve communication between the government and Native organizations.

NOVEMBER 5, 1974   Reid's Art Exhibited. The Vancouver Art Gallery opens a retrospective exhibit of about 200 works produced by prominent Haida artist Bill Reid *(See* biography, January 12, 1920).

NOVEMBER 15, 1974   James Bay Claim. The Indians and Inuit of northern Quebec sign an agreement-in-principle with the Quebec and Canadian governments to settle their land claim in northern Quebec. Cree Chief Billy Diamond of the Waskaganish band and Inuk Charlie Watt lead the negotiations for the Natives.

DECEMBER 22, 1974   Hopi and Navajo Relocation Act. Congress passes the Hopi and Navajo Relocation Act providing for negotiations between the two tribes over their dispute concerning the Joint Use Area. The bill provides for the partition of the 1.8 million-acre Joint Use Area between the Hopi and Navajo and for $16 million to compensate 800 Navajo families who will be required to relocate as a result of the partition. This legislation is the latest attempt by Congress to deal with the longstanding Hopi-Navajo land dispute.

The conflict between the Hopi and the Navajo is complex. The Hopi have never signed a treaty with the United States, largely due to the fact that there has never been open fighting between the tribe and the U.S. Hence, the tribe possesses no legal document proving its title to aboriginal lands. In contrast, the Navajos entered into a treaty with the United States in 1868, following years of hostility and relocations. The treaty establishes the Navajo Reservation in northwestern New Mexico and northeastern Arizona. Prior to the adoption of this treaty, a number of Navajo families had settled their homes in areas claimed by the Hopi.

In response to Hopi complaints about Navajo encroachment on their lands, the president issues an executive order on December 16, 1882, establishing the Hopi Reservation. Hopi lands continue to be settled by Navajo families as well as Mormon settlers.

In an effort to solve the growing conflict between the two tribes, Congress authorizes the courts to make a determination as to the competing land claims. In response, the courts create the Joint Use area, comprised of 1.8 million acres, while allotting only 650,000 acres of the 1882 reservation for the exclusive use of the Hopi.

The Hopi and Navajo Indian Relocation Commission, pursuant to this legislation, issues a plan for relocation of individuals of each tribe residing on lands partitioned to the other pursuant to a court order resulting from the 1974 statute. Dissatisfaction with implementation of the legislation is expressed by the Navajo, who comprise the great majority of relocates, and by some members of Congress. The Hopi tribal government rejects any attempts by the Navajo to negotiate changes in the provisions of relocation mandated by current law.

1 9 7 5

1975   *Arnett v. Five Gill Nets.* In *Arnett v. Five Gill Nets,* the California Court of Appeals affirms a lower court decision that the state cannot regulate Indian fishing on the Hoopa Valley Reservation since the Indian fishing rights are derived from Congress.

1975   *Carriers of the Dream Wheel* Is Published. *Carriers of the Dream Wheel,* edited by Duane Niatum, is published. It is the first substantial collection of Native American poetry.

1975   Council of Energy Resources Tribes (CERT). Tribal leaders from 25 reservations

Creek actor Will Sampson starring with Jack Nicholson in the movie, *One Flew Over the Cuckoo's Nest*, 1975. Courtesy of The Saul Zaentz Company.

containing energy resources agree to establish the Council of Energy Resources Tribes. The organization, known as CERT, has its headquarters in Denver, Colorado. Its primary function is to assist tribes in the development of their energy and mineral resources and to promote the welfare of member tribes through protection, conservation, control, and careful management of their oil, gas, shale, uranium, geothermal, and other energy resources.

1975 Northern Mining. Uranium mining begins near Wollaston Lake in northeastern Saskatchewan, disrupting the hunting and trapping way of life of the Chipewyan residents. The Chipewyan are not informed of the development, and few find employment in the mines.

1975 *Our Brother's Keeper* **Is Published.** Janet McCloud's activist work takes on broader national issues such as Indian education, Indian rights regarding the preservation and maintenance of Native cultures, languages, and religions, and the political conditions of American Indian prisoners. Her work with the Native American Rights Fund (NARF) results in both a book, *Our Brother's Keeper* in 1975, and in the organization of the Brotherhood of Indian Prisoners.

1975 *Passamaquoddy Tribe v. Morton.* The U.S. Court of Appeals, First Circuit, upholds Judge Edward Gignoux's decision in the case of the *Passamaquoddy Tribe v. Morton.* The Passamaquoddy and Penobscot of Maine, two non-federally recognized tribes, successfully argue that the 1790 Trade and Non-Intercourse Act establishes a trust relationship between them and the federal government. The 1790 act forbids the sale of Indian lands without the approval of the federal government. The colony of Massachusetts (later divided into Massachusetts and Maine) purchased land from the Passamaquoddy and Penobscot tribes via an illegal colonial treaty. The federal government responds that it holds no obligations to repre-

sent the tribes in their suit against the state of Maine because the tribes are not federally recognized. Judge Gignoux's decision upholds the principle that the federal government has an obligation to protect the land rights of all tribes, whether recognized or not.

JANUARY 1–FEBRUARY 4, 1975 Menominee Warrior Society Seizes Catholic Novitiate. Forty-five Indians of the Menominee Warrior Society seize a Catholic novitiate in Gresham, Wisconsin. The Warrior Society demands that the Alexian Brothers give the 225-acre complex to the tribe for use as a hospital. The compound, comprised of a 20-room mansion and another 64-room building, is currently unused by the religious order. *(See also* entry, July 10, 1975.)

JANUARY 2, 1975 American Indian Policy Review Commission Act. Congress, pursuant to a joint resolution of both houses, agrees to review the government's historical and special legal relationship with Indian people. The American Indian Policy Review Commission (AIPRC) includes a task force of three senators, three House representatives, and five tribal representatives and is chaired by Sen. James Abourezk of South Dakota.

JANUARY 4, 1975 Indian Self-Determination and Education Assistance Act. Congress passes Public Law 93-638, the Indian Self-Determination and Education Assistance Act, which expands tribal control over tribal governments and education. This act also encourages the development of human resources and reservation programs and authorizes federal funds to build needed public school facilities on or near Indian reservations. Hailed as the most important piece of legislation passed since the 1934 Indian Reorganization Act, the Self-Determination Act's goal is to give governing authority over federal programs to the tribes and to inhibit the pattern of further federal dependency and paternalism.

JANUARY 8, 1975 Pine Ridge Oglala Sioux Tribal Chairman Election Ruled Invalid. The U.S. Commission on Civil Rights issues a report reviewing the results of the election for tribal chairman on the Oglala Sioux Tribal Council. The election race involves Richard Wilson and Russell Means. The commission finds that the elections are invalid and recommends a new election. They report that "almost one-third of all votes cast appear to have been in some manner improper.... The procedures for ensuring the security of the election were so inadequate that actual fraud or wrongdoing could easily have gone undetected." The Justice Department, however, takes no action on the commission's finding.

FEBRUARY 25–MARCH 3, 1975 The American Indian Movement Takes Over the Fairchild Camera and Instrument Corporation Electronics Plant. The American Indian Movement (AIM) takes over the Fairchild Camera and Instrument Corporation electronics plant on the Navajo Reservation at Shiprock, New Mexico, from February 25 through March 3. Armed AIM members, including John Trudell (Santee), protest the company layoff of 140 underpaid Indian employees who had organized a union to represent their worker rights. On March 13, the plant announces the closing of its Shiprock plant. The company, which produces semiconductors and integrated circuits for computers, employed approximately 600 Navajos before the layoffs took effect in February. Assessing the takeover damage, a Fairchild spokesperson states, "Fairchild has concluded that it couldn't be reasonably assured that future disruptions wouldn't occur."

MARCH 3–JUNE 8, 1975 Berger Inquiry. The Mackenzie Valley Pipeline Inquiry (Berger Inquiry), headed by Vancouver lawyer and judge Thomas Berger, holds hearings. The inquiry has a mandate to make recommendations regarding the social and economic implications of the construction of a pipeline to convey gas from Prudhoe Bay (Alaska) and the Beaufort Sea to southern markets via the Mackenzie River Valley. The hearings, some of which are televised nationally, greatly increase public awareness of the concerns of northern aboriginals regarding economic development in their traditional homelands. Thomas Berger often has defended Native interests in court. For example, he represented the Nishga in the landmark *Calder v. Attorney General* case in 1973.

MARCH 14, 1975 The American Indian Film Festival. The American Indian Film Festival opens in Seattle, Washington, to enthusiastic audiences. The festival, the oldest and most recognized international film forum, is dedicated to the presentation of American and Canadian Indians in the cinema. The festival moves to San Francisco in 1977 (now its permanent home) and initiates an annual awards' ceremony in 1978 honoring its filmmakers and actors. Its founder and current director is Michael Smith (Dakota Sioux).

APRIL 22, 1975 Violence on Pine Ridge Reservation. The *New York Times* reports that violence on the Pine Ridge Reservation continues despite the end of the Wounded Knee occupation and its subsequent government negotiations. According to one FBI report, 6 people are killed and 67 assaulted since January 1 of that year. The story attributes the violence to the 1973 takeover that divided the reservation into two opposing groups.

JUNE 16, 1975 AIM National Convention. The American Indian Movement (AIM) ends its national convention in Farmington, New Mexico. AIM issues a statement declaring that the U.S. government, religion, and education are the most potent enemies of Indian people.

JUNE 24, 1975 British Columbia Reserves. The British Columbia government and the Indians of British Columbia (B.C.) agree to negotiate to settle the issue of "cut-off" (removed) reserve lands. Following the recommendations of the McKenna-McBride Commission, the B.C. government "cut off" land from 22 B.C. bands in 1919 and 1920, without their consent. Where feasible, lands will be returned, otherwise financial compensation will be arranged.

JUNE 26, 1975 Shoot-Out on the Pine Ridge Reservation. A shoot-out on the Pine Ridge Reservation in South Dakota between AIM members and the FBI results in the death of two agents. Leonard Peltier *(See* biography, 1944) is charged and convicted for the murder of the FBI agents and is presently serving two life-sentences in prison.

JULY 10, 1975 Alexian Brothers Roman Catholic Novitiate. The Alexian Brothers Roman Catholic order rescinds its offer to deed to the Menominee tribe of Wisconsin its novitiate in Gresham, Wisconsin, for use as a tribal hospital. *(See also* entry, January 1–February 4, 1975.)

JULY 19, 1975 Dene Declaration. The Indian Brotherhood of the Northwest Territories and the Métis Association of the Northwest Territories issue the "Dene Declaration" declaring that the aboriginal peoples of the Northwest Territories form a nation with the right to self-government. "Dene" means "people" in most Athapascan (Dene) dialects.

AUGUST 6, 1975 The Voting Rights Act Amendment. President Gerald Ford signs into law an act designed to protect the voting rights of non-English-speaking citizens by permitting voting in more than one language. This act specifically addresses the rights of non-English-speaking American Indians.

AUGUST 13, 1975 The Farmington Report. The New Mexico advisory committee to the U.S. Civil Rights Commission issues "The Farmington Report: A Conflict of Cultures." The study concludes that Navajos in San Juan County, New Mexico, including Farmington, are subject to a wide range of injustices and mistreatment. Discrimination, according to the

report, is intensified by poverty, severe alcoholism, and substandard health care. The committee points out that the county has no detoxification or rehabilitation centers, despite the fact that alcohol related offenses are involved for 85 percent of the 21,000 Navajos arrested between 1969 and 1973. The report also takes note of the inadequately staffed and funded Indian Health Service Hospital in Shiprock, and the lack of cooperation and commitment evinced by local doctors responsible for the care of the Navajo population.

SEPTEMBER 10, 1975 Dene Declaration Rejected. Indian Affairs minister Judd Buchanan rejects the concept of separate Native government in the Northwest Territories. He describes the Dene Declaration as "gobbledygook" and compares the position taken by the Dene to that of Quebec separatists. Indian leaders respond by calling for Buchanan's resignation, saying that he does not understand the declaration.

OCTOBER 1975 World Council of Indigenous Peoples. George Manuel *(See* biography, February 17, 1920), president of the National Indian Brotherhood, is selected to head the World Council of Indigenous Peoples at its founding conference in Port Alberni, British Columbia. George Manuel believes that indigenous peoples in various modern countries constitute a "Fourth World" of "internal colonies." He feels that by joining together they can better fight against the problems they all face.

OCTOBER 23, 1975 Federal Trade Commission Report. The Federal Trade Commission issues a report criticizing the Bureau of Indian Affairs's failure to adequately live up to its trust responsibility when negotiating with energy companies on behalf of tribes.

OCTOBER 27, 1975 Alberta Land Claim. Seven Indian bands, including the Lubicon Cree band, submit a *caveat* (a declaration that ownership of land is in dispute) on land in northern Alberta covered by Treaty 8. The ruling in *Re*

Paulette et al. and Registrar of Titles in the Northwest Territories suggests that such a caveat would be accepted by an Alberta court.

NOVEMBER 11, 1975 The James Bay and Northern Quebec Agreement. The East Main Cree, Montagnais, Naskapi (6,500 people), and Inuit (4,200 people) bands of northern Quebec sign the James Bay and Northern Quebec Agreement with the federal and Quebec governments and three Quebec Crown Corporations, the first land surrender agreement signed in Canada in over 50 years. In this way Quebec finally keeps its 1912 agreement with the federal government to negotiate land surrender agreements with Natives. According to the agreement, the Natives surrender their claims to 1,062,000 square kilometers (410,000 square miles) of land for a cash settlement ($225 million over 20 years) and surrender their aboriginal rights in exchange for rights granted them in the agreement. These rights include significant control over their political, economic, and social affairs. The agreement creates three land categories in northern Quebec— Natives will own 14,000 square kilometers (5,408 square miles), and will enjoy exclusive hunting, fishing, and trapping rights on an additional 62,160 square kilometers (24,000 square miles). The general public will have equal access to the rest of the land. The agreement also includes income security for Cree hunters and trappers. Many Natives groups criticize the deal, claiming it compares poorly with a land claims settlement in Alaska (The Alaska Native Claims Settlement Act) in 1971, which gave the Alaska Natives 44 million acres of land and $962.5 million. *(See* map of Comprehensive Land Claims in Canada, pp. 483–85.)

NOVEMBER 25, 1975 Four Indians Indicted on Charges of Premeditated Murder. A federal grand jury indicts four Indians—Leonard Peltier, Robert Eugene Robideau, Darrelle Dean Butler, and James Theodore Eagle—on the charges of premeditated murder of two FBI officers. The officers are killed on June 26 in a shoot-out on the Oglala Sioux Indian Reservation near Pine Ridge, South Dakota *(See also* entry, June 26, 1975.)

1 9 7 6

1976 The Council of Energy Resources Tribes (CERT). CERT, representing 22 tribes, visits Washington and attempts to coordinate federal and private leasing policies. Several long-term leases are renegotiated as Indian concern over the depletion of nonrenewable resources grows.

1976 Manitoba Hydroelectric Projects. A hydroelectric development on the Churchill River in northern Manitoba floods half the Cree community of South Indian Lake, causing significant damage to fishing, hunting and trapping in the region. Indians affected by diversions and flooding were promised compensation in 1974. The flooding follows the relocation of Indians from Chemanwawin, on Cedar Lake in central Manitoba, to nearby Easterville in 1965 to make way for another hydroelectric project that raised the level of Cedar Lake by 3.7 meters. The community was beset by significant social and economic dislocation after that relocation.

1976 Yuroks' Land Claims. A court decision confirms an 1890 award to the Yurok of northern California. The decision involves residual property rights to a 30-mile corridor along the Klamath River. Legal conflicts with non-Indians arise repeatedly due to timber operations in the watershed and the local Indian practice of net fishing in the river.

FEBRUARY 24, 1976 Indian Protesters. Madison, Wisconsin, city police remove 175 protesters demanding the firing of the Menominee tribal police chief in the killing of two tribal members in a shoot-out.

FEBRUARY 27, 1976 Inuit Land Claim. The Inuit Tapirisat of Canada present their claim to an immense area in Canada's arctic. The claim, on behalf of all the Inuit of the Northwest Territories (N.W.T.), follows a unique federally funded study of Inuit land use and occupancy in the N.W.T. This claim proposes to establish Nunavut (our land) as a new territory covering most of Canada north of the tree-line. The territory, which would be taken from the N.W.T., would be controlled by the Inuit who comprise over 80 percent of the population of that region. *(See* map of Comprehensive Land Claims in Canada, pp. 483–85.)

MARCH 2, 1976 *Fisher v. District Court.* In *Fisher v. District Court,* the Supreme Court rules that the Northern Cheyenne tribe of Montana has exclusive authority over adoption proceedings in which the participants are all tribal members and residents of the reservation.

APRIL 27, 1976 *Moe v. Salish and Kootenai Tribes.* In *Moe v. Salish and Kootenai Tribes,* the Supreme Court rules that the states may not tax either personal property on the reservation or cigarette sales by Indians to Indians on the reservation. In a blow to tribal economic development, however, the Court rules that tribes must collect cigarette sales tax on the reservation on sales by Indians to non-Indians.

MAY 1976 **Indian College Organized.** The Saskatchewan Indian Federated College, an independent college integrated with the University of Regina, is organized as the first Canadian college under Native control. The college, intended to encourage Native socioeconomic development and to contribute to the general academic community, will accept aboriginal and nonaboriginal students.

MAY 1976 **Yukon Land Claims.** The Council of Yukon Indians (formerly the Yukon Native Brotherhood), reorganized to include status and non-status Indians, reaches an agreement-in-principle with the Canadian government to settle its land claim. The Indians will retain title to 52 hectares (128 acres) per person, and exclusive hunting, trapping and fishing rights on an additional 44,000 square kilometers (17,000 square miles). They will surrender subsurface rights to all the land. The membership of the organization rejects the deal because they believe it compares unfavorably with the Alaska Native Claims Settlement of 1971.

MAY 29, 1976 **Indian Crimes Act of 1976.** Congress passes Public Law 94-297, the Indian Crimes Act. The act ensures that all individuals, Indian and non-Indian alike, will receive equitable treatment for violating crimes in all territories under federal supervision, including Indian reservations, military installations, and national parks. The act itself "provide[d] for the definition and punishment of certain crimes in accordance with the Federal laws in force within the special maritime and territorial jurisdiction of the United States; when said crimes are committed by an Indian, in order to insure equal treatment for Indian and non-Indian offenders."

JUNE 8, 1976 **AIM Members On Trial for Murder of FBI Agents.** American Indian Movement (AIM) members Robert Robideau and Darrelle Butler go on trial for the murder of two FBI agents on Pine Ridge Reservation in South Dakota *(See* entry, June 26, 1975).

JUNE 15, 1976 *Bryan v. Itasca.* In a victory for tribes, the U.S. Supreme Court rules that Public Law 280, a statute giving six states criminal and civil jurisdiction over Indian reservations, does not give the states the authority to levy state property tax on Indians living within their reservation boundaries.

JUNE 22, 1976 **Mercury Poisoning.** A team of doctors recommends closing the English/Wabigoon River systems in northern Ontario to all fishing because of mercury pollution. The Reed Paper Company in Dryden, Ontario, dumped mercury into the English-Wabigoon River between 1962 and 1970. The Ojibway of

Grassy Narrows have been told not to eat fish from the rivers, but they continue to eat them because the rivers remain open to sport fishermen. Experts find evidence of Minimata disease (mercury poisoning) among the Indians. In 1985, the Grassy Narrows people agree to a financial settlement with the Canadian government as compensation for mercury poisoning.

SEPTEMBER 1976 New Indian Leader. Noel Starblanket, a Cree from Saskatchewan, becomes the president of the National Indian Brotherhood (1976–80).

SEPTEMBER 1, 1976 All Indian Pueblo Cultural Center. The All Indian Pueblo Cultural Center opens in Albuquerque, New Mexico. The $2.3 million Indian Cultural Center is a joint effort of 19 pueblos that lie along the Rio Grande. The complex houses a museum, restaurant, and gift shop.

SEPTEMBER 16, 1976 Indian Health Care Improvement Act (IHCIA). Congress passes Public Law 95-195, the Indian Health Care Improvement Act, authorizing seven years of increased appropriations in an effort to improve Indian health care. The bill provides $480 million for the recruitment and training of Indian health professionals; improved health services including patient, dental, and alcoholism care; the construction and renovation of health facilities, and the provision of health services to urban Indians.

SEPTEMBER 17, 1976 Racist Prison Manual. The chief of correctional services in the Northwest Territories resigns after a racist prison manual is made public in Yellowknife.

OCTOBER 8, 1976 Appropriations for Indian Claims Commission Act. Congress approves Public Law 97-164, the Appropriations for Indian Claims Commission Act that provides an additional amount, not to exceed $1,650,000, for the dissolution of the Indian Claims Commission on September 30, 1978.

The U.S. Court of Claims will adjudicate all remaining cases, including Indian claims.

OCTOBER 10, 1976 Native American Awareness Week. President Gerald Ford proclaims the week of October 10 as Native American Awareness Week.

OCTOBER 13, 1976 Mesquakie Land Settlement. The federal government awards $6.6 million to the Mesquakie tribe for lands taken in Iowa, Missouri, Illinois, and Kansas in ten treaties signed between the federal government and the tribe between 1804 and 1867.

OCTOBER 26, 1976 Dene Land Claim. The Dene of the Northwest Territories (N.W.T.) present their claim to much of the land in the western N.W.T. The claim includes a proposal for an Indian government for the N.W.T. with powers like that of a province. Major centers of population would not be included in the territory of the new government. The Métis Association of the Northwest Territories does not support this claim, and instead asks for separate funds from the federal government in order to fund its own claims research.

OCTOBER 29, 1976 Berger Report. Thomas Berger, justice of the Supreme Court of British Columbia, issues a draft report of The Mackenzie Valley Pipeline Inquiry (Berger Inquiry) recommending a 10- to 15-year delay in the construction of a pipeline from Prudhoe Bay (Alaska) and the Mackenzie Delta to southern markets via the Mackenzie River Valley. Oil was discovered in Prudhoe Bay in 1968.

OCTOBER 31, 1976 Puyallup Protesters Occupy Cascadia Juvenile Diagnostic Center. Approximately 60 members of the Puyallup tribe, including members of the tribal council, occupy the Cascadia Juvenile Diagnostic Center in Tacoma, Washington. After a week-long occupation in which the tribe claims title to the building, the governor of Washington announces an agreement to give six acres of land to the tribe.

NOVEMBER 3, 1976 Yukon Indians. Canadian Indian Affairs minister Warren Allmand says that as long as Yukon Indians do not take a meaningful role in Yukon politics, the territory will not be given provincial status. Aboriginals account for half the population of the Yukon but have no representatives in the territorial legislature.

DECEMBER 13, 1976 Navajo Radio Network. On the Navajo Reservation, the Navajo radio network broadcasts its first day of news and public interest programming in the Navajo language.

DECEMBER 20, 1976 The *Paulette* Case. In the case of Re Paulette et al. and Registrar of Titles, the Supreme Court of Canada rules against the Indians of the Northwest Territories who are seeking to file a *caveat* (notice of claim) on land in the territories. This ruling, however, is made on a technicality and does not change the lower court's finding which casts doubt on the legality of Treaty 8 and Treaty 11 as land cession treaties. The earlier ruling already has led the federal government to accept the Dene land claim as a comprehensive claim (a land claim covering land never ceded by the Native inhabitants). The proposed Mackenzie Valley Pipeline would pass through part of the area in question in the case and in the land claim.

As the courts began to restore tribal treaty rights in the 1960s and 1970s, some communities challenged Native claims. Courtesy of Stephen Lehmer.

1 9 7 7

1977 The American Indian Policy Review Commission Report. A report prepared by the Indian Policy Review Commission, the result of two years' work by a select congressional committee, is circulated for Indian review and input prior to its presentation to Congress. The product of 11 study groups comprised of 33 members, 31 of whom are Indian, the report recommends that tribes be recognized as sovereign entities. Moreover, the commission suggests the formation of a separate Department for Indian Affairs with cabinet status and the granting of full "self-governing" power to tribes wherein they can levy taxes on their reservations, try reservation offenders in tribal courts, and control Native resources such as waterways, hunting, and fishing. Despite strong backing for the report's recommendations, Indian affairs remain under the authority of the Department of Interior, although the commission's own authority is increased. A new position, Assistant Secretary for Indian Affairs, is created.

Concerned with his reelection, Rep. Lloyd Meeds (D.-Wash.) denounces his Indian support due to pressures from voters angry over his state's issue of Indian fishing rights. He issues a minority report stating that the task force calls for an "unwarranted extension of the concept of sovereignty which Indians have been trying to forward for some time, and some of its suggestions are so unrealistic as to subject it to ridicule."

The commission's final report also reveals that more than 100 tribes do not have federally recognized status and are, therefore, ineligible for the services, benefits, and privileges accorded to tribes that are federally recognized (of which there are more than 300).

1977 BIA Under Attack by GAO. The administration of the Bureau of Indian Affairs comes under attack by the General Accounting Office (GAO) for its failure to uphold tribal interests in negotiating natural resource leases and for mismanagement of certain tribal trust lands.

1977 Big Mountain Resistance. Pauline Whitesinger, a Dene or Navajo woman, physically confronts a Bureau of Indian Affairs work crew fencing off the joint-use area according to Washington legislation "resolving" the long-disputed Big Mountain area. A few years later, in the summer of 1979, another Dene woman, Katherine Smith, fires a .22 caliber shot at the fencing crew as they begin to cordon off the area. Elder Dene women protestors include Roberta Blackgoat and Ruth Benally; their actions are in response to the forced removal of the Dene from their homelands in the Big Mountain area.

1977 California and Arizona Indian Water Rights. An alliance of several California and Arizona tribes files suit against the government for failure to sustain guaranteed water rights for reservation lands. The Interior Department resumes coal leasing; Congress passes a law to control the environmental effects of coal strip mining as well as providing for tribal control of strip mining upon Indian lands.

1977 *Ceremony* Is Published. Laguna writer Leslie Marmon Silko publishes her widely acclaimed novel, *Ceremony*. Paralleling Momaday's *House Made of Dawn*, Silko's novel (which includes both prose and verse text) tells the story of Tayo, a disaffected World War II veteran who returns to Laguna. Tayo is unable to forget the killing he witnesses in "the White people's big war" or his brother Rocky, who dies in the Philippines. *Ceremony* is the story of how Tayo comes to embrace Laguna traditions in order to recover from his war experience. On the basis of *Ceremony* and her subsequent autobiographical collection *Storyteller* (1981), Silko is awarded a prestigious MacArthur Foundation Fellowship in 1981. She uses the stipend to publish another critically acclaimed work, the lengthy *Almanac of the Dead* (1992).

JANUARY 13, 1977 Crow Mineral Leases. Secretary of Interior Thomas S. Kleppe rescinds a number of coal leases and lease options of coal reserves upon the Crow Reservation. The strip-mining agreements, providing for a royalty payment of 17.5 cents per ton on subtracted coal, come under attack by Crow tribal members, who eventually file suit to revoke the company leases of Shell Oil, AMAX Inc., Peabody, and Gulf Oil.

FEBRUARY 1, 1977 Mackenzie Valley Pipeline. A U.S. Federal Power Commission report recommends approval of a proposed Mackenzie Valley Pipeline. The report suggests that Native land claims should not cause a long delay to the project.

MARCH 5, 1977 First Canadian Native Senator. Willy Adams, an Inuk from Rankin Inlet, Northwest Territories, becomes the first Inuk elected to the Canadian Senate.

MARCH 17, 1977 Canadian Indian Rights Commission. The Canadian government and the National Indian Brotherhood establish the Canadian Indian Rights Commission to replace the federal government's Indian Claims Commission established in 1969.

MARCH 21, 1977 Menominee Warrior Society Occupies Courthouse. Members of the Menominee Warrior Society take over a courthouse in Keshena, Wisconsin, demanding that authorities formally charge the parties responsible for the beating of two women.

APRIL 4, 1977 Catawba Land Claims. In a council meeting the Catawba Indians of South Carolina vote 101 to 2 to ask Congress for settlement of their claim to 144,000 acres in York and Lancaster counties. The tribe requests recognition of a reservation within their former lands, and argues that its 1763 treaty with Great Britain guarantees its ownership to the land. Barring Congressional relief, the tribe agrees to take its suit to court.

APRIL 5, 1977 *Rosebud Sioux Tribe v. Kneip*. The Supreme Court rules that the congressional legislation opening surplus reservation lands to United States settlers in the nineteenth century diminishes the size of the reservation and thereby the tribe's jurisdictional authority over that area.

APRIL 15, 1977 Berger Report. The Mackenzie Valley Pipeline Inquiry (Berger Inquiry) releases its final report, *Northern Frontier, Northern Homeland*, which calls for a ten-year moratorium on construction of any pipeline in the Mackenzie Valley to allow time for the Indian and Inuit to settle their land claims with the government and for the residents to prepare for changes the development would bring. The report points out that residents fear the development, and that aboriginals have not benefitted from northern developments in the past. The Indian Brotherhood of the Northwest Territo-

ries, the Native Council of Canada, and the National Indian Brotherhood endorse the report, but the Northwest Territories Métis Association, which supports the principle of the development, expresses disappointment.

APRIL 18, 1977 Conviction of Leonard Peltier. American Indian Movement (AIM) leader Leonard Peltier is found guilty of two charges of first-degree murder in the June 26, 1975, shooting deaths of two FBI agents on the Pine Ridge Reservation. Despite defense objections that Peltier is entitled to a public trial, the court closes itself to the public for the reading of the verdict by a jury of nine women and three men. Darrelle Butler and Robert Robideau, previously co-charged with the murder, were acquitted of the same charges on July 16, 1976. Peltier is sentenced to two consecutive life terms by a Fargo, North Dakota, court on June 2, 1977 *(See* entry, June 26, 1975; and biography, 1944).

MAY 1977 Alberta Land Claim. The Alberta government passes a law that makes it impossible to file a *caveat* (notice that ownership of land is in dispute) on unpatented Crown land. The law is to be applied retroactively, effectively killing an attempt by several Alberta Indian bands to file such a caveat. The provincial government has been fighting the caveat since October 1975.

MAY 13, 1977 Inuvialuit Land Claim. The Committee for Original People's Entitlement (C.O.P.E.), established in 1969, presents *Inuvialuit Nunangat*, a land claim on behalf of 2,500 Inuit of the western Arctic. C.O.P.E. originally was party to the Inuit Tapirisat claim presented in February 1976, but, because of differences of opinion, withdrew in order to present its own claim. *(See* map of Comprehensive Land Claims in Canada, pp. 483–85.)

MAY 13, 1977 Mohawk Occupation of Adirondack Mountain Site. Militant Mohawk occupy a 612-acre campsite for three years in the Adirondack Mountains, finally reaching a May 13 agreement with the state of New York. In return for a grant of two separate sites, the Mohawk agree to vacate within the next five months the site they have renamed Ganienkeh or "Land of the Flint." The larger of the negotiated sites consists of 5,000 acres and is located within the Macomb State Park. The smaller parcel of 700 acres lies near the town of Altoona, New York. The Mohawk claim this area as a part of the land guaranteed to them per an eighteenth-century treaty.

MAY 31, 1977 Elected Band Councils. The Supreme Court of Canada upholds a federal order to establish an elected system of government at the Six Nations Reserve near Brantford, Ontario. Traditional leaders on the reserve have been resisting the federal government's attempts to establish an elected band council on the reserve since the 1920s.

JUNE 13–17, 1977 Inuit Circumpolar Conference. Two hundred indigenous peoples from Alaska, Canada, and Greenland convene the first Inuit Circumpolar Conference in Barrows, Alaska. The conference is the first attempt to organize the 100,000 Inuits who inhabit the North Pole region. Delegates adopt resolutions concerning the preservation of their cultures, recognition of political rights to self-rule, environmental protection, and the banning of all weapons testing and disposal in the Arctic.

JUNE 17, 1977 Human Rights Abuses. The *New York Times* reports that the International Indian Treaty Council (IITC), representing 97 tribes, announces its intention to provide the Soviet Union with a list of human rights abuses by the United States against American Indian tribes. The list includes treaty violations, the destruction of Native cultures and religions, and federal interference in tribal economic and social life. Provision of this list will allow the Soviets to demonstrate the failure of the United States to uphold global obligations per the

Helsinki Accords. Signed by 35 nations in 1975, the Helsinki Accords pledge signatory states to respect the self-determination and human rights of all peoples.

JULY 4, 1977 Northern Pipeline. The Canadian National Energy Board endorses the Alaska Highway route for a pipeline from Alaska to the south.

JULY 24, 1977 Ute and Comanche Hunting Rights Dispute. The Ute and Comanche nations meet to formally end a 200-year-old dispute over hunting rights in jointly claimed territory. More than 2,000 members from both tribes attend the traditional ceremony which includes the exchange of buckskin scrolls, the smoking of a peace pipe, and the shaking of hands.

JULY 29, 1977 Alaska Highway Pipeline. Kenneth Lysyk, chair of the Alaska Highway Pipeline Inquiry, recommends approval-in-principle of the Alaska Highway Pipeline but recommends that construction be delayed by two years in order to settle Indian land claims before construction begins. The report also recommends that $50 million in advance payments be given to help Indians prepare their claims.

AUGUST 1, 1977 Health Scholarship Act. Congress passes Public Law 95-83, extending the Public Health Service Act through the fiscal year ending September 30, 1978. Special scholarship benefits will continue to be offered to Indians entering the health professions through that date. The original Indian Health Scholarship Program covered all costs for Indian individuals entering professional health fields who upon graduation are obligated, according to a written contract, to work in health service shortage areas.

AUGUST 1, 1977 Seneca Museum Opens. The Seneca Nation holds an opening ceremony for its new $265,000 museum in Salamanca, New York. Designed and constructed by the tribe from federal grants, the museum houses artifacts from the Seneca Nation and the Iroquois Confederacy as well as Indian artwork.

AUGUST 3, 1977 Northern Land Claims. The Canadian federal government rejects the proposals for separate Dene and Inuit governments in the Northwest Territories. These proposals, part of Inuit Tapirisat and Dene Nation land claims, are stalling negotiations on northern land claims.

AUGUST 15, 1977 The Native American Public Broadcasting Consortium (NAPBC) Established. Established in Lincoln, Nebraska, the NAPBC is an educational, nonprofit corporation offering the nation's largest quality library of Native American programs for public television and general use. Consortium services include program development, production funding, and national distribution. All services are consistent with NAPBC's goals to significantly increase multicultural programming on public television. By assisting Indian producers, the NAPBC works to bring a new perspective through American Indian programs to the national public television audience.

AUGUST 24, 1977 Métis Land Claims. The Federation of Saskatchewan Indian Nations and the Canadian and Saskatchewan governments reach preliminary agreement on a formula by which the Indians will receive land promised in treaties. The Saskatchewan Formula will calculate the land still due Indians by using 1976 population figures rather than population figures from when the treaties where signed. In 1930, the three prairie provinces agreed that they would transfer unalienated land to the federal government for the use of Indian reserves in order to fulfill unmet treaty obligations.

SEPTEMBER 1977 Alaskan Eskimo Whaling Commission. The Inuit of northern Alaska form the Alaskan Commission to fight the International Whaling Commission's ban against the hunting of all bowhead whale. The Inuit commit themselves to ensuring that all hunts are conducted in a traditional and non-wasteful manner, to educating non-Alaskan Natives about the cultural importance of whaling, and to promoting scientific research to ensure the bowhead's continued existence.

SEPTEMBER 28, 1977 Northwest Territories Land Claim. The Métis Association of the Northwest Territories presents its claim to land in the Mackenzie Valley to the federal government. This group was part of the Dene claim of October 1976, but withdrew to present its own claim. *(See* map of Comprehensive Land Claims in Canada, pp. 483–85.)

OCTOBER 13, 1977 First Assistant Secretary of Indian Affairs. President Jimmy Carter appoints Forrest J. Gerard (Blackfeet) as the first assistant secretary of Indian affairs. First proposed by President Richard Nixon, the creation of an assistant secretary of Indian affairs position elevates the Bureau of Indian Affairs administration to an equitable level with other agencies within the Department of the Interior.

OCTOBER 31, 1977 James Bay Settlement Act. The James Bay Settlement Act is passed by Quebec and Canadian governments. The James Bay and Northern Quebec Agreement is the only land surrender agreement backed by government legislation. This gives the agreement greater legal force than other Indian treaties in Canada. Courts have ruled that treaties with Canadian Indians do not have the status of international treaties, nor of laws, but are like contracts.

NOVEMBER 18, 1977 Restoration Act of Confederated Tribes of Siletz Indians of Oregon. Congress passes Public Law 95-195, the Restoration Act of Confederated Tribes of Siletz

Indians of Oregon. This act restores "the Confederated Tribes of Siletz Indians of Oregon as a federally recognized sovereign Indian tribe," and "restore[s] to the Confederated Tribes of Siletz Indians of Oregon and its members those Federal services and benefits furnished to federally recognized American Indian tribes and their members."

NOVEMBER 22, 1977 Quebec/Labrador Land Claims. The Naskapi-Montagnais Innu Association of Labrador presents a claim on behalf of the Naskapi (Innu) and Montagnais in the interior of Labrador. The claim includes a declaration of sovereignty similar to the 1975 Dene Declaration. The Conseil Attikamek/ Montagnais, an alliance of Attikamek and Montagnais-Naskapi Indians of Quebec and Labrador, present an overlapping claim to land in Quebec and Labrador in the same year. According to the Quebec government, the land they are claiming is properly covered by the James Bay Agreement; however, these Indians are not party to that agreement.

DECEMBER 1977 Inuit Land Claim. The Inuit Tapirisat of Canada (I.T.C.) present a revised claim to land in the central and eastern Arctic. The revised claim is made necessary by the withdrawal of the Inuvialuit of the western Arctic from the original I.T.C. claim. *(See map of Comprehensive Land Claims in Canada, pp. 483–85.)*

DECEMBER 1977 Labrador Inuit Land Claim. The Labrador Inuit Association, representing Inuit and "Native settlers" in five remote communities in northern Labrador, presents its claim to land and sea-ice in northern Labrador. Earlier in the year it released "Our Footprints are Everywhere," a land use study similar to that done by the Inuit Tapirisat of Canada for their land claim submitted in 1976 in the Northwest Territories. "Native settlers" are longstanding residents in Labrador who are of part-Inuit ancestry. The Inuit and Native settlers, who work as fishermen, sealers, and whalers, are almost the only residents of the sparsely populated region.

DECEMBER 8, 1977 Indians and the Law. A special Native commission created by the Native Council of Canada condemns the effects of the Canadian legal system on Natives. It associates the large number of Indians in jails with high unemployment, little education, pervasive poverty, and lack of opportunities. It also associates a tendency for Natives to become repeat offenders as a result of inadequate rehabilitation programs in correctional facilities.

DECEMBER 16, 1977 Manitoba Hydroelectric Project. The Northern Flood Agreement, signed by the Canadian and Manitoba governments, Manitoba Hydro, and five northern Manitoba Indian bands, establishes a process by which the Manitoba government agrees to compensate northern Manitoba Indians whose reserve lands were flooded by hydroelectric projects in the 1960s and early 1970s.

1 9 7 8

1978 California Indian Fishing Rights. A new federal ruling allowing commercial fishing on the Klamath and Trinity rivers in northern California causes several confrontations between Indians and non-Indians. Previously, state fish and game officials had placed a moratorium on all but Indian subsistence fishing.

1978 Health Care. The Canadian Department of National Health and Welfare announces cuts in free medical services to Indians. Some Indian groups denounce the move as an attempt to implement the policies of the White Paper of 1969.

1978 Indian Land Claims. The U.S. tentatively settles extensive land claims pressed by eastern Indian tribes with compromises from each side, but other such suits remain pending in 14 states.

1978 Washington State Fishing Rights. Expecting to affect other West Coast tribes as a landmark action, the U.S. District Court in Washington State rules in favor of protecting fish allocations awarded to the Washington tribes who signed treaties with the United States during the last century.

JANUARY 2, 1978 Devils Lake Sioux Land Claims. The Bureau of Indian Affairs reports that the federal government has reached an out-of-court settlement with the Devils Lake Sioux Indian tribe for the illegal expropriation of 100,000 acres of land between 1880 and 1890. The tribe receives $8.5 million for land taken from the Fort Totten Indian Reservation.

JANUARY 12, 1978 Northeastern Quebec Agreement. The Naskapi (Innu) and Inuit of northeastern Quebec sign the Northeastern Quebec Agreement, an agreement similar to the James Bay and Northern Quebec Agreement of 1975. (*See* map of Comprehensive Land Claims in Canada, pp. 483–85.)

FEBRUARY 1978 Onondaga and Cayuga Land Claims. Negotiations are held among the federal government, New York State, and the Onondaga and Cayuga nations over the tribes' claims to 275,000 acres in New York State.

FEBRUARY 11, 1978 The Longest Walk. Approximately 3,000 Indians begin a march to Washington, D.C., to protest anti-Indian legislation pending in the Congress. The five-month trek begins on Alcatraz Island, the site of the 1969 Indian occupation that lasted 19 months and gave impetus to many subsequent occupation events. The marchers arrive in Washington, D.C., on July 15, and on July 18, 25 religious and traditional Indian leaders meet for three hours with Vice President Walter Mondale and Secretary of the Interior Cecil Andrus. The

leaders' request to meet with President Carter is denied.

MARCH 2, 1978 Narragansett Land Claims. The Narragansett Indians of Rhode Island receive 1,800 acres in what is the first negotiated settlement between state officials and an eastern tribe. The tribe had filed suit against Rhode Island for the taking of 3,500 acres in violation of the 1790 Trade and Non-Intercourse Act. Eastern tribes have filed 14 land claims against the original 13 states.

MARCH 6, 1978 *Oliphant v. Suquamish Indian Tribe.* The *Oliphant v. Suquamish Indian Tribe* case is brought before the Supreme Court by two non-Indians arrested by Suquamish tribal police for disturbing the peace and resisting arrest during the tribe's annual Chief Seattle Days. Oliphant, one of the non-Indian defendants, argues that Indian tribes do not have criminal jurisdiction over non-Indians. This argument is upheld by the Supreme Court on March 6, in an opinion that undermines the traditional principles of federal Indian law. The court concedes that tribes never gave up this power by treaty, nor had it ever been taken away from them explicitly by an act of Congress. The ruling, however, claims that Indian tribes only "possess those aspects of sovereignty not withdrawn by treaty or statute, or by implication as a necessary result of their dependent status." Indian rights "must be read in light of the common notions of the day," that is, of the nineteenth century—clearly revealing that U.S. citizens never expected to be tried by Indian courts. Hence, "by submitting to the overriding sovereignty of the United States" via the treaty process, "Indian tribes therefore necessarily give up their power to try non-Indian citizens of the United States except in a manner acceptable to Congress." By opening the door to additional judicial limitations upon tribal sovereignty, *Oliphant* poses a significant potential threat to tribal autonomy. Moreover, the ruling also presents tribes with the practical problem of how to protect their lands and citizens from criminal

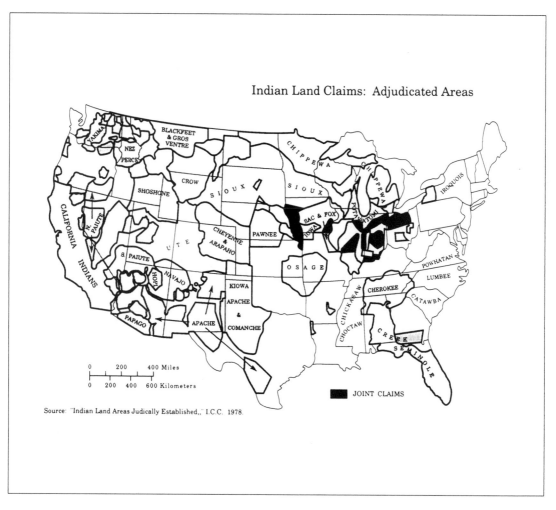

Indian Land Claims: Adjudicated Areas

Source: "Indian Land Areas Judically Established,," I.C.C. 1978.

This map is based on 'Indian Land Areas Judicially Established,' as published in the *Final Report*, Indian Claims Commission, 1978. Courtesy of the University of New Mexico Press.

actions by non-Indians; for the most part, state police officers do not have the authority to maintain law and order on Indian reservations. In a 1978 companion case, *United States v. Wheeler*, the Supreme Court reaffirms the "sovereign power of a tribe to punish its members for tribal offenses."

MARCH 13, 1978 Indian Claims Commission Act. Congress passes Public Law 95-243, the Indian Claims Commission Act, which amends the Indian Claims Commission Act of

1946 and specifically applies to the U.S. government's taking of the Black Hills.

MARCH 22, 1978 *United States v. Wheeler*. The Supreme Court, in an unanimous decision, finds that the U.S. did not violate a Navajo Indian man's protection against double jeopardy by trying him for rape in a federal court when he had been convicted in the Navajo tribal courts on a lesser charge arising from the same incident. In a victory for tribal sovereignty, the court underscores that tribal governments are not creations of the federal government but are separate sovereigns. As separate sovereigns, they retain the power to punish their own members, and they also have the power to tax non-Indians for their activities on the reservation.

MARCH 24, 1978 Mashpee Land Claims. The Mashpee, a village community, claims 11,000 acres in the Cape Cod area of Massachusetts. The U.S. District Court in Boston requires the Mashpee to prove they were a continuous tribal community from the time of early colonial contact. A non-Indian jury, however, rules that the Mashpee constituted a tribe in 1834 and 1842, but lost their tribal status in 1869 when their land "passed" into non-Indian hands. Because the tribe fails to meet the definitions of a tribe during 1869 and today, the court declines to acknowledge their rights to land and self-government. Massachusetts therefore declines to recognize the Mashpee as an Indian community.

MARCH 30, 1978 Dene Nation. The Indian Brotherhood of the Northwest Territories changes its name to the Dene Nation and opens membership not only to treaty Indians but to all Native people, including Métis. The Dene and Métis have claims to the same regions of the Northwest Territories, and differences between the two have complicated negotiations with the federal government since 1976.

APRIL 13, 1978 Native-Government Relations in Canada. The National Indian Brotherhood (N.I.B.) pulls out of a Joint Cabinet-National Indian Brotherhood Committee formed in 1975. Noel Starblanket, president of the N.I.B., cites lack of progress in issues important to the N.I.B., and the N.I.B. belief that the government is attempting to implement the assimilationist aims of the 1969 White Paper.

APRIL 17, 1978 Navajo Occupation of Aneth, Utah, Oilfield Ends. An agreement between four oil companies and the Navajo Nation is reached, ending a 17-day occupation of an Aneth, Utah, oilfield. The four companies involved, Conoco, Phillips, Superior Oil, and Texaco, agree to institute a code of conduct for their oil workers and to establish a hiring preference program for Indian employees. The protesters demand the implementation of a conduct code due to the oil workers' use of alcohol on the reservation and their harassment of Navajo women.

APRIL 19, 1978 Extradition of Dennis Banks Refused. Gov. Jerry Brown of California refuses an official request from Gov. Richard F. Kneip of South Dakota to extradite Dennis Banks, who is to stand trial in South Dakota. Banks, an Anishabe and a leader in the American Indian Movement (AIM), is convicted by a South Dakota court in 1975 of assault with a deadly weapon without intent to kill and rioting while armed. This conviction stems from Banks's involvement in the February 1973 Custer riot over the mistreatment of the mother of homicide victim Wesley Bad Heart Bull. Jumping bail, Banks, 45, flees to Oregon and then to California, where he has been teaching at a Mexican-American and Indian college near Sacramento. In his letter to the South Dakota governor, Brown refers to "the strong hostility there against the American Indian Movement as well as its leaders." Brown's refusal to extradite Banks to South Dakota is upheld by the California Supreme Court.

APRIL 22, 1978 Fort Hall Indian Reservation Denies Access to Non-Indians. The Fort Hall Indian Reservation's business council votes to deny non-Indians access to the reservation for any purpose, including hunting and fishing in the Snake River basin. This action counters the Supreme Court's decision, in *Oliphant v. Suquamish Indian Tribe*, that tribal governments do not possess criminal jurisdiction over non-Indians.

APRIL 30, 1978 Department of Education Established. The Senate passes a bill to establish a new cabinet-level agency, the Department of Education. A provision includes the transfer of Indian education programs from the Department of the Interior to the newly established Department of Education.

MAY 13, 1978 Substandard Housing on Indian Reservations. The General Accounting Office reports that substandard housing for reservation families increases from 63,000 in June 1970 to 86,500 six years later. Concurrently, new housing construction on reservations drops from 5,000 units to 3,500 units. The number of Indian families increases from 46,000 in 1970 to 141,147 in 1976.

MAY 15, 1978 Federal Recognition of Indian Tribes. Congress passes Public Law 95-281, which reinstates the Modoc, Wyandot, Peoria, and Ottawa Indian tribes of Oklahoma as federally supervised and recognized Indian tribes.

MAY 15, 1978 *Santa Clara Pueblo v. Martinez.* *Santa Clara Pueblo v. Martinez* exemplifies the difficult questions raised by the Indian Civil Rights Act of 1968 (ICRA). The Santa Clara Pueblo extend membership to children of male members who marry outside the tribe but denies membership to children of female members who marry outside the tribe. Martinez charges that this tribal ordinance constitutes a denial of equal protection under federal law. The Supreme Court holds that the federal courts do not have jurisdiction to review the alleged violation, since ICRA explicitly authorizes review of tribal ordinances by federal courts only in the context of habeas corpus. The Court determines that if it grants any additional federal oversight of tribal courts and legislatures, Congress would further intrude upon tribal sovereignty.

MAY 20, 1978 Chumash Protest at Little Cohu Bay. Approximately 25 Chumash Indians agree to end their three-day protest at Little Cohu Bay, Point Conception, California. This site, an ancient ancestral burial ground, is one of the proposed locations for a billion-dollar coastal site for the importation of liquefied natural gas. Under the terms of an agreement between the tribe and the utility companies, the tribe has access to the area for its religious practices, safeguarding all ruins and artifacts, and having six tribal members monitor future excavations.

MAY 24, 1978 Indian Activists Found Innocent of Murder. Indian activists Paul Skyhorse and Richard Mohawk are found innocent of murder and robbery in the death of a taxi driver. The driver's body is found on October 10, 1974, near an American Indian Movement (AIM) campsite north of Los Angeles. The case takes 13 months to try and costs $1.25 million to prosecute. Both men remain in jail during the entire three and one-half years that the case languishes within the court system; supporters of AIM argue that Skyhorse and Mohawk are being framed for their AIM activities.

JUNE 1978 Constitutional Reform. The Canadian federal government's discussion paper, *A Time For Action,* calls for Native constitutional issues to be addressed and identified in the upcoming constitutional reform process. Constitutional reform becomes a prominent issue after Quebec elects a separatist government in 1976. Canada's Constitution (the British North America Act) can be amended only with the consent of the British Parliament. Constitutional reform is intended to include "patriation"—bringing the Constitution under the sole control of Canadians.

JUNE 21, 1978 Aleut Awarded $11.2 Million. The *Tundra Times* reports an award of $11.2 million by the Indian Claims Commission to the Aleuts of Pribilof Islands for mistreatment by the federal government in the fur seal monopoly from 1870 to 1946. This award settles a 27-year struggle on the part of the Aleuts for recompense from the federal government.

JULY 16, 1978 Norma Jean Croy Arrested.
A heated exchange occurs in a Siskiyou County convenience store, quickly escalating to an all-out "shoot anything" pursuit of Patrick "Hooty" Crow and his companions, including Norma Jean Croy and her brother Darrell, by Siskiyou County police. Near the cabin of the Croys' grandmother, gunfire is exchanged resulting in the death of one officer and the wounding of two Shasta Indians. Norma Jean is arrested and tried for charges resulting from this event and is sentenced to life imprisonment. Of three adults convicted in this case, only Norma Jean continues to serve time for the offense; in 1990, Hooty Crow was retried and found not guilty by reason of self-defense while Darrell Croy served his time on a six-year sentence. Norma Jean's imprisonment and inability to gain retrial—despite the overturn of her brother's case—raises important questions concerning the treatment of American Indian female prisoners within the American legal system.

AUGUST 11, 1978 American Indian Religious Freedom Act (AIRFA). President Jimmy Carter signs Public Law 95-341, the American Indian Religious Freedom Act. By this act Congress recognizes its obligation to "protect and preserve for American Indians their inherent right of freedom to believe, express, and exercise their traditional religions." The act directs all federal agencies to examine their regulations and practices for any inherent conflict with the practice of Indian religious rights, including, but not limited, to access to sites, use and possession of sacred objects, and the freedom to worship through ceremonies and traditional beliefs. The drafters of this legislation intend the reversal of a long history of governmental actions designed to suppress and destroy tribal religions. Until 1924, for example, the Bureau of Indian Affairs had regulations prohibiting the practice of Indian religion. Violators, if caught, could receive ten days in jail. Many courts find AIRFA to be symbolic in nature and do not require federal agencies to do more than consider American Indian religious

issues, as no federal statutes compel an agency to change a proposed course of action merely because of interference with an Indian custom. More recently, Indians have been prohibited from entering sacred areas, from gathering and transporting sacred herbs, and from obtaining eagle feathers and meats necessary for the conduct of ceremonies. The American Indian Religious Freedom Act becomes law.

AUGUST 24, 1978 The Federal Acknowledgment Program. The Federal Register publishes final regulations regarding a set of "procedures for establishing that an American Indian group exists as an Indian tribe." These regulations become effective on October 1, 1978, and comprise a formalized procedure and set of standards describing the criteria to be used in tracing an "identifiable Indian group containing a membership core which has exercised a governing influence over its members from historic time to the present."

On September 5, the Bureau of Indian Affairs publishes regulations for the newly organized "Federal Acknowledgement Program." The BIA estimates that more than 250 tribes are unrecognized in 38 states. Unrecognized tribes generally do not have a land base and are ineligible for federal services, such as education, housing, and health benefits. The regulations create a Federal Acknowledgement Branch, comprised of a historian, an anthropologist, a sociologist, and a genealogist, responsible for decisions concerning tribal petitions for recognition and tribal compliance to federally stated requirements.

To gain recognition, tribes must prove that: (1) they have continuous existence as an aboriginal tribe; (2) they live in a geographically contiguous area; (3) the group has been under the recognized authority of a governing body from historical times to the present; (4) they are currently governed by a constitution or other document; (5) they have developed membership criteria; (6) they possess a list of current members; and (7) the federal government has not previously terminated its relationship with the tribe.

The 1977 Final Report of the American Indian Policy Review Task Force, created in 1975 to recommend changes in the administration of Indian affairs, strongly urges the establishment of a Federal Acknowledgement Process. Hence, this regulation process is hailed as a victory for tribes although the specific requirements are perceived by many Indian people as unduly complicated and unattainable. Those tribes, maintaining a peaceful existence and virtually unnoticed by their non-Indian neighbors, fear difficulties proving their existence. Similarly, tribes operating under their own governing rules frequently do not possess written documents "officially verifying" their continued political existence.

SEPTEMBER 11, 1978 Yurok Salmon Fishing. Secretary of the Interior Cecil Andrus agrees to personally mediate a dispute between the Yurok Indians and federal officials over a federal and state ban on salmon fishing. The two-week-old ban is in response to a noticeable drop in the salmon spawning population returning to the Klamath River. The ban results in a violent confrontation between the tribe and game wardens on the Klamath River in northern California. The tribe argues that the ban violates it religious rights, given the spiritual importance placed upon fishing within Yurok culture. Reduced salmon runs are attributed primarily to heavy commercial industry fishing, but are also a consequence of pollution caused by heavy regional logging.

SEPTEMBER 28, 1978 Native-Government Relations. The Canadian federal and Ontario governments, together with the chiefs of Ontario, establish the Indian Commission of Ontario to help resolve land claims and other disputes in Ontario. Organization begins after the Canadian Indian Rights Commission dissolves.

SEPTEMBER 30, 1978 Rhode Island Indian Claims Settlement Act. Congress passes the Rhode Island Indian Claims Settlement Act, Public Law 95-395, settling the Narragansett Indian land claims within the state of Rhode Island and Providence Plantations; negotiation results in a confirmed out-of-court settlement between the state and the tribe. The tribe receives $3.5 million to purchase 900 acres, thereby releasing all tribal claims to land within the state.

OCTOBER 17, 1978 Tribally Controlled Community Colleges Act. Congress passes the Tribally Controlled Community Colleges Act, Public Law 95-471, which "provide[s] for grants to tribally controlled community colleges," including any Alaska Native village or village corporation as designated by the secretary of the interior.

OCTOBER 31, 1978 Inuvialuit Land Claim. The Committee for Original People's Entitlement signs an agreement-in-principle with the Canadian government to settle the Inuvialuit (Inuit of the western Arctic) land claim in the western Arctic.

NOVEMBER 1978 Sioux Television. The Oglala Sioux tribe announce plans to construct the first Indian-owned and operated television station. The station will serve 14,000 people who live on the Pine Ridge Reservation in South Dakota.

NOVEMBER 1, 1978 Education Amendment Act. Congress passes the Education Amendment Act of 1978. This act gives substantial control of education programs to local Indian communities.

NOVEMBER 8, 1978 Indian Child Welfare Act (ICWA). Congress passes Public Law 95-608, the Indian Child Welfare Act. The ICWA provides that an Indian tribe will have exclusive jurisdiction over child custody proceedings where the Indian child is residing or domiciled on the reservation, unless federal law has vested jurisdiction in the state. The act also directs a state court having jurisdiction over an Indian child custody proceeding to transfer such proceeding, absent good cause to the contrary, to the appropriate tribal court upon petition of the parents or the Indian tribe. Tribal leaders lobby extensively for passage of this act. Recent surveys conducted by the Association on American Indian Affairs (AAIA) report that 25 to 35 percent of all Indian children are being raised in non-Indian foster and adoptive homes or institutions. The ICWA further establishes standards for the placement of Indian children in foster homes and provides authority for the secretary of the interior to make grants to Indian tribes and organizations for establishment of Indian child and family service programs. The passing of the ICWA alters the prevalence rules made through court decisions in Indian child welfare issues. The underlying premise of the act is that Indian tribes, as sovereign governments, have a vital interest in any decision concerning whether Indian children should be separated from their families.

1 9 7 9

1979   CERT Energy Treaty. U.S. Secretary of Energy Charles Duncan, Jr., meets with representatives of the Council of Energy Resources Tribes (CERT) in Denver; collectively, the CERT tribes are the largest private owners of coal and uranium resources in the United States. They sign an "energy treaty" with ten western state governors in December, pledging to cooperate in the wise use of resources for regional development.

1979   Indian Education. The Bureau of Indian Affairs' educational programs are not transferred to the new U.S. Department of Education, but are administered separately from other programs.

1979   Indian Fishing Rights. Lawsuits over fishing rights are won by Indian groups in the states of Washington, Michigan, Idaho, and Montana.

1979   Indian Land Claims. Land claims based on a 1790 law requiring congressional approval of any sale or cession of Indian lands make slow progress during the year in Rhode Island, New York, Maine, and South Dakota.

1979   Native Declaration of Rights. The Native Council of Canada issues its *Declaration of Métis and Indian Rights*. The document claims Natives have rights to self-determination, to representation in legislatures and in the constitutional reform process, and to recognition of special status in confederation.

1979   Tribal Sovereignty and Treaty Rights. At American Indian conferences, speakers emphasize the need for unity as a means to protect tribal sovereignty and treaty rights. They note a trend in court decisions that favor Indians in reference to land claims, fishing rights, water rights, and mineral rights.

JANUARY 1979   Indian Rights Commission. The Canadian Indian Rights Commission, a joint federal government-National Indian Brotherhood (N.I.B.) commission, is officially dissolved because of dissatisfaction on the part of the N.I.B.

FEBRUARY 5–6, 1979   Constitutional Conference. Canada's First Ministers (prime minister and premiers) meet to discuss constitutional reform. Indian groups are offered observer status, but boycott the meeting to underscore their demands for direct participation in the talks.

MAY 29, 1979   Akwesasne Police Station Takeover. A nine-hour takeover of the Akwesasne police station ends peacefully. The protest stems from the arrest of a traditionalist chief over a property dispute. This dispute is part of a long-standing feud between traditionalists and tribal members who support the elected form of government. The traditionalists do not recognize the authority of either the state police or the Franklin County sheriff's

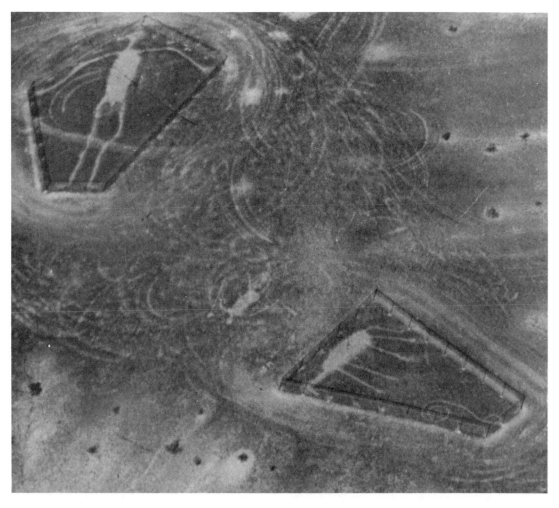

Desert intaglios in the Colorado River region, 1978. These giant figures are rare examples of an art tradition found across much of the desert West. Courtesy of the Phoebe A. Hearst Museum of Anthropology, University of California at Berkeley.

department, despite the latter's force of 16 Indian officers.

JUNE 13, 1979 Black Hills Award. The U.S. Court of Claims awards the Lakota Nation $122.5 million for the federal government's illegal taking of the Black Hills in South Dakota. The Lakota Nation refuses to accept the award and the federal government continues to hold the $122 million, plus accumulating interest, in trust for the Lakota people.

JULY 1, 1979 London Protest. Three hundred Canadian Indian chiefs of the National Indian Brotherhood visit London, England, to press British politicians to block any change to the British North America Act unless Indians are given a greater role in constitutional reform discussions. The Indians are fighting the government's proposed constitution that would recognize the existence of two founding nations (English and French) in Canada, but which would give no special recognition to aboriginals. Aboriginals demand direct participation in constitutional talks.

JULY 21, 1979 Hollywood Walk of Fame. Jay Silverheels, who played Tonto in the television series "The Lone Ranger," becomes the first Indian actor to have a star placed in the Hollywood Walk of Fame. Silverheels is a member of the Mohawk tribe. An actor for more than 35 years, he founded the Indian Actors Workshop.

JULY 31, 1979 Native Participation. The newly elected federal government promises Indians a participatory role in future First Ministers Conferences on the Constitution. (The promise is made moot by the defeat of the minority government in February 1980.)

AUGUST 18, 1979 Dempster Highway. The Dempster Highway, connecting Dawson, Yukon Territory, with Inuvik, Northwest Territories, is officially opened. The highway greatly reduces the isolation of Native villages along its route, but causes concerns about how the highway might disrupt the caribou herds of the region.

AUGUST 19, 1979 Narragansett Land Claims. The 800-member Narragansett Indian tribe of Rhode Island settles its land claim against both federal and state governments, the first of the eastern land claims to reach an agreement. The Narragansett initially filed suit in 1975 for ownership to 3,500 acres. According to the settlement, they will receive 1,800 acres. The tribe will purchase 900 acres with federal funds and receive the other 900 acres from public state lands. While hailed as a victory by some tribal members, others express dissatisfaction with the agreement. They express frustration over the agreement's inadequate compensation in regard to the loss of thousands of acres of land and 300 years of mistreatment.

OCTOBER 5, 1979 Black Hills Demonstration. Two thousand Indian activists and supporters demonstrate against the development of uranium mines in the Black Hills of South Dakota.

OCTOBER 31, 1979 Archaeological Resources Protection Act. Congress passes Public Law 96-85, the Archaeological Resources Protection Act of 1979, providing protection for all important archaeological sites on federal public lands and Indian lands. The act further requires that scientists or lay personnel must obtain a special permit before excavation will be allowed. Indians are exempt from obtaining federal permits for excavations on Indian lands.

NOVEMBER 1979 Ottawa and Ojibway Fishing Rights. The Ottawa and Ojibway (Chippewa) Indians are subject to racist and violent actions as they exercise their inherent right to fish as guaranteed in their treaties with the United States. Indian fishers are fired upon, their tires are slashed, and their boats smashed. Bumper stickers begin to appear with derogatory sayings such as "Spear an Indian—Save a Fish."

NOVEMBER 11, 1979 Indian Fund Accountability. Reporters from six newspapers investigate the tribal government fund expenditures on seven South Dakota Indian reservations. They find that millions of dollars are unaccounted for or misspent. The FBI begins an investigation on the Rosebud Reservation.

NOVEMBER 15, 1979 The *Baker Lake* Case. In the *Hamlet of Baker Lake et al. v. Minister of Indian Affairs and Northern Development* case, Mr. Justice Mahoney of the Federal Court rules that the aboriginal inhabitants of the Northwest Territories have hunting, trapping, and fishing rights to the land based on occupancy, not based on the Royal Proclamation of 1763. The court, however, also finds that governments can extinguish aboriginal title unilaterally. The ruling includes criteria by which the court can determine whether a group has proven to have aboriginal rights to land. According to these criteria, claimants must prove that they and their ancestors were members of an organized society that occupied the claimed land to the exclusion of other organized societies at the time the English asserted sovereignty over the area, in order to establish legal aboriginal title. Notwithstanding the ruling, the Caribou Inuit of Baker Lake lose this case because the court finds that aboriginal rights do not allow them to prevent mining in the area. The Inuit at Baker Lake believe that uranium explorations have disrupted the caribou of the region and are concerned about the effects future exploration and mining might have on their livelihood.

NOVEMBER 23, 1979 Onondaga Sovereignty. The Onondaga Indian Nation claims victory in its dispute against New York State for jurisdictional sovereignty. The dispute arises from the nation's forcible eviction in 1974 of 18 non-Indians living on the reservation. In response to the Onondaga action, the county indicts six Indians on charges of felony coercion. Tribal leaders see the county's request to dismiss the charges against the tribal members as acknowledgment of the tribe's jurisdictional authority within its reservation boundaries per the 1794 Canadiagua Treaty between the United States and the Haudenosaunee or Six Nations confederacy (Iroquois).

DECEMBER 8, 1979 Oneida Land Claims. The Oneida Indian Nation files a class-action suit against New York State, local governments, farmers, and cooperatives in an effort to regain control of 3 million acres illegally taken by the state in violation of the 1790 Trade and Intercourse Act.

DECEMBER 9, 1979 Hopi-Navajo Settlement. The Hopi and Navajo tribes agree to a settlement of a 100-year-old dispute over control of the Joint Use Area. The dispute involves the ownership and use of 1.8 million acres of land within the Navajo Reservation. The dispute between the two tribes stems from an 1882 executive order by President Chester Arthur assigning the land to both tribes for their joint use.

DECEMBER 9, 1979 Western Energy Resource. Tribal leaders whose reservations contain energy resources and the governors of the western states of Alaska, Arizona, Colorado, Montana, Nebraska, New Mexico, North Dakota, South Dakota, Utah, and Wyoming sign an agreement to ensure that tribal concerns will be considered in any national effort to achieve energy independence. Fearing that the more populous eastern portion of the country will enact an energy policy to the detriment of the West, the agreement's objective is to protect western energy resources for the economic benefit of the areas in which they are located. Tribal and state lands in the West contain an estimated 50 percent of the nation's coal, 33 percent of the oil, 22 percent of the natural gas, 92 percent of the uranium, and 100 percent of the most easily developed oil shale.

1 9 8 0

1980   Apache Oil Resources. The Jicarilla Apache tribe take over the ownership of Palmer Oil's wells located on their reservation lands.

1980   Interagency Indian Task Force. An interagency, government-wide Indian Task Force is established by the federal government to "improve social and educational services" for American Indians. After news accounts reveal that administrative problems exist within the Office of Indian Education, Assistant Secretary of Education Thomas Minter begins an internal investigation of the agency and consequently instigates changes in management and policies.

1980   Inuit Land Claims. The Inuit Tapirisat of Canada agree to set aside demands for the Nunavut Territory in order to get negotiations on their land claim (submitted in 1971) started. The federal government refuses to negotiate demands for the territory.

1980   Northern Pipeline. The Dene and Métis of the Northwest Territories approve the laying of a pipeline from Norman Wells along the Mackenzie River to the south. The project is much more modest than that studied by the Mackenzie Valley Pipeline Inquiry in the 1970s.

1980   *Washington v. Confederated Tribes of*

Colville Indian Reservation. The Supreme Court upholds the authority of a tribe to impose a sales tax upon on-reservation sales of cigarettes to non-Indians. In this case, the state of Washington levied a cigarette tax to be enforced by tax stamps; the state sought to enforce its tax by seizure of cigarettes whenever destined to be sold to non-Indians without affixation of the stamps. The Court upholds the right of states to impose a cigarette tax for sales to non-Indians on tribal land.

1980   Yukon Land Claims. Negotiations resume between the Council of Yukon Indians and the federal and Yukon governments. Negotiations broke off after the Yukon Indians rejected a tentative agreement in May 1976.

JANUARY 17, 1980   Omaha Land Claims. The U.S. Court of Appeals sides with the Omaha tribe in their claim to 2,900 acres of land on the Iowa side of the Missouri River. The land, originally on the Nebraska side of the river, initially belonged to the tribe as recognized in their 1854 treaty with the federal government.

JANUARY 23, 1980   Leonard Peltier's Prison Sentence Extended. Leonard Peltier, the American Indian Movement (AIM) activist serving two life terms in prison, is sentenced to an additional seven years' imprisonment for escaping from a federal prison. Peltier, considered by many Indian supporters to be a political prisoner, was convicted of killing two FBI agents on the Pine Ridge Reservation (*See* entry June 26, 1975). Peltier and another inmate escaped from the federal correctional institution in Lompoc, California, in July 1979.

FEBRUARY 18, 1980 Iroquois Meet with European Parliament Representative. The Italian representative to the European Parliament, Mario Capanna, holds a meeting with the Grand Council of the Six Nations Iroquois Confederation on the Onondaga Reservation. Capanna is one of 22 European Parliament members who introduce a resolution in January calling for the parliament's condemnation of New York State's decision to send state troopers into the Mohawk Reservation. On March 13, five members of the Iroquois and Lakota tribes take their case against New York State to the European Parliament. They request the body's support for their efforts at the international and national levels in the hopes of gaining recognition for their own rights and the recognition of tribal sovereignty.

APRIL 1980 Indian Health Issues. The Indian Health Service issues a report stating that tuberculosis and gastroenteritis are no longer the most important problems facing Indians. Indian health priorities now include "accidents, alcoholism, diabetes, mental health, suicides and homicides," stemming from "changes in their traditional lifestyles and values, and from deprivation."

APRIL 3, 1980 The Paiute Bands of Utah Restoration Act. Congress passes Public Law 96-227, the Paiute Bands of Utah Restoration Act, which restores federal recognition and trust relations to the Shivwits, Kanosh, Koosharem, and Indian Peaks bands of Utah, and Cedar City Band of Paiute Indians of Utah. These tribes, whose relationship with Congress was terminated 27 years earlier, will acquire the rights to approximately 15,000 acres in southwestern Utah and access to badly needed educational, employment training, and health benefits. As a consequence federal termination, an estimated 60 percent of Indian adults are unemployed, and 40 percent of Indian children do not attend school regularly.

APRIL 13, 1980 Washoe Hunting Rights. The Washoe Indians win a victory in federal court with the decision that the tribe can enforce its own hunting laws on 60,000 acres of land owned by the tribe, but never recognized as a reservation, in the Pine Nut Mountains of Nevada.

APRIL 15, 1980 Tellico Dam Suit Dismissed. The U.S. Court of Appeals for the Sixth Circuit dismisses a suit brought by members of the Eastern Cherokees to prevent the construction of the Tellico Dam in eastern Tennessee. Tribal members argue that the dam, a project of the Tennessee Valley Authority, will flood ancestral lands sacred to the Cherokees and thus violate their right to freely practice their religion as protected under the free exercise clause of the First Amendment. The Appeals Court, affirming a lower court decision, rules that the plaintiffs are unable to demonstrate that the land in question is indispensable to the practice of the tribe's religion.

APRIL 20, 1980 Mohawk Land Claims. The St. Regis Mohawk tribe (in New York State) and the federal government reach a tentative agreement regarding the disposition of tribally claimed land near the St. Lawrence Seaway. According to the terms of the agreement, the Mohawks of Akwesasne will receive 9,750 acres south of the reservation and $6 million in federal funds.

MAY 28, 1980 Constitutional Reform. Noel Starblanket of the National Indian Brotherhood announces that Indians will push for greater participation at Canadian constitutional talks scheduled for June 9. Prime Minister Trudeau has promised that Indians will be

Health care facility at the Turtle Mountain Chippewa Reservation in North Dakota. Courtesy of Duane Champagne.

given a seat at the table on matters that directly concern them.

JUNE 9, 1980   Constitutional Reform. At constitutional talks among Canada's First Ministers (prime minister and provincial premiers), the premiers agree that Indian groups will be invited to participate only in discussions that directly affect them.

JUNE 14, 1980   St. Regis Mohawk Indian Reservation. New York State sends 70 police to Akwesasne, the St. Regis Mohawk Indian Reservation that straddles the Canadian-U.S. border. The police serve as a barrier between two armed and hostile political groups on the reservation. The rift, in existence for more than a hundred years, has grown to the point of civil war in the last year. One side of the dispute involves traditionalists who argue that the reservation is under the governing authority of the traditional leaders as recognized by the Haudenosaunee, or Iroquois Confederacy; the opposing party supports the elected tribal government originally appointed in the 1880s by the state of New York and recognized by the federal and state governments as the legitimate governing authority. At issue is political control

of the 10,000 Mohawk members, the economic development of the reservation, and the administration of federal grants.

For the previous ten months, in an effort to prevent the arrest of several traditional leaders involved in the 1979 takeover of the Akwesasne police station, approximately 70 traditionalists have maintained an armed camp on 20 acres along the St. Lawrence River.

JUNE 17, 1980   Indian and Federal Trade Act. Congress passes Public Law 96-278, the Indian and Federal Trade Act. The act affects Indian trade with federal employees, and repeals and amends certain laws regulating trade between Indians and some federal employees, in order to protect the interests of Indian people.

JUNE 22, 1980   Kateri Tekakwitha Beatified. The Vatican beatifies Kateri Tekakwitha, a Mohawk-Algonquin Indian who died 300 years before at the age of 24. (The beatification process is the last step before achieving sainthood in the eyes of the Catholic Church.) She is the first American Indian to be beatified by the church. Renamed Kateri at her baptism at the age of 20 (her Indian name being Loragode, or Sunshine), she suffered ridicule by her family, friends, and tribe, actions that ultimately forced her to move 200 miles away from her family and people.

JUNE 24, 1980 Family Breakdown on Reserves. A federal report says alcoholism, unemployment, and poor living conditions are leading to family breakdown on Canadian Indian reserves.

JUNE 24, 1980 Health Care. The federal government announces that Alberta Indians will be given control over their own health care.

JUNE 27, 1980 *White Mountain Apache Tribe v. Bracker*. This U.S. Supreme Court denies state governments authority to impose a motor carrier license and fuel use tax on non-Indian contractors engaged in on-reservation logging operations under a contract with a tribe.

JUNE 30, 1980 *United States v. Sioux Nation*. The Supreme Court upholds the $122 million judgment against the United States by the Court of Claims for the illegal taking of the Sioux Nation's Black Hills. Essentially, the Supreme Court reverses the ruling in *Lone Wolf* that stated that the manner in which the federal government manages tribal property is not reviewable by the courts. The *United States v. Sioux Nation* case dates from 1877 when Congress ratified an "agreement" with the Sioux Nation, or the Lakota, to sell the Black Hills, thereby violating provisions of the 1868 Fort Laramie Treaty. The 1868 treaty clearly guaranteed the Black Hills, or Paha Sapa, to the Sioux Nation as an area of sacred significance to the tribe. The discovery of gold in 1874, however, brought a flood of settlers to the area. After enduring years of war and the intentional killing off of the tribe's staple food, the buffalo, the Sioux sign an agreement in 1876 ceding the Black Hills to the United States.

In 1951, after several unsuccessful attempts to repeal the 1874 legislation, the Sioux make an appeal to the newly created Indian Claims Commission. Brought before the court, the United States argues that the 1868 Sioux Reservation was not "property" in the meaning of the Fifth Amendment and could be disposed of however Congress wished. The court disagrees: Indian treaties create "vested property rights" under the Constitution, and, as such, can be taken away only for a legitimate public purpose. Since the Black Hills was not sold for the benefit of the Sioux, but rather for the profit of U.S. citizens, the United States would have to pay the value of the land in 1877, plus interest. The Sioux Nation does not accept this decision; instead, it demands the return of the land in another lawsuit. Thus, the lawsuit proves unsuccessful, but Congress has since considered legislation to return parts of the Black Hills to the Sioux.

JULY 8, 1980 Hopi-Navajo Relocation Act. Congress passes Public Law 96-306, the Hopi-Navajo Relocation Act, requiring the relocation of certain Navajo and Hopi families in an effort to settle the Joint Use land dispute. The legislation provides for funds to assist in the purchase of additional lands for the Navajo tribe.

JULY 12, 1980 James Bay Agreement. The Cree of northern Quebec file suit against the government of Quebec, claiming that the government has failed to live up to the James Bay and Northern Quebec Agreement.

JULY 17, 1980 Indian Status. Twenty-eight female members of Parliament from all political parties announce that they will fight for the repeal of a section of the Indian Act that denies Indian status to women (and their children) when they marry non-Indians.

JULY 18, 1980 Oglala Sioux File New Black Hills Lawsuit. The Oglala Sioux file a class-action suit against the federal government and the state of South Dakota for $11 billion, seeking $10 billion for the loss of nonrenewable resources from the Black Hills and $1 billion for "hunger, malnutrition, disease and death" incurred by the Sioux resulting from the loss of their traditional lands. The Oglala Sioux contend that they are not the beneficiaries of the award decided by the Supreme Court in the previous month. The Oglala argue that the lawyer's contract with the tribe in the previous case expired three years prior to the decision and had not been renewed by the tribe.

JULY 20, 1980 Maria Martinez Dies. Maria Martinez, age 95, dies at San Ildefonso Pueblo, New Mexico. A world-renowned potter, Martinez and her husband revived the traditional black pottery of the Pueblos. Her pottery is characterized by its perfect craft and shape even though she did not use a potter's wheel. Her pots appear in collections throughout the world.

AUGUST 8, 1980 Kainai Protest. Indian Affairs minister John Munro agrees to investigate Kainai (Blood) grievances. The Indians had set up blockades in Cardston, Alberta in July.

AUGUST 18, 1980 Creek Purchase the Hickory Grounds. The Creek Nation east of the Mississippi, or Alabama Creeks as they are called locally, regains ownership of a 33-acre site known as the "Hickory Grounds." Prior to the Creeks's removal to Oklahoma, Hickory Grounds was revered as a sacred town of refuge in Creek mythology and history. The Creek purchase Hickory Grounds with the proceeds of a $165,000 federal grant.

SEPTEMBER 4, 1980 Reservation for Confederated Tribes of Siletz Indians of Oregon Act. Congress passed Public Law 96-340, the Reservation for Confederated Tribes of Siletz Indians of Oregon Act, which establishes a reservation of 3,663 acres for the Confederated Tribes. Congress terminated its relationship with the confederation of 24 tribes and bands in 1956. The Confederated Tribes, with approxi-

mately 900 members, are restored to full federal recognition.

SEPTEMBER 8–12, 1980 Constitutional Conference. Canada's First Ministers meet to discuss constitutional reform. Representatives of Native organizations attend as observers.

SEPTEMBER 25, 1980 Constitutional Patriation. Canadian Native groups file application in federal court to prevent the patriation of Canada's Constitution (the British North America Act) without their consent. The Constitution can be changed only with the approval of the British Parliament. Patriation is the process by which the Constitution would come under exclusively Canadian control.

SEPTEMBER 26, 1980 Indian Will Act. Congress passes Public Law 96-363, the Indian Will Act, that "permit[s] any Indian to transfer by will restricted lands of such Indian to his or her heirs or lineal descendants." This act amends the Indian Will Act of June 18, 1934.

OCTOBER 11, 1980 Maine Indian Claims Settlement Act of 1980. Congress passes Public Law 96-420, the Maine Indian Claims Settlement Act, which brings to a conclusion the settlement of a large land claim filed by the Maine Indians consisting of the Passamaquoddy tribe, the Penobscot Nation, and the Maliseet tribe. Using a symbolic feather pen, President Jimmy Carter signs the Maine Indian Land Claims Settlement Act, thereby ending the Passamaquoddy, Penobscot, and Maliseet claim to two-thirds of the state of Maine. The settlement provides for an $81.5 million settlement to the tribes. The money includes a $27 million trust fund and $54.5 million to purchase 300,000 acres of illegally taken former tribal lands. The agreement follows the tribes' successful claim that Massachusetts (Maine was formed from part of Massachusetts colony) had taken their aboriginal homeland, now the northern two-thirds of Maine, in violation of

Okanagan Larry Pierre on the occasion of the First Nations Constitutional Conference, 1980, demanding Native participation in constitutional tasks. Photo by Rod McIvor. Courtesy of Canapress Photo Service.

the 1790 Trade and Intercourse Act. The Trade and Intercourse Act granted authority only to the federal government to purchase land from the tribes.

OCTOBER 13, 1980 Native Foster Care. Seven hundred British Columbia Indians protest the number of Indian children placed in non-Native foster homes in the 1960s and 1970s. As a result, the government begins to increase

band control of child welfare services, a trend that also begins in other provinces.

NOVEMBER 1, 1980 U'Mista Cultural Centre. The Nimpkish Kwagiulth of Alert Bay celebrate the opening of the U'Mista Cultural Centre, following the opening of another center by the Nuyumbalees Society of Cape Mudge on June 29, 1979. Both centers display Kwagiulth artifacts confiscated by police during raids on illegal potlatches in the 1920s. The federal government returned the items on the condition that they be housed in museums.

NOVEMBER 7, 1980 London Protest. Canadian Indian leaders hold a press conference in London, England, to explain why they feel threatened by Canada's constitutional proposals. Prime Minister Pierre Trudeau announces that he is willing to include a provision to protect aboriginal rights in the Constitution if such an amendment would be accepted by the premiers. Indian leaders choose to go to London because most Canadian Indian treaties have been with the British Crown, and because the British Parliament has the ability to block changes to Canada's Constitution.

NOVEMBER 8, 1980 Helsinki Conference. U.S. representatives provide the Helsinki conference, meeting in Madrid, Spain, with a federal study on U.S. compliance with the 1975 Helsinki Accords in its treatment of American Indians. The report concludes that the U.S. record is "neither as deplorable as sometimes alleged nor as successful as one might hope."

NOVEMBER 23, 1980 Cayuga Land Claims. The Cayuga Indian Nation files suit against New York State for the taking of former Cayuga lands located in the Finger Lakes region. The tribe demands the return of 100 square miles, payment of $350 million in damages, and the relocation of 7,000 property owners.

NOVEMBER 29, 1980 Tellico Dam. The flood gates of the Tellico Dam on the Little Tennessee River begin to flood the 16,000-acre reser-

Canadian Natives protesting before Parliament for land rights and aboriginal rights within the Canadian constitution. Courtesy of Canapress Photo Service.

voir. Several traditional Cherokees attempt to legally prevent the flooding of their aboriginal lands on the grounds of religious protection. *(See* entry, April 15, 1980.)

DECEMBER 2, 1980 Russell Tribunal Verdict. The Russell Tribunal, an international human rights body located in the Netherlands, finds the United States, Canada, and several countries in Latin America guilty of cultural and physical genocide and of the unlawful seizure of land in their treatment of their Indian popula-

tions. The verdict comes following an eight-day hearing during which the human rights activists received testimony from 14 Indian communities. Many of the "judges" are lawyers who base their decision, which has no legal authority, on the protections afforded to Indian people in the 1975 Helsinki Accords, the International Covenant on Civil and Political Rights, and the Universal Declaration of Human Rights.

DECEMBER 17, 1980 Aboriginal Self-Government. National Indian Brotherhood presi-

Indians gather at the home of Grace McCarthy, British Columbia's Human Resources minister, to protest the government's child welfare policies. Courtesy of Ken Oakes/*Vancouver Sun*.

dent Del Riley, appearing before a parliamentary committee on constitutional reform, protests the lack of Native involvement in the reform process. He says aboriginal peoples want a third level of government that would allow them to control their own land, resources, and people. He also calls for the entrenchment of the Proclamation of 1763 in the new Constitution.

DECEMBER 22, 1980 Salmon and Steelhead Conservation Act of 1980. Congress, primarily in response to the tribes' victories in the *United States v. Washington* and *Sohappy v. Smith* cases, passes Public Law 96-561, the Salmon and Steelhead Conservation Act of 1980. Designed in part to meet the guarantees promised by the federal government in treaties signed with the tribes in the 1800s, the bill provides for the conservation and enhancement of the salmon and steelhead runs in the Pacific Northwest.

1 9 8 1

1981 *Seminole Tribe of Florida v. Butterworth.* The Supreme Court rules that Indian tribes retain vestiges of their original sovereignty to the extent that they have not been divested of it by specific federal statute or by their status as dependent nations within the United States. Since there are no specific statutes addressing the question of gambling on an Indian reservation (except pertaining to gambling devices), Indian bingo experiences a "boom" in development. The Supreme Court holds in *Seminole Tribe of Florida v. Butterworth* that tribes retain the power to regulate gambling on their reservations unless statutes that transfer criminal jurisdiction to states or that assert federal criminal jurisdiction over state offenses committed on Indian reservations apply to gambling. The court says that those laws apply only when the state law at issue contains an *outright prohibition* on gambling, or on bingo, rather than, as is the case with most state laws, a system of regulating gambling or bingo.

1981 Simon Ortiz Wins Pushcart Prize. Acoma Pueblo poet Simon Ortiz wins the Pushcart Prize for poetry for his important collection, *From Sand Creek.* Ortiz, who received a master of fine arts degree from the University of Iowa, has taught creative writing and literature at a number of universities and colleges, including San Diego State, the University of New Mexico, and Sine Gleska College on the Rosebud Reservation in South Dakota. His poetic voice, evoking images of traditional pueblo storytelling, is evidenced in a number of collections, including *Going for the Rain* (1976), *A Good Journey* (1977), and a collection of short stories *Fightin'* (1983). In 1992, a collection of previously published works, *Woven Stone,* is published.

JANUARY 30, 1981 Constitutional Amendments. The federal government accepts a constitutional amendment that would entrench the provisions of the Proclamation of 1763. Another amendment reads: "The aboriginal and treaty rights of the aboriginal peoples of Canada are hereby recognized and affirmed." Del Riley, president of the National Indian Brotherhood, endorses the amendments.

MARCH 3, 1981 San Francisco Peaks Ski Resort. Navajo and Hopi religious leaders request the federal district court to halt the construction of a ski resort in the San Francisco Peaks. Arguing that the First Amendment protects their right to religious freedom, the tribal leaders' suit states that construction would destroy sacred sites and that the desecration would anger their gods.

APRIL 11, 1981 Native Claims. Ontario Indians present "A New Proposal for Claims Resolution in Ontario" to the federal and Ontario governments. They suggest that validity of land claims should be judged on moral, not legal, grounds.

APRIL 18, 1981 Navajo-Hopi Joint Use Area Partitioned. A federal court officially partitions the 1.8 million-acre Joint Use Area equally between the Navajo and Hopi; the court does so under congressional approval. The division forces the relocation of 3,000 to 6,000 Navajo and 100 Hopi tribal members. Four days later, Bureau of Indian Affairs officials begin seizing Navajo livestock for removal.

APRIL 24, 1981 Constitutional Proposal. The Federation of Saskatchewan Indians and the Association of Métis and Non-Status Indians of Saskatchewan reject the proposed new Canadian Constitution, saying that it does not go far enough in protecting Native rights.

MAY 8, 1981 Resignation of Secretary of the Interior Demanded. Attending the National Tribal Government Conference in Washington, D.C., 150 tribal leaders send a letter to President Ronald Reagan demanding the immediate resignation of Secretary of the Interior James G. Watt. The letter cites Watt's unwillingness to consult with tribes as dictated by law. The leaders write: "We find this callous disregard of his lawful function and responsibility as the Federal official with general statutory-delegated authority in Indian matters completely intolerable." Elmer Savilla, spokesperson for the group, calls further attention to Reagan's proposal to cut Indian funds by consolidating the financing of ten Bureau of Indian Affairs programs into one block grant, thereby reducing the allocation of funds by 26 percent. Other administration proposals call for the reduction of adult and child education, housing, employment, assistance, and vocational training programs.

MAY 29, 1981 *Montana v. United States.* In *Montana v. United States,* the Supreme Court rules that the state of Montana has the authority to regulate hunting and fishing on the Big Horn River flowing through the Crow Indian Reservation. The Court rules that the state assumed title to the riverbed, under the "equal footing doctrine," upon its entrance into the Union in 1889. The case is a blow to tribal authority and its efforts to regulate hunting and fishing within its own boundaries. Subsequent-

ly, the state of Montana orders the Crow tribe to open access to fishing on the Bighorn River. Previously, the tribe had closed the river to fishing by non-Indians in 1975 by claiming ownership of the river. In response to the Court's ruling, members of the Crow tribe barricade a highway bridge over the river near Hardin, Montana. Crow members blockade both lanes of Highway 313 with approximately 15 cars, campers, and pick-ups. The barricade is removed 14 hours later when federal marshals serve notice on the tribe that the blockade is an illegal act.

JUNE 11, 1981 Civil Rights Commission Report. The U.S. Civil Rights Commission issues a major report on the federal government's treatment of American Indians. Commission Chairman Arthur Flemming sums up the government's policy toward American Indians as one of "inaction and missed opportunities." After a decade of research, the commission proposes several changes in federal policy regarding Indian tribes. One of its primary recommendations is that Congress apportion, as in the case of states, federal funds to tribes as block grants. The commission also recommends the establishment of an Office of Indian Rights within the Civil Rights Division of the Justice Department. The study further urges that the government act expeditiously and fairly in the resolution of fishing rights disputes and the eastern land claims. Moreover, the report suggests that Congress pass legislation allowing tribes that so choose to assume criminal jurisdiction over all peoples within their reservation boundaries.

JUNE 11, 1981 Restigouche Reserve Raid. About 375 Quebec police raid the Restigouche Micmac Reserve on the Quebec/New Brunswick border, confiscating 250 kilograms of salmon and salmon nets. The raid stems from a dispute over whether the Quebec government has a right to regulate Indian fishing and hunting. Negotiations between the band and the Quebec government broke down on June 8. Police raid the reserve again on June 20. Accusations of police brutality follow the raids.

JULY 10, 1981 Chippewa and Ottawa Fishing Rights. In Michigan, the Bay Mills and the Sault Ste. Marie Chippewa and the Grand Traverse Tribe of Ottawa Indians win a nine-year court battle in the U.S. Court of Appeals for the Sixth Circuit, recognizing their fishing rights in Lakes Michigan, Superior, and Huron. The federal court lets stand a district court decision in which tribes successfully proved that the treaties of 1836 and 1855 guaranteed their right to fish in the Great Lakes. In addition to acknowledging their fishing rights, the courts rule that tribes may continue to use their traditional gill nets, an apparatus banned under state law. The tribes' next step will be to enter into negotiations with the federal government and the state of Michigan for the development of a fishing management plan.

AUGUST 13, 1981 Omnibus Budget Reconciliation Act of 1981. Congress passes Public Law 97-35, the Omnibus Budget Reconciliation Act of 1981. This lengthy act under Title IX—Health Services and Facilities, authorizes the secretary of health and human services to make community "block grants" to include "the Indian tribe or tribal organization serving the individuals for whom such determination has been made" for a fiscal year. The act, also called the Head Start Act under Sub-chapter B, Sec. 635, implements Head Start programs in Indian communities and aims to improve impoverished areas such as Indian reservations. Also referred to as the Small Business Budget Reconciliation and Loan Consolidation/Improvement Act of 1981, the act allows small business loans to be made for up to 25 years to qualified small businesses owned by Indian tribes.

SEPTEMBER 2, 1981 Indian Status. The United Nations Human Rights Commission rules that Canada's Indian Act violates international human rights because it discriminates on the basis of gender. The ruling is made in regard to Sandra Lovelace, a Maliseet, who had lost her Indian status and the right to live on her band's reserve because she married a non-Indian. Canadian courts have upheld the discriminatory sections in the Indian Act.

OCTOBER 14, 1981 Amnesty International Report. In a 144-page report, Amnesty International charges the U.S. government with retaining as political prisoners Richard Marshall of the American Indian Movement (AIM) and Elmer Pratt of the Black Panther Movement. The report alleges official misconduct in the investigations and trials of both leaders.

OCTOBER 16, 1981 Treaty Rights. In the *R. v. Taylor and Williams* case, the Supreme Court of Ontario finds that the terms of a land cession treaty must be kept even if they do not appear in the treaty document. In this case, the treaty document makes no mention of hunting and fishing rights, but minutes of a meeting clearly indicate that the Indians were specifically promised these rights.

NOVEMBER 2–5, 1981 Constitutional Amendments Deleted. Nine of ten provinces accept an amending formula for the Constitution and a Charter of Rights only after amendments guaranteeing aboriginal rights (agreed upon on January 30, 1980) are deleted from the package. Several premiers oppose the provisions because they find them too poorly defined. The agreement meets with immediate angry denunciation by Indian leaders across Canada.

Negotiations toward a new Canadian constitution begin in earnest after the May 1980 provincial referendum defeats a proposal which would have seen Quebec move toward a limited form of independence. The First Ministers try to devise a constitution which will increase loyalty to Canada in that French-speaking Canadian province. The First Ministers failed to agree on a constitutional proposal at a conference in February.

NOVEMBER 16, 1981 Wildlife Protection. Congressional legislation prohibits the export, import, selling, receiving, acquiring, or purchasing of wildlife in violation of federal law or Indian tribal law.

NOVEMBER 19, 1981 Natives Protest. Three thousand protesters march on Parliament Hill in Ottawa to protest the constitutional proposal agreed upon by Canada's First Ministers on November 5.

NOVEMBER 26, 1981 Amendments Reinstated. The House of Commons reinstates a reworded version of a constitutional provision agreed upon on January 30, 1981. The new amendment recognizes "existing aboriginal and treaty rights." Indian groups call for the removal of the word "existing" despite assurances that the word will not alter the intended meaning of the section. The House of Commons also adds a provision that guarantees a federal-provincial conference, with Native participation, to define these existing rights.

DECEMBER 16, 1981 Comprehensive Land Claims Policy. John Munro, Canadian minister of Indian affairs releases "In All Fairness," a new comprehensive Native claims policy document that implies acceptance of aboriginal land title in areas not covered by treaties and announces the government's intention to negotiate fair and equitable settlements that would allow Native people to live the way they wish. It also promises that the land claims process will be speeded up. Comprehensive land claims are defined as land claims covering land that Native groups have never surrendered in a treaty.

1 9 8 2

1982 *Gallahan v. Hollyfield.* The U.S. Court of Appeals finds that in light of an Indian prison inmate's sincere belief in his Cherokee religion, prison authorities cannot require him to cut his hair without better reasons than those advanced by the state. The state claims that long hair prevents easy prisoner identification, provides a place for hiding contraband, and poses a potential sanitary problem. The court, in a rare refutation of prison limitations, reasons that the state's justifications are overly broad and lacking in cause.

JANUARY 1982 Inuit Broadcasting Corporation. The Inuit Broadcasting Corporation launches programming in the Inuktitut language. Since 1958 the Canadian Broadcasting Corporation has produced a modest amount of Native-language television broadcasting in the far north.

JANUARY 7, 1982 Nuclear Waste Policy Act of 1982. Congress passes Public Law 97-245, the Nuclear Waste Policy Act of 1982. The act calls for the "development of repositories for the disposal of high-level radioactive waste and spent nuclear fuel, to establish a program of research, development, and demonstration regarding the disposal of high-level radioactive waste and spent nuclear fuel." Section 2 of the act allows the administrator of the Environmental Protection Agency to authorize such repositories to be located within the boundaries of Indian reservations "upon the petition of the appropriate governmental officials of the tribe."

Passage of this act draws considerable criticism from several tribes who interpret the act as a federal attempt to desecrate Indian lands. Although the act requires that permission be received from appropriate government tribal officials, concern is expressed that tribal officials may not convey or comply with the opinion or wishes of the tribal majority.

JANUARY 21, 1982 Indian Oil and Gas Royalties. In response to a special commission's sharp criticisms of the Interior Department's collection of royalty money, Secretary of the Interior James G. Watt announces a revision in the department's policy for obtaining royalties on oil and natural gas on federal lands.

JANUARY 25, 1982 *Merrion v. Jicarilla Apache Tribe.* The Supreme Court upholds the right of a tribe to impose a severance tax on oil and gas that is extracted and produced by oil companies on reservation land and under leases approved by the secretary of the interior, even though the tax falls on nonmembers.

JANUARY 28, 1982 **British Court Ruling.** The British Court of Appeals rules that Britain no longer has any responsibility for the protection of Native rights in Canada and that these responsibilities have been handed over to Canada. (Most Canadian Indian treaties were made with the British Crown.) Indian groups appeal to the British court in an attempt to convince the British government to prevent patriation (transfer to Canada) of Canada's Constitution (the British North America Act). The British Parliament has the power to block any changes to this constitution. On March 11, the Indians are denied leave to appeal the ruling.

MARCH 1982 **Penticton Okanagan Band Settles Land Claim.** The Penticton Okanagan band becomes the first band in British Columbia to settle its claim for compensation for land "cutoff" its reserve following the McKenna-McBride Commission report in 1916. The band will receive $14.2 million and 4,855 hectares of land. Twenty-one other bands await compensation. Land was removed from 34 reserves.

MARCH 27, 1982 **Land Claim Settled.** The Wagnatcook Micmac band becomes the first in Atlantic Canada to settle a specific land claim. The Nova Scotia band will receive $1.2 million in compensation for land improperly taken from its reserve.

APRIL 14, 1982 **Northern Referendum.** The people of the Northwest Territories vote to approve the division of the Northwest Territories into Denendeh and Nunavut as proposed in Dene and Inuit claims.

APRIL 17, 1982 **Constitution Act.** Canada's new Constitution and Charter of Rights and Freedoms is proclaimed by the British government despite opposition by Canadian Native groups, fulfilling the aim of Prime Minister Pierre Trudeau of patriating (putting under Canadian control) the Canadian constitution. Section 35 of the Constitution says, "The existing aboriginal and treaty rights of the aboriginal peoples of Canada are hereby recognized and affirmed." (Indians, Inuit and Métis are explicitly identified as aboriginal peoples.) The constitution also guarantees aboriginal participation at a conference to define what these existing rights are. Section 25 of the Charter says that its guarantees of equal rights "shall not be construed so as to abrogate or derogate from any aboriginal, treaty or other rights or freedoms that pertain to the aboriginal peoples of Canada including (a) any rights or freedoms that have been recognized by the Royal Proclamation of October 7, 1763; and (b) any rights or freedoms that may be acquired by the aboriginal peoples by way of land claims settlement." Indian groups boycott celebrations and denounce the new Constitution.

APRIL 21, 1982 **New Indian Leader.** David Ahenakew, a Cree from Saskatchewan, is elected to replace Del Riley as the new president of the National Indian Brotherhood. The National Indian Brotherhood announces its reorganization as the Assembly of First Nations (A.F.N.). The A.F.N. becomes an association of chiefs rather than an alliance of bands.

MAY 13, 1982 **Specific Claims Policy.** Canadian Indian Affairs Minister, John Munro releases "Outstanding Business." The statement expresses the government's aim to meet its legal obligations as set out in post-Confederation treaties and the Indian Act. The government specifically addresses those claims that are based on the position that the federal government has not lived up to its responsibilities as set out in treaties or legislation such as the Indian Act.

JUNE 11, 1982   Tlingit Seek Official Apology for Shelling of Village. Tlingit Indians arrive in Washington, D.C. They seek an official apology from the navy for its shelling of their village in the Admiralty Islands in 1882. The navy's actions were undertaken as a means of forcing the Alaskan Indians to return to work for private whalers.

JUNE 21–26, 1982   Inuit Organization. The Inuit Tapirisat of Canada form the Tungavik Federation of Nunavut to represent them in negotiations for the land claim they presented in November, 1971.

JULY 1982   James Bay Agreement. The federal government announces it will set aside $61.4 million to deal with problems with the James Bay and Northern Quebec Agreement. The announcement follows reviews by the Indian Affairs Department (the Tait Report) and the Justice Department that found that the federal government is keeping the letter but not the spirit of the 1975 agreement. The Cree and Inuit claim that the agreement calls for much more federal money.

AUGUST 14, 1982   National Navajo Code Talkers Day. President Ronald Reagan declares National Navajo Code Talkers Day, commemorating the cadre of Navajo servicemen who relayed military defense messages coded in their tribal language during World War II. The Japanese never deciphered the code.

SEPTEMBER 22, 1982   Indian Status. A Canadian Parliamentary Sub-Committee on Indian Women and the Indian Act releases its report calling for the removal of sections that discriminate on the basis of gender. The Su-

U.S. President Ronald Reagan recognizes Navajo code talkers for dedicated service during WWII. Courtesy of Vee Salabiye.

preme Court upheld the discriminatory section in 1973 but the passage of the Charter of Rights, which guarantees gender equality, has put the law in question once again.

OCTOBER 13, 1982   Return of Thorpe Olympic Medals. The International Olympic Committee announces that it will restore to Jim Thorpe's family the two gold medals he won in the 1912 Olympic decathlon and pentathlon events. Thorpe was stripped of his medals for having played minor league baseball for $2 a game. The two medals were returned in a ceremony to Thorpe's daughter Charlotte during the 1984 Olympics in Los Angeles. *(See also* biography, 1888 and entry, 1912.)

NOVEMBER 2, 1982   Navajo Nation Elects Peterson Zah. The Navajo Nation elects Peterson Zah as new tribal chairman. The 44-year-old Zah defeats Peter MacDonald, 53, chairman of the tribal council for the previous 12 years; Zah wins by a vote of 29,208 to 24,665. Founder of the reservation's legal aid organization, Zah pledges to stop further exploitation of energy, minerals, timber, and wa-

Jerry E. Salabiye (left), flanked by WWII veteran Navajo code talkers and his daughter, Deborah Bitah (far right). Courtesy of Vee Salabiye.

ter resources on reservation lands by non-Indians. Zah's platform also includes a proposal that the Navajo and Hopi seek to mediate their dispute over the Joint Use Area without the interference of the federal government.

DECEMBER 30, 1982 Cow Creek Band of Umpqua Tribe Recognized. President Ronald Reagan signs legislation extending federal recognition to approximately 300 members of the Cow Creek band of Umpqua tribe in Oregon.

DECEMBER 30, 1982 Indian Claims Limita-

tion Act of 1982. Congress passes Public Law 97-394, the Indian Claims Limitation Act of 1982, as a part of the appropriations act for the 1983 fiscal year. The act limits the time in which claims may be filed and reads in part that "claims that are on either of the two lists published pursuant to the Indian Claims Act of 1982, any right of action shall be barred unless the complaint is filed within one year after the Secretary of the Interior has published in the Federal Register a notice rejecting such claims or three years after the date the Secretary of the

Interior has submitted legislation or legislative report to Congress to resolve such claim." This act puts time limitations on Indian claims against the United States, and requires Indians to file complaints after their claims have been filed with the secretary of the interior or with Congress.

1 9 8 3

1983 Jicarilla Apache Oil and Gas Wells. The Jicarilla Apache tribe drills oil and gas wells using tribal funds. Through a joint effort, Fort Peck tribes and the U.S. Department of Energy produce oil from a joint venture well.

1983 Minerals Management Service (MMS). The Minerals Management Service (MMS) is created within the Interior Department to manage and collect oil and gas royalties on federal lands, including most Indian lands.

1983 *She Had Some Horses* Is Published. To great critical praise, Creek poet Joy Harjo publishes her second collection of poetry, *She Had Some Horses.* With photographer Steven Strom, Harjo later publishes a group of prose poems and photographs, *Secrets from the Center of the World* (1989). In 1990 another poetry collection is published, *In Mad Love and War,* again to enthusiastic reviews. Awarded a master of fine arts degree from the Iowa Writer's Workshop at the University of Iowa in 1978, Harjo has received a number of awards including an American Book Award and two National Endowment for the Arts Creative Writing Fellowships.

1983 *Southland Royalty Co. et. al. v. Navajo Tribe et. al.* The Tenth Circuit Court of Appeals holds that Navajo taxation of oil and gas leases is a valid exercise of tribal authority, and that approval by the secretary of the interior of this particular tax regulation is not required.

1983 *Williams v. Lee.* A non-Indian person operating a store on an Indian reservation in Arizona brings a collection suit against a Navajo and his wife who live on the reservation; the couple had bought goods using store credit and never paid the bill. The plaintiff sought to address the issue in the Arizona State Court. The question arises, does the state have jurisdiction on a reservation matter? The Supreme Court decides that state law cannot be applied if it interferes with the right of Indians to make their own laws and be governed by them. The court also holds that if a tribe's authority in regard to reservation transactions is to be diminished, then that is an act falling under congressional jurisdiction.

1983 Woodland School Exhibit. The Art Gallery of Ontario in Toronto holds an exhibit of the "Woodland School" of artists, reflecting the recent exposure that Native artists have received in mainstream art circles. The Woodland School, dominated by Cree, Ojibway, and Ottawa artists, is characterized by a pictographic style and bright colors. Ojibway artist, Norval Morriseau *(See* biography, March 14, 1932) is its leading representative.

JANUARY 8 Texas Kickapoo Apply for Citizenship. Congress passes legislation allowing the Texas Kickapoo to apply for U.S. citizenship and for federal services. The Texas or Mexican Kickapoos lived in southern Wisconsin in the early 1800s. However, as hostilities increased, one band fled to Mexico, settling near Nacimiento Kickapoo, 80 miles from the Texas border. Today, the 600 members of this tribe spend their summers in or near Eagle Pass, Texas, working as migrant laborers. In the winters, they return to their home in Mexico for the tribe's sacred winter ceremonial.

JANUARY 12, 1983 Federal Oil and Gas Royalty Management Act of 1982 (FOGRMA). Congress passes Public Law 97-451, the Federal Oil and Gas Royalty Management Act of 1982. Congressional passage of the act provides for cooperative agreements among the secretary of the interior, Indian tribes, and states for the sharing of oil and gas royalty management information. It directs the secretary of the interior to establish a comprehensive inspection, collection, fiscal and production accounting, and auditing system to provide accurate determination of oil and gas royalties, interests, fines, penalties, fees, deposits, and other payments owed on minerals taken from federal (including Indian) lands pursuant to commercial agreements; and collection of and accounting for such amounts. In essence, the act assures renewed federal attention to the collection of royalties that are owed to tribes and that are derived from oil and gas resource leases on tribal land.

JANUARY 12, 1983   Indian Land Consolidation Act. Congress passes Public Law 97-459, the Indian Land Consolidation Act. This act authorizes the purchase, sale, and exchange of lands by Indian tribes, specifically the Devils Lake Sioux tribe of the Devils Lake Sioux Reservation of North Dakota. Section 203 empowers "the Secretary to adopt a land consolidation plan providing for the sale or exchange of any tribal lands or interest in lands for the purpose of eliminating undivided fractional interests in Indian trust or restricted lands or consolidating its tribal land holdings." Passage of the act serves to assists all tribes experiencing problems created by fractional interests within reservation lands.

Historically, tribal reservation lands were allotted under the federally imposed terms of the 1887 General Allotment or Dawes Act. These tribes now possess, in some cases, allotments owned by over 200 individuals. The original allotments were of 80 to 160 acres; these were divided, according to federal regulations, equally among allottee heirs. The act therefore allows tribes to purchase and consolidate these lands in an effort to make them more economically productive.

JANUARY 14, 1983   Indian Tribal Governmental Tax Status Act of 1982. Congress

passes Public Law 97-473, the Indian Tribal Governmental Tax Status Act of 1982, Title II of the Amendments to the Internal Revenue Code Act of 1954. Passage of this act confirms that tribes possess many of the federal tax advantages enjoyed by states. Like states, tribes are acknowledged to have the power to issue tax-exempt bonds to fund tribal economic development projects.

JANUARY 19, 1983   Indian Reservations Compared to Failure of Socialism. Secretary of the Interior James Watt states during a television interview that Indian reservations are "examples of the failures of socialism." "If you want an example of the failures of socialism, don't go to Russia. Come to America, and see the American Indian reservations. . . . Socialism toward the American Indian," Watt says, "led to alcoholism, unemployment, venereal disease, and drug addiction." Watt's remarks provoke an outcry across Indian Country demanding his resignation.

JANUARY 24, 1983   Reagan's Indian Policy Statement. President Ronald Reagan issues the first Indian policy statement since 1975. Emphasizing that "the Constitution, treaties, laws, and court decisions have consistently recognized a unique political relationship between Indian tribes and the United States," the president states his commitment to deal with Indian tribes on a "government-to-government" basis. This emphasis calls to mind previous efforts to strengthen tribal government, Nixon's in the 1970's and Congress's passage of Indian Self-Determination and Education Assistance Act of 1975. However, Reagan's support of tribal sovereignty is consistent with his conservative political philosophy: "Tribal governments, like State and local governments, are more aware of the needs and desires of their citizens than is the Federal Government and should, therefore, have the primary responsibility for meeting those needs."

The address, also promoting economic development on reservations, states the government's support for industrial development of resources on Indian lands. Tribes and the American society "stand to gain from the prudent development and management of the vast coal, oil, gas, uranium and other resources found on Indian lands."

Reagan's address is met with skepticism by many Indian leaders who fear that the underlying message is terminationist in disguise. Ultimately, shifting costs and accountability for Indian programs to tribes themselves becomes the hallmark of Reagan-Bush Indian policy.

JANUARY 25, 1983 *Lac Courte Oreilles Band of Lake Superior Chippewa Indians v. Voigt.* The U.S. Court of Appeals for the Seventh Circuit affirms that the Chippewa treaties with the United States in 1837 and 1842 preserve the rights of six Chippewa bands to hunt, fish, and cut timber in lands they had ceded to the federal government.

JANUARY 31, 1983 **Reagan Budget Proposal.** President Ronald Reagan sends his first budget to Congress. Proposals include a one-third cut in the total budget for Indians *(See entry, January 24, 1983).*

MARCH 1983 **Dennis Banks Granted Asylum.** The Onondaga Nation, located south of Syracuse, New York, agrees to grant asylum to American Indian Movement (AIM) leader Dennis Banks, who is fleeing charges arising from the February 1973 riot at Custer, South Dakota.

MARCH 1983 **National Métis Organization.** Alberta, Saskatchewan, and Manitoba associations of the Native Council of Canada withdraw to form the Métis National Council.

MARCH 15, 1983 **Pacific Salmon Treaty Act of 1983.** Congressional passage of the Pacific Salmon Treaty Act of 1983 clarifies and protects tribal fishing rights set forth in executive orders and Indian treaties as they relate to treaties between the United States and Canada over Pacific salmon fishing.

MARCH 15–16, 1983 **Canadian Constitutional Conference.** At a conference guaranteed by the 1982 Constitution, representatives of Canadian aboriginal peoples, Canadian First Ministers, and the elected governments of Yukon and Northwest Territories agree to alter Section 25 of the charter to recognize all aboriginal rights acquired in past and future land claims settlements. Section 35 of the Constitution will be amended to guarantee gender equality in the enjoyment of treaty rights. Native groups also are guaranteed participation at two more conferences to define the nature and extent of "existing" aboriginal and treaty rights enshrined in Section 35 of the Constitution. This is the first constitutional conference in which Native groups have had full participation. Indian leaders endorse the amendments but express frustration at the slow progress being made on central issues.

MARCH 30, 1983 *Arizona v. California.* In *Arizona v. California,* the Supreme Court rejects a federally appointed fact finder's reporting that five Indian tribes are entitled to receive a larger share of water allocation in the lower basin of the Colorado River. The five tribes are the Cocopah, Fort Mohave, Fort Yuma, Colorado River, and the Chemehuevi; they requested an enlargement of their water rights, allocated in 1964, on the basis of an increase in their respective reservations' sizes.

Protection of Indian water rights is both a crucial and primary issue facing Indian Country. Seventy-five percent of all Indians live in the arid West. As reservation populations boom and tribes seek to improve their economic status, the question of whether the tribes or the states possess the right to the precious water supply, and in what amounts, and for what purposes, becomes critical.

As early as 1970, water rights experts express public concern over the Bureau of Indian Affairs' inadequate protection of Indian water rights. The National Water Commission issues a report in 1973, criticizing the federal

Indian chiefs open the first ministers' conference on aboriginal issues, March 1983. This conference, guaranteed by the 1982 constitution, marked the first time that aboriginals were given full participation at constitutional conferences. Courtesy of Canapress Photo Service.

government for its failure to protect Indian water rights. Pointing out a conflict of interest between the Department of the Interior and the protection of tribal resources, the commission report details how the department supported the construction of irrigation projects on or near reservations, thus diminishing the amount of water available to tribes for their own needs. "In the history of the United States Government's treatment of Indian tribes, its failure to protect Indian water rights for use on the reservations it set aside for them is one of the sorrier chapters," the report says.

MAY 10, 1983 Imprisoned Micmac Acquitted. Micmac Donald Marshall, from Subenacadie, Nova Scotia, is acquitted of a murder charge by the Supreme Court of Nova Scotia. He was convicted of the murder in 1972, and has spent 11 years in jail. The judges rule that because Marshall lied during the original trial, he must bear part of the blame for the original conviction.

JUNE 2, 1983 President Ronald Reagan Criticized. The National Indian Tribal Chairmans' Association holds a news conference criticizing President Ronald Reagan for his failure to uphold his pledge to free tribes of federal regulations and to provide them with greater self-determination.

JUNE 13, 1983 *New Mexico v. Mescalero Apache Tribe.* In *New Mexico v. Mescalero Apache Tribe,* the Supreme Court rules that New Mexico cannot enforce its state laws against non-Indians hunting and fishing on tribal lands within reservation boundaries. The imposition of state laws in this instance, the court states, would interfere with "Congress' overriding objective of encouraging tribal self-government and economic development."

JUNE 24, 1983 *Nevada v. United States.* In *Nevada v. United States,* the Supreme Court unanimously upholds a lower court ruling affirming the allocation of water rights to the Pyramid Lake Reservation in western Nevada.

JULY 1, 1983 *Rice v. Rehner.* In *Rice v. Rehner,* the Supreme Court rules that states have the authority to enforce liquor laws on reservations. The court holds that Rehner requires a state license to sell liquor. To the extent that Rehner seeks to sell to non-Indians or non-tribal Indians, the court writes, a state may impose a nondiscriminatory tax on non-Indian customers. The court states that application of the state licensing scheme does not impair a right granted or reserved by federal law. Hence, tribes lose any inherent preemptive power to regulate liquor sales on reservations as a result of their domestic dependent status.

JULY 15, 1983 *Arizona v. San Carlos Apache Tribe.* In *Arizona v. San Carlos Apache Tribe,* the Supreme Court rules that state courts have the authority to decide water right disputes involving Indians. The decision is another blow to tribes who seek to preserve their water rights. The San Carlos Apache attempted to prove that water right disputes must be settled in federal courts; many tribes fear that state courts, under pressure to protect the progress and development of major cities and areas throughout the West, will not provide tribes with a fair hearing.

JULY 30, 1983 Seminole Judicial System. Fifteen hundred Seminole tribal members, occupying five reservations in southern Florida, approve a referendum establishing a judicial system that will reflect their traditional values and principles. Tribal leaders carefully examine the neighboring system of the Miccosukee tribe, which operates with two judges, one schooled in modern law and the other in traditional law.

SEPTEMBER 13, 1983 American Indian Movement Co-Founder Dennis Banks Surrenders. American Indian Movement (AIM) co-founder Dennis Banks surrenders to state authorities in Rapid City, South Dakota, following nine years as a fugitive. Banks's surrender allows the state to prosecute him for assault and rioting charges stemming from the February 1973 Custer incident and his subsequent flight to avoid prosecution. Banks, who states that he feared for his life, explains that he gave himself up for the sake of his family. Banks spent six years in California under the protection of Gov. Jerry Brown, fleeing to the Onondaga Reservation in New York after Brown's successor, Gov. George Deukmejian, indicated his willingness to extradite Banks to South Dakota. New York governor Mario Cuomo agrees to return Banks to South Dakota but forbids marshals from entering the Onondaga Reservation near Syracuse, New York.

OCTOBER 1, 1983 American Indian Registry Established. The American Indian Registry for the Performing Arts, a nonprofit organization for Indians in the media, is established in Los Angeles. Its founders include Creek/Muskogee Indian actor Will Sampson. The agency publishes an annual American Indian Talent Directory and works as a liaison with studios, producers, and casting directors to promote the hiring of Native Americans within the motion picture industry. Bonnie Paradise (Shoshoni/Paiute) becomes the registry's executive director in 1990; currently, more than 300 Native American performers and technicians are members.

OCTOBER 20, 1983   Pequot Indians Become a Federally Recognized Tribe. President Ronald Reagan signs legislation acknowledging the Mashantucket Pequot Indians of Connecticut as a federally recognized tribe with all powers of self-government. This legislation also provides for a $900,000 appropriation to the Pequot for the purchase of land near their reservation. The president vetoed a similar bill on April 10, 1983.

NOVEMBER 3, 1983   Aboriginal Self-Government in Canada. The Report of the Special Parliamentary Committee on Indian Self-Government (the Penner Report), headed by Liberal Party Member of Parliament for Kenora Keith Penner, unanimously agrees that the aboriginal right to self-government should be entrenched in the Constitution. It suggests that Indian governments should be formed as a distinct order of government, with authority to control reserve land and resources. It suggests that present reserves are too small. The commission also recommends abolishing the Indian Act and the Indian Affairs Department. The report receives unanimous support in the House of Commons.

1 9 8 4

1984   Environmental Protection Policy and Indian Governments. The Fort Peck tribes produce oil from tribally owned wells. The Environmental Protection Agency (EPA) adopts an Indian policy supporting the primary role of tribal governments in reservation environmental matters.

1984   Indian Education. The Canadian Edu-

cation Association reports that Indian bands that have control of Indian education are witnessing marked improvement in student achievement. Since 1970, increasing numbers of Indian bands have taken over control of Indian education.

1984   Indian Status. The Canadian federal government introduces revisions to the Indian Act to remove sections which discriminate against women. (The bill fails to pass before the next election.)

1984   Saskatchewan Indian Policy. A new government in Saskatchewan announces that it will not negotiate land transfers according to the Saskatchewan Formula of 1977, but according to population figures at the times treaties were signed. This will reduce potential land transfers by about 155,000 acres.

1984   Siksika Claim Settled. A Siksika band of southern Alberta agrees to $1.675 million compensation for cattle promised in Treaty 7 that was never delivered.

JANUARY 26, 1984   Yukon Land Claim. The Council of Yukon Indians sign an agreement-in-principle to settle their land claim with the federal government. The Indians would retain title to 20,000 square kilometers of land and would get $540 million over 20 years to surrender their aboriginal land rights. National Native groups condemn this last provision.

MARCH 8–9, 1984   Canadian Constitutional Conference. The second First Ministers' constitutional conference on aboriginal issues ends with an agreement to amend the Indian Act to guarantee gender equality but without an agreement on the major aim of defining aboriginal rights. Six premiers reject a proposed amendment that would recognize the right to aboriginal self-government, complaining that its wording is too vague. The federal government offers a compromise amendment that would recognize the right of aboriginals to have self-governing institutions to meet their communities' needs, but the amendment is not accepted.

MARCH 25, 1984 Cherokee Joint Council Meeting. Members of the Eastern Cherokee and the Cherokee Nation of Oklahoma hold their first joint council meeting in 146 years. An estimated 10,000 tribal members attend the historic meeting held at the Cherokee's sacred ground in Red Clay, Tennessee.

In the late 1830s, 16,000 Cherokee are forcibly removed from their ancestral lands in Tennessee, North Carolina, Georgia, and Alabama by Andrew Jackson's army. One-fourth of those forcibly relocated died along the route known as the Trail of Tears. Descendants of those who completed the trip now live around Tahlequah, Oklahoma. A few hundred Cherokee successfully eluded removal by hiding in the hills of western North Carolina. Their descendants now form the Eastern Cherokee.

The two tribes, confirming their permanent split, agree to meet annually in the Council of Cherokee to discuss and plan for issues and needs of common concern.

MAY 17, 1984 Indian Status. Alberta Indians walk out of an Assembly of First Nations (A.F.N.) meeting because of disagreement over the gender equality amendment. The Assembly of First Nations supports an amendment that would restore Indian status to many women and their offspring who were affected by a law denying status to Indian women who married non-Indians. Alberta Indian bands oppose the amendment because they fear the effects on their communities should they be forced to accept large numbers of new members.

JUNE 5, 1984 Inuvialuit Land Claim. The Final Agreement is reached on the comprehensive claim of the Committee of Original People's Entitlement (C.O.P.E.) on behalf of the 2,500 Inuvialuit of the Mackenzie Valley. This is the first comprehensive land claims settlement north of the sixtieth parallel. The agreement calls for the Inuvialuit to surrender their aboriginal rights in return for the rights and benefits provided in the agreement. These rights include a cash settlement and provisions regarding wildlife, the environment, and economic development. The agreement is unique in that it gives the Inuvialuit outright ownership of 82,880 square kilometers (32,000 square miles) including subsurface rights in 13,000 square kilometers (5,000 square miles.) It also allows the Inuvialuit to participate in wildlife management decisions. The federal government agrees to establish a 13,000-square-kilometer (5,000 square miles) National Wilderness Area in which the Inuit will enjoy hunting, trapping, and fishing rights. Native leaders criticize the provisions which would have the Inuit give up their aboriginal rights in exchange for the rights specified by the agreement. C.O.P.E. was formed in 1969 to represent the claims of all the aboriginal groups of the Mackenzie Valley, but by 1984 represents only the Inuvialuit. (See map of Comprehensive Land Claims in Canada, pp. 483–85.)

JUNE 8, 1984 Senate Select Committee on Indian Affairs. The U.S. Senate agrees to make the Senate Select Committee on Indian Affairs a permanent body. The body, responsible for the consideration of Indian affairs and oversights, was established on a temporary basis in 1977.

JUNE 12, 1984 Newfoundland Micmac Band. The Micmac, who settled at Conne River, Newfoundland in 1870, are recognized as an Indian band under the Indian Act. This is the only recognized Indian band on the island of Newfoundland.

JUNE 21, 1984 Constitutional Amendments. The first amendments to the Canadian Constitution are proclaimed. The two amendments are provisions agreed upon at the First Ministers' Conference in March 1983.

JULY 3, 1984 James Bay Agreement Implementation. The Canadian government proclaims the Cree-Naskapi (of Quebec) Act according to a provision in the James Bay and Northern Quebec Agreement of 1975. The act gives the Natives of northern Quebec a type of self-government. The Cree and Naskapi (Innu) no longer fall under the jurisdiction of the Indian Act.

JULY 5, 1984 Cayuga Land Claims. The Cayuga Indian Nation agrees to accept approximately 8,500 acres of land in Cayuga and Seneca counties of New York State. This agreement is a final settlement against the state for the illegal appropriation of 64,000 acres.

JULY 22, 1984 Tribes Protest Police Jurisdiction on Reservations. In Connecticut, three of the five local Indian tribes protest the state's assumption of police jurisdiction on their reservations.

SEPTEMBER 2, 1984 Pequot Land Claims. The Mashantucket Pequot Indians from eastern Connecticut take possession of 650 acres of land. Tribal title to the land ends an eight-year struggle by the Pequot to regain former reservation lands.

SEPTEMBER 9–20, 1984 Pontiff Visits Canada. Pope John Paul II visits Canada, but fog forces him to cancel a planned visit to Fort Simpson, Northwest Territories, where he has intended to deliver a speech sympathetic to aboriginal peoples' demands for self-government. He promises to return to Fort Simpson at a future date. Most of the Indians of the Mackenzie Valley are Roman Catholic. The pope keeps his promise to visit Fort Simpson in September 1987.

SEPTEMBER 23, 1984 Santa Fe Newspaper Apologizes. *The New Mexican* newspaper in Santa Fe apologizes to the Santo Domingo Indian community for its publication of two photos of sacred dances. The community posts a policy that forbids the taking of photographs at sacred ceremonies.

OCTOBER 8, 1984 Dennis Banks Sentenced. Dennis Banks is sentenced to three years in prison for his part in the Custer courthouse riot in 1973. (*See* entry, February 6–8, 1973.)

OCTOBER 19, 1984 Indian Education Amendments of 1984. Congress passes Public Law 95-511, the Indian Education Amendments of 1984. Title V of the act contains provisions to improve educational standards, contract schools to local Indian communities in accordance with the Indian self-determination policy, and to extend other Indian programs.

OCTOBER 23, 1984 *Delgamuukw v. The Queen.* The Gitskan and Wet'suwet'en (Western Carrier) Indians of the Skeena and Bulkley River valleys of northern British Columbia (B.C.) initiate a court action to claim over 57,000 square kilometers of northwestern and north-central B.C. (*See* map of Comprehensive Land Claims in Canada, pp. 483–85.)

NOVEMBER 1, 1984 The Musqueam Case. In the *Guerin v. The Queen* case, the Supreme Court of Canada rules that the Canadian government must pay the Musqueam Coast Salish band (Vancouver) $10 million because it violated its legal obligations to the band when it leased out reserve land in 1958 under terms not approved by the band. The court also rules that Indians have special right to the land because they were its first inhabitants, not because of special government legislation such as the Royal Proclamation of 1763.

NOVEMBER 30, 1984 Indian Reservation Economies Report. The Presidential Commission on Indian Reservation Economies presents its report to President Ronald Reagan. Characterizing the Bureau of Indian Affairs' organization and administration as "byzantine" and "incompetent," the report calls for the BIA's replacement with an Indian Trust Services Administration. As an illustration of the BIA's top-heavy administration and over-regulation, the report points out that two-thirds of the BIA's budget goes into administration; less than one-third of the federal funds reach the reservations.

Other recommendations in the report include the placement of tribal businesses in individual hands, the subordination of tribal courts to federal courts in interpreting law, the reduction of tribal immunity, and the allowance of tribal taxation only after the vote of all Indian and non-Indian residents on the reservation. The report further recommends that tribal leaders and federal officials tackle the issue of tribal self-determination through private economic development. The report immediately draws a cool reception from many tribes.

DECEMBER 17–18, 1984 Canadian Constitutional Talks. Federal, provincial, and territorial leaders and Native leaders meet to discuss Native constitutional issues in preparation for a conference in March, where Canada's first ministers will propose and discuss constitutional amendments on Native rights. The meeting focuses on self-government rights of Native communities within a proposed Canadian Constitution. They make little progress.

DECEMBER 20, 1984 Yukon Land Claim. The Canadian federal government announces that the Yukon land-claims agreement has collapsed because several Indian bands want to renegotiate the deal.

---

1 9 8 5

1985 *Love Medicine* Wins National Book Critics Circle Prize. The year after its release, the first novel by Turtle Mountain Chippewa writer Louise Erdrich wins great critical acclaim and several major awards, including the National Book Critics Circle Prize and the Los Angeles Times Book Prize. Actually a collection of integrally related short stories, *Love Medicine* is the tale of several Chippewa families told through multiple generations. In later publications like *Tracks* (1988), Erdrich continues the family stories told in *Love Medicine*. Another novel, *The Beet Queen* (1986), explores the Germanic side of Erdrich's mixed-blood heritage. Prior to her first novel, Erdrich published her first poetry collection, *Jacklight,* which also received much praise from reviewers. In 1992 she completed *The Crown of Columbus,* which she wrote in collaboration with her husband, Modoc author Michael Dorris. In another story about the people and life on the Turtle Mountain Chippewa Reservation, her novel *The Bingo Palace* (1993) gained strong early praise.

1985 Navaho Tribe's Right to Impose Taxes. The U.S. Supreme Court confirms the Navaho tribe's right to impose taxes without approval of the secretary of the interior. The Royalty Management Advisory Committee is created to advise the secretary on royalty valuation issues. At issue are the interrelated and sometimes conflicting goals of economic development of valuable tribal resources balanced by environmental responsibility.

JANUARY 9, 1985 Kickapoo Land Purchase. Charitable contributions provide for the purchase of a 125-acre land parcel on the Rio Grande near Eagle Pass, Texas. The land is intended for the resettlement of the Kickapoo tribe.

JANUARY 11, 1985 The National Tribal Council Association Rejects Private Enterprises. The National Tribal Council Association, a national group comprised of tribal political leaders, votes 84-18 to reject a proposed program for the development of private enterprises on Indian reservations. As explained by NTCA executive director Elmer Savilla, the program's philosophy is in direct opposition to the "Indian way," which is "to go into business to provide income for tribal members," and "to provide employment for as many tribal members as you can."

FEBRUARY 11, 1985 Wyandot Land Claims. The federal government agrees to pay $5.5

million to members of the Wyandot Indians of Kansas and Oklahoma. The payment is retribution for the forced sale of ancestral aboriginal lands, for which the Wyandot originally received purchase amounts far below fair market value in 1842.

FEBRUARY 20, 1985 *Dann et al. v. United States.* The Supreme Court rejects a suit brought by two Shoshoni Indians claiming ownership of 5,100 acres of the tribe's aboriginal homeland. In 1951, the Shoshoni tribe sought compensation for the loss of their lands. Subsequently, they were awarded $26 million by the Indian Claims Commission. The tribe refused payment of the funds, requesting the return of their Native lands instead. The court rules that the Shoshoni, by placing the payment funds in an interest-bearing account, extinguished all claims to their lands.

FEBRUARY 26, 1985 **Grise Fiord Relocation.** Inuit from Grise Fiord, Ellesmere Island, in Canada's high Arctic, meet with Indian Affairs minister John Crosbie to seek help to move south. The Inuit were relocated from Port Harrison (Inukjuak), Quebec, in 1953. The government argues that the relocation was made in the best interests of the Inuit, but the Inuit claim the government moved them to assert its sovereignty over northern Arctic islands.

MARCH 4, 1985 *County of Oneida v. Oneida Nation.* The Supreme Court upholds the right of the Oneida Nation of New York State to sue for lands illegally taken in 1795.

MARCH 5, 1985 **Winnebago Calendar Sticks.** The *Journal of the Society for American Archaeology* reports that scientists, through the analysis of Winnebago calendar sticks, have the first evidence that tribes, using systematic astronomical observations, had developed advanced full-year calendars.

MARCH 15, 1985 **Pacific Salmon Treaty Act of 1985.** Congress passes Public Law 99-5, the Pacific Salmon Treaty Act of 1985, an act

giving effect to a treaty concerning Pacific salmon fishing that was signed on January 28, 1985, and involving the U.S. and Canadian governments. The act passes due to the intervention and support of northwestern tribes dependent upon fishing for cultural and economic survival. The law clarifies Indian treaties and executive orders specifically addressing the matter of Native fishing rights. Many legislators and biologists hail the act as the most important key to saving the salmon runs from extinction.

APRIL 2–3, 1985 **Constitutional Conference.** At a Canadian Constitutional conference on aboriginal issues, four premiers refuse to approve a constitutional amendment that would entrench the Indian right to self-government without a clear definition of such a right. The Assembly of First Nations refuses an amendment that would entrench the principle of self-rule for aboriginals but would not guarantee a process for defining such powers. The proposal is supported by the necessary seven provinces as well as by the Métis National Council and the Native Council of Canada, but is rejected by the Assembly of First Nations. The participants agree to meet again in June.

APRIL 16, 1985 *Kerr-McGee Corp. v. Navajo Tribe.* The Supreme Court unanimously upholds the right of the Navajo Nation to tax businesses located on the reservation without first obtaining federal approval. The decision allows the Navajo to continue taxation of mineral leases on reservation lands.

MAY 7, 1985 **Canadian Funding Cuts Recommended.** Some additional contents of a preliminary report of the Nielson Task Force, commissioned to find ways to reduce government spending and conducted by Member of Parliament Erik Nielson, are leaked less than a month after other contents of the report are revealed. Noting that the Department of Indian Affairs is failing to improve conditions for Canada's Indians, the report recommends the dissolution of the Department of Indian Affairs and the transfer of responsibility for Indian programs to the provinces. It also urges the government to stop negotiating comprehensive land claims and to cut funding to Indian organizations. It explains how the government can save $312.3 million by cutting funding to Native housing, education, medical, economic, and land-claims programs. Indian organizations condemn the report, comparing it to the White Paper of 1969. Prime Minister Mulroney says the report is not government policy.

MAY 16, 1985   Sioux and Assiniboine Water Allocations. Montana Governor Ted Schwinden signs an agreement with the Sioux and Assiniboine tribes guaranteeing water allocations between the tribes and their neighbors.

JUNE 3, 1985   *Montana v. Blackfeet Tribe*. The Supreme Court upholds a Court of Appeals ruling stating that Montana cannot tax the royalty interests earned by the Blackfeet from leases issued in accordance with the Indian Mineral Leasing Act of 1938.

JUNE 5–6, 1985   Canadian Constitutional Conference. Constitutional talks with First Ministers and aboriginal organizations fail to make progress in defining Indian rights to self-government. The federal government announces that it will begin negotiating self-government agreements with individual Native bands.

JUNE 14–17, 1985   Saskatchewan Natives Protest. About 150 Chipewyan Indians and Métis from the area surrounding Wollaston Lake in northern Saskatchewan block access to uranium mines in the region. The 300 residents of Wollaston say that they mines contaminate fish and wildlife but offer the Natives little employment opportunity.

JUNE 28, 1985   Bill C-31. Bill C-31 (Indian Amendment Act, 1985) removes sections of the Canadian Indian Act that discriminate against women. The amendment is made in order to harmonize the Indian Act with the new Charter of Rights and Freedoms. Some Indians protest that the federal government has no right to define who is or is not an Indian. Many Indian bands, concerned about the effect that a sudden influx of new status Indians would have on reserve life and band funds, refuse to accept the so-called "C-31 Women" as band members.

JULY 2, 1985   Apache Offer Tax-Exempt Municipal Bonds. The Jicarilla Apache tribe of New Mexico becomes the first tribe to offer tax-exempt municipal bonds to institutional investors. The tribe issues $30.2 million in revenue bonds.

JULY 29–31, 1985   Indians Split over Strategy. The Prairie Treaty Nations Alliance (P.T.N.A.), accounting for approximately a third of the membership of the Assembly of First Nations (A.F.N.), walks out of an A.F.N. convention in Vancouver over disagreements arising out of the A.F.N.'s negotiating strategy with the government. The Prairie Indians, unlike the A.F.N. leadership, believe that Indians should refuse to negotiate with the provinces. This defection follows earlier defections by Alberta and Atlantic organizations. Incumbent A.F.N. leader David Ahenakew from Saskatchewan, facing questions about the A.F.N.'s $3.6 million debt, becomes leader of the P.T.N.A. Georges Erasmus (*See* biography, August 8, 1948), a Dene from the Northwest Territories, is chosen president of the A.F.N.

AUGUST 15, 1985   Indian Education Technical Amendments Act of 1985. Congress passes Public Law 99-89, the Indian Education Technical Amendments Act of 1985, amending Title XI of 1978's Education Amendments concerning Indian education. This act specifies school boundaries, the functions of the Bureau of Indian Affairs, and the availability of appropriations.

SEPTEMBER 19–21, 1985   International Inuit Organization. The Inuit Circumpolar Conference (I.C.C.) meets in Montreal. Participants from Canada, the United States, Greenland, and Scandinavia discuss issues of mutual concern. The conference calls for the Canadian government to pay more attention to issues important to the Inuit. The I.C.C., first organized in Alaska in 1977, aims to promote Inuit unity, dignity, political rights, and economic self-sufficiency.

OCTOBER 2, 1985 Arapaho and Shoshoni Youth Suicide. A news service reports the suicides of nine young Arapaho and Shoshoni Indians on the Wind River Reservation in Wyoming. In a period of just two months these Indian youths died as a consequence of hanging themselves. The reservation, with 6,000 people and an unemployment rate of 80 percent, reports 48 suicide attempts in 1985. The National Center of Health states that the suicide rate at Wind River, at 233 suicides per 100,000, is almost 20 times higher than the national average of 12 per 100,000.

OCTOBER 3, 1985 Indian Affairs Streamlining. Canadian Indian Affairs Minister David Crombie announces a reorganization of the department in order to reduce manpower and move toward Indian self-government. He says money saved will be used to the benefit of Indians.

OCTOBER 9, 1985 Canadian Religious Leaders Back Native Aspirations. Leaders of the Roman Catholic, Anglican, Evangelical Lutheran, and United churches issue a call for the governments to recognize aboriginal rights, including their right to self-government. They also criticize British Columbia's policy of refusing to recognize aboriginal title.

NOVEMBER 1985 Haida Protest Logging. Seventy-two Haida and their supporters are arrested while trying to prevent logging on Lyell Island (Queen Charlotte Islands, B.C.) The Haida, who have protested logging in the area

since 1974, filed a claim in 1983, and set up a blockade on October 30 after the British Columbia government approved logging on the island. The federal government and environmentalists have expressed interest in establishing a national park in the region.

NOVEMBER 21, 1985 The *Simon* Case. The Supreme Court of Canada, in the *R. v. Simon* case, finds that a 1752 treaty between the British and the Micmac, which granted the Micmac of Nova Scotia certain hunting and fishing rights, still takes precedence over provincial game laws. A lower court had ruled that the peace treaty was nullified when the Micmac killed six Englishmen on a ship in May 1753.

NOVEMBER 22, 1985 Dennis Banks Paroled. American Indian Movement (AIM) leader Dennis Banks is granted parole from the South Dakota Penitentiary. He serves approximately one year of a three-year prison term arising from a 1973 disturbance at Custer County courthouse in South Dakota.

NOVEMBER 22, 1985 Kickapoo Tribe of Texas and Mexico Issue Citizenship Card. The Kickapoo tribe of Oklahoma issues 143 citizenship cards to members of the Kickapoo of Texas and Mexico. These cards acknowledge the latter Indians' status as a "subgroup" of the Kickapoo tribe of Oklahoma.

DECEMBER 1985 Coolican Report. Indian Affairs Minister David Crombie issues *Living Treaties: Lasting Agreements* (the Coolican Report), a report prepared by Halifax consultant Murray Coolican on the government's comprehensive land claims policy. The report notes that little progress has been made in settling land claims. It suggests that the government seek to settle Indian and Métis claims through negotiation rather than litigation. The new policy statement announces that land claims agreements should not necessarily require Natives to surrender their aboriginal rights and should be viewed as flexible over time. The policy also calls for agreements that will allow Native peoples to share in the financial rewards of development in their territories. Native organizations welcome the new policy as a breakthrough.

DECEMBER 1985 Ojibway Compensated. The Ojibway of the Grassy Narrows band and nearby Whitedog Reserve in northwestern Ontario accept an offer of $16.7 million from the federal and Ontario governments as compensation for mercury poisoning on both reserves and for land on the Whitedog Reserve flooded by a hydroelectric project in 1958.

DECEMBER 14, 1985 Wilma Mankiller Sworn In as Principal Chief of Cherokee Nation. In Oklahoma, the Cherokee Nation swears Wilma Mankiller into their council position of principal chief. Mankiller had served as principal chief since 1985 by stepping in for the elected chief from her position as deputy chief; it is not until 1987 that she is officially elected to the position. The nation, the largest Indian tribe in the country after the Navajo, is headed by a 15-member council. Mankiller becomes the first woman in modern history to lead a large tribe.

1 9 8 6

1986 *The Sacred Hoop* Is Published. Written by poet Paula Gunn Allen, this collection of essays has become a standard introduction to the field of American Indian literature. By the time *The Sacred Hoop* is published, Allen is already the author of numerous books of poetry and a novel and has edited *Studies in American Indian Literature* (1983), an influential collection of essays, bibliographies, and course designs published by the Modern Language Association. Of mixed Laguna Pueblo, Sioux, and Lebanese descent, Allen works with concepts and aesthetics distinctive to American Indian

Wilma Mankiller. Courtesy of Cherokee Nation Public Affairs.

culture; she thereby develops a different methodological approach to Indian literary materials. The essays in *The Sacred Hoop* are frequently reprinted, and Allen's approach has had great effect on American Indian literary criticism.

FEBRUARY 14, 1986 Smithsonian Agrees to Return Indian Skeletal Remains. The Smithsonian Institution's Museum of Natural History agrees to return Indian skeletal remains to tribal leaders for reburial, in those instances where a clear biological or cultural link can be established. Several Indian organizations, while applauding the museum's decision, request that all Indian remains be returned for reburial as required by Indian spiritual beliefs. Studies estimate that more than 1 million Indian remains are in the possession of museums and universities.

MARCH 24, 1986 White Earth Reservation Lands Settlement Act of 1985. Congress signs Public Law 99-264, the White Earth Reservation Lands Settlement Act of 1985, settling "unresolved claims relating to certain allotted Indian lands on the White Earth Reservation, to remove clouds from the titles to certain lands," regarding checkerboard Chippewa and non-Chippewa land ownership.

MAY 15, 1986　Lummi Treaty Rights. The Lummi Indian tribe of western Washington fights a demand from the Internal Revenue Service requesting that Indian fishers pay an income tax on the sale of salmon caught by the tribe in Puget Sound. The tribe argues that their natural resources, as guaranteed to the tribe by treaty, are immune from taxation.

JUNE 3, 1986　Catawba Land Claims. The Catawba lose a major case before the Supreme Court in their quest to reclaim 144,000 acres of aboriginal lands now in private hands. The court rules that the tribe lost the opportunity to bring a suit due to a statute of limitations.

AUGUST 27, 1986　Klamath Restoration Act. Congress passes Public Law 99-398, which reinstates its federal relationship with the Klamath, Modoc, and the Yahooskin band of Snake Indians of Oregon. The approximately 3,000-member Klamath tribe was one of the first terminated by Congress in the 1950s. The Klamath, Modoc, and Snake, along with the Menominee of Wisconsin, are the largest tribes to be terminated. The act specifically provides "for the restoration of the Federal trust relationship with, Federal services and assistance to the Klamath Tribe of Indians and the individual members thereof consisting of the Klamath and Modoc Tribes and the Yahooskin Band of Snake Indians." The federal trust relation refers to the U.S. governments' responsibility, spelt out in many treaties and legal cases, to protect the land and political and cultural autonomy of Indian communities from exploitation or encroachment by non-Indian interests.

SEPTEMBER 7, 1986　New Hampshire Reburial of Indian Remains. New Hampshire announces the designation of an official site for the reburial of repatriated Indian remains and artifacts.

OCTOBER 9, 1986　Sechelt Self-Government.

Legislation is passed giving self-government to the Sechelt band of Salish Indians in British Columbia. The band has agreed to a form of self-government akin to a municipal government.

OCTOBER 17, 1986　American Indian, Alaska Native, and Native Hawaiian Culture and Art Development Act. Congress passes Public Law 99-498, an act developing a corporation to be known as the Institute of American Indian and Alaska Native Culture and Arts Development. The institute, to be administered by a board of trustees, will acknowledge and promote the contributions of Native arts to American society.

OCTOBER 27, 1986　Indian Alcohol and Substance Abuse Prevention and Treatment Act. Congress passes the Indian Alcohol and Substance Abuse Prevention and Treatment Act. Under Part 1, General Provisions of the Anti-Drug Abuse Act, this legislation attempts to prevent the trafficking of illegal narcotics in Indian country. It also seeks to develop programs for the prevention and treatment of alcohol and substance abuse. Statistics show that, when adjusted for age, Indians are four times more likely to die from alcoholism than the general population, four of the top ten causes of death among Indians are alcohol related, and Indians between the ages of 15 and 24 years are twice as likely to die from vehicular accidents, 75 percent of which are alcohol related.

OCTOBER 27, 1986　Indian Civil Rights Act. Congress passes an amended Indian Civil Rights Act which allows tribal courts to impose fines of up to $5,000 and one year in jail for criminal offenses perpetrated by Indian people on Indian reservations.

NOVEMBER 4, 1986　Peter MacDonald Reelected as Navajo Tribal Chairman. Peter MacDonald regains his elected position as the tribal chairman of the Navajo Nation, the largest Indian group in the United States. MacDonald, chairman from 1970 to 1982, defeated the incumbent, Peterson Zah.

NOVEMBER 6, 1986   Ben Nighthorse Campbell Elected to U.S. House of Representatives. Ben Nighthorse Campbell, a member of the Northern Cheyenne tribe of Montana, is elected to the U.S. House of Representatives from the third district of Colorado. Campbell is the second Indian elected to the U.S. House of Representatives in recent times. Ben Reifel, a Sioux from South Dakota, served in the House from 1961 to 1971.

NOVEMBER 19, 1986   Grandfather Plaque Dedicated. The Grandfather Plaque, or the American Indian Vietnam Plaque, is dedicated at Arlington National Cemetery in Virginia. The plaque commemorates the service of approximately 43,000 indigenous combatants who served in Vietnam. An estimated one out of every four eligible Indian males served in Vietnam.

DECEMBER 1986   Comprehensive Claims Policy. Canadian Indian Affairs Minister Bill McKnight unveils a new comprehensive land claims policy which announces the government's intention to restrict land claims negotiations specifically to land issues (as opposed to self-government issues). The government will seek to make once-for-all settlements with Indians. The policy differs considerably from the recommendations made in the Coolican Report of December 1985. The government defines comprehensive claims made for land not covered by any treaty.

DECEMBER 1986   Cree Land Claim Resolved. A Cree band at Fort Chipewyan, in northeastern Alberta, settles a claim for treaty land entitlement. For land promised in Treaty 8, the band receives 4,969.5 hectares (12,280 acres) and cash.

DECEMBER 1986   *Loyalties* Opens. *Loyalties* opens in Toronto. A dramatic piece, it focuses upon a tragic liaison between an English family and their Métis neighbors in northern Alberta. Directed by Anne Wheeler, the film features the Cree/Métis actress Tantoo Cardinal in a leading role. Cardinal's stirring performance wins her rave reviews by Canadian critics as well as a Genie Award nomination (the Canadian equivalent of an Oscar) for Best Actress in a Feature-Length Film. One reviewer notes that "she all but steals the film."

1 9 8 7

JANUARY 1, 1987   Isleta Pueblo Elects Female Governor. The Isleta Pueblo elects Verna Olguin Williamson its first female governor. Isleta Pueblo is located near Albuquerque, New Mexico.

FEBRUARY 25, 1987   *California v. Cabazon Band of Mission Indians.* The U.S. Supreme Court holds that California may not regulate bingo and gambling on the Cabazon and Morongo reservations. The Court rules that neither Public Law 280, granting the state of California criminal jurisdiction over offenses committed in Indian country and within the state, nor the 1970 Organized Crime Control Act, which makes certain violations of state gambling laws federal offenses, expresses the consent of Congress to the application of California state statutes or municipal ordinances to such activities.

MARCH 8, 1987   Wampanoag Tribal Council of Gay Head, Inc., Indian Claims Settlement Act of 1987. Congress passes Public Law 100-95, the Wampanoag Tribal Council of Gay Head, Inc., Indian Claims Settlement Act of 1987, an act "to settle Indian land claims in the town of Gay Head, Massachusetts" with the state of Massachusetts surrendering up to $2,250,000 for land purchase in trust for Wampanoag Tribal Council of Gay

Head, Inc., in return for extinguishment of Native land title. On August 23 ceding to the Wampanoag more than 400 acres of undeveloped land located on Martha's Vineyard, Massachusetts, the Bureau of Indian Affairs extends federal recognition to the Wampanoag Indians of Gay Head, Massachusetts.

MARCH 26–27, 1987 Canadian Constitutional Conference. The final Constitutional Conference on aboriginal issues guaranteed by amendments to the Constitution of 1982 ends with no agreement on how to define Indian rights to self-government, and no agreement to meet again. Differences center around the concept of the "inherent" aboriginal right to self-government. Aboriginal groups argue that their right to self-government is inherent—a right they held since before Europeans came to North America, and one which they never relinquished. Several provincial governments and the federal government are willing to recognize a delegated and well-defined right to self-government.

APRIL 30, 1987 Meech Lake Accord. The Canadian prime minister and the premiers unanimously agree on a constitutional reform package that becomes known as the Meech Lake Accord. The First Ministers have sought the new constitutional package because Quebec has refused to sign the Constitution of 1982. This reform package makes no reference to aboriginal issues.

MAY 28, 1987 Meech Lake Accord Denounced. Canadian Native leaders hold a press conference to accuse the First Ministers of holding a double standard in the Meech Lake Accord. They accuse the governments of being willing to enshrine an undefined recognition of Quebec as a distinct society after rejecting amendments guaranteeing aboriginal rights to self-government because they are poorly defined. They also protest that they were shut out of these constitutional talks.

JULY 1, 1987 New National Park. The Canadian federal government announces an agreement with the British Columbia government to establish a national park in the South Moresby region of the Queen Charlotte Islands. The Haida have been protesting logging operations in the area.

SEPTEMBER 18, 1987 Pope John Paul II Speaks to American Indian Leaders. Pope John Paul II speaks to a group of 1,600 American Indian leaders in Phoenix, Arizona. He urges them to forget the past and to focus on the church's current support of Indian rights. An American Indian Catholic attendee responds, stating to the pope that the Catholic Church still has much to accomplish in the United States.

OCTOBER 1987 Lubicon Claim. Negotiations resume between the Lubicon Lake Cree band in northern Alberta and the federal government regarding the band's claim. The Lubicon Lake Cree band was missed when the government and Northern Alberta Indians signed Treaty 8 in 1899. The band launched a claim in 1933 and was promised a reserve in 1940, but no reserve was ever given. In 1980, an access road was built to the band's settlement area, and about 400 oil wells were drilled, seriously disrupting the band's hunting and trapping lifestyle and leading most members to turn to welfare. Negotiations with the government broke down in July 1986.

OCTOBER 9, 1987 Indian Religious Freedom. The U.S. Justice Department formally drops all charges against Seminole Chief James E. Billie, who killed a rare species of Florida panther and was arrested for violating the Endangered Species Act. Billie admitted killing the panther in December 1983. He claimed religious freedom as the basis for this action in addition to rights guaranteed per a Seminole and U.S. treaty of 1842. Billie's first hearing ends in mistrial on August 27. The jury disputes whether Billie could identify the panther while hunting at night. Billie's second trial ends in an acquittal October 8.

NOVEMBER 5, 1987 Indian Tribal Judgment Funds Use or Distribution Act. Congress passes Public Law 100-152, the Indian Tribal Judgment Funds Use or Distribution Act, "to make miscellaneous technical and minor amendments to laws relating to Indians" for clarification. The act is also known as Indian Law Technical Amendments of 1987.

DECEMBER 2, 1987 Cherokee Removal Commemorated. The U.S. House of Representatives passes a bill commemorating the centennial anniversary of the army's forced removal of the Cherokee from the southeastern portion of the United States to northeastern Oklahoma.

1 9 8 8

1988 Natives and the Law. The Canadian Bar Association issues a report denouncing the impact of Canada's justice system on Natives. It calls for reform that would allow for a self-administered aboriginal justice system.

JANUARY 11, 1988 Cheyenne Tribal Sovereignty. In Montana, the Northern Cheyenne tribe proposes to exercise its inherent right to tax by levying a tax on Bureau of Indian Affairs contractors operating within reservation boundaries.

FEBRUARY 1, 1988 Tuscarora Seize Newspaper Office. Two Tuscarora Indians seize the office of the *Robesonian* in Lumberton, North Carolina. The two men hold 17 of the newspaper's employees hostage for ten hours. They demand that the paper investigate local police corruption and discrimination against the African-Americans and Indians living in the area. A standoff ends with an agreement by the governor of North Carolina to investigate the charges. The hostage crisis is simply one inci-

dent reflecting the growing racial tensions in Robeson County, a locale whose population is 40 percent white, with the remaining 60 percent divided evenly between African-Americans and American Indians.

MARCH 17, 1988 Indian Youth Suicide. The Warm Springs tribe of Oregon hosts a conference concerning suicide among Indians. This meeting follows a rash of suicides on a reservation inhabited by 2,800 members of the Washo, Paiute, and Warm Springs tribes. Here six young people killed themselves and 16 others had attempted to do so within the two months preceding the conference. Nationwide, the suicide rate for young Indian men is more than twice the national average. The conference, attended by Indian leaders and families as well as psychologists and social workers, seeks an answer to this recent outbreak by returning to traditional practices and methods of counseling for young Indian people.

APRIL 19, 1988 *Lyng v. Northwest Indian Cemetery Protective Association.* The U.S. Supreme Court holds that the First Amendment's protection regarding free exercise of religion does not prohibit the Department of Agriculture from constructing a road through, and allowing timber operations in, a part of a national forest used for religious purposes by the Yurok, Karok, and Tolowa tribes of California. The Indians claim that the preservation of the area in its natural state is essential for their religious practice. This case may prove important as an authoritative citation for other courts facing similar claims. *Lyng* also may allow the courts to be more expansive in identifying a public interest that would permit the disruption of Native American religious practices.

APRIL 28, 1988 Indian Education Act of 1988. Congress passes Public Law 100-197, the Indian Education Act of 1988. Part C of the act authorizes funding for: local educational agencies that educate Indian children, special educational training programs for Teachers of Indian children, programs for adult Indians, the Office of Indian Education, the National Advisory Council on Indian Education, and the White House Conference on Indian Education.

APRIL 28, 1988 Repeal of Termination Act. Congress signs Public Law 100-297, the Repeal of Termination Act, an act (within the Indian Education Act of 1988) formally repealing the termination policy established by House Concurrent Resolution 108 passed on August 1, 1953. Without tribal approval or input, the resolution instituted the termination of 108 tribes and bands over the following ten years. The new act prohibits the BIA from terminating, consolidating, or transferring BIA-administered schools without the consent of the affected tribes.

MAY 31, 1988 Indian Leader Elected. Georges Erasmus *(See* biography, August 8, 1948) is elected to a second term as national chief of the Assembly of First Nations. He warns Canadians that the present generation of aboriginal people in Canada may be the last that is willing to deal peacefully with the government.

JUNE 2, 1988 Indian Act Amended. The Canadian federal government amends the Indian Act to clarify and expand band councils' powers to levy taxes. This amendment (called the "Kamloops Amendment") is the first amendment of the Indian Act launched by Indians.

JUNE 2, 1988 Mohawk Protest. Mohawk at Kahnawak', a reserve on the south shore of the St. Lawrence River, block two highways and the Mercier bridge (which connects Montreal with its southern suburbs) for 30 hours to protest a June 1 police raid in which 17 Mohawks are charged with smuggling cigarettes from the United States. The Mohawk claim that the Jay's Treaty of 1794 gives them the right to bring goods across the border without paying duty.

JUNE 29, 1988 Indian Housing Act. Congress passes Public Law 100-358, the Indian Housing Act, amending the United States Housing Act of 1937 and thereby establishing a separate program providing housing assistance for Indians and Alaska Natives under the supervision of the secretary of housing and urban development. Previously, Indians and Alaska Natives were not eligible under the 1937 act.

JULY 8, 1988 BIA Contract Services. The Absentee Shawnee and the Citizen band of Potawatomi, both of Shawnee; the Iowa of Oklahoma in Perkins; the Sauk and Fox of Oklahoma in Stroud; and the Kickapoo of Oklahoma in McLoud announce plans to contract with the BIA for all services currently provided by the Shawnee Agency.

JULY 8, 1988 *Oklahoma Tax Commission v. Muscogee (Creek) Nation.* The Supreme Court refuses to overturn a lower court ruling that exempts the Creek Nation from paying a state sales tax on its bingo operations. The gaming operation, located in Tulsa, is built on Creek tribal trust lands.

SEPTEMBER 5, 1988 Dene/Métis Claim. Representatives of 13,000 Dene and Métis of the Mackenzie River Valley reach an agreement-in-principle with the federal government to settle their land claim.

SEPTEMBER 11, 1988 Innu Protest. The Innu (Naskapi) of Northwest River in Labrador begin camping at the end of a runway at a North Atlantic Treaty Organization training base near Goose Bay, Labrador, to protest low-altitude training flights. The Innu claim that the low-level flights, which began in 1980, are causing a reduction of wildlife populations, particularly of the George River caribou herd upon which they depend, and is causing distress to the Innu themselves.

SEPTEMBER 17, 1988 Iroquois Confederacy Commemorated. A ceremony commemorates the origin of the Iroquois Confederacy. The confederacy is an organization of the Mohawk, Seneca, Oneida, Cayuga, and Onondaga tribes formed sometime between 1000 and 1500. The government, in existence since that time, is based on a constitution marked by the separation of political powers and a system of political checks and balances.

OCTOBER 5, 1988 BIA-Tribal Contracting. President Reagan signs Public Law 100-472 into law. Popularly referred to as the 638 amendments, the bill provides for an overhaul of the contracting process between the BIA and Indian tribal governments.

OCTOBER 14, 1988 Mohawk Block Bridge. Mohawk from the Akwesasne Reserve block the Seaway International Bridge between New York and Ontario to protest an October 13 police raid in which seven were arrested on smuggling and weapons charges. The Indians claim that provisions of the 1794 Jay's Treaty exempt them from customs regulations, and that their status as a sovereign nation does not make them subject to the laws of Canada or the United States.

OCTOBER 17, 1988 Indian Gaming Regulatory Act. Congress passes Public Law 100-497, the Indian Gaming Regulatory Act. A late 1980s estimate claims that close to 100 tribes have established some form of gaming facilities as a means of improving tribal economies and providing employment for tribal members; they do so by acting on their inherent sovereignty and freedom from state laws. Concerns expressed by non-Indian neighbors, federal officials, and some tribal officials cause Congress to pass the Indian Gaming Regulatory Act. The legislation provides for the establishment of federal regulations and federal standards regarding the conduct of gaming on Indian lands. To ensure the effective regulation of gaming operations, the act establishes the National Indian Gaming Commission with the authority to monitor class II gaming on Indian lands. The act is designed "to establish federal standards and regulations for the conduct of gaming activities within Indian country"; "as a means of promoting tribal economic development, self-sufficiency, and strong tribal governments"; "to shield it [Indian gaming] from organized crime and other corrupting influences . . . to assure that gaming is conducted fairly and honestly by both the operator and players," and "to establish a National Indian Gaming Commission."

OCTOBER 22, 1988 Lubicon Agreement. Chief Bernard Ominayak of the Lubicon Lake Cree reaches a preliminary agreement with Alberta premier Don Getty on terms to settle the band's long-standing land claim. The agreement would provide the band with a 250-square-kilometer (95-square-mile) reserve. On October 15, the Lubicon set up a blockade on the road leading to their community after negotiations with the federal government broke down. On October 20, 23 Indians are arrested when the Royal Canadian Mounted Police remove the blockade. Millions of dollars worth of oil are removed every day from the land claimed by the Lubicon.

The Lubicon first gained international attention by organizing a boycott of "The Spirit Sings," an exposition of Native artifacts held during the Calgary Olympics in February 1988.

OCTOBER 31, 1988 Native Hawaiian Health Care Act of 1988. Congress passes Public Law 100-579, an act to fund, "or enter into a contract with Papa Ola Lokahi for developing a Native Hawaiian comprehensive health care master plan designed to promote comprehensive health promotion and disease prevention services and to maintain and improve the health status of Native Hawaiians."

NOVEMBER 1988 Yukon Land Claim. The Yukon Council of Indians (6,500 people) reach

The Mesquaki (Sauk and Fox) of Tama, Iowa, casino and bingo parlor, 1993. During the 1980s and 1990s many Indian communities opened gambling establishments under the guidance of the National Indian Gaming Commission. Courtesy of Stephen Lehmer.

an agreement-in-principle to settle their land claim with the federal and Yukon governments.

NOVEMBER 21, 1988 Native Parliamentarians. Wilton Littlechild (of the Progressive Conservative Party), an Alberta Cree, becomes the first treaty Indian elected to the Canadian House of Commons. Ethel Blondin of the Liberal Party, a Dene from the Northwest Territories, becomes the first Native woman Member of Parliament. The former teacher and public servant is elected to represent the western Arctic riding (electoral district).

DECEMBER 12, 1988 White House Meeting. President Ronald Reagan holds a meeting at the White House with 16 Indian leaders. This is the first White House conference between Indian leaders and the president of the United States in modern history. The meeting attempts to smooth over the controversy caused by the president's remarks to Russian students in the Soviet Union in May 1988. Speaking at Moscow University, Reagan states, "Maybe we made a mistake. Maybe we should not have humored them [the Indians] in wanting to stay in that kind of primitive life style. Maybe we should have said: 'No come join us. Be citizens along with the rest of us.'" President Reagan also makes reference to the fact that a large number of Indians became very wealthy due to oil money. Both remarks, which Indian leaders quickly point out as incorrect, raise considerable concern within Indian Country as to the level of knowledge possessed by the Reagan administration regarding the current state of Indian affairs. The 20-minute meeting is viewed as successful by the participants. The vice chairman of the Navajo Nation, Johnny Thompson, says that "there was a spirit of forgiveness by all of us."

1 9 8 9

1989 *The Broken Cord* Published. Harper and Row publishes *The Broken Cord* by Michael Dorris. The book details the struggle of a father and his adopted Indian child, whom he later finds to be afflicted with fetal alcohol syndrome. The book brings to light the increasing-

The Canadian Museum of Civilization in Hull, Quebec, is regarded as an architectural masterpiece. Métis architect Douglas Cardinal has become renowned for his innovative designs inspired by natural forms. Photo by Malak Karsh.

ly devastating impact of alcohol use on reservations, specifically the effect of alcohol use on the unborn.

1989 *Employment Division v. Smith. Employment Division v. Smith* is a Oregon state court case involving a claim by two practitioners of the Native American Church, an Indian and a non-Indian, who are denied unemployment benefits because their religious use of peyote is deemed "unconstitutional." The two men are dismissed from their jobs as alcohol and drug

abuse program counselors for violating a regulation requiring them to abstain from drug use. The men participated in a ceremony involving the ingestion of a small quantity of peyote, deciding to partake although the use of peyote is not a strict part of the ritual. Subsequently, they are denied unemployment benefits as their dismissal interprets their actions as job related misconduct within the meaning of Oregon state statutes. The Supreme Court later upholds this decision in 1990. The court finds that the act of ingesting peyote is not worthy of protection under the First Amendment; specifically, the free exercise clause does not necessarily guarantee religious freedom, especially from government intrusion, unless other rights outlined in the First Amendment are also at issue. The court claims that protecting diverse religions, apart from those of a Judeo-Christian ethic, is a "luxury." Moreover, to include small and obscure faiths under this clause would be like "courting anarchy." The court then states that Native religious practices are subject to individual state supervision and legal codes.

1989 Indigenous Women's Network. Winona LaDuke, Ojibway (Anishinabe), and Ingrid Wasinawatok-El Issa, an Oneida, found the Indigenous Women's Network (IWN). Dedicated to meeting the needs of Native women, IWN publishes a journal entitled *Indigenous Women*. The magazine, like the organization itself, seeks to identify and communicate the issues and concerns of Native women. Specifically, they wish to focus on women working within their Native communities. It is their hope to strengthen these active commitments by offering testimony, interviews, alternative perspectives, critical thinking, and possible strategies to Native efforts everywhere.

1989 *Narrative Chance* Is Published. Edited by Anishinabe author Gerald Vizenor and including essays by various authors, *Narrative Chance* attempts to apply "post-modern" and post-structuralist literary theory to Native American literature. Notable among the essays is Vizenor's own, which examines the trickster as both a theoretical and linguistic phenomenon. Vizenor's numerous modes of writing—journalism, essays, literary criticism, and fiction—represent what he calls "trickster discourse." His work is extremely significant for its intellectual distinctiveness and for its subsequent opening of new avenues for American Indian expression. Other works by Vizenor include *Wordarrows* (1978), *The Darkness in Saint Louis Bearheart* (1978), *CrossBloods-Bone Courts, Bingo and Other Reports* (1976), *The*

Marty Pinnecoose, Southern Ute, performing with the American Indian Dance Theatre. Courtesy of Hanay Geiogamah.

People Named the Chippewa: Historical Narratives (1984), *The Trickster of Liberty* (1988), and *Heirs of Columbus* (1992).

JANUARY 1989   Lubicon Land Claim. The Canadian federal government halts negotiations with the Lubicon Lake band following submission of a final offer of $45 million.

JANUARY 19, 1989   Seneca Tax Settlement. The Seneca Indians of New York agree to the settlement of a dispute over taxes with outside local governments and with the state of New York. The tribe, standing on its sovereign authority to levy taxes, establishes stores selling nontaxed goods on the reservation. Responding to pressures by outside competitors, the tribe agrees to levy its own tribal tax on goods thereby making products comparable in market price. The state agrees to the Seneca keeping all tax revenues for tribal programs and dismisses its suit against the tribe for $10 million in state sales tax for goods sold to non-Indians.

FEBRUARY 27, 1989   Anishnabai Land Claim. The Ontario Court of Appeal upholds a 1984 finding that the Teme-Augama Anishnabai (Bear Island People) band of Ojibway had lost title to its land in 1850 even though they had not signed the treaty. The federal government had granted the Indians a reserve at the south end of Lake Temagami in east-central Ontario in 1885, but the Ontario government refused to transfer the land to the federal government to be used as a reserve. The Indians opened negotiations with the Ontario government in 1973 in order to regain their land, but could not convince the provincial government to transfer the land to Indian control. Consequently, in 1982, the Teme-Augama Anishnabai began legal proceedings, which resulted in the 1984 decision in their favor, and the favorable appeals ruling in 1989.

MARCH 1989   Indian Education. The Canadian federal government announces a ceiling on funding for Indian students attending postsecondary institutions. Indians protest with sit-ins and hunger strikes in Thunder Bay (western Ontario), claiming that the funding is a treaty right. Special funding for Indians in postsecondary education began in 1968 when only a very few attended universities. The number of Indians in Canadian postsecondary institutions has increased from 432 in 1970 to 18,535 in 1989.

MARCH 3, 1989   *Lac Courte Oreilles Band of Lake Superior Chippewa Indians et al. v. State of Wisconsin.* In this case, several Chippewa Indian tribes seek to clarify their rights to hunt, fish, and gather on off-reservation lands, based upon the treaties of 1837 and 1842. Judge Barbara Crabb, presiding over the U.S. District Court for the western district of Wisconsin, rules that the Chippewa are not obligated to negotiate with the state concerning the length of their spearfishing season, the number of lakes to be fished, or the size of the catch. The court further rules that the usufructuary rights of the Chippewa Indians (their rights to use the resources of state lands) may be regulated only if it is shown that such regulation is both reasonable and necessary for public health or the conservation of natural resources. Moreover, it must be shown that such regulation does not discriminate against the Chippewa.

APRIL 3, 1989   *Mississippi Choctaw Band v. Holyfield.* In the case of *Mississippi Choctaw Band v. Holyfield,* the Supreme Court upholds the jurisdictional rights of tribal courts under the Indian Child Welfare Act of 1978. The act addressed problems resulting from the large number of Indian children separated from their families and their subsequent placement in non-Indian homes. ICWA gave sole jurisdiction to tribal courts in child custody proceedings. The case involving the Mississippi Choctaw band concerns their attempt to negate an adoption decree that had been signed by the biological parents of two Indian children. The Supreme Court of Mississippi initially rules that the adoption decree is binding in part because the twins were born off-reservation and had never been "domiciled" there; thus, the decree did not come under the tribal court's jurisdiction. Overturning the lower court's decision, the U.S. Supreme Court rules that the twins were domiciled on the Mississippi Choctaw band's reservation and, therefore, the tribal court has exclusive jurisdiction. *Mississippi Choctaw Band v. Holyfield* is viewed as a watershed case supporting tribal jurisdiction over tribal members.

APRIL 23–MAY 7, 1989 Wisconsin Tribes Fishing Rights. Police arrest more than 100 people protesting against the rights of northern Wisconsin tribes to fish. The northern Wisconsin tribes are guaranteed their fishing rights per their treaties of 1837 and 1842. Almost 900 individuals assemble to protest against the tribes' fishing rights while over 100 people gather in support of the Indians.

MAY 10, 1989 Great Whale Project. Cree of northern Quebec file suit to stop construction of the $7.5 billion Great Whale Project (Phase II of the James Bay Hydroelectric Project) in northern Quebec. Studies by Hydro-Quebec have confirmed that mercury levels in reservoirs created by the first phase of the James Bay project are now up to nine times higher than the federal government's guidelines for safety. The 1975 James Bay and Northern Quebec Agreement made provisions for this second phase, even bigger than the first, but the Quebec government elected to begin construction without the project undergoing the environmental review process established by the agreement.

JUNE 24, 1989 Repatriation of Stanford Ohlone Remains. Stanford University agrees to return and rebury the remains of 550 Ohlone Indians, the descendants of tribes in what is now the northern California area. Stanford is one of the first universities agreeing to a repatriation request by tribal leaders.

JUNE 28, 1989 Coquille Restoration Act. Congress passes the Coquille Restoration Act, providing for the restoration of a federal trust relationship with, and assistance to, the Oregon Coquille tribe of Indians and all individual members of the tribe. This relationship was canceled by the Termination Act of 1954, in an attempt to forcefully facilitate the assimilation of the Coquille into American society. This form of integration strategy failed. Consequently, Congress began to reestablish federal recognition of Indian tribes in the 1970s.

JULY 7, 1989 Eddie Brown Becomes Assistant Secretary for Indian Affairs. Eddie Brown, an enrolled member of the Pascua Yaqui of Arizona, takes the oath of office as assistant secretary for Indian affairs.

JULY 21, 1989 *Brendale v. Confederated Tribes and Bands of the Yakima Indian Nation.* The Supreme Court rules in *Brendale v. Confederated Tribes and Bands of the Yakima Indian Nation* that tribal zoning laws do not apply to non-Indian-owned lands falling within reservation boundaries in the instance where that land is surrounded by other non-Indian-owned lands. However, non-Indian-owned land surrounded by tribally owned lands is subject to tribal zoning laws. The court states that "in their view, tribes can regulate land-use in predominantly Indian parts of a reservation, but not in predominantly non-Indian communities." A result of both the Brendale and the 1978 Oliphant decision is that tribes have lost a great deal of control over the non-Indians in their territories. They now must look to Congress to return, legislatively, the government authority the Supreme Court took away from them.

JULY 21, 1989 FBI and New York Troopers Raid St. Regis Casinos. Approximately 225 state troopers and FBI agents sweep onto the portion of the St. Regis Indian Reservation (Akwesasne) located in the United States around Hogansburg, New York, closing down seven suspected casinos and arresting eight people.

JULY 22, 1989 Navajo Clash between Police and MacDonald Supporters. Two individuals are killed and nine injured in a clash in Window Rock, Arizona. The clash involves police and the supporters of ousted Navajo chairman Peter MacDonald. A tribal council vote on February 17 placed McDonald on involuntary leave in the wake of bribery accusations.

JULY 27, 1989 New York Police Close Roads to St. Regis Indian Reservation. New York State police close all roads to the New York portion of the St. Regis Mohawk Reservation. The Mohawk at St. Regis discuss the legality of gambling on the reservation. Moreover, the matter arises of whether the traditional Mohawk Sovereignty Security Force or the state police properly exercise jurisdiction on the reservation.

AUGUST 4, 1989 Centennial Accord. This accord involves the state of Washington and the federally recognized Indian tribes in the state. The agreement marks the beginning of a new approach to relations between state and tribal governments, one based on negotiated cooperation, rather than confrontation and litigation. The state and tribes agree to develop a "government-to-government relationship," to meet annually to discuss more specific goals and strategies, and to work together to "improve the services delivered to people," Indian and non-Indian, in Washington State. Subsequent agreements agree to share responsibility for the protection of Indian children and the conservation of natural resources. For instance, the "Timber-Fish-Wildlife" (TFW) process is one in which both tribal and state agencies coordinate management of watersheds utilized by Indians and non-Indians.

AUGUST 4, 1989 Tohono O'Odham Land Claims. Tohono O'Odham tribal leaders request that Mexican government officials in Mexico City return thousands of acres of indigenously owned lands to the tribe. The Tohono O'Odham Nation argues that the Gadsden Treaty of 1853 illegally divided its

Most tribal governments have Indian police forces supported by the Bureau of Indian Affairs. Courtesy of Duane Champagne.

tribal lands with the establishment of the international boundary.

AUGUST 10, 1989 Gambling on St. Regis Reservation. State and federally recognized tribal officials report that the St. Regis Mohawk Reservation has voted to allow gambling on the United States side of their reservation.

AUGUST 11, 1989 Washington Indian Tribes Sovereignty Recognized. Washington Governor Booth Gardner and the state's 26 federally recognized tribes sign the Centennial Accord. In the historic agreement, the state recognizes the sovereignty of Washington tribes and agrees to a government-to-government process for solving problems of mutual concern between the two governmental entities.

AUGUST 11, 1989 Working Group on Indian Water Settlements. Secretary of the Interior Manuel Lujan announces the formation of the Working Group on Indian Water Settlements. The group, reporting to the Interior's Water Policy Council, is charged with establishing principles to guide Indian water settlements. It will assist in negotiations with tribes and report to the council on the progress of such negotiations.

AUGUST 13, 1989 New York Agrees to Return Wampum Belts to Onondaga. New York State agrees to return twelve wampum belts to the Onondaga Nation of New York. The wampum belts, woven of shells and beads, signify important historical and cultural events within the history of the Onondaga and Iroquois Confederacy. The New York Senate and Assembly passed legislation in 1971 requiring the return of five wampum belts to the nation.

AUGUST 21, 1989 Omaha Sacred Pole Returned. The Peabody Museum at Harvard University returns a sacred pole to the Omaha tribe. The pole is a symbol of unity to the tribe and has a human scalp on top. It is estimated to be 300 years old. Yellow Smoke, the last pole-keeper, placed this sacred object within the museum's care 101 years ago.

AUGUST 28, 1989 Lubicon Land Claim. The federal government announces that it will settle with a band (the Woodland Cree) composed of Indians that the government claims have defected from the Lubicon Lake band in northern Alberta. This follows the federal government's rejection of an agreement reached between Chief Bernard Ominayak of the Lubicon Lake band and the Alberta premier in October 1988. That agreement would have given the Lubicon a 250-square-kilometer reserve. The Lubicon rejected the government's take-it-or-leave-it offer of $45 million in January 1989.

SEPTEMBER 1989 Nishga Land Claim. The Nishga (Nisga'a) sign a framework agreement with the federal government toward resolving their claim to land in west-central British Columbia, but the British Columbia government refuses to recognize the legitimacy of the claim.

OCTOBER 8, 1989 Inspector General Reports Irresponsible Management of Indian Trust Funds. The inspector general issues a report, detailing the Bureau of Indian Affairs irresponsible management of Indian trust funds. The BIA, as trustee of Indian moneys, handles trust funds for 20 tribes and 200 individuals totaling $1.8 billion. The inspector general report states that some $17 million is missing as a result the BIA's sloppy bookkeeping.

NOVEMBER 2, 1989 National Museum of American Indian Act. Congress passes Public Law 101-185, the National Museum of American Indian Act, establishing a national museum specifically devoted to the preservation of American Indian culture and history. The museum will be located in Washington, D.C.

NOVEMBER 11, 1989 Anishnabai Canadian Land Claim. The Teme-Augama Anishnabai set up roadblocks on a logging road being built to give access to lands they claim near Lake Temagami in northern Ontario. The action follows an Ontario Supreme Court decision not to order a halt to road construction until the court rules on their land claim. The Teme-Augama lost their case in the Ontario Supreme Court in February 1989.

NOVEMBER 17, 1989 Senate Report on Corruption and Mismanagement of American Indian Land and Money. A specially convened Senate panel issues its report following a two-year investigation into the corruption and mismanagement of American Indian lands and money, The report, the first study of its kind in over a decade, uncovers corruption in the administration of tribal governments and failure upon the part of federal trust responsibility. Specifically cited as violating this trust obligation is the Bureau of Indian Affairs management; under this administration, oil companies robbed tribes of proceeds garnered from their natural resources. Likewise, inadequate .nonitoring of teachers in BIA boarding schools resulted in the abuse and sexual molestation of Indian children. The report recommends that tribes be given greater control over their federal

A highlight of American Indian Dance Theatre performances is the *Women's Fancy Shawl Dance*, in which female members of the company exhibit their grace and virtuosity as they spin around the stage, displaying intricate dance steps while twirling colorful shawls to the beat of the drum. Photo by Don Perdue. Courtesy of Hanay Geiogamah.

funds and programs. In particular, the panel proposes that a new executive agency be given responsibility for providing the more than 500 Indian tribes and Alaska Native groups with block grants to administer their own programs.

1 9 9 0

1990 Mohawk Blockade in Oka, Quebec. Canadian plans to extend a golf course onto a sacred burial site near Oka, Quebec, provokes a Mohawk blockade. Kahn-Tineta Horn, then program officer for the Canadian Department of Indian Affairs, is arrested on September 26, 1990, for her involvement in the Oka incident. She claims that she was part of a negotiating team sent into peacefully resolve the blockade matter. Among the casualties of the Oka incident is Horn's 14-year-old daughter, whom Horn states was stabbed by Canadian police while protecting her four-year-old sister. In addition to losing her position, Horn loses custody of her younger daughter. Presently, Horn is challenging her department dismissal, alleging that her firing stems from political and

racial motivations surrounding the Mohawk/ Oka uprising. She also has regained custody of her daughter.

JANUARY 26, 1990 Wrongful Imprisonment. An inquiry in Nova Scotia finds that, because of racism and incompetence in the police force and legal community, Micmac Donald Marshall wrongfully convicted of murder in 1972. (He spent the next 11 years in prison.) The inquiry also rejects the findings of the Nova Scotia Supreme Court that ruled that Marshall was partially to blame for his conviction. The report recommends that the government establish a cabinet committee on race relations and a Native criminal justice system.

FEBRUARY 7, 1990 Government Apology. The Nova Scotia government issues an apology to Donald Marshall and announces that it will establish a cabinet committee on race relations and a Native criminal court as a pilot project.

FEBRUARY 27, 1990 Treaty Rights. Leaders of several North American tribes enter into an agreement to collectively defend rights granted by their treaties with the government of the United States. In accordance with the agreement, several tribes from both the United States and Canada will assist each other with legal services and lobbying and law-enforcement aid. The tribes also agree to work together in attempting to educate the non-Indian public about federal treaties with Indians.

MARCH 2, 1990   Métis Land Claim. The Canadian Supreme Court rules that the Manitoba Métis Federation can take their land claim to court. The federal government has rejected their claim and has been attempting to prevent the case from going to trial. The Métis claim that the federal government made some unconstitutional amendments to the Manitoba Act of 1870 that deprived the Métis of much of the land reserved for them by that act. Their multibillion dollar claim covers some of the most valuable land in Manitoba, including the city of Winnipeg.

MARCH 7, 1990   Micmac Hunting and Fishing Rights. The Nova Scotia Court of Appeal rules that provisions in the Constitution Act of 1982 give Micmac Indians the constitutional right to fish for food, as well as granting them some immunity from government regulations.

MARCH 20, 1990   Native Film and Video Production Center Established. Great Plains Productions Inc., a Native-controlled film and video production center, is established in Edmonton, Alberta. Its co-founders are Native filmmakers Wil Campbell (Métis) and Gil Cardinal (Métis) *(See* biography, July 19, 1950). In 1991, the company's thirteen-part series, *My Partners, My People,* celebrates the rich cultural history and traditions of Canada's Native people and receives a nomination for television's prestigious "Gemini Award." A 90-minute documentary, *Our Home and Native Land,* captures the momentous year (1992) of Canada's constitutional referendum and its implications for the country's aboriginal people. This documentary is produced in association

with the British Broadcasting Corporation in England.

MARCH 25, 1990   Puyallup Land Dispute. The Puyallup tribe of Washington ends a longstanding land dispute with the city of Tacoma and the state. In return for extinguishing its land claims, the tribe agrees to a $162 million package settlement comprised of money, jobs, and education guarantees, and title to a section of the Tacoma waterfront.

MARCH 31, 1990   Yukon Land Claim. The Council of Yukon Indians, representing 6,500 Indians, and the federal government and Yukon governments reach an Umbrella Final Agreement to settle their 1973 land claim. This agreement is designed to serve as the blueprint for negotiations between the government and the 14 First Nations of the council. It is unique in that it offers the Indians a share of federal royalties from mining and exemption from some forms of taxation, although the status Indians will give up their rights under the Indian Act in exchange for rights specified in the agreement. The Indians will retain title to 41,440 square kilometers (8.6 percent of the land in the Yukon) and will receive $242.7 million over 15 years. *(See* map of Comprehensive Land Claims in Canada, pp. 483–85.)

APRIL 4, 1990   Great Whale Project. The New York legislature passes a law that will require an environmental assessment of the Great Whale Project before it signs a contract to buy the power from the project. The legislation follows lobbying by the Cree of northern Quebec who oppose the project. The Cree began fighting the project immediately after the government's 1989 announcement that it would start construction.

APRIL 9, 1990   Dene/Métis Land Claim. The 13,000 Dene and Métis of the Northwest Territories sign a land-claim agreement for the Mackenzie Valley in the western Arctic. The agreement would give the claimants title to

180,000 square kilometers of land. Issues of treaty rights and self-government remain to be negotiated.

APRIL 23, 1990 Anishnabai Land Claim. The Ontario government grants the Teme-Augama Anishnabai (Ojibway) a veto over logging on a tract of land which they claim as theirs.

APRIL 30, 1990 Inuit Land Claim. The Tungavik Federation of Nunavut, established to negotiate the claim of 17,000 Inuit in northern Canada, reaches an agreement-in-principle with the federal government in its claim for an immense area of the central and eastern Arctic. Under the agreement, the Inuit will own 350,000 square kilometers of land and their corporations will be given $580 million for the surrendered land. It also includes provisions for the creation of the territory of Nunavut. Still to be negotiated are provisions concerning the extinguishment of aboriginal rights and conflicting claims of the Dene and Métis of surrounding areas in the Northwest Territories and the northern prairie provinces.

APRIL 30, 1990 Seminole Awards Act. Congress passes the Seminole Awards Act, Public Law 277. The intent of the act is "to provide for the use and distribution of funds awarded the Seminole Indians" from the Indian Claims Commission.

APRIL 30–MAY 3, 1990 Akwesasne Reservation. A dispute between those in favor of gambling and those opposed on the Akwesasne Reservation results in the killing of two men on the Canadian side of the reservation. Hundreds of New York and Canadian police are sent to seal off the reservation, while negotiators sent by Gov. Mario Cuomo attempt to settle the issue.

MAY 1, 1990 Mohawk Deaths. Two Mohawk die in gun battles at the Akwesasne (St. Regis) Reserve. Conflict centers around gambling casinos in the U.S. part of the reserve.

MAY 22, 1990 Seneca Land Agreement. The Seneca Nation, local leaders of Salamanca, New York, and state and federal officials reach an agreement on the land rented by the city of Salamanca from the tribe. Under the terms of the first lease, negotiated in 1892, the town paid the nation $17,000 annually. Ninety percent of the town of 6,600 lies within the boundaries of the Allegany Reservation. According to the terms of the new lease, the town, which is the only city in the United States built on leased Indian land, will pay the tribe $800,000 a year. In addition, state and federal officials will reimburse the tribe $60 million for the inequities of the previous lease.

MAY 24, 1990 The *Sioui* Case. In the case of *R. v. Sioui*, the Supreme Court of Canada rules that a 230-year-old treaty signed by the Huron Indians of Quebec supersedes later legislation that contradicts it. The ruling is based upon Section 35 of the Constitution of 1982, which guarantees aboriginal treaty rights.

MAY 29, 1990 *Duro v. Reina.* The U.S. Supreme Court rules in *Duro v. Reina* that tribes do not possess the authority to exercise criminal jurisdiction over nonmember Indians on the reservation. The decision is a major legal and political blow to tribes in their struggle to regain and protect their inherent right of self determination. The decision also creates a very difficult situation on reservations, where many nonenrolled tribal members have married within the tribe or are working on the reservation. According to the court's decision, no governmental body currently possesses criminal jurisdiction over these individuals.

MAY 31, 1990 *Sparrow v. Regina.* The Supreme Court of Canada orders a retrial for Ronald Sparrow from the Musqueam band (Vancouver), who had been convicted of violating federal fishing regulations. The court rules that Section 35 of the Charter supersedes wildlife regulations.

JUNE 12, 1990   Meech Lake Accord. Following eleventh-hour talks, the Manitoba government seeks leave to debate the passage of the Meech Lake Accord. Debate on such short notice requires unanimous consent of the Members of the Legislative Assembly (M.L.A.s). Ojibway-Cree New Democratic Party M.L.A. (Red Sucker Lake, Rupertsland) Elijah Harper denies leave to debate. Harper's actions are planned in conjunction with the Manitoba chiefs. The Meech Lake Accord will fail if not ratified by the national Parliament and all provincial legislatures by June 23.

JUNE 14, 1990   Meech Lake Accord. Following meetings with constitutional lawyers and experts on parliamentary procedures, Elijah Harper uses more complex procedural tactics to block debate on the Meech Lake Accord, convincing federal politicians that the Canadian aboriginals, through him, can possibly prevent the passage of the Meech Lake Accord before the June 23 deadline.

JUNE 18, 1990   Meech Lake Accord. Senator Lowell Murray, the minister of state for federal-provincial relations, meets with the Manitoba chiefs (led by Phil Fontaine). The chiefs reject the government's offers to deal with aboriginal concerns following passage of the Meech Lake Accord, and promise to kill the accord.

JUNE 22, 1990   Meech Lake Accord Defeated. Elijah Harper, an Ojibway-Cree member of the provincial legislature in Manitoba, is able to use procedural rules to prevent the passage of the Meech Lake Accord in the Manitoba legislature. This effectively kills the constitutional reform package which aboriginals have been opposing since its inception in 1987.

JUNE 23, 1990   Natives Claim Victory. On the day on which the Meech Lake Accord officially dies, Prime Minister Brian Mulroney speaks to Canadians on national television. He blames Newfoundland premier Clyde Wells for the failure of the accord. (When it became apparent that the accord would be blocked in Manitoba, the Newfoundland government elected not to vote on the accord. These are the only two legislatures to fail to ratify the agreement.) Elijah Harper and Phil Fontaine say that Mulroney blames Wells because he refuses to admit that he was defeated by Indians.

JULY 2–3, 1990   Self-Governance Pilot Program. Assistant Secretary of the Interior Eddie Brown signs historic agreements with six tribes: Quinault Indian Nation, Tahola, Washington; Lummi Indian Nation, Bellingham, Washington; Jamestown Klallam Indian tribe, Sequim, Washington; Hoopa Valley Indian tribe, Hoopa, California; Cherokee Nation, Tahlequah, Oklahoma; and Mille Lacs band of Chippewa Indians, Onamia, Minnesota. The tribes are part of a Self-Governance Pilot Program that will ultimately allow up to 20 tribes the authority to administer and set priorities for federal funds received directly from the government.

JULY 11, 1990   Oka Crisis. A police officer is killed after Quebec police storm a barricade on the Mohawk Reserve at Kanesataké (Oka), near Montreal. The Mohawk set up the blockade in March to prevent construction of a golf course on land that they claim. After this failed attempt to remove the barricades, police surround Kanesataké. In sympathy with the Mohawks at Kanesataké, members of the Mohawk Warrior Society at Kahnawak' (Caughnawaga), south of Montreal, block access to the Mercier Bridge, which links southern suburbs of Montreal with the city. The actions initiate a 78-day standoff between the police and military and the Mohawk Warriors of Kahnawak' and Kanesataké, a conflict that draws worldwide attention.

JULY 19, 1990   Dene/Métis Land Claim. The Dene and Métis reject their comprehensive land claim settlement with the federal government because of concern over the provisions that would have them surrender their aboriginal rights.

Elijah Harper, holding an eagle feather for spiritual strength, uses procedural rules to prevent the last-minute passage of the Meech Lake Accord. Courtesy of Canapress Photo Service.

AUGUST 1990 Tutu Visits Canada. Black South African Anglican archbishop Desmond Tutu visits the Osnaburgh Ojibway Reserve in northwestern Ontario. He says Canada's treatment of its indigenous peoples is reminiscent of treatment of blacks under apartheid in South Africa.

AUGUST 1990 White House Conference on Indian Education. Congress passes legislation to convene the White House Conference on Indian Education. The conference is charged with examining the feasibility of establishing an independent Indian Board of Education, which would oversee all federal programs directed at Indian education and recommend improvements to current educational programs.

The Bureau of Indian Affairs currently funds 182 schools, attended by 39,000 Indian children. Seventy of these schools are contracted by tribal education committees. Another 400,000 Indian children attend public schools operated by the states.

AUGUST 3, 1990 American Indian Heritage Month. Congress passes the American Indian Heritage Month Act, Public Law 101-343, designating November as National American Indian Heritage Month.

AUGUST 9, 1990 British Columbia Indian Policy. The British Columbia government announces that it is willing to join Indians and the federal government in land claims negotiations assuming the legitimacy of aboriginal title. The policy reverses the position held by every British Columbia government since 1864. The promise is made after Indians bands block rail lines and roads in the province.

AUGUST 18, 1990 Indian Law Enforcement Reform Act. Congress passes the Indian Law Enforcement Reform Act, Public Law 101-379, to clarify and strengthen the authority of "certain Department of the Interior law enforcement services, activities, and officers in Indian country."

AUGUST 20, 1990 Oka Crisis. Twenty-five hundred Canadian soldiers replace provincial police at Mohawk blockades at Kanesataké and Kahnawak'. Since the conflict began, Indians in several places across the country have demonstrated and blocked roads and railways to express sympathy with the Mohawk and to present their own grievances.

AUGUST 29, 1990 Wood Buffalo Slaughter. A report recommends the slaughter of a herd of wood buffalo in northern Alberta because they risk transmitting tuberculosis and brucellosis to cattle. Indians and Métis, who depend on the herd for food, reject the plan.

SEPTEMBER 7, 1990 Peigan Protest. The Royal Canadian Mounted Police move in on the Peigan Lonefighters (a revived warrior society) camp, ending a month-long attempt by the Lonefighters to divert the Oldman River around the site of a partially completed dam. The leader of the Lonefighters, Milton Born With A Tooth, is arrested on weapons charges. The Lonefighters oppose the dam because it would

A Mohawk warrior and a Canadian soldier engage in a staring match during the 78-day Oka standoff. The conflict at Oka brought unprecedented domestic and international attention to the grievances of Canadian Natives. Courtesy of Canapress Photo Service.

flood land that they consider sacred, and be-cause they fear its environmental effects.

SEPTEMBER 25, 1990 Canadian Land Claims Policy. Prime Minister Brian Mulroney an-nounces a new government agenda to meet aboriginal grievances. He commits the govern-ment to speed up settlement of all land claims and meet all its outstanding treaty obligations. For the first time, the government will begin negotiating more than six comprehensive claims

at a time. He also announces a commitment to improve housing, sewage treatment, and water facilities on reserves, and to increase aboriginal control over their own affairs.

SEPTEMBER 25, 1990 Carl D. Perkins Voca-tional Education Act. Congress passes the Tribally Controlled Vocational Institutions Sup-port Act of 1990, Public Law 101-392. Under Part H of the Carl D. Perkins Vocational Education Act, this act "provides grants for the operation and improvement of tribal controlled post-secondary vocational institutions."

SEPTEMBER 26, 1990   Oka Crisis. The Warriors at Kahnawak' and Kanesataké surrender after an 11-week standoff with police and soldiers. The 78-day armed standoff has attracted international attention and made Canadians more aware of the depth of frustration among many Native Canadians. The federal government has refused to negotiate with the Mohawk while the standoff continues.

SEPTEMBER 28, 1990   Indian Tribal Leaders Conference. Secretary of the Interior Manuel Lujan and Assistant Secretary Eddie Brown call the Indian Tribal Leaders Conference in Albuquerque, New Mexico, to discuss proposals to reorganize the Bureau of Indian Affairs. More than 1,000 Indian tribal leaders attend the first such meeting since 1976.

OCTOBER 4, 1990   Indian Environmental Regulatory Act. Congress passes the Indian Environmental Regulatory Act to reinforce and clarify the authority of Interior officials to protect areas of environmental concern in Indian Country. Congress also passes the Indian Environmental Regulatory Enhancement Act of 1990, Public Law 101-408, the same day "to authorize grants to improve the capability of Indian tribal governments to regulate environmental quality."

OCTOBER 11, 1990   Nishga Land Claim. The British Columbia government signs an agreement to join the federal government in land claims negotiations with the Nishga (Nisga'a) Tribal Council.

OCTOBER 30, 1990   Native American Languages Act. Congress enacts the Native American Languages Act, which is designed to preserve, protect, and promote the practice and development of Indian languages. The act is important given the government's historic efforts, especially in the nineteenth century, to eradicate Indian languages. It is estimated that more than half of all Indian languages are now extinct. Approximately 250 Indian languages still exist, although some are spoken by only a few individuals.

OCTOBER 31, 1990   Ponca Restoration Act. Congress passes the Ponca Restoration Act, Public Law 101-484, "to provide for the restoration of Federal recognition to the Ponca Tribe of Nebraska." Federal recognition of the tribe had been taken away in 1962. As with other Indian tribes, the termination policy had negative ramifications for the Ponca both economically and culturally.

NOVEMBER 1990   Lubicon Claim. Thirteen Lubicon Lake Cree are arrested after logging equipment located near their homes is damaged. The provincial government has approved logging on land that the Lubicon Cree claim as theirs.

NOVEMBER 2, 1990   Native American Languages Act. Congress passes the Native American Languages Act, Public Law 101-477, to preserve, protect, and promote the practice and development of Native American languages as deemed also by federal policy.

NOVEMBER 6, 1990   *Duro v. Reina.* President George Bush signs a defense appropriations bill that includes an amendment to delay enforcement of the *Duro* decision until September 30, 1991. The amendment, according to the bill's authors, fills the vacuum created by "an emergency situation": "Throughout the history of this country, the Congress has never questioned the power of tribal governments to exercise misdemeanor jurisdiction over non-tribal member Indians in the same manner that such courts exercise misdemeanor jurisdiction over tribal members." *(See* entry, May 29, 1990.)

NOVEMBER 7, 1990   Dene/Métis Land Claim. The federal government announces that as a result of the rejection by the Dene and Métis of their land claims settlement in July, the government will begin negotiating with individual

Indian groups in the western Arctic, saying that such groups have indicated their desire to negotiate separately. Indian leaders accuse the government of adopting a "divide and conquer" strategy. (See map of Comprehensive Land Claim in Canada, pp. 483–85.)

NOVEMBER 16, 1990 Fallon Paiute Shoshoni Indian Tribe Water Rights. Congress passes the Fallon Paiute Shoshoni Indian Tribe Water Rights Settlement Act of 1990, Public Law 101-618. The act appropriates a total sum of $43 million for fiscal years 1993–97 for economic and tribal developments on the reservation in Nevada.

NOVEMBER 16, 1990 Fort Hall Indian Water Rights. Congress passes the Fort Hall Indian Water Rights Act of 1990, Public Law 101-602, describing and quantifying tribal water for Shoshoni-Bannock tribes in the state of Idaho.

NOVEMBER 16, 1990 Native American Graves Protection and Repatriation Act. Bowing to intense lobbying efforts by individual tribes and national and local Indian organizations, Congress enacts the Native American Graves Protection and Repatriation Act, Public Law 101-601. The act provides for the protection of American Indian grave sites and the repatriation of Indian remains and cultural artifacts to tribes.

NOVEMBER 20, 1990 Navajo Nation Elects Zah. The Navajo Nation elects Peterson Zah as tribal president. Zah takes over leadership of the tribe from Peter MacDonald, who was convicted of taking bribes by the Navajo tribal court in October.

NOVEMBER 21, 1990 Indian Policy Recommendations. The Canadian Human Rights Commission condemns the Indian Act and the Indian Affairs Department. It calls for a new land claims policy to speed up the land claims process and for a Royal Commission on Native issues. Indian Affairs minister Tom Siddon rejects the recommendations.

NOVEMBER 28, 1990 Indian Child Protection and Family Abuse Prevention Act. Historically a rare problem, child abuse is increasing on tribal reservations. Congress passes the Indian Child Protection and Family Abuse Prevention Act, which requires tribes to report abusive situations and to establish tribal programs to treat and prevent future abuse.

NOVEMBER 28, 1990 National Indian Forest Resources Management Act. Congress passes the National Indian Forest Resources Management Act, Public Law 101-630. The act provides for improved protection and coordination between the Department of Interior and Indian tribes in the management of Indian forest lands and allows the secretary of the interior to participate in the management of Indian forest lands, to the land owner's benefit, and to be consistent with the trust responsibility of the secretary.

NOVEMBER 29, 1990 Indian Arts and Crafts Act. With the increase in value of tribal artwork and jewelry, tribal artists have faced competition from non-Indian, machine-manufactured art works. Now, under the terms of the Indian Arts and Crafts Act of 1990, Public Law 101-644, Congress gives the Indian Arts and Crafts Board, first established by the 1935 Indian Arts and Crafts Act, expanded powers to bring civil and criminal jurisdiction for civil violations against American Indian craftsmanship.

NOVEMBER 30, 1990 Eastern Land Claim. The Naskapi-Montagnais Innu Association (N.M.I.A.) of Labrador; the Conseil Attikamek/Montagnais (C.A.M.), an alliance of 12 Indian bands in Quebec; and the Labrador Inuit Association (L.I.A.), representing 1,600 Inuit and "Native settlers" in Labrador sign framework agreements toward the settlement of their claims in Labrador and Quebec. The three claims, all presented in 1977, have proceeded together because they overlap. Negotiations were slowed by the N.M.I.A. claim to sovereignty, by acrimonious relations between the Quebec and

Newfoundland governments, by Innu protests of low-level military training flights at a North Atlantic Treaty Organization base at Goose Bay in 1989, and by the fact that the Quebec government has insisted that the land the C.A.M. is claiming is already covered by the 1975 James Bay Agreement. Negotiations will now begin on agreements-in-principle.

DECEMBER 1990 Reorganization Plans for the Bureau of Indian Affairs. Secretary of the Interior Manuel Lujan announces the formation of a 43-member advisory task force to recommend reorganization plans for the Bureau of Indian Affairs. The task force is composed of 36 Indian tribal leaders and seven Department of Interior and Bureau of Interior representatives. Although the BIA reports that tribes have contracted to administer approximately one-third of all BIA programs, the secretary of the interior has urged the reorganization so that funding can be reduced for administering tribal programs. By contracting with the BIA, tribes are free to operate and manage federal programs, some $415 million annually, as they perceive to be in the tribe's best interest.

DECEMBER 19, 1990 Lubicon Claim. The federal and Alberta governments reach a land claim agreement with the Woodland Cree, formed in 1989 as a breakaway band of the Lubicon Lake band that has been seeking a settlement since the 1930s. They also reach agreement with a band of Stoney (Assiniboine) for compensation for land flooded by the Bighorn Dam on the North Saskatchewan River in the foothills of the Rocky Mountains.

DECEMBER 29, 1990 Centennial of the Wounded Knee Massacre. Approximately 400 people attend the centennial of the Wounded Knee Massacre. On October 19, the House of Representatives provides the final approval needed for a resolution expressing "deep regret" over the Seventh Cavalry's massacre on the Pine Ridge Reservation. The Seventh Cavalry

rounded up and killed more than 300 women, men, and children at Wounded Knee, South Dakota, in 1890.

1 9 9 1

JANUARY 1991 Cree Trapper Killed. Cree trapper Leo LaChance is shot and killed after walking into a gun shop in Prince Albert, Saskatchewan. The owner of the shop, a known white supremacist, is convicted in April of manslaughter and sentenced to four years in prison. The police say that they do not believe the killing was racially motivated. Outrage in the Native community leads to the establishment of an inquiry.

JANUARY 29, 1991 Peter MacDonald. The former Navajo Nation chairman, Peter MacDonald, is convicted by a tribal court on charges of conspiracy, fraud, and ethics violations. The tribal court had previously convicted him and his son of accepting bribes and violating the tribe's ethics code. At that time, the tribal court suspended McDonald from tribal office and barred him from holding tribal office for four years. In addition, he was sentenced to almost six years in prison and fined $11,000. His son was sentenced to 18 months in prison and fined $2,500.

FEBRUARY 13, 1991 _Dances with Wolves._ Graham Greene _(See_ biography, 1950), an Oneida Indian from Canada's Six Nations Reserve, is nominated by the Academy of Motion Picture Arts and Sciences as Best Supporting Actor for his performance in Kevin Costner's sweeping epic, _Dances with Wolves_ (1990). Greene receives tremendous acclaim for his role as the Lakota medicine man, Kicking Bird, and the film wins seven Oscars, including one for Best Picture of the Year. Other Indian actors in the cast include Rodney Grant (Omaha), Floyd Red Crow Westerman (Dakota Sioux), and Tantoo Cardinal (Cree/Métis) _(See_ biography, July 20, 1950).

Morgan Tosee, a member of the Comanche tribe of Oklahoma, is a champion *Southern Men's Traditional* dancer with the American Indian Dance Theatre. Photo by Don Perdue. Courtesy of Hanay Geiogamah.

MARCH 1991   Nishga Land Claim. The Nishga (Nisga'a) and the federal and British Columbia (B.C.) governments reach a framework agreement to settle the longstanding Nisga'a land claim. The agreement follows B.C.'s decision to negotiate with its Indians.

MARCH 5, 1991   Museum of the American Indian. The new Museum of the American Indian, under the auspices of the Smithsonian Institution, announces its policy for the return of Indian artifacts. Tribes may formally request

the return of all sacred objects, funerary artifacts, communally owned tribal property, and illegally obtained objects.

MARCH 8, 1991   *Delgamuukw v. The Queen.* Chief Justice McEachern of the British Columbia Supreme Court rules in *Delgamuukw v. The Queen* case that the Gitksan-Wet'suwet'en of west-central British Columbia do not hold aboriginal title to 57,000 square kilometers that they claim because such title was extinguished by British Columbia before it entered Confederation, and because the Proclamation of 1763 does not apply to British Columbia. The Indians announce that they will appeal the decision. The British Columbia government announces that the decision will not change its policy of negotiating with Indian claimants. The Gitksan-Wet'suwet'en submitted its formal claim in 1977 and began litigation in 1984. *(See* map of Comprehensive Land Claims in Canada, pp. 483–85.) The case is appealed to a higher court.

MARCH 25, 1991   Indians and the Law. A federal-Alberta task force finds that Canadian Indians suffer racist treatment in the justice system. It recommends the establishment of Native courts and police forces. The task force was prompted by the fact that aboriginals, who are less than 5 percent of the population of Alberta, are about a third of its prison population.

APRIL 1991   Specific Claims Policy. Canadian Indian Affairs minister Tom Siddon announces changes to the federal government's policy of dealing with specific claims. The new policy would accept some pre-Confederation claims and would inject more money and manpower into the process in order to speed it up. The government defines specific claims as claims which argue that the government is not living up to its responsibilities as set out in treaties or legislation.

APRIL 4, 1991   Census Indian Population. The Census Bureau announces that 1,959,234 American Indians and Alaska Natives live in the United States. Of these numbers, 1,878,285 are American Indian; 57,152 are Eskimo; and 23,797 are Aleut. These figures represent a total increase in population of almost 40 percent since 1980. The increase is attributed to improved census taking and a greater willingness on the part of individuals to be identified as American Indian.

Included in these numbers are 510 federally recognized tribes in the United States and approximately 200 Alaska Native villages and communities.

MAY 1991   Ontario Indian Policy. Ontario premier Bob Rae announces that the Indians of Ontario will be given immunity from provincial wildlife laws.

MAY 20, 1991   Chippewa Treaty Fishing Rights. Members of the Chippewa tribes of Wisconsin and the state of Wisconsin announce an agreement that ends a 17-year dispute over treaty fishing rights in Wisconsin. Based on previous court decisions, the tribes and the state agree to compromise on a number of issues that have divided them for more than a decade. Under the terms of the agreement, tribes will continue to spearfish in Wisconsin lakes, but only according to strictly held conservation limits. The Chippewa also agree not to appeal a ruling that prevents them from harvesting timber in off-reservation areas.

MAY 24, 1991   Mashantucket Pequot Casino. Secretary of the Interior Manuel Lujan approves a request from the Mashantucket Pequot to operate a gambling casino on tribal lands. Permission is granted under the terms of the 1988 Indian Gaming Regulatory Act, which permits Indian gaming if generally legal under state law. Connecticut state officials had sought to block approval. The Pequot casino becomes the only casino on the East Coast besides those in Atlantic City, New Jersey.

MAY 24, 1991   Special Native Seat. The Nova Scotia Legislature endorses the concept of creating a special seat in the provincial legislature reserved for Micmac Indians.

MAY 31, 1991   Elected Band Council. The residents of the Kanesataké Mohawk Reserve vote in plebiscite to hold direct band council elections rather than following the traditional selection of leaders by hereditary clan mothers. The federal government ordered the plebiscite, saying that its negotiations on Mohawk claims following the conflicts of the summer of 1990 could not be successful until it could negotiate with one group which had the support of the entire community. The traditional leadership unsuccessfully tried to block the plebiscite through court action.

JUNE 6, 1991 All-Indigenous Film Studio Created. The National Film Board of Canada announces the creation of Studio One, an all-indigenous studio located in Edmonton, Alberta. Studio One's purpose is to counter the misrepresentation of Canada's aboriginal people in mainstream media by providing production facilities and training for Indian independent filmmakers. Its first producer is Carol Geddes (Tlingit) *(See* biography, November 17, 1945); in 1993, Michael Doxtater (Mohawk) is appointed her successor.

JUNE 12, 1991 New Indian Leader. Ovide Mercredi *(See* biography, 1945), a Cree lawyer from Manitoba, is chosen as the new grand chief of the Assembly of First Nations. He promises to take a tough stand with the government in his calls for a constitutionally entrenched recognition of the inherent aboriginal right to self-government.

JUNE 14, 1991 President Bush's Indian Policy. President George Bush issues his policy statement on American Indians in which he reaffirms the government's commitment to the government-to-government relationship between the federal government and the Indian nations.

JUNE 26, 1991 Residential Schools. Canadian Indian Affairs minister Tom Siddon announces that the government will seek to ameliorate damage done to Indian societies by residential schools. For many years Indian children at residential schools were punished for retaining aspects of Native cultures. Evidence of physical and sexual abuse at residential schools has been revealed in the past few years. Native leaders say that high rate of family breakdown, physical and sexual abuse, depression, alcoholism, and suicide are related to damage done by residential schools.

Grand chief of the Assembly of First Nations Ovide Mercredi. Courtesy of Canapress Photo Service.

JULY 5, 1991   Native Constitutional Hearings. Canadian Constitutional affairs minister Joe Clark and Ovide Mercredi *(See* biography, 1946) agree that the Assembly of First Nations (A.F.N.) should hold its own hearings and constituent assemblies in an effort to reform Canada's Constitution. The A.F.N. would then share its information and proposals with the federal government. The constitutional reform process was prolonged after Manitoba Indians engineered the failure of the Meech Lake Accord in June 1990.

JULY 6, 1991   Woodland Cree Claim. The Woodland Cree band, a band created by the Canadian federal government in 1989, votes to accept the government's offer to settle its land claim.

JULY 10, 1991   Great Whale Project. The Canadian federal government decides to hold its own full environmental review of the Great Whale Project in northern Quebec according to the Environmental Assessment Review Process (E.A.R.P.), a process established to study the environmental impact of resource development projects. The federal government announces its own assessment because it cannot agree with the Quebec government on a joint review process. Native groups denounce federal review as a betrayal because it allows construction on the project to continue while the review is being done. The federal government claims that its E.A.R.P. guidelines do not give it power to halt the project. The Natives of northern Quebec are soliciting a review based on the more rigorous guidelines of the James Bay and Northern Quebec Agreement of 1975.

JULY 13, 1991   Gwich'in Claim. The Gwich'in (Kutchin), Dene Indians of the Mackenzie River Delta, reach a land claims settlement with the federal government based on the agreement rejected by the Dene and Métis of Northwest Territories (N.W.T) in April 1990. The agreement gives the Indians 15,000 square kilometers in the N.W.T. and the Yukon. Negotiations began in November 1990 when the government announced that it would no longer negotiate with the Dene and Métis Association of the N.W.T.

JULY 24, 1991   Oblate Apology. Rev. Douglas Crosby, president of the Oblate Conference of Canada, the largest Roman Catholic missionary order in Canada, asks Natives to forgive the order for the abuses that Indians suffered at its residential schools. The apology follows allegations that aspects of Indian cultures were repressed and that Indians suffered physical and sexual abuse at many residential schools.

JULY 30, 1991   Quebec Native Announcement. Quebec Natives announce that they will determine their own course if Quebec separates from the rest of Canada.

AUGUST 6, 1991   Aboriginal Self-Government. Bob Rae, premier of Ontario, signs an agreement with Indian chiefs committing Ontario to push for the entrenchment of the aboriginal right to self-government in the Constitution.

AUGUST 12, 1991   Manitoba Aboriginal Justice Inquiry. The report of the Manitoba Aboriginal Justice Inquiry finds that aboriginal peoples suffer discrimination in the legal system. It recommends the establishment of a separate aboriginal justice system that would give the aboriginal people the right to enact and enforce laws in their own communities. The inquiry finds that racism played an important part in the deaths of Helen Betty Osborne, a Cree woman murdered by non-Natives in The Pas, in northern Manitoba, and J.J. Harper, a Cree man killed by a Winnipeg police officer. Although aboriginal people account for only 12 percent of Manitoba's population, they account for over half the people in Manitoba's correctional institutions.

AUGUST 15, 1991   Anishnabai Land Claim. The Supreme Court of Canada rules that the Teme-Augama Anishnabai do not hold aboriginal title to land they claim near Lake Temagami in Ontario. The court rules that aboriginal rights do exist in law but that because these Ojibway had accepted treaty rights, they had become party to the Robinson-Huron Treaty (1850) even though they did not actually sign it.

AUGUST 27, 1991   Great Whale Project. The Quebec government announces that construction of the Great Whale Project (Phase II of the James Bay Hydroelectric Project) will be delayed one year. The announcement follows negotiations between Quebec and the state of New York. The Quebec government hopes to sell most of the electricity to northern states of the United States. The Cree of northern Quebec have lobbied New York legislators to refuse to buy the power.

SEPTEMBER 7, 1991   Indians and the Law. Canadian Federal justice minister Kim Campbell announces that she is willing to consider fundamental changes in Canada's justice system in an effort to solve the problems faced by aboriginal peoples. Campbell, however, rejects the concept of a separate Native justice system. The comment follows several provincial and federal reports calling for a separate Native justice system.

SEPTEMBER 10, 1991   Great Whale Project. A Federal Court judge orders the Canadian government to carry out an environmental review of the Great Whale Project according to the guidelines set down in the 1975 James Bay and Northern Quebec Agreement, not those set down in the government's Environmental Assessment Review Process (E.A.R.P.). The terms of the James Bay and Northern Quebec Agreement, unlike the E.A.R.P. guidelines, allow the federal government to halt the development until the review is finished. The federal government appeals the ruling.

SEPTEMBER 18, 1991   Indian Seats in House of Commons. A Canadian Royal Commission on Electoral Reform recommends that a number of seats in the House of Commons be set aside for aboriginal peoples, to ensure that Native Canadians are adequately represented in the House. Because Natives are a minority in almost every constituency (electoral district) in the country, most are unable to elect Native politicians.

SEPTEMBER 24, 1991   New Constitutional Proposal. The federal government releases *Shaping Canada's Future Together*, its first constitutional proposal since the Meech Lake Accord collapsed in June 1990. The document proposes to entrench the aboriginal right to self-government within ten years. Leaders of Canada's treaty Indians denounce the proposals because the government refuses to recognize this right as an inherent one. Ovide Mercredi *(See* biography, 1946) says the Assembly of First Nations will consider boycotting the parliamentary committee that will seek input. Métis leaders respond more positively to the proposal.

OCTOBER 28, 1991   Criminal Jurisdiction Act. Congress passes the Criminal Jurisdiction Act, Public Law 102-137. The act establishes that Indian tribes have the power to exercise criminal jurisdiction over Indian people on Indian reservations. *(See* entry, May 29, 1990 and November 6, 1990.)

NOVEMBER 26, 1991   Custer Battlefield Renamed. Congress passed a bill, after considerable debate, renaming the Custer Battlefield National Monument in eastern Montana as the Little Bighorn Battlefield Monument. At the Little Bighorn site in 1876, Colonel George Armstrong Custer and more than 250 soldiers of the Seventh Cavalry lost a battle against allied groups of Sioux and Cheyenne. The well publicized battle was known as "Custer's Last Stand."

DECEMBER 1991   Federal Government Trusteeship Responsibility. According to *American Indians Today*, a publication by the Bureau of Indian Affairs issued in the winter of 1991, the BIA is responsible in its trusteeship capacity for 278 reservations comprising some 56.2 million acres. (The term reservation includes reservations, pueblos, rancherias, communities, etc.)

The federal government's trusteeship responsibility currently extends to 510 federally recognized tribes, including approximately 200 village groups in Alaska. Since the establishment of the Federal Acknowledgement Program in 1978, the BIA has received 126 petitions for federal recognition; it has extended recognition to 8 tribal petitions and denied recognition to 12. The U.S. Congress during this time has legislatively recognized 12 groups.

The same publication reports that the Bureau of Indian Affairs currently provides grants for the operation of 22 tribally controlled community colleges, enrolling approximately 7,000 students. The BIA further estimates that more than 70,000 Indian students are attending colleges and universities. More than 400 Indian students are known to be pursuing graduate or law degrees.

DECEMBER 4, 1991 Tribal Self-Governance Demonstration Project. Congress passes legislation to amend the Indian Self-Determination and Education Assistance Act. Entitled the Tribal Self-Governance Demonstration Project Act, Public Law 102-184, the act includes feasibility consideration of demonstration projects and extends the number of tribes taking part in the tribal self-governance pilot project from 20 to 30. *(See also* entry, July 2–3, 1990.)

DECEMBER 7, 1991 Yukon Land Claim. The Council of Yukon Indians votes to accept a land claims agreement negotiated with the federal government in March 1990. The agreement establishes guidelines for settlements with the each of Yukon's 14 First Nations. The Indians will receive title to 41,440 square kilometers (8.6 percent of the Yukon) and $257 million. The agreement includes provisions for self-

government for the Indians. *(See* map of Comprehensive Land Claims in Canada, pp. 483–85.)

DECEMBER 11, 1991 Indians and the Law. The Law Reform Commission of Canada recommends the establishment of a separate Native justice system in Canada.

DECEMBER 16, 1991 Inuit Land Claim. Indian Affairs minister Tom Siddon announces that the government has reached a final agreement with the Inuit (Tungavik Federation of Nunavut) of the eastern Arctic. The agreement follows 15 years of negotiations. The agreement would create a new territory of Nunavut in the eastern Arctic. The new territory would be publicly governed although Inuit presently account for 80 percent of the area's population. The provision resembles part of the Inuit's original claim, but had been rejected earlier by the federal government. The agreement also calls for the Inuit to surrender their aboriginal rights. The Inuit would be given cash ($580 million over 14 years) in exchange for title to most of the land, but would retain 350,000 square kilometers of land (approximately 17.5 percent of the territory). Dene in the western Arctic and in Manitoba and Saskatchewan challenge the agreement because it covers land they claim as theirs. Other aboriginal leaders call for the Inuit to reject the deal because it calls for the Inuit to surrender their aboriginal rights. The settlement includes provisions that would give the Inuit a voice in wildlife management. The agreement will be the subject of a plebiscite in 1992. *(See* map of Comprehensive Land Claims in Canada, pp. 483–85.)

1 9 9 2

JANUARY 1992 Native Prison. The federal government announces that it will build Canada's first Native minimum-security prison on the Samson Cree Reserve near Hobbema, Alberta. Some residents of the reserve oppose the decision.

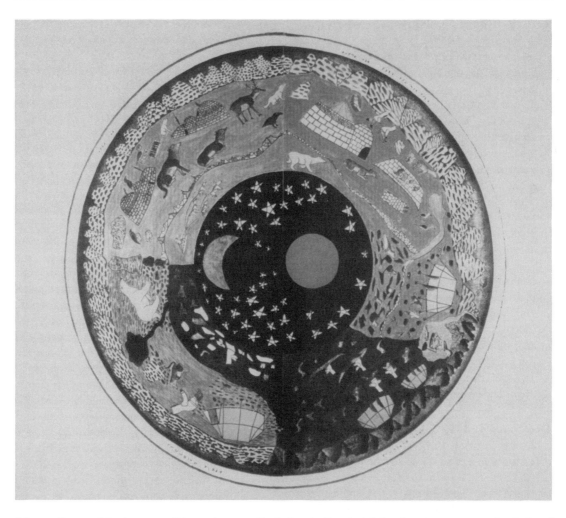

'Nunavut' is one of the three stone lithographs created by Inuit artist Kenojuak Ashevak to commemorate the signing of the Tungavik Federation of Nunavut claim in the eastern Arctic. Courtesy of the Dorset Fine Arts, Inuit Art Section.

JANUARY 24, 1992   Great Whale Project. The federal and Quebec governments, together with the Cree and Inuit of northern Quebec, agree on a environmental review process for the Great Whale Project in northern Quebec. The agreement follows Cree litigation, and a delay in the start of construction.

JANUARY 28, 1992   Indians and the Law. Responding to the report of the Manitoba Justice Inquiry, the Manitoba government announces that it will hire more Native judges and im-

prove legal services to Indians in the provinces, but rejects the suggestion that a separate justice system be established in Manitoba.

FEBRUARY 1992   Compensation for Flooded Reserves. The Cree of South Indian Lake, Manitoba, vote to accept a tentative settlement of $18 million in compensation for land flooded by a hydroelectric project in the 1970s. Critics call the offer inadequate.

FEBRUARY 14, 1992   Aboriginal Self-Government. Following a meeting with Ovide

(left to right) Chester Mahooty of the Zuni tribe of New Mexico, Morgan Tosee of the Comanche tribe of Oklahoma, and Ramona Roach of the Navajo tribe of New Mexico—all-Native American dancers and musicians with the American Indian Dance Theatre. Photo by Don Perdue. Courtesy Hanay Geiogamah.

Mercredi *(See* biography, 1946), leader of the Assembly of First Nations, Constitutional affairs minister Joe Clark suggests that the government may be prepared to consider recognizing a limited inherent aboriginal right to self-government. In turn, Mercredi says the Assembly of First Nations will consider dropping demands that aboriginals be recognized as a distinct society. Two days earlier Clark had suggested that inflexibility on the part of Indian leaders could lead the government to make a constitutional deal without them.

FEBRUARY 15, 1992 Indian Police Force. The Micmac of Cape Breton agree with the federal and Nova Scotia governments to establish an all-Native police force for Micmac on the island.

MARCH 9, 1992 Court Orders Retrial. The Alberta Court of Appeals orders a retrial for Alberta Cree Wilson Nepoose who has spent five and a half years in jail after being convicted of murder. The court rules that his conviction may have been a miscarriage of justice. Nepoose's family calls for a public inquiry, claiming that Nepoose was framed by police. The Crown announces that they probably will not retry Nepoose, and the provincial government rejects calls for an inquiry.

MARCH 12–13, 1992 Canadian Constitutional Conference. At a constitutional conference sponsored by the federal government, participants agree that aboriginal self-government should be entrenched in the Constitution, but differ on the issue of what powers such a government should have. Representatives of federal and provincial governments and Native organizations participate in the conference.

MARCH 26, 1992 Human Rights Commission Report. For the third year in a row, the Canadian Human Rights Commission's annual report lists the injustices faced by aboriginal

groups as the most important human rights issue in Canada. The Commission recommends that the inherent right of aboriginal self-government be entrenched in the federal Constitution.

MARCH 31, 1992 Great Whale Project. The Quebec government blames the Cree of northern Quebec for New York State's decision to cancel a contract to buy power from the Great Whale Project, putting the project in jeopardy. The Cree have lobbied against the project.

APRIL 1992 Canadian Constitutional Agreement. Representatives of the Canadian federal government, nine provincial provinces, two territories, and four aboriginal groups (Assembly of First Nations, Métis National Council, Native Council of Canada, and Inuit Tapirisat of Canada) unanimously agree that the Constitution should recognize the inherent aboriginal right to self-government. The exact powers of Indian governments that would form a third level of government have not been negotiated, but aboriginal leaders and government describe the agreement as the beginning of a new era for Canada's Natives. The Assembly of First Nations announces the creation of a women's committee on constitutional matters to meet criticism that it is ignoring the concerns of Native women. The Native Women's Association of Canada (N.W.A.C.) has argued that Native governments must be bound by the Charter of Rights to protect aboriginal women. On March 31, the organization was refused a court order to force the government to include them in constitutional talks. N.W.A.C., the Women of the Métis Nation, and Pauktuutit, the National Inuit Women's Association, argue that their respective national organizations do not represent their needs and desires.

APRIL 21, 1992 First Nations Aspirations. The Assembly of First Nations advisory body on the Constitution labels constitutional recognition of the inherent aboriginal right to self-government as its key demand. Other demands include the recognition of aboriginal societies

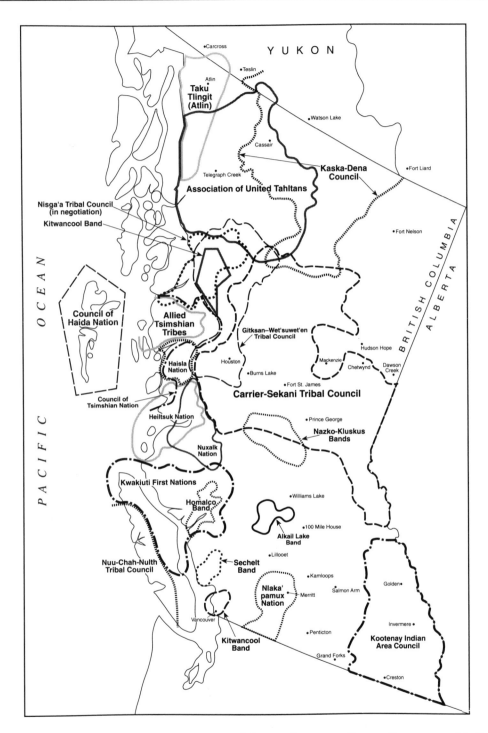

Detailed land claims in British Columbia. Courtesy of Duane Champagne. Source: Department of Indian and Northern Affairs, Ottawa.

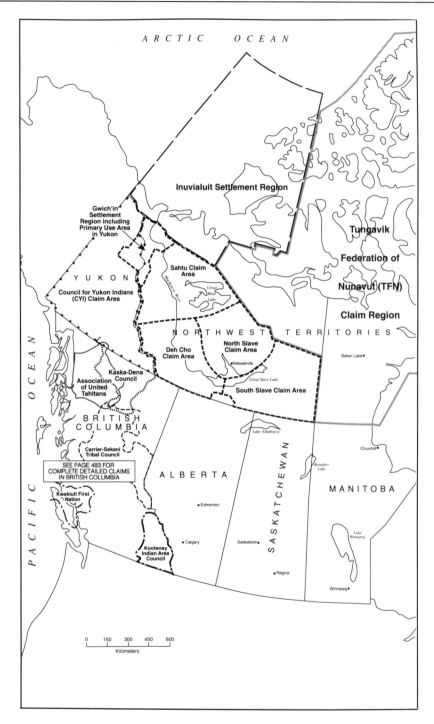

Comprehensive land claims in western Canada. Courtesy of Duane Champagne. Source: Department of Indian and Northern Affairs, Ottawa.

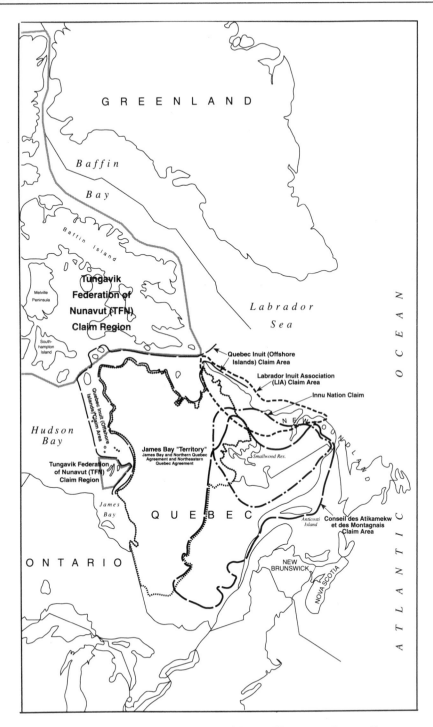

Comprehensive land claims in eastern Canada. Courtesy of Duane Champagne. Source: Department of Indian and Northern Affairs, Ottawa.

as distinct societies, and increased Native control over resources on and off reserves.

APRIL 21, 1992 Royal Commission on Aboriginal Peoples. Georges Erasmus *(See biography, August 8, 1948)*, former head of the Assembly of First Nations, and René Dussault, a Quebec judge, begin their work as co-chairs of the Royal Commission on Aboriginal Peoples. The Royal Commission has a broad mandate to deal with issues affecting aboriginal peoples, including self-government, land claims, justice, and education. The work will take several years.

MAY 4, 1992 Nunavut Territory. Residents of the Northwest Territories narrowly approve the boundary of Nunavut in a plebiscite. The territory will be established by 1999.

MAY 21, 1992 Oldman River Dam Review. A Canadian federal government environmental review panel (Environmental Assessment Review Process) recommends that the nearly completed Oldman River Dam in southwestern Alberta be shut down. The panel cites environmental concerns and the lack of an agreement with the nearby Peigan Indian band. The federal and provincial governments reject the panel's recommendation. Chief Leonard Bastien says the Peigan will continue to fight the dam or seek compensation for environmental damage and flooding of sites they consider sacred.

MAY 22, 1992 Native Women's Prison. The federal government announces that it will build a healing lodge (federal prison) at Maple Creek, Saskatchewan, allowing western Canadian Native women prisoners to be kept nearer their communities. Up to now all women in federal prisons have been housed in one facility in Kingston, Ontario. While only 3 percent of Canada's population is aboriginal, 15 percent of the female prison population is aboriginal.

SUMMER 1992 Salmon Catches. Many thousands of salmon never reach their spawning grounds in British Columbia. Commercial fishermen blame a new federal government-Native agreement that allows Natives to sell their catches commercially.

JUNE 15, 1992 Innu Hold Inquiry. The Innu of Davis Inlet, on the central coast of Labrador, release the findings of an inquiry they carried out following the deaths of six Innu children in a house fire in February. The children had been left alone while their parents were drinking. The Innu acknowledge that most of the residents of Davis Inlet abuse alcohol or sniff gasoline. They admit that they must take control of their lives. They identify the despair caused by the loss of their traditional lifestyle as a central cause of this dependence. They call on the federal government to return them to the mainland where they would be better able to hunt. The Innu were relocated to the island community by the federal government, but shifting ice isolates them from the mainland for most of the year. Indian Affairs minister Tom Siddon says the government must study the issue before funding the relocation.

JUNE 27, 1992 International Platform for Native American Cinema. The Tenth Annual Munich Filmfest in Germany hosts the first major international platform of Native American cinema. The event attracts German media and a large turnout of patrons to its screenings. George Burdeau's (Blackfeet) documentary, *Surviving Columbus* (1992), is a program highlight. Also honored are Gary Rhine and Fidel Moreno (Yaqui/Huichol) for *Wiping the Tears of Seven Generations* (1990); Victor Masayesva Jr. (Hopi) for *Itam Hakim, Hopiit* (1984); and Phil Lucas (Choctaw) for *The Honor of All* (1987). The international film jury awards the "One Future" prize to the entire program of Indian filmmakers.

JULY 7, 1992 Constitutional Accord. Canadian Constitutional affairs minister Joe Clark, nine premiers, two territorial leaders, and aboriginal leaders agree unanimously on a constitutional proposal to present to Quebec. The proposal includes provisions guaranteeing aboriginal self-government as a third level of government. The agreement is followed during the next several weeks by informal meetings with all premiers, including Quebec premier Robert Bourassa. Bourassa publicly expresses concern over the self-government proposals, which he believes may threaten Quebec's "territorial integrity." Some aboriginal leaders, including Ovide Mercredi *(See* biography, 1946) of the Assembly of First Nations, express anger at not being invited to these informal meetings.

JULY 24, 1992   Lubicon Land Claim. Indian Affairs minister Tom Siddon offers $73 million to settle the Lubicon land claim. Negotiations between the federal government and the Lubicon had resumed in November 1991 after a two-year interruption. Lubicon chief Bernard Ominayak rejects the offer.

AUGUST 1992   Tekakwitha Conference. Dissidents at the 53rd Tekakwitha Conference accuse the group's leaders of selling out to a church associated with the conquest of the Americas. Bishop Donald Pelotte, the first Native American to hold such a position, walked out of the final day's discussion. Father John Hascall, a Franciscan and a Native American shaman, led the procession. He stated that the conference had become part of a church "that holds us down as Indian people. . . ."

AUGUST 17, 1992   Native Church Leader. Stanley J. McKay, a Cree from Beausejour, Manitoba, is elected moderator (national leader) of the United Church of Canada, the country's largest Protestant church denomination.

AUGUST 20, 1992   The Charlottetown Accord. Canadian Prime Minister Brian Mulroney, Canada's ten premiers, and the leaders of the Assembly of First Nations, the Native Council of Canada, the Métis National Council, and the Inuit Tapirisat of Canada reach unanimous agreement on provisions that would entrench

aboriginal self-government in Canada's Constitution (the Charlottetown Accord). The provisions are based on the consensus reached on July 7. All agree that laws passed by aboriginal governments will have to be consistent with laws passed by the federal and provincial governments and with Canadian standards of peace, order, and good government. While most Canadians and Natives greet the agreement enthusiastically, there are also immediate voices of criticism.

SEPTEMBER 3, 1992   Referendum on Charlottetown Accord. Prime Minister Brian Mulroney announces that a national referendum will be held on October 26 on the Charlottetown Accord, a proposed new Constitution for Canada that includes provisions that will grant a form of self-government for Canada's aboriginal peoples.

SEPTEMBER 4, 1992   Lubicon Land Claim. Indian Affairs minister Tom Siddon meets with the chief of the Lubicon Cree, Bernard Ominayak, over the question of band membership. They cannot agree on how to determine who is a member of the band. Ominayak insists that the band has 500 members but Siddon argues that the establishment of the Woodland Cree and Loon Lake bands has reduced the Lubicon Lake band to 250 members.

SEPTEMBER 4, 1992   Retrial Ordered for Peigan. The Alberta Court of Appeal orders a new trial for Milton Born With A Tooth because the judge in the previous trial disallowed the presentation of certain relevant evidence. In his previous trial, Born With A Tooth was convicted on weapons charges related to the Peigan protest at the site of the Oldman River Dam in southern Alberta during August and September of 1990.

SEPTEMBER 21, 1992   British Columbia Land Claims. Canadian Prime Minister Brian Mulroney, British Columbia (B.C.) Premier

Mike Harcourt, and B.C. Indians agree to establish a British Columbia Treaty Commission to facilitate the settlement of land claims in the province.

OCTOBER 4, 1992 Canadian Native Response to Columbus Quincentenary. The Canadian Broadcasting Corporation aired "The War Against the Indians," a two-and-a-half-hour documentary commemorating Columbus's voyage. It provides a Native perspective as presented by such notable Canadian Natives as George Sioui, Graham Greene, Tomson Highway, Jim Logan, and Chief John Snow. The 1992 commemoration is in marked contrast to the celebrations held in 1892 (See entry, 1876–1915).

OCTOBER 7, 1992 Royal Commission Report. The Canadian Royal Commission on Aboriginal Peoples issues its first report. It calls for the establishment of aboriginal self-government as a crucial first step in the creation of a completely new relationship between the government and Canada's aboriginal people.

OCTOBER 12, 1992 Native American Response to the Columbus Quincentenary. The Public Broadcasting System (PBS) airs "Surviving Columbus," a documentary produced in co-operation with KNME television in Albuquerque, New Mexico, and the Institute of American Indian Arts in Santa Fe. The two-hour special represents the Native American response to the Columbus Quincentenary, and traces Pueblo history from European contact to the present. Production includes an all-Indian crew consisting of Edmund Ladd, producer (Zuni); George Burdeau, co-executive producer (Blackfeet); Diane Reyna, director (Taos Pueblo); and Simon Ortiz, writer (Acoma Pueblo).

OCTOBER 26, 1992 Charlottetown Accord Defeated. In a national referendum, Canadians reject the Charlottetown Accord. Included in the proposal for a new Constitution are sections that would grant aboriginals a form of self-government. Pollsters suggest that most Canadians did not reject the proposal because of its provisions regarding aboriginal self-government. Nevertheless, status Indians do not appear to have supported the proposal. Sixty-two percent of those on Indian reserves who vote reject the Accord. Many Natives complain that the self-government provisions were not adequately spelled out. Seventy-five percent of the Inuit vote for the agreement. Native leaders announce that they will use general public support for the idea of aboriginal self-government to continue their struggle through other means.

NOVEMBER 20, 1992 James Bay Project. The Federal Court of Appeals rules the federal government of Canada does not have to do an environmental assessment of the Eastmain hydroelectric project because it is authorized by the 1975 James Bay and Northern Quebec Agreement.

DECEMBER 10, 1992 Human Rights Day. The secretary general of the United Nations welcomes more than 200 representatives of indigenous peoples to the New York City, UN headquarters. They gather to mark 1993 as the International Year of Indigenous Peoples. For the first time, indigenous people are invited to address the UN General Assembly. The proceedings begin with a prayer offered by Avrol Looking Horse, keeper of the Lakota sacred pipe.

1 9 9 3

JANUARY 13, 1993 Sahtu Land Claim. The Sahtu Tribal Council, representing 2,200 Sahtu (Bearlake) Dene and Métis, reach a land claims agreement with the Canadian federal government. The agreement will give the Sahtu $75 million dollars over 15 years. The agreement also grants the Sahtu ownership of over 41,00 square kilometers, including subsurface rights to over 1800 square kilometers of land. It also gives them a share of royalties for resources extracted from the region. The Sahtu people emerged as a distinct group in the mid-nineteenth century. Their population probably is derived from Hare and Dogrib Dene bands that resided near the Great Bear Lake and traded at Fort Norman.

JANUARY 19, 1993   Police Raid Gambling Establishments. Police seize unlicensed gambling equipment on five reserves in Manitoba. The Indians and the provincial government have disputed the legality of the gambling establishments.

JANUARY 25, 1993   Court Rules on Jay's Treaty. The Ontario Court of Appeals rules that the Jay's Treaty of 1794 does not exempt Canadian Indians from paying duties on goods imported from the United States. The case is of special interest to Iroquois in Ontario who have been charged with smuggling cigarettes into Canada from the United States. Smuggling as escalated as Canadian taxes have made cigarettes sold in Canada much more expensive than those in the United States. Police estimate that seventy percent of the contraband cigarettes sold in Canada arrive via the Akwesasne Reserve that strattles the international border.

JANUARY 26, 1993   Innu Despair. Television news reports show six Innu children aged 12 to 14, at the remote village of Davis Inlet in Labrador, sniffing gasoline in an apparent suicide attempt. The Innu at Davis Inlet say the level of substance abuse in the village, which has no sewage treatment facilities or running water, reflects the community's despair. The story captures national and international attention and reflects the problems in Native communities across Canada. In December 1992 the *Canadian Journal of Public* reported that Canadian Natives under the age of 65 are two-and-a-half times as likely to commit suicide as non-

Natives. The Innu of Davis Inlet moved to their island village off the Labrador coast in a government-sponsored relocation in 1967. At that time the Newfoundland government had encouraged the Innu to move to a larger population center in Labrador. Health workers estimate that as many as 25 percent of the Innu at Davis Inlet have attempted suicide.

FEBRUARY 6, 1993   First Annual Totem Awards. The First Annual Totem Awards are presented to outstanding Native American artists in film, television, theater, and music. The event is organized by First Americans in the Arts, a nonprofit organization dedicated to encouraging the participation of Native Americans in the entertainment industry. The lavish dinner and awards ceremony is held in Beverly Hills, California. Recipients include John Trudell (Santee Sioux), Graham Greene (Oneida), Sheila Tousey (Menominee), Wes Studi (Cherokee), and Hanay Geiogamah (Kiowa), artistic director of the American Indian Dance Theatre.

FEBRUARY 9, 1993   Davis Inlet. Tom Siddon, Canadian minister of Indian Affairs announces that the government will pay for the relocation of the Innu village of Davis Inlet to the nearby mainland location at Sango Bay. The government is also paying for seven Innu children who are receiving substance abuse treatment at Poundmaker's Lodge, a Native-run addictions treatment center. The seven children return to Davis Inlet on September 2. By that time, the negotiations toward the relocation of the village have become difficult. The Newfoundland government refuses to cooperate unless the Innu are willing to consider other moving to other locations.

FEBRUARY 18, 1993   Suicides at Big Cove. Officials from the federal and provincial governments meet with the Micmac of the Big Cove Reserve in New Brunswick to discuss what can be done about the rash of suicides and suicide attempts there in the past nine months.

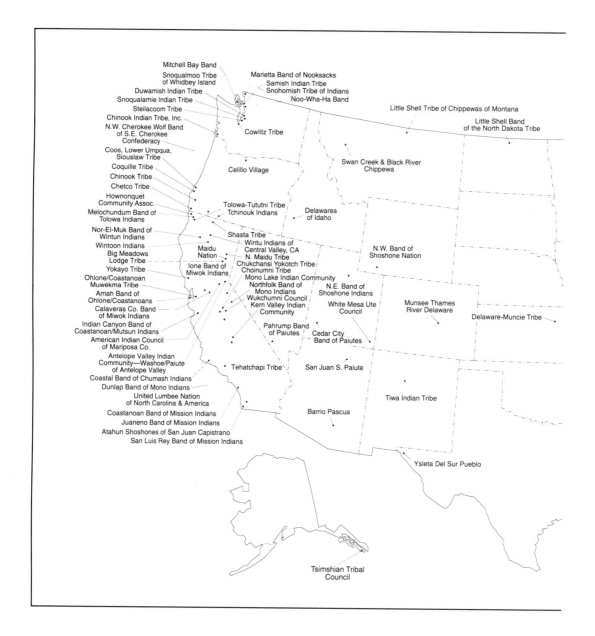

Non-recognized communities with application for federal recognition pending.   Courtesy of Duane Champagne. Source: Bureau of Indian Affairs.

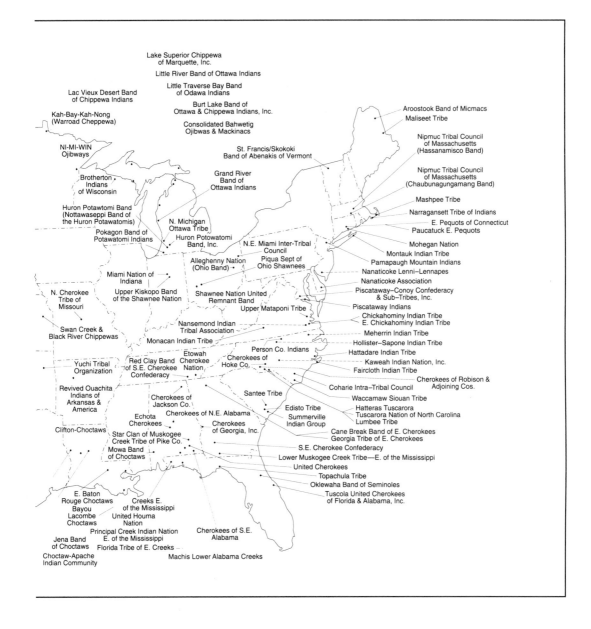

Lake Superior Chippewa
of Marquette, Inc.

Little River Band of Ottawa Indians

Little Traverse Bay Band
of Odawa Indians

Lac Vieux Desert Band
of Chippewa Indians

Burt Lake Band of
Ottawa & Chippewa Indians, Inc.

Kah-Bay-Kah-Nong
(Warroad Cheppewa)

Consolidated Bahwetig
Ojibwas & Mackinacs

Aroostook Band of Micmacs

Maliseet Tribe

Nipmuc Tribal Council
of Massachusetts
(Hassanamisco Band)

NI-MI-WIN
Ojibways

St. Francis/Skokoki
Band of Abenakis of Vermont

Nipmuc Tribal Council
of Massachusetts
(Chaubunagungamang Band)

Brotherton
Indians
of Wisconsin

Grand River
Band of
Ottawa Indians

Mashpee Tribe

Narragansett Tribe of Indians

Huron Potawtomi Band
(Nottawaseppi Band of
the Huron Potawatomis)

N. Michigan
Ottawa Tribe

E. Pequots of Connecticut
Paucatuck E. Pequots

Pokagon Band of
Potawatomi Indians

Huron Potowatomi
Band, Inc.

Mohegan Nation

N.E. Miami Inter-Tribal
Council

Montauk Indian Tribe

Alleghenny Nation
(Ohio Band)

Piqua Sept of
Ohio Shawnees

Pamapaugh Mountain Indians

Miami Nation of
Indiana

Nanaticoke Lenni–Lennapes

Nanaticoke Association

N. Cherokee
Tribe of
Missouri

Upper Kiskopo Band
of the Shawnee Nation

Shawnee Nation United
Remnant Band

Piscataway–Conoy Confederacy
& Sub–Tribes, Inc.

Upper Mataponi Tribe

Piscataway Indians

Chickahominy Indian Tribe
E. Chickahominy Indian Tribe

Swan Creek &
Black River Chippewas

Nansemond Indian
Tribal Association

Meherrin Indian Tribe

Monacan Indian Tribe

Hollister–Sapone Indian Tribe

Person Co. Indians

Hattadare Indian Tribe

Yuchi Tribal
Organization

Etowah
Red Clay Band Cherokee
of S.E. Cherokee Nation
Confederacy

Cherokees of
Hoke Co.

Kaweah Indian Nation, Inc.

Faircloth Indian Tribe

Revived Ouachita
Indians of
Arkansas &
America

Cherokees of Robison &
Adjoining Cos.

Coharie Intra–Tribal Council

Cherokees of
Jackson Co.

Santee Tribe

Waccamaw Siouan Tribe

Echota
Cherokees

Cherokees of N.E. Alabama

Hatteras Tuscarora
Tuscarora Nation of North Carolina
Lumbee Tribe

Edisto Tribe
Summerville
Indian Group

Clifton-Choctaws

Cherokees
of Georgia, Inc.

Cane Break Band of E. Cherokees
Georgia Tribe of E. Cherokees

Star Clan of Muskogee
Creek Tribe of Pike Co.

S.E. Cherokee Confederacy

Mowa Band
of Choctaws

Lower Muskogee Creek Tribe—E. of the Mississippi

United Cherokees

Topachula Tribe

Oklewaha Band of Seminoles

E. Baton
Rouge Choctaws

Creeks E.
of the Mississippi

Tuscola United Cherokees
of Florida & Alabama, Inc.

Bayou
Lacombe
Choctaws

United Houma
Nation

Jena Band
of Choctaws

Principal Creek Indian Nation
E. of the Mississippi

Cherokees of S.E.
Alabama

Florida Tribe of E. Creeks

Choctaw-Apache
Indian Community

Machis Lower Alabama Creeks

Government officials offer funding for counseling and for improved housing on the reserve.

FEBRUARY 26, 1993 Assistance for Davis Inlet. The Canadian government promises $315,000 in immediate emergency assistance for the 500 Innu at Davis Inlet.

MARCH 5, 1993 Métis Politician. Yvon Dumont is sworn in as the first Métis lieutenant-governor in Canada. Gerald Morin, leader of the Saskatchewan Métis, replaces Dumont as president of the Métis National Council.

MARCH 9, 1993 Labrador Inuit Land Claim. William Anderson, president of the Labrador Inuit Association, presents a proposal to Newfoundland premier Clyde Wells which he hopes will break the impasse in negotiations.

MARCH 22, 1993 Gambling Equipment Seized. The Royal Canadian Mounted Police seize gambling equipment on the White Bear Indian Reserve in southeastern Saskatchewan.

MARCH 29, 1993 Canadian National Native Newspaper. *Windspeaker,* published in Edmonton, Alberta, becomes the first national Native newspaper in Canada.

APRIL 2, 1993 Royal Commission Report. The Canadian Royal Commission on Aboriginal Peoples releases its second report about a year after beginning its hearings. It identifies four "touchstones for change," calling for a relationship of respect, the granting of aboriginal self-determination with provisions for self-sufficiency, and healing of years of neglect and abuse. Ovide Mercredi *(See* biography, 1946), national chief of the Assembly of First Nations, condemns the commission for studying Native problems without offering solutions.

APRIL 9, 1993 Canadian Native Protest. Residents of 16 Micmac and Maliseet reserves in New Brunswick and Quebec protest the New Brunswick government's March 31 budget that extends the province's sales tax to Indians when they purchase goods off their reserves. Residents of some reserves blockade major highways in the province for over a day. Nineteen Indians and two non-Natives are charged with obstructing the Trans-Canada Highway on the Kingsclear Maliseet Reserve near Fredericton.

JUNE 1993 Navajo Illness. Twelve Indian people die and others are gravely ill as a result of an illness on the Navajo Reservation. No linkage is made between the disease and the poverty imposed on Indian Country or the lack of adequate care provided by the Indian Health Service.

JUNE 1, 1993 Canadian Census. According to a Canadian census, 783,980 people in Canada identify themselves as Indian (626,000 are status Indians); 212,650 as Métis; and 49,255 as Inuit. Sixty-five percent of Canadian Natives live west of Ontario.

JUNE 3, 1993 Native American Film and Media Celebration. "Wind and Glacier Voices: The Native American Film and Media Celebration" opens at the prestigious Lincoln Center for the Performing Arts in New York City. It is the first film festival showcasing works produced solely by the American (and Canadian) Indian community. The five-day event includes an awards ceremony honoring Native filmmakers and performers, panel discussions on contemporary Indian issues, and daily screenings of independent films. The festival highlights key Indian filmmakers and their works: Dean Curtis Bear Claw (Crow) for *Warrior Chiefs in a New Age* (1991); Bob Hicks (Creek/Seminole) for *Return of the Country* (1984); Loretta Todd (Métis) for *The Learning Path* (1991); Alanis Obomsawin (Abenaki) for *Incident at Restigouche* (1984); and screenwriter Gerald Vizenor (Chippewa) for *Harold of Orange* (1983).

JUNE 25, 1993 *Delgamuukw v. The Queen.* The British Columbia Court of Appeals rules in the *Delgamuukw v. The Queen* case that the 8,000 Gitksan-Wet'suwet'en claimants do enjoy some rights to land that they are claiming in west-central British Columbia. The ruling overturns portions of a March 1991 British Columbia Supreme Court ruling which said that any land rights the Gitksan-Wet'suwet'en may have had were extinguished before British Columbia entered the Canadian Confederation. The claimants welcome the decision as a victory. The British Columbia government expresses its commitment to resolve the claim through negotiation. *(See* map of Comprehensive Land Claims in Canada, pp. 483–85.)

JUNE 25, 1993 **New Minister of Indian Affairs.** Prime minister Kim Campbell announces her new cabinet. Pauline Browes becomes the new minister for Indian affairs and northern development. Native groups complain that the new prime minister has remained quiet about her policy toward indigenous peoples.

JUNE–JULY 1993 **Hantavirus Causes Death on Navajo Reservation.** During the months of June and July, the hantavirus, a rodent-borne disease, is responsible for the deaths of 16 Indian people, primarily Navajo, in the Four Corners region of the southwestern United States. Initially specialists from the Indian Health Service in Albuquerque, New Mexico, stated, "We don't know what causes it," but guided in part by Navajo medicine men, researchers soon traced the contagion to a burgeoned population of rodents. While the majority of deaths have been Navajo, Indians of other tribes, and non-Indians as well, have contracted the fatal disease.

JULY 1993 **Ada Elizabeth Deer, Assistant Secretary-Indian Affairs Confirmed.** Following confirmation hearings, the U.S. Senate confirms Ada Elizabeth Deer (Menominee) as President Bill Clinton's choice for assistant

secretary of Indian affairs in the U.S. Department of the Interior. She is the first woman—and the sixth Indian—to fill the post. (*See also* entry, August 7, 1993.)

JULY 9, 1993 **Sahtu Dene Land Claim.** The Sahtu Dene of the Northwest Territories vote to ratify their land claims agreement with the Canadian government. The agreement is reached in January.

JULY 9–10, 1993 **Simon J. Ortiz Receives 1993 Returning the Gift Lifetime Achievement Award.** The Native Writers' Circle of the Americas presents a lifetime achievement award to Simon J. Ortiz at the 1993 international Returning the Gift conference, attended by nearly 400 Native American poets, fiction writers, and playwrights. His published work includes a volume of stories, *Fightin': New and Collected Stories,* and his most recent, *Woven Stone.* Twenty years ago, he was the editor of *Americas Before Columbus,* the newspaper of the National Indian Youth Council, and the editor of the *Earth Power Coming* anthology.

AUGUST 7, 1993 **Ada Deer Sworn In as Head of the Bureau of Indian Affairs.** Ada Deer, a Menominee and alumna of the University of Wisconsin-Madison and Columbia University, is sworn in as the new head of the Bureau of Indian Affairs. During the inauguration ceremony, tribal leaders from across the country praise her and present her with gifts. At a news conference, she states that she wants Native American communities to have more autonomy in the use of BIA funding.

AUGUST 18, 1993 **Royal Commission Reports.** Canada's Royal Commission on Aboriginal Peoples issues a report that arguing that the aboriginal right to self-government is already recognized in Section 35 of the Canadian constitution. The Charlottetown Accord proposed that the inherent aboriginal right to self-government be recognized in the constitution, but

Ada Deer. Courtesy of Jon Holtshopple and Associates.

was defeated in a referendum in October 1992. Since then the national and provisional governments have refused to discuss further constitutional amendments. Instead, the government has been seeking to negotiate self-government agreements with individual Native communities.

SEPTEMBER 6, 1993   Sahtu Dene Land Claim. George Cleary, president of the Sahtu Tribal Council, and representatives of the Canadian and Northwest Territories governments sign a land claims agreement.

SEPTEMBER 24, 1993   Assembly of First Nations Cuts Staff. The Assembly of First Nations announces that it will lay off about a quarter of its staff. It says the layoffs are necessary because the Canadian government has reduced funding to the organization by about 15 percent in each of the last three years. The organization, which has been involved in a costly land claims court battle, expects that its deficit for this year may reach $1 million.

OCTOBER 23, 1993   First Native American Is Inducted into the Softball Hall of Fame. Ed Morrissette, an Ojibway, is inducted into

the Minnesota Softball Hall of Fame. As a fourth-grader, he remembers his teacher encouraging him to excel in team sports. When Mr. Morrissette told his father that he wanted to try out for the football team, his father advised him that he had to be twice as good as the non-Indian players. Although he encountered racism from his teammates, he did not let them discourage from playing in team sports. He felt that he would prove them wrong by giving 100 percent to the game. He recalls, "The easiest way to quiet them was to hit one over the fence." Because of his experiences, he encourages young people to pursue their sporting interests and try to accomplish their dreams.

OCTOBER 27, 1993   President Clinton Signs the Catawba Land Claim Settlement Act. President Clinton signs the "Catawba Indian Land Claim Settlement Act of 1993," restoring the Catawba tribe's government-to-government relationship with the United States and ending the 153 years of conflict with the state of South Carolina. The act provides a total of $30 to $40 million in benefits and contributions and a payment of $50 million over five years from federal, state, and local governments and private contributors. These monies will be placed in trust funds for land acquisition, economic development, education, and social services for the Catawba tribe.

OCTOBER 28, 1993   Lumbees of North Carolina Are Recognized by Congress. The House of Representatives votes to recognize the 40,000-member Lumbee tribe of Cheraw Indians of North Carolina. After filing their federally recognized status with the Interior Department, the Lumbee Indians can adopt a constitution and by-laws. However, the tribe is not entitled to federal services provided by the Bureau of Indian Affairs and Indian Health Service until Congress appropriates funds for that purpose. Although the state of North Carolina formally recognized the Lumbee Indians as a tribe in 1885, numerous bills in Congress to obtain

The Redstar family tipi encampment at Crow Fair (Crow Agency, Montana), August 1993. Courtesy Stephen Lehmer.

federal recognition have been opposed by the Interior Department since 1890.

NOVEMBER 1993 First Native American Memorial Honors Ute Warriors. About 1,000 people in Meeker, Colorado, gather to honor the Ute warriors who died at the battle of Milk Creek in 1879. This is the nation's first memorial dedicated to Native American warriors and erected by Native Americans.

NOVEMBER 4, 1993 Mercredi Criticizes Choice of Minister. Ovide Mercredi, Grand Chief of

the Assembly of First Nations, criticizes prime minister Jean Chrétien's choice of Ron Irwin as the new minister of Indian affairs and northern development. Mercredi, who calls Irwin "a nobody," says that Ethel Blondin-Andrews, a Dene from the Northwest Territories, would have been a more appropriate choice. The new liberal government was elected on October 26.

NOVEMBER 11, 1993 Aboriginal Self-Government. Canadian minister of Indian affairs Ron Irwin meets with Indian chiefs in an effort

Preparing for the parade at Crow Fair (Crow Agency, Montana), August 1993. Courtesy of Stephen Lehmer.

to begin negotiations toward an agreement that would establish aboriginal self-government in Canada.

NOVEMBER 22, 1993 Inquiry Reports. An inquiry established to examine the case of the murder of Leo LaChance issues its report. It recommends that the Prince Albert police department have a Cree-speaking police officer on duty at all times, and that police officers be trained to be more racially sensitive. It also questions the belief on the part of the police

that the murder of Leo LaChance by Carney Nerland, a known white supremacist, was not racially motivated. Nerland argues that he killed LaChance by accident.

DECEMBER 1993 Cherokee Chief Wilma Mankiller Tours United States to Promote Autobiography. Cherokee Nation principal chief Wilma Mankiller, the first woman chief of a large tribe to be elected, and one of the most progressive Native American leaders, tours American cities to promote her autobiography,

Mesquaki adoption ceremony (Tama, Iowa), 1993. Courtesy of Stephen Lehmer.

Mankiller: A Chief and Her People, co-authored by Michael Wallis. Her autobiography depicts her early years as well as the history of the Cherokee and their problems with the U.S. government in maintaining their identity and culture. In order to continue to work for the Cherokee Nation, she plans for the tour appearances and events to be held in Oklahoma and only on weekends.

DECEMBER 9, 1993 Western Shoshoni Sisters Win the Alternative Nobel Peace Prize. Carrie and Mary Dann are recipients of the 1993 Right Livelihood Award, also known as the "alternative Nobel Peace Prize." According to the Right Livelihood Foundation, the Dann sisters were honored for "their courage and perseverance in asserting the rights of indigenous people to their land." Accompanying this honor is a $200,000 award which the sisters will share with three other recipients from Israel, Zimbabwe, and India.

1 9 9 4

JANUARY 7–9, 1994 Historic Meeting between Oneida Groups. For the first time in seven generations, leaders of the Oneida Business Committee, the Onyota'aka Chiefs Council, and the Elected Council of the Oneidas of the Thames meet in Oneida, Canada, to develop a united front in support of the Oneida land claims. Throughout the discussions, the groups find a common ground—Oneida land is not for sale to any non-Oneida. They plan to meet quarterly to continue building a strong coalition for the cultural and political survival of all Oneida peoples.

JANUARY 10, 1994 Fon du Lac Community College Creates Telecourse in History. Fond du Lac Community College creates a telecourse called "The History of American Indians," covering the social, economic, and political aspects of American Indian communities. Students from Little Hoop Community College in Fort Totten, North Dakota; Deganawida-Quetzalcoatl University in Davis, California; and Fort Belknap Community College in Harlem, Montana, participate in the course via telecommunications technology. This pilot course, the first of several courses to be offered, will allow tribal colleges to share their academic faculty and resources.

JANUARY 14–24, 1994   Native American Performers Travel to Rome for Festival. Native American performers and scholars travel to Rome to participate in the festival, "The Feather, the Flute, The Drum" (La Piuma, Il Flauto, Il Tamburo), featuring music, dance, and storytelling performances; an art installation; video programs; a panel discussion of history and culture; and demonstrations of herb use and cooking. The festival begins with a traditional procession and prayer led by Ken Ryan, Assiniboine spiritual leader. Other participants include Litefoot, a Cherokee musician; Kevin Locke, a renowned Lakota flutist and hoop dancer; Sharon Burch, a Navajo musician; and Sara Bates, a Cherokee visual artist.

JANUARY 18, 1994   Aboriginal Self-Government. The Canadian government announces that it will work with Natives to implement aboriginal self-government as an inherent right. It also announces that it will speed up the land claims process, increase funding for aboriginal post secondary education, and introduce an aboriginal head-start program.

JANUARY 19, 1994   Fon du Lac Community College to Receive Books. The Center for Health, Education and Economic Research, Inc. (CHEER) will donate 10,000 books to the Fon du Lac Community College library. This gift, valued at $500,000, will greatly enlarge and enhance Fon du Lac's library holdings, making it an important educational resource throughout the region.

JANUARY 19, 1994   University of Oklahoma Approves Native American Studies Program. After months of negotiation and community pressure, the Oklahoma State Board of Regents approves a Native American Studies Program at the University of Oklahoma. As an interdisciplinary program, it offers students a wide range of courses, including fine arts, anthropology, and sociology. Students may use the program to work with Native American community organizations or perform library and museum work.

JANUARY 30, 1994   Native American Woman Is the Eleventh to Die from Hantavirus. A 30-year-old Native American woman dies from hantaviral pulmonary syndrome, a disease carried by airborne particles of the urine and feces of rodents. Twenty cases have been reported in New Mexico. The Health Department warns the public to keep rodents out of their homes and to use gloves and disinfectant spray when cleaning infested areas.

FEBRUARY 1–2, 1994   Talks on Self-Government. Leaders of Canada's Native organizations meet with Indian affairs minister Ron Irwin to discuss the implementation of aboriginal self-government. Ovide Mercredi, of the Assembly of First Nations, withdraws from the talks to protest the government's refusal to enshrine the right to self-government in the constitution. Irwin says talks are based on the belief that the right already exists. Ron George of the Native Council of Canada expresses satisfaction regarding the talks. Irwin expresses hope that talks can be completed in about six months.

FEBRUARY 1–4, 1994   Mescalero Apache Sign Nuclear Waste Storage Agreement. Mescalero Apache leaders sign an agreement with Northern States Power, a Minnesota utility, to negotiate the construction of a private nuclear waste storage facility on their reservation in south-central New Mexico. According to Mescalero Apache president Wendell Chino, the proposed nuclear waste storage complex will provide jobs and other economic benefits for approximately 40 years. At a press conference, Governor Bruce King and Democratic Senator Jeff Bingaman voiced their opposition of this agreement due to the health and safety concerns of New Mexico residents. Likewise, Tom Goldtooth, a Dene/Dakota spokesman for the Indigenous Environmental Network, an international alliance of grassroots Native groups, cited the consistent lack of accountability from the nuclear industry and the documented increases in cancer deaths occuring in Native communities. The Mescalero Apache leaders, however, feel confident that their decision to enter into an agreement with Northern States Power has been made after a close study of nuclear technology and its potential economic benefits for their reservation.

FEBRUARY 4, 1994 Mohawk Leaders Fear Police Raids. Akwesasne, Kahnawak', and Kanesataké leaders announce that any attempt by police to raid their reserves will be met with force. The leaders fear that police will raid the reserves in response to the smuggling of cigarettes from the United States to Canada. Cigarette taxes in Canada make U.S. cigarettes much cheaper than Canadian cigarettes. Police estimate that 70 percent of contraband cigarettes in Canada move through the Akwesasne Reserve that straddles the U.S.-Canadian border.

FEBRUARY 7, 1994 President's 1995 Budget Proposes to Eliminate BIA Economic Development Funds. The Clinton administration's 1995 budget plan proposes significant cuts in three BIA economic development grant programs. The $2.5 million direct loan program, $4.3 million in technical assistance grants, and $1.4 million for special tribal courts funding are scheduled to be eliminated. According to BIA spokesman Carl Shaw, the direct loan program is a failure because it has experienced a 70 percent default rate. Ada Deer, assistant secretary for Indian affairs, says that the administration's budget proposal continues the transfer of resources from the BIA to tribal governments and strengthens the federal government and Indian trust relationship.

FEBRUARY 11, 1994 Winnebago Nation Funds Cultural Preservation Projects with Casino Profits. The Wisconsin Winnebago Nation purchases about 600 acres of land on the Wisconsin River for $1.2 million with their casino profits for. The Winnebago elders and others are convinced that this land was once the site of a Winnebago village and contained at least 64 sculptured earthen mounds that have spiritual significance in the Winnebago culture. The Winnebago plan to find and mark all locations of the original mounds. With the approval of the Winnebago elders, they may restore some of the mounds to their original size and shape. Although this land was mainly purchased for a cultural center in which to display and store cultural artifacts the Winnebago are reclaiming from local and national museums, they are also planning for a youth camp, prairie restoration, and a buffalo farm on this site.

FEBRUARY 11–APRIL 3, 1994 Exhibit Exposes Native American Stereotypes. Charlene Teters, Spokane, creates a thought-provoking exhibit, "It Was Only an Indian: Native American Stereotypes" that explores how Native Americans have been and continue to be objectified and dehumanized in popular culture. She exposes racism toward Native Americans by asking: "What does it mean to be the brunt of stereotyping? How would you feel to be examined, probed, and mocked in this manner? Why does this continue to be acceptable?" For several years, she has been collecting and studying apparently innocuous objects such Indian head cigarette ashtrays, toilet paper, and potbellied Indian planters; all of which promote stereotyping. She works as a placement and alumni director for the Institute of American Indian Arts in Santa Fe, while continuing to actively put racism under public scrutiny.

FEBRUARY 11–JULY 15, 1994 Walk For Justice 1994. AIM co-founders Dennis Banks and Mary Jane Wilson-Medrano lead a "Walk For Justice" from Alcatraz Island in California to Washington, D.C., bringing public attention to Native issues and collecting signatures requesting executive clemency for Leonard Peltier, who has served 18 years in prison for allegedly shooting two FBI agents on the Pine Ridge Reservation in South Dakota in 1975.

Other issues brought to public attention by the walk are the James Bay Great Whale Project, where an expanding hydraulic dam threatens fishing and hunting rights of the Cree and Ojibway tribes; the fishing treaty rights struggle in Wisconsin; continued nuclear testing which is destroying water, land, and health for the Western Shoshoni in Nevada; the Dann family (Shoshoni) conflict over land and treaty rights with the Bureau of Land Management; the Big Mountain issue involving involuntary relocation of Navajo from disputed land with the Hopi; and the return of the Black Hills to the Lakota.

FEBRUARY 19, 1994 Innu Protest Government Position. Leaders of the Innu protest Indian affairs minister Ron Irwin's position that the Canadian government will pay for the relocation of Davis Inlet only if the Newfoundland government provides the land for the new Innu settlement. The Innu say that they had understood during a meeting with Irwin in Halifax on February 12 that the federal government would pay for the relocation regardless. They also argue that, since the Innu have never signed a land cession treaty, the land for the new settlement is still theirs.

FEBRUARY 27, 1994 Native Council of Canada Reorganized. The Native Council of Canada reorganizes as the Congress of Aboriginal Peoples. James Sinclair, former leader of the Saskatchewan Métis and of the Métis National Council, is elected its president. Sinclair indicates that he intends to take a more assertive stance toward the Canadian government than that adopted by Ron George, his predecessor.

MARCH 1994 The National Congress of American Indians (NCAI) and the National Black Caucus of State Legislators Join Forces. The NCAI, a confederation of 162 tribal governments and the nation's oldest and largest Indian organization, agrees to support the Black Caucus of State Legislators, a caucus of 540 African American state legislators from 42 states,

in their struggles for African-American rights. In December 1993, the Black Caucus of State Legislators passed a similar resolution to support Native American tribal sovereignty. Both groups agree that since they share similar histories of economic and political oppression in the United States, they need to build coalition networks to fight for basic economic and human rights.

MARCH 9, 1994 Geronimo Scholarship Winners Announced. Greg Powderface, a Gros Ventres graduate student at the Stanford University School of Business, and Wendy Wisdom, a Hopi, Choctaw, and Chickasaw third-year college student majoring in social welfare and Native American Studies, were winners of a scholarship and internship program sponsored by Columbia Pictures and Sony Pictures Entertainment in connection with Columbia Pictures' December 1993 release of *Geromino: An American Legend*. They, along with several hundred American Indian college student applicants, submitted an essay addressing the question, "How can the media better highlight and honor American Indian culture and heritage?" These essays were evaluated by Wes Studi, Cherokee, star of the film, and Sonny Skyhawk, Rosebud Sioux, the consultant for the film. The program provides summer 1994 internship employment in the Columbia Pictures marketing department and a $2,500 scholarship to each winner.

MARCH 11, 1994 Roessel Appointed Deputy Assistant Secretary for Indian Affairs. Mrs. Faith Roessel, a member of the Navajo Nation and former staff attorney with the Native American Rights Fund, is appointed deputy assistant secretary for Indian affairs. In her new post, she continues her work of assisting tribal governments in their efforts to protect their trust assets.

MARCH 16–18, 1994 Indian Country Tourism 200 Conference. A national policy planning conference takes place in Denver, Colorado, and addresses the issues and problems of developing a tourist market in American Indian communities. The feature speakers include Senator Ben Nighthorse Campbell; Calvin Tafoya, New Mexico's Indian tourism program director; and Manley Begay, executive director of the Project on American Indian Economic Development at Harvard University. The speakers present topics such as "Our Responsibility to the Land," "Indian Tourism Networks," and "Using Public Resources to Support Indian Tourism."

American

INDIAN ORATORS

DEKANAWIDAH (Huron and Founder of the Iroquois League) probably sometime between 1300 and 1500. "I am Dekanawidah, and with the Five Nations confederate lords I plant the Tree of the Great Peace. . . . I name the tree the Tree of the Great Long Leaves. Under the shade of this tree of the Great Peace we spread the soft white feather down of the globe thistle as seats for you, Atotarho and your cousin lords. There shall you sit and watch the council fire of the confederacy of the Five Nations. Roots have spread out from the Tree, and the name of these roots is the Great White Roots of Peace. If any man or any nation shall show a desire to obey the laws of the Great Peace, they shall trace the roots to their source, and they shall be welcomed to take shelter beneath the Tree of the Long Leaves. The smoke of the confederate council fire shall pierce the sky so that all nations may discover the central council fire of the Great Peace. I, Dekanawidah, and the confederate lords now uproot the tallest pine tree and into the cavity thereby made we cast all weapons of war. Into the depth of the earth, down into the deep underearth currents of water flowing into unknown regions; we cast all weapons of war. We bury them from sight forever and plant again the tree."

POWHATAN (Powhatan confederacy leader) in a speech made at Werowocomico (Gloucester County) in 1609. "Why will you take by force what you may obtain by love? Why will you destroy us who supply you with food? What can you get by war? We are unarmed, and willing to give you what you ask, if you come in a friendly manner. . . . I am not so simple as not to know it is better to eat good meat, sleep comfortably, live quietly with my women and children, laugh and be merry with the English, and being their friend, trade for their copper and hatchets, than to run away from them. . . . Take away your guns and sword, the cause of our jealousy, or you may die in the same manner."

MIANTUNNUMOH (Narragansett Sachem) c. 1642. "Brothers, we must be one, as the English are, or we shall soon all be destroyed."

PHILIP, OR "KING PHILIP" (Wampanoag Sachem), shortly before the war of 1675, to the ambassador of the governor of Massachusetts. "Your governor is but a subject of King Charles of England. I shall not treat with a subject. I shall treat of peace only with the king, my brother. When he comes, I am ready."

CORNPLANTER (Seneca leader) to George Washington in 1790. "When your army entered the country of the Six Nations, we called you *Caunotaucarius*, the Town Destroyer; and to this day when that name is heard, our women look behind them and turn pale, and our children cling to the knees of their mothers. Our counselors and warriors are men and cannot be afraid; but their hearts are grieved with the fears of the women and children, and desire that it may be buried so deep as to be heard no more. When you gave us peace, we called you father, because you promised to secure us in possession of our lands. Do this, and so long as the lands shall remain, the beloved name will remain in the heart of every Seneca."

RED JACKET (Seneca warrior) in 1792 at a conference with other Seneca chiefs. "Brother! Listen to what we say. There was a time when our forefathers owned this great island. Their seats extended from the rising to the setting of the sun. The Great Spirit had made it for the use of Indians. He had created the buffalo, the deer, and other animals for food. He made the bear and the deer, and their skins served us for clothing. He had scattered them over the country, and had taught us how to take them. He had caused the earth to produce corn for bread. All this he had done for his red children because he loved them. If we had any disputes about hunting grounds, they were generally settled without the shedding of blood. But an evil day came upon us. Your forefathers crossed the great waters and landed on this island. Their numbers were small. They found friends and not enemies. They told us they had fled from their own country for fear of wicked men, and had come here to enjoy their religion. They asked for a small seat. We took pity on them, granted their request and they sat down amongst us. We gave them corn and meat. They gave us poison in return. The white people had now found our country. Tidings were carried back and more came amongst us. Yet we did not fear them. We took them to be friends. They called us brothers. We believed them and gave them a large seat. At length their numbers had greatly increased. They wanted more land. They wanted our country. Wars took place. Indians were hired to fight against Indians, and many of our people were destroyed. They also brought strong liquors among us. It was strong and powerful and has slain thousands. Brothers! Continue to listen. You say that you are sent to instruct us how to worship the Great Spirit agreeable to his mind; and if we do not take hold of the religion which you white people teach we shall be unhappy hereafter. You say that you are right, and we are lost. How do you know this to be true? We understand

that your religion is written in a book. If it was intended for us as well as for you, why has not the Great Spirit given it to us; and not only to us, but why did he not give to our forefathers the knowledge of that book, with the means of understanding it rightly? We only know what you tell us about it. Who shall we know to believe, being so often deceived by the white people?"

LITTLE TURTLE (Miami leader) in council before the battle of Fallen Timbers in 1794. "We have beaten the enemy twice under separate commanders. We cannot expect the same good fortune always to attend us. The Americans are now led by a chief who never sleeps; the day and the night are alike to him. And, during all the time that he has been marching upon our villages, notwithstanding the watchfulness of our young men, we have never been able to surprise him. Think well of it. There is something that whispers to me, it would be prudent to listen to his offers of peace."

TECUMSEH (Shawnee leader) in 1810 to the messenger of the president of the United States. "These lands are ours. No one has the right to remove us, because we were the first owners. The Great Spirit above has appointed this place for us, on which to light our fires, and here we will remain. As to boundaries, the Great Spirit knows no boundaries, nor will his red children acknowledge any."

TECUMSEH also in 1810. "Sell a country! Why not sell the air, the clouds and the great sea, as well as the earth? Did not the Great Spirit make them all for the use of his children?"

TECUMSEH in 1811 at a council with the tribes in the southern part of the country. "Will we calmly suffer the white intruders and tyrants to enslave us? Shall it be said of our race that we knew not how to extricate ourselves from the three most dreadful calamities—folly, inactivity, and cowardice? But what need is there to speak of the past? It speaks for itself and asks, Where today is the Pequot? Where the Narragansetts, the Mohawks, Pocanokets, and many other once powerful tribes of our race? They have vanished before the avarice and oppression of the white men, as snow before a summer sun. In the vain hope of alone defending their ancient possessions, they have fallen in the wars with the white men. . . . So it will be with you Choctaws, and Chickasaws! Soon your mighty forest trees, under the shade of whose wide spreading branches you have played in infancy, sported in boyhood and now rest your wearied limbs after the fatigue of the chase, will be cut down to fence in the land which the white intruders dare to call their own. Soon the broad roads will pass over the grave of your fathers, and the place of their rest will be blotted out forever. The annihilation of our race is at hand unless we unite in one common cause against the common foe."

ONGPATONGA (Omaha leader) in an oration at the burial of a Sioux chief in 1811. "Do not grieve. Misfortunes will happen to the wisest and best men. Death will come, and always comes out of season. It is the command of the Great Spirit, and all nations must obey. What is past and cannot be prevented should not be grieved for."

RED JACKET (Seneca orator) during the War of 1812. "If the British succeed, they will take our country from us; if the Americans drive them back, they will claim our land by right of conquest."

RED JACKET also during War of 1812. "The paper then tells a lie. I have it written here (placing his hand, with great dignity, upon his brow). You Yankees are born with a feather between your fingers; but your paper does not speak the truth. The Indian keeps his knowledge here—this is the book the Great Spirit gave us—it does not lie!" (said, when putting forward his memory against an alleged written statement).

WEATHERFORD (Creek chief) to General Jackson at Fort Mims in 1814. "I am in your power; do with me as you please. I am a warrior. I have done the white people all the harm I could; I have fought them; and fought them bravely; if I have any warriors left, I would still fight, and contend to the last. But I have none; my people are all gone;

and now I can only mourn over the misfortunes of my nation."

MACKATANAMAKEE (Fox leader) at Portage in 1815 to the American commissioner. "Again, I call heaven and earth to witness, and I smoke this pipe in evidence of my sincerity. My only desire is that we should smoke it together—that I should grasp your sacred hand, and I claim for myself and my tribe the protection of your country. When this pipe touches your lip, may it operate as a blessing upon all my tribe. May the smoke rise like a cloud, and carry away with it all the animosities which have arisen between us."

RED JACKET (Seneca orator) in 1820 to Rev. Mr. Brackenridge. "Brother, if you white men murdered the Son of the Great Spirit, we Indians had nothing to do with it, and it is none of our affair. If he had come among us, we would not have killed him; we would have treated him well. You must make amends for that crime yourselves."

PUSHMATAHA (Choctaw leader) to the Secretary of War at Washington in 1824. "I can boast and say, and tell the truth, that none of my fathers, or grandfathers, nor any Choctaw ever drew bow against the United States. They have always been friendly. We have held the hands of the United States so long, that our nails are long like birds' claws; and there is no danger of their slipping out."

PUSHMATAHA (Choctaw leader) to some Indian friends shortly before his death in 1824. "I shall die, but you will return to our brethren. As you go along the paths, you will see the flowers and hear the birds sing, but Pushmataha will see them and hear them no more. When you shall come to your home, they will ask you, 'Where is Pushmataha?' and you will say to them 'He is no more.' They will hear the tidings like the sound of the fall of a mighty oak in the stillness of the woods."

LITTLE BLACK (Winnebago) in 1832. "My father, I ask nothing but a clear sky above our heads, which have been hanging down lately, and the sky has been dark, and the wind has been blowing continually and trying to blow lies in our ears, but we turn our ears from it. But when we look toward you, the weather is clear and the wind does not blow."

BLACK HAWK (Sac leader) in 1832 when he was turned over to the Indian agent at Prairie du Chien. "You have taken me prisoner, with all my warriors. I am much grieved; for I expected, if I did not defeat you, to hold out much longer, and give you more trouble before I surrendered. I tried hard to bring you into ambush, but your last general understood Indian fighting. I determined to rush upon you, and fight you face to face. I fought hard, but your guns were well aimed. The bullets flew like birds in the air, and whizzed by our ears like the wind through the trees in winter. My warriors fell around me; it began to look dismal. I saw my evil day at hand. The sun rose dim on us in the morning, and at night it sank in a dark cloud, and looked like a ball of fire. That was the last sun that shone on Black Hawk. His heart is dead, and no longer beats quick in his bosom. He is now a prisoner to the white men; they will do with him as they wish. But he can stand torture, and is not afraid of death. He is no coward. Black Hawk is an Indian!"

JOSEPH BRANT (Mohawk leader) in 1833 to Colonel Eustis. "The Great Spirit punishes those who deceive us, and my faith is now pledged."

SITTING BULL (Sioux leader) in 1833. "If the Great Spirit had desired me to be a white man he would have made me so in the first place. He put in your heart certain wishes and plans, in my heart he put other and different desires. Each man is good in his sight. It is not necessary for eagles to be crows. Now we are poor but we are free. No white man controls our footsteps. If we must die we die defending our rights."

KEOKUK (Sauk leader) to Governor Everett at Boston in 1837. "The Great Spirit, as you have said, made us the same; we only speak different languages."

OSCEOLA (Seminole leader) when arrested and taken to prison in 1837. "The sun is so high! I shall

remember the hour! The agent has his day—I will have mine."

CHIEF SEATTLE (Suquamish and Duwamish leader) as spoken by Seattle and recorded by Dr. Henry Smith in 1854. "Yonder sky that has wept tears of compassion of our fathers for centuries untold, and which to us looks eternal, may change. Today is fair, tomorrow it may be overcast with clouds. My words are like stars that never set. What Seattle says, the great chief, Washington can rely upon, with as much certainty as our paleface brothers can rely upon the return of the seasons. The son of the white chief says his father sends us greetings of friendship and good will. This is kind, for we know he has little need of our friendship in return, because his people are many. They are like the grass that covers the vast prairies, while my people are few, and resemble the scattering trees of a storm-swept plain. The great, and I presume also good, white chief sends us word that he wants to buy our land but is willing to allow us to reserve enough to live on comfortably. This indeed appears generous, for the red-man no longer has rights that he need respect, and the offer may be wise, also, for we are no longer in need of a great country.

There was a time when our people covered the whole land, as the waves of a wind-ruffed sea cover its shell-paved floor. But that time has long since passed away with the greatness of tribes now almost forgotten. I will not mourn over our untimely decay, nor reproach my pale-face brothers for hastening it, for we, too, may have been somewhat to blame.

When our young men grow angry at some real or imaginary wrong, and disfigure their faces with black paint, their hearts, also, are disfigured and turn black, and then their cruelty is relentless and knows no bounds, and our old men are not able to restrain them.

But let us hope that hostilities between the red-man and his pale-face brothers may never return. We would have everything to lose and nothing to gain.

True it is, that revenge, with your braves, is considered gain, even at the cost of their own lives, but old men who stay at home in times of war, and old women, who have sons to lose, know better.

Our great father Washington, for I presume he is now our father as well as yours, since George has moved his boundaries to the north; our great and good father, I say, sent us word by his son, who, no doubt, is a great chief among his people, that if we do as he desired, he will protect us. His brave armies will be to us a bristling wall of strength, and his great ships of war will fill our harbors so that our ancient enemies far to the northward, the Simsiams and Hydas, will no longer frighten our women and old men. Then he will be our father and we will be his children.

But can this ever be? Your God loves your people and hates mine; he folds his strong arms lovingly around the white man and leads him as a father leads his infant son, but he has forsaken his red children; he makes your people wax strong every day, and soon they will fill the land; while my people are ebbing away like a fast-receding tide, that will never flow again. The white man's God cannot love his red children or he would protect them. They seem to be orphans and can look nowhere for help. How can we become brothers? How can your father become our father and bring us prosperity and awaken in us dreams of returning greatness?

Your God seems to us to be partial. He came to the white man. We never saw Him. We never even heard His voice; He gave the white man laws but He had no word for His red children whose teeming millions filled this vast continent as the stars will the firmament. No, we are two distinct races and must ever remain so. There is little in common between us. The ashes of our ancestors are sacred and their final resting place is hallowed ground, while you wander away from the tombs of your fathers seemingly without regret. Your religion was written on tables of stone by the iron finger of an angry God, lest you might forget it. The red-man could never remember nor comprehend it. Our religion is the traditions of our ancestors, the dreams of our old men, given them

by the great Spirit, and the visions of our sachems, and is written in the hearts of our people.

Your dead cease to love you and the homes of their nativity as soon as they pass the portals of the tomb. They wander far off beyond the stars, are soon forgotten, and never return. Our dead never forget the beautiful worlds that gave them being. They still love its winding rivers, its great mountains and its sequestered vales, and they ever yearn in tenderest affection over the lonely hearted living and often return to visit and comfort them.

Day and night cannot dwell together. The red man has ever fled the approach of the white man, as the changing mists on the mountain side flee before the blazing morning sun.

However, your proposition seems a just one, and I think my folks will accept it and will retire to the reservation you offer them, and we will dwell apart and in peace, for the words of the great white chief seem to be the voice of nature speaking to my people out of the thick darkness that is fast gathering around them like a dense fog floating inward from a midnight sea. It matters but little where we pass the remainder of our days. There are not many.

The Indian's night promises to be dark. No bright star hovers about the horizon. Sad-voiced winds moan in the distance. Some grim Nemesis of our race is on the red man's trail, and wherever he goes he will still hear the sure approaching footsteps of the fell destroyer and prepare to meet his doom, as does the wounded doe that hears the approaching footsteps of the hunter. A few more moons, a few more winters and not one of all the mighty hosts that once filled this broad land or that now roam in fragmentary bands through these vast solitudes will remain to weep over the tombs of a people once as powerful and as hopeful as your own.

But why should we repine? Why should I murmur at the fate of my people? Tribes are made up of individuals and are no better than they. Men come and go like the waves of the sea. A tear, a tamanawus, a dirge, and they are gone from our longing eyes forever. Even the white man, whose God walked and talked with him, as friend to friend, is not exempt form the common destiny. We may be brothers after all. We shall see."

CHIEF SEATTLE (Suquamish and Duwamish leader), as spoken to Isaac Stevens, Governor of Washington Territory, in 1854. "When the last red man shall have perished, and the memory of my tribe shall have become a myth among the white men, these shores will swarm with the invisible dead of my tribe. . . . At night when the streets of your cities and villages are silent and you think them deserted, they will throng with the returning hosts that once filled and still love this beautiful land. The white man will never be alone. Let him be just and deal kindly with my people, for the dead are not powerless. Dead, did I say? There is no death, only a change of worlds."

COCHISE (Apache leader) in a speech made early in September 1866 at a council that was held at the agency at Canada Alamosa. "When God made the world he gave one part to the white man and another to the Apache. Why was it? Why did they come together? Now that I am to speak, the sun, the moon, the earth, the air, the waters, the birds and beasts, even the children unborn shall rejoice at my words. The white people have looked for me long. I am here! What do they want? They have looked for me long; why am I worth so much? If I am worth so much why not mark when I set my foot and look when I spit. . . . When I was young I walked all over this country, east and west, and saw no other people than the Apaches. After many summers I walked again and found another race of people had come to take it. How is it? Why is it that the Apaches wait to die—that they carry their lives on their finger nails? They roam over the hills and plains and want the heavens to fall on them. The Apaches were once a great nation; they are now but few, and because of this they want to die and so carry their lives on their finger nails. Many have been killed in battle. You must speak straight so that your words may go as sunlight to your hearts. Tell me, if the Virgin Mary has walked throughout all the land, why has she never entered the wigwam of the Apache? Why have we never seen or heard her? I have no father or mother; I am

alone in the world. No one cares for Cochise; that is why I do not care to live, and wish the rocks to fall on me and cover me up. . . . I have drunk of these waters and they have cooled me; I do not want to leave here."

TALL BULL (Cheyenne leader) in a speech made to Major General W. S. Hancock on May 22, 1867, at a treaty session at Fort Leavenworth, Kansas. "Great Spirit, I want no blood upon my land to stain the grass. I want it all clear and pure, and I wish it so, that all who go through among my people may find peace when they come in, and leave it when they go out."

SATANK (Kiowa leader) in a speech made at Medicine Lodge Creek in 1867. "It has made me glad to meet you, who are commissioners of the Great Father. You no doubt are tired of the much talk of our people. Many of them have put themselves forward and filled you with their sayings. I have kept back and said nothing, not that I did not consider myself still the principal chief of the Kiowa nation, but others, younger than I, desired to talk, and I left it to them. Before I leave, however, as I now intend to go, I come to say that the Kiowas and Comanche have made with you a peace, and they intend to keep it. If it brings prosperity to us, we, of course, will like it better. If it brings poverty and adversity we will not abandon it. It is our contract and it shall stand."

KICKING BIRD (Kiowa leader) in a speech at Medicine Lodge Creek in 1867. "I long ago took the white man by the hand; I have never let it go; I have held it with a strong and firm grasp. I have worked hard to bring my people on the white man's road. Sometimes I have been compelled to work with my back towards the white people so that they have not seen my face, and they may have thought I was working against them; but I have worked with one heart and one object. I have looked ahead to the future, and have worked for the children of my people, to bring them into a position that, when they became men and women, they will take up the white road. I have but two children of my own, but have worked for the children of my people as though they had been mine. Five years I have striven for this thing, and all these years Big Bow worked against me to keep my people on the old bad road. When I brought in and delivered up white captives to the agent, Big Bow had taken more. Now for a little while he comes on to the good road. The agent has taken him by the hand, and thrown me away after my many years' labor. I am as a stone, broken and thrown away—one part thrown this way, and one part thrown that way. I am a chief no more; but that is not what grieves me—I am grieved at the ruin of my people: they will go back to the old road, and I must follow them; they will not let me live with the white people. I shall go to my camp, and after a while I shall go a little farther, and then a little farther, until I get as far away as is possible for me. When they show me the big chief they select, I shall follow him wherever he leads. When you take hold of my hand today you have taken it for the last time; when you see me ride away today, you will see Kicking Bird no more. I shall never come back to this place."

CHIEF JOSEPH (Nez Percé leader) in a speech made to Generals Howard and Miles, October 5, 1877, on the occasion of the Nez Percé surrender. "Tell General Howard I know his heart. What he told me before, I have in my heart. I am tired of fighting. Our chiefs are killed. Looking Glass is dead. Toohoolhoolzote (Too-hool-hool-suit) is dead. The old men are all dead. It is the young men who say yes and no. He who led on the young men is dead. It is cold and we have no blankets. The little children are freezing to death. My people, some of them, have run away to the hills and have no blankets, no food; no one knows where they are—perhaps freezing to death. I want to have time to look for my children and see how many I can find. Maybe I shall find them among the dead. Hear me, my chiefs. I am tired; my heart is sick and sad. From where the sun now stands I will fight no more forever."

SMOHALLA (Wanapum Indian prophet) in 1884. "You ask me to plough the ground! Shall I take a knife and tear my mother's bosom? Then when I die, she will not take me to her bosom to rest. You ask me to dig for stone! Shall I dig under her skin for her bones? Then, when I die, I cannot enter her body to be born again. You ask me to cut grass and make hay, and sell it, and be rich like white men! But how dare I cut my mother's hair?"

TOOHOOLHOOLZOTE (Nez Percé priest) in 1877 to General Howard. "We never made any trade. Part of the Indians gave up their land. I never did. The earth is part of my body, and I never gave up the earth. So long as the earth keeps me, I want to be let alone."

CRAZY HORSE (Sioux leader) on September 5, 1877, to Indian agent Jesse M. Lee on the night of Crazy Horse's death. "My friend, I do not blame you for this. Had I listened to you this trouble would not have happened to me. I was not hostile to the white men. Sometimes my young men would attack the Indians who were their enemies and take their ponies. They did it in return. We had buffalo for food, and their hides for clothing and for our tipis. We preferred hunting to a life of idleness on the reservation, where we were driven against our will. At times we did not get enough to eat, and we were not allowed to leave the reservation to hunt. We preferred our own way of living. We were no expense to the government. All we wanted was peace and to be left alone. Soldiers were sent out in the winter, who destroyed our villages.

Then Long Hair [Custer] came in the same way. They say we massacred him, but he would have done the same thing to us had we not defended ourselves and fought to the last. Our first impulse was to escape with our squaws and papooses, but we were so hemmed in that we had to fight. After that I went up on the Tongue River with a few of my people and lived in peace. But the government would not let me alone. Finally, I came back to the Red Cloud Agency. Yet I was not allowed to remain quiet. I was tired of fighting. I went to the Spotted Tail Agency and asked that chief and his agent to let me live there in peace. I came here with the agent to talk with the Big White Chief but was not given a chance. They tried to confine me. I tried to escape, and a soldier ran his bayonet into me. I have spoken."

SITTING BULL in 1889. "Indians! There are no Indians left now but me!"

KICKING BEAR (Dakota warrior) in a speech given in 1890 to a council of Sioux Indians. Short Bull, who was in attendance, related the speech to Major James McLaughlin. "My brothers, I bring to you the promise of a day in which there will be not white man to lay his hand on the bridle of the Indian's horse; when the red men of the prairie will rule the world and not be turned from the hunting grounds by any man. I bring you word from your fathers the ghosts, that they are now marching to join you, led by the Messiah who came once to live on earth with the white men, but was cast out and killed by them. I have seen the wonders of the spirit-land, and have talked with the ghosts. I traveled far and am sent back with a message to tell you to make ready for the coming of the Messiah and return of the ghosts in the spring."

AMERICAN HORSE (Sioux leader) in 1890. "We were made many promises, but have never heard from them since."

MANUELITO (Navajo leader) in 1893. "It is as though the whites were in a grassy canyon and there they have wagons, plows, and plenty of food. We Navajos are upon the dry mesa. We can hear them talking but we cannot get to them. My grandchild, education is the ladder. . . ."

CANONICUS (a Narragansett Sachem) to Roger Williams (date unknown). "I have never suffered any wrong to be done to the English, since they landed, nor ever will."

PEZHEKEZHIKQUASHKUM (Ojibway leader) in answer to Reverend Peter Jones, the Indian missionary (date unknown). "How can I, who have grown old in sins and in drunkenness, break off from these things, when the white people are as bad and wicked as the Indians?"

RED JACKET (Seneca orator) (date unknown). "A warrior! Sir, I am an orator!"

WAKAUN HAKA (Winnebago leader) (date unknown). "The Great Spirit has made the skin of the Indian red, and soap and water can not make it white."

HANDSOME LAKE (Seneca orator) related part of his code of conduct (date unknown). "Whisky [is] a great and monstrous evil and has reared a high mound of bones. . . . You lose your minds and whiskey causes it all. . . . So now all must now say, 'I will use it never-more'. . . . The married should live together and . . . children should grow from them. . . . Man and wife should rear their children well, love them and keep them in health. . . . Love one another and do not strive for another's undoing. Even as you desire good treatment, so render it."

Documents

OF HISTORY

ROYAL PROCLAMATION OF 1763, "And whereas it is just and reasonable, and essential to our Interest, and the security of our Colonies, that the several Nations or Tribes of Indians with whom We are connected, and who live under our protection, should not be molested or disturbed in the Possession of such Part of Our Dominion and Territories as, not having been ceded to or purchased by Us, are reserved to them or any of them, as their Hunting Grounds. . . ."

"And we do further declare it to our Royal Will and Pleasure, for the present as aforesaid, to reserve under our Sovereignty, Protection, and Dominion, for the use of the said Indians, all the lands and Territories not included within the Limits of Our Said New Governments, or within the Limits of the Territory granted to the Hudson's Bay Company, as also all the lands and Territories lying to the Westward of the Sources of the Rivers which fall into the Sea from the West and the North West as aforesaid."

". . . We do, with the Advice of our Privy Council, strictly enjoin and require, that no private Person do presume to make any Purchase from the said Indians of any Lands reserved to the said Indians, within those parts of our Colonies where, We have thought proper to allow Settlement; but that, if at any Time any of the said Indians should be inclined to dispose of the said Lands, the same shall be Purchased for Us, in our name, at some public Meeting or Assembly of the said Indians. . . ."

PROCLAMATION OF THE CONTINENTAL CONGRESS, September 22, 1783: "Whereas by the ninth of the Articles of Confederation, it is among other things declared, that 'the United States in Congress assembled have the sole and exclusive right and power of regulating the trade, and managing all affairs with the Indians, not members of any of the states, provided that the legislative right of any State, within its own limits, be not infringed or violated.'"

TREATY WITH THE SIX NATIONS, October 22, 1784: [Typical of treaties signed by the United States with Indian nations following the Revolutionary War] "The United States of America give peace to the Senecas, Mohawks, Onondagas, and Cayugas, and receive them into their protection upon the following conditions:

Article I. Six hostages shall be immediately delivered to the commissioners by the said nations, to remain in possession of the United States, till all the prisoners, white and black, which were taken by the said Senecas, Mohawks, Onondagas, and Cayugas, or by any of them, in the late war, from among the people of the United States, shall be delivered up.

Article II. The Oneida and Tuscarora nations shall be secured in the possession of the lands on which they are settled.

Article III. A line shall be drawn, beginning at the mouth of a creek about four miles east of Niagara, Called Oyonwayea, or Johnston's Landing-Place, upon the lake named by the Indians Oswego, and by us Ontario, thence southerly in a direction always four miles east of the carrying-path . . . so that the Six Nations shall and do yield to the United States, all claims to the country west of the said boundary, and then they shall be secured in the peaceful possession of the lands they inhabit east and north of the same, reserving only six miles square round the fort of Oswego, to the United States, for the support of the same.

Article IV. The Commissioners of the United States, in consideration of the present circumstances of the Six Nations, and in execution of the humane and liberal views of the United States upon the signing of the above articles, will order goods to be delivered to the said Six Nations for their use and comfort. . . ."

NORTHWEST ORDINANCE, July 13, 1787: "The utmost good faith shall always be observed towards the Indians, their lands and property shall never be taken from them without their consent; and in their property, rights and liberty, they never shall be invaded or disturbed, unless in just and lawful wars authorized by Congress; but laws founded in justice and humanity shall from time to time be made, for preventing wrongs being done to them, and for preserving peace and friendship with them. . . ."

CIVILIZATION FUND ACT, March 3, 1819: "Be it enacted . . . that for the purpose of providing against the further decline and final extinction of the Indian tribes, adjoining the frontier settlements of the United States, and for introducing among them the habits and arts of civilization, the President of the United States shall be, and he is hereby authorized, in every case where he shall judge improvement in the habits and conditions of such Indians practicable, and that the means of instruction can be introduced with their own consent, to employ capable persons of good moral character, to instruct them in the mode of agriculture suited to their situation; and for teaching their children in reading, writing, and arithmetic, and performing such other duties as may be enjoined. . . . And be it further enacted, that the annual sum of

ten thousand dollars be, and the same is hereby appropriated, for the same purpose. . . ."

ACT FOR REGULATING THE INDIAN TRADE, May 6, 1822: "Be it enacted . . . that the seventh section of the act, entitled 'An act to regulate trade and intercourse with the Indian tribes and to preserve peace on the frontiers,' shall be, and the same is hereby, repealed; and from and after the passing of this act, it shall be lawful for the superintendents of Indian affairs in the territories and Indian agents, under the direction of the President of the United States, to grant licenses to trade with Indian tribes; which licenses shall be granted to citizens of the United States, and to none others, taking from them bonds with security in the penal sum not exceeding five thousand dollars. . . . And be it further enacted, That all purchases for and on account of Indians, for annuities, presents, and otherwise, shall be made by the Indian agents and governors of territories acting as superintendents, with their respective districts. . . ."

CREATION OF A BUREAU OF INDIAN AFFAIRS IN THE WAR DEPARTMENT, March 11, 1824: "Department of War, March 11, 1824. Sir: To you are assigned the duties [of] the Bureau of Indian Affairs in this Department, for the faithful performance of which you will be responsible. . . . You will take charge of the appropriations for annuities, and of the current expenses, and all warrants on the same will be issued on your requisitions on the Secretary of War, taking special care that no requisition be issued, but in cases where the money previously remitted has been satisfactorily accounted for. . . ."

AUTHORIZATION OF TREATIES: TRADE REGULATIONS, May 25, 1824: "Be it enacted. . . . That the sum of ten thousand dollars be, and the same hereby is, appropriated, to defray the expenses of making treaties of trade and friendship with the Indian tribes beyond the Mississippi: and that the said sum shall be paid out of any money in the treasury not otherwise appropriated. . . . And be it further enacted, That, for the purpose of negotiating said treaties, on the part of the United States, the President shall be, and he hereby is, authorized to appoint suitable persons for commissioners, and to fix their compensation, so as not to exceed what has been heretofore allowed for like services. . . ."

MESSAGE OF PRESIDENT MONROE ON INDIAN REMOVAL,

January 27, 1825: ". . . On the contrary, that the removal of the tribes from the territory which they now inhabit to that which was designated in the message at the commencement of the session, which would accomplish the object for Georgia, under a well-digested plan for their government and civilization, which should be agreeable to themselves, would not only shield them from impending ruin, but promote their welfare and happiness. . . . The great object to be accomplished is the removal of these tribes to the territory designated on conditions which shall be satisfactory to themselves and honorable to the United States."

PRESIDENT JACKSON ON INDIAN REMOVAL,

December 8, 1829: ". . . The condition and ultimate destiny of the Indian tribes within the limits of some of our States have become objects of much interest and importance. It has long been the policy of Government to introduce among them the arts of civilization, in the hope of gradually reclaiming them from a wandering life. . . . Thus, though lavish in its expenditures upon the subject, Government has constantly defeated its own policy, and the Indians in general, receding farther and farther to the west, have retained their savage habits. A portion, however, of the southern tribes, having mingled much with the whites and made some progress in the arts of civilized life, have lately attempted to erect an independent government within the limits of Georgia and Alabama. Those States, claiming to be the only sovereigns within their territories, extended their laws over the Indians, which induced the latter to call upon the United States for protection. . . . I informed the Indians inhabiting parts of Georgia and Alabama that their attempts to establish an independent government would not be countenanced by the Executive of the United States, and advised them to emigrate beyond the Mississippi or sub-mit to the laws of those States. . . . This emigration should be voluntary, for it would be as cruel as unjust to compel the aborigines to abandon the graves of their fathers and seek a home in a distant land. But they should be distinctly informed that if they remain within the limits of the States they must be subject to their laws. In return for their obedience as individuals, they will without doubt be protected in the enjoyment of those possessions which they have improved by their industry."

INDIAN REMOVAL ACT,

May 28, 1830: "Be it enacted . . . that it shall and may be lawful for the President of the United States to cause so much of any territory belonging to the United States, west of the river Mississippi, not included in any state or organized territory, and to which the Indian title has been extinguished, as he may judge necessary, to be divided into a suitable number of districts, for the reception of such tribes or nations of Indians as may choose to exchange the lands where they now reside, and remove there; and to cause each of said districts to be so described by natural or artificial marks, as to be easily distinguished from each other. And be it further enacted, that it shall and may be lawful for the President to exchange any or all of such districts, so to be laid off and described, with any tribe or nation of Indians now residing within the limits of any of the states or territories, and with which the United States having existing treaties, for the whole or any part or portion of the territory claimed and occupied by such tribe or nation, within the bounds of any one or more of the states or territories, where the land claimed and occupied by the Indians, is owned by the United States, or the United States are bound to the state within which it lies to extinguish the Indian claim thereto. And be it further enacted, that in the making of any such exchange or exchanges, it shall and may be lawful for the President solemnly to assure the tribe or nation with which the exchange is made, that the United States will forever secure and guaranty to them, and their heirs or successors, the country so exchanged with them; and if they prefer it, that the United States will cause a patent or grant to be made and executed to them for the same. . . ."

AUTHORIZATION OF A COMMISSIONER OF INDIAN AFFAIRS, July 9, 1832: "Be it enacted . . . that the President shall appoint, by and with the advice and consent of the Senate, a commissioner of Indian affairs, who shall, under the direction of the Secretary of War, and agreeably to such regulations as the President may, from time to time, prescribe, have the direction and management of all Indian affairs, and of all matters arising out of Indian relations, and shall receive a salary of three thousand dollars per annum."

EXTRACT FROM THE ANNUAL REPORT OF THE COMMISSIONER OF INDIAN AFFAIRS, November 22, 1832: ". . . Some of the Indian tribes have proceeded to hostile acts, in the course of the year past, against each other, and conflicts have ensued, in which blood has been spilt in defiance of the obligation imposed by the guarantee of the United States, for the preservation of peace and tranquility among them. The instigator of such unwarrantable proceedings, as well as the chief actors in every instance of ascertained outrage, are justly considered responsible to the Government for the transgression, and are invariably required to be given up to its authority to answer for the offenses.

It is difficult to restrain such aggressions, growing out of ancient feuds, prompted by an unchecked spirit of rapine, and a thirst for warlike distinction, and, particularly, when probable impunity furnished an additional incentive. To prevent outrage, is however, far better than to punish the offenders; nor should the expense attendant on the remedy to be found in the employment of a sufficient body of mounted rangers preclude its exercise. A display of military force, and the certainty of speedy punishment, can alone prevent a ready resort to rapine and bloodshed on the part of those who recognize no restraint on plunder, no bounds to the gratification of revenge."

TRADE AND INTERCOURSE ACT, June 30, 1834: "Be it enacted . . . that all that part of the United States west of the Mississippi, and not within the states of Missouri and Louisiana, or the territory of Arkansas, and also, that part of the United States east of the Mississippi river, and not within any state to which the Indian title has not been extinguished, for the purposes of this act, be taken and deemed to be the Indian country."

PRESIDENT JACKSON ON INDIAN REMOVAL, December 7, 1835: ". . . The plan of removing the aboriginal people who yet remain within the settled portions of the United States to the country west of the Mississippi River approaches its consummation. It was adopted on the most mature consideration of the condition of this race, and ought to be persisted in till the object is accomplished. . . . All preceding experiments for the improvement of the Indians have failed. It seems now to be an established fact that they can not live in contact with a civilized community and prosper."

TRANSFER OF INDIAN AFFAIRS TO THE DEPARTMENT OF INTERIOR, March 3, 1849: "Be it enacted . . . that, from and after the passage of this act, there shall be created a new executive department of the government of the United States, to be called the Department of the Interior; the head of which department shall be called the Secretary of the Interior, who shall be appointed by the President of the United States, by and with the advice and consent of the Senate. . . . And be it further enacted, that the Secretary of the Interior shall exercise the supervisory and appellate powers now exercised by the Secretary of the War Department, in relation to all the acts of the Commissioner of Indian Affairs. . . ."

TREATY OF FORT LARAMIE, September 17, 1851: ". . . Article II. The aforesaid nations [Sioux, Dakota, Cheyenne, Arapaho, Crow, Assiniboine, Gros-Ventre, Mandan, and Arikara] do hereby recognize the right of the United States Government to establish roads, military and other posts, within their respective territories.

Article III. In consideration of the rights and privileges acknowledged in the preceding article, the United States bind themselves to protect the aforesaid Indian nations against the commission of all depredations by the people of the United States, after the ratification of this treaty. . . ."

CREATION OF AN INDIAN PEACE COMMISSION, July 20, 1867: "Be it enacted . . . that the President of the United States be, and he is hereby, authorized to appoint a commission . . . to call together the chiefs and headmen of such bands or tribes of Indians as are now waging war against the United States or committing depredations upon the people thereof, to ascertain the alleged reasons for their acts of hostility, and in their discretion, under the direction of the President, to make and conclude with said bands or tribes such treaty stipulations, subject to the action of the Senate, as may remove all just causes of complaint on their part, and at the same time establish security for persons and property along the lines of the railroad now being constructed to the Pacific and other thoroughfares of travel to the western Territories, and such as will most likely insure civilization for the Indians and peace and safety for the whites."

REPORT OF THE INDIAN PEACE COMMISSION, January 7, 1868: ". . . In making treaties it was enjoined on us to remove, if possible, the causes of complaint on the part of the Indians. This would be no easy task. We have do the best we could under the circumstances, but it is now rather late in the day to think of obliterating from the minds of the present generation the remembrance of wrong. Among civilized men war usually springs from a sense of injustice. The best possible way then to avoid war is to do no act of injustice. When we learn that the same rule holds good with Indians, the chief difficulty is removed. But, it is said our wars with them have been almost constant. Have we been uniformly unjust? We answer, unhesitatingly, yes! We are aware that the masses of our people have felt kindly toward them, and the legislation of Congress has always been conceived in the best intentions, but it has been erroneous in fact or perverted in execution. Nobody pays any attention to Indian matters. This is a deplorable fact. . . . [W]hen the progress of settlement reaches the Indian's home, the only question considered is, 'how best to get his lands.'"

TREATY OF FORT LARAMIE, April 29, 1868:

Article I. "From this day forward all war between the parties to this agreement [the U.S. government and the various bands of the Sioux nation] shall forever cease. The Government of the United States desires peace, and its honor is hereby pledged to keep it. The Indians desire peace, and they now pledge their honor to maintain it.

If bad men among the whites, or among other people subject to the authority of the United States, shall commit any wrong upon the person or property of the Indians, the United States will, upon proof made to the agent and forwarded to the Commissioner of Indian Affairs at Washington City, proceed at once to cause the offender to be arrested and punished according to the laws of the United States, and also reimburse the injured person for the loss sustained.

If bad men among the Indians shall commit a wrong or depredation upon the person or property of any one, white, black, or Indian, subject to the authority of the United States, and at peace therewith, the Indians herein named solemnly agree that they will, upon proof made to their agent and notice by him, deliver up the wrong-doer to the United States, to be tried and punished according to its laws; and in case they willfully refuse so to do, the person injured shall be reimbursed for his loss from the annuities or other moneys due or to become due to them under this or other treaties made with the United States. . . .

Article VII. In order to insure the civilization of the Indians entering into this treaty, the necessity of education is admitted, especially of such of them as are or may be settled on said agricultural reservations, and they therefore pledge themselves to compel their children, male and female, between the ages of six and sixteen years, to attend school; and it is hereby made the duty of the agent for said Indians to see that this stipulation is strictly complied with; and the United States agrees that for every thirty children between said ages who can be induced or compelled to attend school, a house shall be provided and a teacher competent to teach the elementary branches of an English education shall be furnished, who will reside among said Indians, and faithfully discharge his or her duties as a teacher.

Article XI. In consideration of the advantages and benefits conferred by this treaty . . . the said Indians, further expressly agree:

1. That they will withdraw all opposition to the construction of the railroads now being built on the plains.

2. That they will permit the peaceful construction of any railroad not passing over their reservation as herein defined.

3. That they will not attack any persons at home, or traveling, nor molest or disturb any wagon-trains, coaches, mules, or cattle belonging to the people of the United States, or to persons friendly therewith.

4. They will never capture, or carry off from the settlements, white women or children.

5. They will never kill or scalp white men, nor attempt to do them harm.

6. They withdraw all pretense of opposition to the construction of the railroad now being built along the Platte River and westward to the Pacific Ocean, and they will not in future object to the construction of railroads, wagon-roads, mail-stations, or other works of utility or necessity, which may be ordered or permitted by the laws of the United States. . . .

Article XIII. The United States hereby agrees to furnish annually to the Indians the physician, teachers, carpenter, miller, engineer, farmer, and blacksmiths as herein contemplated, and that such appropriations shall be made from time to time, on the estimates of the Secretary of the Interior, as will be sufficient to employ such persons. . . .

Article XVI. The United States hereby agrees and stipulates that the country north of the North Platte River and east of the summits of the Big Horn Mountains shall be held and considered to be unceded Indian territory, and also stipulates and agrees that no white person or persons shall be permitted to settle upon or occupy any portion of the same; or without the consent of the Indians first had and obtained, to pass through the same;

and it is further agreed by the United States that within ninety days after the conclusion of peace with all the bands of the Sioux Nation, the military posts now established in the territory in this article named shall be abandoned, and that the road leading to them and by them to the settlements in the Territory of Montana shall be closed."

PRESIDENT GRANT'S PEACE POLICY. EXTRACT FROM GRANT'S SECOND ANNUAL MESSAGE TO CONGRESS, December 5, 1870: ". . . Reform in the management of Indian affairs has received the special attention of the Administration from its inauguration to the present day. . . . I determined to give all the [Indian] agencies to such religious denominations as had heretofore established missionaries among the Indians, and perhaps to some other denominations who would undertake to work on the same terms—i.e., as a missionary work. The societies selected are allowed to name their own agents, subject to the approval of the Executive, and are expected to watch over them and aid them as missionaries, to Christianize and civilize the Indian, and to train him in the arts of peace. . . . I entertain the confident hope that the policy now pursued will in a few years bring all the Indians upon reservations, where they will live in houses and have schoolhouses and churches, and will be pursuing peaceful and self-sustained avocations, and where they may be visited by the law-abiding white man with the same impunity that he now visits the civilized white settlements. . . ."

INDIAN COMMISSIONER PRICE ON CIVILIZING THE INDIANS, October 24, 1881: ". . . It is claimed and admitted by all that the great object of the government is to civilize the Indians and render them such assistance in kind and degree as will make them self-supporting, and yet I think no one will deny that one part of our policy is calculated to produce the very opposite result. It must be apparent to the most casual observer that the system of gathering the Indians in bands or tribes on reservations and carrying to them victual and clothes, thus relieving them of the necessity of labor, never will and never can civilize them. Labor is an essential element in producing civilization. If white men were treated as we treat the Indians the result would certainly be a race of worthless vagabonds. The greatest kindness the government can bestow upon the Indian is to teach him to labor for his own support, thus developing his true manhood, and, as a consequence, making him self-relying and self-supporting. . . . I am very decidedly of the opinion that ultimate and final success never can be reached without adding to all other means and appliances the location of each family, or adult Indian who has no family, on a certain number of acres of land which they may call their own and hold by title as good and strong as a United States patent can make it."

PROGRAM OF THE LAKE MOHONK CONFERENCE,

September 1884: ". . . The motive, therefore, which has urged the members of the Mohonk Conference to issue their address to the public is twofold:

1. To inform the people of the United States as to the most direct practicable way in which the Indian question may be solved.

2. To stimulate the thoughtful and right-minded citizens of the country to take immediate steps toward the solution of the problem.

It was felt by all those who took part in the work of the conference that a calm, definite, and earnest appeal made to the conscience and intelligence of the country in behalf of a poor and helpless people, and for the righting of a national wrong, would not be uttered in vain. . . .

1. Resolved, that the organization of the Indians in tribes is, and has been, one of the most serious hindrances to the advancement of the Indian toward civilization, and that every effort should be made to secure the disintegration of all tribal organizations. . . .

2. Resolved, that to all Indians who desire to hold their land in severalty allotments should be made without delay. . . .

3. Resolved, that lands allotted and granted in severalty to Indians should be made inalienable for a period of not less than ten or more than twenty-five years.

4. Resolved, that all adult male Indians should be admitted, to the full privileges of citizenship by a process analogous to naturalization. . . ."

GENERAL ALLOTMENT ACT [DAWES ACT], Feb-

ruary 8, 1887: "Be it enacted . . . that in all cases where any tribe or band of Indians has been, or shall hereafter be, located upon any reservation created for their use, either by treaty stipulation or by virtue of an act of Congress or executive order setting apart the same for their use, the President of the United States be, and he hereby is, authorized, whenever in his opinion any reservation or any part thereof of such Indians is advantageous for agricultural and grazing purposes, to cause said reservation, or any part thereof, to be surveyed, or resurveyed if necessary, and to allot the lands in said reservation in severalty to any Indian located thereon in quantities as follows:

To each head of a family, one-quarter of a section;

To each single person over eighteen years of age, one-eighth of a section;

To each orphan child under eighteen years of age, one-eighth of a section; and

To each other single person under eighteen years now living, or who may be born prior to the date of the order of the President directing an allotment of the lands embraced in any reservation, one-sixteenth of a section. . . .

That upon the completion of said allotments and the patenting of the lands to said allotees, each and every member of the respective bands or tribes of Indians to whom allotments have been made shall have the benefit of and be subject to the laws, both civil and criminal, of the State or Territory in which they may reside. . . . And every Indian born within the territorial limits of the United States, to whom allotments shall have been made under the provisions of this act . . . is hereby declared to be a citizen of the United States, and is entitled to all the rights, privileges, and immunities of such citizens, whether said Indian has been or not, by birth or otherwise, a member of any tribe of Indians within the territorial limits of the United States. . . ."

ANNUAL REPORT OF THE COMMISSIONER OF INDIAN AFFAIRS, September 21, 1887: ". . . Longer and closer consideration of the subject has only deepened my conviction that it is a matter not only of importance, but of necessity that the Indians acquire the English language as rapidly as possible. . . . In all schools conducted by missionary organizations it is required that all instructions shall be given in the English language. . . . Your attention is called to the regulation of this office which forbids instruction in schools in any Indian language. . . . You are instructed to see that this rule is rigidly enforced in all schools upon the reservation under your charge. . . ."

MARRIAGE BETWEEN WHITE MEN AND INDIAN WOMEN, August 9, 1888: An Act in relation to marriage between white men and Indian women. "Be it enacted . . . that no white man, not otherwise a member of any tribe of Indians, who may hereafter marry, an Indian woman, member of any Indian tribe in the United States, or any of its Territories except the five civilized tribes in the Indian Territory, shall by such marriage hereafter acquire any right to any tribal property, privilege, or interest whatever to which any member of such tribe is entitled. That every Indian woman member of any such tribe of Indians, who may hereafter be married to any citizen of the United States, is hereby declared to become by such marriage a citizen of the United States, with all the rights, privileges, and immunities of any such citizen, being a married woman. . . ."

RELIEF OF THE MISSION INDIANS, January 12, 1891: "Be it enacted . . . that immediately after the passage of this act the Secretary of the Interior shall appoint three disinterested persons as commissioners to arrange a just and satisfactory settlement of the Mission Indians residing in the State of California, upon reservations which shall be secured to them as hereinafter provided. That it shall be the duty of said commissioners to select a reservation for each band or village of the Mission Indians residing within said State, which reservation shall include, as far as practicable, the lands and villages which have been in the actual occupation and possession of said Indians, and which shall be sufficient in extent to meet their just requirements, which selection shall be valid when approved by the President and Secretary of the Interior."

ARMY OFFICERS AS INDIAN AGENTS, July 13, 1892: ". . . Provided, that from and after the passage of this act the President shall detail officers of the United States Army to act as Indian agents to all Agencies where vacancies from any cause may hereafter occur, who, while acting as such agents, shall be under the orders and direction of the Secretary of the Interior, except at agencies where, in the opinion of the President, the public service would be better promoted by the appointment of a civilian. . . ."

CURTIS ACT, June 28, 1898: [applied to the Cherokee, Choctaw, Chickasaw, and Seminole] "That when the roll of citizenship of any one of said nations or tribes is fully complete as provided by law, and the survey of the lands of said nation or tribe is also completed, the commission heretofore appointed under Acts of Congress, and known as the 'Dawes Commission,' shall proceed to allot the exclusive use and occupancy of the surface of all the lands of said nation or tribe susceptible of allotment among the citizens thereof, as shown by said roll, giving to each, so far as possible, his fair and equal share thereof, considering the nature and fertility of the soil, location, and value of same; but all oil, coal, asphalt, and mineral deposits in the lands of any tribe are reserved to such tribe, and no allotment of such lands shall carry the title to such oil, coal, asphalt, or mineral deposits; and all town sites shall also be reserved to the several tribes, and shall be set apart by the commission heretofore mentioned as incapable of allotment."

MERIAM REPORT, THE PROBLEM OF INDIAN ADMINISTRATION, February 1928: "Whichever way the individual Indian may elect to face, work in his behalf must be designed not to do for him but to help him to do for himself. The whole problem must be regarded as fundamentally educational. However much the early policy of rationing may have been necessary as a defensive, preventive war measure on the part of the whites, it worked untold harm to the Indians because it was pauperizing and lacked an appreciable educational value. Anything else done for them in a way that neglects educating them to do for themselves will work in the same direction. Controlling the expenditure of individual Indian money, for example, is pauperizing unless the work is so done that the Indian is being educated to control his own. In every activity of the Indian Service the primary question should be, how is the Indian to be trained so that he will do this for himself. Unless this question can be clearly and definitely answered by an affirmative showing of distinct educational purpose and method the chances are that the activity is impeding rather than helping the advancement of the Indian."

JOHNSON-O'MALLEY ACT, April 16, 1934: "Be it enacted . . . that the secretary of the Interior is hereby authorized, in his discretion, to enter in a contract or contracts with an State or Territory having legal authority so to do, for the education, medical attention, agricultural assistance, and social welfare, including relief of distress, of Indians in such State or Territory, through the qualified agencies of such State or Territory, and to expend under such contracts or contracts moneys appropriated by Congress for the education, medical attention, agricultural assistance, and social welfare, including relief of distress of Indians in such State. . . ."

WHEELER-HOWARD ACT (INDIAN REORGANIZATION ACT), June 18, 1934: "Be it enacted . . . that hereafter no land on any Indian reservation, created or set apart by treaty or agreement with the Indians, Act of Congress, Executive order, purchase, or otherwise, shall be allotted in severalty to any Indian.

Sec. 2. The existing periods of trust placed upon any Indian lands and any restriction on alienation thereof are hereby extended and continued until otherwise directed by Congress.

Sec. 3. The Secretary of the Interior, if he shall find it to be in the public interest, is hereby authorized to restore to tribal ownership the remaining surplus lands on any Indian reservation heretofore opened, or authorized to be opened, to sale, or any other form of disposal by Presidential proclamation, or by any of the public land laws of the United States. . . .

Sec. 16. Any Indian tribe, or tribes, residing on the same reservation, shall have the right to organize for its common welfare, and may adopt an appropriate constitution and bylaws, which shall become effective when ratified by a majority vote of the adult members of the tribe, or of the adult Indians residing on such reservation, as the case may be, at a special election authorized and called by the Secretary of the Interior under such rules and regulations as he may prescribe. Such constitution and bylaws when ratified as aforesaid and approved by the Secretary of the Interior shall be revocable by an election open to the same voters and conducted in the same manner as hereinabove provided. . . ."

INDIAN ARTS AND CRAFTS BOARD, August 27, 1935: Section 6. "Any person who shall willfully offer or display for sale any goods, with or without any Government trade mark, as Indian products or Indian products of a particular Indian tribe or group, resident within the United State or the Territory of Alaska, when such person knows such goods are not Indian products or are not Indian products of the particular Indian tribe or group, shall be guilty of a misdemeanor and be subject to a fine not exceeding $2,000 or imprisonment not exceeding six months, or both such fine and imprisonment. . . ."

INDIAN CLAIMS COMMISSION ACT, August 13, 1946: "Be it enacted . . . that there is hereby created and established an Indian Claims Commission, hereafter referred to as the Commission.

Sec. 2. The Commission shall hear and determine the following claims against the United States on behalf of any Indian tribe, band, or other identifiable group of American Indians residing within the territorial limits of the United States or Alaska: (1) claims in law or equity arising under the constitution, laws, treaties of the United States, and Executive orders of the President; (2) all other claims in law or equity, including those sounding in tort, with respect to which the claimant would have been entitled to sue in a court of the United States if the United States was subject to suit; (3) claims which would result if the treaties, contracts, and agreements between the claimant and the United States were revised on the ground of fraud, duress, unconscionable consideration, mutual or unilateral mistake, whether of law or fact, or any other ground cognizable by a court of equity; (4) claims arising from the taking by the United States, whether as the result of a treaty of cession or otherwise, of lands owned or occupied by the claimant without the payment for such lands of compensation agreed to by the claimant; and (5) claims based upon fair and honorable dealings that are not recognized by any existing rule of law or equity. . . ."

HOUSE CONCURRENT RESOLUTION 108, August 1, 1953: "Whereas it is the policy of Congress, as rapidly as possible, to make the Indians within the territorial limits of the United States subject to the same laws and entitled to the same privileges and responsibilities as are applicable to other citizens of the United States, to end their status as wards of the United States, and to grant them all of the rights and prerogatives pertaining to American citizenship; and Whereas the Indians within the territorial limits of the United States should assume their full responsibilities as American citizens: Now, therefore be it resolved by the House of Representatives, that it is declared to be the sense of Congress that, at the earliest possible time, all of the Indian tribes and the individual members thereof located within the States of California, Florida, New York, and Texas, and all of the following named tribes and individual members thereof, should be freed from Federal supervision and control and from all disabilities and limitations specifically applicable to Indians: The Flathead Tribe of Montana, the Klamath Tribe of Oregon, the Menominee Tribe of Wisconsin, the

Potawatomi Tribe of Kansas and Nebraska, and those members of the Chippewa Tribe who are on the Turtle Mountain Reservation, North Dakota. . . ."

PUBLIC LAW 280, August 15, 1953: "Each of the States listed in the following table shall have jurisdiction over offenses committed by or against Indians in the areas of Indian country listed opposite the name of the State to the same extent that such State has jurisdiction over offenses committed elsewhere within the State, and the criminal laws of such State shall have the same force and effect within such Indian country as they have elsewhere within the State:

State	Indian Country Affected
California	All Indian country within the State
Minnesota	All Indian country within the State, except the Red Lake Reservation
Nebraska	All Indian country within the State
Oregon	All Indian country within the State, except the Warm Springs Reservation
Wisconsin	All Indian country within the State, except the Menominee Reservation

TRANSFER OF INDIAN HEALTH SERVICE, August 5, 1954: "Be it enacted . . . that all functions, responsibilities, authorities, and duties of the Department of the Interior, the Bureau of Indian Affairs, Secretary of the Interior, and the Commissioner of Indian Affairs relating to the maintenance and operation of hospital and health facilities for Indians, and the conservation of the health of Indians, are hereby transferred to, and shall be administered by, the Surgeon General of the United States Public Health Service, under the supervision and direction of the Secretary of Health, Education and Welfare. . . ."

PRESIDENT JOHNSON, SPECIAL MESSAGE TO CONGRESS, March 6, 1968: ". . . I propose a new goal for our Indian programs: A goal that ends the old debate about 'termination' of Indian programs and stresses self-determination; a goal that erases old attitudes of paternalism and promotes partnership self-help. Our goal must be:

—A standard of living for the Indians equal to that of the country as a whole.

—Freedom of Choice: An opportunity to remain in their homelands, if they choose, without surrendering their dignity; an opportunity to move to the towns and cities of America, if they choose, equipped with the skills to live in equality and dignity.

—Full participation in the life of modern American, with a full share of economic opportunity and social justice.

I propose, in short, a policy of maximum choice for the American Indian: a policy expressed in programs of self-help, self-development, self-determination. . . ."

PRESIDENT NIXON, SPECIAL MESSAGE ON INDIAN AFFAIRS, July 8, 1970: "The first Americans— the Indians—are the most deprived and most isolated minority group in our nation. On virtually every scale of measurement—employment, income, education, health—the condition of the Indian people ranks at the bottom.

This condition is the heritage of centuries of injustice. From the time of their first contact with European settlers, the American Indians have been oppressed and brutalized, deprived of their ancestral lands and denied the opportunity to control their own destiny. Even the Federal programs which are intended to meet their needs have frequently proved to be ineffective and demeaning. . . .

It is long past time that the Indian policies of the Federal government began to recognize and build upon the capacities and insights of the Indian people Both as a matter of justice and as a matter of

enlightened social policy, we must begin to act on the basis of what the Indians themselves have long been telling us. The time has come to break decisively with the past and to create the conditions for a new era in which the Indian future is determined by Indian acts and Indian decisions."

RETURN OF BLUE LAKE LANDS TO TAOS PUEBLO, 1970: "Be it enacted . . . that section 4 of the Act of May 31, 1933, providing for the protection of the watershed within the Carson National Forest for the Pueblo de Taos Indians in New Mexico, be and hereby is amended to read as follows:

Sec. 4. That, for the purpose of safeguarding the interests and welfare of the tribe of Indians known as the Pueblo de Taos of New Mexico, the following described lands and improvements thereon, upon which said Indians depend and have depended since time immemorial for water supply, forage for their domestic livestock, wood and timber for their personal use, and as the scene of certain religious ceremonials, are hereby declared to be held by the United States in trust for the Pueblo de Taos:. . . ."

ALASKA NATIVE CLAIMS SETTLEMENT ACT, December 18, 1971: "Be it enacted . . . that this Act may be cited as the 'Alaska Native Claims Settlement Act.'

Sec. 2. Congress finds and declares that (a) there is an immediate need for a fair and just settlement of all claims by Natives and Native groups of Alaska, based on aboriginal land claims; (b) the settlement should be accomplished rapidly, with certainty, in conformity with the real economic and social needs of Natives, without litigation, with maximum participation by Natives in decisions affecting their rights and property, without establishing any permanent racially defined institutions, rights, privileges, or obligations, without creating a reservation system or lengthy wardship or trusteeship, and without adding to the categories of property and institutions enjoying special tax privileges or to the legislation establishing special relationships between the United States Government and the State of Alaska:. . . ."

INDIAN EDUCATION ACT, June 23, 1972: "Sec. 302 (a) In recognition of the special educational needs of Indian students in the United States, Congress hereby declares it to be the policy of the United States to provide financial assistance to local educational agencies to develop and carry out elementary and secondary school programs specially designed to meet these special educational needs. . . ."

INDIAN FINANCING ACT, April 12, 1974: "Sec. 2. It is hereby declared to be the policy of Congress to provide capital on a reimbursable basis to help develop and utilize Indian resources, both physical and human, to a point where the Indians will fully exercise responsibility for the utilization and management of their own resources and where they will enjoy a standard of living from their own productive efforts comparable to that enjoyed by non-Indians in neighboring communities. . . ."

ESTABLISHMENT OF THE AMERICAN INDIAN POLICY REVIEW COMMISSION, January 2, 1975: "The Congress after careful review of the Federal Government's historical and special legal relationship with American Indian people, finds that—

1. The policy implementing this relationship has shifted and changed with changing administrations and passing years, without apparent rational design and without a consistent goal to achieve Indian self-sufficiency.

2. There has been no general comprehensive review of conduct of Indian affairs by the United States. . . .

3. In carrying out its responsibility under its plenary power over Indian affairs, it is imperative that the Congress now cause such a comprehensive review of Indian affairs to be conducted. . . . Congress declares that it is timely and essential to conduct a comprehensive review of the historical and legal developments underlying the Indians' unique relationship with the Federal Government in order to determine the nature and scope of necessary revisions in the formulation of policies and programs for the benefit of Indians. . . ."

INDIAN SELF-DETERMINATION AND EDUCATION ASSISTANT ACT, January 4, 1975: "Sec. 2. (a) The Congress, after careful review of the Federal Government's historical and special legal relationship with, and resulting responsibilities to, American Indian people, finds that—

1. The prolonged Federal domination of Indian service programs has served to retard rather than enhance the progress of Indian people. . . .

2. The Indian people will never surrender their desire to control their relationships both among themselves and with non-Indian governments, organizations, and persons.

(b) The Congress further finds that—

1. True self-determination in any society of people is dependent upon an educational process which will insure the development of qualified people to fulfill meaningful leadership roles;

2. The Federal responsibility for assistance to education of Indian children has not effected the desired level of educational achievement. . . .

3. Parental and community control of the educational process is of crucial importance to the Indian people.

Sec. 3. (a) The Congress, hereby recognizes the obligation of the United States to respond to the strong expression of the Indian people for self-determination by assuring maximum Indian participation in the direction of educational as well as other Federal services to Indian communities. . . ."

INDIAN HEALTH CARE IMPROVEMENT ACT, September 30, 1976: "Sec. 2. The Congress finds that—

1. Federal health services to maintain and improve the health of the Indians are consonant with and required by the Federal Government's historical and unique legal relationship with, and resulting responsibility to, the American Indian people.

2. A major national goal of the United States is to provide the quantity and quality of health services which will permit the health status of Indians to be raised to the highest possible level and to encourage the maximum participation of Indians in the planning and management of those services. . . ."

ESTABLISHMENT OF ASSISTANT SECRETARY-INDIAN AFFAIRS, September 26, 1977: ". . . Sec. 2. An Assistant Secretary-Indian Affairs is hereby established to administer the laws, functions, responsibilities, and authorities related in Indian affairs matters. In addition to serving as an Assistant Secretary of the Department, The Assistant Secretary-Indian Affairs will assume all the authorities and responsibilities of the Commissioner of Indian Affairs pending subsequent organization and position realignments. . . ."

AMERICAN INDIAN RELIGIOUS FREEDOM, August 11, 1978: ". . . Resolved by the Senate and House of Representatives of the United States of America in Congress assembled, that henceforth it shall be the policy of the United States to protect and preserve for American Indians their inherent right of freedom to believe, express, and exercise the traditional religions of the American Indian, Eskimo, Aleut, and Native Hawaiians, including but not limited to access to sites, use and possession of sacred objects, and the freedom to worship through ceremonials and traditional rites. . . ."

FEDERAL ACKNOWLEDGMENT OF INDIAN TRIBES, October 2, 1978: ". . . The purpose of this part is to establish a departmental procedure and policy for acknowledging that certain American Indian tribes exist. Such acknowledgment of tribal existence by the Department [of Interior] is a prerequisite to the protection, services, and benefits from the Federal Government available to Indian tribes. Such acknowledgment shall also mean that the tribe is entitled to the immunities and privileges available to other federally acknowledged Indian tribes by virtue of their status as Indian tribes as well as the responsibilities and obligations of such tribes. Acknowledgment shall subject the Indian tribe to the same authority of Congress and the United States to which other federally acknowledged tribes are subjected. . . ."

TRIBALLY CONTROLLED COMMUNITY COLLEGE ASSISTANCE ACT, October 17, 1978: ". . . Sec. 101. It is the purpose of this title to provide grants for the operation and improvement of tribally controlled community colleges to insure continued and expanded educational opportunities for Indian students. . . ."

INDIAN CHILD WELFARE ACT, November 8, 1978: ". . . Sec. 3. The Congress hereby declares that it is the policy of this Nation to protect the best interest of Indian children and to promote the stability and security of Indian tribes and families by the establishment of minimum Federal standards for the removal of Indian children from their families and the placement of such children in foster or adoptive homes which will reflect the unique values of Indian culture, and by providing for assistance to Indian tribes in the operation of child and family service programs. . . ."

ARCHAEOLOGICAL RESOURCES PROTECTION ACT, October 31, 1979: ". . . The purpose of this Act is to secure, for the present and future benefit of the American people, the protection of archaeological resources and sites which are on public lands and Indian lands, and to foster increased cooperation and exchange of information between governmental authorities, the professional archaeological community, archaeological resources and data which were obtained before the date of the enactment of this Act. . . ."

INDIAN GAMING REGULATORY ACT, October 17, 1988: ". . . The purpose of this Act is—

1. To provide a statutory basis for the operation of gaming by Indian tribes as a means of promoting tribal economic development, self-sufficiency, and strong tribal governments.

2. To provide a statutory basis for the regulation of gaming by an Indian tribe adequate to shield it from organized crime and other corrupting influences, to ensure that the Indian tribe is the primary beneficiary of the gaming operation, and to assure that gaming is conducted fairly and honestly by both the operator and the players.

3. To declare that the establishment of independent Federal regulatory authority for gaming on Indian lands, the establishment of Federal standards for gaming on Indian lands, and the estab-

lishment of a National Indian Gaming Commission are necessary to meet congressional concerns regarding gaming and to protect such gaming as a means of generating tribal revenue. . . ."

Excerpts

FROM SIGNIFICANT LEGAL CASES

JOHNSON V. M'INTOSH, 21 U.S. (8 Wheat.) 543, 5 L.Ed. 681 (1823): "Conquest gives a title which the Courts of the conqueror cannot deny, whatever the private and speculative opinions of individuals may be, respecting the original justice of the claim which has been successfully asserted. The British government, which was then our government, and whose rights have passed to the United States, asserted a title to all the lands occupied by Indians, within the chartered limits of the British colonies. It asserted also a limited sovereignty over them, and the exclusive right of extinguishing the title which occupancy gave to them. These claims have been maintained and established as far west as the river Mississippi, by the sword. The title to a vast portion of the lands we now hold, originates in them. It is not for the Courts of this country to question the validity of this title, or to sustain one which is incompatible with it."

CHEROKEE NATION V. GEORGIA, 30 U.S. (5 Pet.) 1,8, L.Ed.25 (1831): "Though the Indians are acknowledged to have an unquestionable, and, heretofore, unquestioned right to the lands they occupy, until that right shall be extinguished by a voluntary cession to our government; yet it may well be doubted whether those tribes which can reside within the acknowledged boundaries of the United States can, with strict accuracy, be denominated foreign nations. They may, more correctly, perhaps, be denominated domestic depen-

dent nations. They occupy a territory to which we assert a title independent of their will, which must take effect in point of possession when their right of possession ceases. Meanwhile they are in a state of pupilage. Their relation to the United States resembles that of a ward to his guardian."

WORCESTER V. GEORGIA, 31 U.S. (6 Pet.) 515 (1832): "Indian nations are distinct political communities possessing internal sovereignty. They are capable of self-government and are completely independent of and separate from the states. Hence, state laws cannot be extended into Indian Country nor may states exercise civil or criminal jurisdiction in Indian Country."

THE KANSAS INDIANS, 5 Wall. 737 (1866): "If the tribal organization is preserved intact, and recognized by the political department of the federal government as existing, then the Indians are a people distinct from others and to be governed exclusively by the federal government."

UNITED STATES V. MCBRATNEY, 104 U.S. 621, 26 L.Ed. 869 (1881): "The Circuit Courts of the United States have jurisdiction of the crime of murder committed in any place or district of country under the exclusive jurisdiction of the United States; and, except where special provision is made, "the general laws of the United States as to the punishment of crimes committed in any place with the sole and exclusive jurisdiction of the

United States, except the District of Columbia, shall extend to the Indian country."

EX PARTE CROW DOG, 109 W.S. 556, 3 S.Ct. 396, 27 L.Ed. 1030 (1883): "The nature and circumstances of this case strongly reinforce this rule of interpretation in its present application. It is a case involving the judgment of a court of special and limited jurisdiction, not to be assumed without clear warrant of law. It is a case of life and death. It is a case where, against an express exception in the law itself, that law, by argument and inference only, is sought to be extended over aliens and strangers; over the members of a community separated by race, by tradition, by the instincts of a free though savage life, from the authority and power which seeks to impose upon them the restraints of an external and unknown code, and to subject them to the responsibilities of civil conduct, according to rules and penalties of which they could have no previous warning; which judges them by a standard made by others and not for them, which takes no account of the conditions which should except them from its exactions, and makes no allowance for their inability to understand it. It tries them, not by their peers, nor by the customs of their people, nor the law of their land, but by superiors of a different race, according to the law of a social state of which they have an imperfect conception, and which is opposed to the traditions of their history, to the habits of their lives, to the strongest prejudices of their savage nature; one which measures the red man's revenge by the maxims of the white man's morality."

THE MAJOR CRIMES ACT, 18 U.S.C.A. Section 1153. Within two years after *Ex Parte Crow Dog,* Congress passed the original Major Crimes Act, 23 Stat. 385 (1885) to provide for federal jurisdiction over seven enumerated crimes. The act excludes state jurisdiction in those cases. The Major Crimes Act has been amended several times to cover a total of fourteen crimes and now reads: "Any Indian who commits against the person or property of another Indian or other person and of the following offenses, namely, murder, man-

slaughter, kidnapping, rape, carnal knowledge of any female, not his wife, who has not attained the age of sixteen years, assault with intent to commit rape, incest, assault with intent to commit murder, assault with a dangerous weapon, assault resulting in serious bodily injury, arson, burglary, robbery, and larceny within the Indian country, shall be subject to the same laws and penalties as all other persons committing any of the above offenses, within the exclusive jurisdiction of the United States."

UNITED STATES V. KAGAMA, 118 U.S. 375, 6 S.Ct. 1109, 30 L.Ed. 228 (1886): "The power of the General Government over these remnants of a race once powerful, now weak and diminished in numbers, is necessary to their protection, as well as to the safety of those among whom they dwell. It must exist in that government, because it never has existed anywhere else, because the theatre of its exercise is within the geographical limits of the United States, because it has never been denied, and because it alone can enforce its laws on all the tribes."

In *Kagama* the court confirms the power of Congress to extend federal criminal laws over Indian country. The case sets forth the "plenary power" of Congress in Indian country and upholds the constitutionality of the 1885 Major Crimes Act.

TALTON V. MAYES, 163 U.S. 376, 16 S.Ct. 986, 41, L.Ed. 196 (1895): "By treaties and statutes of the United States the right of the Cherokee nation to exist as an autonomous body, subject always to the paramount authority of the United States, has been recognized. And from this fact there has consequently been conceded to exist in that nation power to make laws defining offenses and providing for the trial and punishment of those who violate them when the offenses are committed by one member of the tribe against another one of its members within the territory of the nation."

LONE WOLF V. HITCHCOCK, 187 U.S. 553, 23 S.Ct. 216, 47 L.Ed. 299 (1903): "The power exists to abrogate the provisions of an Indian treaty, though presumably such power will be exercised only when circumstances arise which will not only justify the government in disregarding the stipulations of the treaty, but may demand, in the interest of the country and the Indians themselves, that it should do so. When, therefore, treaties were entered into between the United States and a tribe of Indians it was never doubted that the *power* to abrogate existed in Congress, and that in a contingency such power might be availed of from considerations of governmental policy, particularly if consistent with perfect good faith towards the Indians."

WINTERS V. UNITED STATES, 297 U.S. 564, 28 S.Ct. 207, 52 L.Ed.340 (1908): "The case, as we view it, turns on the agreement of May, 1888, resulting in the creation of Fort Belknap Reservation. In the construction of this agreement there are certain elements to be considered that are prominent and significant. The reservation was a part of a very much larger tract which the Indians had the right to occupy and use and which was adequate for the habits and wants of a nomadic and uncivilized people. It was the policy of the Government, it was the desire of the Indians, to change those habits and to become a pastoral and civilized people. If they should become such the original tract was too extensive, but a smaller tract would be inadequate without a change of conditions. The lands were arid and without irrigation, were practically valueless. And yet, it is contended, the means of irrigation were deliberately given up by the Indians and deliberately accepted by the Government. The lands ceded were, it is true, also arid; and some argument may be urged, and is urged, that with their cession there was the cession of the waters, without which they would be valueless, and "civilized communities could not be established thereon." And this, it is further contended, the Indians knew, and yet made no reservation of the waters. We realize that there is a conflict of implications, but that which makes for the retention of the water is of greater force than that which makes for their cession. . . . The Government is asserting the rights of the Indians. . . . On account of their relations to the Government, it cannot be

supposed that the Indians were alert to exclude by formal words every inference which might militate against or defeat the declared purpose of themselves and the Government, even if it could be supposed that they had the intelligence to foresee the "double sense" which might some time be urged against them."

The Supreme Court decides that Indians on reservation lands retain the right to sufficient access to water to provide for agriculture. The "Winters" doctrine is designed to preserve water and is a decision in favor of conservationists, who think Indians would not use as much water as free market users. The doctrine guarantees Indian reservations rights to water for economic and agricultural use.

SEMINOLE NATION V. UNITED STATES, 316 U.S. 186, 62 S.Ct. 1049, 86 L.Ed. 1480 (1942): ". . . this Court has recognized the distinctive obligation of trust incumbent upon the Government in its dealings with these dependent and sometimes exploited people. In carrying out its treaty obligations with the Indian tribes, the Government is something more than a mere contracting party. Under a humane and self imposed policy which has found expression in many acts of Congress and numerous decisions of this Court, it has charged itself with more obligations of the highest responsibility and trust. Its conduct, as disclosed in the acts of those who represent it in dealing with the Indians, should therefore be judged by the most exacting fiduciary standards."

ACOSTA V. SAN DIEGO COUNTY, 126 Cal.App.2d 455, 272 P.2d 92 (1954): " From the conclusion reached that Indians living on reservations in California are citizens and residents of this state, it must therefore follow that under section 1, Amendment XIV of the Constitution of the United States they are endowed with the rights, privileges and immunities equal to those enjoyed by all other citizens and residents of that state."

WILLIAM V. LEE, 358 U.S. 217, 79 S.Ct. 269, 3 L.Ed.2d 251 (1959): "There can be no doubt that to allow the exercise of state jurisdiction here would undermine the authority of the tribal courts over Reservation affairs and hence would infringe on the right of the Indians to govern themselves. It is immaterial that respondent is not an Indian. He was on the Reservation and the transaction with an Indian took place there. The cases in this Court have consistently guarded the authority of Indian governments over their reservations. Congress recognized this authority in the Navajos in the Treaty of 1868, and has done so ever since. If this power is to be taken away from them, it is for Congress to do it." In *Williams*, the Supreme Court states that individual state laws may be applied in Indian country only where no federally-defined crime covering a defendant's conduct exists, and in that event, is only applicable to interracial crime.

ARIZONA V. CALIFORNIA, 373 U.S. 546, 83 S.Ct. 1468, 10 L.Ed.2d. 542 (1963): "The Court in *Winters* concluded that the Government, when it created the Fort Belknap Indian Reservation, intended to deal fairly with the Indians by reserving for them the waters without which their lands would have been useless. *Winters* has been followed by this Court as recently as 1939 in *United States v. Powers*, 305 U.S. 527. We follow it now and agree that the United States did reserve the water rights for the Indians effective as of the time the Indian Reservations were created."

PEOPLE V. WOODY, 61 Cal.2d 716, 40 Cal.Rptr. 69, 394 P.2d 813 (1964): "We have weighed the competing values represented in this case on the symbolic scale of constitutionality. On the one side we have placed the weight of freedom of religion as protected by the First Amendment; on the other, the weight of the state's 'compelling interest.' Since the use of peyote incorporates the essence of the religious expression, the first weight is heavy. Yet the use of peyote presents only slight danger to the state and to the enforcement of its laws; the second weight is relatively light. The scale tips in favor of the Constitutional protection."

In *Woody*, the court leans toward protection of culture and religion. The record did not support

the state's chronicle of harmful consequences of the use of peyote. The decision also supports the use of eagle feathers and parts, and the wearing of long hair in prison, by Indian people.

SENECA NATION OF INDIANS V. UNITED STATES, 338 F.2d 55. Certiorari denied 380 U.S. 952, 85 S. Ct. 1084, 13 L.Ed.2d 969 (1965): "It is our responsibility to see that the terms of the treaty are carried out, so far as possible, in accordance with the meaning they were understood to have by the tribal representatives at the council and in the spirit which *generously recognizes* the full obligation of this nation to protect the interests of a dependent people."

WARREN TRADING POST V. ARIZONA TAX COMMISSION, 380 U.S 685, 85 S.Ct. 1242, 14 L.Ed.2d 165 (1965): "We think the assessment and collection of this tax [gross proceeds of sales, or gross income] would to a substantial extent frustrate the evident congressional purpose of ensuring that no burden shall be imposed upon Indian traders for trading with Indians on reservations except as authorized by Acts of Congress or by valid regulations promulgated under those Acts."

NAVAJO TRIBE OF INDIANS V. UNITED STATES, 364 F.2d 320 (1966): "Since the Department of the Interior had an obligation to safeguard the property of the Navajos when they were dealing with third parties, it is clear that an even greater duty existed when the Department itself entered into transactions with the Indians. . . . Because of this and because of the Government's special duty toward the Indians, the various dealings must be carefully scrutinized. In considering the claims of the plaintiff, we have endeavored to give adequate weight to 'fiduciary standards.'"

In *Navajo*, the court was asked to determine if the requirement that "the most exacting fiduciary standards" be applied in the leasing of certain oil and gas rights on land within the Navajo Indian reservation. The court held that it was clear that when dealing with Indian property that an even greater duty existed when the Department of Interior itself entered into transactions with the Indians.

PUYALLUP TRIBE V. DEPARTMENT OF GAME, 391 U.S. 392, 88 S.Ct. 1725, 20 L.Ed.2d 689 (1968): "The treaty right is in terms the right to fish 'at all usual and accustomed places.' We assume that fishing by nets was customary at the time of the Treaty; and we also assume that there were commercial aspects to that fishing as there are at present. But the *manner* in which the fishing may be done and its purpose, whether or not commercial, are not mentioned in the Treaty. We would have quite a different case if the Treaty had preserved the right to fish at the 'usual and accustomed places' in the 'usual and accustomed' manner. But the Treaty is silent as to the mode or modes of fishing that are guaranteed. Moreover, the right to fish at those respective places is not an exclusive one. Rather, it one 'in common with all citizens of the Territory.' Certainly the right of the latter may be regulated. And we see no reason why the right of the Indians may not also be regulated by an appropriate exercise of the police power of the State. The right to fish 'at all usual and accustomed' places may, of course, not be qualified by the State, even though all Indians born in the United States are now citizens of the United States. . . . But the manner of fishing, the size of the take, the restriction of commercial fishing, and the like may be regulated by the State in the interest of conservation, provided the regulation meets appropriate standards and does not discriminate against the Indians."

In *Puyallup*, the court was asked to determine if the Puyallup tribe's use of gill nets fell within the provisions of Article III of the Treaty of Medicine Creek, which states in part "that the right of taking fish, at all usual and accustomed grounds and stations, is further secured to said Indians. . . ." The court ruled that the right of taking fish, at all usual and accustomed grounds and stations, could not be regulated by the State of Washington; however, since the treaty did not address "usual and accustomed manner" in which fish could be taken, the State could regulate, in the interest of

conservation, the manner in which fish are taken as long as the regulation did not discriminate against the Indians. The use of set nets was barred not only to Indians, but to all others as well.

McCLANAHAN V. ARIZONA STATE TAX COMMISSION, 441, U.S. 164, (1973): "The concept of sovereignty is to be used only as a 'backdrop' against which applicable statutes and treaties are to be read. If the statutes and treaties give rise to the fact that the federal government has 'preempted' the field, states may not exercise jurisdiction or otherwise intrude into Indian Country."

MESCALERO APACHE TRIBE V. JONES, 411 U.S. 145, 93 S.Ct. 1267, 36 L.Ed.2d 114 (1973): "Absent express federal law to the contrary, Indians going beyond reservation boundaries have generally been held subject to nondiscriminatory state law otherwise applicable to all citizens of the State. That principle is as relevant to a State's tax laws as it is to state criminal laws . . . and applies as much to tribal ski resorts, as it does to fishing enterprises."

PYRAMID LAKE PAIUTE TRIBE OF INDIANS V. MORTON, 354 F. Supp. 252. (1973): "The United States, acting through the Secretary of Interior, 'has charged itself with moral obligations of the highest responsibility and trust. Its conduct, as disclosed in the acts of those who represent it in dealing with the Indians, should therefore be judged by the most exacting fiduciary standards.'"

DE COTEAU V. DISTRICT COUNTY COURT, 420 U.S. 425, 95 S.Ct. 1082, 43 L.Ed.2d 300 (1975): "[T]he Court requires that the 'congressional determination to terminate . . . be expressed on the face of the Act or be clear from the surrounding circumstances and legislative history.' . . . In particular, we have stressed that reservation status may survive the mere opening of a reservation to settlement, even when the moneys paid for the land by the settlers are placed in trust by the Government for the Indians' benefit."

In *De Coteau*, the court states that the intent of Congress to terminate the federal relationship and responsibility of a tribe must be clearly stated. The mere payment of money does not establish clear and compelling Congressional intent.

UNITED STATES V. MAZURIE, 419 U.S. 544, 95 S.Ct. 710, 42 L.Ed. 2d 706 (1975): "Article I, Section 8, of the Constitution gives Congress power '[t]o regulate Commerce with foreign Nations, and among the several States, and with the Indians Tribes.' This Court has repeatedly held that this clause affords Congress the power to prohibit or regulate the sale of alcoholic beverages to tribal Indians, wherever situated, and to prohibit or regulate the introduction of alcoholic beverages into Indian country."

BRYAN V. ITASCA COUNTY, 426 U.S. 373, 96S.Ct. 2102, 48 L.Ed.2d. 710 (1976): "[W]e conclude that construing Public Law 280 in *pari materia* with these Acts shows that if Congress in enacting Public Law 280 had intended to confer upon the States general civil regulatory powers, including taxation, over reservation Indians, it would have expressly said so."

Bryan presents the question, whether the grant of civil jurisdiction of the States conferred by Public Law 280, was a grant of power to the States to tax reservation Indians except where expressly excluded by the terms of the statute. The court stated that if Congress had intended to confer the power of taxation on Indian people, on reservation, it would have expressly said so.

MOE V. CONFEDERATED SALISH AND KOOTENAI TRIBES OF FLATHEAD INDIAN RESERVATION, 425 U.S. 463, 96 S.Ct. 1634, 48 L.Ed.2d 96 (1976): "The State's requirement that the Indian tribal seller collect a tax validly imposed on non-Indians is a minimal burden designed to avoid the likelihood that in its absence non-Indians purchasing from the tribal seller will avoid payment of a concededly lawful tax. . . . We see nothing in this burden which frustrates tribal self-government . . . or runs afoul of any congressional enactment dealing with the affairs of reservation Indians. . . . We therefore agree with the District Court that to

the extent that the 'smoke shops' sell to those upon whom the State has validly imposed a sales or excise tax with respect to the article sold, the State may require the Indian proprietor simply to add the tax to the sales price and thereby aid the State's collection and enforcement thereof."

UNITED STATES V. WASHINGTON, 520 F.2d 676, certiorari denied, 423 U.S. 1086, 96S.Ct. 877, 47 L.Ed.2d 97 (1976): "We affirm the conclusion of the district court that the fundamental principle to be applied in a judicial apportionment is that treaty Indians are entitled to an opportunity to catch one-half of all the fish which, absent the fishing activities of other citizens, would pass their traditional fishing grounds. This conclusion follows naturally from the circumstances in which the treaties were signed. . . . [A] 50-50 apportionment reflects the equality existing between the two bargaining parties and best effectuates what the Indian parties would have expected if a partition of fishing opportunities had been necessary at the time of the treaties."

In *Washington,* the litigation involved the extent of off-reservation treaty rights. The court listed six treaties, between the United States and a total of fourteen tribes in western Washington, which were entered into between 1854 and 1859. Each of the treaties contains a provision securing to the Indians certain off-reservation fishing rights. The state argued that the treaty right to fish "in common with all citizens of the Territory" meant that the small number of Indian fishers would be subject to all state regulations, including seasons and bag limits. The court rejected the argument, construing the treaty provisions liberally and as the Indians themselves would have understood them. The judge ruled in favor of the tribes.

UNITED STATES V. WINNEBAGO TRIBE OF NEBRASKA, 542 F.2d 1002 (1976): "Rights secured by treaty will not be deemed to have been abrogated or modified absent a clear expression of congressional purpose, for 'the intention to abrogate or modify a treaty is not to be lightly imputed to the Congress.'"

CONFEDERATED BANDS AND TRIBES OF YAKIMA INDIAN NATION V. WASHINGTON, 552 F.2d 1332 (1977): "We can detect no rational connection between the stated purpose and the distinction based on land title within the reservation. The state's interest in enforcing criminal law is no less 'fundamental' or 'overriding' on non-fee lands than on fee lands.... Moreover, no relationship has been suggested or shown between the interest and ability of the state to provide law enforcement and the fee—non-fee status of the land within the reservation. This checkerboard jurisdictional structure based on a selection by land title is the 'very kind of arbitrary legislative choice forbidden by the Equal Protection Clause.'"

In *Confederated Bands,* the state of Washington attempts to assume partial jurisdiction of reservation land under Public Law 280. The court holds that Washington's partial assumption of jurisdiction could not withstand the Yakimas' constitutional equal protection defense.

CONFEDERATED TRIBES OF COLVILLE INDIAN RESERVATION V. WASHINGTON, 446 F.Supp. 1339 (1978): "As an alternate ground for relief, we hold that as applied to non-Indians as a result of their on-reservation purchases from Dealers, the State's cigarette taxing scheme constitutes an interference with tribal self-government."

OLIPHANT V. SUQUAMISH INDIAN TRIBE, 435 U.S. 191, 98 S.Ct. 1011, 55 L.Ed.2d 209. (1978): "We recognize that some Indian tribal court systems have become increasingly sophisticated and resemble in many respects their state counterparts. We also acknowledge that with the passage of the Indian Civil Rights Act of 1968, which extends certain basic procedural rights to anyone tried in Indian tribal court, many of the dangers that might have accompanied the exercise by tribal courts of criminal jurisdiction over non-Indians only a few decades ago have disappeared. Finally we are not unaware of the prevalence of non-Indian crime on today's reservations which the tribes forcefully argue requires the ability to try non-Indians. But these are considerations for Congress to weigh in deciding whether Indian tribes should finally be authorized to try non-Indians. They have little relevance to the principles, which lead us to conclude that Indian tribes do not have inherent jurisdiction to try and punish non-Indians."

RED FOX V. RED FOX, 23 Or.App 393, 542 P.2d 918 (1978): "While the decisions of tribal courts are not ... entitled to the same 'full faith and credit' accorded decrees rendered in sister states, the quasi-sovereign nature of the tribe does suggest that judgments rendered by tribal courts are entitled to the same deference shown decisions of foreign nations as a matter of comity."

SANTA CLARA PUEBLO V. MARTINEZ, 436 U.S. 439, 98 S.Ct. 1670, 56 L.Ed.2d 106 (1978): "As we have repeatedly emphasized, Congress' authority over Indian matters is extraordinarily broad, and the role of courts in adjusting relations between and among tribes and their members correspondingly restrained.... Congress retains authority expressly to authorize civil actions for injunctive or other relief to redress violations ... in the event that the tribes themselves prove deficient in applying and enforcing its substantive provisions. But unless and until Congress makes clear its intention to permit the additional intrusion on tribal sovereignty that adjudication of such actions in a federal forum would represent, we are constrained to find that section 1302 does not impliedly authorize actions for declaratory or injunctive relief against either the tribe or its officers."

In *Santa Clara,* the court was required to decide whether a federal court might pass on the validity of an Indian tribe's ordinance denying membership to the children of certain female tribal members. The court's decision was that "membership rules were no more or less than a mechanism of social ... self-definition, and as such were basic to the tribe's survival as a cultural and economy entity." Accordingly, the court deferred to the validity of the tribe's ordinance.

UNITED STATES V. WHEELER, 435 U.S. 313, 98 S.Ct. 1079, 55 L.Ed.2d 303 (1978): "Indian tribes are, of course, no longer 'possessed of the full attributes of sovereignty.' Their incorporation within the territory of the United States, and their acceptance of its protection, necessarily divested them of some aspects of the sovereignty, which they had previously exercised. By specific treaty provisions they yielded up other sovereign powers; by statute, in the exercise of its plenary control, Congress has removed still others."

SMITH V. EMPLOYMENT DIVISION, 301 Or. 209, 721 P.2d 455 (1986): "The denial of unemployment benefits significantly burdened Smith's free exercise rights. The employer does not question the sincerity of Smith's religious beliefs. The Board's finding demonstrate that peyote is the sacrament of the Native American Church. The fact that some Church members may not ingest peyote is irrelevant to our inquiry.... We are not to examine the tenets of a religion once the sincerity of the claimant's belief has been demonstrated, because to do so would improperly involve the courts in theological disputes."

In *Smith*, the court was asked to decide if the withholding of state unemployment benefits significantly burdened Smith's religious beliefs. Smith had been terminated from his employment after using peyote in a non-work related religious ceremony. Because Smith had been terminated for the use of an "illegal substance," he was denied state unemployment benefits. The court held that denial of the benefits significantly burdened Smith's free exercise rights.

CALIFORNIA, ET AL., APPELLANTS V. CABAZON BAND OF MISSION INDIANS, ET. AL., 480 U.S., 94 L. Ed.2d. 244, 108S.Ct.(1987): "The decision in this case turns on whether state authority is pre-empted by the operation of federal law. State jurisdiction is pre-empted if it interferes or is incompatible with federal and tribal interests reflected in federal law, unless the state interests at stake are sufficient to justify the assertion of state authority. The federal interests in Indian self-government, including the goal of encouraging tribal self-sufficiency and economic development, are important, and federal agencies, acting under federal laws, have sought to implement them by

promoting and overseeing tribal bingo and gambling enterprises. Such policies and actions are of particular relevance in this case since the tribal games provide the sole source of revenues for the operation of the tribal governments and are the major sources of employment for tribal members. To the extent that the State seeks to prevent all bingo games on tribal lands while permitting regulated off-reservation games, the asserted interest in preventing the infiltration of the tribal games by organized crime is irrelevant, and the state and county laws are pre-empted. Even to the extent that the State and county seek to regulate short of prohibition, the laws are pre-empted since the asserted state interest is not sufficient to escape the pre-emptive force of the federal and tribal interest apparent in this case."

RICHARD E. LYNG, SECRETARY OF AGRICULTURE, ET. AL., PETITIONERS V. NORTHWEST INDIAN CEMETERY PROTECTIVE ASSOCIATION ET AL., 1988 U.S. Lexis 1871 (1988): "This case requires us to consider whether the First Amendment's Free Exercise Clause forbids the Government from permitting timber harvesting in, or constructing a road through, a portion of a National Forest that has traditionally been used for religious purposes by members of three American Indian tribes in northwestern California. We conclude that it does not."

OREGON V. SMITH, April 17, 1990: The Supreme Court rules, 6–3, in *Oregon v. Smith*, that a state ban against the use of peyote by American Indians did not violate the plaintiffs' First Amendment rights. The decision represents another blow to tribes in their efforts to protect their religious freedoms. The case involved the firing of two Indian drug counselors after testing positive for drug use. As members of the Native American Church, the two men had ingested peyote as part of the church's ritual. Founded in 1916, the church's beliefs are a mixture of traditional beliefs and Christianity. Members believe that the taking of peyote allows them to communicate more closely with God. This case overturned and reversed the 1986 *Smith v. Employment Division* ruling.

GENERAL BIBLIOGRAPHY

A

Abbott. Elizabeth, ed. *Chronicle of Canada*. Montreal: Chronicle Publications, 1990.

Ahenakew, Edward. *Voices of the Plains Cree*. Toronto: McClelland & Stewart, 1973; rpt.

Albers, Patricia and Beatrice Medicine. *The Hidden Half: Studies of Plains Indian Women*. Washington, DC: University Press of America, 1983.

Alexie, Sherman. *The Business of Fancydancing: Stories and Poems*. Brooklyn, NY: Hanging Loose Press, 1992.

———. *Old Shirts and New Skins*. Los Angeles: American Indian Studies Center, University of California, 1993.

Allen, Paula Gunn. *Sacred Hoop: Recovering the Feminine in American Indian Traditions*. Boston: Beacon Press, 1986.

———. *Shadow Country*. Los Angeles: American Indian Studies Center, University of California, 1982.

———, ed. *Spider Woman's Granddaughters: Traditional Tales and Contemporary Writing by Native American Women*. New York: Fawcett Columbine, 1990.

———, ed. *Studies in American Indian Literature: Critical Essays and Course Designs*. New York: Modern Language Association of America, 1983.

Archuleta, Margaret and Rennard Strickland. *Shared Visions: Native American Painters and Sculptors in the Twentieth Century*. Phoenix: Heard Museum, 1991.

Armstrong, Virginia Irving. *I Have Spoken: American History Through the Voices of the Indians*. Athens, OH: Swallow Press, 1971.

Astrov, Margaret, ed. *The Winged Serpent: An Anthology of American Indian Prose and Poetry*. New York: The John Day Company, 1946; rpt. 1972.

Aveni, Anthony F., ed. *Native American Astronomy*. Austin: University of Texas Press, 1977.

Axelrod, Alan. *Chronicle of the Indian Wars*. New York: Prentice Hall General Reference, 1993.

Axtell, James. *The Invasion Within: The Contest of Cultures in Colonial North America*. New York: Oxford University Press, 1989.

B

Bailey, Alfred G. *The Conflict of European and Eastern Algonkian Cultures: 1504–1700*. Toronto: University of Toronto Press, 1969.

Barman, J., Y. Hebert, and D. McCaskill, eds. *Indian Education in Canada. 2 Vols.*

Vancouver: Nakoda Institute and University of British Columbia Press, 1986.

Bataille, Gretchen M., ed. *Native American Women: A Biographical Dictionary*. New York: Garland Publishing, 1993.

Bataille, Gretchen M. and Kathleen M. Sands. *American Indian Women, Telling Their Lives*. Lincoln: University of Nebraska Press, 1984.

Bataille, Gretchen M. and Charles L.P. Silet, eds. *The Pretend Indians: Images of Native Americans in the Movies*. Ames: Iowa State University Press, 1980.

Beck, Peggy V. and Anna Lee Walters. *The Sacred: Ways of Knowledge, Sources of Life*. Tsaile, AZ: Navajo Community College Press; Flagstaff: Northland, 1990.

Berkhofer, Robert F. *The White Man's Indian: Images of the American Indian, from Columbus to the Present*. New York: Knopf, 1978.

Berlo, Janet C. *The Early Years of Native American Art History*. Seattle: University of Washington Press, 1992.

Bierhorst, John. *The Mythology of North*

America. New York: William Morrow, 1985.

Black Elk. *Black Elk Speaks: Being the Life Story of a Holy Man of the Oglala Sioux.* Lincoln: University of Nebraska Press, 1979.

————. *The Sixth Grandfather: Black Elk's Teachings Given to John G. Neihardt.* Edited by Ray J. DeMallie. Lincoln: University of Nebraska Press, 1984.

Black Hawk (Ma-ka-tai-me-she-kia-kiak). *Black Hawk, an Autobiography.* Edited by Donald Jackson. Urbana: University of Illinois Press, 1955; rpt.

Blowsnake, Sam. *Crashing Thunder: The Autobiography of an American Indian.* Lincoln: University of Nebraska Press, 1983.

Boas, Franz. *Race, Language, and Culture.* New York: Macmillan, 1940.

Boas, Franz and Ella Cara Deloria. *Dakota Grammar.* Washington: U.S. Government Printing Office: National Academy of Science Memoirs, vol. xxiii, 1941.

Bowden, Henry Warner. *American Indians and Christian Missions.* Chicago: University of Chicago Press, 1981.

Boxberger, Daniel L., ed. *Native North Americans: An Ethnohistorical Approach.* Dubuque, IA: Kendall/Hunt, 1990.

Brave Bird, Mary with Richard Erdoes. *Ohitika Woman.* New York: Grove Press, 1993.

Brody, J.J. *Anasazi & Pueblo Painting.* Albuquerque: University of New Mexico Press, 1991.

————. *Indian Painters & White Patrons.* Albuquerque: University of New Mexico Press, 1971.

Brown, Dee. *Bury My Heart at Wounded Knee.* New York: Holt, Rinehart, & Winston, 1970.

Brown, Jennifer. *Strangers In Blood: Fur Trade Company Families in Indian*

Country. Vancouver: University of British Columbia, 1980.

Bruchac, Joseph. *Survival This Way: Interviews with American Indian Poets.* Tucson: University of Arizona Press, 1987.

Brumble, H. David. *American Indian Autobiography.* Berkeley: University of California Press, 1988.

Burton, Lloyd. *American Indian Water Rights and the Limits of the Law.* Lawrence: University Press of Kansas, 1991.

C

Calloway, Colin G., ed. *New Directions in American Indian History.* Norman: University of Oklahoma Press, 1988.

Castile, George Pierre and Robert L. Bee. *State and Reservation: New Perspectives on Federal Indian Policy.* Tucson: University of Arizona Press, 1992.

Champagne, Duane. *American Indian Societies: Strategies and Conditions of Political and Cultural Survival.* Cambridge, MA: Cultural Survival, Inc., 1989.

————. *Social Order and Political Change: Constitutional Governments Among the Cherokee, the Choctaw, the Chickasaw, and the Creek.* Stanford, CA: Stanford University Press, 1992.

————, ed. *The Native North American Almanac: A Reference Work on Native North Americans in the United States and Canada.* Detroit: Gale Research Inc., 1994.

Chartkoff, Joseph L. and Kerry Kona Chartkoff. *The Archaeology of California.* Stanford: Stanford University Press, 1984.

Coe, Michael, E.P. Benson, and D.R. Snow, eds. *Atlas of Ancient America.* New York: Facts on File, 1986.

Cohen, Felix. *Felix Cohen's Handbook of Federal Indian Law.* 2d ed. Char-

lottesville, VA: Michie/Bobbs-Merrill, 1982.

Coffer, William E. (Koi Hosh). *Spirits of the Sacred Mountains: Creation Stories of the American Indian.* New York: Van Nostrand Reinhold, 1978.

Coltelli, Laura. *Winged Words: American Indian Writers Speak.* Lincoln: University of Nebraska Press, 1990.

Confederation of American Indians, comp. *Indian Reservations: A State and Federal Handbook.* Jefferson, NC: McFarland, 1986.

Cook, Sherburne F. *The Conflict Between the California Indian and White Civilization.* Berkeley: University of California Press, 1976.

————. *The Population of the California Indians, 1796–1970.* Berkeley: University of California Press, 1976.

Copway, George (Ka-ge-ga-gah-bowh). *The Traditional History and Characteristic Sketches of the Ojibway Nation.* London: Gilpin, 1851; rpt. Toronto: Coles Publishing Company, 1972.

Cordell, Linda. *Prehistory of the Southwest.* New York: Academic Press, 1984.

Cornell, Stephen E. *The Return of the Native: American Indian Political Resurgence.* New York: Oxford University Press, 1988.

Costo, Rupert and Jeanette Henry Costo. *The Missions of California: A Legacy of Genocide.* San Francisco: Indian Historian Press, American Indian Historical Society, 1987.

Cronyn, George W. *American Indian Poetry: An Anthology of Songs and Chants.* New York: Liveright, 1968.

Crosby, Alfred W., Jr. *The Columbian Exchange: Biological and Cultural Consequences of 1492.* Westport, CT: Greenwood Press, 1972.

Crow Dog, Mary and Richard Erdoes.

Lakota Woman. New York: Grove Weidenfeld, 1990.

Crowe, Keith J. *A History of the Original Peoples of Northern Canada.* (Revised edition.) Montreal & Kingston: McGill-Queen's University Press, 1991.

Cuero, Delfina. *The Autobiography of Delfina Cuero, a Diegueno Indian.* Banning, CA: The Malki Museum Press, 1968.

Cumming, Peter A. and Neil H. Mickenberg, eds. *Native Rights in Canada.* Toronto: Indian-Eskimo Association of Canada/General Publishing, 1972.

Curtis, Edward S. *The North American Indian: Being a Series of Volumes Picturing and Describing the Indians of the United States and Alaska.* Seattle: E.S. Curtis, 1907–1930.

D

Daniels, Richard C. *A History of the Native Claims Process in Canada, 1869–1979.* Ottawa: Research Branch, Department of Indian and Northern Affairs, 1980.

Debo, Angie. *A History of the Indians of the United States.* Norman: University of Oklahoma Press, 1971.

Dejong, David H. *Promises of the Past: A History of Indian Education.* Golden, CO: North American Press, 1993.

Deloria, Ella Cara. *Dakota Texts.* New York: Publications of the American Ethnological Society, volume 14, 1932.

———. *Speaking of Indians.* Vermillion, SD: Dakota Press, 1979.

———. *Waterlily.* Lincoln: University of Nebraska Press, 1988.

Deloria, Vine, Jr. *Behind the Trail of Broken Treaties: An Indian Declaration of Independence.* Austin: University of Texas Press, 1985.

———. *We Talk, You Listen: New Tribes, New Turf.* New York: Macmillan, 1970.

———, ed. *American Indian Policy in the Twentieth Century.* Norman: University of Oklahoma Press, 1985.

Deloria, Vine, Jr. and Clifford M. Lytle, eds. *American Indians, American Justice.* Austin: University of Texas Press, 1983.

Dickason, Olive Patricia. *Canada's First Nations: A History of Founding Peoples From Earliest Times.* Toronto: McClelland & Stewart, 1992.

Dippie, Brian. *The Vanishing American: White Attitudes and U.S. Indian Policy.* Middletown, CT: Wesleyan University Press, 1982.

Dobyns, Henry F. *Their Number Become Thinned: Native American Population Dynamics in Eastern North America.* Knoxville: University of Tennessee Press, Newberry Library Center for the History of the American Indian, 1983.

Dockstader, Frederick. *Indian Art in America: The Arts and Crafts of the North American Indian.* Greenwich, CT: New York Graphic Society, 1966.

Dorris, Michael. *The Broken Cord: A Family's Ongoing Struggle with Fetal Alcohol Syndrome.* New York: Harper & Row, 1989.

———. *Working Men.* New York: Henry Holt, 1993.

———. *A Yellow Raft in Blue Water.* New York: Henry Holt, 1987.

Dorris, Michael and Louise Erdrich. *The Crown of Columbus.* New York: Harper Collins Publishers, 1991.

Duffy, John. *Epidemics in Colonial America.* Baton Rouge: Louisiana State University Press, 1953.

E

Eastman, Charles Alexander. *From the Deep Woods to Civilization: Chapters in the Autobiography of an Indian.* Lincoln: University of Nebraska Press, 1977.

———. *Indian Boyhood.* Boston: Little, Brown and Co., 1922.

———. *Old Indian Days.* New York: Doubleday, Page & Co., 1910.

———. *Wigwam Evenings: Sioux Folktales Retold.* Boston: Little, Brown, 1909; rpt. Lincoln: University of Nebraska Press, 1990.

Eccles, W.J. *The Canadian Frontier: 1534–1760.* New York: Holt, Rinehart and Winston, 1969.

Edmunds, R. David, ed. *American Indian Leaders: Studies in Diversity.* Lincoln: University of Nebraska Press, 1981.

Ehle, John. *Trail of Tears: The Rise and Fall of the Cherokee Nation.* New York: Doubleday, 1988.

Erdoes, Richard and Alfonso Ortiz, eds. *American Indian Myths and Legends.* New York: Pantheon Books, 1984.

Erdrich, Louise. *Jacklight.* New York: Holt, Rinehart, and Winston, 1984.

———. *Love Medicine: A Novel.* New York: Holt, Rinehart, and Winston, 1984.

———. *Tracks: A Novel.* New York; Henry Holt, 1988.

F

Falkowski, James E. *Indian Law/Race Law.* New York: Praeger, 1992.

Fagan, Brian. *Ancient North America: The Archaeology of a Continent.* New York: Thames and Hudson, 1991.

Feder, Norman. *Two Hundred Years of North American Indian Art.* New York: Praeger, 1971.

Feest, Christian. *Native Arts of North America: The Arts and Crafts of the North American Indian*. New York: Oxford University Press, 1980.

Fisher, Robin. *Contact and Conflict: Indian-European Relations in British Columbia, 1774–1890*. Vancouver: University of British Columbia, 1977.

Fleming, Paula Richardson and Judith Luskey. *The North American Indian in Early Photographs*. New York: Harper & Row, 1986.

Fowler, Melvin L. *The Cahokia Atlas: A Historical Atlas of Cahokia Archaeology*. Springfield: Illinois Historic Preservation Agency, 1989.

G

Geronimo. *Geronimo: His Own Story*. Edited by S.M. Barrett. Introduction by Frederick Turner III. 1906; rpt. New York: Dutton, 1970; New York: Ballantine, 1978.

Gibson, Arrell M. *The American Indian: Prehistory to Present*. Lexington, MA: D.C. Heath, 1980.

Gill, Sam D. *Native American Religions: An Introduction*. Belmont, CA: Wadsworth, 1982.

Grant, Campbell. *The Rock Art of the North American Indians: The Imprint of Man*. New York: Thomas Y. Crowell, 1967.

Grant, J.W. *Moon of Wintertime: Missionaries and the Indians of Canada in Encounter Since 1534*. Toronto: University of Toronto Press, 1984.

Green, Donald E. and Thomas V. Tonnesen, eds. *American Indians: Social Justice and Public Policy*. Milwaukee: University of Wisconsin System, 1991.

Grinde, Donald A., Jr. and Bruce E. Johansen. *Exemplar of Liberty: Native America and the Evolution of Democracy*. Los Angeles: American Indian Studies Center, the University of California, 1991.

Guillemin, Jeanne. *Urban Renegades: The Cultural Strategy of American Indians*. New York: Columbia University Press, 1975.

Gunther, Erna. *Indian Life on the Northwest Coast of North America, as Seen by the Early Explorers and Fur Traders During the Last Decades of the Eighteenth Century*. Chicago: University of Chicago Press, 1972.

H

Hamilton, Charles, ed. *Cry of the Thunderbird*. Norman: University of Oklahoma Press, 1972.

Harjo, Joy. *In Mad Love and War*. Middletown, CT: Wesleyan University Press, 1990.

———. *She Had Some Horses*. New York: Thunder's Mouth Press, 1983.

Harjo, Joy and Stephen Strom. *Secrets from the Center of the World*. Tucson: Sun Tracks, University of Arizona Press, 1989.

Hertzberg, Hazel. *The Search for an American Indian Identity: Modern Pan-Indian Movements*. Syracuse: Syracuse University Press, 1971.

Hittman, Michael, for the Yerington Paiute Tribe. *Wovoka and the Ghost Dance: A Sourcebook*. Carson City, NV: Grace Dangberg Foundation, 1990.

Hogan, Linda. *Calling Myself Home*. Greenfield Center, NY: Greenfield Review Press, 1978.

———. *Mean Spirit*. New York: Atheneum, 1990.

Hopkins, Sarah Winnemucca. *Life Among the Piutes: Their Wrongs and Claims*. Edited by Mrs. Horace Mann. New York: G.P. Putnam and Sons, 1883.

Horsman, Reginald. *Expansion and American Indian Policy, 1783–1812*. East Lansing: Michigan State University Press, 1967.

Hoxie, Frederick E. *A Final Promise: The Campaign to Assimilate the Indians, 1880–1920*. Lincoln: University of Nebraska Press, 1984.

———, ed. *Indians in American History: An Introduction*. Arlington Heights, IL: Harlan Davidson, 1988.

Hultkrantz, Ake. *Native Religions of North America: The Power of Visions and Fertility*. San Francisco: Harper & Row, 1987.

Hurt, R. Douglas. *Indian Agriculture in America: Prehistory to the Present*. Lawrence: University Press of Kansas, 1987.

J

Jacka, Lois Essart and Jerry Jacka. *Beyond Tradition: Contemporary Indian Art and Its Evolution*. Flagstaff, AZ: Northland Publishing Company, 1988.

Jaimes, M. Annette, ed. *The State of Native America: Genocide, Colonization and Resistance*. Boston: South End Press, 1992.

Jenness, Diamond. *The Indians of Canada*. Ottawa: Supply and Services Canada, 1932; rpt. 1977.

Jennings, Francis. *The Ambiguous Iroquois Empire: the Covenant Chain Confederacy of Indian Tribes with English Colonies from its Beginnings to the Lancaster Treaty of 1744*. New York: Norton, 1984.

———. *The Invasion of America: Indians, Colonization and the Cant of Conquest*. Chapel Hill: University of North Carolina Press, 1975.

Jennings, Jesse D. *Prehistory of North America*. New York: McGraw-Hill, 1968.

————, ed. *Ancient Native Americans*. San Francisco: W.H. Freeman, 1978.

Joe, Jennie, ed. *American Indian Policy and Cultural Values: Conflict and Accommodation*. Los Angeles: American Indian Studies Center, University of California, 1986.

John, Elizabeth Ann Harper. *Storms Brewed in Other Men's Worlds: The Confrontation of Indians, Spanish and French in the Southwest 1540–1795*. College Station: Texas A & M University Press, 1975.

Johnson, E. Pauline (Tekahionwake). *Canadian Born*. Toronto: Morang, 1903; rpt. Toronto: Canadian House, 1981.

————. *Flint and Feather: The Complete Poems of E. Pauline Johnson*. Toronto: Mission Book Company, 1924; rpt.

————. *Legends of Vancouver*. Vancouver: Saturday Sunset, 1911.

————. *The Moccasin Maker*. Tucson: University of Arizona Press, 1987; rpt.

Jonaitis, Aldona. *From the Land of the Totem Poles: The Northwest Coast Indian Art Collection at the Museum of Natural History*. New York: American Museum of Natural History; Seattle: University of Washington Press, 1988.

Josephy, Alvin M., Jr. *The Patriot Chiefs: a Chronicle of American Indian Resistance*. New York: Viking Compass, 1961.

————. *Red Power: The American Indians' Fight for Freedom*. New York: American Heritage Press, 1971.

————, ed. *America in 1492: The World of the Indian Peoples Before the Arrival of Columbus*. New York: Knopf, 1992.

K

Karamanski, Theodore J. *Fur Trade and Exploration: Opening the Far Northwest, 1821–1852*. Norman: University of Oklahoma Press, 1983.

Kehoe, Alice. *North American Indians: A Comparative Account*. Englewood, NJ: Prentice-Hall, 1981.

Kelly, Lawrence C. *The Assault on Assimilation: John Collier and the Origins of Indian Policy Reform*. Albuquerque: University of New Mexico Press, 1983.

Kroeber, Theodora. *Ishi, the Last of His Tribe*. Berkeley, CA: Parnassus Press, 1964.

Krupat, Arnold. *For Those Who Come After: A Study of Native American Autobiography*. Berkeley: University of California Press, 1985.

L

La Flesche, Francis. *The Middle Five: Indian Schoolboys of the Omaha Tribe*. Lincoln: University of Nebraska Press, 1978.

Lame Deer, John (Fire). *Lame Deer: Seeker of Visions*. New York: Simon and Schuster, 1972.

Landes, Ruth. *The Ojibwa Woman*. New York: Columbia University Press, 1938.

Leacock, Eleanore Burke and Nancy O. Lurie, eds. *North American Indians in Historical Perspective*. Prospect Heights, IL: Waveland Press, 1988.

Leitch, Barbara. *A Concise Dictionary of Indian Tribes of North America*. Algonac, MI: Reference Publications, 1979.

Lesley, Craig, ed. *Talking Leaves: Contemporary Native American Short Stories*. New York: Dell, 1991.

Lincoln, Kenneth. *Native American*

Renaissance. Berkeley: University of California Press, 1983.

Lowie, Robert. *Indians of the Plains*. Garden City, NY: American Museum of Natural History, Natural History Press, 1963.

Lyden, Fremont J. and Lyman H. Legters, eds. *Native Americans and Public Policy*. Pittsburgh, PA: University of Pittsburgh Press, 1992.

M

McLoughlin, William, Walter H. Conser, Jr., and Virginia Duffy McLoughlin. *The Cherokee Ghost Dance: Essays on the Southeastern Indians, 1789–1861*. Macon, GA: Mercer, 1984.

McNickle, D'Arcy. *Indian Tribes of the United States*. New York: Oxford University Press, 1962.

————. *Native American Tribalism: Indian Survivals and Renewals*. New York: Oxford University Press, 1973.

————. *They Came Here First: The Epic of the American Indian*. New York: Farrar, Straus & Giroux, 1975.

————. *Wind From an Enemy Sky*. San Francisco: Harper & Row, 1978.

McPherson, Robert S. *Sacred Land, Sacred View*. Salt Lake City, UT: Signature Books, 1992.

Margolin, Malcolm, ed. *The Way We Lived: California Indian Reminiscences, Stories, and Songs*. Berkeley, CA: Heyday Books, 1981.

Marriott, Alice Lee. *Maria, the Potter of San Ildefonso*. Norman: University of Oklahoma Press, 1948.

Mathews, John Joseph. *The Osages: Children of the Middle Waters*. Norman: University of Oklahoma Press, 1961.

————. *Sundown*. Norman: University of Oklahoma Press, 1988.

————. *Wah'kon-tah: the Osage and the White Man's Road*. Norman: University of Oklahoma Press, 1932.

Mathews, Zena Pearlstone and Aldona Jonaitis. *Native North American Art History: Selected Readings*. Palo Alto, CA: Peck Publications, 1982.

Matthieson, Peter. *In the Spirit of Crazy Horse*. New York: Viking Press, 1983; rpt. 1991.

Miller, J.R. *Skyscrapers Hide the Heavens: A History of Indian-White Relations in Canada*. Revised edition. Toronto: University of Toronto Press, 1991.

Momaday, N. Scott. *The Ancient Child: a Novel*. New York: Doubleday, 1989.

————. *House Made of Dawn*. New York: Harper & Row, 1968.

————. *The Names: a Memoir*. Tucson: University of Arizona Press, 1976; rpt. 1987.

————. *The Way to Rainy Mountain*. Albuquerque: University of New Mexico Press, 1969.

Mooney, James. *The Ghost-Dance Religion and the Sioux Outbreak of 1890*. Lincoln: University of Nebraska Press, 1991.

Morgan, William N. *Prehistoric Architecture in the Eastern United States*. Cambridge, MA: MIT Press, 1980.

Morse, B.W., ed. *Aboriginal Peoples and the Law: Indian, Métis and Inuit Rights in Canada*. Ottawa: Carleton University Press, 1991 (revised edition).

Mourning Dove. *Co-ge-we-a, The Half Blood*. Boston: The Four Seas Company, 1927; rpt. Lincoln: University of Nebraska Press, 1981.

N

Nabokov, Peter. *Native American Architecture*. New York: Oxford University Press, 1989.

————, ed. *Native American Testimony: A Chronicle of Indian-White Relations from Prophecy to the Present, 1492–1992*. New York: Viking, 1991.

Newcomb, Franc Johnson. *Hosteen Klah: Navajo Medicine Man and Sand Painter*. Norman: University of Oklahoma Press, 1964.

Niatum, Duane. *Harper's Anthology of 20th Century Native American Poetry*. San Francisco: Harper & Row, 1988.

O

Olson, James S. and Raymond Wilson. *Native Americans in the Twentieth Century*. Provo, UT: Brigham Young University Press, 1984.

Ortiz, Alfonso. *The Tewa World: Space, Time, Being, and Becoming in a Pueblo Society*. Chicago: University of Chicago Press, 1969.

Ortiz, Simon. *Fightin': New and Collected Stories*. Chicago: Thunder's Mouth Press, 1983.

————. *From Sand Creek: Rising in This Heart Which Is Our America*. New York: Thunder's Mouth Press, 1981.

————. *Going for the Rain: Poems*. New York: Harper & Row, 1976.

————. *A Good Journey*. Tucson: Sun Tracks, University of Arizona Press, 1984.

————. *Woven Stone*. Tucson: University of Arizona Press, 1992.

P

Parker, Arthur. *Parker on the Iroquois*. Syracuse, NY: Syracuse University Press, 1968.

Patterson, E.P. III. *The Canadian Indian: A History Since 1500*. Don Mills,

Ontario: Collier-Macmillan Canada, 1972.

Penney, David W. *Art of the American Indian Frontier: The Chandler-Pohrt Collection*. Detroit: Detroit Institute of Arts; Seattle: University of Washington Press, 1992.

Philp, Kenneth R. *John Collier's Crusade for Indian Reform, 1920–1954*. Tucson: University of Arizona Press, 1977.

Porter, Frank W. III. *The Art of Native American Basketry: A Living Legacy*. Westport, CT: Greenwood Press, 1990.

Powers, William K. *Oglala Religion*. Lincoln: University of Nebraska Press, 1977.

Price, H. Marcus III. *Disputing the Dead: U.S. Law on Aboriginal Remains and Grave Goods*. Columbia: University of Missouri Press, 1991.

Prucha, Francis Paul. *Atlas of American Indian Affairs*. Lincoln: University of Nebraska Press, 1990.

————. *Documents of United States Indian Policy*. 2d ed. Lincoln: University of Nebraska Press, 1990.

————. *The Great Father: The U.S. Government and the American Indians*. Abridged ed. Lincoln: University of Nebraska Press, 1986.

R

Riggs, Lynn. *Green Grow the Lilacs: a Play*. New York: S. French, 1931.

————. *The Iron Dish, a Play*. Garden City, NY: Doubleday, Doran, 1930.

Rose, Wendy. *The Halfbreed Chronicles and Other Poems*. Los Angeles: West End Press, 1985.

————. *Lost Copper: Poems*. Banning: Malki Museum Press, 1980.

S

Sando, Joe. *Pueblo Nations: Eight Centuries of Pueblo Indian History.* Santa Fe, NM: Clearlight, 1992.

Sarris, Greg. *Keeping Slug Woman Alive: A Holistic Approach to American Indian Texts.* Berkeley: University of California, 1993.

Satz, Ronald N. *American Indian Policy in the Jacksonian Era.* Lincoln: University of Nebraska Press, 1975.

Sauer, Carl Ortwin. *Sixteenth Century North America: The Land and the People as seen by the Europeans.* Berkeley: University of California Press, 1971.

Seaver, James. *A Narrative of the Life of Mrs. Mary Jemison.* Syracuse, NY: Syracuse University Press, 1990; rpt.

Shaw, Annie Moore. *Pima Indian Legends.* Tucson: University of Arizona Press, 1968.

Sheehan, Bernard W. *Seeds of Extinction: Jeffersonian Philanthropy and the American Indian.* Chapel Hill: University of North Carolina Press, 1973.

Silko, Leslie Marmon. *Almanac of the Dead: a Novel.* New York: Simon & Schuster, 1991.

———. *Ceremony.* New York: Viking Press, 1977.

———. *Storyteller.* New York: Seaver Books, 1981.

Snipp, C. Matthew. *American Indians: The First of this Land.* New York: Russell Sage Foundation, 1989.

———. *Public Policy Impacts on American Indian Economic Development.* Albuquerque: Institute for Native American Development, University of New Mexico, 1988.

Snow, Dean R. *The Archaeology of North America.* New York: Viking, 1976.

Spencer, Robert F. and Jesse D. Jennings, et al. *The Native Americans: Ethnology and Backgrounds of the North American Indians.* New York: Harper & Row, 1977.

Spicer, Edward H. *Cycles of Conquest: The Impact of Spain, Mexico, and the United States on the Indians of the Southwest, 1533–1960.* Tucson: University of Arizona Press, 1962.

Spittal, W.G., ed. *Iroquois Women: An Anthology.* Ohswekan, ON: Iroqrafts, 1990.

Standing Bear, Luther. *Land of the Spotted Eagle.* Lincoln: University of Nebraska Press, 1933; rpt. 1978.

———. *My People the Sioux.* Boston: Houghton Mifflin, 1928; rpt. Lincoln: University of Nebraska Press, 1975.

Stands in Timber, John. *Cheyenne Memories.* New Haven, CT: Yale University Press, 1967.

Stedman, Raymond W. *Shadows of the Indian: Stereotypes in American Culture.* Norman: University of Oklahoma Press, 1982.

Stuart, Paul. *Nations Within a Nation: Historical Statistics of American Indians.* Westport, CT: Greenwood Press, 1987.

Sturtevant, William C. *Early Indian Tribes, Culture Areas, & Linguistic Stocks.* Reston, VA: Dept. of Interior, U.S. Geological Survey, 1991.

———. *Handbook of North American Indians.* Washington, DC: Smithsonian Institution Press, 1978.

Sullivan, Lawrence E., ed. *Native American Religions: North America.* New York: Macmillan, 1987.

Swann, Brian and Arnold Krupat, eds. *I Tell You Now: Autobiographical Essays by Native American Writers.* Lincoln: University of Nebraska Press, 1987.

———. *Recovering the Word: Essays on Native American Literature.* Berkeley: University of California Press, 1987.

Swanton, John R. *The Indian Tribes of North America.* Washington, DC: Smithsonian Institution Press, 1968.

———. *Indians of the Southeastern United States.* Grosse Pointe, MI: Scholarly Press, 1969

T

Tanner, Clara Lee. *Southwest Indian Painting.* Tucson: University of Arizona Press, 1957; rpt. 1973.

Tanner, Helen Hornbeck, et al. *Atlas of Great Lakes Indian History.* Norman: University of Oklahoma Press, 1986.

Tennant, Paul. *Aboriginal Peoples and Politics: The Indian Land Question in British Columbia, 1849–1984.* Vancouver, University of British Columbia, 1990.

Thornton, Russell. *American Indian Holocaust and Survival: A Population History Since 1492.* Norman: University of Oklahoma Press, 1987.

———. *We Shall Live Again: The 1879 and 1890 Ghost Dance Movements as Demographic Revitalization.* Cambridge: Cambridge University Press, 1986.

Thrapp, Dan. *The Conquest of Apacheria.* Norman: University of Oklahoma Press, 1967.

Trigger, Bruce G. *Natives and Newcomers: Canada's "Heroic Age" Reconsidered.* Kingston and Montreal: McGill-Queen's University Press, 1985.

Trimble, Stephen. *The People: Indians of the American Southwest.* Santa Fe, NM: School of American Research Press, 1993.

U

Underhill, Ruth. *Papago Woman.* New

York: Holt, Rinehart, and Winston, 1979.

Upton, Leslie F.S. *Micmacs and Colonists: Indian-White Relations in the Maritimes, 1713–1867.* Vancouver: University of British Columbia, 1979.

V

Verano, John W. and Douglas Ubelaker. *Disease and Demography in the Americas.* Washington, DC: Smithsonian Institution Press, 1992.

Vecsey, Christopher, ed. *Handbook of American Indian Religious Freedom.* New York: Crossroads, 1991.

Vecsey, Christopher and William S. Starna. *Iroquois Land Claims.* Syracuse, NY: Syracuse University Press, 1988.

Vizenor, Gerald. *Crossbloods, Bone Courts, Bingo and Other Reports.* Minneapolis: University of Minnesota Press, 1990.

———. *The Darkness in Saint Louis Bearheart.* St. Paul, MN: Truck Press, 1978.

———. *The Heirs of Columbus.* Middleton, CT: Wesleyan University Press, 1991.

———. *People Named the Chippewa: Narrative Histories.* Minneapolis: University of Minnesota Press, 1984.

———. *Trickster of Liberty: Tribal Heirs to a Wild Baronage.* Minneapolis: University of Minnesota Press, 1988.

———. *Wordarrows: Indians and Whites in the New Fur Trade.* Minneapolis: University of Minnesota Press, 1978.

———, ed. *Narrative Chance: Postmodern Discourse on Native American Indian Literatures.* Albuquerque: University of New Mexico Press, 1989.

Voices from Wounded Knee, 1973, in the Words of the Participants. Rooseveltown, NY: Akwesasne Notes, 1979.

W

Waldman, Carl. *Atlas of the North American Indian.* New York: Facts on File, 1985.

Wallace, Anthony F.C. *Death and Rebirth of the Seneca.* New York: Knopf, 1969.

Washburn, Wilcomb E. *Red Man's Land/White Man's Law: A Study of the Past and Present Status of the American Indian.* New York: Scribner, 1971.

Weibel-Orlando, Joan. *Indian Country, L.A.: Maintaining Ethnic Community in Complex Society.* Urbana: University of Illinois Press, 1991.

Welch, James. *The Death of Jim Loney.* New York: Harper & Row, 1979.

———. *Fools Crow.* New York: Viking, 1986.

———. *The Indian Lawyer.* New York: W.W. Norton, 1990.

———. *Winter in the Blood.* New York: Harper & Row, 1974.

White, Richard. *Land Use, Environment, and Social Change.* Seattle: University of Washington Press, 1992.

———. *The Middle Ground: Indians, Empires and Republics in the Great Lakes Region, 1650–1815.* New York: Cambridge University Press, 1991.

———. *Roots of Dependency: Subsistence, Environment, and Social Change among the Choctaws, Pawnees, and Navajos.* Lincoln: University of Nebraska Press, 1983.

Wilkinson, Charles F. *American Indians, Time and Law: Native Societies in a Modern Constitutional Democracy.* New Haven, CT: Yale University Press, 1987.

Williams, Walter. *The Spirit and the Flesh: Sexual Diversity in American Indian Culture.* Boston: Beacon Press, 1986.

Y

Yerbury, J.C. *The Subarctic and the Fur Trade, 1680–1860.* Vancouver: University of British Columbia Press, 1986.

Z

Zitkala-Sa (Gertrude Bonin). *Old Indian Legends Retold by Zitkala-Sa.* Boston: London Ginn & Co., 1901.

ILLUSTRATIONS CREDITS

p. lxxvi: Federal and state recognized reservations in the United States. Courtesy of Duane Champagne. Source: Bureau of Indian Affairs; p. lxxviii: Canadian Native culture groups. Courtesy of Duane Champagne. p. 1 large photo: Pueblo homes; p. 1 small photo: Pottery of the Casas Grande people. Courtesy of the Library of Congress; Source: Department of Indian Affairs and Northern Development; p. 4: Sandia stone point. Courtesy of Molly Braun; p. 5 : Clovis stone point. Courtesy of Molly Braun; p. 6: Stone projectile point found at Folsom, New Mexico. Photo by Thane L. Bierwert. Courtesy of the Department Library Services, American Museum of Natural History; p. 7: A monolithic stone axe from Georgia engraved with Southeastern Ceremonial Complex iconography. Courtesy of the National Anthropological Archives, Smithsonian Institution; p. 10: Stenciled handprints designed on a shelter wall at Sliding Rock, Canyon de Chelly, Arizona. Photo by Earl H. Morris and A.V. Kidder. Courtesy of the Department Library Services, American Museum of Natural History; p. 12: Mississippian marble mortuary figure. Courtesy of Molly Braun; p. 13: Adena burial ground in Miamisburg, Ohio. Courtesy of Dean R. Snow; p. 15: The Serpent Mound, an effigy mound of the Adena or Hopewell culture, about the first century B.C. Courtesy of the

Archives-Library Division, Ohio Historical Society; p. 16: Hohokam stone palette, fashioned in impressionistic human figure, used for mixing pigments. Courtesy of the Photographic Collections, Arizona State Museum, University of Arizona, Tucson; p. 17: Reconstruction of a Mogollon pithouse village from the Pine Lawn phase. Courtesy of the Field Museum of Natural History, Chicago; p. 22: Map of the Athabascan migrations from the sub-Arctic to the Southwest and Pacific Northwest. Courtesy of Duane Champagne; p. 23: Anasazi human effigy jar (A.D. 900–1150) from Chaco Canyon, New Mexico. Photo by Hillel Burger. Courtesy of the Peabody Museum, Harvard University; p. 23: Pottery of the Casas Grande people. Courtesy of the National Anthropological Archives, Smithsonian Institution; p. 24: One of the two ball courts excavated at Snaketown, Arizona. The court is 100 by 130 feet and was constructed between A.D. 600 and 900. Courtesy of the Photographic Collections, Arizona State Museum, University of Arizona, Tucson; p. 25: A series of doorways joining the multi-storied rooms and ceremonial chambers of Pueblo Bonito at Chaco Canyon. Courtesy of Troy Johnson; p. 27: Etowah Mound, important Mississippian center in present-day Georgia. Courtesy of Molly Braun; p. 28: Cahokia Mounds, c. A.D. 1100–1150. This painting by

Lloyd K. Townsend is a reconstruction of the site from across Twin Mounds and Central Plaza to Monk's Mounds. Courtesy of the Cahokia Mounds State Historic Site; p. 29: Great Kiva, Chetro Ketl community, Chaco Canyon, New Mexico. Courtesy of Dean R. Snow; p. 30: Notched staff used by Iroquois sachem to list the members of the Great Council. Each peg represents a council member. Courtesy of the Cranbrook Institute of Science; p. 32: Earthen pyramids in Moundville, Alabama. Courtesy of Dean R. Snow; p. 40: The Micmac were among the earliest Indians to meet the European traders. This painting of a Micmac encampment completed between 1820 and 1830 suggests that they retained much of their earlier culture. The guns provide the clearest evidence of cultural adaptation. Courtesy of the National Archives of Canada; p. 41: An early view of Native Americans in Florida, rowing a canoe and showing a communal house for storage of food, c. 1590. These engravings were based on watercolors by Jacques Le Moyne, now lost. Engraving by Bry, Theodor de, [America]. Frankfurt, 1590-part 2, plt.22. Courtesy of the Rare Books & Manuscript Division of the New York Public Library—Astor, Lenox, and Tilden Foundations; p. 43: A five-story Pueblo building. Courtesy of the National Anthropological Archives, Smithsonian Institution; p. 46: An early view of American Indians in the Southeast and Florida. Engraving by Bry, Theodor de, [America]. Frankfurt, 1590-part 2, plt.23. Courtesy of the Rare Books & Manuscript Division of the New York Public Library—Astor, Lenox, and Tilden Foundations; p. 47: On April 30, 1562, two small French ships cast anchor and met with Indians near present-day St. Augustine, Florida. Theodore de Bry's engraving of the French Colony in Florida made from the paintings of Jacques Le Moyne. Courtesy of the Rare Books & Manuscript Division of the New York Public Library—Astor, Lenox, and Tilden Foundations; p. 48: An early view of American Indians, cooking fish. Engraving by Bry, Theodor de, [America]. Frankfurt, 1590-part 2, plt.14. Courtesy of the Rare Books & Manuscript Division of the New York Public Library—Astor, Lenox, and Tilden Foundation; p. 51 : French artist's view of American Indians used as illustration to *Les Voyages du Sr. de Champlain*, c. 1615–18. Reprinted by permission of the Houghton Library, Harvard University; p. 52: Indian method of hunting deer, from *Les Voyages du Sr. de Champlain*, c. 1615–18. Reprinted by permission of the Houghton Library, Harvard University; p. 53: This portrait of Pocahontas was made in London in 1616, one year before her sudden death. Courtesy of the National Anthropological Archives, Smithsonian Institution; p. 58: French engraving of a 'Sauvage Iroquois.' Courtesy of the Library of Congress; p. 70: Ojibway shelter frame. Courtesy of the American Indian Studies Center, University of California at Los Angeles; p. 75: 1775 engraving of William Penn, founder of Pennsylvania, concluding a treaty with the Delaware Indians. Courtesy of the Library of Congress; p. 80: Green quartzite effigy found in east-central Alberta that hints at the central role that buffalo played in Plains Indian societies. The buffalo was the source of food, clothing, and shelter. Courtesy of the Glenbow Museum, Calgary, Alberta; p. 85: Miniature model showing Natchez

life, with a house for corn storage on the left, and a mound temple in the back. Photo by Thane L. Bierwert. Courtesy of the Department of Library Services, American Museum of Natural History; p. 90: By 1750 the horse had spread throughout the plains, greatly easing the quest for food. Particularly in western regions, where steep river valleys and cliffs abounded, large herds of buffalo were driven over 'buffalo jumps,' to be butchered by the women. Courtesy of the National Archives of Canada; p. 93: Cherokee visitors to London in 1762. Courtesy of the National Anthropological Archives, Smithsonian Institution; p. 94: Ottawa chief Pontiac encountering Robert Rogers on his way to occupy Detroit in November 1760. This engraving shows the two men smoking the calumet, or the so-called peace pipe. Courtesy of the Library of Congress; p. 99: April 1778 drawing of the interior of habitation at Nootka Sound by John Webber. Photo by Hillel Burger. Courtesy of the Peabody Museum, Harvard University; p. 101: A group of Plains Cree driving buffalo into a 'pound.' Mounted hunters and a row of waving Indians guide the herd toward the enclosure (constructed of branches), where the buffalo can be slaughtered. Notice that the bow and arrow remains the weapon of choice even though the Cree own guns. Courtesy of the Glenbow Archives, Calgary, Alberta; p. 102: Mohawk Chief Thayendanegea (Joseph Brant). Courtesy of the National Gallery of Canada, Ottawa; p. 117: Native American revitalization movements. Courtesy of Duane Champagne; p. 122: Shoshoni arriving at camp for meeting at the Green River. 1837. Courtesy of the Walters Art Gallery, Baltimore; p. 127: Comanche feats of horsemanship. Courtesy of the National Museum of American Art, Washington D.C./Art Resource NY. Gift of Mrs. Joseph Harrison Jr.; p. 132: Mounted warriors rout a party of Red River colonists at a shootout at Seven Oaks. The Métis victory, captured in song, did much to crystallize a Métis sense of nationhood on the northern plains.

Courtesy of the National Archives of Canada; p. 137: *Interior of a Cree Tent*, by Robert Hood, 1820. The painting shows a Creek party near the important fur trade post at Cumberland House. A number of the most sought-after trade items are evident in the tipi: a gun, a metal kettle, and tobacco. Courtesy of the National Archives of Canada; p. 142: A hunter family of Cree Indians at York Fort, Manitoba, c. 1821. Courtesy of the National Archives of Canada; p. 144: Photo of Cherokee tribal leader John Ross, taken in the 1860s. Courtesy of the National Anthropological Archives, Smithsonian Institution; p. 147: Crowfoot was commemorated in a 1986 Canadian postage stamp. Courtesy of the Canada Post Corporation; p. 148: *Indian Encampment on Lake Huron*, c. 1845–50, by Paul Kane. This painting shows the typical Ojibway birch bark tent and canoe. Courtesy of the Art Gallery of Ontario; p. 149: Homelands of Indian nations that were forced to migrate after 1830 to Indian Territory in present-day Kansas and Oklahoma. Courtesy of Duane Champagne; p. 153: Four Bears, the last of the great Mandan chiefs. Courtesy of the National Museum of American Art, Washington D.C./Art Resource, NY; p. 157: Artist George Catlin portrayed the Choctaws playing games by observing them for hours in their new 'home' in Indian territory. This scene represents a ball game, c. 1834–35. Courtesy of the National Museum of American Art, Washington D.C./Art Resource, NY; p. 159: Osceola, the Black Drink, a warrior of great distinction. Courtesy of the National Museum of the American Art, Washington D.C./Art Resource NY. Gift of Mrs. Joseph Harrison, Jr.; p. 163: Painting of the Cherokees' Trail of Tears. Courtesy of the Woolaroc Museum, Bartlesville, Oklahoma; p. 169: Canada Post issued this stamp honoring Louis Riel in 1970—85 years after he was executed for treason. Courtesy of the Canada Post Corporation; p. 172: *Captain Cold, or Ut-ha-wah*. Painting by William John Wilgus, c. 1838. Captain Cold was the Onondaga keeper of the Iroquois League Fire at Buffalo Creek. The Buffalo Creek Reservation was sold as a consequence of the Compromise Treaty of 1842, and when Ut-ha-wah died in 1847, little was left of the once powerful league. Courtesy of Yale University Art Gallery. Gift of de Lancey Kountze, B.A. 1899; p. 178: *Panorama of the Monumental Grandeur of the Mississippi Valley, 1850,* by John J. Egan. Courtesy of the St. Louis Art Museum; p. 179: The semiannual buffalo hunt was the main event in the Plains Métis community. Note the two-wheeled Red River cart and oxen, both Métis innovations. Courtesy of the Royal Ontario Museum; p. 189: Westward expansion until the 1860s. The land cessions map is based on the Indian Claims Commission Final Report, 1978. Courtesy of the University of New Mexico Press and Imre Sutton; p. 194: Navajo woman, with her baby in a cradleboard, at Bosque Redondo. Courtesy of the Museum of New Mexico; p. 195: Depiction of the Sand Creek massacre by artist Robert Lindneux. His depiction includes the American flag that Chief Black Kettle raised above his tipi in a vain attempt to signal his allegiance and peaceful intentions. Courtesy of the Colorado Historical Society; p. 196: A sketch of Fort Laramie, the site of major treaties with the northern plains Indians, about 1863. Courtesy of the American Heritage Center, University of Wyoming. *Copyright Restricted;* p. 199: Red Cloud. Courtesy of the National Anthropological Archives, Smithsonian Institution; p. 201: Sauk and Fox tribesmen posing for a picture with Louis Bogy, commissioner of Indian Affairs. Third from the left is Fox chief Chekuskuk, and second from the left, seated, is Sauk chief Keokuk. Bogy here pretends to read the treaty specifying that the tribes cede 157,000 acres of land along the Mississippi and the Missouri rivers in exchange for $26,574 and a 750 square-mile reservation territory in present-day Oklahoma. Courtesy of the National Anthropological Archives, Smithsonian Institution; p. 203: Major General William Tecumseh

Sherman presides with commissioners over the signing of a treaty with chief Red Cloud at Fort Laramie, Wyoming Territory, on April 29, 1868. Courtesy of the National Anthropological Archives, Smithsonian Institution; p. 204: Navajo prisoners of war at Fort Sumner, New Mexico, c. 1866. This picture shows Indian captives building an adobe under military guard. Courtesy of the Museum of New Mexico; p. 205: Ely Parker, first Indian commissioner of Indian affairs. Courtesy of the National Anthropological Archives, Smithsonian Institution; p. 206: Oil painting by Louis Didier Guillaume showing Gen. Robert E. Lee (right) surrendering to Gen. Ulysses S. Grant. Behind Grant stands his chief secretary, Ely Parker, a full-blood Seneca of the Wolf Clan. Courtesy of the National Park Service, Appomattox Court House National Historical Park; p. 207: Members of a Blackfoot Confederacy gather in front of Fort Whoop-up (Lethbridge, Alberta), the best known whisky post in Canada. Courtesy of the Glenbow Archives, Calgary, Alberta; p. 208: Members of the Métis Provisional Government at Red River. Louis Riel is seated in the center. Courtesy of the Glenbow Archives, Calgary, Alberta; p. 209: Comanche leader Quanah Parker. Courtesy of the National Anthropological Archives, Smithsonian Institution; p. 210: *Plains Indians.* The Great Plains travois was the principal mode of transportation used by Plains Indians to move their shelter and household and personal effects. Photo by E. Curtis. Courtesy of the George Eastman House; p. 211: Captain Jack. Courtesy of the National Archives; p. 212: Sitting Bull, Hunkpapa Sioux tribal leader. He was killed in October 1890 by government-paid Indian police over a dispute that erupted during a Ghost Dance ceremony at Standing Rock. Courtesy of the Library of Congress; p. 213: The first session of the General Council in Indian territory was held at Okmulgee (Oklahoma), capital of the Creek Nation, in 1870. The meeting gathered delegates from twelve different tribes, and a committee of Indian

leaders framed a constitution for the new territory. This photograph shows the Creek log building and all the delegates of the council, c. 1875. Photo by Jack Hillers, C.W. Kirk Collection. Courtesy of the Archives & Manuscripts Division of the Oklahoma Historical Society; p. 216: Geronimo and three of his warriors in 1886, after their defeat. Courtesy of the Southwest Museum, Los Angeles; p. 218: The view of the Little Bighorn Valley from the position of the Seventh Cavalry looking in the direction of the Sioux, Cheyenne, and Arapaho encampments. Courtesy of Stephen Lehmer; p. 221: Crowfoot, the leading spokesman for the Blackfoot Confederacy, addresses representatives of the Canadian government at the negotiations for Treaty 7 at Blackfoot Crossing near Calgary in 1877. Courtesy of the Glenbow Archives, Calgary, Alberta; p. 222: Dull Knife and Little Wolf, 1880s. Courtesy of the National Anthropological Archives, Smithsonian Institution; p. 225: Indian student at the Carlisle Indian School before matriculation. Courtesy of the National Anthropological Archives, Smithsonian Institution; p. 225: Indian student at the Carlisle Indian School after matriculation. Courtesy of the National Anthropological Archives, Smithsonian Institution; p. 227: Group of Omaha boys in cadet uniforms, Carlisle Indian School, Pennsylvania, 1880. Courtesy of the National Archives Trust Fund Board; p. 228: Sun Dance Lodge. Each lodge had a defined structure, celestially oriented, with the entrance facing east. Courtesy of the Glenbow Archives, Calgary, Alberta; p. 229: Masked dancers participating in a Kwakiutl winter ceremonial. Courtesy of the National Anthropological Archives, Smithsonian Institution; p. 231: Surveyors for the Canadian Pacific Railway meet an Ojibway band in northern Ontario in the early 1880s. The Indians are still living a nomadic subsistence and trapping lifestyle. Courtesy of Canadian Pacific Limited; p. 232: Northwest Coast Indians have become famous for their totem poles.

In this late nineteenth-century photograph, totem poles front the large houses of the Haida village of Skidgate, on the Queen Charlotte Island. Courtesy of the Royal British Columbia Museum, Victoria; p. 233: A band of Plains Cree led by Big Bear (standing center) trade at a Hudson's Bay Company post at Fort Pitt shortly before members of the Big Bear's band join the North-West rebellion. Courtesy of the National Archives of Canada, Ottawa; p. 236: Louis Riel rises in his defense at his trial in 1885. Courtesy of the National Archives of Canada; p. 238: Spring Rancheria (Cahuilla) in southern California, c. 1886. Courtesy of the Riverside Municipal Museum, Riverside, California; p. 240: Wovoka, the prophet of the second Ghost Dance. Courtesy of the Nevada Historical Society; p. 241: The massacre at Wounded Knee. One hundred and forty-six bodies were interred in a mass grave on a small hill. Photo by G. Trager. Courtesy of the Nebraska State Historical Society; p. 242: Crow Indian woman carrying a child. Courtesy of the National Museum of the American Indian, Smithsonian Institution, Charles Rau Collection; p. 243: In 1680, the Pueblo Indian town of Zia was destroyed by the Spanish as a result of the Pueblo's revolt against them. Hundreds of Pueblo Indians were killed in battle, and the Pueblo of Zia were thought to have 'disappeared.' This picture was taken two hundred years later in a 'kiva,' or ceremonial chamber. It shows a Pueblo Zia ceremony for the treatment of a sick boy. Courtesy of the National Anthropological Archives, Smithsonian Institution; p. 245: Tsimshian bear mask, Queen Charlotte Islands, British Columbia. Photo by Melinda McNaugher. Courtesy of the Carnegie Museum of Natural History, Pittsburgh; p. 246: Late nineteenth-century Iroquois false face mask of painted wood with metal eyes, human hair, and a shark's snaggle tooth. Photo by R.P. Sheridan and D. Bauer. Courtesy of the Department Library Services, American Museum of Natural History; p. 252: Boy in

traditional dress with Lacrosse stick and girl with burden basket. Seneca, Iroquois, Cattaraugus Reservation, New York, 1901. Courtesy of the National Museum of the American Indian, Smithsonian Institution; p. 253: Chief Shake's house at Wrangell, Alaska, around the turn of the twentieth century. Courtesy of the National Anthropological Archives, Smithsonian Institution; p. 256: Navajo riding to Tesacod Canyon, 1905. Photo by Edward Curtis. Courtesy of the Library of Congress; p. 257: Earth lodge of the Hidatsa tribe, photographed at the beginning of the twentieth century. Photo by R.H. Lowie. Courtesy of the Department of Library Services, American Museum of Natural History; p. 258: Virginia Rosemyre Hunt (1875–1921), a Gabrielino-Serrano. In her lifetime she completed several hundred paintings. Family folklore states that she always worked with a loaf of French bread which she used to blend areas and create textures. Courtesy of Wallace Cleaves; p. 260: Chief Joe Capilano (center, holding robe) on the north Vancouver Ferry wharf before leaving for London in 1906. Courtesy of the City of Vancouver Archives; p. 262: Kwakiutl maiden and her kinfolk in a canoe going to meet her intended husband, c. 1907. Courtesy of the Rare Books & Manuscripts Division of the New York Public Library—Astor, Lenox, and Tilden Foundations; p. 264: Sewing class in an Indian boarding school in Genoa, Nebraska. Courtesy of the National Archives; p. 265: Fourth-graders in an Indian boarding school in Genoa, Nebraska, 1910. Courtesy of the National Archives; p. 266: School band, c. 1910, at an Indian boarding school in Genoa, Nebraska. Courtesy of the National Archives; p. 267: Kwakiutl canoes with an upright bear effigy arriving for a festival in 1910. The Kwakiutl, of British Columbia (Northwest Pacific Coast), are predominantly fishing people. Courtesy of the Philadelphia Museum of Art, purchased with funds from the American Museum of Photography; p. 268: In 1911, Ishi left his homeland

in the foothills of Mount Lassen in northern California and gave himself up to local townsmen. He was the last member of the Yahi tribe. Courtesy of the Phoebe A. Hearst Museum of Anthropology, University of California at Berkeley; p. 273: The Quaker City banquet of the Society of American Indians, Hotel Walton, February 14, 1914. Courtesy of the National Archives; p. 274: A remarkably high number of Indians enlisted for service in World War I and World War II despite their status as noncitizens. Here young men from File Hills Indian Colony in southern Saskatchewan pose with their fathers before leaving for duty. Courtesy of the National Archives of Canada; p. 275: Chief Raven, a Skidgate-Haida, c. 1915. His family emblem is carved at the center of his headgear, while ermine, feathers, and sea lion whiskers adorn the rest. Courtesy of the Rare Books & Manuscripts Division of the New York Public Library—Astor, Lenox, and Tilden Foundations; p. 276: John Wilson, of mixed Delaware, Caddo, and French heritage, was responsible for creating many of the current peyote doctrines and for helping spread the religion among the Plains Indians around the turn of the century. Photo by G.W. Parsons. Courtesy of the National Museum of the American Indian, Smithsonian Institution; p. 279: Hopi woman making pottery in Oraibi village using a coiling technique. Courtesy of the Field Museum of Natural History, Chicago; p. 289: Early twentieth-century Navajo sandpainting rug woven by Altnabah. Courtesy of the National Anthropological Archives, Smithsonian Institution; p. 306: Indian airmen performing a mock Indian dance for their fellow servicemen during World War II. Courtesy of the Archives Trust Fund; p. 312: During World War II, Ira Hayes took part in a forward attack on Mount Suribachi and was one of the six marines who raised the United Stated flag on the summit of the peak. Courtesy of the National Archives; p. 322: An Inuit family receives its family allowance check at the Hudson's Bay

Company Store at Read Island (near Victoria Island) in the Canadian arctic in 1950. The extension of Canadian government social security payments and other public services to remote regions of Canada after World War II encouraged the movement of Indian and Inuit groups toward permanent settlements. Note that the 'Family Allowance' poster on the counter includes messages printed in Inuktitut syllabics. Courtesy of the National Archives of Canada; p. 334: Tuscarora protest against the New York State Power Authority's condemnation of their lands for a reservoir, 1958. Courtesy of the Buffalo and Erie County Historical Society; p. 343: *Two Bull Moose Fighting*, by Norval Morisseau. In this painting Morisseau's name is signed in syllabic characters. Courtesy of the Glenbow Museum Collection, Calgary, Alberta; p. 345: Billy Mills at the 1964 Olympic Games. Courtesy of 10K Gold; p. 357: Members of the Iroquois League protesting their right to cross the U.S.-Canadian border in accordance with 1794 Jay's Treaty, July 1969. Courtesy of the Buffalo and Erie County Historical Society; p. 359: Harold Cardinal, twenty-four-year-old president of the Indian Association of Alberta, led the Indian resistance to the Canadian government's White Paper (policy papers) of 1969. Courtesy of Canapress Photo Service; p. 360: View of Alcatraz Island in late November 1969 soon after the occupation by American Indian students. Courtesy of Stephen Lehmer; p. 361: Indians of All Tribes pow wow singers at Alcatraz, San Francisco, California, 1969. Courtesy of Stephen Lehmer; p. 362: Indians of All Tribes protester John Trudell at Alcatraz, San Francisco, California, 1969. Courtesy of Stephen Lehmer; p. 368: First Annual War Dance Ceremony pow wow, Vancouver, British Columbia, 1970. Courtesy of Stephen Lehmer; p. 370: 'Declaration of the Return of Indian Land,' Indians of All Tribes, Alcatraz, San Francisco. Courtesy of Stephen Lehmer; p. 371: Indians protesting discrimination in hiring at the Bureau

of Indian Affairs (BIA), Denver, Colorado, March 1970. Photo by D.F. Barry. Courtesy of the Denver Public Library, Western History Department; p. 373: Indians of All Tribes gather for a festival during the occupation of Alcatraz Island. Courtesy of Stephen Lehmer; p. 377: Nooksack Indians gathering for a salmon bake to discuss fishing rights, Deming, Washington, 1970. Courtesy of Stephen Lehmer; p. 379: 'Indian arrested,' Puyallup fishing rights protest, Tacoma, Washington, 1970. Courtesy of Stephen Lehmer; p. 380: *Alcatraz Is Indian Land Forever*, located at pier 40, receiving depot, San Francisco, California, 1970. Artist unknown. Courtesy of Stephen Lehmer; p. 381: Indian encampment at Pendleton Roundup (Pendleton, Oregon), September 1970. Courtesy of Stephen Lehmer; p. 383: Dennis Banks. Courtesy of Alice M. Lambert. p. 394: Map of Indian treaty areas in Canada, by Brian McMillan. Reprinted by permission from *Native Peoples and Cultures of Canada*, by Alan D. McMillan, c. 1988, published by Douglas & McIntyre; p. 401: Creek actor Will Sampson starring with Jack Nicholson in the movie, *One Flew Over the Cuckoo's Nest*, 1975. Courtesy of The Saul Zaentz Company. Copyright 1975. All rights reserved; p. 408: As the courts began to restore tribal treaty rights in the 1960s and 1970s, some communities challenged Native claims. Courtesy of Stephen Lehmer; p. 415: This map is based on 'Indian Land Areas Judicially Established,' as published in the *Final Report*, Indian Claims Commission, 1978. Courtesy of the University of New Mexico Press; p. 421: Desert intaglios in the Colorado River region, 1978. These giant figures are rare examples of an art tradition found across much of the desert West. Courtesy of the Phoebe A. Hearst Museum of Anthropology, University of California at Berkeley; p. 426: Health care facility at the Turtle Mountain Chippewa Reservation in North Dakota. Courtesy of Duane Champagne; p. 429: Okanagan Larry Pierre on the occasion of the First

Nations Constitutional Conference, 1980, demanding Native participation in constitutional tasks. Photo by Rod McIvor. Courtesy of Canapress Photo Service; p. 430: Canadian Natives protesting before Parliament for land rights and aboriginal rights within the Canadian constitution. Courtesy of Canapress Photo Service; p. 431: Indians gather at the home of Grace McCarthy, British Columbia's Human Resources minister, to protest the government's child welfare policies. Courtesy of Ken Oakes/ *Vancouver Sun*; p. 437: U.S. President Ronald Reagan recognizes Navajo code talkers for dedicated service during WWII. Courtesy of Vee Salabiye; p. 438: Jerry E. Salabiye, veteran of WWII and Navajo code talker, and his daughter, Deborah Bitah. Courtesy of Vee Salabiye; p. 442: Indian chiefs open the first ministers' conference on aboriginal issues, March 1983. This conference, guaranteed by the 1982 constitution, marked the first time that aboriginals were given full participation at constitutional conferences. Courtesy of Canapress Photo Service; p. 451: Wilma Mankiller. Courtesy of Cherokee Nation Public Affairs; p. 458: The Mesquaki (Sauk and Fox) of Tama, Iowa, casino and bingo parlor, 1993. During the 1980s and 1990s many Indian communities opened gambling establishments under the guidance of the National Indian Gaming Commission. Courtesy of Stephen Lehmer; p. 459: The Canadian Museum of Civilization in Hull, Quebec, is regarded as an architectural masterpiece. Métis architect Douglas Cardinal has become renowned for his innovate designs inspired by natural forms. Photo by Malak Karsh; p. 460: Marty Pinnecoose, Southern Ute, performing with the American Indian Dance Theatre. Courtesy of Hanay Geiogamah; p. 463: Most tribal governments have Indian police forces supported by the Bureau of Indian Affairs. Courtesy of Duane Champagne; p. 465: A highlight of American Indian Dance Theatre performances is the *Women's Fancy Shawl Dance*, in which female members of the company exhibit their grace and virtuosity as they spin around the stage, displaying intricate dance steps while twirling colorful shawls to the beat of the drum. Photo by Don Perdue. Courtesy of Hanay Geiogamah; p. 469: Elijah Harper, holding an eagle feather for spiritual strength, uses procedural rules to prevent the last-minute passage of the Meech Lake Accord. Courtesy of Canapress Photo Service; p. 470: A Mohawk warrior and a Canadian soldier engage in a staring match during the 78-day Oka standoff. The conflict at Oka brought unprecedented domestic and international attention to the grievances of Canadian Natives. Courtesy of Canapress Photo Service; p. 474: Morgan Tosee, a member of the Comanche tribe of Oklahoma, is a champion *Southern Men's Traditional* dancer with the American Indian Dance Theatre. Photo by Don Perdue. Courtesy of Hanay Geiogamah; p. 476: Grand chief of the Assembly of First Nations Ovide Mercredi. Courtesy of Canapress Photo Service; p. 480: 'Nunavut' is one of the three stone lithographs created by Inuit artist Kenojuak Ashevak to commemorate the signing of the Tungavik Federation of Nunavut claim in the eastern Arctic. Courtesy of the Dorset Fine Arts, Inuit Art Section; p. 481: (left to right) Chester Mahooty of the Zuni tribe of New Mexico, Morgan Tosee of the Comanche tribe of Oklahoma, and Ramona Roach of the Navajo tribe of New Mexico—all-Native American dancers and musicians with the American Indian Dance Theatre. Photo by Don Perdue. Courtesy Hanay Geiogamah; pp. 483–85: Comprehensive land claims in Canada. Courtesy of Duane Champagne. Source: Department of Indian and Northern Affairs, Ottawa; pp. 490–91: Nonrecognized communities with application for federal recognition pending. Courtesy of Duane Champagne. Source: Bureau of Indian Affairs; p. 494: Ada Deer. Courtesy of Jon Holtshopple and Associates; p. 495: The Redstar family tipi encampment at Crow Fair (Crow Agency, Montana), August 1993. Courtesy Stephen Lehmer; p. 496: Preparing for the parade at Crow Fair (Crow Agency, Montana), August 1993. Courtesy of Stephen Lehmer; p. 497: Mesquaki adoption ceremony (Tama, Iowa), 1993. Courtesy of Stephen Lehmer.

INDEX

A

Aaninena, 63. *See also* Atsina; Gros Ventre
Abegweit (Prince Edward Island), 50, 95
Abenaki, 47–50, 71, 83, 89–91
Aboriginal Native Rights Committee of the Interior. *See* North American Indian Brotherhood
aboriginal rights, 436, 441, 444, 450, 454
Aborigines Protection Society, 159–60
Abourezk, Sen. James, 402
Acadia, 56
Acolapissa, 78
Acoma Pueblo, 42, 48, 56, 77
Act for the Gradual Civilization of the Indian Tribes, 184
Adams, Alfred, 290
Adams, Hank, 305, 384
Adams, Willy, 409
Additional Land for Havasupai Reservation Act, 307
Additional Land for Kiowa, Comanche, and Apache Reservation Act, 313
Additional Land to Navajo Reservation Act, 308
Adena culture, 14–20
adobe, 24, 26
Adult Indian Vocational Training Act, 331
Agate Basin, Wyoming, 6
Agnew, Spiro, 364, 377
Agua Caliente Indian Reservation Jurisdiction Act, 320

Aguilar, José Vincente, 292
Ahenakew, David, 449
Ai, 37
Ak ko makki (Old Swan), 118
Akaitcho, 135, 139
Akwesasne Notes, 386
Akwesasne Reserve, 89, 355, 426, 457, 462, 467
Alabama and Coushatta Termination Act, 329
Alaska Allotment Act, 259
Alaska Federated Natives (AFN), 336, 389
Alaska Highway, 303
Alaska Highway Pipeline, 411
Alaska Industrial School, 284
Alaska Native, 86, 348; education, 339; land claims, 335, 348, 388; protest oil pipeline, 362; subsistence, 348, 389; Alaska Native Brotherhood, 269, 283. *See also* Alaska Native Claims Settlement Act; Aleut; Athapascan; Inuit; Tlingit
Alaska Native Business Credit Fund, 342
Alaska Native Claims Settlement, 406
Alaska Native Claims Settlement Act (ANCSA), 336, 385, 389, 405–06
Alaska Native Reorganization Act, 296
Alaska Native Service, 331
Alaska Native Sisterhood, 269
Alaska Purchase, 198
Alaska Reindeer Act, 297

Alaskan Eskimo Whaling Commission, 412
Alaskan Federation of Natives, 348
Alaskan Refuge, 3
Alaskan Statehood Act of 1959, 348
Albany Congress, 72
Albany Plan, 88
Alberta: province created, 257
Alberta Indian franchise, 350
Albuquerque Vocational Technical School, 364
Alcatraz Island occupation, 365, 369
Aleut, compensation for fur trade, 417; education, 251; housing program, 349; rebellion of 1761–62, 86
Alexie, Sherman, 346
Algonkian, 35, 39, 44, 50–54, 60–61, 64, 67–76, 89
Algonquin, 44, 53, 57, 66
All Indian Pueblo Council, 364
All Indian Pueblo Cultural Center, 407
All-Indian Education Association, 349
Allegheny, 344
Allegheny Seneca, 341. *See also* Iroquois; Seneca
Allen, Paula Gunn, 451
Allied Tribes of British Columbia, 234, 244, 272, 275, 285
allotment, 57, 181, 261, 278
Allotted Lands Selling Act, 263
Alvarado, Juan Bautista, 156
American Association on Indian Affairs (AAIA), 301
American Fur Company, 151, 161
American Horse, 164, 214

American Indian Achievement
  Award, 360
American Indian Affairs Association
  Education Conference, 349
American Indian, Alaska Native,
  and Native Hawaiian Culture and
  Art Development Act, 452
American Indian Arts Center, 343
American Indian Civil Rights
  Act, 353
American Indian College
  Committee, 340
American Indian Community
  University Pilot Project, 355
American Indian Defense
  Association (AIDA), 282
American Indian Federation, 290
American Indian Film Festival, 403
American Indian Heritage
  Month, 469
American Indian Higher Education
  Consortium (AIHEC), 397
American Indian Historical Society,
  344, 371
American Indian Magazine, 268
American Indian Movement (AIM),
  298–300, 366, 379, 390–93,
  406, 416–17; convention, 389,
  403; and Dennis Banks, 443,
  450; founded, 287, 354; and John
  Trudell, 315; and Leonard Peltier,
  307, 410, 424; occupations, 381,
  382, 385, 388; police brutality,
  354, 391; protests, 354, 374, 382,
  387, 390; and Russell Means,
  382; urban Indians, 388; women,
  397. *See also* Indian Activist
  Movements; Red Power
  Movement
American Indian Policy Review
  Commission (AIPRC), 402, 408
American Indian Registry for the
  Performing Arts, 443
American Indian Religious Freedom
  Act (AIRFA), 418
American Indian Studies. *See* Native
  American Studies
American Indian symbol, 390
American Indian Theater
  Company, 294
American Indian Youth
  Council, 367
American lions, 3
American Revolutionary War, 76,
  80, 83–87, 90–91, 95, 101–05,
  127–29, 159, 167

American War for Independence.
  See American Revolutionary War
AMERIND, 363
Amnesty International, 434
Anasazi, 19–20, 24–27, 30
Anderson, Mad Bear, 332, 335
Anderson, Sen. Clinton, 346
Anderson, William, 492
Andrus, Cecil, 414, 419
Anglican Church Missionary
  Society (C.M.S.), 134–35
Anglicans, 160
Anishinabe (Anishinaabe), 68, 287,
  416, 460. *See also* Chippewa;
  Ojibway
Anishnabai, 461, 464, 467, 477
Anne (Queen Anne), 83, 150
annuities, 177, 181, 197, 211
antipoverty programs, 345
Apache, 21, 29–30, 46, 59, 67–
  71, 77, 116, 141–43; issue tax-
  free municipal bonds, 449; Kinya-
  ani clan, 27; migration, 69; nuclear
  waste storage, 498; oil
  development, 424, 439; Pueblo
  trade, 67; raid pueblos, 69; U.S.
  attacks on, 184; war of the 1860s,
  141; warfare, 67, 127, 189–
  90, 220
Apache Pass Reservation, 215
Apalachee, 80
Apalachukla, 62
Apash Wyakaikt, 138
Apes, William, 145, 155, 157,
  159, 229
Apfel, Oscar C., 271
Appomatuck, 71, 74
Appropriation Act for Treaties with
  Indians, 116
Appropriation of Indian Affairs
  Supervision Act, 344
Appropriations for Indian Claims
  Commission Act, 407
Arapaho, 126, 164
Arawak, 37
Archaeological Resources Protection
  Act, 422
archaeology, 4, 8
Archaic period, 6–16
Arctic, 5
Arctic communities, 27
Arctic Islands, 226
Arctic Slope Native
  Association, 388
Arctic Small Tool tradition, 12
Arctic Winter Games, 369

Arendaronon (Rock People), 53–
  54. *See also* Iroquois
Arikara, 31, 84, 154
Arikara, Gros Ventre, and Mandan
  Reserve, 206
Aripeka, 158
Arizona Printers, Inc., 281
Arizona v. California, 441, 342
*Arizona v. San Carlos Apache
  Tribe*, 443
Armer, Laura Adams (Hosteen
  Tsosi), 287
Armijo, 170
Army scouts, 197, 244, 275, 314
Arnett v. Five Gill Nets, 400
arroyo, 6
art, 452, 489, 498; Canada Council,
  311; Northwest Coast, 226;
  Oklahoma style, 291; San
  Ildefonso School, 257; Santa Fe
  Studio style, 281, 291; Tribal
  Arts Exposition, 288; Woodland
  School, 291, 439
Art Linkletter Show, 360
Arthur, Chester A., 219, 228
Articles of Confederation, 88, 102
artifacts, 3–7, 10–11, 14
Asah, Spencer, 279
Asia, 3–4, 14
Assembly of First Nations, 476–
  78, 492–95; Constitution, 487,
  498; gender issues, 445, 482;
  and Georges Erasmus, 318, 456;
  Prairie Treaty Nations Alliance,
  449; reorganized, 436; and
  William Mercredi, 309
Assiginack, Jean-Baptiste, 160
assimilation policies, 241, 345, 386;
  boarding schools, 224–25;
  Canadian Indian Act, 217, 313
Assiniboine, 59, 74, 86, 114, 123,
  151, 161; Bighorn Dam, 473;
  Cypress Hill Massacre, 211; fur
  trade, 100; middlemen, 89; signing
  of Treaty 4, 211; trade with the
  French, 86. *See also* Sioux; Stoney
Association of Métis and Non-
  Status of New Brunswick, 391
Association on American Indian
  Affairs (AAIA), 282, 323, 331,
  342, 420. *See also* American Indian
  Defense Association (AIDA)
Astrov, Margaret, 312
Atakapa, 38
Ataronchronon, 54. *See also* Iroquois

Athapascan, 3, 21, 73, 78, 193. *See also* Apache; Diné; Navajo
Atkinson, Henry, 152
atlatl, 5, 8, 19
Atsina, 74, 80, 114, 119, 123, 151, 161. *See also* Gros Ventre
Attignawantan (Bear), 54
Attigneenongnhac, 54
Attikamek, 57
Attiwandaronk, 60–64
Attorney General Canada v. Lavell, 396
Attucks, Crispus, 97
Auchiah, James, 279
Augustine Pattern, 19
Austin, Mary, 277
Awashonks, 68
Awatovi Site, Arizona, 28
Aztec, 37, 40

B

Babbitt, Bruce, 493
Baccus, Maj. Electus, 186
Bacon, Nathaniel, 65, 71
Bacon's Rebellion, 71, 83
Bad Heart Bull, Wesley, 393
Badlands National Monument, 379
baggataway. *See* lacrosse
Bagot, Charles, 168
Bagot Commission, 167
Banks, Dennis, 287; Alcatraz "Walk for Justice," 499; American Indian Movement (AIM), 354, 382; protest in Custer, South Dakota, 393, 398–99, 416, 441, 443, 446, 450
Bannock, 195, 223, 472
Barber, James Nelson, 124
Barber, Lloyd, 366
Barboncito, 133, 170
Barbout, George W., 176
Bascom, Lt. George N., 190
basketry, 8
Bastien, Leonard, 486
Bat Cave, New Mexico, 14
Bates, Sara, 498
Battle at Frenchman's Butte, 234
Battle of Clearwater, 138
Battle of Cut Knife Hill, 234
Battle of Fallen Timbers, 105
Battle of Little Bighorn, 177, 214, 290, 478
Battle of Milk Creek, 495
Battle of Seven Oaks, 113, 131

Battle of Slim Buttes, 214
Battle of the Rosebud, 214
Battle of Tippecanoe, 95, 103
Battle of Tres Castillos, 221
Battle of Warbonnet Creek, 214
Battle of Wolf Mountain, 214
Baumgartner, Leona, 341
Baylor, Lt. Col. John R., 188
beadwork, 226
Beale, Edward Fitzgerald, 200
Bear Claw, Dean Curtis, 492
beaver, 54, 57, 60–61, 72, 88, 123
Beaver Wars, 61
Begay, Harrison, 292
Begay, Manley, 501
Bell, John, 165
Bell, John Kim, 325
Bella Bella, 13, 155
Bella Coola (Nuxalk), 114
Bellecourt, Clyde, 287, 298, 354. *See also* American Indian Movement
Benally, Ruth, 409
Bender, Charles, 254
Benedict, Ernest M., 359
Bennett, Ramona, 340
Bennett, Robert LaFollette, 269, 348, 358, 360
Beothuk, 36, 53, 145
Berger, Thomas, 403, 407
Bering Sea, 3, 86
Bering Strait, 3, 14, 86
Bering Strait Land Bridge, 3–4
Bering, Vitus, 86
Beringia, 3
Berkeley, Gov. William, 65
Berkeley Pattern, 13, 19
Big Bear, 139–40, 218, 228–30, 233–35, 238, 321
Big Eyes, 41
Big Foot, 240
Big Mountain dispute, 409, 500
Big Tree, John, 270
Bill C-31, 309, 316
Billie, James E., 454
Billie, Susan, 250
Bingaman, Sen. Jeff, 498
bison, 3, 5–6, 21, 28. *See also* buffalo
Bison antiquus. *See* bison
Bissonette, Gladys, 393
Black Caucus of State Legislators, 500
Black Elk, Nicholas, 290
Black Elk, Wallace, 387
Black Fish, 101, 103–04

Black Hawk, 94–95, 108, 152, 154
Black Hawk War, 95, 161
Black Kettle, 120, 164, 193
Black Minqua (Erie), 67
Black, Samuel, 141
Black Warrior River, 31
Blackfeet, 167
Blackfoot, 89, 130
Blackfoot Confederacy, 79, 89, 123, 146, 151, 161
Blackgoat, Roberta, 409
Blackwater Draw, New Mexico, 5
Blanshard, Richard, 176
block grants, 433–34
Blondin, Ethel, 458, 495
Blondin-Andrews, Ethel. *See* Blondin, Ethel
Blowsnake, Sam, 284
Blue Cloud, Peter, 379
Blue Jacket, 102, 109, 114
Board of Indian Commissioners, 203, 237
boarding schools, 349. *See also* residential schools
Boas, Franz, 162, 180, 239
Bodmer, Karl, 154
Bole Maru (Dream Dance), 260
Bonfire Shelter, Texas, 6
Bonneville, Gen. Benjamin, 184
Bonnin, Gertrude Simmons (Zitkala-Sa), 217, 251, 258, 284
Boone, Daniel, 102
Born With A Tooth, Milton, 469, 487
Bosomworth, Thomas, 87
Bosque Redondo, 133. *See also* Navajo
Boston Massacre, 97
Boston Treaty, 84
Boudinot, Elias, 123, 139, 144
Bourassa, Robert, 487
bow and arrow, 19
Bowlegs, Billy, 125, 183
Bowstring Soldiers, 134
Bozeman Trail, 164, 197
Bozeman Trail War, 146
Braddock, Edward, 89
Brady, Jim, 291
Brand Site, 8
Brando, Marlon, 394
Brant, Joseph (Thayendanegea), 85–87, 90, 101, 103–04, 107
Brant, Molly, 90–91
Brave Bear, 155, 181
Brave Bird, Mary, 389

Brendale v. Confederated Tribes and Bands of the Yakima Indian Nation, 462
Brightman, Lehman (Lee), 354, 355, 364, 369
British Columbia Association of Non-Status Indians, 366
British Columbia Gold Rush, 186
British Columbia Treaty Commission, 488
British North America Act, 421
British Virginia Company, 50
Brodhead, Col. Daniel, 104, 106
Broken Arrow, 323
Bronson, Ruth Muskrat, 288
Brooks, Maj. Thomas H., 186
Brotherhood of Indian Prisoners, 402
Browes, Pauline, 493
Brown, Eddie, 462, 468, 471
Brown, Gov. Jerry, 416
Brown, Dr. John F., 178
Brown, John F. Jr., 178
Brown Paper, 389
Bruce, Louis R., 360, 362–64
Bruyere, Louis (Smokey), 316
Bryan v. Itasca, 406
Bryce, Dr. Peter H., 256
Buchanan, Judd, 404
Buell, Col. George, 220
buffalo, 63, 66, 74, 210–12, 469. *See also* bison
Buffalo Bill's Wild West Show, 161
Buffalo Bird Woman (Waheenee), 162
Buffalo Calf Road, 218
Buffalo Head Indian nickel, 270
Buffalo Hump, 125
Buffalo Jim, 250
Buffalo meat, 214
Bull Bear, 136, 146
Burch, Sharon, 498
Burdeau, George, 486, 488
Bureau of American Ethnology, 215
Bureau of Indian Affairs (BIA), 340–49, 418–20, 493–94, 499; activism against, 370–72; Civil Service Act, 252; contracts with tribes, 456–57; criticized, 404, 409, 441; economic development, 354; education, 339, 349, 358, 389; and Ely Parker, 144; Employment Assistance Program, 325; employment policies, 363, 370–71, 398; federal benefits for Indian people, 349;

Five Civilized Tribes, 261, 382; mismanagement, 464; occupation of, 299, 315, 366, 370, 371, 392; Office of Indian Education, 390; paternalism, 345–46; protests, 364; reorganization, 312, 348, 446, 473; schools, 346, 351; structural changes, 355; stripmining leases cancelled, 395; trust responsibility, 478–79; urban relocation, 386. *See also* Department of Indian Affairs; Office of Indian Affairs
Bureau of Land Management (BLM), 335, 500
Burke Act, 237, 259
Burnett, Gov. Peter H., 175
Burnette, Robert, 332, 392
Bush, George, 476
Butler, Darrelle Dean, 405–06, 410
Butler, William, 109

C

Cabinet-Native Council of Canada Committee, 400
Cabot, John, 32
Cabrillo, Juan Rodriguez, 43
cacique (leader), 31
Caddo, 20–21, 30, 156, 164, 170; ancestors, 43; land cessions, 156; trade, 30
Cahokia, 26, 31. *See also* Mississippian culture
Calder, Frank Arthur, 272, 319, 331
Calder v. Attorney General, 273, 393, 395
Calhoun, John C., 133
caliche-adobe walls, 24
California Commission on Indian Affairs, 354
California Indian Education Association (CIEA), 349, 351, 355
California Indian Education Centers Program, 397
California Indian Legal Services (CILS), 351, 383
California Indians, 44, 139, 143; abused and killed by miners, 172; attack missions, 96–98; educational funding of, 351; fishing rights, 413; genocide, 176; gold mines, 172; land cessions, 173; land claims, 286, 298, 304–

05, 320, 345; massacres of, 175; minority research, 368; missions, 96–97, 100–01, 104, 106, 109–10, 113, 116; slavery of, 176; treaties, 173, 176; water rights, 355
California missions, 126, 132, 142, 155, 173. *See also* California Indians
California Trail, 129
California v. Cabazon Band of Mission Indians, 453
Callihoo, John, 298, 313
Calusa, 35, 37, 263
camels, 3
Cameron, Louis, 399
Camp Verde Reserve, 214
Campbell, Ben Nighthorse, 292, 453, 501
Campbell, Kim, 478, 493
Campbell, Robert, 162, 173, 177
Campbell, Tom, 355, 384
Campbell, Will, 321, 466
Campbell tradition, 10
Canada, 200; British Columbia joins, 209; constitutional amendments, 432, 446, 447; constitutional reform, 417, 420, 422 425–26, 428–30, 433–36, 441, 448–49, 454, 477–78, 482, 486; Prince Edward Island joins, 211
Canada's Royal Commission on Aboriginal Peoples, 493
Canadiagua Treaty, 423
Canadian Department of Northern Affairs, 347
Canadian Human Rights Commission, 482
Canadian Indian (Native) 144; ancestors, 35; assimilation policy, 202; education, 387; federal funding, 347, 367; foster care, 429; franchise, 339; health care, 347; land claims, 389; legal definition of, 176; mistreatment of, 348; multicultural policy, 388; opposition to White Paper, 359; police 146, 350; provincial franchise, 356; reserves, 147; timber, 124; underemployment, 386
Canadian Indian Act, 217
Canadian Indian Affairs, 347
Canadian Indian Affairs Department, 358

Canadian Indian Rights
Commission, 410, 419–20
Canadian Métis Society, 352. *See
also* Native Council of Canada
Canadian Native Arts Foundation
(C.N.A.F.), 325
Canadian Royal Commission on
Aboriginal Peoples, 488, 492
Canadian Royal Commission on
Electoral Reform, 478
Canassatego, 88
Canby, Edward R.S., 170, 211
Cannon, T.C., 312, 341
Caonabo, 31
Cape Breton Island, 32
Cape Denbigh, Alaska, 16
Cape Verde Islands, 32
Capilano, Joe, 259
Captain Jack, 211
Cardinal, Douglas Joseph, 294
Cardinal, Gil, 321, 466
Cardinal, Harold, 310, 359, 368
Cardinal, Tantoo, 322, 453, 473
Cargo, Gov. David, 362
Carib Indians, 56
Caribbean, 36
Cariboo Gold Rush, 191
caribou, 9–10, 14–15, 74, 82, 139
Carl D. Perkins Vocational
Education Act, 470
Carleton, Gen. James, 190, 192
Carlisle Indian School, 217, 224,
242, 286
Carnegie Report, 358
Carolina, Queen, 62
Carr, Emily, 255
Carrier, 114, 123, 151, 155. *See also*
Wet'suwet'en
Carroll, Don, 370
Carson, Christopher (Kit), 124,
132, 134, 181, 190, 192
Carson National Forest, 380
Carter, Jimmy, 418
Cartier, Jacques, 39, 43
Casa Grande, 24, 31
Castro, Fidel, 332-33
Catawba, 62, 410, 452, 494
Catawba Land Claim Settlement
Act, 494
Catholic Church, 36, 137
Catholicism, 57, 72, 129, 156
Catholics, 56, 161
Catlin, George, 152
Caughnawaga, 84
Cayuga, 64, 67, 69, 75, 88, 414,
429, 446

Cayuse, 172
Census Bureau, 385
Centennial Accord, 463
Center for Health, Education and
Economic Research, 498
Central Intelligence Agency
(CIA), 380
Central Plains Tradition, 25
Certain Lands Sale of L'Anse
Chippewa Act, 317
Certain Pueblo and Cañoncito
Navajo Lands in Trust, 320
Cession of Rights-of-Way on
Wind River Reservation, 325
Cestcine, 29
Chaco Canyon, 26–27
Champlain, Samuel de, 50, 53–54
Chance, Eugene, 339
Chance, James, 339
Charbonneau, Toussaint, 107, 121
Charles Camsell Indian
Hospital, 313
Charles, Curtis, 187
Charlottetown Accord, 310, 328,
487–88, 493
Chato, 215
Chatot, 74
Chee Dodge, Henry, 311
Cherokee, 68–71, 74–76, 80–
82, 347, 451, 496; ancestors, 43;
census, 140; *Cherokee Phoenix*, 156;
and Chief Bowles, 130;
constitution, 143, 158;
constitutional government, 97,
112, 248; culture and religion,
175; First Cherokee Mounted
Rifles, 123; Five County Cherokee
Organization, 346; French and
Indian War, 89; gold, 145;
government, 123, 154; government
abolished, 144; Hopewell Treaty,
108; joint council meeting, 445;
lands, 140, 145; and Major Ridge,
97; migration, 130–31;
publications, 135; regulation of
cattle grazing, 198; relocation to
Indian Territory, 175; removal,
143, 145, 150, 158, 162, 75, 455;
role in Civil War, 189, 191; slave
holders, 143; slaveraids, 68; Tellico
Dam, 425, 429; Texas Cherokee,
164; Trade and Intercourse Act,
120; Trail of Tears, 97, 162; tribal
lands, 175; wampum belts, 167
Cherokee Foundation, 261
Cherokee Hymn Book, 145

Cherokee Land Allotment Act, 254
Cherokee Nation v. Georgia, 150
Cherokee Phoenix, 123, 135, 139,
144, 156
Cherokee syllabary, 135, 144
Chewie, John, 347
Cheyenne, 63, 120, 126, 134, 137,
164; Crooked Lance Society, 146;
flight of, 221; military society,
134; strip-mining, 395, 398;
Sun Dance Ceremony, 63; Sweet
Medicine, 100; tax BIA
contractors, 455; traditions, 134,
146; warfare, 212; warriors, 166.
See also Northern Cheyenne;
Southern Cheyenne
Cheyenne River Sioux, 349. *See
also* Sioux
Cheyenne-Arapaho Tribes Lands
Act, 303
Cheyenne-Arapaho War, 120, 125
Chiaha, 41
Chicago American Indian
Village, 376
Chicago Indian Conference, 340
Chichén Itzá, Yucatan Peninsula, 20
Chickahominy, 55–56, 64, 66, 68,
88, 261
Chickasaw, 41, 69, 71, 83–84,
150; alliance, 83; ancestors, 43;
constitutional government, 183,
248; removal treaty, 183; villages,
83; wars, 82
Chicora, 38
Chief Bowles, 130
Chief Joseph. *See* Joseph
Chihuahua, 67
Chilcotin, 114, 155, 193
children, 419, 461, 464, 472,
476–77
Chilicothe, 104
Chilili, 71
Chilkat, 167, 178. *See also* Tlingit
Chilocco Industrial School
Reserve, 231
Chino, Wendell, 498
Chinook jargon, 10
Chipewyan, 74, 82, 84, 103, 135,
139; Dene dialect, 84; trade
middlemen, 82; uranium
mining, 402
Chippewa, 65–66, 133, 140, 143–
44, 452; fishing rights, 390, 434,
441, 461, 475; Fox Wars, 81;
French and Indian War, 89; fur
trade, 53; hunting rights, 441,

461; Iroquois attacks, 62; King William's War, 76; land cessions, 155, 179; lands, 141; treaties, 133, 182; treaty rights, 390; treaty with Sioux, 72; war with Sioux, 69. *See also* Anishinabe; Ojibway
Chippewa Treaty, 182
Chiquito, 67
Chiricahua, 352
Chiricahua Apache, 165, 352. *See also* Apache
Chisca (Yuchi), 73
Chivington, Col. John M., 165, 193
Choctaw, 84, 87, 135, 143, 148, 150; ancestors, 43; Civil War, 87; constitutional government, 188, 248; English alliance, 78; French alliance, 68; "people of the long hair," 87; political relations, 87; potato people, 87; removal, 148; slave raids, 68; slaves, 78; territory, 135; voting, 387
Choctaw Academy, 160
Choctaw and Chickasaw Land Allotment Act, 254
Choctaw Nation et al. v. Oklahoma et al., 374
Choctaw Reservation, 346
Chona, Maria, 296
Choris Peninsula, Alaska, 14
Chrétien, Jean, 358, 376, 385, 395, 495
Christian churches, 340
Christianity, 119, 122, 130, 155; Delaware Prophet, 91; Indians worthy of conversion, 39; Law of Burgos, 36; and Mikak, 85; and Pocahontas, 48; Puritans, 59; schools, 55
Christians, 56, 60, 73, 121, 145
Christy, Carmen, 357
Chumash, 28; ancestors, 11; archaeological remains, 31; demonstrations, 417; religious rights, 417
Church, Benjamin, 68
Church of England, 53
Churchill, Winston, 280
Citizens Crusade Against Poverty, 292
Citizens Plus, 376. *See also* Red Paper
citizenship rights, 205, 272, 283, 295, 313, 316
civil disobedience, 175
civil rights, 223

Civil Rights Amendment, 196
civil rights movement, 367
Civil Service Act, 252
Clamorgan, 118
Clark, George Rogers, 110
Clark, Joe, 477, 482, 486
Clark, William, 118, 120–21, 154
Clarke, Gen. Newman S., 186
Classic period, 24. *See also* Formative period
Classic Thule, 27
Classification and Appraisal of Unallotted Indian Lands Act, 270
Clear Lake, 374
Clearwater Creek, 138
Cleary, George, 494
Cliff Palace, 27
Clinton, Bill, 493–94, 499
Clovis culture, 4–5
Clutesi, George, 255
Coahuiltecan Tradition, 9, 11
Coast Salish, 13, 244; land cession treaties, 176, 183; land rights, 447; relocation, 267
Coast Tlingit, 167. *See also* Tlingit
Coastal Miwok, 45. *See also* Miwok
Cocacoeske, 65. *See also* Anne (Queen Anne)
Cochise, 116, 126, 184, 190
Cochise culture, 9, 11
Cochití Pueblo, 73, 357. *See also* Pueblo
code talkers. *See* Navajo code talkers
Cody, William, 150
Coeur d'Alene War, 185
Cohen, Felix, 301, 353
Cohn, Abram, 157
Coldwater Experiment, 147
Cole, Douglas, 215
Coles Creek culture, 23, 30
colleges, 388
Collier, John, 282, 293
Colonial period, 24
Colorado River Indian Reservation Lease Act, 330
Colorado River Indians, 28
Colorado River Treaty, 196
Columbus, Christopher, 29, 31, 32, 37
Columbus Quincentenary, 488
Colville. *See* Confederated Tribe of Colville
Comanche, 77, 125, 134, 147, 164, 169; acculturation problems, 245; culture, 169; hunting rights, 411; peyote religion, 169; warfare, 212

Commission on Civil Rights, 392
Commissioner of Indian Affairs, 173, 348
Committee for Original People's Entitlement (COPE), 300, 368, 410, 419, 445
Committee for the Great Council Fire, 343
Committee of One Hundred, 281
Commonwealth Club of San Francisco, 284
communications codes based on Indian languages, 243
Community Action Programs (CAP), 345
Company of New France, 56
Competency of Certain Osages Act, 317
Competent Crow Tribe Act, 320
Comprehensive Employment and Training Act, 396
Conestoga, 71, 93
Conestoga Mission Indians, 93
Confederated Tribe of Colville, 345, 382
Conference on the Future of the American Indian, 301
Congress of Aboriginal Peoples, 500
Connor, Gen. Patrick E., 195
conquistadors, 36
Conrad, G.M., 179
Conseil Attikamek/Montagnais (C.A.M.), 472
Constitution Act, 466
Continental Congress, 99, 102
Convocation of American Indian Scholars, 371
Cook, Tom, 386
Cook Inlet Native Association, 348
Cooke, Lt. Col. Philip, 181
Coolican, Murray, 450
Coolican Report, 450
Cooper, James Fenimore, 171
Coosa, 41, 44
Coosaponakeesa, 87
Cope, Jean-Baptiste, 89
Copena, 24
Copper Inuit, 274
copper trade, 12
Copway, George, 171, 175, 229
Coquille Restoration Act, 462
Corn Mesa, 56
Cornelius, Laura, 268
Cornoyea, Nellie, 300, 369
Cornplanter, 104, 159
Cornstalk, 101

Coronado, Francisco, 38–42
Cortés, Hernando, 37–38
Cost of Indian Wars, 201
Costo, Jeanette Henry, 344
Costo, Rupert, 344
Costs on Flathead Indian Irrigation Project, 317
Costs Related to Crow Irrigation Project Act, 313
Cosumnes culture, 14
Cosumnes period, 20
Council of Energy Resources Tribes (CERT), 400, 405, 420
Council of Yukon Indians, 406. See also Yukon Native Brotherhood
Council on Indian Affairs, 292
Country-born, 100, 135, 136, 137, 166, 171, 205, 207, 223. See also Métis
County of Oneida v. Oneida Nation, 448
coureurs de bois, 63, 68
courts on reservations, 229
covenant, 56
Cow Creek Indians, 152
Cowasuck, 83
Coweta, 73
Cowichan, 124
Coyote, 376
Crazy Horse, 125, 134, 158, 166, 214, 217, 220
Crazy Horse Monument, 317
Crazy War Hunter. See Menawa
Credit Mission (Mississauga, Ontario), 119
Credit River Reserve, 164
Cree, 82–86, 130–31, 466, 478, 480; and Alexander Isbister, 137–38; attacks, 233; bands, 35; and Big Bear, 139–40; English Expeditions, 45; fur trade, 68, 74, 100, 114; hydroelectric projects, 405; James Bay Project, 385, 391; land cessions, 131; land claims, 400, 453; Lubicon land claims, 454, 457, 461, 464, 471, 473, 487; Métis, 161; middlemen, 89; schools, 378; syllabics, 166; trade with British, 62; trade with French, 65–66; 86; warfare, 123, 234; Woodland land claims, 477
Cree Council, 230
Cree Home Guard, 82
Cree-Naskapi (of Quebec) Act, 446

Creek, 72–73, 80–83, 90–93, 108, 126–28; ancestors, 43; civil war, 128; constitutional government, 200, 248; council, 93; Creek Mary, 87; and David Moncock, 137; famine, 159; fur trade 68, 76; government, 128; and Hernando de Soto, 41, 45; land cession, 100; land rights, 295; lands, 128, 159; leaders, 82, 90, 159; national council, 90, 136; neutrality, 82; political rights, 143; purchase Hickory Ground, 428; and Red Sticks, 130; and Tomochichi, 62; Trade and Intercourse Act, 120; removal, 150, 159; slave raids, 68; war of 1836, 132, 137, 159; warriors, 87
Creek Confederacy, 82
Creek Land Allotment Act, 253
Creek Mary. See Coosaponakeesa
Creek Snake Indians, 261
Crenshaw Site, Arkansas, 20
Criminal Jurisdiction Act, 478
criminal justice, 413, 455, 465, 475–82, 496
Crombie, David, 450
Cronyn, George, 277
Crook, Gen. George, 145, 150, 213, 215, 220
Crosbie, John, 448
Crosby, Rev. Douglas, 477
Crow, 136, 138, 146, 148, 154, 167, 409
Crow, Patrick "Hooty," 418
Crow Dog, 155, 229
Crow Dog, Leonard, 326, 387
Crow Dog, Mary, 326
Crow Tribe Buffalo Act, 320
Crowfoot (Isapo-Muxika), 145, 230
Croy, Darrell, 418
Croy, Norma Jean, 418
Cuarac, 71
Cuero, Delfina, 351
Cumberland House (Saskatchewan), 137
Cupa, 251
Curley, Tagak, 388, 396
Curtis Act, 248
Curtis Bear Claw, Dean, 492
Curtis, Charles, 260, 286
Curtis, Edward S., 180, 247, 271
Curtis, Natalie, 258
Cusabo, 68
Cusick, David, 143

Custer, George Armstrong, 164–66, 478; Black Hills, 198, 202, 212, 217; Little Bighorn Battle, 137, 150, 158; and Washita, 120
Cutbank Canal, 258

D

da Verrazzano, Giovanni, 38
Dabuda. See Dat-So-La-Lee
Dade, Francis, 158
Daganett, Charles, 268
Dakota, 59, 81, 154, 161, 191. See also Lakota; Sioux
Dalles Site, Oregon, 7
Dalton culture, 8
Dance Camp, 30
Danger Cave, Utah, 6, 8
Dann, Carrie, 497, 500
Dann, Mary, 497, 500
Dann et al. v. United States, 448
D'Arcy McNickle Center, 255
Dartmouth College, 96, 365
Darwin, Charles, 246
Dat-So-La-Lee, 157
Davidson, Bill, 340
Davidson, Joe, 340
Davidson, Robert, 162, 314
Davis, Alice Brown, 178
Davis, George, 178
Davis, Jefferson, 152
Dawes Act, 237, 251, 254, 259. See also General Allotment Act
Day, A. Grove, 344
Daybreak Star Cultural Center, 372
de Alvarado, Pedro, 37, 42
de Avilés, Pedro Menéndez, 45, 64
de Balboa, Vasco Nunez, 37
de Chomedey, Paul, 60
de Cruzate, Domingo Jironza Petriz, 74
de Groseilliers, Sieur, 66, 68
de Guzman, Diego, 39
de La Rocque, Jean-François, 43
de La Salle, Rene Cavalier, 72–74
de las Casas, Bartolome, 31, 36
de Leon, Juan Ponce, 37
de Luna, Tristan, 44
de Maionneuve, Sieur, 60
de Montesinos, Antonio, 36
de Moscoso, Luis, 41
de Narvez, Panfilo, 38
de Niza, Marcos, 39, 42
de Oñate, Juan, 48

de Otermìn, Gov. Antonio, 73
de Roberval, Sieur, 43
de Sola, Gov. Vicente, 132
de Soto, Hernando, 40, 42, 44, 64
de Toqueville, Alexis, 140
de Vaca, Cabeza, 38
de Vargas, Diego, 73, 77
de Vitoria, Francisco, 39
de Zaldivar, Juan, 48
de Zaldivar, Vincente, 48
Declaration of Allegiance to the
    Government of the United States
    by the North American
    Indian, 270
Declaration of Métis and Indian
    Rights, 420
Declaration of Policy
    Statement, 276
DeCora, Angel, 257
Deer, Ada Elizabeth, 295, 367,
    493, 499
Deganawida, 29
Deganawida-Quetzalcoatl
    University (DQU), 368, 376, 380–
    81, 384–87
degikup, 157
Deiter, Walter, 352, 359, 368
Delaware, 91–92, 120–26, 150,
    164; Big House Religion, 103;
    chiefs, 84; European contact, 38;
    massacred at Gnadenhutten, Ohio,
    106; migrations, 84, 130; in Ohio,
    80; in Pennsylvania, 72; selling
    land, 197; Treaty of Fort Stanwix,
    95; treaty rights, 113–14
Delaware Big House Religion, 122
Delaware Prophet, 91–92, 122
Delaware Treaty, 133
Delaware "Walking Purchase," 84
Delgamuukw v. The Queen, 446,
    474, 493
Deloria, Ella Cara, 239, 292
Deloria, Vine, Jr., 290, 292
DeMille, Cecil B., 271
demographics, 276, 301, 395,
    475, 492
Dempster Highway, 422
Dene, 74, 82–84, 112, 166–
    67, 416, 479; infanticide, 308;
    influenza epidemic, 286; land
    claim, 466; land claims, 407, 408,
    412, 436, 456, 468, 471, 477, 488,
    493–94; language, 35. See also
    Athapascan; Navajo
Dene Declaration, 404

Dene Nation, 416. See also Indian
    Brotherhood of the Northwest
    Territories
Denver, Commissioner, 178
Department of Citizenship, 348
Department of Education, 416
Department of Game of Washington
    v. Puyallup Tribe, 396
Department of Indian Affairs,
    156, 226
Department of Interior, 369, 372
Department of Interior Act, 173
Department of Justice, 369
Department of War, 154, 156
Deposit and Investment of Indian
    Funds Act, 298
desegregation, 364
Deserontyon, Capt. John, 85, 107
Desert culture, 6–9
Deskahe, 283
Determination of the Rights and
    Unity for Menominee, 367
Devils Lake Indian Reservation
    Jurisdiction Act, 313
Dewdney, Edgar, 230
Dewey Flat, 30
Diamond, Billy, 319, 400
Diefenbaker, John, 333
Diego, Juan, 195
Dieguño, 351
Digger Indians, 173. See also
    California Indians
Diné, 170. See also Navajo
Dion, Joseph, 238, 291
disease, 55–57, 66, 145–46
Distant Early Warning (D.E.W.)
    radar stations, 330
Division of Shoshoni and Arapaho
    Trust Funds Act, 315
DNA-People's Legal Services,
    Inc., 287
Doanloe, Etahdleuh, 214
Dodge, Henry L., 152, 184
dog sled, 14
Dog Soldiers, 146, 202
Dogrib, 135, 139, 178. See also
    Athapascan; Dene
Domagaya, 39
Dominion Franchise Act, 235, 248
Doniphan, Col. Alexander W., 170
Donnacona, 39
Dorion, Henri, 385
Dorion Commission Report, 384
Dorris, Michael, 309, 328, 447, 458
Dorset culture, 15, 21. See also
    Kapuivik site, Canada

Douglas, Lt. Gov. James, 193
Doxtater, Michael, 476
Drake, Francis, 45
Dreamer Religion, 130
Duck Lake, 233
Dufferin, Lord, 216
Dull Knife, 125, 134, 214, 221
Duluth, Daniel Greyson, 72
Dummer's War, 83
Dumont, Gabriel, 161, 233–34
Dumont, W. Yvon, 323, 492,
Duncan, Charles Jr., 420
Duncan, William, 191, 237
Dunn, Dorothy, 272, 277, 291, 341
Duro v. Reina, 467, 471
Dussault, René , 486
Duwamish, 111
Dvôrák, Anton, 245

E

Eagle, James Theodore, 405
Eastern Indian tribes, removal, 146
Eastern Kutchin (Gwich'in),
    121, 165
Eastern Shore Indians, 150
Eastman, Charles A., 185, 253, 268
Eastman, Elaine Goodale, 258
Echo-Hawk, Walter, 316
Echohawk, John E., 309
economic development, 268, 347,
    354, 369, 440, 447
Edenshaw, Charles, 162, 278, 340
Edison, Thomas A., 245
education, 247–48, 276–77, 281–
    82, 320–21, 344–46, 419–
    20, 497–98; adult education,
    331; adult literacy rates, 263;
    Alaska Native education, 290;
    boarding schools, 224, 244, 290;
    California Indian education,
    349, 397; Calusa education, 263;
    Choctaw Academy, 160; college
    education, 340; criticism of Indian
    education, 383–84, 391;
    demonstrations, 461; Department
    of Education, 416–17; dropout
    rate, 349; education in treaties,
    114; Federal Industrial Schools,
    205; Hopi forced education, 244,
    266; Johnson-O'Malley Act, 293;
    Kaskaskia Treaty, 120; Indian
    control, 388, 395, 397, 402, 444,
    446, 455–56, 479; residential

schools, 230; schools, 82, 230; White House Conference, 469
Education Amendment Act, 419
Education Appropriation Act, 247
Educational Times, 138
Eel River, 125
egalitarian societies, 18
Ehrlichman, John, 385
El Chilmo, 67
El Paso del Norte, 73
Electrical Lines Right-of-Way Parker Dam Project Act, 304
Elementary and Secondary Education Act, 384
Elk, John, 230
Elk v. Wilkins, 230
Ellis Island, 371
Emperor of Coweta, 72
Employment Division v. Smith, 459. *See also* Native American Church; peyote religion
empty quarter, 31
Encinitas Tradition, 9–10
encomiendas, 36
energy policy, 423
enfranchisement, 278
English General Court, 71
environmental policy, 444, 471, 477
Environmental Policy Act, 391
epidemics, 57, 64, 79, 133; cholera, 125; diphtheria, 79; measles, 79; Northwest Coast, 166; pneumonia, 79; smallpox, 104, 118, 154, 158, 161
Episcopalian, 121
Erasmus, Georges, 318, 449, 456, 486
Erdoes, Richard, 389
Erdrich, Louise, 327, 447,
Erie, 60–64
Eriksson, Leif, 26
Ervin, Sen. Sam, 353
Eskimo, 3, 23; education, 251; Indian status, 299; mission school, 167; soapstone carving, 316. *See also* Inuit
Esopus, 61, 65
Espionage Act, 371
Estate Sale of Crow Tribe Act, 318
Estevánico, 38, 40
eulachon (candlefish), 109
Eulogy on King Philip, 159
Evans, James, 166
Evans, Gov. John, 193
Ewing, A.F., 296

Ex Parte Crow Dog, 233
Exchange of Navajo Tribal Lands Act, 320
The Experiences of Five Christian Indians of the Pequot Tribe, 155

F

Fairchild Semi-Conductor Corporation, 351, 362
Falcon, Pierre, 131
Fallon Paiute Shoshoni Indian Tribe Water Rights Settlement Act, 472
Family Allowance Act, 308
Fantleroy, Moore, 66
The Farmington Report, 404
Father Allonex, 66
Feast of the Dead, 54
Federal Acknowledgement Program, 418, 479
Federal Indian Irrigation Act, 298
federal lands, 369, 379
Federal Oil and Gas Royalty Management Act (FOGRMA), 439
federal recognition, 391, 418, 479
Federal Trade Commission, 404
Federated Indian Tribes (of Los Angeles), 333
Federation of Mission Indians, 280
Federation of Saskatchewan Indian Nations, 412
Federation of Saskatchewan Indians, 332, 341, 352
Fee Patent Allotments for Mission Indians Act, 329
Ferrelo, Bartolome, 43
Ferris, Michael, 369
Ferris, Tom, 390
Fetterman, Capt. W.J., 197
Fetterman Fight, 125, 136
Fewkes, J. Walter, 187, 250
Fewkes Canyon settlements, 27
Fidler, Peter, 118
Figueroa, Gov. José, 155
Filing of Actions to Quit Land Titles Act, 317
Fillmore, Millard, 179
film, 265, 270–71, 281, 291, 294, 321, 466, 476; protest against Indian images, 268
Final Disposition of Affairs of Five Civilized Tribes Act, 259

Fine Day, 234
First Americans in the Arts, 489
First Annual Totem Awards, 489
First Seminole War, 131. *See also* Seminole; Seminole War
Fisher v. District Court, 406
fishing rights, 180–82, 450; Alaska Native Brotherhood, 269; British Columbia, 486; and Dennis Banks, 288; Lac Courte Orielles, 441; Northwest Coast, 375, 414, 420, 441, 448; *Sparrow v. Regina*, 467; Treaty 3, 211; Restigouche Reserve, 433; Wisconsin, 462, 499–500
Five Civilized Tribes, 180, 382
Five Civilized Tribes Citizenship Act, 251
Five Civilized Tribes Contracts Act, 325
Five Civilized Tribes Council Act, 259
Five Civilized Tribes Heirship Act, 276
Five Civilized Tribes Restrictions Act, 292
Five Civilized Tribes Restrictions Extension Act, 330
Five County Cherokee Organization, 346
Five Nations, 50, 53–54, 57, 60–76, 80–81; fur trade, 71; make peace with Shawnee, 77; neutrality policy, 75. *See also* Iroquois; Iroquois Confederacy; Six Nations
Fléché, Jessé, 50
Flemming, Arthur, 433
Fletcher, Alice, 251
Folsom culture, 4–5
Fon du Lac Community College, 497–98
Fond du Lac Treaty, 143
Fonda, Jane, 369
Fonseca, Harry, 311
Fontaine, Phil, 468
Foraging period. *See* Archaic period
Forbes, Jack D., 340, 355–59, 368, 376, 384
Ford Foundation, 365, 383, 387
Formative culture, 14
Formative period, 13. *See also* Classic period
Forsyth, George A., 202
Forsyth, Col. James, 240

Fort Belknap Reservation, 183, 262
Fort Berthold Indian Awards Act, 313
Fort Berthold Reservation, 242
Fort Elliot Treaty, 111
Fort Good Hope, 121
Fort Hall Indian Reservation, 130, 416
Fort Hall Indian Water Rights Act, 472
Fort Laramie Treaty, 134, 145, 150, 155
Fort Larned Council, 146
Fort Lawton, 369, 370, 372, 374
Fort Lewis, 369
Fort Macleod, 211
Fort Nelson, 128
Fort Orange, 55
Fort Peck Reservation, 182
Fort Peck Reservation Fee Patents Act, 329
Fort Ross (Rus), 127, 166
Fort Rupert, 173
Fort Selkirk, 173
Fort Totten Indian Reservation, 391
Fort Yuma Reservation, 230
Foundation of Iroquois and Allied Indians, 356
Fountain of Youth, 37
Four Corners, 19
Four Mothers Society, 175
Fourteenth Amendment, 205
Fox, 61–62, 66, 81, 148, 150, 152, 155
Fox, Luke, 56
Francis, Josiah (Hillis Hayo), 132
Franciscans, 28, 45
Franklin, Benjamin, 88, 99
Franklin, John, 135, 143
Fraser, James Earl, 270
Fraser, Simon, 124
Freedoms Award, 360
Fremont, Capt. John C., 170–71
Fremont culture, 20, 31
French and Indian War, 129
Frobisher, Adm. Martin, 45
fur trade, 53–57, 64–75, 86, 119, 123, 165–67; competition, 99-100; Fox Wars, 81; monopolies, 46; Russians, 86; Salish, 136; Sekani, 141; Tlingit, 155. *See also* American Fur Company; Hudson's Bay Company (HBC); North West Company,

G

Gadsden Purchase, 179
Gadsden Treaty, 463
Gaiwiio (Good Word), 129. *See also* Handsome Lake
Gall (Pizi), 134, 158, 164, 166
Gallahan v. Hollyfield, 435
Gallup Inter-Tribal Indian Ceremonial, 280
gambling, 457, 462–63, 467, 492, 489, 499
Ganado Mucho, 124, 132, 170
Garland, Brig. John, 181
Garment, Leonard, 377, 392
Garrison, Rep. James, 210
Geddes, Carol, 311, 476
Geiogamah, Hanay, 489
Gemmill, Mickey, 375
gender discrimination, 417
General, Emily, 282
General Accounting Office (GAO), 417
General Allotment Act, 181, 237, 250, 293
General Appropriation Act, 254
General Citizenship Act, 283
General Federation of Women's Clubs, 281
genocide report, 350
George II, 62
George III, 92
George, Dan, 248, 384
George, Ron, 498
Gerard, Forrest J., 283, 412
Geronimo, 142, 165, 184, 215, 258
Getty, Don, 457
Ghost Dance, 184, 239. *See also* Wovoka
Gibbon, Col. John, 213
Gila Mountain Apache, 69
Gitenmaax School of Northwest Coast Indian Art, 378
Gitskan, 123, 151; land claims, 446, 474, 493
Gitksan-Carrier Tribal Council (Gitksan-Wet'suwet'), 352
Gladstone, Charles, 278
Gladstone, James, 313, 333, 368
Gobernador Canyon, New Mexico, 21
gold rush, 111, 129, 145, 172, 186, 191, 198, 211–12, 217; Klondike, 247
Goldtooth, Tom, 498
Gorman, Carl, 340

Gorman, Mary, 340
Gradual Civilization Act, 202
Gradual Enfranchisement Act, 204
Grandfather Plaque (American Indian Vietnam Plaque), 453
Grant, Cuthbert, 113, 131
Grant, Rodney, 473
Grant, Ulysses S., 239, 348; and Ely Parker, 144, 203–04; and Manuelito, 132–33; peace policy, 126, 205; and Red Cloud, 136; and Washakie, 121, and Winnema, 160
Grassy Narrows Ojibway Reserve, 374
Grattan, Lt. John L., 181
Great Basin, 6
Great Lakes tribes, 175
Great Law, 29
Great Plains culture, 152
Great Plains Productions Inc., 321, 466
Great Sioux Reservation, 145, 155. *See also* Sioux
Great Society legislation, 344
Great Spirit, 29, 125, 126
The Great Sun, 84
Great Whale Project, 466, 477–78, 480, 482, 500
Greene, Graham, 321, 473, 488–89
Greenville Treaty, 120
Gregory, Dick, 347, 354
Griffith, D.W., 263
Grinnell, George Bird, 247
Grise Fiord, 326
Grossman, Aubrey, 381
Guale, 73
Guanahani, 31
Gucinges, 103
Guerin v. The Queen, 446
Gunther Pattern sites, 17

H

H.B.C. *See* Hudson's Bay Company (HBC)
Haida, 86, 143, 151, 158, 234; art and culture, 162; protest logging, 450, 454
Haisla, 155
Halifax Treaty, 89
Halkomelem Coast Salish, 143
Hamlet of Baker Lake et al. v. Minister of Indian, 422
Hammond, 66

Han, 177, 247
Hancock, Gen. Winfield Scott, 146, 198
Handsome Lake, 116, 129, 159. *See also* Iroquois; Longhouse religion; Seneca
Handsome Lake Church, 129
Hanyerry, 104
Haozous, Bob, 272
Harcourt, Mike, 488
Harden, Ross, 372
Hardin, Helen, 277, 304
Harding, Warren G., 178
Hare, 112, 121, 139
Harjo, Chitto, 261
Harjo, Joy, 323, 439
Harmer, Gen. Josiah, 105, 110
Harney, Gen. William S., 155, 182
Harper, Elijah, 468
Harper, J.J., 477
harpoons, 12–15
Harrison, Benjamin, 261
Harrison, Gov. William Henry, 103, 120, 124, 126
Harrison v. Laveen, 316, 342
Harvey, Byron, 369
Hascall, John, 487
Haskell Institute, 231, 244, 341
Haskell Institute National Guard, 300
Hauptman, Laurence, 386
Haury, Margery, 359
Havasupai, 299, 348
Haven, Jens, 85, 98
Hawthorn, Dr. Harry B., 348
Hawthorn Report, 348, 358, 376
Hayes, Ira Hamilton, 282
Hayes, Col. Jack, 188
Hayfield Fight, 136
Head, Francis Bond, 119, 160, 163
Head Start Programs, 434
health care, 329–31, 411–13, 425–27; and Annie Dodge Wauneka, 263; Canadian Indian health service, 310, 313; *Dreaver v. Regina*, 295; Government Medical Service, 256; Indian Health Care Improvement Act, 407; Indian Health Service, 325; Native Hawaiian Health Care Act, 457; Navajo Illness, 492; Treaty 6, 218
Hearne, Samuel, 84, 97
Helsinki Accords, 411
Helsinki Conference, 429
Henday, Anthony, 89

Henry III, 46
Henry, Patrick, 99
Hendrick, 72
Hernandez, Juan Pérez, 98
Herrera, Joe H., 292
Herrero, 170
Herring, Elbert, 154
Hewett, Edgar, 235
Hiawatha, 29
Hiawatha National Forest, 375
Hickel, Walter, 360, 364, 378
Hickory Ground, 90
Hicks, Bob, 492
Hidatsa, 25, 31, 154, 160
High Forehead, 181
Highway, Tomson, 324, 488
Hill, David, 284
Hillis Hayo. *See* Francis, Josiah
Hind, Henry Youle, 185
Hinmahtooyahlatkekt, 219
Hispañola, 31, 36, 38
History of the Ojibway Indians (1861), 119
Hitchcock, Ethan Allan, 150
Hitchiti, 82
Hochelaga (Montreal), 50, 60
Hogup Cave, Utah, 8
Hohokam, 11, 18, 24, 28
Hokeah, Jack, 279
Holcombe, Western Great Lakes, 7
Hole-In-The-Day, 140, 141
Home Guard Indians, 68, 74
Hoopa Valley Reservation School Act, 325
Hoopa Valley Reserve, 193
Hoover, Herbert, 188
Hoover Commission Report, 318
Hopewell culture, 14, 17, 20–23
Hopi, 28, 30, 56, 73, 132, 229; acculturation pressure, 258; art, 250; Black Mesa, 385; clash with Navajo over Joint Use Area, 394, 400, 423; and Coronado, 42; culture, 385; education, 258; hostile to Spanish reconquest, 77; meet United Nations officials, 335; pottery, 226; religion, 385; silversmithing, 187; strip mining, 385
Hopi-Navajo Relocation Act (Public Law 96-306), 400, 427
Hopkins, Sarah Winnemucca, 229
Horn, Kahn-Tineta, 392
Horse, Michael, 298
Horse culture, 79, 167
Horseshoe Bend Battle, 92

Hosteen Klah, 198
Hotchkiss period, 20
Hothlepoya, 92
House Committee on Interior and Insular Affairs, 347
House Concurrent Resolution 108, 345
Houser, Allan, 272, 292, 341
Houston, James, 316, 335
Howard, Gen. Oliver O., 138, 184, 219, 223–24
Howe, Joseph, 166
Howe, Oscar, 292
Howling Wolf, 214
Hualapai (Walapai), 301
Hualapai (Walapai) Reserve, 229
Huasteca, 31
Hubley, George, 352
Hudson, Henry, 52
Hudson's Bay Company (HBC), 82–86, 113–14, 138–43, 161–67; Battle of Seven Oaks, 131; Blackfoot, 89; chartered, 68; Coast Salish, 176; Cumberland House, 98–99; Fort Good Hope, 121; Fort Simpson, 151; health care, 308; Inuit, 279; North West Company merger, 136; Palliser/Hind Expeditions, 185; Peigan, 117; Red River Colony, 128; removal of, 171; smallpox vaccinations, 158; Tlingit, 155; treaties, 209; York Factory, 74
Hueco Tradition, 11
Huguenots, 45
Hukueko Indians, 127
Hull, William, 127
Hunkpapa Sioux, 150, 158. *See also* Sioux
Hunt, George, 180
Hunt, Henry, 227
Hunt, Tony, 227, 340
hunting rights, 180, 211, 269, 288, 433, 450
Hupa, 355
Huron, 29, 35, 39, 50, 53–54, 57–66. *See also* Wyandot
Huronia, 54, 57, 59, 62

I

Ice Age, 3
idolatry, 73
igloos, 36
Iglulik Inuit, 136

Ihonatiria, 57

Illiniwek. *See* Illinois

Illinois, 62, 69–71, 74–75; traditions, 60; warriors, 72

Immediate Relief of Navajo and Hopi Act, 315

Inca, 40

Ince, Thomas H., 270

Indian Achievement Award, 354

Indian Act, 230, 234, 358, 366, 456, 472; gender discrimination, 434, 437, 444, 449; Indian consultation, 324

Indian Act Amendment, 269

Indian Activist Movements, 367–71, 375, 378, 386–88. *See also* American Indian Movement; Red Power Movement

Indian Actors Association, 296

Indian Actors Workshop, 422

Indian Advancement Act, 230

Indian Affairs Department, 472

Indian Affairs Supervision Act, 344

Indian Agencies, 254

Indian Agent Act, 244

Indian Alcohol and Substance Abuse Prevention and Treatment Act, 452

Indian and Federal Trade Act (Public Law 96-278), 426

Indian Appropriations Act, 209, 244

Indian Arts and Crafts Board, 472

Indian Arts and Crafts Board Act, 296, 472

Indian Association of Alberta, 237–38, 298, 359, 368, 376

Indian Boundaries Act, 131

Indian Boundary Markers Act, 339

Indian Brotherhood of the Northwest Territories, 318, 369, 404, 410, 416.

Indian Child Protection and Family Abuse Prevention Act, 472

Indian Child Welfare Act (ICWA), 419

Indian Citizenship Act, 276

Indian Civil Rights Act, 396, 417, 452

Indian Claims Commission, 343, 346, 352, 374–75, 376, 382, 410, 417, 427; creation, 307, 314; restructuring, 350

Indian Claims Commission Act, 314, 415

Indian Claims Limitation Act, 438

Indian Claims Settlement Act, 453

Indian Commission of Ontario, 419

Indian Confederation of American Indians, 307

Indian Council Fire, 354

Indian Crimes Act, 406

Indian Day, 275

Indian Defense League, 284, 331

Indian Department, 109

Indian Depredations Act, 243

Indian Desk, 345

Indian Education. *See* education

Indian Education Act, 455

Indian Education Act of 1972, 355, 389, 390

Indian Education Amendments, 446

Indian Education Technical Amendments Act, 449

Indian Elementary and Secondary Education Act, 372

Indian Employment Training Center, 362

Indian Environmental Regulatory Act, 471

Indian Environmental Regulatory Enhancement Act, 471

Indian Financing Act, 398

Indian Gaming Regulatory Act, 457, 475

Indian Health Care Act, 365

Indian Health Care Improvement Act (IHCIA), 407

Indian Health Care Transfer Act, 329

Indian Health Law, 348

Indian Health Scholarship Program, 411

Indian Health Service (IHS), 367, 404, 494,

Indian Highway Act, 290

The Indian Historian, 344

Indian Housing Act, 456

Indian Insurance Act, 285

Indian Irrigation Act, 291

Indian Land Consolidation Act, 440

Indian Land Jurisdiction in New York Act, 323

Indian Lands Leasing Act, 330

Indian Lands Mining Act, 298

Indian Lands Rights-of-Way Act, 317

Indian Law Enforcement Reform Act, 469

Indian Liquor Act, 247

Indian Lumber Products Act, 300

Indian Major Crimes Act, 233

Indian Mineral Leasing Act, 298

Indian Monies Due Act, 292

Indian New Deal, 293, 314. *See also* Indian Reorganization Act

Indian Nullification of the Unconstitutional Laws, 157

Indian Oil Leasing Act, 283

Indian police, 151

The Indian Princess, 124

Indian Property Protection Act, 191

Indian Protection Committee, 224

Indian pueblos, 142. *See also* Pueblo

Indian Removal Act, 148

Indian removal policy, 180

Indian Reorganization Act (Wheeler-Haward Act), 293, 296, 372, 393, 402

Indian Rights Association, 224, 292, 340

Indian School Property Act, 326

Indian Schools, 156. *See also* education

Indian Schools Act, 242

Indian Schools in South Dakota Act, 320

Indian Self-Determination and Education Assistance Act, 307, 402, 440

Indian Shaker Church, 177, 246. *See also* Slocum, John

Indian Territory, 93, 123–25, 134, 158–59, 162, 165, 175; Oklahoma, 126, 132, 135, 145, 148, 156; Oklahoma and Kansas, 150

Indian Timber Act, 344

Indian Timber Contracts Act, 292

Indian trading houses, 136

Indian Tribal Governmental Tax Status Act, 440

Indian Tribal Judgment Funds Use or Distribution A, 455

Indian Tribal Leaders Conference, 471

Indian Unity Conference, 361

Indian Voter Project, 341

Indian Welfare League, 280

Indian Wife, 141

Indian Will Act, 428

Indians and the Law, 350

Indians of All Tribes, 303, 369–74, 381, 386–87, 394. *See also* Alcatraz Island occupation; Indian Activist Movements

Indians of Quebec Association, 350

Indigenous Environmental Network, 498
Indigenous Women's Network (IWN), 460
individual land title, 202, 223, 237
Industrial Revolution, 159
infant mortality, 346
Inland Tlingit, 167
Innu (Naskapi), 456, 486, 489, 492, 500; land claims, 413–14, 472,
Institute for the Development of Indian Law, 292
Institute of American Indian and Alaska Native Culture and Arts Development, 452
Institute of the American Indian Art (IAIA), 295, 297, 341
Inter-Tribal Indian Ceremonial, 388
Interagency Indian Task Force, 424
Interest of Trust Funds Act, 288
Interior Salish, 124, 126
International Indian Treaty Council (IITC), 411
International Year of Indigenous Peoples, 488
Intoxication in Indian Country Act, 244
Inuaina Arapaho, 63
Inuit, 18, 35–36, 143–45, 165–66, 226, 239, 347; ancestors, 12; art, 383; Chipewayan trade, 85; cooperatives, 335; early encounters, 45; executions of, 282; housing program, 349; James Bay Project, 385, 391; land claims, 308, 400, 405, 412–14, 424, 436–37, 467, 472, 479, 492; land rights, 422; measles epidemic, 254; Moravian missionaries, 98; Nunavut, 406; printmaking, 335; relocation, 326, 448; Siberia, 18; snowmobiles replace dog sleds, 343; sub-arctic 14; Thule expansion, 23; trade, 12, 103–04; trapping, 279; Tungavik Federation of Nunavut, 437; voting rights, 321; warfare, 135; whaling, 188, 412. See also Eskimo
Inuit Broadcasting Corporation (I.B.C.), 328, 435
Inuit Circumpolar Conference (I.C.C.), 328, 411, 449–50
Inuit Committee on National Issues, 308

Inuit Tapirisat of Canada (I.T.C.), 300, 328, 388, 395–96, 405, 412–13, 482, 487
Inuk, 85
Inuktitut, 35, 383
Inuvialuit, 239, 368; land claims, 300, 410, 419, 445,
Iowa Jurisdiction over Sac (Sauk) and Fox Reservation Act, 317
Ipai, 96
Iron Tall, 270
Iroquois, 53–71, 74–76, 80–92, 107, 128–29, 159, 167; Algonkian-speaker invasion, 44; ancestors, 35; appeal to League of Nations, 281; archaeological remains, 27; buffer zone, 72; Champlain, 50; citizenship, 301; Confederate Council, 80; and Cornplanter, 159; culture, 159; declare war on the Axis powers, 304; defeat, 75; and Deganawida, 29; disease, 67; dominance, 80; formation of the Confederacy, 81; French peace, 80; fur trade, 119; and Handsome Lake, 116; and Jacques Cartier, 39; lacrosse, 184; leadership struggle, 335; meet European Parliment officials, 425; neutrality, 80; Owasco period, 26; reserves established, 147; resist the English, 82; retreat, 75; right of free travel between U.S. and Canada, 284; seek United Nations membership, 309; Six Nations pageant, 282; sovereignty, 314; trade, 63, 80; tribes, 50; waging war over the St. Lawrence region, 72; warfare, 67; warriors, 72. See also Five Nations; Iroquois Confederacy; Six Nations
Iroquois Confederacy, 60–67, 378, 456, 464; Albany Plan, 88; and Cornplanter, 159; divisions, 101; fur trade, 53, 57; and Handsome Lake, 129; power and influence decline, 80; and Samuel de Champlain, 50. See also Five Nations; Iroquois; Six Nations
Iroquois League, 30, 67, 72, 88
Irwin, Ron, 495, 498, 500
Isbister, Alexander Kennedy, 137, 165, 171
Ishi, 266
Isleta Pueblo, 73, 374
Iteshicha (Bad Face), 136

J
Jackson, Andrew, 95, 100, 128, 131–32, 146, 154
Jackson, Helen Hunt, 195, 228
Jackson, Sen. Henry, 369
Jackson, Dr. Sheldon, 230
Jackson, Tom, 319
James I, 50
James, Arlene Wesley, 325
James, Charlie, 226
James, Thomas, 56
James Bay and Northern Quebec Agreement, 308, 319, 405, 412, 427, 446, 473, 477–78, 488; Tait Report, 437
James Bay Hydroelectric Project, 385, 396, 462, 478, 488
James Bay Settlement Act, 412
James Gladstone (Akay-na-muka), 237
Jamestown, 44, 50, 53, 55
Jamieson, Elmer, 243
Janos, 78
Japanese Americans, 320
Jarvis, Annie, 252
Jay's Treaty, 105, 115, 362, 392, 456, 457, 489
Jefferson, Thomas, 83, 109, 120–21
Jémez, 50, 77
Jemez Cave, New Mexico, 14
Jemison, Alice Lee, 289
Jemison, Mary, 139
Jesuits, 45, 57–59, 67
Jicarilla Apache, 78, 181
John Paul II, Pope, 446, 454
John Work Expedition, 152
Johnson, E. Pauline (Tekahionwake), 188
Johnson, Sir John, 104
Johnson, Leo, 333
Johnson, Lyndon B., 344, 348–49, 352–54
Johnson, Chief Ray, 335
Johnson, William, 90
Johnson v. M'Intosh, 139
Johnson-O'Malley Act, 293, 384
Johnson-O'Malley Funds, 351
Joint Cabinet-National Indian Brotherhood Committee, 400, 416
Joliet, Louis, 68
Jones, David E., 246
Jones, John, 119
Jones, Peter, 119, 147, 160, 163
Jones-Miller Site, 4

Joseph (Chief Joseph), 138, 164, 193, 221
Josephy, Alvin M., Jr., 355
Josephy Report, 355
Juh, 215
Julius II, Pope, 37
jurisdiction, 332, 414–15, 439, 443, 446, 453–55, 461–62, 463, 467

K

Kabotie, Fred, 250, 275
kachina masks, 66
Kah-ge-ga-bowh, 171
Kahkewaquonaby ("Sacred Feathers"). *See* Jones, Peter
Kainai (Blood), 74, 79, 123, 145, 161, 428
Kamaiakin, 182, 186
Kaministikwia, 76
Kamloops Amendment, 456
Kanatewat et al. v. James Bay Development Corporation, 396
Kanesataké or Oka, 84
Kansas, 178
Kaposia Band of Mdewakanton Santee, 125. *See also* Dakota; Sioux
Kappler, Charles, 353
Kapuivik site, Canada, 14
Karankawa, 38
Kashaya Pomo, 127
Kashia, 382
Kaska, 123, 167, 211
Kaskaskia Indians, 120
kayak, 10, 14, 45
Keam, Thomas, 226
Kearny, Col. Stephen Watts, 171
Keeler, William W., 261, 341
Kekewepellethe, 109
Kelley, Col. James, 182
Kellogg, Minnie, 268
Kelly, Peter, 233, 244, 272, 275, 313
Kenekuk, 108, 161, 192
Kennebec, 83
Kennedy, Sen. Edward, 364–65
Kennedy, John F., 341, 342
Kenojuak Ashevak, 285
Keokuk, 106
Keres, 63, 77
Kerr-McGee Corp. v. Navajo Tribe, 448
Ketcher, John, 310

Key Marco, 35
Kichai, 170
Kickapoo, 61–62, 81, 92, 125, 130, 161, 164, 450; apply for citizenship, 439; flight from Texas, 189; migration, 192, 257, 259; purchase land, 447; warfare in Texas, 196
Kicking Bear, 240
Kicking Bird, 126
Kieft, Gen. William, 61
Kieft's War, 61, 65
Kilatica, 74
Kincaid Site, Ohio, 21
King, Bruce, 498
King, Robert W., 305
King, Thomas, 305
King Philip (Metacom), 46, 59, 70, 71, 158–59
King Philip's War, 68, 70
King William's War, 76, 87
Kinishba, 30
Kintpuash. *See* Captain Jack
Kinya-ani people (Tall House People), 27
Kinya'a, 27
Kinzua Dam, 341, 344
Kiowa, 125–26, 134, 146, 164
Kiowa Medicine Lodge Council, 146
Kiowa Reservation, 147
Kiowa-Apache, 125, 164
Kirke, David, 56
Kittigazuit Inuk, 143
kivas, 20, 26, 27, 66
Kizer, Charley, 157
Kizer, Louisa (Louisa Keyser). *See* Dat-So-La-Lee
Klamath, 345, 358, 452
Klamath County School Facilities Act, 320
Klamath Restoration Act, 452
Klamath Termination Act, 329
Klamath Welfare Act, 317
Kleppe, Thomas S., 409
Kneip, Gov. Richard F., 416
Knight, Yvonne, 386
Knox, Henry, 111
Kodiak Island, Alaska, 10, 13
Kolomoki Site, 20
Kootenay (Kutenai), 117, 123, 183
Kootenay House, 123
Koster Site, Illinois, 10
Kroeber, Alfred, 267
Ksan Village, 378
Kuptana, Rosemarie, 328, 383

Kutchin (Gwich'in, Loucheux), 112, 165, 172
Kwagiulth (Kwakiutl), 205, 176
Kwakiutl (Kwagiulth, Kwakwaka'wakw), 155

L

"La Chason de la Grenouillére" (The Ballad of Frog Plain), 131
La Flesche, Francis, 180, 251, 258
La Flesche, Joseph, 180
La Flesche, Susette (Bright Eyes), 180, 227
Labrador Inuit Association (L.I.A.), 308, 396, 413, 472
Lac Courte Oreilles Band of Lake Superior Chippewa, 441, 461
Lace Site, 8
LaChance, Leo, 473, 496
lacrosse, 74, 184, 200
Ladd, Edmund, 488
LaDuke, Winona, 460
Lakota, 154, 196. *See also* Sioux
Lame Deer, John Fire, 387, 389
Lamere, Oliver, 284
Land, Franklin, 276
Land Allotment Act, 242
land cession treaty, 92
land claims, 261–63, 282–84, 403–04, 408–10, 432–35, 470–72, 487; British Columbia, 285; California, 272; Canada, 285; Coolican Report, 450; Cree, 453; *Delgamuukw v. The Queen*, 474–75; Eastern Indians, 413, 420; Indian Claims Limitation Act, 438; Indian Lands Mining Act, 298; Innu, 413; Inuit, 413; South Dakota, 420
Land Exchange North Carolina Cherokees Act, 320
Land Lease Act, 285
Land Purchase Act, 282
land rights, 396, 440; British Columbia, 193, 216; Cherokee, 254; Chickasaw, 254; Choctaw, 254; Delaware, 197; and Joseph Dion, 239; Location tickets, 217; Nova Scotia, 187; Oregon, 182; and Peter Kelly, 233–34; and Pontiac, 94; Reconstruction, 197; Restricted Trust Lands Act, 264; Salt River Reserve, 187; Saskatchewan, 444; Sioux, 329;

Tee-hit-ton Indians v. United States, 329; Washington treaty, 182
Lands of Klamath and Modoc Tribes and Snake Indian Act, 303
Lane, Gov. William Carr, 181
LaPena, Frank, 297
Largos, Zarcillas, 186
Laroque, François, 148
Las Salinas Senecu, 71
The Last of the Mohicans, 171
Late Woodland period, 19–20
Laws of Burgos, 36
Le Claire, Antoine, 155
le Moyne, Jacques, 45
Le Quier, Francis, 343
Lea, Luke, 177
League of Indians of Canada, 278
League of Nations, 283
League of North American Indians, 331
Leasing of Indian Lands in Washington Act, 313
Leavitt Act, 291
ledger drawings, 214
Left Hand (Nawat), 164
Legaic, 151
Lego, Marie, 375
Lemhi, 121
Lenni Lenape, 160. *See also* Delaware
Levi, John, 280
Lewis, Lucy, 245
Lewis, Meriwether, 118, 120–21
Lewis, Rev. Dr. Roe B., 354
Lewis and Clark Expedition, 107, 121
Life among the Paiutes, 168
Life and Journals (1860), 119
Life of Ma-ka-tai-me-she-kia-kaik or Black Hawk, 154
The Life of Mary Jemison, 139
Lillooet, 124
Lincoln, Abraham, 120, 134, 152, 192
Lincoln, Kenneth, 351
Lindenmeier Site, Colorado, 4, 5
Line of Demarcation, 31
Lipan, 170, 352. *See also* Apache
Litefoot, 498
literary criticism, 460
Lithic Indians. *See* Paleo-Indian (Paleo-Siberian)
Little Bad Man (Ayimisis), 140
Little Beard, 103

Little Bighorn, 125, 150, 158, 164, 166
Little Crow, 125, 191
Little Ice Age, 31
Little Pine (Minahikosis), 140, 233
Little Raven, 165
Little Talisee, 90
Little Thunder, 155, 182
Little Turtle, 105, 109, 113
Little Turtle's War, 109, 114
Little Wolf, 125, 134, 221
Littlechild, Wilton, 458
Littlefeather, Sacheen, 394
Llano culture. *See* Clovis culture
Loan Fund Act, 343
Lock, Grey, 83
Locke, Kevin, 498
Loesch, Harrison, 388
Logan, Jim, 488
Logan, John (Tachnechdorus), 83
Loisel, Regis, 118
Lone Wolf (Guipago), 134
Lone Wolf v. Hitchcock, 254
Long Walk (March of Tears), 192. *See also* Navajo
Longboat, Tom, 261, 269
Longhouse religion, 116. *See also* Handsome Lake; Seneca
longhouses, 54
Looking Glass (the elder), 138, 219
Looking Glass (the younger), 138
Looking Horse, Avrol, 488
Lord Dunmore's War, 83, 98
Louisiana Purchase, 120, 121
Lower Brulé, Crow Creek Sioux, and Yankton Sioux Act, 328–29
Lower Creek (Apalachicola), 72. *See also* Creek
Lozen, 165
Lucas, Phil, 486
Lujan, Manuel, 463, 471, 475
Lumbee, 332, 339, 391, 494
Lummi, 452
Lummis, Charles, 251
Lurie, Nancy Ostreich, 284
Lyng v. Northwest Indian Cemetery Protective Association, 455
Lysyk, Kenneth, 411

M

Macaulay, James Buchanan, 163
MacDonald, Peter, 287, 452, 463, 473
Macdonnell, Miles, 129

Machemanet, 192
Mackenzie, Alexander, 112, 114
Mackenzie Highway, 316
Mackenzie River Valley depopulation, 133
Mackenzie Valley Pipeline, 318, 409
Mackenzie Valley Pipeline Inquiry (Berger Inquiry), 403, 407, 410
Mackinac, 60, 74
Mad Bear, Anderson, 335
Mahican, 55, 61, 67, 72
Maidu, 11, 157
Maine Indian Claims Settlement Act, 428
maize, 11, 14, 18–20, 23, 24, 26–30
Major Crimes Act, 236
Major Ridge (Nunna Hidihi), 97
Makah, 88
Maliseet, 82, 84, 91, 106, 167, 492
Mallory, Phillip, 66
Malpeque, 82
Mamanti, 134
mammoths, 3–5
Man Afraid of His Horses, 136
Manakin, 68, 71
Manchester Rancheria Act, 304
Mandan, 25, 31, 121, 154, 160
Mandeville, Sir John, 37
Mangas Coloradas, 116, 127, 141
Manitoba Act, 206, 466
Manitoba Hydroelectric Project, 356
Manitoulin Indian Reserve, 160
Manitoulin Island Treaty, 191
Mankiller, Wilma P., 310, 451, 496
manos, 5, 9
Mansos, 67
Manuel, George, 278, 367, 395, 404
Manuel, Victor, 281
Manuelito, 132, 170, 186
Many Treaties, 296
Manypenny, George, 180–81
Maquinna, 109, 120
Marchand, Leonard, 354
Maricopa, 187
Marin, 156
Marksville culture, 18, 23
Marmes Rock Shelter, Washington, 6
Marquette, Jacques, 68
Marriage and Divorce among Klamath, Modoc, and Snake Indians Act, 308
Marshall, Donald, 442, 465

Marshall, James, 172
Marshall, John, 139, 150, 154
Martin, Kenneth, 376
Martin, Mungo (Nakapenkim, "Chief Ten Times Over"), 226, 340
Martinez, Crescencio, 276
Martinez, Jesusa, 190
Martinez, Julian, 235, 275
Martinez, Maria Montoya, 235, 333, 428
Martinez, Paddy, 362
Martinez, Popovi Da, 235
Martyr, Peter, 38
Marvin, Dr. James, 231
Masayesva, Victor, Jr., 486
Mascouten, 81
Mashpee, 157, 416
Massachusetts General Court, 58
Massasoit, 45, 47, 55, 70
Master of Life, 124. *See also* Great Spirit; religion
mastodons, 3–4
Mather, Cotton, 56
Mathews, John Joseph, 294
Matonabbee, 84, 97
Mattaponi, 88
Maximilian, Alexander Phillip, 154
Maya, 10
Mayflower, 55
Mayo, 86
McClanahan v. Arizona State Tax Commission, 392
McCloud, Janet, 340, 402
McCurely, Ella, 335
McDougal, Gov. John, 179
McDougall, William, 205
McDowell, Malcolm, 277
McEachern, Chief Justice, 474
McGillivray, Alexander, 90, 105
McIntosh, William, 92, 100, 136
McKay, Mabel, 260
McKay, Stanley J., 487
McKay v. Campbell, 205
McKee, Reddick, 176
McKenna-McBride Commission, 271, 274, 278, 403
McKenney, Thomas L., 138
McKnight, Bill, 453
McLaughlin, James, 164, 240
McLaughlin, Marie, 275
McNickle, D'Arcy, 254, 296, 307
Mdewakanton Santee, 125–26. *See also* Dakota; Sioux
Means, Lanada, 357
Means, Lorelei DeCora, 397

Means, Russell, 300, 382, 397, 403. *See also* American Indian Movement
Medal of Freedom Award, 342
Medicine Lodge Council, 126, 146
Medicine Lodge Treaty, 126, 134, 146
Medina, Juan B., 292
Meech Lake Accord, 309, 454, 468
Meeds, Rep. Lloyd, 409
Meeker, Nathan, 223
Megumaage, 50
Membertou, 50
Memorial Museum on Fort Hall Reservation Act, 315
Menawa, 92
Menendez, Lucas, 64
Menlo culture, 9
Menominee, 66, 151; federal recognition restored, 396; restoration, 367; school district, 344; termination of tribal status, 326, 328, 345, 351; tribal status restored, 295
Menominee Restoration Committee, 295, 367
Menominee Tribe of Indians v. United States, 351
Menominee Warrior Society, 402, 404, 410
Mercredi, Ovide William, 309, 321, 476–78, 482, 487, 492, 495, 498
Meredith, Henry, 188
Meriam Report, 253, 278, 286, 293
Merligueche, 82
Merriam, C. Hart, 247
Merrion v. Jicarilla Apache Tribe, 436
Mesa Verde, 26, 27
mesas, 27
Mescalero Apache, 352. *See also* Apache
Mescalero Apache Tribe v. Jones, 395
Mesoamerica, 20, 24
Mesquakie, 81, 407. *See also* Sauk
mestizo, 76
Metacom. *See* King Philip
metates, 9
Métchif language, 136
Methodists, 119
Métis, 76, 100, 128–31, 135–36, 166–68, 246, 341; army, 161; battle with Dakota, 177; buffalo hunts, 136, 161; community, 168; economy, 136; Ewing Commission, 296; flight

from Manitoba, 207; fur trade, 173; land claims, 324, 412, 456, 466, 468, 471, 488; land rights, 204; nationhood, 177; provisional government, 205, 206, 233; removal of Hudson's Bay Company, 171; settlements, 161; warfare, 234
Métis Association of Alberta, 238, 291
Métis Association of the Northwest Territories, 404, 407, 412
Métis Commission, 233
Métis National Council, 441, 482, 487
Métis Population Betterment Act, 238, 298
Mexican-American War, 170
Meyer, Dillon S., 320
Miami, 60, 68–69, 72–73, 88–92, 95, 125–26, 133, 150; land cessions, 155; land claims, 346; treaties, 133
mica, 41
Miccosukee, 82, 332, 335, 339, 443
Michelson, Truman, 276
Micmac, 32, 35, 50, 53, 84, 88–91, 106, 145, 211; British peace, 91; disease, 54; epidemic, 87; fishing rights, 466; fur trade, 39; homeland burned, 141; hunting rights, 466; land claims, 436; land losses, 166; lands, 167; opposing French, 82; population decline, 166; recognized under the Indian Act, 446; reserved seat in Nova Scotia legislature, 475; suicide, 489; tax protest, 492
microblades, 5
Middle Missouri tradition, 24
Middle period, 14
Midwestern Inter-Tribal Council, 332
Mikak, 85, 98
Mikasuki. *See* Miccosukee
Miles, Col. Dixon S., 184, 186
Miles, Gen. Nelson, 134, 138, 184, 212–15, 219
military service, 272, 282, 292; draft registration, 301; refused, 302; Vietnam, 453; World War I, 276; World War II, 299, 301, 303
Mills, Billy, 297, 344
Mimbres culture, 26
mineral rights, 288, 298, 330
Mingo (Cayuga), 83

mining, 186, 285
mining rights, 449, 466
Minnesota Chippewa Allotment
    Act, 239
Minority Fellowship Program, 365
Minter, Thomas, 424
Minuit, Peter, 55
Mirabel, Vince, 292
Miranda, Governor, 69
Miss Indian America Pageant, 325
Miss Indian America XVI, 359
Mission Indian Federation, 278
Mission Indian Reserve, 205
Mission Indians, 79. *See also*
    California Indians
Mission La Purísima, 110
Mission San Antonio de Padua, 97
Mission San Buenaventura, 106
Mission San Carlos, 79, 96
Mission San Fernando, 116
Mission San Francisco, 138
Mission San Francisco de Asis, 100
Mission San Gabriel, 97
Mission San Jose, 116
Mission San Juan Bautistais, 116
Mission San Juan Capistrano,
    101, 126
Mission San Luis Obispo, 98
Mission San Miguel, 116
Mission San Pedro, 64
Mission San Rafael, 131, 156
Mission Santa Barbara, 109
Mission Santa Clara, 79, 101
Mission Santa Cruz, 113
Mission Santa Ines, 121
Mission Soledad, 113
missionaries, 82, 216; Anglican,
    165; Catholic, 130; education, 45;
    Franciscan, 79; Jesuit, 79;
    Methodist, 163, 165; Moravian,
    144; Mormon, 121, 129; Native
    health, 79; Protestant, 165; Roman
    Catholic, 135, 165; Spanish, 79
missionary schools, 194, 200, 251
Mississauga, 76, 107, 119, 147,
    160, 164
*Mississippi Choctaw Band v.
    Holyfield,* 461
Mississippian culture, 14, 19, 21–
    23, 42, 84; chiefdoms, 21; diseases,
    42; maize, 21; Southeastern
    Ceremonial Complex, 21
Mississippian period, 20, 27, 31
Missouri, 175, 228
Missouri Fur Company, 118

Missouri-to-Columbia road, 186
Mitchell, George, 287
Mitchell, Stanley, 29
Miwok (Me-Wuk), 11, 156, 176
mixed-blood, 69, 76, 100, 135,
    136, 207, 223, 263, 285, 296, 329
Moapa River Reserve (Muddy
    Valley Reserve), 214
Mobile, 41
Moctezuma, 37
Model Urban Indian Center, 386
Modoc, 160, 211, 417, 452
Modoc War, 160
*Moe v. Salish and Kootenai
    Tribes,* 406
Mogollon, 11, 18, 24–25
Mohawk, 58, 61, 64–67, 72, 75–
    76, 85–90, 101, 499; activism,
    375, 410, 420; Akwesasne, 355,
    467; demonstrations, 357, 456–
    57, 465, 468–71; elected band
    council, 475; fur trade, 80; Jay's
    Treaty, 355; land claims, 331, 410,
    425, 465, 468; language, 87; Oka
    crisis, 291; political divisions, 426,
    462–63, 467; protest, 355, 375,
    388; steelworkers, 186; warriors
    against the French, 72
Mohawk, Richard, 417
Momaday, N. Scott, 294, 351,
    356, 358
Moncock, David, 137
Mondale, Walter, 414
Monks Mound, 26
Monroe, James, 133
Montagnais, 44, 53, 56–58, 63
Montana v. Blackfeet Tribe, 449
Montana v. United States, 433
Montauk, 61
Montezuma, Carlos, 268, 270, 276
Montoya, Domingo, 364
Montoya, Sen. Joseph M., 362–63
Montoya v. Bolack, 342
Montreal Native Friendship
    Centre, 311
Moore Fantleroy, 66
Moorehead Cave, Texas, 9
Mopope, Stephen, 279
Moqui Reserve, 229. *See also* Hopi
Morattico, 63, 66
Moravians, 85, 98, 284
Moreno, Fidel, 486
Morgan, J.P., 247
Morgan, T.J., 239
Morin, Gerald, 492

Mormon Trail, 177
Morrisseau, Norval, 291, 342, 439
Morrissette, Ed, 494
Morse, Jedidiah, 133
Morton, Rogers C.B., 388, 398
Morton v. Mancari, 398
Morton v. Ruiz, 398
mounds, 14, 16, 19–21, 31
Mount Rushmore National
    Memorial, 378–79, 386
Mountain Dene, 121
Mountain Wolf Woman, 284
Mourning Dove (Humishuma), 285
Moves Camp, Ellen, 393
Muckleshoot, 375
Mulroney, Brian, 449, 468,
    470, 487
Mundus Novus, 32
Munich Filmfest, 486
Munro, John, 436
Munsee, 77, 122, 124
Munsee Prophetess, 103, 121
Murphy, Sen. George, 380
Museum of the American
    Indian, 474
Muskogean, 84
Muskwakiwuk, 70
Myrick, Andrew J., 192

N

Naches, 168
Naiche, 184, 215
Nailor, Gerald, 292
Nakai (Spanish), 170
Nakai, R. Carlos, 312
Nakai, Raymond, 363
Nakaidoklini, 215
Nambé, 77
Nampeyo, 187
Nanagoucy, 72, 74
Nanzattico, 74
Napoleon, 120
Narragansett, 38, 57–59, 71; land
    claims, 414, 419, 422
Nash, Philleo, 341–42, 348
Naskapi. *See* Innu
Naskapi-Montagnais Innu
    Association (N.M.I.A.), 472
Nat Turner's Rebellion, 150
Natchez, 41, 43, 83–84
Natchez (Naiche), 184, 215
National Advisory Council on
    Indian Education, 390, 456

National American Indian
Council, 390
National Association for the
Advancement of Colored People
(NAACP), 350
National Association on Indian
Affairs, 282
National Committee to Save the
Menominee People and Forest,
Inc., 295
National Congress of American
Indians (NCAI), 347, 360, 364,
500; business, 353, 358; Chicago
Indian Conference, 340; and
D'Arcy McNickle, 296; formation,
284, 288, 307; termination, 327,
345; and Vine Deloria, Jr., 292
National Council on Indian
Opportunity, 352–54
National Indian Brotherhood
(N.I.B.), 410, 416, 420–21, 436;
education, 392, 395; and George
Manuel, 278-79, 367; and Noel
Starblanket, 407; Status Indians,
352; White Paper, 359. See also
Assembly of First Nations
National Indian Council, 341, 350,
352, 368
National Indian Defense
Association, 224
National Indian Education Advisory
Committee, 349
National Indian Education
Association (NIEA), 349, 365
National Indian Education
Association Conference, 355
National Indian Forest Resources
Management Act, 472
National Indian Youth
Conference, 364
National Indian Youth Council
(NIYC), 340, 363
National Museum of American
Indian Act, 464
National Museum of the American
Indian, 295
National Navajo Code Talkers
Day, 437
National Office for the Rights of
the Indigent, 292
National Tribal Chairmen's
Association, 384, 447
National Water Commission, 441
Native American: adult education,
352; agricultural production, 346;
desegregated schools, 364;

diseases, 46; education, 160, 354,
355, 358, 362, 365; employment
discrimination, 363; fishing rights,
344; funds, 159; health care, 347;
hunting rights, 347; legal
definition, 108; population decline,
36; population-U.S. Census, 339;
slaves, 46, 113; technical job
training, 360; timber industry, 363;
treaty rights, 354; water rights,
342; youth, 360. See also Alaska
Native; American Indian;
Canadian Indian
Native American Awareness
Week, 407
Native American Church, 208, 277
Native American Graves Protection
and Repatriation Act, 317, 472
Native American Indian Early
Childhood Education Program,
390
Native American Languages
Act, 471
Native American Movement
(NAM), 342. See also American
Indian Movement; Indian Activist
Movements
Native American Public
Broadcasting Consortium
(NAPBC), 412
Native American Renaissance, 351
Native American Rights Fund
(NARF), 309, 316, 383, 385,
402, 500
Native American Student
Union, 356
Native American Studies, 303, 357,
362, 498
Native Brotherhood of British
Columbia, 234, 244, 272, 290,
302, 319
Native Caravan, 399
Native Council of Canada, 316,
352, 410, 420, 441, 482, 487,
498, 500. See also Congress of
Aboriginal Peoples
Native Earth Performing Arts,
Inc., 324
Native Hawaiian, 457
Native Hawaiian Health Care
Act, 457
Native North American Women's
Association, 302
Native Women's Association of
Canada (N.W.A.C.), 482

Natural Parents v. Superintendent of
Child Welfare, 398
Navajo, 21, 26–30, 50, 67, 73,
124, 132–33, 399, 463; art,
332; Centennial of Peace Treaty,
353; clash with Hopi over Joint
Use Area, 394, 400, 423; conflict
with U.S. Army, 170; economic
development, 287; education, 312,
351; first U.S. treaty, 170; grazing
allotments reduced, 288;
hantavirus ("Navajo illness"), 492,
493, 498; Harrington-LaFarge
alphabet, 288; illiteracy, 202;
kidnapping of children, 288; land
claims, 297; land claims
settlement, 376; land rights, 287;
livestock, 170; local economy, 170;
mineral contracts, 390; mineral
rights, 287; Mountain Chant, 287;
Naat'aanis (headmen), 170; Navajo
Radio Network, 408; occupy
oilfield, 416; oil and gas leases,
363; oil rights, 439; prisoners,
133; raids, 170; ranchers, 124;
relocation plan, 133; removal
policy, 191; reservation, 125;
resistance, 170; right to tax, 447;
Rough Rock Demonstration
School, 347; silversmithing, 187;
slavery of, 170; trade relations,
170; tribal council, 281, 342;
wars, 67, 170, 186; weaving, 42,
198, 214
Navajo code talkers, 287, 302, 437
Navajo Community College,
356, 363
Navajo Community College
Act, 389
Navajo Eastern Boundary
Association, 297
Navajo Education and Scholarship
Foundation, 287
Navajo Gas Lands Lease Act, 315
Navajo Irrigation Project, 356, 363
Navajo Reservation, 133, 202
Navajo War, 132
Navidad Colony, 31
Neamathla, 131
Negro, Chuchillo, 184
Neighborhood Friendship
House, 354
Neihardt, John G., 290
Nepoose, Wilson, 482
Nerland, Carney, 496

Neutral, 35, 54, 57, 60–63. *See also* Iroquois
neutrality policy, 92
Nevada v. United States, 443
New Caledonia, 123
New Credit, 119
New Mexico Enabling Act, 264
New Mexico v. Mescalero Apache Tribe, 443
Newberry Library, 296
Newcomb, Frances, 198
Newfoundland, 36, 319
Nez Percé, 138, 164; exile and return, 221; land settlement, 382; "Thief Treaty," 193; wars, 219
Niatum, Duane, 400
Nicoleño, 179
Nicolet, Jean, 57
Nidever, Capt. George, 179
Nielson Task Force, 448
Nighthawk Keetoowah Society, 175, 261
Nihewan Foundation, 302
Nipmuck, 59, 71
Nishga (Nisga'a), 151; land claims, 271, 393, 464, 471, 474; land rights, 237; tribal council formed, 331
Nishga Tribal Council, 272, 352
Nispissing, 57, 59, 63, 67
Nisqually, 111, 340, 347, 375
Nixon, Richard, 356, 360, 365, 377, 382, 385, 389, 391
noble savage, 85
Nocona, Peta, 169
Nootka (Nuu-chah-nulth), 98, 143, 151
Norquay, John, 166, 223
Norris, Malcolm F., 291, 298
North American Indian Brotherhood, 244, 272, 279, 304, 319
North American Indian Traveling College, 359
North American Indian Unity Convention, 375
North West Company, 123–31, 136. *See also* Hudson's Bay Company (HBC)
North-West Mounted Police, 237
North-West Rebellion, 161, 168, 233, 234, 235
North-West Rebellion of 1885, 140, 146
North-West Territories, 161, 168. *See also* Northwest Territories

Northeast Indian art, 59
Northeastern Quebec Agreement, 414
Northern Archaic Tradition, 9–10
Northern Cheyenne, 125, 134. *See also* Cheyenne
Northern Cheyenne Allotment Act, 285
Northern Cheyenne Reservation, 232, 288
Northern Flood Agreement, 413
Northern Flood Committee, 398
Northern Maritime Tradition, 23. *See also* Thule Tradition
Northern Quebec Inuit Association, 308, 385
Northern Sekani bands, 123
Northern States Power, 498
Northwest Coast Art, 162, 165, 378; cultural renaissance, 340; silver engraving, 118
Northwest Ordinance, 102, 110
Northwest Passage, 136
Northwest Territories, 113; Indian Brotherhood of the Northwest Territories (Dene Nation), 369, 404, 416; land claims, 406, 407, 412, 436, 466, 477, 493; *Paulette* case, 396, 408
Northwest Territories Métis Association, 410
Norton Tradition, 14, 23
Notti, Emil, 348
Nova Scotia's Indian Act, 167
Nuclear Waste Policy Act, 435
Numaga, 168, 188
Nunavut Territory, 486

O

Oacpicagigua, Luis, 86
Oakes, Richard, 303, 371, 375, 381–82
Obomsawin, Alanis, 291, 492
obsidian, 3, 11, 17
Occaneechi, 68, 71
Occum, Samson, 96, 98
Ocita, 41
Ocmulgee Mounds, 13
Office of Commissioner of Indian Affairs, 154
Office of Economic Opportunity (OEO), 344, 354, 363, 386
Office of Education, 358

Office of Indian Affairs, 133, 138, 240, 241, 268, 286; assimilation policies toward Indians, 177; Education Division, 288; Indian Arts and Crafts Board, 288; Montezuma advocates abolition, 270; reform, 287. *See also* Bureau of Indian Affairs; Department of Indian Affairs
Office of Indian Education, 456
Office of Indian Rights, 395
Office of Minority Business Enterprise, 356
Office of Native Claims, 395, 399
Office of Superintendent of Indian Trade, 123
Ogden, Peter Skene, 155
Ogden Land Company, 185
Oglala Sioux, 136, 378. *See also* Sioux
Oglala Sioux Civil Rights Organization (OSCRO), 393
Oglethorpe, James, 62, 87
Ohlone, 11
Ohlone College, 349
oil, 283, 457; discoveries, 280–81; pipelines, 424; royalties, 435, 439
Ojibway, 59, 72, 76, 92, 119, 133, 147, 160; baggataway (lacrosse), 74; dialect, 59; fishing rights, 422; fur trade, 68; intermarriage, 69; land cessions, 131; mercury poisoning, 406; middlemen, 69; mineral exploration, 176; occupation of Anicinibe Park, 399; receive compensation, 451; relocation of Grassy Narrows, 343; Robinson Treaties, 176. *See also* Anishinabe; Chippewa
Ojibway Warrior Society, 399
Ojo Caliente (Warm Springs), 141
Okanagan, 126, 436
Oklahoma, 239, 240, 261
Oklahoma Indian Welfare Act, 296
Oklahoma Tax Commission v. Muscogee (Creek) Nation, 456
Old Briton, 88
Old Joseph, 130, 138
Old Northwest, 127
Oliphant v. Suquamish Indian Tribe, 414, 416
Ollikut, 219
Olsen-Chubbock, Colorado, 6
Olympic Games, 261, 269, 284, 292, 297, 344

Omaha, 175; land claims, 424; sacred pole returned, 464; treaty, 181; war dance, 342
Ominayak, Bernard, 464, 487
Omnibus Act, 263
Omnibus Budget Reconciliation Act, 434
Oneida, 67, 75, 81, 88, 101; American Revolution, 115; education, 114; land claims, 397, 423, 448, 497; protests, 388. *See also* Iroquois
Onion Portage, Alaska, 10
Onondaga, 50, 64, 75, 88, 101; Dennis Banks granted asylum, 441; jurisdiction, 423; land claims, 414; protests, 388; sovereignty, 423; wampum belts returned, 464. *See also* Iroquois
Ontario Métis and Non-Status Indian Association, 316
Opechancanough, 48, 55, 61. *See also* Pamunkey; Powhatan Confederacy
The Open Door. *See* Shawnee Prophet; Tenskwatawa
The Orator of the Plains. *See* Satanta
Oregon Boundary Treaty, 170
Oregon Indians, 154
Oregon Territory, 172
Oregon Trail, 121
Ormsby, Maj. William M., 168, 188
Ortiz, Alfonso, 355, 371
Ortiz, Simon, 432, 488, 493
Osage, 69, 175; land settlement, 379; mineral rights, 270; oil, 270
Osborne, Helen Betty, 477
Osceola, 119, 125, 158
Oshara Tradition, 11
Osif, Philip, 284
Oskison, John, 285
Oswalt, Robert, 253
Otermín, 73
Otis, Morgan, 355
Oto, 70, 175, 228
Ottawa, 53, 57–59, 62–67, 72–74, 89–92, 128, 144, 150–51, 160; federal recognition restored, 417; fishing rights, 422, 434; land cessions, 155
Ottawa Termination Act, 331
Ouabona, 74
Ouray, 134, 223
Owasco period, 25

P

Pacific Coast Native Fisherman's Association, 296, 302
Pacific Fur Seal Convention, 269
Pacific period, 13
Pacific Salmon Treaty Act, 441, 448
Paiute, 26, 31, 168; effort to oust squatters, 299; hunting rights, 358; Pyramid Lake, 371, 392; tribal council formed, 323; war with U.S. Army, 188
Paiute Bands of Utah Restoration Act (Public Law 96-227), 425
Paiute War, 168
Paleo-Indian (Paleo-Siberian), 3–9
Paleoarctic, 5
Palliser, Capt. John, 185
Pamunkey, 52, 56, 64–65, 88, 150
pan-Indian activism, 372
pan-Indian alliance, 92, 128, 140
pan-Indian confederacy, 124, 126
pan-Pueblo revolt, 77
Panton, Leslie & Company, 90
Papago, 18, 297. *See also* Tohono O'Odham
Papago Minerals Lands Act, 330
Papago Reservation, 228
Paquime. *See* Casa Grande
Paradise, Bonnie, 444
Parent Consent for Education Act, 245
Parker, Arthur C., 268, 295
Parker, Cynthia, 169
Parker, Ely Samuel (Do-Ne-Ho-Geh-Weh), 144, 203, 348, 360
Parker, Quanah, 125, 134, 169, 212, 277
Parrish, Essie, 252
Passamaquoddy, 84, 106; British peace, 91; land rights, 402
Passamaquoddy Tribe v. Morton, 402
Patayan Tradition, 19
Path Killer, 112
Patterson, Brad, 392
Paul III, Pope, 39
Paull, Andrew, 244, 272, 275, 304, 313
Pawnee, 31, 43, 77, 84, 136
Pawnee Treaty, 185
Paxton Boys' Massacre, 94
Peabody Museum, 464
Peace Commission Act, 200
Peace of Paris, 102

Peace Preservation Act, 118
Peach Wars, 65
Pecos, 77
Peguis, 131
Peguis Saulteaux, 275. *See also* Chippewa; Ojibway
Peigan, 74, 79, 117, 121–23, 126, 130, 145, 161, 469; Oldman River Dam, 486, 487. *See also* Blackfeet; Blackfoot
Pelotte, Donald, 487
Peltier, Leonard, 306, 369, 404–05, 410, 424, 499
Peminuit, Paul, 166
pemmican, 104, 128–31
Pemmican Proclamation, 129
Penacook, 83
Penateka Band of Comanche, 125
Penn, Gov. John, 93
Penn, Thomas, 84
Penn, William, 74, 84
Penner, Keith, 444
Penobscot, 83, 402
Peo-Peo-Mox-Mox, 182
Peoria, 150, 417
Peoria Termination Act, 331
Pepikokia, 74
Pequot, 57–58, 145; federal recognition, 444; gambling, 475; land claims, 446
Pequot War, 57, 58
Percy, George, 51
Perrot, Nicholas, 75
Perry, William, 136
Peters, John, 372
Peters, Susan, 279
Petun, 35, 54, 57, 59, 62–63
peyote religion, 169, 208, 277, 284, 459. *See also* Native American Church
philanthropic liberalism, 159
Philip. *See* King Philip
Phillips Petroleum Company, 341
Piankashaw, 74, 89, 139
Piapot, 130–31
Pickawillany, 89
Pickens, Andrew, 104
Picosa culture, 11
Picurís, 77–78
Piedmont, 71
Pigwacket, 83
Pilgrims, 45, 47, 55, 56, 58, 159
Pima, 18, 75, 77, 187; revolt, 86; traditional tales, 352
Pima-Papago culture, 28
Pinchot, Gifford, 247

Pine Lawn phase, 18
Pine Ridge Reservation, 137, 393, 403–04
Pinto Basin culture, 9
Pinto Basin Tradition, 11
Pipelines Act, 255
Piros, 67
Pit River: land reclamation, 375; lawsuits, 389; occupations, 386, 390; protests, 367, 379; reclaims tract, 387. *See also* California Indians
pithouse, 20
Pizarro, Francisco, 40
Place of the Bow Can People. *See* Awatovi Site, Arizona
Plains Cree, 139, 140, 211
Plains Indians, 63, 89, 140, 141, 169, 177
Plains Village Tradition, 21
Plains Woodland culture, 16
Plano culture (Plainview culture), 4, 7
plant domestication, 12, 16
Platero, Dillon, 356
plaza, 21, 25–26, 30
Pleistocene, 3–6
Pleistocene Overkill, 6
Plymouth, 46
Pocahontas, 44, 48, 53
Pocatello, 129
Point of Pines, 30
Pokagon, Simon, 248
Policha, J.M., 347
Pomo, 127, 157, 381; activism, 374, 375; land claims, 255; protests, 367
Ponca, 141, 145; federal recognition, 471; land claims, 180; removal, 180
Ponca Restoration Act, 471
Ponca Treaty, 141
Pond, Peter, 103
Pontiac, 91–92, 94, 141
Pontiac's War, 92, 129
Poor People's Campaign, 340
Poor People's March, 353
Poor Sarah, 139
Popé, 73
Posey, Alexander, 251
post-Archaic period. *See* Formative period
Potawatomi, 53, 60, 74, 89, 92, 125, 144, 150, 162; creation of Potawatomi Nation, 170; land cessions, 154–55; treaties, 170

potlatch, 109, 166, 226; banned in Canada, 230; participants arrested, 280
pottery, 11–26
Potts, Jerry (Bear Child, Ky-yokosi), 211
Potts, Marie, 315
Poundmaker (Pitikwahanapiwiyin), 140, 233–35
Poundmaker's Lodge, 489
poverty, 346, 368
Poverty Point Site, 14, 20
pow wows, 307, 385
Powderface, Greg, 500
Powell, Capt. J.N., 197
Powhatan, 44–45, 48, 51, 53, 61, 76, 83
Powhatan Confederacy, 44–45, 48, 50, 55–56, 61, 65–66, 71
Practice of Medicine and Surgery in Indian Territory Act, 255
Prairie Treaty Nations Alliance (P.T.N.A.), 449
Pratt, Capt. Richard H., 224
Pre-Projectile Point Stage, 3
preemption principle, 129
Presbyterians, 93
presidio soldiers, 79
Prince Edward Island Indians, 343
Prince Maximilian. *See* Maximilian, Alexander Phillip
Principal Dogs military society, 126
Probate of Deceased Indians of Five Civilized Tribes Act, 304
Proclamation of 1763. *See* Royal Proclamation of 1763
Project on American Indian Economic Development, 501
Project Own, 352
promyshlenniki, 86. *See also* fur trade: Russians
Prophetstown, 95, 103, 124. *See also* Shawnee Prophet; Tenskwatawa
Protestants, 161
Proto-archaic culture. *See* Plano culture
Provencher, Joseph Norbert, 135
Public Health Service Act, 411
Public Law 280, 327
Public Schools Tuition Act, 283
Pueblo, 30–31, 60, 66, 77, 453; American Indian Civil Rights Act, 353; Bursum Bill defeated, 281; early Spanish contact, 46, 48; introduction of horses, 73; refugees, 50; religion, 66;

resistance leaders, 73; tax exemption, 256; voting, 299; watercolor painting, 275; weaving, 42
pueblos, 20–21, 24, 27–28, 56, 71
Pueblo Bonito, 26
Pueblo Industrial School Reserve, 232
Pueblo Land Sale to Navajo Tribe Act, 330
Pueblo Lands Act, 283
Pueblo Lands Board, 281
Pueblo Lands Board Appropriation Act, 293
Pueblo of Los Angeles, 156
Pueblo Revolt, 73, 78
Pulitzer Prize, 358
Purchase from Indian Service Appropriations for Alaska Native Act, 303
Puritans, 45, 56–59, 70
Puyallup, 375; demonstrations, 407; fishing rights, 378, 384, 396–97; land claims, 466
Puyallup Tribe v. Department of Game, 353
Pyramid Lake, 371

Q

Quacka'n (Yucca people), 28
Quakers, 74, 93, 129
Qualchin, 182
Quapaw, 69
Quarterly Journal for the Society of American Indian. See American Indian Magazine
Quebec, 477
Quechan (Yuma), 105, 175
Queen Anne's War, 80
Quetzelquatl, 24
Quinault Tribe, 360
Quinnipiac, 59
Quintana, Ben, 292
Quivira, 42

R

R. v. Drybones, 366
R. v. Johnston, 347
R. v. Simon, 450
R. v. Sioui, 467
R. v. Taylor and Williams, 434
Radin, Paul, 284
Radio Corporation of America, 346

Radio Tuktoyaktuk, 383
Radisson, Pierre Esprit, 66, 68
Rae, Bob, 475, 477
Rafinesque, Constantine, 160
Rain-In-The-Face, 158
Rainbow, 219
Raleigh, Sir Walter, 46
ramada, 19
Ramah Chalcedony, 12
Ramona, 195
ranchos, 156
Range Site, Southern Illinois, 21
Rappahannock, 61–62, 66, 71, 74
Raritan, 60–61
Rattlesnake Island, 374
Re Eskimos, 299
*Re Paulette et al. and Registrar of
    Titles*, 396, 404, 408
Reagan, Ronald, 437, 443–44, 458;
    budget cuts for Indians, 441;
    Indian policy statement, 440
Real, Gaspar Corte, 36
Rebolledo, Gov. Pedro, 64
Reckgawawanc, 56
Recognition of Keetoowah Indians
    Act, 314
Récollets, 57
Red Cloud, 136, 150, 155, 164,
    166, 197
Red Cloud's War, 158, 164
Red Jacket, 159
Red Leggings, 165
Red Paper, 376
Red Pheasant Band, 368
Red Power Movement, 340, 399.
    See also Indian Activist
    Movements; American Indian
    Movement
Red River Cart, 136
Red River Colony (Selkirk
    Settlement), 113, 128, 136
Red River Resistance (Red River
    Rebellion), 161, 168
Red River War, 134, 147
Red Shoes, 87
Red Stick War, 100
Red Sticks, 128–32
Red Tipi, 146
Redbeard, Lucy, 178
Redstar, Kevin, 302
Registered National Historical
    Landmark, 341
Rehabilitation of Navajo and Hopi
    Indians Act, 321
Reid, William Ronald "Bill," 278,
    314, 340, 400

Reifel, Ben, 453
religion, 228, 281, 382, 418, 425,
    432, 435, 454–55, 459
relocation policy, 145, 221, 323
Removal of Restrictions from Some
    Lands of Allottee of Five Civilized
    Tribes Act, 263
Reneros de Posada, Gov. Pedro, 73
repatriation, 452, 472, 474;
    Smithsonian, 451; Stanford
    University, 462
Repeal of Termination Act, 456
Report of the Special Parliamentary
    Committee on Indian Self-
    Government (The Penner
    Report), 444
Requerimiento, 36
Reservation for Confederated Tribes
    of Siletz Indians of Oregon
    Act, 428
residential schools, 476–77. *See also*
    boarding schools
Residential Training Opportunity
    Center, 346
Resolute Bay, 326
Restigouche Micmac Reserve, 433
Restoration Act of Confederated
    Tribes of Siletz Indians of
    Oregon, 412
Restricted Trust Lands Act, 264
Révillon Fréres, 280
revitalization movements, 73,
    92, 124
Revolutionary War. *See* American
    Revolutionary War
Revolving Loan Fund Act, 343
Reyna, Diane, 488
Rhine, Gary, 486
Ribaulty, Jean, 45
Rice v. Rehner, 443
Rickard, Clinton, 284
Ridge, John, 143
Ridge, John Rollin, 143, 180, 202
Ridge, Major, 143
Riel, Louis, Jr., 161, 168, 204–06,
    232–35. *See also* Métis; North-
    West Rebellion
Riel, Louis, Sr., 173
Riggs, Lynn, 290
Right Livelihood Award, 497
Riley, Del, 432
Rincon Band of Mission Indians
    Land Act, 301
Rio Grande pueblos, 27, 41, 56
Risling, David, Jr., 349, 355, 376
Roanoke Colony, 46

Robideau, Robert Eugene, 405–
    06, 410
Robinson, Tina, 371
Robinson-Huron Treaty, 478
Roessel, Faith, 500
Rogers, William Penn Adair (Will),
    224, 281
Rogue Indians (Takelma and
    Tututni), 183
Rogue River War, 183
Rolfe, John, 44, 48, 53
Roman Catholic, 50, 120, 135,
    156, 160
Roman Nose, 146, 202
Roosevelt, Franklin D., 293
Roosevelt, Theodore, 247
Rosebud Sioux Tribe v. Kneip, 410
Ross, John, 112, 143, 189
Rough Rock Demonstration
    School, 347
Round Valley Reserve, 184, 193
Royal Canadian Mounted Police,
    211, 233, 333, 457, 469, 492
Royal Commission on Aboriginal
    Peoples, 486
Royal Proclamation of 1763, 83,
    92, 167
Royle, Edwin Milton, 271
Russell, John, 85
Russell Tribunal, 430
Russian American Company,
    162, 163
Russian-Greek Orthodox Church,
    86, 167
Russians, 86, 127, 151, 155
Ryan, Ken, 498

S

saber-toothed tigers, 3
Sacajawea, 107, 121
sachem, 129
Saconnet, 68
Sacred Arrow Bundle Dance, 100
Saginaw, 155
Sahtu Dene, 139
St. Clair, Gov. Arthur, 105, 113
St. Laurent, Louis, 321
Sainte-Marie, Buffy, 302, 375
Sainte-Marie-Among-the-
    Hurons, 59
Salinero Apache, 63
Salish, 452. *See also* Coast Salish;
    Interior Salish

Salmon and Steelhead Conservation Act, 432
Salt River Reserve, 187
Samaria Indian Baptist Church, 251
Samoset, 47
Sampson, Will, 294, 443
Samson Cree Reserve, 479
San Carlos Reservation, 141
San Cristóbal, 77
San Diego de Jémez, 77
San Diego Mission, 95, 96
San Dieguito-Pinto Tradition, 11
San Felipe, 77
San Ildefonso, 77
San Juan drainage, 27
San Juan Pueblo, 46
San Juan River basin, 29
San Luis Obispo, 79
Sanapia, 245
Sanchez, Abel, 275
Sand Creek Massacre, 120, 126, 193, 195
Sandia culture, 4, 5
Sandia Mountains, New Mexico, 4
Santa Ana, 77
Santa Barbara Channel, 28
Santa Clara Pueblo v. Martinez, 417
Santa Fe Studio, 341
Santa Fe Trail, 146
Santa Ysabel Indian Reservation Land Exchange Act, 301
Santee Sioux, 125. *See also* Sioux
Saponi, 68
Sarcee, 88, 123, 151, 161
Saskatchewan: province created, 257
Saskatchewan Indian Association, 307
Saskatchewan Indian Federated College, 406
Satan, 56, 59
Satank (Sitting Bear), 126
Satanta, 126, 146, 147, 212
Saturiwa, 37
Sauk, 61–62, 66, 81, 148, 150, 152, 155
Sauk (Sac) and Fox, 161
Sault Ste. Marie, 76
Saulteaux (Ojibway), 76, 131; signing of Treaty 1, 209; signing of Treaty 2, 210; signing of Treaty 3, 211; signing of Treaty 4, 211; signing of Treaty 5, 215. *See also* Anishinabe; Chippewa; Ojibway
Sawyer, Joseph, 164
Sayer, Pierre-Guillaume, 173
scarlet fever epidemic, 196

Scholder, Fritz, 297, 341
schools, 372
scientific racism, 246
Scott, Thomas, 206, 208, 372, 374
Scott, Winfield, 162
scrapers, 5–8
sea otter, 120, 151
sea otter trade, 108
Seattle (Sealth), 111
Seaver, James E., 139
Second Seminole War. *See* Seminole
Seekaboo, 126
Seitz, George B., 284
Seix (Shakes), 155
Sekani, 35, 114, 123, 141, 151, 350
self-determination, 366, 377, 385
Self-Determination and Educational Assistance Act, 283, 345; amendments (Public Law 100–472), 457
Self-Determination Policy, 345
Self-Governance Pilot Program, 468
self-government, 396, 430, 444–54, 467–68, 476–79, 482, 487–88, 493–95, 498
Sells, Cato, 276
Seminole, 82, 125, 136, 150; constitutional government, 248; Creek Nation, 183; First Seminole War, 131; government formed in Oklahoma, 183; judicial system established, 443; land, 127; land claims, 350; reparations, 375; resist removal, 119; resistance, 158; Second Seminole War, 158; sovereignty, 432; Third Seminole War, 183; villages, 127, 131; war chiefs, 158; warriors, 125; wars, 93, 119, 125, 131, 158
Seminole Awards Act, 467
Seminole Nation v. the United States, 303
Seminole Tribe of Florida v. Butterworth, 432
Seminole War. *See* Seminole
Senate Select Committee on Indian Affairs, 445
Senate Subcommittee on Indian Education, 365
Seneca, 63–71, 74–76, 159, 185, 341; attempt to collect back rents, 267, 299, 467; and Canassatego, 88; and Ely S. Parker, 144; Fox Wars, 81; Iroquois Confederacy

dispersed, 101; lands, 341; and Mary Jemison, 139; museum, 411; and Pontiac, 92; removal, 150; Seneca Arts Project, 295; taxation, 461; Termination Act, 344; treaty at Buffalo Creek, 143; Turtle Clan, 129. *See also* Iroquois
Separate Settlement Contracts for Sioux Act, 323
Sequoyah, 96, 135
Sequoyah League, 251
Seri, 86
Serpent Mound, 17
Serra, Junipero, 96, 101, 179
Seven Cities of Cíbola, 40, 42
"Seven River" Apache, 69
Seven Years' War. *See* French and Indian War
Seventh Cavalry, 120, 158. *See also* Custer, George Armstrong
Sevier, John, 104
Shakes, 162
Shanawdithit, 145
Shasta, 154
Shasta Community Action Project, 386
Shaw, Anna Moore, 352
Shaw, Col. Benjamin Franklin, 183
Shaw, Carl, 499
Shawnee, 71–77, 89–92, 125–26, 151, 164; Lord Dunsmore's War, 98; Five Nations, 74, 77; Iroquois neutrality, 80; and John Logan, 83; migration, 62, 130; Munsee Prophetess, 121-22; Susquehannock War, 67; and Tecumseh, 95. *See also* Shawnee Prophet; Tecumseh; Tenskwatawa
Shawnee Prophet, 122, 126. *See also* Prophetstown; Tecumseh; Tenskwatawa
Shawnee Treaty, 181
Sheepeater War, 224
shell money, 27. *See also* wampum
shell mounds, 13
Sheridan, Gen. Philip, 210
Sherman, Gen. Philip, 204
Sherman, Gen. William Tecumseh, 147, 191, 219
Shinnecock, 56, 391
Shipek, Florence, 351
Short Bull, 240
short-faced bears, 3
Shoshoni, 31, 79, 121, 129, 148, 168; Carlin Farms Reservation,

220; uprising, 268; water
rights, 472
Shoshoni and Arapaho
Compensation Act, 327
Shubenacadie, 82, 89
Shuswap, 124
Siberia, 4, 18
Sibley, Col. Henry Hastings, 192
Sibley, Gen. Henry Hopkins, 190
Siddon, Tom, 472, 475, 479, 486,
487, 489
Siksika, 74, 79, 114, 123, 145-46,
161, 444. See also Blackfoot
Siksika Reserve, 230
Siletz, 412
Silko, Leslie Marmon, 316, 409
Sillery, 58
Silvas, Patty, 357
Silver Rush, 186
Silverheels, Jay, 298, 422
Sinaloa, 75
Sioui, George, 488
Sioux, 65-66, 69-72, 130, 138,
145, 148, 152, 164-67; activism,
379; agency, 137; allotment, 255;
Black Hills, 379, 421; buffalo-
hunting horse culture, 66;
introduced to European goods, 65;
land cession, 160; land claims,
350, 414, 427; land rights, 155;
lands, 134, 151, 158; language, 59;
mass execution, 192; television
station, 419; treaties, 161; tribal
police, 344; uprising, 140, 191;
warfare, 197, 198, 212; wars, 125,
181. See also Assiniboine; Dakota;
Lakota
Sioux Claims Awards Act, 310
Sioux Indian Act, 242
Sioux Museum and Crafts
Center, 299
Sioux (Standing Rock) Reserve, 219
Sioux Treaty of 1876, 388
Sitting Bull, 125, 138, 150, 158,
164, 214, 217, 220
Six Nations, 83, 88, 95, 99, 143,
151, 335; treaties, 115. See also
Five Nations; Iroquois; Iroquois
Confederacy
Six Nations Reserve, 107, 119, 283,
333, 411
Sky World, 177
Skyhawk, Sonny, 500
Skyhorse, Paul, 417
Slave, 139
slave raids, 71, 75-77, 127

slaves, 68, 70-74, 77, 81, 84, 86
Sloan, Thomas, 268
Sloan Site, 8
Slocum, John, 246. See also Indian
Shaker Church
small business loans, 352, 434
smallpox, 36, 38, 54-57, 152, 191,
204. See also epidemics
Smart, Stanley, 358
Smith, Capt. Andrew Jackson, 183
Smith, E.P., 178
Smith, Elijah, 393
Smith, Finis, 346
Smith, Jedediah, 144
Smith, John, 48, 52, 55
Smith, Katherine, 409
Smith, Michael, 403
Smith, Redbird, 175, 261
Smithsonian Institution, 215,
317, 474
Smohalla, 130, 177. See also
Dreamer Religion
Smoke, 136
Smoke Signals, 315
Snake War, 168
Snaketown, 24
Snow, John, 488
Snyder Act, 280
Sobaipuri, 78
social programs, 318
Society of American Indians (SAI),
253, 258, 268, 275
Society of Northern California
Indians, 278
Sohappy v. Smith, 432
Sokoki, 83
Son of the Forest, 145
Songhee Coast Salish, 167. See also
Salish
South America, 3, 4, 32
South Carolina Indians, 74
Southeastern Ceremonial
Complex, 21
Southeastern peoples, 44-45
Southern Arapaho, 125, 165. See
also Arapaho
Southern Cheyenne, 125, 164, 165.
See also Cheyenne; Dog Soldiers
Southern Tlingit, 151
Southern Tutchone, 167
Southern Ute Agency, 134
Southland Royalty Co. et. al. v.
Navajo Tribe et., 439
Southwestern Indian Polytechnic
Institute, 388
sovereignty, 102, 301, 415, 463

Spain, 31, 55, 135
Sparrow, Ronald, 467
spear thrower. See atlatl
Spencer, Horace, 357
Spiro Site, Oklahoma, 21
Spokane, 346
Spotted Tail, 155, 220, 225, 229
Squanto, 45, 47, 55
St. Augustine settlement, 45
St. John's Island, 95
St. Lawrence Iroquois, 35, 39,
43, 53. See also Iroquois;
Neutral; Petun
St. Lusson, Sieur 69
St. Regis, 151
Stadacona (Quebec), 50
Stand Watie, 123
Standing Arrow, 331
Standing Bear (Mochunozhi), 145,
181, 230
Standing Bear, Henry, 268
Standing Bear, Luther, 224,
286, 296
Standing Bear v. Crook, 223
Standing Rock Reservation, 150,
158, 164
Starblanket, Noel, 407, 416, 425
steatite, 14
Steinhauer, Eugene, 298
Steinhauer, Ralph, 399
Stephens v. Cherokee Nation, 248
Steptoe, Lt. Col. Edward J., 185
stereotyping exhibit, 499
Stevens, Gov. Isaac, 138, 182
Stigler, William, 307
Stockbridge, 114, 115
Stone, John, 57
Stoney, 59. See also Assiniboine
Stony Mountain Penitentiary, 140
Strait of Georgia Tradition, 12
Strickland, Rennard J., 299
strip mining, 409
Strom, Steven, 439
"Strong Hearts," 150
Studi, Wes, 489, 500
Studio One, 476
Stuyvesant, Peter, 65
suicide, 450, 455, 489
Sullivan, Gen. John, 104
Sumas Apache, 78
Sun Dance, 230, 374, 387; banned,
226, 264; revival among
Sioux, 321
Supplemental Appropriations
Act, 354

Survival of the American Indian
　Association (SAIA), 306, 354, 384
Susquehannock, 62, 67–71, 74, 93
Sutter, John, 166
Sutter's Mill, 172
Swampy Cree, 209–10, 215
Swanton, John, 162
Sweet Grass, 218
Sweet Medicine, 63, 100
Swimmer, Ross O., 304
syncretic movements, 177. *See also*
　religion; revitalization movements

T

Tobacco People. *See* Iroquois; Petun
Tabeau, Pierre-Antone, 118
Tadoussac, 50
Tafoya, Calvin, 501
Tagish, 167, 248
Tahltan, 141, 155, 162–63, 211
Tahoma, Quincy, 292
Tahontaenrat, 54
Tai-me, 146
Taignoagny, 39
Tailfeathers, Gerald, 283
Taino, 31
Taino Rebellion, 38
Takayren (Noise-In-The-House).
　See Edenshaw, Charles
Tall Bull, 146, 202
Talton v. Mayes, 246
Tamahita, 69
Tammany, 74
Tano, 77
Taos Blue Lake Act, 382
Taos Land Bill, 382
Taos Pueblo, 59, 73, 77, 171, 346;
　Blue Lake, 346, 366, 377, 380,
　382; land restoration, 377; pueblo
　council imprisoned, 284; religious
　sanctuary, 346; return of sacred
　lands, 388
Tax, Sol, 340
Tax of Ceded Indian Irrigated
　Lands Act, 288
Taylor, Richard, 260
Taylor, Zachary, 160
Tecumseh, 95, 103, 114, 120–27,
　128, 132
*Tee-Hit-Ton Indians v. United
　States*, 329
Tejas, 41
Tekakwitha, Kateri, 305, 426
Tekakwitha Conference, 487

Temple Mound Civilization, 30
Tennessee Valley Authority, 425
Tenochtitlan, 37
Tenskwatawa, 95, 103, 108, 122–
　23, 126. *See also* Prophetstown;
　revitalization movements; Shawnee
　Prophet; Tecumseh
Teotihuacan, 24
Termination Act, 367
Termination of Certain Federal
　Restrictions Act, 327
termination policy, 326, 329–31,
　345, 364, 378; California, 327,
　332; end of, 327, 456;
　reversed, 425
Terrazas, Col. Joaquin, 220
Terry, Gen. Alfred, 213, 217
Tesuque, 77
Teters, Charlene, 499
Teton Sioux, 136
Tewa, 77; art, 250; pottery, 187
Tewanima, Louis, 261
Thanadelthur, 82
Thayendanegea. *See* Joseph Brant
Thiokol Chemical Corporation, 360
Thirst Dance. *See* Sun Dance
Thom, Melvin, 340
Thompson (Ntlakapamux), 124
Thompson, David, 126
Thompson, Johnny, 458
Thompson, Wiley, 119, 158
Thorpe, Grace, 375, 381, 387
Thorpe, James Francis, 237, 269,
　296, 437
Three Affiliated Tribes, 31
Thule culture, 14, 18, 23, 27. *See
　also* Northern Maritime Tradition
Thule Inuit, 21, 25, 27
Thunder Cloud, 298
Thunderhawk, Madonna, 397
Tibbles, Thomas H., 181
Tiguex, 41–42
Timucua, 37, 41, 64, 75
Tipai, 96
tipis, 36, 74, 167, 379
Tippecanoe, 126. *See also*
　Prophetstown; Shawnee Prophet
Tisquantum, 55
tiswin, 215
Title XI, 449
Tiwa, 42, 63
Tlastcine, 29
Tlaxcala, 37
Tlingit, 86, 162, 167; control of
　European trade, 211, 247; culture,
　167; language, 167; Russians, 118;

seek apology for shelling, 437;
　trade, 155, 162–63
tobacco, 25, 35, 54, 56, 167
Todd, Loretta, 492
Tohono O'Odham, 18, 77, 228,
　297, 463. *See also* Papago
Toledo, José Rey, 292
Toltec, 24
Toltec Site, Arkansas, 21
Tomochichi, 62, 248
Tompiros, 67
Tonawanda, 144, 299. *See also*
　Seneca
Tongue River Reservation, 125. *See
　also* Northern Cheyenne
Tonkawa, 41
Toohoolhoolzote, 219
Tootoosis, John, 307
Topiltzin, 24
totem poles, 109, 166, 314
Totopotomoi, 65, 83
Tousey, Sheila, 489
Towa, 63
Trade and Intercourse Acts, 112,
　114, 117, 120, 156, 171
Trading Houses Act, 115
*The Traditional History and
　Characteristic Sketches of the
　Ojibway Nation*, 175
Trail of Broken Treaties, 315, 384,
　391, 393
The Trail of Tears, 148, 162
Trans-Canada Highway, 492
transcontinental railway, 230
Transfer of Indian Health Care
　Act, 325
Transfer of Power to Commissioner
　of Indian Affair, 313
trapline registration, 300
Treaty 1 (Stone Fort Treaty), 209
Treaty 2 (Manitoba Post
　Treaty), 210
Treaty 3 (North-West Angle
　Treaty), 211, 232
Treaty 4 (Qu'Appelle Treaty), 211
Treaty 5, 215
Treaty 6, 140, 217, 228, 347
Treaty 7, 146, 220, 444
Treaty 8, 248, 396, 404, 408,
　453, 454
Treaty 9, 257
Treaty 10, 259
Treaty 11, 280, 396, 408
Treaty at Dancing Rabbit Creek,
　148, 374
Treaty at Doak's Stand, 135

Treaty of 1646, 61
Treaty of 1677, 76
Treaty of Aix-la-Chapelle, 87
Treaty of Bosque Redondo, 202
Treaty of Box Elder, 129
Treaty of Fort Harmar, 111
Treaty of Fort Jackson, 128, 130
Treaty of Fort Laramie, 136, 177, 197–98, 242, 394; violations, 202, 212
Treaty of Fort Stanwix, 95, 98, 104
Treaty of Fort Wayne (1809), 124-25
Treaty of Ghent, 127–30
Treaty of Greenville, 95
Treaty of Guadalupe Hidalgo, 171, 173
Treaty of Hell Gate, 183
Treaty of Hopewell, 108
Treaty of Indian Springs, 93, 100
Treaty of Lancaster, 98
Treaty of Medicine Lodge, 254
Treaty of Mendota, 125
Treaty of New Echota, 97, 123, 143, 145, 158, 374
Treaty of Paris, 92, 107
Treaty of Payne, 158
Treaty of Pontotoc, 374
Treaty of Saint Germain-en-Laye, 56
Treaty of San Lorenzo, 115
Treaty of Spring Wells, 130
Treaty of Utrecht, 82
Treaty of Versailles, 107
Treaty with the Navajo at Cheille, 173
Tribal Acquisition of Deceased Members' Land Act, 304
Tribal Funds Act, 260
Tribal Self-Governance Demonstration Project, 479
Tribally Controlled Community Colleges Act, 419
Tribes and Loans Consolidation Act, 372
Trois Riviéres, 54, 57
Troyville culture, 23
Truckee River Decree, 307
Trudeau, Pierre Elliott, 362, 376, 436
Trudell, John, 315, 382, 391, 403, 489
Trust Conveyance of Indian Lands, 335
Trutch, Joseph, 193
Tsatoke, Monroe, 279

Tsejinciai, 29
Tsimshian, 143, 151; establishment of Metlakatla, 191
Tsinahjinnie, Andrew, 292
Tula, 24
Tulalip, 340
Tulalip Tribe Land Sale Act, 308
Tungavik Federation of Nunavut, 467, 479
Tunica, 41
Tupatu, Luis, 78
Turner, Nat, 150. See also Nat Turner's Rebellion
Tuscarora, 81, 83, 88, 101, 143, 455; activism, 378; American Revolution, 115; education, 114; protests, 388; war with English, 81
Tuscarora Reservation, 331, 333
Tutchone, 167, 177
Tutu, Desmond, 469
Tuzigoot Pueblo, 31
Two Moons, 270
Twohy, Julius, 335

U

U.S. Citizenship for Indian Veterans of World War, 278
U.S. Citizenship for Metlakahtla Indians Act, 295
U.S. Civil Rights Commission, 399, 404, 433,
U.S. Civil War, 158, 170
U.S. Constitution, 88, 145, 156, 158; Iroquois influence, 110
U.S. expansion, 105
U.S. Military Academy, 137
U.S. sale of Indian land, 106
Udall, Morris, 348
Udall, Stewart L., 336, 341, 347
Udall Task Force, 341
Uhlman, Wes, 369
Uintah and Ouray Indian Reservation Boundaries Act, 317
umiak, 14
U'Mista Cultural Centre, 429
Umnak Island, Alaska, 11
Umpqua, 438
Uncas, 171
Underhill, Ruth, 296
Union of British Columbia Indian Chiefs, 389
Union of Ontario Indians, 335
Union Pacific railroads, 130
Unitah Reservation, 134

United Church of Canada, 487
United Indians of All Tribes, 369. See also Alcatraz Island occupation; Indians of All Tribes
United Native Americans (UNA), 354, 355, 364
United States and Delaware Tribe Treaty, 103
The United States as Guardian of Hualapai v. Santa Fe Pacific Railway Company, 301
United States v. Creek Nation, 295
United States v. Kagama, 236
United States v. Nice, 275
United States v. Sandoval, 271
United States v. Shoshoni, 298
United States v. Sioux Nation, 427
United States v. Washington, 397, 432
United States v. Wheeler, 415
United States v. Winans, 256
urban Indians, 384, 390; federal aid, 377; migration, 333; service centers, 386
Ute, 31, 59, 77, 120, 124, 132; hunting rights, 411; land claims, 190; memorial to warriors, 495; uprising, 134; war, 223
Ute Per Capita and Division Act, 324
Ute Tribe Termination Act, 329

V

Valentine, Robert G., 266
Van Dyck, Hendrick, 65, 72
Vancouver, Capt. George, 114
Vancouver Island Treaties. See Coast Salish
The Vanishing American, 284
"Vanishing Americans," 241
Veeder, William, 369
Velarde, Pablita, 277
Vespucci, Amerigo, 32
Victoria, Queen (of England), 166
Victorio (Beduiat), 141, 220
Vietnam War, 365
Vigil, Romando, 275
Ville Marie, 54
Virginia Assembly, 65, 66
Virginia War, 55
Vizenor, Gerald, 460, 492
voting rights, 196, 251; Manitoba, 326; non-English-speakers, 404; Ontario Indians, 330

W

W.A.C. Bennet Dam, 350
Wabakinine, 107
Wagon Box Fight, 136
Waheenee (Buffalo Bird
   Woman), 280
Wahunsonacock, 44, 51, 55. *See also*
   Powhatan
Walam Olum, 160. *See also*
   Delaware
Walapai, 31. *See also* Hualapai
Walk for Justice, 499
Walla Walla Council, 138
Wallis, Michael, 497
Wampanoag, 38, 55, 59, 68, 70;
   early English contact, 45, 47; land
   claims, 453; tribal status, 453
wampum, 57
Wampum Belts, 50, 167
Wanamaker, Rodman, 271
Wanapum, 130
Wandering Spirit
   (Kapapamahchakwew), 140,
   233, 235
Waptashi (Feather Religion). *See*
   Shaker Church
War Department, 138
War for the Black Hills, 125, 134
War for the Bozeman Trail,
   134, 155
War of 1812, 76, 103, 108, 127–
   30, 160–61
War of Independence. *See* American
   Revolutionary War
Ward, John, 190
Warpath, 354
Warren Trading Post, 345
*Warren Trading Post v. Arizona Tax
   Commission*, 345
Warrior, Clyde, 340
Washakie, 121, 130
Washington, George, 90, 104–
   05, 111
Washington and Oregon Indian
   Treaties, 182
*Washington v. Confederated Tribes of
   Colville Indian Reservation*, 424
Washita River phase, 28
Washoe (Washo), 157, 378, 425
Washoe Reserve, 196
Wasinawatok-El Issa, Ingrid, 460
Wassaja, 270
water rights, 261, 307, 369, 409,
   441, 443, 449

Watt, Charlie, 308, 385, 400
Watt, James G., 433, 440
Wauneka, Annie Dodge, 263,
   323, 342
Wayne, Gen. Anthony, 105,
   113–14
Wea, 74
Weatherford, William, 132
Weeden Island culture, 19
Weeden Island sites, 19
weirs, 11
Weiser, Conrad, 88
Welch, James, 397
Wells, Clyde, 468, 492
West, John, 134
West Baffin Island Eskimo
   Cooperative, 335
West Indies, 32
Westerman, Floyd Red Crow, 473
Western Apache, 30–31, 66. *See
   also* Apache
Western Archaic culture, 9
Western Cree, 74
Western Land Acquisition, 120
Western Oregon Indians
   Termination Act, 329
Westo, 68, 70, 73
Wet'suwet'en (Western Carrier),
   446. *See also* Carrier
whaling, 27, 31, 239
Wheeler, Anne, 453
Wheelock, Eleazor, 96
Wheelwright, Mary C., 198
whisky trade, 146, 205, 211
White Bear Indian Reserve, 492
White Bird, 219
White Eagle, Philip, 374
White Earth Reservation, 141. *See
   also* Anishinabe; Chippewa;
   Ojibway
White Earth Reservation Allotment
   Act, 255
White Earth Reservation Lands
   Settlement Act, 451
White House Conference on Indian
   Education, 456, 469
White Men and Indian Women
   Marriage Act, 238
White Mountain Apache, 350
*White Mountain Apache Tribe v.
   Bracker*, 427
White Paper, 273, 358, 366, 376,
   395, 413; opposition to, 310;
   retraction, 367, 385; support
   of, 368

White River Ute, 134
White Sticks, 128. *See also* Creek;
   Red Sticks
Whitebear, Bernie, 369, 372
White's Indiana Manual Labor
   Institute, 217
Whitesinger, Pauline, 409
Whitman, Marcus, 172
Wichita, 42, 170
Wickanish, 109
wigwams, 36
Wild Cat, 158
Wild West Show, 150, 161
wildlife protection, 435
Williams, Basil, 341
Williams, Roger, 46, 56, 58
Williams Treaties, 282
Williams v. Lee, 332, 439
Williamson, Col. David, 106
Williamson, Verna Olguin, 453
Wilson, Gilbert, 162, 280
Wilson, James, 99
Wilson, Mary Jane, 287, 354, 499
Wilson, Richard (Dicky), 393, 403
"Wind and Glacier Voices: The
   Native American Film," 492
Wind River Indian Lands Act, 301
Windmiller culture, 11, 14
Windspeaker, 492
Winema, 160
Winnebago, 57, 60, 81, 144, 151;
   calendar sticks, 448; land cessions,
   154, 170; purchase land, 499
Winnemucca, Sarah, 168
Winters v. United States, 261
Winthrop, John, 56
Wintu, 386
Wintun, 11
Winyah, 74
Wisdom, Wendy, 500
Withhorn, Harold, 393
women: activism, 380, 397, 460;
   employment discrimination, 370;
   occupations, 375; in Parliament,
   458; prisoners, 418, 486;
   representation in national
   organizations, 482; tribal
   leadership, 310, 323, 451, 453,
   496; in U.S. government, 493;
   voting, 374
Women of All Red Nations
   (WARN), 397
Women's National Indian
   Association, 224
Woodland culture, 14, 18

Worcester, Samuel, 154
Worcester v. Georgia, 154
Work, Hubert, 281
Working Group on Indian Water
  Settlements, 463
World Council of Indigenous
  Peoples, 279, 404
World's Fairs, 218–19
Wounded Knee Massacre, 239, 253,
  290, 473
Wounded Knee occupation
  (Wounded Knee II), 288, 300,
  315, 366, 387, 393, 395–96
Wovoka (Jack Wilson), 183, 239.
  See also Ghost Dance
Wozencraft, Oliver, 176
Wrangle Institute Boarding
  School, 290
Wright, Col. George, 186
Wuttunee, William, 341, 368
Wyandot, 53, 62–67, 74, 89,
  91–92, 111, 128, 150; federal
  recognition restored, 417; land
  cessions, 155; land claims, 447. *See
  also* Huron
Wyandotte Termination Act, 331

Y

Yahi, 267
Yahooskin, 452
Yakima, 391
Yakima Agency Boarding
  School, 188
Yakima Land Exchange Act, 330
Yakima Land Lease Act, 330
Yakima War, 111, 182
Yakotglasami, 226
Yamasee, 73, 76–77, 81–82
Yamasee War, 82
Yaqui, 38–39, 86
Yatza Haida, 162. *See also* Haida
Yavapai, 31, 355
Yellow Bird, 240
Yellow Smoke, 464
Yellow Thunder, Raymond,
  300, 390
Yellowknife, 135, 139
Yokut, 11, 176
Yolo Native American
  Association, 376
York, 121
Young, Brigham, 121

Young, Phyllis, 397
Young Deer, James, 265
Yuchi, 76, 82
Yukioma, 270
Yukon land claims, 393, 406, 424,
  444, 447, 457, 466, 479
Yukon Native Brotherhood,
  393, 406
Yukon Territory, 3–4
Yuman, 28
Yuquot Nootka (Nuu-chah-
  nulth), 120
Yurok, 405, 419

Z

Zah, Peterson, 287, 437, 453, 472
Zarcillas, 132
Zebree Site, Arkansas, 21
Zephier, Ramona, 349
Zia, 77
Ziolkowski, Korczak, 317
Zo-Tom, Paul, 214
Zuni, 40, 42, 56, 132, 187, 219